Gisela Holfter, Hermann Rasche (Hgg.):

Exil in Irland

John Hennigs Schriften
zu deutsch-irischen Beziehungen

Gisela Holfter, Hermann Rasche (Hgg.)

Exil in Irland

John Hennigs Schriften
zu deutsch-irischen Beziehungen

ωωτ Wissenschaftlicher Verlag Trier

Die Deutsche Bibliothek - CIP-Einheitsaufnahme

Exil in Irland.
John Hennigs Schriften zu deutsch-irischen Beziehungen /
Gisela Holfter, Hermann Rasche (Hgg.).-
Trier : WVT Wissenschaftlicher Verlag Trier, 2002
    ISBN 3-88476-506-X

Umschlaggestaltung: Brigitta Disseldorf
(M. Nottar, Werbeagentur, Trier)

Textbearbeitung und -gestaltung:
Markus Nußbaum

© WVT Wissenschaftlicher Verlag Trier, 2002
ISBN 3-88476-506-X

WVT Wissenschaftlicher Verlag Trier
Bergstraße 27, 54295 Trier
Postfach 4005, 54230 Trier
Tel.: (0651) 41503 / 9943344, Fax: 41504
Internet: http://www.wvttrier.de
e-mail: wvt@wvttrier.de

Inhaltsverzeichnis

I Vorwort

John Hennig (1911-1986) kann als 'Vater der deutschen Irlandkunde' bezeichnet werden. 1939 musste er mit seiner jungen Familie aus Deutschland nach Irland fliehen. In seinem Exil verfasste er neben Beiträgen zu liturgiewissenschaftlichen und benachbarten Themen zahlreiche Artikel zu deutsch-irischen Beziehungen. Seine wichtigsten Schriften dazu erschienen in über dreißig wissenschaftlichen Zeitschriften und Journalen. Sie werden hier gesammelt und wieder zugänglich gemacht, ergänzt durch Auszüge aus seiner bisher nur im Privatdruck erschienenen Autobiographie 'Die bleibende Statt', sowie bislang nicht veröffentlichte Aufsätze und journalistische Arbeiten.

Eine ausführliche Einleitung in Leben und Werk John Hennigs ermöglicht es, die Hintergründe seiner Arbeiten zu verstehen und unterstreicht die zentrale Stellung seiner bislang unübertroffenen wissenschaftlichen Beschäftigung mit den deutsch-irischen Beziehungen.

Bei dieser Arbeit, die wir den Töchtern John Hennigs widmen möchten, wurden wir von vielen Seiten unterstützt. An erster Stelle muss dabei John Hennigs Tochter Monica und ihr Mann Dian Schefold in Bremen genannt werden. Ohne ihre großartige Unterstützung und stete Anteilnahme wäre dieses Buch nicht entstanden. Thanks a million! Danke auch an John Hennigs Neffen Wolfgang Hennig, Stolberg, der uns Briefe, Photos und Familiendokumente zur Verfügung stellte. Danke ebenfalls an John Hennigs einzige noch lebende Schwester, Erica Becker (Australien), und seine jüngste Tochter Margie Landolt.

Weiter danken wir Hennigs früheren Freunden, Nachbarn und Bekannten, Mrs Sheila Harbison und ihren zwei Söhnen, Dr. John Harbison und ganz besonders Dr. Peter Harbison für das Interesse und seine Hilfe. Ann Gallagher, Paula Sheehan, Noel und Thelma Sheehan, Father Maloney, Sister Ines, Sister Assumpta (Santa Sabina), Kitty O'Sullivan, Elisabeth O'Neill und Katherine Meenan (Bord na Mona), Desmond Fennell, John Hyland, Des Reynolds, Sean Schütte, Charlie O'Connor (ehemalige Schüler des Belvedere College) und Father Patrick Twohig (früher Maynooth College).

Ebenso danken wir Ruth Braunizer, Prof. Angelus A. Häußling OSB, Dr. Suzanne Kirkbright, Prof. Hans Reiss, Prof. Michael Richter, Dr. Hans Saner und Prof. Ian Wallace in Deutschland, Österreich, England und der Schweiz.

Für ihre Unterstützung bei der Materialbeschaffung danken wir Sylvia Asmus und Marie-Luise Hahn, Exilarchiv Frankfurt; den Mitarbeitern des Universitätsarchivs Leipzig und des Archivs des Deutschen Bundestags Bonn, Victor Laing und seinen Kollegen in den Military Archives, Dublin, den National Archives und der National Library, Dublin und Miriam Tiernan, Department of Foreign Affairs.

Besonders geholfen bei der Vorbereitung des Buchs für die Veröffentlichung (speziell beim Einscannen der Artikel) haben an der University of Limerick Daniela Schäffer,

2

Johanna Petters, Gillian Edgeworth, Andreas Hüther, Laura Little, Sabine Besenfelder, Dr. Marieke Krajenbrink, Claire O'Reilly, Leonie Kelly und Brendan Bolger.

Für die finanzielle Unterstützung sind wir dem Staff Development Grant for Research Projects for Humanities, dem University of Limerick Seed funding, dem Millenium Research Grant, National University of Ireland, Galway und dem Forschungsstipendium des DAAD dankbar.

Danke auch an Glenn und unsere Freunde und Kollegen an der University of Limerick und der National University of Ireland, Galway, für Verständnis und Unterstützung.

Anmerkung zu dieser Edition:

Sämtliche Artikel wurden eingescannt bzw. neu eingetippt. Dabei wurde großer Wert darauf gelegt, die originale Schreibweise beizubehalten, nur offensichtliche Druckfehler wurden der besseren Lesbarkeit wegen korrigiert und bestimmte formale Aspekte wie Fußnoten standardisiert. Alle Endnoten wurden einheitlich in Fußnoten umgewandelt.

Wir haben uns bemüht, die wichtigsten Aufsätze und gerade auch die zum Teil schwer zugänglichen persönlich gehaltenen Artikel aufzunehmen. Dennoch sind in dieser Sammlung nicht alle Schriften John Hennigs, die deutsch-irische Themen berühren, enthalten. Das hätte einen zweiten Band erforderlich gemacht (und schon dieser Band nahm einen wesentlich größeren Umfang an als geplant) und zu viele inhaltliche Wiederholungen mit sich gebracht. Nicht enthalten sind neben Rezensionen (die aber in der angefügten Auswahlbibliographie aufgeführt sind) insbesondere die Artikel, zu denen man in anderen Sammlungen von Hennigs Schriften Zugang haben kann, dies gilt in besonderem Maße für Arbeiten zu Goethe und seine irischen Beziehungen, die in *Goethe and the English Speaking World*, Bern/Frankfurt u.a.: Peter Lang 1988 (mit einem Vorwort von Hans Reiss) erschienen sind. Nur 'Goethes Irlandkunde' und 'Goethe's Personal Relations with Ireland' wurden als unverzichtbare Grundlagenaufsätze aufgenommen, die anderen hier abgedruckten drei Artikel zu Goethe sind nicht in der Sammlung von 1988 erschienen.

Mit der Bezeichnung 'deutsch-irisch' übernehmen wir die Definition vom Zentrum für deutsch-irische Studien an der Universität Limerick, die ausdrücklich erklärt, dass dieser Ausdruck alle Kontakte zwischen Irland und den deutschsprachigen Ländern einschliesst, also insbesondere Österreich, Deutschland und die deutschsprachige Schweiz.

Wir wünschen allen Lesern dieser Ausgabe von John Hennigs Schriften viel Vergnügen bei der Lektüre.

Limerick und Galway, Oktober 2001

Gisela Holfter und Hermann Rasche

II Versuch einer Annäherung

> *John Hennig, who to all intents and purposes*
> *created the field of Irish-German literary relations*
> P. O'Neill, Ireland and Germany, 1985

In diesem Buch geht es um einen in vieler Hinsicht bemerkenswerten Menschen. John[1] Hennig zeigte offensichtliches Interesse und große Begabung für wissenschaftliche Arbeit, unterrichtete und forschte gerne und veröffentlichte hunderte von Schriften. Viele von ihnen schaffen Grundlagen auf verschiedenen Wissensgebieten, vor allem in der Geschichts-, Literatur- und Liturgiewissenschaft. Ein Akademiker par excellence – der diese Arbeit aber lebenslang nur als Nebenbeschäftigung betreiben konnte.

Nachdem er wegen Hitler 1939 ins Exil gehen musste und in Irland Aufnahme fand, wurden die vielfältigen Beziehungen zwischen der neuen Heimat und dem Herkunfts-land zu einem seiner Forschungsschwerpunkte.

Seine Schwester Erica erinnert sich an gelegentliche Äußerungen John Hennigs, der sagte, dass er "eigentlich nicht recht wüßte, warum er soviel schriebe, da ja so wenige Leute daran interessiert wären (…) und er ja doch bald mit seiner Forschungsarbeit in Vergessenheit geraten würde".[2]

Das ist jedoch zum Glück nicht der Fall. Es gibt verschiedene Sammlungen seiner Aufsätze.[3] Auch auf dem hier genauer beleuchteten Gebiet der deutsch-irischen Stu-dien gibt es Verweise auf ihn.[4] Trotz dieser begrenzten Anerkennung sind jedoch die

---

1   Unmittelbar nach seiner Ankunft in Irland anglisierte Hennig seinen Vornamen Johannes (Hans) zu John.

2   Brief Erica Becker, Ardross, Western Australia, 4.12.2000.

3   Eine davon, John Hennig, *Literatur und Existenz – Ausgewählte Aufsätze* (Heidelberg: C. Winter 1980) wurde noch von ihm selbst zusammengestellt. Weitere Sammlungen sind: John Hennig, *Goethes Europakunde*, Amsterdam: Rodopi 1987 (mit einem Vorwort von Karl Pesta-lozzi und einer Einleitung von John Hennig), John Hennig, *Goethe and the English Speaking World*, Bern/Frankfurt u.a.: Peter Lang 1988 (mit einem Vorwort von Hans Reiss); John Hennig: *Medieval Ireland, Saints and Martyrologies,* hrsg. v. M. Richter, Northampton: Variorum Reprints 1989; John Hennig, Liturgie gestern und heute, Bd. 1 u. 2, o.O. 1989 (Privat-druck, 1184 Seiten, mit Einführung von Angelus Häußling 'John Hennigs Beitrag zur Liturgie-wissenschaft' und dem Kapitel zur Liturgie aus John Hennigs im Privatdruck erschienenen Autobiographie *Die bleibende Statt*). Eine große Hilfe bei allen Arbeiten über Hennig ist die von Emanuel v. Severus OSB erstellte Bibliographie Dr. phil. Dr. phil. h.c. John Hennig 1932-1970, *Archiv für Liturgiewissenschaft*, Bd. 13, 1971, S. 141-171, die 1978 auf den aktuellen Stand gebracht wurde (*Archiv für Liturgiewissenschaft*, Bd. 19, 1978, S. 98-105) mit der Ergänzung von Angelus A. Häußling OSB zu 1971-1976 und Hennigs Veröffentlichungen von 1977-1986 sowie einem Register der behandelten Themen (*Archiv für Liturgiewissenschaft*, Bd. 28, Heft 2, 1986, S. 235-245).

4   Z. B. Patrick O'Neill, *Ireland and Germany. A Study in Literary Relations*, New York: Peter Lang 1985; Joseph Leerssen, *Mere Irish & Fíor Ghael.* Amsterdam/Philadelphia: John Benja-mins 1986; Timothy Jackson, Die getouften von über mer – Zum Irland-Bild im deutschen

4

meisten seiner Aufsätze nur unter großen Schwierigkeiten zu bekommen und seine Forschungsleistungen finden sich gerade noch in den Verweisen auf ein paar – wenngleich grundlegende – Artikel. Die Anzahl und Vielfalt seiner Publikationen ist nur sehr wenigen Fachleuten bekannt, oft ist selbst den an deutsch-irischen Themen Interessierten sein Name nicht geläufig. Das hat verschiedene Gründe – so zum Beispiel die zahlreichen Publikationsorte (allein in die vorliegende Sammlung haben wir Artikel aus rund vierzig Zeitungen und Zeitschriften aufgenommen, dazu kommen Buchauszüge und unveröffentlichte Schriften); auch seine freischaffende Tätigkeit, ohne den Rückhalt einer akademischen Institution, kam erschwerend hinzu.

Max und Johanna Hennig im Jahr ihrer Silberhochzeit, Leipzig 1926 (von W. Hennig, Stolberg)

Bemerkenswert ist ebenfalls die Bandbreite der Themen in seinen Schriften. Ein Leser seiner wissenschaftlichen Arbeiten würde kaum vermuten, dass er auch Verfasser von Traktaten war, in denen man Tipps für Krankheitsfälle oder die bevorstehende Hochzeit finden konnte ("… don't forget to brush your eyebrows and lashes as a very last contribution to perfect grooming" aus: *The Bride's Book*, Dublin). Hennig selbst

---

Mittelalter, in: Y. Shichiji (Hg), *Orientalismus, Exotismus, koloniale Diskurse*, Bd. 7, München: Iudicium 1991, S. 263-274; Doris Dohmen, *Das deutsche Irlandbild*, Amsterdam/Atlanta: Rodopi, 1994; Gisela Holfter, *Erlebnis Irland – Deutsche Reiseberichte im 20. Jahrhundert*, Trier: WVT 1996; Joachim Fischer, *Das Deutschlandbild der Iren 1890-1939*, Heidelberg: C. Winter 2000.

spricht in seiner im Privatdruck veröffentlichten Autobiographie *Die bleibende Statt*[5] von einer "bedenklich vielseitigen nebenberuflichen schriftstellerischen Tätigkeit" (Statt, 11).

Das Haus in der Auenstraße 2 (von W. Hennig)

Hennig kam am 3. März 1911 als viertes Kind seiner Eltern Max Hennig (geboren 10.12.1871 in Meißen an der Elbe) und Johanna Clemen (geboren 12.6.1877 in Grimma an der Mulde) in Leipzig zur Welt und wurde auf die Namen Paul Gottfried Johannes getauft – und meist Hans genannt. Die Familie wohnte bei seiner Geburt in der Funkenburgstraße und zog im Oktober 1912 in die Auenstrasse 2. Vater Max Hennig hatte vor seiner Lehrertätigkeit über A.E. Biedermanns Psychologie der religiösen Erkenntnis promoviert, er bekam Titel und Rang als Professor in der 4. Klasse der Hofrangordnung und war als Religions- und Hebräischlehrer am König Albert Gymnasium tätig. Seine Mutter, die Max Hennig über seinen Studienfreund Otto Clemen kennengelernt hatte, war Diakonisse gewesen und hatte eine Vorliebe für

---

5   Von der Familie zum 76. Geburtstag am 3. März 1987 veröffentlicht. Der Titel bezieht sich auf eine Bibelstelle, Hebräerbrief, 13,14 "Denn wir haben hier keine bleibende Statt, sondern wir suchen die zukünftige". Für Hennig war die Kirche seine einzige 'bleibende Statt' in den vielfachen Wendungen seines Lebens (Statt, 9). Die darin enthaltenen zwei Kapitel über Irland werden in diesem Band abgedruckt, siehe Kap. III.

pietistische Gottesdienste. Das Familienleben war geprägt von großer Religiosität, Büchern und Sparsamkeit.[6]

Als Kleinkind erlebte Hennig den 1. Weltkrieg, später gehörte er als Schüler der berühmten Thomasschule dem Schulchor der Externen an. Herausragende Wesenszüge sind sein Talent, sein Fleiß und eine enorme Arbeitsfähigkeit. In den Erinnerungen seines sechs Jahre älteren Bruders Ernst heißt es, dass "der sehr begabte 'kleine Bruder' die letzte Grundschulklasse 5 übersprang und im Gegensatz zu seinen Brüdern in nur 12 Jahren das vorgeschriebene Pensum bis zum Abitur absolvierte".[7] Auch nach Meinung seiner vier Jahre jüngeren Schwester Erica war er der "weitaus klügste von uns 5 Geschwistern, in allem was er tat und sagte, reif und sicher, überaus selbständig und sicher denkend, kritisch analysierend schon als junger Mensch".[8] Aber Hennig merkte auch, dass er oft nicht Teil seiner gleichaltrigen Umwelt war. Schon in der Jugendbewegung fühlte er sich vereinsamt (Statt, 53), in der Schule war er sich "seiner Isolation schmerzlich bewusst". Er sah sich aber nicht als den "Eigenbrötler", für den ihn seine Klassenkameraden hielten (Statt, 58). In einem Brief an seinen ältesten Bruder Karl im Jahr 1981 schreibt er: "Es kam aber auch die politische Isolierung dazu, denn (…) ich [war] ja seit 1924 (Jamboree in Kopenhagen) radikaler Pazifist."[9] Nach seiner inneren Distanzierung von der Jugendbewegung, in die er durch seine älteren Brüder gekommen war, begann er auf eigene Faust Radtouren zu unternehmen. Die erste große Fahrt mit 15 Jahren führte durch die sächsische Schweiz nach Böhmen. Im Jahr darauf folgte eine Radtour durch Nordbayern und das Rheinland ('Deutsche Dome'),[10] dazu kamen sonntägliche Radtouren, als Ausgleich zur anstrengenden Woche. Die war neben der Schule schon früh ausgefüllt mit Extraarbeiten – ab dem 14. Lebensjahr gab Hennig täglich zwei bis vier Stunden Privatunterricht an Jüngere, und erinnert sich später, dass er bereits mit 16 Jahren in die Deutsche Bücherei durfte, wo er oft bis 10 Uhr abends las und dann erst die Hausaufgaben machte (Statt, 56). Und man spürt noch seine Freude darüber, nach dem Abitur in den Ferien "ganz der Deutschen Bücherei zu leben", er las erstmals Jaspers' *Philosophie* und Joyces

---

6   "'Kinder, lasst nichts umkommen!' Wie oft haben wir das zu hören bekommen. Alle Rester (sic) wurden verwertet, und die unglaublichsten Gerichte entstanden dann noch, um die vielen hungrigen Münder sattzumachen. (…) Nicht anders war es bei unserer Kleidung. Vater und Mutter trugen ohne Rücksicht auf die Meinung ihrer Mitmenschen jahrelang längst verbrauchte Mäntel, Hüte (!) und Schuhe, nur um uns Heranwachsenden das dringend Nötige zu ermöglichen", Ernst Hennig, *Wir fünf Henniggeschwister und unsere Mutter*, S. 11 (19 Seiten, ohne Jahr, maschinenschriftlich (dankenswerterweise von Wolfgang Hennig, Stolberg, zur Verfügung gestellt worden).

7   Ernst Hennig, *Unsere Eltern – Ein Lebensbild niedergeschrieben von Ernst 1978*, S. 12, o.O. o.J. 42 S. maschinengetippt (Privatbesitz Wolfgang Hennig, Stolberg).

8   Brief Erica Becker, 4.12.2000

9   Brief John Hennig an Karl Hennig, 19.2.1981 (dankenswerterweise von Wolfgang Hennig, Stolberg überlassen).

10 Seine Fahrtenbücher mit Erlebnisbeschreibungen, Skizzen und vielen historischen Beobachtungen sind im Exilarchiv Frankfurt im Nachlass von John Hennig erhalten.

Ulysses, zwei Werke, die aus sehr verschiedenen Gründen sein Leben mitbestimmen sollten (Statt, 64).

Studienzeit

In Bonn, seinem ersten Studienort, verbrachte er das Winter- und Sommersemester 1929/30. Hennig begann mit dem Studium der neuen Sprachen, Deutsch, Englisch und Französisch, sein Hauptinteresse aber galt der Philosophie. Unterkunft "in dem wunderbar am Rhein gelegenen Hause" (Statt, 70) bot ihm die Familie seines Onkels Paul Clemen. Während seiner Studienzeit in Bonn, Berlin und Leipzig erlebte er zahlreiche Kapazitäten der universitären Welt; die Liste seiner akademischen Lehrer liest sich wie eine Auflistung bekannter Wissenschaftler seiner Zeit.[11] Und während seines Studiums in Bonn lernte er bei seinen Verwandten auch viele Größen aus Kunst, Wissenschaft und Wirtschaft kennen – sein Onkel Paul Clemen, war vielseits geachteter Professor für Kunstgeschichte an der Universität – aber er blieb "bedrückt" (Statt, 70). Allerdings muss es auch sehr positive Erlebnisse gegeben haben, denn in seiner Bonner Zeit kam es zu der schicksalhaften Begegnung mit Kläre Meyer, die dort Kunstgeschichte studierte und über eine Verwandte mit Paul Clemen bekannt war. An seinen Bruder Karl[12] schrieb er darüber kurz vor seinem siebzigsten Geburtstag,

---

11 Eine Auflistung in dem Lebenslauf, der seinen Promotionsunterlagen beigefügt ist, gibt genaue Auskunft: Evangelische Religionskunde: Hoelscher (Bonn), Stoltenburg (Berlin), Leipoldt, Alt (Leipzig) / Philosophie: Rothacker, Landsberg (Bonn), Spranger (Berlin), Driesch, Litt, Wach (Leipzig) / Pädagogik: Feldmann (Bonn), Spranger (Berlin), Boehm, Litt (Leipzig) / Psychologie: Graf v. Duerckheim (Leipzig) / Deutsch: Walzel, Quint (Bonn), Hermann, Petersen, Alewyn (Berlin), Frings, Karg, Korff (Leipzig) / Englisch: Quint, Schirmer (Bonn) / Französisch: Menzerath, Curtius (Bonn) / Geschichte: Levison, Braubach (Bonn), Oncken (Berlin), Berve, Brandenburg, Hellmann, Scholz, Stimming (Leipzig) / Kunstgeschichte: P. Clemen (Bonn), Waetzoldt, Woelfflin (Berlin), Beenken (Leipzig). Universitätsarchiv Leipzig, Phil Fak Prom 1430.

In der *Bleibenden Statt* werden auch seine Beziehungen zu Levison hervorgehoben, der später ebenfalls ins Exil flüchten mußte. In einem privaten Rückblick schreibt er seinem Bruder Karl: "Von meinen Universitätslehrern hat mich am meisten Erich Rothacker, der leider später ein Nazi war, beeinflusst. Litt überhaupt nicht, obwohl er mein "Doktorvater" war, Wach kaum. Ein grossartiger Mann war der Historiker Hellmann, und auch der Alttestamentler Alt. Dankbar für Verständnis bin ich Leipoldt und Witkowski (Germanist)." Brief John Hennig an Karl Hennig, 19.2.1981 (Privatbesitz Wolfgang Hennig, Stolberg).

12 Karl Hennig (1903-1992), evangelischer Theologe, studierte Theologie, Philosophie, Germanistik und Geschichte in Leipzig und Köln, zusätzlich zum Abschluß seiner Promotionen in Philosophie und Theologie im Jahr 1929 erwarb er den Master of Sacred Theology während seiner Zeit in Hartford/Conneticut, wo er 1930/1931 Austauschtheologe war. Nach drei Jahren als Pfarrer und Religionslehrer in Leipzig übernahm er eine Stelle in Antwerpen, 1938 dann die Pfarrstelle der Gemeinden Eupen-Malmedy und St. Vith. 1945 mußte er Belgien verlassen trotz der Anstrengungen von Nicole Limbosch, einer Freundin von John Hennigs Schwiegervater Felix Meyer. Von 1946-1968 war er Pfarrer in Stolberg, Aachen. Vgl. Matthias Wolfes, Karl Hennig, in: Biographisch-Bibliographisches Kirchenlexikon, Bd. XVII, Herzberg: Traugott Bautz 2000, Sp. 637-638 (www.bautz.de/bbkl) und Briefe Felix Meyer, 30.7., 12.8., 24.8., 26.8.1945 (Exilarchiv Frankfurt). Vgl. auch Amelis von Mettenheim, *Felix Meyer 1875-1950 – Erfinder und Menschenretter*, Peter Lang: Frankfurt a.M. 1998, S. 114.

"das für meinen Lebensweg entscheidendste Ereignis war natürlich die Begegnung mit Claire" und betrachtete das Ganze als "wie der gute Adalbert Stifter sagt, reine Fügung".[13] Zu dem Zeitpunkt der Begegnung stand Hennig gerade erst vor seinem 19. Geburtstag, Kläre war vier Jahre älter. Vom Familienhintergrund her waren beide sehr verschieden – Claire, wie sie ab der Dubliner Zeit hieß, kam aus einer gut situierten jüdischen Familie, die ihre finanzielle Sorgenlosigkeit den ca. 250 Patenten und technischen Entwicklungen des Vaters Felix Meyer verdankte.[14] Trotz aller Unterschiede war es für Hennig schon nach wenigen Monaten klar, dass er die Frau seines Lebens gefunden hatte und schrieb entsprechend nach Hause (er hatte Claire bereits beim ersten gemeinsamen Tanz gesagt, sie wüsste wohl nicht, dass er sie heiraten wolle, worauf er die kaum überraschende Antwort bekam "Du bist wohl verrückt?" (Statt, 95).

John und Claire Hennig, geb. Meyer, ca. 1936 (von M. Schefold)

---

13   Brief John Hennig an Karl Hennig, 19.2.1981, s.o..

14   Vgl. Amelis von Mettenheim, *Felix Meyer 1875-1950 – Erfinder und Menschenretter*, Peter Lang: Frankfurt a.M. 1998, S. 21ff. Er entwickelte u.a. die Rotameter, die die Durchflussmenge und -geschwindigkeiten von Gasen und Flüssigkeiten genau ermittelte, sowie die automatische Herstellung von Ampullen, Serülen und Venülen (vgl. ebd. S. 25f).

Aber schon nach einem Semester der Bekanntschaft ging Hennig nach Berlin, wo er sich auf Anraten seines Vaters, aber sicherlich auch aus eigenem Interesse, für evangelische Religionskunde einschrieb, um ein eventuelles Ausweichen in den Kirchendienst möglich zu machen. Die Beziehung zu Claire wurde durch sporadische Besuche und vor allem durch zahllose Briefe aufrecht erhalten.

Ein weiteres Beispiel seiner zuvor erwähnten Außenseiterrolle im politischen Bereich wird in seiner Autobiographie beschrieben in seiner Zeit an der Berliner Universität (wenige Jahre vor der Machtergreifung), als Gruppenbildung und Radikalisierung unter den Studenten fast selbstverständlich waren, gehörte er keiner Gruppe an, auf Werbungsversuche antwortete er unwillig: "Lassen Sie mich, ich bin ein Einspänner" (Statt, 75).

Nach seinem Studienaufenthalt in Berlin kehrte Hennig im Wintersemester 1930/31 nach Leipzig zurück um dort sein Studium fortzusetzen. Es kann als sicher angesehen werden, dass er zu dieser Zeit eine akademische Laufbahn anstrebte. Der frühe Tod des Vaters, nach unglücklich verlaufener Gehirntumoroperation am 5.7.1931, traf ihn sehr, und er beschloss der beruflichen Absicherung wegen zusätzlich zur Promotion seine Staatsexamina abzulegen. Am letzten Tage seines achten Semesters, wenige Wochen nach Anbruch des 'Dritten Reiches', reichte er zum frühestmöglichen Termin seine Staatsexamensarbeit und seine Dissertation ein. In seiner Promotion hatte er sich mit "Lebensbegriff und Lebenskategorie – Studien zur Geschichte und Theorie der geisteswissenschaftlichen Begriffsbildung mit besonderer Berücksichtigung Wilhelm Diltheys" auseinandergesetzt. Diese Arbeit hatte er beim Religionsphilosophen Joachim Wach[15] begonnen und bei Theodor Litt[16] zu Ende geführt. Litt äußerte sich sehr wohlwollend in seiner Beurteilung, allerdings mit kritischen Anmerkungen:

> Es liegt hier eine Dissertation vor, die, was den Umfang des verarbeiteten Stoffs und wohl auch die Bedeutung der behandelten Probleme angeht, sich der Höhenlage einer Habilitationsschrift anzunähern scheint. (...) Indem er aber, auf Grund einer bei einem 8. Semester kaum glaublichen Belesenheit, in allen Epochen der Philosophie –, ja der ganzen Wissenschaftsgeschichte Parallelen, Vordeutungen, Fortbildungen aufzuspüren weiss, breitet er sehr viel mehr an Materialien und Zusammenhängen vor dem Leser auf, als das Thema vermuten lässt. (...) Insoweit scheint also die Arbeit der höchsten Prädizierung würdig zu sein. Allein es läßt sich nicht leugnen, dass man der gerühmten Vorzüge nicht immer recht froh werden kann. Es ist nicht zu übersehen, dass dieses Herumwühlen in einem massenhaften ideengeschichtlichen Material in mehr als einer Hinsicht etwas Unjugendliches hat. Man möchte einem so begabten jungen Menschen etwas weniger Materialbeherrschung und etwas mehr Mut zu einer eigenen Entnetzung wünschen. Nicht als ob es an geistiger Durchdringung des Stoffes fehlte! (...) So hinterlässt die Arbeit einen zwiespältigen Eindruck, und es fällt schwer, ihr in der Prädizierung wirklich gerecht zu werden.

---

15   Joachim Wach (Chemnitz 1898 - Orselina 1955), deutscher Religionssoziologe; 1929-1935 Professor für Religionswissenschaft an der Universität Leipzig, 1935 vorzeitig emeritiert (seine Mutter war eine geborene Mendelssohn-Bartholdi), ging ins Exil in die USA, zunächst an die Brown University in Providence/Rhode Island und 1945/6 an die University of Chicago.

16   Theodor Litt (Düsseldorf 1880 - Bonn 1962), deutscher Philosoph und Pädagoge; 1920-1937 und 1945-1947 Professor der Philosophie an der Universität Leipzig; wurde 1937 vorzeitig emeritiert.

Ermisst man die <u>Gesamtleistung</u> als solche und zieht man zum Vergleich heran, was sonst in Dissertationen geleistet wird, so scheint mir, trotz der geäusserten Bedenken, die Zensur

I (Sehr gut)

dem Kand. nicht verweigert werden zu dürfen. Eine Umarbeitung zu fordern scheint mir unmöglich, da diese bei der Überfülle des verarbeiteten und mit unendlichem Fleiss zusammengetragenen Materials eine untragbare Mühsal bedeuten würde. 25.3.33 Litt[17]

Der Zweitgutachter Felix Krueger[18] hatte allerdings in wichtigen Punkten andere Auffassungen. Zwar gibt es am Anfang weitgehende Übereinstimmung in der grundsätzlichen Einschätzung der Fähigkeiten des Kandidaten,[19] aber er kommt bei der Beurteilung der Arbeit zu einem deutlich anderen Ergebnis. Krueger kritisiert, dass die "Vielwisserei" in Missverhältnis zu Lebensalter und Studienzeit Hennigs stände, und spricht von seiner "schwache(n) Gestaltungskraft," seiner geringen "geistige(n) Kapazität" (was eigentlich seiner ersten Einschätzung widersprach). Besonders übel nimmt er eine angeblich mangelnde Kenntnis der Fortschritte der "psychologische(n) und biologische(n) Forschung. Hinter seinen vielen Büchern, zumeist über Bücher, wirft er kaum einen Blick auf die zugehörenden <u>Wirklichkeit</u>."[20] Ob man hier schon einen Einfluss nationalsozialistischer Ideen erkennen kann, ist kaum mehr festzustellen, sicher kann man aber vermuten, dass Krueger als Gründer der "Leipziger Schule" der Psychologie eng definierte Meinungen seines Spezialgebiets vertrat. Hennig schreibt von den möglichen politischen Hintergründen der kritischen Beurteilung, von denen er über seinen Bruder hörte, und zwar, dass Krueger die von dem "'Halbjuden Wach' inspirierte" Promotion ablehne (Statt, 100). Die Kritik Kruegers, Hennigs Darstellung erzeuge beim Leser "das Gefühl des Gehetztwerdens" klingt nachvollziehbar. Man muss sich dazu nur die Umstände vergegenwärtigen, unter denen sie verfasst wurde. Eine systematische Überarbeitung war für ihn überhaupt nicht möglich (man sollte sich auch erinnern, dass man im Zeitalter bevor Computer vieles erleichterten, keine schnellen Verbesserungen einfügen konnte), denn er war unter extremer Zeitnot, gleichzeitig das Staatsexamen zu machen, und außerdem betrafen ihn die politischen Veränderungen unmittelbar im persönlichen Bereich. In *Die bleibende Statt* beschreibt er, wie die Dissertation entstand. Er hatte sie zuletzt direkt in die Maschine diktiert. Die Frau, die für ihn tippte, sagte eines Tages: "Sehen Sie da, die Frau? Die hat einen Juden zum Geliebten". Zwei Tage später berichtete sie, die Frau und ihr Geliebter seien verhaftet worden (Statt, 97). Für Hennig, der natürlich an seine jüdische Verlobte dachte, muss dieser zusätzliche Druck enorm gewesen sein. Es muss ihm klar gewesen sein, dass er nach einer Heirat mit Claire keine Chance auf eine akademische Karriere

---

17 Universitätsarchiv Leipzig, Phil Fak Prom 1430 Johannes Hennig.

18 Felix Krueger (Posen 1874 - Basel 1948), deutscher Philosoph und Psychologe, Gründer der Leipziger Schule der Psychologie; 1917-1938 ordentlicher Professor der Philosophie und Psychologie an der Universität Leipzig.

19 "Der Charakteristik des I. Referats kann ich großenteils zustimmen. Der Candidat ist über Durchschnitt begabt, sonderlich mit geistiger Beweglichkeit und Ansprechbarkeit, zumal auf neueste kulturphilosophische Lehrmeinungen und ihre vielerlei Farben. Er hat ungeheuer viel, auch mit Verständnis gelesen." Universitätsarchiv Leipzig, Phil Fak Prom Hennig 1430.

20 Ebd.

mehr haben würde (bereits 1932 war ihm klar, dass auch der Kirchendienst mit einer jüdischen Pfarrersfrau nicht möglich war (Statt, 97)). Als er kurz darauf ein Photo in einer Zeitung sah, das einen Mann mit dem Schild zeigte: "Ich habe eine Judensau gehurt", schrieb er ihr, es sei höchste Zeit, wenn sie noch heiraten wollten. Mitten in den Vorbereitungen für das mündliche Staatsexamen fuhr er am 10.4.1933 mit dem Nachtzug nach Aachen, heiratete Claire am 11.4. auf dem Standesamt und fuhr alleine mit dem nächsten Nachtzug zurück nach Leipzig (Statt, 97f).

Inwieweit Krueger von der anstehenden Hochzeit wusste, ist nicht bekannt.[21] Er beantragte die Rückgabe zur Umarbeitung am 13.4.1933. Daraufhin beantragte Litt seinerseits, die Arbeit mit der Note II anzunehmen und dementsprechend wurde die Dissertation der Philosophischen Fakultät zur Abstimmung vorgelegt. Die daraufhin folgenden Stellungnahmen der Professoren sind erhalten und sind eine aufschlussreiche Lektüre. Die Zustimmungen für den Antrag Kruegers, dass die Arbeit zurückgegeben werden sollte, klingen ebenso interessant wie die Befürwortungen der Annahme. So heißt es beispielsweise: "Nach langem Überlegen und vielem Herumlesen in der Arbeit muss ich mich im Ganzen dem Urteil und der Forderung der Herren Krueger, Volkelt und Junker anschliessen" aufgrund des "Schwelgen(s) in Gedankengespinsten, dem sich der mir persönlich bekannte, als Mensch ganz treffliche junge Verfasser hingegeben hat". Auch die Befürwortungen klingen ambivalent:

> "Der K. ist mir als Teilnehmer meiner Uebungen und aus persönlichem Verkehr ziemlich gut bekannt. Die gegen seine Arbeit vorgebrachten Einwände decken sich mit meinem Eindruck von seiner Persönlichkeit (...) Aus diesem Grunde kann ich aber nicht für "Rückgabe zur Umarbeitung" stimmen, denn keine Umarbeitung kann die Anstöße, die nur scheinbar äußerer Art sind, beseitigen. Der K. müßte sich selber verleugnen, wollte er den ausgesprochenen Wünschen wirklich Rechnung tragen (...) Es ist daher über die Arbeit in der vorliegenden Form zu entscheiden: Annahme oder Ablehnung? Da die unbestritten hohen geistigen Qualitäten des K. und die anerkennenswerte Größe seiner Leistung eine Ablehnung, wie mir scheint, unmöglich machen, stimme ich dem Antrag des Herrn Litt zu."[22]

Am häufigsten aber waren Enthaltungen ("Da ich über die Arbeit, auch bei eingehender Beschäftigung mit ihr, schwerlich ein Urteil gewinnen kann, enthalte ich mich der Stimme").

Das Ergebnis waren 12 Stimmen für die Annahme mit der Note II, 6 Stimmen für die Rückgabe zur Umarbeitung und 26 Professoren enthielten sich. Die mündliche Prüfung am 20.7.1933 war danach, wie sich Hennig erinnert, "eine Farce" (Statt, 100). Bei Helmut Berve bekam er ein 'gut' in Alter Geschichte (die Kenntnisse der Augustinischen Zeit scheinen nicht so hervorragend gewesen zu sein), während Litt bei seiner Note ("Sehr gut") noch einmal schriftlich niederlegte, dass auch die mündliche Prüfung sein günstiges Urteil über die Dissertation "durchaus bestätigt" (Hervorhebung im Original). Auch in Deutsch bei Georg Witkowski, dem Doktorvater Erich Kästners,

---

21 Hennig hatte an Wach geschrieben und ihm mitgeteilt, warum er eine akademische Laufbahn nicht mehr ins Auge fasste, über Wach hatte sich die Nachricht schnell in der Universität herumgesprochen (Statt, 99).

22 Universitätsarchiv Leipzig, Phil Fak Prom Hennig 1430.

schloss er mit "sehr gut" ab (die Erinnerung an gerade diese Prüfung, die für Witkowski, der danach aus politischen Gründen entlassen wurde, die letzte war, kann in *Die bleibende Statt* nachgelesen werden).[23]

Nachdem also keinerlei Aussicht auf eine akademische Karriere mehr bestand, ergab sich für Hennig die Notwendigkeit der Arbeitssuche. Sein Schwiegervater bot ihm an, in seine Firma in Aachen einzutreten. Die Familie Claires bot Hennig "freundliche aber zurückhaltende" Aufnahme. Der Vater wünschte seinen Töchtern eigentlich jüdische Männer, "da er der festen Überzeugung war, dass nur bei ihnen eine Frau davor sicher sein kann, nicht geprügelt zu werden" (Statt, 96). Auch Hennigs Studien hatte er kritisch gegenübergestanden, er brachte ihnen "eine nur schlecht verhehlte Verachtung entgegen" (Statt, 98). Die Aufnahme Claires in die Hennigfamilie scheint problemlos gewesen zu sein – "Claire became soon the darling of all of us. Her precious personality, warm, generous, very understanding, loving. We adored her ...".[24] Auch die Briefe von Mutter Hennig aus den 30er Jahren klingen sehr herzlich und lassen eine große Nähe erkennen, beispielsweise wenn sie an Claire ("mein Klärchen") schreibt: "Deine Schilderung über Hans' Begeisterung, als er in dem Jesuitenseminar die wunderbare Bibliothek entdeckte, kann ich mir lebhaft vorstellen. An Deiner Stelle hätte ich auch Sorge gehabt, ob er sich überhaupt von dort trennen würde!"[25] Ein Interesse an anderen Religionen und philosophischen Fragestellungen hatte es auch schon beim Vater gegeben, der, wie sich Ernst erinnert, lebhaft am jüdischen Geistesleben interessiert gewesen war.[26]

Hennigs neues Arbeitsumfeld, die Firma Deutsche Rotawerke GmbH, die sich auf die Fertigung von Präzisionsmaschinen spezialisierte und viele von Felix Meyers Patenten produzierte, war 1909 von diesem gegründet und 1937 in 'Rota Apparate- und Maschinenbau Felix Meyer KG' umgewandelt worden. Felix Meyer, Claires Vater, war ge-

---

23 Hennigs eigene Erinnerungen an die Umstände seiner Promotion sind unscharf. In *Die bleibende Statt* erklärt er: "Ich bin sicher, dass nicht einer der Befragten auch nur eine Zeile meiner Arbeit gelesen hat. Es war eine Abstimmung Nazis gegen Nichtnazis. Mit einer Stimme Mehrheit wurde meine Dissertation angenommen." (Statt, 100). Dagegen schreibt er in der Betrachtung 'Some Thoughts on Examinations' (in der vorliegenden Sammlung in Kapitel IV enthalten): "No less than three of the professors under whom I had made special studies, were thus liquidated. They were permitted though to finish the examination of candidates they had already taken on. In my thesis I had voiced some criticism at Rosenberg's theory of history, and one of the two referees refused to accept my thesis on political grounds. In accordance with the university rules, a thesis on which the referees failed to agree had to be submitted to the whole staff of that particular faculty or school. This happened very rarely, but, in my case, as this was a secret ballot it afforded an unexpected chance of expressing academic disapproval of the new masters. (...) The great vote, which of course was ridiculously in my favour, made the subsequent oral a mere farce." *Hibernia*, Mai 1949, S. 13f.

24 Brief Erica Becker, 12.7.2001.

25 *'Unsere Eltern' – Ein Lebensbild niedergeschrieben von Ernst* (Hennig) 1978, S. 34f (Anhang mit Briefen) Brief Johanna Hennig 5.12.1935 an die drei Söhne und Schwiegertöchter (Privatbesitz Wolfgang Hennig, Stolberg).

26 Ebd., S. 22.

schätzt und geachtet als ein ideenreicher Erfinder und Kaufmann, er entstammte einer seit dem 16. Jahrhundert in Westfalen nachweisbaren jüdischen Familie, die seit dem frühen 19. Jahrhundert in Aachen ansässig war. Er war aufgewachsen in einem liberalen jüdischen Elternhaus, eingebettet in der "Tradition der klassischen deutschen Kultur" (Statt, 98). Selbst als die Anti-Judengesetze verschärft wurden, wollte er bis zur 'Reichskristallnacht' nicht glauben, dass ihm etwas passieren könne. Auf Hennigs Vorschlag, auszuwandern, hatte er nur unwirsch reagiert.[27] Für Hennig war klar, dass er mit der Annahme des Angebots, in die Firma des Schwiegervaters einzutreten, schweren Jahren entgegengehe, "unvorbereitet, abhängig und hoffnungslos" (Statt, 98). Der Kontrast zwischen seinem bisherigen Leben und Hintergrund und dem neuen Leben im großbürgerlichen Hause seiner Schwiegereltern war beträchtlich. 1935 zog das junge Paar dann in den schlossähnlichen Besitz Bodenhof[28] gegenüber dem Haus seiner Schwiegereltern, wo die beiden ersten Töchter Gabriele und Monica 1936 und 1938 geboren wurden. Hennigs hatten zwei Hausmädchen und es gab auch einen zur Firma gehörenden Chauffeur (Statt, 106).

Dieser begüterten und scheinbar sorgenlosen Situation, wenngleich für Hennig mit großer Abhängigkeit verbunden, stand der spürbar wachsende politische Druck entgegen. Im Frühjahr 1938 musste Claire ihren Anteil an der Firma auf ihren nicht-jüdischen Ehemann übertragen; im Juli 1938 trat Felix Meyer als Komplementär aus und Hennig und eine langjährige Mitarbeiterin in der Firma wurden stattdessen zu Komplementären. Die nationalsozialistischen Machthaber verlangten, dass im Zuge der ‚Arisierung' auch ein ihnen Nahestehender in die Gesellschaft aufgenommen würde. Felix Meyer wurde am 10. November kurzzeitig verhaftet, das Betreten des Betriebes, auf dessen Eingang Angestellte schon ein großes Hakenkreuz gemalt hatten, wurde ihm verboten. Anfang Februar 1939 gestattete man ihm die Ausreise nach Belgien, woher seine Gattin stammte. Sie ließen sich in Le Zoute nieder. Die Auflage war, dass Hennig und seine Familie dafür zu bürgen hatten, dass Felix Meyer im Ausland kein Konkurrenzunternehmen aufziehen würde. Am 6. Februar wurden in dem Firmennamen die Worte 'Felix Meyer' durch 'Dr. Hennig' ersetzt.[29]

In den Jahren seit seinem Eintritt in die Firma hatte es Hennig vermocht, auch neben seinem Beruf und der wachsenden Familie seinen Forschungsinteressen nachzugehen. In der evangelischen *Zeitschrift für Theologie und Kirche* veröffentlichte er 1936 eine

---

27   Vgl. Amalis von Mettenheim, *Felix Meyer*, S. 31.

28   In einem Aufsatz erinnert sich Hennig an das Haus folgendermaßen: "(...) it dated from the six-
       teenth century, with stucco ceilings and a lovely staircase" (The love of books, hier in Kap IV
       abgedruckt). Ein Photo des Bodenhofs ist neben dem Original des in diesem Buch abgedruckten
       Artikels 'Irish Footsteps in Aachen' zu sehen mit der Erklärung "Bodenhof, one of the castles
       characteristic of the Eifel mountains on the main road from Eupen to Aachen", Irish Library
       Bulletin, April 1948, S. 65.

29   Amalis von Mettenheim, Felix Meyer 1875-1950, Erfinder und Menschenretter, Frankfurt: Peter
       Lang 1998, S. 38ff.

Auseinandersetzung mit Karl Jaspers'[30] *Vernunft und Existenz.*[31] Er schickte Jaspers diesen Artikel und fuhr dann von einer Handelsmesse in Frankfurt nach Heidelberg, einer Einladung Jaspers folgend. Man verstand sich auf Anhieb. Es kam sogar zu privaten Besuchen; das Ehepaar Jaspers, für das es aufgrund der jüdischen Herkunft von Gertrud Jaspers unmöglich geworden war, anderswo Ferien zu machen, verbrachte einige Tage im Bodenhof bei Hennigs im Sommer 1939[32]. In seiner Autobiographie erklärt Hennig, dass nächst seinem Vater und Bruder Karl kein Mann auf sein Leben größeren Einfluss gehabt habe als Jaspers (Statt, 116).

Einen weiteren lebensbestimmenden Kontakt knüpfte Hennig über einen anderen ehemaligen Schüler der Leipziger Thomasschule, Heinrich Keller, der Rektor der jesuitischen Hochschule in Valkenburg in Holland (1894 - 1942) war. Hennig fasste 1936 den Entschluss zu konvertieren. Mit der Geburt der zweiten Tochter (Monica) entschloss sich auch Claire katholisch zu werden. Hennigs Konversion war für sie nicht leicht gewesen: "Als sie das Schriftstück unterzeichnen sollte, in dem wir katholische Kindererziehung versprechen mussten, war sie in Tränen ausgebrochen" (Statt, 111f). Für beide war und blieb das unterschiedliche kulturelle Erbe wichtig, etwas worauf sie stolz waren.

Über Heinrich Keller kam es zu dem ersten Kontakt mit Irland. Zu diesem Zeitpunkt war es klar, dass sie auswandern mussten und Irland bot sich als eine Möglichkeit an. Keller stellte einen irischen Jesuiten vor, der nach einem kurzen Gespräch Hennigs Englisch für ausreichend hielt, um dort Deutsch zu unterrichten, und der sich für ihn einsetzen wollte. Ein paar Tage später wurde Hennig über Valkenburg eine Karte des Rektors von Belvedere College, einem von Jesuiten geführten Jungengymnasium in Dublin, weitergeleitet: "Wenn Sie ein paar Deutschstunden bei uns geben können, zahlen wir Ihnen dreissig Schillinge pro Woche" (Statt, 117). Auf dem britischen Konsulat in Köln erhielt er ein Visum für eine Erkundungsreise nach Irland und sein Besuch in Dublin erfolgte Ostern 1939. Die ersten Eindrücke waren nicht unbedingt positiv:

> "Natürlich regnete es in Dublin. Alles war klamm und, wie mir schien, schmutzig. Der Rektor zeigte mir die Schule. Das Glanzstück war das Labor, in dem es eine richtige Wage (sic), einen Ständer mit verstaubten Reagenzgläschen und ein paar Kästen mit exotischen Pflänzlein gab. Auf dem Aussenministerium erhielt ich einen Fragebogen mit dem Bescheid, den solle ich ausfüllen, an die zuständige irische Gesandtschaft in Paris senden, dort werde man ihn prüfen und nach Dublin weiterleiten. Ich werde dann hören." (Statt, 117f)

---

30 Karl Jaspers (Oldenburg 1883 - Basel 1969), Professor für Philosophie und Psychologie in Heidelberg, 1937-1945 Lehrverbot, ging 1948 nach Basel, neben Heidegger einer der führenden Vertreter der Existenzphilosophie.

31 Das neue Denken und das neue Glauben. Eine Studie zu Karl Jaspers' "Vernunft und Existenz" in: *Zeitschrift für Theologie und Kirche*, N.F. 17, S. 30-52.

32 In *Die bleibende Statt* (S. 116) beschreibt Hennig, dass der Besuch ein Jahr nach dem Kennenlernen 1937, also im Jahr 1938 stattfindet. Dank der Auskunft von Dr. Suzanne Kirkbright, die an einer Biographie über Jaspers arbeitet und Einblick in den Briefnachlass hat, läßt sich aber mit Sicherheit sagen, dass der Besuch 1939 erfolgte.

Der angegebene Zeitraum von einigen Monaten bevor er eine Antwort erwarten könne, war für Hennig angesichts der zunehmenden Kriegserwartungen verständlicherweise keine Beruhigung. Außerdem wurde Irland nicht unbedingt empfohlen als Auswanderungsland. So traf Hennig zum Beispiel einen Geistlichen, dem er anvertraute, er beabsichtige nach Irland auszuwandern. "Sind Sie verrückt? (...) Dort haben die Leute in der rechten Rocktasche die Schnapsflasche, in der linken den Rosenkranz und in der Gesässtasche den Revolver" (Statt, 117). Ende August spitzte sich die Situation so zu, dass Claire sich zur Flucht nach Belgien entschließen musste, am 26.8.1939, wenige Tage vor Kriegsausbruch, verlässt auch Hennig Aachen und geht nach Belgien, bewusst legal, denn, wie er sagte: "Ich glaubte noch an Gesetze" (Statt, 118). Während des bedrückenden Wartens auf die längerfristige Aufenthaltserlaubnis für Irland zog er ins Haus seines Bruders Karl, der Pfarrer in Eupen war und wollte sich stellen, sobald sein Jahrgang aufgerufen würde. Am Morgen nachdem dies geschah, kam, gerade als er sich schweren Herzens nach Deutschland aufmachen wollte, die Nachricht, das Visum sei in Paris eingetroffen (vgl. den Abdruck aus den zwei Irlandkapiteln aus *Die bleibende Statt* in diesem Band).

Dieses Visum war das Ergebnis eines intensiven und ausführlichen Schriftverkehrs, der die Schwierigkeiten und bürokratischen Hürden belegte und von dem Hennig – vermutlich zu seinem Glück – nicht wusste.

Das 'Irish Co-ordinating Committee for Refugees' stellte im Sommer 1939 einen Antrag auf Gewährung einer Aufenthaltsgenehmigung für Hennig, unterzeichnet von seinem Sekretär Colum Gavin Duffy. Am 31. Juli erfolgte daraufhin eine Benachrichtigung des Justizministeriums an das Außenministerium, dass ein solcher Antrag vorläge. In dem Brief wird erklärt:

> "The Irish Co-ordinating Committee have satisfied the Minister that Johannes Hennig is a suitable person for admission and I am accordingly to request you to authorize the Legation at Berlin to grant a visa to Johannes Hennig.
>
> The Department of Industry and Commerce are granting a permit for the employment of Dr. Hennig in Belvedere College during his temporary residence in this country. The permit will be sent to the Department of External Affairs and I am to suggest that you forward it to the Legation in Berlin when informing the Legation of the authorisation for the granting of the visa."[33]

Im Brief ist Berlin nachträglich unterstrichen und an den Rand der handschriftliche Vermerk "Paris?" hinzugefügt. Auch den irischen Behörden war inzwischen klar geworden, dass ein Besuch Hennigs in Berlin wahrscheinlich nicht ratsam gewesen wäre. Hennig wiederum schreibt an die 'Irish Legation' in Paris, ob die Visa auch in Belgien ausgestellt bzw. nach dort geschickt werden könnten, so dass er sie in Brüssel abholen könne. Zusätzlich benötigte er ein Transitvisum für Großbritannien – und das würde von den britischen Stellen in Belgien nur dann gewährt, wenn die Iren ihrerseits ein Aufenthaltsvisum in die Pässe eingetragen hätten. Während für Claire die Ungewissheit zunahm – sie befand sich noch in Belgien, der Krieg war inzwischen ausgebrochen und die Gefahr, dass Belgien von deutschen Truppen besetzt würde, war groß – bekam John ein Visum ausgestellt. Er wird registriert unter der Nummer G.S.

---

33   National Archives, Department of Foreign Affairs, 202/417 (Hennig).

14548, mit der Bemerkung "permitted to land in Ireland on condition that he remains therein not later than 8. Aug. 1940".[34]

Irland

Hennigs Tagebucheintrag vom 6. Oktober 1939 beschreibt die Überfahrt nach und die ersten Eindrücke in Irland (und zwar interessanterweise auf Englisch):

> "I got a splendid berth, Schrödinger travelled 1st class. On deck people were first singing and blowing bagpipe, then they all felt seasick (...) appointment with Fr.Rector. Studienleiter. Seen the schoolhouse. I have agreed to teach interesting and objective political opinions. Letters. Supper (eggs)."[35]

Sowohl für Claire, die auf die Visa wartete, als auch für John, der sich alleine in einem fremden Land um Unterkunft und Verdienst kümmern musste und nicht wusste, wann und ob Frau und Kinder aus Belgien nachkommen konnten, müssen diese Wochen sehr schwierig gewesen sein. Irland war sicherlich kein Land, das Hilfesuchende bereitwillig aufnahm, sondern nur eine sehr begrenzte Zahl und unter bürokratischen Erschwernissen.[36]

Ein Brief Johns an Claire, datiert vier Tage nach seiner Ankunft in Irland, der teilweise auf Deutsch und teilweise auf Englisch geschrieben ist, gibt Einblick in seine damalige Situation, die offensichtliche Einsamkeit, die politische Unsicherheit und auch die Wahrnehmung erster kultureller Unterschiede:

> Darling,
> I hope my letter of this afternoon telling that your visa will be granted this week reach you in due course. I shall try to get the official statement or the certificate of the committee as quickly as possible.
> By the way, I hear that Ireland has admitted till now in the whole 110 (hundred and ten) immigrants from Central Europe of which 40 are Catholics (I know already 5 of them!). So it seems that the danger, had [unleserlich] to be kicked out is not urgent.
> I do not understand the consequences of the last political events. In any case, it seems the best we come here. What people is fearing is that if the war will be more vehement over England, thousands and thousands of Irish refugees will come back to Eire and increase the unemployment. (...)
> Im Gang habe ich von dem Leben hier auch – allerdings vorsichtig – von den Möglichkeiten einen etwas besseren Eindruck als das letzte Mal. Es gibt sehr schöne Türen in der Stadt.
> Ich sehne mich so sehr nach Post von Dir. Natürlich wirst Du mir ein Telegramm schicken, wenn etwas ist, aber ich kann ja gar nichts machen. Der Weg zurück ist ja so zu wie nur etwas zu sein

---

34   Military Archives, G2/0467 Dr. Johannes Hennig.

35   Exilarchiv Frankfurt, John Hennig Nachlass. Das Tagebuch ist eine Kladde im A5 Format. Die handschriftlichen Einträge der ersten Wochen sind relativ ausführlich und geben Aufschluss über Termine, Tagesroutine, Begegnungen und ähnliches. Viele der stichwortartigen Notizen sind allerdings kaum zu entziffern (wir danken an dieser Stelle herzlich für die Hilfen dabei von Monica Schefold).

36   Zur irischen Einwanderungspolitik, insbesondere auch jüdischer Bürger, siehe Dermot Keogh, *Jews in Twentieth-Century Ireland – Refugees, Anti-Semitism and the Holocaust*, Cork: Cork University Press, 1998, besonders S. 115-194.

kann. Liebste, ich habe das Gefühl daß es ein gutes Leben ist, was Dich hier erwartet, wenn auch nicht leicht. I am deeply prepared to do my ever best in all times.
The boy-teachers whose acquaintance I made today make the impression 2-3. Mr. Gavan Duffy is a splendid man of one of the best families. I am on best speaking terms with him and he will help me a lot. I make the experience Vati made too: We have quite another tempo of living as this people. The end of the week is for them what for us is the next hour.
All my love to you all. Kiss the chicken. Her photograph decided the official to give the visa.
Thousand kisses

Hans

[*am Rand dazugeschrieben*]
(…) Can you send me the type writing paper at least 300 pages (<u>nicht</u> Durchschlag!). It is so expensive here.
This is my fourth letter from Eire. It contains 2 pages and one annex and is posted Monday night.[37]

Gerade die Bemerkung, die John über die Gewährung des Visums für Claire und die Kinder macht, zeigt die Zufälligkeit mancher Entscheidungen, die Machtlosigkeit Hennigs, der gänzlich auf den guten Willen anderer angewiesen war. Etwas Hilfe gab es, neben dem erwähnten Gavan Duffy und dem Committee, wahrscheinlich durch den auf der Überfahrt geknüpften Kontakt mit dem gleichfalls nach Irland ins Exil gehenden österreichischen Nobelpreisträger Schrödinger.[38] Auch in den nächsten Tagen wird Schrödinger im Tagebuch erwähnt, es gab Anrufe und Einladungen zum Abendessen für den jungen deutschen Schicksalsgefährten, dessen erste Sorge seiner Familie galt und der neben der ungewohnten Umgebung auch sofort mit einer neuen beruflichen Tätigkeit zurechtkommen musste.

"Twenty-four hours after my arrival in this country I stood before a class of boys and started teaching."[39] Der Arbeitsvertrag mit dem Belvedere College, zu dessen illustren Schülern bekanntlich auch einmal James Joyce gehört hatte, war – genau wie seine Aufenthaltsgenehmigung – vorerst auf ein Jahr terminiert. Deutschunterricht zu er-

---

37 Military Archives, G2/0467 Dr. Johannes Hennig. Dieser Brief, der offensichtlich erst von der Zensur abgefangen wurde, befindet sich in den Unterlagen mit der Notiz "Letter, scribbled, English and German, from Henning (sic) to wife (then in Belgium) posted Dublin 10.10.39". Die deutschen Passagen sind übersetzt, wobei Teile für den Übersetzter offensichtlich nicht verständlich waren, so z.B. Hennigs Beurteilung der 'boy-teachers' nach dem deutschen Notensystem, was mit "L-B (?)" wiedergegeben wurde. Zwei weitere Seiten des Briefes, die hier nicht zitiert werden, geben Informationen für Claire, wie sie die Reise am besten mit Gepäck bewältigen kann, außerdem werden Abmeldungs- und Vermögensfragen angesprochen.

38 Erwin Schrödinger (1887-1961), stand, wie in dem in diesem Band abgedruckten Kapitel aus *Die bleibende Statt* beschrieben, zufällig in derselben Reihe, die vom Immigrations Officer in England aufgerufen wurde. Er war 1938 von Wien nach Rom geflohen, schrieb an Eamon de Valera (1882-1975), der an der Spitze der irischen Regierung stand und zu der Zeit Präsident des Völkerbundes war. De Valera, ehemals Mathematiker, bevor er sich ganz der Politik zuwandte, hatte ihm eine Stelle in Dublin in dem neuentstehenden Institute for Advanced Studies angeboten.

39 Schoolboy in Germany, in *Irish Monthly*, September 1946, S.384-392, 384 (abgedruckt im vorliegenden Band in Kap. IV).

teilen war relativ problemlos, da Irland sich erfolgreich um Neutralität bemüht hatte und es keine ausgesprochenen Antipathien gegen Deutschland gab; in weiten, nicht nur nationalistischen Kreisen der irischen Bevölkerung war, zumindest anfangs, sogar in eine mehr oder minder unverhohlene, z. T. naive und unreflektierte Unterstützung Deutschlands im Kampfe gegen England festzustellen.[40]

In Belvedere College scheint der Kontakt zwischen Schülern und Lehrern oft herzlich gewesen zu sein,[41] in *Die bleibende Statt* kann man sogar von der Ermahnung lesen, die Jungen sollten nicht zu hart arbeiten. Hennigs Klassen scheinen auch Verständnis für sein, wie er schreibt, "mangelhaftes Englisch" gehabt zu haben und verkniffen sich das Lachen. Einer seiner Schüler, der irische Autor Desmond Fennell, der 1945/46 am Deutschunterricht teilnahm, erinnert sich an Hennig als einen sehr guten Lehrer (Fennell bekam eine Auszeichnung für seine Deutschkenntnisse und studierte danach in Dublin und Bonn), den einzigen, der ihn je zu sich nach Hause einlud.[42] Inhaltlich folgte Hennig den vorgeschriebenen Schulbüchern, sprach wenig über Deutschland, sondern vor allem über Literatur. Auch andere frühere Schüler von Belvedere College erinnern sich noch an den jungen Lehrer, der auffiel aufgrund seiner Intensität, seiner Kleidung – "you noticed him in a crowd" und der während seiner Anfangszeit – nicht weiter verwunderlich – auch etwas nervös wirkte. Generell sind die Erinnerungen sehr positiv.[43]

Die Sprache in der Familie war – zumindest in den späteren Jahren – Englisch. Hennig schreibt in der *Bleibenden Statt*: "Muttersprache war in unserer Familie die Sprache, die die Grosseltern mühsam von den Enkeln lernen" (Statt,175).

In der Anfangszeit in Irland scheint zumindest Claire Wert darauf gelegt zu haben, mit den Kindern Deutsch zu sprechen, was bei der 2jährigen Tochter Monica zu einem

---

40 Vgl dazu Hennigs Aufsatz 'Irland und der Nationalsozialismus', *Schweizer Rundschau* 47, 1947 (in diesem Band Kap. V.5):
"Unter den zwanzig Kollegen, die ich an einem von Geistlichen geleiteten Gymnasium hatte, war nur einer, der nicht den Sieg Deutschlands wünschte. Einer meiner Kollegen bekannte: 'Es ist uns ganz recht, wenn die Deutschen möglichst viele englische Schiffe in den Grund bohren'. Meine Wirtin: 'Wir werden schon dafür sorgen, dass die Briten nicht den Krieg gewinnen.' Ein hochgebildeter, aktiv im katholischen Leben stehender Herr: 'Ich bete jeden Abend für den Sieg Hitlers.' Ein Ordensgeistlicher: 'Wenn Hitler sich nicht an der Kirche vergriffe, wäre er ein ganz großer Mann.' Ein höherer Regierungsbeamter: 'Hitler hat ganz recht; natürlich steckt er nur Kommunisten in die Konzentrationslager.' Ein Siebzehnjähriger in einem deutschen Schulaufsatz: 'Die Juden sind ein Ungeziefer, man muß sie erlegen, wie Hitler es tut' (drei Monate später trat der Junge bei der R.A.F. ein)."

41 Vielleicht halfen dabei anfangs auch die Briefmarken, die Felix Meyer seinen Briefen aus Belgien beilegte, damit Hennig Sympathien bei seinen Schülern gewinnen konnte. Vgl. Felix Meyer an Hennig, 1.2.1940, Exilarchiv Frankfurt, Nachlass Felix Meyer.

42 Telefonat mit Desmond Fennell, Rom, 13.7.2001.

43 Telefonate, emails und Gespräche mit Sean Schütte, Des Reynolds und John Hyland, ehemaligen Schülern von Belvedere College, Juni/Juli 2001.

"tollen Kauderwelsch" führte.[44] Offen bleibt, wie Hennig es schaffte, schon bald, wenige Monate nach seiner Emigration nach Irland, dort Artikel auf Englisch zu verfassen. Er war natürlich nicht ohne Kenntnisse nach Irland gekommen – schon als Kind hatte er durch Verwandte und Bekannte seiner Eltern Kontakte mit Englisch und lernte es auch außerhalb der Schule.[45]

Auch während des Studiums, zumindest in seiner Bonner Zeit, hatte er weiter englische Sprachstudien getrieben, wie sich durch die Studienunterlagen nachweisen lässt. Die ersten Eintragungen in sein Tagebuch, das er bei seiner Überfahrt nach Irland beginnt, sind auf Englisch abgefasst, später finden sich aber auch Eintragungen auf Deutsch. Es ist zu vermuten, dass – neben den sowieso üblichen Korrekturen durch die Lektoren der Zeitschriften – auch irische Kollegen oder Bekannte durch Korrekturlesen seiner Artikel aushalfen. Einen interessanten Hinweis gibt ein Schreiben, in dem Hennig über einen potentiellen Schüler informiert wird, der aber nicht genug Geld hätte, für die Stunden zu bezahlen und daher zum Ausgleich auf Englisch geschriebene Artikel Hennigs Korrektur lesen könne.[46]

Einen Einblick in seine Arbeitsverhältnisse ein halbes Jahr nach der Ankunft in Irland gewährt der folgende Auszug aus einem Brief an seine Schwiegermutter Marguerite Meyer vom 5. Mai 1940:

"Ihr fragt nach meiner Arbeit. Ich habe ein paar mehr Privatschüler. Es ist jetzt kaum möglich welche zu bekommen, ersten (sic) wegen der Jahreszeit und zweitens wegen des Überangebotes seitens sich gegenseitig unterbietender Emigranten. Ich hoffe, im College im neuen Schuljahr einige Stunden mehr zu bekommen. Ich gebe auch Französisch und würde gerne Latein geben. Jetzt kommen bald 2 ½ Monate Ferien, in denen mich aber das College durchbezahlt.[47] Ich schreibe an einem deutschen Lehrbuch für irische Schüler mit Bezug auf die hiesigen Schulverhältnisse, auf Irland und vor allem auf das Irische, das ich etwas lerne. Es ist sehr interessant, weil es uralte in allen anderen Sprachen verloren gegangene sprachliche Erscheinungen erhalten hat und als keltische Sprache natürlich eigentümlich ist. Es bestehen aber viele interessante Vergleichspunkte mit dem Deutschen, die bisher wenig ausgewertet worden sind.
Seitdem ich hier bin habe ich eine grosse Arbeit vor, die sehr viel Zeit in Anspruch nimmt, eine Untersuchung des von der Kirche gesprochenen Lateins. Diese Arbeit hat ziemlich verschiedenartige Aspekte, nicht nur sprachwissenschaftliche, sondern auch philosophische und natürlich theologische und kulturhistorische. Es ist ein wenig bearbeitetes Gebiet. Allerdings braucht man dazu eigentlich das ungestörte und geruhsame Leben eines Mönchs.
Mit Philosophie kann man hier garnichts (sic) anfangen. Kein Mensch interessiert sich dafür, eine gute Vorübung, wenn man nach USA kommen sollte. Momentan ist aber natürlich in der ganzen Welt im Geistesleben und besonders in der Philosophie Flaute."[48]

44 Brief 2.5.1940 John Hennig an Marguerite Meyer. Vgl. auch Brief 5.5.1940 an Margot Junod (Exilarchiv Frankfurt, Nachlass Felix Meyer).

45 Vgl. How I learnt English, in *Irish Rosary*, March-April 1945 und in diesem Band, Kap IV.

46 Vgl. Military Archives, Akte Hennig.

47 Vgl. dazu den im vorliegenden Band abgedruckten Auszug aus *Die bleibende Statt*, wo Hennig beschreibt, wie ihm eröffnet wird, dass er die Ferien über "natürlich nicht" bezahlt würde. Es ist anzunehmen, dass Hennig seine Schwiegermutter nicht unnötig belasten wollte mit dem Hinweis auf die schwierige finanzielle Situation der Familie.

48 Exilarchiv Frankfurt, Nachlass Felix Meyer, Brief John Hennig 2.5.1940 an Marguerite Meyer.

Im Schriftverkehr finden sich ab September 1940 häufiger wie schon im Brief an Marguerite angesprochene Überlegungen, nicht in Irland zu bleiben, sondern weiter in die USA auszuwandern, aus Angst vor einer möglichen Invasion. Schwierigkeiten bei der Ausführung dieser Pläne bereitete die Bedingung, eine eidesstattliche Erklärung (Affidavit) und Bürgschaft eines US-Bürgers vorzulegen.[49] Im Februar 1941 sah John Hennig allerdings die noch größere Schwierigkeit darin, eine Schiffsmöglichkeit nachweisen zu können, was mittlerweile ebenfalls vorgeschrieben, aber praktisch unmöglich war.[50] Eine besondere Tragik erhielt die Situation dadurch, dass eine Auswanderung 1938 nach einem USA Besuch von Felix und Marguerite Meyer möglich gewesen und sehr von John begrüßt worden wäre, der dort Chancen sah. Felix Meyer aber lehnte die Idee rundweg ab[51] und erinnert sich daran 1941 mit schlechtem Gewissen in einem Brief nach Irland:

> Seid geküsst und umarmt von Eurem blöden Vati, der durch sein Deutshfühlen (sic) all Euer Unglück schuld ist. Wenn ich den Menschen hier erzähle, dass ich in 38 in USA mit der Mutti war und dort glänzend hätte leben können, aber aus Heimweh zurück nach Deutschland gegangen bin, dann sagt man mir, es gehe mir noch viel zu gut für solche Idiotie und man hat vielleicht Recht.[52]

Im Mai 1940 stand ein Umzug für die Familie von Clontarf an, wo sie seit November 1939 gewohnt hatten, da die Situation mit den Vermietern unhaltbar wurde (die ersten Wochen nach seiner Ankunft hatte Hennig im Belvedere Hotel, Great Denmark Street, verbracht). An seinen Bruder Karl schrieb er darüber auf einer Karte, die von seinem privaten und seinem 'wirklichen' Leben, seiner Forschung erzählte:

> (...) It is a pity that we have to leave this flat as our landlord behaved impossibly towards us. We hope we find a place by the sea, but it is hard as this is the most expensive season. Weather is lovely, we had again marvellous impressions from the scenery round Dublin. My work is rather delayed as I have to do some housework. Thanks ever so much for the Lesebuch which will be of tremendous help to me. Could you send me once a small Luther-bible? Thanks too for the K.d.U. it is the first time I really understand Kant. This work appeared 150 years ago and I think it is the first "philosophical anthropology". In spite of these times I remain philosopher, but it is hard to see no outlook. Claire and the children are alright, but Claire needs badly a recovery time. Let me

---

49   "Provided we have an affidavit, we can have our emigration visa for USA in a couple of months. I enclose a form which you will gather that the matter is terribly involved. Most Americans refrain from giving the required details about their financial situation to third persons, quite apart from the risk. Even if, say Herman or Max would be prepared to give us their guarantee (sic), which, indeed, would not be too dangerous for them, as I surely would find a job, I doubt whether they would like to give sufficient details to make the affidavit valid. As it would be a non-relative-affidavit this point is essential (...) As a matter of fact, economical possibilities in this poor countries (sic) become more and more restricted, while all people who go to US, find decent jobs." John Hennig an Margot Junod, 6.9.1940, Exilarchiv Frankfurt, Nachlass Felix Meyer.

50   Vgl. Brief Hennig an Felix Meyer, 16.2.1941, Exilarchiv Frankfurt, Nachlass Felix Meyer.

51   Vgl. Amalie von Mettenheim, *Felix Meyer*, S. 31.

52   Brief von Felix Meyer an John Hennig, 13.2.1941, Exilarchiv Frankfurt, Nachlass Felix Meyer.

have all news about mother and the geschwister. Give my love to Trudel and the kids. With all our love, Hans.[53]

Gerade Claire war in dieser Zeit nicht in bester Verfassung. Der erste Frühling in Irland hatte auch Erkrankungen mit sich gebracht, die in *Die bleibende Statt* geschildert werden. Beide Kinder und Claire waren an Keuchhusten erkrankt, bei der ältesten Tochter Gabriele entwickelte sich eine lebensbedrohliche Lungenkomplikation.

Nachdem diese Schwierigkeiten überwunden waren und Hennigs auf fast wunderbare Weise eine viel angemessenere Wohnung in der Burrow Road in Sutton gefunden hatten, entwickelte sich das Einleben in Irland positiv. Haus und Garten boten für die Kinder viel Freiraum zum Herumtoben, und direkt hinter dem Garten lag der herrliche Strand der Dublin Bay. Als eine Erleichterung für Claire, die gesundheitlich immer noch nicht wieder ganz hergestellt war, half ein Hausmädchen aus[54] – ein Umstand, der vermutlich in der nächsten Umgebung den Eindruck eines gewissen Wohlstands vermittelte. Dies wurde ermöglicht durch sporadische Zahlungen der Firma Jorgensen & Johnson an John Hennig für die Nutzung der Patente von Felix Meyer. Es ist allerdings bezeichnend, dass Hennig dieses Geld als geliehen ansah und offensichtlich möglichst kaum anbrach, sondern sich bemühte, selbst für den Lebensunterhalt der Familie aufzukommen.[55]

Wichtig für das Einleben war die Zunahme der sozialen Kontakte, so zum Beispiel mit dem Historiker Ludwig Bieler,[56] den Hennig in seiner Autobiographie erwähnt als einen der wenigen, die ihn in seiner schriftstellerischen Tätigkeit ermutigten (Statt,

---

53 Karte John Hennig an Karl Hennig, 5.5.1940, Exilarchiv Frankfurt, Nachlass Felix Meyer.

54 "I do hope that I can arrange any kind of holidays for Claire. Although we have a very nice maid from10-6, Claire has always to bother about the children and they are a hard strain. Sometimes Mrs. Hopf's daughter helps Claire with the kids but she is very unexperienced." Brief John Hennig an Margot Junod, 29.7.1940, Military Archives, Dublin, Akte Hennig G2/0467.

55 Vgl. dazu auch die Briefe von Felix Meyer nach Irland vom 22.1.1945 ("Schrecklich, diese Familienzwistigkeiten in Geldsachen! Glücklicherweise sind sie nicht so wie in den meisten Familien, sondern mit umgekehrten Vorzeichen.") und 16.6.1945 ("Rereading your husbands letter I find, that he writes a very good English and I hope, I shall be able to hear him tomorrow on the wireless, but he made one great mistake, when he wrote about money which I had entrusted to you or to him. There has never been a question of enthrusting. Everything what was sent to you, is your and John's property and there has never been a question of paying back. Please dispose of everything you have left from such assets. Never there will come a moment when Mutti nor I will claim a farthing from such money.") Schon im Januar/ Februar 1940 hatte Felix Meyer Tochter und Schwiegersohn sehr ans Herz gelegt, ein weiteres Bett zu kaufen (Briefe 24.1.; 1.2. und 10.2.) und nach Gabrieles Erkrankung schrieb er eindringlich: "(...) this is the moment for spending the extra shilling" (Ostersonntag 1940), Exilarchiv Frankfurt, Nachlass Felix Meyer.

56 Ludwig Bieler (1906-1981) war Professor am University College Dublin für Mittellatein und Paläographie. Zu seinen Forschungsschwerpunkten gehörten Heiligenviten (besonders das Leben des Hl. Patrick).

143). Darüber hinaus gab es auch Kontakte mit anderen Exilanten, so zum Beispiel dem Bakteriologen Hans Sachs und seiner Frau Lotte,[57] die auch Claire zu guten Freunden wurden und den Töchtern eine Art Grosselternersatz. Man besuchte sich oft gegenseitig:

> Claire and I are on very good terms with Prof. and Mrs. Sachs, a famous physiologist from Heidelberg, a friend of our friends Jaspers, we see them at least twice a week. Prof. Sachs is very musical and every Monday they have a little concert in their house, attended by Prof. Sachs and Dr. Bieler, another friend of ours, a palaeographist from Vienna, who sings very nicely. Often he sings Schubert songs. He and his wife as well as a young doctor, born in Neuss, and his wife come often to us.[58]

Hennig, der von seinem Bruder Ernst für den Musikalischsten unter den fünf Geschwistern gehalten wurde,[59] spielte selbst in seiner Jugend Geige und scheint davon auch während der Jahre in Irland noch ab und zu Gebrauch gebracht zu haben.[60] Auch in anderen Aspekten entwickelte sich das Eingewöhnen in Irland gut, es gab sogar die Möglichkeit für Hennig, das neue Heimatland näher kennenzulernen. In einem Brief über den Umzug nach Sutton an seine Schwägerin Margot Junod schwärmt er geradezu von seiner ersten größeren Erkundung Irlands bei einem mehrtägigen Ausflug nach Connemara:

> I was taken for the caravan-trip by the brother of one of my pupils, who is now one of our best friends. We were five in the caravan, all belonging to the Oxford-Group, of which you will perhaps have heard as it is rather strong in your country. I had the most marvellous impressions not only of these companions but of the scenery and the countryfolk. We spent a week in Connemara, the outskirts of Europe, w[h]ere people live in the same conditions as thousand years ago, and we had the most brilliant contact with them especially by splendid campfires. I have learnt in these few days more than else in years. The scenery is undescribable, the beauty of Norway combined with that of Italy. I could not imagine a landscape more appealing to me. The combination of mountains, woods and water (sea, lakes, torrents rivers in steep valleys etc.) and the wonderful character of the people is most impressive.[61]

Als möglicher Spion unter Beobachtung

Während Hennig von dem Aufenthalt in dem Westen Irlands begeistert war und sich noch lange an diese Reise erinnerte (vgl. dazu auch seine Schilderung in *Die bleibende*

---

57 Hans Sachs (1877-1945), Leiter des serologischen Instituts in Heidelberg; der "erste Serologe Deutschlands", so der Dekan Richard Siebeck 1933. 1935 musste er wegen seiner jüdischen Abstammung in den Ruhestand treten und im folgenden Jahr emigrieren. Das Institut wurde geschlossen.

58 Brief John Hennig an Margot Junod, 29.7.1940, Military Archives, Akte Hennig.

59 Ernst Hennig, Unsere Eltern, S. 18.

60 Peter Harbison erinnerte sich an eine Geige, die an der Tür hing (Interview 19.1.2001) und Thelma Sheehan, Schulkameradin der Hennigtöchter, erwähnte eine andere Freundin, die, als sie ca. 6 Jahre alt war, zu einer kleinen Feier bei Hennigs ging, bei der Vater Hennig den Kindern etwas auf der Geige vorspielte und sie alle einmal das Instrument ausprobieren ließ (Gespräch mit Noel und Thelma Sheehan, 9.2.2001).

61 John Hennig an Margot Junod 29.7.1940, Military Archives, Akte Hennig.

Statt), ahnte er kaum, dass er die gesamte Reisezeit hindurch unter Beobachtung stand. Verdacht erregte er offensichtlich, nachdem die irische Überwachungsstelle (G2 - Military Intelligence) von einem "friendly German national" Ende April 1940 den Hinweis erhalten hatte, dass

> Joannes (sic) Hennig, German (...) was worthy of attention. This information was not elaborated upon by informant. Henning (sic) is ostensibly a refugee. He arrived in the country on 6/10/39. His movements are now being subjected to surveillance.[62]

Bereits in der Woche darauf stand er mit drei bis vier anderen Deutschen auf der Überwachungsliste:

> Attention was given to the movements etc. of Johannes Hennig, German National residing in 11, Copeland Ave, Clontarf. Subject was not observed to engage in any suspicious activities. He called to the 'Evening Herald' offices on a number of occasions but it is believed the reason for his visits there is due to the fact that he is seek (sic) house accommodation through the advertising columns of that paper.[63]

Der Bericht 18719 fand es auch wichtig festzustellen: "Not in possession of a car."

So war es kein Wunder, dass Hennigs pflichtbewusste Benachrichtigung bei der örtlichen Polizeidienststelle, er werde für 2 Wochen mit Bekannten in den Westen aufbrechen, beachtliche Betriebsamkeit auslöste und zur Kontaktierung eines Reisegefährten führte, damit dieser ein Auge auf Hennigs Aktivitäten werfen könnte.[64] Erst am 9. September gab es dann die Unbedenklichkeitserklärung:

---

62 Weekly Miscellaneous Report, D.M.D. – Week ended 29th April 1940, Military Archives, Akte Hennig.

63 Weekly Miscellaneous Report, D.M.D. – Week ended 6th May 1940, Military Archives, Akte Hennig.

64 " (...) I beg to report that above named Alien reported at Howth Garda Station on 13th July 1940, his intention of proceeding on a holiday tour to Connemara, County Galway of 14 days duration on 14th July 1940. He stated that he would be accompanied by the following persons: -
(1)   Sydney Gibson, "Rockford", Temple Rd, Rathgar
(2)   Harry Nelson, 16 Royal Terrace, Fairview Dublin
(3)   James Guttrie, 11 Clareville Rd, Rathgar, Dublin and
(4)   Leslie Horton, 10 Furrypark Rd, Raheny, Co. Dublin. [Namen rot unterstrichen]
The party will travel in a Terraplane Motor Car No-Z. A. 8843 from Dublin to Fermoy, Co. Cork, where they will collect a living Caravan and then proceed direct to Connemara, County Galway.
HENNIG is not actually suspect at present but it would be of interest to know whether he or his associates make suspicious contacts in Galway West Division during their holiday there. The Ard Cheannphort Galway has been informed of the contents of this report for guidance in the matter if supervision.
A copy of this report is being furnished to Leas Coimisineir D.M.D. to ascertain if any of the present associates of HENNIG have come under notice of Special Branch in any subversive or suspected activities. I am calling for report regarding Leslie HORTON the only associate of HENNIG who resides in this division."
ARD Cheannphort W.P. Quinn (Military Archives, Akte Hennig, 16.7.1940). Am 29.7.1940 wird dann genauer über den ausgesuchten Informanten berichtet.

Re: Supervision of Aliens – Hennig, Johannes, German National, The Burrow, Sutton, Co. Dublin

Reference previous reports on above named, I beg to state that Hennig and party returned from the tour towards the end of July. The Alien did not engage in suspicious activity of any kind during his absence.

The question raised in last paragraph of minute of Ard-Cheannphort at Bray was dealt with in report furnished on 12th July, 1940.

The delay in returning this file is regretted and was brought about by reason of illness of member of party who accompanied Hennig on the tour and who had promised to supply information if he acted suspiciously.[65]

Zeitweise glaubte man gar, Hennig hätte Kontakt mit Kommunisten, was sich jedoch bald als unzutreffend herausstellte. Besonderen Verdacht löste dabei auch Claires Religionszugehörigkeit aus. In den Military Archives findet sich eine handschriftliche Notiz, die nicht namentlich gekennzeichnet ist, auf einem kleinen DinA 6 Zettel:

Dr. Johannes Hennig: a German. Here 2 weeks before the war. Claims his wife is a Jewess, but she is not. Comes from Aachen. Staying with Dyer, an officer in the L.S.F. at Sutton (Carramore, The Borough). Very suspect.

[*weiter unten, in anderer Handschrift*] arrd. 6.10.39. Age 29. Dr. Phil. Teaching Belvedere Collge. Address given Belvedere Hotel Gt. Denmark Street. Wife arrd. 22/11/39. Age 33 Wife address 11, Copeland Av., Clontarf.[66]

Auch im Jahr 1942 ist Hennig noch von Interesse für die irischen Behörden. In der Hennig-Akte der Military Archives findet sich eine handgeschriebene Notiz vom 2. Februar zu ‚Hennig – Sutton': "A friend who has been on a visiting terms with the above told me 'it is a meeting place for many Germans' Including Sachs of TCD and Bieler".

Auf dem selben Zettel findet sich eine Ergänzung durch eine weitere handschriftliche Notiz "Sachs / Bieler – both ok as far as known". Dennoch war 1942 das Jahr, in dem Hennig selbst Aufmerksamkeit auf sich zog und zwar durch seine Veröffentlichungen. Diesmal kam er in Konflikt mit der Zensurstelle aufgrund eines Artikels, der für eine englische Zeitschrift bestimmt war und anscheinend durch zumindest "milde" Kritik an Deutschland und seinen Verbündeten auffiel. Der Artikel wurde von der Postzensur

---

65   Military Archives, Akte Hennig. M.J. Wymes, Sair 7845.

66   Military Archives, Akte Hennig. Eine ähnliche Notiz findet sich in den Akten mit dem Datum 10.3.41: "Would you please get the particulars of this man? His date of arrival is given as 6/10/39. can this be correct? When did his wife arrive? I have an idea he was here before then. If 6.10.39 be correct, how did he get here? As he then could hardly have contacted Clissmann, the story of his getting Cls pupils can hardly be likely." Helmut Clissmann war Vertreter des DAAD in Irland gewesen und vor Kriegsausbruch nach Deutschland gegangen, er wurde von den Behörden verdächtigt, Spionageaufgaben zu verfolgen, vgl. Horst Dickel, *Die deutsche Außenpolitik und die irische Frage von 1932-1944*, Wiesbaden: Steiner 1983, S. 77. Eine ähnliche Notiz gibt es bereits vom 11. Juli 1940, dort werden auch schon Clissmanns Schüler erwähnt von G2 an P. Carrol, Chief Supt. Garda Siochana Headquarters, Kilmainham – und es werden genauere Informationen angefordert.

abgefangen und von der Zensurbehörde in Dublin Castle[67] mit folgendem Brief von T.Coyne an J.E. Duff vom Justizministerium weitergeleitet:

9 Meitheamh, 1942

Dear Duff,

Please see the attached papers which include a letter which has been intercepted by the Postal Censorship containing a contribution from Herr Dr. John Hennig to the Catholic Times, London. I know Hennig myself and took German lessons from him and he is, as far as I know, a perfectly harmless alien. At the same time I feel that aliens of German nationality who have left the Fatherland should be discouraged from carrying on anti-Axis propaganda even of so mild a kind as this contribution from here through the medium of the English press. In a previous case (your reference 69/80/93)[68] you served an Order on another alien prohibiting him from writing for publication. I don't think it is necessary to go quite so far in this case but, perhaps, you would take some action short of this, such as a warning Hennig off the English papers. We have no objection to his occasional contributions on various topics of non-controversial kinds to Irish publications.

> Yours sincerely,
> (So -?) Thomas J. Coyne[69]

Es ist bemerkenswert, dass Thomas Coyne Hennig persönlich kannte, Deutschstunden bei ihm genommen hatte und ihn als "harmless" einstufte, aber dennoch eine Verwarnung für nötig hielt. Der Artikel, um den es ging, wurde nicht gedruckt und ist auch unseres Wissens nach nicht erhalten. Duff stimmte mit der Einschätzung überein und arrangierte "to have him warned in the manner suggested by you".[70] Diese Einschränkung seiner Publikationsmöglichkeiten traf Hennig sehr, und er bemühte sich um eine Aufhebung des Verbotes in englischen Zeitschriften zu veröffentlichen. Am 24. Juni 1942 schrieb er direkt an den Justizminister:

A Chara,

The Alien Officer has communicated to me the warning regarding my contributions to British periodicals.

Whilst apologizing for all the inconvenience I have caused in this matter, I would like to point out that all my contributions to the Catholic press in England dealt with religious subjects exclusively, and that only in one case where the editor of a paper had appealed to Catholics to discuss a controversial subject, I sent a contribution, which incidentally was not printed. Other-

---

67　Nähere Informationen zur Zensur in Irland während der Kriegsjahre siehe Donal Ó Drisceoil, *Censorship in Ireland 1939-1945*, Cork: Cork University Press 1996.

68　Diese Akte bezieht sich auf Kurt Werner, einen anderen Deutschen in Irland, der an Schweizer Zeitschriften geschrieben und ihnen seine Berichte über Irland angeboten hatte. Dies wurde strikt abgelehnt und Werner bekam Veröffentlichungsverbot und die Auflage sich jeglicher Korrespondenz mit Zeitschriften zu enthalten. (Military Archives, OSS 7/31 - Controllers office / Information regarding aliens)

69　Military Archives, OSS 7/31 - Controllers office / Information regarding aliens. Thomas J. Coyne war seit September 1941 'Controller of Censorship', vgl. Dermot Keogh, Twentieth Century Ireland, Dublin 1984, S. 125. In der Akte findet sich auch eine Kopie des Briefes (ohne Unterschrift) mit kleineren Abweichungen, u.a. heißt es dort statt "anti-Axis propaganda" "anti-German propaganda".

70　Military Archives, OSS 7/31, Duff an Coyne, 11.6.1942

wise I have never been interested in writing on controversial subjects. My contributions to the press are confined to religious subjects, resulting mainly from the research on liturgy, in which I am engaged for some years past. Fr. Stephan Brown, S.J. Miltown Park, Dublin, Fr. Casey, Editor The Irish Rosary, or Mr. O'Curry, Editor The Standard, would be able to testify that I am a specialist in that line. It is mainly due to my publications in the Catholic Press of England (The Universe, The Catholic Herald, Catholic Times, Blackfriars, and Music and Liturgy) that I have succeeded in getting articles published in U.S.A., a fact which is of great importance with a view to my eventual emigration to America. Moreover, those occasional contributions are a small but valuable source of income for me.

It would be a very severe handicap to me if I would be no longer permitted to contribute articles on liturgical subjects to the Catholic press in England, and I would be most grateful if the Minister for Justice would mitigate his warning to that effect that, whilst being prohibited to contribute in controversial subjects, I may continue contributing articles on religious subjects.

> Mise, le meas,
> J. Hennig

Ob zu diesem Zeitpunkt noch wirklich eine Immigration in die USA in Erwägung gezogen wurde, mag dahingestellt bleiben, aber sein Argument, durch ein Veröffentlichkeitsverbot für England eine wichtige Einnahmequelle zu verlieren, hatte sicherlich unmittelbare Bedeutung für Hennig. Nach weiteren Briefwechseln zwischen Duff und Coyne wurde ihm die Erlaubnis erteilt.[71] Für seine nächste Veröffentlichung ging Hennig in die Offensive – er schickte sie direkt ans Justizministerium in der ausdrücklichen Hoffnung, dadurch Zeit zu sparen:

> Since I fear that my letter and the title of my article may give the misleading impression that I am dealing with a controversial political subject, I would like to point out that I am exclusively concerned with a liturgical and historical subject. In order to avoid any delay which otherwise might have been caused, I take the liberty of sending you the letter and article, and I would be grateful if you would kindly forward it in the enclosed envelope.[72]

Duff schickte daraufhin Brief und Artikel an Coyne (vielleicht kann man in seinem beigefügten Brief eine gewisse Erschöpfung anmerken: "If you see no objection to the issue of the enclosure, perhaps you would send it on direct as we do not wish to see it again"[73]), der es seinerseits am 28. August an Joseph Walshe[74] weiterleitete, von dem auch keine Einwände kamen. Dementsprechend meldete Coyne am 1. September an Duff, der Artikel sei ohne Änderungen an The Tablet abgeschickt worden.

---

71 Brief an J.E. Duff vom 30. Juni 1942 (ohne Unterschrift, aber sehr wahrscheinlich von T. Coyne): "In reply to your letter of yesterday's date (69/80/477) we have no objection to Dr. Hennig's continuing to contribute articles on liturgical subjects to the English Catholic Press. I have no doubt that he knows very well the type of stuff we don't want him to write and that the warning he has received will be efficacious." Military Archives, OSS 7/31.

72 Brief John Hennig, 17. August 1942 an das Justizministerium, Military Archives, OSS 7/31. Leider war es uns nicht möglich herauszufinden, um welchen Artikel es sich handelte.

73 J.E. Duff an T. Coyne 27. August 1942, Military Archives, OSS 7/31.

74 Joseph Walsh ( )

Vielerlei berufliche Tätigkeiten

Hennig bemühte sich seit Beginn seiner Zeit in Irland das Familieneinkommen zusätzlich zu dem Schulunterricht und den Veröffentlichungen durch Privatstunden in Deutsch aufzubessern. Besonders zu Beginn der vierziger Jahre gab es mehrmals Anzeigen in verschiedenen Tageszeitungen, so z.B. "German Intensive Courses by experienced Native Teacher. – Dr. Hennig, 28 Parnell Square" in der *Irish Times* am 13. und 15. Januar 1941. In den akademischen Jahren 1943/44, 1944/45 und 1945/46 war Hennig als 'Lecturer' (Dozent) in Maynooth im Priesterseminar tätig und unterrichtete jede Woche während der Vorlesungszeit Deutsch.[75] Außerdem hielt er Vorträge im Radio, gab Abendkurse und Vorlesungen wie z.B. im Februar 1943 'A series of six lectures dealing with the place of Missal in the Liturgy, with special reference to the liturgy of Lent'. Das Familienleben hatte sich eingerichtet, die beiden älteren Kinder Gabriele und Monica besuchten die Santa Sabina Vor- und Grundschule, und seit dem 24.11.1942 gab es noch eine Dritte im Bunde – Margaret Mary Joan ('Margie').[76] Auch der Kontakt mit den Nachbarn war gut. Hennig wird als fleißig in Erinnerung behalten, sich in seine Arbeit zurückziehend und vertiefend, der freundliche Gelehrte, der sehr gut mit Kindern umgehen konnte.[77] 1943 begann er nebenbei noch ein Architekturstudium am University College Dublin, das er nach 1945, unter anderem wegen einer auch noch verlangten Mathematikprüfung nicht fortsetzte (Statt, 153). Im Jahr 1945 gab es weitere Veränderungen und unvorhergesehene berufliche Belastungen für Hennig. Der Tod von Hans Sachs im März 1945 traf die ganze Familie Hennig sehr. Das Kriegsende bedeutete keinen wesentlichen Einschnitt im Leben der Bevölkerung, da Irland zwischen 1939 und 1945 offiziell neutral geblieben war und daher kaum in Kriegshandlungen verwickelt wurde, sondern meist indirekt,[78] wie z. B. durch Rationierungen, betroffen war. Für Hennig persönlich hieß es allerdings, dass er zusätzliche Deutschstunden, die er am University College Dublin gegeben hatte, nicht weiterführen konnte und seine Mitarbeit am *Standard* wurde ebenfalls beendet (Statt, 153). Im September 1945 wurde Hennig von dem Dun Laoghaire

---

75   Auskunft der Personalabteilung von National University of Ireland Maynooth, 19.9.2001. Pfarrer Patrick Twohig, ehemaliger Student des Priesterseminars, erinnert sich auch noch gut an Hennig Treffen 4.2.2001), allerdings in einem rätselhaften Kontext: er habe seinen Schülern die Striemen auf seinem Rücken gezeigt, die noch von einem KZ Aufenthalt stammten (vgl. dazu auch J. Fischer, *Das Deutschlandbild der Iren*, S. 491). Sowohl in Hennigs eigenen Äußerungen (vgl. Statt, 153), als auch den Erinnerungen seiner Tochter lassen sich dafür keinerlei Anzeichen finden.

76   Thelma Sheehan, eine frühere Mitschülerin der älteren Hennigtöchter, erinnert sich noch gut an das Ereignis, da Hennig, der in der Zeit als Claire im Krankenhaus war, einsam wurde, die Töchter aus der Schule holte und nach 1-2 Stunden zurückbrachte – sehr zur Erschütterung der Priorin. Interview mit Thelma Sheehan 9.2.2001.

77   Interview mit Prof. John Harbison, 9.2.2001.

78   Es wurden im Mai 1941 (wohl versehentlich) von der deutschen Luftwaffe Bomben über North Strand in Dublin abgeworfen, es gab über 30 Tote. Die deutsche Regierung entschuldigte sich offiziell und bezahlte Reparationen in Höhe von £327,000 im Jahr 1958. Vgl. Dermot Keogh, *Twentieth Century Ireland*, Dublin: Gill & Macmillan 1994, S. 123.

Vocational Education Committee als Teilzeitkraft eingestellt, dies half wenigstens etwas, die Verluste durch den Wegfall der anderen Einnahmequelle auszugleichen.

In dieser Zeit gab es auch Überlegungen, Kinder aus Bergen-Belsen zu adoptieren. Dr. Robert Collis,[79] der in der Anfangszeit bei der schweren Erkrankung der Tochter Gabriele kostenlos geholfen hatte, war nach dem Krieg einer der ersten alliierten Ärzte, die nach Bergen-Belsen kamen. Er brachte von dort, wie Hennig in *Die bleibende Statt* beschrieb, einige Kinder aus dem Lager nach Dublin. Hennig beschrieb auch, wie er bei einem der Kinder die Religionszugehörigkeit herausfinden sollte. Er erwähnt nicht, dass er und Claire längere Zeit darüber nachdachten, eines dieser Kinder zu adoptieren. Felix Meyer riet ihnen davon eindringlich ab.[80] Auch wenn es zu keiner Adoption kam, kümmerten sich John und Claire um die Kinder, die aus dem KZ nach Irland gekommen waren und luden sie z.B. zum Essen ein.

Am 22. September 1945 gab es in der *Irish Press* folgende Veröffentlichung:

> Notice of application of naturalisation
> Notice is hereby given that PAUL GOTTFRIED JOHANNES HENNIG, of 'Walmer' Sutton, Co. Dublin is applying to the Minister for Justice for a certificate of naturalisation, and that any person who knows any reason why a certificate of naturalisation should not be issued to the applicant should send a written and signed statement of the facts to the Secretary, Department of Justice, Dublin.[81]

Da es offensichtlich keine Einwände gab, wurde John Hennig im Januar zum "New Irish Citizen".[82] Eine Rückkehr der Familie nach Deutschland war offensichtlich nie für die Hennigs in Frage gekommen, man hatte sich in Irland eingelebt, dazu kam die Überzeugung, nach den Schrecken der NS-Zeit nicht mehr in Deutschland leben zu wollen.

Im Juli 1946 kommt es zum langersehnten Besuch von Felix und Marguerite Meyer. Felix Meyers einfühlender Brief an seine andere Tochter Margot in der Schweiz gibt detaillierten Einblick in die Lebensbedingungen der Hennigfamilie:

> Wir sind hier restlos gluecklich und begeistert. Und wenn wir nicht vier liebe Geschoepfe in der Schweiz haetten, so blieben wir gerne immer hier. Alles ist prima. Klaere und Hans sind fabelhaft und die drei kleinen Maedchen sind ueber alle Massen erfreulich. Die Mutti wird Euch wohl alle Einzelheiten berichtet haben. Der einzige Kummer ist, dass Klaere sich zu sehr ermuedet, um uns das Leben hier angenehm zu machen. Sie ist ein fabelhafter Wirt und Hans ist Wirt und Wirtin zugleich. Dass wir, weil die Sache mit dem Bungalo (sic) nicht klappte, bei den Kindern wohnen, macht das Familienleben natuerlich viel enger als wenn wir uns nur hie und da sehen wuerden, bringt aber fuer Hans und Klaere grosse Beschraenkungen mit sich. Der Umstand, dass Hans fast

---

79   Robert Collis (1900-1975), Kinderarzt und Autor, gründete die Cerebral Palsy Ireland Society im Jahr 1948.

80   "Ihr habt einmal unsre Meinung darueber gefragt, ob Ihr ein Kind nehmen solltet. Darf ich Euch sagen, dass ich sehr dagegen waere. (...) Ich hoffe, Ihr begeht nicht, um Eures Arztes willen, eine solche Torheit. So etwas kann schlimmere Folgen haben als eine unueberlegte Ehe." Brief 6.10.1945 Felix Meyer an John und Claire Hennig, Exilarchiv Frankfurt, Felix Meyer Nachlass.

81   Military Archives, Akte Hennig.

82   Vgl. *Irish Independent*, 2.1.1946.

immer zuhause arbeitet, bringt es auch mit sich, dass man viel voneinander hat. Die Kinder kennen unendlich viele und nur nette, sympathische Menschen. Fast jeden Nachmittag und Abend ist Besuch da, es wird musiziert, und die beiden erwachsenen Toechter sind immer dabei und stoeren nie. Das ganze Leben ist hier so frei und ungezwungen, wie wir es nie gekannt haben. Jeder tut was er will. Die Kinderchen haben eine Hetze von Freunden und Freundinnen. Die saemtlichen Nachbarskinder an dem oder jenen Platz, im Sand, im Garten, im Hause und in den Nachbarshaeusern, ohne dass sich die Erwachsenen um sie kuemmern. Wenn Essenszeit ist, wird gerufen und sie kommen aus irgendeinem Haus oder aus dem Wasser oder aus den Gaerten heraus. Oft sind fremde Kinder mit zu Tisch, zum Beispiel eine Anzahl Kinder, die ueber Schweden aus Bergen hergekommen sind und hier von irischen Familien adoptiert werden sollen. Die Erwachsenen haben eine Menge Freunde aus allen Schichten, teils Emigranten, mit denen sie schwerste Jahre geteilt haben.

Hans ist ein im Lande bestens bekannter Mann mit einer m. E. grossen Zukunft. Er vereinigt mit seinem unerhoerten Wissen, seiner Bescheidenheit, seiner riesigen Arbeitskraft, seinem Unterhaltungstalent, seiner Heiterkeit und seinem versoehnlichen Character unerhoerte haeusliche Tugenden. Er kuemmert sich um Kueche und Haushalt, bringt Lebensmittel aus der fernen Stadt herein, erteilt dauernd Unterricht in den verschiedensten Kreisen, schreibt fuer x Zeitungen und Zeitschriften, hat mehrere Buecher herausgegeben und ist bekannt und geachtet. Klaere hat eine zwanglose Gastlichkeit. Sie ist nie so entzueckend gewesen wie jetzt. Die schweren Jahre die die Beiden erlebt haben, haben sie reifer gemacht und staerker. Klaere ist sehr gesund. Hans leider viel von Kopfschmerzen geplagt, sodass Klaere Sorgen um ihn hat. In ein bis zwei Jahren hat Hans es geschafft, so hoffen Beide, und dann wird er ein leichteres Leben haben. Momentan bin ich hinter ihm her, dass er seine Taetigkeit aendert indem er sie auf eine zukunftsreichere Basis stellt. Ich moechte, dass er einen Verlag gruendet. Er kann dabei viel mehr verdienen als wenn er fuer andre Zeitungen schreibt, und er hat soviel Material, dass er mit eignen Artikeln und Abhandlungen noch fuer Jahre genug Stoff besitzt, um seine Spalten zu fuellen. Geld kann er finden so viel er will und technische Mitarbeiter sind genuegend zu haben. Er zoegert noch. Heite (sic) abend kommt sein Freund, der engste Mitarbeiter von De Valera zum Abendessen und wir wollen mit ihm, der selbst einen Zeitungsverlag hat, die Frage einmal ventlieren (sic). Ich moechte, dass Hans nicht lange zoegert und, dass die Sache gegruendet wird so lange ich noch hier bin und ihn beraten kann. D.h. er braucht mich nicht als Berater, ich muss ihm nur Mut machen und er muss sich mit mir klar sprechen (sic). Dann koennte er sich Personal und Auto leisten, und er haette ein leichteres Leben und waere nicht der wurzellose und von allen ausgenutzte Artikelscgreiber (sic). Ich haenge sehr an dem Gedanken, ihn selbstaendig zu sehen.[83]

Der von Felix Meyer erwähnte "engste Mitarbeiter von De Valera" war Frank Gallagher[84], langjähriger Herausgeber der Irish Press, 'special adviser' für de Valera und Direktor des 'Government Information Bureau'. Ihm verdankt Hennig, dass er "einer der ersten war, der nach dem Kriege in das irische Bürgerrecht aufgenommen wurde" (Statt, 144). Die geplante Selbstständigkeit konnte aber nicht so verwirklicht

---

83   Exilarchiv Frankfurt, Nachlass Felix Meyer, Brief Felix Meyer an Margot Junod, 11.7.1946.

84   Frank Gallagher (1898-1962), erster Herausgeber der von de Valera gegründeten 'Irish Press'. Direktor des Government Information Bureau 1939-48 und wieder 1951-54. Arbeitete dann bei der Nationalbibliothek in Dublin. Seine Tochter Ann erinnert sich noch lebhaft an häufige Besuche Hennigs bei Frank Gallagher und die ungewöhnlichen Parties bei Hennigs mit Milch und 'Madeira bisquits' (vermutlich Spekulatius). Die Freundschaft erstreckte sich nicht nur auf Hennig und Frank Gallagher, sondern es gab auch enge Kontakte zwischen den Kindern, Tochter Ann war eine Schulfreundin der beiden älteren Hennigtöchter. Interview mit Ann Gallagher und Paula O'Kelly, 9.2.2001.

werden, wie Felix Meyer es gerne gesehen hätte. Dennoch gab es eine drastische Änderung in Hennigs Berufsleben. Auf eine Zeitungsanzeige hin bewarb sich Hennig bei der staatlichen Torfgewinnungsgesellschaft Bord na Móna, die einen 'Records Officer' mit deutschen und französischen Sprachkenntnissen suchte. Er nahm die ihm angebotene Stelle im 40 Meilen von Dublin entfernten Newbridge im County Kildare an. Erleichtert über eine feste Anstellung, die zumindest ein regelmäßiges Einkommen gewährleistete, schrieb er Anfang Dezember 1946 eine Karte an seinen Bruder Karl: "Meine Anstellung bei Bord na Móna ist inzwischen offiziell bestätigt worden. Ein full-time job, Gott sei Dank."[85]

Familie Hennig mit Felix und Marguerite Meyer: (von l. nach r.) Monica, Marguerite Meyer, Margie, Felix Meyer und Gabriele, dahinter John und Claire Hennig, in Sutton, Co. Dublin, Sommer 1946

Für die nächsten dreieinhalb Jahre war er praktisch nur an den Wochenenden bei seiner jungen Familie zu Hause. Hatte Felix Meyer 1946 noch geschrieben, er arbeite viel zu Hause,[86] so musste Hennigs Schwester Erica bei ihrem Aufenthalt in Dublin im Dezember 1947 feststellen, dass er fast nie zu Hause war,[87] sondern in Newbridge,

---

85   Karte John Hennig an Karl Hennig, 6.12.1946, Privatbesitz Wolfgang Hennig.

86   Brief Felix Meyer an Margot, 11.7.1946, Exilarchiv Frankfurt, Nachlass Felix Meyer.

87   Brief Erica, Ardross, Western Australia, 4.12.2000.

"wo ich meine Abende in dem öden Büro möglichst mit Korrespondenz aufzuheitern versuche, auch schon, um die kostbaren Stunden in Sutton zu sparen."[88]

Es war eine notgedrungene Tätigkeit (ein "oller Briefmarkenleckerjob"[89] wie er selber recht drastisch ausführt), die dem Unterhalt seiner jungen Familie diente, aber ihm natürlich auf Dauer keine berufliche Befriedigung und Erfüllung seiner geistig-intellektuellen Fähigkeiten und Ansprüche bieten konnte.

Hennigs Arbeitsbereich wird beschrieben in einer Passage aus dem Buch *Bord na Móna – Peat Research Centre*:

> The Experimental Station was comprised of five sections. In the Library and Records Section the plentiful and ever-increasing flow of foreign peat handbooks, scientific papers and patents that became available after the war was acquired and indexed by John Hennig who translated and made them available not only to Bord na Móna staff but to Irish industry in general. He also started issuing summaries at regular intervals of current peat research reports that, entitled "Peat Abstracts", later became a publication with a world-wide circulation.[90]

Anerkennend äußerte sich später C.S. Andrews, der damalige Direktor von Bord na Móna, in seinen Memoiren *Man of no Property* über Hennig:

> As a starting point for these investigations (i.e. 'the study and testing of new natural and artificial drying methods') a comprehensive study was made of world literature on current turf production and utilisation techniques and the latest advances in machine design. Much of this desk research was the work of John Hennig, a German who left Germany because of the Nazi regime. With his remarkable grasp of foreign languages, he built up a comprehensive library and information service, establishing connections with practitioners in bog work in many countries.[91]

Die Hochachtung beruhte offensichtlich auf Gegenseitigkeit. Hennig schätzte Andrews seinerseits als den herausragenden Vertreter einer neuen Generation "begeisterter, aber wirtschaftlich nüchterner irischer Patrioten" (Statt, 160).

In der Zeitschrift *Architectural Design*, die eine Sondernummer über Irland herausbrachte, wird John Hennig als "an eminent scientist in charge of technical research"[92] bezeichnet. Hennig machte das Beste aus der Situation, und zumindest gewährte ihm seine Tätigkeit die Zeit, seinen wissenschaftlichen Studien nachzugehen, wenn auch in beschränktem Rahmen und weitgehend entfernt von einer größeren Bibliothek und regelmäßigem Gedankenaustausch. So vertiefte er sich u.a. in Jaspers' monumentales Werk *Von der Wahrheit*, das der befreundete Philosoph ihm zugeschickt hatte, und erforschte die *Berichte der Antiquarischen Gesellschaft*. Über seine Erfahrungen in Newbridge während der gut drei Jahre dort und seine Einblicke in das damalige Leben der irischen Provinz, die Enge und "abgründige Trostlosigkeit einer irischen Kleinstadt", berichtet Hennig anschaulich in seiner Autobiographie. Er schreibt aus der Per-

---

88   Brief Hennig an Felix Meyer, 5.11.48, Exilarchiv Frankfurt, Nachlass Felix Meyer.

89   Brief Hennig an Felix Meyer, 10.8.1949, Exilarchiv Frankfurt, Nachlass Felix Meyer.

90   John Cooke, *Bord na Móna Research Centre*. Bord na Mona, Kildare 1991, S. 67.

91   C.S. Andrews, *Man of No Property – An Autobiography* (Volume Two), Dublin/Cork: Mercier Press 1982, S. 196.

92   *Architectural Design*, Vol 17, July 1947, S. 195f.

spektive eines immigrierten Deutschen über das Land, das ihn aufnahm, dem er sicherlich große Sympathien und Dankbarkeit entgegenbrachte, das er aber nicht unkritisch sah.

Für ihn war das Leben (trotz der in Irland gewonnenen Erkenntnis, dass es besser ist, zu arbeiten um zu leben, als umgekehrt, Statt, 177) ein täglicher Kampf, eine andauernde Anstrengung, seiner Verantwortung gegenüber Claire und den Töchtern so gut wie nur irgendmöglich gerecht zu werden. Aufopferung und enorme Sparsamkeit hatte er ja schon durch seine Eltern prägend erfahren. Ausgelassenheit und gelöste Heiterkeit gehörten nicht so sehr zu seinen Stärken, ein stiller Humor schon eher.[93] In einem Brief vom Anfang des Jahres 1947 redet Schwiegervater Felix Meyer seinem Schwiegersohn freundschaftlich, aber nachdrücklich-bestimmt ins Gewissen:

> Nichts hat mich mehr ergriffen bei unsrem Besuch dort als die Behauptung, Ihr hättet keinen Spass mehr an der Freude, und ich bin glücklich über jeden Leichtsinn, den Ihr begeht und jede Erleichterung, die ihr Euch schaffen werdet. Ihr könnt ja doch nichts daran ändern, dass in Berlin 20 Grad unter Null sind. Wenn es bei Euch warm und gemütlich und nicht radikal ist, dann friert man darum in Berlin nicht weniger und nicht mehr. Ihr habt so unendlich schwere Jahre hinter Euch, dass Ihr die Pflicht habt, Euch und Euren Kindern gegenüber, vergnügter zu werden, immer vergnügt zu sein und ausgeglichen, selbst wenn mal etwas schief geht. (...) Nehmt Euch an Mönchen ein Beispiel! Leistet Euch etwas, was Euch Freude macht! Es ist das easy going viel wichtiger und für Körper und Geist von viel grösserem Wert als das verdammte Pflichtbewusstsein. (...) Wenn ich denke, wie verkrampft Du warst, lieber Hans, als wir die ersten Tage da waren, und über welche Kleinigkeiten du Dich geärgert hast, mit dem Essen und der Sparsamkeit und dem Kampf gegen das waste (sic!), dann bin ich ganz traurig und habe nur den Wunsch, Du mögest diese fanatische Einstellung Dir ganz und gar abgewöhnen. Freude ist notwendig, notwendiger als alles andere. Ich muss es immer wiederholen. Nehmt das Leben nicht so tragisch! Und ich muss es einmal offen sagen, erwartet nicht soviel vom Jenseits und nehmt Euch mehr von diesem Leben! Ihr habt ja beide Anfälle von Fröhlichkeit, und es steckt sicher in Euch Beiden das Talent sich freuen zu können. Dieses Talent sollt Ihr entwickeln, und was Ihr sonst an Talenten haben möget, vernachlässigen.[94]

Ähnlich klingt es zwei Jahre später zu Hennigs Geburtstag:

> Liebes Hänschen! Als Geburtstagsgeschenk gebe ich Dir schriftlich, dass wir Dich leiden mögen. Auch dass uns deine Frau und Kinder nicht unsympathisch sind (...) und schenke dir zu Deinem Geburtstag selbst eine heitere Lebensauffassung (...) Es wird in der Welt niemand satter oder glücklicher, wenn Du aus dem Mülleimer Brot oder Kartoffeln heraussuchst. Lehren eines Vaters an seinen geliebten Sohn![95]

Es ist anzunehmen, dass hier gewisse unterschiedliche Lebensauffassungen, die sich durch die jeweiligen Erfahrungen während der Kriegsjahre noch verstärkten, aufein-

---

93 Auf seinen 'lausbübischen Humor' verwies Dr. Peter Harbison, der auch verschiedene Episoden und Geschichten erzählte, die dies beweisen (wahrscheinlich allerdings vor allem aus der Zeit nach den Kriegsjahren), Interview mit P. Harbison, 19.1.2001. Auch Prof. Hans Reiss erinnert sich an Hennigs Humor, email 27.9.2000.

94 Exilarchiv Frankfurt, Nachlass Felix Meyer, Brief Felix Meyer an John & Claire Hennig, 6.1.1947. 'Mönchen' war Hennigs zweite Tochter Monica, zum Zeitpunkt des Briefes knapp neun Jahre alt.

95 Exilarchiv Frankfurt, Nachlass Felix Meyer, Brief an John Hennig, 20.2.1949.

andertrafen. Hennig war sicherlich kein "Lebenskünstler", der in der Lage war, Dinge leicht zu nehmen, und hinzu kam, dass die besonderen Umstände seines Lebens in der Emigration offensichtlich ihre Spuren hinterlassen hatten.

Die anhaltende Reduzierung seines Familien- und seines Bibliotheklebens auf das Wochenende, die langen einsamen Abende mit ihren "inkommensurablen Beschäftigungen" forderten ihren Tribut. "So kann es nicht weitergehen" war jedenfalls auch Hennigs Reaktion (Statt, 161). Außerdem hatte seine Aufbauarbeit bei Bord na Móna einen gewissen Abschluss gefunden. Eine Alternative bot sich in Form eines Angebots einer anderen staatlichen Einrichtung, der Elektrizitätsgesellschaft ESB, an. Dort versah Hennig eine ähnliche Stellung wie bei Bord na Móna, nämlich die des Bibliothekars in ihrem Hauptbüro mitten in Dublin.

Die Arbeit bei der ESB brachte einige positive Veränderungen mit sich. Er war sowohl näher an der Familie, als auch näher an den wissenschaftlichen Quellen. Der regelmäßige Arbeitsschluss um 5 Uhr nachmittags und die zentrale Lage seiner Arbeitsstelle ermöglichten ihm konzentriertes Arbeiten in Dublins Bibliotheken. Hans Reiss, der schon in seiner Jugend ins Exil nach Irland und später Professor der Germanistik in Bristol wurde, erinnert sich:

> Oft sah ich ihn entweder im Reading Room der Trinity College Library oder in der National Library. Er arbeitete hart, war sehr fleißig und arbeitete anscheinend sehr konzentriert und systematisch; denn er hatte fast immer einen Zettelkasten bei sich.[96]

Bekanntschaft machte Hennig zu dieser Zeit auch mit dem Theaterkritiker und -chronisten Joseph Hone, der ihn dem Schriftsteller Arland Ussher (*Face of Ireland*) vorstellte, und mit Josephs Kusine, der Künstlerin Evie Hone. Joseph Hone hatte Hennig auch zur Mitarbeit an einem von ihm und Lennox Robinson geplanten 'Dictionary of Irish Writers' aufgefordert; er schrieb 50 Artikel von denen aber nur einer gedruckt wurde, das Lexikonprojekt kam nicht über den Buchstaben 'C' hinaus (Statt, 167).

Den wissenschaftlichen Kontakt hatte er, so gut es ging, auch während seiner Zeit im Berufsleben in Newbridge aufrechterhalten. Als Anerkennung für sein fortwährendes wissenschaftliches Schaffen wurde er Anfang 1947 als Kandidat der Royal Irish Academy in Betracht gezogen. Als Qualifikationen wurden neben seiner Dissertation und zwei noch 1936 in Deutschland erschienenen Artikeln neun Aufsätze (einge davon zu deutsch-irischen Beziehungen)[97] aufgeführt im 'Certificate of Candidate' der Royal Irish Academy. Als Befürworter seiner Aufnahme unterzeichneten der Keltologe Gerard Murphy und der klassische Philologe Michael Tierney ("from personal knowledge") und u.a. noch J.H. Delargy, Erwin Schrödinger und der in der *Bleibenden*

---

96 Hans Reiss (geb. 1922) kam als jugendlicher Exilant nach Dublin, um dort seine Schulbildung abzuschließen, studierte dann in Trinity College Dublin und bekam dort eine Stelle, auf die sich auch Hennig beworben hatte, email 27.9.2000.

97 Z. B. Goethe's friendship with Anthony O'Hara, *MLR* 1944, Jean Paul in Ireland, *MLR* 1945, The Brothers Grimm and T. Crofton Crocker, *MLR* 1946. Siehe Royal Irish Academy 'Certificate of Candidate, John Hennig', unterschrieben 19. Januar, am 27. Januar 1947 wurde es der Academy vorgelesen.

Statt erwähnte Anwalt Arthur Cox.[98] Ludwig Bieler und John Hennig wurden am 10.2.1947 in einem Eintrag erwähnt, der die zur Wahl anstehenden Kandidaten nennt. Bieler wurde am 15.3.1947 Mitglied der Akademie. Bei Hennig dauerte es ein wenig länger; am 16.2.1948 wurde er vorgeschlagen und gleichzeitig vom Rat der Akademie empfohlen, am 16. März wurde er zum neuen Mitglied erklärt und einen Monat später unterschrieb er die *roll* (Mitgliederliste).

Trotz der Hochachtung, die Felix Meyer mit den Jahren vor Hennigs Wissen gewonnen hatte ("fabelhaftes Wissen (...) klare[n] Ausdrucksformen. Es ist fabelhaft, ein solches Universalgenie zu sein")[99], sah er Hennigs Konzentration auf wissenschaftliches Arbeiten auch kritisch, denn er glaubte daran, dass Hennig sein Schreibtalent "gewinnbringender" einsetzen könne – "schreibe Kurzgeschichten".[100] Hennig meinte allerdings, er sehe durchaus seine spezifische Begabung, aber auch seine Begrenzung, ihm fehle der Wortschatz und die Leichtigkeit etwa eines William Saroyan in der *Human Comedy*.[101] Bei dieser immer enger werdenden und vertrauensvolleren Beziehung mit seinem Schwiegervater muss ihn der unerwartete Tod Felix Meyers am 14. April 1950 besonders getroffen haben. Neben dem großen persönlichen Verlust für Hennig und seine Frau bedeutete es auch, dass Hennig von nun an noch stärker für die Angelegenheiten der Firma Rota, die bei Kriegsende ins badische Säckingen ausgelagert worden war, zuständig sein musste. Außerdem galt es auch, sich um Marguerite Meyer zu kümmern, sie zog zumindest für einige Zeit zu der Hennig Familie nach Sutton. Seit 1949 war die Frage eines eigenen Hauses diskutiert worden (sehr empfohlen von Felix Meyer), schließlich kauften Hennigs wenige Kilometer von der Burrow Road ein Haus in der Kilbarrack Road in Sutton. Marguerite lebte zeitweise im Haus gegenüber. Das verstärkte Engagement für die Firma und Familie führte schließlich dazu, dass die Familie Hennig im Jahr 1956 nach Basel zog, von wo Hennig wieder die Leitung der Fabrik übernahm. Er überquerte jeden Tag die schweizerisch-deutsche Grenze, eine Rückkehr nach Deutschland war für die Familie nicht vorstellbar gewesen.

Neben dem Gefühl dem Andenken seines Schwiegervaters verpflichtet zu sein gab es wohl noch andere Gründe für den endgültigen Fortgang aus Irland und den Umzug auf den Kontinent. So spielten Gedanken um die Zukunft der drei Töchter eine Rolle bzw. der Wunsch, ihnen in Bezug auf weitere Ausbildung und Partnerwahl mehr Möglichkeiten zu bieten.

---

98   Das Protokollbuch der Royal Irish Academy enthält auch den folgenden Eintrag vom 27.1.1947: "The Secretary read the certificates of the following candidates for membership." Unter den acht Namen befinden sich die von Ludwig Bieler und John Hennig.

99   Felix Meyer an Claire und John Hennig, 29.5.1949, Exilarchiv Frankfurt, Nachlass Felix Meyer.

100 Brief Felix Meyer an Hennig, 27.2.1949, Exilarchiv Frankfurt, Nachlass Felix Meyer.

101 Brief Hennig an Felix Meyer, 9.12.1948, Exilarchiv Frankfurt, Nachlass Felix Meyer.

Die Schweizer Jahre

In der Schweiz waren Hennig nach Angaben seiner Tochter Monica neben seinen beruflichen und familiären Verpflichtungen in erster Linie seine Forschungen wichtig. Der Umzug in die Schweiz eröffnete in viel stärkerem Maße als zuvor die Möglichkeit, auf Deutsch zu veröffentlichen. Thematisch blieb er Irland noch lange verbunden, dazu kamen weiterhin Arbeiten zu Goethe und geschichtsphilosophischen Fragen und noch stärker liturgische Themen. Auch sprachphilosophische Fragen und begriffsgeschichtliche Studien interessierten ihn. Sein Kontakt mit dem Zentrum für Liturgiewissenschaft in Maria Laach vertiefte sich über die Jahre; 1967 wurde Hennig zum außerordentlichen Mitglied des Abt-Herwegen-Instituts für Liturgische und Monastische Forschung gewählt. Am 14.1.1971 wurde Hennig offiziell Bürger der Schweiz. Das Einleben war in den ersten Jahren nicht ganz problemlos gewesen. Wieder gab es eine deutliche Trennung zwischen (offiziellem) Arbeitsbereich, der Leitung der Firma Rota, zu der Hennig jeden Tag fuhr, und dem Wohn- und Forschungsbereich. Die finanzielle Absicherung der Familie war endlich kein Problem mehr, aber immer noch verbrachte Hennig seine Hauptarbeitszeit mit einer Erwerbstätigkeit, die nicht seinen eigentlichen Interessen entsprach. Dazu kam die Schwierigkeit, in Basel integriert zu werden. Hans Reiss erinnert sich an eine Begegnung mit Hennig in den Jahren 1958-1962, bei der Hennig darüber klagte, er werde als ‚Usländer‘ (Ausländer) angesehen.[102]

Doch es gab Kontakte mit Gleichgesinnten, wenn vielleicht auch nicht in dem Maße, wie es von Hennig erhofft worden war. Mit Karl Jaspers, der seit Juli 1947 in Basel Gastvorlesungen gehalten und im Frühjahr 1948 den Ruf an diese Universität angenommen hatte, pflegte Hennig nach seiner Übersiedlung in die Schweiz wieder engeren Kontakt, als es während der Kriegszeit und der anschließenden Jahre in Irland möglich gewesen war. Hennig trug auch zu dem Sammelband *The Philosophy of Karl Jaspers* einen Aufsatz mit dem Titel 'Karl Jasper's Attitude towards History' bei. Der persönliche Kontakt zwischen den Familien blieb so eng, dass Gertrud und Karl Jaspers bei der Hochzeit der Tochter Monica mit Dian Schefold als Gäste geladen waren. 1970, ein Jahr nach Jaspers Tod, erhielt Hennig in Anerkennung seiner wissenschaftlichen Leistungen die Ehrendoktorwürde von der Philosophischen Fakultät der Basler Universität verliehen. Hans Saner, der Herausgeber der Jasperschen Schriften,[103] erwähnt, dass Jaspers auf die Verleihung der Ehrendoktorwürde vielleicht einen "indirekten, posthumen Einfluss" gehabt habe. Auf alle Fälle, so der Eindruck, den Saner aus Gesprächen mit Jaspers gewann, war dieser von John Hennigs Arbeit- und Schaffenskraft sehr beeindruckt:

> Er hat ihn als vorzüglichen Goethe-Kenner und als Geschichts-Philosophen sehr geschätzt und auch als Erforscher der Liturgie. Über religionsphilosophische Fragen dürfte es hin und wieder Auseinandersetzungen gegeben haben. Jaspers liebte den Streit mit Argumenten, und er schätzte die Menschen, mit denen er streiten konnte.[104]

---

102 email Hans Reiss, 27.9.2000.

103 Hans Saner, Philosoph, Publizist, letzter Assistent Karl Jaspers, Herausgeber von dessen Werken.

104 Brief Hans Saner, 6.8.2001.

Wissenschaftlichen Umgang in Basel pflegte Hennig auch mit dem Basler Germanisten Karl Pestalozzi, der sich in einem Brief an Hennig für dessen Aufsatzsammlung *Literatur und Existenz* bedankte und seine Bewunderung "für die grosse Spannbreite Ihres Interesses und für die Treue im einzelnen, die auf den Feldern, die Sie bearbeiten, oft mühevoll ist" ausdrückte. Pestalozzi beurteilte Hennigs Arbeiten als "stets streng sachlich und ganz persönlich zugleich. Dass Goethe einen grossen Raum einnimmt, stimmt ganz damit überein, kam es doch immer auch darauf an, im Erforschten auch die Forscherindividualität zu erkennen".[105] Die in der erwähnten Sammlung vereinigten Aufsätze Hennigs wurden in ihrem jeweils ursprünglichen Schriftbild reproduziert und spiegelten dadurch auch zugleich die zeitlichen Hintergründe ihres ursprünglichen Entstehens wider. Pestalozzi sprach diesen Umstand an, indem er ausführte, er habe noch nie ein Buch gesehen,

> das Aufsätze verschiedener typographischer Physiognomie vereinigt. Das hat seinen besonderen Reiz. Die unterschiedliche Herkunft ist so erkennbar, jede Arbeit bekommt ein zeitliches Timbre. Ich wüsste nicht, wie man die interne Geschichtlichkeit besser in der Buchgestaltung zum Ausdruck bringen könnte, obwohl wahrscheinlich profanere Ueberlegungen dazu geführt haben.

Hennig hatte sich auch bei Pestalozzi erkundigt, ob "man in Basel 1982 etwas zu Ehren Goethes unternehme", worauf dieser sich mit Kollegen und dem Rektor der Universität besprach. Ein Ergebnis war, dass Hennig dazu eingeladen wurde, bei einer zu Goethes 150. Todestag veranstalteten Reihe einen Vortrag in der Universität zu halten. Er wählte dazu ein ihm sehr am Herzen liegendes Thema – "Goethes Kenntnis der nichtdeutschen europäischen Welt". Irland wird mit Sicherheit dabei eine wichtige Rolle gespielt haben.[106] In seinen späteren Jahren trat Hennigs Beschäftigung mit der Liturgie ganz hinter der mit Goethe zurück. Für ihn – der selbst noch mit über 70 Jahren noch die Geschicke der Firma lenkte neben seiner wissenschaftlichen Arbeit –

John Hennig starb am 16.12.1986 an einem Tumor in der Brust, eine einige Jahre zuvor durchgeführte Operation hatte keinen Erfolg gebracht. An seinen Bruder Karl schrieb Hennig fünf Jahre vor seinem Tod, er fürchte alle Wiederbegegnungen, und nannte dabei Dublin als Beispiel.[107] Nach seiner Übersiedlung in die Schweiz kehrte er nie mehr nach Irland zurück. Trotzdem – nach der Erinnerung seiner Tochter Monica, die in seinen letzten Stunden bei ihm war, lautete einer der letzten Sätze, den er auf dem Totenbett gesprochen hat, folgendermaßen: "Die Iren sind ein besonders begabtes Volk, denn sie sprechen andauernd eine Fremdsprache." Seine letzten Gedanken gingen sehr oft nach Irland zurück.[108]

---

105 Brief Karl Pestalozzi an John Hennig, 2.8. 1981, Privatbesitz Monica Schefold.

106 Er widmete den am 3. Juni stattfindenden Vortrag (der "im Unterschied zu den sicher sehr ideologischen Vorträgen der anderen Teilnehmer" positivistisch gehalten war) seinem Bruder Karl, der einen Tag später seinen 79. Geburtstag feierte. Vgl. Brief John Hennig an Karl Hennig, 23. April 1982, Privatbesitz Wolfgang Hennig.

107 Brief John Hennig an Karl Hennig, 19.2.1981, Privatbesitz Wolfgang Hennig.

108 Brief Monica Schefold, 17.8.2001.

John Hennig, der die anglisierte Form seines Namens, die er unmittelbar nach der Ankunft in Irland angenommen hatte, auch in der Schweiz beibehielt, verfügte seinen Leichnam zu kremieren. Die Urne mit seiner Asche wurde im Gemeinschaftsgrab des Friedhofs am Hörnli in Basel beigesetzt. Kein Hinweis markiert diese Stelle. Auch Claire Hennig wurde dort nach ihrem Tod 1990 bestattet. Die Wahl des Gemeinschaftsgrabes war durch den Wunsch entstanden, sich mit den vielen Namenlosen zu identifizieren, in Erinnerung an den Holocaust. Ein Grabstein mit Namen war nicht in ihrem Sinn.

John Hennig in Basel im Jahr 1984

Das anfangs erwähnte Gefühl, auf sich selbst gestellt zu sein, mag mit zu Hennigs frühen Selbständigkeit und dem geradlinigen Verfolgen seines eigenen Weges beigetragen haben. In allen Lebensbereichen folgte er seinen Überzeugungen, was sich in privaten, religiösen, politischen und beruflichen Entscheidungen widerspiegelt. Diese konsequente Lebenshaltung und seine tiefe religiöse Bindung führten allerdings nicht zu einem ausschließlich befriedigenden und erfüllten Leben. Trotz der immer wieder erfahrenen Anerkennungen und Ehrungen beispielsweise in Form der Aufnahme in die Royal Irish Academy, der Ehrendoktorwürde in Basel und der erfolgreichen Fürsorge für seine Familie unter schwersten Bedingungen, hatte er immer wieder das Gefühl, seine eigentliche Arbeit – seine Forschung und zahlreichen Publikationen – seien nie wirklich auf Interesse gestoßen. Als er kurz vor seinem 70. Geburtstag von den Plänen seines Bruders Karl hörte, noch ein Buch zu schreiben, erwiderte er: "Mir geht der Mut und die Kraft allmählich aus (...) da ich keinen Menschen kenne, der sich dafür interessiert."[109] In schweren Zeiten half ihm vor allem seine Familie.[110] Dennoch – die politischen Umstände in Deutschland, die ihm eine seinem Interesse und Können entsprechende berufliche Entwicklung verwehrten, und das aufgezwungene Exil ließen John Hennig gegen Ende seines Lebens folgendes Resümee ziehen: "Das [Konvertitendasein] ändert jedoch nichts daran, dass ich nicht nur gesellschaftlich, beruflich, politisch und sprachlich, sondern auch religiös entwurzelt bin" (Statt, 211). Aber er beendete seine Autobiographie versöhnlich und wies darauf hin, dass er zwar als Konvertit, Ausländer und Nichtprofessioneller Beschränkungen unterlag, aber dafür auch ungewöhnliche Freizügigkeit genießen konnte. In unserem Kontext gibt es noch einen anderen Grund, ein positives Fazit zu ziehen: Ohne die 'Entwurzelung' John Hennigs, die ihn aus dem deutschen akademischen Kontext riss, wären die hier gesammelten, wieder zugänglich gemachten Forschungen und die vielen persönlich gehaltenen Beobachtungen auf dem Gebiet der deutsch-irischen Verbindungen kaum entstanden. Die Geschichte der 'Irlandkunde', wie Hennig es als erster benannte, wäre mit Sicherheit eine andere, und ob deutsch-irische Studien auf dem selben Stand wären wie heute, wäre sehr fraglich.

---

109 John Hennig an Karl Hennig, 19.2.1981, Privatbesitz Wolfgang Hennig.

110 "(...) habe mich jetzt einigermassen gefangen, vor allem in Dankbarkeit dafür, dass ich leben darf und zwar von soviel Liebe umgeben", Brief John Hennig an Karl Hennig, 12.11.1980, Privatbesitz Wolfgang Hennig.

III Auszug aus *Die bleibende Statt*

Die bleibende Statt[1]

V. Krieg

Als ich im Morgengrauen die Treppe hinunterschlich, klopfte es an der Haustür. Noch ein Telegramm. Das Flüchtlings-Kommittee in Dublin teilte mit, das Visum für mich sei erteilt und läge in Paris zur Abholung bereit. Dass meine Familie weit gefährdeter war als ich und dass es nach Ausbruch des Krieges kaum möglich war, das Visum in Paris abzuholen, hatten die Guten nicht bedacht. Die Ahnungslosigkeit der Glücklichen wie der Gesunden, der Reichen wie der Erfolgreichen hat mich immer wieder bedrängt. Später einmal in Irland besuchte ich eine Freundin, die an Tuberkulose erkrankt war. Ich sagte zu ihr: "Es hat keinen Zweck, dass ich dir gut zurede, denn du wirst bei jedem Wort, das ich sage, erwidern: Aber du hast keine Tuberkulose". "Du bist der erste vernünftige Mensch, der zu mir kommt", erwiderte sie, "und du hast mir mehr geholfen als alle Trostsprüche".

Ich drahtete zurück nach Dublin, was aus meiner Familie werden solle. Antwort: Ich solle nur erst mal kommen, das weitere werde sich finden. Erst später lernte ich, dass eine solche Antwort im englischen Sprachbereich so gut ist wie die wortreichste Zusage anderswo. Ein Schmuggler fand sich bereit, gegen eine für uns in den neuen Verhältnissen riesige Summe mit meinem deutschen Pass nach Paris zu reisen und das Visum zu holen. Zwei schlaflose Nächte, die ich durchbetete. Dem Schmuggler könnte der Pass mehr wert sein als die Belohnung. Mein Schwiegervater hatte mich einfach gezwungen, Vertrauen zu haben, und behielt recht.

Es war gut, dass wir auf dem Schiff damit beschäftigt wurden, das Anlegen von Schwimmwesten zu üben, so dass keine Zeit blieb, die Küste verschwinden zu sehen. Bei der Landung in Folkestone nahm sich ein jüdischer Mann das Leben, als ihm verboten wurde, das Schiff zu verlassen. Ich wurde in das Bureau des Einwanderungsbeamten geführt. Mit mir war eine Familie. Der Mann wurde zuerst aufgerufen. "Schrodinger". "Erlauben Sie eine dumme Frage", sagte ich, als er zurückkam, "sind Sie etwa der grosse Schroedinger?". "Ob ich gross bin", war die Antwort, "weiss ich nicht. Aber ich bin Physiker und reise wie Sie weiter nach Dublin". Kein schlechtes Omen, dachte ich, in solcher Gesellschaft auszuwandern. In London liess man uns in jenen ersten Kriegstagen mit rührender Unbesorgtheit herumspazieren. Ich fuhr zur Westminster Kathedrale und betete am Altar des hl. Patrick, unter dessen Schutz ich mich nun stellte.

In Dublin bewahrte mich die Sachlichkeit, die ich bereits als Merkmal der Jesuiten erkannt hatte, vor unnützen Träumereien. Am Morgen nach meiner Ankunft stand ich vor einer meiner Klassen. "Ihnen als Deutschen muss ich sagen: Wir glauben nicht

---

1   Hier abgedruckt sind die unmittelbar Irland betreffenden Kapitel 'V. Krieg' (S. 122-152) und 'VI. Friede' (S. 153-176).

daran, die Jungens zu hart arbeiten zu lassen", war die einzige Anweisung, die ich mitbekam. Auf dem Schulhof stand ein Junge und sprach mit einem der Kleriker; er hatte das lose Ende von dessen Gürtel in der Hand und schlenkerte damit hin und her, während sie sich offensichtlich Witze erzählten. Vom Lehrer erwartete man, dass er sich zu Beginn der Stunde neben dem Katheder hinkniete und ein Ave Maria sprach. Das waren die Dinge, die mir zunächst auffielen. Deutsch nahmen in den beiden letzten Klassen Privilegierte. Ich hatte daher mit einer Elite zu tun. Später hat mir einer von den Jungens erzählt, welche Mühe sie sich gaben, nicht über mein mangelhaftes Englisch herzlich zu lachen.

Mit dem kleinen Vorschuss, den mir mein Schwiegervater in die Hand gedrückt hatte, konnte ich mir gerade ein Zimmerchen in einem viertklassigen Hotel in den slums leisten. Die erste Kälte setzte ein; nur in der Halle des Hotels brannte abends ein Torffeuer im Kamin. Ich sass am Fenster meines Zimmers, blickte auf die Reihe der aus dem 18. Jahrhundert stammenden Häuser und beobachtete die am Tor des Schulhofs gegenüber Vorbeigehenden, wie sie sich bekreuzigten, weil sie wussten, irgendwo da hinten war eine Kapelle.

An einer Hauswand sah ich ein Plakat, das zu einer Mission einlud. Ich fragte die Hotelwirtin, wo diese Kirche läge. "Das ist kein anständiger Bezirk", sagte sie. Das Wellblechkirchlein lag inmitten des durch James Joyces Portrait und Ulysses berühmt gewordenen Stadtteils; die erste Tat der Legion of Mary war gewesen, die Schliessung der dortigen Bordelle zu erreichen. Man hatte, so wurde erzählt, die Mädchen zu Exerzitien eingeladen, und sie waren gekommen. – Das Kirchlein war gefüllt von einer nach Lauch und Schmalz riechenden Menge. Die nassen Wollkleider dampften. Reihen von Frauen in schwarzen Kopftüchern. Zwei Redemptoristen liessen es an Eindringlichkeit nicht fehlen. Die Methode wurde mir später klar: Immer wurde ein Donnerer mit einem Säuseler gepaart, so dass die Gläubigen abwechselnd mit eiskaltem und mit lauwarmem Wasser begossen wurden. Auch die Büchlein sollte ich kennen lernen, aus denen die Anekdötchen – angeblich alle selbst und gerade erst kürzlich erlebt – entnommen waren. Aber was bedeutete das alles? Wer wissen will, was der Rosenkranz eigentlich sein sollte, muss ihn in einer Dubliner slums-Kirche mitgebetet haben. Wenn ich heute das (aussterbende) sentimentale Lied: "Mother of Christ, Star of the Sea, pray for the sinners, pray for me" höre, kommt mir die ganze Kümmerlichkeit unserer festländischen Intellektualität zu Bewusstsein.

Nach dieser Mission nahm ich an einer in der von Newman gegründeten Kapelle der Nationaluniversität teil. Studenten und Studentinnen standen Kopf an Kopf, auch den langen Gang hinunter, der von Stephen's Green auf diese Kapelle zuführt. Der Franziskanerpater sagte: "Ich sah neulich ein junges Mädchen unaufmerksam auf eine Hauptverkehrsstrasse laufen. Ein Auto quietschte. Sie schrak auf – und bekreuzte sich. Sehen Sie, die hatte die richtige Einstellung". Es gibt wenige Festländer, die mir auf diese Geschichte hin nicht erwidern: Na, noch besser wäre es gewesen, sie hätte aufgepasst.

Mein erster Gang war zum Justizministerium gewesen, um das Visum für meine Familie zu erlangen. Im Aufzug hing über der Tür mit einer Reißzwecke befestigt ein Bildchen. Ein Porträt DeValeras oder eines anderen Nationalhelden? Nein, das in jedem katholischen Heim in Irland anzutreffende Bild des Herzens Jesu mit der Umschrift: "Ich will das Haus segnen, wo mein Bild geehrt wird". Hier im Regierungsgebäude war dieses Bildchen nicht auf Anordnung hin angebracht worden, wie im Schuschnigg-Österreich die Heiligenbilder in den Amtsstuben.

Dass man sich bei Vorübergehen oder -fahren an einer Kirche bekreuzigt, wurde uns im Lauf der Jahre zur Selbstverständlichkeit. Auch der Billeteur in der Tram lüpfte seine Mütze. Erklang am Mittag oder Abend der Angelus, so sah man viele Menschen stehen bleiben, die Männer den Hut abnehmend. Einmal sah ich einen Verkehrs-polizisten auf seiner Kanzel den Helm abnehmen. Aus allen vier Richtungen warteten die Verkehrsteilnehmer ruhig. In der Staatsbibliothek kniete sich manch einer beim Angelus neben sein Lesepult hin. Niemand beachtete es auch nur. In den Büros hörten die Schreibmaschinen auf zu klappern, in den Schulen unterbrach man den Unterricht. War man bei jemand zu Besuch, so konnte es einem passieren, dass der Gastgeber sagte: "Lassen Sie uns eben zusammen den Engel des Herrn sprechen".

Nicht nur das Beten miteinander, sondern noch mehr das füreinander war ungeniert. Wie oft schüttete einem ein Mensch das Herz aus und wenn man am Schluss sagte: "Ich wünschte, ich könnte etwas für Sie tun", bekam man zur Antwort: "Aber na-türlich können Sie es, beten Sie für mich". Meine Mutter sagte, sie sei für schlaflose Nächte dankbar, dann habe sie Zeit, für all die Menschen zu beten, für die sie beten müsse. In Irland überreichte man zu Anlässen dem zu Beschenkenden ein Bukett von Gebeten, gewiss oft etwas mathematisch bestimmt, aber immerhin, eine wirkliche Arbeit.

Eine irische Freundin kam einmal zu mir und sagte: "Heute habe ich etwas Trauriges erlebt. Ich ging in die X-Kirche hinein und fand unsern Herrn ganz allein". Das war in der Tat selten. Neben dem Dankgebet und dem Bittgebet – vor allem auch für andere – war das Anbetungsgebet noch ganz lebendig. To drop in, die kurze Besuchung, ge-hörte für Tausende zur täglichen Routine. Mitten in der Stadt liegt die Karmeliter-kirche. Ständig schwenken Einkaufende von der Hauptstrasse ab, um dort ein paar Mi-nuten zu verbringen.

Später in unserer ersten Wohnung hörte ich am ersten Abend durch die dünnen Wande ein Gemurmel von nebenan. Erst nach einiger Zeit wurde mir klar, dass die ganze Familie zusammen den Rosenkranz sagte. Man sagt ihn in Irland in der Form, das vor jeder Dekade das Geheimnis kurz genannt wird. Das Einflechten eines entsprechenden Relativsatzes in jedes Ave Maria würde dem Iren als teutonische Bewusstheit er-scheinen. Wenn ich berichte, dass es in Irland viele Menschen gab, die vom 1. No-vember mittags bis zum 2. November abends mehrere hundert Seelen aus dem Feg-feuer herausbeteten oder dass auf der Wallfahrt in Lough Derg, von der ich noch er-zählen werde, man bis zu 1500 Ave Marias innerhalb 72 Stunden sagte, wird mir klar, wie unmöglich es ist, dem Festländer die Wirklichkeit zu vermitteln. Les Irlandais sont très superstitieux, sagte mir ein ausgezeichneter belgischer Katholik. Wer vier Wochen lang sich als Tourist in Irland aufgehalten hat, schreibt ein Buch über die Geheimnisse der grünen Insel (wie es derer ja jetzt Dutzende gibt). Wer ein paar Jahre dort gewohnt hat, schreibt einen Artikel "Meine Erlebnisse in Dublin"; wer 17 Jahre dort gelebt hat, möchte am liebsten schweigen.

Ich erhielt die Erlaubnis, mein "Gehalt" von Belvedere College durch Privatstunden-gelder his zu max. einem Pfund die Woche aufzubessern. Meine erste Schülerin war ein älteres Fräulein, Verkäuferin in einem Warenhaus. Sie gehörte zu der kleinen Schar katholischer Iren, die nicht den Sieg Deutschlands wünschten. Sie wolle Fran-zösisch lernen – dreist hatte ich angegeben, auch das könne ich lehren (Not lehrt auch schwindeln) – denn sie wolle einmal nach Lourdes pilgern. Sie habe im Gebet die Mutter Gottes gefragt, ob sie bei mir als Deutschem Stunden nehmen dürfe. Als Lek-türe brachte sie eine Biographie der hl. Terese von Lisieux, aber meist schlitterte der Unterricht in Privatunterhaltung hinein. Als Vollwaise lebte sie in einer der unsagbar tristen digs, die für unverheiratete Menschen die letzte Zuflucht sind. Was sie tun sol-le? Try to become a Saint, fuhr es mir heraus – unübersetzbar: Schon im Mittelalter kam Irland an seinen Titel "Die Insel der Heiligen" durch die irrige Annahme, das irische Wort für "heilig" bedeutet einen Kanonisierten. Meine Schülerin verstand na-türlich. Sie klatschte in die Hande. "Ja, das ist es" rief sie. "The Holy Ghost is a pet, er gibt mir alles". Pet ist das Liebkosungswort für Haustiere: die davon abgeleitete Ver-balform hat weniger mit dem Heiligen Geist zu tun.

Als nächstes kamen gleich drei junge Mächen, die in Amtstuben ein kümmerliches Da-sein als Stenotypistinnen fristeten. Sie hatten schon gut Deutsch gelernt, so dass wir sogar Gedichte lesen konnten. Nach zwei Jahren rief mich eine von ihnen an. Sie müsse aufhören, sie ginge nach England. Wohin? Sie nannte eine Industriestadt, die zu jener Zeit allnächtlich, damals noch schutzlos, dem Bombenregen ausgesetzt war. Ich bat sie, mir zu erlauben, ihr Aufwiedersehen zu sagen. Warum sie ginge? Ich wusste, dass sie nicht unbedingt auf Arbeit angewiesen war. Sie zögerte. "Ich erwarte ein Kind". "Das ist doch schön", sagte ich naiv. "Warten Sie". Wieder zögerte sie. "Der Mann ist jüdisch". Ein Orthodoxer, dem seine gute Mutter sagte, er solle schleunigst das Mädchen quitt werden. Sie wolle gern das Kind behalten, aber der Priester habe ihr gesagt, so ein Kind gehöre in ein Heim. Ich kämpfte wie ein Löwe, redete mit dem Mann, redete mit Priestern, aber ich war in einem Käfig. Wir waren gerade im tiefsten Dunkel. Jeden Tag konnten die Deutschen landen. – Beide mit dem Rücken gegen eine Wand stehend, blickten diese Frau und ich einander auf den Grund der Seele. Ich habe das Patenkind, dem sie dann in England das Leben schenkte, nie gesehen. Die Freun-din fand einen guten Mann, der sie mit Verständnis und Liebe geschützt hat. Die beiden sind in der Diaspora der Mittelpunkt eines Kreises edelgesinnter Ehepaare ge-worden.

Zu der äusseren Erbärmlichkeit des kirchlichen Lebens in Irland trägt bei, dass sich praktisch alle alten Gotteshäuser, sofern sie nicht in der Reformationszeit zerstört wurden, in protestantischer Hand befinden. In Dublin drängten sich in der katholischen Pro-Kathedrale jeden Sonntag die Massen in halbstündigen Messen zwischen 6 und 12 Uhr, oft mehrere Messen gleichzeitig an Seitenaltären, während sich zu den ein oder zwei Gottesdiensten in den beiden mittelalterlichen Kathedralen ein Trüpplein Angli-kaner einfand. Die neuen Kirchenbauten waren, mit Ausnahme der klassizistischen Pro-Kathedrale, unschilderbar hässlich, am schlimmsten die neuesten, in denen sich der taufrische bescheidene Wohlstand in marmornen Statuen, Fussbelägen und Wand-dekorationen ausdrückte. Zu meiner Zeit wohnten 85% der Katholiken jeden Sonntag der Messe bei, 70% erfüllten ihre Osterpflicht, 50% beichteten einmal im Monat, 30% allwöchentlich, um täglich kommunizieren zu können. 95% assen am Freitag kein Fleisch. Wir mussten radikal umlernen. Wenn am Heiligabend in der Pro-Kathedrale vor zehn Beichtstühlen jeweils zwei Reihen von bis zu dreissig Beichtkindern warteten, klapperten die Schieber vor den Fensterchen der Beichtstühle alle Minuten. Seelenführung konnte man zu anderen Zeiten, vor allem in den Klosterkirchen haben; hier galt nur das himmelstürmende Verlangen, mit Gott in Ordnung zu kommen. Nur wer hier nicht eingetreten ist, redet von Absolutionsautomaten.

Die Kehrseite der Medaille war unvergleichlich leichter zu sehen. Die typische Sklavenmentalität, gezüchtet durch beispiellose, jahrhundertelange Unterdrückung, Trunk- und Wettsucht, Arbeitsscheu, Schwindeleien und Mausereien, Unzuverlässigkeit in menschlichen Beziehungen, trockene Routine, kläglichste Perversionen, Heuchelei – keine Erfahrung davon blieb uns erspart. Und doch ist es nicht nur die unaussprechliche Dankbarkeit gegen das Land, das als einziges uns das Leben rettete und in dem unsere Kinder in Frieden aufwachsen durften, die uns all diese Dinge nicht in die Waagschale fallen lässt. Die Menschlichkeit reichte weit hinter die konfessionellen Trennungen zurück.

Während der ersten Monate, da wir mit Kleidung unzureichend versehen, einen nasskalten Winter in einer winzigen Wohnung überstehen mussten, erkrankten meine Frau und die beiden Kinder an Keuchhusten, zu dessen Heilung es damals noch kein Mittel gab. Bei unserer Ältesten entwickelte sich eine Lungenkomplikation. Unsere Hauswirtin bot zuerst Whiskey, dann Lourdeswasser als Heilmittel an. Als das Kind verloren schien, wandten wir uns an den grössten Kinderarzt der Stadt. Ohne einen Penny von uns zu verlangen, behandelte Dr. Collis unsere Tochter wie eine Patientin erster Klasse. Sie verdankt ihm ihr Leben.

Später war dieser Arzt der erste, der mit den Alliierten nach Bergen-Belsen kam. Er brachte von dort einige der überlebenden Kinder nach Irland. Man suchte Adoptiveltern. Bei einem achtjährigen Kind war nicht sicher, ob es jüdisch sei. Als Protestant bat der Arzt, es durch einen Katholiken prüfen zu lassen. Da das Kind etwas Deutsch sprach, wurde ich beauftragt. Ich nahm es mit in eine Kirche, es zeigte keinerlei Zeichen des Wiedererkennens. Beim Anblick eines Kruzifixes schien es mir eher abweisend zu blicken. Ich berichtete, es schiene mir unwahrscheinlich, dass das Kind katholisch sei. Unser katholischer Distriksarzt sagte zu mir: "Das war nicht die Antwort, die das Kommittee erwartet hatte. <u>You are an honest man</u>". Die Worte sind mir im Gedächtnis geblieben, nicht weil ich sie gerechtfertigt fand, sondern weil sie eine Freundschaft für mich begründeten. Dieser Arzt hat mich oft gestützt, wenn ich mich durch Engstirnigkeit bedrückt fühlte. Ich habe von ihm so gute Witze über Geistliche gehört, wie sie nur die erzählen können, die im Tiefsten die Kirche lieben.

Gerade in den kritischen Tagen der Erkrankung unserer Tochter wurde mir eine Tutorenstelle in einer adligen Familie in Westirland angeboten. Ich sollte in drei Wochen zwei Studenten in Deutsch auf ein Cambridge-Examen vorbereiten. Am ersten Morgen führte mich der zu einer efeuumrankten Ruine, die neben dem Herrenhaus lag. Wir kletterten hinauf. "Soweit Sie sehen können, gehörte dieses Land meiner Familie seit den Tagen der Normannen". Und doch waren sie Ausländer in Irland, kaum weniger als ich. Am Sonntag morgen bat ich, in der fünf km entfernten Pfarrkirche der Messe beiwohnen zu dürfen. Mit dem Hauspersonal und einigen Landarbeitern fuhr ich auf einem Pferdewagen hin. Es war die Atmosphäre, die ein anderer Leipziger, Goethes Freund Küttner, in dem ersten Buch eines Deutschen, das ausschliesslich Irland gewidmet ist, beschrieb.

Trotz unserer Angst, unsere eiserne Geldration anzubrechen, entschlossen wir uns, der Kinder wegen eine bessere Wohnung zu suchen. Überall waren die Türen verschlossen, wenn wir erwähnten, dass wir zwei kleine Kinder hatten. Endlich las ich eine Anzeige aus dem Vorort Sutton, der auf der Landzunge liegt, die den Hill of Howth (berühmt durch das Schlusskapitel von Joyces Ulysses) mit Dublin verbindet. Das baufällige Hüttchen kam als menschliche Behausung kaum noch in Frage. Auf dem Rückweg zum Bahnhof betrat ich das Wellblechkirchlein am Wegesrand. Dann wandelte ich noch, in Erwartung des nächsten Zuges, sehnsüchtig durch die Hecken in die herrlichen Gärten blickend, eine Villenstrasse entlang den Strand hinunter. Plötzlich entschloss ich mich zu einem verzweifelten Versuch. Ich klopfte an einem der Häuser und sagte, ich habe gehört, hier sei eine Wohnung zu vermieten. Ja, das stimme. Die Frau zeigte mir die Wohnung. Sie war ideal für uns geeignet, der Preis erschwinglich. Ja, wir hätten aber Kinder. Jungen oder Mädchen? Zwei Mädchen. Ach, das träfe sich ja bestens; sie suche Gesellschaft für ihr Töchterchen. Psychologisch ist es wahrscheinlich eine Perspektivenfrage, ob man Zufälle als Gebetserhörungen interpretiert oder nicht. Aber nachdem man einige Dutzend solcher Zufälle erlebt hat, hört man auf, sie noch als Zufälle zu bezeichnen. Ich meine allerdings, es geht dabei wie bei dem Volksglauben an den hl. Antonius. Er tut nichts mehr für einen, wenn man sich ihm nicht erkenntlich erzeigt. Meine Mutter pflegte zu sagen: "Vergiss über dem Bitten das Danken nicht".

Der erste Sommer kam. Ich konnte kaum an mich halten, nicht zu weinen, als mir der Rektor von Belvedere College eröffnete, während der – zwei Monate – Sommerferien könnte man mich natürlich nicht bezahlen, er wünsche mir vergnügliche Ferien. – Wenn ich auf meine Zeitungsannonce für Privatstunden einmal eine Antwort bekam, machte ich immer gleich einen Besuch, um den Fisch ans Land zu bekommen. Bei einem Herrn war ich kaum ins Zimmer getreten, als ich einen Wandspruch sah, der zeigte, dass er der Oxford Group angehörte. Ich hatte von ihr im Zusammenhang mit dem Treffen in Utrecht 1938 und durch Emil Brunners Zustimmung gehört. Nach wenigen Worten waren wir handelseinig. Das weitere Gespräch ergab, dass wir beide unseren Glauben ernst nahmen, er als Anglikaner, ich als Katholik. Ein paar Tage später besuchte er uns. Mit drei Kameraden wolle er im Auto mit Anhänger Westirland bereisen. Im Wagen sei Platz für vier. Sie hatten aber den hunch (Eingebung) bekommen, es müsse ein Fünfter mitgenommen werden. Immer wolle einer im Zelt schlafen. Er habe mich vorgeschlagen. Ich verlebte unvergessliche Tage am äussersten Westrand Europas. Eines Morgens baten mich die Freunde, einmal mit ihnen zu beten, wie ich es gewohnt sei. Ich hatte in einem trefflichen liturgischen Gebetbüchlein The Voice of the Church (wer kennt es heute noch?) ein Textchen gefunden, in dem das Wort quiet times vorkam (die Beobachtung der "stillen Zeit" jeden Morgen hatte

Frank Buchman empfohlen). Wir knieten nieder im Freien, im Anblick des Ozeans, und ich las. Nachher schrieben sich die Freunde das Gebet ab.

Zu unseren abendlichen Lagerfeuern stellten sich allmählich Eingeborene ein, Menschen, die in selbstgebauten Steinhütten zwischen Feldern wohnen, auf denen in Seetang ein paar Kartoffeln und etwas Hafer gezogen wird, deren Hauptnahrungsmittel im Winter das Seemoos Carageen ist und die sich vom Hummerfang kümmerlich ernähren. Wir sangen zusammen die schmissigen Lieder des Moral Rearmament und schlossen mit einem Gebet. Wir besuchten die eine oder andere Familie in ihrem Heim, das aus einem Raum besteht, halb unterteilt durch die Wand, an der dauernd das Torffeuer brennt, über dem der Wasserkessel oder Brotbacktopf hängt. Wir sassen auf Schemeln am Feuer, dem Ehrenplatz. Auf blitzblanken Tellern wurde uns frisches Brot mit Zucker bestreut, wohl auch ein Trunk Milch offeriert. Ein uraltes Grammophon wurde angestellt zum königlichen Willkommen.

Ein Mädchen aus einer der ärmsten Familien schrieb mir nach unserer Rückkehr, sie habe geweint, als wir abgereist seien, so schön sei es immer mit uns gewesen. Es entwickelte sich ein Briefwechsel. Ein Jahr später riss sie mit ihrem Freund aus. Heute ist sie Mutter von acht Kindern, das jüngste bekam sie zur gleichen Zeit, als ihre Tochter ihr erstes Kind gebar. Ausser vom Wetter, dem Fischfang und dem Vorankommen der Kinder schreibt mir die Frau regelmässig von ihrer Teilnahme an Rosenkranzkreuzzügen, Novenen und Missionen. Einmal in den seitherigen dreissig Jahren habe ich sie wiedergesehen, aber wenn ich von einem lebenden Menschen sicher sein kann, dass er für mich betet, ist sie es.

Der Freund, dem ich es verdankte, dass ich auf jene Reise mitgenommen wurde, begleitete mich am Sonntag in die Messe. Dörfer gibt es dort nicht. An einer Strassenkreuzung steht neben der Kirche der Allerweltsladen verbunden mit einer Gastwirtschaft, die leider meist zugleich als Bankfiliale fungiert, und dem Postämtchen. Nirgendwo, nicht einmal im Veitsdom in Prag, der Dionysiuskriche in Athen oder der Dormitiokirche in Jerusalem ist mir deutlicher zu Bewusstsein gekommen, wie stark der Gebrauch des Lateins dazu beitrug, mich die Kirche als Heimat empfinden zu lassen. Diejenigen, die heute so schnell das sog. Touristen- und Gastarbeiterargument unter den Tisch wischen, haben das Problem offenbar nie am eigenen Leibe zu spüren bekommen. Irland ist einer der wenigen Teile der englischsprechenden Welt, wo die Einführung der Volkssprache (wie auf dem europäischen Festland und in Afrika) nicht einigend gewirkt hat. Einerseits war es der Wunsch der irischen Regierung, dass die Leute im Westen die irische Sprache beibehalten sollten. Sie konnten es so schon kaum im Hinblick auf die für die Jungen unausweichliche Notwendigkeit, nach Grossbritannien oder Amerika auszuwandern. Andererseits ist die Vorschrift, mindestens eine der sonn- und festtäglichen Messen in irischer Sprache abzuhalten, weithin eine Farce; die meisten verstehen vom Irischen noch weniger als vom Lateinischen. Von einem Mädchen aus Westirland wurde folgende Geschichte erzählt: Sie kam als Dienstmädchen in eine Familie nach England. Am ersten Sonntag bat sie darum, in die Kirche gehen zu dürfen. Die Dame des Hauses schickte sie in die nächste anglikanische Kirche. Als das Mädchen zurückkam, sagte die Dame: "Nun, wie hat es dir gefallen?" "Ganz gut, nur habe ich nichts verstanden, es war alles in Englisch". Die

Pointe versteht man nur, wenn man berücksichtigt, dass nach dem Wunsch der irischen Regierung dieses Mädchen Irisch als Muttersprache gehabt haben sollte, aber natürlich voll englischsprechend war. Ich habe in keinem irischen Heim den – überall den Ehrenplatz einnehmenden – päpstlichen Hochzeitssegen in einer anderen Sprache als englisch oder lateinisch gesehen.

Am letzten Abend vor unserer Heimreise besuchten wir das Haus eines Jungen, der sich zu unserem Betreuer aufgeschwungen hatte. Er verschaffte uns Lebensmittel und Benzin. Die neue Generation: Er war zu Wohlstand gelangt, als ein Fass Azeton aus einem gesunkenen Schiff angespült worden war, Mangelware erster Ordnung, die unter Umgehung von Zoll und Polizei an den Mann gebracht worden war. Seine Mutter nahm den unerwarteten Segen Gottes hin, ohne unnütze Fragen zu stellen. Sie fragte uns nach dem Leben im fernen Dublin, und ich als sogar von jenseits England Gekommener wurde als Wundertier angestaunt. Die Frau liess mich niederknien und segnete mich speziell. Ich hatte keinen Grund, den Leuten zu sagen, es sei besser, sie schmuggelten nicht.

Von den vier, die mich mitgenommen hatten, gehörte jeder einer anderen Kirche an – Methodist, Anglikaner, Presbyterianer und Plymouth Brüder (hier naturlich die mildere Richtung, denn die strengen hätten ja nicht mit Unreinen verkehren dürfen). Naturgemäss nahm Religion in unseren Gesprächen einen breiten Raum ein. Die Vorschriften bezüglich <u>communio in sacris</u> waren für irische Katholiken äusserst streng. Als ich zum Begräbnisgottesdienst eines presbyterianischen Freundes gegangen war, sagte mir ein katholischer Freund, nur der Erzbischof könne mich von dieser Todsünde losen. Moral Rearmament, dem meine vier Freunde angehörten, war eine der für Katholiken verbotenen Bewegungen.

Ich fürchte, sie nahmen an, dass ich unter äusserem Zwang handelte, als ich mich der Bewegung nicht anschloss. Meine Gründe dafür aber waren anderer Art. Gerade der Ethizismus meines Vaters hat mich hellhörig gemacht gegen moralische Parolen. Die vier <u>standards</u> des Moral Rearmament – absolute Ehrlichkeit, absolute Reinheit, absolute Selbstlosigkeit und absolute Liebe – erschienen mir ebenso banal, wie mir heute die sozialpolitischen Programme erscheinen. Wer will das nicht?, würde ich mit meinem Vater sagen. Was wird mit diesen Manifesten wirklich erreicht? Habt Ihr auch nur eine blasse Ahnung, wie hart im Raume sich die Sachen stossen? Vor allem: Habt Ihr schon einmal mit dem Rücken gegen die Wand gestanden, wo Ihr erkennt, wie dünn diese Art von Moralismus ist?

Umso strahlender ging mir die konkrete Betätigung wirklicher ethischer Grundsätze auf. Ausser von Quäkern, habe ich von Mitgliedern der Oxford Group hierfür die grossartigsten Beispiele gesehen. Der einzige Tag im Jahr, an dem uns Heimweh überkam, war Weihnachten. In den meisten irischen Familien war der Heiligabend ein Trinkgelage. Mitternachtsmessen konnten nur in ganz beschränkten Maßstab vorgesehen werden, da zu viele der Gläubigen voll des süssen Weines ankamen. Der Weihnachtstag selbst wurde mit Papierschlangen und Luftballons, vor allem einem unerträglich schweren Mittagessen gefeiert. Neue Freunde aus Moral Rearmament lehrten uns, dass auch schönere Formen der weihnachtlichen Feier bekannt waren, vor allem durch Heranziehung Bedürftiger zum Familienmahl. Diese Freunde waren schottischer

Abstammung und hörten nach dem Essen mit Andacht die Ansprache des britischen Königs im Radio an. Georg VI wird erinnert werden als der Mann, der seinem Volk nicht ein tausendjähriges Reich versprach, sondern, als viele ohne Hoffnung waren, sagte: "Ich trat hinaus in das Dunkel und streckte meine Hand aus". Die Töchter dieser Freunde weihten ihr Leben Gott und waren vollamtlich für die Gruppe tätig mit dem Eifer, durch den kleinere religiöse Gemeinschaften so oft die Kirche beschämen.

Noch tiefer beeindruckte mich aber die Tätigkeit unseres Freundes für eine arme katholische Familie aus Westirland. Der Vater arbeitete in Dublin, hatte sich aber, getrennt von seiner Familie und schlecht untergebracht, dem Trunk ergeben. Eines Tages erschien er im Büro unseres Freundes, wieder einmal ausgebrannt. Unser Freund nahm ihn mit in eine katholische Kirche und liess ihn dort eine Weile beten. "Nach einiger Zeit merkte ich, dass er wieder seinen Frieden mit Gott gefunden hatte". Durch Beziehungen verschaffte unser Freund dem Mann eine Stellung in der Nähe seiner Familie. – Der junge Mann, der mich nach Westirland mitgenommen hatte, besass ein Wochenendhäuschen in den Wicklowbergen nahe Dublin. Als er einmal hinauskam, sah er dass es grauenhaft verwüstet worden war. Die Übeltäter wurden gefasst. Mein Freund erreichte, dass der Richter die bislang Unvorbestraften mit folgender Strafe entliess. Sie mussten drei Wochenenden dafür opfern, in dem Häuschen eine Krippe aufzubauen für das kommende Weihnachtsfest und dort mit ihm armen Kindern der Gegend bescheren.

Die Gattin eines hohen Beamten wurde zu dieser Zeit ebenso wie ich durch Wohltaten, die sie von Mitgliedern des Moral Rearmament geschehen sah, angezogen. Auch sie war Konvertitin. Wir fanden uns in der Notwendigkeit, einerseits die Gruppe gegen Verdächtigungen durch Katholiken zu verteidigen, andererseits aber unseren Freunden in der Gruppe begreiflich zu machen, dass wir einen anderen Weg zu gehen hatten. Als diese edelgesinnte Frau ihren Mann verlor, durfte ich ihr etwas behilflich sein. Ihre Ehe war nicht glücklich gewesen, und sie konnte nicht, wie manche andere in ähnlicher Lage, posthum den Gatten vergöttern. In ihrem Leben wie in dem meinen brachten äussere Eingriffe die Lösungen. Sie zog mit ihrer Tochter nach Neuseeland und hat dort in Frieden ihr Leben beschlossen. Aus ihrer evangelischen Jugend hatte sie sich eine Nüchternheit in der Selbsteinschätzung bewahrt, welche ihre Seelengröße umso deutlicher hervortreten liess.

Ähnlich wie mit Moral Rearmament ging es mir mit der Legio Mariae: Auch ihr konnte ich mich trotz hervorragender Beispiele einzelner Mitglieder, ja grosszügiger Freundschaftsbeweise durch mehrere vor ihnen, nicht anschliessen. Die Einladung dazu kam von höchster Stelle. Ein junger Privatschüler hatte mir begeistert von seiner Tätigkeit in der Organisation erzahlt. Ebenso wie Moral Rearmament gibt die Legion dem kleinen Mann eine Chance und damit Selbstbewusstsein. In eine Sitzung der Gruppe sei unangekündigt der (gefürchtete) Erzbischof gekommen, er habe aber ganz bescheiden Platz genommen und das Geschäft sei weitergegangen. Von dem Geschäft dieser Sitzungen hatte uns eine kleine Laienaufführung in der Legionshalle unseres Bezirks eine Vorstellung gegeben. Mit irischer Ironie hatte man dort die kleinen Fehlleistungen in solcher Arbeit gezeigt, persönliche Eitelkeit, Geschwätzigkeit, Liebesbeziehungen udgl. Mein Freundchen führte mich bei Frank Duff, dem von seinen Anhängern als Heiligen verehrten Gründer der Legion, ein. Auf meine Bedenken hin, als Ausländer hätte ich doch kaum eine Möglichkeit mitzumachen, schlug er mir vor, eine katholische Untergrundorganisation im Nazideutschland aufzuziehen. Ich könnte sie doch als Goethegesellschaft tarnen. Entscheidender war, dass er, als ich ihm einen konkreten Notfall, der mir bekannt geworden war, vortrug, diesen zu verstehen trachtete, indem er ihn mit einem äusserlich ähnlich gelagerten Fall verglich, dabei aber, wie mir schien, die entscheidende Eigenart des von mir vorgetragenen Falls verfehlte. Seit meiner Dissertation habe ich die Ansicht vertreten, dass Vergleichen zwar eine praktisch unvermeidliche Eselsbrücke, aber eine im geistigen Bereich letzten Endes lebensgefährliche Methode sei. In dem Streit zwischen nomothetischer und idiographischer Geschichtsbetrachtung stehe ich absolut auf dem idiographischen Standpunkt. Mit Jaspers verband mich die Aversion gegen die nomothetische Psychiatrie. In der karitativen Arbeit war mir von Kindertagen her das unlösbare Problem, sachgemäss wirksame und individuelle Behandlung zu verbinden, bewusst. Duff traf also ahnungslos auf einen neuralgischen Punkt bei mir.

Noch peinlicher berührte mich in späteren Jahren die Behandlung, die die Legion einer jungen Griechin angedeihen liess, die in unsere Gegend zog. Sie war an einen in der britischen Armee dienenden Iren geraten, der sie aber, nachdem sie ihm drei Kinder geboren hatte, sitzen liess. Von dem Grundsatz der Legion, "jede Hilfe ausser materieller zu gewähren", trennte mich mein Wirklichkeitsbewusstsein und meine Lebenserfahrung. In diesem konkreten Fall folgten die Mitglieder der Legion diesem Grundsatz auch nicht unbedingt. Als aber die junge Frau sich weigerte, römisch-katholisch zu werden, wurde über sie in einem Ton gesprochen, der mir missfiel. Gewiss hatte sie ruppig und wohl sogar undankbar reagiert, aber ist es nicht das Normale, dass ein geprügelter Hund auch die Hand, die ihn streicheln will, beisst? Zudem fühlte ich mit der Griechin, dass ihr ihre Kirche die letzte Heimat war, die sie noch hatte.

Das Manuskript eines Büchleins, das ein Dubliner Verleger angenommen hatte, über die Geschichte und die Liturgie des Festes Maria Mittlerin aller Gnaden legte ich Duff vor. Er bemängelte meine Übersetzung der Oratio und schlug eine Fassung vor, die m.E. eine Dogmatisierung antizipierte. Ich nahm sie nicht an. Duff war verschnupft. — Den Haupteinwand, den ich immer wieder gegen die Legio hörte, ihre Methode, bei Hausbesuchen schnurstracks aufs Ganze zu gehen, sei taktlos, habe ich nie akzeptiert. Die Frage: Wann haben Sie Ihre Frau zum letzten Mal geschlagen? ist gar nicht so schlecht. Die ständigen Siegesmeldungen der Legion hatten mich etwas ermüdet, aber dann hörte ich von dem Märtyrertum der Legionäre in China. Immer wieder habe ich mich bei der Begegnung mit solchen tatkräftigen und opferfreudigen Gruppen gefragt, ob es der den Intellektuellen nachgesagte Mangel an echtem Engagement ist, der mich zurückhielt. Ich war dankbar, wenn äussere Umstände mir die Entscheidung abnahmen, etwa durch echte Überbürdung mit naheliegenderer Arbeit oder durch erforderlichen Ortswechsel. Da ich auf der kleinen Reise nach Westirland endlich einmal einige Wochen lang nur Englisch gesprochen hatte, fühlte ich mich befähigt, durch kleine schriftstellerische Arbeiten meine kärglichen Einkünfte aufzubessern. Eins der religiösen Blättchen, die Missionsorden verbreiten, nahm meine erste Arbeit an. Das Honorar betrug zehn Schillinge. Eine katholische Wochenzeitung, der Standard, fand an anderen meiner Artikel Gefallen und erklärte sich bereit, allwöchentlich 1000 Worte abzunehmen. Die Presse spiegelte die geistige Situation des Katholizismus in Irland wieder. Die einzige ernstzunehmende Tageszeitung war die Irish Times, ein betont protestantisches und englandfreundliches Blatt. Als katholisch waren allenfalls die Wochenzeitungen anzusprechen, von denen der Standard sozial und nationalistisch, der Irish Catholic devotionell eingestellt waren. Meine Lage beim Standard war peinlich. Am Tage nach der ersten Bombardierung von Coventry wurde ich dort zu den wackeren Taten meiner Landsleute beglückwunscht. Ich spezialisierte mich darauf, über jedes neue Land, das Hitler überfiel, einen Artikel zu schreiben, in den ich hineinpackte, was über die Lage der katholischen Kirche dort zu sagen war. Mir kam zu statten, dass ich eine Wendigkeit im Aufspüren von möglichen Informationsquellen besass und nicht auf englischsprachige Literatur beschränkt war. Von 1944 an erschien dann eine entsprechende Artikelserie über die Länder, aus denen die Deutschen weichen mussten. Es war ein makaberes Geschäft.

Einmal schrieb ich auch einen Artikel über die Lage der Katholiken in Indochina. Der Standard bekam einen wütenden Brief von einem Pater, dessen Name, Graf Spreti, tiefen Eindruck machte; die Informationen seien total veraltet. Natürlich waren sie es. Ich hatte sie aus einem Buch aus dem Jahre 1937 entnommen. Ich entschuldigte mich bei dem Schreiber des Briefes und erklärte meine Lage. Prompt erhielt ich eine Einladung, ihn und seine Gemeinschaft, die Steyler Patres, inmitten Irlands zu besuchen. Ich werde später von diesem Besuch erzählen.

Auf dem Schweizer Konsulat durfte ich jede Woche zwei Nachmittage die Neue Zürcher, die Tat und die Schweizer Rundschau lesen und konnte dadurch Nachrichten sammeln, die keine andere Zeitung brachte. In dem damaligen Gesandten, Herrn Dr. Benzinger, und in seinem gepflegten Heim trat mir das Beste von dem Lande, in dem ich eines Tages leben sollte, entgegen, und das zu einer Zeit, in der ich es gebrauchen konnte, zu erfahren, dass irgendwo die Welt noch heil sei. Die Überlegenheit, mit der Benzinger die Situation des Katholizismus in Irland beurteilte, liess mich ahnen, dass ich es nicht leicht haben würde, sollte ich mich eines Tages wieder ausserhalb dessen bewegen müssen, was mich im Augenblick in seinen Bann gezogen hatte. Aber ohne die mir glücklicherweise in die Wiege gelegte Gabe, nach Möglichkeit an den jeweiligen Umständen nur das Gute zu sehen, hätte ich meine Lage kaum so gut ertragen, und die Dankbarkeit, die ich gegen Irland fühle, ist ausreichende Entschuldigung für eventuellen Mangel an Objektivität.

Meine wirtschaftliche Existenz war insofern besonders prekär, als ich weder in meinem ursprünglichen noch in dem späteren wirtschaftlichen Beruf äusserlich qualifiziert war. Betätigung in der Wirtschaft war in dem an Arbeitslosen reichen Lande unmöglich, solange ich Ausländer war. Meine Lehrtätigkeit wurde etwas erweitert, indem mir einige Sprachstunden an Deutschstudenten auf der Nationaluniversität übertragen wurden. Nur auf Grund persönlicher Empfehlung – das einzige Mal in meinem Leben, dass ich davon Gebrauch machte – wurde ich zum deutschen Lektor an dem nationalen Priesterseminar in Maynooth bestellt. Kurz zuvor hatte ich mich in meiner Verzweiflung entschlossen, das Studium der Architektur zu beginnen. Da ich gleichzeitig eine Reihe Vorträge an der Central Catholic Library halten durfte, ergab es sich, dass ich mich von 9 - 12 mit den Unterschieden zwischen sash-windows und casement-windows, von 2 - 3 mit dem Unterschied zwischen trennbaren und untrennbaren Verben und von 4 -5 mit dem zwischen Benediktionen und Konsekrationen befasste, wenn ich nicht Abends noch einen Artikel über das Verhältnis zwischen Tschechen und Slowaken schrieb.

Meine Klerikerstudenten in Maynooth brachte ich jedes Jahr in wenigen Stunden soweit, dass sie einigermassen das Neue Testament in Deutsch lesen konnten. Die Exemplare holte ich mir in der protestantischen Bibelgesellschaft; ich war zu jener Zeit wohl der einzige Katholik, der diesen Laden betrat. Ich richtete meine Fahrten zu dem 30 km von Dublin gelegenen College so ein, dass etwas Zeit blieb, um auf der Bibliothek zu arbeiten. Hier wie in der Nationalbibliothek genoss ich das Vorrecht, an die Regale herangehen zu dürfen. Ich musste die begrenzten bibliothekarischen Möglichkeiten geschickt ausnützen, um meine wissenschaftlichen Arbeiten zu fördern. Mein Hauptquartier war Trinity College Library, eine der copy-right Bibliotheken von Grossbritannien, aber für Theologica war ich auf andere Bibliotheken angewiesen. Ich fand heraus, dass der erste Band des Jahrbuchs für Liturgiewissenschaft sich in der Nationalbibliothek befand, die weiteren Bände bis Kriegsausbruch standen in Maynooth. Eine für mich wichtige Zeitschrift entdeckte ich endlich in der Bibliothek der Jesuiten in Rathfarnham. Eine Pontificale und die Konkordanz zur Vulgata entlieh ich von einem Ordensgeistlichen. Die blosse Organisation der unentbehrlichsten Unterlagen verschlang viele Stunden.

Meine Produktion reichte von his heute noch bei Woolworth verkauften Heften der Irish Home Handbook Series betitelt "Der Hausarzt", "Mutter und Kind", "Die frohe Braut" und "Moderne Jugend", wofür ich je sechzig Pfund bekam (ich vermischte munter Zusammengelesenes mit Selbsterlebtem) bis zu Abhandlungen über abgelegene kirchengeschichtliche und theologische Fragen, die ich auf gut Glück an Zeitschriften sandte, die ich oft nur dem Namen nach kannte, in Grossbritannien, den USA und Kanada, wo ich für die Sonderdrucke bezahlen musste. Bis an die zehn Mal kam ein Artikel mit dem "Der Herausgeber bedauert"-Zettelchen zurück, oft so zerknittert, dass ich ihn neu schreiben musste. Ich entdeckte, dass zwischen den keltischen Philologen, die von Liturgie keine Ahnung haben, und den Liturgiewissenschaftlern, die Irland für einen Teil von England halten, noch Raum war für einen, der auf beiden Gebieten Halbwissen besitzt. Auf eine Abhandlung über das dem alten Irland eigene Fest aller Heiligen Europas bin, in welchem ich erstmalig meine inzwischen selbst in Liturgischen Wörterbüchern angenommene These vertrat, dass die alte irische Liturgie auf einem anderen Zeitbewusstsein beruhte als die römische, sprach mich der Keltist Gerard Murphy an. "Da haben Sie eine wirkliche Entdeckung gemacht", sagte er. "Sie haben mir überhaupt erst das Verständnis für unsere irischen Martyrologien erschlossen". Murphy beantragte dann meine Aufnahme in die Royal Irish Academy. Verpflichtet in diese illustre Gesellschaft wurde ich durch Monsignore Boylan, den grossen Exegeten, der damals ihr Präsident war. Einmal stand ich im Lesesaal der Akademie an dem Tisch, auf dem Neueingänge aufliegen. Es lagen da auch zwei neue Sonderdrucke von mir. Ich hörte wie ein Besucher zum anderen sagte: "Wer ist eigentlich dieser Hennig?"

In einem etwas weiteren Bereich rückte ich unter die Spezialisten für irische Heilige – wirkliche und, wie Louis Gougaud gesagt hatte, "sogenannte" – auf dem Festland auf, aber ich stellte die Betrachtung dieses Gebietes in einen grösseren Zusammenhang. Mich interessierte an den Heiligen nicht wie die meisten anderen Bearbeiter des Themas die Historizität, sondern die Tradition und zwar insbesondere als Träger oder Ausdruck festländischer "Irlandkunde". Ich prägte dieses Wort im bewussten Gegensatz zu dem von meinem entfernten Verwandten Walter Hofstätter erfundenen Worte "Deutschkunde" und freue mich, dass es nun sogar von einem Universitätsinstitut in seinen Titel aufgenommen worden ist. Die Geschichte der festländischen insbes. deutschen Irlandkunde hat wohl niemand ausgiebiger durchforscht als ich. Ihr sporadischer Charakter eignet sich für die mir allein mögliche Behandlung in Zeitschriftenartikeln. Das Thema ist eine traurige Illustration des im katholischen Bereich verwunderlichen Continentozentrismus, vor allem in dem Mangel an Bereitschaft anzuerkennen, dass Grundkonzeptionen unseres Denkens anderswo nicht passen. Die Erfahrung, dass hinter jenen Bergen auch noch Leute wohnen, anders als ich bin oder auch je sein kann, ist mir in Irland so massiv zuteil geworden, dass ich mich einer gewissen Verärgerung nicht erwehren kann über die Selbstverständlichkeit, mit der heute mitteleuropäische Mittelbürger annehmen, sie wären der alleingültige Maßstab.

Die wenigen, von denen ich in meiner schriftstellerischen Tätigkeit, deren Ertrag meine Familie vor dem Schlimmsten rettete, Ermutigung erfuhr, waren besondere Menschen. Gleichzeitig mit uns und aus dem gleichen Grunde wie wir war Ludwig Bieler nach Irland gekommen. Durch Arbeiten zur irischen Kirchengeschichte ausgewiesen, wurde ihm zunächst eine bescheidene, dann aber verdientermassen stetig in Glanz steigende akademische Laufbahn eröffnet. Er wurde Spezialist für den Nationalheiligen, und DeValera betraute ihn mit dem Sammeln von Nachrichten über irische Handschriften, die sich ausserhalb Irlands befinden. Bieler legte die Grundlage für die einzigartige Mikrofilmsammlung in der Nationalbibliothek zu Dublin. Mit ihm und seiner Frau verbindet uns Freundschaft in fester Verwurzelung im Glauben und in Bereitschaft für Neues, das an uns herantritt.

Eoin McNeill, einer der ersten Kenner des alten Irland, war der erste, der mich ermunterte, die Beziehungen Irlands mit dem frühmittelalterlichen Festland über die üblicherweise in der Kirchengeschichte behandelte sog. Missionszeit hinaus zu verfolgen. Bei meinen Studien über die Beschäftigung des jungen Goethe mit einer keltischen Sprache, Macphersons "Originalen" der Dichtungen Ossians, gab er mir unschätzbare Hinweise. Meines Lehrers Witkowski eingedenk, betrachtete ich die zahlreichen Bezugnahmen auf Irland in der mittelhochdeutschen Literatur nicht, wie bislang üblich, motivgeschichtlich, sondern als Ausdruck des Wissens von einem entlegenen Land, mit dem keinerlei materielle Verbindungen bestanden. Mit dieser Studie stellte ich mich zuerst bei der Akademie vor.

Ein anderes Mitglied der Akademie und zugleich mein Rechtsberater, Arthur Cox, nahm Interesse an dieserArbeit. Er war wohl der ausserordentlichste Ire, den ich gekannt habe. Verheiratet mit der Witwe des im Bürgerkrieg von DeValeras Anhängern getöteten Ministers Kevin O'Higgins, war er doch auch den Regierungen der Partei DeValeras ein unentbehrlicher Ratgeber. Sein Büro am Stephen's Green sah so aus, wie man sich die englischen Anwaltsbüros zur Zeit Dickens' vorstellt. Er sass immer im Halbdunkel. Ob er einem zuhörte, war nur an einem gelegentlichen Grunzen, das er äusserte, zu entnehmen. Wenn er dann aber etwas sagte, so war es schlechthin Gold. Ich habe zunächst bei ihm gelernt, dass der beste Anwalt der ist, der einen so lange wie möglich von Streitigkeiten abhält. Einmal fragte er mich: "Ja, wollen Sie den Mann zum Feind haben?" Diese Frage hat mich seither an vielen Stellen vor Dummheiten bewahrt. Waren wir mit dem geschäftlichen Teil fertig, lud mich Cox oft zu einer Tasse Tee in einem kleinen Café ein. Dann fragte er: "Und was machen Sie wirklich?", wobei er praktisch der einzige war, der unter "wirklich" meine wissenschaftlichen Interessen verstand. Es gab kein Thema, zu dem er nicht sachkundig und weise Stellung nehmen konnte. Zufällig entdeckte ich, dass dieser vielbeschäftigte Mann täglich eine Stunde am Bett seiner schwer leidenden Mutter verbrachte. Mehr als sechzigjährig gab er seine glänzende Praxis auf, trat bei den Jesuiten ein und ging in die Mission nach Afrika. Er starb, wie er gelebt hatte: Er fiel einem Unfall zum Opfer, als er in Ausübung seines Berufs unterwegs war.

Unserem Nachbarn Frank Gallagher, als Schriftsteller (vor allem durch sein Tagebuch über seinen Hungerstreik 1916) unter dem Namen David Hogan bekannt, Propagandaminister von DeValera, verdanke ich, dass ich einer der ersten war, der nach dem Kriege in das irische Bürgerrecht aufgenommen wurde. Gallagher war sich darüber im Klaren, dass mir viel zu einem richtigen Iren fehlte. Vor allem hatte ich nicht die Zeit gefunden, Gerard Murphys Rat zu folgen, Altirisch zu lernen. Modernes Irisch erlernte ich nur in den Anfangsgründen mit meinen Kindern. Gallagher sah aber, dass ich eine einigermassen erträgliche wirtschaftliche Existenz nur finden konnte, wenn ich das Bürgerrecht besass. Und selbst dann noch blieb ich natürlich benachteiligt als Papierire.

Von diesem echten Patrioten habe ich mehr von der jüngsten irischen Geschichte gelernt als durch alle Bücher. Die Schreckensjahre hatten ihm nicht seinen goldenen irischen Humor geraubt. Sein Glück waren seine zwei Adoptivtöchter. Vor allem habe ich selten einen Menschen gesehen, der so von natürlicher Frömmigkeit überströmte wie er. Die daraus resultierende fundamentale Menschenfreundlichkeit drückte sich in den Geschichten aus, von denen er voll steckte. Dass schon durch die Übersetzung der eigentliche Charme, den sie in seinem Munde hatten, verloren geht, ist selbstverständlich.

Den Unterschied zwischen der englischen und der irischen Sprache illustrierte Gallagher wie folgt: "Ich musste neulich eine Familie in der Gaeltacht (dem Bezirk, wo noch Irisch gesprochen wird) besuchen. Als ich ins Haus kam, sagte die Grossmutter der Familie zu mir: "Hallo, Frank, Du hast einen hübschen fetten Wanst". Hätte sie Englisch gesprochen, so hätte sie gesagt: "Guten Tag, Herr Minister!" Wenn ich von meinen Töchtern sage: "Ich habe sie alle gleich gern, besonders die Jüngste", so schaut mir Frank über die Schulter. Leute auf dem Festland, zu denen ich diesen Satz sage, sehen mich verwundert an und erwidern: "Aber das ist doch ein Widerspruch!".

Um die Eigenart der Iren zu kennzeichnen, erzählte Gallagher gern die schon in der älteren Literatur festgehaltene Geschichte von den zwei Iren, die einem der verhassten englischen Landbesitzer auflauern, um ihn bei der nächtlichen Rückkehr von der Stadt zu ermorden. Es wird zehn, es wird elf, kein Hufschlag zu hören. Halb zwölf endlich sagt der eine Ire zum andern: "Dem armen Kerl wird doch nichts zugestossen sein?" Um die Zeit, da ich diese Geschichte von Gallagher erzählt bekam, las ich in einer Zeitung, dass Frank, der Naziherr in Polen, einmal in Lodz eine Rede gehalten hatte, worin er sagte: "Ich sehe hier gar keine Plattfüssler mehr. Ihr werdet doch nicht unsanft mit ihnen verfahren sein?"' Die Iren sagen: Es bedarf vieler Narren, die Welt zu machen.

Geistliche, die sich oft in Gallaghers Haus einfanden, schonte der Hausherr nicht. In Irland gibt es keine Kirchensteuern, sondern empfangen die Geistlichen zu Weihnachten und Ostern dues, freiwillige Geldgaben nach Selbsteinschätzung. Gallagher pflegte zu sagen: "Bis zu zwei Pfund hinunter wird bei der Verlesung der eingegangenen Beträge in der Kirche "Mister" gesagt, bis zu einem Pfund hinunter der Familienname genannt, darunter heisst es nur noch "John ... Peter ... usw.". "– Ein Pfarrer in einem an sich einigermassen wohlhabenden Dorf", so erzählte Gallagher, "hatte Mühe, auch nur das Lebensnotwendigste zu erhalten. Eines Tages bat ihn das Factotum, das ihm als Sakristan diente, ihn einmal mit der Einziehung der dues zu beauftragen. Nach langem Zögern gab der Pfarrer für einmal nach. Einige Tage später begann es, ins Pfarrhaus Briefe zu schneien, die Schecks und Banknoten enthielten. In einem Kouvert aber steckte ein Zettel, auf dem stand: 'Hochwürden, einl. sende ich wie verlangt die dues, aber bitte vormerken, dass 'dreckig' mit ck geschrieben wird und 'Lump' nur mit einem p.' "

Die Charakterunrerschiede zwischen richtigen Iren und den Engländern sind so gross, dass ich mich nicht genug wundern kann über die Naivität festländischer Zeitungen und Rundfunkgesellschaften, die sich aus London über Irland berichten lassen. Bis vor kurzem gab es in England hauptsächlich zwei Klassen katholischer Geistlicher, aus Irland importierte und in England geborene Konvertiten. Gallagher erzählte von einem aus Irland stammenden Pfarrer in Liverpool, der unter der Sauertöpfischkeit der Konvertiten litt, die man ihm als Vikare schickte. Auf seine Beschwerde schrieb ihm der Bischof, beim nächsten Vikar werde er hoffentlich zufrieden sein. Der junge Mann wurde ins Zimmer gebeten. "Konvertit?". "Ja". Der Pfarrer konnte einen Seufzer nicht unterdrücken. "Eine Zigarette?". "Gern". "Ein Gläschen Bier?". "Warum nicht?". "Ein Schnäpschen dazu?" "Mit Vergnügen". "Nun sagen Sie mir, mein Lieber, was hat Sie solange aus der Kirche fern gehalten?".

Endlich eine letzte Frank-Geschichte. Eine Frau trifft auf dem Weg zur Messe eine Nachbarin, mit der sie verfeindet ist. "Leider bin ich jetzt im Stand der Gnade", ruft sie ihr zu, "aber warte nur, wenn ich von der Kommunion zurückkomme, dann gebe ich es dir". – Die gegenwärtige Kritik an der Kirche könnte durch eine gesunde Dosis Humor an existentiellem Ernst gewinnen.

Irland konnte seiner Armut wegen nur wenige Emigranten aufnehmen. So deutsch war man geblieben, dass man schleunigst einen Verein gründete. Die paar orthodoxen Juden unter den deutschen Emigranten hielten sich fern. Einen trafen wir zufällig. Zögernd nahm er unsere Einladung an, aber er lehnte jede Nahrungsaufnahme bei uns ab. An der Vorschrift, dass ein Jude keinen Wein trinken darf, wenn die Flasche von einem Nichtjuden geöffnet worden ist, kommt mein Verständnis an eine Grenze. – Ich schrieb dem Vereinsgründer, es schiene mir, dass wir wenig gemeinsam hätten ausser dem passiven Schicksal, und selbst damit müsste jeder von uns auf je ganz eigene Art fertig werden. Gerade dieser Brief begründete eine Freundschaft, die his zum Tode des edelmütigen Mannes anhielt. Er war einer von den still Leidenden, bei denen sich der traditionelle Halt im Übernatürlichen in die tiefsten Seelenwinkel zurückgezogen hatte.

Nicht eigentlich Emigrant, sondern auf Wunsch seiner amerikanischen Gattin bei Kriegsausbruch in Irland hängen geblieben war Dr. Josef Grabisch, der sich durch Hamannstudien einen Namen gemacht hatte. Er hatte katholische Theologie studiert, sich aber von der Kirche abgewandt. Sein grüblerisches Wesen, sein oft abstruser Tiefsinn erinnerte an seinen Landsmann Jakob Boehme. Er verbrachte seine Tage damit, an den Kais die Ramschbuchhandlungen nach deutschen und auf Deutschland bezüglichen Büchern abzugrasen. Grundsätzlich zahlte er nicht mehr als sixpence pro Band. Wahllos sammelte er Schulbücher, Klassikerausgaben, Reisebeschreibungen und Übersetzungen. Die Manuskripte seiner Vorarbeiten zu einer Würdigung von Mangans Bemühungen um die Verbreitung der Literatur der deutschen Klassik und Romantik im englischen Sprachbereich harren in der Nationalbibliothek Dublin eines, der in der Lage ist, die alte deutsche Handschrift zu lesen.

Als es deutlich wurde, dass Deutschland den Krieg verlieren würde, war Grabisch einem Nervenzusammenbruch nahe. Seine Frau flehte mich an, ihn auf ein paar Tage aufs Land zu bringen. Die oben erwähnte Einladung zu den Steyler Patres kam mir gelegen. Beim ersten Spaziergang durch den Garten geriet Grabisch mit einem der Patres aneinander. "Ich verstehe nicht, wie der Papst behaupten kann, der Zölibat liesse sich aus der Schrift rechtfertigen". Nächst meiner Beschäftigung mit Hermes und Günther hat mein Umgang mit Grabisch mich mit den historischen Wurzeln des aggiornamento vertraut gemacht.

In dem Haus der Patres wurde noch das Viertelstundengebet praktiziert. Alle Viertelstunden Tag und Nacht schlugen sämtliche Uhren im Haus. Während des Tages wurde jede Arbeit, Vorlesung oder Lektüre beim Glockenschlag unterbrochen und ein kurzes Gebet gesagt. Ich erlaubte mir den Patres vorauszusagen, das mit dieser teutonischen Disziplin sie kaum viele Iren gewinnen würden. Ich weiss nicht, ob ich recht behalten habe. – Einer der Patres nahm mich mit auf einen seelsorgerlichen Gang durch die Umgebung, die zu den armseligsten Moorgegenden zählte. Wir traten in eine halbverfallene Kate ein. Eine Frau mit ihrer halbblöden Tochter hauste darin. Die Würde des geistlichen Standes ermisst man an dem Empfang, der dem Priester an einer solchen Stelle zuteil wird.

Grabischs waren umsorgt von Iren, die sich vorgenommen hatten, ihre Seelen zu retten. Wir standen Grabisch innerlich am nächsten, besonders in den letzten Tagen seines qualvollen Siechtums. Er starb an Kehlkopfkrebs. Die Nachricht, er habe auf dem Totenbett den Weg zur Kirche zurückgefunden, nahmen wir mit Zweifel auf. In unserer Erinnerung lebt er als ein Gerechter, der die Wahrheit ernst gesucht hat. Alles andere ist Gottes Sache. Seine Gattin wurde nach seinem Tode in die Kirche aufgenommen, aber ich habe nie gewagt, sie auf religiöse Dinge anzusprechen. Sie bewahrte bis zuletzt die unnahbare Würde einer Dame aus der aristokratischen Gesellschaft der

Südstaaten. Sie und ihr Gatte hatten 1916 in Berlin eine Gesellschaft zur Unterstützung Roger Casements gegründet. Es wurde daraus eine kurzlebige deutsch-irische Gesellschaft, der Kuno Meyer nahestand. Grabisch aber hatte ein eigentümlich zwiespältiges Verhältnis zu Irland. Er behauptete, die leichte Bauart der üblichen Bungalows zeige, dass die Iren noch nicht gelernt hätten, Häuser zu bauen. Er hatte eine panische Angst davor, in irischer Erde begraben zu werden (er hielt den Boden für giftig, ganz im Gegensatz zu der schon in der Antike begründeten Sage, dass irischer Boden Heilkraft besäße), und er verachtete die irische Sprachbewegung. Nationalisten haben auf seinem Grab in Dublin ein keltisches Kreuz mit einer Inschrift in irischer Sprache errichtet.

Noch in einem geistlichen Hause durfte ich einmal in Irland Ferien verbringen. Bei den Zisterziensern in Roscrea nahm ich einige Tage lang an dem ganzen, um zwei Uhr morgens bereits beginnenden Gebetsleben teil. Das Herz des Gastpaters hatte ich mit einem Aufsätzlein über die liturgische Stellung der Verehrung des Herzens Mariä gewonnen. Die damals eben ausgesprochene Weihe des Menschengeschlechtes an das Herz Mariä bezeichnete er als das wichtigste Ereignis unserer Zeit. Wenn ich an die heutige Beurteilung Pius XII – nicht nur durch Hochhuth – denke, kommt mir immer wieder die Erinnerung an die Inbrunst, mit der wir während des Krieges an jedem Wort hingen, das zu uns drang von dem, den wir noch ohne jede Bedenken als den Heiligen Vater verehrten.

Ich durfte tagsüber in der Bibliothek arbeiten und die Grundlagen für mehrere Arbeiten über die Geschichte des Menologiums der Zisterzienser sammeln. Das Entscheidende an dieser Einkehrwoche aber war die Einführung, die ich durch einen alten Pater in das betrachtende Gebet erhielt. Diese Einführung war einzigartig insofern, als sie vor allem in einer rückhaltlosen Beschreibung persönlichster Schwierigkeiten bestand. Der Satz: "Ich habe bei solchem Gebet oft physische Schmerzen gelitten" prägte sich mir ein. Diesen Unterricht teilte ich mit einem jungen Architekturkommilitonen, der mit mir von Dublin gekommen war. Ich hatte ihn daheim in unserem Pfarrkirchlein zuerst gesehen, wo er mir durch seine Sammlung aufgefallen war. Auf seinem Leben lag ein Schatten. Die Trunksucht des Vaters hatte seine Mutter grenzenlos verbittert.

Im Laufe der Jahre hatte ich bei praktisch all den wichtigeren Zeitschriftlein, die Jesuiten, Dominikaner, Karmeliter, Franziskaner und Passionisten herausgaben, Beiträge unterbringen können. Meine Spezialität waren hier Einzelstudien über die Texte der Segnungen im Rituale Romanum, vor allem auch der Laien betreffenden, wie der Segnungen von Werkzeugen, Gebäuden, Lebensmitteln udgl. Einigermassen einwandfrei und angemessen für diese Leser schreiben zu können, hatte ich auf ungewöhnliche Weise gelernt. Auf meiner Jagd nach Privatschülern war ich im Frühjahr 1940 in einem boarding house auf Erina Brady gestossen, die mich umarmte, als ich erwähnte, dass ich ihre Lehrerin Mary Wigman gesehen habe und verehre. Auf dem Festland erzogen von einem hochgebildeten Vater, hochgewachsen und von stolzem Gang, mit seidigem kohlschwarzen Haar und weit aufgerissenen Augen verkündete sie eine neue Ordnung, die die Sklaverei ebenso überwunden hatte wie den Krämergeist. Dem irischen Katholizismus stand sie mit der gleichen Hassliebe gegenüber wie es James Joyce, Frank O'Connor und viele andere taten und tun. Ihr Widerstand galt der fadenscheinigen und repressiven Moral. Die Tanzkunst wollte sie jungen Iren und Irinnen nahe bringen als Selbstausdruck, jenseits des traditionellen steifen Volkstanzes und der erbärmlichen Nachahmung des Amerikanismus. Sie scheiterte. Sobald der Krieg zu Ende war, zog sie sich wieder auf das Festland zurück. Ich schrieb ihr, wie tief es mich bekümmere, dass sie gegangen war, während uns – vorerst – zu bleiben vergönnt war. Sie antwortete nicht. Es war ein schlechtes Zeichen. Auf dem Flughafen in Zürich, wo sich bei Ankünften oder Abfahrten irischer Flugzeuge leicht Iren treffen, hörte ich viele Jahre später, dass sie einsam in einer Klinik in Lausanne gestorben war. In Erinnerung an eine Darlegung der Bedeutung der verschiedenen Bewegungsrichtungen habe ich ihr dann eine kleine Arbeit über das Thema "Raum und Bewegung in der Liturgie" gewidmet. Dass, wer Kunst hat, schon Religion hat, ist mir an keinem Menschen deutlicher geworden als an ihr.

DeValera hatte gelobt, er und seine Amtskollegen würden die Wallfahrt nach Lough Derg machen, wenn Irland unversehrt durch den Krieg komme. Zu dieser Wallfahrt fährt man morgens früh nüchtern von Dublin ab, kommt gegen Mittag an den "roten See" im Nordwesten des Landes und setzt in einem Boot über auf eine Felseninsel, auf der man dann zwei volle Tage bleibt. Auf der Insel zieht man Schuh und Strümpfe aus; die Bussübungen bestehen im Umschreiten uralter Steinringe sowie der Kirche unter vorgeschriebenen Gebeten. Nur einmal am Tage geniesst man schwarzen Tee und trockenes Brot. Die erste Nacht wird im Gebet durchwacht. Während der Sommermonate fahren täglich Sonderzüge aus allen Teilen des Landes, um die Pilger heranzuführen. Manche Geschäftshäuser schliessen für drei Tage, um dem gesamten Stab Gelegenheit zu geben, an der Wallfahrt teilzunehmen. Der alte DeValera löste sein Versprechen ein. In Lough Derg traf man Universitätsprofessoren, Beamte, Fabrikdirektoren, Angestellte, Arbeiter, Studenten, Bauern und Leute aus den slums, denen ein Wohltätiger die Reisekosten geschenkt hatte. Eine alte Frau aus einem entlegenen Bergdorf sagte zu mir: "Ich komme seit 40 Jahren und habe noch nie das erhalten, um was ich gebetet habe". Auf der Rückkehr von dieser einzigartigen Wallfahrt herrscht fröhlichste Stimmung. Es heisst, dass eine Bekanntschaft, die auf dieser Fahrt geschlossen wird, eine gute Ehe sichert. Bei der Ankunft in Dublin hörte ich, wie ein junges hübsches Madchen zu der sie in Empfang nehmenden Mutter sagte: "Oh, it was great gas" – es war ein grosser Spass. Nach 1500 Ave Marias.

Ich schrieb nach meiner Rückkehr von dieser Wallfahrt meine Eindrücke nieder. Im nächsten Jahr ging ich wieder. Wenn die Sonne hinter den Bergen untergeht, sitzen die Pilger auf dem Landungssteg. Die Stille der einsamen Landschaft legt sich auf die Menge. Neben mir sassen zwei Mädchen. In das Schweigen hinein sagte die eine: "Das ist genau das, was Hennig beschrieben hat".

VI. Friede

Wenige Tage nach Kriegsende erhielt ich zwei Briefe von der Universität. Im ersten stand, dass ich zur Fortsetzung meines Architekturstudiums noch ein Mathematikexamen nachmachen müsse, im zweiten, dass man nun nach Beendigung der Notsituation meine Deutschstunden beenden wolle. Der Standard teilte mir mit, er brauche meine Beiträge nicht mehr. Aus Maynooth kam die Mitteilung, man müsse meine Stelle mit einem Kleriker besetzen. Obgleich diese Hiobsbotschaften nichts waren im Vergleich zu dem Entsetzlichen, das wir vom Festland hörten, brachten sie mich an den Rand der Verzweiflung. Ein drittes Kind war uns geschenkt worden, und vielleicht war es diese Tatsache, die meiner Frau ermöglichte, mir zuzureden den Mut nicht sinken zu lassen.

Ich ging allein auf ein paar Tage in ein kleines Hotel in den Bergen. Eines Abends trat ich bei einer uns bekannten Bauernfamilie ein. Der kleine Sohn war krank gewesen und lag noch zu Bett. Ich setzte mich zu ihm und, um ihn zu amüsieren, formte ich ihm aus Plastilin Männchen mit langen Beinen. Seine Mutter kam herein: "Ach, wie drollig. Gerade wie die Leute aus den Konzentrationslagern".

Unter den Hotelgästen war ein Ehepaar aus einem Vorort von Dublin. Sie erzählten, in der Technischen Schule sei eine Lehrstelle für Deutsch frei; sie wollten sich für mich verwenden, obgleich ich als Ausländer ... Ich erhielt die Stelle.

Die ersten Wochen nach unserer Ankunft hatte ich nächtelang wachgelegen, weil ich das Schreien aus den Konzentrationslagern hörte. Freunde redeten mir damals gut zu, ich male mir alles zu schlimm aus, jedenfalls habe es keinen Zweck sich abzuquälen. Wenn ich heute an allen Orten höre, man habe nichts gewusst, frage ich mich, wieso ich davon gewusst hatte. Während des Krieges hatten wir mit den Kindern jeden Abend das liturgische Gebet für die Lebenden und die Verstorbenen gebetet, denn ob unsere Lieben, auf welcher Seite sie auch lebten, "das zeitliche Leben noch im Fleische zurückhielt oder das ewige sie bereits, frei vom Erdenleibe, aufgenommen habe", wussten wir nicht. Jetzt kamen Schlag auf Schlag die Nachrichten. Wir hatten die Mitte unseres Lebens überschritten, denn die Liste der Toten, für die wir zu beten hatten, wurde länger als die der Lebenden. Nur im allerengsten Kreise der Eltern und Geschwister hatten wir wunderbarerweise keinen Verlust zu beklagen. Es begann die grosse Hilfsaktion. Victor Gollancz rief auf. Aus Belfast wurden wir um Anschriften Hilfsbedürftiger gebeten. Unsere eigene Hilflosigkeit drückte mich zu Boden.

Auch in der Nähe wurde mir ein Maßstab gesetzt, an dem ich die eigene Lage messen sollte. Bei einem Gottesdienst in der Pro-Kathedrale sprach uns eine alte Frau an. Sie habe gesehen, dass meine Frau ein lateinisch-deutsches Messbuch benutze. Sie sei früher in Böhmen Gouvernante gewesen. Unter Verlust ihrer Ersparnisse hatte sie auf Umwegen zurück in die Heimat flüchten können. Im Kellergeschoss eines abbruchreifen Hauses lebte sie nun in einem Zimmerchen, in dem ein Bett, ein Waschtisch und ein Stuhl Platz hatten. Sie kochte auf einem Gasring in leeren Konservenbüchsen. Die staatliche Rente langte kaum, um die Miete für dieses Lokal zu bezahlen.

Aber wenn jemand eine Dame war, war sie es. Sie sprach ein gepflegtes Englisch, ohne die Geziertheit vieler Gebildeter, las nur die besten Bücher, die sie sich von

Freunden lieh, verstand jedes Problem und vor allem fühlte mit jedem Leiden. Wenn immer wir sie später trafen, hatte sie gerade einen Betrunkenen nach Hause geleitet, eine unverheiratete Schwangere vom Selbstmord zurückgehalten, einem Mann gut zugeredet, bei der Familie zu bleiben, oder ein Kind mit einem Bonbon getröstet. Oft sahen wir sie wochenlang nicht, aber wenn wir uns wiedertrafen, wusste sie über alles Bescheid; sie hatte uns auf betendem Herzen getragen.

Eines Tages rief die Polizei an. Ob wir Miss Smyth in Gardiner Street Nr. 34 kennten. Sie sei aufgefunden worden, schon drei Tage tot. Auf ihrem Tisch habe ein Brief von uns an sie gelegen. Wir halfen entfernten Verwandten, das Begräbnis auszurichten, und erbaten als Andenken eine Muttergottesstatue aus dem Besitz der Verstorbenen. Wahrscheinlich sind wir heute die Einzigen, die sich ihrer noch erinnern.

Wenige Tage, nachdem ich mein Naturalisationszertifikat erhalten hatte, las ich in der Zeitung eine Anzeige, die staatliche Torfgewinnungsgesellschaft suche einen Records Officer, der deutsche und französische Sprachkenntnisse hatte. Was ein Records Officer war, wusste ich nicht. Ich ging zum Interview und wurde genommen. Die Arbeitsstätte war aber zwei und eine halbe Autobusstunden von meinem Heim. Drei Jahre lang konnte ich nur an den Wochenenden zu Hause sein. Von Montag bis Freitag verbrachte ich die Abende in den verlassenen Büroräumen, die in Kasernen aus der Zeit Napoleons lagen. Ich erinnere mich, wie ich mitten im Tippen einer Abhandlung über die Tradition des hl. Cataldus von Tarent innehalten musste, weil eine der das Zimmer mitbewohnenden Ratten es gar zu toll trieb. Meine Schlafstätte hatte ich bei einer alten Betschwester, die das Zentrum des Stadtklatsches war und mich abwechselnd damit oder mit mütterlicher Fürsorge übergoss.

Die abgründige Trostlosigkeit einer irischen Kleinstadt überfiel mich. Aus der Abendandacht ging man ins Kino, wo der letzte Abhub der amerikanischen Filmindustrie lief, zum Hunderennen oder in die Kneipe. Mein Trost war die morgendliche Messe, zu der mich meine landlady unerbittlich weckte, nachdem sie einmal gemerkt hatte, dass ich, wie es hiess, attentive war. Der Verwalter der kleinen Leihbibliothek überliess mir einen Schlüssel und erlaubte mir, spät abends noch dort zu arbeiten; er besass erstaunliche Dinge, z. B. einen ganzen Satz der Berichte der Antiquarischen Gesellschaft, die ich von A-Z durcharbeitete, um eine Kartothek der mit Heiligen zusammenhängenden Örtlichkeiten, Kirchen, Kunstwerke usw. anzulegen, eine der vielen Arbeiten, die ich nie habe auswerten können.

Der Trennung müde, beschlossen wir ein Grundstück zu suchen, auf dem wir in dem Ort, wo meine Arbeitsstätte lag, ein Häuschen bauen lassen könnten. Ich begann mit einer Frau zu verhandeln. Wir kamen nicht recht voran, aber hatten auch Wichtigeres zu bereden. Sie zog mich zu Rate wegen ihrer Tochter, die ihr Herz an einen während des Krieges in dem nahegelegenen Militärlager internierten Deutschen gehängt hatte. Nach seiner Rückkehr in die Heimat hatte sie ihn unter Opfern mit Lebensmittelpaketen unterstützt. Dann kam der Brief, in dem es hiess, die Mutter verlange wegen der Religionsverschiedenheit Lösung des Verhältnisses. In Irland war in jenen Jahren das Durchschnittsalter, in dem Frauen heirateten, 35 Jahre; die Zahl der unverheiratet bleibenden war grösser als in irgendeinem Lande. Irisches Schicksal: Der Vater hatte sein Leben in Kneipen und auf Rennplätzen vergeudet und war früh gestorben; die ganze Last hatte auf den Schultern der Mutter gelegen. Nun sass sie in ihrem Hüttchen mit zwei enttäuschten Tochtern. Als sie mir ihre Geschichte erzählt hatte, zeigte sie auf das Herz-Jesu Bild über dem Kamin und sagte: "Ohne Den hätte ich es nicht ausgehalten". Wenn Marx' Wort vom Opium für das Volk richtig zitiert wird, hat es einen guten Sinn; man konnte von den Kindern der Finsternis lernen, was sie alles anstellen, um in den Besitz des kostbaren Gutes zu gelangen.

Bei meinen abendlichen Spaziergängen durch die Moorfelder entdeckte ich mein in Kindertagen durch den Besuch der Sternwarte in Leipzig gewecktes astronomisches Interesse wieder. In der Astronomischen Gesellschaft in Dublin fand ich Interesse für eine nachdenkliche Betrachtung des Gegenstandes. Ich sprach über das Grunderlebnis der Spannung zwischen der Erkenntnis der Winzigkeit unserer Erde und dem Bewusstsein für die Würde des Menschen, der befähigt ist, diese Winzigkeit wahrzunehmen. Während des Krieges waren mir die steil in den Himmel gerichteten Scheinwerfer, die wir jenseits der Irischen See sehen konnten, als Sinnbilder der Engel erschienen; der Vergleich wäre mir wahrscheinlich vergangen, hatte ich am eigenen Leibe erfahren müssen, was diese Scheinwerfer bedeuteten.

Die Gefangenheit in der Perspektive, die durch die Lebensumstände aufgezwungen wird, kam mir in den ersten Jahren nach dem Kriege besonders zu Bewusstsein. Im Anschluss an ein Buch des Niederländers Nico Rost, der in Dachau inhaftiert war, schrieb ich eine Arbeit "Goethe in der Grenzsituation", in der ich mich vordergründig mit Goethes letztem Aufsatz über Plastische Anatomie (angeregt durch die Nachricht von den unter einem Iren für Anatomen tätigen Auferstehungsmännern, d.h. Leichenstehlern) befasste, im Grunde aber das Messen kultureller Werte an Grenzsituationen meinte. Zwar muss ich die stehen lassen, die zu mir sagen: "Da haben Sie aber Glück gehabt, dass Sie den Krieg nicht miterlebt haben", aber ich konnte auch nicht in die unter Emigranten nur allzu begreifliche "Geschieht Euch recht"-Haltung eintreten. In der Isoliertheit während der Woche empfand ich oft meine Existenz ganz absolut, auf einen Punkt reduziert oder besser auf einen ganz dünnen Geigenton. Die materielle Aussichtslosigkeit war nur Chiffre.

Jaspers sandte mir als erstes Zeichen einer Freundschaft, die überdauert hatte, sein Monumentalwerk <u>Von der Wahrheit</u>. Wenige seiner Leser dürften es unter so extremen Umständen durchgearbeitet haben wie ich in meinem Kasernenbüro am rauchigen Torffeuer. In der Auseinandersetzung mit diesem grössten Werk der deutschen Nachkriegsphilosophie spürte ich, dass mein geistiges Leben nicht ganz erdrückt worden war. Ich war insoweit jung geblieben, dass ich nicht Bestätigung, sondern Veränderung ersehnte.

Meine Mitarbeiter in der Torfgesellschaft waren durchweg Persönlichkeiten. Unser Leter – wir waren die Versuchsstation, und ich hatte Literaturinformationen zu beschaffen – war ein englischer Konvertit; ich war Pate bei seiner Firmung. Er hatte in der britischen Armee in Burma Menschenführung gelernt. Ergreifend war der Kampf unseres Chemikers, der hinter einer reichlich rauhen Schale eine ungebrochene natürliche Frömmigkeit verbarg, der es gelegentlich gelang, mit seinem Hang zum Alkohol fertig zu werden. Die ersten Wochen musste ich mit einem kleinen technischen Zeichner die Schlafkammer teilen. Ich hörte sein Beten und sagte zu ihm, er müsse eine gute Mutter haben. Er seufzte. Ach, die guten irischen Mütter, wieviel Unheil konnten sie anrichten. Unselbständig, zaghaft, ziellos trotteten ihre lieben Söhne dahin. Wer Glück hatte, wie unser Laborassistent, fand noch rechtzeitig den Weg in eine geistliche Gemeinschaft. In der Mission sollte er aufblühen.

An innerer Kraft standen die weiblichen Mitarbeiter meist weit über ihren Kollegen. Einer aus Urzeiten bewahrten Hochachtung vor der Frau stand eine Missachtung des psycho-physischen Lebens gegenüber. Die Kneipen waren der äussere Rahmen für die niedrigste Form einer rein männlichen und daher in Rüdheit versinkenden Gesell-schaft. Frauen durften nur in unbeschreiblich trübseligen Gelassen am Eingang der Kneipen Alkohol zu sich nehmen. Die Enttäuschten unter ihnen gaben den Ton an in zynischer Lebensweisheit. Unsere Mitarbeiterinnen konnten wohl auch, weil wir eine gut gemischte und fröhliche Gruppe waren, ihre natürliche und übernatürliche Qualität erhalten. Unter der Last des Lebens würden sie früh altern. Um so dringender war ihr Wunsch, die kurzen Jahre der Blüte auszunützen. Lobte man eine von ihnen wegen ihres guten Geschmacks in Kleidung, Schmuck oder Haartracht, so bekam man zur Antwort: "Man sieht, dass Sie ein Ausländer sind". Die bäuerliche Selbstverständlich-keit dem Geschlechtlichen gegenüber war schwer mit dem Jansenismus, der von den Kanzeln verkündet wurde, zu vereinigen. Irland ist wohl das Land in Europa, das die geringste Zahl von Sexualverbrechern hat.

Schlüssellochjournalisten behaupteten zwar, das sei nur Fassade; im Geheimen ginge es umso toller zu. (Eine alte Geschichte: Den Schweizer Ziegenhirten sagten die Deut-schen schon im Mittelalter nach, sie fröhnten dem Bestialismus.) Ein als obszön gel-tendes Buch <u>The Ansty and the Tailor</u> fiel der strengen Sittenzensur zum Opfer und wurde dadurch zum bestseller. In einem Klub aufgeklärter Katholiken in Dublin wohnte ich einer der endlosen Diskussionen über die Zensur bei. Am Ende meldete ich mich zum Wort. Ich begann: "Ich habe das Unglück gehabt, Jahre lang in einem Lande leben zu müssen, wo es keine Zensur gab" (ich erinnerte mich grauenhafter Eindrücke, die ich als Kind an Zeitungskiosken empfangen hatte). "Noch einmal", rief jemand da-zwischen, "was sagen Sie: Unglück?". Ich verteidigte, vielleicht ohne genügende Kenntnis der behördlichen Technik, eine vernünftige Zensur. Nach der Veranstaltung wurde ich umdrängt von Leuten, die nicht gewagt hatten, den Mund aufzumachen: "Natürlich stimmen wir Ihnen restlos zu". Der Vorfall kam mir kürzlich wieder ins Gedächtnis, als ich mich in einem Brief an eine Tageszeitung über die beleidigenden pornographischen Zuschriften beschwerte, die – offenbar im Zeichen der geistigen Freiheit – nicht behindert werden können.

An den Mitarbeiterinnen, die ich im Laufe meiner wirtschaftlichen Tätigkeit in Irland hatte, müsste ich zunächst ihr hohes Niveau religiösen, ja theologischen Verständ-nisses rühmen. Eine Fünfzehnjährige fuhr auf, als einer unserer nichtkatholischen Mit-arbeiter sagte, die Kirche lehre, dass durch den Ablass Sünden getilgt werden. Sie rat-telte nicht einfach die präzise Katechismusdefinition des Ablasses herunter, sondern fügte eine tadellose Erklärung bei. Ich nahm diesen Vorfall zum Anlass, einen Artikel unter dem Titel "Der Ablass in der Sicht eines Laien" zu schreiben. Heute wäre ein solcher Artikel kaum noch anzubringen. Gewiss, wir verschwätzten auf Kosten unserer Arbeitgeber viel Zeit, aber ich meine heute, vieles davon hat sich letzten Endes auch für die Wirtschaft gelohnt. Ich habe in solchen Gesprächen eine gewisse Dreistigkeit im Aufbringen religiöser Gegenstände gelernt; kaum je sind mir dabei grössere Widerstande begegnet.

Nur mit Schweigen hinnehmen konnte man die Beispiele für Ertragen von Leiden; die irischen Frauen haben darin eine geradezu elegant zu nennende Technik entwickelt. Selten habe ich Klagen gehört. Kranke und Arme galten als verehrungswürdig. Das Mass an Aufopferung in hoffnungslosen Situationen war doch wohl noch grösser als anderwärts, besonders unter Frauen. Was müssen viele mir bekannt Gewordene heute denken, wo die Maßstäbe zusammenbrechen, denen sie ihr Glück geopfert haben? Geburtenverhütung, Mischehe, Scheidung – Menschenopfer unerhört. Sind sie ein Irrtum gewesen? Ich glaube zu oft gespürt zu haben, dass den Leidenden und den Umstehenden bewusst war, dass jeweils weit mehr auf dem Spiel stand als die Sache selbst. Hier zählten noch andere Werte, als was die Humanisten das höchste Glück der Erdenkinder nennen.

C. S. Andrews, der damalige Direktor der Torfgesellschaft und für mich der grösste Vertreter der neuen Generation begeisterter, aber wirtschaftlich nüchterner irischer Patrioten, fragte mich, als ich ihm meinen Abschiedsbesuch machte, was mich an Irland am meisten beeindrucke. Ich brauchte keinen Moment zu zögern: "Die Einstellung zum Tode". "Das ist merkwürdig", erwiderte er. "Gestern sagte mein Sohn zu mir, als wir am Friedhof vorbeifuhren: Vater, ich glaube du wirst gar nicht so traurig sein, wenn du mal dort deine Ruhe gefunden hast". Dabei trieb uns dieser Mann mit seiner Energie manchmal zur Verzweiflung. Er tobte gegen die It-will-do ("es geht auch so")-Haltung, die sich seine Landsleute unter der Fremdherrschaft angewöhnt hatten. Ja, er genoss sein Leben, den Kampf gegen die Benachteiligung seines Landes durch die Natur, die Aussicht auf ein freies Volk auf freiem Grund, menschenwürdig, in Wohlstand. Aber der Tod war allgegenwärtig. Das Wissen von ihm stand bereits in den Augen der Kinder. Hier gab es nicht die fein säuberliche, hygienische Eliminierung des Todes aus dem Strassenbild, ja aus dem Familienkreis. Die wake (bekannt aus dem Titel von Joyces letztem Werk, aber auch schon aus Goethes Nachdichtung Irische Totenklage) hat seit Jahrhunderten ihren festen Platz im Leben des Iren. "Ich glaube, Sie haben recht", sagte Andrews, die höchste Zustimmung, zu der sich ein Ire herbeilässt.

Es hatte sich gefügt, wie so oft schon: Wenn ich mir sagte: So kann es nicht weitergehen, trat von aussen eine Änderung ein. Die Zusammendrängung meines Familien- und Bibliothekslebens auf das Wochenende, die langen einsamen Abende mit ihren inkommensurablen Beschäftigungen und ein gewisser Abschluss einer Aufbauarbeit waren Gründe genug, um mich freudig das Angebot der Staatlichen Elektrizitätsgesellschaft annehmen zu lassen, die Stellung des Bibliothekars in ihrem im Herzen von Dublin gelegenen Hauptbüro zu übernehmen. Zudem lockte es mich, nun nochmals auf einem Gebiet, auf dem mir die elementarsten Kenntnisse fehlten, von Grund auf anzufangen.

Am schwersten fiel mir der Abschied von dem Oberingenieur. Er war in seiner Jugend nach Amerika ausgewandert und hatte dort jahrelang an Tunnelbauten gearbeitet. Seine Gesundheit war angegriffen, dadurch lag über dem an sich spröden Mann eine eigentümliche Hartheit. Einmal sprach ich mit ihm über einen begabten älteren Mitarbeiter. "Seine erstaunlichste Eigenschaft", sagte ich, "ist seine Bescheidenheit". "Bescheidenheit", erwiderte der Oberingenieur, "ist alles". Es war keine Lehre, die er mir erteilte, eine Sentenz, sondern die letzte Wahrheit eines Weisen. Viele Jahre später sah ich ihn noch einmal. Ich sagte ihm, was dieses Wort von ihm mir bedeutet habe. Er aber wehrte lachend ab: "Na, habe ich nicht auch manches von Ihnen gelernt?". Mir war, als würde mir ein Orden auf die Brust geheftet.

Ein anderer mir durch die Arbeit in der Torfgesellschaft nahe gekommener Weiser war Kotri Hangelaid, ehemaliger Direktor der estnischen Torfindustrie. Er war unter dem Zaren Kadett gewesen. Mit seiner Gattin und dem jüngeren Sohn gelang ihm 1940 die Flucht nach Schweden. Der ältere Sohn verschwand in Sibirien. Man holte ihn auf einige Zeit nach Irland als Berater. Ich wurde ihm als Dolmetscher und Hilfsarbeiter beigegeben, um eins der riesigen Moore in der Grafschaft Mayo, der armseligsten des Landes, auf Eignung für Frästorfgewinnung zu prüfen. Wir standen oft an einer Stelle, von der aus man, soweit das Auge reichte, nichts als Moor sah. Hangelaid machte mich aus seinem tief religiösen Naturverständnis auf wunderbare Eigenheiten der Flora und Fauna aufmerksam. Es gab da Vögel, die, wenn man sich ihren schutzlosen Brutnestern näherte, vortäuschten, flügellahm zu sein und auf dem Boden dem Menschen vor den Füssen her hinhuschten, um ihn vom Nest wegzulocken. Nach ein paar Schritten schon konnte man das Nest nicht wiederfinden. Es gab Pflanzen, die durch die Moorschicht hindurch ihre Wurzeln bis in die tief darunter liegende Lehmschicht hinuntersandten. Sinnbilder des Lebens ...

Hangelaid war geformt von evangelischer Lebensart, selbstbewusst, von adligem Stolz, hart mit sich und anderen, ehrlich und fleissig. Er setzte Maßstäbe. An ihm wurde mir die nationale Aufspaltung im kirchlichen Bereich deutlich. In den anglikanischen Kirchen konnte er wegen ihrer politischen Ausrichtung auf England keine Heimat finden. Er war zerrissen. Sein Land war eins der am wenigsten antisemitischen der Welt gewesen, andererseits konnte ihn der Sieg der Russen nicht erfreuen. Er litt darunter, dass er sein geliebtes Orgelspiel nicht weiter pflegen konnte. An der katholischen Kirche stiess ihn das proletarische ab. Er meinte, man verfolge ihn als Nichtkatholiken. Alter und Lebensumstände verhinderten ihn, hinter die Fassade zu schauen. Ich versuchte, ihm verständlich zu machen, wie tief sich die Achtung vor den Dingen, aus der er lebte, in den Segnungen wiederspiegelt, aber er liess mich nicht an sich herankommen. Unwillig wurde er, als ich in den Diskussionen um den Plan der Prinzessin Margaret, einen geschiedenen Mann zu heiraten, den konservativen Standpunkt einnahm. Verbittert schied er, als man ihn nicht mehr benötigte. Wir besuchten ihn noch einmal in seiner letzten Zuflucht in Uchte, am Rand der oldenburgischen Moore; er zeigte uns eine Goldmedaille, die ihm für sein Orgelspiel in der Ortskirche verliehen worden war.

Die engeren Mitarbeiter fühlten die Unwürdigkeit der Verabschiedung dieses Mannes. In Irland war nicht nur der reiche Mann, sondern auch der Erfolgreiche mehr eine lächerliche Figur als Gegenstand der Bewunderung. Der Spruch: "Nur der Gnade Gottes ist es zu verdanken, dass ich nicht in seinen Schuhen stecke" war ebenso verbreitet wie der: "Gott hat ihn nun mal so gemacht". Beim Eintritt in die Elektrizitätsgesellschaft glaubte der Oberingenieur dort mir sagen zu müssen: "Wir müssen hier einander das Leben so angenehm wie möglich machen. Das Leben ist zu kurz. Einmal müssen wir doch gehen". Diese Lektion hatte ich längst gelernt. Mein Schwiegervater hatte in seiner Fabrik einen schlechten Menschen geduldet, weil er meinte, er sei wegen seiner technischen Tüchtigkeit unentbehrlich. Dieser Mann hatte dann 1939 die Gestapo aufgehetzt, Gott Lob, zu spät, um meinem Schwiegervater noch etwas antun zu können. Ich würde heute in meinem Betrieb grosse wirtschaftliche Einbussen hinnehmen, wenn ich zwischen Tüchtigkeit und Anständigkeit eines Mitarbeiters zu wählen hätte.

Kurz nachdem ich durch meine Anstellung bei der Elektrizitätsgesellschaft wieder etwas Boden unter den Füssen hatte, sagte mir ein Beamter, der mich nun täglich in seiner Bibliothek arbeiten sah: "Mein Gott, das Leben, das Sie in den letzten Jahren gehabt haben, hatte manch bessern Mann als Sie zerbrochen". Er wusste nur die Hälfte. In meinem doppelberuflichen Leben hat immer die Linke nicht gewusst, was die Rechte tat. Manchmal aber juckte mich der Affe. In einer Akademieabhandlung über altenglische Martyrologien machte ich eine Anmerkung, in der ich darauf hinwies, dass einer gewissen Form der Zeitberechnung in mittelalterlichen Kalendarien die gleiche Denkweise zugrundeliegt wie der Berechnung von Elektrizitätstarifen für Stoss- und Nichtstoss-Stunden. Und wie oft habe ich andererseits schon Worte aus der "Segnung für jegliches Ding" zitiert, wenn es mich wieder einmal beglückte, ganz im Sinn Rilkes der Sache dienen zu können in der Unterordnung unter das Eigengesetz etwa eines Werkstoffs.

Dem Hauptbüro der Elektrizitätsgesellschaft gegenüber lag eine Kapelle der Ewigen Anbetung. Meine Sekretärin machte von ihr ausgiebigen Gebrauch und entschuldigte spätes Kommen und frühes Gehen mit Gebet. Ich wies sie zurecht. Sie begann zu weinen. Heraus purzelte ein irisches Schicksal. Auf dem kleinen Gehöft der Eltern war gerade Platz für eins der Kinder. Der Sohn hatte geheiratet und die Schwägerin duldete keine andere Frau im Haus. So, ab mit dir in die Stadt. Natürlich von einem Mann enttäuscht, verblühte das Madchen; sie entwickelte die aggressive Haltung, in die sich so viele Verbitterte flüchten. Man hatte mir die allerseits Unbeliebte aufgehängt. Als sie einmal ernstlich krank war, besuchte ich sie. Ein dumpfes, in einen trüben Hinterhof gehendes Zimmerchen angefüllt mit Devotionalien, streng bewacht von einer Megäre von Wirtin. Es bestand ein circulus vitiosus zwischen den mangelhaften Leistungen und der erbärmlichen Bezahlung. Als ich kündigte, rief sie mich abends privat an. Ob ich ihretwegen gekündigt hätte? Sie wüsste, sie hätte mir das Leben zur Hölle gemacht. Nach meinem Weggang folgte sie dem allgemeinen Trend und nahm eine Stelle in England an. Hoffentlich ist sie dort glücklicher geworden.

Die Veränderung, die in Iren vor sich geht, sobald sie im Ausland tätig sind, liess mich später italienische Gastarbeiter besser verstehen lernen. Sie haben zwar das zusätzliche Handicap der Sprache, aber verfügen im Allgemeinen von Haus aus über eine grössere innere Robustheit. Später hörte ich auf den Zusammenkünften am St. Patricks Tag auf der irischen Botschaft in Bern viele Klagen von Mädchen, die als Stenotypistinnen, Krankenpflegerinnen, Hausangestellte oder im Hotelbetrieb auf dem Festland arbeiten, über die Schwierigkeiten, die sich für sie aus dem Zusammenstoss nicht nur ihrer heute als repressiv verschrienen Erziehung sondern ihrer innersten Wesensart mit der sich gross nennenden Welt ergaben. Ein Offizier der irischen Armee sagte einmal zu mir: "Wer befehlen muss, hat eigentlich schon verloren". Das irische Volk hat 2000 Jahre Geschichte hinter sich gebracht ohne militärische Siege.

Die Elektrizitätsgesellschaft entliess mich um fünf Uhr. Von dann an konnte ich, ohne noch einen weiteren Gedanken an die berufliche Arbeit wenden zu müssen, dem leben, was Arthur Cox das Wirkliche genannt hatte. Schon während des Tages konnte ich in den Bibliotheken dafür sorgen, dass am Abend die von mir benötigten Bücher bereitstanden. Ich wurde Mitarbeiter am Radio besonders auch für kirchenmusikalische Themen. Die zahllosen Debattierklubs luden zu Mitarbeit ein. Schon vor Jahren hatte ich einmal mit Grabischs einen Klub besucht, der sich mit der Beförderung der Rechte der Frauen befasste, ein etwas antiquiertes Geschäft, da Frauen in die höchsten Stellungen in Wirtschaft und Staat gelangt waren. Es wurde ein Referat gehalten über Gertrud von LeFort, den meisten Anwesenden ein völlig unbekannter Name. Die erste Diskussionsrednerin sagte: "Einige der vorgetragenen Gedichte waren schlecht, so schlecht, dass sie von einem Mann sein könnten". Ich hatte längst gelernt, dass alles darauf ankommt, die Lacher erstmal auf seine Seite zu bringen. (Ernst Lewy, der grosse Sprachforscher, sagte: Die Iren nehmen nichts ernst ausser ihren Witzen). Dann aber folgte eine ergreifende Darlegung des Schicksals der alleinstehenden Frau, ihrer Abspeisung mit Devotionen, der Mangel an schöpferischen Ausdrucksmöglichkeiten. Mein Vater hatte sich immer gewünscht, an einer Mädchenschule lehren zu dürfen. Mir hatte das Leben drei Töchter geschenkt. Meine berufliche Tätigkeit in der Wirtschaft führte mich viel mit Frauen zusammen. Aber in jener Diskussion begegnete mir die Situation, die mich immer wieder zum Schweigen verurteilt hat: Noch mehr als die Farbigen oder die Juden sind Frauen so desillusioniert, dass sie es einem Mann einfach nicht glauben, er könne sich ernstlich für sie einsetzen. Es ist die Unübersteiglichkeit der menschlichen Daseinsgrenzen, die ich später in Darlegungen über die Beziehungen der Engel untereinander (ein wenig durchdachtes Thema) zum Ausgangspunkt nahm. Erfahrung hat mir jeden missionarischen Eifer geraubt. Es bleibt mir nichts übrig als zu beschreiben. Nur ganz selten gelingt es für einen Moment, die Schallmauer zu durchbrechen.

Das letzte Mal, dass ich der Einladung eines Debattierklubs folgte, sprach ich über den Existentialismus, worunter man in Irland eine Art geistigen Halbstarkentums verstand. In der Diskussion stand eine alte Dame auf: "Der Redner hat gesagt, Wahrheit sei auf Wahrhaftigkeit begründet. Wahrheit besteht doch aber an sich und ist von Wahrhaftigkeit, so wünschenswert diese auch ist, unabhängig." Ich spürte die ganz aus der Tiefe kommende Beunruhigung, ja Bestürzung, und kam mir als Brandstifter vor.

In Irland wurde das Wort "Existentialismus", dessen bin ich ziemlich sicher, erstmalig in meinem Vortrag im Juni 1940 vor der sich grossartig Metaphysical nennenden Studentengesellschaft in Trinity College erwähnt. Als Joseph Hone erfuhr, ich kenne Jaspers persönlich und habe Heidegger gelesen, lud er mich ein, um mich mit seinem Freund Arland Ussher bekannt zu machen, Ussher gab mir das Manuskript, das später unter dem Titel "Das Gesicht Irlands" erschien – er hatte wenig Freude am geistigen Leben Irlands. Es stand mir nicht zu, dem in irischer Sprache und Literatur tief verwurzelten Mann zu sagen, dass mir Aussenstehendem seine Ansicht weder umfassend noch tief erschiene. Ussher bat sich einige der mir zur Verfügung stehenden Bücher, vor allem Jaspers' Geistige Situation aus. Nach wenigen Monaten erschien sein Büchlein "Nachwort zum Existentialismus". Es war ein bisschen früh dafür.

Dem feinsinnigen Literaturhistoriker Hone war äusserer Erfolg versagt geblieben. Die Nationalisten lehnten ihn als Angloiren ab. Bei den Modernisten spielte wohl die Erinnerung daran mit, dass Hone für die Verzögerung in der Veröffentlichung von Joyces Dubliners verantwortlich gemacht wurde. Die erste Seite seiner Biographie George Moores ist nicht nur ein klassischer Text der englischen Literatur, sondern auch eine der grossartigsten Selbstdarstellungen des Schicksals der Angloiren, das man am ehesten mit dem der Deutschbalten vergleichen kann. Hone lud mich ein, an einem von ihm und Lennox Robinson geplanten Dictionary of Irish Writers mitzuarbeiten. Ich spezialisierte mich darauf, den Beitrag anglikanischer Geistlicher zum Geistesleben Irlands darzustellen. In den meist absonderlichen Schicksalen dieser Männer wurde mir deutlich, welche Umstände die eigentümliche angloirische Geistesverfassung geformt haben, der wir doch bis heute immer noch die bedeutendsten Beiträge Irlands zur Weltliteratur verdanken. Mangel an Interesse brachte das Unternehmen zum Erliegen. Wir kamen nicht über den Buchstaben C hinaus. Nur einer meiner fünfzig Artikel erschien im Druck. Wo die restlichen 49 geblieben sind, habe ich nie erfahren.

Durch Joseph Hone lernten wir seine Kousine Evie kennen. Sie war Konvertitin und Schülerin von Gris und Braque. Ihre Buntglaskunst begann endlich die Anerkennung höchster Stellen auch im kirchlichen Bereich zu finden. Sie wohnte und arbeitete in ein paar Zimmern in einem Landsitz in der Nähe von Dublin. Ihr Wesen und ihre Umgebung strahlten eine Kultur aus, die inmitten der oft bedrückenden Mittelmässigkeit eine Oase für uns war. Auf dem Weg zur hl. Messe ereilte sie der Tod. Der Entwurf zu einem die Kreuzigung darstellenden Glasfenster gehört zu unseren kostbarsten Besitztümern.

Weder der Existentialismus noch irgend ein anderer -ismus (nicht einmal der Nationalismus) hat in Irland tiefere Bedeutung. Das liegt z. T. an der Geschichte. Hier passt keine der traditionellen Kategorien, angefangen von "Mittelalter" und "Neuzeit" bis zu "Revolution" und "Demokratie". Noch wichtiger aber ist der unwiderstehliche Drang des Iren zu widersprechen, nicht zuletzt sich selbst. Nicht nur nimmt er for argument's sake grundsätzlich die gegenteilige Position zum Gesprächspartner ein, sondern vermag er auch mitten in einer Diskussion umzukippen, und sei es nur mit einem lässigen: I suppose, you are right. Die Grundkonzeption des -ismus, womöglich aufgebläht zu "Bewegung", scheitert an der Ironie fast greisenhafter Weisheit. Mein Nachbar, ein hoher Regierungsbeamter, hatte sich einmal einen Abend lang mit einem Bahai-Anhänger unterhalten. Am nächsten Morgen sagte er zu mir: "Das sind rührende Leute. Sie reden im Grunde von Dingen, die so alt sind wie jene Hügel" – und er zeigte auf die Granitberge jenseits der Bucht. Ich meinte, ich hörte meinen Vater.

Den Unterschied zwischen objektivem und existentiellem Denken braucht man sich in Irland gar nicht erst bewusst zu machen. Das, was den Fremden als keltisches Zwielicht erscheint, ist nur eine Abwandlung davon. Die den Fremden überwältigende Redseligkeit der Iren verdeckt mehr als sie enthüllt. Irland ist das einzige Land Westeuropas, bei dessen Christianisierung es keine Märtyrer gab. Die Botschaft traf hier auf eine einzigartig entsprechende Disposition, oder wenn man will, sie hat sich hier in einzigartiger Weise dem Vorhandenen angepasst. Die Zerstörung der Geistesverfassung, deren Ausdruck die irische Liturgie war – der zentrale Gegenstand meiner historischen Forschungen –, hat überlebt. Ich bin allerdings nicht sicher, ob ich hier nicht das Plusquamperfektum gebrauchen sollte. Sollte es Irland gelingen, den Sprung ins technische Zeitalter ohne Verlust seiner Seele zu machen, so würde es der ganzen Menschheit einen unschätzbaren Dienst leisten. Einige meiner irischen Freunde berechtigten mich zu dieser Hoffnung.

Als ich vor Jahren diese Aufzeichnungen begann, beabsichtigte ich an dieser Stelle einen Überblick über die Erscheinungsformen gottesdienstlichen Lebens, wie sie mir in Irland entgegengetreten waren, zu geben. Das meiste davon wäre wohl heute Geschichte, aber noch nicht entfernt genug, um von Interesse zu sein. Über die Trennung in Zeit und Raum hinweg wage ich kein Urteil über die seitherige Entwicklung, besonders über die auch in Irland bemerkbare Tendenz, das 2. Vatikanische Konzil links zu überholen. Kurz nach Beginn des Konzils nahm ich in Basel an einer Tagung teil, in der Mario von Galli über das zu Erwartende sprach. Ich erlaubte mir zu sagen, dass ich in Irland ein Glaubensleben kennengelernt habe, von dem sich der Durchschnittsfestländer nichts träumen lasst. Unwillig erwiderte von Galli: "Na, auf dem Konzil spielen aber die Iren keine erfreuliche Rolle".

Angesichts solcher Urteile ziehe ich mich auf meine anspruchslosen, ganz persönlichen Erfahrungen zurück. Das Wort: Wenn ihr nicht werdet wie die Kinder, ist in Irland keine sentimentale Forderung, sondern die Feststellung einer allen bewussten Tatsache. Als das Dogma von der Himmelfahrt Mariä verkündigt wurde, schrieb mir meine Mutter, sie bedaure, dass dadurch der Graben zwischen evangelischen und katholischen Christen vertieft würde. Ich erzählte ihr, wie am Morgen der Promulgation wir alle am Radio gesessen haben und wie in dem Augenblick, da das Dogma verkündigt wurde, in allen Häusern eine ins Fenster gestellte Kerze angezündet wurde. Ich traf eine Stenotypistin auf dem Weg zur Arbeit: "Jetzt wissen wir wieder, wozu der Mensch berufen ist", sagte sie. Dass meine Mutter mir antworten konnte, jetzt habe sie besser verstanden, worum es uns ginge, beglückte mich tief.

An dem inneren Frieden, in dem unsere Kinder aufwachsen durften, hatten die Dominikanerinnen, bei denen sie zur Schule gingen, nicht geringen Anteil. Natürlich war das intellektuelle Niveau mit einer mitteleuropäischen oder englischen Schule nicht zu vergleichen. Es wirkt his heute nach, dass jahrhundertelang die katholische Schultradition in Irland zerschlagen war. Man kann es als Zeitverschwendung ansehen, dass die Kinder als Hauptfach die völlig nutzlose irische Sprache lernen müssen. Aber dass einmal irgendwo ein anderer Maßstab zählt als die materielle Brauchbarkeit, ist schon viel wert. Im Erlernen dieser unweigerlich eine Kultur vermittelnden Sprache haben meine Kinder eine Bildung mitbekommen, die anderwärts bestenfalls das Erlernen des Griechischen vermittelt. Latein lernten sie bei mir privat; sie wissen, wie jammervoll die volkssprachlichen Übersetzungen hinter dem Original liturgischer Gebete zurückbleiben. Nachdem ich einmal als Lehrer und als Vater gesehen habe, was eine wirkliche Durchdringung des ganzen Schulgeistes durch eine auf das Göttliche ausgerichtete Menschlichkeit bedeuten kann – nicht in der künstlichen Pensionatsatmosphäre sondern mitten im Gemeinde- und Familienleben –, kann ich Diskussionen über die sog. Konfessionsschule nicht mehr ohne eine gewisse Ungeduld zuhören.

Ebenso wie meine Arbeitskollegen waren die Lehrerinnen meiner Kinder jede eine Persönlichkeit. Dass das Klosterleben nicht uniformiert, konnte ich sehen, wenn ich über fünfzehn Jahre hinweg verfolgte, wie die Schwestern, Mütter und Oberinnen kamen und gingen und wie sie auf die Kinder in ihren verschiedenen Stadien und Verhältnissen reagierten. Die Schwestern brachten Kindern den Rosenkranz dadurch nahe, dass sie jedem Kind ein Geheimnis anvertrauten. Unsere zweite Tochter kam strahlend nach Hause: "Ich habe die Geisselung bekommen". Aber sie erfuhr den tiefen Sinn dieses Zufalls. Wir hatten unseren Kindern, so weit wie es vertretbar war, die Belastung durch das Furchtbare, das ihnen der himmlische Vater erspart hatte, ferngehalten. Ich hatte mir den Vorschlag einer englischen Ordensgemeinschaft zu eigen gemacht, den Kreuzweg, eine in Irland überaus beliebte private Andachtsform, mit dem Gedächtnis an gepeinigte Menschen zu verbinden. Unserem Kind ging dieser Zusammenhang spontan auf. Ich kann das zweite der schmerzensreichen Geheimnisse nicht bedenken, ohne für diese Tochter zu beten und für ihre Lehrerin. Als dieses Kind zu seiner Firmung ging, sagte sie an der Haustür zu uns: "Wenn ich wieder heimkomme, bin ich ganz rein".

Fürbitten waren unseren Kindern vertraut, längst ehe man an die Wiederbelebung in der Liturgie dachte. Der Bitte des Papstes, in aller Welt der Opfer einer Überschwemmungskatastrophe in Italien zu gedenken, wurde spontan und umfassend, natürlich auch mit praktischer Betätigung, entsprochen. Als ich am Abend mit den Kindern betete, piepste das Jüngste damals Sechsjährige plötzlich: "Daddy, floods" (Vati, die Überschwemmung). Das Hervorstechendste an dieser religiösen Erziehung war die Heiterkeit. _Laetatus sum_ ... die Freude am Verweilen im Hause des Herrn, die Juden und Christen eint, war das oberste Ziel. Es wäre uns nicht eingefallen, den sonntäglichen Gang zur Messe oder die Osterbeichte als "Pflicht" zu bezeichnen.

Meine Frau hatte auf einer Auktion einen ausgestopften Alligator gekauft. Wir befestigten ihn auf einem Brett mit Rädern. Die Kinder zogen damit jubelnd zur Schule. Eine Schwester fing sie vor der Schule ab. "Oh, da machen wir was draus", rief sie. Das Viech wurde im Garten vor einen Busch gestellt. Die Schwester stellte sich hinter den Busch und hielt den Strick in der Hand. "Nun ruft die Mutter Oberin und sagt ihr, ein grässliches Tier sei im Garten". Als die ehrwürdige Mutter den Weg heraufgewatschelt kam, zog die Schwester am Strick. Der Jubel war gross, als die Oberin in einen Schreckensruf ausbrach. Der ganze Ort sprach tagelang von dem Mordsspass. Das war Autoritätserziehung.

Über Zeit und Raum hinweg haben unsere Kinder mit den alten Lehrerinnen warmen Kontakt aufrecht erhalten. In regelmässigen Abständen kommen Briefchen in gestochener Handschrift, Agnus Dei, Heiligenbildchen, wohl gar ein Stücklein Tuch, das die Gebeine des Reformationsmärtyrers Oliver Plunkett berührt hat, fehlen nie darin. Es wird geschrieben von Versetzungen, Krankheiten, Bischofsbesuchen, Erweiterungsbauten; es wird gefragt nach den Kindern unserer Tochter, nach den Eltern. In einer Studie über das Beten pro se suisque omnibus habe ich gesagt: Welcher Abstand zwischen dem vagen: "Ich denke an dich" und dem erfüllten: "Ich bete für dich". In einer der dunkelsten Nächte meines Lebens habe ich mir sagen können: Jetzt ist es zwei Uhr; wenigstens die Zisterzienser fangen jetzt an für uns zu beten.

Mein Freund Heinrich Keller erzählte mir einmal, dass seine Mutter regelmässig eine Karmeliterin besuchte, mit der sie nur durch einen Vorhang sprechen durfte, die sie aber in allen wichtigen Fragen um Rat bat. Mein Freund hatte selbst diesen Rat gelegentlich gesucht. Unterricht, den ich in Dublin einer Sacre-Coeur-Nonne erteilen durfte, brachte mich in eine ähnliche Lage. Einmal erzählte sie mir von ihrer Schwester. Sie war in Sorge um sie und hatte sie längere Zeit nicht gesehen. "Da geht sie gerade am Haus vorbei", rief sie plötzlich. Es war mir, als habe sie sie herbeigebetet. Das Ganze trat plötzlich in eine neue Dimension von Wirklichkeit.

Die Schwestern, bei denen unsere Kinder zur Schule gingen, zeichneten sich vor vielen katholischen Laien durch ihr Verständnis für die besondere Lage aus, in der wir uns befanden. Es wurde ein Passionsspiel eingeübt. An einer Stelle sollte gesagt werden: "Alle liebten den Heiland, nur die Juden hassten ihn", und diese Worte sollten mit allen Zeichen des Abscheus vorgetragen werden. Spontan ging unser damals zehnjähriges Töchterchen zur Oberin. Die Oberin entschuldigte sich bei dem Kind und ordnete sofortige Änderung an. Am Sonntag zuvor war uns am Kirchenausgang Fiat, die Zeitung der von Ordensgeistlichen inspirierten antisemitischen Organisation angeboten worden, welche sich geschmackvollerweise Maria Duce nannte. Ich war zu dem Verkäufer hingegangen und hatte ihm gesagt: "Für mich, der ich ein Dutzend mir nächststehender Menschen in den Gaskammern verloren habe, ist Ihr Erscheinen eine Beleidigung". Der junge Mann packte seinen Kram zusammen. Meine Kinder hatten die Szene zitternd vor Aufregung miterlebt.

Wir luden einen Nachkriegsflüchtling, einen baltischen Grafen, in unser Haus ein. "Und da haben sie mich eingesperrt", berichtete er, "aber ich habe ihnen gesagt: Das sind doch hier alles Juden, mit denen können Sie mich doch nicht zusammenstecken". Unsere Kinder verliessen wortlos das Zimmer. Conrad Ferdinand Meyer war weise genug, den Titel seines Gedichtes von Der Hugenot in Die Füsse im Feuer umzuwandeln.

Die Problematik kam nicht nur zu uns. Wir mussten sie nun auch selbst aufsuchen. Bei dem ersten Besuch, den ich nach Erwerb eines irischen Passes in England machen konnte, kam mir erst recht zu Bewusstsein, was uns erspart geblieben war. Einmal waren aus Versehen drei Bömblein auf Dublin gefallen. Unsere Kinder hatten in der Schule das Liedchen "Oranges and lemons say the bells of St. Clement's" gelernt, welches die Glocken der alten Pfarrkirchen der Stadt London durchgeht. Von diesen Glocken läutete keine mehr. Die Kirche der hl. Brigida, der Nationalheiligen von Irland, in dem Bezirk, wo ich wegen meiner journalistischen Tätigkeit zu tun hatte, war zu einem winzigen Kapellchen zusammengeschrumpft, allerdings als Stätte stillen Gebets den ganzen Tag offen.

Endlich musste ich auch meine Scheu überwinden und den Fuss wieder aufs Festland setzen. Ich traf meine Schwiegereltern in dem Häuschen in LeZoute, wo wir uns 1939 getrennt hatten. In der Kirche betete ich um Mut. Am nächsten Tage fuhr ich allein nach Brügge. An einem der Kanäle entlang spazierend, hörte ich aus einem Trödlerladen aus einem quäkenden Grammophon den Schlager "Schöner Gigolo". Man spielte ihn auf dem Karnevalsfest in Bonn, als ich dort meiner Frau den absurden Heiratsantrag machte. Gottes Wege sind merkwürdig. Das Leben schien doch noch zu einer Einheit zusammenwachsen zu können.

Im folgenden Jahre starb mein Schwiegervater. Seitdem er uns nach dem Kriege in Irland besucht hatte, hatte sich von Jahr zu Jahr unser Verhältnis vertieft. Wir hatten beide durch Leiden gelernt. Er hatte während der Besatzungszeit durch einzigartigen Mut Hunderten von Leidensgefährten das Leben gerettet, indem er sie mit Hilfe einiger anständiger Militärs den Krallen der Gestapo entriss. Die Nachricht von seinem Tode löste Beileidsbezeugungen aus aller Welt aus. Einer der von ihm Geretteten schrieb aus Australien: "Er war ein Gerechter", eine feste Kategorie im jüdischen Denken.

Familienangelegenheiten, deren Ordnung nun mir oblag, führten mich dann zum ersten Male wieder nach Aachen. Langsam fuhr der Zug von der Grenzstation ins Tal hinunter. Unser früheres Haus war auf die Grundmauern heruntergebrannt. Ich ging in die eben kümmerlich wiederaufgebaute St. Foillanskirche; der irische Patron dieser Kirche war von Räubern erschlagen worden, weshalb ihn sinnigerweise die Aachener Stadtwache zu ihrem Patron erhob. Inzwischen hatte ich mehrfach über seine Legende geschrieben. Von St. Johann in Burtscheid, wo ich gefirmt worden war, wusste ich inzwischen durch Bellesheims Forschungen, dass dort einmal irische Mönche gehaust hatten. Die Kapelle, wo meine Frau getauft, das Kirchlein, in dem unsere zweite Tochter getauft worden war, lagen in Schutt und Asche. Auf dem jüdischen Friedhof war das jüngste Grab – aus dem Jahre 1943 – das der Mutter eines früheren Arbeitskollegen, der umgekommen war.

Eine Freundin – ich habe ihrer früher gedacht – begleitete mich nach Maria Laach. Meine liturgiegeschichtlichen Arbeiten führten mich bei den gelehrten Patres ein. Es begann sich die Möglichkeit abzuzeichnen, dass über die Anerkennung des Leides, durch das wir – gleich auf welcher Seite – gegangen waren, die Hoffnung auf wiedererstehende Güte erwachsen könne. Der Weg war mühsam; immer wieder steigen Schatten auf, angesichts derer es fast unerträglich scheint, überlebt zu haben oder so zu tun, als sei nichts geschehen.

Im folgenden Jahr wagte ich es, meine älteste Tochter dorthin mitzunehmen, wo sie geboren war. Das Münster in Aachen, der Dom in Köln (im Mittelalter waren Iren dorthin zu den hl. drei Königen gepilgert) waren ihre ersten Berührungen mit einer Kultur, aus der abzustammen ihr bisher nur aus Wort und Schrift bekannt war. Auch für sie wurde die Kirche der Träger der Kontinuität des Lebens, dessen Zerrissenheit sie besonders im Sprachlichen empfinden würde. Muttersprache ist in unserer Familie die Sprache, die die Grosseltern mühsam von den Enkeln lernen.

Von Köln führte mich die Reise allein ostwärts. Die Mustermesse bot Gelegenheit, meine Mutter wiederzusehen. Sie hatte aus Bombennächten das nackte Leben gerettet und in einem evangelischen Altersheim Aufnahme gefunden. An der Mauer des Johannesfriedhofs stand an der Stelle, hinter der Käthchen Schönkopf ruht: "Ruhm und Ehre der glorreichen Sowjetarmee". Über dem Tor zum Südfriedhof, wo mein Vater begraben war, stand: "Im Zuge des sozialistischen Aufbaus haben wir das Plansoll um 20% überschritten"; man hatte übersehen, dass sich diese Inschrift nur auf die Gärtnerei beziehen sollte. In der Universitätskirche hatten die Katholiken Unterschlupf gefunden, aber nur <u>eine</u> Messe konnte am Sonntag gehalten werden. Dicht gedrängt standen die Menschen, die meisten Ostflüchtlinge. In der russischen Kirche hinter der Deutschen Bücherei wurde im Schutze von Sowietuniformen ein orthodoxer Gottesdienst abgehalten. Ich betete für meine teuren Freunde, seit 25 Jahren über den Erdball gehetzte Flüchtlinge, in einem Altersheim in Dublin, bei denen ich russische Stunden nehmen durfte.

Als mich zwei Jahre später in Dublin die Nachricht vom Hinscheiden meiner Mutter erreichte, war das letzte Band zur alten Heimat durchgeschnitten. Meine Mutter hinterliess einen Brief an ihre fünf Kinder. Mir sagte sie darin, sie habe ständig an Gewissheit gewonnen, dass Gott mich geführt habe.

Wirtschaftliche Anforderungen, die über den Kreis der engsten Familie hinausreichten, und die Sorge um die Zukunft unserer Töchter, deren Grundausbildung einen gewissen Abschluss erreicht hatte, riefen uns aus Irland weg. Ein treuer rechtskundiger Freund hatte uns über alle Gefahren hinweg die Grundlage bewahrt, auf der wir auf dem Festland eine neue Existenz aufbauen konnten. Das Flugzeug stieg steil auf, so dass ich die Augen schliessen musste. Als ich wieder um mich schaute, waren wir über den Wolken. Land und See waren den Blicken entzogen, und der Horizont lag vor uns offen und unabsehbar.

IV Persönliche Schriften und Städtebeschreibungen

Living with Books

Leipzig, my native town, was for the last two hundred years the publishing centre of the greatest book producing country in the world. Of the fifty or sixty publishing firms which were established there in 1935, only the biggest three, Insel, Brockhaus and Reclam, have been allowed by the Russians to continue their activities. Scarcely any other industry in Germany has at present a greater percentage of unemployment than the publishing industry.

From my childhood days I heard as much of the producing of books as a Belfast boy hears of shipbuilding. Books, I think, generally play a greater part in German houses than they do in Irish homes. The difference starts right from the use of the word "book". In this country, a periodical is frequently referred to as "a book"; in Germany, even a Penguin would not be granted that name. The point is not so much the size or the binding but the permanent value attributed to a real book. A book is not a thing which is out of date after a fortnight. You do not keep a book in a corner of your wardrobe or on the shelf of a kitchen-dresser. Even in an ordinary German household, in farm-cottages and tenements you would find a book-case (used for no other purpose than that of keeping books), with a stately row of "classics" in artistic bindings, a concise Cyclopedia, a Bible, a dozen of modern novels, a dictionary of at least one foreign language, an Atlas, a spelling-dictionary, manuals for home-nursing, first-aid and cooking, and – in a special corner – books borrowed from the local library. As the average German goes just one tenth as often to the pictures as the average Dubliner he has a little more time for reading.

In my parents' home books occupied certainly the highest position among all our belongings. My father's study offered the sight typical of the study of a German scholar, shelves all around the walls, even over the door, from the floor to the ceiling, tilled with books, well arranged in sections. My father could find any of his 4,000 books in the dark. The library was the main problem in the annual spring-cleaning. My father used to supervise the procedure, so that the books would be replaced in the correct order.

Practically all books published in Germany are sold either bound or unbound, the latter at about two thirds the price of the former. Unbound books were bought not only by those who could not afford the bound edition, or by those who just felt the unbound edition would do, but more frequently by those who got their books bound in homogenous private bindings. Among my earliest memories are the visits I paid with my father to the workshop of his book-binder. Having brought there another batch of newly acquired unbound books, my father often left me there while he was doing messages. Then Mr. Kummer used to show me the stitching of sheets, the casing of books, the gluing and tooling of backs; and technical terms, such as "clew", "trimmer", "folder", attained an early place in my vocabulary.

My father was in charge of the library in his school. Many of the ancient secondary schools had libraries of international reputation, with rare books and manuscript treasures. My father's school had actually two libraries, one for the teaching-staff and one for the boys. The latter contained seven thousand books. Every pupil had a printed catalogue of it. At the age of seven, I was admitted as a "constant reader" to this library. I think this was the first of 26 libraries of which I have been a constant reader. In the holidays, while my father was arranging new entries, I used to roam for hours through the high shelves and return home with an armful of books.

My parents made it a point that each of us children and also the maids should receive at least one book for every Christmas and birthday, and they exercised infinite care in the choosing of these books. They never gave us a book which they had not read themselves. My father was naturally very widely read, as he had to comb the book-market for books suitable for his school-library. My mother was keenly interested in the modern literatures both of Central and Western Europe. Needless to say that books "dangerous to faith and morals" never crossed our doorsteps; but my parents' censor-ship started much earlier: We were never allowed to read books which were beneath the standards of taste and intelligence according to our age. Good aunts and uncles followed the example of our parents and helped us in building up a library of our own, the centre of that private sphere which each of us was allowed and even expected to create within the common home.

Both my father and my brothers spent most of their leisure time in reading. In the night, we four "men" were often sitting for three hours in succession around the table, each of us pouring over a book, and only occasionally one of us children would ask: "Father, what means ...?" In the adjoining room, my mother would be sitting reading to my sisters or making one of them read aloud, while they were doing some handi-craft. She had an ingenious way of having one eye on the book and the other on the stocking she was darning. When my father found the time to read to us, it was a feast-day. On New Year's Eve he always had a funny story for us, which he, otherwise a stern and remote man, would read in such a lively mirthful manner that we laughed away all the worries even of the gloomiest post-war years. One whole winter we had one poetry-night every week, when he read and explained to us the treasures of our national literature.

At a very early age we were trained to treat books with respect. My father made us wrap our schoolbooks just as he wrapped books for his school-library. Thus my brothers could hand down to me the textbooks they had used in school. To this day it causes me physical pain to see a person writing with a pen in a book. I often remember my father's rage at people scribbling silly remarks in library-books, tearing out half pages, making inkspots or jam-stains in them. I inherited from him the feeling that a book is the nearest thing to a living being. I feel personally ill-treated when I see the state in which books from my own library are returned to me. I could beat people who make an ear-mark in the page of a library-book. Once I saw a girl using her book as an ash-tray; she squeezed the buts between the pages!

Leipzig offered unlimited possibilities of buying books at reduced prices, not only just second (or fiftieth) hand but brand new copies, old stocks, rests, returns or copies with slight faults in the binding. From my tenth year, all my little earnings went to the book-shops. At the age of sixteen, after two years of my early career as tutor to younger school-mates, I owned over a thousand books, sub-divided into twelve sections. Besides my schoolbooks I always took a book for private reading to school, and (I hope my boys in Belvedere won't read this) whenever class became too boring, I started reading. I attributed my deficient knowledge of Greek to the fact that I spent a substantial part of my Greek lessons in reading the novels of Leo Tolstoi.

For several years after, I had been a constant reader in two school-libraries and two or three municipal libraries, I was admitted, at the age of sixteen, at the German Library at Leipzig, the only copyright-library of Germany. Perhaps the most unusual thing about this library was that the reading-room opened at 7 a.m. and closed at 11 p.m., and believe it or not, on some holidays I spent there six hours in the morning and seven in the evening. I wonder has the subject-catalogue of that library been destroyed; it was a masterpiece of scholarly industry and organisatory talent. My sorrow at the complete destruction of the University Library of Bonn (where I spent my first two "semesters") will have been shared by many of the former pupils of the late Prof. Thurneysen. One of the first German libraries to be severely damaged in air-raids was the Prussian State Library, the largest library of Germany, where I spent some months of hectic research-work for my thesis. A heap of rubble marks the site of the Aachen Municipal Library, my head-quarters during my last years in Germany, one of the oldest municipal libraries North of the Alps; its organisation on modern lines had been the life-work of Prof. Kuetgens, a fine scholar. Sic transit gloria mundi.

Whenever I see visitors from the country in the reading-room of the National Library, I remember my early travels in Italy, France, Belgium, Holland and England, when I too counted libraries among the important "sights". I owe some of my finest travel acquaintances to the reading-rooms of the great libraries of those countries. Dublin is almost the same size as Leipzig, but I think, still superior to that Mecca of book-lovers in library-facilities. In proportion to its size, its variety of libraries is amazing. What a difference between the Swiftian sombreness of Marsh's and the flood of light streaming through the Georgian windows of the Central Catholic, between the comfortable fire-place of the Academy and the cool stream-line functionalism of Milltown Park, between the Gothic wooden vaults of Maynooth and the flat steel-bars of the R.D.S., and above all between the oaken structure around the Book of Kells and the noble dome of the National. What a wealth of historical associations and of scholarly interests is represented by these libraries. There have been few things for which from the first weeks of my life in Ireland I have been more grateful than the unfailing kindness with which I was admitted to these sources of knowledge.

When I hear modern writers abusing "mere" book-knowledge, I often wonder have they ever made the uplifting experience of obtaining, through the "mere" mental effort of reading, through the "mere" association of meaning with the black signs on white paper, real experience, experience just as striking as that conveyed through personal contact? I think this experience is most impressive when one reads in a foreign language and when books have to supplement the many personal contacts which the non-native has not got. In such cases, the leisurely living with books often becomes necessarily living through books, and the book then attains to its vital and original significance for intellectual and spiritual life.

(Quelle: Hibernia, May 1946, S. 11f)

The Love of Books

One of the most painful memories of my school-days is an incident which took place in my final year. Right up to that time my form had been carrying on a feud with our "parallel" form, and on that day once again we had spent our recreation in a brawl. Now we were back in our class-room, awaiting the entrance of the master. Just for a second, the door was half opened and something was flung into our midst. A heavy book, so vigorously thrown that its pages were scattered through the whole room. It happened to be a Bible. I am not ashamed to admit that to this moment just as much as this fact it grieves me that it was a book that was thus degraded and wantonly destroyed. We were breathless at the insolence of our adversaries.

They should have known better. After all, we were all sons of the city of Leipzig, then the largest book-producing town in the world. Some of us bore the names of Brockhaus and Kippenberg, household-words to book-lovers all over Europe. One of our enemies was the son of the owners of Messrs. Karl Krause, the most highly specialised manufacturers of bookbinding machines in the world. One day his father had arranged for us a guided tour through his factory, where we had gazed in wonder at the ingenious machines for stitching, trimming and binding.

Indeed from early childhood we were as familiar with the art of the makers of books as Dublin boys seem to be nowadays with that of the bookmaker. In my parents' house I heard not only of the material foundations of that art, of the various makes of paper, of lettering, illustrating, printing and binding, but also of the actual production of the books, since many of our relatives were either authors, or librarians, publishers, editors or professional readers. With that knowledge the love of books was instilled into us.

Five shelves seven feet high and six wide lined the walls of my father's study. At the annual spring-cleaning he would not entrust anyone else with the cleaning of these books. One by one he would take them down, heavy tomes they were most of them, lovingly dust them and gently replace them. My mother's book-case occupied a place of honour in our drawing-room. It was not a dead show-piece but a living record of the continuity of her interests from the classics of German and English literature she had studied in her youth to medical works, biographies (especially of the great leaders of the women's movement), and then a series of religious books to which one or two were added every Christmas.

Even before we children were granted the privilege of a room of our own, each of us had his own shelf or case, in which she or he arranged a collection of books with German thoroughness. When I left school I owned more than 2,000 books, mostly Reclam brochures to be sure (comparable to the Penguin series), but still quite a respectable library with its fourteen sections, German, French, Scandinavian, English, Slavic and classical literatures, history, philosophy, psychology, sociology, religion, science, geography and – schoolbooks. I think, in case of a fire, even my sisters would have saved first of all their books. Those of us who left their native land tried to take with them above all the nucleus of their library. In 1945 when I was told that our country-house — it dated from the sixteenth century, with stucco ceilings and a lovely staircase — had been destroyed, my first, in fact my only, thought was: "What a pity, 10,000 books gone." We used to keep them in the eastern wing; remnants they were of a high-class second-hand book-business we had been running for some time, specialising in first editions of English, German and French literatures. *Habent sua fata libelli.*

For one who has the love of books at his heart, it is a comfort to live in a country, the greatest intellectual and artistic triumphs of which are associated with the art of making books, which once upon a time was to Europe what Edinburgh and Leipzig together were during the nineteenth century. Reading a recent article on the future of publishing in Ireland, I could not help thinking of *Nieuwe Uitgaven,* the monthly list of Dutch publications, which I am now receiving again regularly. Outside the Dutch Commonwealth, these books are hardly read except in Flanders. Still, that monthly list contains twenty pages with more than twenty titles each. Nothing could make me more hard-currency-conscious than the reading of that list. Gorgeous luxury editions, scientific publications in three or four volumes, three or four pages of books translated from the cream of English, Nordic, French, Italian and German, etc., etc.

I am often tempted to believe that the future of publishing not only in this country but in the world in general is far less a matter of external conditions than we usually believe. Colgan wrote, produced and published the greatest work of Irish ecclesiastical history in the very middle of a war during which, in that part of Europe where he lived, one-third of the people were killed and half of the towns were destroyed. About the same time an Irish Augustinian wrote (and got published) the largest theological work ever produced by an Irishman, and a hundred years later, this work was once again reprinted.

I still hope for a book, an exhibition, a series of lectures on the Radio, in schools or at least in technical schools, that would deal with the tradition of Irish book production and lead to a survey of the present-day stage of making books right from paper-making up to the writing, preparing, editing, publishing and selling of books. One of the reasons why fairly good second-hand books can still be bought at 2d. or 3d. each, that is the price of a child's handful of toffees, is that we have become largely oblivious of the fact that a book is a marvel, a marvel of comprehensiveness in both time and space. It embodies the constant tradition of more than 2,000 years, and it is the fruit of a co-operation between the technical and intellectual capacities more intensive than found in the production of any machine. Is it not one of the few facts on which rests the very dignity of man, that from a concoction of wood, glue and rags, sprinkled with some colouring material he can build up realities dead and decayed many hundreds of years ago, hundreds of miles away, or even not accessible to any natural sense? The word "reading" is related with the word "riddle". Only in the religious sphere, some of us perhaps also in poetry, are still aware of this fundamental meaning of reading and of books.

Those of us in whose intellectual constitution the book still holds a central position, have a duty, I am not afraid of calling it a sacred one, to convey the realisation of the unique dignity of the book to those who come after us. Lasting love of books will not be regenerated by exhibitions, lectures or objective education, but is the fruit of living example and intimate communication on the foundation of a wide and real personal relationship.

Consciousness and love of books is one of the strongest bulwarks against mechanical mass-existence. Reading is essentially a one-man business; it is infinitely superior to the mass-consumption of pictures or the spoon-feeding entertainment of the wireless. The reader must make a much greater contribution to his entertainment than gazing and listening. While holding the book and turning the pages, he must reconstruct, from a material basis unbelievably frail, sense, meaning and significance of that spiritual reality which has been miraculously embodied in it. In contrast to the picture-goer and the wireless-listener, the reader can take his own time, the greatest privilege of a free man. He is not urged on by merely sensual impressions, but allowed to slow down, to stop and ponder, to dwell upon an association or memory evoked, an outlook opened, to go back and re-read, compare and mark. He is given the even more dangerous freedom to skim and skip and to look at the last page. Above all, it is almost invariably himself who through his own efforts evokes the dead signs, meaningless to the un-taught, to life and reality, various grades of reality, corresponding to the grades of un-derstanding, until finally the climax is reached in understanding the author better than he did himself. That absolute triumph of reading conveys a feeling of happiness, scarcely reached in artistic enjoyment, and shared only by artistic creation. It is this sublime happiness which must be realised and spread before we can hope to regenerate a real and discreet love of books. It is by this lofty standard that the external restric-tions in publishing possibilities may be turned into a blessing, leading to a stronger concentration and condensation. Is it lack of appreciation of the hard facts of life when it is suggested that it is with an eye to that creative happiness and responsible freedom, which is the privilege of the reader, that technicians (who provide the material basis for book-production), authors, publishers, editors, librarians and the book-loving pub-lic should strive for close co-operation.

(Quelle: Irish Library Bulletin, April 1948, S. 65-67)

Schoolboy in Germany

Twenty-four hours after my arrival in this country I stood before a class of boys and started teaching. Quite apart from the language, there were many things so strange to me, and this feeling of strangeness has worn off but little during these seven years.

For at least four generations past we have been a family of teachers, and my two brothers and my two sisters, as well as three brothers of my mother, still carry on this tradition. Methods of teaching and the organisation of schools were among the chief topics of table talk in my parents' home. During my school years, the educational system of Germany underwent one of the greatest changes in its history.

Every German child has to go to school at the age of six, not earlier and not later. It happened to be the "turnip winter" of 1917 when I had to start. The scholastic year in Germany is subdivided into two terms, the first beginning after the Easter holidays, the second after Michaelmas holidays. In ordinary times on the first day after the Easter holidays one could see in the streets of German towns and villages the toddlers trotting along by the side of their mothers, a little felt-lined satchel on their back, from which a sponge (for cleaning the slate) was swinging, and a huge coloured paper-bag in their hands. The first day in school was customarily spent in showing the teacher the "sweets bag", traditionally given to comfort the children when their mothers would leave them in the school-room. When I went to school, there were no sweet bags, no sweets at all; in fact, we had seen no sugar for six months. My parents anyway objected to this custom. A child, they felt, should not start out with the belief that school was such a horrible thing that you must be rewarded for enduring it. Moreover, they had seen too often that a comparison between the sizes and weights of the sweets bags introduced early social distinctions in the classroom.

The primary school where I started was a school where a slight fee was charged in contrast to the district schools. There were practically no private establishments among the primary schools in our province, at least not for boys. My elder sister attended one of the private schools for girls which then still existed; she was most unhappy there, as this school, like most others of its kind, were nurseries of social snobbery, one of the chief causes of the socialist revolution in 1918. The fee charged in the type of school to which I went was so low that it made only a very small distinction from the free district schools. Still, even this distinction was abolished under the Republic. Under the new national school system, every German boy and girl had to attend for the first four years the local district school. This rule at first led to a decrease in the intellectual standard of the primary schools, as the usually more advanced children of the middle and upper classes were kept back by their less intellectual companions. On the whole, however, it worked out very well; the extirpation of snobbery, which had started in the trenches of Flanders and Poland, was carried on through these "unity schools".

After four years, the child was permitted to enter a secondary school, the vast majority of which again were public, that is, owned by the State or by the municipal authorities. Gifted children of the poorer classes were assisted by scholarships and a generous allowance system to enter on higher education. Even when staying (for another four years at least) in the primary school they had various means of acquiring a higher education. There were special classes in modern languages and science, which gradually led up to the technical and vocational schools or even to the university. On the other hand, there were special classes for less gifted pupils, whose practical abilities were developed. At the end of the minimum of eight years of regular schooling, every child had to attend night-classes, on a vocational basis, for another two years. In 1935 it was made illegal to educate a child without preparation for a definite vocation; unskilled labour was then abolished.

I received my instruction in the three R's from a typical specimen of a German school-master, an old white-bearded man of universal education, keen understanding of children and thorough knowledge of educational methods, though he was not quite able to follow the change then taking place from the traditional system of parrot-like learning by heart to the systems which allow for the development of the child's own initiative. Anyway, during the first three months, he had got us so far that during my summer holidays I could write to him a message of greetings, and by the end of the year I successfully passed the reading test to which my stern grandfather subjected me.

I have often heard people holding up the Germans as particularly industrious because schools start at 7 a.m. in summer and at 8 a.m. in winter. Actually, children over here start practically at the same time, deducting double summer-time. The difference is rather that German schools close at 1 p.m. in summer and 2 p.m. in winter. After lunch, children are free for play, at four they have a light meal, after which the elder ones start their exercises. When I started school, we had only one or two lessons a day, and these at rather erratic hours, on some days at 9 a.m., at others at 4 p.m., and every week in a different building. Only one school out of five was heated, and that one was filled to the limits of its capacity.

Another point often raised as a proof of the superior industry of Germans is the shortness of their summer holidays. In reality, Irish children have hardly more holidays than German children, who have a fortnight for Christmas and Easter, a week for Whit and Michaelmas and six weeks in summer. We received reports at the end of each of the two terms. In the primary schools we had report books for the whole four or eight years, so that our progress (if any) from term to term could be seen at a glance. At the beginning of the new term, reports had to be brought back to school signed by the parents. Marks ranged from 1 to 5, 1 being the highest. There were intermediary marks, "a" standing for "better than", and "b" for "less than". Marks for "diligence" and "conduct" as well as for "religious knowledge" were very strict; 1b was already pretty bad, and 2a the first step to jail! At the end of the report, the average figure was given, which determined the place in class. At the beginning of the new term we were placed in class according to our totals; the best boy took his place in the last row in the right-hand corner. The advantage of having the lower orders of the class near to the teacher's desk is obvious.

School discipline was maintained chiefly by means of a well-graded scale of punishments. Corporal punishment was abolished under the Republic, but reintroduced under Hitler. The use of instruments in meting out corporal punishment to children was generally regarded as unworthy of parents, teachers and children alike. Apart from the usual punishments for idlers and talkers, such as "a few lines" of classical poetry, or detention, there was first of all the entry in the class-book. This class-book, usually kept by the top-boy of the form, was presented to every teacher before class. It contained the names of boys absent, the themes set for the day, the subject of the last class, and the dreaded fourth column, in which were listed the names of pupils who had seriously offended. Two or three such "entries" usually meant "1b" in conduct or diligence, in the next term reports. After the second entry you had to expect the arrival on the next morning of a registered letter from the Rector to your father. For still more serious offences, instead of being detained in the usual detention class on Wednesday afternoon, the culprit went into *carcer* (the Latin word for jail), that is solitary confinement. In olden times, the *carcer* had been a dark hole in the cellar of the school, and boys were locked up there for many hours. I was once in *carcer*, for having eaten a sweet in class (I shall never be able to punish a boy for this offence!). I had to call at the janitor's lodge and to request him to lock me up. The worst part in the whole procedure was that I had to pay this hated individual one mark "for his trouble"; that was the rule. And I had to pay it from my pocket-money!

In those rare cases when even *carcer* would not lead to amendment, *consilium abeundi* was given, that is, the unfortunate parent was advised to take away his promising offspring; otherwise the Rector would have to strike his name from the roll. As schools were not private establishments, Rectors had little hesitation to use *consilium* or even dismissal as a weapon against obstinate offenders. Dismissal was usually pronounced when a boy had failed three times to obtain promotion which took place at Easter.

Up to 1936, education was one of the spheres of public life which were withdrawn from the influence of the Reich Government and left to the provincial or "land" Governments. In no other sphere of life was it so obvious that up to that time Germany was merely a military confederation of States.

As a native of Saxony, I was a foreigner in Prussia, only a six miles' tram-ride from my home. Instead of the usual one pound per month, I had to pay two pounds school fee. In the universities outside Saxony, I could not sit for an examination or if so, this examination was invalid in Saxony and would not qualify me for Civil Service in the "land" where I passed it. Imagine a boy from Longford having to pay double fees in Athlone, or a girl from Monaghan unable to take a degree in Galway; and imagine if the Dublin Civil Service had to do without Cork men – and girls!

The most conspicuous sign of the dependence of education on the provincial Governments was the different treatment of religion in the various "lands". We in Saxony lived from 1920 to 1980 under a Red Government, strongly opposed by the majority of the secondary teachers, who were monarchist or nationalist. For our teachers, religion was mainly a weapon in their fight against the Red hand. In the primary schools, most of the teachers were redder than the Government, and only some of the old teachers preserved that minimum of religious atmosphere which had survived the war. It was left to the individual teacher whether he would start class with a prayer or not. At any rate, it was only at the beginning of the first period of the day a prayer was said. In some schools, a short service at the beginning of the week and of each term was tolerated. This service was held in the school hall, where also at the end of term the distribution of prizes was sometimes given a certain religious solemnity. School service consisted of some hymn (of which we Lutheran boys knew by heart many dozens, each with six or seven verses), a short allocution by one of the teachers who gave religious instruction, a prayer and another hymn.

While I was at school a great change in the internal organisation of schools was brought about through the introduction of the democratic system. On the one hand, the autocratic power which the Rector had enjoyed up to then was limited by the weekly staff conference. On the other hand, the pupils were granted a certain amount of influence on the running of the school. Every class elected by secret ballot a captain (rarely the top boy). All the captains of the school formed the Pupils' Council, presided by the *primus omnium,* the captain of the highest form. This council had considerable power. It was permitted to make suggestions regarding school discipline, curriculum, examinations and holidays. On the whole, these councils behaved quite reasonably. They did not suggest that boys should be allowed to smoke in class or that summer holidays should be extended to 26 weeks. I saw this council's working only in my secondary school, where it laboured under great disadvantages. The teachers ridiculed it as an anti-national imitation of "Western" customs; many of the boys, who were secretly members of the para-military organisations of the totalitarian extremists, described any attempt of democracy as "ochlocratic" (the forerunner of "plutocratic"). Still the Pupils' Council in my school obtained the introduction of voluntary instruction in botany, the replacement of the written examination by an oral one in geography, and the establishment of a library of modern literature for the two highest years. At the height of its power, the Pupils' Council succeeded in getting one of the teachers sacked for having beaten a boy unjustly and in a fit of temper.

Our Pupils' Council also organised voluntary help in the school-meal scheme. Thanks to the Society of Friends in America and England, in the early twenties, ten thousand of German school-children received a hot meal in school. There were three teams of helpers recruited from the boys of the upper forms. One would collect the soup cans from the central kitchen. One would distribute the soup during "long recreation" (10 to 10.15 a.m.). The third would take back the cans to the depot.

Also the planning of the monthly "hiking-days" (when under the guidance of a teacher each class had to go for a long walk) was frequently left to the captains and the council. I used to hate those walks. It took us three hours to do five or six miles and, unless the teacher was in a particularly bad humour, the walk ended in a beer-garden, where the differences in our financial resources would become all too apparent.

Under the influence of the Youth Movement and finally the Hitler Youth, school hiking, camping and physical training in general attained great significance. At my time, we had only two lessons in drill per week, in the gymnasium or in the playground, and one afternoon of games. The latter was quite uninteresting, as all real training for games was done in private clubs, completely distinct from the school. Through their membership fees these clubs managed to keep up an amazing social grading. There were clubs where a boy whose father did not own at least one car (at that time only every thousandth German had a car) was not admitted. Of one of our literary clubs it was said that it admitted boys "from three servants at home upwards".

The happiest day of my school career was certainly the day when, having passed in our final examination, we appeared for the last time in school, in dinner-jacket and top-hats. Each of us had a button-hole of snowdrops. In one long row we walked in goose-step through the far-flung building. Every teacher whom we met was offered by the captain a button-hole. We passed through all the rooms in which we had studied and where now small boys gazed at us with envious eyes. From the zoological museum we would bring all the stuffed birds and animals down to the detention room. On the roof of the school we would hoist a white flag. The janitor would be treated to a bottle of champagne. In the gymnasium we climbed the rope for the last time and did a last grand circle on the bar. Then the bell would ring for the final dismissal by the Rector, and off we went to the photographer in an open bus.

The longer I have been teaching in this country, the more I have realised the total neglect in my school education of the formation of character, of the training in elementary virtues and a definite spiritual influence. And I went through one of the most renowned public schools of Germany; its name is well known to all students of the life and work of Johann Sebastian Bach. In recent months, I have often been asked: "Tell me, how was it possible that such things were done in the country which produced Goethe, Beethoven and Kant?" Looking back at my school memories, I have to admit that I know where and when the foundations were laid of what to my mind was first of all due to a complete lack of personal responsibility.

For the last seven years I have been looking forward to each September, when I would meet "my new boys", and not once I have left the room after my first class of the new year without the feeling of gratitude that I am allowed to work with the youth of this country.

(Quelle: Irish Monthly, September 1946, S. 384-392)

When I Started Writing

My first contribution to the press appeared in the same newspaper where eleven years before my name had for the first time appeared in print, in a short note announcing my birth. That I started off by writing a letter to the Editor, will not appear as something extraordinary in a country where to this day the art of writing such letters is so flourishing that newspapers manage to fill regularly many columns with these unpaid and yet highly popular contributions. In my native country, and at the time when I wrote my first letter to the press, this was something rare. Only in the Sunday issue, two or three letters were published, usually of a stern censorious note. In my letter I took the director of the public works to task for the way in which he was running the Municipal Bath, which I used to frequent twice a week on a season ticket for school-boys, working out at 2 1/2 d. per bath.

I did not expect that my letter would be accepted or that it would run to almost two-thirds of a column. There was nothing unusual in my brother's snatching the paper from the breakfast-table on the sunny Sunday morning, to get a first view before my father would take possession of it. He turned the pages. Suddenly he screamed, roaring with laughter: "Goodness gracious, look here, would you believe it?" My mother, of course, could not find her glasses, so Charley had to read the whole sorry story to her. "Public Bath Scandal." Signed by John Hennig, with full address, my penname "disgusted citizen" had been dropped.

My mother decided that father would feel the scandal in the public bath much less keenly than the scandal that it had been exposed by a little schoolboy, who happened to be the son of an official of the self same municipal administration on which that savage attack was aimed. However, as we anticipated, father as usual passed in contempt over the letter-page.

The next morning in school I realised that the storm would not pass me. When I entered the classroom, I was given a great clapping. My letter was pinned on the blackboard. The first master came in. He walked right up to the blackboard and, tearing down my precious work, turned to me saying: "You would not believe it, such cheek." Then followed morning prayer. I failed to derive edification from it. When I came home, mother said quietly: "Father wants to see you in his study. You better go there at once." Father's study was behind the dining-room. Twelve steps it took from the hall door to his study. I entered. Father was reading. He continued reading. I knew what that meant. Then he slowly raised his head and looked at me over the rims of the strong glasses he used to wear at work. "Did you by any chance write that letter?" I did not like that "by any chance", besides he knew just as well as I that there was no one of the same name in our whole province. "I did", I mumbled. I remember exactly six boxes on the ear I received from my father during my childhood. Each of them was perfectly aimed, commensurate to both my capacity and my crime. That bang, anyway, finished the first stage of my journalistic career.

Stage No. 2 was more successful, so far as my father is concerned. In 1924 the International Boy Scouts Movement invited German scouts to take part in the Jamboree to be held at Copenhagen. This was the first time after the European War that Huns were invited to an International youth meeting. There were at that time two branches of German scouts; one nationalist, one neutral. The nationalists refused; the group to which I belonged accepted, and I was among the lucky 50 who were picked out of 800 of us to go. After two glorious weeks we returned with that somewhat light-hearted message of goodwill which was characteristic of the Briand-Macdonald-Stresemann period of European politics. My father, a zealous pacifist on religious grounds, fervently supported the new mission which I felt in me. Should I write about my experience to the German Youth Magazine? Of course, I should. I wrote in my somewhat wild boyish hand, ten, twelve pages of letter-paper – most unorthodox size, but at least only on one side, in spite of the paper shortage. A week later, my script came back. The next day my father said: "Why won't you show me that letter? I am sure you need not be so depressed about it." "We were kindly received by all nations", I had written, "even by the French". Margin note to my editor: "Would you believe it, German youth associating with members of the sadistic nation of born murderers!" I could still show you the place where these awful words were written. "They were all sincere pacifists", I had written. Margin note: "Even worse. Never war again / means never victory again / means never free again / means slavery." This slogan has cost some hundred thousands of lives, and possibly will cost another few millions of lives.

My father advised me not to reply. I wished I had always followed his advice never to argue with editors. What my father said to me to comfort me at that first "The Editor regrets" was the beginning of a long conversation over many years, during which I learnt from him to look at politics with a philosophical mind. Some German newspapers and periodicals shared my fathers view and I managed to contribute to them with better success.

In the second year of my university studies, my eldest brother suggested I should start writing on the subject of my studies by helping reviewing new books for a historical periodical. Being a clergyman, he had long been disgusted with what he denounced as my "crypto-Catholic" leanings. Reviewing The History of the Popes, by an eminent Protestant Church historian, would cure me. It took me a fortnight to review that book of a hundred pages in 25 lines, but re-reading that review after twenty years I am amused at the blows I managed to deal. "K.'s summary of the history of Papacy since 1870 suffers from his ignorance of the great Encyclicals ... His verdict on Leo XIII's attitude to Thomas Aquinas can hardly claim to have attained that freedom from bias which the author claims for himself." My last paragraph was rather nasty. I drew the author's attention to a minor inaccuracy in translating in the Bull suspending, in 1773, the Society of Jesus: "because the Society does no longer produce such good fruit" rather than as the Latin text says: "because the Society can no longer produce such good fruit". My professor, I replied, laid the blame on the Jesuits, whereas the Pope, of course, blamed Josephinism and similar trends. Only a student of history can realise what a triumph it was for a boy of 18 years to show that even a great professor can be misled by his bias, and that the modest study of the sources is always the surest foundation of historical truth.

Looking back at these, my earliest journalistic attempts, I realise that they brought me into conflict with my origin in both the political and the religious sphere, and from my experience I can only say that this is not a very fortunate start for a writer.

(Quelle: Hibernia, July 1948, S. 9)

Some Thoughts On Examinations

I suppose I have to call it good luck that each of the examinations I have had to pass was overshadowed by some event which to both examiners and candidates made the examinations a thing of secondary importance.

At the age of nine I had to pass my first examination by which I was to qualify for admission to a public school. At the time when these examinations should have been held my native city was the scene a civil war hardly less fierce than that at the same time raging in Ireland. The Communists had seized power and the Reich's army, supported by some right-wing citizens' forces, tried to recapture the city. The school to which I hoped to be admitted was situated right on the border of the red and the "white" area; it was a strong fortification in the red defence line. We prepared for that examination while the tac-tac-tac of the machine-guns was in our ears; in the night, though there was no electric light available, the sky was red, from various fires. When a few months later, we were admitted for examination, only just the examination hall had its windowpanes refitted. The walls of the school-building bore innumerable bullet marks, and in a corner of the yard we were shown a heap of rusty barbed wire fences.

In the examination-hall the dusty busts of the Kaiser and of Bismarck had not yet been removed, and one of our examiners, we noticed, had a swastika badge on the reverse side of the lapel of his coat. Hitler's movement had just been banned for the first time. Even to us boys this was not a congenial atmosphere for displaying our knowledge of orthography and grammar, of geography and mathematics. Yet, at the end of our ordeal, the head-master, whose sternness was proverbial, had to congratulate us on the good work we had done in spite of adverse conditions.

My leaving certificate examination was overshadowed in a more literal sense of the word, by a partial eclipse of the sun. The first minutes allotted to the examination were spent in peeping through smoke-blackened bits of glass, at that strange phenomenon, which even our examiners regarded as more important than a translation of some passage from Livy.

Our examinations were very much different from leaving certificate examinations in Irish schools. An important part in the examinations was the year's work, especially a sort of thesis, the subject of which had to be chosen by each of us, from history, literature or science, with the approval of the headmaster. The examination papers themselves were set and marked by each master for his own subject and pupils, uniformity in standard being guaranteed solely by the supervision of the examination through a State Commissioner, usually a retired headmaster or high civil servant. The oral, the most important part of the examination, also taken by our own teachers, was overshadowed by another natural event. As the school year ended at Easter, these examinations were taken in early March, and in that year, those were the coldest days I have ever experienced. The first morning most of us arrived with ears and noses numb and swollen, and the school doctor had to be called in to administer to us a special ointment relieving pain and preventing inflammation.

Dialectics

Our school had picked one of the severest State Commissioners, the mere name of whom had put the fear of God into us. However, when he saw us sitting there in the hall with our purple ears and shining noses, dotted with yellow ointment, there was a twinkle in his eyes which bode us good. In contrast to his usual manner, he did not interrupt the quiet flow of questions and answers between our masters and us. This benevolence lasted through the four days of our oral, and I still recall with distinct pleasure the thirty minutes I was "in the mill". In history, each of us had to take a lucky dip in our master's hat; my slip of paper bore the words "Karl Marx". A few days before, my father had explained to me about "dialectics" — as only my father could explain philosophical terms — and this knowledge stood me in good stead. Afterwards my master came to me and said: "Where did you get that from? That was not what I told you, but, mind you, it was the first time I realised what 'dialectic' really means."

In Greek, we were expected to recite forty verses from the Iliad or Odyssey by heart. Each of us had chosen a different passage. In contrast to my classmates who had chosen passages of the speeches and monologues, I had memorised the description of one of the gorgeous banquets, where the very language of Homer suggests the sizzling of fat dripping from the roasts. At the end of my recitation, the State Commissioner rose: "Now let's have some lunch, after this." The lay-out and timing of the examination was entirely his responsibility.

My degree examination at the university coincided with Hitler's accession to power. One of the first measures of the new government was the suspension of all professors suspected of being unfavourably disposed towards the Third Reich. No less than three of the professors under whom I had made special studies, were thus liquidated. They were permitted though to finish the examination of candidates they had already taken on. In my thesis I had voiced some criticism at Rosenberg's theory of history, and one of the two referees refused to accept my thesis on political grounds. In accordance with the university rules, a thesis on which the referees failed to agree had to be submitted to the whole staff of that particular faculty or school. This happened very rarely, but, in my case, as this was a secret ballot it afforded an unexpected chance of expressing academic disapproval of the new masters.

I was on my honeymoon in Rome when I heard that my thesis had been submitted to what was known as "the great vote". With that news on my mind, I watched a demonstration at the Piazza Venezia to celebrate the conclusion of the three-power agreement between Italy, France and England to prevent German aggression. In the morning, I had looked at the world from the point-of-view of the question whether I would get my degree or not: A few hours later, I knew again that the world would go on without my degree. And on it went.

The great vote, which of course was ridiculously in my favour, made the subsequent oral a mere farce. In principle, these oral examinations were open to the public, but during those months very few took an interest in such matters as academic examinations. When I presented myself to my philosophy professor (one of those under suspension), he found that we had no audience. "That's grand, we are alone. We can freely abuse the government." So he did, in a manner though which compelled me to take together all my wits and my knowledge of the history of philosophy. In history, I was the very last candidate of one of the great masters of the craft, also condemned, and he took the opportunity to draw in that hour the balance of his teaching, at the same time chasing me up and down through European history from West to East and from Alexander the Great to Adolf Hitler. Yet I trembled more for his safety than for my success, as his questions more and more pointedly implied the damnation of our rulers from the point-of-view of historical science and experience.

In Ireland I had finally the somewhat unique experience of, in the same year, sitting for an examination, setting an examination paper and marking, in an official capacity, a few hundred papers. That was in the year of Stalingrad, and I am afraid that in all three capacities my mind was not as fully on my work as it should have been. May God grant peace of mind to the boys and girls who are now preparing to sit for examinations!

(Quelle: Hibernia, May 1949, S. 13f)

Remembering the Dead

Travelling through Germany in the night from the 1st to the 2nd of November one could frequently see to the right or the left of the road or railway track a cluster of numerous tiny red lights. In the afternoon of All the Saints, which used to be a State holiday, the people used to go out to the cemeteries with wreaths or bunches of fir, holly, ivy and white chrysanthemums to cover the graves of their beloved ones for the winter. When the grave had been set, a pole, a yard high, was stuck into the ground and a lantern fixed to it in which a nightlight was lit. "And let perpetual light shine upon them."

This was the Catholic custom. For Protestants, too, November was the month of the Dead, the last Sunday before Advent being observed as Sunday of the Faithful Departed, one of the few days of the year when almost everybody would attend service. From my childhood days, long before my father died, I was accustomed to visit the cemetery on that day. In the course of the years the round which my mother used to make with us on that day became longer and longer. Almost every year a new grave was included, often a grave by which we had been standing when the coffin was lowered into it and when we, too, were allowed to throw a spadeful of earth into the open grave. "Earth to earth and dust to dust." Many years later, when for the first time I received the cross on Ash Wednesday, I understood the origin of this custom: "Remember, man, that thou art dust, and unto dust thou shalt return."

All the Saints and the Sunday of the Dead were not the only days when German families would visit "their" graves. The care of graves is a distinctively German custom. Foreign visitors of churchyards in Germany used to express their astonishment at the devotion with which the graves were cared for. As long as a direct descendant was alive, a grave would rarely be seen without fresh flowers in summer, neatly covered with fir in winter, and the tombstone or cross cleaned at regular intervals. During the month of November, German Catholics frequently recite in church and at home a beautiful, if unliturgical Litany of the Dead, which includes a special petition for "those souls of whom none thinks any more". My mother was not a Catholic, yet she made us pray every night for the repose of the souls of our friends "and all the faithful departed". When she took us to the churchyard and we had put flowers on the graves of our relatives and friends, she made us weed a forgotten grave here and there. Whether there was any actual belief in prayers for the dead or not, there was always some prayerful atmosphere about these people, busying themselves about graves.

To this day, cemeteries, even the sad deserted ones in other countries, have a peculiar fascination for me. Is it just the morbid enjoyment of the vicinity of decay which 18th century poets experienced in their musings on churchyards? I like to decipher the half-effaced inscriptions on tombstones, and to build up from them some pictures of lives long forgotten. I enjoy the tracing of the history of a family from inscriptions on collective tombstones. I am interested in the development of sepulchral art, in this country, for instance, from the sober classicism of the forties to the flowery Neo-Gothicism of the late 19th century and the revival of the national Romanesque style. Tombstones of the Penal Times, not to speak of the rare relics of mediaeval churchyards, are a fascinating study to me. Glasnevin and Mount Jerome have been to me invaluable textbooks of Irish history during the last hundred years. Every time I visit these cemeteries, I am glad to discover that more and more of the names I see on the tombstones begin to mean something to me too.

From my early youth, visits to cemeteries have played an important part in my travel experiences. When I was five years old, we spent one summer in a village in the mountains on the Saxo-Bohemian frontier, near the place where my ancestors had been gamekeepers. In the churchyard of that village my brother introduced me to the peculiar rustic sculpture of that district whose tradition could be traced in the ornamentation of the tombstones and crosses. In later years, when we spent our holidays cycling through the various provinces of Central Germany, we used to rest on a warm day in shady churchyards, quietly roaming between the grass-covered graves, establishing from the frequency of certain surnames on the tombstones the racial background of the people of the district.

The graves of our ancestors had naturally a special attraction for us. Like my brothers, I once planned a tour of our native district from the sole viewpoint of visiting all the graves still in existence of our ancestors. Some of them were situated in out-of-the-way villages deep in the mountains. I always experienced a curious feeling of satisfaction when I stood by another of those worm-eaten crosses or moss-clad tombstones bearing the same name which I am bearing. Many of the villages had scarcely changed since the days when my ancestor had lived there. Leaning against the whitewashed wall of the church in whose shadow he rested, I tried to picture to myself from my knowledge of local and national history the background of his life. This great-grandfather of mine must have heard as a child the distant rumbling of the guns of the battle of Jena, while as a man he took a part in the weavers' rising against the establishment of the textile factory, whose humming now filled the valley.

Twice a year my father used to travel 200 miles to his birthplace for no other purpose than to visit his parents' grave. He was not satisfied with just paying the fee for its perpetual care. From these journeys he often brought a sprig of ivy which he used to keep carefully in a vase upon his desk. Was it just sentimentality, some remnant of paganism, an unchristian clinging to the earthly relics of those who had gone before us? We planted the last sprig my father had brought, on his own grave. A few weeks ago, my sister sent me a photograph to let me know that the ivy had spread over the whole grave.

This care of his parents' grave formed a strange contrast with my father's Puritanical contempt of the physical and material side of life. The only stipulation he made regarding his funeral was that he did not want a tombstone but a simple wooden cross, because, he said, the memory of man does not last longer than a wooden cross. How right he was. Even to his grand-children he is but a distant name. A friend of mine, whom I venerate as the greatest living philosopher, when I told him of that wish of my father's, confessed that it had taught him more than the reading of many a deep treatise on the meaning of life.

My interest in the graves of famous people has been no less personal than that in the graves of my own ancestors. I spent a whole day on the Père Lachaise, made a religious study of Westminster Abbey, and still try to understand even the last historical association of St. Patrick's Cathedral. Poor though it was in living traditions, my native town was surrounded by memories of the dead. Eastward in the plain of Lützen, there was a chapel which enshrined the body of Gustavus Adolphus, the

Swedish king, at whose name the whole of Europe had trembled. A little further on was the village of Röcken. I remember one lovely summer morning when once again I had cycled out there. Once again I stood beside the simple marble slab bearing in golden letters the name of Nietzsche, one of the many great philosophers who originated from clergyman's families of our district. When death released him from the night of insanity, he returned to his father's house. There was just a service going on in the church. Through the open hoppers of the church windows I heard some shreds of the sermon: "I am the Resurrection and the Life." The twittering of the swallows under eaves and the buzzing of bees in the lilac-bush drowned the rest.

(Quelle: The Leader, 23.11.1946)

Catholics and Protestants in Germany

According to statistics lately published and confirmed through investigations made among prisoners-of-war, ninety-three per cent of the German people are still members of Christian denominations. Whilst it is hardly necessary to discuss the political aspects of this fact, I should like to make a few points regarding practical religious life in Germany which might contribute to an appreciation of that figure.

In justification of my venture, I may say that I am an off-spring of a family which for several generations past has played a prominent part in German Protestant church life and scholarship. I myself, through the study of Protestant theology, have become a Catholic. Educated in a purely Protestant part of Germany, I lived and worked for the last seven years previous to my emigration in one of the Catholic centres of the country. Living as I do at present in, I dare say, fairly close contact with Catholic life in these countries, I feel that perhaps the most important point in appreciating the religious situation in Germany is an understanding of the relations between Protestants and Catholics in that country. I must confine myself to some points which incoherent in themselves are all still up-to-date.

Roughly speaking and from a merely statistical view-point, Germany can be sub-divided into a Protestant North and a Catholic South and West. However, whole provinces of Southern Germany, such as Württemberg and the Palatinate, are predominantly and most actively Protestant, whilst Münsterland, Ermland and Silesia have been, especially during the last twenty years, leading centres of Catholic life in Germany.

The idea of subdividing Germany from a religious point of view implies that there is an antagonism between Protestantism and Catholicism on which such a subdivision could be based. However, unlike other countries, Germany's ecclesiastical history knows hardly any religious mass-persecutions and penal laws, and deeply rooted bitterness does not exist on either side. The Thirty Years' War is not remembered in Germany as a religious war. The extirpation of one third of the country's population during that war is traditionally attributed to political rather than religious reasons.

For the decisive period of 150 years after the Reformation, the German peoples strictly adhered to the principle *cujus regio ejus religio,* as to a certain extent they still do. The bishoprics of Münster and Hildesheim like the city of Erfurt (which belonged to the realm of the archbishop-Elector of Mayence) were up to 1803 under Catholic princes and accordingly the inhabitants of those districts are to this day mainly Catholic, islands a hundred and more miles away from the Catholic 'mainland'. In those parts of Germany the observant traveller could pass within one hour's walk from a purely Protestant to a purely Catholic village, the two standing close together and maintaining friendly relations in all respects, though not inter-marrying.

There exists only one Protestant organisation, known as the Evangelical League, which is pugnaciously 'Anti-Popish'. Originating as it did from the anti-ultramontanism of the Kulturkampf-period, it has never gained ground outside the clergy, and its attacks have always been confined to writing and speech. The Gustavus-Adolphus-Verein, on the other hand, rather resembles its Catholic counterpart, the Benno-Verein, two organisations devoted to the cultural support of their respective co-religionists. It may be mentioned that both of these organisations served national purposes, the Gustavus-Adolphus-Verein assisting the Germans in Poland and Yugoslavia, the Benno-Verein those in Italy.

There is no other country in the world where Catholics and Protestants form (if for technical purposes we include Austria and Sudetenland), roughly speaking, one half of the population each, and where they are so closely intermingled as they are in Germany. Even before the great industrial migrations, not to speak of compulsory labour-service, evacuations and other changes brought about by the war, the religious map of Germany was incredibly dappled, the proportion of Catholics ranged from one per cent up to ninety-nine per cent.

Perhaps the most interesting districts are those where the proportion between Catholics and Protestants was between seventy and thirty per cent. In fact, it was an established fact that in those districts both Catholic and Protestant religious life was best. Whereas, according to a statement made by Cardinal Innitzer in a letter to Chancellor Schuschnigg, in the first and fashionable district of Vienna more dogs were found than children, places in the dispersion like Dortmund and Beuthen were, in spite of the absence of a glorious medieval tradition, radiant centres of Catholic life. Likewise, the very parts of Germany where the Reformation was first and most firmly established, such as Saxony and Mecklenburg, were also the first to collapse in their religious structure under the new Church regime, while the Protestant churches in the dispersion, e.g. in Bavaria and Württemberg, took the lead in the movement of resistance known as the Confessional Church.

My survey of interdenominational relations would be incomplete without a short reference to the unique privilege which, much to the annoyance of their bishops, Germany enjoyed in having her Catholic clerics educated at State universities. The early history of Modernism and of Central European reaction to the Vatican Council cannot be understood without an appreciation of that fact. At Bonn, Münster, Tübingen, and Breslau there existed side by side Protestant and Catholic Schools of Divinity. I myself was received as a student of Protestant theology in the University of Bonn by Dr. Rademacher, one of the finest writers on Catholic apologetics in Germany. At Bonn, incidentally, the mingling of Protestant and Catholic theologians was intended by Prussia to bring about a weakening of ultramontanism. Although this plan was successful during the last century, in recent years the distinction between Catholics and Protestants in that university became even more marked than elsewhere through the establishment of the school of Karl Barth, who till 1934 was a professor at Bonn, and through the conversion to the Catholic Faith of Prof. Peterson, one of his early followers.

On account of the close external mingling, together with the strict internal separation between Catholics and Protestants, their mutual ignorance of one another was more marked. Ignorance rather than genuine hostility was the most prominent feature in the Kulturkampf-period and in the more recent controversies on the Concordats. The Catholic party, known as the *Zentrum*, was from 1918 to 1933 the only political party to be represented in all the numerous cabinets formed during that period. The central position of that party enabled it to redeem to some extent the wrong done to the Catholic part of the population in Prussia with regard to higher appointments in the civil service. Thus it became quite a common feature for a Catholic to be appointed President of one of the predominantly Protestant provinces. Even under Bismarck an institution such as the Imperial High Court established at Leipzig, then a 95 per cent. Protestant city, brought many prominent Catholics into Protestant parts. There was often a certain clash between the 'old' local Catholic element, mostly consisting of Polish labourers or Czech artisans, and the newly arrived intelligentsia.

My father was a clergyman, acting as professor of religious instruction in one of the State colleges of Leipzig. In 1929, the Government appointed to his school a new Rector, who happened to be a Catholic. My father already knew him, since he was at that time my teacher in another college. The staff of my father's school, including my father, protested against the appointment, but without avail. Eventually my father was deputised to approach the newly-appointed rector with a view to extracting from him a firm undertaking that he would not use his new position for proselytizing. My father returned from that conversation to tell his colleagues that they could not have a finer Rector and that he had met the best Christian of his life. A few weeks later my father died. At his funeral his Catholic Rector wept like a child, saying that he had lost a friend. I can not think of a better illustration of the fact that ignorance is at the root of interdenominational relations, perhaps not only in Germany. And I very much doubt whether things have changed through the common plight. It suffices to say that the dogmatic background of the Confessional Church is pronouncedly Calvinistic, and that on the other hand, Catholics have begun to realise that they are harvesting the fruit of three centuries of toleration and silent adherence to a cultural system heading towards religious disaster ever since the fateful 31st of October, 1517.

This brings me to my last point. Comparing Irish or English Catholics with German ones, we should not forget that, especially in the predominantly Catholic districts, German Catholicism had been watered down to a merely cultural tradition. 'Packed' churches, with which, even in recent years, foreign trippers used to be so much impressed, are by no means an indication of actual religious life. The true state of the people in those predominantly Catholic districts reveals itself once they have emigrated to a district where they are scattered. Seventy per cent of Berlin Catholics (mainly from Rhineland and Bavaria) married non-Catholics, and only twenty per cent of those mixed marriages were ecclesiastically solemnized. Of their children only thirty per cent were baptized in a Catholic church. The number of divorces in which one of the partners was a Catholic was great.

Yet unlike German Protestantism which has become exclusively a matter of the lower middle class, Catholicism still embraces virtually all sections of the people, and, especially in recent years, it was hard to say which social class stood up best to the trials of the times.

It was the purpose of this paper to point to some of the highly involved problems looming behind the words '93 per cent of the German people still Christian', problems which are bound to play a prominent part in the future of Europe.

(Quelle: Blackfriars 25, 1944, S. 336-341)

My Tale of Three Cities
Condensed from the Irish Rosary[1]

Life has made me in succession a citizen of three cities particularly rich in historical associations.

Leipzig, my native city, has been for centuries an important place of commercial and intellectual exchange between Eastern and Western Europe. An ancient road, on which primitive traders used to import salt from the open case mines in Poland, ran north of that town through the wide plain where, in 1631, one of the momentous battles of European history took place, in which Irish contingents fought on both sides.

On Sundays my father took me for trips in the surroundings of Leipzig. In a church nearby, in Zschernowitz, we would inspect a crude baptismal font in which seven centuries ago our forefathers had been reborn while the frontiers of the Holy Roman Empire were still as far in the West as is now the Iron Curtain.

I was a pupil of a public school founded 750 years ago by the Dominicans, and in the "Preachers' Church" we would see the tomb of Tetzel, one of the promoters of the great indulgence of St. Peter's in 1517, who provoked Luther, our countryman, into his "Reformation".

The city hall housed a local history museum, displaying folklore, housecraft, furniture and dress from more than five centuries. The highlight was a 15 x 15 feet model of the battle of Leipzig in 1813, when an All-European alliance inflicted the final defeat on Napoleon Bonaparte.

In the heart of that industrial town there was a proud consciousness of a great past, of an unbroken tradition of a steady increase in material and cultural wealth, the foundation of a peculiar self-reliance in its burghers, who on many occasions, abandoned by their prince and his government, had to fight, or more often to pay, their way out of the claws of some beleaguerer, Slav, Swede, Prussian or Russian. Our city churches

---

1   Published at St. Saviour's, Dublin C.16 1/- bi-monthly.

illustrated the development of architecture from Romanesque to baroque, and there was still a fair sprinkling of grand residences of the 17th and 18th centuries. A deep feeling of tradition was instilled into us from childhood days.

Later years brought me from the East to the extreme West of the Reich. Aix-la-Chapelle or Aachen is one of the oldest and most venerable towns of Germany, its name recalling the setting up there by Charlemagne of his palace and chapel in the vicinity of the Aquae or hot-springs.

In Aachen, for many centuries, the kings had been crowned. Amidst the ruins of the last war, the cathedral of the city has stood up uninjured, and in it the plain marble seat on which the great emperor used to attend Mass still occupies its traditional place. Just across the street the church bearing the name of our St. Foillan (a brother of St. Fursey) has been completely destroyed.

On January 31 we celebrated the feast of Charlemagne, venerated by an old privilege, as a saint in his city only, and the invocations traditionally recited at the coronation of the Emperor were sung. Whole streets or even quarters of the city had retained their architectural appearance from the 17th century and we ourselves inhabited a mansion, surrounded by a mote, of which we had the title deeds as far back as the early 16th century.

The local museum, housed in a fine baroque city residence, told a tale of wealth and industry of this free imperial city. My kinsfolk had taken a prominent part in building up the modern textile industry which made that district a serious competitor to Lancashire.

There have been few things which made me feel more quickly at home in Dublin than this thorough training in local history. In Dublin too, historical tradition is largely a matter of atmosphere, rather than of the museum. Even though I have by now passed a few thousand times under the railway bridge at Howth Road, I cannot help experiencing a feeling of awe at reading the word "Clontarf" on the notice at the Great Northern Railways station.

Whenever I succeed in crossing Merrion Lane where it empties into Lower Baggot Street, I remember the martyrs who were executed on that spot. It scarce required much effort to meet Fitzgibbon and Grattan in the winding corridor of the Bank of Ireland headquarters.

Overlooking the Four Courts from the library of the Franciscan Convent in blazing sunlight at noon, or Dublin harbour from Butt Bridge on a quiet summer evening, "doing" the seven churches on Holy Thursday in the very heart of Dublin between Clarendon Street and Thomas Street or strolling through Stephen's Green pondering over its mixed bag of historical monuments, I still find it hard to realise that all this should have really become mine.

There are those who study history in order to learn from it for the future, to derive some enthusiasm from its great examples, to pick out what was really important (and to forget the rest as quickly as possible).

I am afraid I scarcely see any other sense in history but that it just happened as it happened. You can hold your ear most closely to its throbbing heart when you modestly confine yourself to what is nearest. The past is great wherever we can lay hands on it.

In the study of local history you will rarely experience the feeling of frustration that "all history is just a bag of lies".

At the age of fifteen I became a member of the local history society of my native city. There I experienced for the first time that friendly family atmosphere which seems to be inherent to local history societies all over the world, welcoming in particular the – unfortunately rare – young newcomer. The core of such societies is usually a small band of enthusiasts firmly rooted by family ties in their town or county, carrying on, without the slightest hope of material profit, the good work of keeping alive the tradition by which we are carried whether we realise it or not.

(Quelle: Irish Digest, April 1952, S. 40-42)

The Voice of German Catholics
An Echo from Before the War

Almost one half of the German-speaking population of the Continent are Catholics. Latin Catholics form by far the largest body among the Christian denominations in Central Europe. In no other denomination is the proportion of active members higher. Even non-Catholics will agree on these three facts. If there is any future for Christianity in Central Europe, the active part of the Catholic population will be both its spearhead and its main body, and its spiritual conditions will be a factor of greatest importance.

The Encyclical *Mystici Corporis Christi* recently drew the attention of the whole Church to some dangerous trends in Catholic theology and devotions in Central Europe. It told us of false and of wrong conceptions of the Mystical Body of Christ – errors in modern times scarcely heard of outside Germany, but obviously of such importance as to be given world-wide publicity by the Encyclical.

Most of these heretical tendencies are to be ascribed to the conditions under which Catholic life and thought on the Continent has been labouring during the past twelve years. At a time when the need for spiritual guidance in public life was most keenly felt, the separation between the religious and political spheres naturally led to most unwholesome conditions. Foreign observers of Catholic life had, in recent years, to rely frequently on sources which neither did nor could claim to be more than private and subjective. The smothering, lately complete, of Catholic publishing and of the Catholic Press, led to the discontinuance of objective information and of the control exercised on waywardness by such means of international and national communications. The dangerous tendencies denounced by the Encyclical were naturally found among the younger generation of Catholics rather than among those who had received their education at a time when matters were still comparatively stable.

One of the most active groups of young German Catholics used to be led by Romano Guardini, well-known in this country as the author of various spiritual and philosophical works, who was, up to 1933, professor of Catholic philosophy in Berlin. *Werkblätter*, a monthly published by this group, was, for many years, one of the most influential organs of young Catholic activists in Central Europe. In the spring of 1939 the editor of *Werkblätter* was informed by the authorities that he would be allowed to publish a final issue. This issue of the last periodical of young German Catholics to be suppressed was a comprehensive manifesto. Though I contributed to it, it was only quite recently that I secured a copy of it, probably the only one existing in this country. Introducing the final parade of former contributors, the Editor said:

> "These contributions were made in reply to the following questions: What do you think of the duties of the individual and of the community in the general human-Christian and the more definitely ecclesiastical spheres? If you are the head of a family, say what, in your opinion, is the place of the young family in the Church of our days? What are the duties of modern Catholic education? I you live in the world, say how you stand in your parish, and what parochial work you are doing? If you are a priest, treat these questions from your special experiences. How can we, as Catholics, serve our people?"

(Quelle: The Tablet, 28.4.1945, S. 197f)

Fruit

I clearly remember the overwhelming impression which even in happy pre-war times the first meal in Ireland made on me. It was a Sunday dinner in a County Dublin home. There was a ham on the table. I had never seen a bigger one, and beside it a no less monumental joint; there were potatoes as tasty as you could dream of, and the cabbage simply melted on your tongue. Sometimes, perhaps, I wish in our restaurants vegetable would not be cooked until it has lost its colour and that there would be a little more imagination in the variety of dishes, but what is all that in consideration of the quality and the abundance of raw materials with which this country is blessed?

There is but one thing I shall always miss in the diet of my adopted country. Sometimes I am dreaming of that midsummer noon when, after a couple of hours of cycling over dusty roads, I arrived at Mayence. On the square beneath the cathedral the weekly market was held. Under large multi-coloured sunshades fat women were sitting amidst dozens of baskets heavy with fruit. There were pears, plums, grapes, loganberries, currants, and so on. I bought a sixpence worth of plums. I could barely carry it to the fountain in the centre of the square where, sitting on the edge and enjoying the cool breeze from the water-spout, I began to eat, one pound, two pounds, three pounds. What a feast! And what plums! The size of a hen egg, with velvety purple skin almost burst by the swelling golden flesh, from which the stone came off like nothing. I must not think of those plums, when I get my daily allowance of a dozen of Irish damson, small and hard like a pebble, and oh, so sour.

Up and down the Rhine Valley near Mayence is the vine district. Asmannshausen, Ruedesheim, Boppard and St. Goar. Irish St. Disbod had not made a bad choice when settling there. An Irish monastic community once owned a vineyard there. There was little temptation in walking up the winding paths leading from the orchards in the plain to the vineyards; the grapes to the right and the left were unfit for direct consumption, being sprayed with some chemical substance to keep away philloxera. Still it was most appetising to see, about the autumn time, the vintagers gathering the yellow and purple grapes in their tubs and emptying them into the funnel of the wine-press. A certain amount of grapes was grown in that district for direct consumption, but most of the grapes sold on the market came from Italy. In early autumn many people used to go to the Meran district in South Tyrolia for a grape-cure. I think much of the sentimental attachment of Germans and Austrians to that province (recently once again in the news) was due to their love of the grapes and of the sunshine stored up in them.

One of my earliest memories – I can hardly have been more than two and a half years old – is attached to the fruit-bowl of Dresden china which my father had brought from Meissen, his native-town (near Dresden), where it was made. My parents were expecting visitors one night. When the finishing touch had been applied to the table set for dinner, I was allowed to have a peep at it, just before being stuffed away into bed. The central piece was the three-storied fruitbowl, loaded with oranges, bananas, pears, apples, and hanging down from the top to the lower storeys glowing purple grapes. For many years this picture remained to me the image of peace-time. I have never seen our fruit-bowl filled again like that.

One day in 1920 or so, my sister came home with the news that, at Felsche's, the fashionable sweet shop in town, the first orange to arrive after the war was exhibited in the main window. While enviously gazing at this wonder, we noticed a smart lady walking out of the shop. "Oh, is it not disgusting, it is not for sale, the girl says", she told her husband who had been waiting outside. The land where the oranges grow, of which Goethe's Mignon had sung, was lying far, far away from us.

Memories of pre-war abundance of fruit came back to my mind in Windsor Hotel, Assisi, just beneath the walls of St. Francis's Monastery. At the end of a splendid lunch, the waiter appeared with a large basket, in which I noticed at once at least twelve different kinds of fruit. We thought this basket was for all the guests, and just ventured upon one orange and a couple of figs. However, similar baskets were placed on each table, each basket containing at least six pounds of choice fruit. Next day, I confined my lunch to the soup, and then made straight for the fruitbasket, to the delight of the waiter. It was a symphony of colours, perfumes and flavours. What a revelation to feel a large, ripe peach in one's hand; to bury oneself in its perfume, to study its red cheeks fading out on its golden skin, and then to apply, with slow surgical cruelty, a silver knife (what else than silver?) to rip off the whole skin and to relish the juicy flesh.

Even the ancient Greek poets derived inspiration from such meditation upon the colour, touch, perfume and taste of their fruit, and good fruit they had. Did you ever see a pineapple being sliced up? Is it not almost as lovely as a sunset in Killary Bay?

When a few months ago the first consignment of oranges arrived in Dublin sales began in the late afternoon. Crowds of children were hanging round the shop doors to inhale the smell unknown to most of them, and watching the fortunate purchasers. "Go and have a few for yourself and your pal", I told a laddie, slipping a shilling into his dirty little paw. I remembered a story I had once read of a German schoolmaster who, whenever the first cherries were for sale, treated some poor little children to them, as they reminded him of his father's orchard. At the beginning of the cherry season, the fabulous sum of two shillings was charged per pound, but we knew they were bound to come down to our level. Cherries have the nasty habit of becoming ripe all at once and then go bad within a few days. By the middle of June they were simply thrown off the market, and I still remember the time when they used to go down to twopence a pound. Then we would come home, each of us with a couple of twins or triplets of those black diamonds hanging over our ears, holding out to our mother an open bag: "Here, mummy, have a handful. Summer is incumen."

Clergymen were among our chief growers of choice fruit. Was it the old tradition of the Benedictines who taught the wild Teutonic tribes the art of fruit-growing? I had a clergyman-uncle, right in one of the cherry districts. Every year we received his S.O.S. for the cherry-harvest. Then he would be in arms all day to frighten away hosts of blackbirds, while we boys were gathering the fruit from the branches hanging down to the ground with their heavy load. Later in the year, other friends of ours would employ us in the still more profitable business of gathering plums. It usually took us three days to clear their orchard. Basket after basket full of purple and golden eggs went into the kitchen, where they were working, five of them, to slice, to mash and to unstone the fruit for preserves and for jam. What a sight, the huge kettle with the plums bubbling in the brown sugar-juice!

To the south of my native town in the wide plain we had hundreds and hundreds of acres planted with apple trees for the cider factories. We would set out on a fine Sunday morning in October when the haze was still hanging between the trees, and would wander for hours through that grand orchard. We had seen it in May when the white blossoms had thrown a veil of immaculate snow on the trees. Now the branches were heavy with apples. We picked up the wind-fall, hefty red-cheeked ones up to five inches in diameter. An Austrian poet described our feelings as the realisation of the very essence of autumn: "And I set my teeth in a juicy apple, my cheeks warm with the new wine." Oh, that crisp heartening apple-juice, this bitter-sweet hardness, the picture of healthy life. No banana, orange, fig, grape-fruit, date or pineapple brought us down to the earth like that.

I love the walk over the Featherbed toward Powerscourt in the autumn. Sitting down in the bilberry-bushes on the mountainside (how poor the crops were last year!) I lift up a twig and take just one berry between my fingers. Then suddenly my mother, brothers and sisters are sitting around me, as they did twenty-five years and more ago, in the mountains of my home district, each of us with a bowl beside him, picking and picking the precious fruit, which together with some milk and sugar and with dry bread would make a gorgeous dinner for us. Those berries by the roadside have become the only food, the right on which has not yet been reserved by the strict rules of ownership. They will never become commercialised. There among the blackberries and bilberries in the mountains I forget even the last bit of longing for all the fruit of the world.

(Quelle: The Leader, September 1947, S. 15f)

Forests

Since my childhood days I have regarded it as one of the most important points in the character of persons what scenery they like most or into what scenery they would fit best. I think that in the character of most persons one can trace a peculiar bent for one particular scenery, in most cases, naturally, the scenery in which they were born. I have become accustomed to distinguishing roughly between mountain-men and seamen. One peculiar group, standing perhaps just half way between these two, are forest-men.

I think I have seen the most beautiful scenery of Europe between the Vistula and the Loire, the Tiber and the Skageragg. I have not yet kissed the Stone of Blarney, so I may claim that it is not an empty phrase when I say that, to my mind, Ireland is the most beautiful country. She comprises the sweetness of the South with the harshness of the North, the barrenness of the East with the friendliness of the West. There is but one thing I shall always miss in this country, a real forest. In my studies of Irish history, I have found no chapter more heartrending to me than the destruction of the forestrial beauty of this country. My first walk in the surroundings of Dublin was to what I had heard being praised as the Pine Forest. What a disappointment! What a miserable grove by comparison with what I would call a forest!

Long after I had realised that I was a forest-man, I learned that I am so by race. My name is supposed to be derived from the same root as the word "hedge" and "The Hague". Actually the first ancestor of ours whom we managed to trace was a game-keeper in the *Erzgebirge*, the mountain range between Saxony and Bohemia. When I was there for the last time, I stood on the top of a mountain, 3,000 feet high, from where so far as you can see there is nothing but forests.

Trying to understand the great poets or the chief periods of the history of literature, I feel, it is of great help to keep in mind the scenery typical for them. What would be Homer without the blue Aegean sea and the rocky isles on a summer morning. Ossian, to his Continental admirers at least, is characterised by a wild mountain scenery in a stormy autumn night. Corneille and Racine stand out against the background of the park of Versailles in its early stage. Dante's *Comedia* begins with a description of a "wild forest". So does Wolfram's *Parceval,* the greatest work of German mediaeval literature. In Goethe's *Faust,* the decisive scenes play in the forest.

As for Germany, the forest-background is essential not only in works of literature. Nothing was more shocking to me in Walt Disney's *Fantasia* than the ridiculous stage-forest in which he pictured to us Beethoven's Pastoral Symphony. My dear sir, Stephen's Green is not a forest.

Right behind the house in which I spent my childhood days, the Rosenthal, the central park of Leipzig, began. It consisted mainly of a fine large meadow, in the middle of which huge oak trees, many centuries old, stood out against the sky, surrounded by a forest belt. The great thing about this park was that though reaching right up to the centre of the city, it extended into the open countryside, uninterrupted by suburbs. Every Sunday afternoon we set out from our house for a walk through the forests stretching along the numerous small rivers meandering through the great Leipzig plain, the scene of so many battles of International significance. For three or four hours we could walk without ever seeing anything but trees. And what trees. To be sure, the oak has often been the source of inspiration for false blatant patriotism. "Hearts of oak." "The God, who made our oak-trees grow." Yet is the oak not really the very image of lasting strength, standing up to all storms with its weather-beaten bark! Walking through an oak forest always gave me that feeling of awe which otherwise only the open sea and high mountains convey to us. The right time to walk through one of those German oak-forests, some square miles in extent at least, is a stormy late autumn afternoon. Putting your ear to the stems of the trees you hear the roaring of the storm in the top branches, the hissing of the rain through the dense foliage. Yet the huge stems remain unshaken. They do not even shiver. Beneath the soft velvet carpet of moss, gigantic roots fix the tree with iron clamps to the ground.

In the front garden of St. Patrick's College, Maynooth, is one of the finest chestnut trees I know. Every year when that tree is in full bloom, I know my term is up. I like to look closely at one of the marvellous candles with the glorious red lights on the petals. They conjure up before me a forest of chestnut trees forming part of the park of Weimar, one of the most beautiful sights in that extraordinary place. Close beside the chestnut tree in Maynooth is a gorgeous copper beech. Of these again I saw a whole forest in Erimitagesletten, belonging to the King of Denmark. What would Copenhagen be without the belt, many miles deep of beech-forests, rising right by the side of the Baltic on the cliffs of Zealand? It was so fascinating to walk through those forests for hours, then suddenly to come to a point where it became thinner, and deep beneath lay the green sea. The whiteness of the rocks falling steeply down into the sea contrasting with the brownish grey of the high stems of the trees, the light green of the foliage through which the sun shed a gentle light, what a symphony of light and colour.

The most glorious effects of light, however, I saw in the birch-forests of the North German plain. Actually though there were thousands and thousands of birches standing close beside each other, it was hard to get the actual feeling of forest. The foliage was nothing but a light veil, supported by slender stems of immaculate white.

For six or seven years I spent most of my holidays hiking through the various parts of Central Europe, first with a youth group, in later years by myself. Many a day we were walking through pathless forests, without a map, just following one straight line. In the night we put up our tent, wherever we liked, possibly under some beeches, whose soft dry leaves offered the ideal foundation for our "beds". There would be a stream breaking its way through rocks. Our supper would consist of fried trout, fresh trout from that mountain brook. In the morning we would have a dip in a pond hidden under the high trees. At the edge of some bogland we would have a camp fire, around which we would sit long after midnight, singing ancient folk songs celebrating the beauties and mysteries of the forest, its symbolism, that message of lasting truth and sincerity which we heard in the monotonous rustling above us. He who has never spent a whole night deep in a forest will never know those mysterious voices which to us were the source of inspiration for endless reveries. I think only the grand bogs of Ireland have a similar richness in voices.

The youth group to which I belonged had hired from the district gamekeeper a hut in which he kept hay for feeding the deer at winter time. Week-end after week-end we went there. Thirteen miles from the nearest railway station, six miles from the nearest village, three from the nearest house. It was not that civilised romanticism of the boy scouts at Powerscourt. It was something more remote, wilder, harsher. Though we stayed there as a group, we all felt the great power of the forest absorbed us each separately. One summer night, I felt I could no longer sleep in the hut with the crowd. I made my bed outside, burying my sleeping-bag under the dry leaves. For hours and hours I lay on my back, my eyes wide open, watching the stars through the swaying tops of the pine trees. Neither the sea nor the bog can give me the same feeling of isolation and utter loneliness. Both the sea and the great plain, as well as the high mountains just dwarf you, reduce you to nothing, almost depriving you of personality. In the forest, however, the view is restricted. You are confined in a living cell.

One of the mediaeval churches of our town had been redecorated towards the end of the 18th century. Following the example of some Flemish wood-carvers, the architect on this occasion had stuck on to the high Gothic vaults a kind of palm foliage in plaster. It sounds awful, but the effect was really magnificent. In fact, I think it emphasised the forestrial nature of Gothic architecture. I could compare each of the great mediaeval cathedrals to some tree. In the exterior of the cathedrals of Milan, Amiens, Paris and Cologne, motives taken from trees play a great part and the whole has doubtless the effect of a cluster of trees. That amazing effect of the interior of those grand cathedrals, the pillars rising us up towards heaven, the vaults however keeping us from just flying away, all this is found in real forests.

One often hears people discussing the question whether animals have a soul or not. Owners of pet dogs regard it as a blasphemy to deny their "Robby" has got a soul. I would maintain the belief that trees have a soul. Indeed I would regard it as the surest sign of barbarism to regard trees merely from the point of view of the timber merchant. No sort of hooliganism can infuriate me more than the wanton destruction of trees, whether fruit trees or not. As a child I cried when our landlord cut down a beautiful acacia behind our house, because, as he said, it made his bedroom too dark. The noise of a saw in the stem of a tree still causes me physical pain. The worst, however, is the sight of branches pulled down, perhaps in order to get a few unripe apples, or from sheer vandalism.

In Bismarck's Memoirs there is an impressive passage where, after speaking of the pains caused to him by the unwarranted dismissal by the Emperor, the author says: "Nothing, however, could grieve me so much as the fact that the first act of my successor was to cut down the old lime trees in front of the Reich's Chancery, the trees under which the late Emperor had played as a child." Bismarck expressly stipulated in his will that he did not want to be buried in any other place than under the old oak trees of the Saxon forest (near Hamburg), where he had spent his last years.

One of the most interesting sights in this country was to me the forestry school in Avondale. Planning afforestation, I feel, is one of the most important points in reas-suring the continuity of nationhood. As we no longer build houses that are going to last longer than twenty years, afforestation is really the only positive work which our marvellous civilisation is capable of doing for the benefit of future generations. The sight of hundreds of acres of seedlings which will grow into forests covering the barren hills of Ireland is a real comfort in this world of exploitation and destruction.

(Quelle: The Leader, September 1946, S. 16f)

House and Home in Germany

Attempts to understand a foreign people should start with a study of the simple foundations of their natural and daily life. Unfortunately in many countries foreigners will find it most difficult to gain access to the best source of knowledge of the national characteristics, the home and the family. In France for instance, even after many years of friendship with a native, the foreigner will not be admitted to his friend's home, but the café will continue to remain the usual meeting place. In Germany, on the other hand, the circle of family life is less restricted, and many foreigners owe their happiest remembrances to a holiday spent in that country in a German home. There are few countries where the home and the family play such an important part as in Germany, whilst at the same time, in this intimate sphere of life, foreigners will most easily realize how differently people live in other countries.

Can you imagine a home without a fireplace in the sitting room? Do you realize how different life looks when the day starts at 6 or 7 a.m. and ends at 10 or 11 p.m.? Could you think of enjoying a family meal without a cup of tea? These are just a few points where the difference between an Irish and a German home is most striking. Before having lived in a foreign country we scarcely realize how much these simple things matter.

One of the first things a foreigner would notice in a German town is the absence of single-family houses. In fact, 90 % of German townsfolk live in flats. On account of the high ground rents only very few people can afford a detached house. In some medieval cities such as Hildesheim and Braunschweig, ground rents were so high that people built houses on a very small ground, but made the higher stories project the lower ones, so that in some cases, the space between the top stories of two opposite houses is so small that people can shake hands across the road. Every German house has a cellar. The first floor is usually a little above street level. This floor is not very popular being in easy reach for burglars, but it is usually inhabited by families with many children, who, on account of the noise, are less welcome in the upper stories. The second story is the most fashionable and accordingly the owner of the house likes to keep it for himself. Every flat has one detached room in the cellar for storing fruit and coal, and one semi-detached room in the attic for drying the laundry on wet days. In the cellar there is also the wash-house, which is used in turn by the different tenants of the house. Many flats have fairly large balconies, mostly with glass-partitions and overgrown with ivy or wild vine. On a warm summer night thousands of families sit in their balconies, and, in the absence of gardens, these balconies are often the only open-air play-ground for children.

German houses have no knockers but bells. At the front door of the house there is a board of bells, one bell for each flat. In better class houses, the front door is always locked, but can be opened electrically from the flat. In some modern houses, beside the front door there is a microphone connected with the flats and after having rung the bell, the visitor is asked for his name and then admitted (or not). In more ancient houses, especially in country cities, outside the windows of the sitting room there is a 'spy', a mirror placed in such a way that it reflects the front door, so that, without opening the window, people can see who is at the door. The advantage of this system is, of course, that unwelcome visitors can easily be kept away.

I mentioned that German houses have no fire-places. Accordingly, family-photo-graphs, knick-knacks and Christmas-cards are not placed on the mantle-piece but on the dresser. In modern houses central heating is almost general. Either the whole house is heated from a central furnace worked by the house-keeper, who usually lives in the attic-flat – in this case the heating is included in the rent – or the single flat is heated from a smaller boiler in the kitchen. In some places the French system of heating whole blocks of new houses from one central plant has been adopted. Fuel for central heating is either coke or oil. The heat is conveyed through the pipes by warm air, warm water or steam. Gas or electric fires are fairly unusual. The ordinary type of heating is the stove. Especially in the Central and Eastern provinces, where winter is long and severe, every room, at least every sitting room, has a stove, a kind of funnel built in glazed tiles and standing in the inner corner of the room. The stove reaches from the floor to the ceiling and is about one yard broad. On the floor there is the grate in the stove in which in the morning the fire is made with briquettes, made out of the dust of lignite. (Lignite, the ordinary fuel for domestic purposes, is something between turf and coal.) When the coal is red, the grate is tightly closed by means of an iron door. The tiles keep the heat for many hours, so that only on a very cold day a second charge is required in the afternoon. In peasant houses, the stove stands a little more in the middle of the room, so that behind the stove there is some space for a bench or a bed on which the old people sleep. When a German speaks of an unconvincing cause, he says that 'it won't attract anyone from behind the stove.' In the Middle Ages the production of stove-tiles was a great art. World-famous are tiles from Delft in Holland. Some of these tiles are painted, others show sculpturesque work. Sometimes events from the Bible or from the national history are depicted on the tiles. Modern stoves display the usual empty ornamentalism of manufactured art.

In many houses the bench standing round the stove is the centre of family life. In the night the family gathers there practising music, telling stories, playing games or doing needle-work. In other houses, family life concentrates round the central table in the living room. Most families have not a separate living and dining-room, but even the poorest families have, what is called 'a good room,' like the west-room in an Irish country house or the usual parlour in our city houses. If possible each member of the family has a bed-sitting-room for him- or herself. For some years past the craze for privacy within the families has increased.

In Germany, schools and offices start in summer at 7 a.m. and in winter at 8 a.m. Accordingly, school-children return from school at 1 or 2 p.m. and have no classes in the afternoon. Offices close at 3.30 or 4.30 p.m. Shops and stores are open from 8 to 6 or 7 p.m. Only in the country, provision stores are open until 9 p.m. and on Sundays.

People used to go to bed about 10 or 11 p.m. when the stove becomes cold. Theatres and cinemas close by 10 p.m. Accordingly there is no late meal in the night. The average German has only three meals, breakfast, dinner and evening-meal. Children, who, by the way, are never sent to school before the age of 6 or 7, have a light meal about 4 p.m. Only on Saturday and Sunday afternoon many families have, what we would call, a light tea at 5 or 6 p.m. Breakfast is much plainer than in this country. Bacon and egg is an unknown dish. A boiled egg for breakfast is regarded rather as a luxury. The usual drink is coffee, or rather a mixture of real coffee and a substitute such as burned barley. White loaves are practically unknown, but the usual 'rolls' consist of white meal. Fresh crispy rolls are delivered three times a day. In the morning as early as 6 o'clock the baker's boys bring their wares in huge baskets and, at each flat door, they find a linen bag in which they put the number of rolls as ordered. In some hotels, no less than 6 different kinds of rolls and four kinds of bread used to be offered for breakfast. Many people eat cheese with their breakfast. Dinner is the main meal. Many people prefer a vegetarian or semi-vegetarian diet, and in all cities there are numerous restaurants catering for vegetarians. Especially in summer, fruit is comparatively cheap. The evening meal is the only meal with which many people drink a cup of tea. A very common dish for the evening meal is chips and cold meat or sausages. Only in Western and Southern Germany beer or wine is frequently drunk with a meal.

House-music is a remarkable feature in German family life. In many families the children learn to play different instruments, so that a family orchestra can be formed. It is a well-known fact that many great German composers such as Bach and Schumann wrote special music for families. Especially at Christmas-time music plays a prominent part in German homes. Every German knows dozens of hymns for the different seasons and occasions of the liturgical year. These hymns are sung not only in church, where on every Sunday there is at least one sung Mass, but also in the homes.

Another characteristic of German family life is its close connection with nature. Whilst only wealthy people can afford a garden by the house, everybody can rent very cheaply a plot in one of the famous garden-colonies found on the outskirts of the cities. In the last war, these garden colonies saved a great part of the civilian population from starvation. On Sunday morning, from the great cities dozens of excursion trains leave between 6 and 9 a.m. bringing thousands of families to the excursion places in the neighbourhood from where they set out for walks for many hours. The German railway company issues special family excursion tickets. A striking feature in German cities is the absence of squares closed to the public, such as Merrion Square in Dublin. On the other hand, a city as Berlin has at least three hundred parks which are open all day and accessible to everybody. In some of these parks, there are paddling pools and sand plots for the children and a small restaurant.

(Quelle: The Leader, 2.5.1942, S. 327f)

Music in the Home

The leading part, which the wireless has to play in modern music life has recently been acknowledged by various talks and interviews by Captain Michael Bowles. It is generally recognised that in no other sphere the wireless can exercise a more favourable influence than with regard to musical education. Whilst we are all aware of the disastrous effects of the indiscriminate all-day use of the Radio on family-life and intellectual activities, it is doubtless one of the few advantages yielded by modern civilisation that the treasures of our musical tradition have become easily accessible to practically every social group and to every part of the world. On the other hand, Captain Bowles demanded that the wireless must not lead to, but rather actively prevent the extermination of direct concerts by professional and amateur musicians and of music life in our families and homes.

It is one of the few consolations which the international character of the wireless offers in these days, that in the sphere of music, to which in all countries up to 80 per cent of the programmes are devoted, a certain sense of appreciation of the common in-heritance of mankind still preserved. The names of Beethoven, Mozart and Schubert figure as prominently as ever in the broadcasting programmes of Britain and America, whilst the German wireless is indebted to foreign contributions made to modern music, from Debussy and Elgar right down to American jazz. Whilst the prominent position held by Germany and Austria in the history of music is an established fact, also with regard to the problems of organisation and education in musical life, Central Europe offers some interesting aspects.

When we consider that the word 'Chamber-music' still points to its origin from the domestic sphere and that the German 'Lied' (Schubert, Wolff, Loewe, Brahms) was and still is based on Folksongs as living in German families, the part played by the home in the history of music is evident. In no part of the world the domestic tradition of music is stronger and more lively to this day than in Germany.

One of the greatest powers in the early history of German music was the religious life of the family. The amazing fertility of musical talents in the family of the great Johann Sebastian Bach is mainly attributed to the fact that at that time German children received from their early youth a very careful musical education. Each child in Bach's family played two or three instruments and their vocal training was not neglected either. This part of their education was, however, most closely connected with their religious upbringing. Every morning and every night the Bachs gathered for a kind of musical home service consisting of the reading of a short passage of Scripture and the singing of various hymns accompanied by various instruments. The great part played by the singing of church-hymns in German life is well known to every visitor to the country, whether Protestant or Catholic. The boys' choirs attached to the Protestant Cathedrals, such as Bach's famous St. Thomas's choir at Leipzig, are well known, from recording and broadcasting. In the Catholic churches the performance of the classical Missae solemnes sometimes seems to overshadow the religious character of the sacred ceremonies, whilst the 'singing Masses,' where the congregation ac-companies the various parts of the Holy Sacrifice by appropriate hymns in the vernacular, are most puzzling for a Catholic visitor from this country. The beautiful hymns composed by Luther, Schütz and Bach have attained world-wide reputation; several National Anthems have been derived from them. For every season of the year there exists a dozen and more appropriate hymns which the congregation usually know by heart. However, if the singing of hymns had been confined to the Church, it would never have attained that tremendous influence which to this day it exercises on the cultural life of the nation. The solemn occasions of family life such as birthdays and feast-days (or name's-days) of the various members of the family, weddings, Christening-parties, first Holy Communions or Confirmations, are surrounded by a wreath of religious songs which are handed down by family tradition. On such days, the piano in the sittingroom becomes the very centre of the family. The mother usually takes her place at it, playing and leading the singing while the father and the children join in with their instruments and voices.

Even in this time of gramophones and loudspeakers, in a fine summer night in the small towns and villages of Western Germany the air sometimes seems to be filled with gentle tunes of guitars, violins and flutes intermingled with the more vigorous chords of the piano or harmonium resounding from the open windows of houses where the tradition of family concerting is still kept up. There is hardly an autobiography by a writer of the classical and modern period of German literature which would not refer to the decisive influence by this home training on the spiritual and intellectual development of youth. The great advantage is that these domestic performances are not confined to social evenings; in fact in the presence of strangers, a certain reluctance to reveal the true genius of the family may be noticed. They are rather regular features in family life, and their educational value is even higher in virtue of the fact that they form an essential part of the domestic 'routine.'

No foreigner should claim to understand Germany and the Germans unless he has witnessed the celebration of Christmas in a German home. Throughout the time of Advent, when the wreath of fir branches bound up with a red silk ribbon and adorned with four red candles is hanging from the lamp in the sittingroom, and when in the night the homely light of the Advent star greets the visitor in the hall, the family are engaged in practising carols. On Christmas Eve, with the Germans the principal part of Christmas, many hours are spent in the playing of 'shepherd-music' from the Christmas oratorios by Bach and Mendelssohn, and with the singing of hymns and religious songs. When I was a child, I used to know up to fifty of these carols, each of them having six or seven verses. I heard Luther's 'From heaven high an Angel came' sung in Cologne Cathedral in the presence of the Cardinal-Archbishop, whilst 'Silent Night,' the immortal Christmas song, the words and music of which were composed by a priest in Tyrolia, will be heard of in all parts of the world where Germans are celebrating Christmas. More than in any other country, this is a family-feast, and music far more than a good dinner is the main attraction in these family reunions. In many families the long nights before Christmas are spent by, the children, especially when the parents are out, in practising more difficult pieces of instrumental music, solo or for the family orchestra, by which the parents will be 'surprised' on Christmas Eve. Bach wrote a whole book of easy music for his dear little daughter Magdalen, to be played on the various solemn occasions of the year. The idea that on Christmas, not only the parents should give presents to their children but also the children to their parents, gives to these efforts a higher significance, since it is obvious that a well-done piece of music is more acceptable to the elders than any purchased present.

One of the most remarkable features in German educational life is the high standard of musical instruction. This standard has been raised in recent years by the formation of the National Music Chamber, the only body authorised to grant licences to music teachers, unlicensed teaching being forbidden. Whilst a definite course of studies was prescribed for the younger members of the Chamber, those who at its establishment were over forty were allowed to continue their work since it could be assumed that, if their education had been insufficient, experience had given them the required qualification. In the present system of total state-control in all spheres of education, musical education is the only line which has not yet been separated, from the domestic sphere. Music lessons in school are rare, for the simple reason that there is no time for them, and that, on the other hand, due to the early closing of schools (in winter at 2 and in summer at 1 p.m.), they are naturally assigned to the afternoons. Thus, amidst cultural destruction and decay, one of the most precious inheritances of European civilisation will be faithfully preserved in the home.

(Quelle: Hibernia, February 1948, S. 12f)

Christmas in a German Home

In his autobiography (which is a prescribed text-book for this year's Leaving Certificate Course) Hans Carossa, a modern German Catholic writer, rightly stated that the splendour with which some of the church feasts were celebrated in Germany had almost something painful, originating as it did from the desire to drown the feeling of unreality at the meaning of those feasts. Throughout the world this disparity between the external splendour and the internal reality is most noticeable in the celebration of Christmas. Christmas is a comparatively young feast and not one of the church's highest feasts. From the business point of view, however, it is the feast of all feasts.

From my earliest days I remember the desperate fight which my parents put up to keep Christmas busyness out of our house. The Advent-star, a large paper star with many multi-coloured points, put over the bulb of the lamp in the hall, was a symbol of those homes where the season of Christmas was not a period of rush but one of peace. With the Protestants, Advent is a season of joyful expectancy rather than of penance. A few days before the first Sunday, my mother used to bring from the market a large bunch of fir twigs which she would shape in a large thick wreath wound with a broad red silk ribbon and on which four thick candles were fixed. For the next four weeks this Advent wreath occupied the middle of the dining-room table, which is the centre of German family life, just as the fireside is in an Irish home. On each of the four Sundays, in the evening, one more of those candles was lit, and then my mother would gather us around the piano, and we would sing to her accompaniment some of the numerous beautiful hymns for Advent and practise our Christmas carols.

Both Protestants and Catholics had an abundance of such hymns for the seasons of Advent and Christmas, and they knew them well. There was one, composed by Martin

Luther (I heard it sung in the presence of the Archbishop in Cologne Cathedral) of which I still remember all the twelve verses.

With us children preparations for Christmas started long before the first Sunday in Advent. In fact, by that day we were supposed to have finished with them. We had to prepare presents not only for our parents, brothers and sisters but also for the maids, close friends and god-parents (of whom each of us was blessed with four!).

When I was sixteen I remember I had to prepare presents for twenty-two persons, including my first lady friend. The rule was that these presents had to be either hand-made or purchased from one's own earnings. Experience had taught us that it was unwise to postpone purchase of presents or of materials for presents until December, when prices showed a decided tendency to double. In fact, throughout the year we were on the look-out for bargains suitable for conversion into Christmas presents. Each of us had his own haunts for bargains which we used to visit at frequent intervals. Mine was a department store, which occupied the house in which Richard Wagner was born.

Though not each of the five of us had a room for himself, we had at least each a corner, strictly respected as our private sphere. In the corner formed by the big linen press, behind a thick curtain, my brother had his workshop. He was a real genius in handicraft. One year he produced for me a grocer's shop fitted into a butter box with shelves made of match boxes, the drawers containing real sugar, flour, peas, salt and coffee, a counter with scales and cash box, and even a neatly written price list.

I was not more than four years old when my mother made me prepare my presents. At first it was the usual rubbish in paper-work, book tokens, match patches, calendars and note-books. Then came a few years of embroidering. At nine I was able to knit for my mother a nice pair of face cloths. In later years I attended in school special handicraft lessons and learned to bind books and to build useful cardboard boxes.

Secrecy and originality were the chief features in our preparations. You were not allowed to ask the prospective recipient of your present what he wished for Christmas. Accordingly, the recipient had to express surprise and delight, even at the most useless present, as long as it had been given by a child. After my father's death we found several drawers of his desk stuffed with presents of former years; he had kept them religiously. Also, it was not the custom to ask for help or even advice unless you were very young. It was important that not only the recipient but also the other members of the family should be surprised. Lack of funds was usually made up for by ingenuity. "You should not have spent so much on me." – "If you knew what it had cost!"

Having completed our preparations, we were ready to enjoy with a good conscience the Christmas rush. Aimlessly wandering among the crowds thronging the streets, the stores and the Christmas market on market square, we realised how wise we had been. The fortnight before Christmas was with us one great musical festival. There were Christmas oratorios and carol services in the churches and schools; our domestic carol practices became more frequent and each of us secretly practised a piece of music he would perform at the concert we would have on Christmas night. There was an abundance of good, easy Christmas music. For some years we had every year a trio, piano, violin and flute.

In most parts of Germany it is Christmas Eve rather than Christmas Day that is regarded as the chief part of the feast. Shops close at 5 p.m. At 6 p.m. the streets are deserted; it is the hour of "Bescherung", the ceremonial giving of the presents. In the afternoon we had attended a short service. Now we were waiting in the hall under the Advent star, lit there for the last time, while our parents were busy in the dining-room. At 6 o'clock sharp my father would ring a silver hand bell used only on this one occasion of the year, and, widely opening the door, he would say slowly and quietly: "Come in, children, the Christ Child has come to us." We were never made to believe in Santa Claus; we received our presents, through our parents and friends, from the Holy Child in the manger.

I can really say we lived all year for that moment. I think each of us realised that he had lost the innocence of childhood when saying for the first time: "What a pity, it is over so quickly." There was the Christmas tree with all its splendour, and beneath it, sheltered by its heavy branches, the crib, our crib, handed down in our family from generation to generation, augmented by ever new figures and animals. Slowly we entered the room, in the traditional order, the younger ones first. For a few minutes we stood in silence around the crib. Then my mother's clear voice would ring out like the voice of the Angel of the Lord *Adeste Fideles*.

Then only we would turn towards the large white clothed table, where each of us would quickly find his place, with a plate full of sweets and the presents from our parents. I remember one year, I could not help noticing when I entered the room, that the long-wished-for toy sword was there on my place right enough; I had a distinct feeling of guilt at having stolen that glance from the time which I owed to the Holy Babe.

After we had examined our parents' presents, my eldest brother and each of us in succession would go out to his corner and gather up his presents. One year my generous sister had to bring hers in two large baskets. Then we opened the various parcels which our friends and relatives had sent for us. In the beginning the table had looked bare. Every year our father apologised to us for his bareness. But then when all our own and our friends' presents had been laid out, there was hardly any room left, and, taking our parents by their hands we would dance round the table.

At eight o'clock supper was served, cold supper, so that our mother and the maids would not have to spend too much time in the kitchen. All our meals at Christmas were simpler even than ordinary Sunday meals, because my parents rightly felt that through the seasonal supply of sweets and cakes we were over-fed anyway. Incidentally, pubs and restaurants were closed for Christmas night. The mere idea of a person getting drunk on Christmas Eve was simply unheard of (the chief reason why midnight Mass is more common in Germany than it is – elsewhere).

After supper, we had my father's hour. Quietly sitting around him, we would listen to his reading the Christmas story from our large family-Bible. Then he would "give out" one or two of the more heavy, philosophical type of hymns, and each of us in succession would propose his favourite carol, until my little sister would start singing *Bah, bah, black sheep*. Interspersed between the carols and more readings from the Bible we had our instrumental music. At ten o'clock the younger children went to bed, but the rest of the family used to stay up for the reading of Christmas letters from friend and relatives far away. In later years, when our family gradually became almost as scattered as many Irish families are, this reading of the letters became on of the more prominent features in our Christmas Eves. The sad Christmas after my father's death was the last Christmas we were all together. Since then, each of us had to try to continue for himself the Christmas tradition of our home. Every Christmas, however, we realise anew how little we have succeeded.

(Quelle: The Leader, 14.12.1946, S. 7f)

How I Learnt English

Apart from the innocent questions: "What do you think of the war?" and "What do you think of this country?" no question is more often put to the foreigner at present living in Ireland than: " Did you know any English before you came over here?"

"I did." I should say, "Of course, I did." Among the comparatively few Continental persons who during the last hundred years put their foot on Ireland's shores, there will not have been many who had not a fair knowledge of English. The one thing on which those of my Irish friends, who, in happy pre-war times, toured the Continent, are unanimous, is that they were amazed at the number of people who could speak to them in tolerable Bearla.

In Germany, in particular, the tradition of learning English is one of the most significant phases in the history of her national culture. A hundred and fifty years ago, classical German literature was born when German writers, freeing themselves from French influence, up to then predominant, adopted Shakespeare as their great master. From that time there was a steady increase in German interest in English literature and in the countries in which it originated. Ireland was known in that connection as the country of Goldsmith, Swift and Sterne. Nineteenth century industrialism gave a broad material basis to this new English influence on the Continent, which after the last war was further reinforced by the blind adoption of all things bearing the trade-mark "Made in U.S.A.".

Yet, up to 1920, the first and principal foreign language in German schools was French. The change over to English was made during my school-days, and, so far as I know, to this day English has preserved its prominent position in the curriculum of German schools. When I was going to school, this change had not yet been completed. In my school, for example, apart from Latin, French was still the first foreign language, and, in fact, the only modern language being taught for no less than seven years four hours a week. English was not included in the regular curriculum. It was an optional subject, to be studied for two hours a week during the last three years at school. Those of us (I lived in a predominantly Protestant district) who went on for the Church took Hebrew instead. English was a despised and ridiculed subject. The teacher to whom was entrusted our initiation into the language of Shakespeare had no other qualification for doing so than having spent three years behind barbed wire on the Isle of Man. In the second year we were in the hands of an energetic young man who tried to persuade us that English public schoolboys were the paragons of honesty. In the final year an elderly embittered gentleman tried to read Shakespeare with us in the original. After the first lesson of the year he realized that most of us were incapable of reading, not to mention translating, even a simple sentence. The next class started with a written test-translation. The result was crushing. One boy wrote across the page "I *weiss* (know) not."

I was in a different position from my fellow students. Trying to trace the reasons for my parents' early interest in my English studies, I can discover in my memory a surprisingly large number of English associations during my childhood-days, which, after all, coincided with the last war, when in every German home a box was kept in which members of the family or visitors had to put a penny whenever they dared to use a word of English or French origin.

By far the earliest of my English associations is connected with a picture of Our Lord which used to hang in our bedroom. It was entitled "The Great Healer". Heaven only knows how an English reproduction of that famous picture had found its way into our house.

Both my father's and my mother's parents had insisted on their children's learning English. My mother had learnt English in an excellent private establishment in a remote country-town directed by a lady who had lived for many years in Scotland and who instilled into her pupils a real love and appreciation of the great novelists of the nineteenth century English literature. Their works, like the works of modern poets and writers (including Yeats) are, on the Continent, easily available in the well-known Tauchnitz edition, sold at two shillings per volume at every bookshop. Bound in red cloth, a series of almost a hundred of those Tauchnitz volumes were one of the most cherished assets in my mother's library. Living now in retirement, my mother's teacher extended her affection to her former pupils' children. I was her guest on several occasions, and she relished talking English with me, presenting me at my departure with a number of English books, including one bearing the author's dedication to her.

My father's knowledge of English was less literary. Its foundation had been laid by an uncle of his, one of the first teachers in Germany to specialise in the teaching of English. I remember some of my grand-uncle's accounts of his early travels in Britain. The English books which my father used to read were mainly works of nineteenth century philosophers and historians. After the war, however, my father became a member of an extreme Christian pacifist movement, spreading from England under the name of Fellowship of Reconciliation. This organisation supplied its members with a monthly published in English, which was amongst my earliest English reading-matters.

As a matter of fact, this periodical was also one of the sources from which my father drew his knowledge of what was going on in Ireland after the war. While he had not shared the exaggerated hopes fostered by some of his compatriots regarding the results of Roger Casement's undertaking, he took a keen interest in the postwar history of Ireland, which was, to his mind, one of the outstanding illustrations of what he regarded as the law of modern history: the cause of justice rests with those which are materially weak, while the powerful make evil use of what is entrusted to them. In his interest for the rise of Ireland my father was an exception. Most people were, at that time, too much concerned with what was going on around them to be interested in such out-of-the-way places as Ireland.

My interest in the English language was also instigated by other relatives of ours. My mother's father had travelled in the Near East, where his knowledge of English had been of great use to him. My mother's eldest brother was before the last war pastor of the German congregation at London; in later years he published numerous articles and books in English. Her second brother was sometime exchange professor in Harvard, and her third brother was a doctor in Egypt. All this naturally created in my parents' home a general interest in the English language.

In 1924 I was one of the two hundred German boy-scouts to go to the International Jamboree in Copenhagen. This was the first time after the war that a German youth-group was invited to take part in an International meeting. Our greatest success was the hearty welcome tendered to us by the English-speaking boyscouts. One English "chum" took a fancy to me, inviting me to tea in the Rovers' Camp, where, for the first time in my life, I tasted "real" tea and sandwiches. On that occasion I became bitterly aware of my ignorance of the English language. At my return I found a letter from my new English friend inviting me to start a regular correspondence with him (which, incidentally, we kept up to this day). My father rejoiced in this undertaking, which he regarded as a tiny step towards promoting mutual understanding between the nations.

One of my father's colleagues was at that time starting a correspondence scheme between German and English school-children, in which, gradually, a few thousand of boys and girls on both sides of the North Sea took a part. Hearing of my correspondence, that gentleman became so much interested in me that he offered to teach me the rudiments of English. He was one of the pioneers of the teaching, on modern lines, of the English language. He believed in the direct method. I still see him sitting in his dusty study, looking at me with his keen grey eyes over the rims of his professorial glasses and, slapping his right knee, exclaiming: "This is my right knee! Repeat!" And slapping my right knee and saying: "*Tis* is my right *k-nee*", I set out to reach that goal which now seems to me more distant than ever.

Professor Hartmann, that was my teacher's name, was also one of the first to introduce into Germany the Anglo-American anti-alcohol and anti-nicotine movement. The former was known as the Blue Cross, the latter as the Green Cross. At his hall-door he had a notice saying: "I am a member of the Green Cross (anti-tobacco) Movement. Please do not smoke!" (Try that in Belfast).

After a few weeks Mr. Hartmann started me on a text. The first and, for some time, the only texts he used were leaflets published by the supporters of American Prohibition, then still in force. Thus one of the first words I had to look up in a dictionary (the direct method was not much use on that occasion) was "cirrhosis of the liver". I shall never forget that word. We also read leaflets in which you were promised eternal salvation and a happy home if you did not smoke. "Do you smoke?" – this question was bound to come up in each lesson. And on my answering in the negative, the invariable reply followed triumphantly: "Neither do I." I have never made the mistake very common with Germans to say in that case: " I also not," and to this day, whenever I light a cigarette, I hear someone whispering in my ear: "That little white slaver, another nail to your coffin", one of Mr. Hartmann's favourite slogans.

One of the greatest promoters of English literature in Germany, apart from Tauchnitz, were the Twietmeyers, secondhand booksellers, also established in Leipzig, my native town; this latter firm is internationally known for its specialisation in English literature. From my childhood days, one of the Twietmeyer brothers was a friend of our family. Known to us by his Anglicised name as "Uncle Charles", he had been head of the branch-office of his firm in England. After recovering, in virtue of the peace settlement, some of the money he had left in England at his sudden departure in 1914, he now lived in retirement together with his sister. He loved to speak English, and his delight, when he heard that I was taking up the study of that language, was touching. Henceforth I spent one night every week at his flat to talk English. While for those two aged persons these evenings became the highlights of their social life, I have gradually realised the value of the training I received thereby. Whole phrases beautifully put and rendered in perfect pronunciation (not Prof. Hartmann's strongest side) are still sticking in my ear. Nothing is more beneficial in learning a foreign language than such exemplary phrases picked up from a fluent or native speaker.

After getting my Matric, I decided to study modern languages in Bonn University (thus taking up residence halfway between my native district and Ireland). I had, therefore, to take leave of Uncle Twietmeyer. We both realised that it was a departure for ever. He was sitting there on his shabby couch under the illustrated English calendar showing the faded page for August, 1914, and in front of him on the table was a leather bound edition of Shakespeare's works with which he presented me at this leavetaking. In his quiet, unobtrusive way he gave me some valuable advice, and then he said a kind of prayer for my future life – all this in English. My apprenticeship had come to an end, henceforth I had to try to work as a clerk, "*ein Geselle*".

Two months later, I received the news of his death. He left me in his will 300 marks (with which I made my first journey to London) and his golden pocket watch. Sometimes I take this watch from its velvet-lined box, and, winding it up, I hold it to my ear. Shutting my eyes, I see before me a gentleman bent and greyhaired, opening a hall-door and greeting me with a cheerful "Hulloh!" I am still unable to get the characteristic English intonation of that word.

(Quelle: Irish Rosary March-April 1945, S. 121-125)

My Early Irish Associations

In his *Personal Recollections* Lord Cloncurry told us of an interview which Lawlor and Wolfe Tone had with Napoleon. Bonaparte complained that "such a fine country as Ireland was still horribly infested with wolves". When his Irish interlocutors stated that this was not the case, the Emperor deigned to reply nothing but "Bah!" The more I read of Continental books on Ireland, the more this Imperial "Bah!" seems to me characteristic of an attitude towards Ireland which has not even yet died out.

What is the reason for the strange anomaly that while being represented as the Island of Saints and Scholars, Ireland is the least known part of Europe?[1] In 1806 the author of the first history of Ireland written by a Continental scholar – a professor at Kiel – stated that there were three reasons for Continental neglect of Ireland. She is regarded as a mere province of England. Her history appears to be of interest only so far as it is an appendix to British history. Irish proper names and place-names offer too many difficulties in pronunciation and spelling. This statement I have tried to verify from my own experience.

Searching in my memory for traces of what I knew of Ireland before I came here, I am struck by the absence of school-knowledge of this country. In fact, among the Continental travellers who wrote up their experiences in this country, there is hardly one who did not admit that when coming here he knew practically nothing of Irish things. Was I absent or did I sleep when Ireland was treated in our geography lessons? I do remember, from our school-maps, that "Ireland is one of the British Isles". Full stop. The names of Dublin or Belfast, of the Shannon or the Boyne, of Croagh Patrick and Lugnaquilla were certainly never mentioned in my school. As for history, England did hardly exist for us up to the period of the Reformation. In the later centuries the Irish appendices to English history were hopelessly overshadowed by events nearer to us, the Thirty Years' War, the rise of Prussia, the French Revolution and the German Revolutions of 48. When our history course prescribed "the 19th and 20th centuries", teachers took great pains to see that the term ended before they had reached the beginning of the World War; the later period was altogether too hot. I am quite certain that up to the twenty-second year of my life I never heard of the existence of Partition.

The other day a friend of mine presented me with a pre-(European) war guide-book of Leipzig, my native town; he had picked it up on the 2d. shelf at Greene's. There I read that Leipzig had an "Irish bath". I only remember the demolition of the old "bath-house" in Dorothy street, but it must be on that occasion (when we were playing hide-and-seek among the rubble) that I heard the word "Irish" for the first time. I understand that the association between these baths and Ireland is just as close as that between German measles and Germany. In another connection the word "Irish" attained really nation-wide popularity in Hitler Germany. German re-armament since 1933 was largely financed by an ingenious scheme of levying "voluntary" taxes under

---

1   A few weeks ago, a band of French children came for a holiday to Ireland. Arriving at Dun Laoghaire the children were met by a reporter who asked them if thex had ever read anythimg about Ireland. Françoise, the 16 years old leader of the group said: "O yes. The father in 'Gone with the Wind' was Irish."

the title of "Winter-help for the Needy". One of the features in that scheme was the institution of a one-pot Sunday-dinner once a month in every German household, the savings thus being made were to go to the "Winter-help". Irish stew was the ideal solution for the problem of one-pot-dinners. To this day Germans will associate the smell of "Irish stew" (this name always kept its English form) with the jingling of collection-boxes, and, perhaps, the beating of big drums.

My earliest associations of modern Irish history are connected with the unforgettable turnip-winter of 1916, when in the windows of grocers' shops we saw nothing but charts proving irrefutably the deteriorating food-position in the Entente countries, and large pictures of the Emperor Francis Joseph and Tsar Ferdinand of Bulgaria, "our gallant Allies", and, occasionally, of Sir Roger Casement.

At that time my elder brother took a keen interest in politics. The walls of our study were plastered with printed lists of the principal events of the war, half-yearly published by the newspaper concerns. Even before I went to school I knew whole columns by heart, including a reference to the Easter Rising. There was also a map of Europe, in which Ireland was given a green colour, distinctive from Britain's red colour. It was from this map that my brother taught me that Dublin is the capital of Ireland.

Then came the collapse of Germany, revolution, general strikes, civil war, inflation. My father whose whole life was devoted to the promotion of charity and justice among classes and nations was one of the few who amidst those ordeals realised that other parts of the world had their worries too. He took to his heart particularly the case of small suppressed nations, and it was from him that I heard the name of Sinn Féin (which he took great pains to pronounce correctly), and its translation "Wir selbst". It was only quite recently that I learnt that it had been a man of German descent, Dr. Henebry, who had suggested this name to Arthur Griffith for his new movement.

Though not having travelled much in his life, my father was very fond of reading travel books. There were always illustrated travel books in our house, especially the various volumes of Sven Hedin's excellent series *From Pole to Pole*. When I first began to think of going to Ireland, I realised to my surprise that from those books I had gathered subconsciously a definite picture of Ireland, green grass, frequent rain, the smell of the sea, a strange mixture of cheerfulness and melancholy. At any rate, something altogether different from an English drawing-room.

Like many German children, I would have scarcely survived the period of 1919 to 1924, had we not been helped by the Society of Friends. They supplied us with a hot meal in school and established holiday-homes for underfed children all over the country. In summer 1921 I spent some weeks in one of those homes. We were entrusted to a kind elderly school-master, who had a splendid means of rocking us thirty youngsters asleep in the night. Sitting at the bed-side of one of us, he would tell us of happy pre-war times when he had travelled through all parts of Europe. The remarkable thing, even more remarkable at that time, about those travels was that he had made them on a bicycle. I remember the storm of laughter I produced from my sisters and brothers when at my return I told them that Herr Raschke had cycled as far as Ireland. He was the first traveller to this country I ever met. I remember only that he spoke with great warmth of the Irish.

It was many years later that I again met a person who had been in Ireland. Returning from my first visit to London, in the train to Dover, a small sturdy country-man addressed me: "Misther, how do you fill up them landing-cards?" He was one of the Siemens-Schuckert boys who built the Shannon scheme. He showed me a photograph of the sweetheart he had left behind, the first picture of an Irish colleen I ever beheld.

In school, in what was known as religious instruction, we were told of the "Iro-Schottische Mission" who, had wicked St. Boniface not intervened, would have made Germany "Rome-free" a thousand years before Martin Luther. I discovered the other day, that the very teacher who dished up to us that old fairy-tale, was the author of the article on the old Irish church in *Religion past and present,* the German Protestant counterpart of our *Catholic Encyclopedia.* This article may be characterised by the following statement: "Among the chief reasons for the failure of Protestantism in Ireland is Emigration, because most of those who emigrated were just those who had been won over partly or even completely to Protestantism." As two-thirds of Germany are Protestant, it is not astonishing that the religious bias plays an important part in the preservation of ignorance on Ireland.

I gained a more correct picture of the significance of Irish monastic activities in Germany through frequent visits to those sacred places in Western and Southern Germany which were the centres of the work of Ss. Kilian, Virgil, Gall and Marianus. There I saw that just because of the foundation laid by those Irish Apostles the people were still *Roman* Catholics.

My first literary contacts with Ireland were concerned less with the Golden Age than with later periods. In many of the editions of *Gulliver's Travels* for German children, it is stated that the author was "Dechant an der St. Patricks Kathedrale in Dublin". On my 14th birthday a friend gave me an edition of Oscar Wilde's lovely fairy tales, which two years later I studied in the original, as *The Happy Prince* and *The Rose and the Nightingale* were prescribed texts in school. Exceedingly popular though these stories were, it was little known that the author was a native of Ireland. His surname O'Flaherty struck me as Irish allright, but I was never told more of the Wildes in Ireland. One of the first school-performances I saw was Shaw's *St. Joan;* a few years later I saw the great Elizabeth Bergner in the title part. *The Doctor's Dilemma* was played for fifty nights in succession in our local theatre. Shaw was at that time, next to Shakespeare, the author most frequently produced on the German Stage.

Of real Irish literature I never heard until I started my university studies. The earliest piece of Irish I came across was in my International driver's licence were the words "M.......... authorised to drive a car, is deprived of this right in (country)" are repeated in 24 languages. I could work my way through that text in a dozen or so of those languages, but the Irish text was as incomprehensible as the Polish or Turkish. Still stranger than the spelling were the sounds of Irish, as we heard them occasionally when we succeeded in getting Radio Eireann on the air. Even in the Nuacht we were quite unable to make out what they were about. It was something very very far away from us.

I received the most extensive account of Ireland during the short period of instruction before my reception into the Church. My prospective "Rektor" had been on a cruise around "the British Isles". He had visited Dublin and he showed me a piece of tweed which the late Mrs. Fylan, Matt Talbot's sister, had given him, an ex indumentis of her saintly brother. Whenever I pass through Granby Lane, Dublin, I remember "my first curate". He was deeply impressed with religious life in Dublin. "When you go there", he said, "don't miss 11 o'clock Mass on a week-day in the Pro-Cathedral. There you can learn what devotion is."

In one of his sermons he referred to his Irish memories. It was on the feast of the Exaltation of the Holy Cross. In German churches from this feast up to the feast of the Finding of the Holy Cross, the Blessing against Storms is administered (a custom from which originated the universal custom of reading at the end of Mass the Gospel of St. John, originally a blessing against storms). Speaking, in connection with the harvest, on our dependence on God, he said that "the best Catholic nation in the world" should teach us how to look upon the vicissitudes of weather. "I mean little Ireland", he exclaimed, pointing to the West, "there the people never complain of the weather (do they?), but when a person says: 'This is a wet day', they answer: 'It is, thanks be to God.'"

It was a nice, soft day when I arrived in Ireland. When the coastline appeared dimly in the morning haze, a memory flushed through my mind, one of those strange little things which have been lying hidden in some corner of your subconscience for twenty years or more and suddenly miraculously emerge. *Gudrun,* one of the national epics of medieval Germany begins with the words: "Once upon a time there was a rich king in Ireland." In the juvenile edition of that epic which had been in the book-case of our nursery, there had been an illustration of the shore of Ireland, on which, according to the poet, King Sigebant's castle towered up. Whether at that moment I mistook the steeple of the parish church of Dun Laoghaire for the turrets of Sigebant's Castle, I do not know. The mountains, the sea, the sky and the sea-gulls, all that had been in my book.

(Quelle: Irish Rosary, Christmas 1945, S. 366-370)

Fáilte *or:* I Boarded the Boat for Ireland

There are two main gateways to Ireland.

The vast majority of visitors to this country arrive by boat. After a few hours train-journey through England, mostly in the company of industrial workers, nurses and "domestics" looking forward to a well-earned holiday at home, they meet on the boat Irish priests and nuns, possibly shepherding a flock of children to (or from) their boarding-schools, business-men returning from a visit to their British "principals", journalists, doctors and engineers. The visitor, especially when by his speech dis-covered as being from the Continent, will soon get the first glimpse of some characteristics which he will readily set down as "typically Irish" contrasting them with what during his brief encounter with the sternness of metropolitan life he had set down equally readily as "typically English".

A Mayo lad will show him how to get a berth even though he had been officially informed that no berths were available. An alert intellectual will literally draw him into a conversation, through which he will learn something of the unpredictable paradoxes of young Ireland's opinions on any conceivable subject. The sweet smile of what the visitor proudly terms a colleen will cheer him in the bleak morning on deck.

If our friend is wise or poor, or as it happens both, he will travel third-class right through, and for some slight lack of the more sophisticated comforts be compensated by a richer atmosphere of Irish accents, more conspicuous in mirth and song than in mere speech. "Walking about on the mail-boat when closing in at Dublin bay". Has no one ever written on this subject? While the Hill of Howth and the Dublin mountains grow, there also grows a family atmosphere embracing "native" and visitor alike. We have plenty of time to ponder over the various feelings the coast-line evokes in the hearts of our fellow-travellers, but there are few sea-passages in the world where at landing the feeling of peaceful gratitude is more prominent. While most of us will give thanks for being home again, the visitor either looks forward to quiet or at least enjoyable holiday or to the thrill of a tour of this mysterious Western outpost of Europe.

Every year growing numbers of visitors however arrive by a less traditional though allegedly more comfortable way. They have boarded a plane in the dehydrated atmosphere of an air-port in Britain or even worse on the Continent, even worse, because thus they miss the slow transition to this country provided by a rail-journey through England. Irish tourists to the Continent rarely specify the country to which they go, and in fact in most cases, cover in a fortnight several countries. While perhaps sometimes irritated at the somewhat indiscreet lumping together of Western Europe as "the Continent", the visitor to Ireland will soon recognise how right the English and the Irish are in referring to the Continent as "Europe" (excluding "these countries" – a convenient term covering inoffensively a multitude of sins). The difference between Germany and France would appear to be smaller than that between Belgium and England, not to speak of the difference between England and Ireland. But how will the air-traveller see that, having missed even the exciting transition from Victoria to Euston?

To him the Aer Lingus hostess is distinguished from her K.L.M. or Swissair colleague only by her green uniform and her shamrock badge. His journey has been a perfect one if he had not to draw comfort from the outstanding qualities of these girls, their gentleness and – their bravery. He is possibly addressed by them in his own language and is served with meals faultlessly stereotype to suit International tastes. He has no contact with his fellow-passengers, or if in one of the twin-seats his neighbour is communicative and talks of Ireland, he is surely not Irish. It always strikes me how unnaturally aloof air-travellers behave at the very point when the common risk should establish some human contact between them. Also the air-traveller has little chance of viewing the physical features of Ireland, as they present themselves at his arrival, except perhaps that he notices that even in periods of drought or in winter Collinstown airport is verdant.

The main difference between our two lots of visitors however appears at their arrival. (I do not count of course the July crowds arriving at Amiens Street; in spite of their strange rapacious solidness in pursuit of happiness we like to think of them as home-comers rather than visitors). The peace of Ireland invades you right from the moment when you awake after sound sleep in your berth, because the rocking of the boat and the throbbing of the engine has ceased. There is the screeching of gulls, the creaking of ropes being tied to the capstans, and the English accents of stewards and waiters become drowned by the morningfresh shouts of porters and newsboys as unmistakably Irish as is the fresh wind referred to in the opening lines of Wagner's "Tristan".

I do not know how our customs authorities manage to get always the right men to the right spots. At Collinstown there is obliging politeness with just a sprinkling of supercilious distrust. At Dun Laoghaire everything is plain human, any unavoidable roughness tempered by a joke, a down-to-earth search for "presents", not entirely deprived of a soothing wink of the eye when the shaving of truth becomes too obvious.

While the name of Collinstown offers no linguistic difficulties to the foreigner, that of Dun Laoghaire-Kingstown at once implies a first lesson in Irish history from Laoghaire to George IV, and the Irish language lesson is continued when, with the peculiar curiosity of the foreigner, our visitor tries to decipher the destinations inscribed in old-fashioned Gaelic letters on the old G.S.R. carriages.

In spite of all its striking architectural beauty, Collinstown cannot boast of special national characteristics. Place a man into the entrance-hall and let him guess where he is. It may be anywhere in the white-race world. But put him on the platform at Dun Laoghaire quay when the mail-boat has arrived, and bless him, if blind, deaf and unfeeling as he may be, this does not knock down Ireland on him. The usual means of conveyance to Dublin is the train. It seems to be a definite C.I.E. policy to break even the last stay of conceit in the visitors by crowding them in dilapidated carriages which have become available presumably by the closing of some branch line in the wild West. Still, here again, the family spirit will wipe out all annoyance. Has ever a visitor been refused admission to a compartment on the grounds that it was already over-crowded? Has he not been squeezed in by hook or by crook, even at the – sometimes not unwelcome – risk that someone had to sit on someone else's knees? The first package of cheap cigarettes is handed around or the first box of point-free chocolates is displayed, and there is no difference between those who wear an Anthony Eden and those who have not even a cap, between the stylish hat and Holy Year scarf.

I remember the dreary April day when I first made that journey. When at last we rambled into Westland Row, I asked: "Is this Dublin?" Westland Row and Collins-town, what a world between the two main gateways to Ireland! Though often in-furiated by the lack of amenities at both the departure and arrival end at Westland Row, I hope and pray that whatever improvements An Tóstal may suggest the unique character of this station should be preserved. If our visitor has not yet got an inkling of the spirit in which the Irish workers, male and female, in England and their families at home are united, he will get it now. Right into Pearse Street we find the groups of grandparents, mothers, wives, children, sweethearts, sisters and friends waiting for, or crowding around, a young man, somewhat dishevelled, but beaming with happiness, between a decrepit fibre-case with a crudely inscribed cardboard label and a roughly packed parcel holding the overflow and some presents for young and old. Already some of the hardness of Coventry and Wolverhampton has gone out of his looks and he is again – the good lad from Tipperary, Leitrim or Drumcondra, hiding some embarrassment at this transformation behind a barricade of rollicking laughter.

Westland Row would not be what it is without the vicinity of St. Andrews', the largest city church. If the statues and pictures in that church could speak, they could tell a moving story of prayers connected with the departures and arrivals at Westland Row. The last time I arrived it was a holiday. At the large holy-water font outside St. Andrews' an Englishman tipped me on the shoulder: "Oh, is this a church? I thought it was some office to which all passengers had to go. I just followed the crowds."

From Collinstown the air-traveller is conveyed to O'Connell Street by a bus, passing new housing estates, middle class residential areas and slums. There is nothing distinctive in all this; the Georgian background of the slums will scarcely be appreciated at this stage. Clearing of the luggage, a taxi to a hotel, and there you are in Dublin. Are you really?

Our mail-boat traveller wanted a taxi too? You can join two or three other parties hiring a pre-historic cab to take them to the long distance buses along Aston's Quay. Perhaps you better wait till one of the sleek modern taxis returns. Meanwhile you may watch the arrival of a wedding party at St. Andrews'. You want to take a chance and walk to your destination? I warn you. There is hardly a Dublin street more depressing than the stretch from Westland Row to D'Olier Street at seven o'clock on a nice soft morning. You are greeted by a wall decorated with out-of-date posters partly torn down. The fish-and-chip shops are still shuttered up. Only some dusty lemonade bottles displayed between Gold Flake dummies under faded paper decorations tell of Dublin night-life. Cats amuse themselves with what the dogs have left when overthrowing the dust-bins. Shivering house-wives creep along from hall-door to hall-door to have their milk-jugs filled at the dairy-shop.

To most of those arriving from the mail-boat, these things appear transfigured, as reassuring signs of being back to *terra firma* or simply of Dublin's still following its familiar pattern of life. Crowded buses pass us in the direction of Ringsend, and shoals of cyclists, holding hands or three abreast, unconcerned about the language of motorists. The intermingling between boat-train passengers and early workers is a feature in the morning life of that part of Dublin. Let the foreigner try to obtain directions, and no matter how hurried his prospective informant may be, a generous if not always pertinent reply will be received, frequently amplified by useful lore on the sights and history of the city.

The Liverpool boat no doubt is the most enjoyable means of arriving at Dublin. On that journey the foreigner has the best chance and more time to mingle with what he then may still describe as "the Irish element". The journey up the Liffey (to a place only a little below that where for hundreds of years travellers to Ireland used to disembark) affords some of the glorious views of the sky-line, its ancient and modern features. On walking down the gangway, the B. & I. traveller is almost in the heart of Dublin, and through a bustle of literally goods and chattels he winds his way to the Customs House and the Bridge.

A few years ago I unearthed what I believe is the only travel book on Ireland written by a Dane. The unusual interest of this book seemed to me to be largely due to the fact that the writer had started his tour at Derry. Similarly the few foreigners and first visitors to Ireland arriving nowadays at Rosslare or Cork not to speak of ports in the North are saved from the fatal error of considering Ireland as an appendix to Dublin. At the other end of the scale, we have the globe-trotters who, after an hour's landing at Shannon for refuelling man and machine, "files" a dictaphoned article on the mysteries of the Emerald Isle to an American or Continental newspaper.

Let us return to our ordinary foreign visitors, now safely installed in their temporary abodes between Terenure and Glasnevin, suited to their tastes and their purses. Let us bid them *fáilte*, asking them what they have learnt of Ireland since their departure from home. Our air-travellers probably set out with a greater store of book-learning. Bored with the monotony of the cloud scenery through which they had been journeying they had perhaps studied a guide-book. Our train-and-boat travellers had no time to do so, but they have taken in a good share of Irish life. Could we get them to pool their knowledge and, during their stay in Ireland, build it up in conjunction and mutual understanding? They would no doubt return to their countries with a picture more real and comprehensive than they had ever hoped for. May a good spirit guide them on every step in this land.

(Quelle: Irish Rosary March/April 1953, S. 71-76)

The Lough Derg Pilgrimage
Dr. Hennig describes his visit and makes a suggestion

A few weeks after my arrival in Ireland, I received, in the house of some "native" friend, my first account of St. Patrick's Purgatory, to my standards of Continental Catholicism a strange and horrible story. Bare feet on cutting stones, icy winds and slashing rain, or scorching sun without a tree to shelter you, 40 hours of sleeplessness, ravenous hunger, and the Prior a pitiless task-master. None of the realtors had actually been there. Later in the evening, a girl turned up. The night before she had returned from Lough Derg. "And how did you find it?" I asked her, gasping with curiosity at the sight of my first real pilgrim. "Oh, it was great fun", she said with an unforgettable twinkle in her eyes.

I gradually begin to realise how thoroughly Catholic was this summary of what Lough Derg means. "When thou fastest, anoint thy head, and wash thy face." For the next ten weeks, every night at 6.30 p.m. we will be able to see the same grand spectacle at Amiens Street or Westland Row. The Bundoran express arrives. Out pour the pilgrims. In sack and ashes, worn out with fatigue? No, spick and span. Cheerfully breaking up this grand family party. Till next year! I should like to see the man who has regretted that he went. "It was great fun", some of us might find just a bit too smart, too little respectful. Well, it is only another way of putting it when you say: it's heaven on earth.

It starts, of course, at home, when you refuse your breakfast. You have to leave, when bacon and egg are just nice and crisp on the pan. In the train, you examine your fellow-travellers. Who of them is Pettigo-bound, who will travel on to Bundoran? This young lady over there? Her handbag does not look like vigil and fasting. Wait, till we come to Pettigo. Getting out we bestow a compassionate glance at the young man in the corner. On the platform we meet pilgrims returning to Dublin, waiting for their train. "Is this your first time?" You will hear this question another hundred times. "It is", you dare to admit. "Oh, then you better come home with us, you don't know what's in store for you." But you have spotted the twinkle in his eyes: "And how many times have you been there?" – "Oh, I go every year, this is my eighth."

You remember the evenings on the jetty, when those who are one day older than you on the island are preparing for their well deserved rest while you wait for the beginning of your ordeal? The soft barren hills gradually sink into shadow. A boat takes gently off from the island, the figure of a fisherman stands out black against the blue water. At this hour there is not a moment that you do not hear laughter somewhere. All the harshness of business and worry seems to have been left behind. We have resigned the world, withdrawn from the world, still we are of the world, and this is one of the few spots in the world whose beauty is perfect, unstained, lasting. During those first eight hours you have been walking twenty, thirty times around the island, still you have not yet seen your fill. It is as if you held the hand of an angel, and thus for the first time you learnt what is the serene beauty of God in His creation.

Every hour in Lough Derg has its own sweetness and depth. The grand experience of the first circuits. Your first meal. A fireside chat in the kitchen. A close-net of criss-cross relations is being woven: "What, you here? I never ..." Stations, evening-prayers, the great tuning in. The night deepens and with it our thoughts and prayers. Holy Hour, the first interval. The world has gone asleep but we are awake under the starlit sky. Cold mists are rising from the lake, creeping along over the concrete floor, even over the soft warm wooden floor of the basilica. The great wrestling begins. Do not sit down, walk around, or demon sleep will grip you.

Even before the sun has broken through the clouds we are at Holy Mass. The Prior's Hour, Confession, and then the grey, dull, fitful, unending struggle, for ten hours. You wonder how on earth you could have gone again. But wait, victory is near. In the afternoon when you see the newcomers at work, you feel again your strength, and when you look back, during the Stations, you begin to realise that it has been a glorious battle.

The greatest artist, the most experienced psychologist, the wisest philosopher could not have planned a more perfect retreat than is the pilgrimage of St. Patrick's Purgatory, the work of many centuries of hundreds of thousands of pilgrims. It is just so much as any healthy adult can bear. You are on an island, but the land is not out of sight. There are all the essentials of life, fresh air, clear water, a countryside unspoilt by civilisation, just as much food and sleep as is necessary for the sustenance of man, and in each and everything there is God, almost visible, almost palpable. Kneeling at St. Patrick's Cross, you feel that this is sacred ground.

Whoever has been in Lough Derg, naturally feels he would like to convey to others the experience of this sublime happiness. Lough Derg is not an organised pilgrimage. There are no Committees, Leagues and Hon. Secretaries connected with it. You just buy your rail-ticket and go. There are, however, a few small points which people do find difficult. Do not think that you are a coward or a bad Catholic if you feel you would rather not go. Have a look at the people returning from Lough Derg. Many of them thoroughly town-bred, overworked business-girls, civil servants, house-wives etc., none of them endowed with an exceptionally strong physique or a miraculous facility of going without food or sleep. Still there *are* people whose health does not permit them to go. Ask any Lough Derg pilgrim whether he regards himself as a particularly good Catholic, and you will receive a good Catholic answer. If you went, and did not like it, just leave it for a year or two.

If you possibly can, do avoid the overcrowded week-ends in Lough Derg. Unfortunately most of our a-fortnight-a-year-holidays-workers cannot. In fact, many of them are deterred by the necessity of sacrificing three out of those precious fifteen days. May I make a suggestion? Would Catholic employers be prepared to grant an additional day or Friday to Saturday morning, to employees who would thus be enabled to make the National pilgrimage?

If for one reason or other you seriously feel you cannot go, what about endowing one who would like to go but simply has not got the funds to do so. Of course, you cannot send another one to do your bit of penance, but you can help one of your fellow-creatures to see real happiness, for himself *and* for you. For the average Dubliner, for instance, the pilgrimage to Lough Derg costs roughly two pounds. This, it must be recognised, is too much for many of those who perhaps would like best to go. Here again I have a suggestion. This time I will not trespass upon the employers' generosity. I appeal to pilgrims who used to travel first-class to remember that by travelling third class (in nice comfortable carriages, I can assure them), they could pay the rail-fare for a less fortunate fellow-pilgrim. Could I induce you to make a vow not to go this year without bringing someone else with you, someone whom you have helped to do this glorious pilgrimage? Would this not be a very practical way of showing how we are looking forward to that font of graces on the rocky island in Lough Derg?

(Quelle: The Leader, 21.06.1947, S. 14f)

On the German Frontier – City of the Siegfried Line
Irish Footsteps in Aachen

I remember one fine Sunday afternoon in the summer of 1936 when the Olympic Games were being held in Berlin, we stood in front of our house in Aachen and watched the increasing procession of foreign cars filing down from the nearby frontier-barrier.

There was a stir from the crowd each time there appeared between the numerous Dutch, Belgian, French and British cars one of the international signs less frequently seen on the Continent – U.S.A., South Africa, Siam and even Ireland. I say "even Ireland" because this was for many of us the first occasion we realised that Ireland was something more than just "one of the British Isles".

Was it the ivy-clad ruins or the artistic treasures, or was it the gaiety of the vine-villages which again and again attracted Irish visitors to the Rhine? Or was it some-times the desire to trace there the footsteps left by Irishmen over a period of 1,500 years?

Before the war Irish travellers to the Continent could leave Dublin at 6 p.m., and on the next day at 4 p.m. board at Ostende one of the trans-European expresses which were bound for Stockholm, the Baltic countries, the Russian frontier or Istanbul. When, about midnight, passing through the ordeal of passport, customs and currency control at Aachen, few travellers felt inclined to alight at this German-Belgian frontier town. Yet a stroll through there would have been amply rewarded.

In Maw of War

To-day the war boils around this ancient city that was my home for several years.

Come with me on a spiritual tour through peace-time Aachen. The French name of the city – Aix-la-Chapelle – recalls the historical fact that it was there Charlemagne built his Imperial Chapel, near the spas which to this day give forth their healthy, warm water.

Many venerable historical memories are attached to the narrow streets and the lovely squares around the Cathedral, the main relic of the palace where the great Charles resided with his court. The famous Irish scholars belonging to that court laid the foundations on which the culture of medieval Europe was to rest.

Some of the Continental scholars and artists belonging to Charles's court were trained in Ireland, and Alcuin, the greatest of them, gratefully remembered Irish influence when composing verses in honour of the patrons of Ireland.

The Cathedral Chapter of Aachen to this day preserves the tradition of their city's association with Ireland. The most extensive history of the Irish church was written by Dr. Bellesheim, Canon of the Cathedral of Aachen, who concluded his voluminous work by the same famous words which are now found on the stamps issued recently in commemoration of Brother Michael O'Clery: Do chum glóire Dé agus onóra na hEireann.

Riflemen's Tribute

The first Irishman I ever met was one of the Jesuit scholastics who, studying in Valkenburg, near Aachen, sometimes came for a visit to Aachen.

Every year, in August, the guild of riflemen, formerly the civic guard of Aachen, used to hold a procession round the Cathedral, invoking St. Foillan in protection against tribulation and war. Close by the Cathedral stands the ancient parish church bearing the name of this Saint, who was an Irishman.

The wall-paintings behind the high altar depict St. Foillan embarking in a skiff, crossing the sea and preaching the Gospel to the pagans. Like others of his country-men labouring in Western Europe he suffered martyrdom from the hands of brigands. Strangely enough, this is the reason why the Aachen riflemen chose him as their patron.

After showing you through the cathedral and St. Foillan's I would take you to the *Maus*, Aachen's famous mediaeval public house.

Then we would set out to see *Burtscheid*, a suburb, where I could show you the church of St. John's Abbey, which, during the Middle Ages, was for a long time entrusted to Irish monks. *Burtscheid* used to be the centre of the fashionable life around the spas in which 18th century Aachen vied with Bath.

In 1820 the statemen of Europe gathered at Aachen to shape there what they thought would be a better future for Europe. In the retinue of English statesmen and princes, Irish nobility and gentry took a part in the splendid life around the *Elisenbrunnen*, the central spa, where those once famous names are engraved on the walls.

Right down to the beginning of the present war Irish visitors were frequently seen among the *Kurgäste* thronging Aachen's *Kurhotels*.

All this splendour has now gone. I remember the day when they started to dig up our garden to build the first pill-boxes of the Siegfried Line. The lovely hedges of our fields were replaced by barbed wire fences, much to the disgust of our cattle. Dark shadows fell on the traditional gaiety of the Rhenish people.

[(Quelle: nicht bekannt, o.J.) article includes photograph of Bodenhof]

Irish Links With Cologne

Eleven hundred years ago the Emperor Charlemagne wrote a letter to Offa, King of the Mercians, requesting him to forward on his way the bearer of that letter, an Irish priest from Cologne, who had been accused of eating meat in Lent and was being sent home to his own bishop for judgment. Heavy punishment it was that an Irish cleric at that time had to expect for such an offence. There is a note of pity on the unfortunate man, in the letter which the great Charles wrote for this first Irish priest of whom we know in the history of Cologne.

From the time of Charlemagne (whose close associations with Ireland have been restated by Dr. Douglas Hyde in his edition of the Irish translation of a medieval account of the Emperor's exploits), we can trace an almost continuous tradition of Irishmen at Cologne for more than a thousand years.

St. Brigid's Feast

The other day I was looking through the latest edition of the Breviary for the archdiocese of Cologne and I discovered that this is one of the few dioceses on the Continent where St. Brigid's feast is still celebrated. The relic of a finger of St. Brigid of Kildare, the Cologne Breviary says, is preserved in St. Martin's, Cologne, and attracts the devotion of the faithful. The steeple of St. Martin's, now the parish-church of the harbour slums of Cologne, used to stand out in the fine skyline of the city beside the splendid silhouette of the grand Cathedral. No wonder that St. Martin's was, and still is, the centre of Cologne's associations with Ireland, for this church and monastery attached to it were entrusted to Irish monks for more than a century.

In the 10th century the archbishops of Cologne were so highly satisfied with the work done by the Irish community of St. Martin's that it was decided to entrust them with still another monastery. Archbishop Bruno, St. Bruno, one of the city's patrons, and brother of the Emperor Otto I (the founder of the Holy Roman Empire of the German Nation), founded specially for the Irish monks the monastery of St. Pantaleon's in the southern parts of the old city. From his early youth, Bruno had been attached to the Irish community at Cologne. Of his Irish teachers, one named Israel seems to have been particularly eminent. This Israel played a leading part on the Council of Verdun, and his name occurs in a book of obits in Echternach in Luxemburg, a place now frequently mentioned in war-news.

Union of Church and State

Bruno did all honour to the education he received from the Irish monks. He reformed the monasteries of the whole country, raised the standard of education of clergy and people and founded many schools and churches. "In his personality", a modern writer says, "he represented the perfect union of Church and State which was the cornerstone of the policy of the mediaeval Reich". Though he died at Reims, he was buried at St. Pantaleon and Ruontger, a member of the Irish community, of that monastery, wrote his life.

It is interesting to note that the earliest mention made in Irish literature of the name of the city of Cologne occurs in an entry made in the 12th century Calendar of saints by Marianus Gorman, abbot of the monastery of the Hill of the Apostles in Co. Louth, for the commemoration on April 11 of Helias *abb mainstre naomh Martain i gUoloin*, abbot of St. Martin's monastery of Cologne.

The university of Cologne was during the Middle Ages one of the great centres of learning on the Continent. St. Thomas Aquinas finished there his studies under St. Albert the Great. Duns Scotus, the eminent philosopher, according to many authorities an Irishman by birth was buried in the Franciscan church of Cologne (now not far from the central station). Many of the Irish exiles during the 16th and 17th centuries studied at Cologne or made Cologne the headquarters of their extensive research work on Irish Saints and missionaries of the early Middle Ages. In one of the churches of the city they traced the tomb of the two Ewalds, the Irish-trained Apostles of what is now the Ruhr-district. They also noticed the large number of churches in the arch-dioceses bearing the name of St. Brigid.

Those who are interested in early Irish Catholic book-production will have noticed that famous books such as David Rothe's *Analecta Sacra* and De Burgo's *Hibernia Dominicana* give Cologne as the printer's place, although they were actually printed in a secret place in this country. This goes to show that the name of Cologne sounded familiar to Irish ears.

In Modern Times

In modern times an ever-increasing number of tourists from these countries used to visit Cologne every year. Most of them will have made the experience that the people there were just as little aware as they had been themselves of Cologne's numerous links with Ireland. In summer time one could hear in the main street of Cologne just as much English as German. In the Cathedral, the principal sight of the city, all notices were in German, Dutch, French and English. A visitor from this country had little difficulty in making his way through the town, then the fourth largest of the Reich.

In spite of Cologne's many associations with Ireland, Irish visitors found it was a hopeless undertaking to make hotel receptionists or guides understand that an Irishman was not just "English".

(Quelle: Irish Catholic, 08.03.1945)

Sir Francis Cruise Street

The little town of Kempen, on the Dutch-German frontier, captured last week by the Allied armies, is the only place in all Germany to have a street named after a Dublin man. One of the streets in Kempen is called Sir Francis Cruise Street.

Sir Francis Cruise was born in 1834. He was educated at Clongowes and Trinity. Sixty years ago he was President of the Royal College of Physicians, and in that time wrote many books upon medical subjects.

Later, however, he began to devote his whole time to the subject of proving that Thomas à Kempis was the author of the "Imitation of Christ". To this end he spent many years in visiting various libraries on the Continent. In the course of his travels he came to Kempen. Here his researches proved to the townspeople of Kempen that they had every right to consider Kempen to be the birthplace of Thomas à Kempis. In gratitude, they named a street after Sir Francis.

Curiously enough, when all street names throughout Germany having the least French or English sound about them were changed during the last war, Sir Francis Cruise Street was allowed to remain untouched.

(Quelle: Irish Times 06.03.1945)

Capital of the British Occupation Zone
Hamburg and its Catholic story

During the last few months I had often reason to remember my last visit to Hamburg, shortly after my reception into the Church. I was staying with Protestant friends of mine, who were not only shocked at my announcement on a Saturday evening that I would go to Mass the following morning, but who also protested that there was such a thing as a Catholic church in their city. It took me some time to find the name of a Catholic priest in the telephone directory. Soon, however, I heard a cheerful Bavarian voice "on the other end" saying: "Make sure that you come for the 8 o'clock Mass. You will like to meet some of the people."

Next morning, with the assistance of dairymen and postmen (as there used to be on a Sunday morning), I found my way to St. Ansgar's, the only medieval church of Hamburg still in Catholic hands. Indeed, there was an interesting gathering. Before and after Mass in the square in front of the main gate the various nationalities of whom Hamburg's Catholic community used to consist assembled. Czechs, Poles, Dutch, Austrians, Bavarians, Silesians and Rhinelanders, linguistically, racially, culturally and socially separated but closely united in their faith. Before the Mass, Confessions were heard in four languages.

I do not know what Catholic life is like in present-day Hamburg when it is the capital of the British occupation-zone. We have heard something of Catholic life in the great metropolis of Western and Southern Germany, but I have been wondering how the small Catholic community of Hamburg fared, the second largest town of Germany.

A Long Tradition

Though before the war less than five per cent of the population were Catholics, Hamburg can boast of a long and interesting Catholic tradition. Founded by Charlemagne as a bulwark against the pagan Saxons and Danes, eleven hundred years ago, "Hammaburg", the city of the forests, became a missionary archbishopric under St. Ansgar, the national saint of Denmark, and obtained ecclesiastical jurisdiction over all the Northern missions as far as Iceland and Northern Russia. In later years, when the Danes continuously raided the mouth of the river Elbe, this see was transferred to Bremen.

In the thirteenth century Hamburg became the centre of Gothic brick architecture, one of the finest achievements of medieval Christian civilisation in Northern Europe. All along the North and Baltic Sea, cathedrals were built in that style. The cathedral of Hamburg remained in the possession of the Catholic archbishop of Bremen, even after the city of Hamburg had officially declared its allegiance to the Reformation in 1529. In later years, this cathedral came into the possession of the kings of Hanover, but in 1802 George III gave it back to the citizens of the Free Imperial City. Unfortunately this venerable building had fallen into decay and had to be demolished.

The Jesuits

Among the Catholics who in the 17th century settled in Hamburg to develop the city's trade, a mission was started by the Jesuits. For many years the chapel of the French envoy and of the representative of Queen Christina of Sweden were the only places where Catholic worship was permitted. In the eighteenth century the Emperor caused a larger chapel to be built for his ambassador. This church, dedicated to St. Ansgar, has henceforth been the centre of Catholic Hamburg.

In 1784 the Catholic religion attained public recognition. A few years later the Prefecture Apostolic of the mouth of the River Elbe was raised to the rank of a parish. Before the war, Hamburg was part of the Vicariate Apostolic of the Northern German Missions under the Bishop of Osnabrück. Pope Gregory XVI had intended to make Hamburg the see of the Vicariate, but the Hamburg Senate protested.

Before the abolition of Catholic schools in 1936, Hamburg had seven Catholic primary schools subsidised by the State and directed by nuns. There was also a college for boys and a secondary school for girls directed by the Ursulines. The Catholic parish of Greater Hamburg was administered by a board of representatives of the clergy and the laity.

Catholic Works

Among the numerous social charitable institutions of Hamburg, the Catholic Orphanage at Bergedorf, the hospital of St. Joseph and St. Mary's Hospital were well known. The sodalities of Catholic artisans, Fr. Kolping's famous *Gesellenvereine* were of special importance for the large section of foreign Catholic workmen employed in Hamburg shipyards and chemical industries. The *Bonifatiusverein*, Germany's great diaspora organisation, and the societies of St. Elizabeth and of St. Vincent of Paul devoted themselves to those in spiritual and material distress. It is interesting to note that it was in Hamburg that the first attempt was made to start the Legion of Mary in Germany.

A special line of Catholic work in Hamburg was the Apostleship of the Sea. The A. M. Club in Hopfengasse near the ports was a centre of widespread activities among Catholic sailors of all races and nations.

Hamburg was also the headquarters of the *Raphaelsverein*, Germany's central organisation for Catholic emigrants. In normal years, up to 100,000 emigrants used to pass through Hamburg. During the last few months before the outbreak of war, this organisation saved the lives of hundreds of Catholics of non-Aryan descent by assisting them in emigrating.

(Quelle: Catholic Herald, 10.08.1945)

Catholic Berlin

Corpus Christi fifteen years ago was, I think, the first occasion on which a Catholic procession was held in public in the capital of modern Germany. Taking place on the square formed by the Catholic Cathedral, the State Opera House and the Old and New University, this procession was given wide publicity in the press, as some of the political leaders of the country took this opportunity to bear testimony to their Catholic faith.

Apart from such official demonstration, the Catholic community scarcely played a very conspicuous part in the life of Berlin. Yet, as ten per cent out of the seven million peace-time population of Berlin were Catholics, this was one of the largest Catholic communities of the Reich. However, scattered as they were over the whole area of 350 miles forming what is known as Greater Berlin, the forty or fifty Catholic churches were hardly able to represent Catholic life in an adequate manner. In fact, the Catholic community was hardly a unit.

Sunday Morning in St. Hedwig's

I realised the lack of coherency among Berlin Catholics whenever on a Sunday morning I watched the people at and after Mass in St. Hedwig's Cathedral. The different nationalities kept together, not only the Czechs, the Poles and the French, but also the Rhinelanders, Bavarians, Silesians and East Prussians. After all, the language spoken by the Ermlander is hardly less different from that of the Tyrolian than are Polish and Czech. The Wends (members of that curious Slavic minority living almost in the very heart of the Reich) always stood out by their colourful Sunday-wear in which they continued to appear at church, even when otherwise they had become thoroughly "Berlinerised".

Of the capitals of Europe Berlin is one of the youngest. Although recognised as a township since the Middle Ages, it was not until the end of the 17th century that it attained some political significance as the residence of the Electors of Brandenburg. One or two fine medieval brick churches in the heart of Berlin used to recall the fact that this had been a Catholic town.

The history of Prussia was determined by her ambition to join her possessions in the East (what is now known as East-Prussia) and those gradually acquired in the West along the Rhine, with her mainland. Even in 1866 when this ambition was fully satisfied, Prussia (and Berlin) remained interested exclusively in its West-East-axis. Travelling from Ostend or Paris to Warsaw, one could pass through Berlin without changing train; but travelling from Munich or Leipzig to Stettin, one had to alight at one of the Southern stations of the capital, and to make a tedious walk or drive to one of the stations on the North side of the city.

Between 1740 and 1815 Prussia acquired large territories with Catholic populations. The Cathedral, since 1930 the see of the bishop of Berlin, was the first Catholic church built in Brandenburg after the Reformation. Frederick the Great erected it to ingratiate himself with his new Catholic subjects in Silesia. It was dedicated to St. Hedwig, patron of Silesia and secondary patron of Poland. (St. Hedwig, whose feast is universally celebrated on October 16, was married to a Prince of Poland.)

Berlin's commercial and industrial life benefited from Frederick's proclamation of religious freedom. It was the first capital of Europe to do away with the Ghettos for the

Jews, and received with equal hospitality Huguenot and – during the Revolution – Catholic refugees from France. By the end of the 18th century, every second Berliner was either a Frenchman or a Jew; the Catholic population of Berlin must have been something like 20 per cent at that time.

In Potsdam, his favourite residence, Frederick the Great built a Catholic chapel in which, it is said, a Franciscan ministered to the Catholic soldiers in the garrison, among whom there was a fair contingent of Irishmen, John O'Keeffe, an 18th century Irish Catholic playwright (as successful as worthless) described in one of his plays the life of Irish soldiers in Frederick's army.

In 1821 Berlin became the see of a Delegate Apostolic. When, as the capital of the Second Reich, Berlin rose to the position of the largest city of the Continent (it is now the fourth largest city of the world) new problems arose for the ecclesiastical administration. From 1870 to 1930 the population increased by five hundred per cent and the area by two thousand per cent.

Mixed Marriages

Forty per cent of Berliners are non-Berliners by birth, and with the Catholic population of Berlin the proportion is still higher. Unlike the now well-established Catholic communities of London, Liverpool, New York and Chicago, Berlin Catholics are on the whole unsettled. Wartime conditions, not to speak of the influx of refugees from the Eastern provinces (many of which have large Catholic populations) will have increased the problems resulting from this state of affairs.

Speaking of Catholic Berlin one cannot help recalling the fact that seventy per cent of Berlin Catholics married non-Catholics, and only twenty per cent of those mixed marriages were solemnised. Of the offspring of those marriages, only thirty per cent were baptised in a Catholic Church. The clergy, of whom there were only 160 secular and forty regular in Berlin, were faced with enormous difficulties.

Of two of the finest manifestations of Catholic life in Berlin, namely, the schools and the press, one can only speak in the past tense. Up to 1937, Berlin Catholics had seven secondary schools, three training colleges and one chair for Catholic *Weltanschauung* in the University (this chair was occupied by Prof. Guardini, the great leader of the German Catholic youth movement and well-known also in these countries as the author of fine studies on the liturgy). Of the Catholic press, the *Germania* was for some time something like the organ of the Government, while the *Märkische Volks-zeitung* was the voice of the whole diocese of Berlin, which comprises the whole of North Eastern Germany, up to the Polish Corridor.

As it may be safely said that what is left of Catholic life in Eastern Germany is now concentrated in Berlin, the future of Catholic Berlin is a problem significant far beyond the frontiers of the Reich.

(Quelle: Irish Catholic, 19.04.1945)

Salzburg, its Primate and Ireland
by "Peregrinus"

Vatican Radio recently announced that Mgr. Andreas Rohracher, Titular Bishop of Isba and Vicar Apostolic of the diocese of Gurk, Austria, has been appointed archbishop of Salzburg, to succeed the Archbishop Waitz.

I remember well the opening of the Salzburg University Weeks in 1932, that splendid meeting of Catholic scholars and scientists from all parts of the world, when the Archbishop preached a fine sermon on the task of Catholics in intellectual life. At that time, I wondered why the Archbishop of Salzburg, though not being a Cardinal, wore red robes. I then learnt that this is a centuries old privilege enjoyed by the Archbishop of Salzburg who to this day has the title of Primate of Germany, a title which, however, is not recognised by Canon Law, and gives no precedence outside the country. Like many other bishops of Central Europe, the archbishops of Salzburg were originally the secular rulers of their dioceses, and in Austria, some of the bishops, including those of Salzburg and Gurk still are called "prince-bishops".

One of the chief aims of the late Archbishop Waitz and of his predecessor, Dr. Riedl, was the re-establishment of a Catholic University for Central Europe. Inspired by the example of Cardinal Mercier, the founder of the Catholic University of Louvain in Belgium, and of Fr. Gemelli, O.F.M., the first Rector of the Catholic University of Milan, Archbishop Waitz tried to revive the tradition of the Benedictine University of Salzburg of the 17th century, when incidentally, some Irish exiles held professorships in Salzburg and when numerous Irish Franciscans made their theological studies there. The annexation of Austria frustrated Archbishop Waitz's plans, and in the meantime the venerable abbey of St. Peter, the see of the Catholic University of Salzburg, was confiscated and converted into a political training-centre.

Work of Irish Monks

The Archbishopric of Salzburg is of special interest to Ireland. In the lessons proper to the Breviary for Ireland no German city is more frequently mentioned than Salzburg. When in the middle of the 18th century the first liturgical calendar for All Ireland was set up the only non-Irish Saint whose name was inserted therein, apart from Pope St. Celestine who sent SS. Palladius and Patrick to this country, was St. Rupert, the founder of the see of Salzburg, to this day the only German Saint to be locally venerated in Ireland. On March 29th, in the Proper for Ireland, the lessons (originally taken from the Breviary of the Benedictines of Salzburg) relate the establishment of St. Rupert's see "on the shores of the *Waller See*" and the foundation of St. Peter's Church. When in happy pre-war times Irish visitors spent their summer holidays in the lovely mountains of Berchtesgaden, and attended the glorious festival plays at Salzburg or called at the famous inn of The White Horse on *Wolfgang-See*, only few of them realised that the foundations of the Christian culture of that remote district were laid with the help of early Irish missionaries. St. Rupert made his see a centre of Irish monastic activities, which from Salzburg extended all over Southern Germany and, in the East, as far as Hungary and Yugoslavia.

On November 27, Ireland and Salzburg join in the commemoration of St. Virgil, the renowned Irish scientist, one of St. Rupert's successors. To this day the Office for this feast is taken from the local Breviary of Passau in Germany. In Salzburg, however, the lessons of the Office contain a few passages which though of special interest to Ireland, are omitted in this country. Here we read that St. Virgil was a monk and later Abbot of the Monastery of Aghaboe, and that, following the example of many of the Saints of his country, he went abroad to preach the Gospel. "In Salzburg, St. Virgil did not give up his native rite and, following the example of his native country, he ruled his bishopric through an administrator, a country man of his." These are perhaps the most expressive official pronouncements concerning the traditional relations existing between Ireland and the see of Salzburg, which has recently received its new ruler.

(Quelle: Standard, 04.06.1943)

V   Literarische Beziehungen

Irish Literature on the Continent

For some decades past, the tradition of Irishmen on the Continent has been studied more than ever before, and it has been found that this tradition can be traced in practically all parts of Europe. The vestiges of Irish influence, or actual footprints, of the ubiquitous Celt are found from Norway down to Portugal, and in the East as far as Finland and the Ukraine. Whilst, however, in many of those distant parts the Irish influence was only accidental and transitory, at all times the Irish activities were concentrated in Northern France, Belgium, the Rhine Valley and Bavaria-Austria. Far from being confined to the Golden Age, when the great missionary saints re-established or preserved Christianity in these parts of Europe, Irish activities have left their traces in all periods of the literature of Central Europe. In fact, Irishmen were instrumental in reconstructing the foundations of the splendid traditions of ancient Rome and Greece on which the glorious edifice of the literary culture of the Christian Middle Ages was to rest. At the palatial University of Charlemagne in Aix-la-Chapelle, Irishmen taught Continental students the Greek language and philosophy. At the same time, they gave to the Continent the material possibility of building up a literary tradition by conveying to them the knowledge of artistic book-writing. Thus the great Irish missionaries of the 6th and 7th centuries were followed by the scholars and artisans of the 8th century. During this Silver Age of Irish cultural activities on the Continent, the Roman Empire of the German nation received its intellectual found-ations. Even when the Continent had become capable of developing these foundations in the great synthesis of medieval philosophy, poetry, sculpture and architecture, Ire-land still played a prominent, though less conspicuous part. In the 11th and 12th centuries especially, there is a continuous influx of Irish clerics and monks, who came to the Continent partly like their great forefathers to live in the wilderness as hermits or pilgrims, partly to seek a living which they could not find in their home country. These representatives of the Bronze Age of the Irish tradition had no longer the glory of the early missionaries whom the people often venerated from mere awe at the fact that they had come across the ocean from distant Ireland. They were scarcely received with honours like the scholars of the Carlovingian period; they had to wander from monastery to monastery and from bishop to bishop, searching for work as scribes, but, to this day, all over the Continent, manuscripts written or illuminated by those la-bourers are still extant. In many cases they finally settled in a hospitable place where they were enabled to found a monastery, which, however, was no longer a spiritual or cultural centre in a barbarian district as were the early Irish foundations, but merely a refuge for Irish supernumerary clerics, who now engaged in religious or cultural activities abroad. The significance and lastingness of the Irish tradition established at that time is most obvious in Cologne, and even more so in Ratisbon.

As early as the 7th century the two Ewalds had come from Ireland to Cologne, and what is to-day known as the Ruhr district, and here their apostolic work and martyr-dom is still faithfully commemorated. The preservation of their tradition is partly due to the Irish community established in St. Pantaleon's and St. Martin's in the 10th century. Among the disciples of this community was Bruno, one of the most famous archbishops of Cologne, and for some years Chancellor of the Reich. Bruno's life, written by a member of the Irish community, holds a prominent place among the sources of medieval history and is annually read in the Office of St. Bruno's feast, observed locally in Cologne. An even greater part in the preservation of the Irish literary tradition of Cologne was played by the generation of Irish exiled scholars who, in the 17th century, traced the footprints of their saintly countrymen through all parts of Europe. In Cologne, they re-discovered the life-story of the Ewalds and also of Marianus Scotus. They then also published books, which were either actually printed in Cologne or, like the famous *Hibernia Dominicana* of Thomas de Burgo, O.P. – later Bishop of Ossory – gave Cologne as the printer's "place of residence".

Similar, and at least for the 17th century, even broader literary traditions have been traced in connection with the history of the Irish colleges in Belgium, France, Spain and Italy. The Catalogue of Irishmen in France, which Dr. Richard Hayes is at present publishing in Studies, enables us for the first time to restate this tradition in its full extent.

With regard to the geographical and historical extent of the literary tradition of Ireland on the Continent, perhaps no place has more interest than Ratisbon. The lives of Saints Albert and Erhard, Irish bishops who, from the 7th century, are venerated as the apostles of that religious centre of Southern Germany, were written by Irish scribes, who settled there in the 11th century and retraced by Irish scholars who, in the 17th century, carefully searched the libraries of that city for traces of the Golden Age. In the Middle Ages, Ratisbon was the centre of a community of Irish monasteries which spread all through Central Europe and to which, for a short time, houses in Silesia and in Kiev were attached. As for the literary significance of Ratisbon, it is not accidental that Friedrich Pustet, the most important Catholic publisher, has his office in that city. His marvellous prints of liturgical text-books are well known in all parts of the world. This firm was the first to print the supplement of the Breviary and Missal for Ireland in its present-day form (1903), and we may safely assume that the tradition of issuing religious books from Ratisbon originated with the Irishmen. Whilst the Missal as we have it to-day was first composed by Alcuin, the leader of the Palace University of Charlemagne, after his return from studying at Clonmacnoise, the first manuscript of what is known as a plenary Missal is that written by an Irish monk for St. Emmeran, the famed bishop of Ratisbon. Other most important fragments of early liturgical books from Ratisbon, showing the characteristics of Irish script and ornamentation, have recently been discovered. It is a well-known fact that Ratisbon is the only place on the Continent where Irish book ornamentation has influenced or rather expressed itself in architecture.

In Ratisbon we can study the whole history of the Irish tradition on the Continent from the early Middle Ages down to the 19th century.

Whilst the early Irish missionaries owed a good deal of their reputation to the fact that they came from distant Ireland, up to the 12th century the mere fact that a pilgrim or monk came from this country was sufficient to gain for him worship as a saint. The scholars and scribes of the 9th and 10th centuries were admired as sons of what was then already known as "the Island of Saints". The cultural labourers of the later Middle Ages, however, were often rather handicapped than helped by their Irish descent. The Continental peoples had become oblivious of the graces bestowed on them by the great predecessors of the hosts of unemployed Irish clerics who then swarmed over Europe. The word "Irish" became synonymous with "vagabond", whilst the early Irish missionaries were reputed for the rigidness of their discipline, the decay of the great Irish monastic organisations on the Continent was mainly due to the ill-fame attached to the Irish name in those times.

Already in the famous lives of Saints Columbanus and Gall, written by Wetti and Jonas respectively, we see how, from the very beginning, the Continental people were struck by certain national characteristics of the Irish, such as their recklessness and wilfulness, at times shown in their dealings with their ecclesiastical authorities. It would be interesting to explore how far this reputation of the Irish was due to the fact that they spoke a language unknown on the Continent. In the life of Saint Fintan – a hermit of Rheinau, near Basle – written by one of his followers and countrymen in the 8th century, we see that Irish monks on the Continent faithfully clung to their native language. Whenever they had an opportunity of doing so, they inserted Irish "glossae" in the texts they had to write. It is a well-known fact that such "glossae", found in Continental manuscripts, still form the basis of our knowledge of the ancient Irish language.

In Ratisbon and Würzburg Scotch monks continued the Irish tradition down to the second half of the 19th century. In many places in Germany the names of Scotch Church and Scotch streets still recall the Irish tradition in later years erroneously attributed to the Scotch.

Whilst the Irish monks of the 17th century failed to recover their former residences in Central Germany, they set up new centres of cultural activities in Louvain, Douay, Rheims, Paris, Salamanca, Rome, etc. From the literary viewpoint, the Irish Franciscan monastery founded in Prague deserves special interest. One of the most famous teachers attached to that monastery was Father Broudin, O.F.M. In his defence of the Catholic Faith he left one of the most important collections of records of the Irish martyrs, at the same time conveying to Continental readers a considerable amount of information regarding Irish affairs. Paris and Prague were the first places where Offices of Irish Saints were printed. This goes to show that whilst Paris was the centre, Prague was the most easterly outpost of the scholarly activities carried out in the search of the footprints of the Irish missionaries of the Golden Age. In this research the Irish scholars displayed such an outstanding amount of modern historical training that they naturally gained the esteem of contemporary Continental scholars, such as the Bollandists. This scholarly intercourse is actually the first sign of a more serious interest about Ireland on the Continent.

The scholarly study of Ireland and her tradition, as initiated in the first half of the 17th century, was carried on in an unbroken tradition to the 19th and 20th centuries, when research on the Irish tradition of the Continent became a recognised branch of European history – a branch resplendent with the glorious names of Wilhelm Wattenbach, Heinrich Zimmer, Dom Gougaud, etc. Whilst this tradition was mainly concerned with Irish ecclesiastical history, the study of the literary and political history of the country received its greatest impulse from what is known as the Ossianic Movement, originating from the famous edition of *Relics of Ancient Poetry* by Bishop Percy and from the grand forgery of MacPherson. The significance of this movement can hardly be overrated, not only for the history of Ireland's place in the literary tradition of the Continent, but also for the decisive development of Continental and modern minds. Neither the "back-to-nature" movement and the philosophy of life underlying the French Revolution nor the "Sturm and Drang", the basis of the classical period of German literature, can be thought of without the Ossianic enthusiasm. Fundamental concepts and ideas proper to modern philosophy and poetry are first found in that movement. Speaking from the viewpoint of cultural history, this second gift made by the Celtic West to the Continent was hardly less important than the first, the preservation of the Christian tradition.

The more definite significance for Continental relations to Ireland of the great cultural break made in the middle of the 18th century is made lucid by Herder and Goethe, the former the pioneer of what is known as German idealism – the intellectual movement, to this day, the basis of the whole of modern philosophy outside neo-scholasticism. In Herder's *Voices of the Nations in Songs,* "old Hibernian" poetry holds a significant place and his ideas on European history for the first time open the possibility of facing the extraordinary position held therein by Ireland. In Goethe's earliest novel, *The Sorrows of Werther,* the Ossianic influence is so obvious that we are hardly surprised to encounter in his notes of that time serious attempts to study the Irish language. Goethe's close relations with Ireland are perhaps the most conspicuous sign of the new high position assigned to Ossian's country in the mind of Continental Europe at the end of the 18th century.

In 1801 appeared the survey of Irish history made by D. H. Hegerisch for the purpose of promoting "a correct understanding of the Rebellion, the Union and Catholic Emancipation". This is probably the first book written by a German author on Irish history from an Irish viewpoint. It is hardly necessary to say that in Germany, in the 20th century particularly, there originated an abundant literature on Irish politics.

In 1830 Goethe enthusiastically reviewed the journal of a tour undertaken by Count Pueckler through Ireland with a view to studying Irish parks and scenery in general. In his review, Goethe emphasised the significance of that book as a source of information on recent Irish political history (Count Pueckler was a personal friend of Daniel O'Connell). In the year of Goethe's death another Continental tourist published an anonymous *Survey of the Present-Day State of Ireland.* Thus was started the very extensive travel literature by means of which perhaps the most knowledge of modern and ancient Ireland was conveyed to the Continent.

In 1838 Diefenbach's *Celtica* made a first attempt at collecting Irish linguistic monuments, whilst Franz Bopp delivered his famous address to the Berlin Academy on the position of Irish among Indo-Germanic languages. These were the foundation stones for the glorious edifice of Celtic studies on the Continent. It is not necessary to recall the lasting significance of the life-work of Casper Zeuss and of his disciples. It suffices to state that in 1882 the Cambridge University Press did not hesitate to publish a translation of Ernst Windisch's Irish Grammar, which three years previously had appeared in German, the first scholarly Irish grammar written in a modern language.

When in 1851 the first, and so far the only, complete history of the Irish Church, both in this country and on the Continent, was published by A. Bellesheim, it was hardly realised what a strange accident it was that the author of that gigantic work was a member of the Collegiate Chapter of the Cathedral of Aix-la-Chapelle, a place where, more than 1,100 years before, the foundation was laid of the literary tradition of Ireland on the Continent. Perhaps more clearly than Ireland's own literature this tradition demonstrates the inseparable inter-linking between the spiritual and the national aspect which seems to he the most outstanding and unique characteristic of Irish history in general. It is mainly due to that inter-linking that that literary tradition itself has something unique and almost miraculous!

In the absence of geographical or political connections consisting entirely of the personal contact made by missionaries, scholars, swordsmen and tourists, this tradition rests on a natural foundation of an almost incredible feebleness, which, however, in the light of 1,500 years of history appears as the expression of a strength never given to any other nation.

(Quelle: Irish Art Handbook 1943, S. 107-113)

Irish-German Literary Relations
A Survey

The only instance in which it has been proposed to study Irish-German literary relations as an historical unit was a popular article in *Irische Blätter,* a short-lived magazine which during the European War tried to establish a cultural foundation for the co-ordination then attempted of Irish-German nationalist interests. From the point of view of that periodical, the writer of that article was bound to overlook the very characteristic of Irish-German literary relations, namely that their tradition does not rest on any community of interests, whether political or economical, between the two countries geographically so wide apart. In fact, the few political contacts that existed between Ireland and Germany were anything but liable to produce cultural relations. In the nationalist conceptions of both Irish and German history, Germany and Ireland respectively appear mainly as serving the antinational cause. The only exception to this rule is the attempt, made in the early nineteenth century and revived in recent years, to describe the early Irish missionaries to Germany as exponents of a Rome-free Church.

The word *Irland* was first recorded by Adam von Bremen in one of the numerous references made in German annals of the time to the invasions of Ireland by the Norsemen. The name of the capital of Ireland was first mentioned in Continental literature by Gottfried von Strassburg, in one of the passages in which he enriched the Tristan tradition by information on early post-Norman Ireland. The first German book to deal exclusively with Ireland was written in connection with Schomberg's campaign in Ireland. The Danes, William and, we may add, the Hassians (who helped to quench the rebellion of 1798) still figure prominently in Irish curses.

In Germany, the word *Scotus,* which originally denoted the nationality of the Irish Saints, scholars and monks, gradually became a synonym for vagabond. The earliest representation in German art of an Irishman as such is the sketch which Dürer made in the Netherlands of a wretched raggy *krigsman in Irlandia hindr Engeland,* an early representative of the Irish soldiery whose sinister part in German history has become, through Schiller, common knowledge of every German schoolchild. Even the most sympathetic among the early German travel-writers on Ireland failed to see in the native anything but Paddy with the whisky bottle. Immermann, Freiligrath, Weerth and others tried in vain to raise famine-stricken Ireland to the rank of a poetical subject; Karl Marx more realistically depicted her as one of the typical victims of capitalist exploitation.

This bird's-eye view may have shown that in the study of Irish-German literary relations the words 'literary relation' must be taken in a wider sense than e.g., in the study of Irish-French or German-English literary relations. Thus study would have but little subject-matter, if it were confined to *Motivforschung* or to the study of purely literary influences. That, in spite of the absence of geographical and historical connections, these relations existed at all, is remarkable. We have to study German personal contacts with Ireland, knowledge of, references to and interest in Ireland, Irish localities, personalities and conditions, as reflected by German literature in the widest sense, including religious, historical and geographical works, and the influence of Irish writers and Irishmen in general in Central Europe, in order to gauge German *Irland-kunde* and vice versa Irish knowledge of Germany.

The study of Irish-German literary relations can rarely be separated from that of German-Irish literary relations. The earliest Irish association in any work of German vernacular literature is the reference to *chrihshha sancti kiliânes* in the late eighth-century description of the Würzburg March, the earliest record of the cult of St. Kilian, the sixth-century Irish martyr. The earliest German association in any work of Irish literature occurs at the same time in the *Martyrology of Tallaght*, when the entry of St. Kilian's death stated that this *Scotus martyr* was beheaded, together with his brethren Aed and Tadg, 'in the hippodrome of the royal palace'. The only definite place in Germany mentioned in the *Martyrology of Tallaght* was that of *Treveris* (Trier), which the writer of that work, however, regarded as the name of another Saint.

Our bird's-eye view of Irish-German literary relations has shown that in their first period the central figure is the cleric, in the second the soldier and in the third the tourist. During the first thousand years of these relations Ireland has been the creditor, and up to the end of the twelfth century Ireland's place in German literature is confined to hagiography. The Vita of St. Fintan of Rheinau was the first work written on the Continent, in the context of which occur some Irish sentences. Wetti's Vita of St. Gall was the source of Ratpert's *Lobgesang auf den Heiligen Gallus,* the first known vernacular work of German literature to be devoted to an Irish subject. Apart from these two Saints none of the twenty or more Saints in Germany to whom medieval tradition attributed Irish associations has escaped modern criticism with regard to these associations or even his very existence. In the study of literary relations, however, we are not concerned with historical facts but with cultural traditions and their signi-ficance. That so many local patrons in Germany were given Irish associations, is due in the first place to the deep impression made by the early Irish missionaries and anchorites, but still more to Irish monastic activities in Germany from the eleventh century.

The tradition of the Irish missionaries is more conspicuous in the liturgical than it is in the strictly hagiographical tradition. Hrabanus Maurus's epigram on the collective dedication of an altar at Fulda to Ss. Brigid, Columbanus and Patrick was the first work of poetry written by a German on an Irish subject. In the Office of the feasts of those Saints, short summaries of their lives were read every year, by every priest of the dioceses in which those feasts were kept. While at present none of the native Saints of Ireland is in the universal calendar of the Catholic Church, in the Middle Ages on more than twenty days of the year the local Breviaries of many dioceses in Central and Western Germany spoke of Irish associations (birth, early life, education, episcopacy and emigration) of the Saint of the day. The feasts of Ss. Columbanus, Gall and Kilian are still celebrated in the dioceses where they had laboured. St. Brigid's feast, once celebrated throughout Europe, is still kept at Cologne, in some parts of France and in one or two dioceses in England. Devotion to St. Brendan was spread by the Normans all along the North and Baltic Sea coasts. The feasts of Saints reputed to be of Irish origin, such as Ss. Rumbold, Livinus and Erhard, patrons of Mechlin, Ghent and Ratisbon respectively, spread through a large part of the Empire. The patronage and cultus of these Saints exercised influence on church-dedications, place-names, folk-lore, arts and of course religious and secular literature except in liturgy and local histo-ry, however, their Irish associations gradually fell into oblivion.

The fact that the original lives of those Saints were frequently distinguished by an introductory summary of the geographical and historical tradition of their reputed native country, shows that, while exercising great spiritual influence, Ireland was materially little known. Most of those summaries were derived from the classical ac-count by Solinus, handed down by Isidor of Sevilla, slightly modified by Dicuil (the only one of the Irish scholars in the Carlovingian Renaissance to refer to his nation-ality) and more radically by the *Visio Tundali*, the most prominent work of Irish-Continental literature of the Middle Ages. Ireland frequently ranks with Egypt as a country full of wonders, far away across the sea. The fabulous longevity of the Irish (of which Hebel still speaks in his *Schätzkastlein*), the natural curiosities of Ireland (barnacle geese growing from rotting timber, miraculous wells and trees, sunken cities, islands of death) were salient points in Continental *Irlandkunde*. There was on the one hand the tradition of Ireland's being the island of Saints, a purely Continental tradition originating from the misinterpretation of the Roman expression *Insula Sacra* and from the erroneous identification of the Irish word *noibh (illustris)* with *sanctus*. On the other hand, we have the classical tradition of the Irish being brutes and the later medieval tradition (probably a Norman fabrication) of their cowardice, the latter exercising great influence on Ireland's place in chivalresque literature, from Tristan's adversary ('a haughty man, Irish by descent, evil-minded, crafty and mendacious' in the Nordic version) to the ludicrous Irish knights performing at the Stuttgart court feast in 1617 (described by Weckherlin).

Continental ideas of Ireland were based on those foreign interpretations (summarized by *Lucidarius* and surviving in the *Kleine Cosmographien* and *Weltkunden* right to the nineteenth century) rather than on the few attempts made by natives of Ireland to criticize this tradition (as was done by Dicuil and by Marcus, the author of the *Visio Tundali*). The spreading of Irish manuscripts, Irish book-illustrations and other works of art showing Irish influence, however, testified more eloquently to the historical truth. The *Visio Tundali*, written in Latin by an Irishman at Ratisbon – at the request of a German abbess, then translated into the Hessian, Bavarian and Low-German dialects, was the first work of German literature inspired by the establishment of a separate monastic organization by Irish clerics in Germany. Under the leadership of St. James's, Ratisbon, this congregation extended from Erfurt to Lake Constance, and for a hundred years had an affiliated house at Kiev, where Irish monks ministered to the Ratisbon merchants. The Vienna house of this congregation figures prominently in the rhymed Chronicles of Austria, and to this day in Vienna, Würzburg, Ratisbon and Nuremberg the names of *Schottenkloster*, *Schottengasse*, etc., recall this tradition. While this congregation gradually decayed, it found a definite place in local histories.

The position which Ireland occupied in the German mind at the late twelfth century can be illustrated by the frequent references made to Ireland in the epic literature of that time. Traditional ignorance of, or lack of interest in, German-Irish literary relations can be seen from the fact that in such a comprehensive work as Gertrude Schoepperle's *Tristan and Isolt, a study of the sources of the roman* (1913), no mention was made of the fact that Gottfried's work is distinguished from the earlier Tristan-tradition by the references made in it to historical Irish place-names and to social and cultural conditions in contemporary Ireland. A considerable part of the tradition on *Kudrun* has been devoted to the suggestion that by *Îrlande,* in the opening line, the Dutch province of Eirlandt is meant rather than Ireland! On the other hand, one writer has set out to prove that *Baljân* in *Kudrun* is 'of course' a typical Irish place-name starting with Bally-. It may be mentioned at this point that even those who do not share the belief that Irish-German literary relations as such are a subject worthy of investigation will derive some benefit from considering these relations at least as one new point of view liable to open interesting vistas on traditional problems.

While from the later thirteenth century German knowledge relapsed into pure fabulation and definite interest in Ireland decreased, a sustained tradition of Irish associations was maintained through the influence of the story of St. Brendan the Seafarer and the accounts of St. Patrick's Purgatory. The oldest manuscript of the *Navigatio Brendani* originally belonged to St. Maximin, Treves. The first – Middle Frankish – translation of this text has been preserved in the Middle German thirteenth-century poem, the Middle Low German poem of the same period and the High German prose version of the fourteenth century, but all these German versions left little of the Irish associations. Still, reference to *Schottenlant* or *das land Ybernia* being St. Brendan's country frequently occur in the thirteenth century.

The earliest existing work of German vernacular literature to deal with an Irish subject was the Alemannic poem of St. Patricius written about 1160, that is, thirty years before the famous account by Henry of Saltrey of Owen's descent into St. Patrick's Purgatory. The German tradition of this latter work (one of the earliest manuscripts of which was at Bamberg) becomes more evident towards the end of the Middle Ages, when Germans were among the first to doubt the veracity of the visions alleged to have been granted to pilgrims. In 1480 appeared at Augsburg two accounts of the pilgrimage, in 1496 at Memmingen Burchard von Horneck's *Carmen de Purgatorio divi Patricii*, but the most interesting reflection of this tradition was the Volksbuch of *Fortunatus* (first published in 1509 at Augsburg). It contains a curious rationalist account of St. Patrick's Purgatory, which it says was situated near Waldrich, a place-name suggesting that this section of the work at least was of German origin. In a later passage, *Fortunatus* tells of an anchorite in Ireland cultivating trees, the fruit of which have miraculous powers.

Between 1400 and 1600 mutual knowledge of Ireland and Germany was at its lowest. The association of the Irish and German 'nationalities' at the university of Paris and the few Irish students whom we can trace at German universities apparently conveyed little first-hand knowledge of the two countries to each other. One literary fruit of this academic intercourse, however, may have been the publication in 1496 at Lübeck of one of the theological treatises by Thomas Hybernicus of Johnstown, Co. Kildare.

While this was the first work by an Irishman printed in Germany, the first book written in German and printed in the Reich to deal exclusively with an Irish subject was *Die Wahrhaffte Historie von dem berümbten Abbt Sankt Fridolin* (Fribourg, 1586). Written by St. Peter Canisius, 'the second Apostle of Germany', and dealing with one of the most shadowy 'Irish' Saints in Germany, this book paved the way for a number of more scholarly works, chiefly by Bavarian historians, on the tradition of Irish Patron Saints. Heinrich Canisius, the cousin of the Saint, published in 1601 some of the fundamental records of Irish hagiography such as Cogitosus's Life of St. Brigid and Adamnan's Life of St. Columba, adding numerous records relating to the first millenium of Irish monastic activities on the Continent. One of Heinrich Canisius's colleagues at Dillingen was Stephen White, S.J., of Clonmel, the chief contributor on Germany to the *Acts of the Irish Saints*, which during the Thirty Years War were compiled by the great John Colgan, O.F.M., and his fellow workers at Louvain.

Fr. White's own work, entitled Apologia pro Hibernia, was not published until 1849; it was directed against the Scots who in Germany claimed for themselves the whole tradition going under the name of the Scoti, thus preventing the restoration of the Schottenkloster to the Irish. While for the German Catholic historians the rediscovered Irish tradition was a powerful weapon against the Reformers, the Irish exiled scholars had to support this tradition (most of which had been completely unknown in Ireland) in their own interest. For the subsequent 300 years, both in Germany and in Ireland the study of the literary tradition of Irish Saints in Germany was burdened with this twofold tendency. The efforts spent on supplying a scholarly foundation for this purely practical tradition were not entirely wasted, as they kept alive a certain minimum of mutual interest between Ireland and Germany.

In Germany this new interest in Ireland did not remain confined to the historical sphere. When Thomas Carve, the self-styled chaplain of the Irish forces serving in the Imperial army, published his Itinerarium from Ireland to Vienna and during the war, a German translation was demanded, which was to become one of the most important sources on the assassination of Wallenstein. Carve after all was the man who had the pleasant task to decide whether Butler's dragoons had been murderers or not. Carve then engaged in a bitter controversy with Anthony Bruodin, O.F.M., on some points in the latter's *Propugnaculum Veritatis* (Prague, 1643), the most comprehensive statement on Irish history ever published by an Irishman in the Reich. Though written in Latin this controversy cannot have failed to spread some knowledge of, or at least interest in, Irish affairs.

During the seventeenth century numerous Irish exiles were appointed to professorships in Central Europe. In 1625 appeared at Frankfurt on Main a commentary of more than 700 pages on the works of Aristotle, by Bernardus Morisanus, of whom little seems to be known beyond the fact stated on the title-page of his work that he was *Derensis Ibernus* (from Derry). Apart from Bruodin (who also wrote several theological manuals), the most prolific among the seventeenth-century Irish writers in the Reich was Augustine Gibbon de Burgo, O.S.A., who lectured at Würzburg and Erfurt, and whose works remained classics with his order right to the date eighteenth century. These refugee writers were naturally too preoccupied with the happenings in their native country not to take every opportunity to refer to them. However, their readers were not likely to take more than a theoretical interest in these matters.

There are but few attempts during that period made by Germans to obtain first-hand knowledge of Ireland. In 1572 three German counts arrived at Dublin, but Fitz-William took good care to prevent them from proceeding beyond the city walls. In his *Itinerary*, Fynes Moryson speaks of a Bohemian Baron who out of curiosity ventured into Ireland in the heat of the rebellion. Arriving at the court of Tyrone, he related 'for a miracle' that for eight days he had no food but porridge. About the same time Weckherlin visited Ireland, where he picked up a few Irish phrases which he inserted in one of his odes. Grimmelshausen says that he saw in Ireland the two wells, one of which conveys beauty, the other ugliness, a typical example of secular *Irlandkunde* of that period. When the great Dutch cartographers set to work, Ireland was the last country they considered worth obtaining first-hand knowledge of, but in 1642 Arnold Boate, one of their countrymen serving with the Cromwellian army, compiled a *Natural History of Ireland* – to attract foreign planters. A few years later a Frenchman wrote up his experiences in Ireland. These first autoptical accounts of Ireland by Continental travellers are still invaluable.

The first German to record his experiences in Ireland was Schomberg who, commanding the Williamite army, was killed at the Boyne. His tomb in St. Patrick's Cathedral, Dublin, is the first grave of a German in Ireland preserved to this day. In the inscription given to this tomb, Swift complained that Schomberg's relatives had shown no interest in his memory. However, Schomberg's activities in Ireland produced a large literary reaction in Germany, notably Happel's *Hibernia Vindicata* (Hamburg, 1691), the first German book to deal exclusively with the history and geography of

Ireland. A curious reflection of Schomberg's activities were the *Memoirs de Montcal*, one of the Abbé Prévost's Irish novels. Sacrificing the last shred of historical truth to frivolous imagination, this work marks the transition from the second to the third period of Irish-Continental literary relations.

With the exception perhaps of the twelfth and early thirteenth century this is the only period where Irish-German literary relations were mutual. That Swift, Steele, Goldsmith and Sterne were Irish, their contemporaries on the Continent realized more clearly than their countrymen do today. In conjunction with the Ossianic movement, the international influence of those writers put Ireland again on the literary map of Europe. The archaeological notes in Macpherson's *Ossian* revived the study of Irish antiquities, a subject in which the Continent soon became interested too. While Gabriel Béranger co-operated with General Vallancey in – somewhat fantastic – studies of this kind in Ireland, Goethe read O'Halloran's *Antiquities of Ireland* and Walker's *Irish Bards*, two standard works with whom Anthony O'Hara, the last Knight of Malta, had presented him.

Goethe, of course, is the pivot-point of German-Irish literary relations. At 21, he translated for Herder some passages from the 'original' of Ossian, the first translation of a Gaelic text into German, and thus, as already recognized by Stern, the foundation-stone of the impressive edifice of German Celtic studies. Through his friend Giesecke, a native of Augsburg, then professor of mineralogy at the Royal Dublin Society, Goethe received a fine collection of the stones of Ireland. He was interested in the fauna and the climate of Ireland. He was far ahead of his time in the appreciation of the political situation created by O'Connell, and above all, through close acquaintance with the numerous Irishmen staying at Weimar (and, as Goethe wrote to Boisseree, of all foreigners liked best in his house), he attained to a knowledge of their national characteristics unsurpassed by any German writer on Ireland. Des Voeux, one of the Irish lovers of his daughter-in-law, was the first English translator of Tasso. Downes and Swifte (a descendant of the Dean) placed on record their experiences in gay Olympic Weimar.

Translations and imitations of Werther had been among the earliest Irish prints of Continental literature. In 1799 William Blaquiere, the son of the Viceregal secretary, published simultaneously at London and Dublin his excellent translation of Schiller's *History of the Thirty Years War*. A few months later, however, William Preston, the playwright, delivered at the Royal Irish Academy a lecture in which he accused Goethe and Schiller of establishing cannibalism on the stage. Yet twenty years later, Goethe was the first German to become a Hon. Member of the Academy. Right from its foundation, the *Dublin University Magazine* made it its special object to promote knowledge of contemporary German literature, by articles on German conditions, reviews of German books, and in particular translations of poetry, notably Mangan's series *Anthologia Germanica* (which also included the best English translation of *Wallensteins Lager*). The subsequent publication of this series in book form and the masterly translation of *Faust*, through Anster, also a contributor to the *Dublin University Magazine*, mark the climax of Irish interest in German literature.

The first German travel-book on Ireland was written in 1783 by Volkmann (whose book on Italy was extensively used by Goethe). The author had never been in Ireland, but gave a balanced compilation of the sources available to him. A few months later, Kuettner wrote his *Briefe aus Irland*, to this day perhaps the best German travel-book on Ireland. Kuettner had the advantage of being tutor to the sons of Lord Tyrone, the brother of John Beresford, then virtually the ruler of Ireland. His modesty and restraint compare most favourably with the sweeping superficiality of Pueckler's *Briefe eines Verstorbenen*, which, through Goethe's review, became the best known German book on Ireland. In the year of their publication, the first German translations of works of nineteenth-century Anglo-Irish literature (Moore's memoirs of *Captain Rock* and Whitty's *Irish Tales*) were published by Messrs. Manz, the leading Catholic publisher, at Breslau. Of Moore's *Lalla Rookh* we have three German translations, not counting Flechsig's translation of *Paradise and Peri*, underlying Robert Schumann's 'secular oratorio'. The publication of Whitty's *Tales* was followed up by the translation, with a beautiful preface *Ueber die Elfen*, by the Brothers Grimm of Croker's *Fairy Legends of the South of Ireland*, and later by von Killinger's series *Erin*, including also Griffin's *Collegians*.

During the years 1830 and 1845 more books on Ireland were published in Germany than during the rest of the century together. The place which Ireland then occupied in German thought may be gauged from the fact that at O'Connell's trial in Dublin, several German newspapers sent special reporters, whose verbatim reports were subsequently published in book form.

O'Connell marks the beginning of the fourth period of German-Irish literary relations, which is outside the scope of this survey. Its central figure is the scholar, Zeuss, followed by two great generations of German Celtists, Lassaulx, the geologist, Bellesheim, the historian of the Irish church, and perhaps Bonn, the best German writer on the political problems of modern Ireland. In 1916, Sir Roger Casement wrote *Irland und Deutschland*, to my knowledge the only book in the title of which the names of the two countries were linked.

In this survey, I have confined myself to offering some evidence of the extent of Irish-German literary relations and their significant implications. As, to my knowledge, I am the only one who has so far systematically devoted himself to this study, I need not apologize for lacunae of which I am only too well aware. The present survey was based almost exclusively on work already published or in hand. I should be glad if my notes would evoke interest in similar studies among those who are in a bibliographical position more favourable than one who works right in the middle of deep Irish bogs.

(Quelle: German Life and Letters, N.S. 3, 1950, S. 102-110.)

Studien zur Geschichte der deutschsprachigen Irlandkunde
bis zum Ende des achtzehnten Jahrhunderts

Die deutsche Irlandkunde[1] entbehrt so sehr der historischen und systematischen Kontinuität[2], daß sie sich nur in der besonderen Lage eines nach Irland verschlagenen deutschsprachigen wissenschaftlich Interessierten, der sein Schicksal zu ergreifen suchte[3], als Forschungsgebiet darstellen konnte. Wenn ich das Thema dieses Aufsatzes fast ausschließlich in Form einer Übersicht über eigene Arbeiten mit einigen Ergänzungen sowie Hinweisen für Weiterarbeit behandle, so geschieht dies aus drei Gründen. Ich bin m. W. der einzige, der das Gebiet der deutschen Irlandkunde wenigstens nach seiner Länge und Breite auszumessen versucht hat. Vorwiegend während des Krieges und der Nachkriegsjahre und mangels Ermutigung z. T. an sehr entlegenen Stellen veröffentlicht, sind meine Arbeiten weit verstreut und mindestens deutschen Lesern vielfach schwer zugänglich. Ein gewisser Abschluß wurde soweit erreicht, daß ein Überblick versucht werden kann.

Das Fehlen geschichtlicher und inhaltlicher Stetigkeit ist selbst ein Stück der deutschen Irlandkunde. Intensive Anteilnahme und beträchtliche Sachkunde im ganzen wie im einzelnen, wie im 13. und 19. Jahrhundert erreicht, haben Wiederabsinken in Oberflächlichkeit, Interesselosigkeit, Mißverstehen und Ignoranz nicht verhindern können. Das hervorstechende Merkmal ist immer die Überwindung der räumlichen Entfernung und des Fehlens an materiellen Berührungen gewesen. Zwar meinte das Kudrunlied, man könne von Skandinavien nach Irland reiten[4], aber im allgemeinen war doch

---

1   Es gibt neuerdings ein Institut für Keltologie und Irlandkunde an der Universität Würzburg. Das Wort »Irlandkunde« wurde m.W. zuerst von mir im Anschluß an, und in bewußt verschiedener Bildung zu, Walter Hofstätters Begriff »Deutschkunde« benutzt.

2   Versuche von Gesamtübersichten: Unabhängig von meinem Artikel in Irish Ecclesiastical Record (IER) 65 (1946) 392-400 über die monastische Tradition von Kolumban bis zur Auflösung der sog. Schottenklöster in Bayern im 19. Jahrhundert schlug der St. Gallener Stiftsbibliothekar P. Duft in 'Iromanie und Irophobie' (Z. f. Schweiz. Kirschengesch. 50 [1956] 241-262 u. 51 [1957] 147-150) eine Periodisierung der irisch-festländischen Kulturbeziehungen vor. Die Perioden sind repräsentiert durch Heilige (Frühzeit), Kulturtechniker (9.-12. Jhdt.), Ritter (13. u. 14. Jhdt.), Soldaten (16. u. 17. Jhdt.), Touristen und Gelehrte (18. u.19. Jhdt.), neuestens Geschäftsleute. J. H., 'Irish-German literary relations' (German Life and Letters N.S. 3 (1950) 102-110), auch 'Irische Frauen in der Weltliteratur' (außerhalb Irlands, Großbritanniens und Nordamerikas) Basler Nachrichten 23.5.54; dazu J. H., Besprechung von M.-L. Portmann, Die Darstellung der Frau in der Geschichtsschreibung des früheren Mittelalters, Diss. Basel 1958, in: Theol. Lit. Ztg. 1959, 367. Der großartigste Versuch einer Gesamtgeschichte der festländischen Kulturbeziehungen mit Irland ist enthalten in A. Rivoallan, Présence des Celtes (Paris 1959). Randgebiete unseres Themas behandeln die Veröffentlichungen des unter dem Namen A. O'Flanders schreibenden Prämonstratensers von Tongerloo zur Geschichte der flämischen Irlandkunde (s. J. H. in Irish Book Lover 32 [1952] 16) und J. Hs. Arbeiten zu irisch-schweizerischen Literaturbeziehungen (Z. f. Schweizer. Kirchengesch. 46 [1952] 204-216 u. 48 [1954] 17-30 und Die Tat (Schweizer Tagesztg.) 24.6.1947).

3   J. H., Irland und der Nationalsozialismus, Schweizer Rundschau 47 (1947) 518-525.

4   J. H., Ireland's place in the chivalresque literature of mediaeval Germany, Proc. Royal Irish Academy 53 C (1950) 279-298.

wenigstens die Tatsache stets bekannt, daß Irland eine Insel ist, und zwar am Rande von Europa, ja der Oikumene. Mit keinem europäischen Lande hat Deutschland weniger politische Kontakte gehabt als mit Irland. Deutsche Soldaten in Irland – am Ende des 17. und am Anfang des 19. Jahrhunderts[5] – und irische Soldaten auf deutschem Boden[6] waren Söldner in fremden Diensten[7]. Die intensivsten Berührungen fanden auf geistigem Gebiete statt. Die Erinnerung an die sogenannten irischen »Glaubensboten« war nicht nur die lebendigste Grundlage deutscher Irlandkunde, sondern vor allem auch eine der wichtigsten Quellen, aus denen sich die eminenten deutschen Beiträge zur Irlandwissenschaft, besonders auf den Gebieten der Kirchengeschichte und Sprach- und Literaturforschung, speisten.

Als das früheste Zeichen von Irlandkunde in deutscher Sprache darf die Eintragung *chrishha sancti kilianes* in der 'Würzburger Markbeschreibung' (Ende des 10. Jahrhunderts) betrachtet werden[8]. Das früheste literarische Zeugnis dessen, was man als irische Deutschkunde ansprechen darf, ist die Eintragung im 'Martyrologium von Tallaght' (Anfang des 10. Jahrhunderts):

Sancti Celiani Scotti martiris cum suis fratribus Aed is Tadg et Amarma conjuge regis Gothorum truncati a preposito domnus regiae in ippodoronia palatii regis[9].

Diese Eintragung ist merkwürdig wegen ihrer Länge und wegen des einzigartigen historischen Details, aber vor allem wegen der sonstigen Kärglichkeit irischer Hinweise auf das, was man in Deutschland als irische Mission bezeichnet hat, im mittelalterlichen Irland selbst. Von den meisten der sogenannten »irischen« Heiligen auf dem Festland hörten die Iren zum ersten Male im 16. Jahrhundert, als sie, aus ihrem Heimatland vertrieben, auf dem Festlande Teilnahme für ihr Schicksal zu erwecken

---

5   Hierzu vor allem F. Hering, Erinnerungen eines Legionärs. Nachrichten von den Zügen der deutschen Legion des Königs in England, Irland ... (Hannover, 1826). Das Hannoveranische Kontingent war vom April 1806 bis zum Juni 1807 in Irland, vor allem auch westlich des Shannon. S. 111 der entscheidende Satz: »In Irland schienen die vorgefallenen Unruhen andere Vorkehrungen nötig zu machen.«

6   J. H., Irish soldiers in the Thirty Years War, Journal Royal Soc. Antiquaries of Ireland 82 (1952) 28-36. Das kleine Kontingent langer Kerls aus Irland in der friderizianischen Armee hat kaum einen literarischen Widerhall gefunden, jedoch beruht die von A. Streckfuß, 500 Jahre Berliner Geschichte (1978), 310, berichte Geschichte, wie Friedrichs Versuch, einen Iren mit einem preußischen Mädchen zu paaren, vereitelt wurde, scheinbar auf Tatsachen, denn sie ist der Vorwurf zu John O'Keefes Lustspiel 'Patrick in Prussia' (1785) gewesen. Zum Ende des 18. Jhdts.: J. H., German literature on Napper Tandy (den irischen Revolutionär, der in Hamburg Asyl suchte), Irish Book Lover 31 (1951) 108f.

7   Die einzigen mir bekannten Artikel, die den Titel 'Irland und Deutschland' tragen, sind E. v. Schultzes in 'Irische Blätter' 2 (1918) 376, dem Organ der zur Unterstützung Casements gegründeten Deutsch-Irischen Gesellschaft in Berlin, und Frank (später Lord) Pakenhams in 'Ireland Today' I (1936) 13, ein Versuch, Hitler den Iren begreiflich zu machen. Man vergaß immer wieder, daß Pearse, der Führer der irischen Revolution von 1916, in sein Tagebuch schrieb: »Germany is no more to me than English is. My object was to win Irish freedom.«

8   J. H., Irish saints in German literature, Speculum 22 (1947) 358-374.

9   J. H., Ireland and Germany in the tradition of St. Kilian, IER 78 (1952) 31-33.

suchten durch systematische Sammlung festländischer Traditionen irischer Heiliger[10]. Schon im elften und zwölften Jahrhundert hatten allerdings Iren, vor den Dänen auf das Festland flüchtend, an solche Traditionen angeknüpft oder sie weitergesponnen, z.B. in den bis ins 19. Jahrhundert (nach der Reformation allerdings von Schotten besetzten) bestechenden Irenklöstern in Würzburg und Regensburg. In Würzburg holte sich dann Kaspar Zeuß entscheidende Anregungen für seine 'Grammatica Celtica' (1853), das Grundwerk der deutschen Keltologie.

Hinsichtlich der auf dem Festland mit Irland in Zusammenhang gebrachten Heiligen ist zu unterscheiden zwischen solchen, deren Verbindung mit Irland als einigermaßen gesichert angesehen werden darf (im deutschen Sprachbereich vor allem Gallus und Fintan von Rheinau[11], aber auch Kilian) und solchen, denen zweifellos erst spät Verbindung mit Irland zugeschrieben wurde[12] (wie Fridolin von Säckingen[13]) oder deren Existenz überhaupt als festländisches Erzeugnis bezeichnet werden darf (im Falle von Albert von Regensburg allerdings unter deutlichem irischem Einfluß). Für die Geschichte der deutschen Irlandkunde ist diese Unterscheidung jedoch weitgehend irrelevant, da gerade auch die weniger historischen Überlieferungen bedeutsame Träger deutschen Interesses an Irland gewesen sind, ja, die Aktivität, die das Festland hinsichtlich der Schaffung von Beziehungen mit Irland entfaltete, Ausdruck nicht nur lebendiger Anteilnahme sondern auch konkreter Kenntnis von Irland gewesen ist.

In Koordination mit meinen liturgiegeschichtlichen Studien habe ich die auf diesem Gebiete besonders wichtigen Kalendarien, Martyrologien und sog. historischen Lesungen des Breviers allgemein als spezifische Literaturgattungen gewürdigt und nach ihrer gesamten Tradition verfolgt und zeigen können, welche eminenten Beiträge zur Irlandkunde durch diese pflichtgemäß mindestens einmal jährlich von einem großen Kreis Gebildeter gelesenen Texte geleistet wurden[14]. Dieses ganze Gebiet, wie überhaupt die Fülle lateinischer Belege deutscher Irlandkunde im Mittelalter, muß ich hier unberücksichtigt lassen. Als wichtigste Aufgabe möchte ich nur eine Sammlung aller (durch die Register leicht festzustellenden) Bezugnahmen auf irische Dinge in den 'Monumenta Germaniae Histor.' nennen, eine Aufgabe, die allerdings nur einer unternehmen kann, der das Glück hat, zu allen Bänden direkten Zugang zu haben.

Die deutsche Irlandkunde hat vorwiegend von drei großen Legenden gezehrt, der von Irland als »Insel der Heiligen«[15], der durch Macpherson geschaffenen »Ossianischen«

---

10   J. H., St. Albert, Mediaeval Studies 7 (1945) 21-39.

11   J. H., The liturgical veneration of Irish saints in Switzerland, Iris Hibernia (Fribourg) 3 (1957) 23-32.

12   J. H., The place of the archdiocese of Dublin in the hagiographical tradition of the Continent, Reportorium Novum (Dublin) I (1955) 46-63.

13   J. H., The Irish monastic tradition on the Continent, IER 87 (1957) 186-193.

14   Meine Arbeiten zu diesen Themen wurden zusammengefaßt in 'Kalendarium und Martyrologium', Archiv f. Liturgiewissenschaft 1961.

15   S. die Titel der Irlandbücher von J. Rodenberg (1873), J. v. Dewald (1934) und R. Bauer (1938).

und der durch die moderne Touristik kolportierten. Zu der ersten dieser Legenden ist Folgendes zu sagen. Das Irische war die älteste Volkssprache, in der eine kirchliche Terminologie geschaffen wurde. Die Eigenart der altirischen Kirche läßt sich am klarsten daran zeigen, daß die meisten Grundbegriffe dieser Terminologie (Bischof, Abt, Fest, Fasten, Buße, Märtyrer usw.) dort eine andere Bedeutung hatten als im Lateinischen oder als auf dem Festland. Das irische Wort *noibh* z. B. heißt nicht (liturgisch verehrter oder gar kanonisierter) Heiliger, sondern »herrwürdig«. Daher vermochte z. B. das schon genannte 'Martyrologium von Tallaght'[16] eine unverhältnismäßig große Zahl irischer »Heiliger« aufzuführen (u. a. ganze Klostergemeinschaften). Als im 10. Jahrhundert irische Flüchtlinge auf das Festland kamen, verbreiteten sie systematisch die Kunde von dem ungewöhnlichen Reichtum ihres Heimatlandes an Heiligen, wobei sie allerdings an solche Äußerungen anknüpfen konnten wie die um 850 in der 'Epistola Ermenrici' gemachte:

Sed neque de Hibernia insula silendum censeo, unde nobis tanti luminis iubar processit[17].

Einige der in Lokalkalendarien durch Iren bewirkte Eintragungen irischer Heiliger, z.B. des hl. Canice, des Patrons des heutigen Kilkenny, in einem Kalender von Basel im 10. Jahrhundert, waren so erfolgreich, daß sie bis heute im 'Martyrologium Romanum' ihren Platz haben[18]. In seinen 'Tituli Ecclesiae Fuldensis' erwähnte Hrabanus Maurus die Weihung von Altären an Kilian, Kolumban sowie an Brigid und Patrick, die beiden Patrone Irlands, die als erste Iren im 'Martyrologium Hieronymianum' Aufnahme gefunden hatten[19]. Walafrid Strabo schrieb ein Gedicht über das Martyrologium des Iren Blathmac und seiner Mönche in Iona[20]. Dies sind die ersten Dichtungen von Deutschen, die sich mit irischen Gegenständen befassen.

Das Leben des hl. Gallus von Wetti, der 824 als Mönch auf der Reichenau starb, war die Grundlage von Ratperts 'Lobgesang auf den hl. Gallus' der nur in der lateinischen Übertragung durch Ekkehard IV. erhalten ist. Ratperts Werk ist der erste deutsche Versuch gewesen, der Hymnendichtung (ein Gebiet, das, wie wir u.a. aus dem Kodex von St. Paul in Kärnten wissen, von Iren besonders gepflegt wurde) Raum zu geben, bezeichnenderweise an Hand eines irischen Gegenstandes. Ratpert scheint sich mehrfach auf die irische Herkunft des Heiligen bezogen zu haben (*Gallus filius Hiberniae - pergunt - tranant maria*, Wetti sprach von einem *portus Hybernicus*).

Die literarische Überlieferung der irischen Heiligen im deutschen Sprachbereich ist in den verschiedensten Kanälen zu verfolgen. In dem deutschen 'Martyrologium' von Straßburg 1484 heißt es im Kalender von Brigida »junckfrau«, im eigentlichen Martyrologium dagegen »innige andechtige chloster junckfrau«; Patricius ist im Ka-

---

16   Henry Bradshaw Society 68 (London 1931).

17   MGH Ep. V, 534f.

18   J. H., Z. f. Schweiz. Kirchengesch. 48 (1954) 26.

19   J. H., Studia Patristica = Texte u. Untersuch. z. Gesch. d. altchristl. Literatur 63 (1957) 104-111.

20   B. Bischoff, Das irische Mönchtum in seinen Beziehungen zum Kontinent, Settimane di studio del Centro Italiano di studi sull'alto medieavo (Spoleto 1957) 136 f.

lendar von Gertrud verdrängt, das Martyrologium aber berichtet von ihm: »ein heiliger bischof und beichter in schottenland, darinn er zum ersten den christglauben gepredigt hat«, und von Foilan, der auch im Kalender fehlt: »zu Vosis (d. i. Fosse in Belgien), kam von Hibernia ...«. Die Überlieferung der Eintragungen in den Kalendarien und Martyrologien ist von mir literarisch in Einzelstudien z. B. über das 'Martyrologium' Wandalberti[21], über die außergewöhnlich reichhaltigen Eintragungen des Hrabanus für den hl. Furseus oder des Notker für Columba[22] bis zu den spätmittelalterlichen Lokal- und Ordensmartyrologien und endlich zu des hl. Petrus von Canisius deutschem Martyrologium, der reichsten Sammlung irischer Heiliger in deutscher Sprache verfolgt worden[23].

Die von mir angeführten Bezugnahmen auf Heilige aus »schottenland« in den Predigten Hermanns von Fritzlar[24] sind eng verwandt mit Eintragungen im Märtyrerbuch von Klosterneuburg[25]. Nur als Beispiel einer deutschen Biographie eines zweifellos unhistorisch mit Irland in Verbindung gebrachten Lokalheiligen nenne ich, außer des hl. Petrus Canisius Fridolinsbiographie[26], 'Das Leben der Heiligen S.S. Marini Bischoues Martyres und Aniani Archidiaconus Bekenners, die auss Irrland in Bayrn kommen des Gottshauses Rodt Patronen worden seiend' von Johannes a Via (München 1579, gleichzeitig mit dem lateinischen Original), angeblich »auss drey wol alten geschriebenen buechern, darinnen sie unordentlich hin wieder vermischet, ausgezogen und ordentlich gestellt«:

> »Warlich unsere Teutsche nation hat in Religionssachen sich wol was zu bedanken gegen denselben wie wol ferne gelegenen Inseln, die offt heilige und hochgeleerte Männer ausgesant, das liecht des Evangelii diesen landen fürtragen.«

Da sind ferner die Segnungen (wie die des Weins zu Ehren des hl. Gallus) oder Schwurformeln (noch in Immermanns 'Tristan' schwören die Iren beim hl. Patrick[27]) und andere gelegentlichere Erwähnungen irischer Heiliger[28].

Auch für die deutsche Irlandkunde sind die Hauptträger volkstümlicher Information über Irland auf dem Festland, die 'Navigatio S. Brandani', das 'Purgatorium S. Patricii' und die 'Visio Tundali', von größter Bedeutung gewesen. Meine Aufforderung, die festländische Tradition der Brandanslegende als Träger der Irlandkunde zu

---

21 Mediaeval Studies 17 (1955) 219-226.

22 S. meine [in] Anm. 14 genannte Arbeit.

23 IER 89 (1958) 173-182.

24 Speculum 22 (1947) 361.

25 Ed. E. Gierach, Deutsche Texte des Mittelalters (Berlin 1928).

26 J. H., Irish Monthly 74 (1946) 129-135.

27 J. H., Modern Language Review 44 (1429) 249f. Vgl. auch Georg Weerths erbärmliches Gedicht 'Gebet eines Irländers' (1846) (J. H., German Life and Letters 8 [1955] 204 f.).

28 Etwa in Stifters Hagestolz.

studieren, hat Prof. M. Draak willkommen geheißen[29]. Dem Auslaufen der Überlieferung vom Fegefeuer des hl. Patrick in der Fortunatustradition bis Tieck bin ich nachgegangen[30]. Aus dem Schreibfehler *Artinacha* für *Artmacha* (Armagh) in der Erlanger Hs. der 'Visio Tundali' konnte ich die praktisch zur gleichen Zeit, am gleichen Ort und aus der gleichen Quelle stammende 'Vita S. Albarti' erstmalig richtig deuten[31]. Mit diesem Schrifttum um das Regensburger »Schottenkloster« ist, wie auch wieder durch den Zusammenhang mit der 'Visio Tundali' zu zeigen ist, das an irischen Eintragungen reiche Kalender verwandt, über dessen Herausgabe DDr. Alban Dold starb.

Den wahren Charakter der deutschen Irlandkunde versteht man erst ganz, wenn man seiner ephemeren Natur in untergeordnetem Schrifttum nachgeht. So ist z.B. Scheffel durch seinen 'Trompeter' und vor allem die, heute nur selten abgedruckten Fußnoten seines 'Ekkehard' einer der wichtigsten Vermittler populärer Irlandkunde in der deutschen Literatur gewesen[32]. Die Überlieferung der historischen und fiktiven Verbindungen von Heiligen mit Irland lebt aller historischen Kritik zum Trotz in Traktätchen weiter. Der irische Gesandte erscheint alljährlich zur Fridolinsprozession in Säckingen. Noch 1930 wurde das für das Sängerfest zu Arbon 1842 von dem streitbaren Thomas Bornhauser verfaßte Epos über den hl. Gallus nachgedruckt, das eine für die deutsche Irlandkunde geradezu exemplarische Verbindung zwischen der Überlieferung der »Glaubensboten« und der Ossianischen Legende herstellt[33].

Daß der volkssprachliche (nicht notwendig deutsche) Name von Hibernia Irland sei, sagte zum ersten Male Adam von Bremen[34]. In einem Werk in deutscher Sprache wurde Irland m. W. erstmalig im 'Rolandslied' erwähnt. Wieder bietet sich eine Parallele in der irischen Deutschlandkunde an: In 'Gabhaltais Shearluis Mhoir', der mittelirischen Übersetzung (aus dem Lateinischen) des 'Chanson de Roland' findet sich erstmalig in der irischen Literatur eine detaillierte Liste der Teile Deutschlands (*i Saxa ocus in Fhrainge ocus in Almain ocus in Baignine* [Bayern?]). Es gibt keine

---

29 Brandaan en Vigilius (Amsterdam 1957) 6 und 17 zu meiner 'Note on Ireland's place in the literary tradition of St. Brendan', Traditio 8 (1952) 397-402.

30 Ulster Journal of Archaeology 13 (1950) 93-104. C. Kraus, Deutsche Gedichte des 12. Jhdts. (1894) konnte das merkwürdige Zusammenspiel von Informationen in der Irlandkunde des 'Patricius' nicht voll verstehen. Die Bezugnahme auf St. Patricks Fegefeuer bei Cäsarius von Heisterbach wäre zu erwähnen. Wir wissen von Ungarn und Schweizern, die diese schwere Pilgerfahrt machten. Henry Jones, St. Patrick's Purgatory (1647) erwähnte in diesem Zusammenhang Albert Krantz (gest. 1517), ADB 17, 43 f.).

31 S. Anm. 10. Über die deutschen Drucke der 'Visio Tundali' und ihre deutschen Übersetzungen s. R. Verdeyen, Van alte Tijden 4 (Groningen 1921) 24. Außer Marcus' Werk war das erste Buch eines Iren, das in Deutschland gedruckt wurde, 'De tribus punctis religionis Christianae' von Thomas de Hybernia (Lübeck 1496, s. M. Esposito in Studies I [Dublin 1913] 511).

32 S. Anm. 13.

33 Vgl. Herders Gedicht 'Die Fremdlinge' (dazu J. H., German Life and Letters 8 [1955] 201 f.)

34 J. H., Proc. Royal Irish Acad. 53c (1950) 279 u. 292. Zum folgenden diese ganze [in] Anm. 4 genannte Arbeit.

Gruppe ausländischer Heiliger, deren literarische Überlieferung in gleicher Weise wie die der Iren (oder mit Irland in Verbindung gebrachten) Träger deutscher Kenntnis ihres Heimatlandes gewesen wäre und deren Heimatland außerhalb dieser Überlieferung den Deutschen so unbekannt gewesen wäre. In entsprechender Weise erschien zwar Irland als eins unter anderen ritterlichen Ländern in der deutschen Epik des späteren Mittelalters, aber diese (angesichts des fast völligen Fehlens irischer Quellen über die ritterliche Betätigung von Iren im Ausland merkwürdige) Tatsache ist Träger sehr spezifischer Information gewesen. Die historische Unwirklichkeit dieser Information weist gerade auf einen eigenen und begreiflichen Zug deutscher Irlandkunde hin: Die ferne Insel erscheint in zauberhaftem Lichte (diesen Zug kann man bis in die moderne Touristenlyrik, etwa die Irland gewidmeten Gedichte von Otto zur Linde[35] und Reinhold Schneider verfolgen).

Den Stand der deutschen Irlandkunde vor dem Einfluß der Irenmönche (um Regensburg, in Würzburg, Nürnberg, Memmingen, Kelheim, Konstanz, Wien, Erfurt und zeitweilig in Kiew[36]) und vor der ersten Welle weltlichen Interesses an Irland im Zusammenhang mit der Normanneninvasion kann man an der Bemerkung im 'König Rother' ermessen, daß Rother saß auf »gestôle daz verre was gevoret von Irlande iz trôgin elphande wilen in den gebeine« - man denkt an die herrlichen phantastischen Elephanten, die um jene Zeit am Münsterchor zu Basel entstanden. Ich habe diese Bemerkung mit der Erwähnung von *helfenbein* in Albers Übersetzung der Beschreibung von Cormacs Schloß in der 'Visio Tundali' in Verbindung gebracht[37].

Die Tradition von Irland als einem Lande, in dem wegen seiner exzentrischen Lage alles möglich ist, reicht ins Altertum zurück. Eine Zusammenfassung von Solinus' Bericht über Irland findet man in Hrabanus' 'De Universo' und in Walafrids 'Vita S. Galli', später auch in Thierrys 'Vita S. Rumoldi' (des mit Irland in Verbindung gebrachten Patrons von Mechelen[38]), und sogar in der 'Visio Tundali', obwohl hier doch direkte und zeitgenössische Information von Irland zur Verfügung stand. Balthars 'Vita S. Fridolini' und die 'Passio II S. Kiliani' bezogen geographische Informationen über Irland aus anderen zeitlich und räumlich vergleichbar entlegenen Quellen. Die 'Visio Tundali' und Rudolf von Ems erwähnen die Abwesenheit von giftigen Tieren in Irland[39]. Rudolf von Ems läßt Brendan, den Abt, zur Zeit Noahs leben, vielleicht ein früher Hinweis auf die spätere Assoziation der *Hiberni* mit den *Hebrei*. Der 'Lucidarius', bis zum Beginn des 19. Jahrhunderts in sog. Kleinen Cosmographien nachlebend, begründete wohl die längste und wirksamste Unterrichtung der Deutschen über Irland. In Ms. Berlin germ. oct. 26 (Anf. d. 14. Jh.) ist nach Britannia und Engelant die Rede von Tybernia (sic), »uz der insulen swaz holzes braht wirt, das vetribet daz eitergift war es iemer kumet. In dem lande ist ein gegene

---

35   J. H., German Life and Letters 8 (1955) 206.

36   J. H. IER 65 (1945) 394-400, auch Irish Book Lover 31 (1950), 79-81.

37   In der [in] Anm. 4 genannten Arbeit S. 280.

38   S. meine [in] Anm. 12 genannte Arbeit.

39   J. H., Besprechung von L. Thorndike, History of magic, in: Irish Book Lover 29 (1944) 21ff.

heizet Schocia (andere Ms: schotenlant, scotia). Ob dem lande wendet sich die sunne.« Der erste Teil dieser Information stammt über Honorius Augustodunensis aus der spätantiken Überlieferung[40]. Der mit dieser Überlieferung verbundene Glaube, daß in einzelnen Teilen von *schottenlant* es keinen Tod gibt oder jedenfalls die Menschen sehr alt werden, spricht sich noch in einer der Kalendergeschichten von J. P. Hebel aus. In Grimmelshausens Simplizissimus heißt es:

> »Ich hatte die zween Brünnlein in Irrland gesehen, daraus das eine Wasser wan es getrunken wird, alt und grau, das andere aber hübsch jung macht.«[41]

Carves 'Reyssbüchlein' (s.u.) berichtet von Dingen in Irland, die (nach dem Original) »omnem prope fidem excedunt«, wie der Insel der Lebendigen oder den Brunnen, die Ebbe und Flut haben.

Da ich mich hier auf Literatur im engeren Sinne des Wortes beschränken muß, bemerke ich nur nebenbei, daß eine Geschichte des enzyklopädischen Schrifttums reizvoll als eine Geschichte der geographisch-historischen Irlandkunde geschrieben werden könnte. Irland würde dabei als eins der unbekanntesten Länder unseres Kulturkreises erscheinen. In Alsteds 1608 erschienenem und erstmalig den Namen Encyclopaedie tragendem Werk herrscht das traditionell-mythische Element noch vor. In der Kartographie hat sich erst durch Ortelius gegen die traditionelle Vorstellung von der Gestalt Irlands als Parallelogramm die richtigere von der Eiform durchgesetzt. In Ortelius' Karte ist der Name der Zisterzienserabtei Mellifont mit Mylisand wiedergegeben, m. E. die Quelle für den »König Milisint« in Mörikes Gedicht 'Die traurige Krönung'[42]. Entscheidend ist die Wendung der deutschen Irlandkunde in dem ersten deutschen Konversationslexikon (Zedler 1735, Bd. 14, 1274):

> »Irland ist vor die Teutschen nicht von sonderlicher Wichtigkeit, außer daß zu Weilen in denen See-Städten ein oder ander Schiffs-Gefäß mit Irrländischer Butter, eingesaltzenem Fleisch oder trockenem Lachs ankommt, und daß von Teutschen Cram-Waren wieder mit sich zurückführt oder auch Ladung auf Engelant oder Schottland einnimmt, bis sie solcher Gestalt wieder nach Haus gelangen.«[43]

Meine Übersicht über Irlands Platz in der ritterlichen Literatur des deutschen Mittelalters[44] plädierte dafür, die umfangreichen Forschungen über irische Motive in der Epik des Hochmittelalters durch das Studium des Verhältnisses zu ergänzen, in dem diese Motive zu den offensichtlichen konkreten Mitteilungen über Irland stehen, denen wir dort in so reichem Maße begegnen. Meine Übersicht ging den Erwähnungen Irlands u.a. im 'Parceval', 'Karlmeinet', den 'Haimonskindern', dem 'guten Gerhart', bei Rudolf von Ems, in Pleiers 'Tandareis', Konrads 'Partonopier', dem 'Buch von

---

40 S. Schorbach, Studien über das deutsche Volksbuch L. (Stuttg. 1894) u. F. Heidlauf, Deutsche Texte des Mittelalters 28 (Berlin 1915).

41 J. H., Modern Language Review 40 (1945) 40.

42 J. H., German Life and Letters 8 (1955) 203.

43 Zum Handel Irlands mit Deutschland um die Wende von 18. zum 19. Jahrhundert bieten die handschriftlichen Aus- und Einfuhrlisten in der National Library of Ireland Materialien.

44 S. Anm. 4.

Troj', dem 'Rosengarten', der 'Kreuzfahrt Landgraf Ludwigs', der 'Rabenschlacht' und 'Kudrun' nach. Den prägnantesten Ausdruck der Vorstellung von Irland als einem Wunderland findet man im 'Wigalois', wo unter anderen Schätzen aus Irland ein herrliches Pferd mit Sattel, vom König von 'Irlant' gegeben, vorkommt, welches von einem Zwerg geführt wird, der dem Helden die Zeit vertreibt mit Erzählungen aus Irland.

Der Hauptteil meiner Untersuchung war dem steilen Anwachsen konkreter Information über Irland in der Tristanüberlieferung gewidmet, ein Punkt, der z.B. in dem monumentalen Werk von G. Schoepperle nicht erwähnt wird. Gottfried von Straßburg war der erste, der in einem Werk in einer festländischen Volkssprache historische Ortsnamen in Irland einführte, charakteristischerweise die dänischen Namen *Develīne* (schon als »houbetstat« bezeichnet[45]) und *Weiseforte*. Die spätere Sensualisierung der Tristanüberlieferung geht streng parallel mit der Vernachlässigung dieser historischen Elemente des ersten Teils. Wenn vor einigen Jahren der deutschen Übersetzung eines an der Westküste Irlands spielenden Romans von Walter Macken die Worte vom Anfang von Wagners 'Tristan' »Frisch weht der Wind« als Titel gegeben wurden, so hat sich gleichsam der Kreis wieder geschlossen.

Die Erforschung der spätmittelalterlichen deutschen Literatur nach einem so abgelegenen Gesichtspunkt wie der Irlandkunde illustriert beispielhaft die bekannten Grundzüge der Epigonenliteratur: Die Erwähnungen irischer Dinge werden wirklichkeitsfern, inhaltlich armselig und stereotyp, typisch z. B. in dem 'Trojanerkrieg' des sich Wolframs Namen bedienenden Dichters des vierzehnten Jahrhunderts[46]. Das Fehlen des Nachschubs neuer Kunde und das Erlahmen an Interesse illustrieren ferner die Vernichtung der irischen Kultur und die Abriegelung Irlands vom Festland, der älteste und dauerndste Erfolg englischer Kolonialpolitik. Es besteht bis heute eine genaue Entsprechung zwischen wirklicher Irlandkunde und der Einsicht in die Verschiedenheit Irlands von England.

Ein letzter Nachklang der eminenten Stellung Irlands als eines ritterlichen Landes ist der Abschnitt 'Der Irländischen Ritter Aufzug' in dem dem Fegfeuer des hl. Patrick gewidmeten Teil von G. R. Weckherlins 'Beschreibung dess, zu Stuttgarten, bey den fürstlichen Kindtauf- und Hochzeit, Jüngst-gehaltenen Frewden-Festes' (Tübingen 1618), den ich (angeregt durch Professor L. W. Forster) im einzelnen untersuchte[47].

Ich bemerkte bereits, daß in diesem Bericht die lateinischen Zeugnisse deutscher Irlandkunde kaum berücksichtigt werden können. Sie sind jedoch auch im Spätmittelalter, vor allem in der systematischen Sammlung hagiographischer Überlieferungen

---

45 S. Anm. 12.

46 Deutsche Texte des Mittelalters 29 (Berlin 1926). Die in diesem Werk verwandten phantastischen Namen irischer Ritter sollten mit denen in den Überlieferungen des hibernisierten Heiligen Rumold und Livinus verglichen werden, sowie mit denen in der späteren Ausgestaltung der Überlieferung des hl. Foillan, in der die Verbindung mit der weltlichen Epik der Zeit deutlich ist.

47 J. Royal Soc. Antiqu. Ireland 80 (1950) 158-163.

besonders in Lokal- und Ordensmartyrologien von größter Bedeutung. Dieser Zweig deutscher Irlandkunde wurde ins Volkssprachliche übergeleitet durch des hl. Petrus Canisius Deutsches Martyrologium[48]. Canisius' 'Wahrhafte Historie des hl. Fridolin' (Fribourg 1589) war ein Versuch, der Schweiz im Zuge der Gegenreformation einen Nationalheiligen zu geben[49]. Die Idee des Nationalheiligen wurde in Irland geschaffen und schon früh wurden verschiedenen Teilen Deutschlands Iren als Patrone vorgestellt[50].

Das Weiterleben der Überlieferung irischer Heiliger auf dem Festland bis zum Einsetzen moderner kirchengeschichtlicher Forschung[51] konnte ich im deutschen Sprachbereich verfolgen z. B. in Zelbachers Übersetzung von Henriquez' 'Menologium Cisterciense' (Prag 1731)[52] und der anonymen Verdeutschung von G. Certanis 'Vita di S. Brigida Ibernese' (Augsburg 1735 und 1767)[53].

Außerhalb meiner Übersicht liegen auch die nicht-literarischen Niederschläge deutscher Irlandkunde, angefangen von der Darstellung des hl. Gallus in der Elfenbeinschnitzerei Tutilos (9. Jh.) auf dem Buchdeckel des St. Galler 'Evangelium longum' über die Darstellungen der Leben des hl. Fridolin im sog. Münster von Säckingen oder des hl. Rumold in der Kathedrale von Mechelen bis etwa zu dem 1826 entstandenen Hauptaltarbild der Kirche von St. Gallenkirch in Tirol (der hl. Gallus die Götzenbilder in den Bodensee stürzend)[54]. Der erste irische Laie, der auf dem Festland abgebildet wurde und m. W. der erste Ire, dessen Bild in einem festländischen Druck erschien, war Lupoldus von Waldrick in Irland, der Begleiter des Helden im deutschen Volksbuch 'Fortunatus' (Augsburg 1509)[55]. Der erste deutsche Künstler, der ein historisches Bild von Iren zeichnete, war Dürer; die Eintragungen in seinem Niederländischen Skizzen-

---

48 S. Anm. 23.

49 J. H., Medium Aevum 1957, 17-24 und die [in] Anm. 26 genannte Arbeit.

50 S. meine [in] Anm. 9 genannte Arbeit, S. 23.

51 L. Bieler, Irish manuscripts in mediaeval Germany, IER 87 (1957) 161-167 und Trias Thaumaturga in: Father John Colgan O.F.M. (Dublin 1959) 41-49. S. oben Anm. 10. Der wichtigste deutsche Korrespondent von John Colgan war der Jesuit Stephen White in Dillingen und Ingolstadt, dessen 1615 geschriebene, aber erst 1849 gedruckte 'Apologia pro Hibernia' 24 »irische« Heilige in Deutschland nachwies. Um die gleiche Zeit widmeten die bayerischen Kirchenhistoriker Hund, Rader und Brunner den Iren besondere Aufmerksamkeit. Einer von Whites Dillinger Kollegen war Heinrich Canisius, der 1601 zum ersten Male Cogitosus' Leben der hl. Brigida, Adamnans Leben des hl. Kolumban und andere wichtige Zeugnisse über die frühen irischen Heiligen, sowie die im 15. Jahrhundert entstandene Chronik des Regensburger »Schottenklosters« im Druck veröffentlichte.

52 J. H., Ireland's place in the tradition of the Cistercian Menologium, IER 95 (1961) 306-317, nimmt auch Bezug auf das Martyrologium von Wettingen (Aargau) 1682.

53 Comparative Literature Studies 19 (1946) 17-21.

54 S. meine populäre Übersicht, vorwiegend an Hand von Gougard, in IER 59 (1942) 181-192.

55 S. meine [in] Anm. 30 genannte Arbeit.

buch 1521 »also gand die krigsman in Irlandia hindr engeland« und »also gand dy pawren in Irlandyen« sind Meilensteine am Wege der deutschen Irlandkunde[56].

In wessen Armee dienten jene Soldaten und wie kamen die Bauern nach den Niederlanden? Zwanzig Jahre später hören wir zum ersten Male von konkreten Schicksalen von Iren auf dem Festlande, charakteristischerweise von einem »armen studiosus ex Hibernia, der von sinnen kam und sin rock zerriss«, dem Amerbach in Basel einen neuen Rock machen ließ. Das Ende des ersten (irischen) Abschnitts der Geschichte des Schottenklosters von Regensburg bezeichnet die Mitteilung Amerbachs von einem Almosen, das er 1555 »einem armen priester Hyberno« gab, »dem sin herr abbas Ratisponae, wie er sagt, gestorben und wider in Hiberniam ziehen mußte«[57].

Irland war das erste Land, das eine nationalbewußte Emigranz im modernen Sinne entsandte[58]. Die umfassende Literatur, die diese Emigranten auf dem Festland zwischen Prag, Rom, Lissabon und Antwerpen publiziert haben und die weithin dem Zwecke dienend, die Dankesschuld des Festlands an Irland festzustellen, viel zur festländischen Irlandkunde beitrug, müßte einmal zusammenhängend behandelt werden[59]. Als eins der wenigst bekannten Beispiele dieses Schrifttums erwähne ich den 700 Seiten umfassenden Aristoteleskommentar des Bernardus Morisonus, Derensis Ibernus (also ein Ire aus Derry), der 1625 in Frankfurt erschien.

Eine Sonderstellung nimmt Thomas Carve ein, der sich als Kaplan der englischen, schottischen und irischen Kontingente in der kaiserlichen Armee (im dreißigjährigen Kriege) bezeichnete und damit der Mann gewesen wäre zu entscheiden, ob Deveroux und seine Genossen an Wallenstein einen Mord verübt hatten oder einen legitimen Befehl ausführten[60]. Sein 'Itinerarium' erschien gleichzeitig in der bereits erwähnten deutschen Übersetzung (Mainz 1640) und rief, wegen seiner Behauptung, erst die Engländer hatten Irland zivilisiert, eine Kontroverse mit dem irischen Franziskaner Bruodin in Prag hervor, die bereits die typischen Züge von Emigrantengezänk aufweist. Walter Deveroux' Zeugnis für Carve ist die erste Urkunde eines Iren in deutscher Sprache. Die deutsche Übersetzung von Carves Werk ist m. W. noch nie im einzelnen mit dem lateinischen Original verglichen worden, obgleich längst bekannt ist, daß erstere mehr enthält als letztere. Seite 288 (am Ende des ersten Buches) hat sie z.B. folgenden ihr eigenen Satz:

---

56   S. meine am Anfang von Anm. 6 genannte Arbeit.

57   M. Sieber, Die Universität Basel im 16. Jahrhundert und ihre englischen Besucher, Basler Zeitschrift 55 (1956) 86 und 95.

58   S. meine Besprechung des Katalogs irischer Materialien in der Sammlung Nunziatura di Fiandra (aus der Kölner Nuntiatur hervorgegangen) im Vatikan in 'Collectanea Hibernica' I (Dublin 1958), in Z. f. Kirchengesch. 70 (1959) 186f.

59   S. Anm. 51 und J. H., Augustine Gibbon de Burgo (ein irischer Augustiner in Erfurt), IER 69 (1947) 135-151.

60   Wieder meine am Beginn von Anm. 6 genannte Arbeit.

»Und so viel von meiner Reyse, der Allmächtige Friedfürst und barmhertzige Emmanuel verleihe allen Fürsten und Potentaten dess Heyligen Römischen Reichs seine heilige Gnade, daß sie dermahlen eins gedencken, einen allgemeinen Frieden auszurichten und darbey zu erhalten. Amen. Also vollendet und geschlossen 1636.«

Der Übersetzer P. K. ist, z.b. durch seine Interpretation irischer Namen, ein wichtiger Zeuge für das, was man zu jener Zeit an deutscher Irlandkunde erwarten konnte und was nicht. Im Zusammenhang mit einem Studium der ersten englischen Übersetzung der 'Geschichte des dreißigjährigen Krieges', die ein irischer Offizier Ende des 18. Jahrhunderts veröffentlichte, bin ich Schillers Irlandkunde, vor allem soweit sie sich in diesem Werke zeigt, nachgegangen[61]. Es wäre nachzutragen, daß das von Schiller im Wallenstein von Iren, insbesondere Butler, entworfene Bild mehr Sachkenntnis verrät, als man wohl anzunehmen geneigt ist. Ich habe ferner erstmalig die beiden im Britischen Museum aufbewahrten deutschen Drucke von 1631 wieder veröffentlicht, die sich auf die etwa achthundert Iren in der mit Gustav Adolph nach Deutschland gekommenen Armee beziehen[62].

Das siebzehnte Jahrhundert brachte nicht nur durch die irischen Kontingente in den auf deutschem Boden kämpfenden Armeen – das größte natürlich in denen Ludwigs XIV. – sondern auch erstmalig durch deutsche Kontingente auf irischem Boden neue Impulse für die deutsche Irlandkunde. Ein merkwürdiges Zeugnis ist vielleicht der, in Deutschland z. B. in der Flugschriftensammlung Gustav Freytag in Frankfurt a.M. erhaltene 'Catalogus etlicher sehr alter Bücher,welche newlich in Irrlandt auff einem alten eroberten Schlosse in einer Bibliothek aufgefunden worden' (1663), eine Liste skurriler angeblicher Titel, die einerseits zeigt, daß man von den Kriegen in Irland eine Ahnung hatte, andererseits das Absinken der Tradition von Irland als Wunderland ins Lächerliche (vielleicht angeregt durch die erst mit Schiller ganz überwundene Schreibweise »Irrland«[63]) illustriert. Zudem ist diese Liste wohl nicht einfach eine Verhöhnung des Katholizismus überhaupt, sondern des bis heute als abergläubig verschrieenen irischen Katholizismus. Ein Nachkomme von Tobias Cramer, eines deutschen Soldaten unter James I, war Anfang des 18. Jahrhunderts ein angesehener Bürger in Cork in Irland.

Der Krieg in Irland Ende des 17. Jahrhunderts brachte, insbesondere im Zusammenhang mit der führenden Rolle Schombergs in der Schlacht am Boyne, ein umfangreiches deutschsprachiges Schrifttum hervor, teils Pamphlete, teils dickleibige Werke[64], aber fand – im Gegensatz zu Frankreich[65] – nur geringen Niederschlag in der

---

61 Modern Language Review 55 (1960) 249-254.

62 Nochmals meine am Beginn von Anm. 6 genannte Arbeit.

63 In der Geschichte der deutschen Irlandkunde sind die Geschichten der deutschen Worte für Irland und die Iren von Bedeutung. Das bei Johannes a Via (s. S. 621) und noch bei Grimmelshausen vorkommende Wort »Schotten« für das Land lebt in dem Namen eines ursprünglich zu einem Irenkloster gehörigen Ortes in Hessen nach. Zu »Schottenpfaffa« im 'Volksbuch von Till Eulenspiegel' (1519) merkt K. Pannier (Reclam S. 135) an: »Irischer Benediktiner«. »Schotte hatte zeitweilig die Bedeutung von »Vagabund«.

64 J. H., Ulster Journal of Archaeology II (1948) 65-80.

Literatur im engeren Sinne, etwa in den Gedichten Benjamin Neukirchs auf die Flucht James' II und die Thronbesteigung des Oraniers sowie den Epitaph auf Tyrconnell[66]. Zu den geographisch-historischen Werken von Happel und Baer (1689 und 1690)[67], in denen ich die deutsche Stellungnahme zu diesen Ereignissen untersuchte, kann man die Ausführungen über Irland in Leutholf von Franckenbergs ‚Europäischem Herold' (1735) ii, 234ff. stellen. Hier hört man einerseits immer noch die klassischen Überlieferungen, daß Irland »von giftigen thieren und geschmeiß und fröschen ganz rein« sei und daß dort Holz nicht verrotte[68]. Das traditionelle Bild der Iren als »gute faule Gesellen, aber verwegene schlimme Leute, im Kriege dauerhafftig und tapfer, selten krank« andererseits wird ergänzt durch aus wirklicher Kenntnis geschöpften Informationen: Die Iren sind »leichtsinnig, unruhig und unbeständig in ihrer devotion gegen ihre Oberen«, ja, ein Niveau von Kenntnis, das bereits auf Goethe hindeutet[69], wird erreicht in dem Satze: »Ihre Hoffnung ist offt ohne Vernunft und ihre Furcht ohne Grund«.

Happel, Baer und v. Franckenberg stellen das Schicksal Irlands vom Standpunkt des Protestantismus aus dar. Ein anderer literarischer Niederschlag der Pfälzer Protestantensiedlung in Irland um jene Zeit als der in Dublin 1710 erfolgte Nachdruck der in Frankfurt a. O. 1704 veröfftentlichten deutschen Übersetzung des 'Book of Common Prayer' ist mir nicht bekannt[70]. Die Iren, die in österreichischen Diensten im Laufe des 18. Jahrhunderts hohe Stellungen erlangten, haben erstaunlich wenig zur festländischen Irlandkunde oder zu einer katholischen Stellungnahme beigetragen. Goethe erwähnte z. B. von den O' Donnells nie ihre irische Abstammung[71]. Die 'Historia descriptive Hiberniae' von William O'Kelly, eques Hibernus (Wien 1703), eine Popularisierung der Mitteilungen von Bruodin und O'Flaherty, enthält eine Elegie auf die Leiden Irlands unter Cromwell und die Vernachlässigung Irlands im Frieden von Rijswijk. In seinem Gedicht 'Hibernia', dem ersten Irland selbst gewidmeten Gedicht, das auf deutschem Boden entstand, rief O'Kelly den Kaiser auf, sich Irlands zu erbarmen. O'Kelly erhielt den Titel eines poeta laureatus und Kaiserlichen Rats. Ein Nachfahre von William D. O'Kelly, der 1767 den Maria-Theresiaorden erhielt und in den Grafenstand erhoben wurde, war der Goethe befreundete Beichtvater der Königin von Sachsen. Ein Nachkomme dieser Familie ist Scan T. O'Kelly, weiland Präsident der Republik Irland, und ein Mitglied dieser Familie in Irland trägt heute noch den

---

65   J. H., ibid. 12 (1949) 89-97.

66   G. Waterhouse, The literary relations of England and Germany in the seventeenth century (Oxford 1914) 84.

67   S. Anm. 64.

68   S. Anm. 39.

69   J. H., Goethes Irlandkunde, DVjs. 31 (1957) 70-83.

70   J. H., Irish Book Lover 30 (1946-48) 89-91. S. G. W. Schumacher, The settlement of Palatines in Ireland 1709-15, Bulletin Irish Historical Soc. no. 58 (Mai 1948), 3.

71   Vgl. J. H., 'Mozart and Ireland', Irish Monthly 75 (1947) 377-381 u. 'Beethoven and Ireland', dass. 332-338, sowie 'Trenck and Britain', Mod. Language Review 41 (1946) 397ff.

kaiserlichen Grafentitel. John Talbot Dillon revanchierte sich 1782 für den ihm vom Kaiser für seine Verdienste um seine Landsleute im irischen Parlament verliehenen Feldherrntitel durch ein in London erschienenes 400 Seiten umfassendes Werk über das Heilige Römische Reich. Erst der Anfang des 19. Jahrhunderts brachte literarische Zeugnisse von Interesse an Irland seitens des katholischen Deutschland hervor.

Im Hinblick auf die spätere deutsche Irlandkunde ist einer der wichtigsten Abschnitte in von Franckenbergs Werk der, in dem er über die sprachlichen Verhältnisse in Irland spricht. Die deutsche Kenntnis der irischen Sprache läßt sich sporadisch weit zurückverfolgen. Die 'Vita S. Findani' enthält die ersten auf dem Festland niederge-schriebenen Sätze in irischer Sprache; ihre Wiedergabe in der handschriftlichen Tra-dition und ihre Interpretation u. a. durch einen auf festländische Ignoranz sich ver-lassenden Schotten[72] ist ein amüsantes Vorspiel zur Entwicklung der keltischen Stu-dien in Deutschland[73]. Wir wissen kaum, wie weit die altirischen Eintragungen in dem Münchener Glossar (9. Jh.) im Mittelalter gewürdigt worden sind[74] oder ob das mit irischen Eintragungen durchsetzte Kalendarium im Karlsruher Beda von Deutschen benutzt wurde[75], aber mannigfach sind die Erwähnungen der irischen Sprache in der Hagiographie. Schon in den Viten der hl. Columbanus und Gallus wird das Problem erahnt, daß die Iren auf dem Festland die Landessprachen lernen mußten, um die ihnen zunächst unerwartete Aufgabe zu erfüllen, Glaubensboten zu sein. In der 'Chronik von Waulsort' und der damit zusammenhängenden 'Vita S. Forannani', in Ekkehards Fortsetzung der 'Casus S. Galli', in den Viten der hl. Furseus und Rumold[76] und in der 'Visio Tundali' wird entweder der »barbarischen« Sprache der Iren gedacht oder der Notwendigkeit, aus ihr zu übersetzen. Gottfrieds 'Tristan' enthält den in der deutschen Literatur des Mittelalters einzigartigen Hinweis auf die Verbreitung des Französischen durch die Normannen in Irland, ein Aspekt, der durch Lappenbergs überragenden Artikel in Ersch-Gruber I (1845) xxiv, 56 erstmalig in der deutschen Literatur wissenschaftlich aufgegriffen wurde.

Daß die Tatsache, daß die Deutschen wie keine andere Nation sich des Studiums der irischen Sprache und Literatur angenommen haben, aus dem Ossianismus herzuleiten ist, haben Zeuß und später Stern und in unseren Tagen Thurneysen eindrucksvoll ausgesprochen[77]. Der erste Deutsche, der die irische Sprache an Ort und Stelle studier-te, war Küttner, ein Bekannter Goethes, der, wie ich gezeigt habe[78], in seiner Eigen-schaft als Hauslehrer des Sohnes eines irischen Lords das erste von einem Deutschen

---

72　H. Zimmer, Glossae Hibernicae (1881) 272-274

73　J. H., Besprechung der so betitelten Schrift von H. Bauersfeld, Irish Historical Studies 4 (1944) 119-121.

74　H. Zimmer, Z. f. vgl. Sprachforschung 33 (1893) 274-294.

75　J. H., Mediaeval Studies 19 (1957) 231.

76　MG SS xiv, 512, zu den hagiographischen Texten J. Kenney, Sources for the early history of Ireland I (New York 1929).

77　'Why do Germans study Irish philology', Studies 19 (Dublin 1930) 26.

78　S. meinen [in] Anm. 69 genannten Artikel S. 73.

ausschließlich Irland gewidmete Buch schrieb und darin vollständige irische Texte, z.B. das Vaterunser, abdruckte, so zuverlässig, daß sich die ersten deutschen Keltisten wie Ahlwardt und Vater darauf beriefen. Goethe aber nimmt auf diesem wie auf praktisch allen Gebieten der deutschen Irlandkunde wohl die bedeutendste Stellung ein: Er war der erste Deutsche, von dem wir wissen, daß er einen gälischen Text ins Deutsche übersetzte.

An Goethe kann man auch am besten sehen, wie wenig Irlandkunde der Einfluß der frühen anglo-irischen Literatur den Deutschen vermittelte. Von Swift, Sterne, Goldsmith und Steele wußte man kaum mehr, als daß sie in ihrem äußeren Lebensgang etwas mit Irland zu tun hatten[79]. In seinen Aussagen über Robert Boyle aber hat Goethe bereits Charakterzüge erkannt, die den Anglo-Iren vom Engländer unterscheiden, und das was er im Zusammenhang mit seinen Reflexionen über den Shandeismus über die Iren gesagt hat, ist bis heute unübertroffen[80]. Während Herder nur ganz am Rande auf Irland zu sprechen kam, z. B. in dem Abschnitt über die »Galen« in seinen 'Ideen'[81], und Jean Paul aus seinem Zettelkasten nur ein buntes aber zusammenhangloses Irlandbild hinschüttete[82], ist Goethe der erste Deutsche gewesen, bei dem man von Irlandkunde in dem komplexen Sinne sprechen kann, den das Wort einschließt. Praktisch kein Lebensgebiet ist ihm entgangen, vieles war aus erster Quelle, nichts blieb oberflächlich, trotz der Entlegenheit des Gegenstandes. Goethe stellte den Maßstab auf, an dem auch die im einzelnen natürlich weit über ihn hinausgreifenden Leistungen der deutschen Irlandkunde bis auf unsere Tage zu messen sind.

(Quelle: DVLG 35, 1961, S. 221-233.)

---

79 Dass., 75, ferner J. H., Swift in Switzerland, Irish Book Lover 30 (1946) 54f. und 'Two Irish bulls in Kant's Kritik der Urteilskraft', Modern Language Quarterly 8 (1947) 487f.

80 S. meine [in] Anm. 69 genannte Arbeit S. 74.

81 S. Anm. 33.

82 J. H., Jean Paul and Ireland, Modern Language Review 40 (1945) 190-196 zu ergänzen durch dass. 49 (1954) 352. Eine Geschichte der deutschen Irlandkunde im neunzehnten Jahrhundert würde erst recht die Zusammenhanglosigkeit der deutschen Irlandkunde vor Goethe aufzeigen.

Studien zur deutschsprachigen Irlandkunde im 19. Jahrhundert

Das erste Jahrtausend der Beschäftigung Deutschsprachiger mit Irland[1] fand in Goethe seinen – auch seither – unübertroffenen Höhepunkt[2]: Von keinem Deutschsprachigen, der nicht selbst in Irland gewesen ist, läßt sich eine vielseitigere Kenntnisnahme Irlands (Sprache, Psychologie, Kirchen-, Literatur-, Staats- und Wissenschaftsgeschichte, Geographie, Geologie, Wetterkunde) nachweisen. Goethe war auch der erste Deutsche, der ein Gedicht verfaßte, in dessen Titel das Wort »Irisch« vorkommt[3].

1799 erschien im 'Neuen Teutschen Merkur' ein 'Ossian' betiteltes Gedicht, in dem es nach einer an den dritten Vers von Goethes 'Mignon' erinnernden Naturschilderung heißt:»So greift in mein Inneres mächtig ein die Kühnheit der Dichtung Ossians.« Nicht nur in der Dichtung[5], sondern auch in der Journalistik ist das deutschsprachige Irlandbild weitgehend bis heute von der pseudo-ossianischen Schwärmerei bestimmt geblieben: Man betrachte nur die Titel einiger während der letzten 25 Jahre erschienenen Irlandbücher: 'Die seltsame Insel' (Segner), 'Die Insel der Elfen, Esel und Rebellen' (Grubbe), 'Heimat des Regenbogens' (Johann), 'Im Land der Rhododendren und Harfen' (Feldhoff), welche den Leser kaum auf die harte Realität vorbereiten, die ihm im politischen Bereich entgegentritt.

Schon in dem Gedicht 'Die Fremdlinge' in 'Legenden' (1787)[6] hatte Herder das Ossianische Interesse mit dem um diese Zeit auch auf den nichtkatholischen Bereich übergreifenden Popularinteresse an der Tradition der Tätigkeit der Iren auf dem frühmittel-

---

1   J. H.: DVjs. 35. 1961. S. 617-629.

2   J. H.: DVjs. 31. 1975. S. 70-83. Hierzu jetzt die Bezugnahmen auf Irland und Iren in den Tagebüchern und Briefen von und an Ottlie v. Goethe. Wien 1962ff. Ferner ist aus H. Rupperts Katalog von Goethes Bibliothek. 1958. nachzutragen, daß Goethe besaß: 1. Ancient Histories of Ireland (Spencer, Camden, Hanmer, Marlborough) Dublin 1633; 2. P. A. Nemnich: Neueste Reise [1805-06] durch England, Schottland und Ireland [so durchweg in diesem Buch] hauptsächlich im Bezug auf Produkte, Fabriken und Handlung Tübingen 1807. und im gleichen Jahre von Goethe angekauft; allerdings erwähnt Goethes Tagebuch 4. und 7.8.1807 nicht den (87 von 750 Seiten umfassenden) Teil über Irland, in dem sich bemerkenswerte Urteile finden:»Ireland wird bisher als ein unterworfenes Reich vom Britischen Gouvernement behandelt ... Die Verarmung des Mittelstandes nimmt täglich zu ... Im Ganzen genommen scheint der kultivierte Theil der irländischen Katholiken keine Religion zu besitzen, und der unkultivierte oder größte Theil gar keine Begriffe von Religion zu haben. Von dem Karakter und den Fähigkeiten der katholischen Geistlichen in Ireland wird im Allgemeinen nicht viel Gutes gesagt ... Ungereizt leben die irländischen Katholiken sehr friedlich und beschämen die Protestanten durch ihren Duldungsgeist«; 3. Keightley: Mythologie der Feenwelt. Weimar 1828, s.u. Anm. 26; 4.

3   Siehe meine in Anm. 2 genannte Arbeit S. 73f.

4   Dies in Ergänzung meiner Arbeit über Irlands Stellung in der deutschen Dichtung des 19. Jahrhunderts. In: German Life and Letters. N.S.A. 1955. S. 201-207.

5   Bis zu dem Gedicht von Otto zur Linde (1901), ebd. S. 206, dazu Reinhold Schneiders Sonett 'Irland' (1940). – Beethovens irische Lieder wären nicht nur als Ausdruck (s. J. H.: Irish Monthly 75. 1947. 332-338) sondern als bis heute wirkende Quelle deutscher Irlandkunde zu würdigen.

6   Ebd. S. 201f.

alterlichen Festland verbunden. 1787 waren G. W. Zapfs 'Reisen in einige Klöster Schwabens, durch den Schwarzwald und in die Schweiz im Jahre 1781' erschienen, in denen von Fridolin, Gallus, Kolumban und vor allem Fintan von Rheinau als »aus Irrland gebürtig« die Rede war[7]. 1804 bot Kosegarten in seinem ebenfalls 'Legenden' betitelten Werk u.a. 'Das Gesicht des heiligen Forseus' (ohne Bezug auf die Quellen, vor allem Bedas Bericht über die Vision des Iren Fursaeus), sowie im Anhang 'Die Irrfahrten des heiligen Brandanus' (wieder ohne Bezug auf das Ursprungsland); der letztere Text gab 67 Jahre später Gottfried Keller die (unausgeführt gebliebene) Idee, als achte seiner 'Legenden' eine über Brandanus zu schreiben[8].

Ein weiteres Zeugnis dieses neuen, oft lokalgeschichtlich orientierten Interesses findet man in Johann Peter Hebels 'Fortsetzung der vaterländischen Geschichte' (1815), worin es heißt, daß das Christentum »von England und Irland her sein Lichtlein im Schwarzwald anzündete. Der erste, der aus jenem Land auf einer langen Pilgerreise wahrscheinlich um das Jahr n. Chr. G. 512 in den Schwarzwald kam, war der heilige Fridolin«. Da Hebel fortfährt, daß »auch Trudpert, Pirmin, Landolin u.a. im unteren Munstertal Verehrte aus England gekommen« seien, bezieht sich der Ausdruck »aus jenem Land« auf England, oder faßte Hebel - nach einer bis heute nicht ausgestorbenen Angewohnheit - Irland als Teil von England auf? Letzterer Vorstellung wirkte schon vom Titel her des Kieler Historikers Dietrich Hermann Hegewisch

> 'Übersicht der irländischen Geschichte zur richtigen Einsicht in die entferntesten und näheren Ursachen der Rebellion von 1798, der Union Irlands mit Großbritannien 1801 und der noch nicht erfolgten sogenannten Emancipation der Katholiken' (Altona 1806)

entgegen.

In seiner Vorrede wies Hegewisch mit Recht darauf hin, daß vor ihm noch kein Deutscher (oder Franzose) »die irländische Geschichte in einem eigenen Werke vorgetragen« habe, obwohl es doch sonst kaum eine Nation der alten oder der modernen Zeit gäbe, deren Geschichte nicht von einem Deutschen (oder Franzosen) dargestellt worden wäre. In seiner 'Geschichte Irlands von der Reformation bis zu seiner Union mit England' (Leipzig 1886)[9] nannte R. Hassenkamp Hegewischs Werk einen bloßen Auszug aus Lelands[10], aber bis zu R. Bauers 'Insel der Rebellen' (Leipzig 1938), einer der zahlreichen nationalsozialistische Sympathie für Irland widerspiegelnden Publikationen, findet man Hegewisch zitiert[11]. Insbesondere war Hegewisch der erste, der »das

---

7   In meinen Arbeiten, von denen DVjs. 35. 1961. S. 618ff. eine kleine Auswahl aufführt, habe ich, unbekümmert um die Historizität, die Quellen und die literarische Tradition im liturgischen und historiographischen Bereich als Träger festländischer Irlandkunde zu würdigen versucht.

8   E. Ermatinger: Gottfried Keller. 1916. Bd. I. S.446.

9   Adolf Lindau: Geschichte Irlands. Dresden 1829, war mir nicht zugänglich.

10 Thomas L.: History of Ireland (1773), aber auch aus James MacGeoghegans (Paris 1758). MacGeoghegans Ouevres mêlées waren 1730 in Hamburg gedruckt worden.

11 Neuestens in Karl Holl: Die irische Frage in der Ära Daniel O'Connells und ihre Bewertung in der politischen Publizistik des deutschen Vormärz. Diss. Mainz 1958.

Schicksal der Irländer im Ganzen [...], das Schicksal der eigentlich irischen Nation« (im Unterschied zu den Angloiren, auf die sich etwa das 'Große vollständige Universal-Lexicon', Leipzig 1739, in seinem Artikel 'Irland' in Band XIV, i beschränkte) zu seinem 'Thema' machte. Er versuchte, wie es dem Außenstehenden geziemt, über den Parteistandpunkten zu stehen. So erkannte er den verderblichen Einfluß der Antikatholikengesetze[12] an, meinte aber, sie seien nicht der Staatskirche anzulasten. Er wußte, daß sich die gegenwärtige irische Nationalbewegung auf die große Überlieferung des 'goldenen Zeitalters' (von dessen Auswirkungen auf Mitteleuropa Hegewisch allerdings nur mit einem Satz – S. 16 – Notiz nahm), sah aber ein, daß schon mangels Textausgaben ihm hier wissenschaftliche Kenntnis verwehrt war. Amüsanterweise betrachtete Hegewisch als besonderes Hindernis, daß

>»die irischen Namen schwer auszusprechen und zu behalten sind. Sie beleidigen das Ohr statt es zu bezaubern. Ich nehme an, daß bloß diese unharmonischen, barbarischen Namen manchen Schriftsteller von der Bearbeitung der irländischen Geschichte abgehalten haben. Man will gern gelesen seyn; man sieht aber vorher, kein Mensch wird ein Buch lesen wollen, wo auf allen Seiten solche abschreckende Namen erscheinen«.

Als wenige Jahre später Adelung und Vater das Irische im Rahmen der gesamteuropäischen Philologie berücksichtigten, bezogen sie sich als deutsche Quelle auf Küttners Briefe über Irland (1785)[13], ein Werk, aus dem sich Hegewisch Angaben für die Religionsstatistik von Irland verschaffte. Für die jüngste Geschichte benutzte Hegewisch 'Annual Register', »ein Werk, dem man bekanntlich in der deutschen Übersetzung den Titel 'Weltbegebenheiten im Großen' gegeben hat« und auf Gordons 'History of the Rebellion' (Dublin 1801; G.s 'History of Ireland', Dublin 1805, war Hegewisch noch nicht zugänglich), auf die er aufmerksam geworden war durch eine Besprechung in 'Allg. Literatur-Zeitung' 1802 Nr. 303 (Hegewisch vermutete, daß Küttner diese Besprechung verfaßt hätte, da er schon in seinen Briefen über den Ursprung der irischen Freiwilligenbewegung berichtet hatte, ein Ereignis, von dem er damals angenommen hatte, daß es auch in sächsischen und Schweizer Zeitungen vermerkt worden sei).

Hegewisch erwähnte S. 206f., daß ein wichtiges Dokument der irischen Unabhängigkeitsbewegung, das in einem Bericht an das Secret Committee des britischen Unterhauses enthalten gewesen war, ihm wegen der Kontinentalsperre nur in einem Auszug in der 'Gazette de Leyde' Nr. XXXVI 1798 zugänglich wurde. Die Kontinentalsperre unterbrach, wie man auch bei Goethe feststellen kann, die Nährung des erwachenden deutschen Interesses am zeitgenössischen Irland. Von besonderer Bedeutung in dieser Hinsicht wurden die Übersetzungen von Werken irischer Schriftsteller, welche Kenntnis des Lebens des Volkes vermittelten. Vor allem der Verlag J. Manz in Breslau wollte durch wohlfeile Übersetzungen das Mitgefühl der deutschen Katholiken für

---

12   1688 war in Hamburg unter dem Titel 'Draconia' »ein Ausszug aller englischen Poenal-Gesetze die Sache der Religion betreffend« erschienen. Hegewisch zitiert die Poenalgsetze nach G. F. Martens' Sammlung der Grundgesetze (Göttingen 1791), ein Werk das 1795 in Philadelphia in englischer Übersetzung erschien.

13   Siehe Anm. 17 meiner in Anm. 2 genannten Arbeit.

Irland wecken. 1825 wurde durch den Untertitel 'über den Zustand von Staat, Kirche und Volk in Irland, mit historischen Anmerkungen' eine Übersetzung von Thomas Moores 'Memoirs of Captain Rock' als Informationsquelle vorgestellt, und die katholische Presse pries sie als solche an.

Der Verlag Manz veröffentlichte im folgenden Jahr die Übersetzung von Michael Whittys 'Tales of Irish Life'[14], eine der ersten echten Quellen in englischer Sprache über das erbärmliche Leben des irischen Landvolkes. Damit wird der für die Folgezeit entscheidende neue Aspekt festländischen Interesses an Irland geweckt, nämlich der soziale, und dieser entsprach einem anderen Leserkreis als dem vom Verlag zunächst ins Auge gefaßte. In seiner Besprechung sagte Börne[15], daß diese »Irländischen Erzählungen uns die große Not des Volkes in Irland, dem unglücklichen Stiefkind der englischen Regierung, zeigen«. Börne meinte allerdings, Irland leide »nicht bloß durch die Freiheit, die man ihm geraubt, sondern auch durch die, welche man ihm gelassen – die frevelhaften Neigungen des gereizten Volkes«, eine der frühsten Versionen des ambivalenten Urteils, mittels dessen Außenstehende mit dem unbegreiflichen Irland fertig zu werden suchen. Ohne selbst das Land zu kennen, nennt Börne die Eigenschaften, die vom Festland Kommende bis heute als vorzüglichste an den Iren rühmen: »Gastfreundschaft und gesellige Tugenden«.

Das ossianische Irlandbild war Ausdruck der Sturm-und-Drang-Zeit; in Hegewischs Geschichtswerk kam man Züge des Klassizismus erkennen; das auch über den katholischen Bereich hinausgreifende Interesse an der Kirchengeschichte Irlands entsprach der Romantik und den aus ihr folgenden politisch-gesellschaftlichen Bewegungen. Man kann dies beispielhaft an einem der Hauptgebiete, wo das Festland die Erinnerung an alte Verbindungen mit Irland festgehalten hat, zeigen. Das 'Neujahrsblatt der Zürcher Hilfsgesellschaft für die menschenfreundliche Jugend unserer Vaterstadt' 1826 widmete 13 Seiten Kolumban und Gallus. Diese aus dem »entfernten Irland oder Schotland« Gekommenen »erklärten den Kleinen die Worte des Evangeliums« und erteilten den Erwachsenen »Anweisungen zum Ackerbau, zur Berechnung und Vertheilung der Sämereyen«. »Hier waltete kein erdrückender Zwang, kein leeres Ceremonienwesen, keine Scheinfrömmigkeit [...] und schmähliche Heuchelei« wie in der »Klostererziehung in alten und neueren Zeiten«. Die Einführung der Benediktinerregel ersetzte den »einfachen, gesunden Religionsbegriff, das thätige Christenthum, die anständige Freyheit, welche der ehrwürdige Gallus aus dem kräftigen Norden hervorgebracht hatte« durch »den Italienischen Mönchs-Charakter, mit seinem Sclavensinn, seinen Mauern und Riegeln für Tugend und seinen Märchenkram«. (Der nordisch-antirömische Affekt macht heute die Iren eher verantwortlich für als Mißbildung Verworfenes in Buß- und Beichtpraxis. Sowohl im kirchen- wie im weltpolitischen Bereich wird das entfernte Irland immer wieder demagogisch benutzt).

---

14 Siehe meine Notiz in: Irish Bookman. February 1947. Zur deutschen Übersetzung von Maria Edgeworths 'Castle Rackrent' vgl. Emily Lawless: Maria Edgeworth. 1904, S. 91f., und S. 76 meiner in Anm. 2 genannten Arbeit.

15 Sämt. Schriften. Bd. II. 1964. S. 468ff.

1837 behandelte Caspar Schiesser (Baden/Aargau) den heiligen Gallus in 12 Balladen. Wir hören hier, daß »hoch im ew'gen Norden der Scotten Fürsten« und »weit jenseits Landes und Meeres auf Erin im Norden Irlands damals Scoten wohnten«. 1842 wurde zu einem in Arbon abgehaltenen Sängerfest von dem dortigen reformierten Pfarrer Thomas Bornhauser als Festgabe ein Epos über den heiligen Gallus angeboten, welchem 1930 die Ehre widerfuhr, nochmals abgedruckt zu werden. Bornhauser hatte eine führende Rolle in der Aargauer Bewegung für Aufhebung der Kloster gespielt; als er sich aus der Politik wieder in sein geistliches Amtsleben zurückzog, war es ihm aber doch ein lieber Gedanke, in Arbon Nachfolger der frühmittelalterlichen Missionare zu werden. Im 5. Kapitel seines Werkchens erscheint ganz ossianisch einem auf dem Festland Träumenden »eine große Insel aus den Nebeln des Meeres. Dort herrschte der König Gormal über die Stämme des schottischen Hochgebirges und das schöne Eiland, das man wohl auch das grüne Erin nennt«. In der Vorrede hatte Bornhauser gesagt, daß er, »was die Geschichte verschwieg, nach seiner Weise ergänze«. So hören wir weiter, daß das von Gormal und seiner Gemahlin Minona bewohnte Schloß Kromla (Name eines ossianischen Helden) am Lego-See lag. IV, 12 ist bei Bornhauser von der »schönen Minona« die Rede; »Minona in ihrer Schönheit« ist bekannt aus Goethes Übersetzung aus 'Songs of Selma', und am 2. September 1797 hatte Goethe in Stuttgart auf der Reise in die Schweiz Zumsteegs Cantate 'Colma' »nach meiner Übersetzung« gehört: »Wenn man Minona, die sänge, ... vorstellte, so müßte die Aufführung nicht ohne Effect seyn«. Goethes Übersetzung der Stelle aus dem 7. Buch von 'Temora', wo von dem Legosee die Rede ist, wurde erst 1911 bekannt; Bornhausers Quelle war hier wohl Ahlwardts Übersetzung (in der Vorrede zu der 1839 gedruckten Ausgabe dieser Übersetzung hatte Goeschen gesagt, daß der wohlklingende Name Minona bei uns längst eingebürgert ist). Anderseits kannte Bornhauser natürlich die Ossianstellen im 'Werther'. In Kap. XVIII träumt Gallus, daß ihn Friedeburg, die Tochter des Herzogs, auffordere,

> sein hochländisches Kleid anzuziehen und heimatliche Lieder zu singen. Ich höre die Sagen des Hochlands so gern, und die Lieder von Erin sind meiner Seele, was der Thau des Himmels ist der durstenden Blume. Da griff Gallus nach seiner Harfe und sang von Komlas Tod und Fingals Schmerz (Conlath and Cuthona),

und es folgt eine verkitschte Version der Szene zwischen Lotte und Werther, gewürzt dadurch, daß es sich um den Traum eines Mönchs handelt. Dem von Bornhauser (und seinem Biographen J. Christinger)[16] irrtümlich mit dem in Wales statt dem im Norden Irlands identifizierten Kloster Bangor stand (nach Bornhauser) Kolumban »mit großer Strenge vor« (von dem 1826 gezeichneten Bild irischen Mönchtums ist also nichts übrig geblieben). In der Schweiz wurden die »Männer aus Erin« oder »schottischen Mönche« schlecht aufgenommen. Man sieht die Perpetuierung der aus dem mittelalterlichen Gebrauch von Scotia stammenden Terminologie, die bis heute in dem Ausdruck 'iro-schottisch'[17] nachlebt.

---

16   1875. S. 227.

17   Siehe meine Artikel hierzu im Lexikon für Theologie und Kirche 2. Aufl.

Schon drei Jahre vor Bornhausers Werk »scheint Jakob Burckhardt eine Arbeit verfaßt und veröffentlicht zu haben, die in den Bereich dieses Themas gehört: 'Die schottischen Glaubensboten in der Schweiz' ('Der Wanderer in der Schweiz' VI (1839) 353ff.)«[18]. 1846 folgte dann in dem in 1.300 Exemplaren in der Schule verteilten 'Neujahrsblatt für Basels Jugend' der sicher von Burckhardt stammende Aufsatz 'Die Alemannen und ihre Bekehrung zum Christentum'[19]. »Aus weiter Ferne her, von dem äußersten Ende der gesitteten Welt, berief die Vorsehung diejenigen Glaubensboten, welche unserm Vaterland das Christentum bringen sollten, nämlich aus dem keltischen Irland.« Dort, so hören wir weiter, hatte »das Christentum aus der Römerzeit überlebt [...] abgeschnitten von der römischen Kirche, die Überlieferung, welche an die schönen Zeiten des Urchristentums erinnert, bewahrt: Sie legten z. B. nur mäßiges Gewicht auf Fasten [...] ihre Priester waren verheiratet«. Diese Irländer suchten »ihren Wirkungskreis auf dem Festlande und nicht unter den näher wohnenden Angelsachsen«, weil letztere einen »heftigen Nationalhaß gegen das mit ihnen im Kampf befindliche Keltenvolk« hatten. Mit Hebel betrachtete Burckhardt als »ersten Irländer, welcher als Glaubensbote auf das Festland und zwar gerade in unsere Gegend kam, Fridolin, Sohn eines irischen Grafen«. (Hundert Jahre später waren es) »wiederum Irländer, und zwar diesmal die bedeutendsten, welche die 'grüne Insel' (so nennt man Irland) je ausgesandt hat: Columbanus, Gallus und ihre elf Gefährten«. Es wäre interessant, die Quellen für diese Serie von Fehlurteilen zu ermitteln[20].

Zur gleichen Zeit, als die genannten Übersetzungen irischer Literaturwerke bei Manz in Breslau erschienen, veröffentlichten die Grimms ihre Übersetzung von Thomas Crofton Crokers 'Fairy Lgends' unter dem Titel 'Irische Elfenmärchen'. Was zu dieser Übersetzung Konrad Sandkühler in seinem Nachwort zu der kürzlich[21] im Verlag Freies Geistesleben, Stuttgart, erschienenen Neuauflage gesagt hat – das anthroposophische Interesse an den »hybernischen Mysterien« ist jenseits unserer Themastellung – wäre zu ergänzen aus meinen m. W. erstmalig das Verhältnis der Brüder Grimm zu Croker behandelnden Arbeiten[22]. Schon vor seinem Aufsatz vom Jahre 1846 hatte Jakob Burckhardt erkannt, daß *in Hibernicis* Vorsicht verboten ist. In seinem Brief vom 2. Oktober 1842 an Heinrich Schreiber verglich er dessen damals

18 E. Dürrs Einl. zu Burckhardts Werke. Bd. I. 1930. S. xlvi. – 1840 erschien in Bonn 'De Culdeis' von dem Hermesianer J.W.J. Braun.

19 Werke. Bd. I. S. 327.

20 Diese Jugendsünden machte B. später mehr als gut durch eine Bemerkung Spitteler gegenüber (dessen Werke. Bd. VI. 197. S. 385f.) »bedauernd, im Tone der Hoffnungslosigkeit: 'Ich sehe nicht ein, wo in Europa in all den starren festgefügten Staatengebilden etwas Neues entstehen könnte. Höchstens vielleicht in Irland, das sich von England abtrennte', und sein Achselzucken fügte hinzu: 'Und selbst das wäre mager'«. Zu Viktor Scheffels Irlandkunde siehe meine Arbeit in: Irish Ecclesiastical Record. 87. 1957. S. 186 bis 193.

21 1948 erschien eine Ausgabe in der Sammlung 'für Kindheit und Jugend' in: Weidmannsche Bibliothek Bd. 3.

22 Modern Language Review. 41. 1946. S. 44-54; 42. 1947. S. 237-242 und 43. 1948. S. 62f. Hierzu nun einige Ergänzungen.

gerade in Freiburg erschienene 'historisch-archäologische Monographie Die Feen in Europa' (die Basler Universitätsbibliothek besitzt das von Schreiber Burckhardt geschenkte Exemplar) mit den 'Irischen Elfenmärchen'. Dabei sagte er: »Vor Rezensionen bedeutender Gelehrter Norddeutschlands über Ihre Celtica sind Sie leider sicher, aus dem einfachen Grunde, weil über diesen Gegenstand fast kein Mensch hier zu Lande mitsprechen kann«.[23]

Wenn man, wie Sandkühler, Crokers Werk in die Geschichte der irischen Folklore- und insbesondere Märchenstudien einordnen will, so muß man K. J. Clements 'Reisen in Irland' (Kiel 1845)[24] berücksichtigen, wo auf S. 111 mit ungewöhnlicher Sachkunde Beziehungen zwischen irischen und friesischen Vorstellungen behandelt wurden. Croker dürfte Tiecks 'Elfen' in der ersten, 1823 erschienenen englischen Übersetzungen gekannt haben; Tieck seinerseits besaß ein Exemplar von Crokers 'Researches in the South of Ireland'[25]. Die Grimms wußten, daß 'Fairy Legends' nicht nur von Croker stammten, sondern auch von Thomas Keightley dessen 'Fairy Mythology' 1828 erschien. B. G. McCarthy, Verfasser einer Arbeit über Keightley[26], teilte mir mit, er habe einen Brief von Keightley an Croker gesehen, der diese Mitverfasserschaft beleuchtete. 'Fairy Legends' wurde in 'Göttingener Gelehrte Anzeigen' I, 6 (12.1.1826) von Wilhelm Grimm besprochen; aus dieser Besprechung geht hervor – was wir aus der 'Deutschen Grammatik' wissen –, daß die Brüder Grimm weit über Croker hinaus Kenntnis irischer Dinge besaßen; sie bedürfte gesonderter Darstellung. Croker erwähnt in der Vorrede zur 2. Auflage der 'Fairy Legends' (1826), er fühle sich geschmeichelt, daß sie von den Herren Grimm übersetzt worden seien, er selbst aber habe noch kein Exemplar von ,Mährchen und Sagen aus Süd-Irland' (Leipzig 1825) gesehen (ich auch nicht).

Sandkühlers Ausgabe läßt die Anmerkungen, die Rutz in seiner Ausgabe (München 1913) gekürzt wiedergegeben hat, ganz weg. Diese Anmerkungen waren von den Grimms übersetzt und mit (durch Sternchen bezeichneten) Zusätzen versehen worden; sie sind für Croker, die Grimms und ihr Verhältnis zu Croker interessant, von ihrem Wert für die Geschichte der irischen Märchenforschung und deutscher Kenntnis davon ganz zu schweigen.

Die Grimms hörten von Croker[27] durch einen Iren Cooper anläßlich seines Aufenthalts in Kassel, vielleicht den Astronomen Joshua C., der um diese Zeit Deutschland

23   Jacob Burckhardt: Briefe. Ed. Max Burckhardt. 1949. Bd. I. S. 215. 346. und 369.

24   Meine Arbeit in 'Bealoideas' (dem Organ der Irish Folklore Commission) 16. 1946. S. 251-256 ist m. W. die einzige Studie über dieses Buch.

25   E. H. Zeydel: Tieck in England. 1931. S. 182 und 246.

26   Studies (Dubliner Jesuitenzeitschrift) 1943. S. 547.

27   In ihrer Vorrede zu Irische Elfenmärchen sprachen die Grimms von Irland als einem Land, »an das wir gewöhnlich nur in weniger und gerade nicht erfreulichen Beziehungen erinnert werden«, vielleicht ein Bezug auf die Stationierung der aus Hannover rekrutierten German Legion in Irland, von der man im Erscheinungsjahr der Elfenmärchen durch die in Hannover veröffentlichten Erinnerungen H. Herings (s. DVjs. 35. 1961. S. 618) Näheres hörte. Auch

bereiste. (Ein anderer Ire traf in Dresden einen Herrn »Schr-r«, den sein »unersättlicher Durst nach Nachrichten über England« (!) veranlaßte, Crokers 'Fairy Legends' zu lesen.)[28] Wilhelm Grimm bedauerte, keine eigene Kenntnis von Irland zu besitzen, und erkannte, daß intime Kenntnis dieses eigenartigen Landes für das Verständnis auch seiner Märchen unentbehrlich sei. Croker zitierte diesen Satz aus Wilhelm Grimms Brief an ihn[29]. Zwischen den ersten deutschen Reisebüchern über Irland, denen von Volkmann und Küttner, und den gleichzeitig mit 'Fairy Legends' bzw. 'Irische Elfenmärchen' erschienenen von Georg Depping (deutsch Pesth 1828) und Pückler-Muskau (die von Goethe 1830 besprochenen 'Briefe eines Verstorbenen') verhinderten die politischen Verhältnisse derartige Publikationen. Depping war der erste Reise-schriftsteller, der Irland vom katholischen Standpunkt aus darstellte.

Duncker sagte, daß die Grimms die Übersetzung von Crokers Werk als Erholung vom Abschreiben des Kasseler Bibliothekskatalogs unternahmen. In dem Artikel 'Irland' in Brockhaus' 'Conversations-Lexicon' (1827) wurden Crokers 'Researchers' erwähnt. Die anonymen 'Skizzen aus Irland oder Bilder aus Irlands Vergangenheit von einem Wanderer' (Stuttgart 1838) bezogen offenbar Nachrichten aus Crokers Werken, aber auch der in diesem Werke übersetzte William Carleton hatte Kunde von irischem Glauben an fairies (S.76 f.: »Feen«) gegeben[30]. Lappenbergs Artikel 'Irland' im Ersch-

---

Venedys Irland (1841, s.u.) nahm auf diese unerfreuliche Verbindung zwischen Deutschland und Irland Bezug, und noch 1846 schrieb C. M. O'Keefe in seinem O'Connell (S. 704): »Still in 1846 the king of Hanover placed at the disposal of Queen Victoria 20,000 Hanoverian troops – all Protestants – who by the aid of steam could be transferred from the German to the Irish shore in four days.«

28   S. 47 Anm. 2 meines in Anm. 22 genannten Artikels.

29   In dem 28 Seiten umfassenden Widmungsschreiben an die Brüder Grimm, das er dem 3. Band der Fairy Legends (1828) voranstellte. Der erste Teil dieses Bandes besteht aus einer Über-setzung der vorwiegend von Wilhelm Grimm stammenden 'Einleitung über die Elfen' (Sand-kühlers Ausgabe. S. 9-63).

30   1835 war bei Cotta eine Darstellung des gegenwärtigen Zustandes Irlands erschienen, deren un-genannter Verfasser (s. K. Holl – oben Anm. 11 – S. 71) sich in der Vorrede gegen Kritik verteidigte, die er während langjähriger Beobachtung Irlands erfahren hatte. Er sprach sich für katholischen Loyalismus (England gegenüber) und gegen Gewalttätigkeit aus. Es ist nicht aus-geschlossen, daß er mit dem Verfasser der Skizzen identisch ist, welcher sich z. B. gegen die Methoden der protestantischen Proselytenmacher in Irland wandte (die Gegenseite stellen als Basler Traktate 'Die arme Irländerin' und 'Die Kraft des Evangeliums, aus dem Leben einer Irländerin' (Basel 1840) dar, auf die ich in Basler Nachrichten 23.5.1954 aufmerksam machte). Die Skizzen enthalten S. 71-158 eine Übersetzung von William Carletons Erzählung 'Der Todtboxer' (s.o., Anm. 28) aus »jener Zeit [frühes 18. Jahrhundert!], wo das Irisch noch als Volkssprache bestand«. In Carletons Worten: »Devotion or piety may be frequently found among peasantry associated with objects that would appear to have but little connection with it«, gab der deutsche Übersetzer: »may ... peasantry« wieder mit: »wurden von dem irischen Landvolk, wie von allen rohen Nationen, in jenen Zeiten häufig«. Vier weitere Erzählungen von Carleton, die Lappenberg als »geistreich und wahr« pries, wurden deutschen Lesern durch Helffreich (s.u.) zugänglich gemacht.

Gruber, von dem gleich zu sprechen sein wird, bezog sich ausgiebig auf Crokers Werke und die Grimmsche Übersetzung; das Gleiche gilt von 'Erin, eine Auswahl vorzüglicher irischer Erzählungen und Volkssagen, Mährchen und Legenden' von K. v. K(illinger) (Stuttgart 1847)[31].

A. Helfferich, 'Skizzen und Erzählungen aus Irland' (Berlin 1858)[32] erkannte die entscheidende Rolle der Zusammenarbeit Croker-Grimm für die deutsche Irlandkunde; Helfferich sandte ein Exemplar seines Buches an Jakob Grimm, der ihm am 12. April 1858 dafür dankte. J. Rodenberg sprach in seinem Irlandbuch, dessen Titel, 'Die Insel der Heiligen'[33] (Berlin 1860) ironisch gemeint war, mehrfach (203, 323) von Croker und den Grimms und ließ sich von ihrem Beispiel anregen, in seiner 'Harfe von Erin' (1864) einen Aufsatz über irische Märchen und 14 Übersetzungen irischer Märchen zu bringen. Über die Neuauflagen in unserer Zeit hinaus kann man die Wirkung von 'Irische Elfenmärchen' bis in die jüngste Journalistik verfolgen[34]. Wenn man wie Sandkühler eine Geschichte der irischen Volkskunde und des deutschen Interesses daran skizziert, so darf man nicht Wilhelm Grimms Aufsatz aus dem Jahre 1856 vergessen, der von Bolte in Band V der 'Anmerkungen zu Kinder- und Hausmärchen der Brüder Grimm' (Stuttgart 1932, 55 ff.) mit wertvollen Anmerkungen wiederabgedruckt wurde. In diesem Aufsatz wurden v. Killingers »irische Sagen und Mährchen« genannt. Anderseits war Rodenberg einer der wenigen, die den Wert von Clements Forschungen auf diesem Gebiet anerkannten.

Von Iren verfaßte Literaturwerke in deutscher Übersetzung ist ein Kapital in der Geschichte der deutschen Irlandkunde,von dem man hoffen möchte, daß sich einmal ein Doktorand damit befaßt.

31   C.[sic] v. K. hatte (Berlin 1829) Übersetzungen kleiner Gedichte von Bryon und Moore veröffentlicht. Die Serie 'Erin' begann mit der Übersetzung der Biographie Gerald Griffins von seinem Bruder (das aus dem Besitze von Josef Grabisch – DVjs. 31 1957. Anm. I – in die National Library of Ireland gelangte Exemplar enthielt die handschriftliche Widmung v. Killingers an den Verfasser); es folgte die Übersetzung von Gerald Griffins 'Collegians' (Die Schulfreunde). Die Anmerkungen v. Killingers enthalten Wissenswertes über Volksleben und Literatur in Irland. Bd. III-VI (1849) brachten Sagen und Märchen (hierzu Boltes Anmerkungen zu Grimms Hausmärchen – s.u. – Bd. V. 1932. S. 55, sowie L. Mühlhausen: Die kornische Geschichte von den drei Ratschlägen. 1938. 6.) Vermutlich weil der British Museum Catalogue von v. Killinger nur 'Ausgewählte englische Synonyma (Karlsruhe 1854)' aufführt, bezeichnete Zeydel (s.o. Anm. 25) ihn als »Anglisten«.

32   Wie Venedy – s.u. – ging H., ein schwäbischer Pfarrersohn, auf Father Mathew ein, dessen Verbindungen mit Deutschland (z. B. Vinzenz Prießnitz) ich erforscht habe (Father Mathew Record. Dublin. Juli und September 1947). Nach dem Tode O'Connells und Father Mathews war, wie H. nicht zu unrecht meinte, das politische Leben Irlands tot. H. begann seine Tour nicht in Dublin, wie die meisten Deutschen, sondern in Belfast (s.o. Anm. 30 Ende).

33   In dem Artikel über Rodenberg (der erste Jude, der ein Buch über Irland schrieb) in Jewish Encyclopedia: Die Insel der Seligen.

34   Als jüngstes Beispiel Karl Reyle: Fingerhütchen (kannte C. F. Meyer die Irischen Elfenmärchen?). In: Berner Bund. 24.6., bzw. Basler Nachrichten. 10.7.1966.

Angesichts des sporadischen Grundcharakters deutscher Irlandkunde ist eine innere Verflechtung von Studien auf diesem Gebiete, wie sich an Hand von Grimms Übersetzung und ihren Nachwirkungen zeigen läßt, mindestens von illustrativem Interesse. Daß hier kein abgerundetes Bild, sondern nur eine Sammlung von Notizen aus z. T. weit auseinanderliegenden Quellen zu erstellen ist, liegt in der Natur der Sache. Selbst die historische Anordnung des Stoffes ist unmöglich, da ständig Bezugnahmen auf die Vorzeit (Ossian, Märchen und Legenden) mit Geschichte und Gegenwart vermischt werden. Die neue Sicht wird deutlich in der 'Darstellung des gegenwärtigen Zustandes von Irland, von einem mehrjährigen Beobachter' (Stuttgart 1835)[35], wenn es heißt:

>»Die Übel, worunter die Insel leidet, sind nicht von heute und gestern, sondern alte tiefgewurzelte Schäden, die, im Laufe der Jahrhunderte fortwährend durch neue vermehrt, nach und nach zu einem so complicierten Krankheitszustand gediehen sind, daß Aderlaß und Umschläge nicht mehr helfen, sondern die Heilung nur auf einem langsamen Wege und durch gründliche systematische Behandlungsart bewirkt werden kann.
>
> Alle diese Umstände werden im Ausland gewöhnlich viel zu wenig berücksichtigt. Man studiert die irische Geschichte und, durch den blutigen Codex der alten peinlichen Gesetze[36] schon im voraus gegen England und die protestantische Partei eingenommen, glaubt man um so sicherer in den fantischen und anmaßenden Declamationen überspannter Orangeisten, die Bestätigung der einseitigen Darstellungen O'Connells, die Rechtfertigung seiner Klagen und die Gültigkeit seiner Forderungen zu finden, ohne zu bedenken, daß man bloß ein Extrem verwirft, um dem anderen zu huldigen. Auch in Deutschland scheint der größere Theil des denkenden Publicums, zwar nicht gerade für die Umtriebe der irischen Demagogen, aber doch fast unbedingt zu Gunsten ihrer Beschwerden gegen England und die Tories entschieden zu haben.«

So ein Schriftsteller, der sich als »katholischer Legitimist« bezeichnet. Ähnlich reserviert, aber aus ganz anderen Gründen, urteilte J. Venedy in seinem 1844 von Brockhaus verlegten 'Irland'[37]. Wie William McCabe in seinen Anmerkungen zu der wenige Monate später in Dublin erschienenen englischen Übersetzung ausführte, war Venedys Antiklerikalismus nicht die günstigste Ausgangsbasis für eine Würdigung der Verhältnisse in Irland. Das erste von einem professionellen Reiseschriftsteller in deutscher Sprache geschriebene und durch Übersetzungen auch im englischen Sprachbereich als bedeutsam anerkannte Irlandbuch war das von Johann Georg Kohl (1842). Eine der wenigen Stellen, an denen Kohl aus seiner Reserve heraustrat, war seine Kritik an O'Connell, dem er vorwarf, den Patriotismus seiner Landsleute für seine Zwecke ausgenutzt zu haben.

Es waren weniger die Übersetzungen von Erzählungen wie die Whittys und Carletons als Zeitungsberichte über O'Connell, die die deutschsprachige Welt mit der Lage in Irland vertraut machten. Die Irlandkunde von Heine, Gutzkow, Freiligrath, Georg

---

35 S.o. Anm. 30.

36 S.o. Anm. 12.

37 Holl. S. 101. Der erste Band, die Geschichte von St. Patrick bis zum Repeal behandelnd, baute auf Thomas Moores 'History of Ireland' auf, von der Holl zwei deutsche Übersetzungen im Jahre 1835 nachgewiesen hat. 1846 erschien dann C. Ackens, ebenfalls auf Moore fußende Älteste Geschichte Irlands.

Weerth u.a. kreist um die politischen Ereignisse, die mit O'Connells Namen verbunden sind[38]. Edward A. Moriartys 'Leben und Wirken O'Connells' (Berlin 1843) war das erste Buch eines modernen Iren, das im Original in deutscher Sprache erschien[39]. Von einem Zusammenwachsen der Information aus der schönen Literatur und touristischen Journalistik – gar mit der beginnenden philologischen und historischen Forschung – zu wirklicher Irlandkunde war bislang jedoch wenig zu spüren.

Umso größer, ja, bis heute einzigartig, ist die Leistung, die Johann Martin Lappenberg mit seinem 100 Seiten umfassenden Artikel 'Irland' vollbrachte, welcher Band XXIV der Serie II der 'Allgemeinen Encyklopädie der Wissenschaften und Künste' 1845[40] eröffnete, nach seinem Biographen (ADB XVII), »eine der besten Arbeiten über Irland, seine Geschichte, Statistik, Sprache und Literatur, über Vieles, was gewöhnlich am Wege liegen bleibt, geradezu eine unschätzbare Fundgrube«. Lappenberg war schon 1813 (als Hamburger trotz der Kontinentalsperre) in England und Schottland gewesen. Im Zusammenhang mit seinen Studien zur frühenglischen Geschichte unternahm er 1837 noch eine ausgedehnte Reise nach England und Irland. Allein die hervorragende Dokumentation seines Artikels beweist, daß er in Irland seine Zeit gut genützt haben muß. Er behandelte die natürlichen Grundlagen, den Nationalcharakter (Trunksucht als Folge der Verzweiflung), Industrie und Handel, Religion und Kirchenverfassung (der katholische Klerus lebt ausschließlich von freiwilligen Beiträgen), Wissenschaft und Kultur (ausgezeichnet über Universität und theologische Seminare), Staatsverfassung und -verwaltung, Justiz und Militär, Sprache, Nationalliteratur und irischen Dichtung. Das Herzstück ist natürlich (S. 46-94) ein Abriß der Geschichte Irlands. Lappenberg konnte darauf verzichten, die doch meist nur tertiäre deutsche Li-

---

38 Außer Gutzkow außerhalb von Holls Untersuchung, die durch meine Kapitel 'Continental Opinion' in dem Gedächtnis Daniel O'Connell. 1949; sowie meine Arbeit: 'Daniel O'Connell in the opinion of some German poets of his time'. In: Modern Language Review. 54. 1959. S. 473-578, zu ergänzen wäre. Auch Immermanns Irlandkunde (in: Tristan und Isolde. Siehe meine Notiz in: Modern Language Review. 44. 1949. S. 246 bis 252) gehört hierher. Immermann war m. W. der einzige Deutsche, der einen Reim auf »Ulster« gewagt hat. (»Polster«). Wenn er die mit Isolde eingeschifften Hoffräulein »Miss Elinor, Miss Kitty, Betty, und die kleine schwarze Pretty« nennt, so ist das zwar sprachlich jammervoll, führt aber in das deutsche Irlandbild ein gesundes Element jungdeutscher Ironie ein. (Daß das nationale Young Ireland – jüngste Gesamtdarstellung von T.F. O'Sullivan. 1944 – seine Namen aus Deutschland bezog, sei nur am Rande vermerkt).

39 Holl besprach deutsche O'Connellbücher von L. Schipper (Soest 1844), G. (Dortmund 1844), M. Brühl (Mainz 1845), C. G. N. Rintel (Mannheim 1845) und 96: Moriarty.

40 Kein Jahr hat mehr deutsche Publikationen über Irland hervorgebracht (s. Anm. 24 und 38). Im gleichen Jahre verehelichte sich Leopold v. Ranke mit der Tochter von John Crosbie Graves, einem hohen Beamten in Dublin, und des anglikanischen Geistlichen C. Percival in der Diözese Cloyne (s. Kap. 1 der Autobiographie des Großneffen Robert Graves: Goodbye to all that. 1929). Am 30.11.1849 wurden auf Empfehlung des Committee of Polite Literature, zu dem auch Charles Graves, Frau v. Rankes Bruder, gehörte, Jacob Grimm, Franz Bopp (s.u.) und Leopold v. Ranke zu Ehrenmitgliedern der Royal Irish Academy gewählt.

teratur zu zitieren. Einmal bezieht er sich auf Carves 'Lyra' (Sulzbach 1666)[41], eine Statistik entnimmt er F. v. Raumers 'England' (1835); nur für die Sprache kann er mit Recht auf einen wirklichen deutschen Beitrag verweisen: Bopps 'Keltische Sprachen' (1839)[42]. Lappenbergs Artikel ist nicht nur heute noch lesenswert, sondern sollte einmal detailliert[43] als eminentester Beitrag zur allgemeinen deutschen Irlandkunde gewürdigt werden. Unsere Übersicht könnte unter das Motto (Lappenberg S. 37) gestellt werden:

> »So rätselhaft Irland in seinen einzelnen Charakterzügen häufig hervortritt, so ist dennoch nicht auffallender als die Stätigkeit derselben Erscheinungen in den wechselnden Jahrhunderten unter den verschiedensten Verhältnissen.«

Wie wenig aber solide Irlandkunde[44] in Deutschland durchdrang, kann man beispielhaft an Fontane sehen. 1860 lernte er »jenseits des Tweed« eine Irin kennen, mit der er von dem »romantischen Charakter Irlands« und seinem Wunsche, »die grüne Insel nächstens zu bereisen« sprach. Als die Irin dann ein Lied von Thomas Moore anstimmte, ergab sich für Fontane[45] offenbar die umgekehrte Situation zu der von Bornhausers Gallus erträumten. Die Tradition von »the wild Irish girl«[46] (Titel des Romans von Lady Morgan, den Goethe 1813 las) kann man von Deirdre und Isolde bis zu Edna O'Brien und Bernadette Devlin verfolgen.

> »Die intime, über Jahrzehnte sich erstreckende Beziehung, die Engels mit der jungen irischen Arbeiterin Mary Burns, die ihm den Weg in proletarische Kreise gebahnt zu haben scheint,

---

41 Siehe meine Arbeit: Irish soldiers in the Thirty Years War. In: Journal of Royal Soc. Antiquar. Ireland. 82. 1952. S. 28ff.

42 Erst mit diesem Werk begann H. Bauersfeld seine 'Entwicklung der keltischen Studien in Deutschland' (1937, siehe meine Besprechung in: Irish Historical Studies. 4. 1944. S. 119f.), obgleich, wenn nicht schon Schoepflin (DVjs. 31. 1957. S. 73), so jedoch jedenfalls Adelung, Vater und Ahlwardt hätten berücksichtigt werden müssen. Lappenberg hatte gesagt: »Durch die Anlegung der Schottenklöster, sowie die späteren vielfachen Wanderungen der irischen Geistlichen sind viele Handschriften in ihrer Landessprache auf dem Continent zerstreut und bisher wenig beachtet«. Dies war der Ausgangspunkt der Studien C. Zeuss' (s. A. Dürrwächters Vortrag am 22.6.1906. Z. f. celt. Philol. 6. 1908. S. 202f.). Ebd. S. 215f. der ergreifende Bericht über die Ansprache eines Führers der Gaelic League am Grabe Zeuss, »des Begründers der altgälischen Wissenschaft«.

43 Holl. S. 124 betrachtet natürlich nur einen Aspekt.

44 Skizzen aus Irland (Berlin 1850) von dem 1800 in Stuttgart geborenen, aber in der welschen Schweiz aufgewachsenen Victor Aime Huber war mir nicht zugänglich und wird in dem ADB-Artikel von R. Elvers nicht erwähnt. Nach Rodenberg (s. Anm. 33) ist dieses Buch eine Übersetzung von Mrs. M. Halls Ireland and its scenery. (M.A.Titmarsh, Irländische Zustände (Stuttg. 1843) war eine Übersetzung von Thackerays Irish sketchbook).

45 Schriften und Glossen zur europäischen Literatur. 1965. S. 181f. Um die gleiche Zeit malte Degas seine heute im Metropolitan Museum New York befindliche Belle Irlandaise.

46 Siehe meinen Artikel: Irische Frauen in der Weltliteratur. In: Basler Nachrichten. 23.5.1954, vor allem für die Deszendenz der irischen Lydia in Gottfried Kellers 'Pankraz der Schmoller' (1956).

anknüpfte, gaben seinem Mitgefühl für (Irland), dieses Opfer 'einer fünfhundertjährigen Unterdrückung', eine ganz eigene Wärme.«[47]

1856 bereiste er mit Mary Burns ihr Heimatland. 1863 nahmen dann seine Beziehungen zu ihrer Schwester Lizzy »intimeren Charakter« an, und 1869 begleitete sie ihn auf der zweiten Reise durch Irland[48]. Am 16. Januar 1872 hielt Engels seine Rede über die irische Arbeiterklasse. 1881 noch verkündete er, daß die proletarische Revolution in Großbritannien erst möglich sein werde, wenn Irland und die Dominions befreit sein würden.

Hatte sich Engels 1843 noch sehr reserviert O'Connell gegenüber geäußert[49], so brachte ihn offenbar Mary Burns dazu, sich »mit den wirtschaftlichen Ursachen der ständigen Gärung in Irland« zu befassen[50]. Er scheint Marx auf Irland gelenkt zu haben.

»Doch erst die gewaltsame Zuspitzung, die der Gegensatz (zu England) seit dem Ende des amerikanischen Sukzessionskriegs unter dem Einfluß der Millionen nach Amerika ausgewanderter Iren erfuhr, bildete bei Marx, der wohl darin (Engels) vorangig, die Vorstellung aus, daß es sich in dieser Frage nicht nur um national oder lokal begrenzte soziale Gegensätze handelte, sondern um einen Konflikt, der in seinem Verlauf das Signal zu der allgemeinen sozialen Revolution geben könnte.«[51]

(Das Gegenstück zu dieser heute höchst lebendigen Lehre war die die deutsche Einstellung zu Irland während der beiden Weltkriege weithin bestimmende Vorstellung, man könne Irland benutzen, um das britische Weltreich zu zerbrechen). In 'Das Kapital' zitiert Marx den Bericht des parlamentarischen Kommittees zum Thema 'Irish Labour' 1858-1860 und den Bericht über die Löhne der Landarbeiter in Irland 1870[52]. Der ebenfalls von Engels auf Irland aufmerksam gemachte Karl Kautsky zitierte zu letzterem Thema in seiner (der ersten sozialistischen) Schrift 'Irland, eine kulturhistorische Skizze' (Leipzig 1881) Roschers 'Nationalökonomie des Ackerbaus'[53]. Hatte Helfferich (s.o.) das politische Leben in Irland für tot erklärt, sagte jetzt[54] Kautsky:

47   Gustav Mayer: Friedrich Engels. 1934. Bd. I.S. 128.

48   Ebd. Bd. II. S. 125. 178, dazu Desmond Ryan: Friedrich Engels in Ireland. In: Irish Travel. 20. 1945. S. 155.

49   Gustav Mayer: Engels. Bd. I. S. 127.

50   Einen ähnlichen Aspekt faßte Franz von Hotzendorff in seinem (auch ins Englische übertragenen) Buch. Das irische Gefangenensystem. Leipzig 1859, ins Auge: vgl. Brockhaus: Konversationslexikon 1908. Bd. IX. S. 688 unter Irisches System.

51   Mayer, Bd. II. S. 174.

52   James Connolly: Labour in Irish History. 1910. Im Anschluß an S. F. Blooms Vortrag 'Ireland's destiny as it appeared to Karl Marx' machte R. B. McDowell wertvolle Bemerkungen zur Literatur über Marx und Ireland (Bulletin of the Irish Committee of Historical Studies. Mai 1946).

53   Band 2 von W. Roschers System der Volkswirtschaft. 1854. 7. Aufl. 1873.

54   Ein völlig anderes Bild bieten die Reiseskizzen aus Irland des Geologen Arnold v. Lasaulx. 1878.

»In Großbritannien hat die irische Agrarbewegung eine Stärke erreicht, die sie englischen Staatsmännern bedrohlicher und wichtiger erscheinen läßt als die afghanische, burmanische, transvaal'sche, orientalische und sonstige Fragen zusammen. Es dürfte kaum ein Land in Europa geben, in dem ein Elend herrscht, das dem irischen annähernd zu vergleichen wäre, keins, in dem das Elend über ein Jahrtausend so ununterbrochen am Mark des Volkes zehrte, wie in Irland.«

Es bahnen sich ganz neue Fronten an, wenn Kautsky schreibt:

»Bei den liberalisierenden Historikern unserer Zeit ist es Mode, alle damals (im 17. Jahrhundert) begangenen Unthaten der römischen Kirche in die Schuhe zu schieben. Ein unbefangener Beobachter aber muß zu dem Resultate kommen, daß der Fanatismus der Protestanten dem der Katholiken das Wasser reichen kann.«

Wenn sich Kautsky hier wohl eher auf deutsche Historiographie bezieht, so erkannte er doch auch die weitgehende Befangenheit damaliger deutscher Beschäftigung mit der Geschichte der irischen Kirche in konfessionellen Vorurteilen. Da ist einerseits etwa die 'Geschichte der altirischen Kirche ihrer Verbindung mit Rom, Gallien und Alemannien' (Freiburg 1867) von dem St. Gallener Bischof Carl. Johann Greith[55], anderseits 'Die iroschottische Missionskirche im 6. und 7. Jahrhundert' (Gütersloh 1873), später gefolgt von 'Bonifatius, der Zerstörer des columbanischen Kirchentums' von Johann Heinrich August Ebrard[56]. Alfons Bellesheims 'Geschichte der katholischen Kirche in Irland' (Freiburg 1890), bis heute die umfassendste Darstellung es Gegenstandes[57] durch einen katholischen Autor, erfuhr scharfe Kritik durch Iren,[58] aber den ganzen Abstand zu Vorherigem ermißt man, wenn man den Artikel 'Irland' von dem Jesuiten Zimmermann aus Wetzer-Weltes 'Kirchenlexikon' (Freiburg 1889) daneben hält. Den Abschluß des hier zu betrachtenden Zeitraums[59] bildet Heinrich Zimmers berühmter Artikel 'Keltische Kirche in Britannien und Irland' in der 'Realencyklopädie für protestantische Theologie und Kirche' 3. Aufl. 1901 (der Artikel »Irland« dass. von W. Götz behandelt nur die Staatskirche).[60] In seiner Übersicht 'Irland in der Kirchengeschichte' konnte Ferdinand Kattenbusch noch 1921 schreiben:

---

55 Vorhergegangen waren Greiths Bücher über Gallus und Kolumban.

56 Über E. siehe den Artikel von E. F. K. Müller in: Realencyklopädie für protestantische Theologie und Kirche.

57 Und m. W. das erste in Deutschland gedruckte Buch, das eine Widmung in irischer Sprache und Schrift (»Zum Ruhme Gottes und zur Ehre Irlands«) trägt. Vgl. Alex. Baumgartners Artikel in: Stimmen aus Maria Laach. 23. 1882 S. 395-410. S. 504-519 über altirische Sagen.

58 D. McCarthy. In: The Academy. 23.8.1890.

59 Die Stellung Irlands in deutschen Enzyklopädien, etwa die verschiedenen Auflagen des Brockhaus, von Religion in Geschichte und Gegenwart etc. wäre ein weiteres der Erforschung wertes Kapitel. Es würde die allmähliche Ablösung des konfessionellen durch des politische Interesse zeigen.

60 Theologische Studien und Kritiken. 93. S. 1ff. Gustav Schirmer, dessen Habilitationsschrift die Brandanslegende behandelte, hielt am 7. Juli 1888 in Leipzig seine Antrittsvorlesung über das Thema: Irlands Anteil an der englischen Literatur. Ich habe nicht ermitteln können, ob diese gedruckt wurde. [Anm. d. Herausgeber: Die drei letzten Fußnoten waren im Text nicht markiert und sind sinngemäß eingefügt worden.]

»Ein Ire hat sich beklagt, daß seine Heimat dem Durchschnittseuropäer im Grunde ebenso unbekannt sei wie die entferntesten Teile Zentralafrikas. Das ist kaum eine übertriebene Behaup-
tung. Wer von uns hat bisher etwas von Irlands ruhmreicher, bedeutender Vergangenheit gewußt?
Ein paar Spezialisten für Kunde des Keltenstamms, dieser oder jener Historiker (am ehesten
Kirchenhistoriker), vereinzelte Philologen. Die Vorstellungen von einem Irländer und einem
Trunkenbolde gehen für uns nach englischen Schilderungen ineinander. Und das Land steht uns
vor Augen als ein gänzlich verkommenes, durch die Trägheit und selbstverschuldete Armut seiner
Bevölkerung aller Kultur bares.«

Es wäre die Aufgabe einer Übersicht der deutschen Irlandliteratur des 20. Jahrhunderts zu prüfen, wie weit dieses harte Urteil 1921 berechtigt war und wie weit es
fünfzig Jahre später eventuell noch gilt.

(Quelle: DVLG 47, 1973, S. 617-629)

Mile-stones of German-Irish Literary Relations

The history of Ireland's place in German literature is of interest from three principal
view-points, 1) the preservation in Central Europe of the Irish missionary and
monastic tradition, 2) the foundation of German interest in the language and the
antiquities of Ireland, 3) the development of German political interest in modern
Ireland.

During the Middle Ages, German interest in Ireland was practically confined to the
tradition of the great Irish Saints and of the later scholars and monks labouring on the
Continent. Since the 12th century, however, there was a considerable amount of
secular information on Ireland attached to the spreading of such works as the *Vision of
Tundalus* (the first work by an Irishman written in Germany and translated into
German), *St. Patrick's Purgatory* (and its continental counterpart, the account of the
Visions which the Knight George had in Lough Derg) and the *Journey of St. Brendan*
(a Saint whose cult the Norman and Hanseatic sea-farers introduced into Lower
Germany). About A.D. 1210 Gottfried von Strassburgs's *Tristan* (of which only the
second part, starting with Isolde's departure from Ireland, served as the basis for
Richard Wagner's opera) was the first work of Continental vernacular literature to
mention the name of Dublin and to impart to the Continent some knowledge of
conditions in Ireland just after the arrival of the Normans. It also speaks of something
like the language-question in Ireland ("Isolde knew the Norman tongue but also
understood the language of the people of Dublin"), while still earlier references to the
Irish language are found in Continental biographies of Irish hermits and missionaries
in the Low Countries and in the Upper Rhine valley. In the Annals of both Ireland and
Germany we find some traces of mutual political interest existing between these two
countries during the early Middle Ages.

The first printed work of German literature to refer extensively to this country was
Fortunatus, apart from *Faust* the most successful "Volksbuch". The first print of *Fortunatus* appeared in 1509 at Augsburg a place where a few years earlier two short
accounts relating to St. Patrick's Purgatory had been published, to which Prof. Waterhouse recently drew our attention. *Fortunatus* embodies one of the most interesting
accounts of St. Patrick's Purgatory, namely an account expressive of a completely

secular and rationalist view. After *Tristan, Fortunatus* was the first work of German literature in which Irish characters other than Saints figured prominently. *Fortunatus* also illustrates the development of the legend of Ireland, the wonderland at the outskirts of the inhabited world, where practically anything might happen. Originating from the classical tradition of Ireland (especially the much quoted Solinus), embellished by the Normans and corrupted by the later English writers, this legend overshadowed right up to the late 18th century, the scanty information of real Ireland which the Continent managed to obtain during that period.

Even less than the activities of the famous Saints and Scholars, the permanent establishments of Irish monks during the later Middle Ages conveyed to Germany much of real knowledge of Ireland. Since the 14th century the great organisation of Irish Benedictine monasteries (which at its height numbered a dozen of houses in all parts of the Reich) decayed partly due to lack of connection with the home-country, partly through the general decline of monastic discipline. For the subsequent five hundred years, the word "Schotte" by which those Irish monks had been known, became synonymous with "vagabond". The Gypsies, at their first appearance in Germany, were occasionally described as "Schotten". However, not only does the memory of the "Schotten"-monks survive in names of buildings and streets in many places of Central Europe, but also do we gradually become aware of the important place held by those Irish monks in German literature, especially historiography, of the later Middle Ages.

Irish-German literary relations entered into a new phase when, in consequence of the religious persecution, priests and friars had to flee from this country. From the end of the 16th century, an ever increasing number of these Irish refugees can be traced not only in Portugal, France, the Low Countries and Italy, but also in various parts of Germany, in Bohemia and Hungary. While in Southern and Western Europe the literary tradition of these Irish exiles is mainly attached to the colleges established for and peopled and staffed by them, in the Reich their influence was more subtle, as in most cases it originates from isolated outstanding personalities among Irish exiles who attained to professorships in universities and seminaries. In the Reich, these academic activities of Irishmen seem to have been attached to the older tradition of Irishmen in German universities. We know e.g. of various Irish Franciscans who in the 14th century went for "advanced studies" to the university of Cologne, not to speak of the great influence exercised on scholastic philosophy in general, by Petrus de Hibernia, who together with Michael Scotus (perhaps also an Irishman) figured prominently in the intellectual life around the great Emperor Frederic II in Italy. [When in recent years the university of Cologne was revived, the tomb of Duns Scotus (whose Irish decent is defended by some writers to this day) in the Franciscan Church near the Cathedral attained to new historical significance.]

The first work published by one of the Irish exiles in Germany, in fact, the first work by an Irishman ever printed in Germany, shows us the continuance of the academic tradition of Irishmen in the Reich. In 1625 appeared at Frankfurt on Main a commentary, comprising more than 700 pages, to all the works of Aristotle. Of

Bernadus Morisanus, the author of that work, little seems to be known what the title page tells us in the two words "Derensis Ibernus", "from Derry in Ireland".

Arriving on the Continent, the Irish exiles seem to have been rather surprised at the extent of the tradition of former activities of fellow-countrymen of theirs. As the Continent had its own worries at that time, it did at first take little interest in refugees from distant Ireland. Thus the re-establishment, in terms of modern scholarship, of the tradition of Irelands Golden Age on the Continent became a matter of really vital interest to the Irish exiles. The extensive work on the tradition of Irish Saints outside Ireland which culminated in Colgan's monumental, if fragmentary *Acta* (Louvain 1645 ff) started in Germany, where Stephen White S.J. of Clonmel, a professor in Dillingen and Ingolstadt, began to follow up the tradition of Irish Saints in Bavaria. His work (which though written before 1615 was not published until 1849) bears the title *Apologia pro Hibernia*. It is directed against the Scots who in Germany proceeded from the merely theoretical "stealing of Saints" to the more lucrative activity of claiming for themselves monastic establishments known by the misleading name of "Schotten-kloster". In Bavaria they succeded, and the first rule which the new Scottish abbots made for their communities was that on no condition any of their Irish fellow-exiles should be admitted. Drawing up an impressive list of no less than 24 Saints, whom the German records drescribed as Irishmen, White protested against both Scottish presumptions and German indolence with regard to the Irish refugees.

Even before Stephen White had begun to supply Usher and Colgan with materials on Irish Saints venerated in Bavaria, German scholars had become engaged in similar work. Of several Saints traditionally described as Irishmen the Irish hagiographer learnt first through the works of the great Bavarian historians Hund, Rader and Bruner. One of White's colleagues at Dillingen was Heinrich Canisius, who published in 1601 for the first time such eminent works as Cogitosus's Life of St. Brigid, Adamnan's Life of St. Columba, Bede's Life of St. Cuthbert and important documents relating to Ss. Kilian, Virgil and Gall, the Irish Saints most venerated in Germany. Canisius added extracts from the Chronicle compiled in the 15th century by an abbot of the "Schottenkloster" at Ratisbon, a work which illustrates the preservation of the tradition of the great Irish Saints through later Irish monasticism in Germany.

Heinrich Canisius was a cousin of St. Peter Canisius, who wrote the first book ever published in German on the life of Irish Saints. It is irrelevant that modern scholars reject the tradition of the Irish descent of St. Fridolin, the hero of the *Wahrhaffte Historie* published in 1589 (at Fribourg) by St. Peter Canisius. What matters is that in this work we find a concise if popular account of the prominent position occupied by Irish Saints in early German Church history, and that this account is given by a man who is known as the second Apostle of Germany.

An important record of laymen exiled from Ireland on account of their faith is found in the first book written by an Irishman and printed in Germany, the translation which shortly after the Latin original had been published, appeared of the *Itinerarium*, by Thomas Carve, a priest from Tipperary, of his journey from Ireland, via England and Poland to Wallenstein's Camp, where he became chaplain to the Irish forces serving in the Imperial army. Carve's work contains one of the first accounts of the assassination of Wallenstein by Deveroux and his six Irish helebareers, an event of which few men can have had a closer knowledge than Carve, who had the pleasant duty to decide whether Butler, Deveroux and their companions and assistants were to be regarded as murderers or not. The fact that, unlike many earlier accounts of that event, Carve's book was speedily translated into German, shows what importance was attributed to it by his contemporaries. In accounts of the sources of Schiller's *Wallenstein* (through which those tough Hibernians were immortalised) Carve is scarcely mentioned, since, as is now generally admitted, the earlier German writers of the history of the Thirty Years' War shamefully neglected to acknowledge their indebtedness to Carve's "Reyssbüchlein", which like the Latin original is now extremely rare.

The Vision of Tundalus, Fortunatus, Moisanus's *Controversia*, White's Apologia and Carve's *Itinerarium* are mile-stones in the early history of Ireland's place in German literature. Carve and many other 17th century Irish writers living in the German Empire wrote books stating Ireland's case and drawing, for both Irish and German readers, a picture of Ireland's former glory and her present misery. German reaction to these appeals is not particularly conspicuous. It was not until 1785 that a German wrote a book exclusively dealing with Ireland. This was also the first book in which a German Protestant expressed his views on Ireland. For the subsequent hundred years, Protestants predominated in German literature in general and in German literature on Ireland in particular. Still, Caspar Zeuss, who wrote a hundred years ago the first standard work of modern Celtology (in Latin though), was a Catholic. A Catholic also introduced the German public to Carleton, Banim and Griffin. Towards the end of the 19th century Dr. Bellesheim, a canon of the Cathedral of Aix-la-Chapelle (where a thousand years earlier eminent Irish scholars had been members of the court of Charlemagne) wrote what still remains the largest history of the Irish Church. However, the first book on Ireland written in German under the title "Die Insel der Heiligen" was by one for whom the term "Saint" had no real meaning, Julius Roden-berg, a Jew (1873). The latest German book on Ireland, expressive of the predomin-ance of the political view-point of 20th century German interest in Ireland, bears the title "Die Insel der Rebellen" (by Robert Bauer, 1938).

(nicht veröffentlicht, ohne Jahr [nach 1938])

V.1 Mittelalter

Deutsche Ortsnamen in der martyrologischen Tradition Irlands

Als in seiner Anordnung anniversaristisch, ragt das Martyrologium Romanum in unsere Zeit hinein als Beispiel einer Geschichtsauffassung, die ihre Gegenstände nach einem anderen Maßstab als dem der gesellschaftlichen Wirksamkeit auswählt und die auf einem anderen als dem linearen Zeitbegriff und der sich daraus ergebenden Vorstellung eines Kausalzusammenhangs beruht. Zu den liturgischen Büchern gehörig, d.h. mit dem Anspruch auf pflichtgemäßen Gebrauch durch einen bestimmten Personenkreis und zu bestimmten Zeiten (und zwar täglich), verkündet das Martyrologium weiterhin Verbindlichkeit der Vergangenheit.[1] Durch diese Grundbestimmungen ist es unserer Zeit besonders fremd, so fremd, daß seine Tradition schwerlich überstehen wird. Es besteht heute wenig Aussicht, daß das Lebenswerk von H. Quentin[2], des eminentesten modernen Forschers auf diesem Gebiete, fortgesetzt werden wird, besonders auch im Hinblick auf die Zeit zwischen Usuard und Baronius.

Außer dem Jahrestag (meist des Todes) gibt das Martyrologium im wesentlichen nur zwei Informationen, einen Ortsnamen und einen Personennamen. Der historische Zeitpunkt[3] wird nur selten und dann auch meist nur indirekt durch einen Personennamen, etwa des römischen Kaisers, unter dem der Heilige den Märtyrertod erlitt, angegeben. Die Angabe des Ortsnamens unterscheidet inhaltlich das Martyrologium vom Kalendarium, aus dem es hervorging. In dem die Geschichte des Martyrologiums hindurch zu verfolgenden Gegenspiel von expliziter Aufführung von (allen erreichbaren) Personennamen einerseits und Beschränkung bis auf eine Eintragung pro Tag (oder nicht einmal für jeden Tag) im Interesse einer breiten historia andererseits stellen sich zwei in der allgemeinen Geschichtslehre zu beobachtende Auffassungen vor. Das extremste Beispiel für den ersten Typ von Martyrologium ist dasjenige von Tallaght (T)[4], welches, verschiedene Handschriften des Hieronymianum (MH) zusammenschreibend, für jeden Tag eine fast nur aus Personennamen bestehende Liste erstellte, die (daher)

---

1 Siehe meine Arbeit „Kalendar und Martyrologium als Literaturformen", in: Archiv für Liturgiewissenschaft 7 (1961), S. 1-44.

2 Les martyrologes historiques, Paris 1908 und unten Anm. 13.

3 Daß in der annalistischen Geschichtsbetrachtung der einmalige Zeitpunkt, in der anniversaristischen der im Jahreslauf immer wiederkehrende als entscheidend erachtet wird, unterscheidet in der Perspektive, aber nicht im Wesen: Bei den Betrachtungsweisen ist die Unvertauschbarkeit von Name, Ort und Zeit Felsengrund von history im Unterschied zu story (siehe meine Arbeit „Das Wesen des Gewesenen" – und frühere dort genannte Arbeiten – in: Geschichte in Wissenschaft und Unterricht 18 [1967], S. 673-681).

4 Hg. R. I. B e s t u. H. J. L a w l o r , Henry Bradshaw Society (HBS) LXVIII (London 1931). Zum Folgenden meine Arbeit „Studies in the Latin texts of the Martyrology of Tallaght, of Félire Oengusso and of Félire húi Gormáin", in: Proc. Royal Irish Academy 69 C (1970), S.45-112.

an Umfang nie wieder übertroffen worden ist.[5] Mit diesem Werk beginnt eine Tradition des Martyrologiums in Irland, die aus vielen Gründen einzigartig ist.

1. Die oben genannte Gegenrichtung zeigt sich bereits in T durch spätere erzählende Zusätze, vor allem aber in der Versifikation[6] im sog. Félire (ir. féil von *uigilia* = „Fest") des Oengus von Tallaght um 800 (FO)[7],

2. und zwar in irischer Sprache, womit hier erstmalig eine westliche vernacula in diese Tradition eingeführt wurde[8].

3. Ausdrücklich dem Beispiel Oengus' folgend, kompilierte der Augustiner Chorherr Marianus Gorman von Cnoc-na nApstal („Apostelhügel") in der Grafschaft Louth ein Félire (FG)[9], das nach seinem Inhalt (es handelt sich im wesentlichen um ein Usuardianum), Anspruch (es will liturgisch genau sein) und Zeitpunkt (um 1180) als Schwanengesang der altirischen Kirche zu bezeichnen ist. Aus MH (und T?) sowie anderen Quellen fügte Gorman den Usuard entnommenen weitere Namen hinzu.

4. Félire (andere wesentlich abgekürzte Repräsentanten davon bleiben hier außer Betracht) stellt sich als devotionell vor und ersetzte (bis auf Gorman) als praktisch jeden Tag vollziehbare Andacht zu allen Heiligen die anniversaristische Verehrung der Heiligen in Messe und Offizium (die altirische Kirche kannte praktisch kein Sanctorale).

5. Rund hundert Jahre nach FG wurde für das Haus der Augustiner Chorherren in Dublin (St. Thomas) eine Abschrift des Martyrologiums Usuards geschrieben, ebenfalls mit Hinzufügungen, die sich größtenteils auch in den auctuaria Usuardi auf dem Festland finden.[10] Dieses Werk (ST) ist lateinisch, enthält nur wenige der auch in FG gemachten Zusätze und kannte FG offensichtlich nicht, obwohl dieses Werk in einem Haus der gleichen Gemeinschaft, für die ST geschrieben wurde, nur ein paar Dutzend Meilen nördlich von Dublin entstanden war.

---

5 Am anderen Ende der Skala steht z.B. Ado (siehe unten unter 6, Ausgabe: P. L. 123, 202ff.), aber auch er verläßt nicht den Felsengrund der Geschichte: Die Was-Wie-Darstellung beruht für ihn auf der Wann-Wo-Wer-Feststellung.

6 Hierzu mein Vergleich zwischen dem Megas Kanon des Andreas von Kreta und FO, in Mediaeval Studies 25 (1963) 280-293.

7 Hg. W. S t o k e s , HBS XXIX (London 1905).

8 Hierzu meine Vergleiche mit Martyrologium Wandalberti und mit dem angelsächsischen Menologium, in Mediaeval Studies 14 (1952) 98-105 und 17 (1955) 219-226.

9 Ed. W. S t o k e s , HBS IX (London 1895).

10 Hierzu A. G w y n n , in Journ. Royal Soc. Antiquaries Ireland LXXXIV (1954) 1-35. Die dort S. 29ff. gegebenen Bemerkungen über das Martyrologium bedürfen, wie eine Prüfung der Hs. B 3. 5. Trinity College Dublin (Microfilm frdl. zur Verfügung gestellt) ergab, der Berichtigung. G w y n n erkannte vor allem nicht, daß es sich um ein Usuardianum handelt. Für Usuards Text: J. D u b o i s ' Ausgabe (Brüssel 1965), Auctuaria (AU): S o l l e r i u s ' Ausgabe AASS Boll. Jun. VI.

6. Wiederum rund hundert Jahre später wurde für Christ Church Dublin aus Ados Werk ein Martyrologium (CC)[11] erstellt, indem die (bei Ado extrem) ausführlichen historiae, meist von ihrem Beginn mit dem Relativpronomen an, gekürzt wurden, anderseits Eintragungen hinzugefügt wurden, die entweder auch in festländischen auctuaria Usuardi zu finden sind oder, besonders für die letzten drei Monate des Jahres, auf MH zurückgehen.

7. FO ist nur in Hss. des 14. und 15. Jahrhunderts erhalten, die z.T. ausführliche Randbemerkungen[12] mit zusätzlichen martyrologischen Informationen über die von FO Genannten und einige in FO nicht genannte Feste, offensichtlich unabhängig von FG und CC, aus der irischen Überlieferung (Todd vermutete FO) und aus nichtirischen Quellen bieten.

8. T ist in der Tradition des MH[13] vor allem dadurch einzigartig, daß es jedem Tagesabschnitt einen etwa gleichlangen, teils in lateinischer, teils in irischer Sprache mit etwa gleich vielen irischen Namen beifügte. In FO und FG erscheinen nichtirische und irische Namen bunt vermischt, aber auch diese Werke erwecken den Eindruck, daß Irland so reich an Heiligen gewesen sei wie die ganze übrige Welt. Im 17. Jahrhundert, als unter dem Druck der Verfolgung die Iren ebenso wie ihre auf das Festland geflüchteten Landsleute sich systematisch der Erforschung ihrer Vorzeit zuwandten, wurde in Donegal ein nur auf Iren beschränktes und noch über T hinausgehendes Martyrologium (D)[14] zusammengestellt, in dessen Beiwerk jedoch auch einige Information aus nichtirischen Martyrologien enthalten ist.

9. Die genannten Werke sind kümmerliche Reste einer breiteren Tradition, mit der Irland im Strom der Überlieferung von MH bis zum Martyrologium Romanum (MR) stand.

10. Weder das Britische Museum noch die Bibliotheken in Dublin (Trinity und National) besitzen ein Exemplar von *The Roman and British Martyrology. Now first translated literally, from the Latin edition* (Dublin 1846), und außer meinem (in Originaleinband) ist mir trotz jahrelangen eifrigen Nachfragens kein weiteres Exemplar bekannt geworden. Das Wort *first* ist dann richtig, wenn man es versteht als „zum ersten Male in Irland (erschienen)"[15], und das Wort *Latin*, wenn man es auf MR beschränkt. Das Wort *literally* trifft, wie wir an den hier zu betrachtenden Eintragungen sehen werden, für die MR entnommenen einigermaßen zu. Wenn der „Übersetzer" Ire war, so war er ein Repräsentant der angloirischen Konzeption (*British*), denn er stellt die Iren keineswegs den Engländern, Schotten und Wallisern

---

11   Hg. J. C. C r o s t h w a i t e , Einl. J. H. T o d d (Dublin 1844).

12   In der [in] Anm. 7 genannten Ausgabe.

13   Acta Sanctorum Nov. II, pars posterior (Brüssel 1931), dort auch die nichtirischen Eintragungen aus T mit gelegentlichen Bemerkungen Quentins dazu.

14   Hg. J. H. T o d d und W. R e e v e s (Dublin 1864).

15   Eine (genaue) englische Übersetzung des MR von G. K e y n e s S.J. war 1627 erschienen; das Britische Museum hat auch die 2. Auflage 1667 und den Neudruck (?) Derby 1848.

gegenüber heraus, ja, bezeichnet auf dem Festland genannte Iren gelegentlich als *Scot*[16], was ebenso irreführend ist, wie die im deutschen Sprachbereich bis heute verbreitete Bezeichnung „iro-schottisch"[17]. Da mit diesem Werk die hier zu betrachtende Tradition abschließt, bemerke ich jetzt schon, daß die darin enthaltenen auf Deutschland bezüglichen Eintragungen (weitgehend in Übereinstimmung mit MR) dieses Werk zu demjenigen in Irland erschienenen machen, durch das die breiteste Kenntnis von deutscher Kirchengeschichte vermittelt wurde. Bei den z.T. amüsanten Schreibungen deutscher Ortsnamen handelt es sich weniger um Ausdruck der in Irland besonders verbreiteten *affectation*, deutsche Ortsnamen falsch zu schreiben, als (etwa bei „Cullen" und „Mentz") um phonetische Wiedergaben oder (wie bei „Elbingen") um Lesefehler. Immerhin sieht man ein Bemühen um Identifikation und mehrfach Eigenkenntnis. Das Werk wäre in Verbindung mit der für Irland einzigartigen Deutschlandkunde in J. O'Hanlons monumentalen, leider unvollendet gebliebenen Lives of Irish Saints[18] zu würdigen.

Bis heute ist das Geistesleben Irlands von der Tatsache bestimmt, daß Irland a) eine Insel, b) am Rande Europas ist. Beide Tatsachen begründen einerseits die Sonderstellung Irlands, anderseits die Bedeutung der Beziehungen zum Festland, die immer in ihrer Wechselseitigkeit zu berücksichtigen sind. Sie sind natürlich umso interessanter, je weiter die Entfernungen waren, und diese Entfernungen lassen sich am leichtesten an den Ortsnamen ablesen. Dabei ist es in Hagiographie und insbesondere Martyrologie unerheblich, ob Ortsnamen in einem historischen oder imaginären Zusammenhang verwandt werden. Es werden, wie die anniversaristische Anordnung sagt, nicht Tatsachen sondern Überlieferungen bedacht, die jedoch nicht, wie man heute oft meint, beliebig Gegenwartsinteressen entsprechend interpretiert oder gar „gestaltet" werden können, sondern einen Anspruch haben, der an Härte hinter dem von Tatsachen nicht zurücksteht. Daß z.B. der Bezug auf Kärnten in der Tradition (MR) des Iren Virgil historisch sein dürfte, macht ihn nicht interessanter als den Bezug auf Cashel in der Tradition des Albert von Regensburg[19], obgleich er dort nur Ausdruck festländischer Kunde von der Errichtung des zweiten Erzbistums in Irland ist. In mehreren Arbeiten bin ich der Stellung irischer Ortsnamen in der festländischen Hagiographie und Martyrologie nachgegangen.[20] Wenn ich mich nun hier, schon aus Raumgründen, auf einerseits die martyrologische Tradition Irlands, wie eingangs um-

---

16 Z.B. Alto (siehe unten unter 9.). Ferner nennt er das „Schottenkloster" in Würzburg (siehe unter a) Scots' monastery, obwohl es im 12. Jahrhundert noch rein irisch war. Anderseits werden wir viele Beispiele seiner Vorliebe für Verbindungen zwischen England und Deutschland anführen können. Vgl. Anm. 51.

17 Siehe meinen Artikel unter diesem Stichwort im LThK 2. Aufl.

18 Dublin 1875ff.

19 Hierzu meine Arbeit in Mediaeval Studies VII (1945) 21-39 und meinen Artikel in LThK 2. Aufl. The Roman Martyrology (Dublin 1846, siehe oben) kommemoriert am 8.1.: *St. Albert, bishop of Munster, Ireland.*

20 Die meisten dieser Arbeiten sind deutschen Lesern kaum zugänglich.

rissen, anderseits die Stellung der Namen von Orten im heutigen Deutschland[21] beschränke, so ist dies zu rechtfertigen. Zunächst soll auch einmal für Deutschland an einem extremen Beispiel entgegen der gegenwärtigen Mißachtung[22] der martyrologischen Tradition ihre Bedeutung als Träger von Information illustriert werden: Wo sonst haben jahrhundertelang Tausende von einigermaßen Gebildeten in fernen Weltteilen im Laufe ihres Lebens mehrere Dutzend Male Namen wie Würzburg, Köln und Trier gelesen, von Buraburg, Eibingen und Schönau, deren Lokalisierung auch den meisten Deutschen schwer fallen dürfte, ganz zu schweigen? Es soll hier angeregt werden, einmal der Tradition der auf Deutschland bezüglichen Eintragungen im Martyrologium als Träger ausländischer Deutschlandkunde nachzugehen. Von dem hier Deutschland genannten Gebiet hatten die meisten Iren nicht nur natürlich keine persönliche, sondern auch kaum die elementarste Hörensagen-Kenntnis. Bis heute ist für den Durchschnittsiren der bekannteste deutsche Ort Oberammergau.

Daß den französischen und italienischen Ortsnamen in der martyrologischen Tradition Irlands vielfach Beziehungen zugrundelagen, läßt sich aus der allgemeinen Kirchengeschichte ableiten. Die Grundfrage unserer Untersuchung ist, wie weit dies auch bei den in dieser Tradition vorkommenden deutschen Ortsnamen der Fall ist. Wie weit, so dürfen wir fragen, waren diese Ortsnamen (und die allenfalls mit ihnen verknüpfte sonstige Information) Träger wirklicher Deutschlandkunde?

a) Würzburg

Die Stellung der Eintragung in T 8 / 7: *sancti celiani Scotti martiris cum suis fratribus Aed 7* [das irische Zeichen für „und"] *Tadg et Amarma conjuge regis gothorum truncati a preposito domus regiae in ippodoronia palatii regii* in der martyrologischen Überlieferung Kilians ist von mir anderwärts behandelt worden.[23] Es genügt hier zu sagen, daß sie eine Sonderstellung einnimmt durch ihre Ausführlichkeit und insbesondere die Bezeichnung des Heiligen als *scottus* (ein Wort, das sonst in T nicht vorkommt), die Bezeichnung seiner Begleiter als *fratres*, die irischen Namen dieser (hier: drei) Begleiter, die Bezeichnung des Fürsten, unter dem sie getötet wurden, als *rex gothorum* und vor allem durch die Bezeichnung des Ortes ihres Märtyrertums, wobei die Schreibung *ippodoronia* besonders auffällt. Diese Eintragung ist zweifellos einer der Zusätze, die zu T gemacht wurden, nachdem FO aus T komponiert worden war, denn bei der Ausführlichkeit der Eintragung hätte FO sicher Kilian mindestens er-

---

21　Ich bemerke nur, daß in der Eintragung für Rupert (28.3.) das Roman Martyrology von 1846 schreibt *Saltzburg*, in der für Thiemo (28.9., nicht in MR) *Saltzbourg* und in der für Virgil (27.11.) – mit dem Zusatz: *a native of Ireland – Saltzburgh in Bavaria.*

22　Sie geht über die die ganze Überlieferung durchziehenden *multae gravesque controversiae* (zwischen kritischer und traditionalistischer Betrachtung), von denen Benedikt XIV in Par. II seines dem MR bis heute vorangestellten Brief an den König von Portugal spricht, hinaus.

23　Nur hier nenne ich einmal eine meiner in Irland erschienenen Arbeiten („Ireland and Germany in the tradition of St. Kilian", in Irish Ecclesiastical Record 78 [1952], 21-33), weil sie J. D i e n e m a n n , Der Kult des hl. Kilian (Würzburg 1955), entgangen ist, obgleich er S. 194 auf mich freundlich Bezug nimmt.

wähnt, wenn nicht sogar ihm seinen ganzen Vierzeiler für 8 / 7 gewidmet. Aber auch keiner der spätmittelalterlichen Kommentatoren zu FO hat auf diese Eintragung aufmerksam gemacht, obgleich diese Kommentatoren öfter Ergänzungen aus T machten. Dies ist die einzige Eintragung in T, die sich auf einen der in Deutschland tätigen Iren bezieht, und überhaupt der früheste Bezug in einem in Irland geschriebenen Text auf diesen Gegenstand, dem die Iren erst später Bedeutung zumaßen.[24]

Die achte und letzte Zeile von FG 8.7.: *Céle Clerech cádfer* (das letzte Wort, am besten lateinisch mit *castus vir* wiederzugeben, ist einer der spirituellen Zusätze, die im *félire* oft gemacht werden) kann man als späteren Zusatz ansehen, zeigt aber vielleicht den Versuch, Kilian, von dem es wie von anderen in Deutschland (wirklich oder der Überlieferung nach) tätigen Iren keine von der festländischen unabhängige irische Überlieferung gibt, heimzuholen. Der Mitarbeiter an D, der im 17. Jahrhundert Anmerkungen zu FG machte, sagt hier: „*epscop* (Kilian wird sonst nicht als Bischof bezeichnet), Aed und Tadg (also nur zwei der sonst allein in T bezeugten irischen Namen der Begleiter), diese drei erlitten Martyrium in *Almain in Uairseburg*". 400 Jahre früher begegnen wir auch im Zusammenhang mit Kilian dem Namen „Würzburg" zum ersten Male in einem in oder wenigstens für Irland geschriebenen Text: ST (siehe oben unter 5) stellte Usuards Eintragung: *sancti martyris kyliani colonate presbyteri totnani diaconi* die Worte *ciuitate uuirziburg* voraus, möglicherweise abgeleitet aus Notkers Martyrologium. Niemand hat bisher gesehen, daß dies die erste Erwähnung eines deutschsprachigen Ortsnamens, ja, wohl überhaupt eines deutschen Wortes in einem Text in Irland ist. Hundert Jahre später brachte CC (siehe oben unter 6) die Eintragung nach Ado wieder ohne Ortsnamen, und ebenso fehlt der Ortsname in der Eintragung fur Kilian in D. In MR ist die Eintragung fur Kilian die älteste der drei mit dem Ortsnamen *Herbipolis* beginnenden. Von den durch Sollier angeführten auctuar. Usuard. (AU) stellten das Lübeck-Kölner und Greven (Kölner Karthäuser) diesen Ortsnamen ihrer Eintragung für Kilian voraus.

D hat unter dem 8. Juli die Eintragung *Céle Clerech* mit dem gleichen Zusatz wie zu der Eintragung in FG (siehe oben). In einer späteren Hand wurde hinzugefügt: *Vide aliter apud M. Tam.* (d.h. T). Man war sich damals also der ganzen Länge der irischen

---

24   FG hat am 27.9. *Coluim súi* (=Weiser), und S t o k e s (angef. Ausg. S. 185) meint, man solle hier (wie am 21.11.) „Columban" lesen mit Rücksicht auf T, wo es am 27.9. heißt: *Columbani eliuatio*. Auch die Herausgeber von T (angef. Ausg. S. 238) beziehen diese Eintragung auf den Gründer von Luxeuil und Bobbio. Statt der elivatio eines Columban gedenkt FG der (ir. *tocbail*) eines Finnián. Warum sollte FG am 27.9. Columbanus auf Colum hibernisieren, wo er doch am 27.11. *Columban* hat? Von der eliuatio Columbani am 27.9. ist auf dem Festland nichts bekannt. Der von eh und je mit der Kommemoration Kolumbans verbundene Ortsname Bobbio war CC so wenig vertraut, daß er ihn mit *Euouio* wieder gab. Bei der Kommemoration von Gallus (hier nun am 16.10.) ließ CC die Ortsbezeichnung *In Alemannia* weg, die Ado, wie Usuard und ST mit der Kommemoration am 21.2. hatten, ja, es verkürzte Ados Worte *mirae sanctitatis viri, discipuli columbani abbatis* auf das Wort *confessoris*. Durch Henry F i t z S i m o n s Catalogus praecipuorum sanctorum Hiberniae (1611) wurde der Grund gelegt für die Erforschung der hagiographischen und martyrologischen Tradition der Iren auf dem Festland (siehe J. F. K e n n e y , Sources for the early history of Ireand I (New York 1929) S. 37ff. und unten Anm. 62).

Tradition dieser Eintragung von T über FG bewußt. Nun folgt aber in D die Eintragung: *Cilianus, Colmanus et Colonatus, Totnanus diaconus, in Martirologio Romano etc.*, und danach kommen in irischer Sprache die Worte: „Es gibt einen Cillian, Sohn des Dodhnan [so in D, gemäß T und FG] am 23. Oktober *inde error*". In T gibt es noch zwei weitere Cillians (26 / 3 und 28 / 12 in FG *Culléin*, in D *Cillén* genannt). Die Herausgeber von D merkten an: „Es ist nicht klar, was der *error* sein soll." M.E. meinte der Schreiber, daß Céle clerech irrtümlich aufgrund der Latinisierung des Namens in T (*clerech* ist – aus *clericus* – ein für die hagiologische Tradition Irlands charakteristischer Beiname) mit Cillian (dann entsprechend auch latinisiert) bezeichnet wurde. *Céle* ist das irische Wort für „Sklave" (*céle Dé* - Engl. Culdee, so wird auch der Verfasser von FO bezeichnet - = *servus Dei*): es gibt in T auch einen Céle Christ (3 / 3). Man sieht, wie gerade infolge der (irrigen) Betrachtung der martyrologischen Tradition als historischer Quelle durch D (und seine Herausgeber) die Iren an dem Ortsnamen weniger Interesse nahmen.

D erwähnt sonst keine festländischen Ortsnamen (bei Kolumban nur *Italia*) und holt überhaupt die festländische Irentradition heim (etwa indem bei Rumold nicht seine Verehrung in Mecheln, wohl aber die phantastische Tradition, daß er Bischof von Dublin gewesen sei, erwähnt wird) oder ignoriert sie (er nennt z.B. Fintan von Rheinau und Fridolin nicht). *The Roman and British Martyrology* (Dublin 1846, siehe oben unter 10) erwähnt *Wurtzburg* nicht nur am 8. Juli, wo es die Worte des MR: *a Romano pontifice ad praedicandum Euangelium missus est* mit *apostle of Franconia* wiedergibt, sondern auch am 17. Mai, wo er die heute im MR unter dem 27. Mai stehende Kommemoration Brunos durch den Zusatz *son of Conrad II, duke of Carinthia* ergänzt und die Worte *in Germania*, die MR zu *Herbipoli* zusetzt, unübersetzt ließ, am 14. Oktober, wo er über MR hinaus dem Worte *Burckhard* hinzufügte: *an Englishman, consecrated by St. Boniface* und dem Worte *Wurtzburgh* (nur hier mit h geschrieben): *in Franconia ...* † *752*, über MR hinaus am 19. Dezember: *At Wurtzburg in Germany, holy Macarius*[25], *abbot of the Scots*[26] *monastery in that city ... in the 12th century* und am 25. Dezember: *At Wurtzburg, in the monastery of St. Megingard*[27], *St. Gregory*[28], *priest and monk, of royal English extraction ... in the middle of the 10th century*; diese beiden Eintragungen illustrieren das „britische" Interesse dieses Werkes.

b) Köln

Unter den nichtirischen Heiligen, die T am 8. Oktober aufführt, findet sich *Agripus*, nach Quentin eine der zahlreichen Doubletten, durch die sich T auszeichnet, nämlich

---

25 F. G. Holweck, Biographical Dictionary of the Saints (London 1924) S. 633. Ich zitiere dieses Werk nur jeweils als ersten Hinweis.

26 Siehe oben Anm. 16. Die Tradition in Würzburg ist bis ins 19. Jahrhundert, als dort Caspar Zeuss den Grund für den deutschen Beitrag zur Erforschung der irischen Sprache legte, die wichtigste für die kulturellen Wechselbeziehungen zwischen Deutschland und Irland gewesen.

27 Holweck S. 698.

28 Holweck S. 451.

vom folgenden Tage, wo T wieder in dem Abschnitt für nichtirische Heilige sagt: *Acripini et aliorum cccvii*, nach Quentin eine Misinterpretation von MH: *In galliis ciuitate colonia agrippina sancti gereonis* (der Name dieses Heiligen fehlt in T). Aus dem Wunsch, keinen möglichen Heiligen unerwähnt zu lassen, interpretierte T vielfach Ortsnamen als Personennamen.

Am 15. Oktober bietet T nochmals *Agripini*, eine Misinterpretation von: *In galliis colonia agrippina natale sanctorum maurorum*. Mit dem Wort *Maurorum* beginnt T seine Eintragung für diesen Tag (die Duplikation in MH der den Ortsnamen und (Ms. E) den bzw. (Mss. BW) die Namen der Märtyrergruppe enthaltenden Eintragung am 10. Oktober hat T nicht). Das Wort *Maurorum* ist eins der lateinischen, das Oengus in seine irische Versifikation von T übernahm: Er widmet dieser Märtyrergruppe den ganzen Vierzeiler für den 15. Oktober beginnend mit den Worten *Primchéssad* [= prima passio] *Maurorum*. Die Schreiber von FO verstanden aber dieses zweite Wort schon nicht mehr: LB (die älteste Hs. von FO, 14. Jahrhundert), sowie die wegen ihrer Anmerkungen (siehe oben unter 7.) besonders wichtigen Hss. RI (frühes 15. Jahrhundert) und L (1453) haben, als ihnen wohl richtigeres Latein erscheinend, *Murorum*, während die (von Stokes nicht datierte) Hs. H 3.18 von Trinity College Dublin *Madurorum* schreibt. RI bietet hier die Anmerkung: *Mauri in Gallia passi sunt* (korrigiert also das offenbar – vielleicht aus LB – übernommene *Murorum*), während L, ganz im Geiste von FO, den rein spirituellen Zusatz macht: *cined mór do dáinib* (= ein großes Geschlecht von Leuten). Man sieht also, daß in dieser Tradition der Ortsname Colonia Agrippina nicht verstanden wurde und kaum eine eigenständige Kenntnis der Tradition der Mauri bestand, denn der Zusatz in RI ist einfach aus MH herausdestilliert (unter Auslassung des Ortsnamens).

FG hat am 11. Oktober *Gerion*, wie in diesem Werke naturgemäß, ohne Ortsnamen, und auch der Kommentator, der im 17. Jahrhundert Anmerkungen mit Ortsnamen zu FG machte, hat hier nichts anzumerken (wir haben schon gesehen, daß der Kreis, aus dem dieser Kommentator kam, an festländischen Ortsnamen nicht interessiert war), obwohl er am 11. April zu dem nicht T, geschweige denn FO entnommenen Namen Ailill, dem Marianus Gorman das Epithet *amhra* (wunderbar) beigab, anmerkte: *Ailill Mucnahma, darb ainm Helias, abb mainstre naemh Martain i cColoin* (= Ailill von Mucnam – ein irischer Ort –, dessen Name Helias war, Abt des Klosters von St. Martin in Köln[29]), m.W. die früheste Stelle, wo der Name dieser Stadt in einer nicht latinisierten Form in einem irischen Text genannt wird. Stokes merkte in seiner Ausgabe von FG an, daß die „Annals of the Four Masters"[30] unter 1042 und 1052 und die „Annals of Ulster" unter 1027 und 1052 diese Realbeziehung zwischen Irland und Köln, auf die hier nicht eingegangen werden kann, erwähnen.

---

29 Eine nekrologische Eintragung. Irische Mönche hatten (nach K e n n e y) Sources S. 613: 975, nach W. N e u s s, Das Bistum Köln, (Köln 1964, S. 378f.: 988) das Kloster St. Martin erhalten (siehe auch K e n n e y S. 544, 555 Anm. 163, 606, 610, 615 und vor allem Nr. 439).

30 Im gleichen Kreis wie D entstanden (siehe K e n n e y, Sources S. 43).

ST hat alle Eintragungen Usuards, in denen der Name Köln vorkommt: 10. Oktober (*ciuitas agripinensis*): Gereon; Victor; Cassius und Florentinus (heute in MR unter *Bonnae* figurierend), 15. Oktober (*colonia agripina*): 50 Märtyrer, 20. Oktober (*ciuitas colonia*): Martha und Saula (von Usuard eingeführt, älter als die Eintragung für Ursula und die 11.000 Jungfrauen)[31], 23. Oktober (*ciuitas colonia*): Severin und 12. November (*colonia agrippinensis*): Cunibert (wie Severin von Usuard aus Wandelbert entnommen). Man darf zweifeln, ob die Benutzer dieses Werkes die verschiedenen Bezeichnungen auf den gleichen Ort bezogen bzw. diesen lokalisieren konnten. FG ist eins der ältesten auctuaria Usuardi und der älteste Text in Irland (und natürlich in irischer Sprache), der (am 21. Oktober) auf die Legende von den 11.000 Jungfrauen Bezug nahm (*oenmili diac derbóg* = 11.000 sichere Jungfrauen)[32], und ST ist der älteste Text in Irland, der für diese Eintragung und überhaupt den Ortsnamen *ciuitas colonia* anführt.

CC ist ein frühes außerdeutsches Martyrologium, das die Vermehrung der auf Köln bezüglichen Eintragungen illustriert. Ado hatte für Colonia Agripina nur die Eintragungen für Gereon sowie Mallosus und Victor am 10. Oktober und für die Mauri am 15. Oktober (hier wie MH mit dem Zusatz: *In galliis*). Von den Eintragungen für den 10. Oktober bietet CC die zweite zuerst: *Apud agripinensem urbem s. martyrum Mallosi et Uictoris*, die erste später: *Apud coloniam agrippinam natale s. martirum gereonis cum aliis trecentis decem et octo*, unbeeinflußt davon, daß Usuard Mallosus als Beinamen Gereons betrachtet und die zweite Eintragung nur Victor gewidmet hatte. Während CC für Gereon Ados historia ausläßt, bietet er sie bei der für die Mauri voll, einschließlich dem Bezug auf seine *basilica*.

Darüber hinaus hat CC:

6 / 2: (ohne Ort) Transportatio reliquiarum s. pantaleonis et quirini mart.[33]

16 / 4: In colonia translatio s. albini mart.[34]

23 / 5: In colonia prope murum dedicatio basilice sancti martini conf. in monasterio ejusdem.[35]

10 / 6: In colonia passio s. maurini abbatis et mart.[36] (bis hierhin heute MR). Qui peracto agonis sui triumpho domus tumuli celo tantum notus et angelici tantum obsequii reuerentia ueneranda habitauit, usque ad

---

31 D u b o i s' Ausgabe des Usuardianum S. 325, G. Z i l l i k e n , „Der Kölner Festkalender", in Bonner Jahrbücher 119 (1910) S. 108.

32 Z i l l i k e n , S.108f.

33 Nach H o l w e c k S. 768: Fest in St. Pantaleon Köln.

34 Z i l l i k e n S. 62 Anm.1.

35 Siehe oben Anm. 29. Nicht in Z i l l i k e n und N e u s s .

36 Z i l l i k e n S. 74f. behandelt nur die kalendarische Überlieferung.

incarnati uerbi annum 957. Nam quia non potuit latere sub modio lucerna ardens coram domino, dum ponendo fundamento basilice s. pantaleonis terra effoditur, loculus gloria tibi Christe maurini martiris inuenitur ac primo peruidetur locum lapis claudens inscriptus martiris nomine et officio et martiris eius die et loco. Hic requiescunt ossa bone memorie maurini abbatis, qui in atrio ecclesie martirium pertulit sub die quarto idus iunii.

11 / 10:   Depositio s. brunonis[37] agripinensis archiep. cuius uita gloriosa et illustris fuit.

13 / 10:   In colonia inuentio corporis s. maurini mart.[38]

21 / 10:   In colonia undecim milia uirginum.

23 / 10:   In colonia s. suerini[39] ep. et conf.

1 / 11:   In colonia s. euergisi[40] ep. et conf.

12 / 11:   In colonia s. cumberti[41] ep. et con.

15 / 11:   S. benedicti in colonia.[42]

CC bietet noch nicht die Eintragung für Heribert 16. März, aber unter den am 31. Juli aufgezählten Reliquien, die an diesem Tage in Dublin verehrt wurden, befand sich *uestimentum herberti, coloniensis ep.* (Köln ist die einzige Stadt, die an dieser Stelle außer Dublin genannt wird). Daß CC eigene Information von Köln hatte, geht aus der in AU nicht bezeugten Eintragung für den 15. November, aus der ungewöhnlich detaillierten Eintragung zum 10. Juni und vor allem aus der (nach Zilliken) in Köln selbst nicht bezeugten Eintragung für den 23. Mai hervor. Aber auch *The Roman Martyrology* (1846) verfügte über eigene Information von Köln. Es bietet alle im MR seiner Zeit zu findenden auf Köln bezogenen Eintragungen, wobei es bei Heribert einfügt *count of Rottemberg* (solche Zusätze wurden auch für andere deutsche Heilige

---

37   Z i l l i k e n S. 104. Ein Lehrer Brunos war der irische „Bischof" Israel (K e n n e y , Sources S. 610).

38   Z i l l i k e n S. 104.

39   Dass. S. 108.

40   Nach H o l w e c k S. 356 offenbar der erste der zwei am 24.10. kommemorierten Kölner Heiligen dieses Namens.

41   Siehe unten Anm. 67.

42   Nach Z i l l i k e n S. 114 seit dem 13. Jahrhundert: *Dedicatio s. benedicti in claustro.* Andererseits hat CC am 16.10. Eliphius unter der Ortsbezeichnung *In castro Sollercii* (Soulosse, wo der Heilige sein Martyrium erlitt) und nicht wie AU und MR *Colonia* (wohin Bruno I. seine Reliquien brachte) (Z i l l i k e n S. 106 Anm. 2).

gemacht)[43] und in der stark erweiterten Eintragung für den 21. Oktober und der Eintragung für Cordula (22. Oktober) den Ortsnamen phonetisch mit *Cullen* wiedergibt. Außerdem bietet es mit dem Zusatz *honoured in Cologne* Eintragungen für *St. Gisle* (Gislenus) 6. August[44], *St. Sandraz, abbot* (Sandrad, Reformabt von Gladbach?)[45] 24. August, *Blessed Sigillinde* 30. August[46] und *St. Noitburge* 31. Oktober[47]. Von keiner anderen deutschen Stadt läßt sich so originelle irische Kenntnis nachweisen wie von Köln.

c) Trier

Während alle Hss von MH am 29. Januar sagen: *Treueris depositio beatissimi ualeri ep.*, schließt T seine Liste nichtirischer Namen an diesem Tage mit dem Worte *Treueris*, das er also als Personennamen deutet (Valerius nennt T nicht). Am 31. August kommemorieren alle Hss. des MH: *Treueris depositio s. paulini ep.*, T aber beginnt seine Eintragung mit den Worten: *Paulini ep. nolanae urbis qui se tradidit in seruitutem pro filio uiduae*, und erst nach zwei weiteren Namen kommt (das wieder als Personenname gedeutete) *Triueris*. T. bezog also die Eintragung auf den ihm bekannteren Paulinus von Nola.[48] Diese Interpretation behielt FO bei (Paulín na fedbae = *Paulinus uidúae*), und sogar noch der Kommentar dazu in Hs. L: *Episcopus Nolanae ciuitatis in Italia* hielt daran fest. FG nannte nur den Namen *Paulin*, während Usuard und mit ihm ST, wie schon Ado und mit ihm CC, diese Eintragung auf Trier bezog. Für den 4. September, an dem Ms. S von MH hinzufügte: *Treueris depositio s. paulini ep.*, sind die nichtirischen Eintragungen von T verloren gegangen (weder FO noch FG erwähnen hier Paulinus). Am 19. September bieten alle Hss. von MH: *In treueris ciuitate militi ep.*; T führt unter den Nichtiren lediglich *Militi* auf. Den mit *Treueris* beginnenden Eintragungen in MH für den 29. Januar, 29. Mai (Maximin; auch hier wieder fehlen die nichtirischen Eintragungen in T; jedoch erwähnen auch FO und FG diesen Heiligen nicht)[49] und 31. August fügte Ado und mit ihm Usuard die vom 5. De-

---

43 Ulrich siehe unten unter f. Ferner für Godehard von Hildesheim: count of Scheyren.

44 H o l w e c k S. 437: Ein Schweinehirt in Luxemburg, nach N e u s s , a. a. O. S. 363 besonders in Schlebusch bei Köln verehrt.

45 LThK 2IV S. 906 oder der Kölner Abt im 10. Jahrhundert (N e u s s , a. a. O. S. 173, 465)?

46 H o l w e c k S. 610

47 N e u s s a. a. O. S. 347: Reliquien in St. Maria im Kapitol (Pfarrkirche bis 1802). H o l w e c k S. 748 (die dritte dort erwähnte): Ihre Reliquien wurden nach Koblenz überführt, aber sie wird „noch von den Wallonen in Köln verehrt". Handelt es sich hier etwa wie bei Gislenus (siehe oben Anm. 44) um eine durch Ausländergruppen in Köln gepflegte Verehrung? Im Zeitalter der Gastarbeiter wäre dies ein interessanter Forschungsgegenstand.

48 Siehe meine Anm. 4 genannte Arbeit S. 52 und 56.

49 P. M i e s g e s , „Der Trierer Festkalender", in Trierisches Archiv, Erg.-Hft. 15 (Trier 1915) geht auch der Stellung der Trierer Heiligen in den festländischen Hss. des MH nach (S. 2f.). Über Iren in Trier s. Kenney, S. 614.

zember für Nicetius hinzu. ST hat auch diese Eintragung, CC aber nicht, da es für diesen Teil des Jahres Ado nicht folgte. ST ließ bei der von Usuard eingeführten Erwähnung Goars (6. Juli) die Ortsbezeichnung aus, vielleicht, weil es keine Entscheidung zwischen der in Usuards erster Rezension genannten (*treueris*) und der in der zweiten Rezension genannten (*magensis* = Mayen) treffen konnte. CC nahm hier Usuards Zusatz auf, aber auch ohne Ortsbezeichnung.

Mit 32 Eintragungen ist Trier der in MR meistgenannte deutsche Ort. *The Roman Martyrology* (Dublin 1846) gab alle diese Eintragungen wieder. Darüber hinaus aber hat es am 8. August: *Agapia*, virgin, honoured at Treves (ebenso hatte es für Sigillinde gesagt: honoured in Cologne), und am 5. Dezember fügt es der Erwähnung von *Nicetas* (recte: Nicetius) hinzu: Basilissa, abbess, honoured at Treves.[50] Ferner fügt es am 14. September in die Kommemoration von Maternus ein: first archbishop of Cologne, who converted the inhabitants of Cologne and Treves ... died in 46. His translation the 18th July and 23rd October.[51] Die Trierkunde dieses Werkes ist aber weniger originell als seine Kölnkunde.

d) Regensburg

Am 22. September fügte CC an: *Apud Radisponam ciutatem passio beati emmeranini*[52] *ep. et mart*. Ist diese Hinzufügung dem Einfluß der irischen Benediktiner zu verdanken, deren Zentrum für ihre festländische Tätigkeit seit dem 11. Jahrhundert[53] Regensburg war (siehe das oben, am Ende von a genannte Würzburger „Schottenkloster")?[54] Die Tradition der Verbindung der Regensburger Lokalheiligen Erhard und Albert mit Irland (siehe oben Anm. 19) blieb in Irland bis zum 17. Jahrhundert unbekannt,[55] obgleich sie zweifellos auf Information beruhte, die aus dem Kreis der irischen Benediktiner über Veränderungen in der Diözesanorganisation in Irland im späten 12. Jahrhundert (als jene Tradition entstand) gegeben worden war. Um jene Zeit bestanden noch rege Beziehungen zwischen den Benediktinern auf dem Festland und der Provinz Munster in Irland (zum ersten Inhaber des Erzbischofstums Cashel in Munster machte ja die Legende Albert). Es ist selbst fraglich, ob die von CC am 11. Mai hinzugefügte Eintragung: *Depositio beati gengulfi egregii* (dieses Wort nur hier) *mart*. auf Einfluß aus Bayern zurückzuführen ist: Reliquien des Hl. Gangulf

---

50   Agapia nicht in M i e s g e s und nicht die H o l w e c k 417 (unter Gaulienus) Erwähnte. – *Bassilla uirg.* bei M i e s g e s unter 20.5.

51   Nach M i e s g e s 15.7.: Inventio, 23.10.: Translatio. Siehe auch A. K u r z e j a , Der älteste Liber Ordinarius der Trierer Domkirche (Münster 1970) S. 286f.

52   Die Vita des hl. Alto (siehe unten Anm. 63) wurde vor 1072 von Othlon, Mönch von St. Emmeran (Kenney, Sources S. 515: Emmeramus), geschrieben.

53   Bereits im 8. Jahrhundert sind Iren in Regensburg nachweisbar (K e n n e y , a. a. O. S. 223).

54   K e n n e y a. a. O. S. 606 und 614-618.

55   Sie wurde für Irland von Stephen White entdeckt (siehe unten Anm. 62).

befanden sich nicht nur in Bamberg und Eichstädt sondern auch in Langres.[56] Die Schreibweisen *emmeranini* und *gengulfi* sprechen nicht für sonderliche Vertrautheit mit den Namen der Heiligen.

Am 23. April fügte CC an: *Natalis s. adelberti mart.* (Obgleich kein Ortsname genannt wird, ist diese Eintragung bemerkenswert, denn alle anderen Zusätze für europäische Heilige in CC beziehen sich auf westliche und südliche Länder). Die irischen Benediktiner hatten kurzzeitig ein Haus in Oels[57], und in Schlesien wurde das Fest des Patrons von Prag damals gefeiert.[58] Die am 13. August von CC angefügte Erwähnung für Radegundis ist der Verehrung dieser Heiligen in Poitiers und nicht ihrer Geburt in Erfurt,[59] wo ein Schottenkloster bis ins 17. Jahrhundert bestand,[60] zuzuschreiben.

e) Mainz

Moguntia wird in der von Usuard eingeführten Kommemoration Albans am 21. Juni genannt, und ST ist somit der erste Text in Irland, der dieses dritte Erzbistum von Deutschland erwähnt. *The Roman Martyrology* (1846) bietet diese Eintragung unter dem Ortsnamen *Mentz* und auch alle anderen auf Mainz bezüglichen Eintragungen in MR. Die Eintragung für Bonifatius (5. Juni) hat hier eine ganz andere Form als in MR: At the abbey of Fulda, in Germany, St. Winfrid, alias Boniface, archb. of Mentz, apostle of Germany, who having arrived at Rome from England, was sent by Pope Gregory II to preach the faith in Germany. Having brought a great multitude of persons to the yoke of the Christian religion, principally among the Frisons, he was massacred by the furious Gentiles, in East Friseland, at Dockum, in 755.

Man muß sich die sehr geringe Zahl irischer Druckwerke bewußt machen, die bis 1846 von Deutschland Kunde gaben, um die Bedeutung dieses Berichtes in der Geschichte der irischen Deutschlandkunde zu würdigen. Am 17. September bietet für Hildegard unser Text (statt der Ortsbestimmung des MR: *Apud Bingiam, in dioecesi Moguntinensi*): *abbess of the monastery of Elbingen* [recte: Eibingen], *in* [recte: near] *Mayence* (hier also nicht die phonetische Schreibweise). Am 28. September sagt MR: *Schorneshemi, prope Moguntiam, sanctae Liobae Virginis, miraculis clarae*, unser Text hingegen: St. Lioba, virgin and abbess, at Fulden, in Germany. St. Boniface invited her over from the monastery of Winborn,[61] for the direction of his German converts, of the female sex, in the way of religious perfection; she died renowned for miracles in 779,

---

56   Holweck S. 413.

57   Bei meiner Arbeit in Irish Ecclesiastical Record 65 (1945) 397 wären die Umstände zu berücksichtigen, unter denen sie entstand.

58   Holweck S. 13.

59   Dass. S. 845.

60   Die Schottenkirche zu Erfurt wurde kürzlich unter schwierigen Umständen restauriert.

61   Dazu die mir unklare Eintragung am 6.6.: In Germany, holy Agatha, virgin and abbess, who was one of the English nuns invited by St. Boniface from the monastery of Winborn in Dorsetshire to establish religious discipline among his German converts.

und, noch deutlicher in Verfolgung der britischen Assoziationen, fügt er am 26. Oktober die Eintragung ein: In the monastery of Haresfield, in Germany, St. Witta, an Englishman, disciple and fellow-labourer of St. Boniface of Mentz and consecrated by him, first bishop of Buraberg, which see has been since translated to Paderborn [recte: Fritzlar]; he died in 786. Man muß bei solchen Eintragungen in Rechnung stellen, daß diese Übersetzung des Martyrologiums für des Lateins Unkundige, also ein breiteres Publikum, bestimmt war und daß zur Zeit ihres Erscheinens die Zahl der Gebildeten unter den katholischen Iren noch klein war.

f) Augsburg

MH hat am 5. August die Eintragung: *Ciuitate agustina s. afri.* T führt an diesem Tage unter den nichtirischen Eintragungen *Affri, Augusti* auf, woraus man schließen darf, daß eine seiner Quellen *augustina* geboten hatte. Wieder wurde von T ein Ortsname in einen Personennamen umfunktioniert. Am 7. August hat MH: *Retia ciuitate agusta afrae*: T trägt nur *Affrae* ein (am gleichen Tage läßt T noch drei weitere in MH genannte Ortsnamen aus). Am 9. Oktober hat MH: *Ciuitate agusta natale affreniae*; möglicherweise ist die in T (in MH nicht) zu findende Eintragung *Eufemiae* eine Interpretation dieses ungewöhnlichen Namens. Keine dieser drei Eintragungen in T hat FO benutzt. Dagegen bietet FG am 5. August *Affra imnár* (= sehr schamhaft) und am 12. August *Affra*. ST hat am 5. August: *Apud prouincia, retie ciuitate augustana afrae*, mit der vollen, auch von CC wiedergegebenen historia, die Ado geboten hatte (in CC soll allerdings *rehtia* geschrieben sein). Am 12. Dezember stellte Usuard (und mit ihm ST) Ados Eintragung für Hilaria, die Mutter Afras, die Bestimmung *Apud Augustanam* voraus (nicht so CC), während FG seine Eintragung mit den Worten *Hilair, Affra* beginnt. Die Leser von FG dürften schwerlich gemerkt haben, daß die Hibernisierung *Hilair* nicht wie am 3. November ein Masculinum war, noch daß die hier genannte Affra dieselbe war, die FG am 5. August kommemoriert hatte, während sie am 12. August nur im Bezug auf die zu kommemorierende Hilaria erwähnt wird. Ob die von Ado und vor allem Usuard genannten Ortsnamen den Iren mehr gesagt haben als die in MH T, bleibt verborgen. Jedenfalls klang in Usuards Text den Iren auch das Wort *Rhaetia* an die Ohren, das für die Tätigkeit der Iren auf dem Festland besondere Bedeutung hatte. *The Roman Martyrology* gibt *Augusta Vindelicorum* in allen diesbezüglichen Eintragungen in MR durchweg mit *Ausburg* wieder. In der Eintragung für Narcissus (18. März) übersetzt es (falsch) *Rhaetia* mit „the Grisons" und in der Eintragung für Ulrich (4. Juli) fügt er ein: *count of Dillingen* (siehe oben); daß ihm dieser Ortsname etwa aus der Lebensgeschichte Stephen Whites bekannt gewesen sei,[62] dessen Apologia pro Hibernia 1849 in Dublin neu gedruckt wurde, ist unwahrscheinlich.

---

62   Dieser Jesuit war im frühen 17. Jahrhundert in Dillingen tätig und sammelte dort Material für die Acta Sanctorum Hiberniae (Kenney, Sources S. 38).

g) Sonstige

Über die bereits genannten nicht im MR zu findenden Eintragungen mit deutschen Ortsnamen hinaus bietet The Roman Martyrology noch folgende:

10.2. At Altmünster in Bavaria, St. Alto, a Scot by nation who founded with the help of King Pepin the abbey which is named from him, where he is honoured on this day as patron of the church.[63]

30.1. At Fulden (siehe oben) in Germany St. Amnichad, an Irish monk, disciple of St. Cochran ... he died in 1043.[63a]

29.11. St. Adumada, honoured at Gaudesheim (Gandersheim).[64]

2.3. In Germany [Kaiserswerth][65] St. Willeick, conf., who went from England ...

26.6. In Germany [recte: Niederlande] St. Corbican[66], an Irish priest: 8th age.

27.9. St. Chumald [recte: Chuniald in Salzburg][67], missioner, in Germany.

26.9. St. Guerin, abbot of Corvey in Saxony, died in 840[68]

und

Ven. Menier, abbot of the monastery of Hersfeld, in the diocese of Halberstadt, in Saxony, died in 1059.[69]

15.8. St. Alfred, bishop of Hildesheim[70], in Germany, died in 875.

4.1. St. Neophite, whose relics were preserved in the monastery of Limbourg, in the palatinate of the Rhine.[71]

---

63 K e n n e y , Sources S.514 und H o l w e c k S. 55.

63a H o l w e c k S. 63.

64 Die sel. Hathumod, erste Äbtissin (ADB XI, S. 23f.).

65 Z i l l i k e n S. 141f.: Reliquien im Stift, auch in Düsseldorf; H o l w e c k S. 1035.

66 H o l w e c k S. 237.

67 H o l w e c k S. 213. Vgl. die Lesung *cumbert* fur Cunibert in CC 12 / 11. Auf die Folgen der Lesung *Artinacha* statt *Artmacha* in der Visio Tundali habe ich in meiner Arbeit über St. Albert von Regensburg (siehe oben Anm. 19) hingewiesen. Darf man anderseits bemerken, daß kaum ein deutschsprachiger Radiosprecher den Namen Armagh richtig auszusprechen weiß?

68 = Warim (H o l w e c k S. 1031). Siehe auch LThK IV2 643.

69 Abt Meginher (M a b i l l o n , AASS VI 2, 136).

70 H o l w e c k S. 54.

71 Leider nicht identifizierbar für mich.

10.11.   At Mecklinburg. St. John, bischof and martyr, an Irishman, who preached the faith in the North of Germany ... † in 1066.[72]

10.4.   At Paderborn, in Germany, Paternus, a Scot[73] ... he died in 1058.

16.12.   Blessed Adelaide ... empress of Germany, wife of Otho I, died 16th December 999 at the monastery of Seltz [Elsass].[74]

Es ist hier nicht der Ort zu versuchen, die Quellen für diese Eintragungen festzustellen.[75] Wenn ein heute im deutschsprachigen Bereich Arbeitender hier beträchtliche Schwierigkeiten hat, so wird dadurch das verdeutlicht, worauf es ankam: Das Dubliner *Martyrology* von 1846 ist ein hervorragender Beitrag gewesen, breiten Kreisen in einem entlegenen Land Kunde von Deutschland zu geben.

Über die im Einzelnen gewonnenen Einsichten – insbesondere die Verbindung mit Köln – hinaus dürfte die Bedeutung der martyrologischen Tradition in einer heute besonders interessierenden Hinsicht klar geworden sein: Nicht nur wegen seiner Informationsbreite ist das Martyrologium weltweit, sondern auch durch seine Informationstiefe, in der es von geographischen und historischen Gegebenheiten ausgehend große menschliche Leistungen den Nachfahren zur Betrachtung vorstellt. Das Martyrologium ist ja kein Buch zum einmaligen Durchlesen, auch kein Nachschlagewerk, sondern will ein Betrachtungsgegenstand sein. Sein Anspruch ist immer so bescheiden gewesen wie seine Stellung in der liturgischen und der allgemeinen Literatur. Seine weit über tausendjährige Tradition ist ein kultur- und geistesgeschichtlicher Würdigung harrender Gegenstand. Die Zerrissenheit der martyrologischen Tradition Irlands illustriert die erschütternde Leidensgeschichte eines kleinen Volkes, dessen Teilnahme, wie unvollkommen sie auch sein mag, an der Welt, von der es durch mannigfache Gründe getrennt war, ergreifend ist. Anderseits beleuchtet unser Studium eines Teilaspekts der deutschen Ortsnamen in der martyrologischen Tradition die Stellung

---

72   K e n n e y , Sources S. 614; H o l w e c k S. 547b.

73   H o l w e c k S. 775: an Irish Scot (!)

74   H o l w e c k S. 16.

75   Die Eintragung in MR 25. 2. für Walburga erweiterte unser Text u.a. wie folgt: She was elected abbess of Heideinheim in Bavaria, died 24th February 779. Her relics repose in the cathedral of Aichstadt [so hier stets statt Eystatt im MR] to which city they were translated 80 years after her death, where an oily liquor distils from them, found to be a sovereign remedy for all diseases. Many churches have been erected in her honour in Germany; her festival in several places is ordered to be observed as a holiday of obligation. – CC aber hatte am 1.5. (H o l w e c k S. 1030: Tag der Heiligsprechung) Ados Eintragungen hinzugefügt: *In germania, pago sualauelda, natalis sancte uualdeburgis uirginis cuius uita uirtutibus et miraculis extitit gloriosa et sic in pace ecclesie quieuit. Zu Sualafeldia alias Sualfeldie, regio uicina ad flumen Almonium, in quo Heidenheimense coenobium* s. AASS Boll. Febr. III, 532f.; von den AU nennt nur das Brüsseler am 1.5. die gleiche Ortsbezeichnung wie CC. Man bedenke, daß die Ortsbezeichnungen einen relativ breiten Raum in den martyrologischen Eintragungen einnehmen und daher ihre Schwerverständlichkeit besonders auffallen muß.

des deutschen Sprachbereichs in einer Geschichte, von der man jenseits aller dogmatischen Stellungen anerkennen muß, daß sie in ihrer Grundabsicht der Menschlichkeit dienen wollte.

(Quelle: Archiv für Kulturgeschichte 54, 1972, S. 223-240.)

Die Stellung der Schweiz
in der hagiographischen und liturgischen Tradition Irlands

Für die zweite Nokturn des Offiziums am 16. Oktober schreiben die Proprien für die Diözesen Basel, Chur und St. Gallen Lektionen vor, die die folgenden Worte enthalten:

> Gallus Abbas, nobilibus apud Scotos natalibus ortus, in Hibernia in monasterio Benchor ... studuit ... cum sociis in Alemannia ad lacum Turicinum, deinde vero apud Brigantium oppidum ... consedit ... apud Arbonam expiravit.

Ganz ähnliche, alle diese irischen und schweizerischen Ortsnamen enthaltende Lektionen werden am gleichen Tage in ganz Irland gelesen. Außerhalb Alemanniens und Irlands wird das Fest des hl. Gallus nicht gefeiert. Die Liturgie dieses Festes ist ein einzigartiges Denkmal der engen Beziehungen zwischen Irland und der Schweiz im frühen Mittelalter.

Die Ortsnamen in diesen Lektionen bildeten die Grundlage eines Mindestmaßes an konkreten Kenntnissen, die durch die Jahrhunderte mittels der Liturgie von Irland der Schweiz und, so sollte man annehmen, auch von der Schweiz Irland gegeben worden sind. In den zahlreichen Studien der Tradition der irischen Glaubensboten ist diese Tatsache jedoch kaum je berücksichtigt worden. Ob es sich um irische Heilige handelt, deren Existenz, historische Bestimmtheit und Abstammung so klar sind wie bei Columban und seinen Gefährten, oder um solche, bei denen der eine oder andere dieser Punkte Zweifeln unterliegt, die liturgische Tradition dieser Heiligen ist jedenfalls ein wichtiger Träger festländischer Irlandkunde gewesen, während Zeiten, in denen das Festland sonst wenig Bestimmtes oder Historisches von Irland wußte. Mit institutioneller Regelmäßigkeit ist die Tradition der irischen Heiligen durch die Lektionen des Offiziums oft in reichem historischen Detail einer – jahrhundertelang der einzigen – Schicht von Gebildeten vermittelt worden. Dieser Umstand kann kaum überschätzt werden in der Geschichte des Interesses, das das Festland an Irland, seiner Geographie[1], Geschichte[2] und Sprache[3] genommen hat, ganz zu schweigen von der in

---

1   Jonas *Vita S. Columbani* war das erste Werk mittelalterlicher Literatur, das einen historischen irischen Ortsnamen (Bangor) erwähnt (siehe meine demnächst in *Ulster Journal of Archaeology* erscheinende Studie über frühe Ulster-Ortsnamen in der hagiographischen Literatur des Festlandes).

2   Siehe z.B. die in das zweite Kapitel von Jonas eingeschobene versifizierte Beschreibung Irlands.

3   Siehe z.B. die sich an die Etymologie des Namens Gallus anschließenden Erläuterungen, vor allem die Genealogie des Heiligen (Kenney, *Sources for the early history of Ireland* i [New York 1929], no. 50, IV; von Kenney angeführte Literaturangaben werden hier nicht wiederholt), oder die irischen Sätze in der *Vita S. Findani* (Kenney no. 422).

jener Tradition niedergelegten Erinnerung an die Beziehung von Ländern und Orten, die sonst kaum andere Beziehungen mit Irland hatten, mit dem Heimatlande dieser als Patrone verehrten Heiligen.

Bis zum Ende des Mittelalters sind wir über die Ausbreitung des Kultes der frühen Glaubensboten und anderer irischer Heiliger auf dem Festlande durch Colgan und seine Mitarbeiter, die Bollandisten, und neuerdings O'Hanlon[4], Weale[5] und Gougaud[6] gut unterrichtet. Die nachreformatorische Zeit dagegen ist kaum ernstlich der Erforschung würdig erachtet worden. Die literarische Herkunft der gegenwärtigen historischen Lektionen ist weithin unbekannt, zumal die früher vielfach in Lokalproprien gemachten Quellenangaben neuerdings durchwegs weggelassen worden sind. Die bedeutenden Änderungen, die in vielen dieser Lektionen im Laufe der letzten zwei Jahrhunderte unter dem Einfluß der Fortschritte der Geschichtswissenschaft vorgenommen wurden, sind nie systematisch untersucht worden. Die Auswirkung dieser Lektionen auf die volkstümliche Verbreitung der darin enthaltenen Überlieferung, in Predigt und devotionellem oder lokalgeschichtlichem Schrifttum, ist unerforscht. Gerade in der Schweiz hatte man aber Gelegenheit festzustellen, daß bis heute Versuche, Interesse an Irland zu wecken, erfolgreich an die gleichsam natürliche Kenntnis der Überlieferung der irischen Glaubensboten anknüpfen konnten,

Den Beginn des modernen festländischen Interesses an irischen Heiligen stellt das deutsche Martyrologium (1562) des hl. Petrus Kanisius dar. Wie später Ferrari in seinem *Catalogus generalis sanctorum qui in Martyrologio Romano non sunt* (Venedig 1625) feststellte, führte Kanisius eine große Zahl irischer Heiliger auf, die sonst unbekannt sind. Die Quellen seines deutschen Martyrologiums sind nie untersucht worden. Für den 16. Oktober hat sein Werk eine besonders lange Eintragung, in der «Schweitzerland» als der Ort der Verehrung des hl. «Gall, geborener Schott» bezeichnet wird. In Baronius *Martyrologium* (Rom 1586) sind die Worte «Apud Arbonam in Germania, sancti Galli Abbatis qui fuit discipulus beati Columbani» (wie bis heute im Römischen Martyrologium) die zweitletzte, und in der gleichzeitigen Antwerpener Ausgabe die letzte Eintragung für den 16. Oktober. Das erste in deutscher Sprache gedruckte, ausschließlich von einem irischen Heiligen handelnde Buch war Kanisius[7] *Warhaffte Historie von dem berümbten Abbt S. Fridolino* (Fribourg 1589), in der zweiten Auflage mit dem Leben des hl. Beatus verbunden; diese beiden Heiligen wurden von Kanisius ausdrücklich der Schweiz als Nationalpatrone vorgestellt. Kanisius hatte ebensowenig Zweifel daran, daß «Schottland (Hiberna genannt) an Engelland gelegen, Fridolini Vatterland» war (p. 3 f.), so wie auch das heutige Offizium für den 6. März in den Proprien von Basel und Chur mit den Worten beginnt:

---

4   J. O'Hanlon, *The lives of the Irish Saints* (Dublin 1873ff.), gerade noch bis über den 16. Oktober hinausgehend.

5   W. H. J. Weala, *Analecta Liturgica* (Brugge 1889).

6   L. Gougard, *Les saints irlandais hors d'Irlande* (Löwen 1936), bes. 114ff. St. Gallus.

7   Siehe meine Artikel «St. Peter Canisius and Ireland», in *Irish Monthly*, LXXIV (1946), 129-135.

«Fridolinus regio Hibernorum sanguine procreatus.» Ganz im Sinne der Überlieferung wies Kanisius Zweifel an der irischen Abstammung des hl. Fridolin mit dem Hinweis zurück, daß «Schottland» auch andere Heilige gesandt habe wie Kilian und Colman; des hl. Gallus gedachte er in diesem Zusammenhange überraschenderweise nicht.

Das besondere Interesse, das der hl. Petrus Kanisius den irischen Heiligen entgegenbrachte, hat vielleicht einen Einfluß auf seinen Neffen Heinrich ausgeübt, der in seinen *Antiquae lectiones* (Ingolstadt 1603) die ersten wissenschaftlichen Drucke von Cogitosus Leben der hl. Brigid und der Passionen des hl. Kilian[8] bot. Er schuf damit die Grundlage für die Arbeit Colgans, der Bollandisten und Mabillons hinsichtlich der Koordination irischer und irisch-festländischer Heiliger und der Sammlung ihrer Viten.

Die Entfaltung der irischen Hagiologie erfolgte, als im frühen 17. Jahrhundert irische Gelehrte auf dem Festlande[9] Zuflucht suchten und inmitten der Kriegsstürme sich dort wohlwollende Beachtung zu erkämpfen trachteten, indem sie darauf hinwiesen, was in früheren Zeiten Irland für die Begründung und Bewahrung der christlichen Kultur auf dem Festlande getan hatte. In diesem Unternehmen wurden die irischen Gelehrten engstens durch die erwachende spezifisch katholische Geschichtsforschung auf dem Festlande unterstützt. Auch hier war das Bestreben, die Grenzen des zu sammelnden Materials so weit wie möglich zu stecken. Es ist kaum etwas darüber bekannt, wie weit in diesen Unternehmungen die Werke des W. Petrus Kanisius benutzt wurden.

Die irischen Gelehrten waren offensichtlich überrascht von dem Umfang, in dem sich die hagiographischen und liturgischen Überlieferungen des Festlandes auf Irland bezogen. Es liegen praktisch keine Zeugnisse darüber vor, ob Irland vor dem Ende des 16. Jahrhunderts Kenntnis von dem Ausmaße festländischer Verehrung irischer Heiliger besaß. Von den frühen Glaubensboten finden wir in den alten irischen Heiligenlisten nur Fursa und seine Gefährten Foillan (Zeitgenossen des hl. Gallus), Kilian und seine Gefährten und Columban. Dieser ist der einzige irische Heilige, dessen Name bereits in den Handschriften des *Martyrologium Hieronymianum* vorkommt, wo er jedoch, wie bis heute im Römischen Martyrologium, ausschließlich mit Bobbio und Italien verbunden wird. In dem *Martyrologium van Tallaght*[10], der merkwürdigen irischen Version des *Hieronymianum*, fehlen die Eintragungen für November, aber es ist unwahrscheinlich, daß sich darin der Name des hl. Columban befand oder daß man sich der Verbindung dieses Heiligen mit Irland bewußt war, denn sonst hätte *Félire Oengusso*[11], das (vollständig erhaltene) Extrakt daraus, ihn in seinem Vierzeiler für den 23. November erwähnt, wie Fursa am 16. Januar. Somit ist die Eintragung «Columbanus» (mit dem historisch wertlosen, nur poetischen Rücksichten entspringenden

---

8   Kenney, no. 147 und 317.

9   Kenney, p. 37-41.

10   Seit Kenney (no. 273) mustergültig von Best und Lawlor herausgegeben in Bradshaw Soc. no. LXVIII (1913).

11   Kenney, no. 272.

Zusatz «den ich liebe») in dem *Félire* (oder gereimten «Martyrologium»[12]) des Marianus Gorman (etwa 1170) die früheste Bezugnahme, die sich von einem der irischen Glaubensboten in der Schweiz in der Literatur ihres Heimatlandes erhalten hat. Im Einklang mit der Tradition des *Hieronymianum* und *Usuardianum* hat die Eintragung in Marianus Werk eine spätere, bisher undatierte Fußnote: «abb robhuí isin Ettáil» – «ein Abt der in Italien weilte». Das einzige sonstige Zeugnis aus dem irischen Mittelalter ist die Eintragung, die sich in dem sog. *Drummond Kalender*[13] erstaunlicherweise unter dem 13. November findet: «In Italia sancti Columbani scoti», das erste irische Zeugnis für die Anerkennung des Heiligen als eines Landsmannes. In der dem Ende des 14. Jahrhunderts entstammenden (durch einige irische Heilige erweiterten) Version des *Usuardian* in Christ Church Dublin[14] beginnt die Eintragung für den 21. November mit den Worten: «In Italia, monasterio Euouio, natalis sancti Columbani abbatis.» Die Schreibweise «Euouium» ist von Jonas «Ebobium» abgeleitet ; sie ist sonst kaum bezeugt und deutet auf keine sonderliche Vertrautheit mit der historischen Tradition des Heiligen. Die dann folgenden Worte: «qui multorum coenobiorum fundator extitit monachorum, multisque virtutibus clarus quievit in senectute bona» sind von Florus[15] abgeleitet, der auch als erster das Fest auf den 21. November datierte; in dem Dubliner Martyrologium sind sie nicht als Hinweis auf spezifische Bekanntschaft mit den sonstigen auf den hl. Columban zurückgehenden Klostergründungen zu werten.

Die Beschreibung Irlands als «Insel der Heiligen» entspringt zunächst zwei sprachlichen Mißverständnissen. Der klassische Ausdruck *insula sacra* heißt «von Europa getrennte Insel». Das irische Wort *noib* ist nicht mit *sanctus* in seiner bestimmten mittelalterlichen Bedeutung gleichzusetzen, sondern heißt bestenfalls *venerabilis*, vielleicht aber nur «begnadet»; diesem Mißverständnis entspringt die Aufzählung (besonders im *Martyrologium von Tallaght*) einer ganz unverhältnismäßig großen Menge (meist nur dem Namen nach bekannter) irischer «Heiliger». Auf Grund solcher Aufzählungen wurde angenommen, daß Irland besonders reich an Heiligen gewesen sei. Diese Annahme wurde zum Anspruch erhoben, als im 10. und 11. Jahrhundert Iren – nicht mehr als geehrte Glaubensboten oder Gelehrte willkommen geheißen, sondern durch die dänischen und normannischen Heimsuchungen aus ihrem Heimatlande vertrieben – auf dem Festlande Brot suchen mußten. Die bereitwillige Annahme dieses Anspruchs durch das Festland entsprang dem Geist der Zeit, der Vorstellung von Irland als einem fernen Wunderland (wie sie gleichzeitig in der *Navigatio Brendani*, dem *Purgatorium Sancti Patricii* und der *Visio Tundali* niedergelegt wurde) und endlich auch der Erinnerung an die nie ganz abgerissenen Beziehungen mit Irland auf den durch die frühen Glaubensboten gelegten Grundlagen. So wurde im 10. Jahrhundert in St. Gallen vermutlich durch einen aus Kilkenny stammenden Iren der hl. Canice, der

---

12   Kenney, no. 275.

13   Kenney, no. 566.

14   *The book of obits and martyrology of the Cathedral Church* (Dublin 1854).

15   Quentin, *Les martyrologes historiques*, 347.

Namenspatron dieser Stadt, in festländische Kalendarien (und endlich in das Martyrologiurn) eingeführt. In der Vita des hl. Wiro wird die zur größeren Ehre des Helden festgestellte irische Missionstradition durch die Namen der hl. Patrick, Columban und Cuthbert belegt.[16] Die Einfügung des Namens des hl. Cuthbert als eines Iren weist darauf hin, daß diese Vita später als im 9. Jahrhundert (Kenney) entstand. Die auf diese Namenliste folgenden Worte «patriae columbae, terrae lucernae» haben später dazu geführt, daß man den Namen des hl. Columban Columba las, wie dies heute noch in den für die Diözese Roermond vorgeschriebenen Lesungen für das Fest des hl. Wiro geschieht. Der in dieser Liste gemachte Versuch, die verschiedenen Schichten irischer Missionstätigkeit und Hagiographie zu koordinieren, wurde nicht mehr verstanden.

In der festländischen Tradition der hl. Columban und Gallus wurde ihrer Tätigkeit in der Schweiz oft gedacht. Als einzigen irischen Beitrag zu dieser Tradition im Mittelalter kann man bestenfalls die Chronik des Marianus Scotus (um 1175 im Rheinland entstanden)[17] anführen:

> Sanctus pater Columbanus ex Hibernia insula Scotorum cum sancto Gallo alliisque probatis discipulis venit in Burgundiam ... Alamniam, ubi sanctum Gallum reliquit, in Italiam ...

Das spätere Mißverständnis hinsichtlich der Bedeutung der Worte *Scotia* und *Scoti* in der frühmittelalterlichen Hagiographie wurde bereits vom hl. Petrus Kanisius aufgedeckt. Zu seiner Zeit begannen schottische Flüchtlinge auf dem Kontinent die festländische Tradition der irischen Heiligen in Anspruch zu nehmen und sich in den Besitz der unter dem Namen Schottenklöster gehenden ursprünglich irischen Gründungen zu setzen. In ähnlicher Weise hat das spätere Mißverständnis des Wortes *Alemania* dazu geführt, die Tradition des hl. Gallus mit *Germania* zu verbinden. Im frühen 13. Jahrhundert war Eicke von Repgow berechtigt zu sagen, daß «Sinte Columbanus unde sinte Gallus quamen von Schotlande an Dudeschlant», aber im Jahre 1586 war die Beschreibung von Arbona als «*in Germania*» schon ein Anachronismus.

Der erste irischerseits gemachte Versuch einer Bestandsaufnahme der irischen Heiligen auf dem Festlande und ihrer Zuordnung zu den in Irland vorhandenen Listen der Nationalheiligen ist der *Catalogus Praecipuorum Sanctorum Hiberniae* des Jesuiten Henry FitzSimon (Rouen 1611)[18], wo unter No. 343 (in alphabetischer Anordnung) *Gallus* aufgeführt wird, mit dem Zusatz «16. Octob. – Surius» [1571, vi, 109]; in der zweiten Auflage wurde als weitere Quelle das Kölner Kartäusermartyrologium hinzuvermerkt. In einer handschriftlichen Notiz in dem der Bibliothek von Trinity College Dublin gehörigen Exemplar wies im 17. Jahrhundert Erzbischof Ussher auch noch auf Goldast (1606) als Quelle hin. Da in FitzSimons Katalog die Orte nicht

---

16 Kenney, no. 311. Vielleicht ein Anklang an Alcuins Epigramm auf die hll. Patrick, Kieran, Columban, Comgall und Adamnan (Kenney, no. 340, II).

17 Kenney, no. 443.

18 Seit Kenney (p. 37) in einer ausgezeichneten Ausgabe von P. Grosjean S. J. in *Feil-Sgribhinn Eoin Mhic Neill* (Dublin 1940) zugänglich geworden.

erwähnt werden, wo die betreffenden Heiligen lebten und verehrt wurden, brauchen wir auf die sonstigen darin aufgeführten irischen Heiligen und ihre eventuellen Beziehungen zur Schweiz nicht einzugehen.

FitzSimons Katalog war die Grundlage für die umfassenden Nachforschungen, die Colgan von Löwen aus über West- und Mitteleuropa nach Quellen irischer Heiliger ausführen ließ.

Einer seiner ältesten Mitarbeiter war der Jesuit Stephan White, der von Ingolstadt und Dillingen aus seine besondere Aufmerksamkeit den Bibliotheken im bayerischen Raume widmete. In seiner eigenen *Apologia pro Hibernia*[19] spricht er unter Bezugnahme auf Heinrich Canisius «Antiqu. I» von St. Gallen als «celeberrimum in Germania coenobium» und seiner irischen Tradition.

Der erste Ire, der die hagiographische Tradition der hll. Columban und Gallus erfaßte, war Thomas Messingham, Rektor des Irischen Collegiums in Paris, der in seinem *Florilegium sanctorum Hiberniae* (Paris 1624) Jonas *Vita S. Columbani* und Walafrids *Vita S. Galli* druckte, letztere natürlich die wichtigste Quelle für die frühen Beziehungen Irlands mit der Schweiz; die Ortsnamen sind in diesem Druck gesperrt. Weiterhin veröffentlichte Messingham als erster die *Vita S. Magni*[20], ein Werk, das ebenfalls irische und schweizerische Ortsbezeichnungen verbindet. Am Ende seines Werkes veröffentlichte Messingham das angeblich vom hl. Gallus in der Kirche von Konstanz gesprochene Gebet.

Die Veröffentlichung von Colgans *Acta sanctorum Hiberniae* ist bekanntlich nicht über die drei ersten Monate hinausgekommen, außer in dem dem heiligen Columkille gewidmeten Teil des von den drei Hauptpatronen Irlands handelnden Bande (Löwen 1645 and 1647). Unter dem 20. März hat Colgan jedoch einen Auszug aus Walafrid und einige Bemerkungen über St. Gallen, das ausdrücklich unter Bezugnahme auf Ado als «in Germania» gelegen bezeichnet wird[21].

Die besondere Bedeutung des hl. Columban, ebenso wie des heiligen Rumold, Patron von Mecheln, veranlaßte Mitarbeiter Colgans die auf diese Heiligen bezüglichen Materialien gesondert zur Veröffentlichung vorzubereiten, und diese Veröffentlichungen wurden in den sechziger Jahren von Thomas O'Sher(r)in durchgeführt. Patrick Fleming, der das Material für St. Columban sammelte, war für diese Arbeit durch seine persönliche Verehrung des Heiligen und seine Reisen zu den Wirkungsstätten einschließlich St. Gallen bestens befähigt.[22] 36 Jahre vor der Veröffentlichung seines Werkes erlitt er in Böhmen den Märtyrertod.

Flemings *Collectanea Sacra seu S. Columbani Hiberniae abbatis* (Löwen 1667) sind das hervorragendste Zeugnis irischer Beschäftigung mit der kolumbanischen Mission

---

19   Kenney, p. 38 n. 129.

20   Kenney, p. 205 n. 133.

21   *Acta Sanctorum Hiberniae*, 392 und 877.

22   Siehe *Ir. Eccles. Record I*, VII (1870), 207-216.

geblieben. Das mehr als 450 Seiten umfassende Werk ist heute überaus selten. In der Vorrede hat Fleming eine unschätzbare Sammlung von Erwähnungen dieser Mission in der Literatur des Mittelalters und der frühen Neuzeit geboten. Das Werk selbst ist ein Abdruck mit ausführlichem Kommentar von Jonas *Vita*. Einerseits haben wir eine lange Abhandlung über die Geschichte des Namens Scotia / Hibernia und eine überaus wertvolle Sammlung von Materialien zur Geschichte des Klosters Bangor, anderseits hat Fleming zusammengestellt, was immer er über die Frühgeschichte von Luxeuil und St. Gallen in Erfahrung bringen konnte. Seine Worte «nobile ex Galli nomine in Helvetia coenobium vulgo Sant-Gallum appelatum» sind m.W. die erste Erwähnung des modernen Namens der Schweiz und des Vernakularnamens von St. Gallen durch einen Iren. «Helvetia Gallum Apostolum colit», stellt Fleming lapidar fest.

Im Jahre 1916 wurde Irland das sonst nur Ordensgemeinschaften gewährte Privileg erteilt, ein Fest aller Heiligen Irlands zu feiern (6. November). In der 6. Lektion des Offiziums wird aus einem Schreiben Benedikt XIV. an die irische Hierarchie folgende Stelle gelesen:

> «Quod si recenscre voluerimus sanctissimos viros Columbanum, Kilianum, Virgilium, Rumoldum, Gallum aliosque plures qui ex Hibernia in alias provincias Catholicam fidem invexerunt, plus nimis epistolae modum excederemus.»

Diese Worte darf man vielleicht auf die Vorrede zu Ferraris Katalog der nicht im Römischen Martyrologium erwähnten Heiligen zurückführen :

> «Quis enim Ss. Patricium, Brigidam, Brandanum, Columbam, Columbanum, Gallum, Magnum, Virgilium, Kilianum, Rumoldum, Dympnam, Fiacrium, Furseum, Malachiam, Laurentium et alios Hibernos esse ignorat.»

Das Fest aller Heiligen Irlands ist nicht nur die Anerkennung der Tradition des Ehrentitels «Insel der Heiligen», sondern auch der eigentümlichen Entwicklung der liturgischen Verehrung irischer Heiliger. Einer der entscheidendsten Unterschiede der frühen irischen Liturgie von der Liturgie des Festlandes war das Fehlen eines *Sanctorale*. Die Heiligen wurden nicht einzeln in einer historischen Zeitordnung an ihren Jahrestagen durch Proprien kommemoriert, sondern alle Heiligen, insbesondere auch die einheimischen, wurden in einer spirituellen Zeitordnung täglich in der Messe durch eine umfassende Litanei vergegenwärtigt. Zuerst durch die Martyrologien, später unter normannischem Einfluß auch durch Propria wurde in Irland die Idee des *Sanctorale* eingeführt. Die Vita der hl. Gertrud von Nivelles (die das früheste Zeugnis für das Fest des hl. Patrick enthält)[23], Alcuins Epigramme auf irische Heilige[24], die Vita des hl. Findan von Rheinau (außer dem hl. Gallus der bestbezeugte irische Heilige im alemannischen Raume)[25] und die Kalender in St. Gallen ms. 250 und 459[26] sowie das

---

23   Siehe meine Notiz in *Bealoideas* XII (1942), 180ff.

24   Siehe oben S. 209 Anm. 1.

25   Siehe oben S. 205 Anm. 3.

26   Siehe meine Artikel (c), 323, note 1.

Buch von Fleury[27] sind die hervorragendsten Zeugnisse für die auf dem Festlande von Iren gemachten Versuche, die Verehrung einheimischer Heiliger der auf dem Festlande üblichen Heiligenverehrung anzugleichen. Die Verehrung des hl. Gallus und anderer in der Schweiz verehrter, mit Irland in Verbindung gebrachter Heiliger war rein festländischen Ursprungs.

Für das fast völlige Fehlen irischer Proprien für einheimische Heilige wird meist die Vernichtung kirchlichen Schrifttums im 11. und 16. Jahrhundert verantwortlich gemacht. Tatsächlich ist jedoch, selbst wenn mehr Material erhalten wäre, nicht damit zu rechnen, daß am Ende des Mittelalters in Irland Proprien in der großen Menge irischer «Heiliger» auch nur einigermaßen entsprechender Anzahl vorhanden gewesen wären. Die Kenntnis der auf dem Festland verehrten irischen Heiligen war kaum größer als es nach dem vorhandenen Material erscheint. Die auf solche Heiligen bezüglichen Eintragungen in dem zur Zeit Colgans zusammengestellten *Martyrologium von Donegal* gehen durchwegs auf damals erst kürzlich vom Festlande erlangte Nachrichten zurück.

Im Jahre 1632 erreichten irische Flüchtlinge in Rom die Einführung des Festes des hl. Patrick für die Gesamtkirche; bis heute ist dies das einzige Fest, an dem sich die ganze Kirche der Insel der Heiligen erinnert. Erst um die Mitte des 18. Jahrhunderts wurde ein Nationalproprium für Irland aufgestellt, und zwar von auf dem Festlande tätigen irischen Geistlichen. Außer den Festen der drei Hauptpatrone (Patrick, Brigid und Columba) enthielt dieses erste Proprium für Irland nur die Feste auf dem Festlande verehrter irischer Heiliger. Messingham und Colgan hatten nahezu ergebnislos in Irland nach Proprien irischer Heiliger gesucht, und legten daher fast durchwegs festländische Proprien irischer Heiliger vor. Bei der Genehmigung des irischen Nationalpropriums im Jahre 1741 wurde verlangt, daß eventuelle Sondertexte approbierten Breviarien zu entnehmen seien. Es wurde dabei offenbar in erster Linie an die historischen Lektionen der zweiten Nokturn gedacht. Bezeichnenderweise mußten alle diese Texte festländischen Quellen entnommen werden.[28] Die seit 1765 am Feste des hl. Gallus in Irland gelesenen Lesungen entstammten, wie mehrere andere dieser Proprien[29], dem Benediktinerbrevier. Außer diesen Lektionen sind keinerlei Eigentexte vorgesehen, wie überhaupt bis heute, ganz im Sinne der altirischen Tradition, das irische Nationalproprium ungewöhnlich arm an Eigentexten ist. Die schöne in St. Gallen gebrauchte Antiphon zum Magnifikat am Feste des hl. Gallus, die, Walafrid entnommen, einer der ältesten Ausdrücke des Heimwehs eines *Irish exile* ist, ist in Irland unbekannt geblieben.

Die auf dem Festlande verehrten irischen Heiligen wurden in das Nationalproprium nach Maßgabe der Geschichtswissenschaft der Zeit einbezogen, d.h. Heilige, deren Verbindung mit Irland und deren historischer Hintergrund heute als zweifelhaft

---

27 Siehe meinen Artikel (f).

28 Siehe meine Artikel (b).

29 Z.B. auch dem für das Fest des hl. Columbanus. Der Vergleich mit den für Chur und St. Gallen vorgeschriebenen Lesungen zeigt, daß die auf den hl. Gallus bezüglichen Stellen (einschl. der Erwähnung der Schweiz und des Zürcher Sees) darin fehlen.

anerkannt sind, wie Albert von Regensburg, Cataldo von Tarent, Livinus von Gent und Rumold von Mecheln wurden mit Rücksicht auf die Bedeutung ihres Kultes oder Kultortes gewählt, während so gut bezeugte irische Heilige wie Findan von Rheinau und Colman von Stockerau außer Betracht blieben. Diese Auswahl erreichte immerhin den Zweck, daß sich Irland allgemein des Ausmaßes mittelalterlicher Verehrung irischer Heiliger auf dem Festlande und der sich daraus ergebenden Tradition bewußt wurde. Schriftsteller[30] wie O'Hanlon[31], Healy und Moran betrachteten ganz im Geiste Colgans und seiner Schule diese gesamte Tradition als historisch. Anderseits wurde diese Überlieferung von festländischen, vom protestantischen Liberalismus herkommenden Schriftstellern wie z.B. in Bezug auf den hl. Livinus von Holder-Egger, in Bausch und Bogen verworfen und in durchaus unhistorischer Weise lächerlich gemacht. In der Schweiz hat sich um die historischen Gestalten von Columban und Gallus[32] eine reiche Tradition sekundärer, mit Irland verbundener Heiliger, wie Magnus, Fridolin, Ursus usw. entfaltet, die selbstverständlich auch nicht als direkte Quelle zu betrachten ist, sondern uns mittelbar Auskunft gibt über die Geschichte festländischer Irlandkunde.

Die hervorragende Stellung. die das erste Nationalproprium für Irland den auf dem Festlande verehrten irischen Heiligen einräumte, hat diesen Heiligen aber nicht eine echte Verehrung in ihrem eigenen Volke zu verschaffen vermocht. Solche Verehrung, das wird heute oft vergessen, muß natürlich wachsen. Ist ihre Tradition abgerissen oder war sie nie da, so kann sie nicht durch noch so eifrige Bemühungen organisiert werden. Es gibt m.W. keine Kirche in Irland, die dem hl. Gallus geweiht ist, vom hl. Findan von Rheinau (dessen höchst zuverlässige Vita das erste Zeugnis des Gebrauchs der irischen Sprache auf dem Festlande ist) ganz zu schweigen. Der Name Gallus kommt unter irischen Laien nicht vor. Nur ganz selten, z.B. in der mit der Erinnerung an den späteren Kardinal Newman verbundenen Universitätskirche in Dublin, findet man ein Bildnis des hl. Gallus in einer Kirche seines Heimatlandes, und es ist kaum bekannt, daß der hl. Gallus wohl der erste Ire ist, von dem ein Porträt erhalten ist.[33] Anknüpfend an das, was die Benediktiner für die Bewahrung der liturgischen Tradition irischer Heiliger getan haben, versuchen in neuester Zeit die aus Belgien stammenden Benediktiner der Abtei Glenstal, Grafschaft Limerick, durch neue Offizien der

---

30 Von irischen Schriftstellern des 18. Jahrhunderts, die der irischen Mission in der Schweiz gedenken, ist besonders MacGeoghegan (*Histoire d'Irlande*, Paris und Haag 1758ff., I, 341ff.) zu erwähnen. Für die spätere Literatur siehe Kenney, *op. cit.* 109.

31 *Op. cit.* X, 271-320. In der in diesem Werke üblichen Weise sind belanglose Illustrationen ('The site of old Brigantium', 'The lake of Zurich' und 'The city of Constance') eingefügt.

32 Eine Übersetzung des Lebens des heiligen Gallus von Walafrid veröffentlichte die namhafte Keltistin Maud Joynt (Dublin 1927) in den Publikationen der protestantischen Society for Promoting Christian Knowledge, in der Serie 'Leben keltischer Heiliger'. Prof. Blankes Buch wurde von mir in *Irish Historical Studies* II (1941) 448-451 besprochen.

33 Siehe meinen Artikel «Early representations of Irishmen in German books» in *Proceedings of the Royal Society of Antiquaries of Ireland*, LXXX (1950), 158f.

von den Benediktinern besonders verehrten irischen Heiligen der irischen Verehrung dieser Heiligen aufzuhelfen.

Das Volk fühlt deutlich, daß die Verehrung von Heiligen naturgemäß mit dem Orte ihres Wirkens und Todes oder ihrer geistlichen Bedeutung verbunden ist und daß eine Verehrung, lediglich durch die Geburtsstätte lokalisiert, nicht lebendig ist. Liturgie und Geschichte haben bis heute in Irland nicht die enge Verbindung gefunden, die uns von der römischen Liturgie her vertraut ist. Wie schon Scheffel in den (heute selten mitgedruckten) Anmerkungen zu seinem *Ekkehard* bemerkte, ist das irische Interesse an St. Gallen und anderen Stätten irischer Wirksamkeit auf dem Festlande nicht über einen kleinen Kreis historisch Interessierter hinausgedrungen. Diese Tatsachen lassen sich nicht nur durch die einzigartig schwere Geschichte Irlands erklären, sondern müssen auch verstanden werden als Ausdruck eines von den ältesten Zeiten fast unverändert gebliebenen Geschichtsbewußtseins, durch das sich Irland vom Festlande unterscheidet.

Literatur

(a) «Irish Saints in the liturgical and artistic tradition of Central Europe», in *Irish Ecclesiastical Record* V, LIX (1942), 181-192.

(b) «St. Columbanus in the liturgy», *ibid.* LXII (1943), 306-312.

(c) «Studies in the liturgy of the early Irish Church», *ibid.* LXXV (1951), 318-333.

(d) «A feast of all Saints of Europe», in *Speculum* XXI (1946), 46-66.

(e) «Irish Saints in early German literature», *ibid.* XXII (1947), 358-374.

(f) Besprechung von P.E. Mundings Buch *Die Kalendarien von St. Gallen aus 21 Hss. neuntes bis elftes Jahrhundert*, in *Irish Historical Studies* VII (1951), 203-206.

(g) «St. Albert, patron of Cashel. A study in the history of diocesan episcopacy in Ireland», in *Mediaeval Studies* VII (1945), 21-39.

(h) «Cataldus Rachau. A study on the early history of diocesam episcopacy in Irland», *ibid.* X (1948), 217-244.

(i) «The meaning of All the Saints», *ibid.* X (1948), 147-161.

(j) «Der Geschichtsbegriff der Liturgie», in *Schweizer Rundschau* IL (1949), 81-88.

(k) «Irisch-schweizerische Literaturbeziehungen», in *Die Tat*, 24.06.1947.

(l) «Irish-German literature relations», in *German Life and Letters*, N.S. III (1950), 102-110.

(Quelle: Zeitschrift für schweizerische Kirchengeschichte 46, 1952, S. 204-216.)

Die kulturgeschichtliche Bedeutung der Stellung Irlands in der hagiographischen Tradition – Rückblick und Ausblick

Herrn Pater Prior Dr. Emmanuel v. Severus OSB Maria Laach zum 70. Geburtstag (24. 8. 1978)

Seinen Ehrennamen *insula sanctorum* verdankt Irland[1] vor allem der Tatsache, daß im Irischen, der ersten westeuropäischen Sprache, in der eine kirchliche Terminologie entwickelt wurde, das Wort *noibh* eine weitere Bedeutung hat als das gemeinhin damit gleichgesetzte *sanctus*. Der Reputation der *insula sanctorum* ist es zuzuschreiben, daß im Mittelalter vielen auf dem Festland als Heilige Verehrten, über deren Herkunft man nichts wußte, Herkunft aus Irland zugeschrieben wurde (Fridolin von Säckingen, Pirmin von Reichenau, Cataldus von Tarent, Albert von Regensburg, Wendelin u. a.). Im Martyrologium von Tallaght (MT), einer aus dem „Hieronymianum" mit größtmöglicher Vollständigkeit (mit dem Risiko zahlreicher Doubletten) extrahierten Liste von Namen von (nichtirischen) Heiligen, wurde eine praktisch ebenso viele Namen umfassende Liste irischer „Heiliger" beigegeben. Man tritt den Iren nicht zu nahe, wenn man sagt, daß diese Tatsache weniger bedeutet, daß Irland so viele Heilige hatte wie die übrige Welt zusammen, als daß die Iren eine weitere (die ältere) Konzeption von *sanctus* („ehrwürdig") hatten. Zugleich weist diese Tatsache darauf hin, daß die irischen Listen in MT nicht wie das Martyrologium außerhalb Irlands (weitgehend) auf liturgische Verehrung der Aufgeführten zurückgehen: Liturgische Verehrung irischer

---

1 Da ich den hier zu behandelnden Gegenstand in einer ungewöhnlichen Breite und Länge, wenn auch nicht in der erforderlichen Tiefe, durchforscht habe, möchte ich diesen Aufsatz als Bericht über eigene Arbeiten vorlegen und einerseits weitgehend auf Literaturhinweise verzichten, anderseits summarisch auf meine im Archiv für Liturgiewissenschaft XIII, 1974, S. 141-172, erschienene Bibliographie verweisen. An nach 1970 erschienenen Arbeiten wären noch hinzufügen: Deutsche Ortsnamen in der martyrologischen Tradition Irlands, in: Archiv für Kulturgeschichte 54, 1972, S. 223-240, Grundzüge der martyrologischen Tradition Irlands, in: Archiv für Liturgiewissenschaft 14 1972, S. 71-98, Ireland's contribution to the martyrological tradition of the Popes, in: Archivum Historiae Pontificiae 10, 1972, S. 9-23; Studien zur deutschsprachigen Irlandkunde im 19. Jahrhundert, in: Deutsche Vierteljahrschrift für Literaturwissenschaft und Geistesgeschichte 47, 1973, S. 167-179; The sources of the martyrological tradition of non-Irish saints in mediaeval Ireland, in: Sacris Erudiri 21, 1972/73, S. 407-434, The notes on non-Irish Saints in the manuscripts of Félire Oengusso, in: Proceedings Royal Irish Academy 1975. Außer dem Kernstück der nachstehenden Ausführungen, der Übersicht über die Stellung Irlands in der Tradition der Bollandisten, könnte ich für jeden Absatz auf einen Artikel von mir verweisen. Dies wäre aber wenig sinnvoll. Meine Arbeiten entstanden unter Umständen, die, um das Mindeste zu sagen, auf diesem Gebiet ungewöhnlich sind. Ihre (sich nicht allein daraus ergebenden) Mängel sind niemandem besser bewußt als mir. Die Umstände, unter denen ich gearbeitet habe und arbeite – vor allem außerhalb jeglichen offiziellen Auftrags –, spiegeln sich darin wider, daß meine Aufsätze in vielen Dutzenden von Zeitschriften der englisch- und deutschsprachigen Welt verstreut sind. An eine Zusammenfassung ist nicht zu denken, nicht nur weil sich kein Verleger an diesen entlegenen Gegenstand wagen würde, sondern auch weil – was Iren besser erkannt haben als Nichtiren – noch zuviele Dokumentationslücken bestehen. Immerhin hoffe ich, dem Nichtspezialisten ein Gefühl für die vielseitige Bedeutung des Gegenstands, weit über den materialen Bereich hinaus, und vielleicht auch für seine Würde vermitteln zu können.

Heiliger begann erst lange nach MT. Die Verehrung der Heiligen drückte sich in Irland paraliturgisch aus.

Um 800 brachte Oengus eine verkürzte Liste der Heiligennamen aus MT in metrische Form, das erste Beispiel der von diesem Werk her als *félire* (von *féil* = *vigilia*) bezeichneten Literaturform, die im Rahmen des zu jener Zeit Ost- und Westkirche gemeinsamen Verlangens nach ansprechender Darbietung des an sich spröden Stoffes (Namenslisten) zu betrachten ist. Félire Oengusso (FO) ist das erste Beispiel in einer nichtklassischen Sprache und hatte eine ähnliche Funktion, wie sie der „Megas Kanon" des Andreas von Kreta bis heute in der griechischen Kirche hat. Im Unterschied zu MT differenzierte FO von seiner Natur her (ein Vierzeiler pro Tag) nicht zwischen Iren und Nichtiren, wodurch der Eindruck verstärkt wurde, alle die genannten Iren seien *sancti* auf derselben Ebene wie die Nichtiren. Fast 400 Jahre später verfaßte Marianus Gorman wieder ein Nichtiren und Iren durcheinander aufführendes *félire*, für die Nichtiren vor allem auf Usuard fußend, dessen Martyrologium seinen Siegeszug durch die Westkirche angetreten hatte. „Félire húi Gormáin" (FG) war die Grundlage für das mehr als 400 Jahre später kompilierte Martyrologium von Donegal (MD), das sich auf Iren beschränkte und die umfassendste Liste, die je von irischen „Heiligen" erstellt worden ist, bietet. Dieses Werk war einer der eminenten Beiträge der irischen Franziskaner zur Bewahrung des nationalen Erbes; dem gleichen Kreise gehörte John Colgan an, der erste Ire, der irische Hagiologie wissenschaftlich und systematisch in Angriff nahm.

In Irland und wohl noch mehr außerhalb Irlands hat die Betrachtung irischer Heiliger zentrale Bedeutung für die Beschäftigung mit Irland überhaupt gehabt. An Hand der Geschichte der Beschäftigung mit irischen Heiligen könnte man die Geschichte der Irlandbildes inner- und außerhalb Irlands exemplarisch darstellen. Vom festländischen Standpunkt aus ist dabei das Interessante, daß hier Kunde von einem Lande verbreitet wurde, mit dem man zwar viele spirituelle Verbindungen hatte (oder zu haben meinte), aber nur ganz wenige materielle. Daß Irland eine Insel am äußersten Rande der bekannten Welt war, ist in vielen Viten irischer und – wie Dom Louis Gougaud, einer der größten Kenner der Materie, sagte – „soi-disant" irischer Heiliger der Ausgangspunkt, von dem aus der Leser gespannt gemacht wurde. Bis in die jüngste Zeit hat Irland als ein Land gegolten, wo Dinge möglich waren, die anderwärts nicht möglich sind, ähnlich zauberhaft wie „das Morgenland". Es wäre an diesem Gegenstand aber auch zu zeigen, daß die dadurch angeregte Beschäftigung mit der irischen Sprache – Deutsche haben hier ja seit Goethe Hervorragendes geleistet – unterschwellig von der Ahnung mitbestimmt gewesen ist, daß das, was später fränkisches oder alemannisches Gebiet war, einmal von Kelten bewohnt gewesen war.

Die als wissenschaftlich anzusprechende Beschäftigung mit den irischen Heiligen begann in Irland und auf dem Festlande etwa gleichzeitig. Im deutschen Sprachbereich wäre vielleicht als erstes Beispiel das Buch des hl. Peter Canisius über Fridolin zu nennen.

Die Acta Sanctorum der Bollandisten (ASB) sind wohl dasjenige wissenschaftliche Unternehmen, das sich über den längsten Zeitraum erstreckt hat. Der erste Band erschien 1643, bis heute ist das über 70 Bände umfassende Werk bis zum 10. November (einschl.) gelangt. Größe und Gewicht der einzelnen Bände sind der cauchemar aller mit ihnen Beschäftigten. Die meisten mir bekannten Bibliotheken leihen diese Bände nicht über den Lesesaal hinaus aus, was bei den heutigen Öffnungszeiten von Bibliotheken besonders für einen, der sich nur nebenberuflich mit wissenschaftlichen Studien befassen kann, eine Erschwerung ist – auch ein Stück Wissenschaftsgeschichte. Die Stellung Irlands in ASB hat eine weit über den Gegenstand selbst hinausgehende Bedeutung.

1. Band 1 von ASB umfaßte den ganzen Monat Januar; der Stoff für Oktober wurde in mehr als 12 Bänden abgehandelt. Die einzelnen Iren gewidmeten Kapitel in den Novemberbänden sind relativ länger als solche in früheren Bänden. Im Ganzen wie im Einzelnen ist also der Stoff immer umfangreicher geworden.

2. Das Werk ist von einer verhältnismäßig kleinen Zahl von Mitarbeitern geleistet worden, Angehörigen einer kleinen Nation (die man nun die belgische nennt). Die Weltgeschichte spiegelt sich vielfach in der Geschichte der ASB wider: Die frühen Bollandisten mußten sich noch mit dem Zusammenhang der Niederlande mit Spanien auseinandersetzen. Die französische Revolution verursachte einen Unterbruch auf Jahrzehnte. Der 1910 erschienene Band ist mit einem Bild König Alberts geziert. Unmittelbare Kenntnisnahme von Irland erlaubten erst die Verhältnisse nach dem ersten Weltkrieg.

3. Noch mehr spiegelt sich im Fortgang der ASB die Kirchengeschichte wider. Die frühen Bollandisten mußten sich gegen dogmatische Verurteilungen wehren. Wenn ASB überhaupt eine Vollendung beschieden sein sollte, so wäre dies angesichts der Veränderung des Stellenwertes der Hagiologie im kirchlichen Leben als Wunder zu bezeichnen. In der irischen Hagiologie sind bis heute Einflüsse der Welt- und Kirchengeschichte besonders deutlich.

4. Ein Werk des Inhalts, der Gründlichkeit, des Umfangs und der Dauer von ASB hat mit großen wirtschaftlichen Schwierigkeiten zu kämpfen. Wir werden gleich von dem wissenschaftsgeschichtlich interessanten Notschrei aus dem Jahre 1838 hören, dessen Tenor unserer Zeit nicht unbekannt sein dürfte, sowie von ähnlichen Schwierigkeiten der irischen Hagiographie außer und innerhalb Irlands.

5. Vor allem aber läßt sich an der mehr als 300jährigen Geschichte der ASB die entwicklungsgeschichtliche, insbesondere kirchengeschichtliche und natürlich speziell hagiologische Methodik darstellen. Ich nenne nur zwei ganz spezifische Aspekte:

a. Richtig davon ausgehend, daß auch die wissenschaftliche Betrachtung der Heiligen sich darauf gründen muß, daß es sich um der Verehrung für würdig Befundene und tatsächlich (wenigsten an gewissen Orten und zu gewissen Zeiten) Verehrte handelt und daß diese Verehrung anniversaristisch ist, boten die Bollandisten den Stoff in anniversaristischer Anordnung, was einerseits Verzicht auf die der Geschichtswissenschaft weithin als unabdingbar erscheinende Darstellung von Zusammenhängen oder gar Entwicklungen einschließt (allerdings zeigt die annalistische Anordnung des Stoffes, die 1668 Mabillon für seine „Acta Sanctorum Ordinis Benedicti" wählte, daß diese für die Hagiographie nicht sonderlich viel hergibt), andererseits Anerkennung der (wenigstens zeitweilig) alljährlichen Erinnerung, die dem Gegenstand eine Insistenz verleiht, die kaum sonst historische Gegenstände erreichen, bedeutet.

b. Aus dieser Begründung der anniversaristischen Anordnung hätte sich ergeben sollen, daß primär die Überlieferung (einschl. der des *cultus*) und erst sekundär die (eventuell feststellbare) Historizität Gegenstand der Hagiologie ist. Tatsächlich ergab sich aus der historischen Situation der Bollandisten, daß der Wunsch nach Rechtfertigung der Grundlage der Verehrung in Historizität im Vordergrunde stand, ein auch in der Geschichte der Mentalität gerade der Jesuiten höchst bedeutsamer Punkt (allerdings folgte auch Mabillon hier den Bollandisten mit dem Ergebnis, daß er sich 1677 gegen heftigen Widerstand aus den Reihen seines Ordens rechtfertigen mußte). Leider – so darf der auf diesem Gebiete innerlich Engagierte sagen – zeichnet sich eine dem Gegenstand angemessene Wandlung erst heute ab, da der Gegenstand solcher Rechtfertigung deshalb kaum noch bedarf, weil das vitale Interesse an ihm abgesunken ist.

Der uns hier speziell beschäftigende letztgenannte Punkt läßt sich an der Einstellung zum Martyrologium, dem in der Geschichte der irischen Hagiographie einzigartige Bedeutung zukommt, illustrieren. Mindestens für Irland ist das Martyrologium für die Hagiologie die primäre, Hagiographie dagegen fast durchweg erst die sekundäre Quelle, denn nur von wenigen in den Martyrologien verzeichneten irischen „Heiligen" haben wir individuelle Viten und hat es wohl je solche gegeben. Weit mehr als bei den Nichtiren wissen wir bei der überwiegenden Mehrzahl der in den Martyrologien verzeichneten Iren außer dem Namen (und allenfalls einem oft kaum zu identifizierenden Ortsnamen) nichts. Auch sekundäre Informationen (wie Erwähnungen in Viten anderer Heiliger oder in den für die irische Geschichtskunde so wichtigen Annalen, um die sich die oben genannten Franziskaner auch bemüht haben) sind für irische Heilige seltener als für nichtirische.

Die Tradition des Martyrologiums ist die hervorragendste und längste innerhalb der anniversaristischen Geschichtsschreibung überhaupt. Das Martyrologium ist aber wesensmäßig sekundäre Historiographie, wie der heutige offizielle Name "Catalogus Sanctorum" richtig sagt: Das Martyrologium soll gleichsam ein Register zu den „Acta" sein. Gerade dort, wo es über diese Urform, am deutlichsten repräsentiert durch MT, hinausging wie etwa bei Ado, bekannte sich das Martyrologium am ausdrücklichsten zu seinem sekundären oder sogar tertiären Charakter. Die Bollandisten lösten das Problem in neuerer Zeit dadurch, daß sie die Heiligen, die nur aus Martyrologien bekannt waren, d.h. über die sonst nichts zu ermitteln war, unter „praetermissi" in einem separaten Abschnitt für jeden Tag abhandelten. Auch die ältesten Martyrologisten beanspruchten nicht Originalität, die Tradition, sich als getreue Nachfolger vorzustellen, gehört geradezu zum Wesen der Martyrologien. Auch hier kommt man zu einer sachgerechten Würdigung erst heute, da die mehr als tausendjährige Tradition des praktischen, d.h. täglichen und devotionellen Gebrauchs zu Ende gekommen ist und darüber hinaus Schätzung und Kenntnis des Martyrologiums auf einem sehr niedrigen Stand angekommen sind.

Noch ehe 1658 die (nunmehr schon drei) den Monat Februar umfassenden Bände von ASB erschienen, veröffentlichte der durch die Reformation auf das Festland verschlagene John Colgan den ersten Band seiner „Acta Sanctorum Hiberniae", enthaltend Informationen (vorzugsweise Viten) über irische Heilige der Monate Januar bis März. Dieses Werk wurde schon durch seinen Erscheinungsort (Löwen) den Bollandisten sofort bekannt und blieb ihnen eine wichtige Quelle weit über die behandelten Monate hinaus. Colgan und seine Mitarbeiter erkannten, daß Informationen über irische Heilige weithin eher aus festländischen Quellen als aus irischen zu erlangen waren (dies bereits ein eminentes Stück der Leidensgeschichte Irlands). Sie erfaßten auch erstmalig systematisch die Tradition irischer (oder „irischer") Heiliger auf dem Festland, von denen man bis dahin in Irland sehr wenig gewußt hatte. Hinzu kam, daß sie diese beiden Erkenntnisse benutzten und benutzen mußten, um ihre Position als bedürftige Flüchtlinge auf dem Festland zu verbessern, ja gewisse Ansprüche daraus abzuleiten, ein Emigranten unseres Jahrhunderts nicht unbekanntes Unternehmen. Es ist bezeichnend, daß Colgans Werk nicht wesentlich über das erste Quartal des Jahres hinauskam. Arbeitskräfte und Geld fehlten, Sorgen, die die Bollandisten auch kennen lernen sollten. Colgan hinterließ umfangreiches Material über die irischen Heiligen, die er in den Bänden April-Dezember zu bearbeiten gedacht hatte; nach seinem Tode behielt sich Bolland (gegenüber Henschen) die Bearbeitung der Iren (wie auch der Deutschen) vor.

1838 veröffentlichten die Bollandisten ein Büchlein betitelt „De prosecutione operis Bollandi", im wesentlichen ein Aufruf, die Wiederaufnahme des seit der Veröffentlichung der ersten Oktoberbände 1794 unterbrochenen Werkes. Das Büchlein enthält einen „Elenchus Sanctorum quorum acta in prosecutione operis Bollandiani (also vom 10. Oktober bis Jahresende) elucidanda videntur", einschl. 60 ausdrücklich mit *Hibernia* in Verbindung gebrachten. Als erste von letzteren wurde dann in ASB Oct. VII unter dem 16. Oktober Kiara behandelt (MT: *Ceire filia Duib Raea;* FO: *Ciar,* nach einer Randbemerkung in ms. Rl: *in Affrica,* weil MT am 16. Oktober unter den nichtirischen Heiligen *Caere in Africa* hat; FG: *Cera mathar cloinne Duib in Maigh Ascad;* MD nur: *Ceara o Mhuige Ascad* – ein typisches Beispiel für eine rein martyrologische Tradition in Irland). In den nach 1838 erschienenen Oktoberbänden wurden noch andere als in dem „Elenchus" verzeichnete irische Heilige behandelt. ASB Oct. XII (1873) enthielt S. 429-435 eine Liste der für Januar bis Oktober nachzutragenden Heiligen (hierunter keine Iren) und S. 396-428 eine revidierte Ausgabe des „Elenchus" von 1838, nunmehr nur noch für November und Dezember (8 Iren über den „Elenchus" von 1838 hinaus). Weder 1838 noch 1873 wurden Quellen z.B. für Zuschreibung an *Hibernia* angeführt, aber ASB Nov. 1 (1887) begann mit einer Liste von Quellen, darunter I. E: „Martyrologia Angliae, Hiberniae et Scotiae": Colgans „Acta", W. Stokes' erste Ausgabe von FO (Dublin 1880), Drummond Missale (11. Jhdt., gedruckt Edinburgh 1872), das Martyrologium von Christ Church Dublin (14. Jhdt., gedruckt Dublin 1844), FG (aus dem Brüssler Manuskript, erst 1895 durch W. Stokes veröffentlicht), die „Annals of the four Masters" (ca. 1632, das Hauptwerk der oben genannen irischen Franziskaner, gedruckt Dublin 1848-51), ferner Standardwerke über irische Kirchengeschichte und sogar Caspar Zeuss' „Grammatica Celtica"

(1853), für die man in Erinnerung rufen darf, daß Zeuss nie einem Irisch Sprechenden begegnet ist.

Die Geschichte der Irlandkunde der Bollandisten wäre ein Gegenstand, der ausführlicher Darstellung (möglichst durch einen Bollandisten) wert wäre, denn kein Werk hat über eine längere Periode und über einen breiteren Raum Kenntnis verbreitet von Irlands Stellung in der Geschichte als ASB. Es wurde bereits angedeutet, daß dieses Thema für die allgemeine Kulturgeschichte, insbesondere aber für die Wissenschaftsgeschichte exemplarische Bedeutung hat. Darüber hinaus ist es ein Kapitel in der Geschichte von Irland selbst, denn bis heute hängt ein beträchtlicher Teil ausländischer Kunde von (und Einstellung zu) Irland an dem durch ASB behandelten. Insbesondere werden in ASB die (außerhalb Irlands größtenteils unbekannten) irischen Heiligen in Irland und die (in Irland, außer allenfalls dem durch ASB Vermittelten, kaum bekannt) "irischen" Heiligen außerhalb Irlands auf gleicher Ebene behandelt.

ASB Oct. XII enthielt auch einen Gesamtindex zu den bis dahin erschienenen Bänden. Darin heißt es unter „Hibernia": „tulit olim innumerabilium Sanctorum multitudinem" (t. I Febr. XVIc, naturgemäß im Hinblick auf die in diesem Bande behandelte Landespatronin Brigida). „Inde multi monachi et sancti ad ceteros populos profecti" (ibid.). „Sanctorum Hiberniae Acta multa a Colgano edita" (XVIf). Dann aber folgen zwei bedeutsame Einschränkungen: „Hibernorum Vitae quaedam Sanctorum portentis imperite congestis plenae" (ibid. XVIIb), „litem de Sanctis inter Scotos et Hibernos non decidimus" (t. I Jan. XXXe et I Febr. XVIId).

Wie oben bemerkt, haben wir nur von wenigen der in den irischen Listen verzeichneten „Heiligen" Viten (dagegen von jedem der „irischen" Heiligen auf dem Festland). Mit verschwindenden Ausnahmen sind diese Viten später jedenfalls als MT und FO, meist weit interessanter für Zustände und Ansichten der Zeit, zu der sie verfaßt wurden, jedenfalls für das Bild der Vorzeit, denn als historische Quellen für den jeweiligen Gegenstand. Das Urteil der Bollandisten ist ein typischer Ausdruck des Verständnisses der Hagiographie als Information statt als Tradition, welches besonders im Bezug auf Irland kaum sachdienlich ist. Ebenso abwegig ist aber auch die in jüngster Zeit aufgestellte Behauptung, praktisch keiner der irischen „Heiligen" sei historisch: Es ist ausgeschlossen, daß sich die Kompilatoren der Martyrologien die Hunderte von Personen- und Ortsnamen (s. das oben zitierte Beispiel der Tradition von Ciara) ausgedacht hätten. W. Reeves, C. Plummer und P. Grosjean haben Listen von in Manuskripten vorliegenden Viten irischer Heiliger vorgelegt. Die von C. Plummer 1910 bzw. 1922 herausgegebenen Sammlungen solcher Viten in lateinischer bzw. irischer Sprache sind relativ leicht zugänglich. Letztere sind eine bedeutende Quelle für die Kenntnis der Geschichte der irischen Sprache und werden als solche in den verschiedenen Versuchen historischer Wörterbücher des irischen ausgiebig benutzt. Die in lateinischer Sprache abgefaßten Viten erfreuen sich naturgemäß bei des Irischen Unkundigen besonderer Beliebtheit; die Geschichte des Hiberno-Latin ist praktisch nur durch den aus Österreich nach Irland verschlagenen Ludwig Bieler systematisch erforscht worden. Die philologischen Studien sind die unentbehrliche Grundlage, anderseits aber auch nur die Grundlage für die kulturhistorische Würdigung dieser Texte und der durch sie illustrierten Tradition. Es fehlt u.a. eine Koordination dieser hagiographischen mit der martyrologischen Tradition, am auffälligsten in J. F. Kenneys unentbehrlichem Standardwerk „The sources for the early history of Ireland I: Ecclesiastical" (New York 1929), auf dessen Neuauflage man seit Jahren hofft. Seit dem Tode des Bollandisten Paul Grosjean ist m.w. jedenfalls auf dem europäischen Festland niemand mehr mit voller Kraft auf diesem Gebiete tätig.

Der von den Bollandisten 1873 erwähnte „Streit zwischen den Schotten und Iren" ergab sich aus dem Wort *Scotus*. Vor allem unter den vor der Reformation auf das Festland Geflüchteten ergab sich naturgemäß der Streit, wer der legitime Erbe der alten *scoti* sei, deren Name in Ausdrücken wie „Schottenkirche, -kloster oder -tor" oder selbst dem Ortsnamen Schotten (in Hessen) nachlebt. In Regensburg jedenfalls übernahmen die Schotten das (zweifellos irische) Erbe bis zum 19. Jahrhundert. Die wissenschaftlichen Leistungen der Schotten auf diesem Gebiet blieben weit hinter den der Iren (wie eben Colgan) zurück. Bis heute geistert der Ausdruck „iroschottisch" (ich durfte ihm einen Artikel im Lexikon für Theologie und Kirche widmen) unter Deutschsprachigen umher. Der Streit wurde verschärft durch den konfessionellen und politischen. An der Vorstellung der altirischen Kirche als antirömisch haben deutsche Autoren seit J. A. H. Ebrard (1873) eifrig mitgewirkt. Die irische (oder gar „keltische") Kirchengeschichte wird als Unterteil der „britischen" dargestellt, wobei schon aus sprachlicher Unkenntnis die Unterschiede verborgen bleiben. Allerdings könnte man sagen, daß der Grund für diese Irrtümer gelegt wurde, als in MT die irischen Heiligen als Sondergruppe den nichtirischen jeden Tages nachgestellt wurden, das früheste Beispiel auf diesem Gebiete für Nationalismus, dessen Zusammenhang mit ähnlichen Erscheinungen in der Ostkirche (wie sie der mit einer Irin verheiratete Ranke für Serbien zeigte oder wie man sie heute mit massiven Folgen in Griechenland sieht) zu betrachten wäre. MT wurde in ASB m.W. erstmalig in Oct. VI (1853) im Zusammenhang mit dem *pratermissus* Brocan (S. 46) erwähnt. 1850 war von Eugene O'Curry eine Abschrift des sog. Brussels Abstract von MT gemacht und durch die belgische Regierung in Dublin deponiert worden. Die Bollandisten haben also noch vor dem 1857 in Dublin erfolgten Erstdruck von diesem Manuskript Kenntnis gehabt.

Aus dem in ASB Oct. XII veröffentlichten Register kann man eine Liste der in ASB bis dahin behandelten mit *Hibernia* Verbundenen erstellen. Die Dichte, Länge und quellenmäßige Fundiertheit der betreffenden Eintragungen wäre die Grundlage für die Geschichte der Irlandkunde der Bollandisten. Dabei sind Irrtümer kaum minder interessant als das Richtige (soweit dieses Wort hier überhaupt angemessen ist).

Wir haben gesehen, daß in der Liste der Quellen für ASB 1887 *Anglia*, *Hibernia* und *Scotia* (man beachte die Ordnung) zusammengefaßt wurden. Der chronologische Index zu Alban Butlers „Lives of the Fathers" (ich benutze die Ausgabe Dublin 1866) faßt für das 6. Jahrhundert „England, Scotland and Ireland" zusammen, für das 7., 8. und 9. „Scotland and Ireland", getrennt von „England" und hier sogar unterscheidend zwischen „natives of Ireland" oder „of Scotland". In ASB Nov. III (1910) wurden für den 8. November *Sancti Hiberni* als eine Gruppe zwischen Kapiteln über andere Heilige, in Nov. IV (1925) aber „Sancti qui in utraque Scotia continentur" in einem den anderen Kapiteln nachgestellten Abschnitt abgehandelt. Diese Bände könnten sich nun auf Stokes' zweite Ausgabe von FO (1905) und damit auch auf die dort veröffentlichten Anmerkungen zu FO in allen spätmittelalterlichen Handschriften von FO beziehen, ferner auf den bereits genannten Druck von FG. Die lateinischen Übersetzungen von Vierzeilern in FO durch die Bollandisten haben Kenntnis des Beitrags, der in altirischer Sprache zur martyrologischen Tradition gemacht wurde, unter Nichtkeltisten verbreitet. Durch die Verzeichnung der in MT, FO, FG und MD genannten Iren haben die Novemberbände von ASB erstmalig die ganze Breite der irischen Tradition in die allgemeine Hagiologie einbezogen.

Nach dem 31 Seiten umfassenden Kapitel in Nov. II, 1 über Malachias von Armagh (bis zu der soeben erfolgten Heiligsprechung des irischen Märtyrers der Reformation Oliver Plunket der letzte der wenigen kanonisierten Iren und der jüngste der mit dem Festland verbundenen irischen Heiligen) behandelten die Bollandisten in gesonderten Kapiteln noch 4.11. Tigernach, 9.11. Benignus (33 Seiten, Kenney S. 350), 10.11. Greallanus (12 Seiten, Kenney S. 466) und Aidus (36 Seiten. Kenney S, 393).

Der einzige nach Colgan unternommene Versuch, die hagiologische Tradition Irlands systematisch darzustellen, war „Lives of the Irish Saints", die 1875 in Dublin zu erscheinen begannen – ein Band für jeden Monat – und 1903 mit dem Tod des Autors, John O'Hanlon. mitten im Monat Oktober abbrachen. 1859 hatte O'Hanlon vorab ein Buch über Malamias von Armagh (s.o.) veröffentlicht. Betrachtet man die Umstände, unter denen O'Hanlon arbeitete, so kann man sein Werk nicht genug bewundern. Er mußte es, um ihm die elementarsten materiellen Grundlagen zu sichern, populär halten. Er hat die Bedeutung von ASB umfangreich anerkannt. Da MT von den irischen Eintragungen für den 31. Oktober an bis zu den ersten nichtirischen Eintragungen für den 17. Dezember verloren ist, ist für diesen Teil des Jahres FO unsere älteste Quelle (allenfalls zu ergänzen aus FG). Die „Acta Bollandiana" sind nicht nur eine flankierende Publikation für ASB, sondern auch ein Hinweis darauf, wie die Bollandisten die Chancen für die Vollendung von ASB innerhalb absehbarer Zeit einschätzen. Man vergleiche die Publikationsgeschichte etwa des „Thesaurus Linguae Latinae" oder des Grimmschen Wörterbuchs und der diesen Unternehmen zur Verfügung stehenden Mittel. Die demgegenüber erstaunlich schnell zum Abschluß gelangte „Bibliotheca Sanctorum" füllt gerade für den Zeitraum nach dem 10. November viele Lücken in der irischen Hagiologie aus. Auch hier nehmen Iren einen breiten Raum ein, weil man soweit wie irgend möglich (d.h. soweit etwas mehr als nur der Personenname bekannt ist) auf in irischen Quellen Genannte einging, sogar (z.B. in dem Artikel „Colman" [IV 89-96]) auf lediglich in den Annalen Vorkommende. In vielen der mehrere Gleichnamige zusammenfassend behandelnden Artikeln wird dabei zugegeben, daß die Quellen nicht zu einer vollständigen Unterscheidung ausreichen.

Für den Zeitraum nach dem 10. November spielt das Festland in der Tradition irischer Heiliger eine besonders große Rolle. In das „Proprium pro Clero Hiberniae" (erst im 18. Jahrhundert erstellt) gelangten Livinus von Gent (12.11.), Kolumbanus, der früheste in irischen Quellen verzeichnete der irischen Glaubensboten auf dem Festland (jetzt auch im Kalender der gesamten römischen Kirche 23.11. in Anerkennung der bis heute eminenten Stellung Irlands in der Weltmission), und Virgil von Salzburg (27.11.), hingegen nicht Fintan von Rheinau (15.11.), obgleich er besonders gut dokumentiert ist (seine Vita ist der älteste festländische Text, der irische Sätzlein enthält) und schon Ferrari 1625 bemerkte, daß er erstaunlicherweise nicht zu den im „Martyrologium Romanum" Verzeichneten gehört. „Bibliotheca Sanctorum" hat über jeden der Genannten einen sachkundigen Artikel, ferner über die nach dem 10. November im „Proprium" für Irland kommemorierten Laurentius von Dublin (14.11.), Colman von Cloyne (24.11.), Finian von Clonard (12.12.) und Flannan von Killaloe (18.12.) sowie über die im Elenchus zu ASB 1875 als Iren aufgeführten Berchanus (4.12.), Boetius (7.12.) und Mogenochus (26.12.).

Der wichtigste Beitrag zur Grundlegung der irischen Hagiologie war die wissenschaftlichte Ausgabe von MT durch R. I. Best und H. J. Lawlor; im gleichen Jahre (1931) erschien der Bollandistenkommentar zum Hieronymianum. Zwischen den Herausgebern von MT und den Bollandisten hatte ein Austausch von Informationen stattgefunden. Den Bollandisten entging aber manches aus der irischen Tradition, weil sie unter den Lesarten nur die nichtirischen Teile von MT berücksichtigen (z.B. nicht die Eintragung für Brigida 2.2., geschweige denn irrtümliche „Hibernisationen" nichtirischer Heiliger). Anderseits war die Behandlung des Verhältnisses des nichtirischen Materials (irreführenderweise als „Roman calendar" bezeichnet) zu dem in den anderen Handschriften des „Hieronymianum" gebotenen durch die Herausgeber von MT allzu kursorisch. Die Herkulesarbeit, die Stellung von MT in der Tradition des „Hieronymianum" zu bestimmen, wäre m.E. lohnender als man glaubt.

Was die irischen „Heiligen" angeht, so kann man die Bedeutung der martyrologischen Tradition Irlands auch für den dem Gegenstand Fernstehenden durch zwei Beispiele illustrieren.

1.: 11. November: Carbre: FO, Ms. Rl. *Corphri*. Ms, L: *Cairpre Culae Rathin*, welchen Ort eine Anmerkung in Rl „im Norden von Dalaradia" fixiert. FG hatte C. als „Bischof" bezeichnet und in einer Glosse den Ortsnamen hinzugesetzt; beides übernahm dann die Anmerkung in Rl, MD fügte eine Genealogie hinzu. Murgal: FG mit Glosse: *milidh Críst* (zu diesem Ausdruck W. Stokes in seinem Index zu FG S. 385) = MD, was zeigt, daß FG und seine Glossen die Quelle für MD waren (Stokes, FG xxxix und 1). Cruimthir (Keltisierung von presbyter): FG mit Glosse: Ortsname = MD mit Vermutung, daß diese C. Oiarán (+ Genealogie) sei. Duban: FG mit Randbemerkung in der Hand des Kompilators von MD: *Dubh dubán* (also eine Etymologie des Namens, *dubh* – wie in „Dublin" – heißt „dunkel") und Verweis auf die irische Vita Patricks l. 2, c. 58. MD nennt D. *saccart* (*sacerdos*), fügt eine Genealogie hinzu und vermutet, dieser D. (s. BS IV 844) habe mit Moling (Kenney, Nr. 248-251) zu tun gehabt. Darerca: FG: *fíróg* (*vera virgo*); MD: *Darearcc* (nicht die in BS IV 482 behandelte); dem Elenchus zu ASB erst 1875 zugefügt. Mael Odran: FG: MD: *Maolodhrain* (allein die Verschiedenheit in den Schreibweisen bietet dem des Irischen Unkundigen Schwierigkeiten). Cronan: FG mit Glosse: *mac Sinill* = MD mit dem Zusatz *A.D. 664* und Genealogie (keiner der BS IV 375 ff. Behandelten). Für Nov. 11 hatte der „Elenchus" zu ASB als einzigen Iren Sinell; auch der „Elenchus" von 1875 bemerkte nicht, daß Sinell an diesem Tage nur als Vater von Cronan genannt wird.

2.: 18. Dezember, also den ersten Tag, an dem wir wieder MT vollständig haben: FG führte alle die in MT genannten 14 Iren auf, natürlich in einer ganz anderen Anordnung, wie durch die strengen metrischen Gesetze des *félire* gefordert, und fügte den Namen der Jungfrau Segnat hinzu. FO nannte aus der Liste von MT nur die ersten zwei; zu dem ersten (Magniu) bringt Ms. R 2 die gleichen Ortsnamen bei wie die Glosse in FG, für den zweiten (Dicuill) hingegen einen anderen als die Glosse in FG (FG hat Ortsnamenglossen 10 der hier genannten 15 Iren). Die Eingangsworte des Vierzeilers von FO für den 18. Dezember: „Die grosse Sonne der Sippschaften" bezog Ms R1 auf Flannan, dessen Name in MT den zweiten der Absätze, in welche an diesem Tage MT seine irische Eintragung unterteilt, einleitet, mit dem (für ein *félire* charakterischen) Zusatz: „Herrscher in Milde". In MD wurde nachträglich angefügt „Moelruain von Rath, wie Oengus heute" (der Herausgeber von MD meinte: in seinem *felire*, also FO; dort aber wird außer dem mit Oengus eng verbundenen Maelruain von Tallaght kein Heiliger dieses Namens genannt; Stokes vermutete, daß der in FO Ms. F am 6. März beiläufig genannte Maelruain der von Rath sei). Von den 16 irischen Heiligen des 18. Dezember widmete die „Bibliotheca Sanctorum" außer dem Artikel für Flannan (s.o.) nur Segnat und Rignaige ein paar Worte. Die martyrologische Tradition in Irland illustriert hier eindrücklich das ständige Bemühen um explizite Vollständigkeit, welches von MT an für Hagiologie in Irland und insbesondere irische Hagiologie charakteristisch geblieben ist und für welches man leicht eine Begründung in der Irland eigenen Spiritualität finden kann. Aber eben dieses Bemühen zeigt, daß irische Hagiologie sich auf einer etwas anderen Ebene bewegt als die Hagiologie anderer Teile der Kirche. Die Elenchi zu ASB verzeichnen für den 18. Dezember keine *Hiberni;* das „Martyrologium Romanum" nennt an diesem Tage 14 Namen.

Die beiden hier betrachteten Beispiele zeigen, daß ein näheres Eingehen auf die irischen Namenslisten für den Nichtiren höchstens exemplarisch oder formal Interesse hat. Von den am 18. Dezember Kommemorierten gibt es m.W. nur für Magniu eine Vita, die MD in einer ungewöhnlich langen Eintragung zusammenfaßte, sowie für Flannan die Vita, die die Grundlage für die historischen Lesungen im „Proprium pro Clero Hiberniae" bildete. Bei der großen Zahl von Gleichnamigen ist es, wenn nähere Angaben fehlen, oft schwer, ja nahezu unmöglich festzustellen, welcher gemeint sein könnte. Kenney führt bei kaum einem der von ihm behandelten irischen „Heiligen" den Erinnerungstag auf, d.h. er betrachtete die martyrologische Tradition nicht als materiale „source for the early history of Ireland".

Es war der Sinn meiner Darlegungen, einerseits die allgemeine Bedeutung, die der Gegenstand auch für Nichtiren haben könnte, darzulegen, andererseits aber auch auf die Schwierigkeiten hinzuweisen, mit denen sich der Nichtire konfrontiert sieht, der hier einzudringen versucht. Bei aller Anerkennung der Bemühungen gerade auch Deutschsprachiger um irische Kirchengeschichte – in neuerer Zeit etwa G. Schreiber, W. Delius, R. Kottje und P. Gaechter – muß man doch feststellen, daß ihr Interesse an dem Gegenstand nur vorübergehend war. Anderseits hat sich seit W. Stokes auch kein Vollkeltist mit der hagiographischen oder gar der martyrologischen Tradition Irlands befaßt. Stokes zeigte die ganze Größe seiner Persönlichkeit in dem Satz, er sei sich seiner Ignoranz in hagiographischen Dingen schmerzlich bewußt, wo doch jeder, der hier tiefer eindringt, immer neu erstaunt ist von dem Umfang von Stokes' Kenntnis trotz seiner beschränkten Mittel.[2]

(Quelle: Archiv für Kulturgeschichte, 59, 1977, S. 222-234.)

Ulster place-names in the Continental Tradition of St. Patrick and other Irish Saints

For almost three hundred years past, every Catholic priest in the world has read on March 17th in the historical lessons of the Office that

> Patritius, Hiberniae dictus Apostolus, Armachanam sedem totius insulae principem metropolim constituit sepultusque est apud Dunum in Ultonia.

There is no text through which such concrete information on Ireland has been conveyed on a wider, more sustained and more authoritative scale than these lessons for St. Patrick's feast.

In the martyrology from the early entries in the Echternach and Berne manuscripts of the Hieronymianum the entries for St. Patrick started with the words *In Scotia* or *Hibernia*. Only after 1913 these words were amplified into: *Apud civitatem Dunum, in Hibernia*. At the same time, the traditional beginning of the entry for St. Brigid: *In Scotia* was changed into: *Apud Kildariam in Hibernia*, and in several further entries for Irish Saints a place-name was added denoting the place of the Saint's death. Since dates and names of persons and places are the basis of historical information, we may say that through the introduction of place-names into the entries for Irish Saints (or Saints venerated in Ireland) the historicity of such entries in the Roman Martyrology has been emphasized. Moreover, in contrast to the historical lessons of the Breviary the entries in the Martyrology in general do not state dates. The place-name with which a martyrological entry starts is the decisive basis of historicity.

While with regard to some later entries of Irish Saints into the martyrology, notably that of St. Canice, it can be shown that they were due to Irish influence, for the two earliest entries of Irish Saints into the Hieronymianum no such influence can be detected. In the Martyrology of Tallaght the list of non-Irish Saints for March 17th starts with the words: *Patricii episcopi*. The addition of this entry, in the Brussels abstract of that work, to the Irish section obscures the fact that this entry was, undoubtedly derived from a Continental source. This is also obvious from the surprising sobriety of this entry as compared with the entry for St. Brigid which opening the Irish

---

2   Hauptberuflich im Wirtschaftsleben stehend, erlaube ich mir, der Hoffnung Ausdruck zu geben, daß die nunmehr engere materielle Verbindung Irlands mit dem Festland auch auf ideellem Gebiete belebend wirken möge. Ich habe mich 38 Jahre lang existentiell (in dem heute wieder aufkommenden nüchternen Sinne dieses Wortes) mit dem Gegenstand beschäftigt und mußte ihn an welt- und kirchengeschichtlichen Wandlungen messen. Er hat sich mir als ein klassisches Beispiel dafür erwiesen, wie die Vertiefung in kleinste Details die Aussicht auf weite Bereiche des kulturellen Lebens nicht nur in der Geschichte sondern auch der Gegenwart erschließen kann. Endlich betrachte ich es als legitimen Teil einer wissenschaftlichen Existenz, daß man im unermüdlichen Einsatz für einen Gegenstand eine Dankesschuld abzutragen versucht.

section for February 1st is of a length quite unusual in the Martyrology of Tallaght: *Dormitio sancti (!) Brigitae LXX anno aetatis suae* (the spelling of the Saint's name with *t* indicates that this entry was not derived from the Hieronymianum where this name is always spelt with *d*). Furthermore the words *Patricii episcopi* occur in all the manuscripts of the Hieronymianum which have an entry for St. Patrick and one of them (Senonensis) is confined to these words. Thus the very entry in the Martyrology of Tallaght points to the early recording of St. Patrick in Continental martyrologies.

In the tradition of Irish Saints on the Continent, the early Irish missionaries naturally hold the first place. The oldest reference made in Continental literature to a historical Ulster place-name is the reference to *monasterium cujus vocabulum est Benechor* (var.: *Benichor, Benecor, Bencor*) in Jonas's Life of St. Columbanus. In an earlier passage of his work Jonas stated that Columbanus was born in *quam Lagenorum terram incolae nuncupant*. The names of Leinster and Bangor are clearly described as being rendered in their native form, and these references to Irish place-names in Jonas's work are of significance because:

1. it was written shortly after St. Columbanus's death on the information of his closest fellow-workers,

2. there are comparatively few Continental lives of Saints associated with Ireland which refer to Irish place-names in a strictly historical manner,

3. Jonas's work exercised considerable influence as an exemplar; this work was more widely spread than the Continental life of any other Saint associated with Ireland.

In the summaries of St. Columbanus's tradition the reference to Leinster is scarcely found while that to Bangor is maintained to this day in the historical lessons for his feast as read in Ireland, Switzerland and Italy. The reference to *monasterium Benchor* (in the Proprium for Basle and Chur: *Benchorense*) occurs also in the lessons to this day read on the feast of St. Gall in Ireland and Switzerland. Thus in the living tradition of Irish place-names in the liturgy, Ulster holds a predominant position.

The significance of Jonas's reference to Bangor may be gauged from further points:

1. The earliest reference to Bangor in Irish records occurs about the time of Jonas's writing, in the hymn *Benchur bona regula* in the Antiphonary of Bangor. A note in the Würzburg glossae in an 8th Century hand refers to *scriba et abbas benncuir* (and also to *insola quae dicitur crannach duinlethglaisse*, off Downpatrick), and a further reference to Bangor in a Continental text is the entry made in the Chronicle of Marianus Scotus for 1066: *Re Ulad in templo Bennchuir occiditur* (there are other Irish place-names in that work).

2. No Irish place-names occur in the hagiographical tradition of St. Gall (Wetti merely refers to *portus Hybernicus* where the Saint embarked). The reference to Bangor in the historical lessons for St. Gall's feast is an inference from the tradition of St. Columbanus.

Of the three patrons of Ireland the latest to enter into the martyrologies of the Continent was St. Columba. Only Cod. Cambr. of the Hieronymianum added to the entries for June 9th: "et in Scotia Columcille". Notker's long entry for this Saint starts with the sentence: *In Scotia, insula Hiberniae, depositio S. Columbae, cognomine apud suos Columbkille, contra morem ecclesiasticam primas omnium Hibernensium habetur episcopus.* In this sentence five points must be noted:

1. This is an early record of the distinction between Hibernia and Scotia (the fact that Hibernia is an island is almost the only one which can be regarded as general knowledge of Ireland on the Continent).

2. This is one of the earliest records in the hagiographical tradition of Continental knowledge of the vernacular of Ireland.

3. The difference between the conceptions of episcopacy in ancient Ireland and on the Continent is noted.

4. This is an attempt to give St. Columba (and his see) an ecclesiastical rank even higher than Armagh.

5. Hibernia is described as the resting-place of the Saint.

In the Usuardian tradition, the entry for St. Columba starts with the words *In Scotia*, but in the Roman Martyrology of our days this is another instance where the geographical determination in the entry of an Irish Saint was specified. It now reads: *In Iona, Scotiae insula*, a version clearly inspired by, but correcting, Notker's entry. The biographical tradition of St. Columba is not Continental.

Returning to St. Patrick, I would trespass upon ground which, in particular during this past year, will have been ploughed by specialists if I would try to investigate the position of Irish place-names in lives by non-Irish authors, such as Jocelin of Furnes or the writers of the Vita quarta or the summary in Legendarium Austriacum. Irish place-names have proved a useful guide in the study of concrete information on Ireland conveyed through hagiographical channels to parts of the world where otherwise but the haziest notions of Ireland can be traced.

The earliest reference to Armagh in a work written on the Continent clearly testifies to the connection between Armagh and St. Patrick. It occurs in one of the Irish sentences inserted in the life of St. Findan of Rheinau, written about 900 by one closely associated with that Irish recluse but probably ignorant of the Irish language. Apart from the traditions of SS. Columbanus and Gall, the tradition of St. Findan is the most historical of all the traditions of Irish Saints on the Continent. It is also remarkable for the fact that while confined to one small place, indeed to one Church (for the last 120 years deprived of its monastic background), and scarcely supported from Ireland, it is very much alive to this day. In the Vita of this Saint we hear that he maintained the ancient custom of his native country of commemorating the days of the great Irish Saints by fasting rather than by liturgical celebrations. When on St. Patrick's day fierce hunger was about to make him break his custom *tale oraculum aure percepit propria lingua relatum: Ataich crist ocus Patric Artmache farafeil tam nakisel, teilc bruth is tart duit, teil colc farsykel et ex hoc vicium minimo sensit* (Stokes: *farna feil tam na cisel teilc bruth is tart doit teilc coil far cisel*). Instead of the words *Patric Artmache* in the old manuscript, the two younger manuscripts, dating from the eleventh and twelfth centuries, have *Patria cart macha* and *Patrigartmachiae* (the latter version suggests that it arose from misunderstanding of a dictation). To these words the oldest and the youngest manuscripts have a glossa saying: *Obsecra cristum et patricium-nomen civitatis*, a clear indication that the name of Armagh was not expected to be known to the readers.

In considering the tradition of St. Patrick as a source of Continental information on Ireland, we have to study the tradition of *Purgatorium S. Patricii* rather than that of the Saint's life. An investigation on the literary tradition of the work by Henry of Saltrey being in progress it would be premature to try to establish what information on the geographical position of the famous cave and of Ireland in general and the journey thither was contained in that tradition. *Visio Georgii*, an account of this pilgrimage by a Hungarian knight, which in Central Europe became more popular than Henry's work, is prefaced by a number of letters of introduction to, or of recommendation by, the Irish hierarchy, including *archiepiscopum Armachanum, primatem Yberniae (Richardus Armachanus archiepiscopus*, var *Armatensis, Armatanus, Armethanus*) and *episcopum Clochorensem (Nicolaus Clot(h)orensis, Clochorensis)*. Similarly the later account by Ramon de Perelhos (1397, written in 1466) was prefaced by the permission given for this pilgrimage *del archivesques d'Armanhac que es primat en Yrlanda e lo evesques en la diocesa de qual es lo purgatorio*. Arriving at *la ciutat d'Armach* the pilgrim was received by *rey Yrnel*.

Apart from *Purgatorium S. Patricii, Visio Tundali* was the most important reflection of Irish literature in Continental literature. *Visio Tundali* is the account of a vision which Tnugdal had in 1148 at Cork. This Latin text was written by Marcus, also a native of Cashel, a few months later, shortly after his arrival at Ratisbon (where presumably he joined the existing Irish Benedictine community) at the request of two German nuns. For the convenience of his Continental readers, Marcus refaced his work by a brief account of the geography of Ireland (largely based on Solinus), concluding with the following passage:

> Hec ergo insula civitates habet precipua triginta quattuor, quarum presules duobus subsunt metropolitanis. Artimacha namque septentrionalium. Hybernensium est metropolis, australium autem precelentissima est Caselensis.

Although two of the manuscripts of *Visio Tundali* read *Artinac(h)a*, none of the interpreters of this work ever expressed any doubt that Marcus referred to Armagh. The Hassian version said that *Iberne* had 34 main cities, one of which was named *Archamacha*, the first reference to Armagh in any work of vernacular literature on the Continent. While omitting the reference to Armagh, the Bavarian version added a lengthy reference to the legend of St. Patrick. The fifteenth century French version speaks of *Patric de Ybernia* and *Celestin archiveque de Nasona;* the Toulouse 1903 edition noted: "On se demande d'où peut provenir le nom de Nasona", as if corruptions of Irish place-names were not the rule rather than an exception in Continental writings relating to Ireland. In the Low German versions, the spellings of the Latinised form of Armagh were disfigured to *Arthijmaka, Arthinaka, Archmake* and finally the writer of the Ghent manuscript obviously knocked fun out of that queer Irish place-name, rendering it by *Archimomska*.

I have shown elsewhere that the spelling *Artinacha* (of course derived from *Artmacha*) in the Erlangen manuscript of Marcus's work permits us to establish a close relationship between this work and the *Vita Sti. Albarti*, also written at Ratisbon about the middle of the twelfth century as an extension of the tradition of St. Erard, minor patron of Ratisbon, to this day simply described as *Scotus*. The *Vita S. Albarti* introduced into the tradition of St. Erard the new point that he was *dignitate episcopus in civitate quae dicitur Artinacha*, while Albartus became *metropolitanus* and *archiepiscopus in Caselle quae est civitas metropolis, urbs Hyberniae regalis*. Seventeenth century Bavarian interpreters of this text suggested, presumably on the strength of information obtained from Irishmen, that *Artinacha* stood for Ardagh, and in the late nineteenth century the bishop of Ardagh wrote to the bishop of Ratisbon for information on St. Erard, "patron" of Ardagh. On the other hand, Père Grosjean failed to establish the identity of *Caselle* as associated with St. Albert. While the late Archdeacon Seymour has shown that *Visio Tundali* is the only extant source on the increase in the number of bishoprics in Ireland from 24 (as established by the Synod of Rathbrassail) to 34, I have demonstrated (in a paper published in *Mediaeval Studies* 1945) that the *Vita S. Albarti* was indirectly an attempt by a Munster-man to assert the claim of Cashel of the Kings, the then newly created and of course much less known second metropolitan see of Ireland, in the eyes of the Continent, and that at the expense of Armagh.

While we need not retrace the tradition of the confusion between Ardagh and Armagh arising from the misspelling of *Artinacha* for *Artimacha*, its possible origin may be of interest. In several respects the *Vita S. Albarti* is related with St. Bernard's Life of St. Malachy. St. Bernard's information that Malachy was reared *in civitate Armacha*, trained by Malchus in *Anglia conversatus* (as was St. Albert), *episcopus in Lessmor civitate Mumoniae quae est Hiberniae pars australis*, and became *metropolitanus totius Hiberniae et Ardmacha* bears some resemblance to the *Vita S. Albarti*. It may be that under the influence of St. Bernard's spelling *Ardmacha*, in his reference to *Visio Tundali* Vincent of Beauvais (Spec hist. xxvii, 88, A.D. 1149) spoke of *Ardinacha*. The details of the tradition of the mis-spellings and corruptions of the name of Armagh in Continental literature may appear as trifling. However, they illustrate on the one hand that no other Irish place-name was referred to, in Continental literature of the Middle Ages, more frequently than that of Armagh and on the other hand, that exact knowledge of Ireland was extremely limited.

In my paper on the place of the archdiocese of Dublin in the hagiographical tradition of the Continent (*Reportorium Novum* 1955) I have treated of the introduction to the *Vita S. Kadroe* than which no text is of greater importance to the study of Irish place-names in Continental literature. The account contained in that introduction of the invasion of Ireland says that the first town to be conquered was *Cloin urbs antiqua Hiberniae, super Synam fluvium*, a statement which may be attributed a special affection the writer of that Vita had for Clonmacnoise. Seeing that the country was *lactis et mellis fertilis* (not only an attempt to establish a parallelism between Irish and Jewish history but also a reference to the classical accounts of Ireland), the invaders occupied it as far as *Artmacha metropolem totamque terram inter lacus Erne et Ethioch*, including *Benchor Ulidiae urbem*. The name of *Artmacha* (Colgan:

Ardmacha) occurs again in the account of St. Kadroe's early training where this is the only place-name mentioned. To my knowledge the Vita S. Kadroe is the first work of Continental literature to mention the name of Ulster.

Professor A. Gwynn has pointed out that apart from the *Vita S. Kadroe* the tradition of St. Forannan is the most important source on Irish monks and the Cluniac Reform on the Continent. *Vita S. Forannani* seems to have been composed by a certain Robert with the purpose of restoring the prestige of Waulsort in the Ardennes, one of the centres of Irish monks associated with Cluny, through the glorification of an Irish Saint who was claimed to have been the monastery's first abbot. He is said to have been consecrated at Armagh. What his *Vita* actually says is that he was

> populorum electus caterva, in civitate quae eorum barbarica sermocinatione Domnachmor nuncupatur, quae est metropolis totius Hiberniae, et in basilica genetricis Dei quam propriis ex reditibus possessionibus fundaverat sublimiter in pontificali collocatus cathedra.

This is not the place to examine the historicity of this reference to the foundation, endowment and dedication of the cathedral and to the election and consecration of the metropolitan or to pursue the speculations as to what place may have been meant by Domnachmor if not Armagh. In the Chronicle of Waulsort, St. Forannan is described simply as *Sc(h)ottiae partibus archiepiscopus*. The tradition of this Saint is a reflection of the early mono-metropolitan organisation of the Irish Church. While the later Irish monastic organisation on the Continent, spreading from Ratisbon, was closely associated with Munster (*Visio Tundali, Vita S. Albarti*), the organisation connected with Cluny, spreading from Waulsort to Lorraine, apparently had affiliations with Ulster.

Another person of the name of Forannanus is mentioned in the *Vita S. Mochullei* in the twelfth century *Magnum Legendarium Austriacum* (Kenney, *Sources*, p. 467 says that this Vita has not been published; it has been published in *Anal. Bolland.* 17 (1898), 136 f.; fragments of it are contained in the fourteenth century Codex Salmanticensis). This work primarily refers to *australes* (later: *austrinae*) *Hiberniae populi*. The Saint lived *in Lumbreciae* (Ms. M. *Lumbrice*) *civitatis locis*, described as *locus austris et solibus aestivis acclivus* and subsequently in *haec gena montana quae aquilones Hiberniae populos ab austro sequestrat*, in particular *collis quem tunc regionis illius incolae Dorsum Riscarum, nunc vero Episcopum Collem usu modernorum nominant. In remotis Hiberniae partibus* he was molested by a *regulus nomine Forannanus, vir immitis et immisericors*, holding *meridianos Hiberniae populos* under cruel tyranny, while *Guareus rex, prout veris antecessorum testimoniis accepimus, prae universis Hiberniae et Scotiae principibus*, protected him. Later we hear of *Thatheus, rex universue meridionalis Hiberniae*. All this was at the time when *rex Hiberniae* was *Theodoricus clementissimus* (according to Kenney either Toirdelbach Ua Briain (1073-86) or Toirdelbach Ua Conchubuir (1120-56)). The words *aquilones Hiberniae populi* may be described as the first record, in Continental literature, of what is now known as Northern Ireland.

In the *Vita S. Runani*, another legend of an Irish Saint contained in *Magnum Legendarium Austriacum* (Anal. Boll. 17, 161) we have a interesting record of Continental knowledge of Ireland, her geographical position, her fertility and her people (*quantum ab aliis nationibus distant per locorum spatia tantum etiam ritu atque habitu*), and in particular her conversion through St. Patrick and her richness in Saints. We are told of a nobleman named Dubglinni (Ms. L. Dubglumni), an official of the *rex Uladorum* (Ms. L. *Valdosum*). This Vita more than any other legend of an Irish Saint on the Continent suggests that the study of Irish place-names is a valuable supplement to the study of the names of Irish persons occurring in those texts.

The tradition of St. Forannan is the first example of a Saint associated, in Continental sources, with Ireland and described as an *archbishop* in Ireland. Like the traditions of St. Wire and of St. Silaus (where however the archiepiscopal sees are not mentioned), the tradition of St. Forannan seems to reflect or advocate a strong mono-metropolitan system, of course under Armagh. In the later traditions of Saints described in Continental sources as archbishops in Ireland (St. Albartus, Cataldus, Rumoldus) have a reflection of the organisation of the Irish Church under several archbishops, including in particular Cashel and Dublin. Again and again the earlier Continental sources show awareness of the derivation of claim of Armagh from St. Patrick. While the result of the study of those Continental sources for the student of Irish history may be meagre (although in several instances they do fill gaps existing in Irish records), this study is at least important to the student of the history of Continental knowledge of Ireland. From this point-of-view the corruption of historical and geographical information is perhaps even more revealing than the possible correctness of such information.

The tradition of St. Silao (see my paper in *Mediaeval Studies* 13 (1951)), the origin of which can be closely dated (about 1183), is the latest attempt to support Armagh's claim to exclusive and more than honorary leaders of the Irish Church, by its association with St. Patrick, repeatedly referred to in this tradition as archbishop of Ireland. The association of St. Silao with St. Patrick was of course spiritual rather than historical, a fact which could not be realised as long as such traditions as that of St. Silao were regarded primarily as direct sources (of the events they purported to describe) rather than as indirect sources (of events of the time when they were written and even more so, of Continental reflection on such events). The jurisdiction of Armagh over the whole of Ireland was clearly recognised in that tradition by the account of a synod convoked by St. Patrick on the occasion of the ordination of Silaus, at *Cluen* (by the explicit association with St. Kieran identified with Clonmacnoise) in the province of *Tesmoria*.

It is remarkable that in the tradition of St. Silao no reference is made to the tradition, created, also at Lucca, thirty years earlier, of the Irish associations of St. Frediano. The present-day office for St. Frediano's feast in the Proprium of Lucca (November 18) bears the heading *S. Frigidiani episcopi et confessoris, ejus corpus requiescit in sua ecclesia*. I have not seen a similar sentence in any other local Proprium. The historical lessons start with the words: *Frigidianus Ultoniae Regis, quae pars est Scotiae, filius*. The lessons adopted in 1741 from the Breviary of the Canons Regular of the Lateran for the Proprium of Ireland are only slightly more explicit, stating that the name of the Saint's father was Hultach. Apart from the Office of St. Patrick this is the only instance where outside Ireland the name of Ulster occurs in the present-day liturgy. It would be interesting to investigate how many priests in the diocese of

Lucca nowadays would associate *Ultonia quae pars est Scotiae* with – let us say a newspaper reference to "Ulster."

The absence of references in the tradition of St. Silao to the earlier Hibernisation at Lucca of St. Frediano is even more surprising when we consider that in both traditions (as also in that of St. Cataldo, with which in turn they are related) we hear of secular rulers interfering with church affairs in Ireland. In the tradition of St. Cataldo the interfering secular ruler is located in the Southern part of Ireland, whereas in the tradition of St. Frediano he is described as *Arth, rex Origiall, quae est provincia Hiberniae*, and in the tradition of St. Silao the interference also takes place in the Northern part of Ireland.

The tradition of St. Frediano marks the climax in the early tradition of Ulster place-names in Continental hagiography. Apart from Ulster and Oriel, a third place-name is mentioned. From Candida in England, where he was trained, St. Frediano *abiit in Hiberniam et in loco qui vocatur Machili habitum religiosum sumpsit*. To this passage Colgan noted: *Mendose in exemplari quo usus sum legebatur Machili pro Macbili, cum nulla in Hibernia ecclesia Machili dicta*. Here as in other instances the emendations made by Colgan from his knowledge of Irish topography (a subject recently studied by Father Mooney) obscured the real meaning of the sources. The present "emendation" has been responsible for the identification of St. Frediano with St. Finnian, an identification which as late as 1920 was adopted in the only book ever published in Ireland on St. Frediano. *Machili*, like *Rachau* (in the tradition of St. Cataldo) is a place-name, which, if it was ever Irish, has been corrupted beyond recognition in accordance with the Continental tradition that a typically Irish word must contain a guttural. Hence Domnachmor in the tradition of St. Forannan was a typical example of the *barbarica sermocinatio* of the Irish.

The various degrees of corruptions of both spelling and historical setting of place-names associated with Ireland and the various degrees of mixing historical and corrupted Irish place-names (analogous to the degrees of corruption in chronology) permit us to establish certain layers and stages in Continental writings relating to Ireland during the Middle Ages. Between Jonas's life of St. Columbanus and St. Bernard's life of St. Malachy there has been no life written on the Continent of a Saint associated with Ireland in which Irish place-names occur more strictly and purely in their historical form and setting than in these two works. Apart from SS. Patrick and Brigid, SS. Columbanus and Malachy have been the Irish Saints best known on the Continent. Both Jonas and St. Bernard were in closest contact with their Irish sources and indeed their heroes. Like the traditions of SS. Cataldo, Frediano and Silao, the tradition of St. Malachy in Italy through its revival in the sixteenth and seventeenth centuries became an important carrier of concrete and indeed modern information on Ireland.

In the historical lessons for St. Malachy's feast used by the Canons Regular of the Lateran (adopted by the Irish Proprium in 1741) his birth-place is not stated. In his extracts from St. Bernard in *Vita di tredici confessori* (Brescia 1595), Giovanni Pietro Maffei stated that St. Malachy was born *in Hibernia, o chiamar la vogliamo Irlanda, nella citta de Ardmaca*. While St. Bernard had described *Ardmacha* as *metropolis totius Hiberniae*, Maffei, perhaps under the influence of *Visio Tundali* (the literary tradition of which extends over many parts of Europe), said: *Sono entro a'liti d'Hibernia due sedi metropolitane, l'uno di Ardmaca, ... l'altro* (*di cui non mi è noto il nome*) *di più bassa qualità.* Maffei also recorded from St. Bernard the place-names of *Conneret, Benchor* and *un luogo chiamato Duno.*

I have shown that the first phase of Ireland's place in Continental literature of the Middle Ages is entirely hagiographical. Most of the references listed and discussed in the present paper are the first references to the respective Ulster place-names in Continental literature in general.

An investigation of Irish place-names in the hagiographical literature of the later Middle Ages and in the rising secular, in particular chivalresque literature would show that between the thirteenth and the sixteen centuries[1] there was a steep decrease in Continental knowledge of Ireland. While the relations with Waterford, Wexford and Dublin conveyed a certain minimum of information to the Continent, Ulster as it were was blotted out. It was due to the Irish refugees from the Reformation that Continental knowledge of Ulster received a new and indeed its first modern impulse, and again this knowledge was primarily derived from the interest in the tradition of St. Patrick.

(Quelle: Seanchas Ardmacha, 1962, S. 76-86.)

A bibliographical note on the Schottenkloster of St. James, Ratisbon

The monastery of St. James, Ratisbon, founded shortly after 1067 by Muiredach Macc Robertaig from Tyrone, was for three centuries the head of a congregation of Irish Benedictine monasteries, spreading in the North as far as Erfurt, in the East as far as Vienna with a short-lived off-shoot to Kiev, and in the South to the shores of Lake Constance. The tradition of this congregation survives, notably at Erfurt, Würzburg, Ratisbon, Nuremberg and Vienna, in names of buildings and streets associated with the *Scotti*. St. James, Ratisbon, is the only place on the Continent where distinctively Irish features in architectural remains have been preserved. In the literary tradition of Ireland on the Continent, the Irish congregation under St. James, Ratisbon, and in particular St. James, and – closely associated with it – St. Emmeran, Ratisbon, occupy an important position, as may be seen from Kenney's *Sources* no. 320, 332, 444 and

---

1   Note: A subject which would require special studies is the place of Ireland in the tradition of Breton Saints. The sources of *Les Vies des Saints de la Bretagne* by Albert LeGrand (1636; Kenney, *Sources* 181f.) would have to be established and their treatment by LeGrand be discussed. *La province que l'on appelle à présent Ultonie* is mentioned in the traditions of SS. Sezny (391), Maudez (606) and Briac (714). In the tradition of St. Sezny we hear that the province *en ce temps-là se nommoit Ostrinct* (Colgan: *Ultaigh*). The Saint lived in an island off the coast, then called *Clarac*. He then joined St. Patrick at Rome. Returning to Ireland he set up a diocesan organization, was made bishop of the church of his monastery which was raised to the rank of a cathedral, and established a training college for his clergy (an interesting reflection on the development of episcopacy in Ireland and on the connection between St. Patrick and Ulster).

619 and from Dürrwachter's book on the *Gesta Caroli Magni der Regensburger Schottenlegende* (see my study on St. Albert, venerated only at Ratisbon and since the eighteenth century as patron of the archdiocese of Cashel, in *Mediaeval Studies* vii (1945), 21-39).

The early history of St. James, Ratisbon, has been studied in recent years by Dr. Barry and Dr. Binchy (*Studies* xviii (1929), 195 ff). Mgr. Hogan traced the history of Ratisbon Schottenkloster right to its liquidation about the middle of the nineteenth century (*Ir. Eccl. Rec.*, III, xv (1894), 1015 ff). A short survey of the whole tradition of St. James, Ratisbon, was given by me in *Ir. Eccl. Rec.*, VI, lxv (1945), 394 ff. A few years before the liquidation of the Schottenkloster at Ratisbon, Lappenberg, in his article on *Ireland* in Ersch-Gruber's Cyclopedia (I, xxiv (1845), 33), stated that it was "noch immer mit den heimathlichen Gegenden in Verbindung," although it had long become an exclusively Scottish institution. The last account of the community at Ratisbon so far known (quoted by Hogan) dates from 1723. In the literature on St. James, Ratisbon, so far as I am aware, no reference has ever been made to the curious autoptical account in the supplement to *Bibliographical Tour in France and Germany* (1818) (London 1821, iii, p. viii ff), by Th. F. Dibdin, the founder of the Boxburghe Club.

Dibdin starts by stating that St. James, Ratisbon "may be designated the College of the Jacobites, as the few members which inhabit it were the followers of the house and fortune of the Pretender, James Stuart". He then describes the sculpturesque orna-mentation of the door of the monastery (well-known from the frontispiece of Zimmer's *Irish element*) which appeared to him "of an extremely remote antiquity", resembling the sculpture of the "Mexicans or Hindoes". Dibdin's work includes drawings of details executed by Mr. Lewis and refers us to "drawings of the whole, published as a lithograph and print, by Quaglio". After further study, Dibdin "conjectured the building to be of the twelfth century", and this conjecture was confirmed by one of the members of the college, "either Mr. Richardson or Mr. Sharp", who also drew Dibdin's attention to the fact that "about twenty miles off, down the Danube, there was another monastery, now in ruin, called Mosburg, which was built about the same period, and which exhibited precisely the same style of architecture". [In reality, as the late Professor Georg Dehio, one of the greatest experts on the history of German art has shown, St. James, Ratisbon, erected in 1120 was influenced in its architecture by the Benedictine abbey of Prüfening, a centre of Cluniac reform in Bavaria. The uniqueness of these architectural features was explained by Dr. Dehio by "the relations of the Scottish (Irish) [sic!] monks with the architecture of Western Europe; it is not impossible that artisans from Western Europe collaborated in this work" (*Handbuch der deutschen Kunstdenkmäler* iii (1934), 439).]

"The members of the College, only six or eight in number, and attached to the interest of the Stuarts, have been settled here almost from their infancy, some have arrived at seven and others at twelve years of age. Their method of speaking their own language is very singular, and rather difficult of comprehension." "Their own language" was English; we know of the literary tradition of the Old Irish phrases in the *Vita Sti. Findani* that the Ratisbon *Schottenmönche* had practically no knowledge of Gaelic.

Dibdin's work includes a portrait of Dr. C. Arbuthnot, then the Head of the community. After his death, Dibdin says, the community was to be dissolved and the buildings to be demolished. A foot-note says that Dr. Arbuthnoth died in April, 1820, and it was not until 1862 that St. James, Ratisbon was liquidated by the Bavarian Government's paying £10,000 to the Scottish College at Rome.

The most valuable part of Dibdin's account, however, is that referring to the Library, which was "carefully visited by him". Dibdin was interested in early and valuable prints rather than in manuscripts. Still, it would appear from his account that by that time, the library of St. James had already been deprived of all mediaeval manuscripts. Dibdin found in the library "a few hiatuses, which had been caused by disposing of the volumes, that had filled them, to the cabinet in St. James's Place ... What remained was comparatively mere chaff", Dibdin mentions some prints of Greek, Latin and Hebrew books by Gourmont, Colinaeus and the Stephans in the first half of the sixteenth century. One or two of these books attracted Dibdin's interest, but Dr. Arbuthnot refused to part with them.

Thus it would appear that when compiling his – still not invaluable – survey of "Materials for Irish Saints' Lives in foreign libraries," the Rev. John O'Hanlon (*Lives* I, cl) was right in passing in silence over St. James, and Dibdin's account is really the post-script on what had been a most important centre of Irish literary influence in Central Europe.

(Quelle: Irish Book Lover 31, April 1950, S. 79-81.)

Irische Einflüsse auf die frühen Kalendarien von St. Gallen

In der Einleitung zu seiner Ausgabe der Kalendarien von St. Gallen sagte P. E. Munding[1], daß er sich entschlossen habe,

---

1   *Literatur*:

FELIRE: *Félire Oengusso* ed. W. Stokes, Henry Bradshaw Society XXIX (London 1905).

GOUGAUD: L. GOUGAUD, *Les saints irlandais hors d'Irlande* (Louvain 1936).

HENNIG (m): J. HENNIG, «Die Stellung der Schweiz in der hagiographischen und liturgischen Tradition Irlands», *Z. f. Schweiz. Kirchengesch.* XLVI (1952), 204-216. Hier die unter HENNIG (a) bis (l) angeführten Arbeiten.

HENNIG (n): «The Irish counterparts of the Anglo-Saxon Menologium», *Mediaeval Studies* XIV (1952), 98-106.

HENNIG (o): «A note on Egerton 185», *Eigse* VI (1951), 257-264.

HENNIG (p): «The Irish background of St. Fursey», *Irish Ecclesiastical Record* V, LXXVII (1952), 18-28.

HENNIG (q) «Ireland and Germany in the tradition of St. Kilian», ibid., LXXVIII (1952) 21-33.

HENNIG (r): «Studies in the literary tradition of the *Martyrologium Poeticum*», *Proceedings of the Royal Irish Academy* LVI C (1954), 197-226.

HENNIG (s): Besprechung von P. E. Mundings Beitrag über das älteste Kalendar der Reichenau zu der Festschrift Alban Dold (*Colligere Fragmenta*, Beuron 1952) in *Scriptorium* 1953.

HENNIG (t): «England's contribution to the history of the calendar», *Clergy Review* (London) 1954.

KENNEY: J. F. KENNEY, The sources of the early history of Ireland, I (New York 1929).

alle Kalendarien von Anfang an, also von 800 an ..., als Gesamtheit herauszugeben. Diese Methode hat den Vorteil, daß man an den früheren Kalendarien den Anfangszustand der Kalenderliteratur beobachten kann. Die Tradition ist noch nicht fest. Man hat und benützt noch Kalendarien und Martyrologien, die man von auswärts erhalten oder mitgebracht hat: von Irland, England, Frankreich[2].

Die Beziehungen zu Frankreich sind geographisch ohne weiteres einleuchtend und ausgiebig in den frühen Kalendarien von St. Gallen belegt. Die Beziehungen mit «Irland, England» dagegen bedürfen der Erläuterung. Darum fuhr P. Munding fort:

> Ganz verständlich für St. Gallens Frühzeit, wo das irisch-kolumbanische Element – St. Gallus war Schüler Kolumbans – noch so stark vorwiegend war. Irische Wandermönche brachten zudem viele Handschriften mit nach St. Gallen, woraus sich leicht erklärt, daß das berühmte Martyrologium Bedae, Cod. 451 aus England[3], sich noch heute in St. Gallen befindet.

Sang. 451 ist zwar *scottice* geschrieben, enthält aber im Gegensatz zu Palat. 834, 833 und Veron. LXV gerade nicht die irischen Heiligen Brigid und Patrick.[4] – In der Zusammenfassung seiner Ergebnisse am Anfang und Ende seiner «Untersuchungen» sagt P. Munding[5]:

> St. Gallen wurde ... vom hl. Gallus, einem Iren und Schüler Kolumbans, gegründet ... Die liturgische Festordnung nahm St. Gallen, der Herkunft seines Gründers entsprechend, wohl aus Irland oder England oder auch von Luxeuil, der Gründung Kolumbans. Im wesentlichen diente wohl ein Gregorianum oder Gelasianum s. viii, vielleicht mit gallikanischen und irischen Zutaten ... Am Ende des 7. Jahrhunderts finden wir eine gemischte Liturgie. In England war der römische Ritus ... verbreitet.
>
> St. Gallen benützte von der Gründung bis zu unseren ersten Kalendarien, also rund von 620-800, wohl keine Kalendarien, sondern die Sakramentarien der damaligen Zeit, d.h. gregorianisch-gelasianische Texte ... Dazu kommen noch etliche ambrosianische, gallikanische und mozarabische Einschläge.

Von irischen Texten während dieser Periode, da doch der irische Einfluß wohl am stärksten gewesen sein müßte, ist hier keine Rede.

Von irischen Einflüssen auf den Kalender von St. Gallen läßt sich vor dem neunten Jahrhundert schon deshalb nicht sprechen, weil uns erst von da an irische Kalender vorliegen, nämlich das in irischer Sprache abgefaßte kalendarische Gedicht des

---

MT: *Martyrology of Tallaght*, ed. R. I. Best und H. J. Lawlor, Henry Bradshaw Society LXVIII (London 1931).

MUNDING I und II: E. MUNDING, *Die Kalendarien von St. Gallen* I, II (Texte und Arbeiten ... Erzabtei Beuron I, XXXVI und XXXVII, Beuron 1948 und 1951).

QUENTIN: H. QUENTIN, *Les martyrologes historiques* (Paris 1908).

2   I, 3.

3   MUNDING II, p. XII unter B; KENNEY, p. 479.

4   QUENTIN, p. 48f.

5   II, p. VII und 174.

Oengus von Tallaght[6], das um 800 angesetzt wird, und das Martyrologium von Tallaght, eine Version des *Hieronymianum,* das um 900 angesetzt wird.[7]

P. Munding gebraucht zwar den Ausdruck «Kalenderliteratur» und gibt uns wertvolle Aufschlüsse über den Zusammenhang zwischen Kalender und Martyrologium[8], nach Anlage und Ziel ist jedoch seine Arbeit heortologisch, d.h. die Texte werden nach den einzelnen darin aufgeführten Festen Punkt für Punkt verglichen. Für einen Vergleich der Texte wird lediglich das Rohmaterial geboten; um nur an einem Beispiel das Fehlen einer Durchdringung dieses Materials zu zeigen: P. Munding erwähnt nicht, daß die merkwürdige Fassung des Eintrags für den 1. Januar in Sang. 250 und Turic. 176 (zwei für uns, wie sich gleich zeigen wird, besonders interessante Texte) der erste Vers des sog. *Martyrologium Poeticum* ist.[9] Weiterhin, da es lediglich um die Entwicklung der liturgischen Feste zu tun war, wurde «auf alle komputistischen, nekrologischen, astronomischen und übrigen Einträge in den Kalendertexten verzichtet»[10]; es wird also ausdrücklich davon abgesehen, diese Einträge und ihren Zusammenhang mit den Heiligenkalendern für die Würdigung der Gesamtwerke als Kalender-*literatur* heranzuziehen.

Gerade bei der Erforschung eventueller irischer Einflüsse auf frühmittelalterliche Kalender ist es nun aber mit der Unterscheidung zwischen Kalendern und Martyrologien nicht getan. Man muß zu einer viel grundlegenderen Unterscheidung in der Funktion der Gesamtwerke vordringen, nämlich der zwischen historischer Kommemoration und geistlicher Repräsentation der Heiligen. Die Erwähnungen der Heiligen im Ordinarium und Kanon der römischen Messe, die Akzentuierung gewisser Fastenzeitmessen auf die Heiligen der Stationskirche, die Heiligenlitaneien, die Votivmessen zu Ehren einzelner Heiliger, die ganze volkstümliche Verehrung einzelner Heiliger das ganze Jahr hindurch, all dies sind noch heute lebendige Formen der geistlichen Repräsentation der Heiligen gegenüber (oder besser: längs) der durch *Sanctorale,* Kalender und Martyrologium dargestellten historischen Kommemoration. Die alte irische Kirche kannte, soweit wir wissen, als einzige westliche Liturgie, nur die geistliche Repräsentation der Heiligen, nämlich durch in jeder Messe verlesene lange Listen im Vokativ oder Genitiv. Daneben entwickelte Irland, das erste Land in Westeuropa, in dem eine religiöse Literatur in der Volkssprache entstand, besondere Andachtsformen in irischer Sprache, poetische Litaneien und kalendarische Gedichte zu Ehren aller Heiligen. Trotz ihrer kalendarischen Anordnung sind diese Gedichte (für die nur in Irland ein besonderer Name, *félire,* existiert) eindeutig Ausdruck geistlicher Repräsentation, denn sie waren als geschlossene Gedichte dazu bestimmt, an jedem beliebigen Tag durchrezitiert zu werden, nicht dagegen Vers für Vers an dem jeweils entsprechenden

---

6   Félire; KENNEY, p. 479f.

7   MT.

8   I, 1f. und II, 147f.

9   HENNIG (r).

10   I, 1.

Tag. Die alte irische Liturgie hatte kein *Sanctorale*, ja nicht einmal ein *Sacramentarium,* geschweige denn also einen (liturgischen) Kalender.[11]

Ein eventueller Einfluß von einem *félire* auf einen liturgischen Kalender hat also eine viel weitere Spannung als ein Einfluß von einem Martyrologium auf einen Kalender, geschweige denn von einem Kalender auf einen anderen. Da P. Munding das *Félire* des Oengus, den einzigen Text, der den frühen St. Galler Kalendarien möglicherweise hätte als Quelle dienen können, nicht erwähnt, könnten diese Ausführungen als irrelevant betrachtet werden. Sie sind jedoch für jede Aussage über eventuelle Beziehungen zwischen Irland und dem Festland in der frühmittelalterlichen Liturgie von Bedeutung, und meine Arbeit möchte an P. Mundings Werk die Schwierigkeiten solcher Aussagen darstellen.

In seiner Literaturliste führt P. Munding nur einen Text aus Irland auf, nämlich «T = Martyrolog. des irischen Klosters Tamlachta [besser: aus dem irischen Kloster Tallaght] bei Dublin s. IX. DQ pg. XII. = Breviar. [soll das nicht heißen «Martyrolog.»?] Hieronym»[12]. Während das *Hieronymianum* die Grundlage für das, was Quentin das historische [oder erzählende] Martyrologium genannt hat, gewesen ist, reduzierte das Martyrologium von Tallaght gerade das *Hieronymianum* (wieder) auf eine reine Namensliste, wobei Rangbezeichnungen der Heiligen und Ortsnamen in Namen weiterer Heiliger uminterpretiert wurden. Diese Namensliste ist so öde, daß es eine der strengen Bußübungen, für die die altirische Kirche bekannt war, gewesen sein müßte, sie zu lesen. Im Gegensatz dazu ist das (heortologisch und geographisch mit dem Martyrologium von Tallaght engstens verbundene) *Félire* des Oengus gerade der erste Versuch, den Kalender zur Literatur zu erheben, also mit einigem Genuß lesbar zu machen.[13] Von einem praktischen Gebrauch des Martyrologiums von Tallaght ist schon deshalb nicht zu sprechen, weil dieses Werk von Doubletten, Mißverständnissen und Fehlern wimmelt. Wie stark es in Irland als Fremdkörper empfunden wurde, läßt sich daran ermessen, daß der Liste jener dem *Hieronymianum* entnommenen Namen in einem besonderen Absatz jeden Tag eine etwa gleich lange Liste von irischen Namen angefügt wurde. (Im *Félire* des Oengus dagegen sind irische und nicht-irische Heilige vermischt.) Während die Listen nichtirischer Namen für viele Tage des Jahres verloren sind, sind die Listen irischer Namen wenigstens in einer zuverlässigen Abschrift einigermaßen vollständig erhalten. In Quentins Ausgabe des *Hieronymianum*[14] sind nur die nicht-irischen Namenslisten wiedergegeben. P. Munding kannte die gleichzeitig mit Quentins Ausgabe des *Hieronymianum* erschienene wissenschaftliche

---

11   HENNIG (c), (d), (i), (j) und (o).

12   II, p. XII.

13   Erst wenn man von der heortologischen Betrachtung zur Würdigung der Gesamtcharaktere dieser Werke fortschreitet, zeigt es sich, daß das *Félire* des Oengus und das *Martyrologium* des Wandelbert von Prüm (von dem Sang. 250 eine Abschrift enthält) zusammengehören.

14   MUNDING II, p. XIII unter DQ.

228

Ausgabe des Martyrologiums von Tallaght[15] nicht; die dortigen Erwähnungen irischer Heiliger, die auch im St. Galler Kalender vorkommen, blieben ihm daher unbekannt. Was also die irischen Quellen angeht, so fehlen P. Mundings Untersuchungen über ihren eventuellen Einfluß auf St. Gallen gerade die entscheidenden Grundlagen. Kommen wir zurück zu seinem «Endergebnis»[16]:

> Im 9. Jahrhundert besteht noch keine klare und beständige Tradition. Die ersten Kalendarien sind zum Teil von auswärts: England, Irland und vom Niederrhein [warum nicht auch «Frankreich»?].

Nächst Sang. 914 (um 800, ein *Martyrologium breviatum* aus Burgund, dem *Gellonense* nahe verwandt) ist der älteste von P. Munding betrachtete Text Sang. 878 (c. 850), der «dem Inhalt nach angelsächsisch oder niederrhein. zu sein scheint. Im Kalendar ... werden Bonifacius und Willibrord genannt»[17].

Eine in der heortologischen Erforschung frühmittelalterlicher Kalendare erstaunlich oft unbeachtete Unterscheidung ist die zwischen der Herkunft eines Heiligen und der seines Kultes. Bonifacius und Willibrord weisen zwar ihrer Herkunft nach nach England, aber ihr Platz in einem Kalendar von St. Gallen ist durch die viel näher liegende Herkunft ihres Kultes bestimmt. Noch klarer ist dieser Sachverhalt bei den irischen Heiligen Kilian[18], Columban und Gallus, deren Kult ausschließlich festländisch war, von Heiligen des Festlandes, denen Beziehungen mit der «Insel der Heiligen» zugeschrieben wurden (wie dem hl. Fridolin von Säckingen)[19], ganz zu schweigen. Daß insbesondere Einträge für den hl. Columban in einem St. Galler Kalender nicht auf irischen Einfluß (in diesem Eintrag!) deuten[20], bedarf keiner weiteren Erklärung.

Bei dem dritten von Munding betrachteten Text, Sang. 450 (c. 850), kann man mit Recht sagen, daß die Einträge für die hl. Cuthbert, Melittus, Alban und Editrudis auf direkten englischen Einfluß deuten.[21] Weil in diesem Martyrologium auch gallische und norditalienische Einträge vorhanden sind, glaubt P. Munding, daß es «von

---

15 MT.

16 II, 174.

17 I, 5f.

18 Munding II, 77: «Iro-Schotte [siehe unten Anm. 48] – 8. VII. 689». Bezüglich des Festes ist Hennig (q) durch P. Mundings Bemerkungen zu ergänzen.

19 Kenney, p. 497f.; Munding II, 42: «Ire – 6. III. 540». Vgl. meine Studien über die hl. Albert von Regensburg, Cataldo von Tarent, Frediano und Silao von Lucca etc. in Hennig (g) und (h) und in *Mediaeval Studies* XIII (1951), 234-242.

20 Wie Munding dies für Sang. 250 (I, 8) annimmt, s. unten. Zu Hennig (m) p. 207 ist nachzutragen, daß zu dem Eintrag «Columbani eliuatio», dem zweiten irischen Eintrag in MT für den 27. September, die Herausgeber (p. 288) bemerkten: «Columban ... founder of Luxeuil and Bobbio». Diese *elivatio* findet sich in keinem der St. Galler Kalender und ist mir auch sonst nicht vorgekommen.

21 Munding I, 6f.

England über Frankreich, Italien nach St. Gallen gewandert sein muß, vermutlich durch Kolumbanschüler und -klöster (Luxeuil, Bobbio, St. Gallen)». Wir kommen hier zu der Bemerkung in P. Mundings Einleitung zurück, daß im neunten Jahrhundert in St. Gallen «das irisch-kolumbanische Element noch so stark vorwiegend war». Nun wird mit einem Zusammenhang der kolumbanischen Stiftungen gerechnet, und wir hören von Kolumbanschülern. Gerade die Kalendare zeigen uns aber doch, daß im neunten Jahrhundert St. Gallen ein normales Benediktinerkloster war, und daß in der durch diese Kalendare illustrierten Liturgie die kolumbanische Überlieferung eine reine Erinnerung war. Die irischen Wandermönche setzten die kolumbanische Tradition nicht ohne Unterbrechung fort. Im Gegensatz zu den Glaubensboten des 6. und 7. Jahrhunderts kamen sie als dienende Vermittler oder Techniker der Bildung. Sie sonnten sich wohl gern in der Tradition ihrer großen Landsleute, die sie auf dem Festlande größtenteils erst für sich und ihr Heimatland entdeckten, und bestärkten diese Tradition, wo immer sich eine Gelegenheit dazu bot.[22]

Von Sang. 250 (c. 889, obwohl Schrift des 11. Jahrhunderts) sagt Munding, daß die Zusammenstellung des Kalenders mit Schriften von Beda und Aldhelm «für englische Herkunft spricht», und daß der Eintrag *Cainnichi abb.* «für den irischen Einfluß wie der übrige Teil spricht».[23]

Nach England-Irland weist uns auch das Kalendar: S. Brigida 1.II., S. Athala cf. in Bobbio 10.III., S. Bonifacius et socii 5.VI., S. Columba, Abt. 9.VI., S. Alban Protom. 21.VI., S. Cainnich, Abt in Irland 11.XI. [recte: X], S. Augustin, B. von Canterb. 16.XI., S. Columban, Abt, 23.XI. ... Somit scheint das Kalendar nach irisch-englischer Vorlage geschrieben zu sein in und für St. Gallen. Im 9. Jahrhundert war noch [!] reger Verkehr zwischen England-Irland und St. Gallen, einer irischen Gründung.

Wie in der Einleitung der Zusatz «St. Gallus war Schüler Kolumbans», so ist hier der Zusatz «einer irischen Gründung» offenbar die Grundlage für P. Mundings Gedankengänge über den grundlegenden Einfluß Irlands auf die Entwicklung des Kalendars von St. Gallen. Dabei deutet der wiederholte Gebrauch des Ausdrucks «England-Irland» vermutlich auf das elementarste Mißverständnis der modernen festländischen Irlandkunde, nämlich die Verkennung des Unterschiedes zwischen England und Irland.[24] Im Studium der Periode, in der sich im Gegensatz zur irischen Kirche die angelsächsische Kirche der festländischen Liturgie anglich, verdeckt dieses Mißverständnis entscheidende Sachverhalte.

Näheren Aufschluß über die von Munding für Sang. 250 angenommene «Vorlage» erwartete man von seinen Quellenuntersuchungen.[25] P. Munding gebraucht das Wort

---

22 Mein Artikel «Irish monastic activities in Eastern Europe» in *Irish Eccles. Record* V, LXV (1945), 394ff. ist zwar in den meisten Punkten überholt, aber meine Unterscheidung von vier Perioden ist noch gültig.

23 I, 8f.

24 Hennig (c) und (l).

25 II, 1ff.

«Quellen» in einem ungewöhnlich weiten Sinne. Er führt die Quellen für die einzelnen Feste in vier Gruppen auf:

1. testes principales (urgregorianische und junggelasianische Liturgie),

2. testes secundarii liturgici,

3. Kalendaria,

4. Martyrologia[26].

In jeder der vier Gruppen werden die «Quellen» in der alphabetischen Reihenfolge der Sigel (in Mundings Literaturverzeichnis)[27] aufgeführt. Die *testes principales* sind fast durchweg nicht die direkten Quellen, sondern lediglich die ersten Belege; die direkten Quellen müßten zeitlich und örtlich näher liegen. Die Kalendarien und Martyrologien sind für die frühen Texte meistens gleichzeitig oder sogar später, also Parallelbelege. In keinem Falle wird der Versuch gemacht, wirklich die individuelle Quelle besonders der neu vorkommenden Einträge zu ermitteln.[28] Wie bereits bemerkt, wird für die auf diesem Gebiete so wichtige Vergleichung der Textgestaltung der einzelnen Einträge nur das Rohmaterial geboten.

Wie weit deuten nun die als irisch anzusprechenden Einträge in Sang. 250 auf eine irische Vorlage? Das Fest der hl. Brigid kommt bereits im Gellonense und in Sang. 450 vor; in diesen beiden Texten ist es der erste Eintrag für den 1. Februar, in Sang. 250 aber der zweite (nach Polycarp). Der Eintrag für S. Brigida, selbst mit dem Zusatz «in Scotia» (der in Sang. 250 gerade fehlt), findet sich, was in P. Mundings «Quellennachweis» nicht erwähnt wird, in den Basel, Echternach und Reichenau zugehörigen Hss. des *Hieronymianum*.[29] Das Ausmaß der Verehrung dieser Heiligen auf dem Festland im 9. Jahrhundert, wie es Gougaud gezeigt hat, ist P. Munding scheinbar unbekannt; die von ihm angeführten Quellen sind durchweg nicht früher als Sang. 250; der Hinweis auf Beda ist irreführend, denn die natürlich besonders erwähnte Hs. Sang. 451 enthält den Eintrag für die hl. Brigid gerade nicht.[30] Daß die Heilige im Martyrologium von Tallaght erwähnt wird, entging Munding[31], da dort die (von Quentin nicht wiedergegebene) irische Abteilung für den 1. Februar mit dem ungewöhnlich ausführlichen und historischen Eintrag beginnt: «Dormitatio sancti (!) Brigitae LXX[O] anno

---

26 II, 22.

27 II, XIIff.

28 Vergleiche meine Ausführungen zu P. Mundings Untersuchung des ältesten Kalendars der Reichenau [Hennig (r) und (s)].

29 MUNDING II, XV: «H – Martyrologium Hieronymianum saec. V». Da M. nie auf die einzelnen Hss. eingeht, muß der unerfahrene Leser annehmen, daß die Einträge, bei denen M. unter den Quellen «H» angibt, bereits im fünften Jahrhundert vorkommen (siehe z.B. unten Anm. 52)

30 Siehe oben Anm. 4. Zur Verbreitung der Verehrung der hl. Brigid außerhalb Irlands siehe GOUGAUD, p. 16ff. Nach MUNDING II, 6ff. wurden die Feste der hl. Brigid, Patrick und Columba in St. Gallen liturgisch gefeiert, sind aber St. Gallen nur *late* eigen.

31 Ebenso die schöne Stanze in *Félire Oengusso*.

aestatis suae». Daß sich dieser Eintrag in der irischen Abteilung befindet, deutet darauf hin, daß er in der nicht-irischen Abteilung fehlte (im Gegensatz dazu befindet sich der Eintrag für St. Patrick am 17. März in der nicht-irischen Abteilung). Dieser Sachverhalt deutet darauf hin, daß auch in dem von dem Martyrologium von Tallaght benutzten *Hieronymianum* die hl. Brigid noch nicht aufgeführt worden war, was ein bisher unerkannter Hinweis darauf ist, daß das Martyrologium von Tallaght seinem Inhalt nach vielfach weiter zurückreicht als nur bis 900. In der Tat behauptete ja schon Marianus Gorman, daß Oengus sein *Félire* aus dem «Martyrologium von Tallaght [verfaßt von] Maelruan» hergestellt hätte.[32] Das Martyrologium von Tallaght und die schöne (Munding unbekannte) Stanze für das Fest der hl. Brigid in Oengus' *Félire* können aber schon deshalb nicht die direkte Vorlage von Sang. 250 sein, weil in beiden Werken der Name der Heiligen (wie in der Heiligenliste des Stowe Missale)[33] mit einem t geschrieben ist. Wir haben aber schon gesehen, daß in der Tradition der Kalendarien von St. Gallen selbst die Heilige von Anfang an so wohl bekannt war, daß man im Eintrag der Sang. 250 keinen erneuten direkten Einfluß von Irland suchen muß.

Dagegen sind unter den St. Galler Kalendarien Sang. 250 (und die auch sonst damit eng verbundene Hs. Turic. 176)[34] die ersten, die den hl. Columba am 9. Juni den hl. Primus und Felicianus voranstellen. Spätere St. Galler Kalendare fügten die Worte «In scotia depositio» bei.[35] Hier führt Munding das *Félire* des Oengus und das Martyrologium von Tallaght wieder nicht unter den Quellen an, auch nicht den Kalender in dem Karlsruher Beda (Aug. CLXVII fol. 16v)[36], der von diesen beiden Werken abgeleitet werden kann, da er wie diese mit dem Namen des hl. Columba den seines *cumtha* (Genossen) Baithen aufführt. P. Munding verzeichnet zwar unter den «Quellen» Notker, macht aber nicht auf die außerordentliche Bedeutung gerade dieses Beleges aufmerksam: Er entstand am gleichen Orte und zur gleichen Zeit wie Sang. 250 und zeichnet sich durch ungewöhnliche Ausführlichkeit aus.[37] Die Überlieferung des hl. Columba in St. Gallen geht an sich weiter zurück als Sang. 250 und Notker. Die berühmte Reichenauer Handschrift (jetzt in Schaffhausen) von Adamnans Leben, im frühen achten Jahrhundert in Iona geschrieben, scheint nach der Reichenau gekommen zu sein, ehe dort unter Abt Grimold (841-872) die kürzere Version (Sang. 551) entstand, und diese Quellen waren zweifellos in St. Gallen bekannt.[38] Auch die von Munding vermerkte Tatsache, daß der hl. Columba bereits von Usuard in das Martyrologium eingeführt worden war, setzt für Sang. 250 keine direkte irische Vorlage für

---

32   *Félire húi Gormáin*, ed. W. Stokes (H. Bradshaw Soc. IX, London 1895), 4.

33   Ed. G. F. Warner (H. Bradshaw Soc. XXXII, London 1915), 14.

34   MUNDING I, 9.

35   Ibid., 55f.

36   KENNEY, 481 und 670; GOUGAUD, 168.

37   KENNEY, 597.

38   KENNEY, 429f.

den entsprechenden Eintrag voraus. Bemerkenswert ist jedoch, daß Usuard den Heiligen als «presbyter et confessor» bezeichnete, Sang. 250 dagegen als «abb.»,ein Beispiel dafür, daß es mit einer einfachen Vergleichung des Vorkommens von Heiligen in den einzelnen Kalendern nicht getan ist, sondern auch die Textgestaltung berücksichtigt werden muß.

Von allem, was P. Munding als Spuren einer irischen Vorlage im Sang. 250 aufführt, bleibt also nur der Eintrag «Ciannichi abb.» übrig. Bis zu Sang. 250 war für den 11. Oktober im St. Galler Kalender kein Eintrag vorgesehen. Hier wäre ein Hinweis auf Gougauds Nachweise gleichzeitiger Einträge in liturgischen Quellen im alemannischen Raume von ganz besonderer Bedeutung gewesen.[39] Nach Munding ist der Eintrag für Cainnichus in Usuard ein Zusatz. De Sollier sagt hierüber nichts, macht aber die wichtige Bemerkung[40]:

> A nullo alio nominatum, adducit forte quod ordinis sui abbatem censuerit aut in ipsa Gallia peculiari cultu fuerat celebratum.[41]

Der von Munding wieder nicht erwähnte Eintrag im Martyrologium von Tallaght, der letzte in der irischen Gruppe für den 11. Oktober, ist jenem für die hl. Brigid in Länge und Wortlaut vergleichbar: «Cainnig m. (Sohn des) Daland LXXXIIII anno etatis suae.» Im *Félire* des Oengus ist «Cainnech, der Sohn von Dala» der letzte der drei in dem Vierzeiler für den 11. Oktober genannten Heiligen, alle drei Iren.

Einträge im *Félire* des Oengus bedeuten nicht, daß die genannten Heiligen liturgisch gefeiert wurden, 1. weil die altirische Kirche überhaupt nicht Messen zu Ehren einzelner Heiliger feierte, 2. weil nach Art der *martyrologia breviata* an jedem Tag mindestens ein Eintrag gemacht wird, 3. weil die Auswahl der angeführten Namen weitgehend durch Rücksichten auf die Regeln der irischen Metrik bestimmt war, und 4. (mit Rücksicht auf die Iren) ein wesentlich weiterer Begriff des «Heiligen» zugrunde liegt als in liturgischen Kalendern. Am ehesten läßt noch die Länge des Eintrags für den hl. Canice im Martyrologium von Tallaght darauf schließen, daß er als bedeutend galt. Dieser Eintrag bildet einen besonderen Absatz in der irischen Gruppe und kann vielleicht als Zusatz angesprochen werden; der Heilige wäre also im Laufe des 9. Jahrhunderts zu der Stellung aufgestiegen, die er später als Patron von Kilkenny (*cella Canici*) einnahm (aber, wie gesagt, er kommt auch schon im *Félire* des Oengus vor). Die in ihren Quellen wie die meisten irischen Heiligenviten schwer zu datierende biographische Überlieferung des hl. Canice steht mit der *Vita S. Columbae* des Adamnan in enger Verbindung und zeichnet sich durch reiches historisches Detail aus.[42]

---

39 MUNDING I, 79 und II, 120 (für die später beigesetzte Eintragung für Sigismundus fehlt der Hinweis auf das Bobbio Missale). GOUGAUD, 46.

40 AASS Oct. 11, p. 642.

41 Wahrscheinlich ein Hinweis auf das von Messingham (*Florilegium* [Paris 1620], 87ff.) veröffentlichte Offizium aus dem spätmittelalterlichen Frankreich.

42 KENNEY, 395f.

An dieser Stelle ist allgemein zu bemerken, daß P. Munding die Querverbindungen zwischen seinen Arbeiten über die Heiligenleben und die Kalendare von St. Gallen leider noch nicht hergestellt hat. In den ersteren erwähnt er z.B., daß der verlorene *Codex S. Brigidae* in Sang. 566 unter dem Feste der Heiligen erwähnt wurde und wahrscheinlich ihre Vita enthielt.[43] Der Zusammenhang zwischen martyrologischen Eintragungen und Viten, besonders den für liturgische Zwecke gekürzten Fassungen der letzteren, ist noch weithin unerforscht. Dieser Zusammenhang ist aber von besonderer Bedeutung in der Erforschung eventueller irischer Einflüsse in frühmittelalterlichen Kalendarien des Festlandes. Feste irischer Heiliger sind zweifellos liturgisch zuerst auf dem Festlande gefeiert worden, aber die Kenntnisse, die solchen Festen zugrunde liegen mußten, waren wahrscheinlich eher biographischen als kalendarisch-martyrologischen Quellen entnommen[44].

Ich weiß nicht, ob die beiden wiederholt genannten Hauptquellen unserer Kenntnisse des frühmittelalterlichen Heiligenkalenders Irlands P. Munding unbekannt waren, oder nicht zugänglich waren, oder ob er aus sprachlichen Rücksichten auf ihre Auswertung verzichtete. Wer auf Stokes' englische Übersetzung von *Félire Oengusso* angewiesen ist, geht auf liturgiegeschichtlichem Gebiete leicht fehl.[45] Die Einträge für die irischen Heiligen im Martyrologium von Tallaght sind zur Hälfte in irischer Sprache, und selbst die irischen Eintragungen des Kalenders im Karlsruher Beda sind bisher fast nur vom philologischen Gesichtspunkt aus betrachtet worden.[46] Daß die irische Sprache im frühen Mittelalter auf dem Festland unbekannt war, läßt sich an zahlreichen Stellen in dem, was ich «irisch-kontinentale Hagiographie» genannt habe, vom 9. bis zum 12. Jahrhundert zeigen[47], am deutlichsten in der Wiedergabe der irischen Sätze in der *Vita S. Findani* (von Rheinau).[48] Es ist schon aus diesen Gründen nicht damit zu rechnen, daß die uns bekannten irischen Kalender des 9. Jahrhunderts auf dem Festlande als Vorlage gedient haben, von den anderen genannten Schwierigkeiten ganz abgesehen.

Ganz allgemein scheint es mir irrig zu sein, die Entstehung von Kalendarien nur auf das Zusammenschreiben von Vorlagen zurückzuführen. Bis heute ist der Kalender der römischen Kirche dadurch ausgezeichnet, daß er weitgehend mündliche Überlieferung widerspiegelt; Versuche, Heilige durch Schrifttum zu popularisieren, haben etwas Gewaltsames und oft Ungesundes an sich. Die Geschichte des Auf- und Absteigens

---

43   Hennig (f).

44   Hennig (c), (g), (h) und «Irish influences in the folkloristic tradition of St. Gertrude», *Bealoideas* XII (1942), 180ff.

45   Ein besonders krasser Fall liegt in der von Wilmart und Levison verbreiteten Theorie vor, *Félire Oengusso* sei das erste Zeugnis für das Fest Allerheiligen am 1. November [siehe Hennig (d) und (i)].

46   Siehe oben Anm. 36, auch Hennig (n) Anm. 32 und 45.

47   Siehe oben Anm. 19 und Hennig (p) und (q).

48   KENNEY, 602f. Für das Fest des hl. Fintan, MUNDING I, 85 und II, 19 und 174: «Schotte» (siehe oben Anm. 18).

von Heiligen in der Verehrung des katholischen Volkes zu erforschen, ist so schwierig, weil sie im Schrifttum nur in ihren Endergebnissen, nicht aber im eigentlichen Lebensvorgang studiert werden kann.[49] In der Auswahl der Feste irischer Heiliger, die der hl. Fintan auf Rheinau beging, läßt sich z.B. ein persönliches Element feststellen. Neben den beiden Nationalheiligen seines Heimatlandes, Patrick und Brigid, verehrte Fintan besonders den hl. Aidan von Ferns.[50] Fintan stammte, wie seine besonders zuverlässige *Vita* mitteilt, aus Leinster, und seine Verehrung für den hl. Aidan läßt uns annehmen, daß er entweder aus Ferns (im Süden der Provinz Leinster) stammte oder dort ausgebildet war. Ebenso ist es als ziemlich sicher anzunehmen, daß der Ire, der zuerst die Einführung des hl. Canice in ein festländisches Kalendar erlangte, aus dem Gebiet stammte, wo dieser Heilige besonders verehrt wurde, nämlich Kilkenny. Es gelang zunächst nicht, dem hl. Canice liturgische Verehrung zu sichern.[51] P. Munding erwähnt die entscheidende Tatsache nicht, daß jener Ire es doch erreichte, daß bis heute ein Eintrag für S. Canicus im Römischen Martyrologium am 11. Oktober gelesen wird.

Was am entscheidendsten dagegen spricht, daß Sang. 250 systematisch eine irische Vorlage benutzte, ist der Umstand, daß der hl. Patrick darin fehlt, obwohl sein Fest doch schon in Sang. 914 (= Gellonense), 878 und 450 erwähnt wurde. Für den bereits erwähnten Zusammenhang von Sang. 250 mit Turic. 176 ist es bedeutsam, daß in letzterem dieses Fest nachgetragen wurde. Es findet sich in den meisten späteren Kalendarien von St. Gallen[52].

Was also an der These, daß Sang. 250 «nach irischer Vorlage geschrieben» sei, übrig zu bleiben scheint, ist die Möglichkeit, daß hier zum ersten Male der hl. Canice in ein festländisches Kalendar eingeführt worden ist, aber selbst diese Erstmaligkeit ist äußerst zweifelhaft. Das einzige St. Galler Kalendar, welches eine Sang. 250 vergleichbare Menge irischer Heiliger enthält, ist Sang. 459 (c. 960/1). P. Munding sagt jedoch hier[53]:

---

49 Hennig (j) und (t).

50 KENNEY, 448f. «Aed ferna», ein Eintrag der sich direkt aus dem Félire des Oengus ableiten läßt, ist auch einer der irischen Heiligen in dem Sang. 250 etwa gleichzeitigen hexametrischen *martyrologium breviatum* in Brit. Mus. Galba A XVIII (und Tib. B V, im Gegensatz zu Jul. A VI), siehe Hennig (r). Im Gegensatz dazu sind die Listen frischer Heiliger des Kalenders im Karlsruher Beda, der Litanei von Fleury [Hennig (c), 323, Anm. 1] und – fast gleichlautend – in den Gedichten Alcuins (KENNEY, 535), sowie die Listen irischer Missionsheiliger in der festländischen Literatur [Hennig (m), 209 und 212 und (q), 23] nicht persönlich-lokal, sondern allgemein-repräsentativ.

51 MUNDING II, 17. GOUGAUD, 46, führt eine Heiligenlitanei in einem Basler Pontifikale des neunten Jahrhunderts an.

52 MUNDING I, 45 und II, 43. Wie wenig tief die irischen Heiligen auf dem Festland Fuß gefaßt haben, zeigt sich darin, daß in einigen späteren St. Galler Kalendarien Patricius mit Pancratius verwechselt wurde. Ähnlich wurde der Name des hl. Canice höchst verfälscht wiedergegeben (GOUGAUD, 1. c.) und endlich (durch Florarius) mit dem des hl. Canuthus verwechselt.

53 I, 10.

Wie aus den Heiligenfesten ersichtlich, für St. Gallen geschrieben: S. Brigida vom 1.II. ... S. Athala, Abt von Bobbio, 10.III. ... S. Columba, Abt 9.VI., S. Kilianus et socii 8.VII. ... S. Cainnachus (nach p. 79: *Gainnachus*) ... S. Columbanus 23.XI.

Sang. 250 scheint somit die einzige wirkliche Stütze für P. Mundings Annahme zu sein, daß man in der Frühzeit in St. Gallen «Kalendarien und Martyrologien, die man von Irland ... erhalten oder mitgebracht hatte, benützte».

Es war die Hauptaufgabe meiner Arbeit zu zeigen, in wievielen Beziehungen wir umdenken müssen, wenn wir von irischen Einflüssen auf die frühmittelalterliche Liturgie des Festlandes sprechen. Was ich an P. Mundings Untersuchungen kritisiert habe, sind im Rahmen seines großen Werkes nur Schönheitsfehler. Sein Werk hat uns wertvolles Material verschafft, um ein klareres Bild von der Geschichte des Kalendars im frühen Mittelalter zu gewinnen. Irland hat in dieser Entwicklung eine bei seiner sonstigen Bedeutung im kirchlichen Leben der Zeit erstaunlich passive Rolle gespielt. Von den Hunderten in Irland als *nóibh* bezeichneten Personen fanden nur ganz wenige im Kalender Platz, und dabei ist es in den allerwenigsten Fällen auch nur wahrscheinlich, daß dabei direkter irischer Einfluß mitgewirkt hat.

P. Munding hat uns vor allem das Rohmaterial zum Studium einer örtlich bestimmten Linie in der Entwicklung des Kalendars als Literaturform geboten. In den irisch-festländischen Beziehungen des Frühmittelalters nimmt St. Gallen eine Schlüsselstellung ein. Daß hier von einer systematischen Einwirkung Irlands auf die Kalendarien nichts nachzuweisen ist, bestätigt uns, daß das Fehlen von Kalendarien in der irischen Kirche nicht etwa durch das Abhandenkommen von entsprechenden Texten zu erklären ist.

In Untersuchungen auf diesem Gebiete spielen kirchen-, kultur-, kunst-, literatur-, schrift- und sprachgeschichtliche Erwägungen eine Rolle, aber all diesen Erwägungen gegenüber muß die liturgiewissenschaftliche Forschung sich ihrer Eigenart bewußt bleiben. In der Unterscheidung zwischen den in der Kalenderliteratur besonders greifbaren Grundcharakteren der irischen und festländischen Liturgie werden wesentliche Formen des geschichtlichen Bewußtseins offenbar, auf die sich zu besinnen eine der tiefsten Aufgaben geschichtlicher Forschung sein muß.[54]

(Quelle: Zeitschrift für schweizerische Kirchengeschichte, 48, 1954, S. 17-30.)

---

54 Diese Bemerkungen müßten im Lichte meiner Arbeiten über irisch-festländische Literaturbeziehungen und über die Grundzüge der altirischen Liturgie betrachtet werden.

The Liturgical Veneration of Irish Saints in Switzerland

Uniformity in essentials and diversity in accidentals is a characteristic of Catholicism. Thus the Ordinary of the Mass is the same everywhere, and there is no profession that can boast of a text-book as identical in all parts of the world as the Breviary. On the other hand, both the Missal and the Breviary have appendixes expressly described as Propers, that is, containing texts used by certain religious congregations or in certain dioceses and places only. In the Missal, these Propers contain the variant parts for certain feasts not universally celebrated, the Collect, as usual, relating most distinctively to the Saint or mystery of the day. In the Breviary, the Propers mainly contain the lessons for the second Nocturn of such feasts, which summarising the tradition of the life of the Saint are also known as "historical lessons".

By a unique privilege, Ireland has a Proper on a national rather than on a diocesan basis. This Proper as a whole is an important record of Irish history. The early Irish Church did not know the custom of observing liturgically the feasts of individual Saints, least of all of the national Saints, on their historical dates. Only from the twelfth century on, mostly by the great orders then introduced from abroad, such as the Cistercians and the Canons Regular, special Masses and Offices were composed proper to the feasts of Irish Saints "adopted" by these orders. As far as these offices were accepted by the Irish Church at large, in spite of English opposition, they did not survive the Reformation. Only very few liturgical text-books of the mediaeval Church in Ireland have come down to us. During the Penal Times of course no liturgical text-books were printed in Ireland or for the specific use in Ireland. The initiative for drawing up a Proper for Ireland came from the Irish Colleges abroad who felt the need for co-ordinating the national devotion to the Saints at home with the liturgical veneration paid on the Continent to Saints associated with Ireland. The granting of a Proper was a singular confirmation of the recognition authoritatively given to Ireland by Paul V, Urban VII and Benedict XIV as the leading missionary country. This Proper also was a great sign of hope that the end of the penal days was in sight and that the time had come to restore liturgical life in Ireland.

When about the middle of the eighteenth century a petition for a Proper for Ireland was granted the stipulation was made, usual in such cases but particularly important in that case, that the texts should be drawn from approved breviaries. Offices proper to Irish Saints, however, were extant only in Continental prayer-books, and up to the first decade of the present century in the Proper for Ireland for each feast the (Continental) source was stated from which the texts had been drawn. Only from 1903 on, new texts, composed in Ireland, were added. The texts for the feasts of Ss. Columbanus and Gall used to this day in Ireland were drawn from the Benedictine Breviary, the most important source of the first Proper for Ireland.

In the study of the subject known as Irish Saints on the Continent, we must distinguish between Saints, mainly of the early missionary period, whose coming from Ireland is well testified, whose names are Irish and the greatest of whom at least were known in mediaeval Ireland, and – on the other hand – Saints to whom Irish associations were attributed at a late date, probably in virtue of Ireland's reputation as the island of Saints, whose names cannot be given by any stretch of linguistic fancy an Irish interpretation and who were quite unknown in Ireland until the seventeenth century. Typical examples of the first group are Ss. Columbanus, Fursey and Kilian and of the latter Ss. Rumold, Livinus and Fridolin. There are of course various degrees of historicity of the Irish associations, between these two extremes.

The subject of Irish Saints abroad in general illustrates the important fact that the biographical and liturgical traditions of the Saints are associated with their work rather than with their birth. The cultus of the Irish Saints who laboured and died abroad originated on the Continent, and their biographical tradition has remained, with very few exceptions, Continental. The vita of St. Fintan of Rheinau stands out by the fact that it contains some fragments – indeed the earliest sentences recorded on the Continent – of the Irish language; this important biography must have drawn at least on Irish information. While the proper names accidentally recorded in the traditions of the Irish associations of these Saints are generally fictitious (see e.g. the life of St. Livinus), many of the Irish place-names mentioned are historical, sometimes ingeniously disguised, sometimes grossly disfigured.

The study of the tradition of the historical lessons of the Breviary has been sorely neglected. In fact, these historical lessons have scarcely been recognised as a distinctive source of tradition, or, if we properly understand the meaning of the word "tradition", a source of greatest importance. Let us consider one fact: Since the late seventeenth century, once a year every Catholic priest in the world reads that *Patricius Hiberniae dictus Apostolus ... Armachanam sedem totius insulae principem metropolium constituit ... sepultusque est apud Dunum in Ultonia,* – by far the greatest single contribution to world knowledge of Ireland. On many other days of the year large numbers of priests in various parts of the world, as far apart as Belgium, Switzerland, Southern Italy or even Australia, have read and still read similar references to Ireland, and this reading is by obligation, rather than by individual interest. The question whether these references to Ireland are historical or historically correct is of secondary importance; they should be considered as a general recognition of the eminent and indeed unique position held by Ireland in the spiritual tradition of Christianity. They are read not as dry accounts of facts but embedded in prayer, glorifying God in His Saints, giving thanks for the graces bestowed through Ireland upon other nations, and promising to imitate the virtues represented (whether in material truth or in spiritual legend) by those Saints.

Thus, by way of example in the Irish associations recorded therein the historical lessons of the Breviary can be shown to be a tradition unsurpassed by its repetitive continuity, its geographical and historical extent and its mental insistence. Let us further consider that they have been and are the basis of many sermons and the source of innumerable popular treatises, the influence of which on the formation of the mind and consciousness of the Christian people is a subject worthy of closer study. So far as the place of Irish Saints in the liturgical text-books has been studied at all, investigations have scarcely been extended beyond the end of the Middle Ages (Weale and Gougaud). While it is important to study the origin of the liturgical tradition and its connection with, or growth from, the biographical one, it is at least permissible to start investigations as it were from the opposite end, that is, from the present-day extent of liturgical veneration as a tradition still alive and authoritatively sanctioned.

The tradition of Ireland's place in Continental thought is generally characterised by the disparity between the fewness of material contacts and the richness of spiritual associations. The communication lines connecting the Irish Saints abroad with their native country (whether real or reputed) have been weak or non existent. Present-day liturgical veneration to Irish Saints in Britain is a product of the nineteenth century. The tradition, once so rich, of Irish Saints in Britanny is practically dead. On the other hand, the recent jubilees of Ss. Columbanus, Kilian, Gall and Fridolin have testified to an awareness of their Irish associations by which Irishmen today must feel as overwhelmed as were, three hundred years ago, Colgan and his fellow-workers when first discovering again those traditions. In Ireland, attempts to create devotion to the Irish Saints abroad have failed, a fact to be accepted as part of the sad history of the country and as an illustration of the reality of the liturgy.

In contrast to Ireland, Switzerland has not a national Proper. The present-day extent of liturgical veneration paid to Irish Saints in Switzerland has to be established from the various diocesan Propers. It may be mentioned at this point that one of the difficulties encountered in the study of the historical lessons is that the texts are difficult to obtain, because Breviaries usually contain only one diocesan proper. The British Museum does not own a set of the Propers for Great Britain, and no public library in Switzerland seems to possess a set of the Propers of the Swiss dioceses. For unknown reasons the price of these propers bought separately is exorbitant.

The feast of St. Columbanus is celebrated in the dioceses of Chur and St. Gallen. I have shown elsewhere that the historical lessons for Chur largely agree with those read in Ireland, an interesting difference being that the former omit the reference to the Saint's attempt to return *in Hiberniam* before he came to Switzerland. In Chur and Ireland these lessons start with the words *Columbanus natione Hibernus* and in St. Gallen with the words *Columbanus Hibernus*. In his biography of the Saint, Jonas was the first Continental hagiographer to record a historical Irish place-name, a fact recognised by the reference in both the Chur / Ireland and the St. Gallen version to *Benchor monasterium*. (Hence in the diocese of Down, St. Gall's feast is a double.) Conversely – apart from the historical lessons for the feast of St. Gall – this is the only instance in which a Swiss place-name is mentioned in the Proper for Ireland: The words *ad lacum Brigantinum consedit* are a reduction from what is now found in the Chur Office: *In Helvetiam ad lacus Tigurini superini partes pervenit ... in regione Tuggiensi daemonum simulacris ... in lacum dejectis ... ad lacum Brigantinum se contulit.* (St. Gallen: *profectus Arbonam, indeque Acronio lacu transmisso Brigantiam pervenit.*)

Since 1586 the place-name of *Arbona* has been associated in the Roman Martyrology with St. Gall. The historical lessons for his feast in the Propers for Ireland, the dioceses of Basle, Chur and St. Gallen and for the diocese of Turin differ only in details. "Gallus Abbas (- I) nobilibus apud Scotos (I: in Scotia) natalibus ortus in Hibernia (- I) in monasterio Benchor (B,C: Benchorensi) adulescentulus vitam pauperem cum elegisset, humilitati et (- I) oboedientiae perfectaeque (I: et perfectae) subjectioni semper studuit. Deinde vero cum non morum tantum, set et ingenii laude, ac sanctarum Scripturarum scientia usuque apprime floreret, (+ G: sacerdos Dei unctus) praedicandi Evangelii cause abbatem Columbanum secutus in Britanniam indeque in (- G) Galliam trajecit: ubi Sigeberti regis voluntate (- B: S. r. v.) Luxoviensem solitudinem dum incoleret ad Christi fidem complures multosetiam ad monasticae vitae institute adduxit (I, G: permovit, T: promovit). Sed cum (+ C: impudicos) regis Theodorici concubinatum (C: mores) redarguere Columbanus abbas non desisteret Brunichildis opera (G, I, T: reginae instinctu) Luxovio pulsus, accepta a Theodeberto Austrasianorum rege potestate (+ G: cum Gallo allisque sociis), in Alemannia ad lacumTuricinum (T: Turininum; probably misread in deference to *diaecesis Taurinenis* !) primum deinde (C: ubi in regione quae nunc est capitoli Marchionensis saluti animarum operam indefessam navavit inde vero expulsus) apud Brigantinum oppidum reconciliato sanctae Aureliae templo consedit.

Verum quoniam Gallus idolatriae scelus (B, C: idolatriam) ubique convellebat (+ G: et) fana et simulacra dissipabat, gentium odia cincitavit. Quibus etiam (G: -) cedendum ratus Columbanus in Italiam ipse ad Agilulphum Langobardorum regem profectus, Gallum febribus detentum, una cum Magnoaldo et Theodoro monachis, in Alemannia reliquit. Gallus vero sexagesimum (I, T: octogesimum) quintum circiter (I, T: -) annum agens, mox ut convaluit, eremum cum jam dictis discipulis ingressus, triduano eam jejunio, orationibus ac lacrimis consecravit et monasterium condidit. In quo (B,C: eo) plures fratres monasticis disciplinis divinarumque (I: ac divinarum), scripturarum intelligentia imbuit et (I, T: -) gentes circumpositas Jesu Christi fidem sectari docuit. Corpus suum inedia, frigore, cilico (I, T.: + denique) et catena castigavit, ita secreto, ut de catena ejus aerea (T: aenea) ciliciove quibus ad hujusmodi exercitia utebatur (I, T: uteretur), nec discipuli ejus dum viveret (I: vixerit) quidquam (I, T: -) scirent (I, T: rescirent).

Fridiburgam (T: Fridiburgiam), Alemannia ducis filia, Sigeberti regis sponsam, a saevissimo daemonio cum liberasset, ducis opulentissima done comminuit, et apud Arbonam in pauperes erogavit. Episcopatum constantiensem, (B, C, G: et) abbatiam Luxoviensem suscipere recusavit. Columbanum in Italia vitae munere sanctissime (I: sanctissimae) perfunctum per visionem in Alemannia praecognovit (G: cognovit). Denique cum populos multos ad idolorum culture avocasset (T: revocasset), ipsoque die sancti Michaelis Archangeli apud Arbonam post Missarum solemnia Evangelium praedicasset, febre in jam dicto oppido iterum correptus, circa (I, T: -) annum (I, T: anno Domini) sexcentensimum (I, T: sexcentesimo) quadragesimum (I, T: vigesimo quarto, Bonifacii Papae quinti septimo) aetatis suae (B, C, I, T: s. a.) nonagesimo quinto, die vero decima septima (B, C: decimo septimo) Kalendarum Novembrium inter discipulorum menus exspiravit. Sed cum illic nullo modo potuisset (T: posses) humari, indomitorum tandem (G: -) equorum ductu, ardentibus continuo ad feretrum cereis, in sacram eremum perlatus (I: portatus) in oratorio suo Joannis episcopi Constantiensis, sui olim discipuli, fratrumque manibus sepultus, miraculis claruit."

This is not the place to explore the stemma of these texts or the method illustrated by them of editing liturgical texts. Apart from a local reference introduced in the Chur text, these five versions differ only in one material detail, in so far as to this day the

Irish one maintains (with the Turin one, of which however I have only the 1869 edition) the dating of St. Gall's death to the year 624.

In the 1870 edition of the Proper for the diocese of Milan a brief summary of the tradition of St. Gall is prescribed as the ninth lesson for October 16 starting with the words *Gallus Abbas, nobilibus religiosisque parentibus in Britannia natus*, omitting all references to Ireland and mentioning only the place-name of *Constantia*. The words *multis et illius provinciae* (which ?) *et Germaniae locis peragratis* seem to reflect the entry for St. Gall in the Roman Martyrology which to this day says: "Apud Arbonam, *in Germania*." While in Ireland, Milan, Turino, Basle and Chur the Collect for St. Gall's feast is taken from the Common of a Confessor not a Bishop (*Intercessio nos*) in the diocese of Alba, a suffragan of Turino, it is proper: "Da nobis, aeternae consolationis Pater, per merita beati Galli Abbatis, pacem et salutem mentis et corporis, ut ejus exemplis jugiter inhaerantes quae tibi sunt placita, tote perficiamus virtute", a beautiful illustration of what has been said above of the setting of the historical lessons for the feasts of Irish Saints.

The Office for the feast of St. Gall, principal patron of the abbey, city and diocese of St. Gallen (and thus a double of the first class with common octave) is a fine example of what a full liturgy proper to the feast of a Saint can be like. The insertion of the words *sacerdos Dei unctus* in the historical lessons may have been inspired by the Chapter of this Office (Eccli. 45: 1-2: "Dilectus Deo et hominibus, cujus memoria in benedictione est ...", also used as versicle and responsory after the Vesper and Lauds hymns. The Mattins and Lauds hymns speak of St. Gall's missionary work and anchorite life.

The first antiphon of the first Nocturn mentions *Gallus puer in monasterio*, while the responsory and versicle after the first historical lesson says: "Parentes beati Galli filium suum primae aetatis flore nitentem cum oblatione Domino offerentes in monasterio commendaverunt. Erant enim religiosi atque nobiles (see the Milan lesson) unde et filium suum in monasterio commendaverunt." Similarly the second and third historical lessons are summed up, and other quotations from Wetti form the responsories after the lessons of the third Nocturn. The way in which these quotations were selected, adapted and placed illustrates what may be described as the historical taste of the liturgy. The antiphon to the Magnificat is the earliest record in Continental literature of Irish nostalgia: "Aperiens Jannes sarcophagum, amariores cum hac voce lacrimas dedit: Heu, heu, Pater amate, heu, doctor egregie, cur me de domo patris eductum quasi orphanum dereliquisti?"

The Collect proper to St. Gall's feast in St. Gallen is a counterpart to the Collect used in the whole Church for the feast of St. Patrick: "Deus, qui gentes nostras per beatum Gallum Abbatem ad agnitionem verae fidei perduxisti: concede nobis in ejusdem fidei professione inviolabilem firmitatem; ut cum ipso praemia consequamur aeterna."

On September 6, in the diocese of St. Gallen and in some parts of the diocese of Chur the feast of St. Magnus is celebrated. In St. Gallen the historical lessons for this feast start with the words: "Magnus, qui etiam Magnoaldus vocabatur, beati Columbani abbatis discipulus" and in Chur with the words: "Magnus seu Magnoaldus sanctorum

Christi Abbatum Galli et Columbani fuit alumnus." No indication whatsoever is given that this Saint was of Irish descent; the tradition of his Irish associations was established by Messingham's inserting the *Vita S. Magni* in his *Florilegium insulae sanctorum* (Paris 1624) in deference to the fact that this Vita alleged that Magnus was St. Gall's successor.

The tradition of the Irish associations of St. Fridolin of Säckingen is an offshoot of the Irish tradition in St. Gallen. The Life of St. Fridolin, written by Balther, who had studied at St. Gallen, is a typical example of a belated Hibernisation of a local Saint on the Continent. From its first words: "Beatus Fridolinus ab extremis partibus inferioris Scotiae oriundus esse non ambigitur" the tradition of these Irish associations is subject to doubts. It is interesting because of the considerable amount of geographical information added by Balther to this initial statement, an important record of Continental knowledge of Ireland in the tenth century, and because of the sustained and authoritative sanction it has received. In the Propers for the dioceses of Basle and Chur the historical lessons for March 6 start with the words: "Fridolinus, regio Hibernorum sanguine procreatus" and a leaflet by P. Hieronymus Wilms O.P. in the series *Unsere Namenspatrone in Wort und Bild,* the latest publication on this Saint, says: "Like many other missionaries of that time Fridolin originated from Ireland."

In the lessons for Basle and Chur, St. Fridolin's life in Ireland is not described. In the Office prescribed for the diocese of St. Gallen, however, the first historical lesson is devoted to this subject: "Fridolinus, in Hibernia nobili genere ortus, jam a juventute scientia ac pietate eluxit. Sacerdotio insignitus et maxime agregiis animi dotibus praeditus, verbum Dei cum tanta eloquentia tantoque omnium applausu praedicabat, ut praecipuis honoribus propter suam artis oratoriae peritiam afficeretur. Ast celebritatem humilitati postponens, divitiasque et omnem saeculi pompam spernens, opes paterns inter cognatos, pauperes et ecclesias divisit, sicque sponte pauper factus, patriam reliquit ..."

Visitors to the former abbey of Rheinau near Schaffhausen are offered a splendidly produced history of the abbey published in 1932 by Hermann Fietz. It states that in the ninth century "Fintan a monk is mentioned, later venerated as patron of the abbey and as Saint ... According to the oldest version of his life which has to be classified as a legend, Fintan was born *in der irischen Provinz Laginien*". A hundred years earlier, in what to my knowledge is the only separate biography in modern times of this Saint, Anton Mätzler, Canon of Augsburg, had already identified *Laginia* (mentioned twice in the *Vita S. Findani*) with Leinster. The neglect of St. Fintan in the literature on Irish Saints abroad is due to a very simple fact: His feast being on November 15th neither Colgan nor the Bollandists nor O'Hanlon have dealt with him. In the Proper for the diocese of Chur the texts for this feast are marked by an asterisk, indicating that it is observed only in certain places (presumably Rheinau only). Only the historical lessons are proper to this feast. They start with the word: "Fintanus, genere Scotus, Princeps Laginiae Provinciae in Hibernia." Like the mediaeval versions of these lessons (published by Mone), the present-day lessons are based on the *Vita*, but it should be noted that the description of the Saint as *princeps Laginiae* rather than as (son of) *miles unius principis Laginiae* was initiated by an eighteenth century series of pictures illustrating the Saint's life, one of which (reproduced by Mätzler) shows the Saint as *Laginiae princeps.*

Fietz's verdict on the *Vita S. Findani* would appear to be somewhat harsh. Apart from the Irish sentences embodied in this Vita, also the details of its account of the Saint's youth point to a solid historical background. In fact, outside the traditions of Ss. Columbanus and Gall, no tradition of an Irish Saint on the Continent rests on sounder foundations than that of St. Fintan.

The survey of present-day liturgical veneration of Irish Saints in Switzerland illustrates the fact that devotion to the Saints is a living reality and as such has a soul and a body. Its soul of course is the realisation of the virtues of the Saints and of the graces bestowed through them generation by generation. Its body is what may be described by the term *paruchia* as used in the old monastic Church in Ireland or by the modern term clientele, that is, some form of organisation. Present-day liturgical veneration of St. Gall is stronger than that of St. Columbanus because it has been backed by the abbey, diocese, town and canton of St. Gallen. On the other hand, since the church enshrining the site of St. Fintan's hermitage (now his tomb) is no longer attached to a flourishing abbey (but to a cantonal asylum) the *cultus* of this Saint leads a precarious existence bordering on mere reminiscence. Indeed today, as a living reality the tradition of St. Fintan is more palpable in places like Mariastein than in Rheinau: Every year thousands of pilgrims, not only from Switzerland but also from France and Germany, see in the church of "Our Lady of the Rock" (South of Basle) the wall paintings in the nave representing St. Fintan and St. Gall and in the porch the memorial slab to the builder of the present church, whose name in religion was Fintan.

The study of the liturgical tradition of Irish Saints on the Continent throws some light upon a conception of history which while specifically Catholic had fallen into oblivion. One of the few references made in Batifoll's *History of the Breviary* to the historical lessons reads as follows: "The lessons taken from the lives of saints have always been a stumbling block. I have found on the margins of late copies of the breviaries annotations such as the following written against the legends of the saints: *Neutiquam ... Fabula ... Apocrypha Falsa narratio ... Fabula anilis ... Officium stolidum et ridiculum.* The marginal notes are by clerks of the Renaissance" (London 1912 p. 168). The writing of history during the nineteenth century emphasized the critical attitude to the sources in the belief that by brushing aside tradition, a direct approach could be obtained to the historical facts. Even in studies of the liturgy this erroneous conception has made considerable headway. However, only where the liturgy appreciated as a living reality, linking up, through the ages, the past with the present, in loving memory and devout prayer, this study comes into its own. In the light of this conception of tradition, the historical lessons become from a subject of criticism, from impatient scorn or condescending tolerance, a valuable source of information on the meaning of tradition.

Literature: For earlier literature see KENNEY'S *Sources* and GOUGAUD'S *Les saints irlandais.* Lists of my publications on the tradition of Irish saints on the Continent are available to Swiss readers in *Zeitscbr. f. Schweizer. Kirchengesch.* 46 (1952),

215 f. and 48 (1954), 17 f. and to Irish readers in *Reportorium Novum* 1 (1955) 45. My paper on "St. Columbanus in the liturgy" appeared in *Ir. Eccl. Rec. V*, 62 (1945), 306-312. On the tradition of St. Fintan see my papers in *Z. Schw. Kirch.gesch.* 46, 28 f. and in *Report. Nov.* 1, 62 f. On St. Fridolin see my paper on SCHEFFEL'S *Ekkehard* to be published soon in *Ir. Eccl. Rec.* G. SCHREIBER, *Irland im deutschen und abendländischen Sakralraum* (Köln 1952) neglected – in spite of its title – the liturgical tradition and the literature on this subject.

(Quelle: Iris Hibernia 3, 1957, S. 23-32.)

Irlandkunde in der festländischen Tradition irischer Heiliger

Während das 1925 von Walter Hofstaetter geschaffene Wort „Deutschkunde" die Kunde bezeichnet, die Deutsche von sich selbst haben, meint das (m.w. zuerst von mir vorgeschlagene) Wort, „Irlandkunde" vorzugsweise Kunde von Irland, die Nichtiren erwerben oder besitzen. Daß „Kunde", im Unterschied zu „Wissenschaft", mehr auf Heuristik und Hermeneutik als auf Systematik und Kritik beruht, ist bei festländischer Irlandkunde in dem hier zu betrachtenden Zeitraum besonders bedeutsam: Elementare Verifikation war schwierig; dies ergab sich aus der Eigenart des Gegenstandes: dieser war

1. eine Insel[1],

2. dem Blick des Festlandes in mehr als einem Sinne verdeckt durch eine größere Insel[2],

3. am äußersten Westrande der bekannten Welt gelegen, mithin keine Durchgangs- sondern eine Endstation, und schwierig zu erreichen[3],

4. mit dem Kontinent durch fast ausschließlich nichtmaterielle Beziehungen verbunden (für deren Erkenntnis der hagiographischen Literatur besondere Bedeutung zukommt)[4],

---

1 *Hibernia insula, extremo Oceano sita:* Poetischer Anfang von Jonas' Vita Columbani (Kenney Nr. 48). Im Allgemeinen werde ich es bei der Zitierung *einer* Belegstelle und bei der Benennung des Kapitels in J. F. *Kenney*, The Sources of the Early History of Ireland 1, New York 1929, belassen.

2 *Insula Hybernia, quae inter Britanniam et Hispaniam est sita:* Eintragung für Gallus 16. Okt. in Notkers Martyrologium (*Kenney* Nr. 413) oder: *Ab ipsis Oceani finibus emergens Hibernia, Gallorum insula, quae Britannici maris limite ambitur:* Vita I. S. Foillani (*Kenney* Nr. 298). Siehe auch die später zu erwähnenden Beschreibungen des Seewegs von Irland nach Gallien.

3 Jonas fährt an der (Anm. 1) zitierten Stelle fort: *expectat Titani occasum, dum vertitur orbis, lux et occiduas pontum descendit in umbras ... sinus ultimus terrarum,* bis hin zu Vita S. Gobani (Kenney Nr. 301): *In insula occiduo sita quae dicitur Hibernia incolarum corda corroboravit in fide Catholica.*

4 *De remotis partibus mundi arbiter orbis lumen nostratibus refulgere disposuit:* Wetti, Vita S. Galli (*Kenney*, Nr. 50, II) oder: *Scotia ... nobis lumen nostrum primitivum destinavit Kylianum:* Jüngere Vita Burchardi, AA.SS. Octob. 6, S. 576.

5. wobei diese nichtmateriellen Beziehungen (wenigstens soweit in der hagiographischen Überlieferung berichtet) fast nur von Irland ausgingen[5] und die von ihnen überbrachte Irlandkunde von den Kontinentalen kaum durch eigenen Augenschein zu überprüfen war.

Wir wissen jedoch von kontinentaler Irlandkunde viel mehr als von gleichzeitiger irischer Festlandkunde. Zudem sind die festländischen Zeugnisse weit weniger der Zerstörung anheimgefallen als die irischen. Viele festländische Traditionen irischer (und praktisch aller „hibernisierter") Heiligen wurden in Irland erst im 17. Jahrhundert und weiteren irischen Kreisen selbst geistlichen, sogar erst durch das im 18. Jahrhundert erstellte Proprium Hiberniae zum Breviarium Romanum bekannter.

Unser Thema bedarf der Erläuterung in räumlicher, zeitlicher, gegenständlicher und personaler Hinsicht.

1. In der Geschichte des Begriffs „Europa" nimmt Irland eine eminente Stellung ein. Der Ausdruck *tota Europa* kommt zuerst in einem Brief des hl. Kolumban vor; aber, indem es am 20. April eine *communis sollemnitas omnium sanctorum Hiberniae et Britanniae et totius Europae* kommemorierte[6], erkannte das Martyrologium von Tallaght den „britischen Inseln" eine Sonderstellung zu. Selbst in den in der irischen Annalenliteratur gebrauchten Ausdrücken „West-", ja „Nordwest-Europa" behält Hibernia immer noch einen eigenen Platz.[7] Es ist schon aus diesen Gründen zu rechtfertigen, daß wir unsere Betrachtung auf das Festland beschränken. Ich klammere auch die Bretagne aus, deren Irlandkunde aus geographischen und sprachlichen Gründen von der des übrigen Festlandes verschieden war.

2. Häufiger als bei anderen in dem hier zu betrachtenden Gebiet im Mittelalter tätig gewesenen Fremden (etwa Griechen) ist es bei den Iren, daß entweder die in den Zeugnissen gemachten Angaben über die Lebenszeit unhistorisch sind oder jedenfalls die Viten von Heiligen, bei denen man annehmen kann, daß sie vor dem 11. Jahrhundert – der unserer Untersuchung gesetzten Zeitgrenze – gelebt hatten,

---

5   Dies vor allem im Gegensatz zu gleichzeitiger Palästinakunde. Wandregesilus von Fontenelle wollte, Mitte des 7. Jh., *remotiora loca inhabitare ... disposuit in Scociam* (Hs: *Hiberniam insulam) ambulare*, kam aber nicht dazu (MGH.SS.rer. Merov. 5, S. 18); ebensowenig führte Dido von Poitiers die *directio* einer *peregrinatio in Scociam* (Anm.: *Hibernia*) aus (ebd. 2, S. 316). Vincentius Madelgarius soll nach Irland gegangen sein und von dort Furseus und dessen Gefährten mitgebracht haben, aber dies ist ein später Zusatz zu seiner Vita (*Kenney* Nr. 305). Um 860 schrieb Ermenrich von Ellwangen an Abt Grimald von St. Gallen: „Wie könnte ich je Irlands vergessen, wo die Sonne des Glaubens über uns aufgegangen und die Strahlen des großen Lichtes uns erreicht haben" (*Kenney* Nr. 408). Im 9. Jh. sprach Hildegars Vita des hl. Faro von Meaux (ca. 685) von der großen Zahl von Iren, die damals nach Gallien gekommen seien. Dies wieder ein Beispiel dafür, daß die Zahl der Iren auf dem Kontinent höher gewesen sein mag, als die erhaltene Überlieferung erkennen läßt.

6   *J. Hennig*, A Feast of all the Saints of Europe, Speculum 21 (1946) S. 49-66.

7   Zum 50. Jahrestag des Ausbruchs des 1. Weltkriegs brachte die Neue Zürcher Zeitung *meinen* Artikel „Tota Europa".

später geschrieben wurden und ihre allfällige Irlandkunde diesen späteren Stand wiederspiegelt. Die hier zu betrachtenden vor 1100 geschriebenen Texte[8] beziehen sich für den kirchlichen Bereich auf die Zeit vor der Ersetzung der monastischen Struktur der irischen Kirche durch die diözesane[9] und für den politischen Bereich auf die Zeit vor der Normanneninvasion.

3.   Da es sich bei den hier zu betrachtenden Zeugnissen fast nie um eine dem Festland bewußt von Iren gegebene, sondern oft um eine auf minimaler Realgrundlage ermittelte Irlandkunde[10] handelt, ist das Irrige und Fehlende von kaum minderem Interesse als das Richtige und (wie wir sehen werden, gelegentlich erstaunlicherweise) Vorhandene. Berücksichtigt man ferner die geographischen Verhältnisse sowie die Schwierigkeiten des Verkehrs, so ist es an sich schon beachtlich, daß es festländische Irlandkunde im frühen Mittelalter gegeben hat. Es läßt sich für die Zeit kaum vergleichbares mitteleuropäisches Wissen von oder Interesse an anderen entsprechend weit nach Norden oder Osten entlegenen Gebieten nachweisen.

4.   Der Anteil von „Heiligen" unter den schon im Vergleich zu anderen auf dem europäischen Festland weilenden Fremden verhältnismäßig zahlreichen Iren ist sehr hoch; die Tradition der Heiligen ist daher besonders wichtig für die Irlandkunde, wobei man allerdings beachten muß, daß die Vermittlung solcher Kunde in dieser Tradition naturgemäß nur beiläufig war. Der hohe Prozentsatz von Heiligen liegt zweifellos nicht nur an den Qualitäten jener Iren, die allerdings häufig, wenn auch meist in allgemeinen Ausdrücken[11] gerühmt werden, sondern auch an dem weiteren – dem älteren – Bedeutungsbereich von „sanctus" (oder gar dem entsprechenden gaelischen Wort) in Irland[12]: Das Martyrologium von Tallaght, der um 800 gemachte Versuch, so vollständig wie möglich alle Heiligennamen aus dem Hieronymianum zu extrahieren[13], fügte der Liste jedes Tages eine praktisch gleich lange irischer Namen hinzu; d.h., die kleine Insel beanspruchte, so viele Heilige hervorgebracht zu haben wie die ganze übrige Kirche. Auch das

---

8   Einen ersten Überblick über die traditionelle Behandlung dieses Problems bieten die centenary tables im Anhang zu Alban *Butler*, The Lives of the Saints, Dublin 1866, wo z.B. für das 7. Jh. an irischen Heiligen, neben Columban und Furseus und deren Gefährten, Dympna (*Kenney* Nr. 314) und ihr Begleiter Genebrard sowie Fiacrius (*Kenney* Nr. 283) und seine Schwester Syra und Peregrinus von Modena (siehe unter Anm. 54) aufgeführt werden, deren literarische Traditionen erst nach dem 11. Jh. beginnen.

9   Hierzu *meine* Arbeiten über die Traditionen der hll. Albert von Regensburg und Cataldus von Tarent: Mediaeval Stud. 7 (1945) S. 21-39, 8 (1946) S. 217-244.

10   Sie wäre natürlich aus anderen Quellen als den hagiographischen zu ergänzen; z.B. vgl. zu meinen obigen Anm. 1-3: *finibus occiduis optima tellus Scottica*, Carmen Scottorum, MGH. Poetae 3 S. 691; *ultima terra*, Versus Dungalo (s.u.), Poetae 4 S. 1124 (*Kenney*, Nr. 350).

11   So heißt es von Preacordius: *ex Scotorum genere virtute clarus et per omnia venerabilis vitae*: AA.SS. Febr. 1, S. 196.

12   Siehe oben Anm. 6.

13   Hierzu *J. Hennig*, Proceedings of the Royal Irish Academy 69 C (1970) S. 45-112.

Kommen von der fernen Insel machte die Iren merk- und ehrwürdig. Balthers Vita des Fridolin von Säckingen (Ende des 10. Jahrhunderts) ist ein frühes Beispiel für die Sitte, daß man, wenn bei der Abfassung der Vita eines Heiligen die Herkunft desselben unbekannt war, unterstellte, er sei von der „insula sanctorum" gekommen.[14] Die Manuskripte der Heiligenviten kamen nur einem kleinen Kreis zu Gesicht. Breiter war das Bekanntwerden irischer Heiligennamen durch alljährlich wiederholte Texte wie Martyrologien. Für den von uns zu betrachtenden Zeitraum gelangten nur wenige dieser Namen in festländische Kalendarien, d.h. Verzeichnisse gefeierter Feste. Wie wenig die Liturgie als Träger von Irlandkunde gewürdigt worden ist, kann man an Max Josef Metzgers Ausgabe des Basler Pontifikale (Freiburg Univ.-Bibl. 363, Mitte 9. Jh.) sehen[15], wo Kilian als „Franke", Furseus, Ultan und Foillan ebenso wie Ita und Brigida als „Belgier" bezeichnet werden. Das Basler Pontifikale ist einzigartig, indem in ihm Columbanus zweimal (einmal unter den Märtyrern!) aufgeführt wird und ferner Effrem, Finian und Darerca genannt werden.

Die Verbreitung der Irlandkunde tragenden Texte der Heiligentradition könnte allenfalls aus der Zahl und den Entstehungsorten der Handschriften erschlossen werden, wobei die Frage, wie weit diese Texte bekannt wurden oder gar, wie es Herrad Spilling gut ausdrückte, „Wurzeln schlugen", offen bleiben muß. Andererseits wäre der Stand der festländischen Irlandkunde in dem hier zu betrachtenden Zeitraum an der späterer Zeiten, selbst der Gegenwart, zu messen.[16]

Es ist nicht meine Aufgabe zu prüfen, ob die Heiligen, deren Traditionen hier zu betrachten sind, wirklich existiert haben; Zweifel in dieser Hinsicht hat man weit mehr bei den nach dem 11. Jahrhundert entstandenen Traditionen wie der von Frediano und Silao von Lucca, Cataldus von Tarent, Dympna von Gheel, Livinus von Gent, Rumold von Mecheln und Albert von Regensburg.[17] Es ist auch nicht auf die genaue Datierung der Quellen einzugehen, vielmehr kann der hier zu betrachtende Zeitraum von 650 bis 1100 als eine Einheit behandelt und nach seiner Irlandkunde abgefragt werden, wie sie sich in den in ihm entstandenen Heiligentraditionen zeigt. Ich untersuche auch nicht die Qualifikationen der in Betracht zu ziehenden Vermittler von Irlandkunde, ob sie

---

14   Zu *insula sanctorum* vgl. Margrit *Koch*, Sankt Fridolin and sein Biograph Balther. Irische Heilige in der literarischen Darstellung des Mittelalters, Zürich 1959, S. 63ff.

15   Freiburger Theologische Stud. 17, Freiburg i.Br. 1914.

16   Obgleich kaum Zweifel daran bestehen dürften, daß Frediano von Lucca (*Kenney* Nr. 40; J. *Hennig*, Mediaeval Stud. 13, 1951, S. 234-242) kein Ire war, stattete ihm zu Ehren 1950 der damalige Präsident der Republik Irland, Sean T. O'Kelly, einen Besuch in Lucca ab (vgl. Pellegrino *Puccinelli*, San Frediano, Lucca 1952, S. 20f.). Der irische Botschafter in der Bundesrepublik nimmt gern an der Prozession anläßlich des Fridolinsfestes in Säckingen (6. März) teil. Festländische Irlandkunde wird in solchen Fällen praktisch nicht gefördert.

17   Siehe oben Anm. 8 und 9; J. *Hennig*, The Place of the Archdiocese of Dublin in the Hagiographical Tradition of the Continent, Reportorium Novum 1 (1955) S. 45-63; zu Livinus: W. *Wattenbach-W. Levison*, Deutschlands Geschichtsquellen im Mittelalter. Vorzeit und Karolinger 2, Weimar 1953, S. 171 Anm. 19.

selbst Iren waren, Schüler oder Bekannte von Iren oder Abschreiber insbesondere antiker Quellen.

Ausgangspunkt der Irlandkunde ist das Vorkommen von auf Irland bezüglichen Bezeichnungen, wobei ich einerseits Unterschiede in der Schreibweise (Hibernia oder Hybernia, Scotia mit th oder zwei t), andererseits die in der Hagiologie oft diskutierte Frage des Bedeutungsbereichs von Scotia außer Betracht lasse.[18] Bemerkenswert ist: *Hibernia insula, in qua est Scotia* in der Vita S. Gibriani (10. Jh.)[19] gegenüber: *In Scotia, insula Hiberniae* in Notkers Eintragung für Gallus[20], sowie, wenn auch nicht genau in den von uns zu betrachtenden Textbereich gehörend: *Ab occidua Hierne* in Walahfrids Carmen.[21] Das deutsche Wort „Irlant" ist m.W. zuerst im Rolandslied bezeugt, das zwischen 1150 and 1172 entstand.[22]

Spezifische Irlandkunde beginnt mit Ortsnamen.[23] Jonas teilte mit, daß Columbanus geboren wurde *in solo quem Lagenorum terram incolae nuncupant*[24]; Leinster wird auch in der Vita S. Findani[25] genannt. Ferner berichtete Jonas, daß Columban eintrat *in monasterium cujus vocabulum est Benchor* (in anderen Handschriften auch *Benichor, Benecor, Bencor*); in beiden Fällen wird der irische Name, wenn auch im ersten latinisiert, als fremdsprachig eingeführt.[26]

Der einzige festländische Text, der möglicherweise noch vor Jonas einen irischen Ortsnamen erwähnte, ist die Vita des Samson von Dol, in der *arx Etri* (*Eastri, Etride*) vorkommt, nach Richard Best Dun Eteir, das später unter seinem dänischen Namen Howth bekannte Vorgebirge von Dublin.[27] Wetti nannte weder den Namen des

---

18 *Scottia tellus*: MGH. Poetae 4, 2 S. 24; *Hibernica tellus*: ebd. 2, S. 639. Wolfgang *Zahn*, Schottenklöster. Die Bauten der irischen Benediktiner in Deutschland, Diss. Freiburg 1967 S. 5, meinte: „Bis Ende des 11. Jahrhunderts hat man unter 'Scotus' immer einen 'Iren' zu verstehen".

19 *Kenney* Nr. 39, AA.SS.Mai 2, S. 298.

20 Siehe oben Anm. 2.

21 *Kenney* Nr. 358.

22 Nach Dieter *Kartschoke*, Die Datierung des deutschen Rolandsliedes, Diss. Heidelberg 1963. Zum weiteren Zusammenhang J. *Hennig*, Ireland's place in the chivalresque literature of mediaeval Germany, Proc. R. Irish Acad. 53 C (1950) S. 279f.

23 „A systematic analysis of the geographical and ethnical names in literary documents is particularly missing in the case of the mediaeval works in which such names are conspicuous", F. *Magoun*, Mediaeval Stud. 7 (1945) S. 85.

24 Siehe oben Anm. 1.

25 *Kenney* Nr. 422. Die Namen der Provinzen werden in der Einleitung zur Vita Caddroe genannt (siehe unter Anm. 31).

26 Nicht so in der Würzburger Glosse (8. Jh., *Kenney* Nr. 55): *Scriba et abbas benncuir*, eher noch in der folgenden Nennung von *insola quae dicitur duinlethglaisse* (bei Downpatrick).

27 Zu *Kenney*, Nr. 31: Rev. Celtique 35 (1914) S. 288.

monasterium in insula Hibernia, wo Gallus seine Jugend verbrachte, noch den *portus Hybernicus*, wo Columbanus und seine Gefährten sich einschifften.[28]

Armagh wird auf dem Festland erstmals in dem Text genannt, der zugleich den ältesten nachweislich von einem Kontinentalen geschriebenen gaelischen Satz enthält, nämlich in der um 900 verfaßten Vita des hl. Findan von Rheinau.[29] Die fehlerreiche Wiedergabe dieses Satzes zeigt, daß der Abschreiber des Gaelischen unkundig war. Die den Worten: *Ataich crist ocus patric artmache* beigegebene (korrekte) Übersetzung: *Obsecra cristum et patricium – nomen civitatis* zeigt, daß nicht erwartet wurde, daß der Leser den Namen von Armagh kennen könnte. In den späteren Handschriften der Vita Findani wurden aus den zwei Wörtern *patric artmache* entweder drei: *Patria cart macha* oder eines: *partaigartmachiae*. Die Geschichte der festländischen Armaghkunde ist – bis heute – ein amüsantes Kapitel der festländischen Irlandkunde.[30]

Der an irischen Ortsnamen reichste unter den hier zu betrachtenden Texten ist die von den Bollandisten als apokryph ausgelassene Einleitung zur Vita Caddroae, die um 995 von einem nichtirischen Mitbruder des Heiligen in Waulsort geschrieben wurde. Sie erwähnt, neben Armagh als metropolis, Cloin, Corach – vermutlich die auch in den Versen auf den auf dem Festland ansässigen Abt Dungal in der Reichenauer Handschrift 195 in Karlsruhe erwähnten *Curracha prata* – und Benchor als urbes, sowie Celdar als civitas, wobei fraglich bleibt, ob der Schreiber oder seine Leser sich der Bedeutung von Kildare als Zentrum der Verehrung der hl. Brigida bewußt waren.[31]

Unter den in mittelalterlichen Texten auf dem Festland erwähnten irischen Heiligen sind vier Gruppen zu erkennen:

1. Patrick, Brendan und Brigida, deren hagiographische Überlieferung in Irland begann, deren Einführung in das Martyrologium (Brendan erst in das späte Usuardianum) und in Litaneien auf dem Festland selbständig erfolgte, wobei weitere literarische Information aus Irland übernommen wurde.

2. Heilige wie Columban, Gibrian, Kilian, Furseus und ihre Gefährten, deren Verbindung mit Irland unzweifelhaft ist, deren Verehrung als Heilige auf dem Festland entsprang und nur wenig Nahrung von Irland erhielt.

---

28 Siehe oben Anm. 4.

29 Siehe oben Anm. 25.

30 Wie J. *Hennig*, Mediaeval Stud. 7 (1945) Anm. 41, zeigte, verstieg sich einer der späteren Abschreiber der Visio Tundali zu Archimomska. Vgl. J. *Hennig*, Ulster Place-Names in the Continental Tradition of St. Patrick and other Irish Saints, Seanchas Ardmacha 1962, S. 76-86.

31 Außer der bei *Kenney* Nr. 428 genannten Literatur: A. *Gwynn*, Irish monks and the Cluniac reform, Studies 1939, S. 409ff. Die Vorrede zur Vita S. Caddroe ist der einzige Bericht über die mythische Frühgeschichte Irlands, welcher „moderne" Ortsnamen enthält und das erste Werk festländischer Literatur, das eine systematische Liste der Hauptorte Irlands bietet. Der Verfasser (Reimann oder Ousmann) war Deutscher. Seine Feststellung: *Neque gestorun eius aliquid sciam praeter audita* könnte als Motto unserer Untersuchung dienen. – Zu den Versen auf Dungal vgl. oben Anm. 10.

3. Unzweifelhaft irische Heilige, wie Adamnan, Canice, Darerca, Ita, Kieran und Samthan, die keine materielle Verbindung mit dem Festland hatten und außer deren Namen die festländischen Texte fast nichts erwähnen.

4. Heilige wie Alto, Corbinian, von späteren ganz zu schweigen, denen das Festland erst spät eine Verbindung mit Irland zuschrieb.

Für die Feststellung festländischer Irlandkunde sind diese Unterscheidungen jedoch insofern sekundär, als die Traditionen erfundener oder hibernisierter Heiliger jedenfalls Zeugnisse festländischer Vorstellungen von Irland sind. Ich gehe nicht noch einmal[32] der Frage nach, wer von den festländischen Martyrologisten – Wandalbert, Hraban, Ado, Usuard und Notker – zuerst den oder jenen irischen Heiligen erwähnt hat, sondern es interessiert hier nur allfällige Irlandkunde, die in den Eintragungen zu finden ist. Außer Betracht lasse ich die Liste irischer Namen in dem Reichenauer Codex 167 (836-848) in Karlsruhe, da diese kaum festländischer Information dienen konnte. Als Beispiele für Irlandkunde erwähne ich, daß Hraban als erster in der festländischen Martyrologientradition von Furseus eine längere Beschreibung seiner Jugend in Hibernia bot; er zitierte ferner Ados Worte über Patrick: *qui in Hibernia insula Scothis primus praedicavit nomen DNJCh.* Worte, die noch bei der für das Missale Pauls VI. Neu geschaffenen Oratio für den 17. März Pate gestanden haben. Notkers lange Eintragung für Columba basierte nach Heinrich Zimmer auf einer guten, anderwärts kaum bekannten Quelle[33], doch ist demgegenüber betont worden, daß er im wesentlichen nur Adomnans Vita Columbae benutzt hat. In beiden Fällen ist jedenfalls Notkers besonderes Interesse an dem Heiligen von Iona deutlich. Daß Usuard Canice in sein Martyrologium einfügte, schrieben die Bollandisten Usuards Annahme zu, Canice sei ein Abt seines Ordens (OSB) gewesen[34].

Für die weltweite Verbreitung von Irlandkunde durch die Tradition irischer Heiliger sind die Eintragungen im Hieronymianum, zuerst Patrick und Brigada, später Columbanus (von dem diese Tradition bis heute die irische Herkunft nicht erwähnt), dann, durch Usuard eingeführt, Furseus, Fintan (Abt von Clonenagh), Columba, Kilian, Kieran von Clonmacnoise und Gallus, entscheidend gewesen. Virgil von Salzburg wurde erst durch Gregor IX. um 1230 ins Martyrologium aufgenommen.

Irland war das erste westliche Land, das in einer nichtklassischen Sprache eine kirchliche Terminologie entwickelte. Die irischen Mönche legten sich nicht so sehr von ihren weltlichen Namen völlig verschiedene klassische Heiligennamen bei, sondern gebrauchten ihre weltlichen Namen, oft unter Beifügung eines Patronymiums (wichtig für die Unterscheidung der vielen Gleichnamigen), und allenfalls daneben eine latinisierte Form. Die Vita altera S. Fursei[35] sagt, daß der Name Furseus *ex virtutibus in*

---

32   J. *Hennig*, Ireland's Place in the Tradition of the Martyrologium Romanum, Irish Eccles. Record V 108 (1967) S. 387-401.

33   *Kenney* Nr. 413; Gertrud *Brüning*, Adamnans Vita Columbae und ihre Ableitungen, Zs. f. celtische Philologie 11 (1917) S. 288-291.

34   AA. SS. Dec. Prop.447.

35   *Kenney* Nr. 296 III (s. XI/XII); AA.SS.Jan. 2, S. 46 c.III, 15.

nostra locutione de Scotica lingua interpretatur –, eine Deutung, die freilich mit dem Titel der Virtutes S. Fursei (9. Jh.) nicht viel zu tun haben dürfte, da „virtutes" eine häufige Bezeichnung für die Wunder eines Heiligen war.[36] Notker sagte in seiner Vita S. Galli, daß *Marcellus Scotus Moengal Ibernice vocatus* sei[37], während die "Genealogia Galli et Brigidae" mitteilt, daß *Callech in eorum lingua apud Latinos Gallus* heißt.[38] Jonas nennt Columbanus' Abt in Irland zuerst Sinilis, dann Comgellus. Eine den Kontinentalen auffällige Erscheinung des Gaelischen waren offenbar die Gutturale: Ununchus, Kethernach, Callech sowie Brosach in der Genealogia Galli et Brigidae, oder Ortsnamen, wie Artmacha und Domnachmor in der Vita S. Forananni[39] (ca. 1140), während das durch ein „au" ergänzte „Rach" auf dem Sarkophag des Cataldus in Tarent zu der Annahme führte, er sei aus Irland gekommen.[40] Auf dem Festland einmalige irische Namen – ich nenne natürlich nur solche, die in Heiligentraditionen vorkommen – waren Chaidocus und Fichorius[41], die in gutturalisierter Form in der älteren Vita des hl. Richarius begegnen – Caidocus erscheint auch in der Überarbeitung derselben durch Alcuin[42] – ferner Canicus (im Basler Pontificale verschrieben: Carnacus), Darerca (außer im Pontificale von Basel auch in der Litanei von Köln [9. Jh.][43]), Dichuil, latinisiert Deicolus, der Begleiter Columbans[44], Failbe (im Martyrologium von Tallaght gibt es 15 dieses Namens), der Eligius in der Osterkontroverse gegen die „überseeischen Häretiker" unterstützte[45], latinisiert Falvius[46], Fintan (von dem es im Tallachtense 18 gibt) und viele andere mehr.

Ihnen gegenüber stehen die eindeutig nichtirischen Namen, die schon Flodoard (Ende 9. Jh.) für die sechs Brüder und drei Schwestern des hl. Gibrianus nannte[47], oder die wenigstens weitgehend latinisierten Namen, die Jonas für Begleiter Columbans in dessen Vita (I 13) verzeichnete. Interessant sind die Namen der Begleiter des hl. Kilian (auch Chilianus), weil diese auch im Tallachtense erwähnt wurden: Dort heißen sie

---

36 Die Vita I. Fursei (saec. VII, *Kenney* Nr. 296 I) erwähnt Irland als Herkunfts- und Arbeitsgebiet des Heiligen; die Virtutes (ebd. II) sprechen von Furseus' *ultramarini cognati*; der Verfasser der Vita Adalgisi c. 2, AA.SS.Juni 1, S. 218 (*Kenney* Nr. 303, saec. XI) ließ seinen Heiligen *de Hibernia scilicet, de transmarinis partibus* auf das Festland kommen.

37 MGH. Poetae 4, 2, S. 1095.

38 MGH.SS.rer.Merov.4, S. 241.

39 *Kenney* Nr. 429: gest. 982.

40 Siehe *meine* Anm. 9 erwähnte Arbeit.

41 So bei Alcuin: MGH.SS.rer.Merov.7, S. 445.

42 Die ältere Vita: MGH.SS.rer.Merov.7, S.445; die Überarbeitung Alcuins ebd. 4, S. 390.

43 Siehe oben Anm. 15.

44 *Kenney* Nr. 51.

45 *Kenney* S. 494.

46 MGH.SS.rer.Merov.4, S. 611.

47 *Kenney* Nr. 39.

Aed und Tadg, in der ältesten Passio aber Colonatus, Gallo, Arnuvalis und Totnanus oder Todnadus.[48]

Hibernisierte Heilige lassen meist schon durch ihre Namen wie Chraudingus (Roding), Erhardus, Fridolinus, Frigidianus, Rodpertus, Sydonius, Trudpert[49] und ihre nicht-irischen, besonders germanischen Formen erkennen, daß es sich kaum um Iren gehandelt haben kann.

Ein unerforschtes Gebiet sind die in der hier zu betrachtenden Literatur beiläufig genannten Namen von Iren, die nicht Heilige waren, Vorfahren (wie in der bereits zitierten Genealogie von Brigida und Gallus) oder Herrscher (in der Genealogie von Brigidae z.B. *rex nomine Temeri, filius Tubthac* mit der Gattin *Brosach*, in der Vita S. Germani ep. mart.[50]: *Scotorum gentis princeps ... Audinus nomine* mit Gattin *Aquila* – hier nehmen die Bollandisten[51] allerdings an, daß es sich um Schottland handelt). Selten erwähnen die Heiligenüberlieferungen etwas von der weltlichen Geschichte Irlands. Bezüglich der Mitteilung der Vita Fursei II. (ca. 1100)[52], daß in *Hibernia rex Fundloga Muminensium regna regnabat, et Brendinus rex tertius fratrum Magmutemnica sceptra gerebat*, vertraten die Bollandisten die Ansicht, daß Magmurtemnica ein Personenname sei, während Colgan meinte, daß dies der alte Name der Grafschaft Louth war.

Naturgemäß berichten die Viten irischer Heiliger auf dem Festland mehr von deren Leben auf dem Festland als von ihrem Leben in Irland. Von letzterem sagen sie allenfalls, daß der Heilige in Irland geboren wurde, aufwuchs, Erziehung genoß, am kirchlichen Leben teilnahm und den Ruf zur peregrinatio erhielt. Daß Iren aus anderen als religiösen Gründen (Pilgerfahrt[53], Rückzug in die Unwirtlichkeit, ja, Unzivilisiertheit und erst an dritter Stelle Mission) auf das Festland gekommen sind, läßt sich aus den von uns zu betrachtenden Zeugnissen kaum zeigen. Daß die Iren einen Hang zur peregrinatio gehabt haben müssen, ergab sich schon aus ihrem Kommen aus weiter Ferne und ohne materielle Zielsetzung.[54]

---

48 Passio Kiliani c.2, MGH.SS.rer.Merov. 5, S. 723. J. *Hennig*, Ireland and Germany in the Tradition of St. Kilian, Irish Eccl. Record V, 78 (1952) S. 33.

49 *... duos germanos ... qui ex Hibernia insula orti*: MGH.SS.rer.Merov. 4, s. 357. — Zu Chraudingus vgl. V. *Levison*, Aus rheinischer und fränkischer Frühzeit, Düsseldorf 1948, S. 101f.

50 AA.SS.Mai 1, S. 262 D.

51 AA.SS.Mai 1, S. 263 Anm. m.

52 *Kenney* Nr. 296, III.

53 Etwa Vita S. Agili (*Kenney* Nr. 289): *Hyberni ad limina Apostolurum venientes ad dictum monasterium* (Rebais) *disgrediuntur* (AA.SS.Aug. 6, S. 574). Siehe oben Anm. 5. Neuestens zum gesellschaftlichen Hintergrund der irischen peregrinatio: Th. Ch. *Edwards*, Celtica 14 (1979).

54 Der bereits erwähnte Peregrinus von Modena war ein Rompilger.

In der Vita S. Caddroa[55] ist von der Sitte die Rede, ein Kind nach der Geburt Pflege-eltern (foster-parents) anzuvertrauen. In seiner schon erwähnten Eintragung für Co-lumba sagte Notker, daß der Heilige *contra morem ecclesiasticam primas omnium Hibernorum habetur episcopus.* Besonders inhaltreich waren die späteren Vitae der hll. Disibodus und Albartus, eminente Beispiele für die Einfügung festländischer Kun-den von dem Irland der Zeit des Verfassers und nicht des Gegenstandes.[56]

Völliges Neuland würden m.w. Untersuchungen über Mitteilungen in der hier zu be-trachtenden Literatur über materielle Verbindungen zwischen Irland und dem Festland betreten. Wie schon Jonas beschrieb Notker den Seeweg von Hibernia über Britannia nach Gallia.[57]

Jonas sprach von einer navis quae Scottorum commercia vexerat, Notker erwähnt eine navis quae de Scottorum terra ad litus Galliae cum mercimoniis venerat et redire parabat. Genauer berichtet die Vita Filiberti[58] von der Ankunft einer Scottorum navis diversis mercimoniis plena, die einem Kloster in Gallien calciamenta ac vestimenta large copia ministravit. Jonas[59] verglich die Beredsamkeit eines Hagiographen mit Balsam aus Engaddi und im Gegensatz dazu die eigene Nüchternheit mit ex Hibernia butyrum. Weiter schrieb er die Erfindung des Bieres den am Ozean wohnenden Scor-discis (von späteren Schreibern in Scotis abgeändert) zu und nannte als Absatzgebiete Gallia, Britannia, Hibernia und Germania. Bier wird in der Regula S. Columbani, in Jonas' Vita S. Columbani[60] und in der Vita III. S. Brigidae[61] erwähnt. Bedenkt man, daß auch auf dem Festland die hl. Brigida als Patronin des Viehs bekannt war, so darf man sagen: Bier, Butter, Schuhe, Textilien und Vieh – die Kunde, die das Festland vor rund 1000 Jahren von der Wirtschaft Irlands[62] hatte, war nicht ganz so schlecht.

Die poetische Einleitung zu Jonas' Vita Columbani[63] stellte in einzigartiger Weise die geographischen, physischen und politischen Gegebenheiten Irlands vor: *Insulae situs* – charakteristischerweise fügt Jonas ein: *ut ferunt – amoenus ac adversantium exterorum carens bella nationum.* Er fährt dann in Prosa fort: *Hanc (insulam) Scottorum gens incolit, gens quamquam absque reliquorum (sic) gentium legebus, tamen in christiani vigoris dogmate florens, omnium vicinarum gentium fide praepollet.* Eine ganz ähnlich aufgebaute Beschreibung findet sich in den Versen eines um 800 auf dem Festland le-

---

55 Siehe oben Anm. 31.

56 *Kenney* Nr. 318 und 332 II; dazu oben Anm. 9.

57 MGH.Poetae 4, 2, S. 1105.

58 MGH.SS.rer.Merov. 5, S. 503.

59 Ebd. 4, S. 63; zum Bier als irischem Produkt ebd. S. 82.

60 J. *Hennig*, Besprechung von Fritz *Blanke*, Columban und Gallus, Irish Hist. Stud. 2 (1940) S. 450.

61 J. *Colgan*, Tria Thaumaturga, Louvain 1647, S. 528.

62 Heinrich *Zimmer*, Über direkte Handelsverbindungen Westgalliens mit Irland, SB. Berlin 1910, S. 1032-44.

63 Leider von Dana Carleton *Munro* in der englischen Übersetzung 1895 ausgelassen.

benden Iren.[64] Die Verwunderung über die Verwandlung der Iren durch die Christianisierung spricht auch aus der jüngeren Vita Burchardi[65], des ersten Bischofs von
Würzburg, welche am Ende des von uns zu betrachtenden Zeitraums entstand: *Scotia,
quondam bruta, nunc in Christo prudentissima*. Die Nachricht von der Rohheit der
Bewohner der fernen Insel geht schon auf Pomponius Mela zurück. Die Tradition der
ausführlicheren Beschreibungen Irlands durch Solinus und Orosius, wie zitiert von
Isidor von Sevilla und von Walahfrid in seiner Vita S. Galli, bis hin zur Einleitung von
Balthers Vita S. Fridolini, hat Margrit Koch[66] in ihrem Buch dargestellt; ich habe diese
Tradition in meinen Arbeiten über die späteren Überlieferungen der hll. Cataldus von
Tarent und Albert von Regensburg weiterverfolgt[67]. In der Geschichte der kulturellen
Beziehungen zwischen Irland und dem Festland wird die durch die literarische Tra-
dition der Heiligen vermittelte Irlandkunde, oder sagen wir vorsichtiger: bewirkte
Wahrnehmung Irlands, ein wichtiges Kapitel sein müssen.

(Quelle: Die Iren und Europa im frühen Mittelalter. Hg. von H. Löwe. Stuttgart:
Klett-Cotta 1982, S. 686-696.)

Irish Saints in the Liturgical and Artistic Tradition of Central Europe

For some years past the activities of Irish missionaries on the European Continent have
been more closely studied and it has been found that far from being restricted to the
Golden Age of the seventh and eighth centuries, they continued up to the eleventh and
twelfth centuries. Then Irishmen took a most active part in the great monastic reform
which, indeed, revived the rigid ideals of the early Irish missionaries. About 250
monks, abbots and Bishops, who have worked on the Continent in the course of those
centuries, were or still are venerated as Saints all over Europe. Many of them never
were properly canonized. Some of them are more faithfully commemorated on the
Continent than in their home country. More than a hundred Irish 'Saints' are venerated
in Central Europe, chiefly as patrons of local chapels or churches. Some have been
coupled with non-Irish Saints. The name of others has been preserved only in the name
of a place or of a church. With regard to others again only the fact is known that they
were venerated at a certain period, and in the case of several the Irish descent is doubtful or legendary. The background of the missionary activities of Irishmen on the Continent is being clarified by historians and philologists, but also the liturgical, artistic and
folkloristic tradition of these activities deserve closer study. Here the permanence and
depth of the Irish influence on the Continent becomes obvious. Up to the present, Irish
Saints have been venerated not only where monasteries still exist or once existed,

---

64   MGH. Poetae 3, S. 691. Auch nur für irischen Gebrauch geschriebene Viten irischer Heiliger
     wie die Abbans (*Kenney* Nr. 126) enthalten Beschreibungen, die nach diesem Muster von Hi-
     bernia als einem entlegenen Lande sprechen.

65   AA.SS.Oct. 6, S. 576 D.

66   Siehe oben Anm. 14.

67   J. *Hennig*, Studien zur Geschichte der deutschsprachigen Irlandkunde bis zum Ende des 18.
     Jahrhunderts, Dt. Vjschr. f. Literaturwissenschaft u. Geistesgesch. 35 (1961) S. 617-629.

which were originally founded or influenced by Irish monks, but almost all over the Continent traces of Irish missionary activities are preserved either in the approved form of liturgical tradition, or in religious art and folklore. Fifty years ago, Margaret Stokes, the sister of the great Celtist, as pioneer, traced the tradition of Irish Saints in the mountains of Italy and in the forests of France. The vestiges of Irish Saints in Italy were clarified by Lucy Menzies (*St. Columban of Iona, Saints in Italy*) and even more extensively by Father Tommasini, O.F.M. (*Irish Saints in Italy*), while the complete edition (1936) of the great research work of Dom Gougoud, O.S.B., chiefly concerning Irish Saints in Central Europe, is not yet accessible in English, although, especially under the present circumstances, it should be of general national interest. It is the purpose of this essay to give some glances on the main lines of the tradition of Irish Saints in Central Europe.[1]

I   Switzerland, Bavaria, Austria

St. Columban being the first and the most influential of the early Irish missionaries, it might have been expected that his cult would be the most widely spread on the Continent. The fact that his rule was superseded by the Benedictine rule, however, somewhat dimmed even at his chief foundations, such as the abbey of Luxeuil in the Vosges, the veneration in which he was held. Nevertheless, traces of St. Columban are preserved all over Central Europe. As late as in 1901, in the former abbey of Hirschau in the Vosges, where St. Columban founded several monasteries, an altar was dedicated to St. Benedict, St. Columban, St. Gall and St. Columba. Here, as in many other places, the Benedictines had become the successors of the Irish missionaries, but the extraordinary severity of the rule of St. Columban was commemorated in religious art, where the common attribute of the Saint is the scourge.

Although St. Columban did not live long near Lake Constance, being unable to under-stand the language of the natives, his tradition is well preserved everywhere in the vicinity. His relics are venerated in the Abbeys of Pfäffers and Einsiedeln in Switzer-land. He is co-patron of the Abbey Church of St. Gallen and patron of the parish church of Rorschach, on the Swiss border of the Lake, where a seventeenth-century statue of the Saint is held in great veneration. There are at least twenty churches in Switzerland and Southern Germany still dedicated to him. In his favourite Cathedral of Bamberg, Saint Henry, the Emperor, erected an altar in St. Columban's honour. There is a St. Columban's Well, the water of which is supposed to be miraculous, near Anegary Abbey, founded by the Saint in the French Department of Haute-Saône, and also in Germany St. Columban is frequently found as a well-saint. The Breviary tells that in the Vosges the Saint produced a well 'like another Moses'.

After leaving France and Switzerland, St. Columban went to Northern Italy. Passing through Mombrione, he stopped to preach the Gospel. This town has since been called San Columbano. At Bobbio, St. Columban founded another famous centre of Irish

---

1   See my article 'The Historical World of Louis Gougaud,' in *Irish Historical Studies,* vol. iii. (1942), pp. 180-6.

missionary activities. The Abbey Church there contains the altar he used, and his tomb, ornamented with Irish interlacing, and the tombs of his companions Attala, Bertulf and Cummian. Relics of St. Columban, his skull, his knife, his bell and a wooden cup, are preserved in Bobbio in a precious silver shrine, in a seventeenth-century relic bust and in a reliquary said to have been given to the Saint by Pope Gregory the Great. Close to Bobbio, a cavern in a rock called St. Columban's Cell bears the miraculous impressions of his hands, and overlooking the river Trebbio a grotto is found where the Saint is supposed to have died. In Brugnato (Italy) St. Columban is celebrated as the Titular of the Cathedral on November 21st. Elsewhere, the date having been changed six times, his feast has been finally fixed to November 23rd, and is at Bobbio and St. Gallen celebrated as a double of the first class.

A plaster relief of the eighteenth century in the Cathedral of St. Gallen represents St. Columban's farewell to St. Gall, whom he left behind to christianize the people. St. Gall is venerated in about eighty places throughout Southern Germany and Switzerland. His feast is kept on October 16th in the whole of Switzerland and in the German dioceses of Freiburg, Rottenburg and Munich. At St. Gallen the Saint is the first patron of the Abbey, which, however, was founded only after his death. Here his feast is kept as double of the first class with octave (in Ireland semi-double). Relics of the Saint as well as of St. Brigid are held in veneration in St. Gallen and in Pfäffers. St. Gall also is frequently found as a well-saint. In Bavaria he is also invoked as 'bestower of food'. In Switzerland he is venerated as the national patron, owing to the fact that it is to him that the nation is indebted for Christianity. On a seventeenth-century engraving called 'Helvetia sancta', St. Columban and St. Gall take a preferential place. The bear is the national emblem of Switzerland, being in artistic representation the attribute of St. Gall, as a bear is said to have helped the Saint when building his cell at Steinach. An ivory tablet by Tutilo in St. Gallen represents St. Gall with two bears carrying joists. A similar scene is found on St. Columban's sarcophagus in Bobbio, viz., a young bull drawing a car with beams for the construction of the monastery. Another representation of St. Gall with the bear is found on the altar of a village in Hohenzollern, where the Saint is portrayed as an abbot, a position to which he never attained, having declined both to become Abbot of Luxeuil and Bishop of Constance. Other statues of St. Gall are found in Chur und Zürich, while scenes taken from his life are represented in the above mentioned reliefs in the St. Gallen Cathedral and in a fifteenth-century Manuscript in the St. Gallen Library.

St. Gallen became the centre of Irish missionary activities in Central Europe. The litanies of St. Gallen and other places, such as Basle, used to include up to twenty Irish Saints. Such litanies formed an essential part of the liturgy of the Gallican Mass. The St. Gallen Library preserves precious relics of the early Irish liturgy. During the ninth century the St. Gallen Abbey, which at that time became most important for early German literature, had at least two Irish abbots.

A monk of St. Gallen, St. Magnus, albeit not a disciple of St. Gall, became the Apostle of the Allgäu, the Bavarian district east of Lake Constance. His feast is kept all over Southern Germany on September 6th. Füssen in Bavaria, where St. Magnus founded a famous abbey, keeps his feast as double of the first class. It also keeps the feast of the

Translation of his Relics. The story of St. Magnus' life became intermingled with that of St. Columban's. In artistic representation, for unknown reasons, the Saint is portrayed as a dragon slayer.

Near Lake Constance some other Irish Saints are held in veneration. There is St. Columba's disciple, St. Fintan, at Rheinau, and St. Eusebius, who settled, according to a local tradition, as an anchorite on Victorsberg near Feldkirch. Another even more legendary Irish Saint of that district is St. Fridolin who is supposed to have founded in the sixth century the monastery of Säckingen. He is also said to have built the parish church of Säckingen. There are many other churches in Baden still dedicated to him. He is patron of the Swiss canton of Glarus. In the Middle Ages St. Fridolin was held in veneration all over Germany up to the Baltic Sea (Lübeck). Modern scholars regard him as a Frenchman, whose relics were brought to Säckingen. It seems that medieval writers supposed him to be an Irishman 'on account of his vagabond life'. In St. Fridolin's Church in Säckingen an eighteenth-century relief represents the Saint's departure from Ireland. In other churches the Saint is portrayed leading a human skeleton by his hand, as there was a legend that he raised from the dead a certain Ursus who may be connected with St. Orso d'Aosta. St. Fridolin's feast on March 6th is kept as a double of the first class at St. Gallen, and as a double in Switzerland, Freiburg and Strasbourg (now March 5th).

Up to the present, St. Kilian is the Patron of the North Bavarian diocese of Würzburg, being the Apostle of Franconia. In the cathedral of Würzburg the tombs of St. Kilian and of his companions Kolonat (Colman) and Totnan are found. They suffered martyrdom for having denounced the sinful life of Duke Gozbert. A representation of this martyrdom is found on ivory covers in the Würzburg University Library. Like St. Boniface's tomb in Fulda Cathedral, where the German Hierarchy holds its annual meetings, St. Kilian's tomb in Würzburg has recently become a centre of German Catholicism in its struggle against oppression and persecution. Since 1926, every year there is a mystery play on St. Kilian's Life in Würzburg. The Saint was venerated all over the diocese of Würzburg, which up to the ninth century comprised a great part of Central Germany. St. Kilian is invoked as patron of the vineyards and for healing sore eyes. In the late Middle Ages the Franconians believed that at the Day of Judgment they will be judged by St. Kilian. Whilst in the liturgy the commemoration of St. Kilian is still made, his feast on July 8th being solemnly kept in Würzburg and in many other places, in art many representations of the Saint are preserved. St. Kilian, as well as St. Colman, is represented with a palm symbolical of their martyrdom. The attribute of St. Kilian is a sword, whilst St. Colman carries a book. Altar figures of St. Kilian are to be found all over Central and Southern Germany. An altar-picture of 1480 in the parish church of Fechenheim (near the place where Caspar Zeuss was born) represents St. Kilian preaching in a chapel, his and his deacons' martyrdom, and Gozbert's Judgment. In Würzburg, there is a St. Kilian statue by the famous German wood-carver, Tilman Riemenschneider.

Another part of Bavaria most probably also owes Christianity to Irish Saints. St. Erhard, the great missionary of Ratisbon, is regarded as an Irishman. His feast is closely connected with that of St. Albert, patron of the diocese of Cashel, who is definitely of

Irish descent and died in Ratisbon when on a pilgrimage to Rome. Albert and Erhard are often regarded as brothers, perhaps in order to explain the détour Albert made on his way to Rome. Albert's feast is kept as a double first class with octave in Cashel on January 8th, and outside Cashel on January 19th. Erhard's feast, originally kept in solemn form at Ratisbon on January 8th and still kept as a simple feast in Munich at that date, is now on January 19th at Ratisbon as a double major. The feast of the Translation of St. Erhard's Relics was kept in the fifteenth century in Ratisbon, where the Saint had lived as a hermit, but also in Erfurt, which belongs to the diocese of Mayence, and where up to that time there was an Irish monastery. St. Albert's and St. Erhard's relics rest together in the Lower Munster Church of Ratisbon. In the *Liber Flavus Fergusiorum* in the Royal Irish Academy Albert's activities in Germany are described. Up to the thirteenth century Ratisbon stood in close connexion with Ireland. The Stowe Missal was probably given as a present to the Irish monastery at Ratisbon in 1130, the tradition of which survives in the name of the 'Schottenkirche' (*ecclesia Scotorum*) at Ratisbon.[2]

The missionary activity of Irish monks in Bavaria was of great importance to Austria. Salzburg was founded by Rupert, whose feast on March 29th is celebrated in Ireland, indeed, not on account of the legend that he was of Irish descent, his true name being Ruperteach, but because of the fact that he was a great friend of the Irish missionaries. Two centuries later a list of the dead of the Cathedral of Salzburg mentions twenty Irish Saints, which points to the close connexion between Salzburg and Ireland in the early Middle Ages.

St. Virgil, one of St. Rupert's successors in the ninth century, was an Irishman, his Irish name being Fearghal. On account of his sanctity and learning he was appointed Bishop of Salzburg and became properly the Apostle of Tyrol. He brought from Ireland relics of St. Brigid, which are still venerated in Salzburg Cathedral, founded by St. Virgil in honour of St. Rupert. St. Virgil is one of the few Irish Saints who were duly canonized (in 1233). His feast on November 27th is kept as a semi-double in Ireland, a double of the first class, with octave in Salzburg, where St. Virgil is Co-patron of the Cathedral. At Seckau, another centre of Irish missionary activity, whence Carinthia was christianized, St. Virgil's feast is kept as a double of the second class, while the feast of the Translation of the Saint's Relics on September 26th is kept as a double of the second class at Salzburg and all over Styria and Carinthia. A grotto in the Mönchsberg near Salzburg Cathedral is called 'St. Virgil's cell'. Virgil is a favourite Christian-name in the Salzburg district. There are many valuable altar statues of the Saint of the fifteenth and sixteenth centuries in Bavarian and Austrian churches. Even in the eighteenth-century churches in Salzburg and Carinthia were decorated with paintings representing scenes of St. Virgil's life.

Another Irish Saint, though not properly one of the missionaries, became one of the national Saints of Austria. St. Colman was killed by mistake in Lower Austria when on

---

2   See my contribution 'Irish Literature on the Continent', in *Irish Art Handbook* (1943), and my lecture on 'The Irish Monastic Tradition in Eastern Europe', in *Bulletin of the Irish Committee of Historical Sciences,* No. 23 (January 1943).

a pilgrimage to the Holy Land in 1012, being taken for a spy. His relics are venerated in the famous Benedictine Abbey of Melk, where his feast of October 13th is kept as a double of the first class. His cult, spread also over Hungary and Southern Germany, but chiefly all over Western Austria, where many churches and chapels are dedicated to him. He is frequently found as a well-saint and is, like other Irish Saints, invoked for the protection of cattle and horses. There exists a special Blessing of the cattle in honour of St. Colman, which up to the present is used in some places. St. Colman is also the patron of marriage, being invoked by girls who seek a good husband. In art, St. Colman is represented as a pilgrim with a string in his hand because he was put to death by hanging. Many Bavarian and Austrian churches preserve altar figures of the Saint from the fifteenth and sixteenth centuries. Albert Dürer represented St. Colman with scourge and tongs, perhaps on account of a tradition that the Saint was tortured before his death.

A similar origin has the cult of St. Ursus in the Savoian Alps and in Western Switzerland. He is one of those Irishmen who owe their veneration on the Continent to the fact that they died on a pilgrimage. St. Orso died in the fourth century when travelling through Val d'Aosta, where the College Church of St. Pietro d'Orso keeps his feast on February 1st, the same date as St. Brigid's feast. At Digne the saint's feast is kept on June 17th. There are about ten places all over the western part of the Alps where the Saint is still venerated and where he is invoked against hailstorm and inundations. The question arises if there may be a relationship established between the two facts that the Irish Saints came across the sea and that they are so often invoked for the protection of wells or against inundations, as St. Fursey and St. Frigidian of Lucca. In this connexion, there may be mentioned also the legend of the seafaring Irish Saint Brendan, the patron of sailors, which has been dealt with by various medieval authors, and became very popular in all countries round the North and the Baltic Sea. In Low German countries St. Brendan was invoked against fire, perhaps on account of the relationship between his name and the German word 'Brand', 'fire', and as a patron of the candle-makers. The Christian name Brendan is still found in Northern Germany. St. Fintan, one of the Saints who are said to have travelled on their mantle over a river or even over the sea (like Raymond of Penaforte), will be mentioned below. All these legends point to the strong and general belief that Irish Saints were able to exercise influence on water.

II.   Belgium and Holland

Speaking of St. Brendan's veneration in the Low German districts, e.g., by the candle-makers of Brugge, brings us to the second centre of Irish missionary activity in Central Europe. While the Austro-Bavarian district stands in close connexion to the Irish activity in Upper Italy, the tradition of Irish Saints in Belgium and Holland is closely connected with that in Britanny. However, the relationship between Ireland and Britanny must be dealt with from a completely different view-point owing to the fact that by the racial and linguistic connexion the activity of Irishmen in Britanny was no longer a 'foreign' mission as it was in Central Europe. However, it may be mentioned that both in Bavaria as in the Low Countries the Irish missionary activity embraced districts which perhaps no more than a thousand years ago had been left by the native Celtic population.

St. Livinus, who on November 12th is solemnly venerated as the Apostle of Flanders in the diocese and especially in the City of Ghent, has probably been confused with St. Liafwin, the Apostle of the Frisians. The Prayer proper to his feast contains petitions for 'safety, peace and finally unending joyfulness', petitions which have recently gained in significance for the whole territory which St. Livinus or St. Liafwin's activity embraced. The relics of the Saint are venerated in a precious shrine in the Cathedral of Ghent, world-famous for the altar picture 'The Adoration of the Lamb' by the brothers van Eyck. The Feast of the Elevation of the Relics in 1173 is celebrated in that church as a double major on June 27th.

The liturgical tradition of another Irish Saint, St. Rumold, is even more important for Belgium, as the centre of the veneration of this Saint is the primatial see of Belgium, the Cathedral of Malines. While the Irish descent of St. Rumold is certain, it is a legend that he was an Archbishop of Dublin, as there were no Bishops of Dublin in the eighth century. Like St. Fursey, St. Rumold was killed by brigands. According to the Roman Martyrology his feast is kept on July 1st, while both in Ireland and in Belgium it is kept on July 3rd. The Cathedral of Malines also celebrates the Feast of the Restoration and the Collection of St. Rumold's Relics on the Sunday after Pentecost. According to the legend, St. Rumold's body was thrown by the brigands into a river, but miraculously revealed to his disciples. The Prayer proper to the liturgy of the Saint's Feast makes mention of a similar story, saying that St. Rumold 'by his power gave firmness to the waters and marvellously rescued, dry and sound, from the toils of death and the depth of the flood, one who had been sunk therein for three days' and asks that 'through his prayers and merits we may be delivered from the perilous floods of the world'. The interval of 'three days' is obviously akin to the three days Jonas was in the whale and, of course, to the Resurrection of Our Lord. On September 27th the city of Ghent celebrates the Translation of St. Rumold's Relics.

The small city of Gheel, near Malines, is world-famous for a unique work of charity which is closely connected with a local cult of an Irish Saint. The majority of the inhabitants of this city devote themselves to the nursing of insane by keeping them in their families, trying to bring them to some useful activity. The whole life of Gheel is determined by this work. The anticipation of such modern methods of dealing with mental diseases seems to be linked to the veneration of St. Dympna who, like St. Columban in Britanny, is invoked for the healing of insanity and epilepsy in these parts since ancient times. St. Dympna was the daughter of an Irish King in the seventh century. Having been secretly baptized, she fled from Ireland in order to escape her father's sinful attentions. However, her father found her in Belgium and she suffered martyrdom for her chastity at his hand. On account of this, the prayer proper to St. Dympna's Feast on May 15th begins with the words: 'O God, the lover of Chastity' — *'Amator pudicitiae'.* Though she lived in the seventh century, there are no records of a liturgical veneration of St. Dympna before the thirteenth century, when her body was found. At that time, her cult was already connected with the healing of insane people, who were made to creep under her cenotaph. The cult of St. Dympna became known all over Low Germany. Once, the inhabitants of Xanten, on Lower Rhine, set out and stole St. Dympna's relics from Gheel, which, however, were soon restored on a car drawn by a pair of calves. This and other stories of the legend have been represented by the Flemish painter, Jan van Wave, in 1515 in a great altar picture in the Church of Gheel. Another famous representation of St. Dympna's life by Gosewijn and Roger van der Weyden was in 1913 sold to England by the Abbey of Tongerloo, near Gheel, for which it was painted. St. Dympna's Church in Gheel possesses a precious chasuble of the fifteenth century with a representation of the Saint, while altar statues of the Saint are to be found all over Low Germany as far as Minden-on-Weser.

Also the Wallon part of Belgium is indebted to Irish missionaries. St. Fursy or Fursey founded famous abbeys in Northern France and Belgium, such as Lagny and Peronne. While in the Middle Ages his cult was spread all over Belgium and France, it is now chiefly kept in the diocese of Amiens and in Southern Belgium, his feast being on January 16th. He is represented with cattle, being invoked for the protection of cattle and also on account of the legend that his corpse was brought to Peronne on a car drawn by a pair of bulls without a driver. The cult of St. Fursey's brothers is proper to Belgium: St. Feuillen was a great friend of St. Gertrude of Nivelles, the national Saint of Belgium. He founded the Abbey of Fosse, the centre of Irish activity in Belgium, Irishmen becoming also the superiors of the nuns of Nivelles. The Relics of St. Feuillen are still venerated at Fosse, from where his cult spread all over the diocese of Liège as far as Aix-la-Chapelle. The ancient Parish Church of the city of Aix-la-Chapelle beside the famous Cathedral of Charlemagne is dedicated to 'St. Foillan'. Here, as in Fosse, the Saint is the patron of a confraternity of riflemen, perhaps on account of the legend that he was killed by brigands. These confraternities hold annual processions to avert pestilence, St. Feuillen like St. Columban since the late Middle Ages being invoked against plague. In Aix-la-Chapelle and in Fosse the Feast of St. Feuillen is kept on January 16th, the feast of St. Fursey, when his body was found in the woods, while the diocese of Namur, to which Fosse belongs, celebrates the feast of his death on October 31st. St. Ultain succeeded his brother Feuillen as Abbot of Peronne. Feuillen's death was revealed to him beforehand when he was saying Mass. St. Ultain became even more famous by his prophecy of St. Gertrude's death. He told her that she was to die the following day (which was the feast of St. Patrick) but that she had nothing to fear, as she would be received in heaven by St. Patrick together with the Elect of God. Probably on account of these legends St. Ultain is invoked as a patron for a good death. His relics are venerated in Fosse. It is noteworthy that chiefly on account of her friendship with these three brothers, St. Gertrude was for a long time venerated also in Ireland.

Another Irish Saint whose cult was widely spread in Belgium, although he did not actually work there, is St. Fiacre. He also belongs to St. Gertrude's friends who made it possible for him to found Breuil monastery in France, nowadays called St. Fiacre. In 1568 his relics were brought to the Cathedral of Meaux, where, as in Ireland, his feast is kept on August 30th as a double of the second class. He is the patron Saint of the French province of Brie. All over France and Belgium, where many churches are dedicated to him, St. Fiacre was invoked as the patron of gardeners, because he marked out his garden by his stick. In art, his attribute is the shovel, e.g., in the valuable picture by Hans v. Kulmbach in Karlsruhe Museum. In Paris St. Fiacre was the patron of tin potters and cap makers. The French name for 'cab', 'fiacre' is due to the fact that in 1640 a certain Sauvage kept cabs for hire in a Paris mansion called, 'L'Hotel St. Fiacre'. Therefore St. Fiacre is the patron of cab and taxi-drivers. In Bruges, in the Church of Our Lady, there were guilds of corn-carriers and measurers, which venerated St. Fiacre as their patron. A strange feature in the folkloristic tradition of this Saint is that he was invoked against ficus and tumors, haemorroids even being called 'ficus Sti. Fiacrii'.

Speaking of the prophecy of St. Ultain that St. Gertrude would be received in heaven by St. Patrick, we have already given one instance for the veneration of Irish Saints who have not worked on the Continent. It goes without saying that especially the cult of St. Patrick and of St. Brigid became widely spread in those parts which were embraced by Irish missionary activity.

Up to the eleventh century, St. Patrick's Day was kept in many places in France and Belgium, where his cult was most intensive round the Irish foundations of Luxeuil, Peronne, Fosse and Corbie. Many churches all over the Continent are still dedicated to St. Patrick, as St. Pierre of Rheims, St. Patrice of Rouen, the churches of Lisieux, Pfäffers, Böhmenkirch (Württemberg) and of Heiligenzimmer (Hohenzollern). There is a 'Pozzo (well) di Patrizio' at Orvieto, near Rome, this place obviously having a special devotion to Irish Saints, being the only place outside Ireland where St. Brendan is still venerated. Up to the present, the church of Neubronn (Württemberg) preserves an altar statue of St. Patrick which is the object of great devotion. In High Styria St. Patrick is – like St. Colman – invoked for the protection of cattle. In other places he is invoked for the curing of deaf and dumb people. In some places in Austria, as Weinigzell, there are confraternities of St. Patrick, which pray for the souls in Purgatory. According to a Breton proverb, one who kills an ear wig receives St. Patrick's blessing. This is probably a derivation from the legend that St. Patrick chased all vermin from Ireland. Another proverb says that 'to kindle a fire with snow is one of the miracles of St. Patrick', which means – according to Dom Gougaud – a ridiculous undertaking. It is noteworthy that the spreading of devotion to St. Patrick all over the States and Australasia, especially through churches being dedicated to him, offers a parallel to the liturgical veneration of St. Patrick on the Continent in consequence of the Irish mission.

Also St. Brigid's Feast was kept in many of those parts in which the cult of St. Patrick spread. Relics of St. Brigid were brought to St. Gallen and to Salzburg. Up to the liturgical reform of 1914, St. Brigid's feast was kept in Strasbourg and many other German dioceses. Already in the eighth century, relics of St. Brigid, especially her skull, had been brought to Honau, one of the Irish foundations, whence they came later to Strasbourg, where there are also two ancient pictures of St. Brigid. About twenty churches in Southern Germany are still dedicated to St. Brigid, and this number is known to have been doubled in the late Middle Ages. In the diocese of Cologne, St. Brigid's feast continues to be kept. Up to the thirteenth century Irish monks had an influential settlement in the city of Cologne, owning the monasteries of Great St.

Martin and of St. Pantaleon. The ancient church of Great St. Martin near Cologne Cathedral still preserves relics of St. Brigid. The 'Scots Church' of Mayence was dedicated to St. Brigid. St. Brigid's Church in the Hessian village of Schotten, which was probably a Scots colony, and in two other places in Hessia most likely belonged to those eight churches which were bequeathed to the Irish monastery of Honau near Strasbourg. In Erfurt the 'Scoti' were in the late Middle Ages abused by a poet of the thirteenth century for calling St. Brigid 'Mother of God'. It is noteworthy that in the chapel of Merdrignac in the French Department Côte-du-Nord there is – probably the only – representation of St. Brigid, Mary of the Gaels, carrying the Child Jesus in her arms. It is not impossible that Irish missionaries really called St. Brigid 'Mother', as in some places she is invoked as the patroness of wet-nurses. In Sasbach near Achern in Württemberg, where St. Brigid is patroness of the parish-Church, a relief is found representing the Saint surrounded by the poor and by cripples. Near Sasbach there is a Brigid's Castle. In the seals of the parish church of Iffegheim in Germany, St. Brigid is represented clothing the poor, while in a *Vita Sanctorum* of 1481 she is represented healing the severed hand of a man.

In Belgium and Holland St. Brigid's feast was kept, especially in the diocese of Liège. Up to the present the peasants of this district believe that the earth and the water blessed in honour of St. Brigid heal the cattle, restrain wicked people and witches, and destroy mice and vermin. In other places hazelsticks are blessed in honour of St. Brigid, and are hung up in stables. St. Brigid is also invoked against intemperance. In Bruges St. Brigid's mantle is venerated on one of the side altars of Our Saviour's Church. Up to the nineteenth century here and in many places in Southern Belgium and in Northern France pilgrimages were held in honour of the Saint. It may be assumed that it is from Belgium that the cult of St. Brigid spread to Scandinavia, where it has been traced in Roskilde (Denmark), Lund (Sweden) and Trondhjem (Norway), while to Italy (Forsano, Pinesola) and Portugal (Lumiar) relics and veneration of St. Brigid were brought by Irish missionaries from Bobbio and from France.

In the thirteenth century in the church of Liestal, near Basle, there existed a Blessing of the Light of St. Brigid. In art, St. Brigid is, especially in many Swiss churches, represented as an abbess with a candlestick, or with little cows protected by her mantle. In Southern Germany she is invoked as patroness of poultry-farms, according to the legend that geese and ducks sought refuge with her. It can be assumed that this legend originated from the fact that St. Brigid's feast falls on February 1st when many geese were killed either on account of scarcity of feeding-stuff or before Lent, exactly as geese are connected with the story of St. Martin, whose feast on November 11th was, according to the Gallican liturgy, the beginning of fasting before Christmas.

As St. Brigid was, like St. Colman, regarded as one of the Saints of the Habsburg dynasty, we come back to Irish Saints chiefly venerated in Germany. There is another Irish Saint whose tradition in Germany was chiefly folkloristic, but who did not work on the Continent: St. Columba. The surname of this Secondary Patron of All Ireland, Columcille, Pillar of the Church, was in Germany invoked against fire, storms and rats. It was corrupted to Kakuwilla, and has become a common spell against vermin. The liturgical veneration of this Saint was spread all over the Continent, even in Spain.

St. Fintan, a disciple of St. Columba, in the ninth century was captured in Holland by the Normans when on a pilgrimage to Rome. The Saint escaped and settled on the island of Rheinau, near Lake Constance, where his Relics were taken up in 1446 and held in great veneration until destroyed by fire in 1529.

Rheinau still keeps the feast of its co-patron on November 15th as a double of the first class. A picture of the Saint is preserved in the seal of the monastery and in a relief on his cenotaph in Rheinau. There are also statues portraying St. Fintan as a pilgrim or as a monk with a ducal hat and a book, a dove sitting on his shoulders. The origin of these attributes is unknown.

As we have seen, the liturgical, artistic and folkloristic tradition of Irish Saints on the Continent is not only widely spread and vivid, but also full of interesting and even unique features which well deserve a closer study. The connexion between the Continent and the home country of these venerated Saints thus, perhaps unconsciously, maintained, may become of greater import in the near future, when Christian civilization of these countries is at stake just as it was thirteen centuries ago.

(Quelle: Irish Ecclesiastical Record 59, 1942, S. 181-192.)

A Saint Was Ireland's First Ambassador
Italy, France and Germany commemorate the 14th centenary of Columbanus

There are few saints whose tradition has been as continuously alive, and there is no Irish saint whose tradition has done more to spread the reputation of the Island of Saints and to promote foreign knowledge of Ireland than St. Columbanus.

In 1943 it was not possible to celebrate the fourteenth centenary of St. Columbanus, so this commemoration is being observed in connection with the present Holy Year. In Luxeuil in France, in Bobbio in Italy and other centres of the Saint's activities, special celebrations have been or will be held.

On November 27th, in Ireland and in various dioceses in Germany, Switzerland, France and Italy, the historical lessons of the Office start with the words: "Columbanus was an Irishman." Reference is also made to his entering the monastery at *Benchor*. These lessons are based upon the life of St. Columbanus by Jonas, a 7th-century Italian writer, who stated that Columbanus was born "in what the natives called the country of the Lageni" (Leinster) and that he entered "the monastery named *Benechor*".

Jonas's work was not only the example of many later lives of saints but also the first work of continental literature to record Irish place-names. In fact, it was only about Jonas's time that the name of Bangor was also recorded in Irish literature.

Jonas, moreover, prefaced his work by a brief description of "*Hibernia,* an island situated in the extreme ocean", because he obviously felt that his readers knew so little of Ireland that they could do with some description of the geographical background of the Saint's early life.

This description of Ireland was based on the geographical works of Roman writers rather than on first-hand contemporary information. Henceforth it became a tradition with continental lives of saints associated with Ireland to preface the account of the saint's life with such a description of Ireland from the classical sources. Including such information as that birds were rare in Ireland and that wood or dust from Ireland was an antidote against poison, these accounts did at least so much as to keep alive continental interest in the wonderland at the outskirts of the inhabited world. In later years, Irishmen seem to have deliberately kept up this fantastic tradition so as to make themselves more interesting to their innocent continental hosts.

St. Columbanus was the first Irish saint to be referred to in German literature, e.g., in the *Saxon Chronicle of the World,* written about A.D. 1225, stating that *"Sente Columbanus unde sente Gallus* came from *Schotlande* to *Germany".* St. Columbanus was the first Irish saint whose name was inserted into what was to become the *Roman Martyrology.*

In the early Middle Ages, no Irish saint was more frequently mentioned in local lists of saints and in liturgical calendars than St. Columbanus. His name was also inserted into many litanies of the saints. An altar in his honour was dedicated by the Emperor Henry II in his favourite cathedral at Bamberg. Relics of the saint were venerated in many churches as far to the north as Goslar on the foot of the Harz mountains.

It is all the more surprising that there is little evidence of Irish knowledge of St. Columbanus during the Middle Ages. In fact, the earliest Irish record referring to him is the *Félire* composed in the late 12th century by Marianus Gorman, Abbot of Cnoc na nApstol in County Louth, who, however, confined himself to listing the name of *Columban,* a later footnote adding that he was "an abbot who dwelt in Italy". The later Martyrology of Christ Church, Dublin, said that he was commemorated "in Italy in the monastery *Euaium"* – thus not even the name of Bobbio was properly known in Ireland by that time.

Yet, throughout the Middle Ages, we have records of continental pilgrims visiting Bobbio for the sake of St. Columbanus. His life was widely read (more than 130 manuscripts have been traced) and his works, his letters, poems, sermons and monastic rule, were known. In 1482, his body was placed into a marble sarcophagus adorned with bas-reliefs, depicting scenes of his life. It was not until 150 years later, when the great Franciscan scholars, exiled on the Continent, under John Colgan, started collecting information on the tradition of Irish saints on the Continent, that St. Columbanus became really known in Ireland.

In 1667, Patrick Fleming, one of Colgan's friends, published at Louvain what has remained to this day the basis of studies in St. Columbanus. Some eighty years ago, a collection was made in Ireland for the restoration of St. Columbanus's shrine at Bobbio and some thousand pounds were raised. In 1910, Irish funds helped to restore the crypt and a recent visitor informed us that "a huge marble tablet recounts the donors, from Cardinal Logue of Armagh to the Archbishops of New York and Sydney, flanked by the harp of Ireland and Celtic designs".

St. Columbanus is the patron of seven churches both in Canada and Australia, and of eleven in the United States, to which we may add the colleges of the Maynooth

Mission to China in Nebraska, Silver Creek, N.Y., Bristol (Rhode Island), Essenda (Victoria), Han Yan and Shanghai.

On the Continent, the early Irish missionaries are referred to as "the Columbian mission" and every school-child knows that Columbanus was the first to introduce church bells, using the traditional Irish hand-bell for calling the people to prayer. St. Columbanus was also the first Irish saint portrayed in a work of continental art.

St. Columbanus is one of the few saints associated with Ireland whose Irish descent has never been doubted or forgotten.

He has been the first ambassador of Ireland, and it is in this rank that he is now of 1,400 years' standing. World-wide and 1,400 years old as it is, the devotion to our saint is fittingly summed up in the indulgenced prayer:

> "Assist and protect us, dear St. Columbanus, so to live for God's glory that when our pilgrimage through life is over, we may enjoy with thee the eternal rest of Heaven."

In the calendar of the Universal Church, the Island of Saints is represented by but one saint, and it is only since the end of the 17th century that, on March 17th, every Catholic priest in the world reads in the Office for the day that St. Patrick, "the Apostle of Ireland, was called by Divine intimation to the salvation of the Irish", that he "made Armagh the metropolitan see of the whole island", and that "he was buried at Down, in Ulster". During the Middle Ages, St. Brigid's feast was more widely-spread than St. Patrick's, but in later years it was superseded in the calendar of the Universal Church by the feast of St. Ignatius of Antioch.

The only liturgical book in which native Irish saints are universally commemorated is the *Roman Martyrology*, the list of saints for every day of the year, but this book is now in practical use only with some religious Orders where the Office is recited in choir. There is, however, one prayerbook of the whole Church in which an Irish saint is referred to, namely, the *Raccolta*, the Church's official collection of indulgenced prayers, where we have a prayer for the foreign missions starting as follows: "O blessed Columbanus who, in thy zeal for the extension of Christ's Kingdom and the salvation of souls, didst spend thy life in suffering and exile, assist and protect, we beseech thee, the missionaries of our day ..."

– condensed from the *Father Mathew Record* –

(Quelle: Irish Digest, October 1950, S. 16-18.)

The Irish Background of St. Fursey

Eighty years ago, in what has remained the most extensive account published in Ireland of St. Fursey,[1] Father John O'Hanlon said that this 'celebrated saint attained great celebrity, not only in his own country, but even among people living in more distant regions.' It would be more correct to say that St. Fursey is one of the few early Irish

---

1   Literature listed in J. Kenney, *Sources*, pp. 500ff. will not be repeated; add Thomas Davila, *Historia y vida del admirable y extatico San Furseo, principe heredero de Irlanda, Apostol de muchos Reynos y Naciones* (Madrid, 1699), the most extensive work ever published on St. Fursey; also W. H. Kirwan's article in I. E. Record, 4th Series, xxxii. (1912), pp. 170-87. For later literature see L. Bieler in *Studies* (1946), pp. 543, and my paper in *Speculum*, xxii. (1947), pp. 358 ff.

saints on the Continent who already during the Middle Ages attained some celebrity in his own country. In fact, he and his brother Foillan are the only Irish saints on the Continent whose names appear in the martyrologies of Tallaght, where even the name of St. Columbanus is not found. St. Fursey is also the only Irish saint on the Continent to whose Irish associations specific reference is made in medieval Irish sources. The tradition of his association with Connaill Murtemne (first recorded on the Continent about 1100) is stated also in a marginal note to *Félire húi Gormáin*. Finally, St. Fursey is the only Irish saint on the Continent a vernacular version of whose life was written in medieval Ireland.

Still, to this day, St. Fursey and his companions have not become really popular in Ireland. There are no churches, religious institutions or lay-persons bearing his name. The Catholic Truth Society has published pamphlets on many continental saints whose historical importance is inferior and whose association with Ireland more subject to doubt than that of St. Fursey. When after the middle of the eighteenth century his feast was introduced in Ireland, the historical lessons, to this day the only text proper to his feast, were compiled from St. Bede's *Historia Eccles*, and the only reference to the saint's Irish associations are the introductory words:

> Furseus, cum multis annis in Scotia verbum Dei annuntians tumultusirruentium turbarum non ferret, in provinciam Anglorum devenit.[2]

The biographical and devotional tradition of this great Irish missionary has remained overwhelmingly continental.

We can distinguish two different groups of Irish saints on the Continent, namely those whose associations with Ireland are testified to by an early tradition and those to whom such associations would appear to have been attributed by later tradition.[3] So far as the Irish associations are concerned, the records of the former group can be taken as direct historical sources, while those of the latter group are primarily records of continental ideas on Ireland at the period when those records were written rather than of historical facts at the time to which the saint is assigned. St. Fursey is the only Irish saint on the Continent who belongs to both groups. In the course of his unusually rich and varied literary tradition, the scanty references made in the early sources to his coming from this country became more and more expanded under the influence of later continental ideas of Ireland. It is not the purpose of this paper to engage in the thankless attempt to segregate what in the literary tradition of St. Fursey and his companions can be accepted as direct historical evidence and what has to be described as secondary information on later, indeed much later, continental ideas on Ireland. My object is to show that irrespective of its direct historical value the literary tradition of St. Fursey has been an eminent carrier of information to the Continent on Ireland, her geography and history.

The earliest life of St. Fursey, written in the seventh century, does not refer to Ireland, but the *Virtutes Fursaei* (ninth century), usually combined with it, speak or his coming

---

2   Literally from Bede, V. xix.

3   See my papers on St. Albert of Ratisbon (and Cashel) and St. Cataldo of Taranto in *Mediaeval Studies*, vii. (1945), pp. 21ff. and viii. (1946), 217ff.

de ultramarinis partibus. Literally repeating these words, the eleventh-century life of St. Adalgisius,[4] said to have been one of St. Fursey's companions, found it necessary to add the words *de Hibernia scilicet.*

That the *Vita II* of St. Fursey is certainly not older than the twelfth century is obvious from the reference made in it to the tradition of St. Nicholas. The extensive references made in this Vita to the history of the kings of Ireland, and of Munster in particular, place it into the tradition of twelfth-century Irish-Continental hagiography; the relationship with the tradition of St. Cataldus of Taranto (then for the first time associated with Ireland) is particularly obvious.[5] One remarkable characteristic of twelfth-century Irish-Contenental hagiography was the introduction of Irish place-names, historical, corrupted or fictitious.

In the dedication, Arnulph, the author of the Vita II said that he had been ordered

> ut juxta antiquissimas, quas de pluribus locis collegisti, schedulas, in uno volumine constringam; et quae scriptorum vitio depravata seu vario linguarum genere videntur dissona, sensum servando, illaesum, ex arte ad usque unguem corrigam,

a statement remarkable not only for the tradition of St. Fursey, but for Irish-Continental hagiography, indeed for medieval hagiography in general. Stating that Fursaeus meant *de virtutibus in nostra locutione de Scotica lingua* (an etymology regarded by Colgan as a corruption of Irish *fearta*), Arnulph made it abundantly clear that he was not Irish, but suggested that he drew on Irish sources. Regarding the sources mentioned in that dedication, Colgan assumed that these were mainly the ancient life of the saint on which St. Bede drew, augmented by *quaedam Hibernica et Saxonica saltem nomina propria quae non eodem modo a diversis scribebantur, et quae (timeo) non satis ipse correxit.* This is scarcely a sufficient explanation for the insertion of the story of the saint's descent and of the numerous place-names in the *Vita II.*

The actual biography starts as follows:

> Igitur tempore quo apud Hiberniam insulam quae Scotia est contigua, Rex Fundloga Muminensium regna regnabat, et Brendinus Rex tertius fratrum Magmurtemnica sceptra gerebat. ...

Of the editions of this Vita, Dr. Kenney listed only that by the Bollandists. Colgan has this Vita, too, but his edition is primarily interesting as an interpretation of the original text from the standpoint of seventeenth-century Irish hagiology, which of course considered such works as direct historical sources. Whatever in Irish-Continental hagiography did not fit into the accepted picture of Irish history or the knowledge of Ireland of the Irish hagiologists was acrimoniously criticized and ridiculed by them:

> Auctor licet vel ipse vel eius aliquis descriptor in quibusdam Hibernicis nominibus et locis hallucinatus est. Ego nomina Hibernica reddidi suae integritati ex Hibernicis monumentis.

---

4   Kenney, op. cit., no. 303. Discussed by Colgan, *Acta*, pp. 94f.

5   See my papers, 'Early references to Ulster place-names in continental hagiography,' to be published in *Ulster Journal of Archaeology* and 'The traditions of S. Frediano and S. Silao' in *Mediaeval Studies.*

The devastating effect of the example given by Colgan's procedure to later generations has been demonstrated in numerous instances. This procedure was particularly objectionable when continental 'mis-spellings' were 'corrected' only by halves, e.g. the name of the king of Munster was changed to *Findloga*, to bring it nearer to *Finnloga*.[6] The Bollandists not only preserved those 'mis-spellings' (which, of course, are eminent historical sources) but also added some notes of great value as expressions of seventeenth-century continental ideas of the geography and history of Ireland. *Magmurtemnica*, e.g., they said, is not a place-name but a derivation from *Mac Murchertachi*. Colgan, however, said that this was the ancient name of the northern part of County Louth, formerly belonging to Ulster (and to this day to the archdiocese of Armagh), one of the most conspicuous petty kingdoms in that province.

I suggest that in this point the *Vita II* of St. Fursey was influenced by the later tradition of St. Brigid. According to Animosus (who according to Esposito[7] wrote his life of St. Brigid much later than has been traditionally assumed), St. Brigid was born

> in Fochart Muirthemne quae est in provincia Ultorum, scilicet in regione quae dicitur Conelle Murthemne.[8]

A further parallel between the later traditions of SS. Brigid and Fursey is the account of the illegitimate birth of these saints and the reflections attached to it concerning the clash between the law of nature and of God and the law of the state,[9] and still another parallel is the story of the *rex Hiberniae* and his three sons.

The literary development of the family-story in the biographical tradition of SS. Fursey and Foillan is extremely intricate. Considering it as a direct historical source, Father O'Hanlon straightened it out and tried to synchronize it with Irish genealogies and other native records. The difficulties of this undertaking can be illustrated by the study of the Irish place-names referred to in this tradition.

In the account of the flight of Fursey's father, the *Vita II* referred to *Esbren insula* where he had an uncle *nomine Brendanus antistes, qui in insula quae Clynne-Fearta vocatur monasterium construxerat*. Correcting the mis-spelling, Colgan added that Cluain-fearta was situated on the banks of the Shannon and that the description of this place as an island arose

> ex quadam hallucinatione, ex eo nempe quod S. Brendanus in sua navigatione continue ab insula ad insulam profectus legitur.

---

6   The *Vita V Sti. Foillani* has Funologa. I shall not treat of the various spellings and forms of proper names referred to in this tradition. On the whole, place-names are indicative of geographical knowledge, whereas proper names illustrate historical knowledge.

7   Kenney, op. cit., no. 151, ii., and Bieler, l.c., p. 538.

8   This tradition was referred to in St. Bernard's *Life of St. Malachy*, par. 56. Compare also Windisch's edition of *Táin Bó Cualnge* (Leipzig, 1905), p. 178.

9   See my paper, 'The literary tradition of Irish saints in the Order of Canons Regular of the Lateran', *Comparative Literature Studies*, xvii-xviii. (1945), pp. 20ff., and xix. (1946), pp. 17f.

In the *Navigatio Brendani*, since the tenth century known on the Continent, the name of Clonfert was not mentioned, as St. Brendan's establishment there took place after his return from his journeys. The *Vita II* of St. Brendan and his Irish life[10] which refer to it were contemporary with the *Vita II* of St. Fursey. At this point it can be shown that the description of works of Irish-Continental hagiography as secondary sources by no means detracts from their historic value. The association of St. Fursey with St. Brendan is an important record of early continental acquaintance with the tradition of the great patron of Clonfert. Associations of Irish saints on the Continent with the great patrons of Ireland are a characteristic of later Irish-Continental hagiography, expressive of continental awareness of the spiritual connection between Irish activities on the Continent and the great saints in Ireland, a decisive feature in the development of the connotation of the term insula sanctorum.

When leaving St. Brendan's community, Fursey *ad aliam insulam Rathmat nuncupatam transiit, in qua secus lacum Ersben vocitatum monasterium aedificavit.* In this passage, Colgan changed *Ersben* into *Erbsen*, an approximation to *Orbsen.* Loch Oirbsen is said to be named after Orbsen, son of Allad of the Tuatha De Danann.[11] The topography of Orbsen was first extensively discussed by Roderick O'Flaherty in his celebrated *Description of Hua Connaught*[12] in a commentary upon the reference made in the *Vita Sti. Endei* to *stagnum Orbsen* and its *insula quae Ech Inys dicitur.*[13] The *Vita II* of St. Fursey attributed the name of Esbren to an island and that of Ersben to a lake (the Bollandists' reading *locum Erben* seems to be corrupt). In the first instance, the name of the lake is not mentioned, in the second, the name of *alia insula* is fictitious. (Colgan assumed that Rathmaith – as he spelt it – was identical with Killursa, near Loch Corrib). This confusion may have some connection with the *Vita II* of St. Brendan where we read that the saint *ad Hiberniam terram Connactensem intrans, habitavit in quadam insula quae vocatur insula Maccu Chuind,* Cod. Salimant. adding: *Oirbsen*; in the parallel passage the Irish life has: *co hInis meic hUa Chuinn for Loch Oirbsen.*[14] The name of *Rathmat* seems to be a general term (like that of *Domnachmor* attributed in the life of St. Forannan presumably to Armagh), doubtless of Irish origin. That these details of St. Fursey's life were invented by an Irishman on the Continent rather than in Ireland, is obvious from the Irish life of St. Fursey, which regarding the saint's life in Ireland confines itself to saying that he was *do cenel na nGaoidel.*

---

10   Kenney, op. cit., no. 202, and Plummer's *Vitae Sanctorum Hiberniae,* i. p. 145, and *Bethada name nErenn,* i. p. 87.

11   Keating's *History* (Irish Text Society), i. p. 244.

12   1664 (Dublin, 1845), 79.

13   Par. 29; Kenney, op. cit., no. 164.

14   *Vitae Sanctorum Hiberniae,* i. 143 f., and *Bethada name nErenn,* i. p. 87. This is now Inisquinn in Loch Corrib. A modern 'version' of this tradition was given in R. Hayward, *The Corrib Country* (Dundalk, 1943), p. 27 f. To the instances listed in Hogan's *Onomasticon,* pp. 467 and 503, add the reference to Orbsen (by the adjective *fuar* clearly described as an island) in *The Taboos of the Kings of Ireland* (ed. M. Dillon, Proc., R.I.A., liv. (1951), c. 19).

Among our earliest sources on St. Fursey and his companions are the lives of St. Gertrude of Nivelles.[15] Her *Vita I* is the oldest record of the observance of St. Patrick's feast on 17th March. Referring to St. Ultan's foretelling St. Gertrude's death on that day, the *Vita I*, however, speaks of St. Ultan merely as *ille peregrinus*. Already in the martyrology of Tallaght St. Foillanwas described as *frater Fursu*[16]; later Fursey, Foillan and Ultan were made triplets.[17] The tradition of St. Foillan is an offshoot of that of St. Fursey. As in the latter, the earliest source does not say anything of the saint's descent, but the *Vita I*, written not long after St. Foillan's death, stated that he came 'ab Oceani finibus, Hibernia, Gallorum insula, quae Britannici maris limite ambitur.' The expression *Gallorum insula* may have caused the later tradition of St. Vincentius (then credited with having brought St. Fursey and his companions to the Continent), accordjng to which this relation of St. Gertrude received Ireland as a feud from the Frankish king Dagobert,[18] a tradition, perhaps, connected with the listing, in the *Chanson de Roland*, of Ireland among the countries subject to Charlemagne.[19] The eleventh-century *Vita II* said that Foillan was born *in Hibernia*, while his *Vita III* recasts the story, told by the *Vita II* of St. Fursey, of these children of the son of *rex Muminensium* and the daughter of *rex Magmurtemnicus*. However, in the tradition of St. Foillan this story was co-ordinated with Frankish history ('about the time when *Francia* was ruled by the sons and grandsons of Louis, whom St. Remy baptized') and Fursey's maternal descent transferred to Scotland ('regnabat in Hibernia insula Fundloga ... porro in Scotia quae continua est Hiberniae regnabat Brendinus').[20] This latter change was due, on the one hand, to the incomprehensibility of the term *Magmurtemnica*, and on the other hand, to the limitation – from the late eleventh century – of the term *Scotia* to Scotland.[21] To the word *Fundloga*, the *Vita III* added: 'cujus frater Brendanus Esbrem insulam illustrabat episcopali officio,' but in the later account of the flight of Fundloga, it simply said that he went 'ad patrum suum Brendanum episcopum' without mentioning any place-name.

15   Kenney, no. 299. To the literature listed there add v. Heuck, *A propos de Sainte Gertrude* (Bull. de la Soc. d'anthropologie de Bruxelles, xxxii, 1913), and A.F. Stocq, *Vie critique de S. Gertrude* (Nivelles, 1931, reviewed by P. Grosjean in Anal. Boll., lii. 417), also my note on 'Irish influences in the folkloristic tradition of St. Gertrude' in *Bealoideas*, xii. (1942), pp. 180 ff., and Ed. Panels, *St. Gertrude* (Malines, 1946).

16   *Biographie nationale de Belgique*, vii. (Brussels, 1883), 178 f., boldly identified St. Foillan, *fils de Fintan prince héréditaire de Munster*, who made his studies at Cluain Fearta (based on Vita II S. Fursaei), with the companion of St. Livinus.

17   To the literature listed by Kenney, no. 298, add Ed. Janart, *St. Feuillen, son séjour et son culte à Nivelles* (1879).

18   *Anal. Boll.*, xii. 429, and AA. SS. Boll., 14 Jul., iii. 641, compare the references to Dagobert in the lives of St. Gislen and St. Landulin, by Philippe de Harveng (P.L., cciii. 1337 and 1350).

19   See my paper on 'Ireland's place in the chivalresque literature of mediaeval Germany,' *Proc. R.I.A.*, liii, (1950), C. pp. 279 ff.

20   Compare the association between St. Patrick and Chlodewech in a twelfth-century life of St. Patrick, which claimed that St. Patrick lived for some time among the *Morini* in *Gallia Belgica*, a tradition, according to Dr. Bieler (*Codices Patriciani*, 52) 'quite unique in Patrician legend.'

21   Making Brendinus an uncle of Fursey's mother rather than of his father.

This anticipation of the reference to St. Brendan indicates that the name of that great saint was considered as liable to enhance from the outset the glory of the descent of SS. Fursey and Foillan. This association with St. Brendan was no doubt brought about by the name of the father of the mother of SS. Fursey and Foillan, which in both the *Vita II* of St. Fursey and the *Vita III* of St. Foillan was stated to be Brendinus, according to Desmay and Colgan, identical with 'Brandubh mac Eathach, rex omnium Laginensium non solum totius Hyberniae usque ad Colla Ruaidh.[22] (This Eathach is not to be confused with his name-sake, rex superbus of Connaught, who gave St. Brendan the island in Loch Oirbsen). As in the tradition of St. Cataldo, the Irish-Continental hagiographer was unable to form a clear picture of the relationship between petty kings, such as the *dux Rachau* (in the tradition of St. Cataldo) or the *rex Magmurtemnicus* (in the tradition of St. Fursey), provincial kings, in both traditions of Munster, and the high-king of Ireland (also referred to in both traditions).

That the *Vita III* of St. Foillan made Brendinus, a petty king, king of Scotia, is first of all due to the tendency, arising from the continental aim of this Vita, to replace difficult and obscure place-names by well-known ones, the more so when in doing so the glory of the hero could be enhanced.

The twelfth-century *Vita IV* of St. Foillan by Hillin is remarkable because, versified as it is, it is an important record of the popularity of St. Foillan. Following the *Vita III*, Hillin said that the father of St. Foillan was *principis Hiberniae filius and his mother Schottorum filia regis*. Brendanus is described as *episcopus Hesbrenorum*, which may be a syncopation of Hibernorum and Ersben.[23] According to the late twelfth-century *Vita V* by Phillip de Harvengt, Brendanus 'in terra Herbreniorum episcopali cathedra praesidebat', possibly an association with *Heberus*, a word used for *Scotus* in the Vita of St. Etto,[24] another ramification of the tradition of St. Fursey.

The tradition of St. Fursey and his companions not only lays a cross-section through the whole tradition of Irish-Continental hagiography, but also presents us with the unique opportunity of studying its three principal phases. The first phase is that of direct historical recording with but scanty references to Ireland. The second phase is that of extensive inferences of information on the geography and history of Ireland which, while being useless as a direct source, is of eminent interest to the study of twelfth-century con- tinental knowledge of and ideas on Ireland, illustrating also the establishment of Irish-Continental hagiography as a distinctive type of writing, namely, specifically for continental readers though undoubtedly based on Irish information. The third phase is that of purely speculative evolution of the second phase after both creative interest in and concrete information of Ireland had faded away.

It was not until the early seventeenth century that such interest in and information on Ireland appeared again on the Continent. In his Latin translation *of La vie de Fursey*

---

22   *Vita Sti. Maedoci*, par. 26 and 43 (Kenney, no. 230).

23   Or is this a confusion with *Hesbonia*, the district around Thienen in Belgium, referred to in the tradition of St. Rumold, also mentioned in the Office of St. Rumold's feast in Ireland?

24   Kenney, no. 304.

(Paris, 1607) by Jacques Desmay, Canon of Peronne (the centre of St. Fursey's cultus on the Continent), Colgan restored what he considered to be the historical forms of proper names. In doing so, he took considerable liberties with Desmay's text, rendering, e.g. the words 'Brendinus roi dans toute l'Hybernie' by 'Brandubhius Lageniae rex,' thus making it quite inexplicable why Phyltanus, son of 'Fonloga, roy de Momonie' went to the court of Brendinus.[25] Strangely enough, Colgan did not correct Desmay's place-names. Desmay described *St. Brandanus* as bishop of *Elbréen*, an island in the ocean, but living withdrawn from the world 'dans une petite isle voisine de sa diocese de Clunaferta' (Colgan: 'de insula Cluanfertensi'), where there was a Benedictine monastery, an interpretation of early Irish monasticism in continental terms, showing, moreover, that St. Fursey was one of the many Irish saints on the Continent in whose cultus the Benedictines took a special interest. Colgan preserved Desmay's corruption of Rathmath to *Ratimath*, which may be compared to the corruption, in the *Visio Tundali* and the *Vita Sti. Albarti*, of *Artmacha* to *Artinacha* (which in Ireland has led to regarding St. Erhard, the associate of St. Albert, as bishop of Ardagh!).

A curious addition, expressive of the promotion of continental knowledge of Ireland through hagiographical studies, is Desmay's remark that, preaching in Ireland, St. Fursey used the Irish language. The study of Irish place-names, even more than that of Irish proper names, in continental literature is a fascinating chapter in the early history of continental awareness of the Irish language.

The importance of the literary tradition of St. Fursey to the history of Irish-Continental relations is a reflection of the significance of his mission to early medieval church history in Northern France and the Low Countries. Considering these facts we must describe the devotional tradition of this saint as disproportionately thin. The reason for this lack of proportion is that Peronne, the natural centre of this devotion, almost continuously suffered from the ravages of war from the ninth right down to the present century.

In his fundamental study on *Perrona Scottorum*, the great Ludwig Traube[26] pointed out that 652 is a more likely date of St. Fursey's death than is 648, as stated by the *Annals of Ulster*. The present article is a tribute to the thirteenth centenary of this great Irish missionary on the Continent.

(Quelle: Irish Ecclesiastical Record, 77, Jan-Jun 1952, S. 18-28)

---

25 At this point, Desmay has an elaborate synchronism of the life of St. Fursey with French and English history.

26 Pp. 480 and 490; see Kenney, p. 500.

Ireland and Germany in the Tradition of St. Kilian

In the sixth lesson of the Office for the feast of All the Saints of Ireland passages from a Breve of Benedict XIV are read, which include the following sentence:

> Quod si recensere voluerimus sanctissimos viros Columbanum, Kilianum, Virgilium, Rumoldum, Gallum aliosque plures qui ex Hibernia in alias provincias Catholicam fidem invexerunt, plus nimis epistolae modum excederemus.

Of the five saints mentioned in this passage as the representative leaders of the Irish missions to the Continent, SS. Columbanus, Rumold and Gall were listed in the first Proprium for all Ireland approved in 1741, the name of St. Kilian being added in 1747 and that of St. Virgil in 1780 (first only for Dublin).[1] The approbation of the first national Proprium for Ireland ruled that any texts to be used in the liturgical celebration of the feasts listed in it should be taken from 'approved Breviaries'. The feast of none of the Irish saints on the Continent was then celebrated in Ireland, and in general, there were no 'approved Breviaries' in Ireland containing the feasts of the native saints. When the first Officia for the Irish Proprium were compiled, the proper parts for the feasts of SS. Columbanus, Gall, Kilian and Rupert (the only local German saint specially venerated in this country) were taken from the Benedictine Breviary.

To this day, in the lessons of the second Nocturn for 8th July in all Ireland the following words are read:

> Kilianus, natione Hibernus, nobilibus parentibus est ortus et a pueritia liberabilibus studiis eruditus; divina eum gratia praeveniente, cunctis mundi illecebris spretis, monasticam vitam in Hyensi monasterio professus est ... Solo natali relicto, Herbipolim in orientali Francia cum aliquot sociis pervenit (where at last the hirelings of the duchess Geilana) eos orationi ardentissime instantes interfecerunt.

These lessons are derived from what is known as the *Passio II Sancti Kiliani*,[2] the statement that the monastery where St. Kilian was trained was *Hyense* being an interpretation first introduced by Trithem, the late-fifteenth-century historian, and subsequently adopted by Benedictine writers. The original tradition did not specify any place-names in its account of St. Kilian's life in these countries. The tradition that he was born at Mullagh, Co. Cavan (to which tradition it is due that Mullagh is one of the very few Irish churches to bear the name of St. Kilian),[3] has no foundation in the original records.

No place-names in these countries are mentioned in the historical lessons for St. Kilian's feast proper to the diocese of Würzburg. While formerly celebrated throughout Western Germany, this feast is now confined to this diocese, where however it bears the title of 'Festum SS. Kiliani Episcopi, Colonati et Totnani, martyrum, Franconiae Patronorum', that is, this feast is also observed in honour of the two, out of St.

---

1   See my article, 'St. Columbanus in the Liturgy', in I. E. RECORD, lxii, pp. 306 f.

2   Dr. Kenney, Sources, no. 317; L. Gougaud, *Les saints irlandais hors d'Irlande* (1936), 125ff., and my paper 'Irish Saints in the Liturgical and Artistic Tradition of Central Europe', in I. E. RECORD, lix. p., 184.

3   J. O'Hanlon, *Irish Saints*, pp. 7, 140.

Kilian's reputed eleven, companions who according to the oldest tradition suffered martyrdom with him. In the lessons read in Ireland the name of the first of these two is 'Colomanus,' a re-Hibernization already found in the entries for St. Kilian's feast in some manuscripts of the martyrology of Notker[4] and subsequently inserted in the Bedan Martyrology.[5] This is the only existing feast of three Irish saints. St. Kilian is the only Irish saint venerated outside Ireland, only in what is now Germany. The Office of his feast is the only instance where a place situated in Germany is mentioned in the Irish Proprium.

The traditions of Irish saints on the Continent in general have been studied mainly for the purpose of establishing how far they can be accepted as direct sources.[6] This year, in Würzburg, the twelfth centenary of St. Kilian will be celebrated, namely of the elevation of his relics, an event, which, as in the traditions of other Irish saints (such as SS. Albert, Cataldus, Livinus, Rumold and Silaus) is regarded as the beginning of his *cultus*. However, St. Kilian is one of the few Irish saints on the Continent the chronological background of whose early records is likely to be historical. The passages selected from these records in the lessons read in Ireland refer to his being in Rome under Conon, whose Pontificate lasted only a few months (A.D. 686-7). Although this date is not easily reconciled with the tradition associating St. Kilian with St. Columbanus, it is too definite to be dismissed.

Among the traditions of Irish saints on the Continent, those of SS. Columbanus, Fursey and Kilian and their companions stand out for the early date from which they have been recorded. St. Kilian is the first Irish saint, in fact, the first saint in general, referred to in a vernacular record in Germany.[7]

The beginning of the *Passio I Sancti Kiliani* says: 'Fuit vir vitae venerabilis nomine Killena quem Scottica tellus de magno edidit genere,' words which bear a striking resemblance with the earliest Vita of St. Fursey. Throughout the *Passio I* our saint is referred to as Killena, while the *Passio II* has *Kilianus*, the form found in the earliest secondary records of his tradition in Germany. The *Passio II* said that St. 'Kilian was 'genere Scotorum ortus,' adding the significant note:

> Scotia, quae et Hibernia dicitur, insula est maris Oceani, foecunda quidem glebibus, sed sanctissimis clarior viris; ex quibus quidem Columbano gaudet Italia, Gallo ditatur Alemannia, Kiliano Teutonica nobilitatur Francia,

a passage which for four reasons can be assigned to a late date:

(1) the distinction between Hibernia and Scotia,
(2) the distinction between Alemannia and (implicitly) Germania,
(3) the allocation of one Irish patron to each country,
(4) the reference to the tradition of Ireland's being the *Insula Sanctorum*.

---

4   *P. L.*, 131, 1116.

5   Also in the Rheinau Calendar (Kenney, p. 479).

6   See my various papers listed in my article on St. Fursey, in I. E. RECORD, January, 1952.

7   See my paper 'Irish Saints in Early German Literature', in *Speculum*, 22 (1947), pp. 360 f.

The specific reference to Hibernia made in this note did not prevent Dempster and his followers from claiming St. Kilian for Scotland, on the strength of which claim in the sixteenth century Scottish refugees occupied the *Schottenkloster* at Würzburg. To make Ireland's claim to St. Kilian quite clear the lessons read in Ireland change the words 'Scotorum genere' into 'natione Hibernus.' The reference, added by the *Passio II*, to St. Kilian's travelling 'ad vicinam Scotiae Britanniam quam non longa navigatione praeteriens Galliam attigit'[8] caused the Bollandists some doubts in St. Kilian's association with Ireland.

On the strength of the later application, by foreigners, of the word *Alemannia* to the whole of Germany, St. Gall, e.g. in the tradition of the Roman Martyrology, was associated with Germany rather than with Switzerland; St. Kilian on the other hand was sometimes associated with Austria,[9] and it may be doubted whether those who in the lessons of St. Kilian's feast read that he laboured 'in orientali Francia' thought of a part of Germany.

There is no country other than Ireland whose missionary saints could be, and were as early, assigned to the position of patrons of the chief countries of Europe. St. Columbanus's association with Italy has been confirmed by the Roman Martyrology and lately been ratified by the highest authority. St. Gall undoubtedly stands for Switzerland. St. Rumold is the patron of the metropolitan see of Belgium, and St. Virgil the co-patron of the cathedral of Salzburg, still bearing the honorary title of metropolitan see of Germany. We have seen that what the note in the *Passio II* indicated has become more true than its writer could possibly foresee: St. Kilian is the Irish saint in Germany *par excellence*.

The reference to Ireland's natural and spiritual fertility may be compared with the description of Ireland inserted in the second chapter of Jonas's *Vita Sancti Columbani*. The marvellous fertility of the soil of Ireland had of course been stated already by the classical geographers, and the wonderful news that in this island cattle can be left out all winter and indeed that sometimes they have to be prevented from overfeeding was repeated right to the early nineteenth century in popular Continental descriptions of Ireland.[10]

The history of the compilation and redaction of the historical lessons of the Sanctorale of the Breviary is a subject still unexplored. With regard to the lessons for the feasts of Irish saints, this study would throw much light on the development of Continental knowledge of Ireland, and on the interweaving of devotional tradition and historico-geographical infomation. The Benedictine lessons for St. Kilian's feast were adapted from the *Passio II*, while, e.g., the lessons used in Lambach (one of the many churches

---

8   Compare the account of the journey of St. Kilian of Aubigny (Kenney, no. 282). The accounts of the journeys of Irish saints to the Continent should be studied as records of Continental knowledge of the geographical position of Ireland.

9   The early misinterpretation of Rabanus's entry apparently caused Notker to enlarge on this point.

10   See my review of Thorndike's *History of Magic* in *The Irish Book Lover*, 29 (1945), pp. 21ff.

in Germany where St. Kilian was patron)[11] were based on *the Passio I*. References to the geography (and, we shall see, the history) of Ireland such as in the *Passio II* and more frequent and extensive in the traditions of other Irish saints on the Continent, are expressive of the most striking feature of Ireland's place in the medieval hagiography of Europe: while Ireland's eminent spiritual position was admitted by the faithful preservation of the tradition of historical Irish saints and even more so by the attribution of Irish associations to Continental saints, it was recognized that, by her geographical position (*insula maris Oceani*) and the lack of direct contact with her, Ireland was one of the least-known countries.

By its reference to Bangor, Jonas gave his account of St. Columbanus's youth a sound geographical foundation.[12] By his Vita, the first work written on the Continent actually embodying whole sentences in Irish, St. Fintan of Rheinau was clearly assigned to Ferns.[13] In the tradition of St. Fursey and his companions a broad, if certainly less sound, geographical foundation was laid by later interpretation, and the references to Irish place-names in the tradition of Hibernized saints such as Albert, Cataldus, Frigidinus, Livinus, Rumold and Silaus permit us to gauge the value of these sources for the development of Continental interest in and knowledge of Ireland.[14] The tradition of St. Kilian neither originally contained nor was later enriched by a similar foundation. Still, it too has been an important carrier of Continental information on Ireland.

The tradition of St. Kilian in the vernacular literature of medieval Germany has been outlined elsewhere,[15] but it may be re-stated here that in his sermon on 'Sancte Kylianes Tac', Hermann of Fritzlar (about 1343) said that '*sanctus kylianus* was born from *Ybernia von Schottenlantes* of a noble family and endowed with a rich inheritance,' while in the fifteenth century *Geschichte der Heiligen* St. Kilian and his companions are the only Irish saints given a special chapter: 'He came to Wirtzburg, as St. Gall came to Suebia and Columbanus to Milan', a well-informed derivation from the note in the *Passio II Sancti Kiliani*.

German studies in the tradition of St. Kilian started with Nicholaus Serarius, whose extensively annotated reprint (1598) of the (incomplete) text of the *Passio II* (as published in 1573 by Surius) was often republished. Serarius's derivation of the saint's name from 'Anglice kyl=lex' was repudiated by Henry Fitzsimon's *Catalogue of Irish saints* (1611), which while stating that 'kil' was 'locorum in Hibernia praenomen, cellam significans', suggested that it was related with the name of Cellach. Etymo-

---

11   Printed by the Bollandists.

12   See my paper on 'Ulster Place-names in Early Continental literature' in the forthcoming issue of the *Ulster Journal of Archaeology*.

13   See my review of Dom Munding's edition of the St. Gallen calendars in *Ir. Hist. Stud.*, 7 (1951), p. 206.

14   See above, note 6.

15   See above, note 7.

logies of proper names and place-names in Irish hagiography are an important source of what may be described as rudimentary Celtic studies on the Continent.

The first print of both *Passio I* and *II* was published by Henry Canisius in his *Antiquae Lectiones* (Ingolstadt, 1603), a work whose special interest in Irish saints may have been inspired by the German Martyrology of St. Peter Canisius (Dillingen, 1562). It has scarcely been recognized that St. Peter Canisius laid the foundation-stone of modern Continental studies in the traditions of Irish saints. In his Martyrology, St. Kilian was given an extensive entry stating that he was 'ein edler Schotlender'. Speaking of the feast of St. Kilian 'apostoli Franconiae, in Germania, cum duobus sociis Ibernis Colonato at Totnano', Stephen White[16] quoted as his main sources Rabanus Maurus (see below) and Henry Canisius. Canisius's text of both *Passio I* and *II* was so good that it was reprinted by the Bollandists and by Mabillon; the latter could also draw on the tradition of Benedictine devotion to St. Kilian as recorded by Wion. In the standard edition of the *Passio I* by the late Professor W. Levison, only the principal additions found in *Passio II* are stated in the footnotes, a procedure which does not do justice to the differences between these two works and to the development of Continental knowledge of Ireland illustrated by them.

Let us illustrate this by two points.

(1) To the account of St. Kilian's going to Rome to obtain a licence for preaching the Gospel, the *Passio II* added:

> Hibernia siquidem olim Pelagiana foedata fuerat haeresi apostolicaque censura damnata, quae nisi Romano iudicio solvi non poterat. Idcirco vir sanctissimus coram primate apostolicae sedis eiusdemque ministris, ut sibi semina divini verbi gentilibus erogare liceret, studio divini amoris expetivit.

Professor Levison made the following note:

> De censura illa papale nemo nisi hic auctor quicquam tradidit; cui fides deneganda est (follows reference to Zimmer's *Pelagius in Irland*).

an unsatisfactory recognition of this peculiar late reflection on Pelagianism in Ireland. The whole account in the *Passio II* of St. Kilian's sojourn in Rome and his elevation there 'consensu totius urbis' to the episcopacy is to be studied in conjunction with similar Continental accounts of the elections of Irish bishops and their sojourns in Rome.[17]

(2) The peculiar remark already found in the *Passio I* that St. Kilian was made a bishop so that he could 'krisma conficere et ecclesias dedicare et sacros ordines consecrare inreprehensibiliter' must be considered in the light of the information added by *Passio II* that in Ireland before becoming a bishop St. Kilian entered a monastery (Trithem suggested *Hiense*) and that when his confreres saw his constant progress in virtue

---

16 *Apologia*, pp. 15 and 23.

17 See above, note 6.

primo eum per ecclesiasticos gradus ad presbyteratus officium precibus ascendere deinde eiusdem monasterii regiminis curam sumere coegerunt,

in my opinion a Continental reflection on the Irish monastic system and its conception of episcopacy. According to *Passio II*, Kilian became a bishop by the Roman rather than by this conception, another indication of the lateness of the *Passio II*.

St. Kilian is one of the few Irish saints on the Continent of whom we have a comprehensive. modern monograph in which respect for the tradition and historical scholarship are well balanced (F. Emmerich, Würzburg, 1896).

Apart from St. Columbanus and St. Fursey and their companions, and perhaps the much-neglected St. Fintan of Rheinau, St. Kilian and his companions are practically the only Irish saints on the Continent whose historical association with Ireland has never been seriously questioned. This is remarkable because in contrast to those other unquestionably Irish saints on the Continent, the information supplied on this point by the fundamental records is scanty.

On the other hand, St. Kilian and his companions are the only Irish saints on the Continent to whose tradition we have a definite, explicit and original reference in an early Irish source. Our late-tenth-century *Martyrology of Tallaght* is a copy of the *Hieronymianum* distinguished by the reduction to a mere list of names of saints (placenames being frequently mistaken for names of saints) and the addition for each day of a similar list of names of Irish saints roughly equalling in number the names in the 'Roman' sections. Among the very few narrative entries found in the *Martyrology of Tallaght* we have the end of the entry of the Irish section for 8th July:

> Sancti Celiani Scotti martiris cum suis fratribus Aed 7 Tadg et Amarma coniuge regis Gothorum truncati a preposito dommus regiae in ippodoronia palatii regis.

I am not aware of any attempt to study this entry in the light of the tradition of St. Kilian. Nowhere else is it stated that the names of St. Kilian's companions were Aed and Tadg,[18] that the woman who contrived their death was named Amarma, or that they were beheaded 'in ippodoronia palatii regis'. Let us assume that 'rex Gothorum' is merely a mistake for 'dux Franconiae'. We could account for the translation of the names of the two fellow-martyrs, for the alteration of the name of the duchess and the conversion of the *lictor*[19] into *prepositus dommus regiae*, but it is hard to explain the reference to *ippodoronia regis*. O'Hanlon and Best-Lawlor suggested that we should read *hippodromo*. After all, this entry belongs to that part of the *Martyrology of Tallaght* which has come down to us only in a seventeenth-century copy, and *ippodoronia* is most likely a mere copyist's error. If it was in the *Book of Leinster* or its *Vorlage*, this misspelling would suggest that the compiler colpied this word which he did not understand any more. Is it an attempt to render the German word *Wirziburg* or

---

18 Marianus Gorman, who wrote about the time when the *Book of Leinster* was written, rendered these names by *Tadc is Aed*, Hibernizing also the name of St. Kilian to *Cele Clerech*. A margin note by Michael O'Clery when copying *Félire húi Gormáin* says that 'Cele clerech epscop, Aodh ocus Tadg' underwent martyrdom 'isin Almain (Stokes: "Germany") in Uairseburg.'

19 According to Rabanus *iudex* (named Gozbert as is in other sources the duke).

its – later[20] – translation by *Herbipolis*,[21] or was it suggested by the words 'dum Deus suos finire voluisset milites temporale certamen' (in the *Passio I* account of St. Kilian's martyrdom) evoking, as it were, irresistibly the memory of accounts of martyrs of Roman persecutions? One guess seems to be as good or as bad as another.

At any rate, it would appear that this entry with its five or six deviations from the Continental tradition represents the unique example of a specifically Irish version of the tradition of an Irish saint on the Continent. May we explain the numerous deviations of this tradition by the fact that it came to Ireland by word of mouth[22] and was not written down until it had passed through several stages of interpretation? This interpretation affords an example almost unique in this type of literature of the then Irish knowledge of the Continent. A special point must be made of the word *truncati* which occurs in both the Continental and the Irish accounts (Rabanus and the Roman Martyrology have *trucidati*); if the Irish tradition of St. Kilian was quite independent of the Continental one, it could easily have used any other word for the death which the saint met with. In fact, considering the numerous differences between these two traditions it would not have been surprising to find that according to the Irish tradition the saint was, say, poisoned.

The only other group of Irish missionaries on the Continent whose tradition is recorded in early Irish sources is St. Fursey and his companions. Under 31st October (to this day the feast of St. Foillan), the *Martyrology of Tallaght* has a separate paragraph between the 'Roman' and the Irish sections saying: 'Failani martiris fratris Fursu'. While, at an early stage SS. Foillan and Ultan were described not only as brethren but as brothers of St. Fursey, there is no trace of a Continental tradition regarding St. Kilian's fellow-martyrs as his brothers (as the *Martyrology of Tallaght* possibly suggests).

Apart from the *Martyrology of Tallaght*, the earliest Irish reference to the place of St. Kilian's martyrdom is the statement made by Marianus Scotus saying that he was ordained (in 1059) in the church of the saint at Würzburg.[23] This statement suggests that in the eleventh century Irishmen were well aware of the Irish associations of the patron of Würzburg. It can be shown that narrative passages in the *Martyrology of Tallaght* are generally of a later date than the original body of that work (which in fact must be even prior to *Félire Oengusso*). The only old copy of the *Martyrology of Tallaght* is the mid-twelfth-century *Book of Leinster*. The narrative passages in the

---

20   This point was made quite clear in Rabanus's entry for St. Kilian's feast.

21   The difficulties encountered by foreigners in pronouncing the word Würzburg are illustrated by Michael O'Clery's rendering of it. While much amusement can be derived from Continental ignorance of the Irish language past and present, similar amusement can be derived from such statements as found in Father O'Hanlon's work as: 'By the Germans St. Kilian is called Kulhn', or the references to his veneration at 'Huxar near Corbei' (of course, Höxter near Corvey).

22   That the oral tradition in Irish-Continental relations played a much greater part than is commonly assumed, is obvious also from the examples listed by me in my review of Dom Munding's edition of St. Gallen Calendars (above note 13).

23   Kenney, no. 443.

Martyrology of Tallaght are usually at the end of their respective sections or form separate paragraphs. The fact that, in spite of the prominence given to him in the *Martyrology of Tallaght*, no reference is made to St. Kilian and his companions in *Félire Oengusso* makes it clear that that entry was of a later date.

Eighty years after Marianus Scotus the first branch of the Irish community of St. James Ratisbon was established at Würzburg, undoubtedly attracted by the tradition of St. Kilian.[24] The Würzburg *Schottenkloster* existed right to the nineteenth century. Apart from Ratisbon, there is no place in Central Europe where we can trace a longer and wider tradition of Irish activities than Würzburg. St. Kilian apparently was one of the few Irish saints on the Continent whose tradition remained known in Ireland throughout the Middle Ages; a version of his life (along with those of SS. Fursey, Foillan, Fiacra, Columbanus and Malachy) was incorporated in John of Tynemouth's *Sanctilogium* which drew on both Irish and Continental sources.[25]

The originality of the entry in the *Martyrology of Tallaght* relating to St. Kilian can be measured by comparison with the corresponding entry in the martyrologium of Rabanus, subsequently enlarged by Notker. While giving a very exact description of the position of Würzburg, the latter confined themselves to speaking of St. Kilian's native country as 'Hibernia Scotorum insula'; among the late medieval Usuardian martyrologies some said 'de partibus insularum Oceani maris,' others simply 'de Scotia.'[26] Baronius and the Roman Martyrology do not refer to St. Kilian's native country, but in the prologue to his Catalogue of Saints (Venice, 1625), Ferrari said:

> Quis enim Ss. Patricium, Brigidam, Brendanum, Columbam,Columbanum, Gallum, Magnum, Virgilium, Kilianum, Rumoldum, Dympnam, Fiacrum, Fursaeum, Malachiam, Laurentium et allos Hibernos esse ignorat?

an important statement in the history of early Continental interest in the Irish saints. Moreover, by his reference to Bede (insertion from Rabanus), Ado (*recte* Usuard), Sigebert of Gembloux, Otto of Freising and Trithem as his sources Baronius made it clear that he was aware of the continuous Continental tradition of St. Kilian, in which his Irish associations had been made abundantly clear.

Apart from the name of Gallus, no name of an Irish saint has become more popular on the Continent than that of St. Kilian. By way of contrast, these names are rarely used in Ireland by lay persons. The tradition of St. Livinus refers to a monk Kilian,[27] and an offshoot of the traditions of SS. Fiacre and Faro ist that of St. 'Chillenus ex gente Scottorum' or 'in Ibernia' whose *Vita*[28] bears a clear resemblance with the *Passio I* of

---

24   See my papers on Irish monastic activities in Eastern Europe, in *Bull. Irish Comm. Hist. Stud.*, no. 23 (1945), and I. E. RECORD, lxv, 394 ff.

25   Kenney, no. 117.

26   As edited by de Sollier. The publications by Weale and Gougaud on the place of Irish saints in late medieval Continental calendars do not give any information on such points.

27   Kenney, no. 310.

28   See above, note 8.

St. Kilian of Würzburg. It is curious that when referring to the name of Kilian (Brust-fleck, a popular figure), Goethe's mother still used the traditional spelling of *Chilian*.[29]

The name of Würzburg is associated with some of the most important records of the early Irish language, and the Irish associations of Würzburg caused Caspar Zeuss, a native of that diocese to devote himself systematically to the study of those records. The tradition of St. Kilian stands out for its uncontaminated historicity as a hagio-graphical source. Its value in this respect is enhanced by the fact that it is one of the few practically unbroken sources of Irish information on Germany, while to the Continent it has conveyed knowledge of the geography, history and language of Ire-land.[30]

(Quelle: Irish Ecclesiastical Record 78, 1952, S. 21-33.)

With Irish Saints Along the Alps

A hundred years ago, in his account of Irish monastic activities around Lake Con-stance in *Ekkehard,* one of the most successful novels ever published in Germany, Victor von Scheffel suggested that the Irish had become more conscious of the many links of their country with the Continent. During the subsequent years Margaret Stokes and Monsignor Hogan told us of journeys undertaken by them with the definite purpose of following the footsteps of Irish Saints and missionaries especially in the heart of Europe. Has interest in these matters remained confined to a few scholars? A week ago I received an invitation addressed to Irish tourists to visit Switzerland. No reference whatsoever was made in this invitation to the many points of particular interest Switzerland has to offer to those who love and study Irish history.

On March 6th in Alsace, Northern Switzerland and South Western Germany the feast of St. Fridolin is celebrated. Whether his association with *Scotia* established through later tradition is historical or not, it has been the carrier of a considerable amount of Continental interest in Ireland. One no less than St. Peter Canisius proposed St. Fridolin, "from Ireland behind England", to Switzerland, then (A.D. 1589) attaining to full self-consciousness, as a national patron. St. Peter's work was the first biography of an Irish Saint printed separately in the German language and in fact was the starting point of modern scholarly interest in Irish Saints on the Continent. In one of his poems, Scheffel describes St. Fridolin addressing his native country: "Do not worry, beloved mother. Thy sons will fight for glory with better weapons than with sword and spear. Faith and charity are a better armour. My shield is the Lord. Thus armed I go to the heathens in far away lands, a true Celt. I have dreamt of those lands, of hills and an island in a green river, but none of these scenes could rival thy beauty."

In the early Middle Ages, the tradition of St. Gall had inspired a German poet; his work has come down to us only in a Latin translation. St. Gall and his fellow-mis-

---

29   To Goethe, 19th June, 1781.

30   In his article on St. Kilian in the German national biography (A.D.B. xv, (1882), pp 735f.), Wegele, the great historian, described the saint as 'Britte.'

sionaries are also the subject of a poem written towards the end of the eighteenth century by Herder, a poet much beloved by Canon Sheehan.

When, last year, I visited the cathedral of Säckingen, which for almost a thousand years past has been the centre of veneration of St. Fridolin, I saw his precious reliquary and a relief portraying his departure from Ireland. In some churches in Switzerland St. Fridolin is depicted leading a skeleton by his hand, a reference to the tradition that he raised a certain Ursus from the dead.

To one whose professional work is concerned with electricity supply problems and who in his spare time studies the lives and traditions of Irish Saints, the island of Rheinau some fifty miles up the Rhine from Säckingen, is of twofold interest. For several years past in the daily press of Switzerland the question has been debated whether the beauty and tranquillity of that island should be desecrated by the setting up of a power station harnessing the Rhine. A thousand years ago, an Irishman named Fintan chose this island for his abode. After the death of this hermit, one of his followers wrote his life, a work standing out by sobriety and reliability. To this day this biography has been studied mainly by linguists, since it is the first Continental record of some sentences in the Irish language. Transmitted to us in a badly mutilated form, by Continental scribes wholly ignorant of the language, these sentences have puzzled both Irish and Continental scholars for the last hundred years. However, it is clear that these sentences are to render heavenly voices heard by Fintan when, by Continental standards of his time, his penitential exercises became too rigid. These intimations were given to Fintan by *Patrick Artmache*, Columba, Aidan and Brigid, and it is an early illustration of national self-consciousness that these Saints are represented as speaking in the Irish language. Moreover, this is a very early record of the grouping together of the Saints later venerated as the three patrons of Ireland. We shall presently see why St. Aidan was associated with them.

Of the many Irishmen venerated on the Continent as Saints, Fintan of Rheinau has been one of the least known in his native country. To this day, his feast on November 15th is celebrated only in the diocese of Chur. However, not only the details of his life in Rheinau but also his Irish associations are exceptionally well testified. Indeed, Fintan is practically the only Irish Saint on the Continent whose name is indisputedly Irish and has been preserved in its original form. In fact, no less than twelve namesakes of his are known as saints in this country.

The biography of St. Fintan says that he was "a citizen of the province of Leinster" where his father occupied a high military position under one of the *principes* or petty kings. The lessons at present read on November 15th in the diocese of Chur make Fintan himself a *princeps* (the usual and indeed literal translation of the word *taoiseach*). Since St. Aidan (or Maedoc) along with the three patrons of Ireland is said to have spoken to Fintan, we may assume that Fintan was specially associated with Ferns, the seat of a monastic school established by St. Aidan. Another historical feature in the biography of St. Fintan is the account of his captivity by Danish raiders. Fintan's decision to dedicate his life to God is attributed to the tribulations endured by him in captivity. The biographer tells us that Fintan vowed never to return to Ireland if God would free him.

Not to return to Ireland, therefore, was regarded as a very great sacrifice. A similar illustration of attachment to Ireland is found in a passage in the Life of St. Gall read in St. Gallen, the diocese neighbouring that of Chur, in the office for October 16th as the Antiphon to the Magnificat: When one of St. Gall's disciples heard of his master's death he exclaimed: "Oh, oh, my beloved father! Why, oh learned man, hast thou led me forth from my father's house and now leavest me an orphan ?"

I am not going to speak here of the various places associated with St. Gall and his companions around Zurich. In connection with the recent celebrations commemorating the mission of St. Columbanus and St. Gall this ground has been covered elsewhere, and it is to be hoped that many of those who travel through Zurich will take a day or two off to visit places of Irish historical interest. In his *Ekkehard* Scheffel treats of the Irish monks who five hundred years after St. Gall were associated with the abbey bearing his name.

Travelling eastwards along the foothills of the Alps beyond St. Gallen and Lake Constance into Austria, at the end of March we may celebrate at Salzburg the feast of St. Rupert, otherwise observed only in Ireland. St. Rupert is the only German saint whose feast is found in the calendar proper to Ireland. Whereas elsewhere foreign saints are specially venerated on account of their missionary activities in the respective countries, St. Rupert is venerated in Ireland although he never set foot on Irish soil. His place in the calendar proper to Ireland is due to his associations with our St. Virgil, who succeeded him and raising his relics, laid the foundations of his cultus. Indeed the lessons read on March 29th by all priests in Ireland make no reference to Ireland, but relate exclusively to places and events in what is now known as Austria.

On September 24th in the archdiocese of Salzburg the translation of St. Rupert's relics is commemorated. On the following day is the feast of the dedication of the Cathedral. In the Office for this feast we read that in 1628 the new Cathedral was consecrated to Ss. Rupert and Virgil whose relics are placed under the high altar. Let us remember that the Cathedral of Salzburg occupied a supreme position in the former German Empire; the archbishop of Salzburg bears to this day the title of Primate of Germany.

Last year I spoke to six persons from this country who had been to Salzburg. They had listened to the operas, they had seen the cathedral and the castle, and they had toured the surrounding countryside. I am afraid not one of them was aware of Salzburg's close associations with Ireland. The feast of the translation of St. Virgil's relics coincides with the end of the tourist season in Salzburg. If one of my readers lucky enough to go to Salzburg this year, will take the trouble to read in St. Peter's Abbey the epitaph on St. Virgil relating to the Saint's coming from "Hibernian soil", I shall be well pleased.

(Quelle: Irish Rosary 59, 1955, S. 470-473.)

The Irish Monastic Tradition on the Continent
A German Novel – A Centenary

In studies on the tradition of the Irish saints on the Continent the series of papers published some sixty years ago by Monsignor J. F. Hogan in the I. E. RECORD occupies an eminent position. These articles described what the author had seen in the places visited by him where saints associated with Ireland had lived and where they were still remembered. Moreover, Monsignor Hogan combined in a masterly manner the study of historical records with that of the liturgical, artistic, popular and literary traditions of those saints.

In his article on St. Fridolin, Monsignor Hogan mentioned that to Germans the tradition of this saint is best known through *Der Trompeter von Säckingen,* an epic written about the middle of the last century by Viktor von Scheffel.[1] While in the historical records the associations of St. Fridolin with *Scotia* are so late and vague that modern investigators do not make much of them,[2] the *Propria* for Basle, Chur and St. Gallen, where his feast is celebrated on 6th March, clearly associate him with *Hibernia.* In his poem, Scheffel refers to the saint's yearning for 'Erin, the green island, his native country far away' which he had left urged by the wanderlust characteristic of 'Celtic blood'.

In 1855 Scheffel's novel *Ekkehard* was published, and no work of modern German literature contains more references to Irish monastic activities in Central Europe. *Ekkehard* was the first work of German literature to draw extensively on the *Monumenta Germaniae historica.* Scheffel's principal source was the history of the abbey of St. Gallen, entitled *Casus Sancti Galli,*[3] written in the late ninth century by Ratpert, who also composed a hymn in honour of St. Gall, the earliest German hymn of which we know and the first German poem on an Irish subject.[4] *Casus Sancti Galli* was continued about A.D. 1030 by Ekkehard IV, one of the most colourful works of early German historiography, though not particularly reliable in detail.[5] Scheffel perused this work during the winter of 1853-4 in connection with his studies in the history of German law. In May 1854 he made a journey to the district around Lake Constance, the scene of the *Casus* and of his novel which he had then begun to write.[6]

Ekkehard has been the most successful historical novel in German literature. Up to 1869, 50,000 copies were sold. In 1916 the copyright expired and from that time the

---

1   I. E. RECORD, iii, 14 (1893), 193ff. As Monsignor Hogan pointed out, the name of Fridolin is known to every German child through the beginning of Schiller's poem *Der Gang zum Eisenhammer:* 'A God-revering youth, we learn, was gentle Fridolin' (Mangan's translation).

2   Kenney, *Sources,* No. 292, and Büchi in Buchberger's *Lexikon für Theologie und Kirche,* iv (1932), 182f. For the tradition of St. Fridolin, see L. Gougaud, *Les Saints irlandais hors d'Irlande* (Louvain, 1936). An interesting note on the chronology is found in Lappenberg's article 'Irland' in Ersch-Gruber's *Encyclopädie* (Leipzig 1845), ii, xxiv, 53.

3   Kenney, *Sources,* No. 410.

4   See my paper on ' Irish Saints in early German literature' in *Speculum* 22 (1947), 361f.

5   Kenney, *Sources,* No. 411.

6   Karl Siegen, introduction to *Ekkehard* (Berlin, about 1920), 8.

number of reprints can scarcely be counted.[7] In Nazi Germany, *Ekkehard* was particularly acceptable, because this was 'a poetical version of the past conceived from inspiration through the blood rather than from research and study';[8] moreover, though the offspring of a good Catholic family, Scheffel in this work gave expression to his anti-clerical complex.

As regards the Irish associations, Scheffel's *Ekkehard* cannot be appreciated from the English translation,[9] since they do not contain the 285 notes which were added to the original edition, on the suggestion of the publisher 'to appease those who might be inclined to regard the work as pure fable and fiction'. The hero of this 'tale from the tenth century' is Ekkehard II, described by the *Continuatio Casus Sancti Galli* as a teacher in the schools of the abbey of St. Gallen. The name of St. Gall occurs some sixty times in Scheffel's work, mostly with reference to the monastery. Some of the characters in *Ekkehard* constantly use the exclamation 'By St. Gall' or 'in the name of St. Gall'. In the fifth chapter Thieto bids farewell to Ekkehard saying: 'May St. Gall keep and protect thee', a reference to the blessing of travellers administered in honour of St. Gall, the earliest German text in which the name of this saint occurs.[10] The invocation 'St. Gall, pray for us' (chapter vi) recalls the fact that the name of this Irish saint was inserted in medieval litanies in Southern Germany and Switzerland.[11]

In the 2. chapter, entitled 'The disciples of St. Gall', Scheffel speaks of the saint himself:[12]

> Gall, the Irishman, had chosen a pleasant place when craving for forest air [note: 'silvarum avidus', *Vita S. Galli*] he settled in this lonely part of *Helvetia.* This Irish anchorite followed the strange urge which took those missionaries from *Albion* and *Erin* to the Teutonic Continent. 'With *Briten* the urge to go abroad is innate and irresistible' [note: 'de natione Scotorum, quibus consuetudo peregrinandi jam in nature conversa' – again from Walafrid].[13] They were the forerunners of modern tourists and were known from afar by their usual satchels [note, from a glossa in a ninth-century St. Gallen manuscript: 'Ascopam i.e. flasconem ... sicut solent Scotones habere']. Many of them stayed, although the honest natives scarcely invited them to do so. However their persistency, characteristic of their British nature, made them successful.

When, even in parts of Central Europe with strong Irish associations, Irish tourists nowadays fail to ensure that they are not described as English, they may lay some of the blame on Scheffel. He not only made no difference between the Anglo-Saxon and

---

7   Writing in 1930 Kosch *(Deutsches Literatur-Lexikon,* ii, 2180f) said that this 'most successful novel of the century' had reached its 294th edition.

8   J. Nadler, *Literaturgeschichte der deutschen Stämme,* iv (1928), 622. Nadler gives a good account of Scheffel's studies.

9   Tauchnitz edition and Everyman's Library, the latter abridged for German Classics of the nineteenth and twentieth centuries (see Bayard Morgan, *Critical bibliography of German literature in English translations* (Stanford, 1928), No. 7709-15). The chapter on St. Gall in romance in Dr. J. M. Clark's *The Abbey of St. Gall as a centre of literature and arts* (Cambridge, 1926), 261-6 is the most extensive account in English of the contents of Scheffel's novel, but is also quite unaware of the notes.

10   See above, note 4.

11   Gougaud, op. cit.

12   Hogan, loc. cit., 1057, also *15,* 35ff. and 289ff.

13   *Mon. Germ. hist. Scriptores,* ii, 30.

Irish missions but even translated the word *Scoti* by 'Briten', describing the Irish as heirs of British virtues. It is remarkable, however, that while at Scheffel's time Protestant writers began to suggest that St. Boniface had forced 'Romanism' upon the Teutonic nations, one of the characters in *Ekkehard* states that, when overthrowing the idols at Bregenz, 'St. Gall did not inflict any harm on the people'.

Continuing his comparison with modern 'British' activities Scheffel concludes the passage on St. Gall with the words: 'To-day the descendants of that saint take money from the honest Swiss to construct their railways.' A footnote says that 'looking back upon the activities of well-meaning ancestors, we may agree with the praise given by Herder to "the strangers" (the title of one of his clumsy poems) who *scotice* with Bardic diligence wrote books to preserve our inheritance'.[14] Note 87 speaks of the artistic tradition of St. Gall and of the *Liber Sancti Galli aureus,* without mentioning its Irish associations. The *Vocabularium Sancti Galli*[15] is described as 'a glossary important to German linguists, because it contains the German versions of a basic vocabulary obtained by St. Gall, ignorant of the vernacular spoken around Lake Constance, by the parson of Arbon'. In reality, this *Vocabularium* originated about A.D. 750.

Ekkehard is important because it treats not only of Irish associations at the time of St. Gall but also of their later tradition. At the time of Ekkehard, that is, in the middle of the tenth century, there were many *Schotten* among the 'disciples of St. Gall'. In that community they were distinguished by their tall stature. 'Fortegian, Failan, Dubslan and Brendan, or whatever their names were, were an inseparable national community, zealously guarding their privileges.' One of them, red-bearded Dabduin, had to bear penance for composing defamatory verses on his confrères. In a note, Scheffel states as his source von Arx's *History of the Canton of St. Gallen* (1830); from the same source, Scheffel knew that among the benefactors of St. Gallen there were kings of England.

Near the abbey of St. Gallen, the place where, according to Walafrid (note), 'St. Gall fell into thorns' is known as *Irenhügel*. With this place Scheffel associated 'St. Fintan, a renowned hermit of yore. Throughout the night he was heard to pray in his cell, exorcising the devil in the strange sounds of his Irish tongue.' In chapter xv Scheffel refers to the island of Rheinau, where Fintan lived, then adorned with 'many impressive walls of church and cloister'. When seeing his hut burnt by the Huns, a shepherd exclaims: 'St. Fintan, pray for us.' Scheffel's erroneous interpretation of the Irish sentences in the *Vita S. Findani*[16] can be traced to the faulty translation given of them by an eighteenth-century Scottish Benedictine (published by van der Meer).[17]

The most interesting Irish character in *Ekkehard is* Moengal or Marcellus, the only clerical character who appears in a favourable light throughout that novel.[18] Scheffel

---

14   See my paper on 'Ireland's place in the 19th century German poetry' in *German Life and Letters,* viii (1955), 201-7.

15   G. Ehrismann, *Geschichte der deutschen Literatur* (Munich, 1928), i, 258.

16   Scheffel used Mone's edition. See Kenney, *Sources,* No. 422, Hogan, loc. cit., 384ff., and Gougaud, op. cit., 95.

17   H. Zimmer, *Glossae Hibernicae* (1881), xlif. and 272ff.

18   Kenney, *Sources,* p. 596.

relished Moengal's sense of independence without recognizing that this was a characteristic of Irish clerics on the Continent throughout the Middle Ages.

Scheffel also shared Moengal's love of nature and as a sign of endearment attributes to him considerable freedom in language: 'Pestilence and leprosy! By the beard of St. Patrick of Armagh', he greets Ekkehard when the latter interferes with his deer-stalking.[19]

> On his right arm there was etched-in, in crude lines, the picture of the Saviour surrounded by a snake-pattern with the words *Christus vindex* [note: 'picture in corpore, quales Scotti pingunt' from a St. Gallen manuscript]. The custom of painting eyelashes and of tattooing the arms seems to have pleased the *Scoti* and Irish of that period. Such etched-in pictures must have been of a crude ugliness, beyond words, to judge from extant miniatures of Irish origin in the manuscripts, which by their strange and, if I may say so, Celtic lack of beauty compare most unfavourably with similar works by German hands.

This is an interesting contribution to the history of Continental appreciation of Irish art; it was not until the general revival of the appreciation of Byzantine and Romanesque art – in the second decade of the present century – that this art became generally appreciated or indeed known on the Continent.

Referring to his coming from Ireland to Switzerland, Moengal says: 'It is well known in this country that Ireland breeds piety.' When Moengal returned 'with his uncle Mark from a pilgrimage to Rome, the world was not worth a farthing to him: "Psalms, vigils and spiritual exercises were my fare."' For the sake of their 'holy fellow-countryman', these pilgrims went to St. Gallen. In his hermitage at Radolfzell, Moengal wrote 'several records in neat script, also Cicero's *De Officiis* and Priscian in Latin with interlinear Irish writing'.

However, when Ekkehard drinks the health of 'Marcellus, author of the Irish version of Priscian', Moengal admits:

> 'As regards the Irish translation, there may be a catch.' A catch indeed. Some time ago a learned son of green Erin came to the library of St. Gall to examine more closely the work of his pious ancestor. He had scarcely begun to copy this text when he was heard by the librarian chuckling to himself. The librarian went up to him and the *Rektor von Dublin* translated for him some of the Irish glossae: 'Thanks be to God, it is getting dark! St. Patrick of Armagh, deliver me from this job! Ah, that I had a glass of old wine!' Such was Moengal's 'translation'![20]

---

19 Similar 'invocations' of St. Patrick are found in Immermann's epic *Tristan und Isolde* (1839); (see my paper in *Modern Language Rev.,* xliv (1949), 246-52) and Freiligrath's poem *Irland* (see above note 14). Scheffel's Irish associations must be considered against the background of Ireland's place in German literature and thought of the mid-nineteenth century (see my contribution to *Daniel O'Connell* (Dublin, 1949, 235-69). In 1844, A. Stifter, the great Catholic novelist, referred in *Der Hagestolz*, iv, to 'priests who brought the cross from *Schottenlande*' and who, settling in an island in a mountain-lake in Austria, suffered martyrdom from the people whom they tried to convert.

20 Scheffel's note 112, one of the few notes found in the Tauchnitz edition translation. Kenney, *Sources,* No. 533, ii. Moengal was not one of the scribes of this famous manuscript and its glossae, but this manuscript originated in his lifetime. On the marginalia, see E. Curtis in *Irish Statesman*, viii (2/2/1927), 89f. and L. Gougaud in *Rev. d'Histoire., Ecclés* xxvii (1931), 294f.

Needless to say that these Irish *marginalia* are quite different from the *glossae* on the Latin text.

Moengal's reaction to the news that the Huns were coming appeared to Scheffel more adequate than the 'wailing and praying' of the Reichenau monks. Moengal grips his 'old Cambotta, a huge club cut in the old Irish fashion' [note 179: 'Cambutta, scottica vox, baculum significans', a misinterpretation as Clark was shown.][21] Scheffel had learnt from Walafrid that after St. Columbanus' death his *cambutta* was given to St. Gall. Moengal also takes his Irish satchel and 'an Hibernian flask on top'. On leaving his cell he wrote on the door 'a few words in Irish script which were effaced by the rain but no doubt this was some sort of curse, left there in Irish *Runen*'. Scheffel perhaps had heard something of ogham script. In the battle of the Huns (chapter xiv) 'Dubslan the Scot' is killed, having invoked in vain the help of a St. Minwaloius (one of the many 'funny' names by which at all times, Continental writers have tried to render the strange Celtic sounds). Moengal, however, trusting his *cambutta,* prevails.

The attempt of a German writer to form some idea as regards the possible relations of the Irish monks with their Continental confrères is interesting. With reference to Moengal, the abbot of Reichenau exclaims: 'I wished thou hadst stayed in thy monastery at Benchor in the green island, Irish ruffian' [*Hartknochen*]. The reference to *Benchor* in Walafrid's life of St. Gall was the first reference to an Irish place-name in German literature: Scheffel apparently did not try to establish the identity of this place in modern Ireland.

In general, Scheffel's knowledge of modern Ireland seems to have been inferior to his knowledge of early medieval Irish activities. The reader gets tired of the references to 'the green island'. Still, *Ekkehard* is to be remembered as a popular source of information on the Irish monastic activities during the early Middle Ages. The authoritative summary of Scheffel's life and work in the German national biography rightly states that *Ekkehard's* popularity in Germany was unique. Bismarck and the princes of Germany vied in showering honours upon its author.

Reviewing the possibilities of the historical novel in Germany, Julian Schmidt wrote in the year of the publication of *Ekkehard*:[22] 'Medieval subjects must be excluded, because while being of historical interest they lack in individual colour.' It was Scheffel's merit that he proved that this statement was untrue. He found much 'individual colour' in the Irish characters in early German church history, the local traditions of which were, to some extent, first made known through Scheffel. Scheffel's mother summed up her opinion of *Ekkehard* saying: 'I do not really care to propagate it, because it contains many things distasteful to me. Yet it has some points of truth and beauty.'[23]

(Quelle: IER 87, 1958, 186-193)

---

21   Op. cit., 265.

22   *Geschichte der deutschen Literatur*, iii, 199. In 1852, William B. McCabe had published *Bertha or The Pope and the Emperor, a historical tale* (2nd ed. 1853), which in many respects resembles *Ekkehard*.

23   Siegen, loc. cit.

Irish Saints in Early German Literature

The extensive studies which during the past fifty years have been carried out by American, British, Dutch, French and German scholars on the influences exercised by Celtic mythology on the mediaeval literature of the Continent have been confined almost entirely to *Motivforschung*.[1] That it would be worth studying what the Continent learned, through those influences, of the countries from which they originated, of their geography, history and inhabitants, is a suggestion which may be regarded as a relapse into methods of literary research characteristic of nineteenth-century Positivism. Yet it *is* astonishing that in such a comprehensive work as Gertrude Schoepperle's *Tristan and Isolt, a Study of the Sources of the Roman* (1913) not a single reference was made to the fact that Gottfried's *Tristan* is distinguished from the earlier Tristan-tradition by the references made in it to historical Irish place-names[2] and to social and cultural conditions in contemporary Ireland, and that these references show that Gottfried had more recent and more definite information of Ireland than that embodied in the Irish influences which can be traced in his sources. The Tristan tradition as a whole is an important source of the development of Continental knowledge of Ireland under Norman influence. The definite references made in the epics of mediaeval France and Germany to chivalresque relations with Ireland have not been investigated either, though it might have been expected that these relations have played an important part in conveying Irish influences to the Continent.

The Tristan tradition shows us at its height the connection between Irish literary influence and concrete information on Ireland. An investigation of the development of this connection may offer some contributions to the study of Irish literary influences. It is remarkable that Irish scholars, far from enthusiastically adopting the theory that Ireland was the cradle of basic tendencies of the chivalresque literatures of mediaeval Europe, have emphasized the fundamental weakness of that study, which appears to be based on suggestions rather than facts.[3] The investigation of actual references to Ireland and Irish things in mediaeval Continental literature may not lead to such far-reaching conclusions as the study of Irish literary influences, but it rests on a fairly secure basis.

We may expect that literary works enshrining Irish influences contain a certain amount of information on Ireland, especially of that period when those influences were actually conveyed to the Continent. It would of course be quite erroneous to apply generally vice versa this conclusion by that works enshrining or pretending to enshrine such information, by laying the scene of certain episodes in Ireland or by referring to Irish persons or places, are also literarily influenced by Ireland. The references made

---

1 Notably by Windisch, Thys, Nutt, Bédier, Kittredge, Thurneysen, Kuno Meyer, Loomis, and Arthur C. L. Brown.

2 See below, note 76. So far as I am aware, the only writer who realized the paramount significance of Irish place-names for the study of Irish literary influences was v.d. Zanden. See his *Etudes sur le Purgatoire de St Patrice* (Amsterdam, 1927), p. 50.

3 See, e.g., Prof. Gerard Murphy's review of Professor Brown's *Origin of the Grail Legend* in *Béaloides*, XIII (1943), 295.

to Ireland in *Kudrun,* for example, are not expressive of direct Irish literary influence on that work; they simply show that by the time when the final version of that epic was compiled Ireland – partly due to the extensive literary influences she exercised on contemporary literature in general – had become a country which was bound to interest the reader.[4]

However, when we consider the peculiar position occupied by Ireland in the mediaeval world, her spiritual importance and geographical remoteness from the Continent, we may regard the examination of early references to Ireland and Irish things in the vernacular literature of the Continent as a valuable supplement to the study of Irish literary influences on the classical chivalresque literature.

Taking the history of mediaeval literature on the Continent as a whole, Ireland's influence on it seems to be twofold. There is the literary tradition of Irish monasticism, which is Christian in character, historically pre-Norman and linguistically Latin, and there is the literary influence of Irish mythology and folklore, which is pagan, historically Norman, and vernacular. If we confine ourselves to German (vernacular) literature, we see, indeed, that up to the late twelfth century references to Ireland are based entirely on the hagiographical tradition. Thus, so far as Germany is concerned, the study of early references made in the vernacular literature to Irish saints can be described as the first instalment of the study of the development of both German knowledge of Ireland and of Irish literary influence as reflected in the vernacular literature.

The study of the concrete knowledge of or information on Ireland and things Irish contained in either of the two lines of the Irish tradition in the mediaeval literature of the Continent establishes also the link between those two lines. The first work of Continental vernacular literature to mention Irish place-names is the introduction to the German *Tundalus* where the tendency to convey concrete knowledge of Ireland is obvious. The *Tundalus* is historically just pre-Norman, but reflects the change in Irish cultural, political and ecclesiastical history which prepared the way for the invaders. It tells us expressly how it was translated from the Latin original, written, still in the hagiographical tradition, by a member of the Irish community at Ratisbon, the center of Irish monastic activities in Central Europe throughout the Middle Ages. Still more successful on the Continent than the *Tundalus* were the *Purgatorium sancti Patricii* and the *Navigatio Brendani.*[5] Combining the tradition of Irish saints with Irish mythology and folklore, these works helped to establish, on the basis of the ancient Continental tradition of *Insula Sacra,* the new Norman legend of Ireland.

---

4   See Friedrich Panzer, *Hilde-Gudrun* (Halle, 1901), 435.

5   While the oldest manuscript of the Latin *Navigatio* is of the tenth century, the 'oldest extant version of the Brendan vernacular other than Irish' is the Norman-French poem written about 1121 for Alix of Louvain, second wife of Henry I of England (James F. Kenney, *The Source for the Early History of Ireland,* I [New York, 1929], No. 203: NB 2, p. 416), which was repeatedly retranslated into Latin (*ibid.,* NB 3 and 4). Towards the end of the twelfth century appeared the French prose version (*ibid.,* NB 5). See also Hammerich, *Munken og Fuglen* (Copenhagen, 1933), pp. 58 and 62.

In a purer form this legend was established through the Irish influences on chivalresque literature, which, on the whole, are a Norman interpretation of Irish mythology conveyed to, and digested for, the Continent with a definite political end in view, namely to justify the 'conquest'. More and more crudely distorted, this legend ruled Continental ideas of Ireland right to the late eighteenth century.

From the early seventeenth century on, mainly through the great Irish hagiologists exiled on the Continent, the Continental tradition of Irish saints was re-established in its original purity, but in this process it lost more and more in popular appeal.

* * *

The earliest Irish association found in any work of German vernacular literature is the reference to *chrihshha sancti kiliânes* in a description of the Würzburg March. This is the second of two such descriptions which were entered towards the end of the tenth century in a ninth-century Evangeliary.[6] The first description is in Latin, enlarged by German names of persons and places, and dated October[7] 779; the second is entirely in German, therefore certainly not an official document, undated, but, to conclude from the identity of several names of witnesses, contemporary with the first. This is the earliest literary record of the cult of St Kilian, the sixth-century missionary to Würzburg. The earliest records of his Irish descent, his labors and his martyrdom were written more than half a century later. However, the cultus of St Kilian is certainly older. In 752, Burchard, first Bishop of Würzburg, transferred the relics of St Kilian and his companions to the cathedral.[8]

In his *Tituli Ecclesiae Fuldensis*[9] Hrabanus Maurus mentions collective dedications of altars including Chilianus, also Saints Brigid, Columbanus and Patrick. These epigrams are the first works of poetry written by a German[10] to refer to an Irish subject.

The sermon on *Sancte Kyliânes Tac* by Hermann von Fritzlar (written about 1345)[11] is only one example of the position held by Irish saints in the homiletic literature of

---

6   Müllenhoff-Scherer, *Denkmäler deutscher Poesie und Prosa*, 3rd ed., I, 226, and Ehrismann, *Geschichte der deutschen Literatur bis zum Ausgang des Mittelalters*, I (1922), 350f. References to literature made in passages here noted of Kenney's and Ehrismann's works are not repeated.

  The cathedral of Paderborn was consecrated to the Blessed Virgin and St Kilian. A record of Lewis the Pious A.D. 881 refers to this dedication (P. Kehr, *Urkunden der deutschen Karolinger*, I [Berlin 1934], pp. 141 and 359; *Chilianus*; this is to this day the liturgical spelling in Würzburg; see also the letter of Frau Aja to Goethe, 19 June, 1781, Koester's edition, Leipzig 1912, p. 58). A record of A.D. 844 refers to 'reliquiae beati Chiliani martiris' (Kehr, *ed. cit.*, 44). *Bruniwilarensis Monasterii Fundatio* (*Mon. Germ., Scriptores* XI, 406) reports that in 1061 a new monastery was erected at Würzburg 'in loco ubi santi Kiliani sociorumque eius sacrum erat martyrium'. See also Gougard, *Les Saints irlandais hors de l'Irlande* (Louvain 1936), 125 ff.

7   Kenney, *op. cit.*, 513: 'March'.

8   Gougard, *l.c.*

9   *Mon. Ger. Hist., Poet, Lat.*, II, 208, 221, 230. Kenney, *op. cit.*, 340, ii refers to similar poems by Alcuin (*M.G.H., Poet. lat.*, I, 342).

10   Kenney, *op. cit.*, No. 356, I, does not mention these epigrams.

mediaeval Germany. 'Dirre herre sanctus kyliânus was burte von Ybernia von Schottenland von hoheme geslechte und hate erbegutes vil and vile. Das liz her durch die libe gotis.'[12]

Hrabanus's epigram seems to be also the earliest record we have of a literary reference made by a German to St Columbanus. Devotion to him[13] and still more to St Gall was so extensive in mediaeval Germany[14] that it could not fail to leave traces in vernacular literature. The name of St Gall occurs first in the Tobias blessing, a twelfth century version of the old Teutonic and ancient Christian blessing for travellers.[15] Whether the words 'Sante Galle dîner spîse pflege' were found in the earlier versions of that blessing, we do not know; in some manuscripts the name of St Oswald takes the place of that of St Gall.[15b] From the large number of German manuscripts of the Latin lives of St Gall (especially that by Walafrid, a Suabian)[16] it may be concluded that his story was well known in mediaeval Germany.

On the Life of St Gall by Wetti,[17] who died in 824 as a monk in Reichenau, was based Ratpert's *Lobgesang auf den Heiligen Gallus* which has come down to us only in the close Latin translation by Ekkehard IV.[18] Ratpert's poem was the first known attempt to write German hymns. It is expressive, Professor Ehrisman[19] said, 'of the efforts

---

11 Franz Pfeiffer, *Deutsche Mystiker des 14. Jahrhunderts* (Göttingen 1907), I, 152f. See note 33.

12 In the late fifteenth century *Geschichte der Heiligen* the only Irish saint mentioned is 'sant kilian und seine gesellschaft' ... 'geboren von hydenischem (!) geschlecht von schottenlant' ... 'Er kam gen Wirtzburg. Do kam sant Gallen in schwaben land. Do fuor sant Columbanus gen Meyland.' The 'gesellen' of St. Killian are not identified.

13 See my article St Columbanus's place in the liturgy, in *Irish Ecclesiastical Record*, November 1943.

14 Gougard, *op. cit.*, pp. 53ff. and 114ff.

15 Müllenhoff-Scherer, *op. cit.*, I, No. 47, 4, II, 297; Ehrismann, *op. cit.*, 118f.

15b In his *Nachträge zur älteren deutschen Dichtung* (Stuttgart, 1886) Piper published (p. 201f.) a blessing of travellers from a Munich manuscript in which only female saints including 'Sant Brigida' are invoked (this blessing was also known as St Gertrude's blessing; see my article quoted below in note 28). P. 203f. Piper quotes from a Wolfenbüttel manuscript, 'Sant Oswald dein spies pfleg' and in a note, from a Berlin manuscript, the variant: 'sente galle muse dynis mundys pfleger syn.'

16 Kenney, *op. cit.*, No. 50, III, p. 206. The first Irish reference to this *Vita* was the reprint – from Surius – in Thomas Messingham's *Florilegium* (Paris, 1624).

17 Kenney, *l.c.*, II.

18 Müllenhoff-Scherer, *op. cit.*, No. 12 and II, 78-85. Ratpert also wrote the *Casus Sti Galli*, a history of his monastery, which was continued by Ekkehard IV (Kenney, No. 410f., xxx, p. 595f.), the source for Victor v. Scheffel's *Ekkehard* (1857), the most important modern illustration of the tradition of Irish saints in German literature (see J.M. Clark. *The Abbey of St Gall as a Centre of Literature and Art* [Cambridge 1926], p. 260ff.; Clark did not study the 285 notes which Scheffel appended to his work and which are usually omitted in foreign translations of *Ekkehard*).

19 *Op. cit.*, 217ff.

made in the Carolingian era to introduce Christian spirit into German popular poetry'. Ratpert died towards the end of the ninth century. It seems that his poem repeatedly referred to St Gall's Irish associations. 'Sanctum misit Gallum filium Hiberniae' (I, 3). 'Pergunt – tranant maria' (II, 1); Wetti[20] speaks in the corresponding paragraphs of 'portus Hybernicus' and 'Britannia'. Ratpert also refers to the other Irish companions of St. Columbanus, notably Magnoald and Theodorus.

The *Sächsische Weltchronik,* written about 1225 by Eicke von Repgow, seems to be the only historical work of vernacular German literature prior to the fourteenth century which refers to the Irish missionary activities of the first period. For A.D. 604 Eicke enters: 'Sente Columbanus unde sente Gallus quammen von Schotlande an Dudesch-lant.'[21] This entry is of special interest as the *Sächsische Weltchronik* is the first work of Middle Low German literature which has come down to us. Although Eicke took this entry from one of his Latin sources, we may regard it as characteristic of the tradition of Irish saints in Northern Germany.

Based on Weale's *Analecta Liturgica,*[22] Dom Gougaud[23] has given us a survey of the extent of devotion to Irish saints during the late Middle Ages. The spreading of this devotion to districts which had not even remotely experienced the influence of Irish monastic activities was due to the veneration of relics,[24] to the dedication of churches,[25] especially cathedrals, in honor of Irish saints, or simply to the imitation of the older and richer *Sanctoralia* of the Upper German dioceses. In many districts to which this, what we might call, secondary devotion to Irish saints spread, the reading by the clergy on several occasions during the year in the local *Propria* of the Irish associations of those saints was the principal source of information on Ireland.[26] It is remarkable that even in the lives and offices of saints whose Irish descent was legendary a fair amount

---

20   See note 17.

21   *Mon. Germ., Deutsche Chroniken* (1877), II, 137. A.D. 412 Eike enters: 'do wurden oc de Schotten cristen' (*ibid.,* p. 132; for the sources of this latter entry see Ludwig Bieler, *Codices Particiani* [Dublin 1942], p. 42. and below note 31). – On Eike see Ehrismann, *op. cit., Schluss-band,* p. 437f.

22   Bruges, 1889.

23   *Op. cit.,* especially for St Brigid, p. 30ff.

24   In the *Karlmeinet* (A.D. 1320), we hear of the knights attending Charlemagne's tournament at Aachen taking an oath on the 'gebeine' of St Patrick (Paul Piper, *Höfsche Epik* [Stuttgart, 1884-85], II, 112). On Charlemagne's devotion to St Brigid see John O' Hanlon, *Lives of Irish Saints,* II, 215.

25   See Hrabanus's titulus on St Ignatius's altar in the Cathedral of Fulda (above note 9) and Alcuin's epigram on the saints of Ireland (*ibid*).

26   See note 13. As an illustration of present-day devotion to an Irish Saint who never set foot on the Continent, I may perhaps quote the *Proprium* of the archdiocese of Cologne for St Brigid's feast: 'Beata Brigida circa initium saeculi sexti in Scotia sive in Hibernia christianis orta parentibus ... post mortem per totam Hiberniam, Britanniam, Belgiam et Germaniam evasit celeberrima. Ejus digitus Coloniae in ecclesia Sti Martini asservatur, ubi maxima populi freqentia honoratur' (see O'Hanlon, *l.c.*).

of information on Ireland was embodied.[27] The spreading of the devotion to Irish saints to districts not directly influenced by Irish monastic activities was expressive not so much of the predilection for Irish association which is characteristic of twelfth-century Upper German hagiography, but of the popularity of the cultus of saints in general. Irish associations preserved in the literature attached to this devotion are therefore of special value as they are accidental rather than deliberate.

The predilection for associations with the Island of Saints and the popularity of the cultus of saints in general also were instrumental in continuing the devotion, instituted by the early Irish missionaries, to the great patron saints of Ireland, who had not actually labored on the Continent. I have shown elsewhere[28] that between the seventh and eleventh centuries devotion to Saints Patrick, Brigid and other Irish patrons and to the great Irish missionaries on the Continent was brought into the form of definite historical commemoration, votive dedications of churches and altars and by proper masses and offices for their feasts, a form of liturgical devotion not found in Ireland before the early twelfth century.

The vernacular literature attached to the tradition of devotion to Irish saints was particularly rich during the late Middle Ages, the Counter-Reformation[29] and in the nineteenth century.[30] While this literature has been studied so far as it is of interest to the historian, it has never been investigated from the viewpoint of the development of German interest in, and knowledge of, Ireland. This is even more remarkable when we consider that a side-product of the vernacular tradition of the devotion to Irish saints, namely folklore, has been extensively studied.[31] While the folklore tradition of St Patrick, patron of horses in Austria, or of St Brigid, patron of cattle in the Ardennes and Vosges is certainly expressive of the popularity attained by the devotion to those saints, it naturally neglects their Irish associations.

The literary tradition of St Brigid is of special interest not only with regard to the Europe-wide extent of her cultus during the Middle Ages but also with regard to the ab-

---

27   See below, text for footnotes 94-100.

28   See my articles on 'Irish influences in the folkloristic tradition of St. Gertrude,' in *Béaloides*, (1943), XII, p. 180ff., 'A feast of All the Saints in Ireland,' in SPECULUM, XXI (1946), 49-66, and 'The liturgical tradition of Irish Saints in the order of Canons Regular of the Lateran,' in *Comparative Literature Studies* (1945). See note 29.

29   See my article on St Albert, patron of Cashel, in *Mediaeval Studies*, December 1945. The Bavarian literature quoted in that article deals also with other Irish patron saints in Bavaria (see note 30). For St Ehrhard, see also the literature quoted in the article on him in the *Catholic Encyclopedia*, v, 518.

30   See e.g., Kenney, *op.cit.*, p. 207 (Gall, see above note 18), p. 497 (Fridolin, also Mgr Hogan in *Irish Ecclesiastical Record*, series III, XIV, [1893], p. 193ff.), p. 511 (Wendelin; Marinus and Anianus), p. 512 (Kilian, also Mgr Hogan, *op. cit.*, XI [1890], p. 395, p. 519 (Pirmin, see below note 102), and pp. 616 and 787 (Marianus).

31   See Gougard, *op. cit.*, and the various articles on Irish saints in *Handwörterbuch des deutschen Aberglaubens*, also my article on 'The liturgical and artistic tradition of Irish Saints in Central Europe,' *Irish Ecclesiastical Record*, VI, lxi (1945), 172f.

sence of later mythological influences as in the cases of St Patrick and St Brendan. St Brigid's feast was more widely observed than St Patrick's, as the latter was overshadowed on the Continent by the feast, occurring at the same date, of St Gertrude of Nivelles.[32] In the later Middle Ages St Brigid's feast was superseded by that of St Ignatius the martyr, which was universally prescribed in 1644. The Sermons of Hermann of Fritzlar foreshadow this process. On 'Sente Briden tac' Hermann says:[33] 'Uf unser vrowen âbent lichwîche sô begât man zweier heiligen tac sente Brîden und sante Ignacius. Dise juncvrowe was von Schottenlande und was rîche von gute und edel von geslechte.'

At the same time the earliest German life of St Brigid was entered into the Southern German *Buch der Märtyrer*. This versified Life 'von sand Breide' consists of 500 verses and begins

'Als ich an den puechen las
von schotten lande waz
ein maget Brigide geporen.'[34]

The earliest work of vernacular German literature to deal exclusively with a definite Irish subject is the Alemanic poem of St Patricius written about 1160.[35] The fragments which have come down to us in a thirteenth-century codex of rather bad condition relates the rising of King Echu from the dead and his account of what he has seen of the punishment of the wicked and the bliss of the saints.[36] This story is found in the *Vita Tripartita*[37] and in the *Vita Tertia*[38] of St Patrick. Colgan's copy of the latter was made from a manuscript which Stephen White, S.J., traced for him in the monastery of Biburg in Bavaria.[39]

Dealing with this fragment, Ehrisman[40] expressed some surprise that it did not also contain the story of St Patrick's Purgatory. However, the earliest record we have of the visit which the Knight Owen paid to the cave of Loch Derg dates from about 1190.[41] It

---

32   See above notes 15b and 28.

33   Pfeiffer, *op. cit.* (note 11 above), 76f.

34   Zingerle in *Wiener Sitzungsberichte*, 105 (1883), 70-82.

35   Ehrismann, *op. cit.*, II, 1, 51; Hammerich, *op. cit.*, p. 58f.

36   A little noticed parallel to his story, a still earlier Continental reflection of Irish vision-literature, is found in the *Vita Sti Livini* (Kenney, *op. cit.*, No. 311): *Patrologia Latina*, 87, 333 A. See note 83 below.

37   2068ff. (*saec.* X), Stokes ed. (1887) p. 178ff., Kenney, *op. cit.*, No. 135. The fifteenth century *Austrian Chronicle* (I, fol. 167a., *Deutsche Chroniken* [1909], VI) says that Celestinus 'sant sand Patricium (*Ms. F Patricum*), sande Marteins swester suon, gen Yberniam, der daz lant zu dem christentumb do bechert.' The reference to St Patrick's being a nephew of St Martin is proper to the *Vita Tripartita*.

38   III, 66 (*saec.* IX). Kenney, *op. cit.*, No. 134. Piper, Die *geistliche Dichtung* (Stuttgart 1884-1889), I, 13, assumes that the source for the German Patricius was Jocelin!

39   Reeves, 'Memoir of Stephen White' in *Proc. Royal Irish Academy* (1861), VIII, 29-38.

40   *Op. cit.*, p. 162.

41   Kenney, *op. cit.*, No. 146, p. 354ff.: 'The belief and the practice has made their appearance before 1170.'

is possible that the tradition that David Scotius wrote a work *De Purgatorio Patricii* is correct and that the manuscript existed, and perhaps still exists, at Würzburg, where David was in charge of the cathedral school during the early twelfth century.[42] This would be the first record of the tradition of St Patrick's purgatory. The book written by Henry of Saltrey on Owen's descent was translated into German 'nur in ganz geringem Umfang'[43], and among the later mediaeval pilgrims who placed on record their experiences at Loch Derg, we have no German.[44] The earliest original work written by a German on this subject is Burchard of Horneck's *Carmen de Purgatorio divi Patricii* (Memmingen,[45] 1496).

---

42   Kenney, p. 355, also No. 448; Seymour, *St Patrick's Purgatory* (Dundalk 1918), p. 15.

43   Hammerich in his review of Max Voigt's *Beiträge zur Geschichte der Visionenliteratur im Mittelalter* (Leipzig 1924) in *Zeitschrift für deutsche Philologie*, LIII (1928), p. 26 Ed. Mall, however, pointed to the curious fact that 'ein bemerkenswert gut erhaltener Repräsentant des Urtextes' (of Henry of Saltrey's work) befindet sich in Bamberg' (*Romanische Forschungen*, VI [1891], 141). The chief source of mediaeval German knowledge of St. Patrick's Purgatory were the *Visiones Georgii*, i.e., the account given in 1353 by Georg Crissaphan, a Hungarian, of his descent. The manuscripts on which Hammerich's edition (Copenhagen, 1930) is based, are all from Bavarian or Austrian monasteries. There exist two German translations of the *Visiones Georgii*, one in Rome (Bernadus Montfaucon, *Bibliotheca Bibliothecarum Manuscriptorum nova* [Paris 1739], I, 16b, no. 122), one in Vienna (Denis, *Codices manuscripti theologici Bibliothecae Palatin. Vindel. Lat.*, I [Vienna, 1794], II, 2441-50: this work was not available to me). See my 'Cataldus Rachau', *Mediaeval Studies*, VII (1946), 243.

R. Verdeyen and J. Endepols, *Tondalus' visioen en St Patricii vagevuur* (The Hague, 1914), I, 215, say that the only German translation of *Purgatorium Sti Patricii* which has come down to us, is the fourteenth-century Cologne version to which they refer. However, *Legenda Aurea* (Bieler, *op. cit.*, 42) is found in the fourteenth century *Passionale* of the Teutonic Order (Piper, *op. cit.*, II, 113; Ehrismann, *op. cit.*, II, 1, 162, note 3 and Schlussband, 379f; there also is a reference to the fourteenth-century translation of the whole *Legenda Aurea*, including the section on St Patrick [*ibid.*, 390]).

For the later tradition of St. Patrick's Purgatory in German literature, the *Volksbuch Fortunatus* (Augsburg, 1509; Ehrismann, *op. cit.*, 518) was of greatest importance (see the list of German versions given in Kosch's *Deutsches Literatur-Lexikon* [1930], 474). Thomas Carve's *Reysbüchlein* (Mainz, 1640), the first book by an Irishman ever printed in German, contains a short reference to Loch Derg. For modern German literature on St. Patrick's Purgatory see Shane Leslie, *St Patrick's Purgatory* (London, 1932), p. 204.

44   Lists of mediaeval pilgrims: Leslie, *op. cit.*, p. xxi, Seymour, *op. cit.*, 21f., Verdeyen, *op. cit.*, 257-275 and 307, Grosjean in *Analecta Bollandiana*, XXVII (1908), 36ff. Two accounts of St Patrick's Purgatory printed about 1480 at Augsburg were published by Prof. Gilbert Waterhouse in *Modern Language Review* (1923), XVIII, 317f., and (1934), XXIX, 74f. The first of these two accounts begins with a summary of St Patrick's apostolate who 'in daz land ybernia den cristenlichen gelauben zu bredigen un an zeheben geschickt ward ... von der großen frewd der säligen ward dann das gancz land ybernia zu cristenlichem glauben bekert.' Both accounts conclude with a reference to a German Carthusian; the first account speaks of one who failed to obtain his superiors' permission to go to Loch Derg, the second one who once met a monk of St Bernard's Order who had been there (not necessarily 'a German pilgrim,' as Leslie [*op. cit.*, 42] assumed).

45   The Irish community under St. James's Ratisbon has a house at Memmingen (Kenney, *op. cit.*, 606).

The closing of the cave of Loch Derg by the ecclesiastical authorities in 1497 was due to an unfavorable report which a monk from Eymstadt in Holland had sent to the Pope.[46] A still earlier criticism, hitherto never noticed, is found in an account written about 1480 by Brother Felix, a Dominican from Ulm, on his pilgrimage to the Holy Land. On the authority of Heinrich von Hessen or von Langstein[47] who died at Vienna in 1397, Felix states that 'the horrible sights to which the visitors are submitted in St Patrick's Purgatory, are brought about by natural means rather than by Divine intervention'.[48] Heinrich von Langstein, Felix says, quotes as his authority one Nicholas Ore, 'an extremely learned doctor of natural science'. Thus Continental distrust of the tradition of St Patrick's Purgatory seems to have started in the middle of the fourteenth century. Still, the Normans had succeeded in their attempt to establish, by means of the ancient hagiographical tradition, their new legend of Ireland on the Continent. 'St Patrick's Purgatory did not become famous till the Anglo-Normans added it to their Irish heritage. It was the conquering knight who descended into the cave and their ranks who blazed its fame to Europe. Through Giraldus and Henry of Saltrey, the Purgatory entered literature, and daring visitors began to find their way from all over Europe. During the Middle Ages Loch Derg was far from being a National Pilgrimage. The entrants were foreigners.'[49]

Like the *Purgatorium Sancti Patricii*, the *Navigatio Sancti Brendani* was spread through Europe by Norman influence. Yet the fundamental difference between those two works is that the latter is originally altogether Irish,[50] though the composition of this *immram* in the tenth century may be ascribed to the increase brought about by the Danes in Irish interest in seafarers' stories. In Germany the spreading of the *Navigatio* and of the devotion to St Brendan was due to the combined influence of the Irish monastic establishments[51] and of the Hanseatic seafarers.[52] An early literary record of

---

46 Leslie, *op. cit.*, 61f., *AA.SS.Boll.*, VIII, 588.

47 *Allgemeine Deutsche Biographie*, XVII, 672f.

48 Palestine Pilgrim Text Society, No. 20 (1893), I, 589f. Br. Felix also refers to the tradition that St Mary Magdelen was in Ireland.

49 Leslie, *op. cit.*, XVII, and John Ryan, S.J., in *Studies*, XXI (1932), 441f.

50 See above, note 5, Ehrismann, *op. cit.*, II, 1, 53. Also W. Stammler, *Deutsche Literatur des Mittelalters Verfasserlexikon* (Berlin, 1933), I, 273ff.

51 See the often quoted lines from the *Carmen Satiricum* by Nicolaus de Bibera (*ca.* 1300):
'Sunt et ibi (in Erfurt) Scoti
qui cum fuerint bene poti
Sanctum Brendanum
proclamant esse decanum
in grege sanctorum
vel quod deus ipse deorum
Brendanus frater
sit et ejus Brigida mater ...'
(Carl Schröder, *St Brandan* (Erlangen, 1871), IV and Gougard, *op. cit.*, Appendix, III).

52 Gougard, *op. cit.*, 9ff., and 193, and Carl Steinweg, *Die handschriftliche Gestaltung der lateinischen Navigatio Brendani* (Halle, 1891), 7; Eleven Mss in Germany.

298

German devotion to St Brendan is an episode in the *Orendel* (ca 1190), a work in its subject-matter related with the *Navigatio*[53] where Breide gives Orendel a sword in which a relic of St Brendan is embedded.[54]

The oldest manuscript (tenth century), now in the British Museum, of a Latin text of the *Navigatio Brendani* originally belonged to the abbey of St Maximin[55] at Trèves. The first – Middle Frankish – translation of this text and of the French prose version has been preserved only in the Middle German thirteenth century poem, the Middle Netherlandish poem of the same period and the High German prose version of the fourteenth century. In the Latin original there is 'meisterhafte Lokalisierung', but in the German versions little is left of definite Irish associations.[56] While the Middle German poem says that 'Brandân was geboren von Iberne'[57] and the prose-version 'von dem lande Iberniam',[58] one of the early references to the German *Brandanus,* namely the *Rätselspiel,* the first part of the *Wartburgkrieg* (ca 1230)[59] speaks of 'Schottenlant' as Brandan's homecountry. In the poem Brendan prays for a favorable wind to bring him home 'to Yberniam',[60] while in the prose version he resolves to 'keren in Schottenlant'; at his actual return however the prose version speaks again of

---

53 Piper, *Spielmannsdichtung* (Stuttgart 1884-1889), I, 187.

54 See above note 24.

55 Kenney, *op. cit.,* 414, erroneously: 'Maxim'.

56 The woodcuts in the first printed German versions of *Brandanus* still show islands (Wilhelm Meyer, *Die Überlieferung der Brandanslegende* [Göttingen, 1918], I, 83) See C. Selmer, 'The St Brendan Legend in Old German Literature' in *Journal of the American Irish Historical Society,* XII, (1941), 161-169, and 'St Brendan's Legend on the Continent' in *Catholic Historical Review,* XXIV (1943), 173. For later German tradition of Brandanus see Podleiszek (note 58 below) and G. Schirmer, *St Brendanus Legende* (Leipzig, 1888), 68f. One of the earliest German summaries of the hagiographical background of this tradition is found in v. Killinger, *Sagen und Mährchen-Erin,* II (Stuttgart, 1847) 484ff. Johann Engelbrecht, the Pietist, christened his son Brandanus at a time when he translated Arthur Young's *Tour in Ireland* (Leipzig, 1780), first modern book on Ireland in German (*Allgemeine Deutsche Biographie,* VI, 133).

57 V. 13 Schröder, op. cit., 51 = *Anglo-Normal Voyage of St Brendan,* ed. Waters (Oxford, 1928), p. 4, v. 20. Latin text: 'Stagnili regione Mumensium (or Muminensium or Mimensium) ... in insula occidentali Hybernia' (Schröder, 3); Flemish text v. 19: 'een heere was in Yerlant' (*ibid.,* 94). – In the Old Italian version of the *Navigatio Brendani* (ed. Waters, Oxf., 1921, 41), Irish associations were ruthlessly eliminated: 'dela contrada di Eoginistraguile in Venezia fu.'

58 Schröder, p. 163; 'Yberniam' in the 1481 print republished by Podleiszek in *Volksbücher von Weltweisheit und Abenteurerlust* (*Deutsche Literatur,* ed. Kindermann, Leipzig, 1936), p. 37. The very title of Podleiszek's edition illustrates the general character of the later Brandanus-tradition. 'I Tyskland glider Brandan-traditionerne i baggrunden med Reformaitonstidens kritik' (Hamerich, *Munken of Fuglen,* p. 58).

59 Str. 42.; Str. 108; 'Schotenlant'; Ehrismann, *Schlussband,* 79. The different names for Ireland found in mediaeval German literature will be the subject of special study.

60 V. 1093 = Anglo-Norman poem, v, 1819 (ed. Waters, p. 43). Latin version (Schröder, p. 93), 'ad Hiberniam'. Brendan's companions are 'die allerheiligsten münich, die er zuo Yberniam hat' (Podleiszek, p. 37; Schröder, pp. 120 and 164); Flemish poem, v. 1825: 'heim zû Iberne.'

'Ybernia'.[61] The prose version attained to great popularity. In Germany there exist ten manuscripts of the Latin text of the *Navigatio*. Up to 1521 the German prose version was printed thirteen times.[62]

The traditions of both St Patrick and St Brendan are referred to in the *Tundalus*.[63] In the history of Irish-German literary relations this work holds a unique position. While being Irish in its subject-matter, it received its definite literary shape in Germany at the request of Germans. The author used this opportunity to tell Continental readers something of his home-country. His work stands in the tradition of Irish vision-literature, but at the same time shows certain important changes which, owing to Norman influence, had taken place in Irish eschatology.[64] These changes are another aspect of the reform. The *Visio Tundali* is also an important source of our information on the change brought about by the reform in the ecclesiastical organization of Ireland.[65]

The prologue to the Latin prose[66] version of the *Tundalus* states that an Irish monk named Marcus brought to Ratisbon an account which Tnugdal, an Irish knight, had given him of a vision he had had in 1148. At the request of Gisela, abbess of St Paul's convent at Ratisbon,[67] Marcus undertook 'de barbarico (Irish) in Latinum transferre eloquio' this account. Forty years later, Alber, a monk of the Norbertine abbey of Windsberg near Ratisbon, translated Marcus's work into the Bavarian dialect.[68]

Alber's work may be regarded as the first record in German vernacular literature of the lively intercourse between Ratisbon and Ireland which had resulted in the establishment in 1076 of an Irish monastery at Ratisbon.[69] This monastery became in later

---

61 Schröder, p. 192; Volksbuch 'gen Hyberniam in daz cloister' (Podleiszek, p. 37).

62 Podleiszek, p.11; Piper, *Geistliche Dichtung*, II, 14.

63 Kenney, *op. cit.*, no. 619; Ehrismann, II, 1, § 52. One of the manuscripts of the *Visio Tundali* was in Göttweich (Albr. Wagner, *Visio Tnugdali lat. und altdeutsch* [Erlangen, 1882], XI), where John, one of the companions of Muiredach, the founder of the Irish monastery at Ratisbon, became an incluse (Kenney, *op. cit.*, p. 617). For modern German translations see Emil Peters, *Die Vision des Tnugdalus* (Berlin, 1895), p. 10ff.

64 Seymour, 'Studies in the Vision of the Tundal' in *Proc. Royal Irish Academy* (1926), XXXVII, pp. 87-106, and *Irish Visions of the Other World* (London, 1930), pp. 124-167.

65 See note 29 above.

66 Wagner, *op. cit.*, p. 3.

67 According to Alber, Gisela was joined in this request by the nuns Heilke and Otegebe (Wagner, p. 125).

68 Stammler, *op. cit.* (note 50), col. 24f (Hammerich). The architecture of St James's monastery at Ratisbon and of the abbeys of Windsberg and Biburg (where Colgan's manuscript of the *Vita Tertia Sti Patricii* was preserved) was strongly influenced by that of the Abbey of Prüfening, one of the centers of the Hirsau reform in Germany (Dehio, *Handbuch der deutschen Kunstdenkmäler, Süddeutschland* [Berlin, 1934], pp. 70, 438 and 548, and Aubrey Gwynn, S.J., 'Irish Monks and the Cluniac Reform', *Studies*, XXIV [1940], p. 428ff.).

69 See my article on Irish monastic activities in Eastern Europe in *Irish Ecclesiastical Record*, series VI, LXV (1945), p. 394ff. Of the extensive Bavarian literature on this foundation I quote only one of the earliest examples, namely Andreas of Ratisbon, *Chronicon Episcoporum Ratis-*

years the head of a congregation of Irish monasteries with houses in Erfurt, Würzburg, Vienna[70] and various other places in Germany, and also, for a hundred years, one (ministering to the Ratisbon merchants) at Kiev.

About the time when the Irish monastery at Ratisbon was founded, Othlon, a monk of St Emeran, Ratisbon, wrote a life of St Alto, said to have been in the eighth century an Irish missionary in Bavaria,[71] and Paul, at the request of Heilica, abbess of the Niedermünster convent, Ratisbon,[72] wrote a life of St Erhard, in which he described this traditional patron of the city as 'Scoticus'.[73] A hundred years later this Erhard was further Hibernicized by his association with a thitherto unknown saint named Albartus, described as 'archiepiscopus Casselensis', that is Cashel, the then newly created sec-

---

bonensium (A.D. 1328; in Oefeli, *Rerum Boicarum Scriptores*, I [Augsburg, 1763]), I, 34. The extensive historical literature produced by or attached to the Irish monastic congregation under Ratisbon was probably an important source of information not only on Ireland to the Continent but also on the Continent to Ireland.

70 The foundation in 1155 of the 'munster zu den Schotten ze Wienn' by Duke Henry of Austria is recorded in *Österreichische Chronik*, II, 213 (*Deutsche Chroniken*, VI [1909], 92) and in Jansen Enikel's *Weltchronik, Babenbergische Genealogie* and especially the *Fürstenbuch*, v. 962ff. (*ibid*, III [1900], 545 and 616):

> Der herzoc Heinrich
> der stift zu Wienne ein klôster grôz
> daz guot er sêre von im schôz
> und hiez das klôster bouwen sêre
> zwâr in unser vrouwen êre,
> als ez noch hiut ze Wienne stât
> Schotten sagte er dar in drât
> als si noch hiut ze Wienne sint
> dâr gânt man, wîp und kint.

The 'abt von den schotten' is also mentioned in the *Österreichische Reimchronik* (*ibid.*, V [1908], V, 65798 and 65835) and in *Österr. Chronik*, IV, 363 (*l.c.,* p. 174).

> Wie er (Duke Leopold IV) Stîr gewunnen hât,
> daz wil ich iu sagen drât,
> wan ichz ze Wienn geschriben vant:
> ze den Schotten tat mirz der apt bekant,
> dâ laz ichz…,

says the *Fürstenbuch*, v. 187 and 1115 (*l.c.,* 619). This is a reference to the *Continuatio Scotorum* (*Mon. Ger. Hist., Scriptores*, IX, Index).The Fürstenbuch also states that Duke Leopold was buried in the Schotten monastery at Vienna (*ibid.*, pp. 620 and 681) and that in 1232 the grounds of the monastery were the scene of the knighting of 200 men by Duke Frederick (*ibid.*, p. 642), again from the *Continuatio Scotorum*, also in *Österr. Chronik*, III, 236 (*l.c.*, p.106).

71 Kenney, *op. cit.*, no. 320.

72 In his list of abbesses of the Niedermünster in *Metropolis Salisburgensis*, Wigileus Hund (1620, II, 593ff.), lists one 'Hailke, com. plat. a Wittelsbach,' and 'Helica, com. de Kirchperg'. The *Kalendarium Necrologium Inferioris Monasterii Ratisponensis* (J. Böhmer, *Fonte Rerum German*, III, 483f.) enters on September 23 'Eilika Pataviensis abbatissa'.

73 Kenney, *op. cit.*, No. 322, I.

ond metropolitan see in Ireland.[74] The introduction to the *Visio Tundali* also refers to the short period from 1101 to 1152 when Ireland had only two metropolitan sees and, moreover, describes Tundalus as a native of Cashel. We may safely assume that both Marcus[75] and the author of the *Vita Sti Albarti* were Cashel men who were interested in spreading the new fame of their native town in foreign countries. The relationship between these two works becomes most striking in the fact that the *Vita Sti Albarti* makes Erhard 'episcopus Artinachensis' and that also the *Visio Tundali* renders the name of Armagh by 'Artinacha'[76] or 'Artimacha', a spelling which is the more remarkable as Marcus, on his way to Ratisbon, seems to have visited St Bernard at Clairveaux and supplied him with information for his *Vita Sti Malachiae,* on recent changes in the ecclesiastical organization of Ireland; St Bernard, however, spells the name of Armagh in one of the traditional ways 'Ardmacha.'[76b]

Whatever may have been the reasons for the spelling 'Artinacha', it prevented German readers from understanding the reference made in both works to the bi-metrolitan organization of the Irish church in the first half of the twelfth century. In the Bavarian tradition of St Erhard, 'Artinacha' was eventually identified with Ardagh,[77] an interpretation which in 1903 attained official sanction even in Ireland (through the historical lessons then prescribed for the feast of St Albert, who in the eighteenth century was made 'patron of Cashel'). While Marcus said: 'Hec ergo insula civitates habet precipua tringinta quattuor, quarum presules duobus subsunt metropolitanis. Artimacha magna septentrionalium Hybernensium est metropolis, australium autem precellentissima est Caselensis.'[78] Alber[79] translates:

> Hyberne ist ein kreftig lant
> als ichz an dem buoche vant.
> Ez hât groôzer stete vil,

---

74   For detailed references for this whole paragraph see my article on St. Albert, in *Mediaeval Studies*, December, 1945.

75   Esposito in *Studies*, II (1213), 510. Munstermen played a prominent part in the Ratisbon congregation. In 1148, Christian MacCarthy, a Munsterman as his name says, the eighth abbot of St James's, Ratisbon, dies on his second visit to Ireland. The Ratisbon congregation owned for some time a house at Roscarbery, County Cork. (See Seymour, *Proc. Royal Irish Academy*, XXXVII, 89, and Kenney, p. 617.) The personal intercourse between Ratisbon and Ireland was of course an important means of exchanging general information. As late as 1424, by Papal mandate, Dermot O'Glesayn, a Benedictine of St James's, Ratisbon, was admitted at Holy Cross Abbey, Kilkenny (M. Callanan, *The Abbey of the Holy Cross* [Dublin, 1929], p. 35.)

76   *Manuscript E*(rlangen); *T*(reves): 'Artinaca.' In the reference to Cel(e)s(tin)us (see below), the *Visio* speaks of 'Arthmacha,' that is one of the (rarer) spellings for the name Armagh; this spelling have *Mss. E, Mo*(Munich), and *V*(ienna), while *Ms. G*(raz) has 'Artmanacha', *T*(reves), 'Artinacha', and *M* (another Munich Ms.), 'Artianacha.'

76b   Lawlor's edition (N.Y., 1918), p.x.

77   This erroneous identification seems to be derived from the spelling 'Ardmacha' by St Bernard, and 'Ardinacha' in reference to Tundalus in Vincentius Bellovac., *Speculum histor.*, XXVII, 88 A.D., 1149. For the Bavarian pedigree of this error see my article on St Albert, note 76.

78   Wagner, *op. cit.*, p. 6.

79   V. 171 ff.; Wagner, p. 126.

der zal ich iu sagen wil.
Ir sint drîzec unde viere,
michel unde ziere,
der ieglichiu hât ein bistuom,
si achtent nich ûf ûppegen ruom.
Der stete eine vil gewis
heizet cafelensis.

An earlier Hassian translator of the *Visio Tundali,* whose work has come down to us only in fragments, has here.[80]

Ibernen daz selbe eilant
hat vir un drizcik howbet stede,
di alle stent an irme vriden.
Eine stat heizet Archamache,
di stet Ybernen och wol na,
di saget man daz si vil riche si.
Crocagensis stet och do bi.

Alber omits the reference to Armagh, the Hassian translator that to Cashel. Alber shows that he had never heard the name of Casselensis before when he misreads, as in Irish script is easily possible, *'cafelensis'.* The Hassian translator identified perhaps through St Bernard's *Life of St Malachy,*[81] Marcus's 'Artimacha' as 'Archmacha.' He also refers to Cork,[82] the town where, according to Marcus, Tnugdal had his vision.

In spite of all these misunderstandings the German translations of the introduction to Marcus's work are of greatest importance as the earliest references made in vernacular German literature to Irish place-names. These references are made in an account of the ecclesiastical organization of Ireland and an account of a vision. While they thus stand in the tradition of Irish religious literature, the ecclesiastical organization here referred to is the establishment of the diocesan system, which marks the end, under Continental and English influence, of the tribal system of the Celtic church, and the vision here re-lated is the first vision in Irish literature attributed to a layman rather than a saint.[83] In this latter point, so far never noticed, the *Visio Tundali is* closely related with the *Purgatorium Sti Patricii.* In both works, the hero is a knight, and thus these two works stand at the beginning of the great literary tradition of Irish chivalry on the Continent.[84]

---

80 V. 80 FF.; Wagner, p. 115.

81 See note 76b above.

82 The later Low German tradition of the *Visio Tundali,* studied by Verdeyen and Endepols, *op. cit.* II, no longer refers to Cork.

83 For the difference in their eschatological ideas between the Visio Tundali and the earlier visions of Irish saints (Adamnanus, Furseaus, ect.), see Seymour, *op.cit.,* note 64 above. In the *Vita Sti Livini* (note 36 above), it is a lay-person (Livinus's nurse) who has the vision, but under the in-fluence of a saint.

84 I referred in notes 24, 53 and 54 to examples of the interlinking between the hagiographical and the chivalresque tradition. In the thirteenth-century poem *Moritz von Craon* (v. 890), the hero when going to a tournament looks so splendid that the people think St Brendan comes along (Piper, *Spielmannsdichtung,* II, 304). Also *Pfaffe Amîs* (Stricker), v. 372ff. speaks of Brandan (Ehrismann, II, 2, 127ff.).

Another point, through which the *Visio Tundali* is of outstanding significance in Irish-Continental literary relations, is that it supplied the Continent with the most extensive account up to then of the geography and natural conditions of Ireland. Apart from the reference to the ecclesiastical organization of Ireland, this account takes 23 lines in the Hassian version and 32 lines in Alber's. Marcus's account is mainly based on Solinus.[85] Shorter versions of Solinus's account of Ireland, which, via Isidore of Seville,[86] came into Hrabanus's work *De Universo,*[87] were frequently embodied in the introductions of Continental lives of Irish saints, as e.g., Walafrid's *Vita Sti Galli*[88] and Thierry's *Vita Sti Rumoldi* (ca. 1100).[89] Other *Vitae,* such as that of St Fridolin by Balthar[90] and the *Passio II Sti Kiliani,*[91] give in their introductions short geographical information on Ireland taken from other sources. While the study of the development of Continental knowledge of the geography of Ireland is outside the scope of this paper, it should be noted that the introduction to the *Visio Tundali* is still dependent on the tradition of Continental hagiography of Irish saints. In the translations of the *Tundalus* such a description appears for the first time in German vernacular literature, and it was probably from there that it entered into the German *Lucidarius,*[92] later known as *Kleine Cosmographie,* which was reprinted up to 1806.

In the literary tradition of the Tundalus itself, which is mainly Low German,[93] the connection between the geographical-historical introduction and the vision itself was less and less appreciated; eventually the former was completely suppressed. Similarly, it could be shown that in the hagiographical and chivalresque tradition of the later Middle Ages Irish associations became more and more vague; the purely literary interest triumphed.

Perhaps the most interesting result of the separation of information on Ireland from the hagiographical tradition was the superseding of the picture of the Island of Saints by the gloomy picture which Giraldus and his followers gave of the Irish. In his description of 'mea yens in Hibernia', Dicuil[94] omitted Solinus's reference to its being 'inhospita et bellicosa', 'inhumana, ritu incolarum aspero'. Hrabanus also omitted all

---

85   Kenney, *op. cit.,* no. 11.

86   *Ibid,* no. 22.

87   Patrol. Lat., 111, 354.

88   AA.SS. O.Ben. (Mabillon), II (1936), 329.

89   AA.SS. (Boll.), July, II, 615.

90   AA.SS. (Boll), March, I, 433.

91   AA.SS. (Boll.), July, II, 615.

92   Podleiszek, *op.cit.,* 126f. (from the 1527 print); Ehrismann, *Schlußband,* 436f. The *Lucidarius* was compiled about 1190 at the court of Henry the Lion whose wife Mathild, a daughter of King Henry II of England had just died. It is supposed that the writing of *Tristan and Isolde* was suggested to Eilhart von Oberge by the Braunschweig Court (Ehrismann, II, 2, p. 66).

93   See note 82 above.

94   Kenney, *op. cit.,* p. 545ff. Letronne, *Recherches géographiques* (Paris, 1814), p. 170; G. Parthey, *Dicuili liber de mesura orbis terrae* (Berlin, 1870), VIII, 21.

this.[95] Marcus, the author of the *Visio Tundali*, apparently mitigated Solinus's verdict when describing the Irish nation as 'armis crudelis et inclita'.[96] A few years after Marcus, the author of the Life of St Disibod states for the first time in Continental literature that Ireland is known as 'insula sanctorum', 'insula sanctis viris plena',[97] a statement foreshadowed by Marcus's words 'religiosis viris et feminis satis preclara'.[98] The Hassian version turns Marcus's reference to Irish monasticism into a general description of the Irish national character: 'Da sint gude wib un man'; the subsequent 'si hant gude wapen un gewant'[99] is perhaps a recollection of Solinus's 'bellicosa'. Proper to the Hassian version is the statement: 'Di lude sint da harte milde, irs gemudes sint si vro.'[100] Alber, strangely enough, makes no reference whatsoever to the Irish character. In the *Lucidarius*, Giraldus's verdict is summed up in the words: 'Das volck (of Ireland) ist aber ungezogen, unfreintlich und grausam.'[101] At the same time, we can trace in Continental chivalresque literature, the tradition of the Irish coward (e.g., in the Norwegian *Tristan*, XXXVIII). It was not until the middle of the nineteenth century that the tradition of the Island of Saints was restored in Continental vernacular literature (in France by Montalembert, in Germany by Rodenberg).

In his description of Ireland, Marcus – based on the geographical tradition of late antiquity – says that Ireland is 'serpentium, ranarum, bufonum et omnium amimalium venena fercentium ita inscia, ut ejus lignus aut corrigia aut cornu aut pulvis omnia vincere noscentur venena'.[102] In Alber's translation the reference to the absence of snakes and poison is made the last point in the description of Ireland:[103]

> do enist ouch der slange
> ez gescheiden danne
> swaz gewurmes either truoc
> swaz in dem lande ist,

then follow 63 verses, found in no other version of the *Tundalus,* in which the tradition, recorded in the *Vita Tripartita* and the *Vita Tertia*, of St Patrick's crozier

---

95 *Patrol. Lat.* 53, 354.

96 Wagner, p. 6.

97 AA.SS. Boll., July, II, 594; Kenney, no. 318.

98 Wagner, *l.c.*

99 V. 77, Wagner, p. 115.

100 *Ibid.,* v. 62.

101 See note 92 above.

102 Wagner, p. 6. The Hassian version, v. 68 (Wagner, 115) has: 'slangen, credin, spinnen ist da vile.' Wagner offers three theories for this version. Either 'insita' was read for 'inscia' (p. xxvii f. and xli), or this is a reference to Bede's description of Ireland. Or the Hassian translator knew already of Jocelin's tradition of which however he took only the first part, namely the reference to the abundance of vermin in Ireland prior to St. Patrick; this would mean that the Hassian version is later than is usually assumed. In the Life of St. Pirmians (who in later years was said to have Irish association, Kenney no. 322a: *saec.* VIII) a similar tradition is reported from the island of Reichenau.

103 V. 95 ff., Wagner, p. 124.

piercing King Oengus's foot,[104] is connected with the more recent tradition of St Patrick's freeing Ireland from snakes and vermin. Alber makes it quite clear that he simply repeats a tradition which, in contrast to the 'buoch' from which he collected the tradition of Tundalus, is described as oral.

> Nun hoeret wie daz si komen,
> al wir ez hen vernomen.
> dô sante Patrîcîus
> der der Schotten hêrre ist
> vuor ze alrêrist
> in daz lent Hybernîam ...[105]

Regarding the tradition of St Patrick's expelling vermin from Ireland, it has been traditionally assumed that Anglo-Norman writers such as Jocelin and Giraldus[106] were the first to report it. However, as Dr Bieler[107] has recently shown, this tradition occurs already in the earlier *Vita Cottoniana,* where we read at the end of the fragment: 'Postremo (in monte illo) edito, ut venenata reptilia penitus removeret, nec in partibus Hybernicis aliquod veneni seminarium reliqueret, secundum exemplum Domini ...' The connection of the tradition of King Oengus with that of the expulsion of vermin is Alber's own work and is found in no other source. 'Die Verschmelzung,' Wagner says,[108] 'ist gut gemacht, und Alber fühlt sich teilweise (durch sie) zu weiterer Ausführung angeregt: St Patrick und der verwundete König werden redend eingeführt, und die Situation ist anschaulich und lebendig geschildert.'

In Marcus's text the description of Ireland concludes with a reference to the date when the vision took place. It was in the second year of Conrad's being Roman king, under Pope Eugene II (error for III), in the same year Malachy, bishop of Down, died in Clairvaux, and Nehemias, bishop of Cloyne, died.[109] While in both the Hassian version and in Alber's translation this passage was omitted, it was preserved in the later Low German versions.[110] The co-ordination made by Marcus between events of Continental history and events of Irish church history is interesting, but just about that time frequently found in literary works.[111]

Malachy, one of the few Irish saints properly canonized, is mentioned once more towards the end of the vision. At the end of his journey the soul of Tundalus is addressed

---

104 This is one of the four legends of St Patrick preserved also in the *Legenda Aurea* (see note 43 above). *Vita Tripartita,* 2397 ff. (Stokes, 196); *Vita Tertia,* c. 60 (see notes 37 and 38 above) in both instances I am indebted to my friend Dr Bieler for his kind assistance.

105 V. 107 FF., Wagner, *l.c.*

106 Wagner, p. xliii, refers to AA. SS., March, II, 547 A.

107 Anecdotum Patricianum, in *Miscellany of historical and linguistic studies in honour of Bro. Michael O'Cleirigh* (Dublin, 1944), p. 229.

108 Wagner, lv.

109 *Ibid.,* p. 5.

110 See note 82 above.

111 I shall deal with this point in a special study.

(according to Marcus) by a saint Ruadanus,[112] according to Alber[113] (the Hassian version of this passage is lost) 'ein heiliger hêrre Sante Prandânus.' Then Tundalus 'sach sent Patrîctîum der die Schotten bekêrte und sî den kristentuom lêrte and ander bischove mainic schar ... Er erkande darunter viere die in Hyberne bî sîner zît heten verwandelt den lîp' (that is, had died). Marcus[114] gives the names of all the four of them: 'Celestinus Arthmachanus archiepiscopus (St Celsus), Malachias episcopus (Manuscript T(rier): *archiepiscopus)* qui (ei) successit in archiepiscopatu ... Christianus episcopus Lugdunensis and Nemias Cluanensis'. Of these four names Alber preserves only that of 'Sent Marachyas'.

Thus the *Visio Tundali* leads the hagiographical tradition of Ireland right up to the chief figure of the Reform. That Alber describes 'Marachyas' as 'Saint' shows how quickly – through his *Vita* written by St Bernard (as Marcus had pointed out in the introduction) – the fame of the great Reform Legate to Ireland had spread on the Continent. The formal canonization of Malachias marked the end of the rather loose conception of the term 'Saint' in Irish Church history. Henceforth 'the Island of Saints' was merely a literary tradition.[115]

At the same time, we encounter in Continental vernacular literatures the first indications of a secular view of Ireland. The tradition of Ireland as the Island of Saints became a mere glamour attached to the picture of that fabulous wonderland on the Western outskirts of the inhabited world. This is the picture of Ireland underlying the chivalresque tradition, in which the hagiographical aspect becomes co-ordinated with the newly discovered (pagan) mythological aspect. While in the hagiographical tradition of Ireland in German vernacular literature there had been a steady increase in comprehensiveness from the ninth to the early thirteenth century, the new chivalresque tradition appears almost at its very beginning (in Gottfried's *Tristan* and in *Kudrun*)[116] in its fullest development rapidly declining to a stereotyped pattern gradually losing in consistency and reality.[117]

(Quelle: Speculum 22, 358-374, 1947)

112　Wagner, p. 53.

113　V. 2035, Wagner, p. 181.

114　Wagner, XXV.

115　Even for the more sophisticated Irishman the tradition of St. Brendan has become completely secularized and historical: 'When Drake was winning seas for England / We sailed in puddles of the past / Pursuing the ghost of Brendan's mast' (Partick Kavanagh, 'Memory of Brother Michael O' Clery' [see above note 107] in *Poems from Ireland* [Dublin, 1944], p. 44).

116　See note 4 above.

117　This article does not presume to be an exhaustive study of the subject-matter. It rather aims at pointing to a line of investigation which might be found sufficiently interesting to be followed up by more detailed studies and to be extended especially with regard to English-German literary relations. That I can hardly claim more than to have given the bare outlines, is mainly due to the fact that for the time being my bibliographical sources are restricted. However, I wish to place on record my gratitude towards the National Library of Ireland and the Library of Trinity College, Dublin, for the facilities they have given me.

Ireland's Place in the Chivalresque Literature of Mediaeval Germany
[Read 14th November, 1949. Published 5th July, 1950]

In a previous paper[1], I have shown that, so far as Germany is concerned, the study of early references to Irish Saints in the vernacular literature may be described as the first instalment of the study of Ireland's place in that literature in general, and that, reaching its climax about the middle of the 12th century, this hagiographical tradition began to give way to a secular view.

So far as I am aware, the first explicit reference to Ireland in the vernacular literature of Germany is found in the *Rolandslied,* written about 1131 by Konrad, where, addressing his sword before destroying it in Ronceval, Roland speaks of the countries which he had conquered with it for his king namely "Provincia, Proteganea, Sorbîten, Beire, Sahsen, Alemannia, Ungeren, Pritaniâ, Pôlân, Franken, Friesen, Scotten unt Irlant[2] ... Engellant ... unde anderiu vile manigire rîche". I shall not treat in this paper of either the history of the connotation of the word *Scotia* and its vernacular equivalents (at that time beginning to be restricted to Scotland) or the history of the word *Irland* (first mentioned, in a Latin context, by Adam von Bremen)[3]. Dependent upon the *Rolandslied,* the *Karlmeinet*[4] had a similar list of countries ruled by Charlemagne, and there is a striking similarity between these lists and that of countries subject to Arthur, e.g. in *Die Krone* by Ulrich von dem Türlin (about 1220)[5], where between "Britanje, Gal, Normandie" and "Wales, Engelland", we have a reference to "Scoti, Irland" and other countries as far as the great sea.[6]

The earliest Irish association found in any work of German vernacular literature, namely the reference to *chrihshha sancti kilîânes* in a description of the Würzburg March,[7] is almost contemporary with the earliest reference to Germany in any work of

---

1 "Irish Saints in early German literature", *Speculum* xxii (1947) 358 to 374; hence forth abbreviated SP.

2 6853 ff, ed. Bartsch (Leipzig 1874), in contrast to the identification of "schotten und yberne" in the Dresden und Heidelberg mss. of Eilhart's *Tristan* (see note 18), not to speak of the distinction between "Yberne" and "Irlant" in *Der gute Gerhart* by Rudolf von Ems (Piper, *Höfische Epik* (Stuttgart 1874) ii, 554). Like Eilhart, Gottfried used the word "Iberne" only in one instance (see note 60). *Chanson de Roland* clxxii (2332) has: "Je l'en cunquis Escoce, Guales, Islande" (L. Gautier (Tours 1872) ii, 184; p. 363 G. said he did not know why F. Michel had suggested "Zelande". J. Bedier (Paris 1922) 176 thought that one should read: "Vales islande"). The subsequent reference to "Engleterre" seems to make it clear that the German version is correct.

3 See Emerson's note on "Iraland" in *Modern Language Review* xi (1916) 458f.; C.A. Christensen's ed. (Copenh. 1948), 125.

4 SP note 24.

5 v. 346; Piper, op. cit. 257.

6 I do not concern myself with general references to the parts of the world "westar ubar wentilseo" (*Hildebrandslied*), but it is remarkable that also the *Visio Tundali* and *Lucidarius* refer to this tradition.

7 SP p. 360.

Irish literature, namely the entry relating to St. Killian's martyrdom at Würzburg in the *Martyrology of Tallaght*[8]. Similarly, with regard to the first explicit reference to Ireland in a work of vernacular German literature, an Irish parallel can be produced. There exists a middle-Irish translation (sec. xiv/xv) from the Latin (sec. xi/xii) of the *Chanson de Roland*, entitled *Gabhaltais Shearluis Mhoir*[9], which in chapter iii omits the list of *urbes et majores villae*, but in chapter ix many of the names of countries and kings ruled by Charles, but in chapter i says that he ruled "i Saxa ocus in Fhrainge ocus in Almain ocus in Baignine" (Bavaria ?)[10] and later speaks of "Frisia"; this is the most elaborate enumeration of parts of Germany found in any work of mediaeval Irish literature.

Earlier in the description of the battle of Ronceval, the German *Rolandslied* related the slaying, by Samsôn, of "Scarpulôn then kunine von then Iren";[11] a hundred and fifty years later, Stricker disfigured these words to "den künee von Vantamin", an interesting, illustration of the decay, setting in about the year 1250, of the Irish tradition in Continental literature in general.[12]

About 1150, Marcus from Cork wrote at Ratisbon the Latin account of the visions of his countrymen Tnugdal; this account, subsequently translated into the Hessian and later the Bavarian dialect, was, in German literature, the earliest first-hand description of contemporary Ireland.[13] In 1160, the Alemannic poem of *Patricius* was the earliest work of vernacular German literature to deal exclusively with an Irish subject.[14] During those years an anonymous writer produced the epic of *König Rother,* which contains a curious reference to the reputation of pre-Norman Ireland for her secular civilisation. Describing the banquet given in Rother's honour at the court of Constantine, this poem says, that Rother was seated on "gestôle daz verre was gevôret hei vor / von Irlande iz trôgin elphande / wîlen in den gebeine / darinne lac gôt gesteine / swê diuster die nach was / si lîechte alsô der tae".[15] Rendering the description, given in Marcus's

---

8   Bradshaw Soc. lxviii, 54.

9   Ed. Dr. Douglas Hyde in Early Irish Text Society xix (1917) 85ff.

10 See above in the German version "Beire".

11 Gottfried and most other writers of the time describe the Irish as "Irlandaere"; the word "Iren" was re-introduced by Küttner's *Briefe über Irland* (Leipzig 1785), the first modern travel-book in German literature to deal exclusively with Ireland. Lately, similar to the work "Schottländer", the word "Irländer" has become archaic. See also note 34.

12 Bartsch, ed. cit. 198 note. However, in Stricker's epic on Charlemagne (ed. Bartsch, Quedlinburg 1857), we have v. 350 in an enumeration of the various parts of Europe "über alle schotesch erden wirstu herre genant. sam tuostu über Irlant" (ms D: "eierlant"), and v. 8179 addressing his sword, Roland says: "swaz dannen ist unz zIrlant, daz twanc ich mit mîner hant". For Ireland-Eierland see below note 103.

13 SP 369 and my paper on "St. Albert, patron of Cashel" in *Mediaeval Studies* vii (1945) 28ff.

14 SP 364, see C. Kraus, *Deutsche Gedichte des 12. Jahrhunderts* (Halle 1894); in the few fragments that have been preserved there is no explicit reference to Ireland.

15 Rückert, *Deutsche Dichtung des Mittelalters* (Leipzig 1872) 90, v. 1607; this seems to be a reflection of the Hanseatic influence in the Rother tradition (Ehrismann, *Geschichte der deutschen*

Visio Tundali, of Cormac's castle as "structura ex auro et argento et ex omnibus lapidum pretiosorum generibus," Alber, the Bavarian translator, spoke of "ein hus von silber und von golde und von edelen gesteine" and in a later passage he referred to "helfenbein".[16]

Alber's translation originated about the year 1190. At the same time, at the Braunschweig Court, Mathild, a daughter of Henry II of England, probably induced Eilhart von Oberge to write his *Tristan und Isolt,* which was based on the *Estoire del Tristan et d'Iseut* by Robert of Rheims, known as il Kievres. The Tristan tradition is the most impressive illustration of the fact that the influence of Celtic "Motive" in 12th century Continental literature was naturally combined with an influx of concrete information of the home-countries of those "Motive". In the fragments of Eilhart's original poem, no place-names are mentioned.[17] In the "Bearbeitung", however, we hear in v. 59 of a king "gewaldig zû Iberne"; the Dresden and Heidelberg manuscripts have in this instance "ze schotten und yberne", whereas the earliest prints omitted the word "Iberne",[18] which by that time had become obsolete. In all other instances in Eilhart, the country of Isolt is referred to as *Irlant.* To obtain a complete picture of the tradition and development of the Irish background of the Tristan-tradition, it appears to be desirable to extend our study from its German versions (Eilhart, Gottfried and Heinrich v. Freiberg) to the French prose novel[19] the Norwegian *Tristramsaga,*[20] the

Literatur (Munich 1922 ff), ii, 1,293ff). The name of Lupoldus, the suitor, confirms the connection between *Rother* and *Fortunaus*; in the latter work (see the end of the present paper) this is the name of the Irish servant.

16   A. Wagner, *Visio Tnugdali* (Erlangen 1882) 42f. Anthonie Donker's poems *Tondalus visione* (The Hague 1948) are the latest illustration of the evaporation of the historico-geographical associations outlined in SP 369f.

17   On the difference between *Motivforschung* and *Realienforschung*, as visualized by the series *Stoff- und Motivgeschichte der deutschen Literatur*, in which W. Golther's study on *Tristan und Isolde* appeared (Berlin 1929), see SP 358. The word "motive-grinder", used by Carlyle in *Sartor Resartus*, may be applied to many a student of the Irish background of the Tristan-tradition. It has been left to popular studies such as E. Schultze in *Irische Blätter* ii (1918) 565f. and J. M. Flood, *Dublin in Irish Legend* (Dublin 1919) to point to the striking historico-geographical information on Ireland contained in that tradition. See also H. Küppers, *Bibliographie zur Tristansage* (Jena 1941).

18   Ed. F. Lichtenstein in "Quellen und Forschungen zur Sprach- und Kulturgeschichte der germanischen Völker" xiv (1977) 29; see above note 2.

19   J. Bédier, *Roman de Tristan* ii (1905); English translations by Belloc (illustrated by E. Engels, London 1913) and F. Simmonds (illustr. by M. Lalau, London 1910), Irish translation (Dublin 1934 and 1935), German translation by Binding (1917). The French prose novel (which knows of but one journey of Tristan to Ireland) was the basis for *La Tavola Rotonda* and Malory's books viii and ix (E. Vinaver, *Le Roman de Tristan dans L'Oeuvre de Thomas Malory* (Paris 1925) and George H. Stewart "English geography in Malory's *Morte d'Arthur*" in *Modern Lang. Rev.* xxx (1935) 204ff).

20   Ed. E. Kölbing (Heilbronn 1878); modern English version by Loomis (1923).

North-English poem *Sir Tristrem*[21] and the Oxford MS of *Folie Tristan.*[22] Together with Béroul[23] and the Berne MS of *Folie Tristan*, Eilhart and the French prose novel represent the *Spielmannsepos*, whereas the *höfische Epos*, as established by Thomas[24] ("von Britanje", who this story "in britûnsche buochen las"), is represented by Gottfried, the *Tristramsage, Sir Tristrem* and the Oxford MS of *Folie Tristan*. Considering their breadth and variety, the Irish associations may be expected to throw some new light on the much discussed problems of the development of the Tristan-tradition and its sources.

In most of the early sources, Eilhart's king of *Iberne* (or *Schotten*) is called Gorman (Gottfried: *Gûrmûn*); the French prose novel however calls him Angyn (v. 338), whence Malory's *Anguish*. Gottfried said this king was of African[25] birth and, by permission of the Romans, became king of whatever lands he conquered. Travelling with a strong army over land and sea, he eventually came "zer Irlande", a tradition which, as Bédier stated, is also found in Wace's *Geste as Bretons*:

> Rois venquant, terres conquerant,
> En Irlande vint salvement.
> La terre pris delivrement,
> D'Irlande se fist roi clamer.[26]

This tradition seems to be a corruption of the picture of early Irish history presented by the various Synchronisms (from the 8th century)[27] and in a more elaborate form in *Lebor Gabala* or the *Book of Invasions.*[28] An earlier representative of a Continental version of this tradition is found in the historical introduction to the 11th century *Vita Sti. Kadroe.*[29] The important idea behind those synchronisms is of course not to supply an absolute chronology, but to connect Irish history with Biblical and classical

---

21 Ed. E. Kölbing (1882), dedicated to Sir Walter Scott who had edited this work in 1804, and by McNeill (1886).

22 Ed. J. Bédier (Paris 1907); the Berne Ms of this work contains no references to Ireland.

23 Ed. E. Muret (Paris 1903) and A. Ewert (Oxford 1939).

24 The latest edition by A. Closs (1944) omitted practically all the passages of interest to us; that by E. H. Zeydel (Princeton 1948) was not accessible to me. On Thomas's associations with the English court see Loomis in *Mod. Lang. Rev.* xvii (1922) 24.

25 Heinrich von Freiberg (Bechstein's ed., Leipzig 1877, 82) described Morolt as *Affricân*, probably on account of his name. In *Kudrun, Môrlant*, Siegfried's realm, was "vom Dichter als ein wirkliches Land der Mohren betrachtet, aber ursprünglich eine der Nordsee naheliegende Gegend" (Bartsch's ed., Leipzig 1880, 355). The expeditions of the Gaels were said to have extended as far as Africa (Keating's *History of Ireland*, Early Irish Text Soc. (1902) ii, 397).

26 Bédier, *Roman*, i, 74.

27 McNeill, *Proc. R. Irish Academy* xxviii (1910) 123.

28 Ed. Macalister (Dublin 1944).

29 J. Kenney, *The sources for the early history of Ireland* (N.Y. 1929), no. 428. Only Colgan printed the historical introductions (*Acta Sanctorum Hiberniae*, Louvain 1647, now available in a photostatic reprint, 494ff).

history. The tendency to synchronise events of Irish history with the classical period of the Roman Empire is also noticeable in the tradition of St. Cataldus, one of the most curious productions of 12th century Irish-Continental hagiography.[30] The conception of ideal rather than real synchronism (typical of the Irish conception of historical time in general) is further illustrated by the fact that according to Wace (and Malory) Gorman (and Tristan) were contemporaries of King Arthur, while in the early Tristan tradition they are later.

While the *Tristramsaga* (xxvi) says that "Írir tóku um thann tíma skat af Englandi", which thus became "skattgilt Írlandi", Gottfried states (v. 5880 f) that "Irlande" received "zins von beiden landen, von Kurnewal und Engelant". The French prose novel says that it was "au temps du roy Thonosor d'Irlande" (322) that this tribute was established.

The Saga said that before paying that instalment of the tribute which was due in human lives, the king of England had to go "á Irlandi" to receive new laws. According to Gottfried, the king of England had to go to Rome for this purpose, another instance expressive of Thomas's (and Gottfried's) tendency to reconcile the Tristan-tradition with the conception of early British history established by Wace and Gaufrei of Monmouth. For the same reason, Thomas had altered the ancient tradition according to which the whole tribute was levied in human lives.[31]

This tribute in human lives is called for by Mor(h)olt "ein hêre in Irlant" (Eilhart v. 351), "frere a la royne d'Irlande" (Prose novel 322 ff), "sendimann Írlands konungs" (*Saga* xxvi[32]). The accounts of Tristan's negotiations with Morholt in particular in Gottfried and *Sir Tristrem* abound with references to Ireland, her king and her people.[33] In the Berne Ms of *Folie Tristan* the combat "in Cornuaille" with Mohort (I shall not consider in this paper the various spellings of proper-names) is referred to, but Ireland is not mentioned.

At the point of death, Morholt asks his people (*Saga* xxvii: *Írir*) to take his body "til Írlandes". "Do hûben sie (Gottfried 7113: "die klagende Irlandaere";[34] *Saga* xxviii:

---

30   See my paper on "Cataldvs Rachav" in *Mediaeval Studies* viii (1946) 224ff.

31   Bédier, *op. cit.*, 76.

32   xxvii: "sendimadhr Ira konungs"; see above note 3.

33   Sir Tristram 935, 969 and Gottfried 5867ff. Morolt was also referred to in Wolfram's Parveval i 1445; ii 263 and 705 expressly described "von Yrlant", probably for the sake of the rhyme, as otherwise Morolt's associations with Ireland were common knowledge e.g., in *Younger Titurel* (Piper, *Spielmannsdichtung*, ii, 499 ff, 502 and 509) and in *Rabenschlacht* (v. 806: "von Eierland"; see above note 12). On an old Norwegian parallel (a hero from Bretland fighting an Irish prince and his champion, named Malkus of Sweden) see H. M. Smyser and F. P. Magoun, *Survivals in Old Norwegian of mediaeval English, French and German literature* (Baltimore 1941).

Ireland is referred to also in Parceval ix, 662 ff where we hear that Kyôt read in Latin books "des landes chrônicâ ze Britâne unte anderswâ, ze Franrîche und in Îrlant".

34   Morolt's followers were described by *Sir Tristram* (1092) as "folk of Yrlond", by the French prose novel (322 f) as "ceulx d'Irlande", and by Gottfried as "die leiden gesten von Îrlant".

Írir) sich schîre dan vedir heim zu lande" (Eilhart 942; "til Írlands" *Saga* l.c.).[35] Only the *Saga* said that Morholt's body arrived at *Dyflinnarborgar*, Ireland's finest harbour;[36] Gottfried (7147) simply said that the Irish "ze lande kamen".[37]

According to Gottfried, Morholt told Tristan that wounds inflicted by his sword could only be cured by "Isôt die künegîn von Irlande" (6951). In the earlier tradition, Morholt did not tell Tristan where he could obtain healing and Tristan set out in a rudderless boat which "li veng chaçat en Irlandt" (*Folie Tristan* Oxf. 345ff).[38] Rejecting this tradition, Thomas made Tristan aim his journey at Ireland (Gottfried 7395, 8605 and 8622). While the *Saga* simply says that Tristan came "at Irlandi" (xxx), Gottfried and *Sir Tristrem* state that he landed at Dublin. As this is the earliest mention made in Continental vernacular literature of the capital of Ireland, this passage should be discussed in greater detail. *Sir Tristrem* (1165) says that Tristan landed "in Deuelin ... an hauen in Irland". Gottfried has the following story:

> Und alz das schif begunde
> Irlande also genaen
> daz si daz land wol sahen,
> Tristan den stiurmeister bat,
> daz er sich gein der houbtestat,
> ze Develîne wante (7398).[39]

This, the first reference made in any work of literature to Dublin being the capital of Ireland, is the more curious as it implies that it was a fact well known to *foreigners* that Dublin was the capital.[40] According to Gottfried, Tristan's first journey not only aimed at Ireland in general but at Dublin in particular, where, it must be assumed, the

---

Compare the reference in *Kudrun* (508, 4) to "die von Irrîche" as "dise werden geste" (Martin's note in his ed., p. 119).

35 French prose novel (327): "Yrlande".

36 xxix; Bédier, *op. cit.* 30: "au beau port de Duveline".

37 The same expression is used, probably quite naturally in the description of Brandanus's homecoming, in both the German poem and the prose novel (SP 367).

38 Eilhart 1472ff, Gottfried 8605ff and 11215. See Schoepperle, *Tristan and Isold* (1913), 370 and 389f. Also St. Maughold, the Irish-born patron of the Isle of Man, went there — as a penance — in a rudderless boat (a tradition to this day referred to in the Office of his feast).

39 Compare on the one hand, Eilhart 1483: On his second journey, Tristan "dem stûrmanne entbôt daz er Îrlant vormede" (for the account of the first journey, see below p. 7), and on the other hand, Kudrun 133f: On his return to Ireland, Hagen said: "Ir goute schifliute, ir bringet mich ze lande ... wendet inwer segele, daz man daz schif gein Îrlande kêre".

40 Among the earliest records of the name of Dublin, Lanfrane's letter to Gothric "rex Dubliniae" (Kenney, *op. cit.*, no. 636) is of special interest with regard to the Tristan tradition. The entry for A.D. 291 in the Four Masters can of course not be regarded as the earliest reference to the Danish name (see John Ryan S.J. in *Proc. R. Soc. Antiquar. of Ireland* Sept 1945). The 12th century chronicle of the war of the Gaedhil with the Gail sub A.D. 857 (ed. Todd (London 1867) p. il and 13) and Jocelin's life of St. Patrick clxxiii (see Todd, *St. Patrick* (Dublin 1864) 466) record the name of *Ath Cliath* and *Dublind* or *Dublinia* beside each other (similarly the Life of St. Molaga, in *Irish Rosary* xv (1911) 516).

king resided. In *Sir Tristrem* (1180) it is only through the Irish sailors picking him up that Tristan learns that the town is *Deuelin*. In Gottfriedds epic, Tristan asks the sailors for the name of that town in order to conceal the aim of his journey. The sailors reply:

> So sagen wir dir, daz du bist
> ze Develîne in Irlant.[41]

Tristans reply:

> Daz lobe ich den heilant,
> daz ich doch unter liuten bin,
> wann eteswer ist unter in,
> der sîne guete an mir begât
> end tuot mir eteslîchen rât (7628f),

is perhaps related with the words: "Di lude sint da harte milde", by which the Hassian version of the *Visio Tundali* rendered Marcus's reference to "religiosis viris et feminis" (in contrast to Solinus's description of the Irish as "gens inhospita").[42]

Isold later recalled Tristan's arrival at *Develîne* (11399f.). The news of Tristan's arrival spread through the town of *Develine* (7697 f) and the *burgaere,* especially a priest, take care of the sick stranger. According to the earlier tradition, Tristan did not actually behold Isold, but, at the king's request, the queen sent him the miraculous medicine which cured him. The later tradition, however, not only made Tristan be nursed by princess Isold, but elaborated the descriptions of their relations during that period.[43] According to Gottfried, Isold, far from being merely Tristan's nurse, conveyed to him that knowledge of Ireland and Irish things of which he boasted on later occasions. "Die schoene si kunde ir sprâche da von Develîn", but at the same time she spoke French and Latin (7989); her cultural language was apparently French. "Si sanc, si schreip unde si las in franzoiser wîse".[44] Of Tristan, Gottfried told us in an earlier passage, that he sang songs in "britûnsche und gâloise, latînsche und franzoise" (3624ff and 3689ff). That French of course was the language in the early Norman settlements in Ireland, is testified to by the relics of Hiberno-French literature from that period.[45] *Sir Tristrem* has in this instance a few points illustrated of early English attitude to Ireland. Tristan taught Isold "to rede romances aright" (1258), an accomplishment to which no knight in Ireland had then attained, and the people of

---

41 Compare French prose novel (330): Arriving at Hessedot (see below) Tristan asked "Quelle terre ce est ou il est arrive", and is told by the king: "Parfois, c'est Yrlande."

42 SP 372.

43 Dr. Hanmer's *Chronicle of Ireland* (1571, reprint Dublin 1809, 104f) seems to be the first work to associate the Tristan tradition with "Isod's towre upon the wall of the citie". On Isod's Fount see *Proc. R. Soc. Antiquar. Irel.* xxxi (1901) 387. See above note 17.

44 See Hertz, *Spielmannsbuch* (Stuttgart 1905) 36.

45 See Curtis "The spoken language of mediaeval Ireland" in *Studies* (Dublin 1919) vii, 234ff and Esposito "Hiberno-French literature", ibid. i (1913) 516f, also W. Heuser *Die Kildare-Gedichte* (Bonn 1904).

Dublin swear "bi seyn Patrike"[46] that they have never seen such a wonderful harp[47] as Tristan's (1228).[48] Gottfried's objectivity is most conspicuous when compared with such tendentious information.[49]

The earlier Tristan tradition reflected quite a different picture of English-Irish relations. Eilhart has the story of Tristan's suggesting to send ships to England to relieve the famine in Ireland (1192ff especially 1249ff). When the betrothal between Marke of Cornwall and Isold is announced according to Gottfried, "daz gesinde von Irlande" rejoiced that thus would be brought to an end "langez hazzen" between England and Ireland (11385),[50] or as the French prose novel had put it: The king of Ireland declared: "Nous voulons desormais que le royaume d'Irlande et cil de Cornuaille soient amys et bienveillens lex ungs aux aultres" (333,340). As it must be assumed that Gottfried obtained his information on early Norman Ireland of his time from one of the Irish clerics in Germany, it is to be noted that the interest of the reform movement in the Irish Church in friendly relations with England and the Anglo-Normans is testified to by the *Vita Sti. Albarti*, one of the important works of lrish-Continental hagiography (written about the same time, in the same place, and perhaps by the same writer as the *VisioTundali*).[51]

When after his return to Cornwall, Tristan praised to Marke the attainments of Isold who shines like the sun "dahêr von Develîne" (Gottfried 8285f), it was decided to send him back to Ireland to woo on Marke's behalf for Isold. In the Norwegian *Saga*, at this point, it is expressly stated: "Hann kann ok írsku" (xxxiii). According to Gottfried, Tristan, at this second landing, hides his men in the hold, while he goes ashore to negotiate with the suspicious Irish as he knows the *lantsprache* (8705). Tristan yielded

---

46   Compare the reference made in *Karlmeinet* to the knights attending Charlemagne's tournament after swearing by the "gebeine" of St. Patrick (SP note 24).

47   On Irish music see Giraldus Cambrensis, *Topographia* iii, I and on Celtic harps, Kittredge in *American Journal of Philopogy* vii (1886) 186.

48   Eilhart 2090 we read of the garments which Marke sent for Isold. It was said "daz noch ni quam in Irlant also recht gut gewant" (see *Kudrun* 300ff).

49   Zander, the first professor of German in Trinity College Dublin, so far as I am aware also the first to refer in Ireland to the German Tristan-tradition, said in *Dublin University Magazine* ii (1833) 26: "The Romantic Epic was a foreign importation in German literature, which, however, was nurtured carefully and treated more scientifically than in any other land".

50   = *Saga* xlv. – *Saga* xxxii suggests that marrying "einbeirni Irakonungs", Marke would bring all Ireland under his rule (the corresponding passage in Gottfried (8504 f) says: "Daz Îrland iuwer werden mac". On the other hand, Cornwall is given to Isold as "morgengabe, daz si wesen solde frouwe uber alles Engelant" (11399f). See my article on St. Albert note 69. These references to the king's ruling, from Dublin or Wexford (see below note 59), all Ireland are of interest 1) with regard to the interpretation of *Kudrun* (see below note 105) and 2) with regard to the description of the king of Ireland (who arrives at Lismore by boat) as *rex insule*, in the tradition of St. Cataldo (see my paper quoted above note 30, p. 231 and 239). The combination of reconciliation with Anglo-Normans and centralization of power in Ireland was a significant feature in the ecclesiastical reform in Ireland.

51   See my paper on St. Albert, p. 28ff.

to his king's request: I will go "in daz saelige Irlant, hin wider ze Develîne, gein der sonnen schîne" (Isold, 8574). In the *Saga,* he adds: Known is to me "Írland ok írska manna sidhir" (xxxiv). "Er kunnugt allt Írland" (ibid.); this geographical knowledge stood Tristan in good stead.[52] While according to the *Saga* (and *Sir Tristrem*), travelling across *Irlandshaf* (xxxiv), Tristan landed at *Dyflinnisborg* (Ms: *Diblinis-borg*),[53] according to the French prose novel "Tristan ariva ung jour en Yrlande devant le castle de Hessedot" (330), and according to Gottfried he came "ze Irland ... ze Weiseforte vür die stat". At this point, it is most obvious that the study of Irish place-names occurring in the Tristan tradition can throw some new light on its development. Knowing of but one voyage, the French prose novel doubtless represents the oldest version. In its original form, no definite place-names were mentioned in this tradition. In this respect, Eilhart, though speaking of two voyages, is as ancient as the French prose novel. According to him, at the first voyage, Tristan's boat

> treip in kein Irlant
> und warf in ûz ûf daz sant
> vor einer borg des koningis (1153ff).[54]

At the second voyage, his boat is thrown by a storm "kein Irlant vor eine borg an daz sant" (1499), where he is assured that "diz des koninges borgo is in Irlant". That is to say, in both instances, Tristan lands in the same place. We shall see that also in *Kudrun,* the (principal) castle of the king of Ireland is thought situated by the sea. In the *Saga,* no place-name is mentioned at the first landing, while the second landing is said to have taken place in Dublin, the place where Morholt's corpse was brought by the Irish. Dublin, we may say, was the obvious choice during the time of the Danes. Bédier's suggestion that "Hessedot" in the French prose novel "est une fausse lecture pour Wessefort" has never been contested.[55] "Weisefort(e)", the spelling adopted by Gottfried, shows that the original meaning of "We(y)seford" (Giraldus: "Weisefordia") was no longer obvious.[56] Waesfiord or Weshford, "a bay overflown by the tide", was

---

52   As an example of the ruthless frittering away of this knowledge I refer to *King Arthur's Knight* by Henry Gilbert, where the place of Tristan's landing is named Cro-na-Shee.

53   *Sir Tristram* 1386: "Intil Yrlond thede", 1393: "Develin". *Folie Tristan* (Bern.) 127f said merely that Tristan went across the sea.

54   See above note 39.

55   Bédier, *op. cit.*, 209; this suggestion was adopted by F. Simmonds (above note 19), while Belloc interpreted "Whitehaven" (McDermott in his notes on Connellan's edition of the Four Masters (Dublin 1846, 225) thought that Wexford means "Western haven")! In Hannah Closs's *Tristan* (London 1940), which referring only to one journey seems also to be based on the French prose novel, no place-name is mentioned, but the fishermen picking up Tristan are given the names of Sean and Teag, a typical illustration of the corruption of the historical back-ground.

56   Camden (the publication of whose work in 1610 at Frankfurt marked the beginning of modern German knowledge of Ireland) had stated that "the name of Weisford is but novel and of German original having been given by those Germans whom the Irish called Oustmen". J. C. Behr, *Das neu-geharnischte Gross-Britannien* (Nürnberg 1690) still spoke of "Weisford". On the history of the name of Wexford see above all John O'Donovan's *Letters containing information relating to the County of Wexford* (1840, in the National Library of Ireland, p. 8f). What Ptolemy had called Menapia and what in Irish is known as Loch Garman is first referred

the Danish name given to Loch Garman, and this plate was, if we may say so, in world news in connection with the Norman landing in 1169. Bédier felt that the knowledge of this ancient Irish port was natural with an English writer (if Thomas must be regarded as such), but surprising with an inhabitant of Strassburg. If the insertion of the name of Wexford into the Tristan-tradition was due to Thomas, it was certainly not merely due to the fact that this was an Irish port. Gottfried's knowledge of this Irish place-name is by no means so surprising, when we consider that even before his time Southern Irish places, such as Cashel, Cork and Lismore were mentioned in Continental literature (*Vita Sti. Albarti, Visio Tundali* and the tradition of St. Cataldo).

The neglect of the study of Irish place-names, doubtless the most conspicuous Irish associations, in the Tristan tradition is largely due to the effect even on scholarly studies of the pre-occupation of the later tradition with the adultery-story. The more this pre-occupation grew into obsession, the more the original Irish background faded out.[57]

Not only with regard to the place-name but also with regard to other details of the Wexford-episode Gottfried's information was more exact than that of the French prose novel.[58] The latter confined itself to saying: "le roy d'Irlande et la royne y estoient". According to Gottfried, the whole district *(alles)* stood in the power and hand of the king "von Irlant" (8735).[59]

According to Gottfried, Tristan tells the king that in company of other Norman merchants he had come "ze Iberne" (8818), the only instance where Gottfried uses this word,[60] "allhie her wider Weisefort" (8839). "En ce pais d'Irlande" (Prose novel 332; Gottfried 8908: "dâ ze lande"), there was at that time a monster, which destroyed the

---

to as Weseford in *Pipe Rolls* 18 and 19 *Henry II* (vol. xvii, 119) and in Pseudo-Benedict's *Gesta Henrici II* (about 1195) sub. 1172; *Roturlorum Cancellariae Hiberniae Calendarium* (1825), index sub Weys(e)ford and Calendar of *Documents relating to Ireland* (1875), no. 34.

57   This obsession has always been in strict proportion to the neglect of the historico-geographical background. In Malory no place-names are mentioned and in Rys's edition the sensuous side of the later Tristan-tradition was emphasized by Beardsley's masterly illustrations (London 1893 and 1927). When speaking of "Sir Tristram violer d'amores", James Joyce in *Finnegans Wake* refers to "Dobbelin". The only other Irish writer who, in a literary reference to the Tristan-tradition, mentioned Dublin was An Philibin (J. H. Pollack (*Tristram and Iseult*, Dublin 1924)).

Of the German continuators of Gottfried only Heinrich von Freiberg (about 1290) referred to the Wexford-episode. V. 1055 ff Tristan accounts his adventure "ze Weiseforte in Irlant" ("Weisefort", without the final -e, also 1901ff and 6447ff). In Heinrich von Neustadt's *Apollonius*, Cusanus's *Eriolus et Lucrecia*, the *Heliodorus*, and *Theagenes und Chariklea*, the romantic tendency triumphed. When Tristram Shandy was given his name by his mother, his father was, at his time, quite right when he "demanded categorically whether she had ever heard or even heard talk of a man called Tristram, performing anything great" (I, xix).

58   Bédier (l.c.) said that "Weiseforte is the form used by Anglo-Norman writers of that time". However, it is obvious that Thomas, or whatever was the source for the place-name of "Hessedot" in the French prose novel, has "Wesefort", and this source was Pseudo-Benedict (above note 56).

59   See above note 50.

60   See above note 2.

people and the land (8910: *Saga* xxxvi: the citizens of the town),[61] but none in the whole kingdom had yet been able to conquer it. Tristan saw the Irish (*Saga* xxxv: "Ira", "folkit"; *Sir Tristrem* 1409: "folk of Develin toun")[62] flee. According to the *Saga*, it was on a rock near a lake in a valley and a forest (Wicklow-mountains?) that Tristan killed that monster; Gottfried assigns this combat to the valley of Anfergînan (8944), i.e. "l'enfer guignant".[63]

The man who tried to deprive Tristan of his prize is described by Eilhart as the king's *marschalke* and *trogseze* by Gottfried as *truchsez* and by the *Saga* as a vassal of the Irish king, a haughty man, Irish by descent, evil-minded, crafty and mendacios (xxx viii).[64] The suggestion that he was one of the "mere Irish" is most curious, firstly because it illustrates the close associations at first existing between the Normans and the natives, secondly because this is one of the earliest illustrations of the systematic campaign of defamation of the natives by which the short-lived attempt to supersede the description of the Irish given by the late Roman authors, by a balanced first-hand account (as in the *Visio Tundali*) was frustrated. In the reference made in the *Lucidarius* to the Irish as "ungezogen, unfreintlich und grausam" classical and Norman defamation are blended.[65] Further information on social and political conditions in early Norman Ireland is supplied by Eilhart's reference to "des landes hêren" (2090) and Gottfried's to the convocation of the king's "landbarûne ... des landes cumpanjeîne" (9704 and 9765) or "halfti ríki Írakonungs" (*Saga* xl). Here again, we may compare the tradition of St. Cataldus, where advised by the *senators et religuos principes cititatis*, the *rex insule* appoints a new *dux* to a *provincia*.[66] In this gathering at Weisefort, Tristan discovers amidst the Irish many of the Cornish youth who in former years had been sent to Ireland as a tribute (11177), obviously no longer kept as captives.[67] According to *Folie Tristan* (Oxf. 765), Tristan was greatly honoured at the *curt d'Irlande*.

---

61   "Burgenses Weseford" in *Pipe Rolls* l.c., 157.

62   See note 34.

63   Lexer, *Mittelhochdeutsches Wörterbuch* i, 41. Eilhart 1608ff describes the combat with the dragon, without mentioning a place-name. To the parallels traced by Schoepperle, *op.cit.* see also van Hamel in *Revue Celtique* xli (1924) 331ff. Colgan, *op.cit.*, 135 has the Life of St. Fechin, who by his prayer made a "venenosa quaedam bellua" throw itself into "vicinum lacum Loch Meochra". Among the monsters killed by St. Abban (Plummer) *Vita Sanctorum Hiberniae* (1910) i, 8 note = Lives of Irish Saints (1922) i, 6) there was one in Loch Garman (above note 56).

64   Compare the dux Meltridis in the tradition of St. Cataldo (my paper p. 231ff). Mr. William Larminie traced in Achill a parallel to this story (*West Irish Folk-Tales* (London 1893), 144f and 256). It appears however that the Irish revenged themselves by turning the coward into a "son of the king of Prussia".

65   See my paper on St. Albert, 33, and SP 372.

66   See my paper on St. Albert note 69 and my paper on St. Cataldo note 93. On "Barún" in Irish see *Zeitschrift für celtische Philologie* i, 427 and *Revue Celt.* X, 190, 20.

67   According to Giraldus, a synod at Armagh, considering that the Norman invasion was a judgement on the Irish for formerly buying Englishmen as slaves, proclaimed that all Englishmen who were held in bondage in Ireland should be set free.

Describing the departure of Tristan and Isold from Ireland, Gottfried once more expressly stated that they embarked "ze Weisefort"; the "Irlandaere" (11523f) came to the shore to bid their princess farewell. Both Gottfried and the *Saga* spoke of Isold's homesickness (there are earlier descriptions in Continental literature of the nostalgia of Irish exiles).[68] In *Folie Tristan* (627), Tristan in a later conversation with Brenguain refers to the fact that "ensemble partimes d'Irlande".[69] In the Beroul fragments the Irish background of Isold was borne in mind throughout her later story (2033, 3061, Muret 3065, also 2557 and 2617). In the *Saga* Isold's Irish descent is particularly referred to in the account of the attempt made by an Irish harper to carry her away from Cornwall, an episode proper to the Norwegian tradition Marke promised that harper he would give him whatever he wished if he would sing for him "Írskan slátt" (il). Outwitting the "írski", Tristan scornfully dismissed him: "Go home covered with shame *til Írlands*" (1).

It is from the survey of the principal references made to Ireland in eight of the oldest versions of the Tristan tradition, originating from four different countries between 1150 and 1300,[70] that we can gauge the importance of this tradition as a secular source of popular information of the Continent on Ireland and the neglect of this aspect in the traditional literature on this subject. Like the hagiographical tradition – in vernacular literature notably that of St. Patrick's Purgatory and of St. Brendan's navigation – this secular tradition was doomed to gradual dilution.[71] The tradition of Ireland's place in the chivalresque literature of the Continent illustrates what Jacob Grimm described as "der völlige Verfall einer epischen Zeit" and the dilution of the "erzählende Gedichte durch ... lyrische Episoden".[72] The Tristan-tradition affords the most comprehensive view of this development. The decay of Continental interest in and knowledge of Ireland from the end of the 13th century can be more fully understood when the breadth of this interest between 1150 and 1300 is considered.

At this point it is desirable to throw a glance at Ireland's place in the work of Chrestien de Troyes. One of his first works, according to the famous preface to *Cligès* was entitled *Del roi Marc et d'Iseut la blanche* (about 1170); Isuet is also mentioned v. 3147, 3151, 5260f and 5312f and in *Erec* 424, 2076 and 4944. In *Erec* also we hear of "un cheval d'Irlande" (2176) owned by Orguelleus and among the knights "de mainte diverse contree" of "Escoz et Irois" (6643 ff). In his *Chevalier de la Charette* the king of Ireland and his country are frequently mentioned (5650, 5729, 5929, 5952ff and 6995). While the detailed study of Ireland's place in the chivalresque literature of France is outside the scope of this paper, it is obvious that in France too, references to Ireland are not so much an indication of literary influences as an illustration of contemporary

---

68   See Colman's verses to *Scottigena patriae cupidus* (Kenney, *op. cit.* no. 359).

69   Eilhart 2798ff relates that the putting out of the lights during the wedding-night was represented to Marke by Brangaine as an Irish custom.

70   Gottfried 131f and 18467 refers to numerous other versions of this tradition.

71   SP 374. See my review of Draak's edition of the Dutch version in *Ir. Hist. Studies* (1950).

72   Raumer, *Geschichte der germanischen Philogie* (Munich 1870), 396ff.

knowledge. In this respect the description of Ireland as "une vile" in the late 12th century *Elie de Saint Gille*[73] is particularly remarkable.

The tradition of the *Chanson de Roland* and of Tristan supplied examples of boastful and unsuccessful Irish kings and knights.[74] Erec, the hero of Hartmann's early work (about 1190),[75] derived from Chrestien's epic, is promised by the dwarf of gigantic strength that the land and people of Ireland will be made subject to him.[76] About the same time, Ulrich von Zazikhoven[77] wrote his *Lanzelot,* in which Artus, Tristan and Lanzelot meet the wild knight, the enemy of the king of Ireland; after being conquered, the king of Ireland is compelled to send an army to help Lanzelot in his campaign against Genewis.[78] A still less glorious part is played by the king of Ireland in *Wilhelm von Orleans* by Rudolf von Ems,[79] where Alan, king of Ireland invades Ysales da silwes, where Savine, sister of the king of England, is prioress; conquering Alan, Wilhelm becomes king of England, a curious illustration of Continental awareness of the political connection between the two countries. In *Wigamur*[80], closely connected with the Lanzelot-tradition, among the supporters of the hero's enemy we have the kings of Ireland and Spain, perhaps a reflection of the extensive tradition of the relationship between *Ibernia* and *Iberia*.[81]

We have seen that already in the tradition of the *Chanson de Roland* Ireland appeared as a vassal country. There is an obvious connection between the enumerations of the countries conquered for and subject to Charlemagne and the lists of countries sending knights to tournaments described in the later chivalresque literature. The transition is most clearly illustrated by the *Haimonskinder,* where a tournament at the court of Charlemagne is attended by "Richard von Normandia, Salomon von Brittania, Dessiers uss Hispania, Gödfrid von Avignon, Barthole uss Teutschland, mit schöner gselschafft; wann er bracht mit ihm die uss Irssland und wohl tussend guother schutzen". The author of this version apparently was not certain whether he should read "Iceland" or "Ireland".[82]

The Irish are obviously regarded as vassals in Wolfram's *Parceval.* After the tournament held by Herzeloide, queen of Wallis, Gahmuret is told that everyone who wit-

---

73   Ed. Raynaud (Paris 1879) 895ff.

74   On *milites* in Ireland see my paper on St. Cataldo p. 243. For the later tradition of the *miles gloriosus* in the stage Irishman, see F. Mezger, *Der Ire in der englischen Literatur* (Palaestra 169, Leipzig 1929) 50ff.

75   4268-4629.

76   3663-3928.

77   Ehrismann, *op. cit.*, Schlussband, p. 4 note 1.

78   Piper, *Höfische Epik* ii, 191, 194, suggesting a source in "Celtic-Irish" epics.

79   Piper, *op. cit.* 637.

80   Ibid. 566; Ehrismann, *op. cit.*, 57.

81   See above note 2.

82   Ed. A. Bachmann in Literar. Verein Stuttgart vol. 206 (Tübingen 1905), 90.

nessed his bravery "er si Britûn oder Yrschman od swer hie wallisch spräche kan, Franzois od Brâbant, die jehent und volgent dîner hant".[83]

In *Der gute Gerhart*, written by Rudolf von Ems about 1220 from a Latin *Vorlage* at the request of a St. Gallen *Ministerialen*, we hear of the kings of "Waleis, Scotten, Yberne und Irland, Curneval und Norgaleis" attending the tournament held by Willehalm of England.[84] In most of these tournaments the Irish were no more successful than they were in war. In Pleier's *Tandareis*,[85] the king of Ireland is conquered in a tournament at Arthur's court. This defeat is particularly humiliating because his adversary had to fight under the disadvantage of being demented by a beautiful lady.

Lists of the home-countries of those attending tournaments are staple-ware rather than "willkürliche Erweiterungen"[86] by which Konrad von Würzburg managed to swell *Partonopier* to twice the size it had in the French *Vorlage*. He speaks of the kings of "Ungern, Reussen, Schotten,[87] Norwegen, Orchade, Irland, Britanje und England".[88] In an earlier passage, Konrad mentioned among the supporters of Salruin, Sursin, king of Ireland, probably another alternative for Gorman-Angyn. The complete decay of the historical background of such references to Irish knights is visible in Konrad's last work, the War of Troy (a subject also dealt with in an Irish epic), where the description of battles afforded ample scope for enlargements (from the *Roman de Troie* of Benoit de St. More).[89] Colebrant of Ireland appears among the Trojan heroes, of course on the losing side. On the other hand, the collapse of the geographical background may be seen from *Rosengarten,* an off-shoot of the Nibelung-tradition, where in the Austro-Bavarian Mss A and B the knight Staudenfuss (in the mixed redaction of Ms C: Stuffing) is described as coming from *Irland,* whereas the Thuringian Ms D makes Stuffing come from *Ungerland*.[90]

In lists of countries moving in the orbit of the great kings and heroes of chivalresque literature, Ireland was merely one item in the reference to which the authors could display some cosmographical knowledge. In most cases, Ireland is clearly grouped among the British isles, and the derivation of such references from encyclopedical cosmosgraphies of the time can be demonstrated. It is interesting though that outside this literature there is hardly any evidence of knights from 13th century Ireland taking part in the chivalresque life of the Continent. So far as I am aware, there is, in German literature of the time, only one parallel to the reference made in *Elie de Saint Gille* to Irishmen taking part in the crusades, namely in the *Kreuzfahrt Landgraf Ludwigs des Frommen* v. 551, mentioning Danes, Frisians,

---

83   ii, 800ff. and above note 11.

84   See above note 2. Piper, *op. cit.,* 554, and Ehrismann, *op. cit.* 26.

85   About 1270. Piper, *op. cit.,* 340, 343.

86   Ehrismann, *op. cit.,* 35f.

87   See above note 2.

88   Piper, *op. cit.,* 301; Ehrismann, *op. cit.,* 2.

89   Piper, *op. cit.,* iii, 227.

90   Grimm, *Deutsche Heldensage* (1867), 246.

Normans and "Schotten und noch mê".[91] Irish participation in the crusades however is frequently referred to in the Papal Register of the mid-thirteenth century.

Among all these references to Ireland in German chivalresque literature, apart from the Tristan-tradition the only one to show some awareness of Ireland's special place as one of the home-countries of that folklore upon which the epic literature of mediaeval Europe was largely based, was *Wigalois* by Wirnt von Grafenberg (early 13th century). In that epic we hear of a "hövische mantel ... der hâr daz was weitîn brâht von Iberne" (801ff Ms C. and L: *Ziberne*), of "ein riemen von Iberne" (10555, missing in Ms A; in both instances "Iberne" is rhymed on "sterne"), and of a wonderful horse with a precious saddle given by the "künic von Irlant" as a prize for the most beautiful lady, apparently a chivalresque interpretation of tribute paid by Ireland (2562). After Wigalois had gained this horse for his lady, a dwarf accompanying the horse began

> Sagen schoeniu maere
> we sîn herre waere
> der ez dar hêt gesant
> und wiez stüende in Irlant. (Mss C, K: "in irem land", Ms S: "in seim land")
> Hie mit kürzter in den tac,
> wan man mit guoten maeren mac.

Though unfortunately these *maere* were not specified, these are clear indications to the Irish foundations of *Wigalois*,[92] illustrating the re-lapse of Continental *Irlandkunde* into pure fancy.

Outside the Tristan-tradition, *Kudrun is* the only epic of this period in which Ireland is not only a passive and distant partner but the actual and active scene of happenings. However, while in the Tristan-tradition Ireland represents the oldest stratum, in *Kudrun,* the references to Ireland are obviously a late addition. Still there is one point in common to the Tristan-tradition and *Kudrun.* Considering the eminent position held by women in the history and literature of mediaeval Ireland, we cannot fail to notice how little we hear of women in the references made to Ireland in Continental literature. In *Die Krone,* Ginower of Ireland receives precious jewels from queen Lenomie of Alexandria, her sister,[93] a tradition which may be linked with that reported by Reinfried von Braunschweig (about 1300) of Yrkane, daughter of the King of Denmark, receiving a miraculous ring which came from India through the king of Schottenland to Norway and finally to Yrkane's mother.[94]

---

91 Above note 73. Hans Naumann in the Index to *Monum. Germ. Hist., Deutsche Chroniken* iv, 2 (Berlin 1923) doubted whether this was a reference to Ireland. For the later tradition of Irish knights in German literature see Weckherlin's *Der Irrländischen Ritter Aufzug* of which I have treated in my "Notes on early representations of Irishmen in German books" in *Proc. R. Soc. Antiquar. Ireland* (1950). A very curious account of a chivalresque conversation in Ireland, between Philtanus and Gelgehen, the parents of St. Fursey, is in his Vita II (Kenney, *op. cit.* 296, iii, saec, xi/xii).

92 Piper, ii, 217 and 219, and Ehrismann, 7.

93 Piper, ii, 237.

94 Ibid., 360 and Ehrismann, *op. cit.,* 87f. Heinrich von Frieberg frequently referred to Îsôt as "von Îrlande die bêle", "die blunde bêle ûz Îrlant" "die blunde ûz Irland" distinguishing her from "die nicht ûz Îrlande".

The beginning of *Kudrun*: "Ez wuohs in Irlande ein rîcher künic hêr" is of course an imitation of the beginning of the *Nibelungenlied*,[95] and it was generally admitted that the whole Ger-Sigebant-Hagen story was originally not connected with the Kudrun-tradition.[96] This connection was established in the German epic, where also the Hagen-story was first localised in "Irlant". Panzer[97] was the first to state that this is by no means surprising in view of the extensive references made to Ireland in the chivalresque literature of the time. Panzer indeed was the first to establish at least the outlines of Ireland's position in that literature. The history of the study of the Irish associations of *Kudrun* illustrates the importance of a detailed investigation of Ireland's place in mediaeval literature in general. In 1866, Haupt[98] suggested that "Irlant" in *Kudrun* was Mecklenburg and that Baljàn, Hagen's residence, was Poeley, the island of Poel near Wismar. However as early as 1841, Ettmüller[99] had stated that "Baljàn" was "Bally-glan, ein in Irland öfters vorkommender Ortsname", a theory which was adopted not only by Symons [100] but even by Francis E. Sandbach in his study on *Nibelunglied and Gundrun in England and America* (London 1904)[101]: "Baljân at once reminds one of the ubiquitous Irish prefix Bally-, and the name of Ballyglan is said to be not unknown in Ireland", a statement which shows that foreign knowledge of Ireland had made little progress during the last sevenhundred years. Sandbach was apparently not in a position to establish, from any gazeteer, that there was not, and indeed never had been, a place named Ballyglan in Ireland. The connection between Baljân and the prefix Bally-, the English corruption of Irish *baile*, in the late 12th century, is a ludicrous suggestion.[102]

So far as I am aware, Bartsch[103] was the first to suggest that "Irlant" stood originally for Eyerland, a part of the island of Texel, a suggestion which merely shows that

---

95   Bartsch's edition (1880, reprint 1921), xi, xxv and 1.

96   Piper's edition (1895), xxx, and Ehrismann, *op. cit.,* 149.

97   *Hilde-Gudrun* (Halle 1901), 436.

98   *Untersuchungen zur deutschen Sage*, i, 10.

99   In the introduction to his edition, ix, see also K. Müllenhoft's edition (1845), 75.

100   In his edition (1883), 21.

101   186.

102   On Irish place-names with Bally- see K.J. Clement's *Irland* (Kiel 1845), 88: Clement was the first to make Germanic studies in the various parts of Ireland. In this connection the following note in *Altirische Sagen und Geschichte* (Stimmen aus Maria Laach 1882 = *Geschichte der Weltliteratur* (1912), 696) by Alexander Baumgarten S.J. is of interest to the tradition of Ireland's place in German literature: "Während die keltische Sage von Wales und Schottland einen nicht unerheblichen Einfluss auf die kontinentale Literatur erlangte, ist die keltische Sage der Iren nur mittelbar und in sehr beschränktem Grade über die Inselgruppe ihrer Heimat hinaus-gedrungen. Sie wird vielleicht auch nie eine Macht erlangen, wie sie die Artus-Sage über die Gemüter der mittelalterlichen Dichter erlangte. Dennoch verdient sie Interesse. Sie bildet mit altirischen Ortsnamen und Erinnungen ein anziehendes Ganze".

Baljân is one of the fictitious Irish place-names characteristic of Continental literature of that time (see my papers on St. Albert and St. Cataldo and my forthcoming studies on Irish place-names in Continental hagiography).

103   Ed. cit., 335.

Bartsch was not aware of the place held by Ireland in German literature contemporary with *Kudrun*. However bad the geography of *Kudrun*,[104] the suggestion that in a fraction of the small island of Texel there were seven or even fifteen under-kings (2.2 and 186.2)[105] would have been too much for many readers of that work. I am not aware of any reference in the literature of that period to Eyerland on Texel. To the words "in dem lande" (in 72.4) a marginal note says "In Eyrland";[106] in *Rabenschlacht* 806 Morolt is described as "von Eierlande", obviously approximations – via "Ierlandt" (so to this day in Dutch) – to phonetic spelling.[107] Bartsch's suggestion was partly adopted by Piper:[108] "Hagen heisst zwar durchweg König von Irland, aber welches Irland gemeint ist, ist die Frage. Unter *Irlant, Irriche* versteht man meist die Insel, wo im 9. Jahrhundert wirklich nordische Reiche bestanden."

Willmans[109] had already stated that "die Sage sich zu einer Zeit consolidierte, als die Dänen in England herrschten", namely the late 9th century! It is against the background of such statements that the fundamental significance of Panzer's book on *Kudrun* will be appreciated.

Yet, fifty years before Panzer's work was published, v. Ploennius had already stated:

> Haben auch Irland und die Normandie einen festen Platz in der Sage, so fehlt dieser doch eine speciellere Kenntnis jener Gegenden; finden wir Karadine [=Cardigan in Wales] mit Irland richtig in Verbindung gebracht, so geschieht dies vom Dichter, der seine Kenntnis aus einem ausländischen *maere* geschöpft haben muss. Die ganze Schilderung der Reise nach Irland ist leer und schwach.[110]

While the association between Isold and Ireland was firmly established in the old Tristan-tradition, there is no evidence of Irish associations in the early Kudrun-tradition.[111] While Gottfried marked the climax of the introduction of definite and contemporary information of Ireland into the Tristan-tradition, what *Kudrun* tells us of Ireland is little more than fiction. Of the geography of Ireland, the writer of *Kudrun* did not know more than that it was situated by the sea; some foreigners seem to reach it on horseback (37 and 64). The reference to the reception of Ute on her way from the coast to Baljan, "uf zweier lande marke" seems to be a formula customarily used in the description of such scenes. Ireland lies across the wild sea (287), East of Norway (13), a hundred miles from Griffinsland and a thousand miles from Hegelingen (80 and 288), but near Scotland (9) and Wales.

---

104 On this subject see Frings in *Zeitschrift f. deutsches Altertum*, lxi (1924) 192ff (does not deal with references to Ireland though).

105 The words: "Dem wirte rîten bî, daz ouch künige hiezen, zwelve unde drî" (186.2) are peculiar, because (1) in 2.2 we were told that Ger "hat siben fürsten lant," and (2) in the tradition of St. Patrick's Purgatory, either 12 *or* 15 *viri* accompanying the *dux* were mentioned (on the literary and historical background of this tradition see my paper on St. Cataldo, 243).

106 Simrock's translation, "Irland".

107 Ehrismann, *op. cit.* 167.

108 *Ed. cit.*, xxvf.

109 In his edition of *Kudrun*, 269.

110 *Kudrun* (1859), 305, 330.

111 Bartsch's edition, p. v, Piper's p. xxx.

There is, as has been pointed out, a close relationship between the accounts of Tristan's landings in Ireland and the descriptions of Hagen's and Wate's arrivals. Hagen recognised his father's country by "die vil wîten bürge" (towns) and "einen pales hôhen bî dem fluote" with "dri hundert türne veste unde guote" (138). The "hûs" or "burc ze Baljân" (144, 161) is a few miles from the coast (10, 148ff), and there is a town nearby in which the "burgaere" are under a "rihtaere" (293). There were facilities for ship-building in Baljan (454). The foreign guests had an opportunity of hearing early Mass there, but some of Hagen's under-kings are pagans (441 and 186). The extension of "lêhenlîche rehte" to Ireland (186, 190) was also implied in the description given in the later Tristan-tradition of the court at Wexford. There is scarcely anything specific in the references made in *Kudrun* (49 ff) to musical life in Ireland ("pusûnen unde trumben, floiten unde harphen, rotten unde singen, phîfen unde gîgen"); Bartsch said that "rotte" is "ein Saiteninstrument von keltischem Ursprunge". The words: "Nâch site in Irlande vil dicke man began maniger hande freude" (354) according to Martin refer to the reputation of the Irish for fencing, as testified to by *Biterolf und Dietleib* (2138): "den jungen künec rîche ein meister lêrte uz Irlant".[112] It is curious that Wate expects that the king of Irland understands when he speaks of foreigners in general as "wilde Sahsen oder Franken", according to Bartsch a standard expression in folk-songs, bearing some resemblance to the Gaelic custom of referring to the English as Sassanach.

Comparing the Irish associations in *Kudrun* with the references made to Ireland in other works of the period, the most significant point perhaps is the suggestion that Ireland attracted the knighthood from foreign countries to her tournaments rather than merely sending her knights abroad (37 and 138). Even in *Kudrun*, however, Irish knights are not depicted as particularly clever (28 and 445ff).

By comparison with Ireland's place in the Tristan-tradition, the Irish associations in *Kudrun* are mere patch-work. Gottfried's *Tristan* clearly stands out as the climax of German Irlandkunde as reflected in the epic literature of the 12th and 13th centuries.

It was not until the second half of the 15th century that German knowledge of, and literary interest in, Ireland was revived. The decay during the 14th and early 15th centuries is largely a reflection of the decay of the Irish monastic organization in Central Europe[113] and of the lack of direct intercourse of German merchants with Ireland.

The first period of Irish-German literature relations was that of the clergy, the second that of the knighthood. The third period was that of the *burgaere*, the trader, swords-man and scientist. In German literature it was initiated by the Volksbuch of *Fortunatus* in which the hagiographical and chivalresque traditions of Irish associations in Conti-nental literature are merely a memory.[114]

(Quelle: Proc. Royal Irish Academy 53 C, 1950, S. 279-298.)

---

112 Martin's edition, p. 81 and Ehrismann, *op. cit.* 162f.

113 See my papers "The liturgical and artistic tradition of Irish Saints in Central Europe", "Irish monastic activities in Eastern Europe" and "Augustine Gibbon de Burgo" in *Irish Ecclesiastical Record* (1943), 172f., (1945), 394f. and (1947), 135f., also my paper on "Irish-German literature relations" in *German Life and Letters*, N.S. iii (1950) 102-110.

114 See my paper on "Fortunatus in Ireland" in *Ulster Journal of Archaeology* (1950).

Fortunatus in Ireland

Between the 13th and the 19th centuries, no place in Ireland has been more frequently referred to in Continental literature than St. Patrick's Purgatory. In fact, for long stretches of those five hundred years, the tradition of St. Patrick's Purgatory was the principal source of Continental information on Ireland. While there is ample evidence of the spreading of Hugo of Saltrey's work through all parts of Europe, it is curious that in Germany only one manuscript of this account of the pilgrimage to St. Patrick's Purgatory has been traced, which however seems to be the oldest.[1] Among the earliest references, in the vernacular literature of the Continent, to the tradition of St. Patrick, we have the Alemannic poem of *St. Patricius* written about the year 1160.[2] This work refers to the vision of the other world by Echu, whom St. Patrick raised from the dead. It is said that David Scotus, who in the early 12th century was in charge of the cathedral school of Würzburg, wrote *De Purgatorio Patricii*; if this tradition is correct, this would be the earliest account of St. Patrick's Purgatory.

While Continental interest in accounts of the pilgrimage to St. Patrick's Purgatory was of course primarily devotional or romantic, these accounts occasionally managed to convey to the Continent at the same time some geographical knowledge of Ireland. In the absence of evidence of the spreading of the earlier accounts, it can be assumed that one of the chief sources of German information on this subject was *Visio Georgii,* i.e. the account given in 1363 by Georg Crissaphan, an Hungarian, of his pilgrimage.[3] This work was prefaced by letters of or references to bishops in Ireland, especially *Richardus Armachanus archiepiscopus* and *Nicolaus Clochorensis episcopus,* also to *Dunedalkum* and *Druminiskum* and other places in Ireland. Towards the end of the 14th century, Ramon de Perelhos[4] recorded that he obtained for his pilgrimage the permission "del archivesques d'Armanhac, que es primat en Yrlanda e lo avesque es aquel en la diocesa de qual es lo purgatori". This pilgrim landed at "la vile de Diondan laquel es aussi gran coma Puegsarda [Puycerde in Gironde] o Tarragona" and proceeding via "une vile appelada Dandela" arrived at "la ciutat d'Armach", where he was received by the *rey Yrnel*! I hope to deal with these place-names in a special chapter of my comprehensive study in Irish place-names in the Continental literature of the Middle Ages.

With regard to Irish place-names in Continental literature of the Middle Ages,[5] it is important to bear in mind the three principal groups, namely (*a*) historical place-names, (*b*) mutilated place-names and (*c*) fictitious place-names. The combination of

---

1   See my paper on "Cataldus Rachav. A study in the early history of diocesan episcopacy in Ireland" in *Mediæval Studies*, viii (1946), 243.

2   See my paper on "Irish saints in early German literature" in *Speculum*, xxii (1947), 364.

3   Ibid. 365. Ed. Hammerich (Copenhagen 1930), see index.

4   Ed. Jeanroy and Vignaux (Toulouse 1903), index.

5   See my paper on the tradition of St. Cataldus, my paper on St. Albert, in *Mediæval Studies*, vii (1945), 21-39 and my paper on Irish place-names in early Cistercian records, in *Irish Ecclesiastical Records*, V, lxxiii (1950), 226-231.

truth and fiction in Continental writing on Ireland can be seen in Ramon de Perelhos's coupling the name of Armagh with a fictitious king Yrnel. On the whole, all the great mediaeval traditions associated with Ireland such as the *Navigatio Brendani,* the V*isio Tundali, Purgatorium Sti Patricii* and *Tristan and Isold*[6] suffered from gradual dilution of the historico-geographical elements by romantic fiction. In the tradition of St. Patrick's Purgatory this process is particularly interesting as this tradition was (or pretended to be) constantly revived by new pilgrims from the Continent adding their accounts to it.

In his survey of accounts of the pilgrimages to St. Patrick's Purgatory, Sir Shane Leslie mentioned *Fortunatus,* translated in 1679 from Dutch into English.[7] This is one of the innumerable translations, re-translations, versions and interpretations of the tradition of Fortunatus which started with the Augsburg 1509 print of the *Volksbuch,* of which complete copies are preserved in Berlin, Göttingen, Munich and Zwickau (the copy preserved in the British Museum being incomplete).[8] Most of the *Volksbücher* conveyed, more or less directly, under the cloak of fiction, a certain amount of cyclopedian information, especially in the geographical field. The subject of Fortunatus in particular lent itself to this purpose and right down to Chamisso's *Schlemihl* (1814), the scientific bend of this tradition has been evident. In many other *Volksbücher* we have references to these countries, but in none are they as prominent as they are in *Fortunatus.* With regard to the tradition of Continental knowledge of Ireland, *Fortunatus* occupied an important position, because

(1) Ireland holds a very special place in it;

(2) Several places in Ireland are described in it in some detail, and in particular the two place-names mentioned in this connection shed some light on the much-discussed question of the origin of this curious work;

(3) This is an important link with both the hagiographical and the chivalresque tradition of Ireland in Continental literature (these being the first and the second phases of this tradition);

(4) This is an important contribution to the Continental attitude at that time to St.Patrick's Purgatory and to the tradition of the Island of Saints in general;

(5) The references to Ireland play a certain part in the later tradition of *Fortunatus.*

---

6   *Speculum,* xxii, 358f., and my paper on "Ireland's place in the chivalresque literature of mediaeval Germany" (R. I. A.).

7   *St. Patrick's Purgatory* (London 1932), 108.

8   Ed. Hans Günther in *Neudrucke deutscher Literaturwerke des 16. und 17. Jahrhunderts,* no. 240 and 241 (Halle 1914, reprinted 1933). Günther's Ph.D. thesis (Freiburg 1915) on *Die Herkunft des Volksbuches vom Fortunatus* tried to establish the German origin. The Irish associations are briefly referred to. The information on St. Patrick's Purgatory is "superficial and merely second-hand" (G. thinks it to be derived from Rathold). The place-names occuring in the account of Fortunatus's journey to Ireland are not mentioned. The Irish associations of *Fortunatus* are mentioned in the article "Fortunatus" in Ersch-Gruber, *Allgemeine Enzyklopädie der Wissen-schaften* (Leipzig 1847).

1

Fortunatus, a young fortune-hunter from Cyprus, met in a forest in Brittany, Fortuna who gave him a lucky purse. After equipping himself as a knight, he went to a tournament at Nantes, where he met Lüpoldus, "a nobleman born from *Ybernia*, who had been travelling for seven years, visiting two empires and twenty kingdoms". Fortunatus made him his servant, tutor and guide. After touring Western Europe, they went to ...

... *Lunden, Edinburgh in Schottenlandt* and after another six days' journey on horseback in *Ybernia*,[9] they arrived at a town named *Waldrich*, where there was Lüpoldus's home. As Fortunatus had heard that from there it was another two days' journey to the town where there is St. Patrick's Purgatory (also situated in *Hybernia*), he said: 'We will go there.'

So they rode with joy into the town of W*erniks*, in which there is a large monastery, an abbey, and in the church behind the altar of the Sacrament there is a door through which one enters a dark cave, known as St. Patrick's Purgatory. Now no one is allowed in there without the abbot's permission. Lüpoldus went to the abbot and obtained leave, which was granted, but the abbot asked him whence the master was. He told him he was from Cyprus. Seeing that he was from a distant country, the abbot invited him and his retinue as his guests, a gesture which Fortunatus considered as a great honour. When they were about to go to dinner, Fortunatus bought a casket of the best wine he could find and presented it to the abbot, because wine is dear in that country. The abbot accepted this present most gratefully, because otherwise little wine was used in the monastery except for divine service. When the meal was over, Fortunatus addressed him as follows: 'Sir, if it is not beneath your dignity, I wished to learn for what reason it is said that here is St. Patrick's Purgatory.' The abbot replied: 'I will tell you. Many hundred years ago there was a wild desert where there is now this town and church. Not far from here there was then an abbot named Patrick, a very devout man, who often went into this desert to do penance.[10] On one particular occasion he found this cave, which is both deep and long. He entered it, but lost his way in it. Falling upon his knees he implored God that, if it was not against His will, He should help him out of this cave. While he was still praying with great devotion, he heard in the distance great crying and lamentation as if there was a great multitude. He was much frightened at this, but God helped him to find his way out of the cave. He thanked God for this delivery and returning to his monastery he was more devout than before. Whenever he wished to do penance, he went into this cave. He then built a chapel by the entrance of this cave,[11] which attracted many other devout persons who eventually built this monastery and the town.' Fortunatus said: 'The pilgrims who come here and whom you allow into the cave, what do they say when they come out of the cave?' The abbot replied: 'I do not ask them and I do not allow them to ask. However, some of them stated that they heard crying and lamentation. Others did not hear or see anything, but that they were much frightened.' Fortunatus said: 'I have come here from afar, and if I would not enter this cave, this would be a slight on me. I shall not go from here without entering the Purgatory.' The abbot replied: 'If you desire to enter, do not go too far into the cave, because one easily loses

---

9   So far as I am aware, all the other existing accounts of the pilgrimage to St. Patrick's Purgatory refer to the journey from the South East (Dublin-Dundalk).

10   For the distinction sometimes made between Patrick, the abbot of Lough Derg, and Patrick, the Apostle of Ireland, see Stanihurst's *Life of St. Patrick* (1587); Leslie, *op. cit.*, 46.

11   Compare the account of the Patrician associations of the cave in the first of the Augsburg 1485 accounts published by G. Waterhouse in *Modern Language Review* (1923), xviii, 317f.

one's way in it,[12] as happened to several persons within my memory, whom we found again only after four days' searching.' Fortunatus asked Lüpoldus whether he would go with him, and Lüpoldus replied: 'Yes, I will go with you and I shall stay with you, as long as God grants me life.' Fortunatus was much pleased at this.

How Fortunatus and Lüpoldus his servant entered Patrick's Cave.

On the following morning they went to the church, to receive the Sacraments of penance and of the Eucharist, because the cave was hallowed by St. Patrick. He who has spent a night in it, gains a plenary indulgence.[13] Therefore those who wish to enter it, must first go to Confession. Then the door of the cave was unlocked for them, which is behind the Altar of the Sacrament in the monastery. Behind the door is a small cellar, and when the pilgrim has entered it, the priests bless him and close the door, which is not opened again until the following day at the same time. When they came to the cave and had descended deep down into it, they arrived at its floor. There they took each other's hand, so as not to lose each other. Thus they walked along in the dark, hoping to reach the end of the cave and thence to return again. When they had walked for a long time, they realised that they were going quickly downwards. They therefore decided to return to the entrance, but they could not find it. They walked along until they were tired. Then they sat down to rest and wait until they would be called from the door, and thus would find their way out. Fright had come over them and they did not know how long they had been in the cave.

When on the following morning the hour had come, the door was opened and they were called, but they had gone too far from the door to hear. Therefore the door was locked again. The two of them walked to and fro and did not know what to do. They were hungry and lost all courage and hope. Then Fortunatus began to pray: 'Almighty God, come to our assistance. In this place neither gold nor silver is of any avail.' Then they sat down again in despair, neither hearing nor seeing anything. On the third morning, the priests came again and opened the door of the cave. They called again for the pilgrims, but as there was no answer they locked the door again. They went to the abbot and told him of the misfortune. They were particularly sorry for Fortunatus who had presented them with the excellent wine. Fortunatus's servants too complained and were grieved at their master's fate.

Now the abbot knew an old man, who many years ago had surveyed the cave by means of ropes. The abbot sent for him and asked him, could he promise to bring the pilgrims back from the cave. Fortunatus's servants promised him a hundred sovereigns. The old man replied: 'If they are still alive, I shall bring them back.' Equipped with his ropes he entered the cave. You may ask: Why did they not go into the cave with lights or lanterns? You must know that this cave does not suffer any light. Thus the old man had to use his instruments to survey one part of the cave after the other until he found them. They were very glad at this, for they felt weak, and he told them to hold on to him like the blind to one that can see. Following his instruments and with the help of God, he brought them out again. The abbot was very pleased at this. He was afraid that if these pilgrims had been lost in the cave, no more pilgrims would have come and he and his church would have lost the profits. The servants told Fortunatus that they had promised the old man a hundred sovereigns for his search. He gave him that and more and thanked him very much. He also ordered that the hostel where they stayed should be splendidly arrayed, and invited the abbot and his whole community. He thanked God for his delivery and presented the abbot and his

---

12   According to *Visiones Georgii* (ed. cit., 99), the cave had *"spacium seu longitudinem unius miliaris cum dimidio."* Earlier writers said that it had nine pits (Leslie, *op. cit.*, 8).

13   "Ablass aller seiner sünd." The first of the Augsburg 1485 accounts says that "whosoever is truly sorry for his sins and with firm Christian faith goes through this cave for one day and one night, shall return from it purified of all his sins!" In 1790 the cave was permanently filled up, but the vigil of 24 hours is still the central part of the penitential exercises at Lough Derg.

monastery with a hundred sovereigns that they should pray to God on his behalf. Then they took leave from the abbot and continued their journey on horseback straight to *Callis,* because beyond *Ybernia* it is so wild that one cannot go further.

After various other adventures, Fortunatus and Lüpoldus returned to Cyprus. The journey to *Waldrich in Ybernia* had been undertaken at Lüpoldus's request, who had said that he was old and wanted to see once more his wife and children. Leaving Waldrich again, he provided for them. In Cyprus, Fortunatus offered him to return to Ireland, but Lüpoldus replied: "I am old and weak and might die on the way. Even if I would succeed in making this journey, I would die there soon, for *Ybernia* is a rough, harsh country where there grows neither wine nor precious fruit to which I have become accustomed." Fortunatus set up a house for Lüpoldus, but though enjoying life in comfort, Lüpoldus did not forget to go to church every morning. When, a few months later, Lüpoldus died, Fortunatus was much grieved, and ordered his friend to be buried in a church which he (Fortunatus) had built. Then he set out for another journey, to the East, where he acquired a miraculous cap, by means of which he could travel through the air to any place he wished.

The second half of *Fortunatus* relates the adventures of Andolosia, Fortunatus's son, who had inherited both purse and cap. At *Lunden in Engeland,* he fell in love with Agrippina, daughter of the king. She, however, at the instigation of her parents stole his purse, and as a revenge, Andolosia, by means of his cap, carried her away "to a wild desert, where there is no dwelling-place". This chapter bears the title "How Andolosia took Agrippina to a wild forest in *Hybernia*", for his cap took him to "a wretched island, bordering *Hybernia*". Agrippina managed to get hold of the cap and wishing herself back to London, left Andolosia on this island. Looking for some food, Andolosia came to an apple-tree, but after eating some of its fruit, horns grew on his head. A hermit (*Waldbruder*) who "during thirty years of living in that desert had neither seen nor heard a human being" took him to his hut, "where he had neither bread nor wine, only fruit and water". Seeing that this was not the proper food for him, he directed him to the main land, after giving him another apple which caused the horns on his head to disappear. "Now go straight on and you will come to a wide water, that is a branch of the Spaniolic sea. Wait till the tide has gone, and then walk quickly through towards the high tower which you will see on the far side. Not far from there you will find a good village, where they will have bread, meat and other good food."

After taking a good meal in that village, Andolosia asked "where he would go quickest to *Lunden in Engeland.* He was told that this was a good distance and that he was still in *Hybernia.* He would have to pass through the Kingdom of *Schotten*[14], then England began and *Lunden* was situated well inside. When the people noticed how he longed to be in London, they directed him to a large town not far from their village, which was situated by the sea, being a sea-port, from where boats go to *Engeland, Flandern und*

---

14 *"Schotten"*, originally the dative plural of the name of the inhabitant, used since the 13th century for the country. The very clear distinction between Ireland and Scotland in *Fortunatus* is remarkable.

Schotten. There he found a boat which took him to London." He managed to sell Agrippina one of the apples he had brought from the hermit's island. Two horns grew on her head and Andolosia, disguised as a doctor, promised to remove them. When alone with her, he seized his cap and wished himself "into a wild forest,where there are no people". Arriving there, he disclosed himself to Agrippina. As he refused to remove the horns from her head, she begged him not to take her back to London, but to permit her to withdraw from the world to a convent. Complying with this request, Andolosia took her "to *Hybernia*, near the end of the world, where not far from St.Patrick's Purgatory, in the open country far from inhabited places, there is a large and beautiful convent". Andolosia gives the abbess 600 sovereigns, that is, three times the usual dowry. Agrippina must promise "to be obedient, to attend mattins and all the hours in choir, and to learn whatever is required". However, she is told that otherwise "this order is not harder than others. Those who wish to enter a different order or to take a husband, can do so, only the dowry will be forfeited". She is also given a room and an attendant.

Andolosia then retuns to Cyprus, where the king begs him to obtain for his son the beautiful daughter of the king of England, who unfortunately, has just been kidnapped by a magician to *Hybernia*. Andolosia wishes himself back into the hermit's island, where he gathers a few of the apples which remove the horns. Then he proceeded to *Hybernia* to the convent. He calls all the nuns to come out of the convent to see the miraculous cure of Agrippina. Then he pays the abbess another hundred crowns, thanking her that she kept Agrippina so well. The wedding is held at London.

2

There is no other early travel book in which no less than three different journeys to Ireland are referred to. From the point of view of Irish-Continental relations, *Fortunatus* is further remarkable for the fact that this is the first Continental book in which Irish persons are depicted. The wood-cuts illustrating the chapters, here for the first time translated into English, show:

(1) Fortunatus seated, negotiating with Lüpoldus standing in front of him;

(2) Fortunatus and Lüpoldus walking through the church towards the entrance of the cave;

(3) Andolosia taking Agrippina to the hermit's island (in the background mountains which may be meant to represent Ireland).

(4) Andolosia meeting the hermit.

(5) Andolosia talking to the abbess at the convent-gate.[15]

---

15 Various English translations of the German original, without these illustrations, appeared between 1612 (according to *Cambridge Bibliogr. of English Liter.*, i (1940), 336 by Thomas Churchyard, who, however, died already in 1604) and 1830 (Bayard Morgan, *A critical bibliography of German literature in English translations* (Stanford, 1927), no. A 161ff.); none of them seems to have been published or re-printed in Ireland. In Simrock's edition of *Fortunatus*

The references to Ireland's being situated at the end of the world, beyond which it is so wild that one cannot get any further – 50 years after the discovery of America – once again refer to the oldest references to Ireland in German literature, such as the mention made in the Old-High-German *Hildebrandslied* to the *wendelseo.*

In the many discussions of the origin of *Fortunatus,* scarcely any attention has been paid to the two place-names occuring in the account of Fortunatus's journey to Ireland.[16] The names of both *Waldrich* and *Werniks* (Simrock[17]: *Waldrik* and *Wernich!*) are obviously German, scarcely showing even the guttural character which in Continental literature is often given to fictitious place-names associated with Ireland.[18] The name of Fortunatus's Irish servant, especially in the spelling *Lüpoldus* in the original *Fortunatus,* is also German. In the curious booklet *Aliquot nomina propria Germanorum* (Wittenberg 1537), sometimes, erroneously ascribed to Martin Luther, this was emphatically stated.[19] How the Irish associations, embodied in these names, have fared with later interpreters of the tradition of Fortunatus may be shown by one recent example. In the children's version by Mrs. Clark in *The King of the Golden River* (London 1920), Lüpoldus is named Loch-Fitty and described as a Scot; Fortunatus went with him to Scotland, only to see his family. Simrock apparently knew why in his edition of the *Volksbuch* he added to the first reference to *Ybernia* the words *d.i. Irland.*[20] Lüpoldus is a representative of the long literary tradition of the faithful Irish servant, like Macmorris in Shakespeare's *Henry V,* or similar figures in Thomas Heywood's *Four Prentices of London* and Dekker's *Honest Whore,* down to Farqhar's *Twin Rivals.* There is no doubt from the description given in *Fortunatus* that both *Waldrich* and *Werniks* are supposed to be situated in Ulster, between Scotland and Donegal. Lüpoldus is, to my knowledge, the first layman from Ulster in Continental literature.

The account of Fortunatus's visit to St. Parick's Purgatory is derived from a source different from that of the account of Andolosia's journeys. In the former, St. Patrick's Purgatory is in the town of *Werniks.* In the latter, St. Patrick's Purgatory is not associated with any town but rather imagined to be situated in the open country. In the latter account the geography of Ireland as a whole is more detailed than in the former. There is no reference to sea-crossings in the account of Fortunatus's journey on horseback from Edinburgh to Waldrich and from Werniks to Calais. It is useless to

---

in his collection of "Deutsche Volksbücher nach den älteren Ausgaben", these old woodcuts were replaced by modern ones. On Simrock's edition that in *Deutsche Volksbücher nach den frühesten Drucken* by Peter Jerusalem (Munich 1912) was based.

16   See note 8.

17   See note 15.

18   See my paper on St. Cataldus, p. 224.

19   Raumer, *Geschichte der germanischen Philologie* (Munich 1870), 32. Lupoldus is the name of the faithful servant in the 12th century German epic of King Rother, which in its general character is closely related with *Fortunatus.*

20   See note 14.

speculate about the identities of Waldrich and Werniks, two days' journey on horse-back further inland. In the Andolosia account, the hermit lives on an island from which at low tide one can walk to the main-land, where there is a village and not far from it a sea-port. Writing this paper under the shadow of Ireland's Eye, I am naturally inclined to think of St. Nessan's island, though of course the Andolosia story seems to refer to a larger island. That the Irish sea is described as a branch of the Spaniolic Sea is in keeping with the theory maintained right up to Ortelius that Ireland was nearer to Spain than she is in reality.[21]

Apart from the information which *Fortunatus* gives on religious life in Ireland, the following points of historical information are of interest. (*a*) Lüpoldus says that he would die soon in Ireland, as this is a rough country with no vine or precious fruit. Lüpoldus thus refutes the tradition that in Ireland people reach exceptionally high age, a tradition first stated by Michael Scotus, the court magician of the Emperor Frederick II[22] and surviving in Continental literature down to Hebel's *Schatzkästlein* (1811). (*b*) His statement that there is no fruit in Ireland, is in contrast with Andolosia's experience on the hermit's island. The story of the miraculous apple-trees on the hermit's island may be connected on the one hand with the legend of St. Kevin, reported by Giraldus (*Topographia II*), and on the other hand with the tradition reported in Grimmelshausen's *Simplicissimus* of the two wells in Ireland, the water of the one conferring ugliness and that of the other conferring beauty.[23] Giraldus ascribed the scarcity of apple-trees to lack of industry by the inhabitants rather than to absence of suitable climate or soil.[24] It is not impossible that *oilein na crann ttorthach,* the island of fruitful trees, referred to in the Irish life of St. Brendan par. 140[25] was confused with *Ellanu frugadory* (*oilean a phurgadora*) as described in Camden's *Hibernia* (Frankfurt 1590, p. 710).[26] (*c*) The statement that wine is scarce in Ireland is made in both the Fortunatus account and the Andolosia account. The fact that Fortunatus can buy at Werniks a casket of wine, as a precious gift to the abbot, is in keeping with Giraldus's famous statement: *"Vineis ... semper caruit et caret. Vina tamen transmarina ratione commertii terram replent."*

3

I have shown elsewhere that the first phase of Irish-German literary relations (up to the year 1150) is purely hagiographical, while the second phase covering practically the

---

21   *"Hibernia medio inter Britanniam et Hispaniam"* (Tacitus, Agricola, 24).

22   See my review of Thorndike in *Irish Book-Lover*, xxix (1944), 21.

23   See my paper in *Modern Language Review*, xl (1945), 40. See also the tradition of the magic alder or lime-tree in Inis Cealtra in Lough Derg (Flower, *Catalogue of Irish MSS*, p. 500).

24   See also the classical accounts of Ireland's fertility, especially that in the *Visio Tnugdali* (A. Wagner's edition, Erlangen 1882, p. 6).

25   Plummer, *Bethada naem nErenn* (Oxford 1922), i, 75.

26   See my paper on "Early representations of Irishmen in German books" in *Proc. R.S.A. Ireland* (1950).

rest of the Middle Ages is primarily chivalresque.[27] While still preserving the tradition of St. Patrick's Purgatory, *Fortunatus* is practically the first work to describe this pilgrimage primarily as a secular adventure. Fortunatus does this pilgrimage for no other reason than that he does not wish to be considered as a coward. The contrast between his receiving the Sacraments and praying and, on the other hand, the abbot's view of this pilgrimage is an interesting record of the mentality of the time. The chivalresque tradition of this pilgrimage may be traced right from Hugo of Saltrey's knight Owen to the account of Froissart's pilgrimage while in Dublin with Richard II.[28] That this pilgrimage was both a pious exercise and a daring undertaking is clearly expressed in the Continental accounts of St. Patrick's Purgatory.[29]

Fortunatus's account of this pilgrimage has obviously nothing in common with the two short German texts relating to this subject, published at Augsburg in 1485. These two texts relate to German Carthusians, the first speaking of one who failed to obtain his superiors' permission to go to Loch Derg, the second telling of one who met a Cistercian who had been there (not necessarily "a German pilgrim" as assumed by Sir Shane). The earliest original work written by a German on this subject was *Carmen de Purgatorio divi Patricii* (Memmingen 1496) by Burchard von Horneck; the introduction to this work is based on Solinus and the account of the pilgrimage purely traditional.

That one of the German Carthusians referred to in the Augsburg 1480 texts was refused permission to make the pilgrimage may be due to the criticism then spreading on the Continent of the tradition associated with St. Patrick's Purgatory. I have pointed elsewhere[30] to a German text written in 1480 by a Dominican at Ulm, stating that in the late 14th century Heinrich von Langstein had said that 'the horrible sights to which visitors are submitted in St. Patrick's Purgatory are brought about by natural means rather than by Divine intervention'. Heinrich von Langstein, it is said, quoted as his authority one Nicholas Ore, 'an extremely learned doctor of science'. *Fortunatus* illustrates the collapse of Continental fascination at St. Patrick's Purgatory and in fact the collapse of the Continental tradition of Ireland being the Island of Saints, but it continued the tradition, first established through the chivalresque literature, of Ireland's being a country of natural miracles.

4

Considering the fact that the accounts of Fortunatus's journey and Andolosia's journeys to Ireland are obviously derived from different sources, their agreement with regard to ecclesiastical, in particular monastic life in Ireland is striking.

---

27   See note 6.

28   Leslie, *op. cit.*, 21.

29   Seymour, *St. Patrick's Purgatory* (Dundalk 1918).

30   See my paper in *Speculum*, xxii, 365.

The hermit on the island off Ireland represents the last stage of ancient Irish monasticism, which, as a result of the great Reform of the 12th century, had been superseded by Continental orders. This process is interpreted, subconsciously to be sure, in Continental terms when this hermit is described as *Waldbruder* (as the hermit with whom young Simplicius shelters),[31] though no doubt it is historically true that the system of the ancient Irish anchorites survived longest in the remote parts of the country. In *Fortunatus* the rigidness of the life of the hermit is contrasted with the worldliness of the abbot at Werniks and still more so the convent in which Agrippina is received. By comparison with old Irish monasticism, the rules of the Continental orders generally appeared as soft.

The organising of St. Patrick's Purgatory and the spreading of its fame throughout Europe was one of the numerous attempts to establish a traditional connection between old Irish monasticism and the monastic system introduced from the Continent. The propagation of the pilgrimage to St. Patrick's Purgatory was mainly due to the Canons Regular[32] who in the late 12th century took over the ancient sanctuary of St. Dabheoc, *Termon Daveog*, associated with St. Patrick, in Lough Derg. It was probably under the Canons Regular that St. Dabheoc's seat, on the mainland by the lake, was re-named St. Brigid's seat.[33] I have shown elsewhere[34] that for the subsequent five hundred years the Canons Regular were among the chief promotors of devotion to the patron Saints of Ireland on the Continent.

That the convent to which Agrippina is taken was "not far from St. Patrick's Purgatory" is to be understood in the spiritual rather than the geographical sense. I suggest that this convent is Kildare; the Canons Regular claimed for themselves not only all the Patrician monasteries but also those under *ban-chomhartha Brighde*. In his *Propugnaculum veritatis* (Prague 1669),[35] Anthony Bruodin, the great Irish Franciscan scholar, told Continental readers how Derforgilla eloped with Dermot while her husband made the pilgrimage to St. Patrick's Purgatory. When the two lovers were overtaken by the husband, Derforgilla is sent to St. Brigid's convent Kildare. There may even be a connection between Agrippina's entering that convent because of her horns, and the tradition of St. Brigid being permitted to embrace religious life because God had made her unsightly.

---

31   See my paper in *Mod. Lang. Rev.*, xl, 37f. In her introduction to the Dutch version of the *Navigatio Brendani* (Amsterdam 1948; see my review in *I.H.S.*, 1951), Dr. Draak has drawn attention to the fact that hermits living on islands play a great part in *Immram Maelduin* and – in contrast to the Latin version – in the German tradition of the *Navigatio Brendani*.

32   The first of the Augsburg 1485 accounts expressly says that the monastery built by St. Patrick over the cave was peopled by monks of St. Augustine.

33   See Leslie, *op. cit.*, also A. Curtayne, *Lough Derg* (London 1944), and J. Ryan in Buchberger's *Lexikon f. Theologie und Kirche*, vii (1935), "St. Patrick's Fegfeuer".

34   "Irish Saints in the literary tradition of the Order of Canons Regular" in *Comparative Literature Studies*, xvii/xviii (1945), 20-29, and xix (1946), 17-21.

35   P. 938f.

It is a well-known fact that the closing of the Purgatory in 1497 was caused through the unfavourable report made by the unnamed monk or Canon Regular of the monastery of Eymstadt in Holland, a devout observant of the statutes of his order's chapter at Windesheim. It is usually assumed that the main point in his report was that, as there were no more visions in the cave, this pilgrimage was liable to superstitious abuse. Such abuse, however, must also have been due to some mismanagement by the Canons at Lough Derg, whom the Eymstadt monk attacked for their refusal to adhere to the reform. An interesting link between the report of the Eymstadt monk and that of *Fortunatus* is that in both instances the pilgrims were rescued from the cave by means of a rope.[36] *Fortunatus* seems to represent the conditions at St. Patrick's Purgatory which the Eymstadt monk found.[37] Complaints at lack of edification in the cave had made the abbot cautious. The religious significance of the pilgrimage had become to him a mere tradition and – a source of income. The precarious financial position of the Canons since the decline of the pilgrimage is illustrated in *Fortunatus* by several details which can scarcely be considered as entirely fictitious. It is mainly for this detail that this account of the pilgrimage ranks very high among the sources of the traditions of St. Patrick's Purgatory.

In *Fortunatus* the Purgatory is described as St. Patrick's *Loch*. The German word *Loch* of course means "a hole", but it is quite possible that this description was associated with the Irish word "loch". There is no reference in *Fortunatus* (or the Augsburg 1485 accounts) that St. Patrick's Purgatory was situated on an island, in a lake.

5

In Germany, the historical tradition of St. Patrick's Purgatory was continued through C. Loecher's study *De fabulosos Patricii Purgatorio* (Leipzig 1660) and C. Meiner's *Beschreibung der Höhle des Hlg. Patricius in Irland* (Göttingen 1793). The first description of the pilgrimage in a German travel-book on Ireland is that (entirely based on Inglis) in Knut J. Clement, *Reisen in Irland* (Kiel 1845), one of the few German travel-books on Ireland to start with, and to treat extensively of Ulster.[38] However, the literary tradition of *Fortunatus* provided far more popular information on this subject. In *Fortunatus mit dem Wunschhütlein* (1553), the great Hans Sachs[39] for the first time placed an Irishman on the German stage. V. 250f. Leupolt gives a summary of his life before he met Fortunatus, expressing his desire to settle down for the rest of his life

---

36 William Staunton (1409) was rescued from the pit by a woman who let a cord down into the cave from the top of a tower, but this was part of the vision and a spiritual explanation is given (Leslie, *op. cit.*, 32f.)

37 According to Günther, *Fortunatus* was compiled by a citizen of Nürnberg about 1450. His account of St. Patrick's Purgatory tallies most closely with that of the Canon of Waterford reported by Caxton in *Mirror of the World* (1480).

38 See my paper on this book in *Bealoideas*, xvi (1946), 251ff.

39 *Deutsche Dichter des 16. Jahrhunderts*, ed. K. Goedecke and J. Tittmann (Leipzig 1885), vi, 119ff.

in Hibernia weit hier hinder
darin hab ich mein weib und kinder.

Leupolt promises Fortunatus that he will bring him "through all the kingdoms I know *in Schotten und in Engellant,* France and Spain". There is no reference to a visit to Ireland, but in the account of Andolosia we hear of his taking Agrippina "to a desert, a hundred miles from England, *in Hibernia,* unknown to thee (Agrippina), not far from St. Patrick's Purgatory", and the second time *"in dem land Hibernia* into a rich convent".

There is ample evidence for Goethe's intimate acquaintance with the *Volksbuch* of *Fortunatus,* which he knew from his childhood days.[40] About the same time August Wilhelm v. Schlegel, Adalbert von Chamisso, Ludwig Uhland, Wilhelm Schwab and Matthias C. v. Collin[41] treated of Fortunatus, but the most famous version of this tradition, produced by the Romantic movement in German literature is Tieck's play *Fortunatus* (1815), in which the Irish associations of the *Volksbuch* are not only preserved in all detail but actually extended. When in a scene taking place "near St. Patrick's Purgatory", one of the characters exclaims: "O Ireland! Ireland! sad and gloomy country!",[42] he expresses something of Continental consciousness of the history and geography of Ireland. Indeed Tieck's *Fortunatus* represents the blending, on the one hand, of the traditions of the Island of Saints and of Ossian's country with the new awareness of contemporary Ireland.

It has been due to its incorporation into the *Volksbuch* of *Fortunatus* that the tradition of St. Patrick's Purgatory continued to exercise its influence on the Continent beyond the end of the Middle Ages. This incorporation took place when the religious significance of the tradition of St. Patrick's Purgatory was waning, and in such a form that it was acceptable to the modern mind. In view of the scarcity on the Continent of direct and comprehensive information on Ireland, the importance of such traditions as sources of indirect information on certain aspects of Ireland can scarcely be underrated in the study of Irish-Continental literature relations.

(Quelle: Ulster Journal of Archaeology 13, 1950, S. 93-104.)

---

40 *Aus meinem Leben I,* i (Weimar edition I, xxvi, 51f.); letter from his mother, 2 May 1807; diary 12 April 1808.

41 Kosch, *Deutsches Literatur-Lexikon,* i, 474.

42 *Schriften,* iii (1828), 166. My thanks are due to Dr. Hans Reiss, London, and Dr. Heinrich Haverkamp, Bonn, for assisting me with some bibliographical details.

V.2 16.-18. Jahrhundert

Notes on Early Representations of Irishmen in German Books

The first Irishmen to be represented in Continental Art were, naturally, the saints and missionaries who had come, or were reputed to have come, from Ireland and sub-sequently, Irish saints whose cultus was imported by those missionaries.[1] The first Irish layman who became sufficiently notorious in Continental literature that pictorial representations of him might be expected, was Tnugdal or Tundalus, a knight (*miles*) from Cashel, whose visions of the other world (at Cork) as written up in 1149, by his country-man, Marcus, at Ratisbon,[2] were, apart from the reports on St. Patrick's Purgatory, the chief source of popular information of the Continent on mediaeval Ireland.[3]

The first Irish layman, and I believe the first Irishman in general, to be represented in a book printed on the Continent, was Lüpoldus from "Waldrick" in Ireland, the servant of Fortunatus. I have before me a photostat of the first print of *Fortunatus* (Augsburg 1509), in which the chapter entitled "Wie Fortunatus and seyn diner Lüpoldus in Patricius loch giengen" includes a woodcut showing Fortunatus in conversation with the abbot at St. Patrick's Purgatory; the subsequent chapter entitled "Wie Fortunatus wider gen Venegid kam" begins with a wood-cut showing the embarkation from Ireland, Lüpoldus standing in the ship, while Fortunatus hands him some goods. *Fortunatus* was one of the most popular cosmographies in novelistic form, a type of literature among the earlier representatives of which we have the *Navigatio Brendani* and *König Rother*, one of the first secular works of German literature to refer to Ireland. The "Volksbuch" of Fortunatus was re-printed on the Continent and in England right up to the 20th century; its literary influence – I only mention Dekker, Tieck and Carlyle – has never been fully explored.[4] During the period when Continental knowledge of Ireland was at its lowest, *Fortunatus* was almost the only original expression of Continental "Irlandkunde".

The ebb of Continental knowledge of Ireland during the late 15th and early 16th centuries was due to the lack of direct intercourse. The Irish monastic organisation, during the 13th and 14th centuries the chief source of Continental information on Ireland, had collapsed.[5] The last of the numerous mediaeval records of Irish students at a German

---

1. Some additions to the late Dom Louis Gougard's *Les saints irlandais hors d'Irlande* (Louvain 1936) were made by my article on "Irish saints in the liturgical and artistic tradition of Central Europe," *Irish Ecclesiastical Record* V, lxi (1942), 184 ff.

2. See my article on "St. Albert, patron of Cashel" in *Medieval Studies* vii (1945), 27 and the literature listed there.

3. See my article on "Irish Saints in early German literature", in *Speculum* xxii (1947), 364 ff.

4. See my paper "Fortunatus in Ireland" to be published in *Ulster Journal of Archaeology*. For illustrations in early prints of the Continental versions of the *Navigatio Brendani* see my 'review of Dr. Draak', edition to be published in *Irish Historical Studies*.

5. See my article on "Irish monastic activities in Eastern Europe," in *Ir. Eccl. Rec.*, VI, lxv (1945), 394 ff. and the literature listed there. It is possible that early prints of *Till Eulenspiegel* contain

university so far known dates from 1441.[6] The first book by an Irishman to be printed in Germany was *De Tribus Punctis Religionis Christianae* by Thomas de Hybernia,[7] Lübeck 1496.[8]

The best known representation of Irish laymen during the 16th century are the drawings which in 1521 Albrecht Dürer entered at Antwerp in the sketch-book of his journey to the Low Countries. They are two in number, entitled "Also gand dy krigsman in Irlandia hindr engeland" and "Also gand dy pawren in Irlandyen". So far as I know, these drawings were first reproduced in Ireland by the *Journal of the R.S.A.* July-October 1877, with the notes: "The great artist's own brief words are all we can tell about them." These words hold good to the present day. Reproducing these drawings in his book on *Old Irish and Highland Dress*, H. F. McClintock said that they represented "Irish people, perhaps pilgrims, whom Dürer met on the Continent"[9]. Chotzem felt that while the peasants were Irish alright, the soldiers appeared to be Scottish.[10] In the latest discussion of these drawings, Panofsky[11] stated that it has been suggested[12] to read the words "Irlandia" and "Irlandyen" as "Zelandia" and "Zelandyen" respectively. This reading is impossible, because the word "Irlandia" is followed by the special mention "hindr engeland"[13]. I do not understand why Panofsy continued: "*This proves* that Dürer made costume studies of this type not only from life but also from drawings, for he never went to Ireland." Is it not most unlikely that just on a journey Dürer should have engaged in costume studies from drawings, and this in a place like Antwerp, which afforded ample material for life-studies? Why shall

---

illustrations to the episode in which that famous rogue associates himself with a "Schottenpfaffe", who illustrates the synonymity which by that time the German word "Schotte" frequently has with "vagabond" (see Grimm's *Deutsches Wörterbuch*).

6   Fitzmaurice-Little, *Materials for the history of the Franciscan province of Ireland* (Manchester 1920), 192.

7   Supposed to be from Johnstown near Naas, Co. Kildare, see *JRSAI* v, 65.

8   No less than 19 manuscripts of this work were in the university library of Prague, see Esposito, *Latin writers of mediaeval Ireland* (1913), 511.

9   Dundalk 1943, ill. 19 and p. 26 f. These drawings were also discussed by L. Price in his article on "Armed forces of the Irish chiefs in the early 16th century" *JRSAI* lxii (1932), 201 f.

10   Th.M. Chotzen & A. M. Draak, Lucas de Heerdt's *Beschrijving der Britanische Eilanden* (Antwerp 1937), ixxx.

11   *Dürer* (London 1945), i, 216 and ii, 127.

12   I do not know to which earlier writer on this subject Panofsky refers, Friedrich Lippmann, *Zeichungen von A. Dürer in Nachbildungen* (Berlin 1883/1929), (62) and (129) (quoted by Chotzem strangely enough in a French title), J. Veth and S. Müller, *A. Dürers niederländische Reise* (Berlin 1910) I, p. xliv, Winkler in *Klassiker der Kunst* iv, 825 or L. Tietze's *Kritisches Verzeichnis?*

13   This suggestion is reminiscent of the earlier one that "Irland" as mentioned in the beginning of *Kudrun*, the 13th century epic, was not Ireland but Eyerland, a province of the Netherlands. Quite apart from Panofsky's reference to the words "hindr engeland," in both instances these suggestions are due to ignorance of Ireland's place in Continental thought.

we reject the obvious explanation that in that port he met those strangers? In 1572, Lucas de Heerdt embodied in his *Beschrijving der Britische Eilanden*[14] similar illustrations of the Wild Irish and the Anglo-Irish, of an Irish woman and girl, and of Irish men and women in the attire in which they had appeared before the late King Henry.[15] This may be a reference to the appearance of Irish characters in "mantles according to the Irish fashion" in Masques performed under and before Henry VIII. Irish characters became a standard feature in Masques, and this was one of the sources of the stage-Irishman. The masque of 1557 featured "Almaynes, Pilgrymes and Irishmen, with their insidents and accomplish accordingly."[16] The masque *The Irish Knighte* was shown at Whitehall on Shrove Tuesday, 1577, before Elizabeth.[17]

On the feast of St. Thomas of Canterbury (traditionally a sort of All Fools Day) 1613, Ben Jonson's *Irish Masque at Court* was performed at the wedding of Robert Carr, Earl of Somerset, with the daughter of Thomas, Earl of Suffolk. In this masque appeared the characters of Demnise, from the Pale, Donnell, Dermock and Patrick to announce the arrival of twelve noblemen from Ireland, who then performed a solemn national dance.[18]

An unexpected parallel to this performance is found in *Kurtze Beschreibung dess, zu Stuttgarten, bey den Fürstlichen Kindtauf und Hochzeit, Jüngst-gehalten Frewden-Fests* (Tübingen 1618), by Georg Rudolf Weckherlin, which includes a long description entitled "Der Irländischen Rittern Aufzug". This passage was first mentioned in the study on Weckherlin's life in England (Basel 1944) by Dr. Leonhard Wilson Forster, who kindly supplied me with further information on this subject.[19] In his ode, "Paranesisch, Bacchisch and Satyrisches Gemüss," Weckherlin quoted toasts in German, French, Italian, Welsh, English, Dutch, Spanish and Irish.[20]

In Irland war ich auch einmahl	On one occasion I have been in Ireland,
Und sah dort manche ding verwirren	where I saw many a strange thing,
Doch wissend wohl die rechte wahl	but knowing how to choose from them
Liess ich mich billich nicht verirren	I was not embarrassed:
Schench ein ein wenig Usquebagh	Pour out some whiskey,

---

14   See the review of the Antwerp 1937 edition in *Irish Historical Studies* 1945, 286 f.

15   Table xvi to xviii and lxx.

16   Ben Jonson ed. C. H. Herford and Percy Simpson (Oxford 1925), ii, 293.

17   W. J. Lawrence in *Gentlemen's Magazine* 269, 1890, p. 179.

18   F. Mezger, *Der Ire in der englischen Literatur (Palästra* 169, 1929), 59.

19   Basler Studien zur deutschen Sprache und Literatur, ii, 25 f and notes. A brief reference to Weckherlin in Irland in W. B. Rye, *England as seen by foreigners* (London 1865), cxxv.

20   Hermann Fischer, *G. R. Weckherlins Gedichte* (Bibliothek des Literar. Vereins zu Stuttgart, Tübingen 1894-1907), 199, p. 511, and 200, p. 494. Fischer explained that "Usquebagh" literally meant ""Lebenswasser" (Scottish: 'Whiskey')"; see my paper on "Some early German accounts of Schomberg's Irish campaign" in *Ulster Journal* 1948; p. 70 and 79). Zimmer informed Fischer that the words "sho fed tourim..." stood for "so dhuit tabhrain, dean go sugach."

In Irland überall geliebet	favoured throughout Ireland
Sho fed tuorim; den do sugagh!	
So, dieses haisset wol geübet.	That's the style!

Dr. Forster assumed that Weckherlin's visit to Ireland must have taken place between the years 1607 and 1615, possibly in 1608, when Weckherlin accompanied Prince Ludwig Friedrich of Wurttemberg through Scotland, though in the unpublished diary of this journey there is no reference to Ireland. Reprinting the *Kurtze Beschreibung* in his edition of Weckherlin's works, Hermann Fischer omitted the whole description of the Irish pageant; for Dr. Forster's purposes it was sufficient to print the paragraph relating to St. Patrick's Purgatory. Besides the words "Nu kam daher die Irländische felsige Hölin *Ellanu frugadory*," the original print has the margin note "*Camden de Hibern*".[21] The Frankfurt 1590 print of Camden's *Hibernia*, in conjunction with Ortelius's new description of Ireland, (1577), marked the beginning of a new phase of Continental "Irlandkunde".

Dr. Forster pointed out to me that the only copy of *Kurtze Beschreibung* which, to his knowledge, contained the plates was that in the Bodleian.[22] By kind permission of the Librarian, I obtained a photostat not only of the whole description of "Der Irländischen Rittern Aufzug" but also of these plates, five in number, which will be deposited in the Royal Irish Academy. While I confine myself to drawing attention to the first representation in the book printed in Germany of Irishmen in their national attire, I should be glad if an expert on early 17th century Irish history would examine these plates in conjunction with the description here attached to establish their historical value. (I understand that this will be done by Major H. F. McClintock).

Weckherlin's *Kurtze Beschreibung* was published in the year of the outbreak of the Thirty Years' War. Among the numerous pictorial representations of the assassination of Wallenstein, that in the town-hall of Eger may be specially mentioned this year, when the bi-centenary of the birth of Goethe is celebrated, who gave a fine description of it, mentioning the various Irish characters in that drama by name.[23]

The Pageant of the Irish Knights.

(While the spectators were still laughing at the procession of the Spaniards), their attention was attracted by the ringing of many brightly sounding bells and by pitiful crying and fearful clamouring. After being cheered by so many divine heroes and nymphs, they beheld a group, very strange and curious, but of stately attire, moving into the lists in the following order.

21　P. 34.

22　Selfmark Douce Prints d. 44.

23　Weimer-edition, Diaries (1 July 1806) iii, 133. With regard to the tradition of Irishmen serving in the Württemberg army, it may be noted that the Stowe Missal was once in the possession of John Dowell Grace, of Nenagh, captain of Württemberg dragoons, who retired from service in 1776 and died in Ireland in 1811 (Warner, Bradshaw Soc. xxxii (1915)), p. vii f.

PLATE XXII

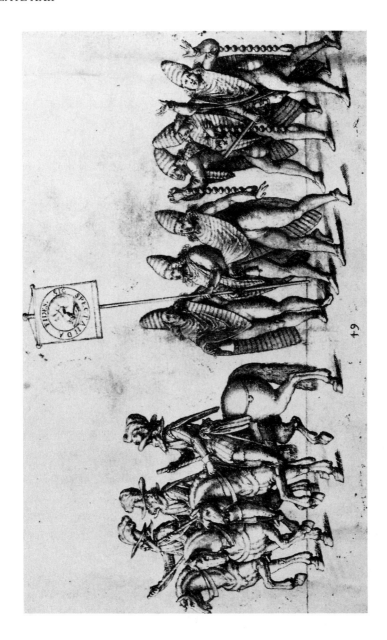

PLATE XXIII

PLATE XXIV

PLATE XXV

PLATE XXVI

In front there rode three noble heralds in stiff brown hats with white and red feathers, in garments of altas with red and white stripes, their standards with their gilt arms of the same colours as also the regiment staffs they carried.

After them came three Irishmen on foot. The one in the centre was dressed in dark brown and carried a yellow flag on which there was painted a hand probing gold on a stone, with the inscription *Sic spectanda fides*. The two Irishmen at his sides were dressed in light gray, with woollen scarfs striped in the Irish fashion, with shaggy caps, equipped with ringing bells to call the people to devotion.

They were followed by three more Irishmen in great devotion, apparently worn out by many a long pilgrimage and vigil, the two outside ones dressed in greyish green, the one in the centre in purple, all the three carrying vials, rosary beads, caps and shaggy scarfs.

Then followed three Irish harpists, playing together in sweet accord, according to their national custom. The first was dressed in yellow, the second in light blue, the third in light green. Their appearance offered a delightful sight to those who preceded them and to those who followed them.

Then, one beheld two Irish footmen in white taffeta with red patterns, walking in front of their master, who was dressed in white atlas embroidered in red and blue, holding a javelin in his hand, galloping on a snow-white steed bedecked with a red cover and bridles in the Irish fashion.

Then followed a cleric. To free the spectators from the pain and torment of what followed him, he sprinkled water on them, which was carried after him by a servant.

Now came the rocky cave of *Ellanu frugadory* in Ireland, in reality situated in a lake, about fifteen miles from Lake *Erne*. In consideration of the Cartel (see below) it should have been called *Knoc Patric, Patricii* Hill [this word in its English form], for *S. Patricius*, the Apostle of Ireland himself was sitting on it. All kinds of vermin crawling upon it, smoke rising from it, fire, howling and screaming indicate the large numbers of souls pitifully tormented inside.

Behind that rock walked a person, most beautifully dressed in blue and red. To warn the mortals and to save them from all fear of the torment represented by the previous scene, he carried a cross with the inscription *Solum Crede*.

He was followed by two footmen dressed in white with stripes in various colours, and thereafter.

Their two masters on horse-back, one in flesh-coloured cloth with blue and yellow, the other in purple-blue material with flower patterns in blue and white, carrying javelins in their hands, their horses bedecked in the same colours, small saddles and covers.

This procession was concluded by four beautiful, well-groomed horses, each one led by a stable-boy in their national costumes in their master's livery.

The cartel which an Irishman handed to the Lord judges and distributed among the spectators read as follows:

Cartel of Irish Knights.

Honoured ladies and renowned knights! Humble your hearts to receive the blessing of our priest so that you may be able to understand that I Con Cochbragan with my brothers Teg Kilmannug and Ned Clochmoga, insuperable Irish Knights of St. Patrick's Purgatory, having travelled though almost all parts of the world, freeing and cleansing it from all vice and vermin, have come here, attracted by the wide-spread fame of this gathering of excellent and insuperable heroes and knights, to obtain from this highly respected gathering new faith in our manly valour and new admiration of our knightly virtues.

That the kind-hearted and benevolent knights here assembled may not be unaware of our insuperable and unconquerable power, we wish to announce (let them beware and take care of themselves) that our heroic fortitude cannot be resisted by any knightly adversary, not even the devil himself, because those who behold us as enemies, even the devil and St. Patrick's whole purgatory (which we have produced here in triumph) are terrified and frightened at our strong hearts and our irrestible blows. Therefore, we kindly admonish and earnestly warm them to join devoutly our procession, promising them that we shall protect and deliver them, in their knightly honours, not only from all temptations by devil and hell, but also from all enemies, whom we may encounter.

We appear in these lists for no other purpose than to prove ourselves true knights defending our honour and our conscience, decided to stake our honour, our possessions and our blood in this profession.

If however any other knight may present himself, who makes so bold of his valour as to contradict us and to have a liking to try either his strength against our power or his cleverness against our lances, we are gladly prepared to meet him.

We do not doubt that our procession will be enlarged with great pleasure and concours, so that after victory has been won by us, our gallantry shall be extolled and praised with even greater admiration.

Con Crochbragan.

Teg Kilmannug.   Ned Clochmoga.

(Quelle: Journal of the Royal Society of Antiquaries of Ireland 80, II, 1950, S. 158-163.)

"German" Script in Irish Printing

Official post-cards now issued by the Allied Military Government for German postal service bear the words: "Written in German. Use only Latin characters!" While this rule was apparently made for the convenience of the censorship, it may be assumed that it also aims at generally discouraging the use of German script, as the use of distinctive characters in writing and in print may be regarded as a nationalist barrier. In this respect the present position, of "German" script may be of some interest to this country.[1]

---

1   The first to offer to the German public a printed imitation of Irish script was J. G. Kuettner in his *Briefe aus Irland* (Leipzig 1785), a book which was still one of the chief sources of in-

The use of German characters, in both printing and hand-writing, was dying out already under the pre-Hitler regime. In the Weimar Republic the teaching of writing and reading started with the Latin script, while the Gothic script was treated as a side-line. In the younger generation it was a sign of lack of higher education (where foreign languages naturally required the use of Latin script) or of extreme nationalism to use the German script. Books of scientific character or with foreign quotations were generally printed in Latin script. Many high-class publishers, such as the Insel, abandoned the use of Gothic characters, while cheaper publications such as the Reclam series appeared in Gothic script.

Newspapers were mostly printed in Gothic characters, except for the sports columns and commercial news. The newspapers of the German speaking parts of Switzerland followed this use. Type-writers were mostly equipped with Latin characters, though with the attenuated broad vowels and German double s (ä, ö, ü and ß) in the place of the keys for fractions in English type-writers.

Apart from the *Book of Common Prayer* 1551, *A Brefe Declaration of certeine principall articles of Religion* 1560 and Franckton's *Almanack* (1612), it seems that only legal texts were printed in black-letter in this country. The earliest example for this practice is the *Proclamation against the Earl of Tyrone* 1585. The various editions of *The Statutes of Ireland* from 1621 (Stationers) to 1723 (Crooke) were printed in black-letter. Black-letter was also used in the prints of the *Proclamation of the Lord Justices* of June 1642 in Coote's *True Relation* (Bladen), in the *Act of Parliament* 1681 (Benjamin Took and John Crooke), the *Acts against Papists* and the *Popish Clergy* of 1695 and 1697 and the Articles of Limerick of 1697 (Crook) etc. A mixture of black-letter and Roman character is found in the *Act of relief for prisoners* (Crook) 1699, as in contemporary German prints, such as Bernhard *v.* Zech's *Europaeischer Herold* (Leipzig 1705), an important source of early German information of happenings of that time in Ireland.

Still in 1799, Grierson printed the *Act for the suppression of the rebellion* in black-letter. Outside legal literature,[2] however, in 18th century[3] printing in Ireland the use of

---

formation of Vater, the first German Celtist. In the Rev. Alex. Dallay's *Points of hope in Ireland's present crisis* (London 1849), there is an invocation of the Holy Trinity in Irish printed in Irish characters whereas the English text is printed in black letters. In his book *Die Insel der Heiligen* (Berlin 1860) I, 139, at Glendalough; the English translation (London 1860) used black-letter in this instance.

2   As a curiosity I may quote from the anonymous *Songs of the Press* (London 1845), the following lines from 'Bibliomaniac Ballad':

To the *Roxburghe Club*, by way of dedication,
And all *black letter dogs* who have passed initiation. . . .
Though born *Georgii primo* he a CAXTON would prize
'Bove ten full-bottom'd Caxons to curl round his eyes:
And the spell of *black letter* he ne'er thought absurd
For young bibliomaniacs love WYNKYN THE WORDE.
(words in italics in the original in black letters).

black-letter was confined to German texts. The first and, to my knowledge, only German book ever published in Ireland was the German translation of the *Book of Common Prayer,* printed *by Crooke* in 1710. The translation itself was not made in these countries, but was a reprint from that published at Frankfurt on Oder in 1704. In this work both the German and the parallel English texts are printed in Gothic characters, but in the beginning a comparative table of the Roman and Gothic alphabet is given, so as to help people not accustomed to the use of Gothic characters.

In 1788, a reprint of the London edition of Thomas Holcroft's translation of *The Life of Baron Frederic Trenck* was published at Dublin (for Messrs. Chamberlaine, Wogan, Byrne, etc.). Like the London edition this Dublin reprint used Gothic characters:[4]

(a) For the title of Fischer Geschichte Friedr. II of which the note London ed. ii, 108 quoted *Theil* (Dublin ed. i, 207: *Thiel) I, S.* 265 and the note London, cd. ii, 124 (omitted in the same note Dublin ed. ii, 22) *Theil II S.246.*

(b) For the two lines from a poem *by* Trenck in the note London ed. ii, 65, Dublin ed. i, 188. In the Dublin ed. the printer mis-read the " b" in selbst and uebel for a "v" and misprinted *unr* for *nur* he certainly knew no German.

In the appendix of Denis Florence MacCarthy's *The two lovers of heaven* (Dublin: Fowler 1870), the extracts from Continental reviews of MacCarthy's *Calderon* begin with a long quotation in German from *Blätter für literarische Unterhaltung* 1862 printed in Gothic characters; the printer had no knowledge whatsoever of the German language, of the difference between round s and long s, of the use of double s or tz or of capitals, also he puts å instead of ä.[5]

(Quelle: Irish Book Lover, January 1948, S. 89-92)

Swift in Switzerland

The Historical Section of the Books of Switzerland Exhibition which was held at Suffolk Galleries, London, from April 26 to May 25, 1946 included three rare Swiftiana.

The first was a reprint of the *édition nouvelle* of the French translation of *The Tale of a Tub* which in 1721 and 1722 and in 1741 and 1742 had been published by Scheurleer in The Hague. The first two volumes are entitled *Le Conte du Tonneau, contenant tout*

---

3   In the beginning of his *Life of Johnson,* Boswell tells that in the late 'teens Johnson was first taught to read English by a lady who could read the black letters and asked him to borrow from his father a Bible printed in those characters.

4   In an article on Trenck in *Modern Language Review,* Sept. 1946, I have dealt with the largest collection of Treckiana in these countries, namely, in the Joly collection now in the National Library of Ireland.

5   This note may be regarded as an addition to Dix's paper on "The earliest printing in Dublin in the Irish, Latin, Greek, Hebrew, French, Italian, Saxon, Welsh, Syriac, Armenian and Arabic languages" in Proc. R.I.A. xxviii (1910), 14-9 ff; on the use of black-letter in the Dublin Almanack of 1612 Dix ibid. xxx, 330. A history of the printing of news-paper head-lines in Ireland may throw some further light on the history of black-letter in Irish printing.

ce que les arts et les sciences ont de plus sublime et de plus mystérieux. What the catalogue of the London Exhibition did not say was that on the title-page Swift is described as *Doien de St. Patrick en Irlande.* The Swiss reprint was published by Marc-Michel Bousquet & Cie., Lausanne-Geneva in 1742. The third volume which appeared in The Hague and the Geneva editions of 1742 under the title *Traité des Dissensions entre les Nobles et le Peuple dans les Républiques d'Athènes et de Rome,* and in 1764 by Marcel Chapuis & Cie. in Geneva. These are apparently the only French translations of works by Swift printed in Switzerland.

The second exhibit was a complete set of eight volumes of Swift's *Satyrische und ernsthafte Schriften,* translated by Johann Heinrich Waser, the curious Zürich writer, revolutionist and impostor. This translation appeared in 1756 to 1766 (that is to say, Waser began it at the age of sixteen!) with the imprint "Hamburg und Leipzig"; the Exhibition catalogue says "*recte* Zürich", probably because Mr. Teerink in his *Swift Bibliography* said that he possessed a copy exactly in the same printing, but with the imprint "Zürich bey Orell und Compagnie 1756". Actually from 1766 to 1772 there appeared another edition with the imprint "Zürich bey Orell, Gessner, Füsslin und Cie.", of which incomplete sets are found in the British Museum, the Bibliotheque Nationale and the Fribourg University Library. The German translation of *The Tale of a Tub,* published in 1767 by Orell, Gessner & Füssli at Zürich seems to belong to this edition.

The third exhibit was the translation listed by Mr. Teerink as No. 433 of *Gulliver's Reisen,* "neu übersetzt von dem Verfasser der Briefe eines reisenden Franzosen durch Deutschland," Zürich, Orell, Gessner & Füssli 1788. (This was not the first translation of *Gulliver* published in Switzerland. In 1772, the same firm had published a translation which according to Mr. Teerink, No. 216 is "no doubt a separate issue of Vol. V of *Satyrische und ernsthafte Schriften* 1772, with an interesting *Vorrede,* defending Swift against Orrery and Young.") In 1787 Orell, Gessner & Füssli published also a new translation of *The Tale of a Tub,* which was expressly described as being made by Risbeck. All these publications are extremely rare.

Johann Caspar Risbeck was born in Höchst on Main, but since 1779 lived in Zürich, from 1783 (when his *Briefe eines reisenden Franzosen* appeared) in Aarau, where he died in 1786. It may be mentioned that the Dublin reprint of the English translation of Risbeck's *Briefe* was the first book on Germany ever published in Ireland.

Thus the Books of Switzerland Exhibition has demonstrated in a comprehensive form the prominent part played by Switzerland in the spreading of Swift's works on the Continent.

It may be added that that Exhibition included also a Basle 1800 edition of the English original and a Neuchatel 1776 issue of Frenais's French translation of Sterne's *Sentimental Journey,* while the majority of the manuscripts exhibited originated from or are owned by the abbey of St. Gallen.

(Quelle: Irish Book Lover 30, November 1947, S. 54f.)

Mozart and Ireland

In her loving memoirs of Ireland in the 'sixties Mary Fogarty told us of a rural violinist who used to come to "the farm by Lough Gur" because the O'Briens shared his taste for classical music. One day he told them he had been deeply offended in the castle of the local squire when he "thought to give his lordship and her ladyship a treat by playing Mozart's Adagio in D" but was requested to "stop and give us *Philip McKeogh*". "We did not dare to laugh at this story," Sissy O'Brien writes, "so deep was the musician's sense of outrage not for himself but for his adored Mozart."

That old County Limerick violinist could hardly know that among the first to adore Mozart, in fact, among the few to appreciate him during his life-time, there had been an Irishman. The importance of this fact is recognised by all the biographers of Mozart, none of whom has failed to place on record the composer's friendship with Michael "O'Kelly".

Kelly's *Reminiscences* which appeared in 1826 a few months before his death are well known as one of the most valuable records of the cultural life of that period. While John O'Keefe's memoirs covered chiefly the history of the theatre of that time, Kelly gave us an account of musical life in Pre-Union Dublin and of the prominent part played by Irishmen in England and on the Continent in that decisive period of history of music. My interest in Kelly's *Reminiscences* was evoked through its numerous references to Irish-German cultural relations at that time in both Ireland and other countries. Kelly was born in 1762 at Dublin as the son of a wine-merchant who, for many years, acted as the Viceregal Master of Ceremonies. His mother was a McCabe. While being brought up by her as a strict Catholic, he was sent to "the best academy of Dublin, kept by Dr. Burke, a clergyman of the Church of England, whose daughter was one of the finest piano-players of the day".

At that time, Italy exercised an unchallenged hegemony in the musical world. In the Italian Opera in Capel Street, Lady Morgan tells us, the works of composers, now long forgotten, such as Sestini and Pinetti "elicited the rapture of the judicious and the applause of the gallery". At an early age, Michael Kelly was trained as a singer by "Signor Passerini, a native of Bologna, Signor Paretti, who was *vero musico*, and Signor St. Giorgio, who was then engaged at the Rotunda". At the Rotunda concerts, however, young Kelly was specially impressed by representatives of a nation who then began to ascend in the musical world, "Ritter, the famous basoonist, and Fischer, the great oboist", the latter probably a member of the famous family of singers.

Having appeared at the age of eleven in several public concerts, Michael was placed under the tuition of Rauzzini, who had sought refuge in Dublin after his expulsion from Munich (where, it was said, one of the princesses had fallen in love with him). Rauzzini prevailed upon Kelly's parents to send the boy to Naples, Mrs. Kelly wisely entrusted her son to a clerical student who was just setting out to pursue his studies at Rome. At Naples, Father Dolphin, O.P., was Kelly's "protector, guardian and guide"; he found lodgings for his ward in the house of an Irish woman, and through him Kelly received his monthly allowance from home. Fr. Dolphin introduced him to two young countrymen of his, cadets in the Irish brigade (on his visit to Palermo he saw at a revue the whole brigade), and to two young Dominicans, "one of them called Plunket, whom I often see in London even now, the other named McMahon, whom I saw the last time I was in Dublin[1] at the Friary in Denmark Street".

At Naples, Kelly saw the ballet *Artaxera* with Richard Blake, an Irishman, who has also gone abroad very young and who was considered the best grotesque dancer of his days. On the other hand, even in the very heart of Italy, he had an opportunity of observing the ascendancy of Germany in the musical world. He studied contemporary German composers[2] and had lessons from Joseph Schuster, the musical director of the Elector of Saxony.

Kelly then proceeded to Rome where he was introduced by Father Dolphin to Father McMahon, an Irish Capuchin, who showed him the sights of the Eternal City, telling him also of a wrecked Irish sailor named O'Flanagan who had just managed to ingratiate himself with Cardinal York, pleading, to the disgust of his countrymen, that he was a loyal subject of His Britannic Majesty. Later, at Leghorn, Kelly witnessed a visit of the Russian fleet under the command of Admiral O'Dwyer, and as an anticlimax, the visit of the *Fame*, a private from Dublin with an all-Irish crew. By that time Kelly had become acquainted with Stephen Storace and his sister Nancy, who had already attained to considerable reputation in the musical world. Stephen was one and Nancy four years younger than Kelly; at the time of their birth, their father, an Italian contrabass-player, was staying in Dublin. Their mother was English, and both children were born in London, where Nancy received her first musical training by Rauzzini who came there from Dublin.

It was probably the Storaces who suggested to Kelly to go with them to Vienna. Passing through Graz, Kelly met "the surgeon of an Irish regiment" (in the Austrian Army) and a great number of Irish officers, among whom were the Generals Dillon, Dalton and Kavanagh. Dalton was "an enthusiast about Ireland and agreed with me that the Irish language was sweeter and better adapted for musical accompaniment than any other, the Italian excepted. And it is true that, when a child, I have heard my father sing many pathetic Irish airs, in which the words resembled Italian so closely, that I did not know the impossibility, the impression on my memory would be that I heard him sing in that language". Later at Vienna, when Kelly in his capacity as court singer, witnessed a parade, Kavanagh addressed him in Irish. When Kelly did not understand, the Emperor turned quickly to him saying: "What is that O'Kelly, don't you speak the language of your own country?" – "Please, Your Majesty," Kelly replied, "none but the lower orders of the Irish people speak the Irish language".

It had been on the advice of Fr. Dolphin that Kelly had prefixed the O' to his name. Fr. Dolphin might have felt that it would stand his ward in good stead to appear as a relative of the famous O'Kellys in Austria. Also, perhaps, he realised that the O's and

---

1   On October 1st, 1811, at Dublin, Kelly made his last appearance on the stage at his own benefit, where he sang *The Bard of Erin* composed by himself.

2   Later he visited Haydn at Esterhazy and witnessed at Vienna the introduction of Gluck which marked the triumph of German music.

Mac's are saved from being regarded as English, and that at that time, in consequence of the Ossianic enthusiasm, it began to become profitable to be regarded as Irish. Finally there is evidence that the O' was generally regarded as a sign of nobility. Franz August Oetzel, the Prussian military expert (1783-1850), was not accepted by his noble fellow-officers until he had changed his name into O'Etzel; he really managed to describe himself as the descendant of an old Irish noble family!

"O'Kelly" had his own opinions on this subject. In spite of the Emperor's suggestion, he did not associate with his fellow-countrymen but preferred to move in the orbit of the British ambassador. When the Duke of York visited Vienna he crouched at him, as in later years John O'Keefe did, describing him as "distinguished by condescension and kindness".

All this we must bear in mind when we consider what Kelly described as "the greatest gratification of his musical life", namely his acquaintance with "that prodigy of genius, Mozart." Kelly was introduced to Mozart at a musical party at Vienna, where Mozart "favoured the company by performing fantasias and capricios on the piano-forte. His feeling, the rapidity of his fingers, the great execution and strength of his left hand particularly, and the apparent inspiration of his modulations astounded me". At dinner, Kelly sat between Mozart and Mrs. Mozart, of whom, he says, the composer "was passionately fond". Mozart conversed with Kelly "a good deal about Thomas Linley, the former Mrs. Sheridan's brother, with whom he had been intimate at Florence and spoke of him with great affection". Mrs. Mozart told Kelly that her husband was fond of dancing. "He was a remarkably small man, very thin and pale, with a profusion of fine fair hair, of which he was rather vain." This is the only description of Mozart penned by one of his Irish contemporaries.

In his *Reminiscences*, Kelly embodied the copy of an operatic melody *Grazie agl'inganni tuoi* which he described as composed by himself and arranged by Mozart for a performance in Vienna in 1787, adding that Mozart "composed variations upon it which were truly beautiful". These variations do not exist but the thematic list of Mozart's work, known as *Koechel-Verzeichnis*, lists an arrangement by Mozart of a melody by "Occhelly" with some improvement of the version published by Kelly, for two soprano and one bass voice, with a wind instrument accompaniment (flute, two clarinets, horn and basoon). So far as I am aware, this curious work has never been deemed worthy of performance at a public concert in this country.

There is evidence that Mozart regarded Kelly as a clever performer rather than a composer. On one occasion Kelly asked him, should he apply himself to the study of counter-point. "By no means," Mozart replied, "Nature has made you a melodist, and you would only distract and perplex yourself. A good melodist is a fine racer, a counter-pointist is a back post-horse." While Kelly took this as a compliment (Mozart apparently knew what a fine racer meant to an Irishman), Jahn, the author of the classical Mozart biography, gives this advice perhaps too censorious a note saying that it implied that Kelly should confine himself to writing "pretty little melodies", an expression, incidentally, showing that the derogatory use of the word "pretty" was not invented, as has been alleged, by the advocates of "modern" art.

That Mozart had a high opinion of Kelly may be seen not only from his friendship with him in general. At Kelly's request, he accepted as his pupil young Attwood, one of Kelly's English friends, and instructed Stephan Storace in the writing of *opere buffe*, such as in later years Storace composed with Kelly's help at London. It may be mentioned that in the history of opera Stephan Storace secured for himself a place not so much through the intrinsic value of his operas, at their time most popular, such as *The Haunted Tower, The Siege of Belgrade* and *No Song no Supper*, but through his maxim that the words of an opera should be written to the directions of the composer rather than the music to the directions of the librettist. This, the *Thespian Dictionary* (that invaluable source of English and Irish theatrical history about 1800) says, "is the modern mode of writing operas, which are therefore deservedly called vehicles for music". It is due to this maxim that Mozart's ecclesiastical music appears to us unacceptable for its purpose.

Mozart himself suffered much from the traditional conception that operas should provide, as the *Thespian Dictionary* put it, "music for the words". For his *Magic Flute*, for example, Schikaneder and Giesecke (who in later years was Professor of Mineralogy at the Royal Dublin Society and supplied Goethe with his fine collection of Irish minerals) forced upon him their political and philosophical ideas through a libretto with which Mozart must by no means be identified. Kelly himself perhaps carried Storace's theory to the extreme by just pilfering in the composition of his librettos foreign works at a rate at which even his contemporaries were scandalised, though they had rather free opinions on the subject of intellectual property. In spite of his prolific output, Kelly was unable to make a living as a composer, so he went back to his father's trade and opened a wine-shop. Sheridan proposed that he should inscribe over his shop "Michael Kelly, composer of wines and importer of music".

Whether Jahn was right in interpreting Mozart's warning to Kelly, it appears that he was greatly pleased with him as a singer. The most valuable part of Kelly's *Reminiscences* is perhaps his description of the first performance of *The Marriage of Figaro*. The *Nouvelle Biographe Générale*, which has an excellent article on Kelly, says that Mozart actually wrote for him the part of Basilio, which at any rate he took on that occasion. Later he took the part of Don Curzio. Against Mozart's advice he stuttered the part of the judge right through, even in the sextet (where Mozart had expected, this would not work); at the end of the performance Mozart expressed his delight at this tour de force.

At Salzburg, Kelly found Mozart's father, "a pleasing intelligent little man", while Leopold Mozart in a letter to his daughter describing this visit, speaks of the "Vienna opera tenor O'Kelly, who is an Englishman by birth". Both Mozart and his father spoke English, but preferred to speak Italian, and we may assume that their conservations with Kelly were mostly carried on in this language.

Of Miss Storace we hear little in connection with this visit. Old Mozart however seems to have taken a fancy to her mother who chaperoned her daughter through the world; he guided her through Salzburg. Kelly's association with the Storaces continued right to the death of the latter. During her years in London, Nancy Storace received seven letters from Mozart, none of which had been preserved. It was only after Mozart's death that she returned to the Continent. Kelly however remained for the rest of his life on this side of the Channel. Considered as a possible source of Mozart's information on Ireland, he is a typical representative of the Dublin in his days. Still he is the focal point of Mozart's associations with contemporary Ireland, and we may be contented with what a hundred years ago William Robson, "the Old Playgoer", wrote of him: "To have been honoured by an intimacy with Mozart he must have been something".

(Quelle: Irish Monthly 75, 1947, S. 377-382.)

Augustine Gibbon de Burgo: A Study in Early Irish Reaction to Luther

On 18th February, 1546, Martin Luther died at his birthplace in Eisleben. Germany to-day is in a state even worse than that in which she was on the first centenary of that day, when, towards the end of the Thirty Years' War, vast portions of her territory were occupied by foreign powers, many of her cities in ruin, and one-third of her po-pulation killed.[1]

In the first years of the sixteenth century when Luther was a student of law in Erfurt, he can hardly have failed to come across some memories, preserved in names of streets and buildings, of the *Schotten*[2] or Irish monks, who had been established there in former centuries. Of the houses belonging to the congregation of Irish Benedictines under St. James's, Ratisbon, Erfurt was the one furtherst to the north. [3] Little is known of that monastery.[4] In the Erfurt Annals it is frequently mentioned in connexion with ordinations held there.[5] Towards the end of the thirteenth century the Ratisbon con-

---

1   Peter Reade, an Irish Jesuit at Salamanca, whose *Commentaria in libros Machabaeorum* (Lug-dun., 1651) frequently refer to Luther (see Index), states that the Lutherans 'saecularem impiae religionis suae numeravere, et ludis et carminibus, numeribus, jubilo, gaudioque ingenti celebra-vere' (p. 335). See my article 'The Machabees and the Irish' in *Irish Monthly*, January, 1947.

2   Duhr, *Geschichte der Jesuiten* (Freiburg, 1907), i.p. 423 shows a plan of Erfurt of 1650, no. 23 'Schottenkloster'.

3   See my article on 'Irish Monastic Activities in Eastern Europe,' in I. E. RECORD, series vi. vol. lxv. (1945), p. 394 f.

4   It is generally assumed that this house was founded in 1136 (Gougaud, *Christianity in Celtic Lands* (London, 1932), p. 183). In Erfurt records, however, it is traditionally stated that this foundation took place in 1036, that would be forty years before Muiredach came to Ratisbon (*Annales Erphesfurtenses*, ed. Holder-Egger (Hanover, 1899), pp. 152, 790 and 810), also Lap-penberg (one of the early co-operators in *Monumenta Germaniae historica*) in his article on Ire-land in Ersch-Gruber's *Encyclopädie* (Leipzig, 1845), i., xxiv. pp. 53 and 61. See also W. Schum, *Verzeichnis der Amplonianischen Handschriften-Sammlung zu Erfurt* (Berlin, 1887), pp. 115 and 239 ('iste liber est puerorum de Scotia').

5   Holder-Egger, op. cit. Index.

356

gregation began to decay. About 1300, Nicolaus de Bibera entered in his *Carmen sati-ricum* the often-quoted[6] lines:

> Sunt et ibi (in Erfurt) Scoti
> qui cum fuerint bene poti,
> Sanctum Brendanum
> proclamant esse decanum
> in grege sanctorum
> vel quod deus ipse deorum
> Brendanus frater
> sit et ejus Brigida mater.
> Sed vulgus miserum
> non credens hoc esse verum,
> estimat insanos
> Scotos simul atque profanos.

The chief cause of the decay of the Irish monasteries on the continent was the discontinuance of intercourse with Ireland. In the twelfth century, this congregation had received supernumerary clerics from Ireland,[7] but in the fifteenth the inmates of those houses tended to go back to Ireland.[8] In the early fifteenth century the Irish monastery at Erfurt had only three inmates.[9]

Luther apparently never referred to the Irish monks or to Ireland. When, in 1522, he wrote his rude answer to Henry VIII, *defensor fidci*,[10] he described him as 'von gotis ungnaden könig von Engellandt' and suggested that his alliance with the Pope was due to his fear that otherwise God might punish him for murdering the other descendants of the royal family. At that time Henry VIII had not yet assumed the title of 'King of Ireland', the reference to which title is in many later German writers the only instance in which Ireland is mentioned.

Due to the later activities of Henry VIII, we have little chance of studying early reaction in Ireland to Luther and his teaching. The subject of my article is the work done on the continent by an Irishman in defence of the Catholic faith against Luther and his followers. The greater part of the life-work of Augustine Gibbon de Burgo was devoted to this object. Several of his great fellow-countrymen at that time, labouring and writing in exile on the continent, occasionally dealt with Luther.

---

6   See e.g. Carl Schröder, *St. Brendan* (Erlangen, 1871), iv. and Gougaud, *Les Saints Irlandais* (Louvain, 1936), Appendix iii. On Nicolaus (probably a native of Geithain in Saxony) and his *Carmen*, see Wegele in *Allgemeine Deutsche Biographie*, ii. pp. 613 f.

7   As late as 1310 a Franciscan from Co. Galway joined the Irish Benedictines at Würzburg (see also below, p. 142, note 2). Fitzmaurice-Little, *Materials for the History of the Franciscan Province of Ireland* (Manchester, 1929), p. 93.

8   M. Callenan, *The Abbey of the Holy Cross* (Dublin, 1929), p. 35.

9   Dr. Binchy in *Studies* (1929), xvii. p. 210.

10   Weimer edition of Luther's works, x., ii. pp. 227 and 262.

The earliest account of Luther's life found in any printed book written by an Irishman[11] is embodied in the *Annnales Hiberniae* which Thomas Carve, a Tipperary man,[12] who styled himself chaplain of all the Irish forces serving in the Imperial Army, wrote under the title *Lyra sive Anacephalaeosis Hibernica*, fist published at Vienna in 1651. Under the year 1517, Carve refers to the beginning of the Reformation: When Tetzel, a Dominican, was entrusted with the propagation of the great indulgence, 'nunnulli Augustini exagitati fuerunt, praecipue Stampitzius [sic] Ordinis superior per partes Germaniae, vir doctrina ac sapientia praestantissimus, nec non Martinus Lutherus, ejusdem Ordinis Theologiae Doctor, qui 95 Theses ad valvas templi arcis Wittembergensis in Saxonia affixit'. Carve gives as his source for this entry Surius and Sleidanus. For 1518, he enters Luther's meeting Cardinal Cajetanus at Augsburg, and for 1521, he says, Luther 'in quandam arce juxta Isennacam detinetur, ubi multa de votis monasticis, de abroganda missa privata, de auriculari Confessione sordide conscripsit' (no reference to Luther's translating the Bible during his sojourn at the Wartburg). 'In hunc quoque Anglorum Rex Heinricus Octavus opusculum omni Religione plenum edidit, in quo Lutheri opera de captivitate Babylonica aptissime refutavit: quare a Leone Papa . . . Catholicae fidei defensor est appellatus'. For 1547, however, Carve enters: 'Heinricus infeliciter vixit, infelicius diem estremum clausit'.[13] Of English descent as he was, Carve tried to take as lenient as possible a view of English activities in Ireland. In 1525, Carve commemorates Luther's 'marriage'.

A comprehensive account of the whole life of Luther is found in the first thirty pages of the second chapter of *Propugnaculum Veritatis*, the celebrated work of Anthony

---

11　An active part in German church politics at Luther's lifetime was taken by Robert Waucop, a Scotchman, who shortly before his being raised to the dignity of Archbishop of Armagh accompanied Campeggio, the Papal Legate, to the Conference of Worms and the Imperial Diets of Ratisbon and Spire (1540 to 1542). See Moran's *Spicilegium Ossoriense*, i. pp. 13 ff.

　　The earliest printed book in which an Irishman dealt with Luther seems to be the famous *Britannomachia* (Douai, 1614) by Henry Fitzsimons, a Jesuit from Dublin (see Index).

　　As a curiosity, I also quote the earliest poetical references made by an Irishman to Luther:

　　　. . . (Germania) nunc ipsa ab avitis
　　　Ritibus, invidia Procerum, et Monachalibus iris,
　　　Defecit patrum : Fovit Lutherus ab inde
　　　Dividium. Augustae Confession Religionis
　　　Facta novae : tandem Transactio Passaviensis . . .
　　　(Carmen saeculare (1711), by William O'Kelly from Aghrim.)

12　On Carve, see the introduction by Kearney to the reprint of Carve's *Itinerarium* (London, 1859).

13　One of the points on which Bruodin (see below) attacked Carve was that he had said that he had prayed for the repose of the soul of Henry VIII. In his *Itinerarium*, chapter xxv, Carve refers to the denial of the belief in the Real Presence by *sectores Lutheri*. Reade (see above, p. 135, note 1) refers to the disturbances caused in Ireland by *Lutheri et Calvini turbulentissima proles* (Preface, § 11).

Bruodin,[14] born in Co. Clare, professor at, and guardian of, the Irish Franciscan house at Prague (ibid. 1669).

'Martinus Lutherus, Europae pestis, mundo datus ad Islebii in Saxonia.' [His name] 'germaniee scurrum, bohemiee latronem significat.[15] Erfordensi in Coenobio Patrum Augustinorum mundo valedixit.'

Bruodin admits that there had been grave abuses in connexion with the preaching of the Indulgence. He gives a list of 43 errors of Luther. In the short summary of his theological lectures given at the Archiepiscopal Seminary at Prague, which Bruodin published for the benefit of his former pupils under the title *Manuale summae totius Theologiae* (Prague 1663 and 1664), he scarcely referred to Luther, not even when discussing indulgences (ii. pp. 83 ff.).

Richard Archdekin or Arsdekin, S.J., from Kilkenny,[16] who for many years taught philosophy and theology in Belgium, wrote a similar work under the title *Theologia Tripartita,* which appeared at Antwerp, 1671; we can trace at least twelve reprints of this work, published at Antwerp, Cologne, Dillingen, Ingolstadt, Prague and Venice; as late as 1860 a reprint appeared in Spain edited by A. J. A. Claret y Clara, Archbishop of Santiago. In vol. i. *Controversiae Heterodoxae et Scholasticae, tractatus* iii. entitled 'De sectis modernis', gives in article 2 a list of Luther's errors with reference to various of his works and pronouncements; article 3 deals with the ramifications of Lutheranism; this treatise concludes with the Bull of Leo X against Luther (Denzinger No. 741-81).

A little-known summary of the life of Luther is found in *Viaggio di cinque anni in Asia, Africa et Europe del Turco* (Milan, 1686) by John Baptist de Burgo, 'abbot of Clare[17] and Vicar Apostolic of Ireland'.[18] In 1672, on his journey from Milan via

---

14   See Gregory Cleary, *Father Luke Wadding* (Rome, 1925), pp. 136 f. and pp. 153 f. In his *Armamentarium Theologicum* (Prague, 1678), ii. 2, p. 62, Buodin refers, regarding Luther, to his *Propugnaculum* ii. p. 4.

15   In his *Responsio Veridica* (Sulzbach, 1672), to Bruodin (p. 226), Carve refers to 'illa puerilis et insulfa inversio et lusus nominum', by which the name of Zwingli was derived from 'swine', an 'etymology' to which the Protestants retorted by calling Dr. Eck 'Dreck' (the German word for 'filth'). By such nonsense, Carve says, 'offenduntur piae aures, obstinantur haeretici'.

16   DeBacker, *Bibliothèque des Ecrivains de la Compagnie de Jèsus,* (Liège, 1834), ii. pp. 33f., vii. 34; Bellesheim, *Geschichte der katholischen Kirche in Irland* (Mainz, 1891), iii. pp. 690 f. and *D.N.B.* i. (1908), p. 540.

17   'Clarense nobile coenobium penes Fergium fluvium Canonicis Regularibus Sti. Augustini ante ingressum Anglorum fundavit Dermotius O'Brien' (Bruodin, *Propugnaculum*, p. 967).

18   I have discussed the place of this work in the literary tradition of Ireland on the continent in my article on 'The Literary Tradition of Irish Saints in the Order of Canons Regular', in *Comparative Literature Studies*, 1945, (xvii.-xviii.), 24. See Todd's manuscript notes to Ware-Harris, *Writers of Ireland* (Dublin, 1764, Trinity College, v.g. 5, p. 256), and below, note 23. In his *Anatomicum Examen* (Prague, 1671), Bruodin quotes some lines dedicated to Carve, his adversary, by ' eximius SS. Theologiae Doctor simul Abbas, Joannes de Burgo, Annae Bruodinae dignissimus filius.'

Hamburg and London to Ireland (where he was to take up his position as Vicar Apostolic of Connaught), de Burgo also visited 'Magdeburg, paese de Lutero, belle città e università ini si mostra il sepolero del rinegato Lutero et della monaca Catarina sue concubina'. De Burgo obviously confuses Magdeburg and Wittenberg. At the end of his chapter *Vita di Luttero,* he says again that after his death, 'l'anno 1546 a 18 di Febraro', Luther was 'sotterato a Magdeburg in Sassonia', whereas he refers to 'Vittenberg' only in connexion with Luther's becoming 'maestro di theologia'. Not only was Luther's body taken at once from Eisleben to Wittenberg and interred there in the Schlosskirche, but also Magdeburg was at that time far from being *bella città,* as in 1631 it had been completely destroyed by Tilly.[19]

In the second volume of his *Viaggio,* de Burgo gives on eight 12° pages[20] an account of 'vita e morte de Martin Luttero Heresiarca naturale di Bay (?) in Sassonia.' As in Bruodin's work this account is followed by a biography of Calvin, to which de Burgo adds that of Mahomet (of whom Bruodin treated in the first chapter of the *Propugnaculum*). De Burgo offers another etymology of Luther's name: 'Il suo cognomine in lingua Saxona fù Leyder, che significa Sordido.' De Burgo refers to Luther's studies *a Exfordia* and later he speaks of the condemnation of his teaching by the universities of Paris, Salamanca, Cologne, Louvain e *Dexfordia* (probably misprint for *ed Exfordia).* While thus ranking Erfurt with the leading universities of the time, de Burgo shows that he did not know the correct name of that town. He also attributes the beginning of Luther's activities to envy. At that time 'some indulgences' were published by Julius II and Leo X, without the intervention of Luther's Order, so 'egli secretemente cominciò a straparlare contro dette indulgenze; dopo publicamente predicà contro esse dichiarandole nulle.' As a zealous Jacobite, de Burgo makes a favourable reference to 'Henrico VIII Re – Dottore d'Inghilterra' for having written against Luther: 'Rispose a questo libro Luttero chiamando Henrico VIII Rè stolido, ignorante & altri titoli impertinent.'

Far more extensive and of lasting significance are the references to Luther in the work of Augustine Gibbon de Burgo.[21] He was born in Connaught in 1613, brought up by

---

19   In the second chapter of his *Itinerarium* (Mayence, 1639), Carve gives an impressive description of this *funesta tragedia* caused by *militum insano furore.* 'Magdeburgium quod olim fuerat universi orbis spectaculum, nunc miseriarum calamitatumque omnium moestissimum visitur amphitheatrum', words which have become once more true in our own time. In chapter viii. Carve speaks of the part played by the Legio Butleri in the atrocities committed at Magdeburg.

    In his *Werner* iv. 1, Byron says:
        'And who loved Tilly ?
        Ask that at Magdeburg !'

20   Pp. 388 f.

21   The first summary of the life of Augustine Gibbon de Burgo seems to have been given by Johannes Moller in his *Cimbria Litterata* (Schleswig, 1687 ; *Allgemeine Deutsche Biographie,* xxii. p. 127), on which are based Jöcher (*Allgemeines Gelehrten-Lexicon,* ii. (Leipzig, 1750), col. 983 f.), and Ossinger (*Bibliotheca Augustiniana* (Ingolstadt, 1768), p. 371). See also Harris, op. cit. p. 191, Bellesheim, op. cit. ii. p. 712 f., Hurter, *Nomenclator* (Innsbruck, 1891), ii. p. 31, and Grabmann, *Geschichte der katholischen Theologie* (Freiburg, 1933), p. 164.

pious parents and received a good education. In his *Thesaurus* (iv. 465) he speaks of the filial love we owe to our parents 'ob magnitudinem incomparabilis beneficii quod accepimus e parentibus tamquam vitae et educationis auctoribus'. At the age of twenty, Augustine Gibbon de Burgo entered the Augustinian Order, probably the Hermits Augustinian who had at that time established themselves at Ballinrobe.[22] He went to Spain where he studied at Salamanca and Valladolid. Of his teachers at Salamanca, he gratefully recalls the names of Franciscus Cornego and Bernardinus Rodriguez, both Hermits Augustinian. He lectured for five years at Valladolid. Then he was called back to Ireland, where he lectured for four years at Tuam, until the war forced him to give up this position. He retired to the monastery of Ballinrobe.[23] However, he did not cease to labour for the faith by word and writing. Thus he came into new danger and had to go into hiding with his community 'in the forests, the mountains and other desert places,'[24] until eventually – in 1652 – he had to leave Ireland altogether. Going to Germany, he became affiliated to the Augustinian monastery at Würzburg; he graduated D.D. in 1656. In the following year he was transferred to Erfurt, where in 1659 he became General-Vicar for Saxony and Thuringia, and in 1668, Provincial of the Suevo-Rhenan province of his order. He was a celebrated professor in the university of Erfurt. He died on 2nd March, 1676, and was buried with great solemnity. The bishop of Meissen[25] preached the funeral sermon.

In Würzburg de Burgo was particularly welcome. Not only was there still in existence the Schottenkloster, originally belonging to the Ratisbon congregation, then however occupied by Scottish Benedictines (who zealously took care that no Irishman should join them), but there was also a lively tradition of St. Kilian,[26] the sixth-century martyrbishop from Ireland, whose tomb is the centre of the Catholic life in Franconia. De Burgo's first work entitled *Amphitheatrum Sapientiae* appeared in 1656 at Würzburg; presumably this was his thesis. In one of the few personal references made in his works (in the dedication of the first volume of his *Theologia Scholastica,* 1669), de Burgo ascribes his obtaining a professorship at Erfurt to the special interest taken in

---

22 D'Alton, *History of the Archdiocese of Tuam* (1928), i. pp. 166 and 173 ff.

23 Twenty years later (see above, note 18), 'Giovanni Abbate de Burgo, Dottore di Sacra Theologia, e Vicario Apostolico della Diocese Aladense nella Provincia di Connacia à Tuam, fù preso da soldati Luterani . . . e condotto alle carceri publiche di Ballenrobe.' Then he was sentenced to ninety-nine years of exile from Ireland. A statement on this sentence signed by the then ecclesiastical rulers of Ireland is found in de Burgo's *Viaggio,* i. p. 103.

24 Jöcher, loc. cit.

25 De Burgo dedicated his *De Luthero-Calvinismo* (see p. 144) to Peter V. Waldenburch, Bishop of Meissen.

26 In this Notationes to the *Passio Kiliani* (Kenney, *The Sources for the Early History of Ireland* (New York, 1929), No. 317, ii.), one of the early printed books in Germany to relate to Irish saints, Nicolaus Serarius, a Jesuit from Lorraine (Wimpfen, 1598), pointed out that St. Kilian, patron of Würzburg, brought Christianity to Franconia as early as the seventh century : *Qui estis vos?* Serarius exclaims, 'o Luthere, Calvine, Zwinglie, Schwenkfeldie, unde et quando venistis? ubi tamdiu latuistis ?' (p. 62). See also above, note 7.

him and the Hermits Augustinian by the Archbishop of Mayence[27]: 'Ego ipse iam ante sexdecim circiter annos paternis laribus Crumvvelliana tyrannide procul in exilium abductus post tot discrimina rerum sorte felici ad tuae celsitudinis ditiones perveni, ibique gressu superiorum interveniente pedem fixi.'

The Augustinian monastery of Erfurt had obtained worldwide reputation for having numbered Martin Luther among its members.[28] Founded in 1273, this was one of the first houses of the Hermits Augustinian in Germany. Staupitz, Luther's friend, was the leader of a reform of this order in the early sixteenth century, and it is assumed that Luther's journey to Rome was connected with that reform.[29] In 1561 the Augustinians were expelled from Erfurt, and their monastery transformed into a secular college.[30] In 1585 the Catholic revival of Erfurt started with the arrival of the Jesuits, who in 1621 opened a college in Erfurt.[31] In 1618 the Augustinians returned to Erfurt and the college was restored to them.[32]

In Luther's time the university of Erfurt was at its height. After Prague had lost its exalted position, in consequence of the Hussite controversy and the exodus of the Germans, Erfurt became 'a new Prague'. Then Erfurt took the lead establishing Humanism in German universities.[33] Erfurt was the only German university to side with Wittenberg in the beginning of the reformation, but, after the first excitement at the

---

27　At that time, an Augustinian, Walter Heinrich V. Strevesdorf, was Rector and Chancellor of the university of Mayence (Erfurt belonged to the archdiocese of Mayence), and had other connexions with Erfurt (Ossinger, op. cit., pp. 877 f.).

28　Like Carve and John Baptist de Burgo, the present-day *Westminster-Catechism* says that one of the causes of the Reformation was that 'Luther was annoyed that the commission to preach the plenary indulgence [of St. Peter's] was given to the Dominicans and not to his own order.' As Augustine Gibbon de Burgo (*De Luthero-Calvinismo*, p. 332), stated, this suggestion was first made by Cochlaeus in his *Acta Lutheri*, 1518, a work which was already quoted in *Disputatio Apologetica de iure Regni Hiberniae*, by C. M. (i.e. Connor O'Mahony, S.J.), 'Francofurti [in reality, presumably, in Portugal], 1645', p. 226.

29　Bruodin, op. cit. p. 124, says that Staupitz and Luther fostered a schism in their Order.

30　Heimbucher, *Die Orden und Kongregationen der katholischen Kirche* (1930), i. pp. 543 and 549 f. The plan of Erfurt mentioned above, note 2, shows no. 16 St. Augustine's Church. In 1803 the Augustinian monastery at Erfurt was converted into an orphanage, but Luther's cell was 'religiously preserved' (see Koenig's illustration ' placed before the British public ' in *The Life of Luther* (London, 1858) by George Croly).

31　Paulsen, *Geschichte des gelehrten Unterrichts* (Leipzig, 1896), i. p. 198. Duhr, op. cit. i. p. 442 and ii., i. pp. 157 f. The introduction into Erfurt of the Augustinians and the appointment of Augustinians to the university seems to have aimed at reconciling the Erfurt citizens to the Counter-Reformation by agreeing to their demand that the Jesuits should not become too conspicuous.

32　Heimbucher, op. cit. p. 554.

33　Paulsen, op. cit. pp. 79 f. and F. W. Kampschulte, *Geschichte der Universität Erfurt* (Trier, pp. 1858 ff.); neither deal with the Catholic revival. A brief survey of the Catholic revival at Erfurt is found in Richard Graf v. Moulin-Eckart, *Geschichte der deutschen Universitäten* (Stuttgart, 1929), p. 82.

innovation had evaporated, both universities rapidly declined. In 1533 the university of Erfurt was practically moribund.[34] It was mainly due to the Archbishop of Mayence (who for some time was chancellor of the university; see above, n. 26), that the Augustinians were called to play a prominent part in the Catholic revival of the university of Erfurt.[35]

In 1663, six years after Augustine Gibbon de Burgo had arrived, there was published at Erfurt: 'De Luthero-Calvinismo, Schismatico quidem, sed Reconciliabili, per Adm. Rev. et Exim. Patrem Fr. Augustinum Gibbon de Burgo, Hibernum, Ordinis Eremit. S.P. Augustini, SS. Theol. Doctorem, Ejusdemque Facultatis in perantiqua Universitate Erfurtensi Profess. Publ. ac Assessorem', etc. In the dedication to the Rector and Dean of the College of the Blessed Virgin Mary at Erfurt, de Burgo expressed his hope to find a protector 'who would be in a position to defend him and vindicate him against the bites of his enemies', an allusion to his theological adversaries rather than to the persecutors of the faith in Ireland. Though the subjectmatter of the book was modern, de Burgo stated that 'meum de stabilienda pace Ecclesiastica opusculum scholasticae principi unice innititur, adeoque illa non potest radicitius discuti, nisi ad hanc referatur'. De Burgo, Heimbucher says,[36] was the last representative of what is known as 'the old Augustinian school', which had been at its height in the late Middle Ages; shortly after him, Cardinal Noris (died in 1704) established 'the new Augustinian school', which distinguished itself from Thomists and Molinists by a particular teaching on the *causa gratiae efficientis.*[37]

De Luthero-Calvinismo is devoted to the refutation of the assertion made by Joseph Hall, *Exoniensis in Anglia,* and Johannes Hülsemann, professor in Halle and Wittenberg, that Catholics are 'irreconcilable'. Right through the three hundred and fifty pages of his work, de Burgo shows that he is widely read in the works of his adversaries. He quotes Calvin's *Institutions,* the various Confessions of the reformers, the Geneva Catechism, various works of Luther and the works of Melanchthon, Gerhard, Beza, Brenz, etc. He is well acquainted with the controversies of the reformers among themselves, such as revealed by the Disputation at Mömpelgard or the fight between the Wittenberg and Jena schools. He establishes no less than seventeen essential points on which the reformed churches disagree among themselves, accusing one another of heresy.

De Burgo, however, is at his best when he demonstrates the Catholic teaching rather than when refuting heresies.[38] His explanation of the teaching on *fides implicita*[39] is not only a masterpiece, but also hits the decisive point of distinction between Prot-

---

34   Paulsen, op. cit. pp. 190 f.

35   Heimbucher, loc. cit.

36   Ibid. p. 555.

37   In *De Luthero-Calvinismo*, p. 725, de Burgo refers to a teaching proper to his order. He speaks repeatedly of theologians of his order as 'noster magister N'.

38   Hurter describes de Burgo's *De Luthero-Calvinismo* as *opus sane praestans et accuratum.*

39   P. 45.

estants and Catholics, namely, the teaching on Tradition. In an article on 'Theological Literature in the Seventeenth Century', in the I. E. RECORD, 1880,[40] attention was drawn to his exposition of the teaching on Papal infallibility in *De Luthero-Calvinismo,* ii. 2.[41] In the last section of his work, which deals with the ways and means of bringing about reconciliation, de Burgo shows that he is not only a learned theologian, but also a keen observer of life.[42] He gives a short history of the attempts to settle the disagreement by means of *colloquia.* Pugil's suggestion that two leading princes of different persuasion should appoint two theologians, 'peaceful, modest and good-natured men' to settle the matter in a manner by which charity is not offended, 'sane modus valde aptus mihi videtur. Per ipsos S. Romani Imperii Principes haec compositio politice tentetur.' Friendly conversations between princes of different persuasion, but of mutual regard, should be held in the presence of approved theologians. The princes might be interested in returning to the Church by a consideration of the following point: 'The most illustrious of the German Protestant dynasties are bound to perish, unless they return to the Catholic Church, because otherwise they will have to continue dividing their territories, as they have no means of disposing of their supernumerary sons in ecclesiastical benefits.' While hardly being very worthy, this argument certainly was based on observation of the mentality and policy of the princes of that time. With an eye to the origin of the reformation in England rather than in Germany, de Burgo adds : 'Nam propter motiva temporalia, voluptates et mundane gaudia coepit hoc Neo-Evangelicorum schisma, et propter eosdem fines finem habere poterit.'[43]

In 1667 appeared at Mayence de Burgo's *Considerationes seu Conciones Praedicabiles, super principales virtutes Christianorum, et Evangelia Dominicalia et Festivalia.* From its title we see that, apart from controversial and (as will be shown) moral and dogmatic theology, de Burgo was also interested in homiletics. Two years later appeared also at Mayence his *Theologia Scholastica in Divum Thomam, juxta illibatam ejusdem Angelici Doctoris Doctrinam et Scholam.*

In addition to de Burgo's titles given on the title-page of *De Luthero-Calvinismo,* he is described on the title-page of this work as 'olim in Hispania et Hibernia professor' and 'Provinciarum Rheni et Sueviae p.t. Rector Provincialis'. The first volume of this work, dedicated to the Archbishop of Mayence, comprises an introduction into theology and

---

40   By J. M. (series iii. vol. i. p. 283 n.).

41   Compare *Securis Evangelica ad haeresis radices posita, Pars Prima : Heterodoxa Religio propriis convicta principiis ex omni vera religione, Pars Secunda : Omnes de Religione Christiana disceptationes in una sola expeditae controversia, de perpetua infallibilitate Romanae Ecclesiae,* by Francis Porter, a Franciscan from Co. Meath, Novae-Domi, 1674 ; several reprints up to 1722.

42   The later reprints of Porter's *Securis* want the very interesting introduction on 'methodus conuincendi heterodoxos modernos ex propriis eorum principiis' (fifteen pages). Both de Burgo and Porter realized that the traditional methods of apologetics are inadequate when Protestants are to be dealt with, and that rational arguments have no longer the last word.

43   P. 332.

the treatise *De Deo* (de attributis divinis in genere, de visione beatifica, de scientia et voluntate Dei); vol. ii. (1670), dedicated to the abbot of Fulda, contains the treatises *De praedestinatione Sanctorum* and *De Trinitate.*

The approbation[44] of this work by the Censor of the Order of Hermits Augustinian says that Gibbon 'nihil magnificentius existimans quam aliis prodesse, optimas profundissimae doctrinae suae divitias quam plurimis annis in Hibernia, Hispania, Germania aliisque Regnis et Provinciis Professor Discipulis communicavit, in aperto nunc totius Qrbis theatro exponit'. It also praises him for his zeal to reconcile the different schools (as testified to also by the subsequent approbations by local superiors of the Franciscans and Dominicans; the Jesuits, strangely enough, are missing). Finally, it describes his work as one 'in quo subtilitati doctrina doctrinae soliditas conjungitur'.

In his own preface, de Burgo distinguishes himself from 'aliquorum rigidorum Thomistarum intricatas vias', and says that he, 'sicut Thomista mollis faciliora et lucidiora principia quibus res melius intelligitur et explicitur, pro mea tenui capacitate seligo et approbo'. On the other hand, in his preface to *De Luthero-Calvinismo,* he had said that 'non solis controversistis aut aliis primae tonsurae theologistris sed et perfectioribus scholasticis placere studui'. Thus, trying to steer a middle course, de Burgo had naturally to experience adversity from both sides, and his description of his adversaries suggests that in these controversies there was ample scope to display his Irish sense of humour.

Even in this work, de Burgo frequently refers to the Luthero-Calvinists. He speaks of the refutation by the university of Paris of Luther's assault on scholastic philosophy, and of the condemnation by the Council of Trent of his teaching on grace. However, the chief object of his work was the discussion of the teaching of sixteenth and seventeenth-century Catholic theologians. De Burgo's intensive knowledge of the great Spanish theologians of that period became still more evident in his most comprehensive work, entitled *Speculum Theologicum.* This work appeared also in 1669 at Mayence, but the copies preserved in this country are of the *editio novissima, correctior et pulchrior,* which was edited by Father Benedictus de Meyrelles, Or.Er.D. Aug., in Sacra Theologia Sector Jubilatus, Bracharensi archiepiscopatu Examinator Synodalis, at Coimbra[45] 1740-45. The subtitle of this edition says that in this work 'universa theologia speculativa mira claritate, methodo, soliditate et subtilitate elucidate conspicitur, aureo exarata calamo', and the title-page of the first volume contains the addition, 'sumptibus Emmanuelis de Meyrelles Freyre, in Ecclesia Sanctae Eulaliae de Godinhacos Rectoris'.

The whole work consists of six volumes (in the original edition seven bound in four), numbering altogether more then 3,200 folio pages; to the last volume of the Coimbra

---

44   The copy preserved in St. Patrick's College, Maynooth, lacks the approbations, etc. (fourteen pages) and the Index (eighteen pages). The copy preserved in Trinity College, Dublin, has also a frontispiece by Nicolaus Person depicting St. Augustine being presented by a Hermit Augustinian with a book. The complete work comprises more than eight hundred pages.

45   See *Catholic Encyclopedia,* iv. pp. 252 f. and Ossinger, op. cit. p. 573.

edition is added a reprint of *De Luthero-Calvinismo* (one hundred and ninety-nine pages without index). De Meyrelles says that the first edition of de Burgo's *Speculum* had been used so much that it had disappeared from the market. 'Gibbonii probatissimum nomen non obscurum fuit umquam in scholis et illum opus Theologicum magnis sapientium praeconiis ubique extollitur. Inclitae familiae Eremitanae Augusanae Gibbon generosum filium esse, qui Africanae Aquilae non modo nomen, sed Aquilinum haereditatvit ingenium, nemo est qui nesciat.'

It was, Meyrelles says, Gibbon's ardent wish that his work should be re-published. The approbations of the Coimbra edition (all dated 1739) also give great praise to this work. The approbation by the Censor of the Hermits Augustinian speaks of 'sapientissimi authoris ex clarissimo angelico fonte faecundatum praeclarissimum opus ab omni theo-literato orbe avide expectatus thesaurus Gibbonicae theologiae'. While vol. i. and ii. of *Speculum Theologicum* correspond to *Theologia Scholastica,*[46] vol. iii. and iv. treat of moral theology.[47] Vol. v. contains the treatises *De Christo, De Immaculata Conceptione,* and *De Sacramentis,* vol. vi. deals with the sacraments of Baptism, Confirmation and Holy Eucharist.

De Burgo's treatises on the sacraments of Penance, Extreme Unction and Holy Orders appeared posthumously under the title: 'Probatica Piscina Naturae per peccatum lapsae morbos sanans sive opus posthumum de Virtute et Sacramento Paenitentio, etc.' (Würzburg, 1687). Nowhere does de Burgo show more clearly his extensive knowledge of contemporary theology than in this work. While repeatedly referring to controversies with the Luthero-Calvinists,[48] he also discusses the teaching of some sixty Catholics theologians of his age. Five hundred and ninety-two out of the seven hundred and twenty-two pages of this work are concerned with the sacrament of Penance, a clear indication of the principal topic of theological controversies at that time. Of special interest is de Burgo's reference to the *Theologi Lovanienses* who, 'adhuc tempore non verentur [namely, in spite of the Council of Trent] resuscitare sententiam attritionem conceptam ex metu gehennae esse insufficientem dispositionem ad justificationem in Sacramento Poentitentiae' (p. 227).

From the copies of de Burgo's works preserved in the libraries of this country, we can see that he was read in the colleges of various parts of Central Europe and of the Iberian Peninsula. The copy of *De Luthero-Calvinismo* acquired in 1936 by the National Library of Ireland bears the hand-written note: 'Ad usum Fr. Ludovici

---

46   Hurter apparently confuses these two works when speaking of de Burgo's *Speculum Theologicum seu Theologia Scholastica.*

47   De Burgo's *Tractatus Schalostico-Morales in Prima Secundae et Secunda Secundae D. Thomae* (Erfurt, 1673) were not available to me.

48   So frequent are the references to Luther in this work, that on p. 266, the printer mis-spells *Concilium 'Luteranense'* for *'Lateranense'.* De Burgo traces the origin of these heresies in Wiclif. P. 444 he refers to Thomas of Canterbury and his disputes with *rex Angliae.* P. 259 he speaks of Theodore of Canterbury (whose *Poenitentiale* was printed in 1677). With regard to lay-confession, de Burgo still believed that *De vera et falsa poenitentia* (one of the main authorities for this practice) was by St. Augustine (see *Catholic Encyclopedia,* ix. p. 94 C).

Osterholt Ord. prov. 1684' and, by a later hand, 'Nunc collegii Pauli 1829'. Of *Theologia Scholastica,* the library of St. Patrick's College, Maynooth, owns both volumes: the first was owned by the Hermits Augustinian at Munich; the second bears the hand-written note, 'De Provincia Bavaric. Ord. Erem'. 1674; the first volume of this work, preserved in the National Library, was owned in 1741 by a monastery of the Hermits Augustinian in Portugal. The copy acquired by the National Library in 1940 of *Speculum Theologicum* bears the hand-written note, 'Fr. Jose de E.M.', while the copy acquired in 1936 of *Probatica Piscina* came from a German Franciscan monastery. The copy of that latter work preserved in Maynooth was acquired by 'Fr. Andrae Parocho in Limburg' for the Benedictine monastery of Amorbach in Odenwald.

It was not the purpose of this paper to discuss de Burgo's place in the history of Catholic theology or of Augustinian theology, but to outline his place as an important defender of the Catholic faith in the very home-country of the reformation. Augustine Gibbon de Burgo realized what he owed to his position as superior in the province of his order to which Luther[49] had belonged, and to his position as a professor in the university where Luther had become imbued with some of the fundamental ideas of his later work. Among the Irish theologians of that time, de Burgo was perhaps not the most original but certainly the most prolific and the most influential. In particular his *Speculum* became a recognized text-book. De Burgo's work gives us a comprehensive picture of the methods, ideas and principal tendencies of seventeenth-century theology.

Thus we may apply with special reason to de Burgo's work what, sixty-five years ago, was written in the I. E. RECORD:[50]

> The work of our theologians are monuments of which as Irishmen we may well be proud. Devoutly orthodox in their matter, clear, able and exhaustive in their manner of treatment, they offer to the searcher after truth most ample facilities for gratifying his desire. Not the least of the services rendered to Ireland by the superiors of Maynooth is that at a very great cost, though from

---

49   In the history of Irish reaction to Luther, the most important work after de Burgo's is Thomas Moore's *Travels of an Irish gentleman in search of a religion* (see my article on 'Thomas Moore as Theologian' in the forthcoming issue of *Irish Monthly*). i. (1833), p. 205, Moore sums up a Protestant sermon on Luther preached in the parish-church of 'Ballymudragget'; ii. p. 91 he speaks of Luther's cell at 'Erfurth' (see above, note 30). The 'Irish gentleman' also visited Wittenberg and the Wartburg, 'places which are now connected immortally with Luther's name'. Moore stated expressly that he himself had never been in Germany.

The only biography of Luther ever written by a modern Irishman is the popular work by the Right Rev. Henry Brann (born 1837 in Co. Meath, died 1921 in New York; see *The Catholic Encyclopedia and its Makers,* p. 17). In *Studies* i. and ii., Professor O'Sullivan reviewed extensively Grisar's *Luther* (English translation).

50   See above note 40: p. 286.

limited resources, they have secured for the College library, and thus brought within reach of the students, most, if not all, of these rare and valuable works.[51]

(Quelle: IER 69, 1947, S. 135-151)

---

51   I should like to place on record my gratitude for the generosity with which I have been permitted to examine the various rare works quoted in this article, in the libraries of St. Patrick's College, Maynooth, and of Trinity College, Dublin, and in the National Library of Ireland, Dublin.
Maynooth College Library owns a copy of Eck's *Opera contra Ludderum* (Ingolstadt, 1530) marked 'colle. S.J. Eystadii 1655' bound together with Eck's *Christenliche Underricht* (Ingolstadt, 1533).

Addendum to note 21:

Since this article was written, Mr. F. X. Martin, O.S.A., kindly supplied me with much further information of Irish Augustinians in seventeenth and eighteenth centuries Germany, a subject on which Mr. Martin is carrying out a special investigation. Mr. Martin has obtained some information from the German Augustinians, though through the destruction of the libraries of their houses at Munich and Würzburg and the complete upsetting of the library at Münnerstadt much material has been lost. The book which contains most on Augustine Gibbon de Burgo was written by a German Protestant theologian, Gisbert Menge (*Versuche zur Wiedervereinigung im Glauben Deutschlands*, 1920). Some notices on de Burgo are found in Clemens Hutters' articles on Scriptores O.E.S.A. in *Rivista Augustiniana* ii. an vii. From 1670 to 1672 Richard Gibbon, an Irishman, studied philosophy and theology at Würzburg (see above, n. 26); in later years he was confessor to the Augustinian convent of St. Catherine's, Constance. William Gibbon, who had been prior at Ballinrobe (see above, nn. 23 and 23), Tullow and Galway, was received in 1705 into the Rheno-Suebian province, and died in 1717 as professor of theology in Breisach. The works by Marcus Forstall (Prague, 1658) and Patrick Raw (Vienna, 1641), both Augustinians from Ireland, were not available to me.

Some Early German Accounts of Schomberg's Irish Campaign

PLUS PUTUIT FAMA VIRTUTIS APUD ALIENOS QUAM SANGUINIS
PROXIMITAS APUD SUOS *Swift's inscription on Schomberg's monument in St.
Patrick's Cathedral, Dublin (1731)*

In his *Itinerary* (1761) Fynes Moryson[1] told us that "a Bohemian Baron having seene
the Courts of England and Scotland would needes out of his curiosity returne through
Ireland in the heat of the Rebellion." Landing somewhere in Ulster, "for eight days he
found no bread, not so much as a cake of Oates, till he came to eate with the Earle of
Tyrone." Later "he related this their want of bread to us for a miracle who nothing
wondred thereat."

This is the first record of a traveller from the German Empire who visited Ireland from
sheer curiosity. This "Bohemian Baron"[2] is also the first person from the German
Empire of whom we hear in connection with the history of the Irish Rebellions. He
himself seems to have left no record of his experiences in Ireland. Yet in seventeenth
century German writings on Ireland, we hear repeatedly of the "want of bread" in the
Irish diet.[3]

The earliest record we have in Ireland of a German taking part in the military and political history of this country during the seventeenth century, and in fact the earliest record printed in Ireland relating to a German and of a writing by a German, is found in

*A Declaration by the Lord Lieutenant of Ireland concerning his resolution for the
peace and safety of Ireland together with copies of several letters taken in Ireland, viz.
the correspondence between Prince Rupert and Ormonde in July, 1649, printed by
special order of Oliver Cromwell, by William Bladen at Dublin, 1649.*

Prince Rupert, "Pfalzgraf vom Rhein" was the third son of Elizabeth, the daughter of
James I and the wife of Frederick V, the ill-fated "Winter King" of Bohemia.[4] Born in
1619 at Prague he was, after the battle of the White Mountain, taken by his mother to
Berlin and subsequently to Holland. In 1636 he followed his father to England,[5] where
he was received with great favour by his uncle. The university of Oxford conferred
upon him the degree of M. A. He was the soul of the royal party in the Civil War, and

---

1   London (1908), iv, 190.

2   John Talbot Dillon of Lismullen, Co. Meath, who in 1782 was made Freiherr of the German
    Empire protested in his *Political Survey of the Sacred German Empire* (London 1782, p. 127)
    against "the universal abuse of every obscure German, styling himself as a baron when distant
    from home."

3   See below.

4   *Dictionary of National Biography*, xvii (1909). 405. In his *History of the Rebellion and Civil
    War in Ireland* (Dublin 1691, ii, 167) Frederick Warner said: "The people who knew prince
    Rupert and the fickle disposition of the Irish knew that no submission to the Lord Lieutenant
    could be expected."

5   In his notes to his translation of Schiller's *History of the Thirty Years War* (London 1799 /
    Dublin 1800), the Hon. William de Blaquere dealt with the history of Frederick V and his sons.

in 1644 made C-in-C. In 1649 he landed at Kinsale, where he opened a correspondence with Antrim and Owen Roe O'Neill, without giving effective aid to Ormonde. In the summer of 1649 the Parliamentary fleet tried in vain to blockade him in Kinsale. His younger brother Maurice stayed with him.

Rupert left a natural son, Dudley Bard, by Frances, daughter of Sir Henry Bard, Viscount Bellamont in the peerage of Ireland. Frances Bard, who claimed to be married to the Prince, lived in later years at the court of the electress Sophie.

The most active part ever played by Germans in the history of Ireland is that which Schomberg and his German officers and troops took in the battle of the Boyne. With regard to the history of the development of German knowledge of Ireland, these events are of the greatest importance as they produced the first German book to deal exclusively with Ireland, namely Happel's *Hibernia Vindicata* (Hamburg, 1691). This work is the most conspicuous illustration of the new interest which Germany took in Ireland in connection with the great political events of that time. Of the numerous pamphlets dealing with those events I mention only

Catalogus etlicher sehr alter Bücher, welche newlich in Irrlandt auff einem alten eroberten Schlosse in einer Bibliothek gefunden worden, 3 pages, s.l. 1663.[6] and

Sr. Hoheit von Gottes Gnaden, Des Hn. Printzen von Oranien Wilhelm Henrichs Declaration In sich begreiffend die Ursachen, die Ihn bewogen, mit den Waffen in das Königreich Engelland überzugehen, Zu Beschirmung der Protestantischen Religion. Und Wiederbringung der Gesetze und Freyheiten von Engelland, Schottland, und Irrland, aus dem Holländischen übergesetzet, 16 pages, Hamburg, 1688.[7]

In 1690 appeared at Nürnberg

Das Neu-Geharnischte Gross-Britannien, das ist: wahre Landes und Standes Beschaffenheit derer drey vereinigten Königreiche Engel-, Schott-, und Irrlands (with special reference to the recent deposition of James II and the coronation of William III)

"represented to curious minds by a truly impartial pen" the events right up to the eve of the battle of the Boyne. The author of this voluminous work (J. C. Baer ?)[8] was a staunch supporter of the orange claims. James II he says in the preface "is hated everywhere", while William's accession was "fervently desired in those three nations by the secular and ecclesiastical states of Reformed Religion." Baer's work commences with a short survey of the natural conditions and subdivisions of the British Isles. Chapter V

6 *Flugschriftensammlung Gustav Freytag in der Stadtbibliothek Frankfurt am Main* (Frankfurt 1925), No. 4070. I have been informed that this catalogue is still in existence; I hope to publish it in the near future.

7 *Ibid.*, No. 6014. See below, note 23. In 1689 appeared at Hamburg a German translation (from the Dutch version) of Pierre Boyer's *La Couronne usurpée*. The British Museum catalogue further lists: *Relation der grossen Victoria, welche König Wilhelm ... bey Übersetzung über den Fluss Boine in Irrland wider König Jacob erhalten* (1690), and *Extract Schreibens aus London vom 7. Juli 1690, die entdeckte Verrätherei in England betreffend* (1690).

8 Catalogue of the National Library of Ireland. Not in the *Allgemeine Deutsche Biographie*.

(pp. 408 to 446) dealing with Ireland in particular is preceded by a good map and followed by an account of the Rebellion of 1641 to 1643. The description of Ireland[9] given in *Das Neu-Geharnischte Gross-Britannien* was used in *Hibernia Vindicata*, the second volume, comprising 280 pages, of *Britannischer Glücks-Wechsel*, of which the first volume entitled *Fortuna Britannica* had been published at Hamburg in 1689 with the author's name Eberhard Werner Happel, who died at Hamburg a few months after the publication of the first volume of this work.[10]

In *Fortuna Britanica* Happel gave a short description of Ireland. He says that like Great-Britain in the narrower sense of the word, Ireland consists of two parts, namely *Irishire*, inhabitated by the wild old Irish, and *The Anglis Pale*, inhabited by more cultured people.[11] Speaking in the general introduction of the character of the peoples of Great Britain, Happel informs us that the Irish are everywhere regarded as daring soldiers, enduring in trials, but unfit for work and obstinate in their actions.[11a] Since Henry II conquered Ireland, the English have multiplied there at such a rate that now only one fourth of the island is inhabited by the old Irish,[12] a statement repeatedly found in German writers on Ireland of that period.[12a] The popish Irishry made a rebellion in 1641, in the course of which they slew 200,000 Protestants. Such fantastic figures were usually given by continental writers on the Rebellion right up to the early nineteenth century.[13] It is remarkable though that the author of *Das Neu-Geharnischte*

---

9   Also with a good and detailed map, different from that however given by Baer. A very poor map of Ireland, supposed to be derived from Mercator, is found in Happel's *Historia* (see below, p. 7), where Dublin is inserted in the place of Limerick and the Arran Islands are described as the "Blasques".

10   Beneke in *Allgemeine Deutsche Biographie*, x, 551. A list of Happel's work is also found in the beginning of his *Historia*. On Happel's novels, especially *Die Insularische Mandorelli* (Frankfurt 1682), see G. Lock's Ph.D. Thesis (Berlin 1939), and Günther Müller, *Deutsche Dichtung von der Renaissance bis zum Ausgang des Barock* (Potsdam 1930, p. 256; the scene of these novels is laid "in foreign countries"). Neither these novels nor Happel's *Grösste Denkwürdigkeiten der Welt* (1683ff) are accessible to me.

11   p. 11 = Baer, *op. cit.*, p. 417. In his *Europäischer Herold* (Leipzig 1705), Bernhard v. Zech, the Saxon diplomatist (*Allg. Deutsche Biographie*, xiiv, 734 f) distinguishes (p. 234) between "the uncouth and rough *Irishire* or *wild Irish*, in which the people formerly did not allow themselves to be bound by laws and the *English pale*, whose inhabitants have received some moral culture" (words in italics are in English in the original). The first continental book to record this distinction is, to my knowledge, Mercator's *Atlas*, ii (Duisburg 1595). In *Memoire donné par un homme du Comte O'Donnel à M. D'Avaux* (1690) in *Negociations de M. le Comte d'Avaux en Irlande* (Dublin 1943, p. 735 f) three groups of inhabitants of Ireland are distinguished.

11a See below, note 19.

12   V. Zech, *op. cit.*, 236, adds that among this old Irish quarter "there are some who speak a language different from Irish".

12a See below, note 45.

13   In D. v. H.'s *Eengeland's Staatsveraandering* (Haarlem 1690; see below, p. 7) there is a gruesome illustration of the "Moort van Yerlant" (p. 7). In the biography of Cromwell (Italian: Amsterdam 1692; French: *Ibid.* 1694) by Gregorio Leti, the Protestant Italian historian, the estimate is 100,000 . This work, not mentioned in the article on Leti in *Nouvelle Biographie*

Gross-Britannien did not give any estimate of the victims of the Rebellion; probably he distrusted the sources from which these estimates were derived. "As the whole nation was so untamed and incorrigible", Happel continues, "Cromwell is said to have planned to destroy it altogether. Had he reached his aim, the Irish would not be able now to engage in such dangerous affairs as the rescue of James II."[14] In his survey of English history, Happel speaks of the conquest of Ireland, of the annoyance caused to the Pope by Henry VIII's calling himself King of Ireland, of Usher, archbishop of Armagh in Ireland, and of the association of the "Norder-Protestants in Ireland". The latest document included in *Fortuna Britannica* is dated March 11, 1689.

In the preface to *Hibernia Vindicata*, Happel gives a summary of the "early history" of Ireland, its colonisation from *Iberia*,[15] Bartholanus, the Belgian, Dananian, and Scottish Kings up to St. Patrick. A more extensive account of these traditions is found at the end of the general description of Ireland, copied from *Das Neu-Geharnischte Gross-Britannien*, where it was stated that the source was "Flahertus, a noble English writer". Between King Laogarius and King William "now happily reigning" there were, Happel states, fifty Christian kings of Ireland. Among the early Christian kings "Donatus O-Brien A. D. 1065" was the most important; Happel gives a full page picture and an enthusiastic characteristic of him:

"My readers may ask whether this work should be called Old Ireland or New Ireland. It is new because through recent events it has come to light in the German language.[15a] It is old because it unearths material from ancient records and histories. Nowhere, especially not in the German Empire, much attention has so far been paid to this kingdom, far away as it is.

The kingdom of Ireland, whose description we present now to the reader, is as it were a newly discovered country to the present-day world, because while we have heard of it and have been

---

Générale, xxx (1859). Col. 1012, is accessible to me only in the German translation, published 1710 at Hamburg under the title *Das Leben des Weltberühmten Protectors Oliver Cromwell von Engelland aus dem Italiänischen des Hn. G. L. wie auch Mehrere Frantzösischen und Englischen Scribenten.* The translator or compiler was M(agister) Ludwig F. Vischer (*Allg. Deutsche Biographie*, xl, 65 ff.) who introduced Defoe's *Robinson Crusoe* into Germany. I, 232 Vischer's translation refers top the confederation of "Kilken in der Provinz Leyster", ii, 91-95 it accounts Cromwell's conquest of Ireland, mentioning "Droghdal". Also Happel in his *Historia* (p. 110) accepted this estimate, adding: "The cause of this cruel massacre was, it is said, the heavy yoke which the English Protestants imposed on both bodies and consciences of the Irish." p. 163 and 513 Happel's *Historia* refers to Cromwell's activities in Ireland, v. Zech, *op. cit.*, 238 stated that 150,000 Protestants and *100,000 Catholics* were killed in the Rebellion.

14   V. Zech, l.c. says that "Cromwell failed to extirpate the Catholic religion in Ireland, because this nation is completely incorrigible. Especially the Northern quarters they live like the dumb beasts, and still they are regarded as staunch upholders of the Romish Church." "The ferocity of the old Irish and their deeply rooted wilfulness could not be extirpated. The Pope made the Irish still more stiff-necked. The zeal for the Protestant religion has brought much severity upon the Catholic Irish, who were incensed to such rage, that the Scots and English had to join in reducing them to reason" (*ibid.*, 234 f.).

15   p. 5. Happel gives as his source the Irish "Time-books" (Annals?).

15a   "The eyes of all Europe were now fixed upon Ireland " (Dalrymple's *Memoirs* (see below, note 75) (Dublin 1771, ed. ii, 137).

aware of its geographical position, no one in these countries has seriously concerned himself with the conditions of this kingdom. It has been regarded as a remote country, inhabited by uncouth people, who have little intercourse with their neighbours as other nations have.

However at present, Ireland is *sedes belli*, and therefore the eyes and ears of all of us are directed towards it. An account of its conditions may therefore be interesting to the present-day world, especially to our neighbours" (the Dutch).

At this point, I may suggest that these German works on Ireland influenced Laurence Eachar[16] of Christ College, Cambridge, to write in 1691 his *Exact Description of Ireland*. While *Das Neu-Geharnischte Gross-Britannien* was "presented to curious minds", Eachard says:

> "Ireland is at present a place of very considerable activities, and of so nigh concern to these nations that I thought a short description of it could not be very unacceptable to so curious an age ... I not only observed those things that were purely Chorographical and Modern, but also such as were Historical and Ancient."

Like Baer and Happel, Eachar deals successively with the names of Ireland, her geography, climate, soil, products, and commodities; like Happel in particular he adds a special description of St. Patrick's purgatory. Only his chapter on the "wild Irish" embodies material not found in the German works. This material, he hopes, "our Irish Schollars will not take amiss and think ill of that Characteristic which no way belongs to them." The passages on Irish superstitions[17] contain much of the curious material found in the German works.

In his description of Ireland, Happel followed literally *Das Neu-Geharnischte Gross-Britannien*, but adds some of his own speculations on the early history of Ireland. Induced by a suggestion made in Sebastian Munster's *Cosmography*, the chief record of sixteenth century German knowledge of Ireland, that the German Saxons helped Ireland to reduce the Scots, Happel embarks on extensive speculations on the early associations of the Irish with the Scyths, who, he suggests, were Germans and occupied Ireland between the times of King Solomon and the Babylonian Exile. Happel was also fascinated by the marvellous capacities ascribed by Giraldus and others to Irish lakes and wells,[17a] especially by the ancient tradition of barnacle geese growing out of rotting wood in the waters of Ireland, a subject to which he devotes a special illustrated chapter.[17b]

Baer had been more critical with regard to what we may call the classical tradition of Ireland. He enlarged the ancient tradition of Ireland's fertility by the remark that Ulster and Connaught must be excepted from this statement, as there is much unbroken land in those provinces. The German descriptions of the fauna and the natural products of Ireland were obviously based on Boate, though his work is never expressly referred to.

---

16   D. N. B.

17   p. 21 ff. Also v. Zech, *op. cit.*, 238 says that the Irish "venerate the moon and the wolves".

17a   See my article on "Simplicius Simplicissimus's British Relations" in *Modern Language Review*, xl (1945), 40 note.

17b   See my review of Thorndike's *History of Magic*, in the *Irish Book Lover*, xxix (1944), 21.

Of special interest is the reference to the fine qualities of Irish horses; other animals though are smaller than on the continent.

Of the Irish both Baer and Happel say that they are

> "a swift and daring people, not afraid of any danger, enduring hunger, cold, and toil in war, inclined to debauchery, though living in a cold and damp climate. They live on bad food, herbs, roots, butter, porridge, milk, a little meat, but no bread in order to save corn for their horses, which they hold in high honour. They often eat meat raw with *Branntwein*[18] poured over it. Although they are so poor that they can hardly support themselves, they are ashamed of work, many think that it is better that they are poor, as wealth would induce them to rebellion."[19]

Happel adds to these quotations from Baer a summary of what Botero, the seventeenth century Italian historian, had said of the natural resources of Ireland. Baer was the first German author to give information on the position of commerce, on the remnants of native government and legislation,[20] and on the English military and secular government in Ireland. The following passages are of special interest with regard to the history of Schomberg.

> "The Irish horse train their beasts to complete obedience; they jump on them in full armour, being swift and agile. They have heavy spears which they seize by the middle of the shaft and throw them at their enemies. Among the foot the *galeglassen* are the strongest; each of them has two sharp knives, called Beiheln (Happel: Beilein), one foot in length, sharper than shearing-knives, tied to a lance-shaft, which they whirl around themselves. The light foot are called *karni;* they do not regard an enemy as dead until they have cut off his head. Thirdly there are 'runners' called *daltin,* unarmed attendents of the horse-men. Their battle-cry is Pharro! Pharro![20a] They regard it as an evil omen when they do not cry very loud at the beginning of a battle. Instead of drums they have bagpipes and fifes ... Ireland is populous and it would be easy enough to raise there a large army, if the people were not so prone to internal strife, a fact which has always given the English a chance of ruling them. The profits the English draw from Ireland are almost completely spent on the English garrison."[21]

---

18 See below.

19 In his *Geographical Dictionary* (of which I consulted the French translation, Brussels, 1783) Laurence Eachar (see above) describes the Irish as "strong, with a lively and subtle mind, but uncouth, lazy, and addicted to drink." The corresponding passage in v. Zech's work reads: "The inhabitants are good-natured lazy fellows, but (!) daring, evil people, enduring in warfare and brave, as recently shown in the battle of Cremona. They spend little time on studies. Their chief art and profession is brigandage. They are easy-going, restless and fickle (see the quotation from Warner, above, note 4) in the devotion to their superiors." Schomberg, we shall see, made an experience to the contrary (see below, p. 9). "Their hope is often without reason, and their fear without foundation. They are irreconcilable in their hatred against the English nation." The gradual increase in details in German knowledge of the Irish is unmistakable.

20 Also v. Zech, p. 237, speaks of the Tanistry system and the Brehon Laws. "Historians, doctors, surgeons and minstrels", he adds, "often receive land-grants from the Irish nobility", a fact to which Jean Paul referred.

20a This whole passage was used by Johannes Buno (*Allg. Deutsche Biogr.*, iii, 540) in his notes to Klüwer's *Introductio ad Universa Geographiam* (Amsterdam 1697), p. 149 f.

21 Baer, 416; Happel, 11.

In both the works of Baer and Happel and in that on Eachar the general description of Ireland is followed by individual descriptions of the various counties. In the passage on Co. Donegal, Happel enlarged Baer's brief account of Lough Derg by a summary of the Patrician tradition of the sanctuary, this summary is given on the back of the plan of the island taken from Carve's *Lyra Hibernica* (Wein, 1651, and Sulzbach, 1666). Baer on the other hand has a map of Dublin.[22] In the chapter on Dublin, both Baer and Happel add a history of the city in the years 1642, 1649, 1655, and 1671. Similarly the account of the rebellion of 1641 is attached to the history of Waterford, the last county of Ireland to be dealt with in this survey.

The account of the Rebellion concludes with the text of the treaty of Siringstown, 1643. While Baer then continues the history of the government of Great Britain from Cromwell to William,[23] Happel continues his account of the events in Ireland. He offers numerous documents relating to the activities of Rinuccini and Ormonde and makes a brief reference to the part played by Prince Rupert in Irish affairs. His description of the arrival of James II in Ireland is no longer dependent on that given in *Das Neu-Geharnischte Gross-Britannien*,[24] also the portraits of Schomberg found in these two works are different.[25] Baer's work concludes with an account of the conquest of Carrickfergus and Charlemont. "How things will go on, we will leave to God."

The most extensive account of the siege of Derry ever given in continental literature is found in D. v. H.'s *Eengeland's Staatsveraanderingen*, published at Haarlem, 1690.[26] Whether Happel used this work,. I do not know. While D. v. H. gave a description of Londonderry with a large plan of the city, Happel has a rather fantastic illustration on the reverse side of which he describes the town. Similar illustrated monographs he gives of Sligo, Charlemont, Drogheda, Dublin, Waterford, Galway, Limerick, Cork, Kinsale, and Athlone. Also his accounts of the battles of the Boyne and of Aughrim are illustrated. It may be mentioned that Happel's description of the battle of the Boyne differs in essential details from that given in Jean de La Brune's *Histoire de la Révolution d'Irlande* (Amsterdam, 1601),[27] which is usually regarded as the continental standard-work on and contemporary to those events.

Apart from those descriptions of the cities of Ireland, there is little general information of Ireland in Happel's account of the years 1688 to 1691. He informs us that the inhab-

---

22   p. 434.

23   The numerous German *Flugschriften* (see above, note 6) on that period and the works of German literature relating to Charles I (listed by Gilbert Waterhouse, *The Literary Relations of England and Germany in the 17th Century* (Oxford 1914) 81 ff. and 159 ff.) refer only accidentally to Ireland. Most of those *Flugschriften* were printed in Hamburg.

24   Baer, 1085; Happel, 74.

25   Baer, 1094; Happel, 83.

26   II, 172-206; see below, note 61 b.

27   p. 120. One of the copies of this work preserved in the National Library of Ireland contains a folding sheet showing the "orde de la bataille d'Agrim". On de LaBrune, a Huguenot, see *Nouvelle Biographie Générale*, xxviii (1859), 423.

itants of Ulster are Protestants and "brave by nature".[28] He gives us the text of the new charter granted to the city of Dublin in 1688.[29] His description of Cork is amplified by an account of the curious "battle of the birds" in that town from 1621 to 1653.[30] It may be said however that, as we are only at the beginning of the study of the history of continental knowledge of Ireland, we are still far from fully realising the important position which Happel's work holds in the development of German interest in modern Ireland.

Numerous references to Ireland are also found in Happel's *Historia Moderna Europae*, which appeared in 1692 at Ulm.[31] These extensive annals for the years 1649 to 1671 are a characteristic example of the unoriginal "pragmatist" historiography of that age. An interesting point is that while, following Baer, Happel in his *Britannischer Glücks-Wechsel* had said that Ireland belonged to "*Gross-Britannien*" in the wider sense of the word, he states in his annals that "by the name of *Engeland* we comprehend also *Schottland* and *Irrland*." It was not until a hundred years later when Professor Daniel H. Hegewisch wrote the first complete German history of Ireland, that it was realised that this application (to this day quite prevalent on the continent) of the words "England" and "English" to Ireland and the Irish implied the idea that this country was merely an appendix of England. This idea naturally precluded any real understanding of the historical foundations and the political conditions of Ireland. It may also be mentioned that, in his *Historia*, Happel used, apart from the mis-spelling Irrland (which Baer and he firmly established in Germany for the subsequent hundred years), the still worse word "Irr-Reich" which suggests even more a connection with the German word "irre", which means "mad", a connection which did not escape James Joyce's attention.[32]

In his *Hibernia Vindicata*, Happel introduced Schomberg as "the brave general". We need not suggest a connection between this expression and the terms in which eighteenth century Orange ballads spoke of Schomberg,[33] but it should be noted that these ballads are the first works of literature in Ireland to refer to a German.

> "Brave Schomberg he was shot
> As he crossed the water.
> And when King William he perceived
> The brave Schomberg falling
> He reined his horse with a heavy, heavy heart
> And the Enniskillen men he called."

Farquhar in his *Ode on Schomberg*[33a] goes further in adulation of the Duke, calling him "godlike" and "mighty". However it seems to be hardly an exaggeration when Farquhar said:

---

28 p. 92.

29 p. 70f.

30 p. 161f.

31 See above, notes 9 and 13.

32 Both Happel and v. Zech speak also of "*die Irren*", a word which definitely means both "the insane" and "the Irish"; the word "*Ire*" gradually superseded the word "*Irländer*".

33 See the Rev. Dr. Hume's article in *U. J. A.*, 1st Ser., ii (1854), 9ff.

33a *Works* (1760), i, 16.

"The Death of Schomberg hung
On every fault'ring tongue."

"I shall not concern my readers with the poems written in various languages[34] on the Victory of the Boyne and on Schomberg's death",

Johann Friedrich August Kazner concluded his *Leben Friedrichs von Schönburg,*[35] a work which, though published in 1789 (at Mannheim), is still "the standard authority" on Schomberg, as Robert Dunlop admitted in the best summary of Schomberg's life, one of the brilliant articles contributed by this expert on seventeenth century history to the *Dictionary of National Biography.*[36] Kazner was "Gräfl. Degenfeld-Schönburgischer erster Hofrath", in which position he had access to the archives of the Schönburg family (now preserved at Frankfurt-on-Main) and other original documents.

Apart from Prince Eugene of Savoy (who, incidentally, had an Irish chaplain), Schomberg was the greatest condottiere of his age.[36a] Born at Heidelberg in 1615, he spent his youth in the service of the king of Sweden and of the prince of Orange. After the death of William II of Orange he joined the French army, where in 1652 he was appointed captain in the Scottish guards with the rank of maréchal-de-camp. Then he raised by his own exertions a regiment of foot in Germany. In 1657 he was governor of St. Ghislan, then besieged by the Spaniards. The Spaniards, Kazner[37] tells us,

"relied on a secret agreement which they had made during the winter with some Irish officers under Schomberg's command, who had promised to instigate a rebellion among the garrison of St. Ghislan. This treachery however was frustrated through the love of the common soldiers for their governor."

This was apparently Schomberg's first encounter with the Irish. Schomberg then distinguished himself in the Portuguese War of Independence. After the revocation of the Edict of Nantes he entered into the service of the Elector of Brandenburg. In

---

34   Benjamin Neukirch, a Silesian, wrote at that time a poem on the flight of James II and on the accession of William and Mary and an epitaph on Tyrconnel (Waterhouse, *op. cit.*, 84).

35   i, 349.

36   See also Poten in *Allg. Deutsche Biographie*, xxxii (1811), 260f. – I cannot deal in this article with Schomberg's place in 18th century German books on England. In his reference to the battle of the Boyne in *Staatsverfassung der heutigen vornehmsten Europaeischen Reiche und Voelker im Grundriss* (Goettingen 1779), 297, the "Koeniglich Grossbritannische und Churfuerstlich Braunschweig-Lueneburgische Hofrath" Gottfried Achenwall, professor of natural law at Goettingen, mentioned Walker and Ginkle (!), but not Schomberg. Achenwall's sources, the German translations of Rapin (by J. J. Baumgarten, Halle 1755-1760, who also published *Sehr merkwuerdige Lebensbeschreibungen groesstentheils aus der Britischen Biographie*, Halle 1754-70) and Hume (Breslau 1762-1772), and *Der Britische Plutarch* (Zuellichau 1764-1768), see also *Allgemeine Geschichte der vornehmsten Staaten* (Heilbronn 1760-1764: vol. iv English history up to 1727) were not available to me. In a note to his paragraph on Henry II (p. 229). Achenwall made a note on Irish history, in which he quotes Ware, Keating "Ma Geoghehan", Warner and Giraldus; there is no reference to the Penal Times. See below, note 75.

36a   In his *Collegians*, ch. ii, Gerald Griffin says that at his time pictures of Prince Eugene and of Schomberg at the Boyne were still "popular prints of the day".

37   I, 44.

accordance with an agreement between the Elector and William III, Schomberg was appointed commander of the 6,000 Brandenburg soldiers who were to take part in William's operations in England. A few months after William had landed, together with Schomberg as second in command, the latter was naturalised and created Baron of Teyes, Earl of Brentford, Marquis of Harwich, and Duke, against the English custom, under his German title, von Schomberg. Kazner edited, described, and annotated the document issued to this effect by William and Mary by the Grace of God King and Queen of England, Scotland, France, and Ireland. Among the illuminations of this patent is found "die goldene Harfe Irlands im blauen Felde."[38]

A curious point in this document is that, passing over in silence Schomberg's eldest son (Otto, whom his father despised on account of his lack of diligence and bravery), it rules that after Schomberg's death the title should go to his youngest son Charles who had become a British subject too and in later years distinguished himself in the wars on the continent. After Charles's death in the battle of Marsaglia (in 1693), his heart was taken to England by the Rev. de Bourdieu.[39] This Calvinist minister had accompanied Schomberg to Ireland as his chaplain. At the Boyne he received him in his arms when he had fallen from his horse "mortally wounded by two sabre wounds on his head and a bullet from the Irish horse."[40]

In compliance with the patent Charles was succeeded in the Dukedom by his elder brother Meinhard, who in the battle of the Boyne led the party crossing "the upper ford at Slainbride towards Dunkert (or Dulaek)"[41] and after his father's death distinguished himself by the fury with which he sought to revenge him. He was naturalised in 1691 and a few months later made Baron of Tarragh, Earl of Bangor, and Duke of Leinster. After a rather wild military career he died in 1719 at Lausanne.[42]

The account of Schomberg's operations in Ireland occupies fifty pages in the first volume of Kazner's work. On July 16, 1688, Schomberg took leave from the House of Commons, "étant sur le point de partir dans l'expédition d'Irlande où j'exposerai fort librement ma vie et pour le service du Roi et pour le Votre".[43] In its reply to Schomberg the Speaker said that "no one in this House doubted that Schomberg would bring the impending war to a successful conclusion". Arriving from Berlin to accompany his father, Meinhard Schomberg conveyed to him the warmest wishes of the Elector of Brandenburg for the affairs *in England, Schottland, sonderlich aber in Irland.*" The Elector expressed the hope that "die Irländische Affaire" may be soon concluded, so

---

38   ii, 369. The blue arms of Ireland with the golden harp are mentioned in Lucas de Heerdt's *Beschrijving der Britsche Eilanden* (1570, ed. Th. M. Chotzen and A. M. Draak, Antwerp 1937, p. xxiv). Par. 1210 of that work in Irish are said to be "like the wild Indians without religion and law".

39   D. N. B., xvii (1909). 920.

40   *U. J. A.*, 1st Ser., I (1853), 291.

41   Kazner, i, 33.

42   D. N. B., xvii, 923f.

43   Kazner, ii, 228.

that William could help him against "the mighty and cruel enemy", that is, Louis XIV, who, with the help of his Irish contingents, had just been ravaging Western Germany.

The chief basis for the story of Schomberg's operations in Ireland up to October 24, 1689, is a diary,[44] found among his papers, though not actually written by himself, published among the documents in the second volume of Kazner's work. Apart from Berwick's Memoirs (published in 1777), this is the most important of the numerous diaries of that campaign which have come down to us. The following extracts do not aim at restating the historical events but at pointing out the amount of information of Ireland conveyed to Germany through this, the first known diary supposed to be written by a German in Ireland. This diary begins by saying that after his flight to France, James had tried to stir up rebellion in England, Scotland, and Ireland, "surtout dans ce dernier royaume, où les trois quarts du pays pour le moins sont Papistes", a statement of particular interest with regard to the fantastic reports spread by Happel and others of the marvellous multiplication of the English in Ireland.[45] The rebellion which James instigated after his return to Ireland, was at first neglected in England, "either because it was assumed that it would abate by itself, or because the government shunned the expenses of a campaign". In the meantime, Protestants in Ireland were ruthlessly persecuted and robbed.

William ordered that the landing should take place as near as possible to Dublin.[46] The Duke wished to land at Carlingford (later: Carlingfort), but the pilots recommended the bay of "Karrikfergus". The Duke agreed, as he would thus have a possibility to join, or at least communicate with the troops in "Londonderry, Iniskilling, et Balichanon". Approaching the coast of Ireland, they met a wretched boat with three men and the wife and daughter of a poor Protestant minister, fleeing to Scotland. Schomberg received them in his boat and took them back to Ireland.

On August 13th he entered Carrickfergus bay after a journey of only thirty-one hours. "He landed at Bangor, a little village on the banks of the bay, belonging to Hamilton, the brother-in-law of Lord Monmouth."

> "Le peuple de ce canton est tout protestant, la plus part presbiterien. Il eut une joie de voir l'armee. Ils étaient auparavant dans des transes continuelles."

They had disobeyed James's order to evacuate the coastal district. Approaching Belfast,[47] Schomberg's troops captured an Irish priest, "qu'on dit être un fort méchant et pernicieux homme, sa phisionomie répondit assez à sa réputation", Schomberg tells him that he has not come to Ireland "to wrong any person but only to confirm the reign of William and Mary, to reduce the rebels, and to protect those who submit, Protestant

---

44 ii, 282-316.

45 Leti (see above, note 13) says that ninety per cent of the Irish were Papists (i, 226).

46 Kazner, ii, 288.

47 *Ibid.*, 302. In his instructions issued from Lisburne, for the journey of the King, Schomberg told the Purveyor of their Majesties train "to buy shipping to Belfast in the Province of Ulster" (*U. J. A.*, 1st Ser., I (1853), 58f.).

and others".[48] There was no question of forcing people to become Protestants. Then the priest was returned his breviary and his knife and scissors, which, Kazner suggests, he had brought to murder the Duke. He was permitted to go where he wished.

The assault on Carrickfergus was conducted by the Count of Solms. The Duke proceeded to "Lisnagarue, Drumore and Briklin dans le comté de Douane", to "la petite ville de Nury" (later: Nevry, Niewry, or Newry)[49] and to Dundalke. This latter town was saved from being burnt by the Jacobites through Schomberg's threatening that he would kill the four hundred Irish prisoners he had from Londonderry and Inniskilling unless the scorched-earth policy was stopped. The news transpired that the enemy would make a stand at "Drogheda ou proche de Dublin". There is a bewildering variety of spelling for the Irish and the Anglicised form of the name of Drogheda.[50] The Orange army proceeded as far as Atterdée (later also spelt Ardée).[51] The Inniskillings gained a victory over the Popish militia near Slego (the usual spelling, also found in Happel's work). The Duke reinforced his troops on the far side of the Shannon by sending detachments to *Jamestown*, *Athlon* and *Galloway*. Among the Protestant refugees arriving by sea, a man was captured who betrayed the town of Kilmore to James.

After this diary, Kazner gives several letters written by William to Schomberg in the autumn of 1689, mainly on the plan to capture Kinsale or Cork before the winter. On November 30 the King wrote to Schomberg to persuade him to desist from his plan to come over to England:

"Si vous abandonnez présentement l'Irlande, tout y est perdu, étant impossible de le maintenir cet hyver si vous n'y restez."[52]

The King agreed however to Meinhard's returning to Brandenburg. On his way "il pourra me donner les lumières nécessaires de cequ'il y a à faire en Irlande."

Then follow four reports by Schomberg justifying his conduct of the campaign up to March, 1690.[52a] One of the reasons for avoiding a battle, Schomberg says, was the appalling condition of the ground between Newry and Ardee. "Le pays est plein de côteaux et de marécages, entre lesquels il y a trois chemins à environ un mille l'un de l'autre."[53] Moreover, Schomberg wished to wait for the troops levied by several "Seigneurs Irlandois." A premature battle would possibly lead "à la perte de toute l'Irlande". Schomberg also includes a report on an action aiming at destroying enemy

---

48   Kazner, ii, 293.

49   *Ibid.*, ii, 331, 341, 348, and i, 308.

50   See above, note 13 middle.

51   Kazner, ii, 333 and i, 308.

52   i, 323.

52a   Among the Irish historical documents recently exhibited in the National Library of Ireland, there was an autograph letter singed by "Schonberg" dated 25 Febr. 1690: "Je ne scay ce que je pouvouy faire quand le Roy viendra en Irlande ..."; later in this letter "Cavan" is mentioned.

53   ii, 334.

watercraft in *Lac Neagh*[54] (of which up to that time Germans had heard only the famous fables repeated from Giraldus by Baer and Happel) and at taking Charlemont, a place defended by "l'Irlandais O-Regan",[55] Dungannon and Caillimote. When the enemy marched on Kells, Schomberg sent detachments to Balturbet, from where one can go on boats "par le Laugh (Erne) à Iniskillin et de là jusques à Ballishannon". These troops were Germans "travaillans mieux que les Iniskillins."[56] Meanwhile an attempt is made to raise the low spirits in the Catholic camp, by a priest who claims to have seen heaven and hell. "In hell he found but Protestants, and in heaven only people who had died for the Catholic faith."[57]

The last document presented by Kazner is a letter by St. Felix, Schomberg's chief aide-de-champ, to the wife of Count Meinhard, dated "du camp à trois milles au delà de la rivière de Drogheda en Irlande, le 2 Juillet 1690", giving an eye-witness account of Schomberg's death. While it was not necessary to enter into the details of Schomberg's fatal accident, it may be mentioned that St. Felix's account does not fully agree with the various accounts found in Irish records.[58]

Apart from these records, Kazner's own account of Schomberg's activities in Ireland is, as he states,[59] based on Leland,[60] Dalrymple,[61] and Larrey's *Histoire de l'Angleterre* (Rotterdam, 1713). Leland's chief source was *The Impartial History of the War in Ireland from the time that Duke Schonberg landed with an army in that Kingdom to the 23rd of March 1691/2* published in London 1693 by George Story, dean of Connor and chaplain to the regiment of the Earl of Drogheda, the earliest counterpart in these countries to the works of Happel and LaBrune.[61b] In the beginning of his work, Story refers to the "Duke Sconberg (*sic*), General of all Their Majesties Forces."

Kazner's history of Schomberg in Ireland begins with an account of the siege of Derry, with special reference to "heroic parson Walker", who was to die also at the battle of the Boyne. It may be mentioned that a medal struck in commemoration of the battle

---

54   ii, 347.

55   i, 328.

56   ii, 350.

57   ii, 315 = i, 316. "They carry about old prophecies which in conjunction with their other super-stitions (see above, note 17) are often detrimental to them, especially before battles as on account of them they have often been more daring than was advisable" (v. Zech, 238. see above, note 19). Examples of "paper charms" used by the Irish Catholic soldiers are given in *The Whole Proceedings of the Siege of Drogheda* (Dublin 1736), p. 101f.

58   *U. J. A.*, 1st Ser., i, 291f, and ii, 272f.

59   Kazner, i, 259f.

60   History of Ireland (Dublin 1773), iii, 536-566 on Schomberg.

61   See below, note 76; Dublin 1771, ed. ii, 137-159.

61b   D. N. B., xvii (1909), 1314; the enlarged version of 1693 contains an excellent map of Derry.

shows on the obverse side two dead bodies lying on the ground, with the words "Schomberg" and "Walker".[62]

Kazner gives a detailed description of the difficulties encountered by Schomberg's advancing army especially in Co. Louth. "Wherever the soldiers turned their eyes, they beheld nothing but a fearful desert and its companion Hunger. Crosses marked the doors and gables of the deserted houses, so that the country-side looked like a churchyard."[63] James's army was reinforced by "the armed rabble of the country".[64] In Schomberg's army several (German?) Officers died after drinking "a certain Irish drink called *Usquebough* and is stronger than our *Brandtwein*. I do not know whether this drink is the same as *Whisskey*, of which we received recently an account in a Göttingen periodical. At any rate, this drink was also responsible for the duel in the course of which two of Schomberg's aide-de-camps wounded one another mortally."[65] In a later passage, Kazner reports that before the battle, (Richard) Hamilton ordered "Brandtwein" for the Irish horse.[66]

During his stay in Ireland, Schomberg was said, Kazner relates, to have fallen in love with the Marquise of Antrim, Helena, the third daughter of Sir John Burke of Derrymaclaghy, Co. Galway.[67] 'When the Count de Bussy heard the rumour of this "match", he is said to have caustically remarked that the Duke's plan to marry at the age of seventy was a clear indication of his imminent death.

Summing up the character of Schomberg, Kazner says, that the Duke was blamed in Germany for having wasted his extraordinary capacities in the service of foreign powers. But, Kazner rightly remarks, at the time "Germany was not as she is now. She did not offer sufficient scope to a man of his ability. Moreover, the battle of the Boyne confirmed the foundations of Protestant Germany and England and the present happy system of Europe."[68] Indeed it was a direct result of Brandenburg's friendship with William III that the Elector who had lent Schomberg to William assumed in 1701 the dignity of King of Prussia. What Kazner wrote at the eve of the French Revolution was inspired by the enthusiastic support which the minor Protestant princes of Germany (such as the Degenfeld-Schönbergs) gave to the rise of Prussia under Frederick the Great.

---

62 *U. J. A.*, 1st Ser., ii, 272f. Carl v. Rosen, probably a relative of the Livonian Baron Reinhold v. Rosen who served under Louis XIV (*Allgemeine Deutsche Biographie*, xxix, 197f.), besieged Derry in vain (Kazner, i, 307f., Walker, *Siege of Londonderry* (1736), 167).

63 i, 305.

64 i, 309.

65 i, 315.

66 i, 338.

67 Lodge's *Peerage*. This seems to be the source of the story of Mlle. Fiedert in the Abbé Prévost's *Memoire de M. de Montcal* (1742). I hope to deal elsewhere with the historico-geographical background of Prévost's Irish novels.

68 Kazner, i, 345.

Kazner did not confine his research to Germany. In the appendix to his work he gives the translation of a letter dated August 3, 1788, from an unnamed friend just returned to London of the present state of the memorial slab which in 1731 Swift had erected in the "Kirche des H. Patrik zu Dublin"[69] to "the brave and exalted German" whose memory, Swift said, had been shamefully neglected in his native country. The inscription, which Kazner had already found in *Europaischer Staats-Secretarius*, was in 1788 "thickly covered with dust".[70] Kazner traced a more elaborate Latin inscription which a contemporary of Schomberg had suggested for the Dukes final memorial.[71] Schomberg's tomb in St. Patrick's Cathedral, Dublin, is, to my knowledge, the earliest tomb of a German in this country to have been preserved to this day. Apart from this tomb, the most conspicuous memorial to Schomberg in Dublin is the tapestry in the Lord's Room of the House of Parliament (now Bank of Ireland) representing his death.[71a]

The memory of Schomberg's Brandenburgers[72] (who gave their name to a type of boot still worn by the military heroes in *Vanity Fair*) and of German officers under his command is inseparable from that of the "god-like Duke" himself. I mentioned Count Solmes, that is, Heinrich Maastricht Graf v. Solms-Braunfels, who was the first to cross the Boyne with his men. When William III left Ireland, Solms was made Commander-in-Chief.[73] As his conduct of the siege of Limerick was not particularly brilliant, he was replaced by Ginkel, a Dutchman, the first Earl of Athlone.[74]

Other major figures in those historic events were the young Dukes Friedrich Wilhelm and Karl Rudolf of Wurttemberg, who came to Ireland with the contingent supplied by the King of Denmark, and fought with distinction at the Boyne, at Cork, "Kinsale", and Ballina. William III is said to have stated that:

> "Next to God I owe the conquest of Ireland to the bravery and prudence of Duke Frederick William and the heroic courage of his brothers."[75]

(Quelle: Ulster Journal of Archaology 11, 1948, S. 65-80)

---

69 i, 348.

70 ii, 359.

71 ii, 361.

71a Referred to in Küttner's *Briefe ueber Irland* (Leipzig 1785), the first German travel-book to deal exclusively with Ireland, p. 46.

72 The "Teutsche Garde" to which Happel (*Hibernia Vindicata*, 105) refers in his description of the battle of the Boyne.

73 Story, 6.; D. N. B., xviii, 623.

74 *Ibid.*, vii, 1265. This title became extinct in 1844. One of the copies of de la Brune's work (see above, note 27) in the National Library of Ireland contains *Relation de la campagne d'Irlande en 1691 sous le commandement de M le Général de Ginkel* (Amsterdam 1693). On Ginkel in Ireland see *Proc. R. S. A. I.*, xvii, 36, and xviii, 48.

75 Kazner, i, 326 mainly based on Dalrymple's *Memoirs Relating to History of Gt. Britain and Ireland* (London 1762, Dublin 1771), also Storey, 94, and *Allg. Deutsche Biographie*, vi, 710 and iv, 373. I hope to treat in a later article of the Williamite war in 19th century German historiography, se above, note 36.

Irish Soldiers in the Thirty Years War

Unlike the story of Irish swordsmen in France, the tradition of Irish soldiers in German armies[1] has scarcely been investigated. Can we consider Dürer's sketch as an early source of this tradition? Were those who took part in the Irish section of the Stuttgart 1618 pageantry soldiers?[2] Perhaps the best known episode in the tradition of Irish swordsmen in Germany is the assassination of Wallenstein[3], a subject on which one of the main sources is Carve's *Itinerarium,* chapter 11:

> Huius tragoediae actores seu spectatores fuerunt e militibus Butlerianis triginta circiter, inter quos duo Scoti, unus Hispanus, reliqui Iberni, qui uno cum Deveroux cadaver mortui tapete obvoluerunt.

A small point not always mentioned is that Deveroux before dealing the fatal blow gave Wallenstein time to say an act of contrition. Carve, the self-styled chaplain of the English, Scottish and Irish contingents in the Imperial army, should have taken the decision, had it presented itself to him, whether the assassination of Wallenstein was foul murder or a lawful action carried out, to use the familiar phrase, by higher orders.

It has been stated that Continental writers on the Thirty Years War rarely admit their indebtedness to Carve's *Itinerarium.* The value of this work as a source of the early tradition of Irish soldiers in Continental armies is not sufficiently recognised either, as will be readily seen when it is considered that, in the absence of an index, no list of the Irishmen mentioned in that work has yet been published. Apart from James Butler, his sons Walter and James, and Walter Deveroux, the following are referred to by Carve as *Iberni:*

> Edmund Borcke, *capitanus*: 11[4].
> Thomas Broone, *locumtenens*: 8.
> Thomas Butler, *vexilliferus*: 8.
> Dermot Carthy: 8 (in the genitive case "Dermitii Carthii", rendered by the German translator: "Dermitz Carthii").
> Desmond, *vice-colonellus*: 20.
> Florinus Fürstenaw: 20 (between Gordon and Gall in a list concluded by the words "omnes Iberni"!).
> John Henry Gall, *vice-colonellus*: 20.
> William Gall, *colonellus*: 6.
> Peter Geraldin: 19 (probably identical with "capitanus noster G.": 21).

---

1   In E. O'Donnell's book, *The Irish Abroad* (London, 1915), this subject is given 10 out of 400 pages, and only the Seven Years' War is dealt with.

2   See my paper on "Early Representations of Irishmen in German Books", *J.R.S.A.I.,* LXXX, 158-163

3   In Mangan's translation of *Wallensteins Lager* by Schiller the passages relating to Butler's dragoons were rendered in a most disappointing manner.

4   Christian names have been de-Latinised, but surnames are given in Carve's spelling, and no attempt has been made to translate the terms for military ranks. The numbers are those of the chapters, because readers might like to refer to either the original edition or the contemporary German translation (both Mayence, 1640), or the modern reprint of Carve's *Itinerarium* (London, 1859).

Robert Geraldin: 11.
James Gordon, *colonellus*: 6, 7 (*Scotus*[5]), 19, 20 (in the list concluding with the words "omnes Iberni"), also his *colonellus* and two *vice-colonelli* or *locumtenentes* (unnamed): 7.
Grase, *Ibernus*: 8 (in the German translation: *Grass*).
Alexander Mac Daniel: 19.
Salomon de la Moville, *colonellus*: 20.
Hugh Onell, *tribunus*: 8.
Barnaby Patrich: 8 (German translation: *Patrirch*).
Patrick Purcel, *supremus vigiliarum praefectus*: 22.
Robert Purcel, *capitanus*: 20, 21.
Stivin, *capitanus*: 19 (in 20 and 21: Stevin).
Worloch, *colonellus*: 20 (in the list concluding with the words "omnes Iberni").

More Irish names, probably mostly Ulstermen, are mentioned in Carve's *Apologia* in a list of those who had accused him of having slandered, in chapter 4 of the first book of his *Itinerarium*, the Irish, in particular the Ultonians, by quoting from St. Bernard's *Life of St. Malachy*. Neither Carve's *Itinerarium*, especially ch. 4, 66 and 72, and the dedications to, and the appendix on the Butlers, nor Carve's controversy with Anthony Bruodin, O.F.M., arising from Carve's *Apologia* have been considered yet as important sources of Continental information on Ireland past and contemporary.

The very presence of Irish contingents in Germany was of course a source of such information. In the course of the war the Irish contingent became more and more diluted with German and other elements. For some time it was under the command of Colonel Mulheim (ch. 19), and the intercourse between Irish and Continental officers must have been close. Let us consider only the linguistic aspect of this intercourse. Walter Deveroux's testimonial for Carve is the earliest record written by an Irishman in the German language. On the other hand, Carve states "Ob linguam commodam peritiam me ad conterraneos Ibernos sub legione Domini Deveroux transtuli" (after Butler's death; ch. 15). To negotiate with the Swedes an "Ibernus Anglicani idiomatis gnarus" (ch. 25) was chosen. So far as not in Latin, the letters protesting against Carve's alleged abuse of Ulster were written in English.

With considerable pride Carve relates instances of the Swedes' respect of their Irish adversaries. When after overcoming Irish resistance, Gustavus Adolphus had conquered Frankfurt (Oder), he asked Walter Butler to supper. In spite of his wounds, Butler ordered himself to be carried on a stretcher into the king's presence. "Are you Butler senior?" the king asked. "I am not", Walter Butler replied. "The gods are kind to you, brave soldier", the king said. "Because if you had been the elder one, my royal right hand would have smitten you" (ch. 8). When the Swedes heard that *Scoti Ibernique* opposed them, they quickly withdrew. Carve occasionally refers to Scots serving with the Swedes, e.g., to "Dromundt", the governor of Garz in Pomerania, "natione Scotorum" (ch. 29), and to the "Scotica legio" in the Swedish army (ch. 45).

---

5   Carve's use of the word "Scotus" is inconsistent. In ch. 3, 4 and 7 we have "Ibernia Scotiave", in ch. 11 "Scoti seu Iberni", but in ch. 8 and 20 "Scoti et Iberni" (see also "Angli et Scoti" in contrast to "Iberni" in ch. 19, 47 and 66). Other *Scoti* mentioned by Carve are Leslie (11, 33, 67), Hebron (19) and Wadt (8).

The presence of a Scottish contingent in the army of Gustavus Adolphus is generally known, because it is well testified to and because to this day Scottish names have been conspicuous in Swedish nobility. In a popular lecture on Gustavus Adolphus[6], delivered on several occasions (also in Ireland), Richard Chevenix Trench, Protestant archbishop of Dublin said:

> The material of Gustavus's army was not rendered worse by including in its making a Scottish brigade, for of his officers are none of whom we hear more often and more honourably than the Seatons, the Leslies, the Mackays, the Monroes....

Of these officers, Sir George Monroe later played a prominent part in Ireland. Robert Monroe published in 1637 *Expedition with the Scots regiment, called Mackey's regiment, landed in August 1626 for his Majesty's Service in Denmark.*
Archbishop Trench stated[7]:

> In the preparation of this lecture I examined in the British Museum a collection of broad sheets, placards, ballads, caricatures, etc., which appeared during the course of the Thirty Years War.

Apparently he did not come across the items listed, for the first and only time in this country, in the *Catalogue of the National Gallery of Ireland* (1914), 456 as

> two curious prints of Irish soldiers in the service of Gustavus Adolphus in German in 1631. Also a German broad-side with a wood-cut of five Irish soldiers, undoubtedly No. 123, 124 and 125 of the *Catalogue of Prints and Drawings in the British Museum, Division I: Political and Personal Satire I* (1870).[8]

These three items refer to a contingent from these countries in the Swedish army different from Mackey's regiment. This second contingent was the result of a compromise by Charles I between his desire to help his brother-in-law and the Protestant cause and his desire to keep out of the war. He tolerated the enlisting in the Swedish army of a contingent[9] under the marquess of Hamilton, assisted by David Ramsay.[10]

---

6   London, 1865, based on a work by Gustav Freytag (whose fine collection of historical brochures, pamphlets, broad-sheets, etc., in the Stadtbibliothek at Frankfurt contains many items of interest to Ireland), p. 22.

7   Ibid., 38 f.

8   As I had to cut the pages in the copy preserved in the library of Trinity College, I note tho following other items of possible interest to Ireland:

no. 305 English soldiers in Ireland under Charles I,
no. 375 The Popish conspirators . . . cruell Irish destroying kingdome, religion and laws, under colour to defend them, especially the Irish . . . the blowdy Irish, 1643
no. 677 Irelandes Lamentation, 1647 (Erin weeping at the cruelties inflicted upon Protestants)
no. 1228 The Royal Courant for the year 1689, no. 4: Macklesfield, no. 5: Lameere.

9   Harte, *Gustavus Adolphus* (London, 1747), 315-326. The number of 8,000 Irish stated in our broad-sheet no. 123 (below) was corrected in no. 124 into 800. See below Burnett's reference to the exaggerated ideas of the Germans on the strength of Hamilton's contingent. The figure of 800 Irish can probably be accepted.

10   Simplicius, the hero of Grimmelshausen's famous novel, was described as a relation of Ramsay and as a Catholic (see below, note 21). (Grimmelshausen's novel was the fore-runner of the type

On 31 May 1630 an agreement was signed at Stockholm, the first article of which said that Hamilton was ready to bring over his forces and that Gustavus Adolphus would assign him a place for his landing.[11] The fifth article said:

> Whatever the illustrious lord marquess shall take from the enemy, the lands and territories shall belong to us (the King), but the revenues and all the emoluments shall go to him and to the relief of his army; yet so as these revenues shall be gathered decently and in order, without depredation and plundering.[12]

Hamilton specially undertook to keep this article

> since the reasons of my expedition to Germany are the same with your Majesty's (namely), to help and relieve the oppressed princes and states of Germany with the ease of all these burdens with which they are now pressed.

Hamilton undertook to land his contingent before the end of June, 1631. Scottish and English officers were appointed and "the levies went on all the winter."[13] Harte stated that "the *cause in itself* (Harte's italics) was so agreeable to the people of England and Scotland that a considerable number of troops" was soon brought together, "partly Scots, partly English". The Scots sailed from Leith and joined the English at Yarmouth, where they left on July 16,1631.

Trench was right in saying that in the accounts of the Swedish war in Germany we hear much of Scottish officers, but not so much on account of their honours, but on account of the trouble they gave to Gustavus Adolphus. This trouble started right from the beginning of the expedition. Gustavus Adolphus had ordered Hamilton to land at Bremen to force the archbishop to join his cause, but Hamilton went via Denmark to the mouth of the Oder. Harte reports that the 6,000, "English and Scots", landed all in good health and spirit; only two had died during the journey. This diminutive army consisted of four regiments, each of which contained ten companies, every company amounting to 150 men. Number of the English perished by eating German bread, which is heavier, darker-coloured and sourer than that of their own country; they suffered too by an immoderate fondness of new honey, of which they found great abundance in those parts, nor did the German beer agree with their constitution. They came fresh likewise and to a country that was infested by the pestilence.[14] Of course this body of troops proved but of little service in the sequel of the war. For they were new-raised recruits, the very off-scouring of the people. Gustavus made no use of them

---

of historical novel developed by the Abbé Prévost, whose Irish associations I have investigated in *Ulster Journal*, 1949.) Simplicius claimed to have been in Ireland, where he "drank from two fountains, the water of one making you old and grey, that of the other making you handsome and young" (see my paper in *Modern Language Review*, XL (1945), 37-45).

11   The Memoirs of the Lives and Actions of James and William Dukes of Hamilton, by Gilbert Burnett (1677, reprint Oxf. 1852), 9 f.

12   Trench, *op. cit.*, 73, stated that the word "plunder" was imported into the English language by soldiers returning from the Thirty Years' War.

13   Burnett, *ed. cit.*, 14 and 20

14   Compare Carve's reference to pestilence among the *legio Colonelli Deverouz* (ch. 26)

upon trying occasions, and about his person, till they had been better experienced and disciplined in the art of war.

Charles did not even send the money for these troops, and Gustavus had to pay them. German recruits were added to them, and Hamilton was denied their command.

> His army, for causes above assigned, was reduced to little more than two complete regiments, and what was worse, had subsisted ever since its arrival in countries infected with the pestilence, and where the provisions had been twice consumed by enemies and friends.

Hamilton "and his Britons" were delighted when they heard that they were to be moved to Silesia. However, Gustavus had promised the conquest of Silesia to the Elector of Saxony, therefore Hamilton and "his 1500 British" were ordered to guard Frankfurt and other passes over the Oder, in case the king would be defeated (at Breitenfeld) and have to flee. In Frankfurt one-third of this contingent was attacked by the plague. In the course of 1632, the contingent was reduced to two regiments, "one English and one Scottish, the former commanded by Bellandin, the latter by Hamilton". Hamilton, Ramsay and Hopkin finally left the Swedish service, and while they returned to England, "the few remaining soldiers incorporated themselves into the Swedish service".

The three German prints illustrate what Burnett said:

> The fame of this army (Hamilton's at its arrival) ran through Germany, being represented to be about twenty thousand men, which struck a great terror into the whole imperial party, so high was the fame of the Scot's valour.

So far as I am aware, the only reference to an Irish selection in Hamilton's contingent is Harte's statement that his account of the levying of this contingent was based on *Military Tables and Diary of the War*, written in 1632, by some English, Scottish and Irish officers in Gustavus's service. Our three prints are therefore of eminent historical value. There is no evidence of pictorial representation of Hamilton's "army", except those of its Irish section.

No. 123.[15]

Curious conversation held in the Royal Swedish camp by two foreign nations, namely a Lapplander with a newly arrived *Irrländer*, on the present state of affairs and the present war.

This is the attire of the 8000 *Irrländer* or *Irren* arrived at Stettin.		This is the dress worn by the Lapplanders.
The Irrländer.	The Lapplander.	The Finlander.

The *Irrländer* are strong enduring people, contented with plain (or little food); when they have no bread, they can endure hunger for three or four days, feeding instead on

---

15   The following translations and descriptions are not meant to replace but merely to supplement the excellent descriptions in the British Museum catalogue. Passages in brackets are summaries.

PLATE V.

No. 123.

water, cress, roots and grass; when necessary, they can walk more than twenty miles a day; apart from their musquets they have their bows and long knives.

(Swarms of insects and strange birds have foreshadowed the arrival of these foreigners in Germany. On the opposite side, a similar description of the Lapplanders. Behind the figures a fortified town by the sea is seen, a historical view of Stettin, as in no. 124, with the sun rising and ships at sea. Underneath a versified conversation between the Lapplander and the *Irrländer*.)

Lapplander: (It is a shame that we have to be here, far from home, in a foreign country. The devil knows who has started this war. I wished the fellow would be hanged. They are grand people who start such a war and raze their own country to the ground).
Behold, what sort of man is coming along here?
You do not look like one who is at home in this country,
Because your attire is almost as strange as mine.
Irrländer: You are right and did not tell a lie,
I have travelled almost as far as you.
What stars are ruling this country
That we poor *Irrn* are sent here,
Far across water and land?
I have never even heard the name of this place.
You have been here longer than I have,
Tell me something of this place.
Lapplander: I do not know exactly who started this game.
The rascal is supposed to be named *Tylli*.
It is he whom we are supposed to smite.
Another section is called the Jesuits,
they are a rare crowd!
Another section is known as Liguists,
all of them are Papists.
These rascals, I have been told,
are striving for all the power and honour,
all the countries and all the money;
They wish to have the world for themselves. ...
It is these people whom our king
wishes to destroy,
to protect the rights of God and His Word.
Therefore he has made us come here.
We shall fight them
with nets and ambushes, with drum-sticks
and daggers[16],

---

16   I am not concerned in this paper with the linguistic aspects of the German text (in this instance, *e.g.*, with the expression "Lappen, Läuschen, Querl und Knittelsäbel"), but a point of interest is the variety of names for the Irish: "Irrländer" *or* "Irre", and "Irreman".

until they run home again to St. Stephen [Vienna]
from this country,
to sell their sins there.[17]
Irrländer: I see how the matter stands.
I am not an ignorant fellow.
For a long time, I have heard of their antics.
It is a shame that these nitwits,
these violators of honour an women
should have a chance to destroy so many countries.
Lapplander: That is true and is grievous indeed.
Oh, we poor Lappland peasants,
Although the world considers us as
daring and bold, we are still gentle and peaceful.
We are not so daring and wild
as to make our own country
the laughing-stock of the world
and to deprive the parts of our country,
our neighbours, friends and brethren of their property.
I am certain that you too
do not do such things to your country. ...
Irrländer: ... if these things are like that here,
I admit, I regret having come here.
I had heard of the Roman Empire,
that things there were straight and right,
that it was the abode of justice,
government and power without wars and feuds.
But now I see that this Empire
is more tyrannical even than the Turks.
Woe to this country, that it must
learn from us how to behave.
I think it would be better if they
went to our country, and if this silly nation   ...
would thus be improved by us.
Lapplander: ... It is not the fault of the people,
but they have been poisoned
by the Spanish and the French.
They wanted to turn this country into a monarchy. ...[18]
Irrländer: If that is so, we will not disturb them,
but we will sharpen our daggers and knives
to destroy *Tylli*, the League
and the Spaniards,

---

17   Apparently a reflection of Protestant misunderstanding of the teaching on indulgences.

18   *i. e.*, to destroy the liberty of the princes.

PLATE VI.

No. 124.

even though we are only rough fellows.
Lapplander: That is right, my dear *Irreman*. ...
   Printed in the year MDCXXXI.

No. 124.

Such dress is worn by the 800 *Irrländer* or *Irren* arrived at Stettin.

(The description of the Irish is almost identical with that in No. 123: "strong enduring
... knives." All the four figures in this print are Irishmen. In the background the
seashore with the same view of Stettin, but the harbour thronged with ships and
"soldiers marshalled and dressed in costumes similar to those of the figures in front,
ranged under the banner of the three Crowns".[19] The faces are cruder than in No. 123.
The engraver's name (G. Köler) is stated.)

No. 125.

Short description of the soldiers of His Royal Majesty in Sweden, arrived from *Irrland*
in Germany, of their country, nature, food, arms and qualities.[20]

(In contrast to Nos. 123 and 124, this is a wood-cut. The two figures at the right and
left largely correspond to the four figures in No. 124, but a beardless man in a different
costume has been included who, apart from bow and quiver, has a spear. The text says
that the arrival of foreign soldiers in Germany is a well-deserved punishment for *alla
modo sins*. The verses specifically referring to the Irish are as follows):

They come from very far, from *Irrland*,
named after their island *Hiberni*.
That nation is enduring and hardy,
swarthy like gypsies,
stocky of build, war-loving,
experienced in the use of musquets,
bows and long knives.
They are so swift, that in one day
they can cover sixteen miles.
Their dress and caps are altogether barbarous,
almost entirely black in colour,
because, as is well known, all the sheep
in their whole country are black.
Their shoes are mostly made of straw.
They are contented with plain (or little) food.
When they have no bread and are hungry,
they dig up roots from the ground
and thus satisfy their hunger.

---

19   British Museum catalogue

20   In the British Museum catalogue "Engenschafft" is a mis-reading of "Eygenschafft".

PLATE VII.

No. 125.

Though in many respects agreeing with the descriptions of the Irish in Nos. 123 and 124, this account has some particularities. The Irish are credited with walking 16 rather than 20 miles a day. Their appearance and dress is referred to, and a curious explanation given of its colour. The discussion of the dress and equipment of the Irish, as shown and described in these prints, is left to experts on this subject.

Considered as its early forerunners, these broad-sides compare favourably with the modern illustrated press, combining as they do information and interpretation[21], instruction and entertainment, aesthetic and moral aspects.

(Quelle: Journal of the Royal Society of Antiquaries of Ireland 82, 1952, S. 28-36)

---

21 Information is what these prints tell us of the external appearance and habits of the Irish soldiers. What the *Irrländer* says in the conversation with the Lapplander is, of course, interpretation. There can be little doubt that the vast majority of the Irish soldiers were Catholics who enlisted in the wedish army merely from force or by dire necessity.

Irland und das Friderizianische Preußen

In meinen Studien zur Geschichte der deutschsprachigen Irlandkunde habe ich wiederholt darauf hingewiesen daß ihr wesentliches Gegenstück die Geschichte der irischen Deutschlandkunde ist. So entspricht der ältesten Erwähnung eines Iren in einem deutschsprachigen Text, der des hl. Kilian in der Würzburger Markbeschreibung, die älteste Erwähnung eines deutschen Ortes, Würzburgs, in der Eintragung für den hl. Kilian im Martyrologium von Tallaght[1], oder Goethes ausgedehnter Irlandkunde der eminente Beitrag, den Iren zur Verbreitung von Goethes Werken in der englischsprechenden Welt geleistet haben[2].

Zwischen der deutschen Irlandkunde und der irischen Deutschlandkunde bestehen allerdings entscheidende Unterschiede.

1. Nach den Heiligen des Mittelalters[3] errang keine irische Persönlichkeit nennenswerte Popularität auf dem Festland[4]. Von Brian Boru, Art MacMurchada, Shane, Hugh und Eoghan Ruadh O'Neill, Red Hugh O'Donnell und Patrick Sarsfield darf man getrost sagen, daß sie dem Durchschnittsdeutschen nichts sagen. Erst die Führer der Rebellion von 1798 und dann natürlich O'Connell[5] wurden als Persönlichkeiten im deutschsprachigen Bereich bekannt, Parnell viel weniger, Casement nur wegen seiner Verbindung mit den Deutschen; eine deutschsprachige Biographie De Valeras gibt es m. W. nicht.

Von irischer Kenntnis deutscher Persönlichkeiten kann erst von Luther an die Rede sein[6]. Daß das Fest des hl. Rupert von Salzburg in Irland gefeiert wird, ist der Verbindung dieses Heiligen mit Iren zuzuschreiben (als im 18. Jahrhundert das Fest in Irland eingeführt wurde, betrachtete man Rupert gelegentlich als Iren). Im 16. und 17. Jahrhundert ist solche Kenntnis vorwiegend in den auf dem Festland erschienenen Werken irischer Flüchtlinge zu finden. In Irland selbst nachzuweisen ist eingehendere Kenntnis Schombergs[7]. Bis heute unerreicht hoch ist die irische Kenntnis der großen und mittleren Vertreter der zeitgenössischen deutschen Literatur im Zeitalter der Klassik und Romantik gewesen. Dagegen dürfte es kaum ein Land in Westeuropa geben, in

---

1   S. meine „Studien zur Geschichte der deutschsprachigen Irlandkunde bis zum Ende des achtzehnten Jahrhunderts", Deutsche Vierteljahrsschrift für Literaturwissenschaft u. Geistesgeschichte 35 (1961) S. 618.

2   J. Hennig, Goethes Irlandkunde, ebd. 31 (1957) S. 70-83 und Frank O'Connor und Goethe, in: Goethe 24 (1962) S. 296-299.

3   Ders., Irish saints in early German literature, Speculum 22 (1947) S. 358-374.

4   In meiner Arbeit „Ireland's place in the chivalresque literature of mediaeval Germany" in: Proceedings Royal Irish Academy 53 C 3 (1950) S. 279-298 habe ich gezeigt, daß entsprechende Personennamen fast völlig fehlen.

5   S. meinen Beitrag „Continental opinion" zu: Daniel O'Connell (Dublin 1949) S. 235-269.

6   Vgl. J. Hennig, Augustine Gibbon de Burgo, a study in early Irish reaction to Luther, in: Irish Ecclesiastical Record V, 69 (1947) S. 135-151.

7   Ders., Some early German accounts of Schomberg's Irish campaign, in: Ulster Journal of Archeology 10 (1948) S. 65-80.

dem der Name Hitler heute dem Durchschnittsbürger weniger sagt, als dies in Irland der Fall ist[8].

2.   In der Geschichte der deutschen Irlandkunde ist bis zum Beginn des 20. Jahrhunderts das vorzugsweise katholische Interesse an der sog. Missionszeit und an der Verfolgungszeit auszusondern. Erst nach dem ersten Drittel des 19. Jahrhunderts entstand ein wirkliches Interesse an Irland auf nicht-katholischer Seite: Die irische Kirche wurde als Vorläuferin eines romfreien Christentums dargestellt; Liberale und anschließend Marx und seine Freunde warben für Verständnis für den Freiheitskampf Irlands.

In Irland gab es bis gegen Ende des 18. Jahrhunderts nur englischstämmige Drucker, Literatur in irischer Sprache blieb praktisch ungedruckt. Kenntnis des Englischen war bis auf kleine Bereiche Irlands unter dem literarischen Niveau. Bislang wurde angenommen, daß erst bezüglich der französischen Revolution Katholiken (= Iren) und Protestanten (= Englischstämmige) einem außenpolitischen Ereignis gegenüber gleich reagierten, teils positiv, teils negativ. Die gleiche Gemeinsamkeit trat noch einmal in den siebziger Jahren des 19. Jahrhunderts ein, als das katholische Irland eher noch mehr als das protestantische franzosenfreundlich war, woraus sich nur sekundär Feindlichkeit gegenüber Preußen ergab, ebenso wie im 20. Jahrhundert die vermeintliche Deutschfreundlichkeit der Iren nur Folge der Gegnerschaft zu England ist.

3.   Daß Irland eine Insel am Rande der Welt ist, war eine der wenigen Tatsachen, die zu allen Zeiten dem Festland bewußt waren. Die materiellen Kontakte zwischen Irland und Deutschland sind während der letzten tausend Jahre minimal gewesen. Bis heute wird Irland nur in der Kirchen- und Literaturgeschichte für ganz wenige Perioden systematisch von Deutschen ins Auge gefaßt.

Die Anglo-Iren waren in ihren Interessen eher noch insulaner als die Engländer; die Iren dagegen hatten seit dem 16. Jahrhundert durch die Flüchtlinge (Soldaten und Geistliche) viele Bande zu den Ländern Westeuropas, zu Italien und auch zum römisch-deutschen Reich einschließlich Böhmen. Ihr Interesse erlangte aber kaum systematisches Niveau. Erst seit Ende des 19. Jahrhunderts hat die Geschichte irischer Kontingente in den festländischen Armeen seit dem Dreißigjährigen Kriege zusammenfassende Behandlung erfahren. Die größte Darstellung der Tätigkeit irischer Geistlicher auf dem Festland seit dem 16. Jahrhundert findet man immer noch in Bellesheims „Geschichte der katholischen Kirche Irlands"[9], dem umfangreichsten Werk über diesen Gegenstand, sie ist natürlich überholt. Die Iren beschränken sich zunächst noch darauf, das Material über dieses interessante Kapitel europäischer Geistesgeschichte zu sammeln[10].

---

8   Hierzu meine Mitteilungen in: Schweizer Rundschau 47 (1947) S. 518-525.

9   A. Bellesheim, Geschichte der kathol. Kirche in Irland (1890-91).

10   S. meine Besprechungen von „Collectanea Hibernica", in: Z. f. Kirchengeschichte 70 (1959) S. 186 f; 72 (1961) S. 417; 73 (1962) S. 399; 74 (1963) S. 201 f; 76 (1965) S. 428 f.

4. Festländische Zeugnisse mindestens des Interesses an der irischen Sprache lassen sich bis zur Vita S. Findani zurückverfolgen und in fast allen Zeiten seither aufspüren[11]. Von Goethes Bekanntem Küttner an läßt sich deutscherseits systematische Beschäftigung mit dem Irischen nachweisen –, bis heute der hervorragendste Teil deutscher Irlandkunde[12].

Bis ins späte 18. Jahrhundert kann weder bei Anglo-Iren noch bei Iren (außer solchen auf dem Festland) Kenntnis der deutschen Sprache nachgewiesen werden[13]. Bis heute spielt in den Lehrplänen irischer Schulen das Deutsche, verglichen mit dem Französischen, eine Aschenbrödelrolle[14].

Nur auf Grund dieser Einleitung, die sich trotz ihrer Länge ihres kursorischen Charakters nur allzu bewußt ist, kann der Gegenstand der folgenden Mitteilung richtig eingeschätzt werden. Friedrich d. Gr. war der erste Deutsche, von dem eine ausgedehnte Kenntnis in Irland nachzuweisen ist. Kein Deutscher hat je auch nur annäherndes Interesse in Irland gefunden. Dieses Interesse verband erstmalig Anglo-Iren und Iren hinsichtlich eines außenpolitischen Ereignisses und erlangte durch Art, Breite und Länge der publizistischen Dokumente systematischen Charakter. Es lassen sich hier auch Zeugnisse in irischer Sprache nachweisen.

Der Name „Preußen" erscheint m. W. erstmalig in einem Text in irischer Sprache in den Annalen von Ulster für 1522[15]: „Ein gewaltiger Krieg brach aus in Westeuropa zwischen den Italienern, *Alamainich, Prusainnich* und *Saxsanaich*". Ein Keltologe sollte einmal die Geschichte der gälischen Deutschland-Terminologie behandeln. „Sachsen" sind an dieser Stelle nicht, wie sonst im Irischen, die Engländer, und „Preußen" bezieht sich natürlich auf den Ordensstaat. Ich überlasse es ferner Kennern der irischen Literatur, festzustellen, wo sich in irischen Texten das Wort „Preußen" nachweisen läßt bis zu dem von Professor M. Tierney veröffentlichten Gedicht aus der Zeit des Siebenjährigen Krieges, in dem von dem ré Pruise (*rex Prussiae*) die Rede ist[16].

---

11 H. Z i m m e r, Glossae Hibernicae (1881) S. 272-274.

12 S. o. Anm. 2.

13 Hierzu auch meine Notiz: German script in Irish printing, in: Irish Booklover 30 (1946-1949) S. 89-91.

14 S. James J o y c e, Stephen Hero (1944) S. 35 f.

15 James F. K e n n e y, Sources for the early history of Ireland 1 (New York 1929) S. 23 und 66.

16 M. T i e r n e y, Studies (Dublin) März 1942. – Auf seiner Fußreise (1782) durch England (London 1798, S. 93) hörte Karl Ph. M o r i t z von dem Landvolke viele wunderbare Geschichten über Deutschland und den König von Preußen. William L a r m i n i e, West Irish folk-tales and romances (London 1893) S. 256 meinte, daß die Geschichte „The sons of the king of Prussia" nicht älter sei als 1870, also die Sympathie mit Frankreich widerspiegele (es handelt sich um die Einkleidung der typischen Geschichte vom Feigling durch einen Geschichtenerzähler auf der Insel Achill).

Manfred Schlenke gab seinem Buch „England und das friderizianische Preußen 1740-1763"[17] eine Liste der einschlägigen Flugschriften in englischer Sprache 1740-1763 (S. 410 ff.) und der Werke Friedrichs, preußischer Staatsschriften und Dienstvorschriften etc. in englischer Übersetzung 1741-1789 (S. 418 f.) bei. Es handelt sich fast durchweg um in London erschienene Schriften; für je eine wird Birmingham und Edinburgh als Druckort benannt. Da S. die Bibliotheken in Edinburgh und Glasgow durchforscht hat, darf angenommen werden, daß tatsächlich nur eine der hierher gehörigen Schriften in Schottland erschien. Aus Irland führt S. drei Drucke auf. Aus eigenen Feststellungen in Dublin kann ich mitteilen, daß es deren einige mehr gibt, und diese Tatsache soll zum Ausgangspunkt einer Ergänzung gemacht werden, die, über die räumliche und zeitliche Begrenzung im Titel von Schlenkes Werk hinausführend, dessen Bedeutung unterstreichen soll.

Die von Schlenke S. 411 aufgeführte Schrift „An Englishman's answer to a German nobleman" (London 1743) dürfte die Antwort sein auf eine von S. nicht erwähnte Schrift „A compleat view of the present politicks of Great Britain. In a letter from a German nobleman to his friend in Vienna, translated from the French original" (Dublin 1743), die erste Dubliner Veröffentlichung, die in diesen Bereich fällt, das erste irische Druckerzeugnis, in dem der Autor im Titel als *German* bezeichnet wird und die erste Dubliner Veröffentlichung zu britisch-deutschen Staatsbeziehungen.

S. 414 erwähnt Schlenke zu 1753 die offenbar nur in Dublin nachweisbare Veröffentlichung „The Duke of Newcastle's letter by His Majesty's order to Monsieur Michell the King of Prussia' Secretary of the Embassy", die S. in Goldsmith's Library London fand; sie befindet sich nicht in den von mir untersuchten Trinity College Library und National Library in Dublin.

S. 416 sagt Schlenke zu „A full and candid answer[18] to a pamphlet entitled Considerations on the present German war": „London 1760, benutzt in der Ausgabe Dublin 1761". Mauduits „Considerations" (bei S. zu 1760) wurden aber ebenfalls 1761 in Dublin nachgedruckt[19], ferner seine „Occasional thoughts on the present German war" (Schlenke: „2. Aufl., London 1761") 1762, auch „A vindication of the conduct of the present war" (Schlenke: „London 1760") („in a letter to the author of the Considerations") und „The case of British troops serving in Germany" (Schlenke: „London 1761") („humbly submitted to the House of Parliament") 1761.

Zu Schlenkes Liste der Werke Friedrichs:

---

17 „Ein Beitrag zum Verhältnis von Politik und öffentlicher Meinung im England des 18. Jahrhunderts". Orbis Academicus Bd. 6 (Freiburg 1963).

18 Zu der Mauduit-Kontroverse ebd. S. 253-265.

19 Für Irland galt besonders, was Mauduit S. 15 sagte, daß nicht einer unter Zehntausenden die Namen der Grafschaften kennt, um die den Schlesischen Kriegen gekämpft wurde. Interessant ist, daß hier (im Gegensatz zu anderen zu zitierenden Stellen) Preußen zu Deutschland gerechnet wird: „Germany has been so unhappy as to have a dispute arise between two of its leading princes".

1. Die in London 1748 u. ö. gedruckten „Memoirs of the house of Brandenburg (from the earliest accounts to the death of Frederick I, King of Prussia) " erschienen auch in Dublin 1750.

2. „The King of Prussia's plan for reforming the administration of justice" (London 1750) wurde im Erscheinungsjahr in Dublin nachgedruckt. Auch die von S. angeführte „weitere Aufl. London 1758" dürfte in Dublin schnell nachgedruckt worden sein, denn in 4. (s. u.) wird dieses Werk als „just published" angezeigt.

3. „New regulations for the Prussian infantry" (London 1757) ist wahrscheinlich der Anhang zu „The exercise of horse, dragoon and foot forces upon the establishment of Ireland. To which is added the manual exercise of the Prussian infantry drawn up by His Majesty Himself" (Dublin 1759); es ist die erste irische Publikation, die von preussischem Einfluß auf das Militärwesen in Irland zeugt (s. u. Anm. 27).

4. „Memoirs of Frederick III [sic!], King of Prussia" (Schlenke: „2. Aufl. London 1757") erschien 1759 in Dublin mit dem etwas anderen als bei S. angegebenen Untertitel „constaining all the military operations of that great prince to the end of the campaign of 1758" (statt wie bei S.: „to the latter end of November 1757"). Diese Veröffentlichung ist interessant, weil erstmals in einem irischen Druck „illustrated with maps of Germany, Hanover and Upper Saxony". Morgan[20] führte hierfür als 3. Auflage Dublin 1758 auf, woraus allgemein zu schließen ist, daß aus amerikanischen Bibliotheken Ergänzungen zu der Liste irischer Drucke, die sich auf das friderizianische Preußen beziehen, zu machen wären.

5. Nicht aufgeführt bei Schlenke und nicht im British Museum Catalogue ist „Royal dissertations by the present King of Prussia, translated from the Berlin copy to which is added his description and character", wofür ich nur die Ausgabe Dublin, Williamson 1758 nachweisen kann. Die ersten dieser dissertations: „On manners, customs, industry and the progress of human understanding in the arts and sciences" und „On superstitions and religion" befindet sich auch in „Memoirs of the house of Brandenburg" (Schlenke S. 382, s. o. 1); ihnen folgen in „Royal dissertations": „On the ancient and modern government of Brandenburg" und „On the reasons for the enacting and repealing of laws, with the Character of the celebrated M. de Voltaire"; S. 3-8 enthält die Lobpreisung Friedrichs.

Erwähnt sei noch, daß 1789 in Dublin erschienen:

Mirabeaus „Secret history of the court of Berlin with numerous anecdotes of... Frederick II and the state of politicks in Prussia, Russia, Germany and Holland" (Th. Holcrofts Übersetzung), John Gillies, „A view of the reign of Frederick II of Prussia", und Joseph Powers, „Memoirs of the life and reign of Frederick III" [sic!], was man als den Höhepunkt irischer Deutschlandkunde bezeichnen darf.

1792 erschien dann noch in Dublin Johann Georg Zimmermanns „Select views of the life, reign and character of Frederick the Great, King of Prussia". Endlich sei erwähnt,

---

20   Bayard Morgan, Critical bibliography of German literature in English translation (Stanford 1938, bei Schlenke nicht erwähnt).

daß in Thomas Moores „Byron" (London 1830) I, 96 Byrons „list of historical writers whose works I have perused in different languages" (1807) abgedruckt ist, worin es heißt: „I have seen at least twenty lives of Frederick II, the only prince worth recording in Prussian annals. Gillies, His own works, Thiebault – none very amusing".

Die Drucker dieser Dubliner Veröffentlichungen gehörten, wie man aus ihren Namen sieht (Exshaw, Powell, Williamson, Wilson) sämtlich der englisch-protestantischen Klasse an[21]. Sie hätten aber wohl kaum so viele Veröffentlichungen unserem Thema widmen können, wenn sie nicht auch schon auf Leser aus dem – trotz der noch bestehenden *penal laws* allmählich wiedererstarkenden – irisch-katholischen Bürgertum hätten rechnen können[22]. Wir werden gleich mehr davon hören.

Es handelt sich durchweg, wohl auch bei den „Royal dissertations", um sog. Piratendrucke, wie damals üblich. Beachtenswert ist, daß diese Nachdrucke meist innerhalb weniger Monate den Londoner Drucken folgten, ein Zeichen für die Lebhaftigkeit des Interesses, das natürlich durch die Aktualität des Gegenstandes (s. die Vervollständigung der „Memoirs" bis zum Ende 1758) begründet war.

Zu den sinnfälligsten Erinnerungen an die – kurzlebige – Begeisterung der britischen Öffentlichkeit für Friedrich d. Gr. gehört der Name *Prussia-Street* in Dublin[23], heute vor allem dadurch bekannt, daß sich dort der für die irische Wirtschaft so wichtige Viehmarkt jahrzehntelang befand. Die Benennung dieser Straße erfolgte am 49. Geburtstag Friedrichs. Am 24. Januar 1760 wurde eine schwarze Tafel mit diesem Namen in goldenen Buchstaben angebracht und im März in einer Nische über dieser Tafel eine Marmorbüste „at the sole expense of the principal inhabitants" (dieser Straße), damals vorzugsweise englischer Abstammung[24], – eine in der Geschichte Irlands einzigartige Ehrung eines Deutschen, der sich um Irland nicht verdient gemacht hatte.

Nirgendwo wird in den genannten Dubliner Drucken erwähnt, daß Iren in der friderizianischen Armee dienten, aber diese Tatsache hat zweifellos mit zu dem irischen Interesse beigetragen. Bekannt waren, wenn auch in dieser Literatur kaum erwähnt, die Namen der großen irischen Generäle in den festländischen Armeen der Zeit, aber eben vorzugsweise den gegen Friedrich stehenden. In der Vorrede zu seiner Übersetzung

---

21 Mauduit, Considerations (Dublin 1761) S. 18 hatte gesagt, daß Friedrich „was described to us as a man void of faith, religion and every good principle. Have his writings made us think better of his religion? ... (He) built a Popish chapel at Berlin, and had the foundation-stone laid in his own name in the midst of his Protestant dominions". Fünfzig Jahre später aber wies Edward Wakefield in seinem „Account of Ireland" II (London 1812) S. 573 auf eben diese Tatsache hin als Beispiel des vorbildlichen Nebeneinanders von Protestanten und Katholiken, das er für Irland wünschte.

22 Schlenke, Kap. I, 2.1.: „Umfang und Struktur des Lesepublikums", wobei für Fieldings „Tom Jones" (S. 55) darauf hingewiesen werden könnte, daß dort in XVII, 8 „the wise King of Prussia" erwähnt wird; ferner Kap. V, 3. 8.: „Das konfessionelle Argument".

23 Vgl. die von Schlenke S. 356 nachgewiesene Londoner Gastwirtschaft „Old King of Prussia" (der Name überlebte zwei Kriege zwischen Deutschland und England).

24 Journal Royal Soc. Antiquaries Ireland 27 (1897) S. 181. Zu der Preußenbegeisterung in jenem Zeitpunkt s. Schlenke S. 237.

von „The posthumous works of Frederick the Great" (London 1789) sagte Thomas Holcroft: „Several English names in the service of Austria and that of Prussia are so disguised by German spelling as not to be known such as marshall Braun (Browne), general Lascy (Lacy), Okelli (O'Kelly), Maquire (Maguire)" – Holcroft betrachtete also diese irischen Namen als „englisch".

Ein zeitgenössisches Gedicht in englischer Sprache erzählt, daß in dem Dubliner Kaffeehaus The Globe „learned politicians assembled round in deep debate/discussed on Prussia's arms and Britain's fate", was einen gewissen Abstand zu *Britain's fate* zeigt, aber noch mehr zu dem Schicksal der Iren, die auf den verschiedenen Schlacht-feldern ihre Haut zu Markte tragen mußten[25]. Aus den Veröffentlichungen von M. Tierney[26] und R. Hayes[27] über Iren, die während des Siebenjährigen Krieges in festländischen Armeen dienten, erwähne ich außer dem bereits zitierten irischen Gedicht, in dem der *ré Pruise* genannt wird, auch das Gedicht des berühmten Raftery

---

25 A. Peter, Dublin fragments (Dublin 1925) S. 56.

26 Studies (Dublin) März 1942.

27 Ebda. Juni und September 1943, sowie „Irish swordsmen of France" (Dublin 1934) und „Biographical dictionary of Irishmen in France" (Dublin 1949). Hayes teilte ein zeitge-nössisches Gedicht mit, in dem „the stout legion of Hibernian blood" gefeiert wird, die „on Rosbach's bloody plain withstood ambitious Frederick's savage troops and Prussian arms", während in „The case of the British troops serving in Germany" (s.o., Dublin 1761) S. 13 gesagt wurde: „His Prussian Majesty's unexpected victory at Rossbach favoured His Britannic Majesty's spirits" (zur Schlacht von Rossbach s. Schlenke S. 235). Auf diese Schlacht bezog sich auch William de Blaquiere, der Sohn des irischen Vizekönigs in seinen Anmerkungen zu seiner (der ersten englischen) Übersetzung von Schillers Geschichte des dreißigjährigen Krieges (1799, s. meine Notiz: Modern Language Review 55 (1960) S. 251), sowie der Ire North Ludlow Beamish in seinen Anmerkungen zu seiner (der einzigen englischen) Über-setzung von „Lectures on the tactics of cavalry, from the German of Count von Bismarck, colonel of the 3rd Royal Wurttemberg regiment of cavalry" (London 1827), S. 26, 43 und 198. - In „General observations on the state of affairs in Ireland in the defence against an invasion" (Dublin 1797) S. 65 ff. bezog sich der als Captain Thomas Blaquiere identifizierte Verfasser ausführlich auf Archenholtzs Beschreibung der Schlacht von Kunnersdorf. Archenholtzs Geschichte des siebenjährigen Krieges erschien aber erst 1843 (in Frankfurt a. M.) in einer eng-lischen Übersetzung (von F. A. Catty), so daß Blaquiere das Werk in deutscher Sprache gelesen haben muß. James F. Mangan, der große irische Vermittler deutscher Literatur (u. Anm. 33), gab seiner Übersetzung von Tiedges Gedicht (Dublin University Magazine 10, 1837, S. 663) eine Anmerkung über Ort und Geschichte der Schlacht von Kunnersdorf bei. Es dürfte in der irischen Literatur keine vergleichbare literarische Tradition auch nur für Waterloo oder Ypern geben. – Über den Wert der preußischen Armee als Vorbild für eine irische waren sich die irischen Nationalisten von 1798 nicht einig. Wolf Tone schrieb unter dem 1. April 1796 in seiner „Autobiography" (London 1893): „We in Ireland should make the French army our model instead of the Prussian". Robert Emmet dagegen studierte Georg Friedrich v. Tempel-hofs „Treatise on winterposts" (s. meine Mitteilung aus Emmets handschriftlichen Notizen in: The Irish Sword 1, 1951, S. 148-150). Nach O'Keeffes Lustspiel (s. u.) kann man annehmen, daß John Mitchell an Preußen dachte, als er in seinem „Jail Journal" (jüngster Druck Dublin 1952) am 12. August 1849 die Bemerkung unterstrich: „In the Irish Army there shall be no scourging".

„Ah Johnny Gibbon, you are a long way from me in Germany"[28] oder die Klage des (unbekannten) irischen Offiziers in der französischen Armee um „die unglücklichen Gälen, die durch das ganze Europa verstreut sind, einige im Dienst der Spanier, andere in *Gearmáine*, in Italien oder unter dem König von Versailles"[29]. Der „Colonel Marlay of Celbridge (einem Dorf westlich Dublin) who gallantly served in Germany up to the peace of 1763", von dem Arthur Young („Ireland" Dublin 1780, I, 14) erzählt, war wohl ein Mitglied der englischen Klasse. Die Iren unter Friedrichs langen Kerls dagegen waren vermutlich vorzugsweise Söhne des armen irischen Volkes. Der (kürzlich verstorbene) große Historiker Pater Canice Mooney, O.F.M. teilte mir mit, daß es in seinem Orden überliefert werde, daß diese Iren bei Potsdam eine Kapelle gehabt hätten, wo sie ein irischer Franziskaner betreute.

Elliott O'Donnell nahm 1915[30] an, es sei unwahrscheinlich, daß Iren in der Armee des als „Tyrannen bekannten" Friedrich gedient hätten; aber ich habe bereits an anderer Stelle darauf hingewiesen[31], daß dem Lustspiel „Patrick in Prussia" von John O'Keeffe, einem der ersten aus dem katholischen Volksteil hervorgegangenen Bühnenschriftsteller Irlands, ein auch von Streckfuß berichteter Vorfall zugrundeliegt, der jedenfalls insoweit historisch ist, wie uns hier interessiert. O'Keeffe gab seinem Stück zunächst den Titel „Love in a camp" (nach den Bühnenanweisungen: „near Breslaw"). Indem er den Titel dann in „Patrick in Prussia" umänderte[32], nannte er erstmalig in einem Werk der „schönen" Literatur Irlands das Wort „Preussen" und verband dieses Wort mit dem charakteristischen irischen Personennamen. Er versprach sich von dieser Änderung, die zwischen 1785 und 1793 vorgenommen wurde, größere Anziehungskraft für sein Stück.

Dies war nicht O'Keeffes erster Versuch, zeitgenössische Geschichte in einem Lustspiel zu verwenden. 1783 hatte er in „The definite treaty" den zwanzig Jahre zuvor geschlossenen Frieden von Paris verulkt[33]. Harris, der Besitzer von Covent Garden,

---

28   R. Hayes, Studies 32 (Dublin 1943) S. 248.

29   Aoidh de Blacam, Gaelic literature (Dublin 1935) S. 275 f. Es bleibe dahingestellt, ob hier Deutschland allgemein oder nur die kaiserliche Armee gemeint ist (s.o. Anm. 19)

30   E. O'Donnell, The Irish abroad (London 1915), im Hinblick auf das Erscheinungsjahr seinerseits ein Beitrag zur irischen Deutschlandkunde. Der Artikel „Six-foot Irish soldiers for the King of Prussia" von M. J. McManus in: The Irish Press 31. Dez. 1950 handelt von den Iren in der preußischen Armee nach 1799; hierzu auch Lord Cloncurry, Personal Recollections (Dublin 1849) S. 207 (für 1805) sowie meine Notiz: German literature on Napper Tandy (den irischen Nationalisten, der in Hamburg Zuflucht suchte), in: The Irish Booklover 31 (1951) S. 108 f. Einen wesentlichen Beitrag zur irischen Preußenkunde erbrachte die umfangreiche Trenck-Literatur, s. meine Arbeit in: Modern Language Review 41 (1946) S.393–407.

31   S. o. Anm. 1.

32   Der bisherige Untertitel wurde somit zum alleinigen Titel erhoben.

33   Ich verweise generell auf den zweiten Band von O'Keeffes Recollections (London 1826) sowie auf Samuel Lover, Poems of Ireland (London 1858) S. 15. O'Keeffe war wie Mangan (s. o. Anm. 27) Schüler einer von dem Jesuitenpater John Austin in Dublin errichteten Schule gewesen.

dem O'Keeffe später das Copyright an „Patrick in Prussia" verkaufte, war erstaunt über die politischen Kenntnisse, die O'Keeffe in „The definite treaty" zeigte. O'Keeffes Kenntnis der preußischen Geschichte zeigt sich auch daran, daß er in „Patrick in Prussia" Preußen mit den Namen Fehrbellin und Olmütz auftreten läßt[34]. Nach Streckfuß hieß der „Irländer", um den es sich an der von Streckfuß berichteten und von O'Keeffe in „Patrick in Prussia" dargestellten Geschichte handelt, „Mac Doll", wohl MacDowell, ein schottischer, in Irland damals noch vorzugsweise bei Protestanten verbreiteter Name. Zwischen der ersten Fassung dieses Stückes, die in Dublin 1786 zweimal gedruckt wurde, und der zweiten, die 1798 in O'Keeffes „Dramatic Works" erschien, bestehen Unterschiede, die darauf zurückzuführen sind, daß O'Keeffe 1793, als George III. nach Wiederherstellung seiner Gesundheit zum ersten Male wieder ins Theater ging und „Patrick in Prussia" zu sehen wünschte, das Stück für diese Gelegenheit herrichtete, u. a. indem er der Abkühlung britischer Gefühle Preußen gegenüber Rechnung trug. Zugleich schloß er sich noch stärker als in der ersten Fassung an das Bild an, das sich die Engländer von den Iren zu machen beliebten. Damit wurde der Gegenstand Träger einer englischen, allenfalls irischen Problematik, wie es für weite Teile des späteren irischen Interesses an Deutschland charakteristisch werden sollte[35].

Immerhin illustrieren die irischen Veröffentlichungen über das friderizianische Preussen gewisse Eigenarten des irischen gegenüber dem englischen Interesse. Gerade wegen der Abgelegenheit Irlands, das zu jener Zeit noch die Rolle der ältesten englischen Kolonie spielen mußte, ist ihre Betrachtung als Anhang zu Schlenkes Darstellung und im Rahmen der Geschichte der Beziehungen zwischen Deutschland und Irland zu rechtfertigen. Friedrich d. Gr. wurde den Iren nicht nur als König, Staatsmann, Feldherr und politischer Denker vorgestellt, sondern auch in seinen philosophischen Ideen. Vor allem aber erweist sich hier an unerwarteter Stelle Friedrich d. Gr. als einflußreiches, ja einzigartiges Thema der deutschen Geschichte[36].

(Quelle: Archiv für Kulturgeschichte 48, 1966, S. 278-286)

Robert Emmet's Military Studies

In his biography of Robert Emmet, Robert Madden wrote a hundred years ago: "In the middle of November 1802 when Emmet was in Ireland, his brother directed Robert's books which bad been left by him in charge of Lawless at Paris, to be sent to Brussels from where they were to be forwarded to him by his brother. One of those books is

---

34 Den seitherigen Rückgang irischer Deutschlandkunde mag man daran ermessen, daß Michail MacLiammoir in einem seiner Lustspiele eine Deutsche als „Gretchen Tannenbaum" einführte. Umgekehrt hätte aber wohl kaum je ein deutscher Bühnenschriftsteller auf historisch-politische Assoziationen in seinem Publikum rechnen können, wenn er einen Iren als „Boyne" eingeführt hätte.

35 S. Anm. 7 meiner Anm. 31 genannten Arbeit, sowie Fritz Mezger, Der Ire in der englischen Literatur, Palaestra 169 (Leipzig 1929) S. 133 ff.

36 Vgl. J. Hennig, Voltaire in Ireland, in: Dublin Magazine, Januar - März 1944 S. 37 f.

now in my possession for which I am indebted to a friend of his in Dublin." The book mentioned by Madden was "Extracts from Colonel Templehoffe's History of the Seven Years War: His Remarks on General Lloyd: On the subsistence of Armies, and on the March of Convoys. Also a Treatise on Winter Posts . . . London 1793."

Owned by Emmet and subsequently by Madden, this book was given to the Royal Irish Academy in 1835 by the latter. The title page of the second volume bears a hand-written note by Madden saying: "This book belonged to Robt. Emmet. The marginal notes in pencil were written by him, and are very curious. This book was given to me by John Patten, his early and dear friend, the brother-in-law of J. A. Emmet."

In his biography of Emmet, Madden gave a short account of these notes. In the table of contents, the reference to Emmet's reading this book is summed up by the words: "E.'s study of works of military science". There is no evidence of Emmet's reading in this work anything but the *Treatise on winter-posts* appended to the second volume, or indeed any other military work. This *Treatise* was by Karl Friedrich v. Lindenau, a Saxon, who had served in the Prussian Army. In 1788, when his Treatise was published he had joined the Austrian Army.

Emmet's notes start with that passage of Lindenau's treatise which deals with the choice of posts in a level country, where Emmet marked as the chief points "posts in defiles", "disadvantages to the enemy", "exposed in the attack of them" and "pre-cautions to be observed in them". Passages making practical suggestions are frequently underlined or marked by strokes in pencil in the margin. In the passage on posts in mountainous country, Emmet established the six advantages pointed out by Lindenau. On Lindenau's remark that "advanced posts in such situations can be easily re-inforced", he noted: "This is to be understood only of advanced posts, for main posts are more difficult." The remark that "a hundred hussards supported by as many yae-gers or other light infantry can effectually perform the service of patrole better than a thousand horse upon the plane" is specially marked. It is obvious that these notes re-flect Emmet's ideas on the possibilities of a small army's taking advantage of a mountainous country side.

Emmet recognised in particular the significance of Lindenau's information on "the conduct to be adopted before the country is reconnoitred" (especially in mountainous regions), "places fitted for the flanc", a problem of special interest to an army with a short line of defence, "conduct to be adopted to obtain information respecting our flanc" (with special reference to the participation of civilians in that work), "conduct to be pursued with respect to the choice of posts near defilés", "advantages of infantry and cavalry, who are to accompany the general in reconnoitring" etc. Emmet did not blindly adopt Lindenau's statements, but modified them when they appeared to him based on conditions other than those he had in mind. For example, he restricted Lindenau's general condemnation of forests, saying: "A forest cannot be occupied from its great extent, but a wood on the other hand is an advantage." Forests, of course, of the extent found in Central and Southern Germany, then no longer existed in Ireland.

The chapter on Advanced Posts is particularly richly annotated. Emmet noted: Fixed advanced posts on all roads leading to the enemy, chain of troops between, patrols in front during the night, difficult to find place for advanced posts in the plain, village houses etc. two miles in front to be occupied by infantry 60 to 80 or 100, block houses in defilés, fortified advanced posts to trace artillery, in night patrols 2 or 3 horsemen (Lindenau had said: one or two mountain yaegers) to be included, their position and hour to be changed every evening and not to be sent out till dark, parallel defilés proper for main posts, perpendicular ones for advanced do., on an alarm at one post the rest to be alert and patrole. A mere list of the points specially marked by Emmet, shows how detailed his studies were, how earnestly he thought of the practical problems of defensive and guerilla warfare.

Emmet did not confine himself to just piecing together some information from single notes. His numerous cross-references show that he tried to obtain a comprehensive picture of the problem of posts. To Lindenau's remark that the rule that fortifications must not be placed so that they may be commanded may suffer some exception with winter forts, Emmet noted:

"The same observation is made with regard to main posts p. 371 par. I." He summed up Lindenau's advice in this respect saying: "Advanced posts may sometimes be placed where they are overlooked, provided not within musquet shot." At this point Emmet again paid special attention to the geographical conditions he had to reckon with: "This is not so dangerous in mountainous countries." In v. Lindenau's remark: "Mountain roads are seldom so good that artillery can pass along them: on the contrary, they are generally narrow paths", Emmet, obviously from his knowledge of conditions in Ireland, underlined the words "so good that", crossing out the words "on the contrary". Several passages were crossed out by him altogether, because he felt that they did not apply to Irish conditions. Summing up v. Lindenau's remarks on Main Posts, Emmet gave in a nutshell his conclusions from the study of the whole work: "In posts among mountains, the general object is to defend the approaches. They must sometimes be placed where they are commanded, in which case mounds must be raised. In Mtns. the work must sometimes be placed down the side of the hill to defend approaches. In such a case we must build block-houses on the top." Such notes throw an unexpected light upon the advanced state of Emmet's military studies.

Speaking in this connection of "our outguards", Emmet seems to make it clear that he was thinking of an Irish army. His notes also show that he was aware of the fact that defensive warfare with a comparatively small army was bound to place much greater strain on the individual soldier than was visualised by v. Lindenau. A point of very special interest seems to me that Emmet envisaged campaigns of this nature to extend over several years.

The realistic attitude in which Emmet carried out these studies is most obvious in the fact that he did not deceive himself regarding the chances of ultimate success. He does not seem to have envisaged anything but delaying the enemy's operations. "Troops should if possible be lodged behind the posts at such distance as to be able to gain their posts before the advanced guards are beaten". The practical importance of his study must not, however, be overrated. In contrast to Madden, I assume that this was the only part of Lindenau's work read by him; this selective reading though is indicative of his eminently practical interest. His study scarcely extended over more than a few days. There is no trace of his pencil's ever having been pared in the writing of these notes, and in the second part of Lindenau's treatise the notes become fewer and more erratic. It appears that Emmet embodied the results of these studies in an essay on the Art of War, the MS. of part of which is now in the S.P. Office, Dublin. See H. Landreth, *The Pursuit of Robert Emmet,* p. 173.

Emmet's notes are a curious illustration of early Irish cognisance of the military tradition of Prussia. During the Seven Years War Ireland largely sided with Catholic Austria. During the last quarter of the 18th century both Loyalists and Nationalists took a keen interest in Prussia as the most advanced military power on the Continent.

(Quelle: Irish Sword 1, 1951, S.148-150)

An Irishman Makes European History

An Irishman who, 150 years ago, helped Russia conquering the Crimea, who was the tsar's last ambassador to the Sovereign Order of the Knights of Malta, who had to flee from the personal hatred of Napoleon Bonaparte, and who, finally, was spoilt favourite of the splendid society gathering in the years after the Congress of Vienna in the watering-places of Bohemia, that is a career of historical significance and of topical interest.

In the 18th century the most renowned names of the Irish nobility appear in the lists of all the armies of the European powers. Perhaps the most interesting of these Irish swordsmen abroad were those selected by Peter the Great to reorganize the army of the Russian Empire. Well known are the names of the two great Limerick men, George Browne and Maurice Lacy who both attained high positions in the service of the Empress Catherine and distinguished themselves in the wars against Sweden and Turkey by which was brought about the extension of Russia's frontiers to the Baltic Sea in the North, the Black Sea in the South and the Dnjester in the South-West. The glory of those generals naturally attracted a great number of others of their exiled countrymen. The service in the army of the great rising power in Eastern Europe apparently offered the most prosperous prospects to military adventurers. Many of the Irish officers who had served in the armies of France and Austria passed to Russian service, and soon the names of O'Connell, O'Donnell, O'Connor, O'Rourke and Taaffe appeared in the Russian army lists. Towards the middle of the 18th century, Charles Hubert O'Hara, an offspring of the Catholic branch of the O'Hara family from Longford, joined the French and later the Austrian army. He had just married a French lady who, in 1751, at Genoa gave birth to their first and only child. When Mary Marcellus Anthony was seven years old, his father passed to the Russian service. In that very year, George Browne had attained the rank of a Field-Marshal after having gloriously distinguished himself in the battles of Kollin and Zorndorf against the army of Frederic the Great of Prussia. (It is strange that practically no Irishmen joined the new Prussian army). Charles O'Hara did not play an active part in those campaigns. With his family he moved to various garrisons in Russia. In 1774 he died in Vyburg, the famous port in Finland, where up to 1917 his name was found on a memorial tablet in the parish church.

At that time, Peter III was engaged in the first war against Turkey in which the Crimea was annexed to the Russian Empire. In that war Anthony O'Hara did his first service. A few years later, he was sent in a diplomatic function to Malta, a place in which, since the beginning of the century, Russia took a lively interest with a view to gaining a footing in the Mediterranean. Since the 16th century, Malta was under the rule of the Military Order of St. John, the wealthiest and most powerful, but also the most exclusive Order of Catholic Chivalry. The Order never amalgamated with the population of Malta, who, in fact, were led by the native clergy to an ever increasing alienation from their rulers. In 1775, the tsar had openly taken the part of the people of Malta against the Order, whose rule was obviously decaying. After the second Partition of Poland, the Empress Catherine sanctioned the establishment of a Polish Province of the Order in order to gain more influence on that powerful institution. Anthony O'Hara's mission was concerned with this new establishment. The Grand Master approved of it at the same time awarding O'Hara with an Order. Dazzled by the splendour of the Order of Malta and hoping for more speedy promotion in the diplomatic service, he applied for admission to the Order. The Cardinal of York, known to the adherents of the Stuart cause as Henry IX King of England, sponsored his application which had to be submitted to the Pope. In search for the required proofs of his noble descent, Anthony O'Hara made first contact with Ireland. He knew so little about her that he had to approach his relatives, the Taaffes in Bohemia (who incidentally, in later years, became so poor that some of them had to seek refuge in Ireland where they joined Irish yeomanry). At Malta, Anthony met a distant relative of his, Hamilton O'Hara of Crebilly, Co. Antrim, and also Mr. La Touche, the famous Dublin Banker. He thus heard of his cousin Charles O'Hara of Ballyhara, Co. Sligo, a Protestant, from 1780-1820 member of the Irish and British Parliament, who, in 1792, presented the famous petition of the Catholics in the British House of Commons, a service which the petitioners had solicited in vain from other members of the house. This was the first petition presented to Parliament by the Catholics of Ireland. It appears that Anthony O'Hara was not aware that he was an offspring of one of the oldest royal families of Europe. Being one of the Milesian Families, the O'Haras has occupied thrones long before the Habsbourgs and Estes were spoken of. Charles (or Cormac) was the traditional Christian name of the O'Haras for twenty-five generations. It is remarkable that in his correspondence with Anthony, Charles O'Hara apparently did not make mention of the ancient connection of his family with the Knights of Malta. Part of the ancient property of the O'Hara Buidhe at Annaghmore had been usurpated by the Knight Hospitallers. In the days of the Confederation of Kilkenny, the O'Haras obtained from Rinuccini, the Papal Legate, a decree granting them 'Templehouse', which in the Reformation had passed in the possession of the Croftons. In this grant it was expressly stated that this part of Annaghmore formerly belonged to the Comandry of Taght of the Knights of Malta.

The documents presented by Anthony concerning his family were examined by a committee of what was known as the Anglo-Bavarian League (or Province) of the Order under Count Preysing, an ancestor of the present-day first Catholic bishop of Berlin. In 1790, Pope Pius VI issued the Bull making Anthony a Knight of Malta. Incidentally, he became not a professed knight, thus being not bound by the vow of celibacy. In the meantime, he had attained the rank of Lieutenant-Colonel, stationed in garrison in St. Petersburg, where he waited for another appointment in the diplomatic service which would allow him to leave the army for ever.

In fact, in 1796, when Paul I had ascended to the throne, he was nominated chargé d'Affaires to the Russian Mission to Malta. He arrived in La Valetta at the death of the Prince of Rohan, who on his deathbed prophesized that he would be the last Grand Master of the Sovereign Order. His successor Count Hompesch, an Austrian, was to die deposed in exile and poverty. Feeling the weakness of the external and internal position of the Order of Malta, Hompesch appealed to Paul to assume the dignity of Grand Protector of the Order, an idea which possibly had been suggested by O'Hara, the only member of the Russian mission to Malta who was also a Knight. On that occasion the golden crown which had been worn by La Valetta, the illustrious founder of the capital of Malta, and the famous relic of the right hand of St. John the Baptist (from which the Order actually took its name) were sent to Russia. The latter relic came after the Bolshevist Revolution to Berlin and, in later years, to Serbia. In the subsequent year, O'Hara succeeded Admiral Psaro as Russian Minister to the Sovereign Order. At the same time Charles O'Hara, another distant relative of his, was Governor of Gibraltar. With his help, Anthony hoped to become also British Minister and, as he said 'thus to be useful to his countrymen'. For that purpose he also sought to become a member of the Irish Province of the Order. His ambition failed to be gratified mainly on account of the objections made by Sir Charles Whitworth, British Minister to Petersburg, whose father had been made Baron of Galway, and who, in later years, became Lord-Lieutenant. (In Dublin he is commemorated in the name of Whitworth Street). He was well-known for his deep distrust of Irishmen. In 1791 he had sent a report on a plot said to have been engineered in Russia to destroy the English Navy in Portsmouth with the help of Irish incendiaries.

On Malta, Anthony was very popular with the inhabitants who looked upon him, a Russian, as their friend and protector against the unreasonable arrogance of the Order. In 1798, however, all the diplomatic cobwebs of Russian diplomacy on Malta were cruelly torn by the bold occupation of the island by the French on their way to Egypt. (The invaders were actually helped by some French Knights and even more effectively by the people themselves.) Anthony O'Hara was the only member of the Sovereign Knighthood to protest against the occupation and to try to induce the Grand-Master to defend the Order's dignity and independence. He was betrayed to the French who gave him three hours notice to leave Malta. (Owing to delay in transmission of the order, only three quarters of an hour remained). Abandoning a fine residence which he had just fitted up and furnished at his own expense, Anthony escaped right through the squadron of the invaders lying in the harbour, and went to Naples. Henceforth he was persecuted by Napoleon's personal hatred. In fact, his ever increasing anti-revolutionary and anti-Napoleonic attitude made O'Hara one of the most vigorous representatives of the *ancient régime*. ('It grieves me sorely,' he wrote to his cousin 'to see that in our own country, the same regicids have succeeded in propagating the infernal spirit of revolution and in seducing some of the people of our province of Connaught for their allegiance. These Irish gentlemen forget their duty and their religion'). A few months later, we find him in Trieste as one of the few Knights who followed their Grand Master into exile. His position became most awkward when the newly established Russian (Orthodox) Province of the Order elected the Tsar as the new Grand Master. Financial distress forced O'Hara to return to Russia, where he encountered not only the increasing hostility of Sir Charles, to whom 'even his Irish name was suspect', but the more serious opposition of Rastoptchin, the tsar's Prime Minister, who in order to flatter his ambitious master made the most extravagant proposals, such as to get him elected Pope, etc. O'Hara not only fought for the rights of Grand-Master Hompesch but also rebuked Rastoptchin's suggestion to send out a military force for the conquest of Malta. At length, his position became almost untenable. After many years of anxiety and poverty, (during which he lived in the mansion of his ancient friend the Grand Mistress of the Court, Countess Mathiushkin), the assassination of the insane Tsar Paul and the ascension to the throne of Alexander I brought brighter days for him. He was granted a pension of about 350 guineas per annum and was permitted to choose his residence abroad after he had refused to become Governor of one of the provinces of central Russia. When England occupied Malta, O'Hara for a short time thought of re-entering the diplomatic career. His idea was that England would 'not keep Malta in her possession without being menaced by never ending wars from all the powers'. He suggested that 'she should return the island to the Sovereign Order and at the same time encourage Catholic Ireland'. We may conjecture how differently the history of Europe would read, had the British followed O'Hara's advice.

Anthony O'Hara went first to Ellischau in Bohemia where the Taaffes had some estates. In later years, he engaged in the splendid social life in the watering-places of Northern Bohemia, being befriended by royalties and diplomats and, in particular, by Goethe, Germany's greatest poet. It is a well known fact that both during the Congress of Vienna and after, the destiny of many countries was decided in the Kurpromenade of Karlsbad and the public gardens of Marienbad. For many a winter, Anthony went to Dresden, where he met Count Marcolini, a Saxon diplomat, who was married to an O'Kelly, another Irish nobleman in Bohemia, and an ancestor of the first Irish minister to France and Belgium and now Minister for Finance. Thus the last years of the eventful career of this wild goose are once more connected with present-day history.

(Quelle: The Leader, 30.12.1944)

V.3 Goethe und Irland

Goethes Irlandkunde

Unter Deutschlands Verhältnissen zu anderen Ländern zeichnet sich das zu Irland durch den Gegensatz zwischen der Vielfalt der inneren Beziehungen und dem Mangel an äußeren Beziehungen aus. Einer der wichtigsten Abschnitte in der Geschichte der deutschen Irlandkunde ist Goethe; der Überblick von den frühmittelalterlichen Heiligenleben zur modernen Reiseliteratur hat gezeigt, daß kein Deutscher, ohne in Irland gewesen zu sein oder sich unmittelbar mit irischen Dingen befaßt zu haben, eine vielseitigere und tiefere Kenntnis von Irland gehabt hat, als Goethe.[1]

Einige Aspekte von Goethes Irlandkunde sind in Untersuchungen über seine Beziehungen zu Iren ins Auge gefaßt worden.[2] In dem einzigen deutschen Kommentar zu Goethes Bemerkung (in einem Brief an Boisserée vom 12. 10. 1828): »Eigentlich finden die Irländer in meinem Hause am meisten Beifall« hat Muncker versucht, Goethes konservative Haltung der katholischen Emanzipation gegenüber auf seine persönlichen Beziehungen mit Iren zurückzuführen.[3] Allerdings gehörten die irischen Bekannten Goethes durchweg der Schicht an, die diese konservative Haltung vertreten mußte, es liegen aber kaum Anzeichen dafür vor, daß er in dieser Sache Kenntnis aus jenen Beziehungen geschöpft hat. Es läßt sich vielmehr zeigen, daß sein Wissen um irische Verhältnisse aus literarischen Quellen stammt. In ihrer Gesamtheit betrachtet, erlaubt uns Goethes Irlandkunde, den Beginn und die Vielseitigkeit des modernen deutschen Interesses an Irland zu beobachten,[4] das dort am echtesten ist, wo es sich auf das literarische Gebiet beschränkt hat.

---

1 Eine Geschichte der deutschen Irlandkunde hätte von Dr. Josef Grabisch, dem Gründer der ersten deutsch-irischen Gesellschaft (1916), geschrieben werden sollen (s. meinen Nachruf in: Irish Bookman, Juli 1948, S. 87-89). Meine Arbeiten dazu sind über mehr als zwanzig Zeitschriften in Amerika und Europa verstreut und werden hinsichtlich Goethes durch meine Arbeiten über seine Beschäftigung mit der englischen Naturwissenschaft und seine Übersetzungen aus dem Englischen sowie zur Geschichte der irischen Deutschlandkunde ergänzt. Kurze Zusammenfassung in: German Life and Letters N.S. 3 (1950) S. 102-110 und 8 (1955) S. 201-207. Wo Fundorte, weitere Belegstellen, Literatur und Ausführungen in meinen Sonderuntersuchungen (H) zu finden sind, werden nach Nennung letzterer jene Angaben nicht wiederholt, ebenso wenn Einzelheiten leicht durch die Register zur W(eimarer) A(usgabe), zu E. v. Keudell, Goethe als Benutzer der Weimarer Bibliothek, und J. Boyd, Goethe's knowledge of English literature (beide 1932) verfügbar sind.

2 G. Waterhouse, 'Goethe, Giesecke and Dublin', in: Proc. R. Irish Acad. 41 c (1933) S. 210-218 und Minutes dass. 1943-1944, S. 18-22. Meine populäre Zusammenfassung in: Dublin Magazine Jan.-März 1943, S. 45-56 ist weithin überholt.

3 Sitzungsber. Bayer. Akad. 1918, 121f.

4 H., 'Continental opinion' in: Daniel O'Connell (Dublin 1949), S. 235-239.

Unter den Ephemeriden für 1770[5] findet sich eine Liste von Namen, die das Register zur W(eimarer) A(usgabe) als irisch bezeichnet: »*Magog – Baath – Finiusa Farsu – Gadel, son of Eathevir of the posterity of Gomer, Cavih Far, son of Neamha the Hebrew.*« In der ersten Veröffentlichung dieser Ephemeriden brachte Schoell eine längere Anmerkung von G. Stickel, in der die Liste als »kabbalistische Zauberformel« hingestellt wird, aber nicht ermittelt wird, wer »der Engländer« ist, dem diese Stelle entnommen ist.[6] In der WA verwies Martin auf d'Arbois de Jubainville, wo jedoch nur die durch jene Liste zusammengefaßte altirische Überlieferung behandelt wird, nicht dagegen die eigentliche Quelle zu finden ist, der Goethe diese Liste entnahm, nämlich die erste englische Übersetzung (1723 u.ö.) von Keatings 'Grundbestandteilen der irischen Geschichte' (Manuscript 1633).[7] Die letzten sieben Worte in Goethes Liste sind eine irrige Zusammenziehung von Keatings Worten: »*Caoi on Judéa nó Iar (nicht: Far) mac Neamha*«. Diese Liste ist der Niederschlag einer Überlieferung des frühmittelalterlichen Irland, nach der, ähnlich wie Vergil die Gründung Roms mit dem Fall von Troja in Verbindung brachte, die Besiedlung Irlands auf die Zerstreuung der Völker nach dem Turmbau von Babel zurückgeführt wird.[8] Man kann diese Ableitung der »*Hiberni*« von den »*Hebrei*« als »Faseleien« abtun, wie Goethe dies in einem Gespräch vom 18.06.1825 mit den späteren deutschen Spekulationen »von einem vor-Noachidischen Zeitalter« tat.[9]

Seit Düntzers Veröffentlichung der Briefe an Herder (1856) war das Fragment des zweiten Briefes bekannt, den Goethe im Herbst 1771 an Herder richtete und das mit den Worten beginnt: »Diese Stellen sind alle aus dem siebenten Buch ... Ossians Schottisches macht ganz verschiedene Würckung auf Ohr und Seele ... im Original hängts fast an jeder Zeile (*na speur, na h'oicha, nach beo, nan teud, nan nial*) ... Wenn Sie noch mehr aus dem Schottischen übersetzt haben wollen, so schreiben Sie's.« Der erste Teil dieses Briefes, der »diese Stellen«, d.h. Abschriften der von Macpherson veröffentlichten Beispiele seiner mysteriösen Originale mit Goethes Übersetzung bietet, wurde erst 1908 durch Heuer bekannt.[10] Es ist hier nicht der Platz zu zeigen, wie unzureichend die einzige dieser Übersetzung bisher gewidmete Sonderunter-suchung ist.[11] Sie spricht mit dem auf diesem Gebiete so häufigen Mangel an histo-rischer Perspektive von »*Goethe's very faulty transcription of Macpherson's itself faulty Gaelic*« und geht nicht auf die Einzelheiten, ja Feinheiten, von Goethes Über-setzung ein, z.B. die Art, wie er den für das Gälische fundamentalen Unterschied

5 WA I Bd. 37, S. 97

6 1846; WA I Bd. 38, S. 231.

7 In der Gaelic Text Society Ausgabe Bd. 1 S. 226 u. Bd. 2 S. 6.

8 Dazu H. in: Traditio Bd. 7 (1951), S. 233-261.

9 Biedermann Bd. 5 S. 219.

10 WA I Bd. 53 S. 152 u. 480.

11 H. T. Betteridge in: Modern Language Review (MLR) Bd. 30 (1933), S. 334 bis 338; bez. Goethes Übersetzungen aus den englischen Texten, H. in: Journ. Eng. Germ. Philology Bd. 45 (146) S. 77-87 u. MLR Bd. 42 (1947) S. 127-130.

zwischen breiten und schlanken Vokalen nachahmt. Thurneysen hat nachgewiesen, daß diese erste uns bekannte unmittelbare Übersetzung eines gälischen Gedichtes ins Deutsche der Grundstein zu dem überragenden Beitrag gewesen ist, den bis heute Deutsche zur gälischen Sprach- und Literaturwissenschaft leisten.[12] Der letzte Artikel, den Stern, der wie andere durch die Ossiankontroverse zur Keltistik kam, sollte das Thema behandeln 'Goethe als Keltist'.[13]

Während in England und auf dem Festland die Ossiankontroverse um die Authentizität von Macphersons »Originalen« ging, ging sie in Schottland und Irland um die Frage, welchem Lande die Weltliteratur diesen Beitrag zu verdanken habe. Daß Goethe dem Schotten glaubte, ändert nichts an der Tatsache, daß der Ossianismus nicht zuletzt durch ihn den Grund für die moderne Irlandkunde in Westeuropa gelegt hat.[14] Goethes Bemerkungen über die Eigenarten der »galischen« Dichtkunst zeigen, daß er Macphersons Anmerkungen gelesen hat. Diese heute ganz vernachlässigten Anmerkungen enthalten auch Macphersons Darlegungen eines geographisch-historischen Hintergrundes der Gedichte mit vorwiegend irischen Orts- und Personennamen. Was Macpherson sagte, war weit weniger phantastisch als was etwas später Vallancey in Irland behauptete. Auf persönliche Mitteilungen Vallanceys bezog sich Küttner, ein Bekannter Goethes[15], in dem ersten deutschen Reisebuch über Irland[16] und gab dadurch den ersten deutschen Sprachwissenschaftlern, die sich speziell mit dem Irischen befaßten, wie Ahlwardt, Material.[17] Mit den ersten Anfängen der wissenschaftlichen Keltistik machte sich Goethe bekannt, als er im Oktober 1812 aus der Weimarer Bibliothek Schoepfelins 'Alsatia illustrata Celtica, Romana, Francisca' (Colmar 1751) entlieh.

Macpherson hielt es für erforderlich, die »uncouth appearance« zu entschuldigen, die ein gälischer Text auf die machen muß, »who are strangers to its harmony«. Bei

---

12   'Why do Germans study Celtic philology?', in: Studies (Dublin) Bd. 19 (1930) S. 26. Siehe auch H., Besprechung von Bauersfeld, Entwicklung der keltischen Studien in Deutschland, in: Irish Histor. Studies Bd. 4 (1944) S. 120.

13   Kuno Meyer in: Z. f. celtische Philologie Bd. 8 (1912) S. 585 u. 587.

14   1776 veröffentlichte Gerstenberg eine Übersetzung von 'Mémoire de M. de C. au sujet des poèmes de M. Macpherson' in: Journal des Sçavans (1746), worin erstmalig die Authentizität von Macphersons Veröffentlichungen und die Ableitung der Gedichte aus Schottland statt Irland bezweifelt wurde (M. de C., nach Gerstenberg »ein Irrländer« von A. Gillies, Herder und Ossian [Berlin 1933] S. 6 mit John O'Brien, kathol. Bischoff von Cloyne, identifiziert). Bei der Ausgabe des englischen Textes, den Merck 1775 veröffentlichte, und der am Ende von Bd. 4 ein Beispiel des Originals von Temora Buch VII bot, half Goethe mit (Ulrich in: Z. f. Bücherfreunde [1906] S. 283-285).

15   Tagebuch 07.05.1798 u. 05.05.1800.

16   Briefe über Irland (Leipzig 1785); die darin nur mit Anfangsbuchstaben bezeichneten irischen Orts- und Personennamen wurden von mir in Irish Times Literary Suppl. 27.01.1945 identifiziert.

17   Der verstorbene Professor Eoin McNeill war der erste irische Gelehrte, der mir bei diesen Studien behilflich war. In seinen Phases of Irish history (1918) S. 6-9 hat er mit einzigartigem historischen Sinn diese Ursprünge der irischen Altertumswissenschaft und ihre Auswirkungen auf dem Festland behandelt.

Goethe hielt die Begeisterung für die Originalität der »Celten ..., so stark, so feurig, so groß«[18], nicht vor. Als er 1787 in Rom dem (bis heute in ähnlicher Weise üblichen) Epiphanie-Empfang auf der Propaganda beiwohnte, nannte er »Hybernisch« unter den exotischen Sprachen, »die ich nicht verstehen konnte« und nach deren »barbarischen Tönen« das Griechische »klang, wie ein Stern in der Nacht erscheint«.[19] Zahlreiche Beispiele aus der Geschichte der deutschen Irlandkunde zeigen, daß der klassische Goethe, indem er die Verachtung der Römer für den gutturalen Klang des Irischen teilte, in einer fast tausendjährigen Tradition steht.

In der Übersetzung aus Lady Lambs 'Glenarvon' (1817), der Goethe den Titel 'Klaggesang, Irisch' gab, bewahrte er aus dem Original die traditionellen Klänge eines »irischen Todtengesangs«[20] auf: »*Och orro orro ollalu*«. Ich habe gezeigt, daß sich in Goethes Übersetzung die Haltung Irland gegenüber aus der romantischen Herablassung, zu der sich damals ein Teil der englischen Herrenschicht durchrang, in das vorsichtige Wohlwollen verwandelte, das bis heute dem Kontinentalen immer noch am besten ansteht. Ich habe ferner gezeigt, daß Goethe, indem er das Wort »zart« auf keinen Menschen häufiger anwandte denn auf den irischen Physiker Robert Boyle, unbewußt ein Merkmal herausgestellt hat, durch das sich die Anglo-Iren entscheidend von den Engländern unterscheiden.[21]

Von den in Irland geborenen Schriftstellern in englischer Sprache hat Goethe nur zwei ausdrücklich als Iren bezeichnet, Sterne und Moore.[22] Als Goethe 1827 in Thomas Hoods 'Whims and Oddities'[23] las, daß der Ire »*wears a flowery had and talks a flow'ry speech*«, hatte er sich schon der englischen Vorstellung vom sog. Bühnen-Iren entwunden. In der Abteilung über Sterne in 'Maximen und Reflexionen'[24] wird der Shandeismus definiert als »schneller Wechsel von Ernst und Scherz, von Anteil und Gleichgültigkeit, von Leid und Freude«.[25] Die Worte »von Anteil und Gleichgültig-

---

18   Macpherson: Einl. zu den gälischen Fragmenten des 7. Buchs von Temora; Goethe: Frankf. Gel. Anz. 1772 (WA I Bd. 37 S. 217).

19   Briefe an Charl. v. Stein, hrsg. Fränkel (1908) Bd. 3 S. 326.

20   Tages- und Jahreshefte 1817. H. in: Monatshefte (Univ. Wisconsin) Bd. 41 (1949) S. 71-76. 1831 studierte Goethe (Tagebuch 30. u. 31.03.) Jamiesons Gälisches Wörterbuch; seine Beschäftigung mit dem Gälischen erstreckt sich somit über mehr als sechzig Jahre.

21   H. in: DVjs. 29 (1955) S. 515.

22   Ich ergänze in Einzelheiten Prof. Boyds Werk (s. oben Anm. I), bes. hinsichtlich der Naturwissenschaften; s. H., 'Goethe's knowledge of books by Irish scientists', in: Irish Booklover Bd. 32 (1955) S. 86f.: Boyle, Molyneux, Kirwan u. O'Halloran (über letzteren s.u.).

23   H. in: Modern Language Quarterly (MLQ) Bd. 12 (1951) S. 57-66.

24   1828. Schon am 23.03.1826 sprach Goethe mit Ottilie über »die verschiedenen Charaktere der Bewohner der drei britannischen Inseln« (vgl.: »eine Colonie junger Engländer, Schotten und Irländer« in Brief an Varnhagen 03.04.1825; »junge Männer aus den drei Königreichen« in Brief an Sterling 30.06. u. 10.07.1826).

25   In der Korrespondenz mit Zelter (04.03.1829) betr. »Irish bulls« sprach Goethe davon, daß letztere ein Ausdruck einer »wunderbaren Unbehülflichkeit des Geistes« seien (H. in: MLQ Bd. 8 [1947] S. 487 f. u. Bd. 15 [1954] S. 366). In Whittys Erzählungen, einem der ersten Werke

keit« (an denen der in Irland lebende Ausländer die Wahrheit von Goethes Beschreibung ermißt) beziehen sich keinesfalls auf Sterne, und die Schlußworte: »soll in dem irländischen Charakter liegen« zeigen in der Tat, daß Goethe hier einmal weit über das Literarische hinausgeht. Die Quelle für jene meisterhafte Zusammenfassung des irischen Charakters war zweifellos der irische Freundeskreis seiner Schwiegertochter. Am 29. März 1828 (Tagebuch) sprach er mit Ottilie »über den Unterschied der britischen Nationen und ihren Charakter, besonders Charakter der Irländer«. Drei Monate später ließ Goethe der eingangs angeführten Bemerkung in dem Brief an Boisserée die Worte vorausgehen: »Junge Männer aus den drei Königreichen[26] leben hier in Pension und so kommt man nicht aus der Gewohnheit über sie nachzudenken.« Wir werden gleich sehen, daß Goethe guten Grund hatte, über diese jungen Iren nachzudenken. Betrachten wir hierbei auch die Verzahnung von literarischen und persönlichen Beziehungen zu Irland in der Woche vor der Unterhaltung mit Ottilie: Am 23. und 24. März las Goethe in Sternes Werken besonders den 'Koran'; am 27. März kam der (unten zu erwähnende) Herr Knox (aus Dublin), »um Abschied zu nehmen. Fortgesetzte Studien des Yorick«.

Von Swifts Geburt und Leben in Irland und seinen Schriften über Irland hat Goethe nie gesprochen. Von Goldsmith sagt er im 10. Buche von 'Dichtung und Wahrheit', daß er »ein Engländer ist, und die Vortheile, die ihm sein Land, seine Nation darbietet, hoch anrechnen« kann.[27] Steele ist ihm »der edle Engländer«.[28] Goethes Bewunderung für Moore ist eine Zeitlang so unbegreiflich erschienen wie seine Bewunderung für Byron.[29] Zwar notierte sich Goethe aus Jacobsens' 'Briefen an eine teutsche Edelfrau', daß Moore »Irländer, geb. 28.03.1780 zu Dublin« war, an anderen Stellen jedoch bezeichnet er ihn (wie auch Sterne) als »Britten«. Goethes Achtung für Moore gründet sich nicht auf dessen 'Irish Melodies' sondern auf 'Odes of Anacreaon' und vor allem 'Lalla Rookh' und die Biographien Byrons und Fitzgeralds, von denen die letztere ihm weniger ihrem irisch-historischen Inhalt als ihrer literarischen Form nach interessant war. Schon anläßlich der Cellini-Biographie von Richard Boyle, dem Bruder des Physikers, war ihm die Kunst der Biographie als spezifisch englisch erschienen.[30]

Wieweit Goethe bei Anthony Murphy (dessen von Schroeder bearbeitetes Lustspiel 'Die Eifersüchtigen' das Tagebuch vom 16.01.1794 erwähnt), James Murphy (dessen

---

aus der anglo-irischen Literatur, die in Deutschland erschienen (Breslau 1826) (H. in: Irish Bookman, Febr. 1947 S. 39-44), hätte Goethe ausgezeichnete Illustrationen dieser Eigenschaften finden können.

26   »Junge Männer Ihrer drei überseeischen Reiche« (Entwurf an Carlyle 16.06.1828).

27   Zur Parallele zwischen der Szene Auerbachs Keller im Urfaust und der Wirtshausszene in 'She stoops to conquer' (letztere auf einer Erfahrung des jungen Goldsmith in einer heute noch bestehenden Landkneipe in Irland beruhend) H. in: Comparative Literature 1955 Bd. 7 (1955) S. 193-202.

28   WA I Bd. 36 S. 322.

29   H. in: MLR Bd. 48 (1953) S. 445-50.

30   WA I Bd. 44 S. 370 und 418.

'Reise nach Portugal' er in einer aus der Weimarer Bibliothek entliehenen französischen Übersetzung im Frühjahr 1801 las)[31], dem Grafen Macartney[32], Leicester Stanhope ('Greece in 1823' entliehen während des Sommer 1825) oder gar bei William Duckett (Tagebuch 22.10.1829: »Duchett«)[33] klar war, daß es sich um Iren handelt, läßt sich nicht ermitteln. Die Agenda für den 16.11.1813 enthält die Eintragung: »Roman der M. Edgeworth«.[34] 'Leonara', das »treffliche Werk einer der vorzüglichsten englischen Schriftstellerinnen«, war 1806 von Hüttner in seinen Goethe bestens bekannten 'Englischen Miscellen' angezeigt worden; es könnte sich auch um 'Castle Rackrent' handeln, ein Werk, das Jean Paul zweifellos gekannt hat.[35] Als Goethe zehn Jahre später in Karlsbad Charles Sneyd Edgeworth und dessen (englische) Gattin kennen lernte, erwähnte er nie, daß dieser ein Stiefbruder der Romanschriftstellerin war; er erschien Goethe entschieden als »Engländer«. Weiterhin in der Agenda für den 16.11.1813 erwähnt Goethe »(Roman) der M. Owenson ... die Stael von England genannt«. Hier handelt es sich wahrscheinlich um die französische Übersetzung von Lady Morgans 'The wild Irish girl', damals gerade unter dem Titel 'Glorwina ou la jeune Irlandaise' erschienen, über Merimées 'Colomba' die Quelle für die irische Lydia in Kellers 'Pankraz der Schmoller'.[36]

Diese Erwähnung der beiden irischen Schriftstellerinnen seiner Zeit ist besonders bemerkenswert, weil das Festland von unmittelbarer Verbindung mit der englischen Literatur abgeschnitten war.[37] 1822 las dann Goethe in deutscher Übersetzung Lady Morgans Buch über Italien, das ihm nach v. Müller verhaßt war. Am 27. Juni 1828 verglich er in einem Brief an seine Schwiegertochter deren Tagebücher mit denen Lady Morgans. Wenige Monate nach Goethes Tod traf Ottilie Lady Morgan. Sie war tief enttäuscht, in ihr eine Dame mit französischen Manieren zu finden. »Ach, mein Gott, hätte sie mich mit [dem irischen Gruß] Cushlamachree begrüßt, ich hätte sie umarmt.«[38] Ich erwähne, daß Ottilie 1830 Campbells 'Exile of Erin' und 1831 Banims

---

31 In WA III Bd. 15 S. 83 werden die beiden Murphys zusammengewürfelt.

32 H. in: MLR Bd. 46 (1951) S. 405.

33 D. war mit den nationalistischen Flüchtlingen in Hamburg assoziiert (H. in: Irish Booklover Bd. 31 [1951] S. 108f.). Er soll auch noch andere deutsche Werke ins Französische übersetzt haben und gab die französische Übersetzung von Brockhaus Conversationslexikon heraus (Dict. of National Biography).

34 H. in: MLQ Bd. 15 (1954) S. 366-371.

35 Zu H. in: MLR Bd. 40 (1945) S. 190 ist hinzuzufügen, daß die Mitteilung, daß in Irland Diener die Häuser mit ihren Perücken fegen, von Jean Paul aus diesem Roman entnommen wurde.

36 H., Irische Frauengestalten in der Weltliteratur, in: Basler Nachr. 23.05.1954.

37 H. in: MLR Bd. 46 (1951) S. 405-406.

38 L. Stevenson, The wild Irish girl (1936) S. 286. Lady Morgans Tagebuch über ihre Begegnung mit Ottilie: Bd. II S. 370.

'O'Hara Stories' las, eindeutig ihres nationalirischen Inhalts wegen[39]; ihr Freund Ferdinand Gustav Kühne schrieb 1840 'Die Rebellen von Irland'.[40]

Die einzigen ausschließlich von Irland handelnden Bücher, von denen wir bestimmt wissen, daß Goethe sie gelesen hat, sind O'Hallorans 'Introduction to the history and antiquities of Ireland' und Walkers 'Irish bards', die Grundbücher der modernen Forschung über irische Volkssagen und irische Volksmusik. Diese Werke wurden ihm 1810 in Karlsbad von Anthony O'Hara, dem letzten russischen Gesandten in Malta, verehrt, der sich später zu einem vergnüglichen Lebensabend in Weimar niederließ. Durch ihn lernte Goethe ein weiteres Mitglied der irisch-katholischen Adelsemigranz[41] kennen, Pater O'Kelly, den Beichtvater der Königin von Sachsen, einen Vorfahren des gegenwärtigen Präsidenten der Republik Irland.

Einige Monate früher (Brief 07.11.1808) hatte Goethe Interesse genommen an Sartorius' »englischen und irländischen Klosterstudien aus jener dunklen Zeit, von der man so wenig weiß«. Von Kindheitstagen war Goethe mit den Namen der frühen irischen Heiligen vertraut. Das St. Gallusthor in Frankfurt wird in 'Dichtung und Wahrheit' erwähnt. Bryd, der Name der Magd in dem von Goethe 1820 besprochenen Straßburger Dialektstück 'Der Pfingstmontag', erinnert an die im Straßburger Gebiet bis heute nachlebende Verehrung der irischen Heiligen Brigid.[42] Unter den Auszügen für die Italienreise findet sich eine Notiz über 'St. Colomban qui avait établi l'abbaye de Luxeuil en Franche Comté'. Im Juni 1826 entlieh Goethe aus der Weimarer Bibliothek Canisius' 'Antiquae lectiones' (Ingolstadt 1601), ein Werk das zum ersten Male in Deutschland Viten irischer Heiliger in wissenschaftlicher Ausgabe bot. In seiner 'Geschichte der Farbenlehre' bespricht Goethe die Werke zweier Insassen des Schottenklosters in Erfurt, einer irischen Gründung des 13. Jahrhunderts.[43] Durch Schiller war Goethe die Rolle der irischen Soldateska im Dreißigjährigen Kriege bekannt.[44] Im Juli 1806 besichtigte er im Rathaus zu Eger das Wandgemälde, das Wallensteins Ermordung darstellt; er erwähnt dabei ausdrücklich Butler. In seiner Besprechung der 'Monatsschrift der Gesellschaft des vaterländischen Museums in Böhmen' (1827) erwähnt Goethe die Geschichte der Carolina in Prag während des Dreißigjährigen Krieges; irische Professoren spielten eine hervorragende Rolle in den von Goethe beschriebenen Ereignissen.[45]

---

39   v. Oettingens Ausgabe von Ottiliens Tagebüchern (Schriften der Goethe-Ges.) Bd. 2, S. 280, 320 und 419.

40   Proels in: A.D.B. Bd. 51 S. 431.

41   H. in: MLR Bd. 39 (1944) S. 46-51. Durch die O'Donnells (R. M. Werner, Goethe und die Gräfin O'Donnell [1884]) lernte Goethe auch die Baronin O'Bryne kennen.

42   WA I Bd. 41, I S. 147. Goethe war diese Beziehung ebensowenig bewußt wie die des Vornamens von Kilian Brustfleck (H. in: Irish Eccles. Record V Bd. 78 [1952] S. 33).

43   Erfurter Schottenkloster: H. in: Irish Eccles. Rec. V Bd. 69 (1947) S. 135f., Grant und Gordon: H. in: Osiris Bd. 10 (1952) S. 60f.

44   H. in: Journal R. Soc. Antiquar. Ireland Bd. 82 (1952), 28-36.

45   WA I Bd. 42, I S. 33, und H. in: Irish Eccles. Rec. V Bd. 63 (1945) S. 400.

Für die neuere Geschichte Irlands kann man den Umfang von Goethes Wissen aus seinen Studien zur britischen Geschichte erschließen. Als er in der Autobiographie, die Luke Howard für ihn schrieb, las, daß einer von Howards Vorfahren mit Jakob II. nach Irland kam, war ihm der historische Hintergrund zweifellos gut bekannt.[46] Die führende Rolle deutscher Kontingente im Kampf gegen Jakob II. in Irland war durch die zeitgenössische deutsche Literatur eingehend dargelegt worden. Z.B. war Goethe mit dem Werke Happels bekannt, der eins der umfassendsten deutschen Bücher über Irland am Ende des 17. Jahrhundert schrieb.[47] Als ihn 1797 Lord Bristol, der Bischof von Derry[48], zu sich zitierte, war ihm sicher die Rolle bekannt, die dieser um jene Zeit in der nationalen Bewegung in Irland spielte. Als 1828 »die Rede auf die irländischen reichen Pfründen kam, die man jetzt zu schmälern beantrage«, äußerte Goethe: »Die dunklen Köpfe. Als ob man der Geistlichkeit etwas nehmen könne«[49], vielleicht eine Erinnerung an den »erbaulichen Bischoff«.

Als Goethe ein Jahr nach der Begegnung mit Bristol Erasmus Darwins 'Botanical Garden' las, übersetzte er die Zusammenfassung des zweiten Gesangs, die die Worte »Freiheit Amerikas, Irlands und Frankreichs« enthält.[50] Die Verbindung zwischen dem Freiheitskampf Amerikas und Irlands mag ihm schon durch das Buch des irischen Nationalisten David Baillie Warden über die Vereinigten Staaten nahegebracht worden sein, das er während des Sommers 1819 studierte und das sich noch 1904 im Goethehaus befand.[51] Das Bild Darwins von der – kurzen – Freiheit Irlands am Ende des 18. Jahrhunderts (»*Liberty helm'd his bold course to Hibernia, Art plies his oar, and Commerce pours her horn*«) lebte wohl noch nach, als sich Goethe in dem Gespräch mit von Ompteda am 22.06.1807 über die Lage der Katholiken in Irland äußerte; sie erschien ihm damals noch als eine interne Angelegenheit Englands.

Die Entwicklung des europäischen Interesses an Irland läßt sich bei Goethe durch die intensive Beschäftigung mit Canning[52] und O'Connell[53] verfolgen, wobei man weiterhin die von diesen beiden Politikern zuerst erkannte Rolle von Zeitungen und Zeitschriften als Propagandaquellen studieren kann. Hüttner und Bran müßten gesondert als Goethes Informationsquellen über Irland studiert werden[54]; in des ersteren 'Eng-

---

46   H. in: MLQ Bd. 10 (1949) S. 322-333 u. Bd. 12 (1951) S. 446-450.

47   H. in: Ulster Journal of Archaeology Bd. 11 (1948) S. 65-80. Goethe entlieh 1801 Happels Thesaurus exoticon (1688) aus der Weimarer Bibliothek.

48   Nicht »Derby«, wie es in den älteren Goetheausgaben heißt, H. in: Ulster Journal of Archaeology Bd. 10 (1947) S. 101-109.

49   S. oben Anm. 4.

50   An Schiller 26.01.1798.

51   Mackall in: Goethe Jahrbuch Bd. 25 (1904) S. 31.

52   H. in: MLQ Bd. 10 (1949) S. 512-516. Castlereagh wurde im Gespräch mit Eckermann 01.09. 1828 erwähnt. Über Goethe und Wellington: H. Landgraf, Goethe und seine ausländischen Besucher (1932) S. 48f.

53   S. oben Anm. 4.

54   H. in: MLR Bd. 46 (1951) S. 405-418.

lischen Miscellen' findet sich z.B. 1806 eine Notiz über eine Bittschrift für die irischen Katholiken[55], während des letzteren 'Minerva' 1819-1821 mehrere den irischen Katholiken äußerst günstige Berichte brachte.[56] 'Le Globe' rang sich trotz seines Antiklerikalismus gerade in den Nummern, von denen wir durch Goethes Übersetzungen bestimmt wissen, daß er sie gelesen, zu einer liberalen Ansicht der Verhältnisse in Irland durch. Am 12.08.1830 las Goethe »in der Revue Française[57] die ältere Geschichte Irlands«, nämlich in einer Besprechung von Shiels 'Scènes populaires en Irlande'[58] eine Zusammenfassung der 'causes historiques de l'état de l'Irlande' seit dem Normanneneinfall, wobei noch rein der britische Standpunkt vertreten wird.

O'Connells Name fällt zwar ausdrücklich nur in der Besprechung von Pücklers 'Briefen eines Verstorbenen'. Eckermann hat uns aber mehrere Zeugnisse von Goethes Interesse am Fortgang von O'Connells Werk aufbewahrt. Goethes Ansicht, daß katholische Emanzipation zwangsläufig zu weiteren Forderungen der irischen Nationalisten führen würde, eilte, jedenfalls auf dem Festland, der Einsicht seiner Zeitgenossen weit voraus. Wenige Tage vor seinem Tod erhielt Goethe von Ottilie Kenntnis »von dem neueingelangten Werke über Irland«, vielleicht Deppings damals gerade erschienenes trocken-zuverlässiges Buch.

Es würde zu weit führen, der Rolle von Ottilies Hibernomanie als Quelle von Goethes Irlandkunde im Einzelnen nachzugehen. Die kürzlich erschienenen Biographien haben keine Auskunft über den Ursprung von Ottilies Hibernomanie gegeben.[59] Das älteste Zeugnis dafür das Billet Goethes vom August 1820[60]:

Seine Herrlichkeit der Vicekönig von Irland
empfiehlt sich und die Natur
der patriotischen Frau v. Goethe
durch das beliebte einheimische Immergrün
mit den besten Wünschen für ihre Genesung

liegt lange vor dem Erscheinen des aus Limerick gebürtigen Sterling, der im März 1823 Goethe den bekannten Brief von Byron brachte, um während zwölf Jahren eine verhängnisvolle Rolle im Leben Ottilies zu spielen. Was sie an ihm als typisch irische Eigenschaften bestrickte, schrieb Goethe Eckermann gegenüber auch den jungen Schotten, im Gegensatz zu dem einseitigen Intellektualismus der Deutschen, zu.

Da Goethes persönliche Beziehungen mit Iren bereits, wenn auch keineswegs genügend, behandelt worden sind, beschränke ich mich auf einige Zusätze von literari-

---

55   Bd. 22 S. 123.

56   1819 S. 95f.; 1820 S. 354; 1821 S.9-26.

57   No. xv S. 152-189; no. xiv hatte er sich im Mai aus der Weimarer Bibliothek geliehen.

58   D. i. die französische Übersetzung von Mrs. Belloe der Sketches of the Irish Bar (1821-1823), die Goethe am 2. u. 3.8.1830 las, aber schon am 8.10.1829 hatte er in sein Tagebuch eingetragen:»Der Irländer Sheil (sic) über den gegenwärtigen Zustand von Irland«.

59   G. H. Needler, Letters of Anna Jamesson to Ottilie v. Goethe (1939), u. D. Zeemann, Ottilie (1949).

60   WA IV Bd. 33 S. 180.

schem Interesse. Der Brief mit dem sich der Rt. Hon. George Knox (Tagebuch 26.05. 1825: »Anmeldung des Herrn Knox aus Dublin. Brief des Herrn von Giesecke von dorther, mit einigen interessanten Mineralien ... Kamen gedachte Engländer, Knox und Söhne«) bei Goethe ansagte, ist zwar literarisch belanglos, mag aber hier als der soweit bekannt einzige erhaltene Brief eines Iren an Goethe Platz finden[61]:

au Prince Hereditaire
Weimar
May 26. 1825

Sir –

I have the honour of sending you a letter from S(i)r Charles Giesecke with some minerals and also a paper of his on Greenland.

I am travelling, as S(i)r Charles probably informs you, with two of my sons. If it should suit your convenience to see us we shall be most flattered by your naming an hour when we can wait upon you. We shall proceed this afternoon to Jena.

I have the honour to be, S(i)r,
Your obediant and humble servant
George Knox

His Excellency
Baron Von Göthe

Die Beziehungen mit Giesecke, der als Professor für Mineralogie an der Royal Dublin Society der erste deutsche Gelehrte war, der in Irland selbst etwas zur Irlandkunde beitrug, führten zu Goethes Ernennung zum Ehrenmitglied der Kgl. Irischen Akademie.[62]

Bereits 1819 hatte Goethe ein Buch von Bernard O'Reilly über Grönland gelesen und mit Giesecke Kontakt aufgenommen. Als er am 22.11.1819 Giesecke für Mineralien dankte, verglich er sie mit Bergkristallen, die er von Mawe aus Schottland (Hs. ursprünglich: »Irland«) erhalten hatte.[63] Auch 1826 erwähnte er wieder mineralogische Parallelen zwischen Schottland und Irland[64], und wenige Monate später zog er in seiner Besprechung von Nöggeraths Geologie des Rheinlands einen Vergleich zwischen der Landeskrone und dem »Riesendamm in Irland«.[65] Man kann den Hochstand deutscher Irlandkunde zu jener Zeit daran ermessen, daß 1787 in Leipzig eine Übersetzung von William Hamiltons 'Letters concerning the North coast of Antrim, containing a natural history of its basaltes' erscheinen konnte. Der Riesendamm, wie überhaupt der Norden Irlands, kommen in den modernen deutschen Reisebüchern kaum noch vor. Wie wenige Besucher des Darmstädter Museums würden heute noch beim Anblick der Zeichnung eines Riesengeweihs an den megacervus Hibernicus denken, wie Goethe dies tat ('Kunst und Alterthum am Rhein und Neckar').[66]

---

61 Photostat der Nationalen Gedenk- und Forschungsstätten, Weimar.

62 Waterhouse, a.a.O., zu ergänzen durch H. in: Irish Naturalists J. Bd. 10 (1951) S. 195f.

63 H. in: Mineralogical Magazine Bd. 28 (1949) S. 534-546.

64 Brief an den Großherzog 30.10.

65 WA II Bd. 9 S. 199.

66 WA I Bd. 34, I S. 153.

Im gleichen Monat wie Knox kam sein Landsmann George Cromie nach Weimar. Auch er wird von Goethe als »Engländer« bezeichnet, obwohl er durch seine frische irische Art die Herzen der Damen bestrickt. August v. Goethes Freundschaft mit Cromie war zweifellos unbelasteter als die mit Sterling; August machte mit Cromie melancholische Spaziergänge, auf denen er seinem Herzen Luft machte[67]. Mr. Blochmann veröffentlichte Goethes Autogramm in Cromies Stammbuch.[68] Als Cromie im Juli 1828 Weimar verließ, nahm der Dubliner George Downes seinen Platz ein. Die Beschreibung, die dieser in der deutschen Literatur wohl bewanderte junge Mann von seinem Besuch bei Goethe gab, ist bisher in Deutschland kaum beachtet worden.[69] Sie enthält die für uns besonders bemerkenswerten Worte: »*Mme v. Goethe is curious about everything relative to England und even to Ireland which is at Weirnar known to be a distinct island, a great stretch of Continental Geography.*« Noch weniger bekannt ist die Beschreibung, die William R. Swifte von Goethe und den Lustigen von Weimar gab;[70] die Artemis-Ausgabe von Goethes Gesprächen gab nur einen kurzen Auszug daraus.[71] In Swiftes Stammbuch schrieb Goethe einige Verse[72]. Goethe bezeichnet ihn als den »Engländer Swift«, obwohl ihm zweifellos bekannt war, daß Prinz Bernhard einmal zu Swiftes Ehren einen Toast ausbrachte »zum Andenken an seinen Verwandten«, Jonathan Swift. Von den späteren irischen Besuchern – im ganzen sind es ja deren 25 – erwähne ich nur noch Randall Edward Plunkett, mit dem Goethe Zeitschriften austauschte; er ist ein Vorfahre von Lord Dunsany, einem der führenden Schriftsteller des heutigen Irlands.

Aus dem Studium von Goethes Irlandkunde kann man einige allgemeine Lehren ziehen. (1) Als ich zu meinem Lehrer Witkowski mit dem Plan einer Arbeit über Herder und das Mittelalter kam und dazu sagte, ich wolle nicht zum wiederholten Male Herders Anschauungen über das Mittelalter darstellen, sondern feststellen, auf welcher Kenntnis diese beruhten, umarmte er mich fast. In meinen Goetheforschungen bin ich auf Schritt und Tritt darauf gestoßen, wie selten die Darstellungen seiner Meinungen auf eine Erforschung des ihnen zugrunde liegenden Wissens aufgebaut worden sind. (2) Bei der Betrachtung eines so abseits liegenden Gebietes wie Goethes Irlandkunde muß man sich besonders bewußt bleiben, daß wir von keinem Menschen umfassendere Nachrichten über die Weite seines Wissens haben als von Goethe. Wieweit sein Wissen einzigartig war, kann nur im Rahmen einer Geschichte deutschen Wissens von dem betreffenden Sachgebiete verstanden werden. Es läßt sich z.B. zeigen, daß Jean Pauls[73] ausgedehntes Wissen um irische Dinge seiner Arbeitsmethode gemäß durchaus anekdotenhaft war, während sich Goethes zu einer rechten Irlandkunde zusammen-

---

67   v. Oettingen, op. cit., Bd. 2 S. 130.

68   In: MLR Bd. 39 (1944) S. 58-62.

69   Letters from Continental countries (Dublin 1832).

70   Wihlhelm's wanderings (London 1878).

71   S. H., Irish descriptions of Goethe, in: Publications English Goethe Society 1957.

72   Aus dem West-östlichen Divan.

73   S. o. Anm. 35.

schloß. (3) Andererseits war Goethes Wissen natürlich viel weiter, als ausdrückliche Erwähnungen in seinen Werken, Tagebüchern, Briefen und Gesprächen zeigen. Nebenbei gemachte Bemerkungen sind oft besonders aufschlußreich, und mittelbares Erschließen von Goethes Wissen, wie gelegentlich hier unternommen, ist zulässig. Man tritt einem großen und universalen Schriftsteller unserer Tage kaum zu nahe, wenn man vermutet, daß er sich nicht, wie Goethe dies tat (Tagebuch 21.05.1827), eine Spezialkarte von Irland hat kommen lassen oder auch nur angesehen hat.

Wem nicht wie einem nach Irland verschlagenen Germanisten Goethes Irlandkunde zu Herzen geht, dem kann sie doch eines der Themen werden, an dem er in bezug auf Goethes Gesamtwerk wieder einmal begreifen kann, welches da ist die Breite, und die Länge, und die Tiefe, und die Höhe.

(Quelle: Deutsche Vierteljahresschrift für Literaturwissenschaft und Geistesgeschichte 31, 1957, S. 70-83)

Goethe's Personal Relations with Ireland

In his paper on Goethe's relations with Sir Charles Ludwig Giesecke, the founder of the mineralogy of Ireland, Professor Gilbert Waterhouse has given as his opinion that "it was neither politics nor literature that roused Goethe's interest in Ireland but natural science".[1] On the occasion of a recent performance of "The Magic Flute" in Dublin, I had an opportunity of pointing out that Giesecke, who became professor of mineralogy in the Royal Dublin Society in 1814, and in later years, was instrumental in getting "the baron de Goethe" elected member of the Royal Irish Academy, was identical with the inferior Viennese actor who, in 1791, was entrusted with the adaptation from Wieland's Oberon of the libretto of Mozart's last Opera. Whilst greatly admiring "the deeper meaning" which had been given to the "tale of Lulu" underlying the libretto of "The Magic Flute", Goethe himself, like most of his contemporaries, was unaware are of the identity of the famous Dublin mineralogist with the author of that libretto.

Professor Waterhouse has collected the various references found in Goethe's diaries and letters to Ireland and Dublin in connection with his relations with Sir Charles Ludwig Giesecke. These relations were mainly based on Goethe's mineralogical and meteorological studies. Giesecke enriched Goethe's extensive collections of minerals by rare specimens collected on his journeys to Greenland, Cornwall and the various parts of Ireland, and on the other hand, procured for Goethe the barometer readings of Dublin of February, 1825, a date chosen by Goethe for a study of the relationship existing between the barometer readings and the altitude of places compared over wide latitudes. I have been told by Professor Pollak that those barometer readings were probably taken in the meteorological observatory in the Botanic Gardens, Dublin. The international extent of Goethe's correspondence may be gathered from the fact, that, whilst Dublin was chosen as the most westerly station, Charkov was the most easterly.

---

1 Proceedings R.I.A., 1933.

Based on these observations, Goethe published his study on "the Causes of barometer fluctuations".[2]

The more interesting points in his correspondence with Giesecke are the various mentions made of Irishmen whom Giesecke sent to him. These were either tourists who, whilst visiting Weimar, wished to meet the great man, or youngsters who were on the Continent for the study of languages. As to the spreading of Goethe's fame to Ireland, I may note that the earliest reaction found in William Preston's "Reflections on the particularities of style in the late German writers"[3] was most unfavourable. In Mr. Preston's opinion, Goethe (of whom he apparently knew only "Goetz", his first drama) was "the great patriarch of the terrific and ferocious school, which established the cannibalism on the theatre". But later on, several Irishmen of distinction visited Weimar for the purpose of acquainting themselves with Goethe. There was the Right Honourable George Knox, the mineralogist, who was there in Spring, 1825, with his sons. Then came "the Irishman Joy" with another collection of "fine minerals from Giesecke", and soon after this, the diploma of the Royal Irish Academy was brought to Weimar by Mr. Knox's son, who was then to study the German language and literature. After his arrival, Goethe wrote: "Your (Giesecke's) countrymen will all be welcome here; these young men are popular with my children (August and his wife, Ottilia) with whom English literature is the order of the day." Goethe adds that he takes "a personal interest in their (the young Irishmen's) progress in acquiring the language and often talks to them". The natives of the three kingdoms formed a kind of colony in that city. In October, 1826, Goethe mentions the visit of "Herr Dutmall, an Irishman". In March, 1829, he refers to a "letter from an Irishman (George) Seymour" who was about to be accommodated in Weimar by Eckermann. A few months later Goethe enters in his diary: "Lunch with Eckermann. The English-man (!) Seymour has started translating my biography. I saw the first half and, so far as can be judged in a foreign language, it is quite readable." (Mr. Seymour apparently did not publish his translation; the first English translation of "Aus meinem Leben" had appeared five years previously). On November 2nd, 1830, Goethe's "Agenda" and diary mention "an Irishman named Archer, who in a short time made himself acquainted with German language and literature".

Writing to Sulpiz Boisserée, the great advocate of the revival of medieval art on the Continent, Goethe said: "The Irish are certainly the most popular in my house." This remark is a sufficient justification of a closer study of Goethe's personal relations with Ireland, a subject, which, moreover, reveals Goethe's true significance as the most universal genius ever produced in any nation. References to Ireland, Irishmen and Irish affairs are found scattered through the 138 volumes of the gigantic edition of Goethe's works, known as the Sophie or Weimar-edition. These references date from practically all periods of Goethe's life and virtually embrace all spheres of life. His references to Irish politics have been collected by Karl Blind in a study inaccessible in this country, whilst his knowledge of English and Irish literature has been investigated by Dr. Boyd.

---

2   Sophie-edition, series ii, vol. 12, p. 59 foll., map. on p. 78.

3   Transactions R.I.A., viii, c. 1800.

It will take a special study to discuss Goethe's knowledge of ancient Ireland as conveyed to him through the Ossianic enthusiasm of his youth and, in later years, through the study of O' Halloran's Antiquities. Goethe's knowledge of Ireland, as in fact his knowledge of most other subjects, was personal rather than book-knowledge. When we consider that Goethe never crossed the English, let alone the Irish Channel, this fact makes his knowledge of Ireland most remarkable.

Goethe has been one of the few Continental scholars who realized that Ireland is something else than "one of the British Isles"; in fact, that there is a fundamental difference between the English and the Irish. In his diary of the Campaign in France (1792) he remarks that he freed himself of the sentimentality of Werther by the study of Sterne, and he hints at the ambiguity of the racial characteristics found in Sterne when saying that he combines "a gentle passionate ascetism with the British sense of humour". In later years Goethe realized more clearly the distinctive character of Irish humour as displayed in "Irish Bulls" (a subject discussed in his letter to Zelter, dated March 4th, 1829): "The very nice story of the servant, who could not imagine how hot and warm water produce luke-warm water, comes just in time. It is like the Irish bulls, which originate from a strange intellectual heaviness and of which much could be said in the psychological sense. There is another one: An Irishman lies in bed; people rush into his room crying: "Save yourself, the house is on fire!" "Why," he replies, "I am only a boarder here." In this second period of his study of Sterne (1825-30), Goethe summarized the difference between the Irish and the English in a concise aphorism on Sterne and Goldsmith, saying: "The highly ironic humour of both of them, Sterne inclined towards formlessness, Goldsmith moving freely in the strictest form."[4] As usually Goldsmith may be regarded as more Irish than Sterne, this statement may seem curious to Irish readers but Goethe had probably been influenced by the fact that Sterne's mother was of Catholic Irish stock, whilst Goldsmith was from both parents an offspring of the ascendancy. (For Goldsmith's Irish relations, see Stephen Gwynn, "Oliver Goldsmith", p. 16). Of Goldsmith, Goethe says: "He is an Englishman and has the advantages offered by his country and his nation",[5] whilst in Sterne he finds "that quick change from seriousness to joke, from interest to indifference, from sorrow to joy, which is said to lie in the Irish character".[6] In the latter statement, the words "is said" call for special attention. A few weeks before writing down those words Goethe entered in his diary: "Went for a walk with Ottilia. About the difference of the British nations and their characteristics, especially the character of the Irish" (March 29th, 1828).

One of the main influences in Goethe's relations to Ireland was Ottilia, who married his ill-fated son, August, and became the devoted nurse and companion of the aged poet. A note written by Goethe as early as summer, 1820, bears testimony to Ottilia's interest or even passion for Ireland:

---

4   See James Boyd – Goethe's knowledge of English Literature, Oxf. (1932), p. 103.

5   Sophie-ed. Series I, vol. xxxvii, p. 343.

6   Ibid., vol.xlii, ps. 204, 353.

"His Excellency the Viceroy of Ireland recommends himself and the nation to the patriotic Madam de Goethe by the well-known Evergreen with best wishes for her recovery."

When in the summer of 1875 "the Irishman Mr. Joy and his ladies" arrived in Weimar, Goethe arranged that they and Ottilia should make an excursion to the castle of Belvedere near Weimar. After that visit Goethe wrote to Giesecke: "Should more such distinguished travellers come to visit this neighbourhood, they will be always welcome. Direct them to me personally or to my daughter-in-law Frau Geh. Kammerrätin v. Goethe, and they will be sure of a hearty welcome." An undated note (No. 107) to Ottilia saying: "What was the name of the young man who brought me the parcel from Dublin?" doubtlessly refers to the above-mentioned son of Mr. Knox. On September 25th, 1826, Goethe wrote to Ulrike, Ottilia's sister, of "the pleasant conversations" they had in his house with "foreigners from the western and northern islands". He makes special mention of the various presents by which these visitors enriched "Ottilia's book-case", and he himself acquired various books on Ireland. In 1810, Anthony O'Hara, who had been Russia's last Minister to the Independent Order of the Knights of Malta, had presented him with O'Halloran's Antiquities. Professor Waterhouse drew attention to the enigmatic entry found in Goethe's diary for October 8th, 1829, on "a book by the Irishman Sheil on the present state of Ireland". Is "Sheil" a mis-spelling for "Shiel"? A few months later, on August 2nd, 1830, Goethe says that he has read "Scenes populaires en Irland par M. Shiel, Paris, 1830", a book in which he notices "inestimable clearness of presentation and style". This is probably a French translation of the famous sketches of the Irish bar, which were published in 1822-'23, and, to this day, are one of the best sources of information concerning the leading celebrities of the time in Ireland. (Though Goethe also took a lively interest in the political life of Ireland, he apparently did not know the "Survey of Irish history" made by D.H. Hegerisch (Altona, 1806) for the purpose of promoting "a correct understanding of the causes of the Rebellion, the Union of 1801 and Catholic Emancipation", probably the earliest work on modern Irish history written by a German author from an Irish stand-point).

In 1827, in the above-mentioned letter to Sulpiz Boisserée, Goethe said: We have here "innumerable Englishmen, men and women. My daughter-in-law made them very welcome and I saw them and talked to them more or less. If you know how to take such visitors, there is no doubt that they give you in the end some idea of the nation, indeed, I might say of all three nations." Here, whilst following the habit, still prevailing on the Continent, of calling "English" all the inhabitants of the "British Isles", Goethe clearly distinguishes the Irish, which, as we have seen, he subsequently calls "the most popular in his house". (Six years previously, when reading Jacobsen's "Letters on the latest English poets", Goethe noted fifteen names and only to that of Thomas Moore he added "Irishman, born at Dublin on March 28th, 1780".) It is obvious that personal intercourse with Irishmen was Goethe's main source of information on Ireland, Irish affairs and the national characteristics of the Irish. In this respect, Ottilia's influence can hardly be over-rated.

On January 22nd, 1832, a few months before his death, Goethe entered in his diary: "Later Ottilia, reporting on some newly-arrived books on Ireland." A similar reference to Ottilia's help in his acquiring a literary knowledge of Ireland is found in 1830/31 when "Ottilia reported on Byron's correspondence edited by Moore", and "on the Life of Fitzgerald" (March 3rd, 1830 and October 13th, 1831). On the latter occasion, the visit of Charles and James Sterling, sons of the English Consul at Genoa (Charles, in later years, was "Wolfchen's" tutor), induced Goethe to remark: "It is most noteworthy how Thomas Moore and the British in general understand how to make such a boor; entirely collective and nevertheless a masterly amiable whole. That comes from their continuously agitated public life."

In December, 1829, Goethe wrote to Thomas Carlyle: "It is well known indeed that the inhabitants of the three kingdoms are not at all living in the best possible agreement."[7] At the same time, in a comparative study of the political events of Europe in 1828 and 1829 he exemplifies his theory that a number of "Krisen", originated in 1828, were partly solved, partly absorbed in the subsequent year: "1828: The crisis of the Irish question – 1829: decided in favour of the Catholics, – new demands: Protestant Church endowment threatened – illness of the King." From Eckerman's Conversations with Goethe we may gather that this study probably originated in April, 1829. Upon April 3, Eckermann enters: "From the Jesuits and their wealth conversation turned upon the Catholic and Irish emancipation. Goethe gave as his opinion that an emancipation 'with preventive clauses' would be 'ineffectual with Catholics'." Upon April 7, Eckermann records Goethe's famous remark: "We cannot get a clear notion of the state of Ireland, and the subject is too intricate. But this we can see, that Ireland suffers from evils which will not be removed by any measure, and therefore, of course, not by emancipation. If it has hitherto been unfortunate for Ireland to endure her evils alone, it is now unfortunate that England is also drawn into them. Then, no confidence can be put in the Catholics. We see with what difficulty the two million of Protestants of Ireland have kept their ground hitherto against the preponderate five millions of Catholics. ... The Catholics do not agree among themselves but they always unite against a Protestant. They are like a pack of hounds, who bite one another, but when a stag comes in view, they all unite immediately to run it down." Goethe's appreciation of the political conditions in Ireland may have had some foundation in his geographical knowledge, unusual on the Continent. Giesecke's various mineralogical gifts had made him acquainted with the names of most of the counties in Ireland, e.g., he makes special mention of Limerick. On May 21st, 1827, Goethe mentions the reception from England of a map of Ireland.

On August 12th, 1822, Goethe entered in his diary: "Received a letter of an Irish lady residing at Bremen." He does not tell us her name, nor can we derive it from the material found in the Sophie-edition. In any case, it was not the great Irish friend of Ottilia. Anna Jameson arrived at Weimar after Goethe's death, but her correspondence with Ottilia is perhaps the most impressive document of Ottilia's sympathy with Ireland.[8] Mrs. Jameson's maiden name was Anna Brownell Murphy. She was born in Dublin as the daughter of a young artist who was connected with the United Irishmen,

---

7   Sophie-ed., Ser. I, vol. xlii, p. 205.

8   Edited by Mr. G. H. Needler, Oxf., 1939.

but, before the rising, he had gone to England in the hope of improving his professional prospects. In 1828 his daughter married Robert Sympson Jameson, a young barrister, from whom she soon separated. Anna Jameson made a brilliant career as a writer, and as a writer she visited various parts of the Continent. Her friendship with Ottilia became very close and their correspondence lasted for the subsequent thirty years. In her Visits and Sketches (1834) the "indefatigable" Anna Jameson has given a lively account of Ottilia's influence on old Goethe: –

> "She was the trusted friend, the constant companion, the devoted nurse of his last years. It accounted for the unrivalled influence which apparently she possessed – I will not say over his mind – but on his mind, in his affections; for in her he found truly *eine Natur* – a piece of nature, which could bear even his microscopic examination. Her mind was like a transparent medium, through which the rays of that luminary passed. For fourteen or fifteen years she could exist in daily, hourly communication with that gigantic spirit, yet retained, from first to last, the most perfect simplicity of character. Sometimes there was a wild, restless fervour in her imagination and feelings. Quick in perception, uniting a soul of restless vivacity with an indolent gracefulness, she appeared to me by far the most poetical and genuine being of my own sex, I ever knew, in highly cultured life."

This passage must be the most notable early Irish appreciation of Goethe: It also indicates Ottilia's Irish affinities as noticed by Goethe.

Ottilia's influence on Goethe gains in significance when we consider the various references to her interest in Ireland shown in her correspondence with Anna Jameson. On August 2nd, 1853, the latter writes to Ottilia: "I told Sir Robert Kane (the great Irish scientist) of your passion for Ireland and all things Irish (excepting Irish men — of which I do not speak) and he promised to send you any publication regarding Ireland, which he thinks might interest you." Two years previous Mrs. Jameson had sent Ottilia a series of books on Ireland, but the exception made by Mrs. Jameson is hardly justified. Ottilia seems to have been attracted by Sir William Wilde, whom she met in Vienna in 1846 and she and he went to "many balls and carnivals, resplendent sceneries of gaiety".[9] That Ottilia's interest in Ireland was sincere and deep, we see from further instances in her correspondence with Anna Jameson. In July, 1843, Anna Jameson writes to her: "Ireland occupies all minds, as well as yours." Then follows a description of Irish debates in Parliament. "Meanwhile", Anna Jameson continued, "the state of Ireland becomes worse and worse. Should there be civil war the community cannot stand against the English power ... I feel it all deeply."

The most expressive document of Goethe's appreciation of Ireland is his review of Prince Pückler-Muskau's famous "Letters of a Deceased", which in 1832 appeared in an abbreviated English translation under the title "Tour in England, Ireland and France in the years 1828 and '29 with remarks on manners and customs of the inhabitants and anecdotes of distinguished public characters, by a German Prince". Prince Pückler was Silesian and was married to the daughter of Hardenberg, the omnipotent chancellor of post-Napoleonic Prussia. He was equally known for the extravagance of his private life and for his merits as a brilliant writer and one of the greatest garden-architects.

---

9   Wilson, Victorian Doctor, 1942, p. III.

The object of his journey through Western Europe was partly to study the parks of France, England and especially of Ireland, partly (it was said) to capture a rich heiress who would marry him after having divorced his first wife. The fact that Princess Hardenberg, the "beloved and adored Lucy", to whom "the letters of a deceased" are written, had consented to that plan was well known and greatly added to the success of Pückler's book. He started his journey by a visit to Weimar, where he met Goethe. A few weeks after the Letters had appeared, Goethe read the book and apparently he immediately decided to review the work which, in his opinion, was "important for Germany's literature". He sent his review to Varnhagen-Ense, who did not hesitate to publish it in his Berliner Jahrbuch. "Here we meet," Goethe says, "a man in his best years, in a high position where one has not to toil before attaining a certain level, but where one has an opportunity of forging one's own fortune. The writer appears a perfect and experienced man of the world, endowed with talents and with a quick apprehension." As for the book itself, Goethe says: –

> "Descriptions of natural scenery form the chief part of the letters, but of these materials he avails himself with remarkable skill. England, Wales and especially Ireland, are drawn in a masterly manner. It is only from his pictural talent that the ruined abbeys and castles, the bare rocks and scarcely pervious moors of Ireland, become remarkable and endurable; poverty and careless gaiety, opulence and absurdity would repel us at every step. The hunting parties and drinking bouts which succeed each other in an unbroken series, are tolerable because the author can tolerate them. He introduces us into distinguished society. He visits the famous O'Connell in his remote and scarcely accessible residence and works out the picture which we had formed to ourselves from previous descriptions of the wonderful man. (Here Goethe doubtlessly refers to personal descriptions). He attends popular meetings (Catholic Association) and hears speeches from O'Connell, the remarkable Shiel (see above), and other strangely appearing persons. He takes the interest of a man of humanity and sense in the great question which agitates Ireland, but he had too clear an insight into all the complicated considerations it involves to be carried away by cheerful hopes."

George Paston[10], the only English biographer of the famous Prince deliberately omits reference to Pückler's adventures in Ireland, but the Letters had undoubtedly a great influence in spreading knowledge and appreciation of modern Ireland on the Continent. The Prince explored all parts of the country and all spheres of social life, by no means confining himself to the ascendancy exclusively. He studied Dublin from top to bottom; explored the Wicklow Mountains and the Hill of Howth; he is interested in the pagan and early Christian traditions of the country; he admires the construction of the harbour of Kingstown; he attends the Galway Races; he rambles through Kerry, where he comes across the Whiteboys, and he inserts dozens of valuable remarks on social, religious and natural conditions. In this book, Goethe read a great number of Irish place-names; here he came across the venerable names of SS. Patrick and Kevin as well as of Fian McCumhall; here he found allusion to the struggle of the great O'Sullivan and O'Donovan and to many other historical events otherwise unknown on the Continent.

---

10   "Little Memoirs of the 19th Century", 1902.

When travelling through Kerry, Prince Pückler was given by a friend "an old English translation of 'the Sorrows of Werther'" (the first English translation appeared in 1780 and reached four editions; in 1789 a new translation from the French was published). Amidst the beauties of Killarney and Kenmare he writes: "you know how highly, how intensely I honour our prince of poets", but, strange to say, on this occasion he read "Werther" for the first time. Did he realize that this was the scenery which Goethe, when young, had believed to have inspired Ossian, that grand forgery which two decades previously the Gaelic Society, Dublin, had unmasked, but which had been the first inducement for Goethe and many of his contemporaries to study ancient Ireland, her culture and even her language? Whole passages from MacPherson's works rendered in Goethe's masterly translation are embodied in the "Werther". What struck Prince Pückler was "the strangeness of the accident which led him to read 'Werther' for the first time in a foreign tongue and in the midst of the wild nature of Ireland". When writing these words, he was not aware that the review of his letters would become the latest and most outspoken document of Goethe's relations with Ireland, and that through his reference to "Werther", he led his readers back; to the earliest stage of these relations which accordingly comprise a period of over sixty years.

Author's Note. – I have confined myself in this paper to Goethe's relations with natives of, or visitors to, Ireland. His relations with the offspring of the "Wild Geese" in Austria, Russia and Germany, such as Anthony O'Hara (see above), O'Kelly, confessor of the Grand-duchess, Amalia, and the Countess O'Donnell would have to form the subject of separate studies, which, as a matter of fact, would be interesting from an entirely different view-point, mainly, the history of the Irish element on the Continent and their influence with regard to the spreading of the knowledge of Ireland and Irish affairs.

(Quelle: The Dublin Magazine, Vol. 18, Jan-March 1943, S. 45-56.)

Irish descriptions of Goethe

Without going into the question whether, by standards past or present, the persons concerned should be described as Irish or how far Goethe was aware of their connection with Ireland, we may list Goethe's Irish contacts as follows:

1771 J. F. O'Feral[1]
1791 Lord Bristol[2]
1801 Hamilton
1811 Anthony O'Hara and the Rev. O'Kelly[3]
1811 the O'Donnells and the Baroness O'Byrne[4]
1813 John Lord O'Carroll, and Miss Dillon

---

1 Erich Schmidt, *Charakteristiken* (Berlin, 1886), 286 and *Goethe Jb.* 9, 242.

2 See my paper in *Ulster J. Archaeol.* III, 10 (1947), 101-9.

3 See my paper in *MLR* 39 (1944), 146-151.

4 R. M. Werner, *Goethe und die Gräfin O'Donnell* (Berlin, 1884). Compare Wilhelm v. Humboldt's associations with the wife and daughter of Andreas Graf O'Reilly (born in 1742 in Ballinlough, from 1763 in Austrian service), (*Ges. Schriften* 15, 185).

1822	"Serenissima, eine in Bremen lebende Irrlanderinn"
1823	Charles J. Sterling
	Sneyd Edgeworth[5]
1825	Henry Joy[6]
	George Knox and his sons Thomas and Henry[6]
	George Cromie[7]
1826	Charles Knox[6]
1826	George Downes
	William R. Swifte
	Dutmal
	Charles Des Voeux[8]
1828	Fitzroy
1829	Charles Lever
	Seymour
	Randall E. Plunkett
	Wellington's sons[9]
1830	Sohnles and Dr. Hauython[10]
1831	Charles Goff

The most outstanding lacuna in the field of studies of these contacts[11] is Charles Sterling, one of Ottilie von Goethe's lovers: From 1835 to 1837 there lived at Vienna a child whose father was Irish, whose mother bore the name of v. Goethe[12] and whose Christian name was that of her Irish godmother (Anna Jameson).[13]

---

5   See my paper in *MLQ 15* (1954), 366-371.

6   G. Waterhouse, "Goethe, Giesecke and Dublin" *Proc. Royal Irish Acad.* 41 C (1933), 210-218 and *Minutes* 1943-44, 18-22. Regarding Charles Knox it has been repeatedly stated that he was the twelfth son of the bishop of Derry. William K., the successor of Lord Bristol (see note 2) and brother of George Knox, however, had only four sons. Charles, the youngest, is the Captain C. K., who translated the first part of *Faust* (Carré, *Goethe en Angleterre* (1920), 58). He died in 1864, as lieutenant-general. Moore (*Byron* I, 675) said that C. K. met Byron in Ithaca. In his letter to Goethe of 22 Sept., 1826, Giesecke spoke of his visit to "Fahan, the country seat of the Lord Bishop of Derry, father of the young Mr. Knox, who is at present in Weimar." William Knox was "delighted to hear of Goethe's interest in his son's progress."

7   Blochmann in *MLR* 39 (1944), 58-62.

8   L. A. Willoughby, *ibid.* 9 (1914), 223.

9   Landgraf, *Goethe und seine ausländischen Besucher* (München, 1932), 48f.

10   Possibly Robert Houghton, B.A., 1828, in Trinity College. Dublin.

11   For general surveys see Alford in *PEGS* (1889), 191f., 6, 132-134 and 7, 8ff., Bode in *Stunden mit Goethe* (1915), xxxviiif. ("Die Franzosen und Engländer in Goethes Leben"), Jones *PEGS* N.S. 9 (1933), 68-91, Landgraf (see note 2), Waterhouse (see note 6) and my papers in *Dublin Magazine,* Jan.-March, 1943, 180-186 and "Goethes Irlandkunde" in *Deutsche Vierteljahresschrift f. Literaturwissenschaft und Geistesgeschichte* 1956.

12   Houben, *Ottilie v. Goethe* (Leipzig, 1929), und D. Zeemann, *Ottilie* (Salzburg, 1949).

13   G. H. Needler, *Letters of Anna Jameson to Ottilie v. Goethe* (Oxford, 1939).

Apart from Goethe's and Ottilie von Goethe's diaries the literary records of these contacts are limited. There are DesVoeux' translation of *Tasso* and his poem "Auf zu den Wohnungen ewigen Friedens", the only German poem by an English-speaking contributor to Ottilie's *Chaos*, and there is the English translation of *Faust 1* (London, 1847), by Charles Knox, who had contributed a poem expressive of Irish sentiments to *Chaos*.[14] I have published the only letter so far known of an Irishman to Goethe[15], and I now add a subsequent note by the same author, George Knox, to Goethe[16]:

> Mr. G. Knox will have the honour of waiting on Baron von Göthe at twelve o'clock – In the meantime he may like to see an account of the Beryl which Sr. Charles [Giesecke] has sent him – it is in a late Dublin publication and the place is marked.

Reference to this correspondence was made in Goethe's diary for 25 May, 1825.

It has never been stated that we owe to Goethe's Irish contacts three accounts of visits to him. Two of these accounts have been republished before, Swifte's in the Artemis-edition[17], apparently from the German edition of Swifte's autobiography (referred to in the English edition), and Downes's first by Biedermann in German without the author's name[18] and lately in the Artemis-edition in English.[19] In the index to the Artemis-edition (where sources have not been stated), Swifte is described as "engl. Schriftsteller und Reisender" and Downes as "reisender Engländer"; in the reproduction of Downes's account after the word "Ireland", the Artemis-edition omitted the words: "which at Weimar is known to be a distinct island – a great stretch of Continental geography". Owing to the fact that also in the index to the Weimar-edition (and indeed by Goethe himself) many of Goethe's Irish contacts were described as English, Goethe's remark to Boisserée: "Eigentlich finden die Irländer in meinem Hause am meisten Beifall" (letter of 12 October, 1828), has not been fully explored.

In Goethe's Agenda for the year 1826, under 19 August, "der Engländer Swift" is mentioned. The author of *Wilhelm's wanderings, an autobiography,* published anonymously in 1878, at London, did not try very hard to conceal his identity. On p. 54 he told of a party at the Weimar court:

> Prince Bernhard himself stood up and proposed a toast to the memory of a namesake and kinsman of mine, Dean –, whose eccentric writings, he said, were universally known, especially in Germany.

Swifte added in brackets: "(see Goethe's Stella)". In his study on Lessing and Swift (1869), G. Caro pointed out that the title and subject of *Stella* suggested close con-

---

14   See note 6 and note 11 above (Jones).

15   "Goethes Irlandkunde", see note 11.

16   Once again I have to thank the Nationale Forschungs- und Gedenkstätten der klassischen deutschen Literatur, Weimar, for supplying me with the photostats. See Weimar-edition III, X, 316.

17   XXIII (1950), No. 1811; not repeated here.

18   V (1890), 1068 from A. Diezmann "Besuch eines Engländers bei Goethe" in *Allg. Moden Zeitung,* 1828, No. 16, Sp. 127.

19   XXIII (1950), No. 1841; not repeated here.

nection with the life and work of Jonathan Swift. The author of *Wilhelm's wanderings* was the first to state that there was in Weimar a definite tradition of Swift's influence on *Stella,* a tradition on which Goethe himself never commented.[20]

That the author of *Wilhelm's wanderings* was William R. Swifte, an offspring of Godwin Swift, Dean Swift's uncle, and a member of the Swift Heath family in Kilkenny, was first established through a brief and not too complimentary note by Edward Dowden in his essay on "Goethe's last days".[21] Dowden referred to Swifte's then recent death near Dublin and repeated Swifte's account of his losing Goethe's medal "in some flying leap in some ditch in the county Kildare".

The colony of young men from these countries to whom Goethe's Irish visitors in the twenties largely belonged goes back to the academy for young Englishmen founded in 1779 at Weimar by Mounier. Dr. Jones stated that they did not take much part "in court society beyond upsetting it with very Britannic horseplay". Swifte claimed (p. 40) that his horsemanship displayed at the Grand-Ducal riding school attracted the attention of the Princess Augusta, the later Empress. Dr. Jones further said that it was "not the presence of Goethe that kept them in Weimar, but the pulsating life of his daughter-in-law and her friends".[22] Swifte dedicated his autobiography "to the ladies of Wiemar (sic) in whose society at a period when I first enjoyed the acquaintance of Goethe I spent many happy days", and his fourth chapter, devoted to Weimar, is prefaced by the cri-de-coeur: "Weimar Ach!!! Dieser Seufzer folgt dir nach" (words to this day adapted on German "fun" post-cards from seaside resorts).

Having spent his childhood in Ireland, Swifte lived with his mother in London and Paris. Destined for the diplomatic career, he was sent to Germany to learn the language. He was boarded with the family of a clergyman in a village near Leipzig, and after seven months was ready to enter into higher society. He told us in great length of the gay life in Weimar. More than thirty pages of his book are taken up by descriptions of balls, sledge-parties, jeux innocents and his various flirtations.

On 16 July, 1827, Goethe entered in his diary: "Herr Swift Abschied zu nehmen." This final visit

> to the aged Goethe was particularly interesting and gratifying; he pasted his portrait as a frontispiece in my album and with his own hand inscribed the following lines in the first page thereof, besides presenting me with his medal in bronze [see above], struck on the occasion of his *Jubileum,* and giving me letters of introduction to several of the leading litterati of that day in Paris (p. 65).

The lines written by Goethe in Swifte's album were "Fünf andere Dinge" from *West-Östlicher Divan* IV. Eckermann also enriched Swifte's album with an *Andenken,* some insipid verses on Swifte's love affairs in Weimar (p. 67).

---

20   See Düntzer, *Goethe Abhandlungen* II (Leipzig, 1885), 302.

21   Additional information kindly supplied by Mr. J. M. Hone, Dublin. (*New Studies in Literature,* (1895), 311).

22   See note 11.

Swifte's references to Goethe's family are of particular interest. Of August he said that "he was considered of no pretentions in point of intellect", while Wolfgang was "admitted by all to be a child of great promise".

> His daughter-in-law, the Graefin Ottilie von Goethe, gebohrene von Bogwisch [Thuringian pronunciation] was a great favourite especially amongst the English. I copy her autograph from a leaf in my album at the end of a page of poetry [not found in the copies of Swifte's work in Trinity College, Dublin, and the National Library of Ireland]. She had been a very pretty woman but being too daring a rider, she was thrown, and dragged by her horse on her face a considerable distance through the streets of Weimar and was fearfully disfigured permanently. Fortunately she possessed in an unusual degree the art of pleasing and did the honours in Goethe's house to perfection.

An account of Ottilie's accident, vital for understanding her development, was given by Goethe in his letter to Sterling, then at Derry, of 30 June, (10 July), 1826.

George Downes came to Weimar at the same time as Swifte. Born in Dublin in 1790, he obtained a good place at scholarship examinations at Trinity in 1812.[23] In 1820 he toured Northern Germany. In 1823 he published a Hebrew Grammar[24] and in the following year *Dublin University prize poems with Spanish and German ballads* (the latter including poems by Stricker, Koerner and Matthison as well as Goethe's "Der Sänger"). In 1825 he set out for another journey to the Continent, which took him through France, Switzerland and Italy to Germany. In 1830 he published a *Guide through Switzerland and Savoy* and in 1832, *Letters from Continental Countries* 1825-1826.[25] In the latter work, letter LVIII (vol. ii, 418ff.) deals with Weimar and Goethe. Here again it was outside the scope of *Goethes Gespräche* to reproduce the account of life in Weimar. Downes referred in particular to Spiegelberg and Froriep whose house was "a most advantageous abode for young foreigners, of whom we have met several, who are here for their education – English, Scotch and Irish". Also in Goethe's house "we found several young British subjects".

> The conversation was desultory – books of prints, or other literary lumber, occasionally furnished the topics. Goethe himself turned over a collection of indifferent views of Bath, from beginning to end, incidentally dropping an observation.

After speaking of Lichtenstein, the African traveller, and v. d. Hagen, Downes continued in a passage that might have interested Thomas Mann:

> The sister of Werter's Charlotte, who resides exactly opposite to our hotel, was also present at Dr. F[roriep]'s. You will be surprised to hear that the heroine of romance is still living. Her name is Madame Kästner, and her abode – Hanover.

---

23 W. B. J. Taylor, *History of Trinity College Dublin* (1845), 498 and *Alumni Dublinenses*.

24 In the previous year, Downes had supplied "copious notes" to George Nelson Smith's *Killarney*.

25 See note 18. On the title-page Downes described himself am Foreign Honorary Member of the Mineralogical Society of Jena (see my paper or Goethe's interest in British mineralogy in *Mineral Magazine*, 28 (1949), 534-546).

In the company of Ottilie and Bettina, Downes drove to Belvedere and inspected the Botanic Gardens, and in the evening he attended, in Goethe's box, a performance of *The Marriage of Figaro.*

> So have been our days at the German Athens, which as Goethe once observed to me, contains many 'ergetzungen' ... He is at present engaged in a general revision (would that I could add *expurgation*) of his works which are to appear in three separate forms, to suit every purse.

Concluding his account, Downes said:

> Goethe is popular in Weimar, and we have found him kind. He has sent us his likeness on a medal, and also as an engraving [reproduced in Swifte's work], together with two printed odes, subscribed with his autograph in both the English and German characters. The medal was struck for his birthday, and the poems were written severally to commemorate the same anniversary and his recovery from a fever.

Like Downes, the third Irish visitor who left us an account of Goethe was not mentioned in Goethe's diaries. In his biography of Charles Lever, Edward Downey (i [1906], 16) said that Lever's *Logbook of a rambler* 1828, then lately presented by Dr. C. Litton Falkner to the Royal Irish Academy, concluded with "an account of a quarrel between the students and the professors of Heidelberg", where after some months in Göttingen Lever pursued his studies, that "after a short sojourn Lever proceeded to Vienna", and that "from Vienna the young student proceeded, early in 1829, to Weimar, and at the Academy made the acquaintance of Goethe". We shall see presently that in actual fact Lever's visit to Weimar took place in September, 1828. Downey continued with a shortened version of the description of Goethe reproduced in W. J. Fitzpatrick's biography of Lever (i [1879], 51f.)[26] from Lever's anonymous contribution entitled "Cornelius O'Dowd upon men and women, and other things in general" in *Blackwood's Magazine* 96 (1864), 291.

Lever's diary (Royal Irish Academy ms. 3/B/52) bears the title "Einige Erinnerungen von Deutschland". One of the fly-leaves contains in pencil an agenda stating:

> 22 Sept., 1828, visited the graves of Schiller and Wieland at Osterode and Weimar
> 24 Sept., was presented at Goethe's
> 26 Sept., spent the day at the Frau von Goethe's ...

On page 3 we find a list of

> German classic authors whose works I have already read
> Schiller
> Goethe
> Kotzebue
> Burgher
> Lessing
> Uland
> Schall[27]

---

26   Ibid., 76f., an important note on Goethe and Wellington, see above note 9. The articles on young Lever in *Dublin Univers. Magazine,* 1880, 465 and 570, do not go as far as Lever's student years.

27   Karl Sch., a writer of comedies.

Voss
Hoffmann
La Motte Fouque P=Prosaists
Pfeffel P[28]
van der Velden P[29]
Körner
Herder P
Tieck P
Jean Paul P
Meissner[30]
Wieland
Schlegel
Boutwerweck
Horn[31]   } Criticists
Luther
Werner.

Then follow copies in German of poems by Werner, "Uland", "Bürger", Goethe ("Der Fischer" and "Erlkönig", the latter with a brief note on the music) and Schiller ("Des Mädchens Klage"), interspersed with fine pencil sketches of a Herder memorial and scenes of the Rhine, and prose quotations from Wieland, "Burgher, Kotzebüe", Bouterweck, Jean Paul[32] and Luther, as well as some German tomb-stone inscriptions.

Lever's diary is prefaced by a few "Maxims", the first of which calls for "a perfect acquaintance with Continental languages", while the third states that "any German of the North who pretends of education can speak English fluently". Lever's knowledge of German can be gauged from the following note, the biographical background of which cannot be explored at this point:

> Ich bin gewiss, dass es viel besser ist noch zuruck nach mein Frau zu gehen für einige Tagen dann nicht – nur einmal jeden Tag, weil ein persone has mir gesaght dass er hat sie gesehen drei mal den Tage in der Stadt hier.

Maxim VI reads as follows:

> Abstain from nationalities of every sort, at the same time denying that you are an Englishman[33], and above all don't fall into the error of the untravelled of our countrymen in supposing that your being English alone is to procure respect and even esteem from the foreigner. The overbearing

---

28   The Alsation playwright and novelist.

29   Karl Franz v.d.V., a popular novelist.

30   August Gottlieb M., poet and novelist.

31   Franz Christoph H., novelist, whose work on Shakespeare (in five volumes) appeared between 1823 and 1831.

32   See my papers on Jean Paul and Ireland in *MLR* 40 (1945), 190 and 49 (1954), 352.

33   See my note on Lever and Toepfer, in *MLR* 43 (1948), 91.

manners of the English abroad are only tolerated from the length of their purses and except in individual instances the English are neither loved nor respected by any nation of the Continent.[34]

It would appear that neither Fitzpatrick nor Downey re-examined Lever's manuscript but relied on the extracts published in the *Dublin Literary Gazette* 1830. Lever's diary concludes with an account of Cassel, and at the end of chapter xxxiii of *Arthur O'Leary* he related the last lap of the journey from Göttingen to Weimar (Erfurt and Weimar). The account of Goethe published in 1864 was obviously written from memory rather than from notes. Nevertheless it is worth being reproduced in full.

> In the evening the [Weimar] "society" rendezvoused in a sombre old house, with narrow windows in front and a small somewhat gloomy-looking garden behind, where lived a large white-haired man with his niece[!]. Being a man of grand presence and imposing mien, with much dignity of address, he was very fond of mixing with the young people of the company, especially with a number of young Englishmen who at that period resided at Weimar for the advantage of military[!] education. ... With them this old gentleman frequently conversed or, more frequently still, discoursed, talking of his travels in Italy, the objects which had held the chief place in his memory, the galleries which he had seen, the society he had frequented, the distinguished men whose acquaintance he had made, and all this with occasional touches of picturesque description, traits of humour, and now and then a deep feeling which held his little auditory in rapt astonishment that he could hold them there entranced, while they could not, when he had done, recall any of the magic by which he had worked his spell. I myself remember to have tried to repeat a story he told, and once, more hazardous still, to convey some impression of how he talked, and with that lamentable failure let my present confession atone. The task would have tried a better man, for him whom I represent was Goethe.

While erring in material detail, this pathetic description of atmosphere is impressive. Lever's account surpasses those of Swifte and Downes in literary quality and psychological understanding.

In many details these three descriptions of Goethe by Irishmen who visited him within a period of a few months confirm each other in a most striking manner. It is safe to assume that they were written independently of each other. They occupy a prominent place in the history of Irish interest in Goethe which cannot be studied without reference to the lively interest taken in Ireland by Goethe and his daughter-in-law.

(Quelle: Publications of the English Goethe Society, 25, 1956, S. 114-124.)

Frank O'Connor und Goethe

In meiner Notiz über Canon Sheehans Interesse an deutscher Literatur (Modern Language Review 49, 1954, S. 352-355) habe ich gezeigt, daß kein irischer Romanschriftsteller weitere und tiefere Kenntnis von Goethe verraten hat als Patrick Sheehan, dessen meisterhafte Darstellungen irischen Lebens zwar zu seiner Zeit auch in deutscher Übersetzung erschienen, heute aber wohl kaum noch in Deutschland gelesen werden. Meine Notiz schloß mit den Worten, daß Sheehans Interesse an deutscher

---

34 One of Lever's maxims dealt with visits of art galleries, a subject on which Downes's *Letters* were most unsatisfactory.

Literatur das Zeugnis einer vorübergehenden Phase in der Geistesgeschichte des katholischen Irland waren.

Aus Frank O'Connors[1] kürzlich erschienener Autobiographie (An only child, London 1961) erfahren wir jedoch, daß Sheehans Interesse an Goethe an unerwarteter Stelle Widerhall gefunden hat. O'Connor erkennt zwar nicht, daß Sheehans Methode, deutsche Brocken und insbesondere Goethezitate in seine Erzählungen einzuflicken, auf Mangan zurückgeht, aber er gibt für diese, heute bei irischen und auch englischen Schriftstellern oft zur Mode gewordene Methode eine einleuchtende Erklärung: "With one half of my mind I regarded it as detestable snobbery, but with the other I think it the only sensible way of influencing young people like myself. If the original monkey had not despised monkeys he would never have invented clothes, and I should not have bothered to learn Goethe's S y m b o l e n by heart." O'Connor leistet hier einen Beitrag zu der ebenfalls schon zur Mode gewordenen Unart, deutsche Brocken fehlerhaft zu zitieren. Von Mangan bis Mac Liammoir könnte man aus der irischen Literatur zahlreiche Illustrationen dieser Unart beibringen.

O'Connor sagt weiterhin: "From Sheehan's novels I had deduced that German was the real language of culture and that the greatest of cultured persons was Goethe, so I read right through Goethe in English and studied German of the Self-Educator so as to be able to read him in the original." Diese Mitteilung muß auf dem Hintergrund der Tatsachen gewürdigt werden, daß außer Mangan die Iren, die englische Übersetzungen von Goethe veröffentlichten, der protestantischen Schicht angehörten (der Tassoübersetzer DesVoeux war ein Hugenotte) und daß die Erwerbung von Kenntnissen deutscher Literatur, geschweige denn der deutschen Sprache, für ein Kind aus einer unbemittelten katholischen Familie in einer irischen Kleinstadt heute noch genau so schwer ist, wie sie es zu der Zeit vor fünfzig Jahren war, von der O'Connor erzählt. Ebenso wie Sheehan war O'Connor fasziniert von einzelnen Zeilen, z.B. den Anfangszeilen von "Mignon" (die er fehlerhaft zitiert). "I knew practically nothing about Goethe, and that little was wrong. In a truly anthropomorphic spirit I recreated Goethe in my own image and likeness, as a patriotic man who wished to revive the German language, which I considered to have been greatly threatened by the use of French. I drew an analogy between the French culture that dominated eighteenth century Germany and the English culture by which we in Ireland were dominated."

---

1   Frank O'Connor (Pseudonym für Michael O'Donovan), geboren 1903 in Cork, gegenwärtig in London lebend, gehört zu den bedeutendsten und in Deutschland am besten bekannten irischen Prosaschriftstellern unserer Zeit. Wie weit seine Erzählungen aus dem Leben in Irland autobiographischen Hintergrund haben, zeigt sein neuestes Werk, mit dem sich diese Miszelle befaßt.

Patrick A. Sheehan (geb. 1852 in Mallow, gest. 1913 in Doneraile) wurde durch seine Priesterromane "My new curate", "Luke Delmege", "The triumph of failure" und "The blindness of Dr. Gray" (hierin die unten erwähnte Stelle über "Heidenröslein") besonders im katholischen Deutschland bekannt. In "Tristram Lloyd" sprach Sheehan mehrfach von "Dichtung und Wahrheit". Systematischer sprach sich Sheehan über die klassische und romantische Literatur Deutschlands in seinen philosophischen Aufsätzen "Under the Cedar and the Stars" und "Parerga" aus. Die Bezugnahme auf Goethes "Symbole" entnahm O'Connor aus dem Kapitel "Spring XXVIII" in letzterem Werk.

O'Connor scheint hier auch eine Abneigung gegen die bis heute im irischen Schulbetrieb bestehende Vorherrschaft des Französischen als erster Fremdsprache zu verraten, und diese Abneigung darf man mit seiner (von so vielen namhaften irischen Schriftstellern geteilten) Gegnerschaft gegen den Einfluß der Kirche im nationalen Leben Irlands in Verbindung bringen. Diese Vorherrschaft stammt z.T. aus der Zeit, während der die Ausbildung von Priestern, ja jede höhere Schulbildung den irischen Katholiken nur auf dem Festland, vorwiegend auf Anstalten im französischen Sprachbereich möglich war. Aus jener Zeit schreibt man auch Grundzüge des Katholizismus in Irland her, die von vielen Intellektuellen, besonders auch den Nationalisten, verurteilt werden, wie die Geringschätzung des Natürlichen und die Unterordnung unter die bestehende Staatsgewalt. Der Geist, von dem die englische Goethebegeisterung im 19. Jahrhundert getragen war, blieb den irischen Katholiken fremd (Sheehan war hierin eine Ausnahme). Während des Ersten Weltkrieges wandten sich irische Nationalisten entschieden Deutschland zu (einer der von O'Connor erwähnten Anhänger DeValeras erzählte mir, daß er mit seinen Kameraden im englischen Kerker die Wärter durch den Gesang der "Wacht am Rhein" geärgert habe; O'Connor erwähnt nur, daß er von seiner Mutter, einer ganz einfachen Frau, die englische Version von "Es zogen drei Burschen wohl über den Rhein" lernte). Die Episode war aber zu kurz. Deutschland erfüllte nicht die Erwartungen, die die Iren auf es gesetzt hatten, und 1921 waren die französischen Sympathien schon wieder vorwiegend auf der Seite der irischen Nationalisten. Zudem fehlten den irischen Katholiken Lehrmittel und -kräfte für deutsche Sprache und Literatur, ganz abgesehen davon, daß Deutsch für die Iren von geringerem praktischen Wert war – und ist, als das Französische.

Bei Sheehan waren nur dort, wo er sich der zu seiner Zeit im katholischen Bereich vorherrschenden Reserven Goethe gegenüber aus moralischen oder konfessionellen Gründen erinnerte, über das Ästhetische hinausgehende Gesichtspunkte aufgetaucht. Im Anschluß an Nico Rosts "Goethe in Dachau" (Amsterdam 1946) sprach ich in "Monatshefte" (University of Wisconsin 42, 1950, S. 101 bis 104) von dem unserer Zeit gegebenen Messen Goethes "in der Grenzsituation". Zu diesem Thema leisten O'Connors Erinnerungen einen Beitrag. Als er im irischen Bürgerkrieg 1921 als Anhänger DeValeras von der den Vertrag mit England befürwortenden Regierung gefangen gehalten wurde, las er, während seine Leidensgefährten gemeinsam den Rosenkranz beteten, "Hermann und Dorothea" (Sheehan waren bei dem Dreimal-Sanctus oft die Worte "Röslein, Röslein, Röslein rot" in den Sinn gekommen, ein Nachklang der für die alt-irische religiöse Dichtung charakteristischen Triaden). Der Schriftsteller Daniel Corkery hatte ihm sein Exemplar geschickt, das die Inschrift trug "Martin Cloyne" (nach einem der Helden eines Romans von Corkery; Rost las in Dachau "Campagne in Frankreich" in einem Exemplar aus der Lagerbibliothek, das die Inschrift trug "Ex libris Moses Mandelbaum"). Allerdings schrieb Corkery an O'Connor bei Übersendung dieses Bandes, daß "Heine was the proper poet for a man in prison", aber während O'Connors Leidensgefährten sich gegenseitig in ihre Stammbücher zur Erinnerung an jene Tage Verse aus der englischen Literatur, vor allem von Shelley, schrieben, wählte er für diese Zwecke meist "a line or two of Goethe", die so ähnlich wie möglich die gleichen Gedanken aussprachen wie die englischen Verse, die seine Freunde eintrugen. So scheint also auch in jenem Lager wie für Rost in Dachau

Goethe die Prüfung an einer der Grenzsituationen bestanden zu haben. O'Connors Lieblingsvers war: "One must be either the hammer or the anvil" (scheinbar war ihm Mangans Übersetzung aus Goethes "Koptischen Liedern" nicht bekannt). Sein Mitgefangener Sean Mac Entee (später Finanzminister unter DeValera) erfüllte ihm seinen Wunsch, einen Band Heine zu besitzen. Bei der Entlassung aus dem Lager packte O'Connor unter seinen wertvollsten Besitztümern eine Groschenanthologie deutscher Dichtung, seinen geliebten Heine und "Hermann und Dorothea" zusammen, "all that had kept me in touch with the great world of culture that I hoped I might some day belong me".

Wie weit sich die irischen Nationalisten unserer Generation bewußt waren, daß ihre Vorfahren vor hundert Jahren, die sich im Anschluß an Jung-Deutschland Young Ireland nannten, eine ähnlich erstaunliche Begeisterung für deutsche Literatur gezeigt hatten, geht aus O'Connors Mitteilung nicht hervor. Die zahlreichen Beiträge zur deutschen Literatur in der Zeitung der Jung-Iren "The Nation" sind bislang keiner (jedenfalls keiner veröffentlichten) zusammenfassenden Würdigung unterzogen worden. Vor allem würde man an die merkwürdige Stelle in dem "Jail Journal" von John Mitchel denken (Kap. VII), wo es im Anschluß an "Wilhelm Meisters Wanderjahre" "with its stately repose and its elegant instrumentalities, material and spiritual" heißt: "Goethe, I think, never tried the galleys". Verglichen mit dem Interesse, das Goethe in anderen Ländern gefunden hat, mag das, was die irischen Nationalisten von ihm sagten, elementar oder ephemer erscheinen. Aber dieses Interesse war realistischer und wahrhaft notwendiger als das ästhetisch-gelehrte glücklicherer Nationen. Dieser Aspekt irischer Goethekunde ist das rechte Widerspiel zu Goethes Irlandkunde (s. meine Übersicht in Deutsche Vierteljahresschr. f. Literaturwissenschaft u. Geistesgesch. 31, 1957, S. 70-83), und an dieser abgelegenen Stelle zeigt es sich einmal wieder deutlich, wie in doppelter Hinsicht Goethe das große Brennglas ist, in dem der Geist die Lichtstrahlen sammelt.

(Quelle: Goethe 24, 1962, S. 296-299.)

John Stuart Blackie's Translation of Goethes's *Jahrmarktsfest zu Plundersweilern*

We can distinguish three phases of early Irish interest in classical German literature. The first was the pre-Union period, when English translations of works of German literature were freely reprinted in Dublin and other places in Ireland. The only original translation of a work of German literature made at that time in Ireland was that of Schiller's *Geschichte des Dreißigjährigen Krieges* by William de Blaquiere (London and Dublin, 1799). The second period was that of the twenties when a large number of young members of the Irish aristocracy were in Germany to study the language and literature of the country, and when especially in Goethe's house they were most welcome. DeVoeux's *Tasso* (1827), Downes's *Letters from Continental Countries* (1832), and Swifte's *Wilhelm's Wanderings* (1878) are the chief literary documents of that phase. The third period of Irish interest in classical German literature may be described as the period of the *Dublin University Magazine,* as even its two principal literary records in book form, namely Mangan's *German Anthology,* and Anster's *Faust,* originated from that periodical. Of the numerous contributors who, during the editorship of Isaac Butt, promoted knowledge of German literature among the Irish public, only a few resided outside Ireland. John Stuart Blackie was one of them.

Of John Stuart Blackie's translations from the German, Bayard Morgan[1] listed only *Faust* (1834, 2nd ed. 1880), *The Wisdom of Goethe* (1863), and *War Songs of the Germans* (1870). In Anna M. Stoddart's biography,[2] Blackie's translation of *Das Jahrmarktsfest* is not mentioned either. This translation appeared in the *Dublin University Magazine,* November, 1836.[3]

When Blackie's translation of *Das Jahrmarktsfest* was accepted for publication in the *Dublin University Magazine,* he was twenty-five years old. At his arrival at Göttingen in 1829 "his capital of German had been small". However,

> he studied with a competent German master for six to eight hours daily. Forbes [Francis, the son of Dr. Forbes] and Blackie spoke German to each other, imposing a fine of two pfennigs for each relapse into English. They read only German newspapers[4]

and eagerly sought the company of their German "Kommilitonen". Among the professors whose lectures Blackie attended at Göttingen, Heeren and Otfried Müller made the deepest impression on him, and of the latter he left us an interesting portrait.[5] In Göttingen Blackie just missed Charles Lever, who had spent there the winter semester 1828/1829, and whose *Log-Book of a Rambler,* published in the *Dublin Literary Gazette,* is an interesting source of our information on the life at Göttingen of students from Great Britain and Ireland among the German "Burschen".[6] At Berlin, however, Blackie met another Irish student, named Jackson[7], to whose influence it was due that the young Scottish Presbyterian overcame his aversion to the theatre and availed him-

---

1   *A Critical Bibliography of German Literature* in *English Translation* (Stanford, 1938), pp. 154 and 636. M. J. Carré's bibliography of Goethe in England was not accessible to me; in his *Goethe en Angleterre* (Paris, 1930) Carré refers only to Blackie's translation of *Faust* (p. 226).

2   J. *St. Blackie* (Edinburgh 1895; new ed., 1896), from which I quote, the chief basis for the article on Blackie in *DNB.* On Blackie's influence on the Irish language revival, see Canice Mooney, "The Beginnings of the Language Revival", *Irish Ecclesiastical Record,* LXIV (1944) 13.

3   VIII, 524-34. In the subsequent issue of the *Dublin University Magazine* appeared the first part of Mangan's translation of *Wallensteins Lager,* the eighth instalment of his Anthologia Germanica, of which the seventh instalment, dealing with some of the Romantics, had appeared in the August issue, while the September issue contained a 16-page review of Sarah Austin's book, *Goethe and His Contemporaries.*

4   Stoddart, *op. cit.,* p. 35f.: "You are now fixed in Germany, and what you have to do, is to attain wholly to those things which are better attained in Germany than elsewhere. ... Speak nothing but German. Live with Germans. Read in German. Think in German. Don't mind a few pounds ... in learning German", Poole wrote thirty years earlier to Coleridge in Ratzeburg (Henry Sandford, *Thomas Poole* [London, 1888], 1,279).

5   Stoddart, *op. cit.,* p. 40f.

6   W. J. Fitzpatrick, *The Life of Charles Lever* (1896), p. 41f. See also Lever's *O'Leary,* ch. xix, and "Göttingen in 1824", in *Putnam's Magazine,* VIII (1856), 608

7   Stoddart, *op. cit.,* p. 58f.

self of the opportunity of seeing good performances of plays by Goethe and Schiller.[8] The lectures of Schleiermacher, Neander, Boeckh, and Raumer also contributed to Blackie's becoming still further imbued with German culture.[9]

After his return from the Continent in 1833, Blackie translated *Faust*. In 1835 he published essays on Jean Paul in *Blackwood's Magazine*, and on Menzel's *German Literature* and on Goethe's *Correspondence with Zelter and Bettina* in the *Foreign Quarterly*, and in the following year he wrote, for the same periodical, reviews of Pückler's *Tour* and of Eckermann's *Conversations with Goethe*. A friend of his at that time said that "his noddle is muddled with German, our wits he'd fain daze with his foreign phrase".[10]

Das Jahrmarktfest zu *Plundersweilern*, written in 1773, appeared in 1774 in *Neueröfnetes moralisch-politisches Puppenspiel*.[11] In 1778 this play underwent a thorough transformation with a view to its performance at Ettersburg,[12] and this new version first appeared in the eighth volume of *Goethes Schriften* (Leipzig, 1789). The manuscript for this edition was corrected by Herder.[13]

Blackie gave his translation the title

The Plundersweil – Fair.

A New Ethico-political puppet-play,[14] from Goethe.

Although, In the 1778/1779 version, this play was given a more general application, it has remained one of the less accessible works of Goethe, owing to the numerous allusions made in it to persons and conditions of the early 'seventies. Moreover, the language of this play offers great difficulties to the foreign translator. There are on the one hand the Knüttelverse of the Schönbartspiel, full of idioms, colloquialisms, and alliterations without definite meaning, and on the other hand, alexandrines, deliberately stilty and pompous. Was it a mere tour de force of the young student of the German language to attempt a translation of this work?[15]

---

8   Ibid., p. 54.

9   Ibid., p. 47f.

10   Ibid., p. 108f.

11   Zeitler in *Goethe-Handbuch,* II (Stuttgart, 1918), 227f., Weimar edition of Goethe's works, I, xvi, 393-406, and Morris, *Der junge Goethe,* III, 142, and VI, 295.

12   Goethe's *Tagebücher,* 2, 5, 6 and 20 October, and 6 November, 1778, and 3 May, 1779.

13   Weimar edition, XVI, 395.

14   In the Ankündigung to the 1816 edition of his works, Goethe called this work a 'Fastnachtsspiel' (*ibid.,* XLI, I, 84), but in all other editions the subtitle is 'Ein Schönbartspiel'.

15   The earliest reference to *Das Jahrmarktfest* in English literature was made by Sarah Austin in her *Characteristics of Goethe* (1833). To Falk's references to 'Lumpen und Quark' (see below) Mrs. Austin made a note in which she quoted the whole conversation between Zigeunerhauptmann and Zigeunerbursch. 'I attempted to translate this' she added, 'but found it impossible to do it in such a way as not to greatly disserve the author'. She then described *Das Jahrmarktsfest* as the opposite of *Iphigenie*, the former work being 'one of the outpourings of that wild, many-coloured fancy to which Goethe sometimes gave the reins'. The scene here especially referred to is, according to Mrs. Austin 'not an expression of Goethe's feelings towards the mass of

In Blackie's life this translation marks the point when

> from Wordsworth he returned with relief to Goethe, recognising in him that Hellenism which he was learning to appreciate at first hand, the large tolerance, the appreciation of 'all things lovely and of good report', the moderation in judgement and in action ...[16]

Blackie was too much rooted in Scottish Presbyterianism to enter, in a purely aesthetical manner, into Olympic Hellenism. That he chose *Das Jahrmarktsfest* as an object worthy of translation shows that he felt that Goethe himself had realised that beneath the golden heights on which the gods and heros are enthroned there are dark valleys in which the mortals are groping, Indeed as John Mitchel entered twelve years later in a log-book somewhat different from that of Lever, "Goethe never tried the galleys"[17] but he never forgot that there were galleys. Goethe was just as old as Blackie was at his coming to Germany, when he wrote the scene in which Marmotte and the Citherspielbub fight for a few coppers which "die Gesellschaft" throws among them. There is, as Blackie probably realised, something like "a third curtain" that opens when the Citherspielbub cries:

> Ai! Ai! meinen Kreuzer! Er hat mir meinen Kreuzer genommen!

Goethe adds the laconic stage direction: "Balgen sich. Marmotte siegt. Citherspielbub weint. – Symphonie." This is no longer a mere Schembart-play.[18] We have here rather a subtle expression of the metaphysical background of the new sense of reality leading up to modern social revolutions.

Still, just as in his translation of *Faust*, so also with regard to the *Jahrmarktsfest*, Blackie was unable to overcome certain limitations in his appreciation, arising from his moral and religious background. On page 534 of the *Dublin University Magazine*, VIII, Blackie's translation concludes with the fourth line of the Marktschreier's epilogue to the second act of the Esther-tragedy; the omission of the final Schattenspiel-scene is justified by the following note:

> Our MS does not conclude, but goes on with a sort of farcical lecture on the creation, by a common showman, which, however characteristic, may be easily dispensed with; and in deference to

---

mankind', but an expression of the universality of his mind. Then Mrs. Austin gave a survey of the cast of *Das Jahrmarktsfest*, omitting, however, the Esther-play. 'Last comes the Schattenspielmann whose description of the creation and deluge shows how perfectly familiar Goethe was with that sort of traditional lore which amused the simple fathers of the German people'; this scene is reminiscent of the *Wunderhorn* (I, 22f. and 20f.). In III, 219, Mrs. Austin gives a translation of the reference made in Brockhaus' *Conversations-Lexicon* to "the wild baroque humour and yet wonderful force of truth" of *Das Jahrmarktsfest*.

16   Stoddart, *op. cit.*, p. 108.

17   *Jail-Journal*, ch. vii.

18   None of Goethe's friends gave a more enthusiastic welcome to *Das Jahrmarktsfest* than did his mother. "Daß uns das Jahrmarkts Fest wieder auf lange Zeit vergnügt und froh gemacht werden Ihro Durchlaucht leicht glauben," she wrote on 24 November, 1778, to Anna Amalia, who had written some music for the Ettersburg performance. Frau Aja and her circle obviously read this play in one of the manuscripts listed in the Weimar edition, XVI, 397f.

religious feeling that ought to be respected, as also with the consent of the translator, we have omitted it altogether.[19]

Though Blackie reinforced the slightly anti-Semitic note in the original (when rendering Haman's words: The Jews feel themselves entitled "die Fremden zu berauben" by "to hate all mankind, and suck our blood like leeches", and Mardochai's exclamation: "Bei Gott!" by "By Father Abraham!", he apparently failed to recognise, or to convince the editor of the periodical, that the Schattenspielmann's parody of sacred history is described as a Jewish performance,[20] with which neither Goethe nor his translator need to be identified.

Blackie's ready compliance with the editor's opinion on the blasphemous character of this scene is foreshadowed by his attitude towards some rather free passages in the fair-scenes. The Broomman's street-call, "Kehrt die Gasse, Stub' und Steiß," is rendered by the words:

> To clean the street
> And to wipe your feet
> And to dust the room.

The Zigeunerhauptmann's comparison of the crowds at the fair with a herd of "Schöpse" is turned into a comparison with "boys running home from school".

Blackie's translation contemplated theatrical performance even less than the original did. The stage directions at the end of the first and second scenes are either shortened or omitted altogether.

As Blackie tells us in his preface to the second edition of his translation of *Faust,* it was only in later years that he realised the necessity, and acquired the ability, to translate freely.[21] His version of the *Jahrmarktsfest* takes very few liberties with the text of the original, although he occasionally adds or omits a line for the sake of rendering the meaning of the original. In the first section of the Marktschreier's speech, for example, the last two lines

> Ich hoff' es soll euch wohl behagen,
> Geht's nicht vom Herzen; so geht's vom Magen

---

19   It is interesting to compare the different attitude which Blackie or Butt and Mrs. Austin took to this scene. In a letter to Graf v. Brühl, the Generalintendant of the Royal Theatres at Berlin, of 3 November, 1825, Goethe referred to the final scene, writing: "Der Jahrmarkt von Plundersweilern war auf einen kleinen Raum berechnet. In einen großen Raum [such as it would be given in at Berlin, as proposed by v. Brühl] versetzt, müßte er nicht hinten so abschnappen, wie mit dem Schattenspiel geschieht. Eine lebhafte und tumultarische Nachtscene würde ... ihm ein auffallendes Ende verleihen." How far is this Romantic suggestion from the spirit in which the original play was written, fifty years before!

20   Düntzer (*Abhandlungen zu Goethes Leben und Werken* [Leipzig, 1785], pp. 141ff.) obiously felt himself that his suggestion that the Schattenspielmann was "ein Deutsch-Franzos" rested on very weak foundations ("er braucht kein einziges französisches Wort als 'Mesdames'").

21   See also Stoddart, *op. cit.,* p. 100f. (Carlyle's criticism of the first edition). The severe criticisms by Lina Baumann (*Die englischen Faustübertragungen* [Halle, 1907], p. 10) and by Bayard Morgan (*op. cit.,* No. 2699f., in contrast to Carré, *op. cit.,* p. 226) are obviously based on the first edition and ignore more or less the preface to the second edition, which contains also an interesting account of Blackie's German studies.

are rather chlumsily rendered by:

> I hope you will like the piece,
> And though our heart, may not inspire us,
> Our belly craves, and that will free us.

A similar enlargement actually leads to a significant change of the meaning:

Hüten uns auch vor Zoten und Flüchen,	Their ears have grown so delicate
Seitdem in jeder großen Stadt	In towns both great and small of late
Man überreine Sitten hat.	The Devil's self more they hate
	Then graceless equivoques are curses.[22]

The words "Wie sie gewöhnlich thun und reden" are even expanded to three lines:

> An honest picture of the age,
> Expose to public profanation
> Their daily life and conversation.

The rhymes of the speech of the Bauer (whom Blackie turns into a Broom-girl) have in the original the form *a b b c1 c2 c3 c1*, but in Blackie's translation the form is *a b c b c d d f e f f*, thus losing in both primitiveness and terseness. A similar enlargement is found in Blackie's version of the Nürnberger's speech. To the word "Nürnberger" Blackie adds the words "with toys". Blackie apparently knew something of Nürnberg toys, but while Goethe described the simple things he had had in his nursery in Hirschgraben, Blackie gives a list of the more sophisticated toys of a hundred years later: "a little French peerie, a Swiss guard and an English hussar."

Also in the speech of the Tyrolerin the description of the goods for sale has become more elaborate and more sophisticated.[23] The only case where Blackie's translation takes up fewer lines than the original is the second section of this speech:

Nicht immer immer gleich	Think not, gentles, to make free
Ist ein galantes Mädchen,	With honest maidens such as me ...
Ihr Herrn, für euch ...	

but actually the number of words is the same. Blackie's translation fails to render the mocking terseness, the tripping lightness of the original. "Ein galantes Mädchen" was simply beyond Blackie's comprehension. He is much more at home when he comes to the Wagenschmiermann (Oilman), whose speech he splendidly renders as follows:

> Oil to smear
> Your axles and wheels
> Squeal and squeak,

---

22   On two or more occasions Blackie reverses the order of the lines:

Unsere Helden sind gewöhnlich schüchtern	We play our drunkards mostly sober,
Auch spielen wir unsere Trunkenen nüchtern.	Our heroes are as soft as mud.
Ich laß sie gelassen sich entzweien	Each day they raise some nouvel route,
Jeden Tag gibt's neue Parteien.	I let them fight their battles out.

   In the last case the reversion was not demanded by the rhyme.

23   Möcht' all das Zeug nicht   Though they should give it me
      Wenn ich's geschenkt krieg   Money and carriage-free.

   in the Zigeunerhauptmann's speech (Blackie obviously tries to render the German idiom "gratis und franko") is still worse.

Creak, creak
No more shall grate the wheels.

The Zigeunerhauptmann's speech may be regarded as a very hard test for any foreign translator:

Lumpen und Quark
Der ganze Mark!

Misreading "Markt" for "Mark," Blackie translates:

Worse than dirt
Is all the fair.

In the Zigeunerbursch's reply:

| Die Pistolen | I would I had |
| Möcht' ich mir holen! | These pistols there, |

Blackie again takes the meaning too directly. Rhymes such as "Quark-Mark", "Pistolen-holen" are mere associations. The rhyme "Kohlen-holen" is actually the last example of "Blumen- und Zeichenwechsel" in the Notes to the *West-Östlicher Divan*.[24] Blackie is much better in his imitation of expressive rhymes such as :

| Weitmaulichte Laffen | Babbling and squabbling all! |
| Feilschen und gaffen, | Higgling and piggling all! |

where he reaches the same freedom as in his version of the Wagenschmiermann's speech. We may compare with these two passages the following passage from the Marktschreier's introduction to the first act of Esther:

| Zahnklappen und Grausen gepaart | With dashing and crashing and hashing |
| | And tearing of hair and teeth-gnashing. |

However, this example shows us again that Blackie's version of the fair-scenes is on the whole characterized by a certain heaviness. This becomes still more obvious at the transition from Knüttelverse to alexandrines, which in Blackie's translation is far less striking than in the original.

Goethe inserted the Esther-play to ridicule the stiltedness and unrealism of the epigones of the classical French tragedy. In contrast to Goethe, however, Blackie makes the ironical meaning of this play far too obvious. When Haman says: "Laß sie durch ein Gesetz--belehren", Blackie gives us:

One only plan, my liege, to cure this great enormity
I see – it is, to pass an act of uniformity.

Still worse is Ahasverus' reply:

Du machst mich lachen	Does the wind blow so
Ein Jude wird dich doch nicht eifersüchtig	... Haman is *geloso* ...
machen ...	

a memory of Blackie's journey to Italy. When rendering Ahasverus' words: "Mir wird ganz grün und blau", by "I am all green and blue", Blackie apparently failed to realise that the original aimed at ridiculing the use of colloquialisms so frequently found in

---

24   In the Weimar edition, VII, 127.

third-rate alexandrine tragedies of that time, rather than at using an almost incomprehensible image.

It is due to this fundamental misunderstanding of the significance of the Esther-interlude that Blackie frequently missed the vigour of the original:

Ahasverus:
Von Mord und Straßenraub hab ich lang' nicht vernommen

The jails are almost empty

Haman:
Tief in der Hölle ward die schwarze That erdacht ...

Deep, deep in night was hatched this deed ...

By rendering, in the initial monologue of Haman, the words "ein Einziger" by "proud Mardocai", Blackie took away the tension in the end of the first act when Haman gradually leads Ahasverus to the resolution to sacrifice Mardochai.

The only instance in the whole translation of *Das Jahrmarktsfest* where Blackie tries to bring in a note more daring than the original is the end of the Ochsenhändler's speech:

Wir trinken eins. Die Heerde ist versorgt.
[i.e., the cattle, just bought in the fair, and now – as implied by the initial words "Die Ochsen langsam zum Ort hinaus" – entrusted to a drover].

... at home our wives may snooze
[to rhyme with "house"].

A rather disagreeable consequence of Blackie's recent sojourn in Germany is his tendency to insert German words. This leads to such inconsistencies as translating the words in the Marktschreier's interval-speech "Es ist so wenig zu verlieren" by "You cannot lose more than a groschen," while at the end of that speech "Batzen" is rendered by "penny", and in the subsequent Milchmädchen's speech "Dreier" by "three farthings".

The words "Geschwind, Herr Pfarrer" are rendered by "Come, Mr. Parson," but in the interval-scene, the doctor's question: "Wie gefällt Ihnen das Spiel?" is translated "Well, Amtmann, how do you like the play?" although in this place "Herr Amtmann" would have been correct and could have been easily fitted in.

Another example is the translation of "Frau Amtmann" by "My lady Amtmännin." Blackie finds it necessary to add the following note:

We have retained [!] the German phrase, in order not to offend against the dignity of the lady, who according to the transcendental principles of German etiquette must be designated by her husband's title. Read Kotzebue's play of the Kleinstaeder,[25] and laugh at this pedantry.

Strangely enough, when the Governante speaks of "Der Doctor und mein Fräulein," Blackie says: "The doctor and Miss B.", for no other reason than to rhyme with the subsequent "and me"!

---

25 "Amtmännin" is taken from the subsequent stage direction, but only this or "Frau Amtmann" is correct. Blackie had seen this play in Berlin, where "at that time Kotzebue was counted of classical rank" (Stoddart, *op. cit.,* p. 54). "How fond these Germans are of titles", Lever remarked in *Harry Lorrequer* (1857), p. 360, a memory of his earlier visits to Germany.

In the Zigeunerbursch's line

| Wetter! Wir wollten sie! | Wetter! we'd give it them! |

Blackie possibly mistakes the curse "Wetter!" for a surname (of the gypsy-captain).

The Hanswurst's speech required again a very intimate knowledge of the German language:

Ihr mehnt, i bin Hanswurst, nit wahr?	I am the clown, you may suppose,
Hab' sei Krage, sei Hose, sei Knopf;	For I have his cap, and I have his hose;
Hätt' i au sei Kopf,	And had I only a head like him,
War' i Hanswurst ganz und gar.	I were the clown in every limb;
Is doch in der Art.	At least 'tis something to that tune;
Seht nur de Bart!	I've got a beard like pantaloon.
Allons, wer kauf mir	Allons! who will buy?
Pflaster, Laxier!	Pills and plasters
Hab' so viel Durst,	Who will buy?
Als wie Hanswurst.	Cures all disasters –
Schnupftuch 'rauf!	Gently my masters!
	Who will buy?
	Up with your handkerchiefs!
	Who will buy?

A fine illustration of the ingenuity of Blackie's translations of colloquialisms is the Tyroler's speech:

Kauft allerhand, kauft allerhand,	Buy, buy! great and small,
Kauft lang' und kurze Waar'!	Long and short, old and new!
Schnupftuch 'rauf!	Gently my masters!
Sechs Kreuzer's Stück, ist gar kein Geld,	Six kreuzers a piece, no money at all
Wie's einem in die Hände fällt.	For high-born gentlemen like you.

Goethe used in this instance the old form "kurze Waar'" – now "Kurzwaren" – for quincaillerie, measured by the inch, while "Langwaren" are measured by the yard.. Blackie seems to apply the terms "long and short" to the customers rather than to the goods. "Wie's einem in die Hande fällt" is an expression for a bargain (= "in den Schoß") rather than for trickery; The general meaning and the linguistic effect of this street call is adequately rendered.

Also Marmotte's song is most successfully translated:

Ich komme schon durch manche Land,	Through many a land come I, come I
Und immer ich was zu essen fand,	Nor ever for want of meat did die,
Ich hab' gesehn gar manchen Herrn,	And many a master I did find
Der hätt die Jungfern gar zu gern.	That was too fond of womankind.
Hab' auch gesehn die Jungfer schön,	And many a fair did I see,
Die thäte nach mir Kleinen sehn.	Though I was small she looked at me
Nun laßt mich nicht so gehn, ihr Herrn,	Ye gentle sirs and dames, 1 pray,
Die Burschen essen und trinken gern ...	O send me supperless not away!

That Blackie is still better in rendering passages in a less light may be seen from the beginning of the Esther-play:

Die du mit ew'ger Gluth mich Tag und Nacht begleitest,
Mir die Gedanken füllst und meine Schritte leitest,
Rache, wende nicht im letzten Augenblick
Die Hand von deinem Knecht! Es wägt sich mein Geschick.

Was soll der hohe Glanz, der meinen Kopf umschwebet?
Was soll der günst'ge Hauch, der längst mein Glück belebet,
Da mir ein ganzes Reich gebückt zu Füßen liegt,
Wenn sich ein Einziger nicht in dem Staube schmiegt?
Thou, who with thoughts of flame my restless spirit feedest,
Both night and day, thou who my feet securely leadest,
Sacred Revenge! that long has blest my sunless lot,
With cheering hope, in this last hour desert me not!
What boots the halo bright, that floats around my head?
The breath of the king's love wherewith my life is fed?
What boots it that to me submit an empire must,
Unless proud Mardocai lies prostrate in the dust?

And may I finally quote the Marktschreier's defence of actors?

Warum will man's uns übel nehmen?	Why then are we, poor actors, blamed?
Tritt im gemeinen Lebenslauf	In common life, we see, each man
Ein jeder doch behutsam auf,	Chalks out his well-considered plan
Weiß sich in Zeit und Ort zu schicken,	Obedient to the moment's wink,
Bald sich zu heben und bald zu drücken	Knows when to rise, and when to sink,
Und so sich manches zu erwerben,	Attains to good, eschews the scaith,
Indeß wir andre fast Hungers sterben.	While we, poor wretches, starve to death.

Thus, on the whole, Blackie's translation of *Das Jahrmarktsfest* may be called a very creditable achievement by a young foreigner with a comparatively short experience of German language and literature, especially in consideration of the particular difficulties of the subject-matter and language of this play. That Blackie's translation has found so little attention is doubtless due to the play itself rather than to his translation. On the other hand, the fact that this translation of the then still little-known Scottish student was published in the *Dublin University Magazine* was an acknowledgement of the qualities of his work and is an illustration of the great interest taken by Isaac Butt and his friends[26] even in the less-known works of German literature.

(Quelle: Modern Language Quarterly, 8, 1947, S. 91-100.)

---

26 Michael Sadler, "Dublin University Magazine," in *The Bibliographical Society of Ireland,* IV (1938), 64 and 75.

V.4 19. Jahrhundert

German Literature on Napper Tandy

In my paper on 'Trenck and Britain' (including also some references to Ireland – in Modern Language Review XLI, 405, note 4 (1926)) and on 'The historical and biographical background of Prevost's Irish novels' (U.J.A. XII, 93 (1949)), I have referred to Hamburg's being, throughout the eighteenth century, a sanctuary of Irish refugees. The most conspicuous of these Irish refugees was, of course, Napper Tandy. The article on him in D.N.B. extensively drew on Karl Wilhelm Harder, *Die Auslieferung der vier politischen Flüchtlinge Napper Tandy, Blackwell, Morris and George Peters* (Leipzig 1857).

The following list of later German literature on Napper Tandy and the Irish nationalists at Hamburg was kindly placed at my disposal by the Staatsarchiv der Hansestadt Hamburg, and as, except for no. 3, these items seem to be inaccesible in these countries, this list may serve as a guide to further investigations on the continent.

1) Adolf Wohlwill, 'Die Verhaftung Napper Tandys und Conflicte Hamburgs mit den Grossmächten 1798-1800, nach den Acten des Geh. Staatsarchivs in Berlin' in *Mitteilungen des Vereins fuer Hamburgische Geschichte*, 33ff (1878). See also the same author's *Neuere Geschichten der Freien und Hansestadt Hamburg insbesondere von 1789-1815*.

2) Heinrich Harkesee, Beiträge zur Geschichte der Emigranten in Hamburg, ii. Madame de Genlis,' in *Programm der Oberrealschule und Realschule vor dem Holstentor* (Hamburg 1900) 42ff (on Lady Fitzgerald).

3) Wolfgang Mettgenberg, 'James Napper Tandy. Ein Beitrag zur Geschichte des Auslieferungsrechts', in *Niemeyers Zeitschrift für Internationales Recht* XXVII (191 S.).

4) Heinrich Reincke, 'Aus dem Briefwechsel von Karl und Diederich Gries 1796-1819', in *Zeitschrift des Vereins für Hamburgische Geschichte* XXV, 2bS ff. (1722).

The Hamburg Staatsarchiv stated that while Harden and Wohlwill made extensive use of the official records, the letters of the refugees, reports by the police and contemporary brochures have not been sufficiently considered in the Geman literature, as it was concerned with the political and legal implications of the extradition rather than with the refugees themselves. See also George Serviere's paper 'L'extradition et mise en líberte de Napper Tandy' in *Revue Historique* XCIII. 46-73 (1907).

(Quelle: Irish Book Lover 31, 1951, S. 108f)

Immermann's 'Tristan und Isolde' and Ireland

To appreciate the position held by Immermann's *Tristan* in the history of Continental interest in Ireland, it may be useful to restate briefly the place which Ireland occupied in the older Tristan tradition. *Motivforschung* has demonstrated the extensive influence which Celtic mythology and folklore exercised in this tradition.[1] *Realienforschung* reveals that especially in its later stages this tradition was strongly influenced by more recent information on Ireland, and that, embodying this information, the story of Tristan became an important expression of Continental knowledge of contemporary Ireland. That this *Realienforschung* is still in its early stage will be realized at the reading of Bédier's[2] remarks on the place-name of Hessedot (according to the French prose-novel, the place of Tristan's landing in Ireland). The use of definite place-names (Dublin and Wexford by Gottfried von Straßburg, Wexford by Heinrich von Freiberg,[3] Dublin by the Norwegian Saga[4]) throws new light on the chronology of the various versions of the Tristan epic, the relationship between Continental and British versions, and above all, the linking of Celtic mythological influences and the new political interest in Ireland in twelfth- and thirteenth-century Continental literature.

Up to that period, the literary tradition of Ireland on the Continent had been exclusively hagiographical.[5] The development of Continental secular literature under the influence of Celtic mythology became connected, by sheer historical coincidence, with the new definite information on Ireland conveyed to the Continent under Norman influence. The spreading of the new secular interest in Ireland throughout the Norman realm from Norway right down to Southern Italy led to a new interpretation of the hagiographical tradition of Ireland, in the new version of the traditions of St Patrick's Purgatory and St Brendan's navigation, and in the Continental lives of saints reputed to be of Irish descent, such as St Livinus in Ghent, St Rumold in Mechlin, St Albert in Ratisbon,[6] St Frigidian in Lucca and St Cataldus in Taranto.[7] It also produced the first up-to-date secular accounts of Ireland, in the *Visio Tundali,* the *Lucidarius* (like Eilhart's *Tristan* inspired by the Brunswick Court which was dominated by a daughter of Henry II of England), Gottfried's *Tristan,* and *Kudrun.* It is curious that all these works belong to German literature. Regarding *Tristan,* even in Germany the Irish associations became more diffuse from the end of the thirteenth century on. As elsewhere, the interest in the mere fable, especially the adultery stories (that is, those parts of the Tristan tradition where definite reference to Ireland is insignificant), overgrew

---

1   Gertrude Schoepperle, Tristan and Isolt, a study of the sources of the roman (New York, 1913).

2   Roman de Tristan (Paris, 1901), I, 76.

3   See the index to Bechstein's ed. (Leipzig, 1869). In Dr. Closs's selection (London, 1944) most of the passages relating to Ireland have been omitted.

4   See Kölbing's ed. (Heilbronn, 1878).

5   See my article 'Irish Saints in early German literature' in Speculum, XXVII (1947), 358 ff.

6   See my article, 'St. Albert, patron of Cashel' in Medieval Studies, VII (1945), 21-39.

7   See my article, 'Cataldus Rachav', ibid. VII (1946), 217 ff.

the definite interest in contemporary Ireland[8] which, in that tradition, had reached its climax in Gottfried's version.

In the English Tristan tradition this specific interest in Ireland had never been so strong. In Malory's version these Irish associations have become vague memories.[9] The Continental prose novel of the later Middle Ages was mostly derived from the French prose version, which told of only one journey of Tristan to Ireland.[10]

The rediscovery of Gottfried's *Tristan*[11] coincided with the general revival of German and Continental interest in Ireland, partly through the Ossianic controversies, partly through political events of that time. In 1785 appeared both Karl Gottlieb Küttner's *Briefe über Irland,* the first German travel book to deal exclusively with Ireland, and the first print of Gottfried's *Tristan* in Myller's *Deutsche Gedichte aus dem 12., 13. und 14. Jahrhundert.* A few years before, Didot had published *Tristan de Leonis* by Louis, Count de Tressan, the last novelistic version of Tristan.[12] In the improved reprint of Paris 1822 the section containing references to Ireland, namely from the combat with Morhoult to the love-potion scene, occupies just nine out of 160 pages, an illustration of the insignificant position to which this part of the story had become reduced.

> Wounded by 'Morhoult d'Irlande, frère de la reine de ce pays' , 'un des plus renommés chevaliers de la Table ronde', Tristan 'par le conseil d'une demoiselle demande permission de son oncle de chercher du secours dans le pays de Logres (Angleterre).... Les vents le jettent enfin sur les côtes d'Irlande.' Standing by the window looking out over the sea, the king heard him playing his harp. On this first journey, Tristan has to dispose of a rival, not an Irishman (as Gottfried says), but a Saracen. The second journey, instead of being without any definite destination, brings Tristan to England rather than to Ireland. At the court of king Artus he meets Argius, king of Ireland, whose friendship he wins by helping him to clear himself from the accusation of having murdered his sister. Then they go to Ireland, where Tristan wins Isold for his uncle.

A few months after the appearance of Tressan's *Tristan,* Wieland[13] decided to compose a Tristan epic in stanzas, but for various reasons he was unable to execute this plan. The first modern German writer to draw poetical inspiration from Myller's edition was August Wilhelm Schegel, whose gigantic plan to write an epic comprising Tristan, the traditions of the Grail and the Round-Table cycle did, however, not proceed further than some 90 stanzas on Tristan's early youth. Brentano and Arnim

---

8   The Tristan-version in Buch der Liebe (Frankfurt, 1587; other editions ibid. 1578; Erfurt, 1619; Nürnberg, 1664) was the chief source for the article 'Schotte' in Grimm's Deutsches Wörterbuch (articles 'Irland' and derivations are missing).

9   See Beardsley's designs to Ryss's edition (London, 1893 and 1927).

10   See above n.2, and Walther Golther, Tristan und Isolde, Stoff- und Motivgeschichte der deutschen Literatur (Berlin, 1929) II, 48.

11   Gustav Ehrismann, Geschichte der deutschen Literatur bis zum Ausgang des Mittelalters (München, 1927), II, 2, i, § 46.

12   Ed. Campenon (Paris, 1822), III, 40 ff. See also Nouv. Biogr. Génér. (1859), XLV, 623ff.

13   Golther, op. cit. p. 49.

planned, on a less ambitious scale, to write a Tristan epic, less sweetish and elegant than Schlegel's.

The Tristan editions by von Groote and von der Hagen are almost contemporary with the travel books on Ireland by Count Pückler, one of the sources of Goethe's information on Ireland,[14] and George Depping, now the least known but at its time the best and most widely read book on Ireland.[15] *Sir Tristrem,* published in 1804, obtained at that time a European reputation, first of all on account of the illustrious name of its editor, Sir Walter Scott.[16] Platen's Tristan poems (1825, 1830 and 1834) are only remotely inspired by the medieval epics.[17] Rückert decided in 1839 to continue Schlegel's work, but he too did not get much further than Tristan's arrival at his uncle's castle in Cornwall.[18]

Karl Immermann was not only the first German writer to give a poetical version of the principal parts of *Tristan,* but he has remained the only modern adapter of the Tristan tradition who preserved, and even increased, the number of references to Ireland.

As early as 1831 Immermann read von der Hagen's edition of Gottfried's *Tristan* 'mit großem Entzücken'.[19] He conceived at once the idea of 'raising this story from the dead' and of rewriting it 'wie Gottfried von Straßburg dichten würde, wenn er heutzutage lebte'. As in Tristan's life the adulterous relations with Isold with the golden hair were followed by the relations with Isold with the white hands, in Immermann's life the association with Gräfin Ahlefeldt (who had divorced for him her husband, the famous General von Lützow) was superseded by the marriage with Maria Niemeyer. It was actually during his engagement to Maria Niemeyer that Immermann began to write his *Tristan;* visiting Dresden on his honeymoon, Immermann discussed with Tieck the first part which had appeared in Freiligrath's *Rheinisches Jahrbuch* of 1839. Though written, as Immermann said, 'unerlaubt rasch', *Tristan* was not finished. It was 'des Dichters Schwanengesang'. Like Gottfried, Immermann was prevented from finishing it by death (23 August 1840). However, he had the satisfaction of seeing the public taking to his work as they did during the last years of his life to his *Münchhausen.* Tieck then suggested to Immermann's widow that he should finish where his friend had left off, but the death of his daughter Dorothea prevented him from doing so.[20]

---

14   See my article, 'Goethe's personal relations with Ireland', Dublin Magazine (Jan.-March 1943), pp. 53f.

15   See my article, 'Goethe and Lord Bristol', Ulster Archaeological Journal, x, 1(1947), 101.

16   Golther, op. cit. p. 50. Kölbing dedicated his re-edition (Heilbronn, 1880) to Sir Walter.

17   Cotta edition (1876), I, 76 f. For further literature on modern versions of Tristan see also Kosch's Literaturlexikon (Halle, 1930), col. 2749.

18   Golther, loc. cit.

19   Robert Boxberger's introduction to his edition of Immermann's Werke, XIII, and Max Koch's introduction to his selection for Kürschner's Deutsche National Literatur.

20   Allg. Deutsche Biog. XIV, 62f. and Schnase in the 'Vorrede' to the first edition of Immermann's Tristan (Düsseldorf, 1841).

In Immermann's *Tristan und Isolde,* references to Ireland occur mainly in Songs V-XI corresponding to Songs X-XVII in Gottfried's work. Immermann is one of the few adapters of the Tristan tradition who were not so much fascinated by the adultery stories to neglect over them the earlier parts which contain the references to Ireland. We shall see though that the poetic value of Immermann's work is lowest in his references to Ireland; it increases undoubtedly in the love-potion scene and the subsequent songs.

In the manuscript, Song V of Immermann's *Tristan* was entitled 'Tristan und Morolt', in accordance with the title given to the corresponding song in Gottfried's work; in the printed edition, however, it was given the title 'St Patricks Schiff'.[21] The beginning

> Vom Abend her, von Irland grün
> Blies steif der Wind gen Cornwalls Dün'....

may have inspired the sailor's song opening Richard Wagner's opera (which, however, starts with Isolde's departure from Ireland):

> Westwärts schweift der Blick,
> Ostwärts streicht das Schiff.
> Frisch weht der Wind der Heimath zu.
> Mein irisch Kind, wo weilest du?

The repeated reference to 'der steife Wind von Irland grün' recalls the Roman tradition of the Irish sea's being particularly rough and of Ireland's being 'pabulosa' and evergreen.[22]

> Mit blauer Flagg' und Segeln weissen
> Fuhr her das braune Sehiff, geheissen
> Der heilige Patrick. Nicht klein
> Kann dieser Männer Herze sein.

We shall see that Immermann mostly uses the word 'Patrick' with the stress on the last syllable, apparently an indication that he had merely book-knowledge of the patron saint of Ireland.[23] In the medieval Tristan tradition, St Patrick is mentioned only in *Sir Tristrem,* v. 1228, where the people of Dublin swear 'bi seyn Patrike' that they have never seen a finer harp than Tristan's. We know that Immermann used also *Sir Tristrem,*[24] but the frequency of references to St Patrick in his work rather points to modern sources of information on Ireland. Note the references to the national symbols of modern Ireland in the description of Morolt's boat:

> Der Spiegel
> trägt ein Heil'genbild, das ist

---

21 Boxberger, op. cit. p. 98.

22 Ptolemy, Pomponius Mela and Solinus, right to the early nineteenth century quoted in descriptions of Ireland in Continental cosmographies. Podleiszek's Volksbücher von Weltweisheit und Abenteuerlust (Deutsche Literatur, ed. Kindermann, Leipzig, 1936), p. 37.

23 'Patrick', Thomas Moore said in his Two-penny Post Bag, IV, 'is a bad name for poetry'.

24 Golther, op. cit. p. 51. Immermann directed the English studies of Countess von Ahlefeldt, who translated Scott's Ivanhoe (Koch, op. cit. p. xxii).

> Der Schutzpatron zu jeder Frist
> Von Irland, Sanct Patrick mit Namen,
> Vergoldet und geschnitzt aus Holz;
> Und drunter in dem weissen Rahmen
> Auf blauem Grund das Wappen stolz
> Hiberniens: Vom Klee, der Stengel
> Die Davidsharfe mit dem Engel,
> So fuhr das Schiff von Irland grün....[25]

In vi. 171, the Irish are actually called 'die Patrickstruppe'. At Marke's court, Morolt asks as tribute for a weight of gold:

> Als lebensgroß mein Sanct Patrick
> Am Spiegel wiegt mit Kutt' und Strick;
> Wagst du mir meinen Schutzpatronen
> Mit Gold nicht auf...
> ... wir legen Tintagel in Graus
> Bei unsres Heil'gen Fegefeuer,
>   Bei goldnen Klee und Davids Harf'....[26]

Of St Patrick's Purgatory, Immermann had probably heard through the new version, given by his friend Tieck, of the old story of *Fortunatus*.[27]

In Song VII when, at the beginning of the combat, Tristan compares himself with David, Morolt replies:

> Ich kam von Irland.... Bei Kreuz und Stern !
> Verläßt du dich auf Gott den Herrn,
> Verlasse ich mich auf ein Paktum,
> Das ich im Himmel bündig schloß;
> Mein Glaube, Junker, ist ein Faktum,
> Nicht so ein luft'ges Bibelschloß.
> Ich habe meinem Sanct Patricke,
> Wenn er mir schirmet das Genicke,
> In jeder Straß', 'nen großen Dom
> Gelobt zu baun am Liffy-Strom.[28]
> Dies weiß ganz Leinster, Mounster, Ulster,
> Und Connaught auch. – Das ist mein Polster,
> Worauf man sicher ruhen kann.
> Patrick läßt keinen Iren sterben,
> Er war ein gar zu braver Mann.
> Hat einst das Land von dem Verderben
> Des giftigen Gewürms errett't
> Und alle Schlangen tot gebet't.

---

25 Boxberger, op.cit. p. 101. Koch did not give Song V; Boxberger did not number the stanzas, I therefore quote from Koch's edition whenever possible.

26 Boxberger, op. cit. p. 109.

27 Schriften, III (1828), 162ff. and 347 ff.

28 Koch's edition, p.208, has a note on 'Liffey'.

Even if caricature of a Catholic is meant as a special hit at Ireland, the intellectual level of this passage is hardly higher than its poetical level. How could the public of that time swallow rhymes like: Patricke–Genicke, Ulster–Polster, and errett't–gebet't? However, since the German *Tundalus*,[29] this is the first reference in German verse to the tradition of St Patrick. The 'Paktum' referred to by Morolt is the covenant of Croagh Patrick. At the actual beginning of the combat, Morolt

> hob den rechten Arm
> Rief: Sanct Patrick, du sitzest warm,
> Bring mich denn endlich auch zum Schlusse!
> Denk deines Doms am Liffy-Flusse!

This invocation, however, does not avail; in the end Morolt lies

> ob dem Hinterdecke
> Zu Patricks Fuß, Sanct Patricks Mann.[30]

This seems to be the only instance where the word 'Patrick' has the accent on the penultimate.

Morolt's companions are mostly called 'die Iren', also 'die Irländer'[31] (now gradually becoming an archaism), 'der Iren Rott',[32] 'der Irenbund'[33] and 'der Iren Schwarm',[34] the last three expressions pointing to the contemptuous treatment of the Irish which Immermann metes out more generously than any of the medieval versions had done. The Irish are dressed 'in Bärenfellen und Eisenhosen',[35] a reflexion of the fantastic descriptions of the battle-dress of the Irish in the sixteenth and seventeenth century Continental accounts.[36] That Morolt's helmet was adorned with a 'Medusenkopf' is one of the numerous clumsy anachronisms in Immermann's work. Among Morolt's companions 'Herr Donegal', a drunkard,[37] 'O'Connor'[38] and 'Gin, ein Hauptmann bei der Irenbande',[39] are named. Morolt himself is 'der Feldherr im Solde der irischen

---

29 See my article quoted above, n. 5. See, however, Buchard von Hornech, Carmen de Purgatorio Sti. Patricii (Memmingen, 1495).

30 Koch's ed. VII, 268f.

31 v, Boxberger, op. cit. p. 105.

32 VII, V. 107.

33 Ibid. p. 242.

34 Ibid. p. 254.

35 V, Boxberger, op. cit. p. 101.

36 See my paper 'Early representations of Irishmen in German books' to be published in Journ. Roy. Soc. Antiquar. Irel. (1949). Like the Norman, the Williamite invasion of Ireland brought about a decisive increase in Continental knowledge of Ireland (see my paper 'Some early German accounts of Schomberg's Irish campaign' in Ulster Archaeol. Journ. XI (1948), 65 ff.).

37 VII, 406.

38 VI, 111, and Boxberger, op. cit. p. 103.

39 VI, 143.

Königin'.[40] He asks for the 'Zins, den Irlands Frau zu heben hat. . .für Irlands Schatz' and which the late King Gorman

> Soweit die ir'sche Welle treibt,
> Soweit sie ir'sche Flaggen träget,
> Einst allen Landen aufgeleget.

The Pope had granted this tribute;[41] this is apparently Immermann's own interpretation of the tradition that Cornwall's tribute to Ireland was fixed by the Romans, a tradition introduced by Gottfried in order to reconcile the Tristan tradition with the conception of British history established by Wace and Monmouth[42] and confused by Immermann with the tradition of the donation of Ireland by Pope Adrian IV to Henry II. Morolt tells Marke that through Gorman's death 'Irlands Reich ist nicht am Sterben' and that he must not 'Dublin Rest verbleiben'.[43]

Like the word 'Patrick', the word 'Dublin' is mostly accentuated on the last syllable, probably in analogy to 'Berlin'. In the night before the combat between Tristan and Morolt, wine is offered.

> Der beste Meister schuf den Krug,
> Der in Dublin je Meisel trug.[44]

At this point, Immermann makes an insertion which is expressive of his indebtedness to both Romantic irony and to modern information on Ireland:

> Zu jener Stund'
> War noch der Whiskey nicht erfunden,
> Der jetzo labt der Iren Kehl'.[45]

The farcical character of Immermann's references to Ireland is also obvious in the ballad sung by the Irish while sitting 'in dem feuchten Kote'.[46] Starting 'Grünes Erin! Stolzes Erin!',[47] it relates the story of 'Dundiridone, der Bauernsohn' who wooed 'die Lady', killed her father and was eventually locked up, a reflexion of the accounts given – from English sources – in seventeenth-century German literature of Irish lascivity and wildness. Though again ironically ending in the reference to 'Stolzes Erin!' this song 'schläfert die Irischen Degen' and soon nothing is to be heard but the 'Geschnarch der Irisch-Men';[48] the use of the English form clearly shows that Immermann drew on the literary tradition of the stage-Irishman.

---

40   Boxberger, op. cit. p. 101.

41   Ibid. pp. 105 and 108.

42   Bédier, op. cit. p. 74.

43   Boxberger, op. cit. p. 109.

44   VI, 369.

45   VI, 351 f.

46   VI, 196.

47   VI, 431 ff.

48   VI, 490 and 506 f.

After the combat, the Irish return 'gen Irland grün',

> Doch als Dublin sie sahen ragen,
> Begann auch wieder laut ihr Klagen.[49]

In Song VIII there is no description of Tristan's journey to Ireland (which in Gottfried's work is perhaps the most interesting reference to Ireland). We find Tristan immediately 'im fernen Irland', 'im Königsschlosse zu Dublin', in a room 'fern vom Schrei der Schlemmer'.[50] When Isolde departs from Ireland, the roofs of the houses of Dublin are

> all besetzt mit treuen Ir'n
> die der Prinzessin salutier'n,[51]

the 'Königstochter Irlands' who is about to entrust herself to 'Hiberniens Wogen'.[52] Immermann gives us a backwash of Romantic irony mixed perhaps with a dose of derision of Anglomania as expressing itself at that time in the craze for English girls' names, when he describes the (with Isolde) 'eingeschiffte Hoffräulein' as

> Miss Elinor, Miss Kitty, Betty
> Und die kleine, schwarze Pretty.[53]

Not much better is his description of the 'Lords'[54] who came with Tristan from Marke's court, 'Lord Triamour von Maidenclung', 'Lord Stonycraft' who is 'genannt der Kühle' for no other reason than to rhyme with 'Graf Moor de la Valpüle'. The rhyming of 'Drywater, der Baron' with 'der alte Ritter John' is hardly better. However, as it is not the purpose of this paper to discuss the literary merits of Immermann's work, I confine myself to quoting Golther's verdict:

> Die Verse sind nicht sonderlich gut gebaut, die Sprache mit .... stilwidrigen modernen Ausdrücken durchsetzt, der Stil mitunter geschmacklos.

If Immermann's *Tristan und Isolde is* nevertheless 'eine hochbedeutsame Schöpfung, der unter den strophischen Nachbildungen Gottfrieds der Preis gebührt',[55] this is due to the more lyrical passages rather than to those containing references to Ireland. In fact, I feel, it would be unfair if my collection of these references should be taken as a basis for judging the poetical value of Immermann's work.

My paper is concerned with the study of the place of Immermann in the literary tradition of Ireland, in particular in the Tristan literature. Apart from Scheffel's *Ekkehard* (which, however, appeared fourteen years later, during which Continental *Irlandkunde* made vast progress), Immermann's *Tristan und Isold is* the work of nine-

---

49   VII, 274 and 279.

50   VII, 236 and 321 f.

51   X, 605.

52   XI, 336.

53   XI, 95 ff.

54   In v, Boxberger, op. cit. p. 105, and X, V. 14 and 145.

55   Boxberger, op. cit. p. 51.

teenth-century German literature most extensively relating to Ireland. Though it leads to many 'Geschmacklosigkeiten', the interweaving – in both these works – of the information on Ireland given by the medieval sources and that drawn from modern sources was an important step in the development of modern Continental *Irlandkunde,* which rests, on the one hand, on antiquarian studies and, on the other hand, on modern ethnographical and political interest.

(Quelle: MLR 44, 1949, S. 246-252)

Pestalozzi in Irland

Die persönlichen Beziehungen Pestalozzis mit Engländern – insbesondere seine Briefe an James Pierrepont Greaves (1818/1819, zuerst veröffentlicht 1827) – und die frühe Verbreitung seiner Ideen in England (durch Charles Mayo 1828 und Edw. Biber 1831) sind vielfach, wenn auch nie zusammenhängend und erschöpfend behandelt worden. Die frühesten Druckschriften in englischer Sprache über Pestalozzi erschienen jedoch nicht in England, sondern in Irland.

Im Jahre 1815 erschien in Dublin «Eine biographische Skizze der Kämpfe Pestalozzis ... zusammengestellt und übersetzt hauptsächlich aus seinen eigenen Werken, von einem irischen Reisenden». Der Verfasser war John Synge, ein Mitglied des irischen Zweigs der Familie Synge, der seit dem 18. Jahrhundert ein großes Landgut in Glanmore, in der Grafschaft Wicklow, besaß. Der Dichter John Millington Synge (1871-1909), von dessen Werk Rudolf Stamm kürzlich den ersten in der Schweiz veröffentlichten Ueberblick gab (Three Anglo-Irish Plays, u.a. Synge's Riders to the Sea, Francke 1943), wuchs in Glanmore auf, wo sich zu seiner Zeit noch Zeugnisse für seines Vorfahren Interesse an Pestalozzi befanden.

John Synge hatte mit Recht das Pseudonym «The Irish Traveller» gewählt. In einer Zeit tiefster politischer Erregung hatte er die iberische Halbinsel bereist. In seiner biographischen Skizze Pestalozzis erzählt er uns, wie er im Jahre 1814 nach Yverdon kam. Als man ihm riet, Pestalozzis Schule im Schloß zu besichtigen, war er zögernd. «Das mechanische System bei uns daheim hatte mich gegen alle Pädagogik eingenommen.» Endlich ging er doch. Der Erfolg war, daß er drei Monate blieb. «Pestalozzi und seine Gehilfen gewährten mir uneigennützig und großzügig ihre persönliche Freundschaft. Pestalozzi erlaubte mir, alle seine Schriften zu benützen, von denen er mir sogar die letzten ihm verbliebenen Exemplare zur Verfügung stellte.»

Synge's Buch über Pestalozzi besteht vorwiegend aus Uebersetzungen von Auszügen aus Pestalozzis Werken und aus De Chavannes Buch. Diese Auszüge, bemerkt Synge, sollen keinen Leser zu der irrigen Annahme verleiten, er könne nun Pestalozzis System lehren. Ihre Veröffentlichung verfolgte nur den Zweck «bei denjenigen nützlichen Mitgliedern der Gesellschaft, denen an der Verbesserung ihrer Mitmenschen gelegen ist», Interesse an Pestalozzi zu erwecken. Am Ende seines Buches wendet sich Synge charakteristischerweise an die *britische* Nation mit der Bitte, Beiträge zur Unterstützung von Pestalozzis Werk an die La Touchesche Bank in Dublin zu überweisen. Die Idee, sich an seine irischen Landsleute zu wenden, ist Synge offenbar nicht gekommen. Soweit sie nicht, wie er, Angehörige der englisch-protestantischen

Herrenklasse waren, konnte er von ihnen auch kaum Geld und noch weniger Interesse erwarten.

Seit Beginn des 19. Jahrhunderts, experimentierte ein anderes Mitglied der anglo-irischen *gentry*, Richard Lowell Edgeworth, der Vater der Schriftstellerin Maria Edgeworth, auf seinem Gute in der Grafschaft Longford mit neuen Erziehungs-methoden, deren Objekt vor allem seine aus vier Ehen stammenden zahlreichen Kinder waren. Edgeworth war ein interessanter Vorläufer Pestalozzis. Obgleich er geistig noch tief in der Aufklärung steckte, erkannte er doch den Wert sinnlicher Anschauung und spontaner praktischer Betätigung für die Erziehung. Edgeworths Vorbild regte wohl Synge an, auf seinem Gut eine moderne Schule zu errichten, die nicht nur seinen eigenen Kindern, sondern auch den Kindern seiner Zinsleute dienen sollte, wobei letztere wahrscheinlich zum Protestantismus bekehrt werden sollten. Der Dichter Synge hat in seiner Jugend noch das Oelgemälde von Taylor gesehen, das das Innere von Synges Schule in Kilfee mit Pestalozzischen Tabellen an der Wand darstellte.

John Synge errichtete auch in Roundwood, in der Nähe seines Gutes, eine Drucker-presse, die offenbar ausschließlich der Verbreitung der Werke Pestalozzis gedient hat. In den Jahren 1817 bis 1819 erschienen drei Bändchen Pestalozzischer Zahlentabellen und ein Band über «Relations and Descriptions of forms», endlich 1820 eine Be-schreibung von Pestalozzis Bohnentafel. Außer diesen Büchern ist scheinbar nie ein druckschriftliches Erzeugnis aus dem Dorf Roundwood, jetzt eine bekannte Sommer-frische in den Wicklower Bergen, hervorgegangen. Im Jahre 1931 erschien in London eine von Synge nach Pestalozzis Methode verfaßte Einführung in die hebräische Sprache «für Eltern, die es für einen wichtigen Teil der Erziehung ihrer Kinder er-achten, daß sie auch die Sprache lernen, in der das Wort Gottes geschrieben ist». Die kleine Druckerpresse in Roundwood hätte für die Herstellung dieses Buches natürlich nicht ausgereicht.

Im gleichen Jahre übergab John Synge seinem gleichnamigen Sohne die Verwaltung seines Gutes. Im Jahre 1842 besuchte J.G. Kohl, der erfolgreiche Reiseschriftsteller, Synges Gut, hörte aber nichts mehr von den Versuchen, Pestalozzi in Irland heimisch zu machen. Im folgenden Jahre verbrachte Graf Joseph d'Avèze, der Schriftsteller der «Revue Britannique» einige Tage in Roundwood; Synges Druckerpresse hatten aber damals schon längst aufgehört zu arbeiten. Bis heute ist der Einfluß von Pestalozzis oder von ihm abgeleiteten Ideen auf die protestantischen Schulen beschränkt. John Synge war einer der vielen Angehörigen der anglo-irischen *gentry* seiner Zeit, die ver-suchten, Irland mit kulturellen Bestrebungen auf dem Kontinent in nähere Beziehung zu bringen. Sein Mißerfolg in dieser Hinsicht war kaum weniger charakteristisch als der Mißerfolg, den achtzig Jahre später sein Nachkomme *John Millington* erlitt. Wenn überhaupt, so erreichen die kulturellen Erregungen des Kontinents diese abgelegene Insel spät und in höchst abgeleiteter Form. Das frühe direkte Interesse, das ein Ire an Pestalozzi nahm, ist daher bedeutsam.

(Quelle: Die Tat, 18.05.1946)

Beethoven and Ireland

The other day, when opening a Thomas Moore Exhibition in Dublin, an Taoiseach said that the significance of Thomas Moore was chiefly that he had been instrumental in gaining for Ireland that world-wide publicity which she wanted at that time. It is curious that in achieving this end, Moore was in a way assisted by the greatest spirits of his age, Goethe and Beethoven. Goethe, of course, had a knowledge of Ireland more detailed than had any Continental person before him. Beethoven's contribution to Continental consciousness of Ireland was less outspoken, though scarcely less significant. To appreciate this contribution, I must ask my readers to retrace with me a chapter of the history of Irish music.

Towards the end of the 18th century, George Thomson of Edinburgh, Secretary to the Board of Trustees for the Encouragement of Arts and Manufacture in Scotland, conceived the idea of publishing some Scottish airs which he had collected. It was a curious undertaking. Scottish poets, including Burns, and Continental composers, including Haydn, were engaged simultaneously to write the words and the accompaniments respectively. They were given just the bare melody with nothing else to guide them in their work than Italian musical terms such as allegro, andante, affettuoso etc.

In the course of their correspondence on this work, Burns wrote to Thomson in September 1793 that some of the airs submitted to him were not Scottish but "rank and downright Irish, though very pretty ... If they were like *Banks of Banna,* for instance, though really Irish, yet in Scottish taste, you might adapt them. Since you are so fond of Irish music, what say you to 25 of them in an additional number? We could easily find this quantity of charming airs; I will take care that you shall not want songs; and I assure you that you would find it the most saleable of the whole." About that time, several collections of Irish airs were undertaken, of which Thomas Moore's was the most extensive, one of the last and in the long run the most popular. It is interesting that it was Burns who induced Thomson to extend his collection of national airs from Scotland and Wales to Ireland and who promised to Irish airs a great success.

It was not until the autumn of 1814 that Thomson was in a position to publish at Edinburgh *A Select Collection of original Irish Airs for the Voice united to characteristic English Poetry written for this work with Symphonies and Accompaniments for the pianoforte, violin and violoncello composed by Beethoven.*

In the preface to this first volume (the second appeared two years later), George Thomson said that "many years elapsed since he had begun to collect Irish Melodies, about twenty of which, the most familiar to music-lovers in Scotland, were interspersed in his collection of Scottish Airs". Thomson, in this instance, did not simply adopt the term "Irish Melodies" which in the meantime Moore's collection had begun to make world-famous, but expressly acknowledged that Moore had stolen the march on him. Still, he could rightly claim that his collection had been started earlier than Moore's. It was to Dr. Latham of Cork, Thomson said, that he was indebted for "this great variety of the finest melodies existing in Ireland, either in print or in manuscript". Thus he could rightly claim that these melodies were "original Irish". Regarding their antiquity he had no illusions; he expressly agreed with Moore's statement that most of this type of melodies were fairly modern. It is curious that Thomson made his collection with an eye to the Scottish rather than the Irish, not to speak of the English or Continental market. In contrast to Moore's collection his collection was made in the first instance for music-lovers. Thomson, therefore, did not hesitate to admit that the words added to, or may we say, superimposed on, these airs were "characteristic English poetry". Apart from Burns, twelve writers had supplied the words, all English and Scottish, except for the Rt. Hon. John Philpot Curran, the father of Sarah Curran. It has been suggested that when some of Beethoven's *Irish Airs* were reprinted in 1855 by the proprietors of Beethoven's manuscripts, an attempt was made to substitute words by Thomas Moore, but this was prevented by Messrs. Power, Moore's publishers.

It should be remembered that the early international reputation of Thomas Moore was based on his *Odes of Anacreon,* on *Lalla Rookh* and his prose-works, while it was only in the late 'thirties that his name became as exclusively associated with *Irish Melodies.* While it is true that to this day Irish melodies have decisively shaped foreign ideas on Ireland, it must not be forgotten that Beethoven's contribution to this source of Continental knowledge of Ireland was no less important than Moore's. Considering the conditions of the time, the writers of the "characteristic English poetry" published with Beethoven's setting of Irish airs had done their best. The opening number entitled "Return to Ulster" by Walter Scott struck the key-note. A large number of Irish proper-names and place-names occur in these poems. However, in accordance with the curious method employed by Thomson in getting together his collections of national airs, Beethoven never saw these words until they were published.

In his preface, Thomson said that the collection of Irish airs which Dr. Latham sent him in 1802 was first submitted to Haydn, and only after his death also to Beethoven. That Haydn had some knowledge of Irish airs is shown by the famous anecdote that at hearing one of them he burst in tears saying: "What an unhappy enslaved nation it must be whose music this is." However, it appears that it was before Haydn's death that Thomson had approached Beethoven. On August 1st, 1806, Beethoven wrote to Thomson that in consideration of the sum of £100 he was "on the whole not indisposed to accept" Thomson's proposition to extend his work from the Scottish airs to the Irish airs. "I shall take care to make the composition easy and pleasing, as far as I can and as far as is consistent with that elevation and originality of style which, you say, characterises my work." Reserving for himself the rights of publication in France and Germany, Beethoven indicated that he saw a Continental market for the *Irish Airs.*

It was not until the autumn of 1809 that Thomson actually sent Beethoven forty-three melodies, Irish and Welsh, with the request to "compose and very quickly ritornelli and accompaniments for pianoforte or pedal-harp". Any student of the life of Beethoven at that period is acquainted with his constant complaints at his financial worries, and there can be little doubt that Beethoven undertook this work, so unsatisfactory for a genius like him, mainly for its financial prospects. Accordingly, in the literature on Beethoven, his *Irish Airs* are usually passed over in silence or dismissed in a few words as a work of inferior quality. I suggest that a purely musical appreciation of this work does not do justice to its significance. Considering the conditions under which

Beethoven wrote this music, even a comparison with the work done by Stevenson and Moore becomes fundamentally unjust. Thomson's method of obtaining words and accompaniment to these airs independently of each other appears as ludicrous from the viewpoint of our modern conception of songs and of national music. Beethoven himself realised this only too clearly.

Shortly after receiving the Irish airs from Thomson, Beethoven asked him to send "the words along with the airs as it is very necessary for me to have them in order to get the correct expression". He added significantly: "They will be translated to me." Beethoven, we must remember, did not understand any English. His letters to Thomson were written in French. Even if mail conditions of the time would have permitted Thomson to fulfil Beethoven's wish, the words to these airs were probably not yet ready by that time. Moreover, they would hardly have been a source of genuine inspiration to Beethoven regarding "the correct expression".

Beethoven wrote the accompaniment to twelve Scottish, twenty-six Welsh and fifty-seven Irish airs. To the latter must be added "The Minstrel Boy" and "By the side of the Shannon" in the Continental publication of *Twelve songs of various nationalities,* in which Ireland is the only country to be represented by more than one melody, and three more songs in *Sixteen national airs with variations as duets for violin or flute and piano,* namely "Last Rose of Summer" (a very incorrect version of the air), "While History's Muse" and "Oh! had we some bright little isle". It may be mentioned that on the other hand Moore wrote, in 1816, three of his *Sacred Songs* to airs by Beethoven.

Looking at the words "Irish" and "Beethoven" side by side on the title page of what I believe is the only copy of the original edition of *Irish Airs* in any public library of this country, I realised that this work occupies an important position in the history of Irish-Continental cultural relations.

On the one hand, Thomson in his preface paid a high tribute to Beethoven, saying that "of all composers that are now living, it is acknowledged by every intelligent and unprejudiced musician that he is the only one who occupies the same distinguished rank as the late Haydn". While Haydn had become famous through his concert tours in England, Beethoven was at that time still far from being well known in these countries. That Beethoven's *Irish Airs* could not be published until 1814 was due to the fact that, though Beethoven had completed his work in 1810, due to the Continental Blockade no less than three copies of Beethoven's *Irish Airs* were intercepted on their way to Edinburgh. For the same reason also, Beethoven's other works had not become so well known in England as could have been expected under normal circumstances. Beethoven's accompaniments, Thomson says, are singularly appropriate to the great beauty of Irish airs, "full of matter perfectly original, and diversified in the most fanciful and striking manner". Modern critics of Beethoven's Irish airs would do well to study these words. They are expressive of an idea of accompaniment to national airs which has become totally inacceptable to us, yet at that time was adopted by the greatest masters as long as it did not interfere with the "elevation and originality" of their own style. Beethoven had refused to write for the pedal-harp, which he regarded as an inferior instrument. Thomson apparently agreed with this verdict, for in his preface he describes it as an advantage not shared by any other collection of Irish airs that Beethoven's accompaniments were written for violin and violoncello. Neither Thomson nor Beethoven regarded national airs as anything else but a raw material for more elevated forms of music. "Amidst the powerful attractions of new und excellent compositions, and the fluctuations and refinements of taste, national melodies would be much neglected, were it not for their union with masterly and beautiful accompaniments." Thus Thomson justifies the undertaking to engage a composer to whom Ireland was practically unknown, to write accompaniments to her airs.

On the other hand, even more than the names of the famous writers like Burns and Sir Walter Scott who sponsored this collection, Beethoven's name carried the fame of Irish airs far afield. Thomson's preface was, for many Continental readers at least, an important source of information on Irish music. Of Beethoven himself there is no record that he ever wrote the words "Ireland" or "Irish".

He regarded his work on Irish airs simply as a continuation of the work in which he had joined in 1803 on Scottish airs. Of Scottish airs he must have had a good initial knowledge, for, writing in October, 1803, he promised Thomson that he would treat "the Scottish airs in such a manner that the Scottish nation would be pleased and which would be in accordance with the spirit of her songs; I am particularly fond of Scottish airs and I shall therefore enjoy working on them". In August, 1806, after receiving the further order for Irish airs, Beethoven repeated this promise (see above) without expressly stating from which nation these songs were derived. In July, 1810, when sending the first batch of *Irish Airs,* Beethoven asked Thomson innocently to accept these *airs écossais* as a tribute to the national genius of the "Scottish and English peoples", repeating at the same time his request to have the words to these "Scottish songs" before they were published in Scotland. Commenting on this letter, Thayer, the great Beethoven expert, noted laconically: "For Beethoven everything was Scotch."

Mr. Thayer could also have said that for Beethoven everything coming from these countries was English. Beethoven took his full share in the Anglomania of his age. We have of him five variations on "Rule Britannia" and seven on "God save the king," which he regarded as "a blessing to the English nation". In 1813 he dedicated to the Prince Regent his Symphony on Wellington's victories and planned to visit England, a plan which had to be given up owing to his increasing deafness.

There are special reasons for Beethoven's confusing the Irish and the Scots. He was deeply indebted to the Ossianic enthusiasm evoked through the grand forgeries of James Macpherson. "Ossian" appeared to the Continent as the ideal of original poetry; whether he was Scottish or Irish, nobody cared. The only one of the *Irish Airs* in Beethoven-Thomson's collection to appear in a German translation was one entitled "The Spirit of the Bards", a typical reflection of pseudo-Ossianic ideas of Caledonia and Hibernia.

In Vienna, where Beethoven lived for the last forty years of his life, the names of *Schottenbastei, Schottentor,* and *Schottenkloster* have preserved to this day the memory of the time when the *Scoti* (mostly Munstermen) established a monastery there. There is little evidence of any attempt by the influential Irish colony in 18th century Austria to claim for themselves this tradition. Beethoven knew particularly well the descendants of Ulysses and George Browne of Limerick, who had left Ireland after the Battle of the Boyne. To one of them, "Brigadier Browne in Russian services", Beethoven dedicated his setting of *Songs by Gellert* including the famous "Die Himmel ruehmen des Ewigen Ehre". In the house of his cousin Philipp George Browne, one of the numerous *salons* of Vienna nobility which Beethoven frequented, one of the famous incidents took place which are invariably quoted in Beethoven biographies to illustrate the eccentricities of the great composer. "At the house of Count Browne," Beethoven's first biographer (who probably witnessed the scene) tells us, "when playing a duet with Ries, a young nobleman at the other end of the room persisted in talking to a lady; several attempts to quieten him having failed, Beethoven suddenly lifted Ries's hands from the keys, saying in a loud voice: 'I play no longer for such hogs!', nor would he touch another note nor allow Ries to do so, though entreated by all." Beethoven, of course, was grenerally known for the liberties he was permitted to take in the houses of his noble friends. Still, it always appeared to me as significant that it was in the house of a man of Irish descent that this scene took place, in which Beethoven asserted the right of the spirit against the presumption of hollow social privileges.

The Brownes and the other Wild Geese among the Vienna nobility on whom Beethoven lived did not make any contribution towards his knowledge of Ireland. We do not know of any visitor from this country who made his acquaintance. When it became fashionable among the Anglo-Irish[1] to tour the celebrities of the Continent, Beethoven was already dead. He had to discover for himself, that Ireland possessed an abundance of melodies, beautiful and rich, "plaintive, spirited and playful," as Thomson put it. In the historical perspective we may perhaps still subscribe to what Thomson said of Beethoven's setting of Irish airs: –

"If Carolan, the Irish Bard, would raise his head, and hear his own melodies sung with Beethoven's accompaniment, he would idolise the artist that, from his design, could produce such exquisitely coloured and highly finished pictures. This is flattering to the melodies of Ireland and will be received no less favourably."

(Quelle: The Irish Monthly, Vo. 75, 1947, S. 832-838)

A Donegal Family in Germany

Manuscript 250 of the National Library of Ireland consists of 81 pages in octavo closely written in ink, described in the catalogue as the 'Diary of life in Germany and

---

[1] Sir John Russell, Moore's friend, toured Germany and Austria eleven years before he paid a visit to Ireland, a country in whose government he was then to play an eminent part. In the account of his Continental tour he gave one of the most interesting descriptions of Beethoven penned by any of his English contemporaries.

This article is an enlarged version of a talk which I gave in Radio Eireann on the occasion of the 120th anniversary of the death of Beethoven.

Switzerland during residence there by "Moll" Hamilton, a daughter of John and Mary Hamilton of St. Ernan's, Co. Donegal, Ireland', and given to the National Library in 1913 by the Howard Memorial Library, New Orleans. This is an account, written shortly after the events recorded had taken place rather than an actual diary, covering the period from 6th December 1838 to the beginning of June 1840. On fol. 8v. it is stated that there was an earlier volume covering the Hamiltons' first sojourn at Neuwied. The present volume concludes with the Hamiltons returning to Neuwied (on Rhine) after their sojourns at Karlsruhe and Lausanne. The Hamiltons' residence in Co. Donegal is stated in the inscription on the tomb-stone of Isabell Hamilton, Moll's sister, at Karlsruhe, as recorded at the end of this diary.

From fol. 12r. we learn that the Hamiltons had with them in Germany their son, James, and four daughters. Isabell, born in 1826, died "in a foreign land" (as is stated on her tomb-stone) on 3rd May 1840. Moll, who was educated together with Isabell and in her diary repeatedly recognised her sister's superiority, was presumably the second; therefore, at the time when this diary was written she was scarcely more than thirteen. The hand of this manuscript, however, is that of an elderly person, and it is suggested that it was written by Miss Bagot, the governess of Bell and Moll Hamilton. Only the last page, perhaps, was written by Moll herself, in a stiff child's hand, paying tribute to the memory of her sister.

Bell Hamilton was buried at Karlsruhe side by side with "Rebbecca McClearn, born at Raphoe in Ireland 1813, a faithful servant and beloved sister," who had died four days before the present diary opens, on the day when the Hamiltons moved into their new house at Karlsruhe. The inscription on that joint grave has been, and possibly still is, a record of a closely knit life of an Irish family.

When visiting Bell's grave, the Hamiltons passed by the grave of the husband and father of their best friends, Mrs. and Miss V. Struve. This was Johann Gustav V. Struve, who in 1817 had become Russian minister to the Karlsruhe court and had died there in 1828. Moll Hamilton referred to the great review held at Karlsruhe on the occasion of the visit of the son of the Emperor of Russia in the spring of the year 1839, an event no doubt of special interest to the V. Struves.

Moll Hamilton's diary is a record of Continental life 110 years ago as seen through Irish eyes and of an Irish family's life on the Continent, especially of their efforts in learning the languages. It suffices to say that this diary contains accounts of Karlsruhe, Baden-Baden, Strassburgh, Freiburg, Basle and Switzerland in general, in particular Geneva and Lausanne, and finally of Heidelberg, Mayence and Neuwied. The detailed descriptions of Christmas and Easter in German families are particularly valuable and of historical interest even to a German.

Regarding Mr. Hamilton's business on the Continent, Moll's diary informs us that "on the first Sunday 1839" he began to hold morning meetings. "At eleven many English and some Germans used to come to our rooms and we had little meetings like at Neuwied, but at Carlsruhe we only knew one or two English people". These were apparently religious meetings. At the end of her diary Moll tells us that on their return to Neuwied the Hamiltons stayed at the 'Brudergemeinde' (Herrenhuthers) Inn and that they took lodgings with two Moravian ladies. The description, on her tomb-stone, of their servant Rebecca as "beloved sister" also points to some sectarian association. On Christmas 1839 Moll was given by her father (nothing but) "a nice German testament". Mr. Hamilton also gave English lessons to the Misses Struve, in exchange for the German lessons given to his ladies though, rather than for money. That the Hamiltons were well-to-do can be gauged from the fact that while bringing their own maid from Ireland, they engaged a German maid and later a second German maid whom they took with them to Switzerland. Moreover, they had a governess (presumably from Ireland) for their daughters and a tutor (one Lauterbach) for their son, who were also among the party on the journey through Switzerland. Thus it would appear that John Hamilton was a free-lance evangelist of independent means, who might be assigned a place in a history of English-speaking sectarian missions in Germany.

Towards the end of 1839, Mr. Hamilton considered taking his family to England "to put James to school, but we did not like this going so near home without getting home", the only note of attachment to Ireland struck in Moll's diary. On their journey to Lausanne, the Hamiltons called at Baden on their friends the Wellesleys, probably Henry Richard W., later British minister to the Frankfurt Confederation, who in 1833 had married Olivia Fitzgerald (D.N.B.). At Strassburg, they called on the Nesbitts and the Bohns, the latter perhaps, James Stuart B., the book-seller (D.N.B.).

While there are numerous English descriptions of the Rhineland and Switzerland at that time (including some by Irish-born authors), Moll Hamilton's diary is an interesting record of how thoroughly many of these visitors applied themselves to the learning of the German language. In conjunction with the records of the various young Irishmen who stayed for this purpose at Weimar, Moll Hamilton's diary is the counterpart of the extensive interest in German literature in Ireland between 1830 and 1850, most noticeable in the *Dublin University Magazin* and *The Nation*. The Hamiltons' example shows that this interest had spread outside Dublin and to the female sex. On their return to Ireland, the Hamiltons, from their blind admiration of everything German, must have been in their circle an important source of information on German life and German letters.

John Hennig.

My thanks are due to the Trustees of the National Library of Ireland for permitting me to publish this note.

(For further particulars of the Hamiltons in Germany see "Sixty Years' Experience as an Irish Landlord – memories of John Hamilton D.L." edited with introduction by Rev. H. C. White. (London, Digby Long and Co.))

(Quelle: Donegal Annual 2, 1950, S. 315-318)

Moore's Influence on the Continent

125 years ago, in the spring of the year 1821, the Grand-Duke Nicholas of Russia and his wife paid a state visit to Berlin. At a gala fete given on this occasion members of the grand-dukal party and of the Prussian Court joined in performing a play entitled Lalla Rookh, based on the "oriental romance" by Thomas Moore. A few weeks later, at one of his earliest visits to the Duchess of Orleans, Thomas Moore heard what he describes as "the most flattering piece of news" of this performance, of which Chateaubriand, the French ambassador had sent an account to Paris. The King of Prussia and his Russian guests were so much pleased by the performance of Lalla Rookh that the producer, a young painter named Hensel, was commissioned with retaining the pictures of the illustrious performers in their oriental costumes. The originals of these drawings were given to the Grand-Duchess as a memory of this visit.

I could hardly think of a better illustration of the early spreading of Moore's fame on the Continent. We must take a few steps back to appreciate the full significance of those few facts. The Grand-Duchess who played the part of Lalla Rookh was the daughter of the King of Prussia. The Grand-Duke who took the part of Feramorz was heir-to-the-throne and brother of Tsar Alexandar, whose influence on the Continent was then practically unchallenged. Prussia and Russia together with Austria were the Big Three of that time, the Holy Alliance. England was represented in this performance by the Duke of Cumberland's playing the part of Aurungzebe. France, we have seen, had been keenly interested in this performance, as it was an essential part in that meeting of greatest international significance. And all this based on a work of Thomas Moore's published just three years before. Byron rightly said to Moore that the Berlin performance of his Lalla Rookh was an honour unknown in the history of literature for many centuries.

Hensel's drawings were probably the first occasion of the spreading of Moore's fame to Russia. A short time later Lalla Rookh appeared in a Polish translation. It was translated even into Persian. It was of course translated into French and German, also into Italian, Dutch, Danish and Icelandic.

The Berlin gala performance is characteristic of what I should like to call the first phase of Continental interest in Moore. During this period, Moore was known on the Continent first of all as the writer of the Odes of Anacreon, The Love of the Angels and Lalla Rookh, and in the second instance, as the author of Irish Melodies. We know that Byron declared he would rather be the author of four of Moore's poems, including "Oh Breathe not his name" and "As a beam o'er the face of the waters" than have written Childe Harold. On the Continent, Byron and Moore were celebrated as the great representatives of Romantic poetry in these countries. However, an early Continental appreciation of the specifically Irish note in Moore's poetical work was not visualized. Whether it was Greece, India or Ireland, he was writing about, did not make much difference to the Romantic critics on the Continent. In fact, while early French criticism of Moore's poetical works called him "the bard of Erin" or "The Irish Anacreon", in later years he was described as the "British Anacreon", and "one of the greatest poets of England". Similarly, Goethe in an early note on the author of Odes of

Anacreon and Lalla Rookh, speaks of him as "Irlander", Irishman, born in Dublin, while in later years he calls him "einen Briten" – a Briton.

It was rather through his prose works that Moore became to the continent the great literary representative of Ireland, and the lasting fame of the Irish Melodies on the Continent was chiefly due to the sympathy and interest in Ireland, which Moore's prose works had evoked. Now, as the study of the influence of Moore's prose works on the Continent is a subject very much neglected by bibliographers, I must ask you to permit me to pester you with some dry names and dates. Moore's Memoirs of Captain Rock, the Life of Fitzgerald and Travels of an Irish Gentleman in Search of a Religion were published simultaneously with the London editions at Paris. Incidentally, all early editions of Moore's poetical works, that of 1819 in 6 volumes, that of 1817 in 7 volumes and that of 1827 in six volumes, also appeared at Paris. In 1826, the Life of Fitzgerald and in 1829 Memoirs of Captain Rock appeared in French translations. The first volume of his History of Ireland was translated into French no less than three times within the year of its publication. Of the Travels of an Irish Gentleman I traced two French translations of which I shall have to speak presently.

In Germany, the first work of Moore's to be translated was Lalla Rookh. The translation published in 1822 by De la Motte Fouque, a well-known Romantic poet, was doubtless caused by the Berlin gala performance; it was reprinted in Vienna in 1825, and six or seven different German translations of that work were subsequently published. The best of these was the one which appeared just a hundred years ago in the Tauchnitz-series, a cheap edition of works of English literature, well-known to everyone who travelled on the Continent. Of the German translations of Irish Melodies, I mention only the most popular one which appeared in Reclam's Universal Library, a cheap and very widely spread series. Germany has the privilege of having produced the first foreign translation of any of Moore's prose-works, namely of Memoirs of Captain Rock. This translation was published in 1825 by a firm in Breslau, an interesting illustration of the early spreading of Moore's fame even to the Eastern parts of the Reich. In 1846, the year of the completion of Moore's History of Ireland, an abridged German translation of that work appeared at Baden-Baden.

We have ample evidence that also those works of Moore's of which no German translations can be traced, were extensively read. In 1829, Crabb Robinson, a friend of John Murray, Moore's publisher, went to Weimar to collect from Goethe some new material relating to his friendship with Byron; Goethe took a keen interest in Moore's Life of Byron, and read both the first and the second edition of that work. A few months before his death Goethe also read Moore's Life of Fitzgerald, which he described in his Diary as "masterly and inspiring." As for German knowledge of Moore's Travels of an Irish Gentleman in search of a religion, it suffices to say that one of the numerous replies which this controversial work provoked, was published in 1835 at Berlin by a German Protestant theologian.

I am afraid I have tired you by all these bibliographical details. However, I felt that without giving you a few details I might be accused of rashness when claiming that the extent of Moore's influence on the Continent is far from being sufficiently realised. The view-point from which I have studied this subject is not the traditional search for literary "influences", but the development of Continental knowledge of Ireland. There has never been a more important period in the history of Irish-Continental relations than that from 1815 to 1845. During that period more books relating to Ireland were written and published on the Continent than during the subsequent hundred years. During that period the traditional idea of Ireland as the remote fog-bound native island of bards, saints, rebels and tough swords-men was replaced by a detailed picture of the true conditions of modern Ireland and of their historical and spiritual foundations.

The first source of this modern interest in Ireland was revolutionary Liberalism, to whom Ireland appeared as the Western counterpart of Poland. The French translator of Memoirs of Captain Rock, for example, said that though he was a staunch anticlerical he was interested in the sufferings of the Catholics in Ireland, because Liberalism had to fight tyranny wherever it was found. Did he know that O'Connell had said in 1823 that "religious liberty meant emancipation of Catholics in Ireland and protection of Protestants in France"?

Freiligrath, the German poet of the revolution of 1848, not only gave us some of the finest German translations of poems by Moore, but, as an American scholar has pointed out, was influenced in his political poetry by no one more than by Moore. In his elegy on An Irish Widow, Freiligrath paid back to Ireland the debt which he had incurred through Moore. This liberal interest in Ireland was often somewhat indirect, Ireland being regarded as just another illustration of the sufferings inflicted by tyranny. The second source of Continental interest in Moore opened a more direct approach to Ireland. It is found in the sympathy which Continental Catholic revival naturally felt with this country. When the German translation of Memoirs of Captain Rock appeared, the Catholic press spoke of it as "a deeply shocking account of the terrible conditions and the cruel treatment of Catholic Ireland," a subject of which up to that time, Continental Catholics had remained incredibly ignorant, in spite of the literary exertions of the Irish refugees. Another German Catholic periodical said that Moore's work gave "a horrifying picture of a nation suppressed by political and ecclesiastical fanaticism. Please God, this book will impress those who rule that nation with an iron rod." While the Memoirs of Captain Rock shook Continental Catholics from their indolent ignorance of contemporary Ireland, Moore's History of Ireland presented them for the first time with the Catholic view of the historical foundations of those "horrifying conditions". The German translation of Memoirs of Captain Rock was the first illustration of the new interest taken by German Catholics in Ireland based on the study of our literature. The same Catholic publisher who produced this translation published a few months later one of the earliest collections of Irish folk-tales; Carleton, Banim and Griffin were also introduced to the German public by Catholics.

In France, Catholic interest in Moore was apparently confined to his Travels of an Irish Gentleman in search of a Religion. The first French translation of that work was made by a countryman of Moore's, who revealed his name only in the handwritten dedication to Moore, in the copy now preserved in the Moore library of the Royal Irish Academy. This translation, as well as the second translation, published also in 1834 (by a French priest) was definitely Catholic in character.

Behind the poetical, the political and the religious interest in Moore, there has gradually appeared what I personally would consider as the most genuine and most adequate
interest which the Continent could take in Moore. Thomas Moore was beyond all
doubt one of the most important sources of modern Continental interest in Ireland.
Some historians may describe his History of Ireland – reckoned by modern standards –
to be an outmoded work. Still, in view of the information available to Moore at the
time, it was a sound work. Captain MacCall rightly reminded us of the fact that just
this most doubtful of Moore's prose works "served the useful purpose of spreading
some knowledge of Ireland's history where, before, there was none.

To my mind it is more than a historical concidence that the completion of Moore's
History and the publication of its German translation were contemporary with the
appearance of Caspar Zeus's Grammatica Celtica the foundation of modern Celtic
studies. The history of modern Celtic studies would read very, very differently had
there not been the popular enthusiams for Ireland which Moore's works nourished
from so many different sources.

I wish to conclude this paper with an apology for its scrappy character. The scantiness
of sources, mainly due to emergency conditions, is the chief reason why I would not
dare to describe this survey of Moore's influence on the Continent as more than a few
hints. I should be glad if one or the other of you would believe with me that in this
study we might be able to raise one of the hidden glories of Ireland, and, if not, I
simply wished to pay, through modest bibliographical research, my tribute to the
genius of Thomas Moore.

> (Quelle: Vortrag, Thomas Moore Society, Dublin 1946, Vorlage von Monica
> Schefold, Bremen)

Thomas Moore and the Holy Alliance

One hundred and twenty-five years ago, in the spring of the year 1821, the Grand
Duke Nicholas of Russia and his wife paid a State visit to Berlin. At a gala fête given
on that occasion, members of the grand-ducal party and of the Prussian Court joined in
performing a play entitled *Lalla Rookh*, based on the "Oriental Romance" by Thomas
Moore. A few weeks later, the Duchess of Orleans told Moore at Paris "the flattering
news "of this performance, which in an official report Chateaubriand, the French
ambassador at Berlin, had described as "the most splendid and tasteful thing he had
ever seen". A gentleman just returned from Berlin told Moore that the Princess of
Prussia had requested him to tell Moore "how beautifully the fête at Berlin, taken from
your *Lalla Rookh*, went off". The Grand Duchess had acted Lalla Rookh, her husband
Feramorz. *Lalla Rookh* had perhaps been chosen for this occasion on account of the
similarity between the alliance confirmed through the marriage of the brother of the
Tsar and heir to the throne of Russia and the daughter of the King of Prussia and the
alliance confirmed between the Emperor of India and the King of Lesser Bucharia
through the marriage between Lalla Rookh and the minstrel prince. In the Berlin
performance the part of King Arungzebe was taken by the Duke of Cumberland, at
that time living at Berlin, as his marriage to a sister of the late Queen of Prussia had

not been approved by the Court of St. James. A sister of Prince Radzivil, another son-in-law of the King of Prussia, played the part of the Peri.

The King of Prussia and his guests were so much pleased with the performance of *Lalla Rookh* that the producer, a young painter named Hensel, was commissioned with preserving the memory of the illustrious performers in their Oriental costumes in drawings, the originals of which were to be given to the Grand Duchess as a memento of her visit. The printed edition of these drawings were the earliest and chief means of spreading Moore's fame to Russia. In 1829, Moore was shown a translation of *Paradise and the Peri* by "the Russian poet who had accompanied the present Empress when she was at Berlin, incorporated in a collection of Russian poetry". Moore's name was spelt Muosou. A Russian friend read to Moore "a good part of that translation which seemed very musical". There existed also at that time two Russian translations of *Irish Melodies*; these were presumably the first works of Anglo-Irish literature to be translated into Russian. The Berlin performance also prompted De la Motte Fouqué, the Romantic poet, to produce the first German translation of *Lalla Rookh*; a reprint of this translation appeared at Vienna.

Russia, Prussia and Austria were the Big Three of that time. In September, 1815, after their second entry into Paris, the sovereigns of these three countries had concluded the Holy Alliance. "In view of the great events which the last three years had brought to pass in Europe and in view especially of the benefits which it had pleased Divine Providence to confer upon their States", they adopted the principle of drawing their inspiration in internal and foreign politics from the Christian religion and of looking upon each other as brothers. "Fraternity, Religion and Peace" were to replace the famous slogan of the French Revolution. "All those Powers who wished solemnly to make avowance of these sacred principles" were promised "to be received into this Holy Alliance with as much cordiality as affection".

The state visit at Berlin took place just between the congresses of Troppau and Laibach, where the Big Three established their right of suppressing democratic and nationalist movements even in those countries which had not availed themselves of the cordial invitation tendered to them. Naples, Sardinia and Spain appeared successively on the agenda.

Let us imagine for a moment that after their gala dinner at Yalta, instead of joining humming *Ol' Man River* to the ethereal sounds of a jazz-band (as press-reports told us), Mr. Stalin and Mr. Churchill had taken part in a performance of a suitable entertainment for their American friend, such as Louis MacNeice's *Columbus* would have been. Can we doubt that, like Moore, Mr. MacNeice would not complain of being robbed of royalties for the right of this performance?

Was it due to ignorance of Moore's attitude towards the Holy Alliance that his *Lalla Rookh* was chosen for the Berlin State performance? Or was this choice due to the well-read leaders of the opposition at the Berlin Court to the reactionary policy of Frederick Wilhelm III? Apart from Prince Radzivil and his wife (the Princess of Prussia who sent Moore a message to Paris), there was Prince Frederick William, who in 1822 sent a message to Moore saying that "he slept with a copy of Lalla Rookh under his pillow", and who twenty years later, after becoming king, made Moore the first knight in the newly established class "for Science and Arts" in the Prussian Order *Pour le Mérite* (Moore read this news in the Prussian State Gazette). Still, I find it hard to believe that a work of Moore's could have been chosen for such a conspicuous occasion as the Berlin State visit, without counting on the broadmindedness, almost incredible to our democratic age, with which the rulers of that time took lampoons. Castlereagh, for example, Moore tells us, declared he "did not mind at all" the nasty things Moore said about him as long as they were "humorous and laughable". The King of Prussia, we shall see, had been the subject of one of Moore's boldest lampoons. However, when Canning, another of Moore's victims, invited Moore in October, 1820, to dinner, Moore entered in his diary: "This is excellent! Can he ever have read the later editions of the *Fudge Family*? I fear not."

The deprecation, now so prevalent, of Moore's poetry is strictly proportional to the neglect of his other works. Giving the *coup de grâce* to Moore's traditional reputation as a champion of Irish Catholics, the late Professor Stockley dismissed his *History of Ireland* as "impossible". Yet, in these countries, and still more on the Continent, what Captain McCall said of this work holds good, "it spread some knowledge of Ireland, where before there was none". Still more unjust is the unhistorical, purely æsthetic disregard shown to Moore's political pamphlets (Mr. Strong, in what has been so far the most extensive biography of Moore, devoted to them two out of more than 300 pages). This disregard is the more surprising as political pamphlets are not only an important source of Irish history, but also a most significant line on Anglo-Irish literature. Whoever had to plough through some volumes of Irish political pamphlets of the 18th and early 19th centuries, will simply sigh with relief when he comes to Tom Moore.

As early as 1808, Moore had started his career as a political pamphleteer with the poems *Corruption* and *Intolerance*, "addressed to an Englishman by an Irishman". In the first sentence of the preface to that work, Moore outlined his programme: "The practice which has been lately introduced into literature, of writing very long notes upon very indifferent verses, appears to me rather a happy invention; as it supplies us with a mode of turning dull poetry to account, and as horses too heavy for the saddle may yet serve well enough to draw lumber, so poems of this kind make excellent beasts of burden, and will bear notes, though they may not bear reading." Thus was anticipated Mr. Garnett's condemning this work of Moore's as "heavy". In *Corruption*, Moore dealt with the Rebellion of 1688, "which to Ireland has brought nothing but injury and insult", but in the final line

O England! sinking England! boast no more

he referred to more recent times, quoting perhaps "the prophetical remarks made by Sir Richard Talbot in 1762: 'In the same proportion as the British increase in riches, they approach to destruction. Europe will remind us of the balance of commerce, as she has reminded France of the balance of power.'" In *Intolerance*, Moore spoke of still more recent sufferings of Ireland when she was "forgot by all but watchful France". In the Epilogue, he stated that his expectancy of Ireland's "having her turn" in European affairs, was based on "the tradition", then by no means very lively, "of days when this island was distinguished by the sanctity of her morals, the spirit of her knighthood, and the polish of her schools".

In 1808, too, Moore wrote *The Sceptic*. Starting with a learned discourse on ancient Scepticism, Moore

> Asks, who is wise? – you'll find the self-same man
> A sage in France, a madman in Japan;
> And *here* some head beneath a mitre swells,
> Which *there* had tingled to a cap and bells:
> Nay, there may yet some monstrous region be,
> Unknown to Cook, and from Napoleon free,
> Where C–stl–r–gh would for a patriot pass,
> And mouthing M–lgr–ve scarce be deemed an ass!

In this work, Moore for the first time makes a reference to definite events in foreign politics of that time. With regard to England's protecting Denmark's neutrality (by the taking of Copenhagen in September, 1807), he says:

> Thus England, hot from Denmark's smoking meads,
> Turns up her eyes at Gallia's guilty deeds;
> Thus, selfish still, the same dishonouring chain
> She binds in Ireland, she would break in Spain;
> While praised at distance, but at home forbid,
> Rebels in Cork are patriots at Madrid!

Moore's attitude to Napoleon is a subject worthy of being studied in detail. How much of this attitude was influenced by Moore's national feelings, may be gathered from the reference he makes in his *Letter to the Roman Catholics of Dublin* (1810) to "Buonaparte, the greatest of all statesmen and warriors." England's war for the freedom of the nations overrun or threatened by Napoleon is sheer hypocrisy, he suggests:

> Let shipless Danes and whining Yankees dwell
> On naval rights, with Grotius and Vattel[1],
> While C–bb–t's pirate code alone appears
> Sound moral sense to England and Algiers!

He predicts that England's "victory will be defeat", her "triumph will be Europe's scorn". Does it not sound like a prophecy of the spiritual development leading right up to the atomic bomb, when Moore writes:

> In science too – how many a system, raised
> Like Neva's icy domes[2], awhile hath blazed
> With lights of fancy and with forms of pride,

---

[1] Hugo Groot, in 17th century Holland, and Emmanual de Vattel, in 18th century Switzerland, expounded the theory of the Droit des Gens. C - bb - t is of course William Cobbett whom Moore attacks in spite of his pro-Irish pamphlets early in the century. The reference to the "whining Yankees" should be studied in connection with Moore's attitude to the States in general. See especially his Epistle to Lord Viscount Forbes, from the city of Washington.

[2] The splendid ball, opening Fables for the Holy Alliance (see below) took place in "a beautiful Ice Palace upon the Neva's flood".

Then, melting, mingled with the oblivious tide!
Now Earth usurps the centre of the sky,
Now Newton puts the paltry planet by;
Now whims revive beneath Descartes' pen,
Which *now*, assailed by Locke's, expire again:
And when, perhaps, in pride of chemic powers,
We think the keys of Nature's kingdom ours,
Some Davy's magic touch the dream unsettles,
And turns at once our alkalis to metals!

Let us remember that it was right at the beginning of the glorious 19th century that these lines were written.

In 1818, Moore published his *Twopenny Post Bag,* the only one of his political pamphlets which has been more extensively dealt with by the biographers of Moore. The passage in the preface to the 14th edition in which the author "pleads guilty to the charge of being an Irishman and a Roman Catholic" has frequently been quoted. Moore ventures upon theological ground when he ridicules "those exclusive patentees of Christianity, so worthy to have been the followers of a certain enlightened Bishop Donatus who held 'that God is in Africa and not elsewhere'". I may mention that one of the finest political books published before the war on the Continent bore the title, *Dieu est-il Français?*

In his *Trifles* (1814) Moore settled down to what became one of the chief objects of his political writings, the castigation of Castlereagh. After his visit with Rogers to Paris, he wrote his largest political pamphlet, *The Fudge Family in Paris.* Philipp Fudge went to France "at the special desire of his friend and patron, my Lord C–stl–r–gh" to help with

The good orthodox work much wanting just now,
To expound to the world the new – thingummie – science
Found out by the –what's-its-name, – Holy Alliance
And prove to mankind that their rights are but folly,
Their freedom a joke (which it *is*, you know, Dolly),

Philipp's daughter Biddy writes to her friend in Ireland. In his first letter to Castlereagh, Fudge sen. tells us

That Poland, left for Russia's lunch
Upon the sideboard, snug reposes,
While Saxony's as pleased as Punch,
And Norway "on a bed of roses".

The Congress of Vienna had allotted the greater part of Poland as a separate kingdom to, but in personal Union with, Russia; under Tsar Alexander, she enjoyed peace and some prosperity, but in 1880 she would again rise out in open. rebellion. Even before the general carving up of Europe, Sweden had made a separate treaty with Denmark and obtained from her Norway (from the middle of the 19th century Norway struggled for independence, which she obtained in 1905). I personally was much interested in discovering Moore's sympathy with Saxony, my native country, half of whose territory was annexed in 1815 by Prussia. Moore was particularly incensed by Castlereagh's letter to Hardenberg, the Prussian Prime Minister

"Which bid the Saxon King go whistle"

by yielding to Prussia's exorbitant demands.

The most interesting passages of *The Fudge Family in Paris* are the letters by Phelim Connor, an Irish nationalist, who boldly describes the Holy Alliance as

> That royal, ravening flock, whose vampire wings
> O'er sleeping Europe treacherously brood,
> And fan her into dreams of promised good,
> Of hope, of freedom — but to drum her blood!
> If *thus* to hear thee branded be a bliss
> That vengeance loves, there's yet more sweet than this, —
> That 'twas an Irish head, an Irish heart,
> Made thee the fallen and tarnished thing thou art ...
> Who say this world of thinking souls was made
> To be by kings partitioned ...

The word "partition" occurs once more in the second letter of Phelim's when he accuses "these Holy Leaguers"

> Who, even while plundering, forge Religion's name
> To frank their spoil, and without fear or shame,
> Call down the Holy Trinity to bless Partition ...

This letter gives us a comprehensive picture of Moore's knowledge of current affairs in foreign politics. Referring to the leading part played by Tsar Alexander, Phelim Connor says that Europe

> Caught wisdom from a Cosack Emperor's mouth
> When monarchs, after years of spoil and crime,
> Met round the shrine of Peace ...

The "hope the lust of spoil had gone" was mistaken. "The game of Pillnitz" (Pillnitz near Dresden, where in 1791 the Ring of Prussia and the Emperor of Austria had concluded an alliance for the protection of 'all the princes of Europe' against the French Revolution) "has been played o'er so oft".

> Let Saxony, let injured Genoa tell,

two of the chief victims of the "new order".

Then Moore holds up to the world the ruling powers:

> Most faithful Russia–faithful to whoe 'er
> Could plunder best, and give him amplest share;
> Who, even when vanquished, sure to gain his ends,
> For want of *foes* to rob, made free with *friends*,
> And, deepening still by amiable gradations,
> When foes are stript of all, then fleeced relations![3]
> Most mild and saintly Prussia–steeped to the ears
> In persecuted Poland's blood and tears.

---

3   Notes in The Poetical Works of T.M. (Warne) say: "At the peace of Tilsit, where Russia abandoned his ally, Prussia, to France and received a portion of her territory" – "The seizure of Finland from his relative of Sweden."

And now, with all her harpy wings outspread
O'er severed Saxony's devoted head!
Pure Austria too–whose history nought repeats
But broken leagues and subsidised defeats ...
And thou, O England!–who ...
Art now *broke in*, and, thanks to C–gh,
In all that's worst and falsest lead'st the way!

Moore's early and spectacular success at the Prussian Court is most astonishing, when we consider the attack upon the person of the king made in *The Fudge Family in Paris*. In Paris, Biddy meets

A fine sallow, sublime, sort of Werter[4]-faced man
With mustachios that gave (what we read so oft)
The dear Corsair[5] expression, half savage, half soft,
As hyænas in love may be fancied to look, or
A something between Abelard and old Blucher![6]
(Oh, Moore!),

and she takes him for "no less than the great King of Prussia",

Pa says he's come here to look after his money
(Not taking things now as he used under Boney),
Which suits with our friend, for Bob saw him, he swore,
Looking sharp to the silver received at the door.[7]
Besides, too, they say that his grief for his Queen[8]
(Which was plain in this sweet fellow's face to be seen)
Requires such a stimulant dose as this car is,
Used three times a day with young ladies in Paris.
Biddy hopes that the newspaper will soon announce that
"Count Ruppin"[9] has taken Miss Biddy Fudge for a drive.

However, soon she discovers

He might be a king, Doll, though, hang him, he isn't
... a Brandenburg–(what is a Brandenburg, Dolly?)[10]

---

4   The name of Werther, the hero of Goethe's famous novel, was usually spelt "Werter" in English translations and imitations, such as frequently reprinted in late 18th century Dublin.

5   In 1814 Dalton gave Moore a description of the King's appearance in London.

6   In 1814 Byron had dedicated his Corsair to Moore.

7   The King of Prussia had inherited from his great-grandfather a miserly disposition.

8   Louisa, she had died in 1810.

9   The King travelled incognito under this name. Ruppin is a Castle near Berlin.

10   A brandenburg was a name for a shopman.

11   See Moore's Lines written on hearing that the Austrians had entered Naples. The last stanza reads:
    For if such are the braggarts that claim to be free
    Come, despot of Russia, thy feet let me kiss–
    Far nobler to live the brute bondman of the,
    Than to sully even chains by a struggle like this!
Paris, 1821.

Would be, after all, not such very great catch.

In 1828, when the publication of the drawings of the Berlin performance of *Lalla Rookh* announced to the world that Thomas Moore was something like the poet laureate of the Prussian Court, Moore published his *Fables for the Holy Alliance*. The Berlin fête might have been the source of inspiration for the dream with which this work opens, of

> a splendid ball,
> Given by the Emperor Alexander,
> To entertain with all due zeal,
> Those holy gentlemen who've shown a
> Regard so kind for Europe's weal,
> At Troppau, Laybach, and Verona.
> (The congresses I referred to above.)
> The Czar, half through a Polonaise,
> Could scarce get on for downright stumbling;
> And Prussia, though to slippery ways
> So used, was cursedly near tumbling.
> Yet still 'twas who could stamp the floor most,
> Russia and Austria 'mong the foremost,
> And now to an Italian air. ...

During the past five years, the Holy Alliance had gained in volume but lost in weight.

> Proud Prussia's double bird of prey,
> (the double eagle in her arms, was now)
> Tame as a spatch-cock, slunk away;
> While–just like France herself, when she
> Proclaims how great her naval skill is–
> Poor (Louis's) drowning fleurs-de lys
> Imagined themselves water-lilies ...
> The great Legitimates themselves
> Seemed in a state of dissolution.
> The indignant Czar–when just about
> To issue a sublime Ukase–
> "Whereas, all light must be kept out"–
> Dissolved to nothing in its blaze.
> Next Prussia took his turn to melt,
> And, while his lips illustrious felt,
> The influence of this southern air,
> Some word like "Constitution", long
> Congealed in frosty silence there,
> Came slowly thawing from his tongue.

The news of the Revolutions in Italy gave new strength to the Liberals in the Reich. It was generally realised that many "kings have been by mob-elections raised to the throne". Moore saw the torch of liberty raised in Naples (where Austria had quenched the democratic movement), Spain (where France was just about to do the same), South America (where Bolivar had succeeded in throwing off the Spanish yoke) and above all – in Greece, not in vain *The Fables* were dedicated to Lord Byron. Finally, from Poland, "where Alexander puts every fire of freedom out", Moore's thoughts turn to Ireland where "we see churchmen, who if asked

'Must Ireland's slaves be tithed and tasked,
And driven, like negroes or Croats,
That you may roll in wealth and bliss?'

answer: 'Yes!' "

Is it possible that Moore's name should be forgotten in a history of democracy in Ireland? Whatever Moore said against the Holy Alliance served in the last end the purpose

> to tell the proud and fair
> Amidst their mirth that slavery had been there
> On all I love,–home, parents, friends–I trace
> The mournful mark of bondage and disgrace.
>
> (*The Fudge Family in Paris*, v.)

(Quelle: Irish Monthly, July 1946, S. 282-294)

Jean Paul and Ireland

The only work of Jean Paul's embodied in Mangan's *Anthologia Germanica* (the centenary of which occurred in June 1945) is 'The New Year's Night of a Miserable Man'.[1] When first publishing this 'admirable versification',[2] Mangan wrote:

> Many of the German prose moralists disfigured their essays or etchings by exuberance of embroidery and decoration. We should, last of any, be disposed to utter a disrespectful syllable against Richter, but that he has now and then squandered the wealth of his mind on fantastic fripperies, none will doubt.[3]

O'Donoghue rightly remarks on this passage:

> It is to be feared that the offence which Mangan alleges against Richter of 'spending the wealth of his mind on fantastic fripperies', though unjustified, may be charged with equal truth to himself.[4]

The only other Irish author who, to my knowledge, has written on Jean Paul, Lady Speranza Wilde, the mother of Oscar Wilde,[5] made the same point, though giving it a more favourable interpretation:

> In his early youth were laid the foundations of that truly wonderful varied extent of knowledge, that unlimited power of illustration from all sciences, all literatures, which is such a distinguished peculiarity of his writings.[6]

For the foreign reader, Jean Paul's continuous digressions, his far-fetched similes and impertinent anecdotes must be one of the most puzzling features in his writings,[7] even

---

1   1, 194: also in Mangan's Poems (Dublin, 1886), p. 132.

2   O'Donoghue, Mangan (1897), p. 81.

3   Dublin University Magazine (1835), V, 400.

4   Loc. cit.

5   On Speranza see Wilson, Victorian Doctor (London, 1942), Appendix.

6   Notes on Men, Women and Books (London, 1891), p. 2.

7   Gervinus, Geschichte der deutschen Dichtung (1874), V, 280 f.; Kurz, Geschichte der deutschen Literatur (1876), III, 573.

when it is realized that in this respect more than in any other Jean Paul imitated the work of a great Anglo-Irish writer, Sterne's *Tristram Shandy*. Even less romantic natures than Lady Speranza's, however, may get some amusement out of Jean Paul's digressions when they regard them as a source of our information on the knowledge which Jean Paul and his contemporaries had on all conceivable subjects.[8]

Examining the 1840 edition of Richter's works preserved in University College, Dublin, I noticed that the only passage relating to Ireland which Miss Maud Joint, tbe great Celtist (who formerly owned that edition), had marked was that in *Flegeljahre*, § 22, where Jean Paul speaks of the custom of servants in Ireland to sweep the stairs of their masters' houses with their wigs. This is a characteristic example of the kind of knowledge of Ireland still prevailing on the Continent during the early nineteenth century, and just this type of information on Ireland must have been particularly attractive for Jean Paul, as it lent itself to merely decorative or illustrative purposes.

To anticipate the result of the survey which I intend to give in this paper of the references made in Jean Paul's works[9] to Ireland, his Irish associations seem to me of greater interest than the references made to Ireland in contemporary travel books or even in the few German books on Ireland published up to his time;[10] the latter show what individual students of Ireland knew, and what their readers could have known, if they had been really interested in Ireland as such.[11] Jean Paul, however, who had no personal relations with, and not even any special interest in Ireland, shows us what an educated man of his time actually knew. The scrappiness of his knowledge shows clearly enough that it was merely incidental. Yet, he marks exactly the point where the legend of Ireland, handed down on the Continent from the late Middle Ages, was superseded by the more serious and scholarly interest in modern Ireland; the growth of this interest was one of the most important factors in the history not only of Celtology but also of political and cultural relations between Ireland and the Continent.

Jean Paul's associations touch a great variety of spheres of Irish life past and present, and it is against this broader background that his literary relations with Ireland should be newly and fully appreciated. The study of the relations between German and English, including Anglo-Irish, literature has hitherto been confined to the study of the mutual appreciation and interdependence of individual writers. So far, none of the numerous books and theses devoted to this subject has proceeded to investigation into the mutual knowledge of historical, social, economic or physical conditions underlying those literary relations.

---

8   J. F. Coar, Studies in German Literature (New York, 1903), p. 5.

9   Of the works quoted in this article, only Hesperus and Levana have so far been translated into English. As E. Berend's critical edition of Richter's works (Berlin, 1927 ff.) is not available to me, I quote from the 1840 edition.

10   Namely, Volkmann's Schottland und Irland (1784) and Küttner's Briefe über Irland (1785).

11   Only the two last pages of Prof. Kelly's study England and the Englishmen in German Literature of the Eighteenth Century (New York, 1921) relate to Ireland.

Miss Philippovic, for example, has collected the references made by Jean Paul and other German writers to Swift, but she has not tried to find out whether the reading of Swift's works conveyed to Germany a knowledge of conditions in Ireland or to what extent Swift's associations with Ireland were realized.[12] Jean Paul has almost a hundred references to Swift; he wrote whole essays on his qualities as a humorist. Once only he calls him 'Dechant Swift' (XIII, 101); that Swift was Dean of St Patrick's Dublin was a fact generally known in eighteenth- and nineteenth-century Continental literature.[13] The only passage where Jean Paul espressly refers to Swift as Irish, and, in fact, to Anglo-Irish literature in general, is his *Untersuchung des Lächerlichen*, § 23 of the *Vorschule der Aesthetik*:

> Ernste Nationen hatten den höheren und innigeren Sinn für das Komische; ... Britten... Spanier... Führt man diese historischen Zufälligkeiten ohne Anmaßung eines scharfen Entscheidens an: so kann man vielleicht fortfahren und sogar dazu setzen, daß das trübe Ireland (sic) meisterhafte Komiker – die mithin eine große Zahl anderer, wenn auch nur geselliger voraussetzt – gezeugt, von welchen nach Swift und Sterne noch der Graf Hamilton zu nennen, welcher, wie der berühmte Pariser Carlin, so still und ernst im Leben gewesen.[14]

The study of the interrelation between climate (and other physical conditions) and intellectual life is a very modern line of study. J. Nadler's *Literaturgeschichte der deutschen Stämme*,[15] perhaps the most advanced work in that respect, gives a fine picture of the influence exercised on Jean Paul's writings by the climate and scenery of central Germany, a district which he practically never left.[16]

With regard to Ireland, a similar study would make contributions to the answering of such interesting and topical questions as what conditions brought about the remarkably quick assimilation to Ireland of the various waves of invaders and settlers, a process doubtless influenced by the land rather than the people. (It is an idea generally accepted that it is due to the different climate that Irishmen abroad are more active than they used to be at home.) And what is an Irish writer?[17] Only the Gaelic-speaking offspring of a Milesian family, or also Swift, Dublin-born of English parents, cursing his exile in Ireland and yet taking up the fight for the rights of his country; or Sterne, Irish-born[18] of an Irish Catholic mother, little interested in his country, and still – as

---

12   See my article, 'Voltaire and Ireland', The Dublin Magazine (January-March 1944), pp. 35 f.

13   See Teerink's Swift Bibliography (The Hague, 1937).

14   Anthony Hamilton, the French classic, was a native of Roscrea, Co. Tipperary (see Dict. Nat. Biog. (1908), VIII, 1019); portrait in Read's Cabinet of Irish Literature, I, 94. On Carlin, the French comedian, see Bibliographie Universelle (1813), VII, 152.

15   Regensburg, 1923 ff., III, 372.

16   As one of the most important facts of Richter's life, Lady Speranza states: 'He never beheld the sea or the mountains' (op. cit. p. 2).

17   See Selections from A Dictionary of Irish Writers, edited by Joseph Hone for the Irsih Academy of Letters (Dublin, 1944). The present writer has the honour of being among its contributors (ibid. pp. 16 f.)

18   Küttner (op. cit. p. 105) visited Clonmel, 'a town which has nothing curious but that it is Sterne's birthplace'.

Goethe noticed – showing the sense of humour characteristic of the Irish?[19] Has Celtic twilight something to do with the haze and mist, which, according to Continental observers,[20] is the outstanding characteristic of Irish climate?

Stories of ghosts, strange crimes and passions, weird fires and feelings, a sombre melancholy, that is what we should expect of *das trübe Irland.* Of Irish ghost stories, Jean Paul seems to have been well aware. Treating of 'organic magnetism', in a note to his *Museum* he quoted from John Aubrey's *De Miscellaneis*[21]

> die merkwürdige Angabe, daß der Irländer in der Stunde, wo er das doppelte Gesicht (*second sight*) der nächsten Zukunft hat, diese prophetische Kraft dem mittheilen könne, auf dessen Fuß er im Schauen trete (XXVII, 22).

Aubrey actually got his information from the Gaelic-speaking parts of Scotland. That Jean Paul speaks of *der Irländer* is probably due to Aubrey's later remark:

'They generally term this second-sight in Irish Taishitaraughk and such as have it Taishatrin from Taish, which is a shadowy substance'.[22] This confusion may have already arisen in the *Monatliche Unterhaltungen vom Reich der Geister*, from which Jean Paul gathered this quotation.

Yet, according to Richter, the Irish climate is to be thanked in the first instance for the masterpieces of humoristic literature produced by writers whose Irish birth may be regarded as merely accidental.[23]

The story of his relations with Sterne is a field still wider than that of his relations with Swift.[24] While Sterne's influence on eighteenth- and nineteenth-century Continental literature has been studied very much indeed, it has, so far as I am aware, never been ascertained whether this influence increased Continental knowledge of Ireland.[25]

Jean Paul says that Irish productiveness in masters of literary humour indicates that sense of humour is a general characteristic of the people among whom those writers lived. He makes it clear that this is a mere suggestion. The things which Continental people do not know of Ireland are perhaps even more interesting than the few things

---

19 See my article on Goethe in The Dublin Magazine (January 1943), p. 48.

20 Küttner, op. cit. pp. 23 ff. Goethe based some of his meteorological research on the fact that Ireland was the country with the highest rainfall in Europe. See my article quoted above, note 18, p. 46.

21 1695. In the London edition of 1784 this passage is found on p. 253. In his own additions to Th. Crofton Croker's notes to Fairy Legends and Traditions of the South of Ireland (London, 1825), in the translation of that work published Leipzig (1826) under the title Irische Elfenmärchen, Wilhelm Grimm quotes p. 216 Aubrey's Miscellen. The article on Aubrey in Jöcher's Gelehrten-Lexicon, I, (1750) states that in 1660, on his way back from 'Irrland', Aubrey was shipwrecked. Incidentally, this article seems to be one of those originally compiled by Jöcher.

22 1784 edition, p. 271.

23 See n. 19 above.

24 See L. M. Price's survey of Jean Paul's relations with Sterne in German-English Literary Relations (Berkeley, 1919) pp. 328 ff. and 476.

25 See n. 18 above.

which they do know. The correctness of Jean Paul's suggestion shows that his 'poly-mathy' was not quite as sterile as has been sometimes alleged.[26]

In the passage which I quoted from the *Vorschule,* the name of Ireland is given in its English form, perhaps an indication of an English source from which Jean Paul quoted. The earliest mention of the German word *Irland* in his works is found in the *Grönländische Prozesse,* the first of his works to show Sterne's influence. He says there (IX, 93) that 'nach Bleskenius[27] kann ein See in Irland das gemeine Holz, das seinen Boden berührt, in Eisen umschaffen'. This story clearly belongs to the Continental tradition of Irish legends. It is related with the story of the generation of barnacle geese from rotting ships in the Irish Sea,[28] and with the reference made in Grimmelshausen's *Simplicissimus* (1669, VI, 14) to 'die zween Brünnen in Irrland,[29] darin das eine Wasser wan es getrunken wird, alt und grau, das andere aber hübsch jung macht'. All these legends relate to water. It is a well-established fact that some of the early Irish missionaries to the Continent were regarded as Saints merely because they had come across the sea from the outskirts of the world, and they were frequently associated with wells.[30] That Ireland is an island is one of the few facts which every Continental school-child knows of that country.

The transition from this purely legendary knowledge of Ireland to a more serious study of modern conditions in that country is marked by another early passage, found in Jean Paul's *Jubelsenior* (X, 147):

Ich finde in Troil's Reisebeschreibung,[31] daß sonst die alten Barden in Irland ganze Strecken Landes geschenkt bekommen haben und daß im 6ten Jahrhundert ein Drittel des irländischen Volkes aus Barden bestand. In den neuen Reiseberichten treffen wir, (hoff' ich), im nämlichen Ir-land dieselbe Anzahl Strassen-Barden an.

As in his reference to Irish humour, Jean Paul in this passage also draws a conclusion from what he is told. Whether his hope was fulfilled or not, I do not venture to decide. The extraordinary number of outstanding street singers, not only in Dublin, but also in the country, for instance at the Galway Races, was noticed by Count Pückler, and still earlier by Küttner. Even in this respect, however, Ireland still is, for Jean Paul at least, a fabulous wonderland.

26 See n. 7 above.

27 Bleskenius? Was Jean Paul's source not rather P. L. Berkenmeyer's Curioser Antiquarius (Hamburg 1720) which attributes this miraculous quality to a lake called Niach near Armagh (Lough Neagh)? See Macallister in Journal of the Royal Soc. of Antiquar. of Ireland, XXXVI (1906), 397, also Kelly, op. cit. p. 142.

28 Lynn Thorndike, History of Magic and Experimental Science (1941), VI, 279 and 288. See my review in The Irish Booklover (1944), XXIX, 21f.

29 See my article, 'Simplicissimus's British Relations', in Mod. Lang. Rev. (1945), XI, 37.

30 See my article, 'Irish Saints in the tradition of Central Europe', Irish Ecclesiastical Record, vth series, LXII, 182 ff.

31 The most important referene made to Irish literature in the Letters on Iceland by Uno von Troil, a high dignitary of the Swedish Church, is found in the Dublin 1780 edition, p. 21 f.

This wonderland and her people show other, less attractive, aspects. Lady Wilde was one of the few writers in English to point to Jean Paul's *Hesperus* as an interesting example of the tradition of the cultural influence exercised by English nobility on the Continent.[32] Prince Januar, a German autocrat, is educated by an English lord in exactly the same sense as is the prince in Schiller's *Kabale und Liebe* by Lady Milford. During his love affairs with Lord Horion's niece, the prince contracts a nervous fever. At the point of death he makes, at the suggestion of his confessor, a vow of continence. No sooner has he recovered from his illness than he realizes how rash this vow was (V, 52):

> Ein geschickter Exjesuit aus Irland, der blos für Gewissenszweifel lebte und selber conscientiam dubiam hatte, sprang dem Zweifler bei und machte ihm faßlich ..., daß er ohne Einwilligung seiner Gemahlin weder geloben dürfte, noch einwilligen könnte.

This acute suggestion facilitates Januar in resuming his adulterous life. What made Jean Paul assume that this ex-Jesuit came from Ireland? Why not from Italy or Spain, where German writers otherwise procure their ubiquitous, sinister Jesuits? Was it just the quaintness and indecency of the argument? The history of Irish monasticism on the Continent as well as the history of the Catholic Church in America offers us many examples of queer Irish characters, causing trouble to the authorities. The Irishman spiritually lapsed and professionally shipwrecked, oftentimes an ex-cleric or an ex-pupil of the Jesuits, has become almost a standard figure in the history of world literature. The story of the generation of barnacle geese was not the only contribution made by queer Irish clerics to the Irish legend on the Continent,[33] nor was the smart advice given to George Primrose by 'the Irish student returning from Louvain'[34] the only mischief done by such odd characters.

The lives of Goldsmith, Sterne, Thomas Parnell and Swift (the latter for example, reflected in Goethe's *Stella*) illustrate the fact that this trend of Irish tradition extended also to the Reformed churches. It is hardly incidental that 'das irländische Wappen, nämlich ein Kleeblatt' is referred to as a symbol of family life in the address delivered at his *Selbertrauung* by the *schottischer Pfarrer Scander-y mit Miß Sucky-z* (XXX, 195), one of the most entertaining pieces of Jean Paul's humour. Such self-weddings wore not unknown in Ireland. The last case of a clandestine wedding in the United Kingdom (discussed by the Lords in 1861) was concerned with the Rev. Samuel Beamish, a Church of Ireland minister, who married in 1831 one Isabelle Frazer at Cork, not only performing the marriage ceremony himself but even bestowing upon himself and his bride the nuptial blessing.

Regarding the rather suggestive reference to the symbolism of the shamrock leaf as well as the spiritual advice given by the Irish ex-Jesuit, it may be mentioned that Jean Paul revered Swift as the pioneer of what Carlyle in his essay on Jean Paul called the fight 'against the French principle of literary jurisprudence', especially, however, the

---

32   Op. cit. p. 9. Mérimée's Colomba shows us an Irish lord on the Continent. See also Kelly, op. cit. p. 123.

33   See, for example, J. Brodrick, S.J., The Origin of the Jesuits (London, 1940), pp. 110 f. and L. Gougaud, O.S.B., Les Saints irlandais hors d'Irlande (Oxford, 1939), Appendix.

34   Goldsmith's Vicar of Wakefield, chap. XX.

ideal of 'decency' established by those whom Carlyle described as 'the Literary Gentlemen' rather than 'Men of Letters'. Richter regarded Swift as the initiator of the literary movement aiming at a more sincere self-exposure of man, a movement which in our days James Joyce has led to its climax.

Jean Paul quotes a more definitely historic example of a queer Irish Protestant clergyman abroad. In one of his literary essays he records that

> ein irländischer Pfarrer, namens Eccles, sich dadurch für den Verfasser von Mackenzie's *Mann von Gefühl* auszugeben gedachte, daß er von dem Buch eine Kopie genommen und sie mit Einschiebseln und Rasuren versehen, um sie als Manuskript zu produzieren (XIV, 232 f.).

This is one of the numerous instances where Jean Paul quotes from Boswell's *Life of Johnson*. What he calls 'ein irländischer Pfarrer', was, according to that work, 'a young Irish clergyman', who died in 1777.[35]

Unlike more superficial, if perhaps more directly informed, writers on modern Ireland, Jean Paul did not draw lighthearted conclusions from those quaint specimens of the Irish people, though the one reference made in his works to the character of the Irish nation as a whole is not too favourable either.

'Der Deutsche', he says in one of his early political essays (1805, XXIII, 244), 'ist redlicher als jede Nation, nur er darf die Phrase "deutsch handeln" für "gerade handeln" nehmen. Italienisch, französisch, englisch, irländisch handeln bedeutet bei den Völkern selbst etwas anderes.'

On what authority did Jean Paul place the Irish on one level with the Italians, French and English whose 'perfidy' is generally assumed by the average German?[36] That the Irish are mentioned in this instance besides the three leading nations of Europe is certainly remarkable, especially when we consider the subsequent words: '... und zugleich ist er (der Deutsche) als Volk von Natur unpoetischer als jedes'.

We may conjecture how far Jean Paul attributed the lack of straightness in the national character to the vicissitudes of Irish history. In *Levana,* his great educational work, he says:

> Es gibt eine höhere Tapferkeit ... die Tapferkeit des Friedens, der Mut zu Haus. Manches Volk [ist] im Vaterlande ein feigduldender Knecht, außer demselben ein kühnfassender Held (§ 102, XXII, 297).

---

35   Hill's edition (Oxford, 1887, I, 360); in Shorter's edition (London, 1924, I, 235), Hill's note has been shortened. This Mr Eccles seems to have been one of the two sons of the Rev. Robert Eccles, of Co. Fermanagh, who were in Trinity College, Dublin. For Mackenzie's relations with German literature see Cooke, Mod. Lang. Rev. (1916), XI, 156f., and Willoughby, ibid. (1921), XVI, 237. Has it ever been noticed that in the introduction to The Man of Feeling the 'editor of Harley's Memoirs' says that while the curate used that manuscript for wadding, he 'had actually in his pocket ... an edition of one of the German Illustrissimi for the same purpose', the earliest reference to Mackenzie's reading of German classics? L. M. Price (see p. 192, n. 8) makes no reference to Mackenzie's influence in Germany.

36   'Nein, ein Deutscher soll nicht lügen/Soll ein Fremder das nicht rügen', lines three times repeated in Goethe's Singspiel, Die ungleichen Hausgenossen.

Comparing this passage with the beginning of Schenk's introduction to Küttner's *Letters on Ireland*,[37] we may assume that Jean Paul refers to the opinion at that time prevailing on modern Ireland:

> Ein Volk, das seit unserem Gedenken in einer sklavischen Abhängigkeit lebt und mit einer sklavischen Feigheit sein Joch zu tragen scheint, ist für uns kein Volk, an dessen Schicksal wir besonderen Anteil nehmen könnten (pp. v f.).

Both Schenk and Richter were well aware of the injustice of this idea, which, as Schenk (and, at the same time, O'Halloran) suggested, was deliberately spread by the English. Applying the idea of magnetism to the political sphere, Jean Paul says later in the same paragraph of *Levana*: 'Der weite Raum löst die britische Freiheit schon in Irland unglaublich auf wie sonst nur in Nordamerika.' What he means is that the British idea of freedom, so much admired on the Continent throughout the eighteenth and early nineteenth centuries, had undergone certain 'modifications' through its application to large spaces:

'Auf dem Meere, in den Kolonien', Jean Paul continues, 'ist sie [die Freiheit] durch die Entfernung bis zu einem Grade weggedünstet, daß nur noch das scharfe Auge eines Kapitäns oder Nabobs sie von gänzlicher Knechtschaft unterscheiden kann.'

Ten years later, in his *Politisches Allerlei*, Jean Paul complains of the general adaptation of this idea of 'freedom' throughout Metternich's Europe. The only partner in this system of oppression who can at least claim to live up to a certain dignified tradition is England, of whom is well known 'der alte Ruhm, mit dem es sein Irland und Ostindien regiert' (XXXII, 169). In a later passage of that essay, Jean Paul says:

> Ein gährendes[38] Volk würde auf einem politisch unzugänglichen Eiland[39] seine kämpfenden Kräfte bald durch die moralischen Schwer- und Anziehpunkte zu einer harmonischen Welt abgerundet sehen.

Continuing: 'Man wende hier nicht England ein', he makes it clear that he does not suggest that the English of his age were a 'fermenting nation'. In fact, he subsequently compares English pseudo-harmony to ale, which 'never bursts its container'. In Ireland, on the other hand, he suggests, the process of national fermentation is always accompanied by the development (as in Continental beer) of an exuberant amount of short-lived froth. While thus anticipating, in this last reference made in his works to Ireland, the doubts regarding the political future of Ireland, which Küttner had expressed with regard to pre-Union Ireland,[40] and which Goethe expressed in reference to Daniel O'Connell,[41] Jean Paul has freed himself from the traditional lore of Ireland and attained to a serious consideration of Ireland's place in the modern world.

(Quelle: MLR 40, 1945, S. 190-196)

---

37   See n. 18 above.

38   'Sie wissen, daß seit ein Paar Jahren hier alles in Gährung ist'; Küttner, op. cit. p. 51 (writing from Dublin).

39   'Eiland', an old-fashioned word, not only suggesting relationship with English 'island', but also implying a certain affectionate note, therefore invariably occuring with regard to Ireland in the more sentimental type of German writings on that country.

40   Op. cit. p. 112.

41   Werke, Sophie-edition, XLII, 1, 58.

The Brothers Grimm and T.C. Crocker

The five biographical articles which have so far appeared on Thomas Crofton Croker[1] are unanimous in regarding it as a conspicuous sign of the immediate success of his collection of *Fairy Legends and Traditions of the South of Ireland* (London, 1825) that within the year they were translated by the brothers Grimm. The relations between Croker and the Grimms, however, have never been studied in detail. I have reason to assume that none of those who wrote on Croker ever saw a copy of the original of the Grimms' translation. In his address at the Annual Meeting of the Philological Society, Oxford, 1915, W. P. Ker did not even mention *Irische Elfenmärchen*.[2] The only one who made a real contribution to the study of Croker's relations with the Grimms was T. F. Dillon Croker who in the second edition of his Memoir of his father, prefacing Wright's edition of *Fairy Legends* (1862), published the letter which Wilhelm Grimm wrote on 29 July 1826 in reply to Croker's letter of 16 June 1826.

The *Fairy Legends* were reviewed in the first issue of 1826 of the *Göttingische Gelehrte Anzeigen* (I, 6, 12 January 1826). This anonymous review was by Wilhelm Grimm, in whose *Kleinere Schriften* (II, Berlin, 1882) it was reprinted. Wilhelm Grimm gives great praise to the external appearance of Croker's collection; Brooke's illustrations reminded him of Cruikschank's (sic). (A few years before, Cruikshank had illustrated Taylor's edition of the *Kinder- und Hausmärchen*.[3] After comparing the Irish fairy legends to the *Arabian Nights*, Grimm continues:

---

1   Apart from the literature on which the article on Croker in D.N.B. v (1908), 133 is based, also Read's Cabinet of Irish Literature, III, 137 ff. and Dr. McCarthy in Studies, XXXVI (1943), 539 ff.

2   Croker's translation of the Grimms' Einleitung and Notes should have been entered into Mr. Bayard Morgan's Bibliography of German Literature in English Translations (Stanf. 1928). In 1913 a reprint of Irische Elfenmärchen with the Grimms' Einleitung was edited by Johannes Rutz and published by R. Piper and Co., München. Rutz says that in his family Irische Elfenmärchen had been read for three generation past. Rutz gives a short survey of the racial, geographical, spiritual and historical background of the fairy-tales, an interesting contribution to German Irlandkunde before it received its new political impulse. Croker's Forschungen (see below, p. 46) are described as 'eine Reisebeschreibung reich an geschichtlichem Wissen und voll Humors'. Of the Fairy Legends, Rutz says that Croker was 'zu deren Herausgabe durch die Grimm'schen Märchen angeregt worden' (see following note): 'Sie erschienen anonym, denn der Verfasser hatte das Manuskript verloren, und Freunde, denen die Märchen bekannt werden, hatten ihm bei der zweiten Aufzeichnung geholfen.' The Grimms' notes were shortened. References to the edition of Moore's Irische Melodien in Reclam's Universalbibliothek and to Kohl's Reisen in Irland (1843) (see below, p. 51, n. 5) were added. My friend Dr. Joseph Grabisch informs me that still another reprint of the Grimms' Irische Elfenmärchen appeared before the European War, published by Diederichs in Jena.

3   Morgan, op. cit. no. 3133. Taylor concluded the second volume of this translation with a note congratulating 'those who have a taste for these subjects (compare 'Wer noch Sinn hat für schuldlose und einfache Poesie...' in the Vorrede to Irische Elfenmärchen) on the publication of Fairy Legends and Traditions of the South of Ireland. It may be referred to throughout, for the curious illustrations which it affords of mutual affinities between the traditionary tales of widely

Irländer[4] werden die dargestellten Scenen, einzelne Züge, sprichwörtliche Redensarten, dem Volke zugehörige Scherze und Gleichnisse, unübersetzbare Bulls schneller und mit besondern Vergnügen wiedererkennen, doch auch Fremde pflegen dergleichen zu fühlen und zu schätzen... Dem Irländer ist eine gewisse Beschränkung des Verstandes, aber innerhalb dieser Grenzen viel List und Gewandtheit angeboren: er ist nicht offenherzig, aber seine Verstellung ohne Bosheit.

This passage shows clearly that, even before reading the *Fairy Legends*, Wilhelm Grimm had possessed a definite idea of Ireland and of the Irish; the attention which he and his brother devoted at once to Croker's collection seems to be expressive of the spontaneous general interest in Ireland of which at that time Goethe especially gave so many proofs.

Grimm accepted Croker's claim that his collection consisted of 'Elfensagen wie sie in Irland bis zur Stunde gehört werden':

Dieser Aberglaube erweitert bald die Seele des Irländers und treibt ihn zu guten Handlungen. ... bald beschränkt und umklammert er ihm mit Angst... Der ungenannte Verfasser[5] [the reprint in the *Kleinere Schriften* adds in brackets: T. Crofton Croker] hat die Überlieferungen an Ort und Stelle mit sichtbarer Treue erfaßt und auf die Darstellung nicht gewöhnliche Sorgfalt verwandt.

After giving a synopsis of the five parts of Croker's collection the review concludes with a demand that the Irish fairy legends be compared with 'Shackespeares Elfenwelt' and the traditions of 'den einsamsten Gegenden anderer entfernter Länder'.[6]

In the preface to the first volume of the second edition of *Fairy Legends* (1826), Croker writes: 'It is flattering to find that these legends have been translated into German by the Messrs Grimm ... I have not yet seen a copy of the Mährchen und Sagen aus Süd-Irland.' A note in Wright's edition (1862, p. xxv) says: '*Mährchen und Sagen aus Süd-Irland. Aus dem Englischen übersetzt und mit Anmerkungen bereichert von den Brüdern Grimm. Leipzig* 1825'.' The title-page of the Grimms' work actually reads: 'Irische / Elfenmärchen. / Übersetzt / von / den Brüdern Grimm. / Leipzig. /

---

separated nations, and it will, it is trusted, give rise to similar endeavours to preserve, while it can yet be done, the popular stories of other parts of the British Empire.' See below, p. 51, n. 2.

On Cruikshank's illustration of the Grimm's Märchen, see D.N.B., v, 253 and 258, and Briefe der Brüder Grimm, ed. A. Leitzmann (Jena, 1923), p. 285.

4   In the Deutsche Grammatik, II (1822), 1005, it had been pointed out that 'man sagt ... irisch ... nicht irländisch ... obgleich ... irland, weil jene adj. aus den alten volksnamen ... iren selbst gezogen sind'. Nevertheless, the Elfenmärchen, from the Vorrede on, speak of 'Irländer'. In his note on Irische Märchen (1856, see below, p. 51), Wilhelm Grimm uses 'Irländer' und 'Iren'.

5   Croker never told the Grimms expressly that he was not 'der Verfasser'. (Cf. in the preface to the second volume: 'my former volume' (see below).) But in the dedicatory letter to Grimm (in vol. III) he says that the Grimm's translation gave satisfaction to 'the writers'. One of the co-collectors of the Fairy Legends was Th. Keightley, who published in 1828 a Fairy Mythology, which even in its external appearance was a sequel to Fairy Legends (Read, op. cit. p. 236). While Keightley quotes in that work the Grimm's edition of Brixener Volksbuch and their Deutsche Sagen, Jacob Grimm 'is said to have praised' Keightley's Mythology (Mac-Carthy, p. 547, repeats this statement (D.N.B.), omitting the words 'is said', but had no additional authority for this).

6   See above, p. 44, n.3.

Friedrich Fleischer. / 1826.' I failed to trace an earlier edition with the title mentioned by Croker[7] and Wright. No copy of any of the Grimms' works was among the books from Croker's library sold after his death (in 1854) by Messrs Puttick and Simpson, London.

In the preface to the second volume, 1828, containing more 'Irish fairy tales', Croker wrote:

> I cannot but feel and express a considerable degree of satisfaction at observing my former volume translated into German by such eminent scholars as the Brothers Grimm, whose friendship and valuable correspondence it has also procured me. Their version, which I had not seen when the second edition appeared, is, as might be expected, faithful and spirited; and to it they have prefixed a most learned and valuable introduction respecting fairy superstitions in general.

(There follows a quotation of twelve lines corresponding to the words 'Wer noch Sinn hat ... Beispiele abgibt', p. iv f. including the Grimms' reference to the country 'an das wir gewöhnlich nur in wenigen und gerade nicht erfreulichen Beziehungen erinnert werden'[8] but which is inhabited 'von einem Volk, dessen Alterthum und frühe Bildung die Geschichte bezeugt und das, wie es zum Theil noch in der eigenen Sprache redet, auch lebendige Spuren seiner Vorzeit wird aufzuweisen haben' – the Magna Charta of modern Irish folklore studies.)

In the Memoir of his father T.F. Dillon Croker said that the Grimm's translation of *Fairy Legends*, vol. I, '*led* to an intimate correspondence between the author (!) and the two eminent German philologists, which *commenced* on their part with a flattering letter from Wilhelm dated 29 July 1826'. This letter was actually an acknowledgement of Croker's letter of 16 June which the Grimms had received through their publisher and in which Croker revealed his identity and bestowed his approbation on the Grimms' translation. It appears that the Grimms did not endeavour to communicate with Croker before publishing their translation. There was, of course, no question of royalties. It is unlikely that the Grimms submitted to Croker (or – as they say in the *Vorrede* that they do not know his name – rather to his publisher) anything but the final edition of *Irische Elfenmärchen* (the title of which was fixed, as we shall see, before the middle of January 1826 and which appeared in February). It is therefore hard to say where the title *Mährchen und Sagen*, quoted by Croker (before he saw a copy) and more extensively by Wright, came from. Wilhelm Grimm wrote to Croker apparently in English; his letter has never been published elsewhere than in T.F. Dillon's Memoir.

In his letter, Wilhelm Grimm tells Croker that the translation of *Fairy Legends* 'occupied us for several months last summer'. As early as 20 April 1825 Jacob Grimm

---

7   Croker's son, in the Memoir of his father, says that the Grimm's translation appeared in 1825.

8   What are these 'gerade nicht erfreulichen Beziehungen'? The unpleasant representatives of the decaying Irish monasticism in fifteenth-century Germany, as referred to in the article 'Schotten' in the Deutsches Wörterbuch, or the participation of German troops in the suppression of the rising of 1798, which for the following hundred years made Germany so unpopular with the Catholic Irish (most of those troops were soldiers pressed from Hesse, of which Kassel was the capital)? In his Irland (Leipzig, 1844, II, 210), Venedy refers to this antipathy.

had written to Lachmann: 'Nebenbei übersetzen wir jetzt[9] *Irish fairytales*, London, 1824,[10] mit Anmerkungen; es sind hübsche und echte volkssagen meist von zwergen und hausgeistern, oft in wunderlicher übereinstimmung mit deutschen märchen'.[11] The additions made by the Grimms in *Irische Elfenmärchen* to Croker's notes – these additions were marked by an asterisk and a translation of them appeared in the Appendix of Croker's *Fairy Legends*, vol. III (1828), p. 295 ff. – are mainly concerned with parallels found in the *Hausmärchen*.

Even before receiving Croker's letter, the Grimms had

> guessed your name from the Researches in the South of Ireland,[12] which a few weeks before reached our Library, as the quotations in the Fairy Legends, pp. 24 and 36[13] authorized us in supposing a connection before the two works … It happened fortunately that a countryman of yours, Mr. Cooper (if I understand his name rightly),[14] who in his travels has been at Cassell,[15] being a friend and acquaintance of yours, was able to give us a more exact account of your literary employments.[16]

---

9 Albert Duncker, Die Brüder Grimm (Kassel, 1884), p. 45, says that the Grimms undertook this translation as a recreation from the drudgery of copying the whole catalogue of the Library of Kassel, a task to which the Duke had set them.

10 Title and date are obviously quoted from memory; still it is remarkable that while Croker dates the Grimms' translation 1825, Jacob Grimm also dates the Fairy Legends one year back.

11 Briefwechsel der Brüder Grimm mit Karl Lachmann, ed. A. Leitzmann (Jena, 1927). Without making a paragraph, Grimm goes on to ask Lachmann for his opinion about the passage from Petronius quoted Elfenmärchen, p. lxxv; Lachmann forgot to answer that query.

12 London, 1824. Tieck owned a copy of this work (Edwin Zeydel, Tieck in England (Princeton, 1931), p. 246).

13 Both passages referring to Lusmore.

14 Is this Edw. Joshua Cooper, the great astronomer, born in Dublin 1798, who travelled in Germany at that time (D.N.B.)?

15 Wilhelm Grimm dated his letter from Kassel in Hesse. Cassell is, doubtless, an Anglicism of the transcriber.

16 The article on Croker in the Dublin University Magazine, xxxiv (1849), for which Croker himself supplied the material, quotes, p. 205, from Souvenirs of a Summer in Germany (a book written by an Irish Lady) a passage relating to a Mr Sch-r whom the authoress met at Dresden and 'whose insatiable thirst for information about England' has induced him to read the Fairy Legends 'over and over again with the genuine German enthusiasm for the wild and supernatural' (see Wilhelm Grimm's reference to the 'wildness' of the Irish in his Survey of Irish fairy-tales, cf. below, p. 52). 'How eagerly he listened while I described the chronicler (!) of Fairie Land'. Later the same article refers to the passage (2 Oct. 1828) in which in his Briefe eines Verstorbenen, Fürst Pückler speaks of Croker's Daniel O'Rourke (Fairy Legends, I, no. 20). See also below, p. 49, n. 3).

 Apart from Grimm's translation of Fairy Legends, the article 'Irland' in Allgemeine deutsche Real-Encyklopädie für gebildete Stände (Brockhaus's Conversations-Lexikon), v (Leipzig, 1827), 574 ff., was one of the chief means of spreading Croker's reputation in Germany. 'T. Crofton Croker', it says, 'hat in s. "Researches in the South of Ireland" (London, 1824, 4) den gegenwärtigen sittlichen und bürgerlichen Zustand, die Alterthümer und die Literatur der Ir-

Grimm regrets that he is 'not intimately acquainted with the country itself', as he is thus unable to understand perfectly 'certain peculiar expressions and turns'. Croker referred to this sentence in the preface to the third volume of the *Fairy Legends* (1828). This preface consists of a dedicatory letter (of twenty-eight pages) to Dr Wilhelm Grimm at Cassel, presenting that volume to the brothers Grimm. The first part of the third volume of *Fairy Legends* consists of a translation of *Einleitung. Ueber die Elfen* = pp. vii-cxxvi of *Irische Elfenmärchen*.[17] This translation had been suggested by Wilhelm Grimm, who in his letter to Croker had said that he was 'vain enough to set some value on the annexed Essay on the Fairies', and that it would help to promote folklore studies in *England*. As Scherer said:

---

länder beschrieben.' Cf. also Lappenberg's article 'Irland' in Ersch-Gruber, Allgemeine Encyclopädie, I, xxiv (1845).

The numerous excursions on Irish fairy legends inserted in the translation of Carleton's story The Dead Boxer (first published in Dublin University Magazine, II (1833), 617-54), in Skizzen aus Irland oder Bilder aus Irlands Vergangenheit und Gegenwart von einem Wanderer (Stuttgart: Cotta, 1838), are obviously derived from Croker, p. 76 f. The translator says: 'Ob Irland auch Abgeordnete zur Blocksbergfeier der Walpurgisnacht gesendet habe, steht zu bezweifeln, weil die dort waltenden Feen der Oberherrschaft Beelzebubs nicht anerkennen; so viel ist indessen gewiß, daß die erste Mainacht [see Fairy Legends, I, 306 f.; Carleton begins the paragraph, Dublin University Magazine, p. 619: "Sometime about the end of April"] auch auf der grünen Insel stets ein grosses Fest für das Geisterreich und seine Geweihten gewesen ist. Selbst heutzutage ist der Feenglaube noch keineswegs aus dem Volke verschwunden, noch immer hegt man gewaltigen Respekt vor den "kleinen Herrschaften" oder "guten Leutchen", und hütet sich sorgfältig vor allem, was sie beleidigen könnte, wär's auch nur das Umhauen eines einsamen alten Dornbusches. Zu jenen Zeiten aber, wo die Welt noch nicht von den Aufklärungsgaslampen solcher Würdigen, wie Ehren [Edward] Nangle [editor of the Achill Missionary Herald (1837 ff.); se W. D. Killen, Eccles. Hist. of Ireland, II (1875), 499 ff.], und Ehren [Robert James] MacGee [author of a great number of tracts against the 'Church of Rome'] erleuchtet war, übten die mannigfachen Ideen von dem geheimen und mächtigen Wirken der Feen noch einen weit bedeutenderen Einfluß auf das Thun und Lassen des Volkes.' These last words seen to be a translation from Croker's Preface to the first volume of Fairy Legends ('... powerfully influence their conduct and manner of thinking').

In his article 'Irland' in Ersch-Gruber, Allgemeine Encyclopädie, I, XXIV 91845) Lappenberg, a close friend of the Grimms, said that Croker's Fairy Legends 'sind bei uns schon durch die treffliche Übersetzung und die gediegenen Erläuterungen der Brüder Grimm sehr vorteilhaft bekannt geworden ... Eine vorzügliche Sammlung humoristischer Einleitungen und zweckmässiger historischer Erzählungen hat T. C. Croker (The popular songs of Ireland, London, 1839) herausgegeben. Dieses Buch enthält auch einige historische Gedichte und biographische Notizen über die Liederdichter. Ihm verdankt man auch die Researches in the South of Ireland and Sayings and Doings in Killarney' (p. 103). Lappenberg also referred to Croker's Narratives illustrative of the Contests in Ireland in 1641 and 1690 (Camden Society of London, 1841) (notes 71 and 82). Later in his article (pp. 340 and 355f.) Lappenberg draws a parallel between Ireland and Germany with regard to 'Sonnendienst', as established by Grimm's Deutsche Mythologie (see below p. 48, n. 1). With regard to my note 1, above p. 45, I may add that Lappenberg wrote the preface to the German translation of Keightley's History of England.

17 'Die zum größten Theil von Wilhelm verfaßte Einleitung war so vorzüglich, daß sie bei der in 1828 erfolgenden neuen Ausgabe (!) des englischen Originals ins Englische übertragen wurde.' Carl Francke, Die Brüder Grimm (Dresden, 1899), p. 51f.

Der Antheil der Brüder an den Irischen Elfenmärchen (1862) läßt sich ebenso wenig sondern (als an den Sagen). Sie übersetzten sie aus dem Englischen und versahen sie mit einer schönen Einleitung über die Elfen in Irland, in Schottland, und über das Wesen der Elfen: eine ganze Naturgeschichte dieser zarten poetischen Gebilde, zugleich eine Vorarbeit zur deutschen Mythologie.[18]

The correspondence with Croker suggests that Francke was right in saying that 'the greater part' of the *Einleitung* was by Wilhelm; it has accordingly been incorporated in his and not Jacob's *Kleinere Schriften* (I, 404-409). The additional notes 'to the authorities from the MS. Communication of Dr. Wilhelm Grimm' (Fairy Legends, III, 146-156) and the Grimms'[19] additions to Cromer's notes (ibid. pp. 295 ff.) have never been reprinted. That in the index to Leitzmann's edition of the Grimm's correspondence with Lachmann *Irische Elfenmärchen* were listed as a work of Jacob's was obviously due to the fact that in that correspondence Jacob happens to make more references to that work than Wilhelm does.

On 14 January 1826 Jacob Grimm writes to Lachmann promising him a copy of the 'Elfenmärchen worin Sie die einleitung lesen können, weil auch ein und das andre mhd. vorkommt'. Lachmann answers twelve days later:

Auf die Elfenmärchen freue ich mich: Nicolovius,[20] der sich auf Volkspoesie versteht, hat sie mir sehr gelobt.

On 25 February Jacob Grimm starts his letter to Lachmann: 'Hier, lieber Lachmann, haben Sie die Elfenmärchen.' Lachmann answers only ten weeks later. He read his book, while he was laid up with gout:

mit vieler Erbauung. Nur das gefällt mir nicht, daß sie so systematisch geordnet sind: anders gestellt wären sie anziehender für jemand der nach der Reihe liest. Die weitläufige zerlegende Art ist wohl in der Übersetzung gemildert? denn ganz unangenehm habe ich sie höchst selten gefunden, bei Walter Scott ist sie mirs oft sehr. Das Compliment für Scott iv unten[21] scheint mir daher eine Ungerechtigkeit gegen den Verfasser, wenn es nicht ein wohlverdientes Compliment für die Übersetzung versteckt.

---

18   Allgemeine Deutsche Biographie, IX (1879), 693. Scherer's idea of Elfen is not in keeping with Grimm's statement: 'Aus elben elfin machen heißt unserer Sprache gewalt thun' (Deutsche Mythologie, II (1835) Vorr. Chap. XVII deals with Elben), a fact which was obviously not yet recognised when the title Elfenmärchen was chosen and the Einleitung written. For Elfen see, for example, the beginning of Faust, II.

In Grimm's Deutsche Mythologie (1854) the word 'Irland' seems to occur only once, namely, in a reference (based on Acta Sanctorum) to 'die heilige Brigida in Irland (†518 oder 521)', in whose honour, as in that of Vesta, there was 'bei Kildare ewiges feuer unterhalten' (p. 578; p. 636 a short reference to St. Gall).

19   In the Anmerkungen zu Kinder- und Hausmärchen (1856) – see below, p. 51 – Wilhelm refers to these notes as 'his'.

20   The husband of Goethe's niece Luise Schlosser. He was at that time chief of the department for religious affairs in the Prussian Government (see Friedländer in Allg. Deutsche Biogr.XXIII (1886), 639 and Dilthey's famous article on 'Süvern', ibid. XXXVII (1894), 211 ff.)

21   See below, p. 51.

Als ein gründlicher Leser habe ich auch die Einleitung gelesen, die andre zu gelehrt finden. Ich finde sie so schön in der ganzen Weise und in der Ausführung, daß ich sie mir garnicht besser wünschen kann. Anmerkungen habe ich nur ein Paar (*sic*), die nicht sagen wollen.[22]

Jacob answers a week later:

Die Ordnung ist wie im Original, es wurde stückweise übersetzt und gleich abgeschickt, so daß der Gedanke an eine andere Stellung weder aufkommen noch gut ausgeführt werden konnte.

This also explains how the German translation could appear so shortly after the original had been published. The French translation took a much longer time.

In Wilhelm's correspondence with Lachmann the *Elfenmärchen* are not referred to until 21 April 1827 when Wilhelm writes:

Habe ich Ihnen schon gesagt, daß der Vf. der irischen Märchen (Crofton Croker heißt er) die Abhandlung über die Elfen nicht bloß übersetzen, sondern durch neue Beiträge aus Wales und England zu einem eignen Werke erheben will? Verstehe ich ihn recht, so will auch Walter Scott, der doch auch über diesen Gegenstand geschrieben hat, Theil daran nehmen.

There has been, as T.F. Dillon Croker also suggested, a lively correspondence exchanged by Grimm and Croker between Wilhelm's letter of July 1826 and Croker's dedicatory letter of 1828. In that correspondence Wilhelm communicated to Croker the 'additions to the authorities' (quoted in the *Einleitung*), in which he dealt with parallels from the folklore of various European countries, America and Africa.[23] What was Croker's part in the essay on *The Mabinogions and Fairy Legends of Wales* forming the second part of *Fairy Legends*, vol. III, is a much-debated point.[24] The Grimm's study of the works of Scott should be made the subject of a special investigation.[25] One of the additions made by the Grimms to Croker's notes on no. 14 of the *Fairy Legends* is taken from the second volume 'der altschottischen Balladen' (p. 216). On 20 February 1828 Wilhelm Grimm sent the second part of the 'englischen Märchen' (which was dedicated to Scott) through Professor Phillips[26] to Lachmann.

---

22 7 May 1826. Lachmann explains two passages quoted in Elfenmärchen, p. lvi f., from Rüdeger, adds an early reference to 'elvesce', rejects Grimm's suggestion that 'tiuvel' could be a neuter (ibid. lviii), and expresses his surprise at Grimm's quotation (lxxii) from Berthold's sermons (A.D. 1272) referring to five-year-old Angels. 'Soviel ich mich erinnere', Lachmann writes, 'sagt man gewöhnlich Engel als Kinder vorzustellen habe erst Raphael (oder Perugino) aufgebracht.'

23 See below, p. 52, n. 4.

24 MacCarthy, loc. cit. p. 547, says that 'the whole essay was written by a lady of unspecified name and given by her to Croker'. See, however, Croker's references to Dr. Owen Pughe (e.g. Fairy Legends, I, 195), and, apparently independent of Croker, the addition from Welsh folklore made in Elfenmärchen, 209.

25 Apart from Stewart (see below), Scott is the principal authority for the section 'Die Elfen in Schottland' in the Einleitung.

26 'George P. – so schrieb er regelmässig, Georg auf dem Titel des Kirchenrechts [Regensburg, 1845 ff.], – Germanist und Canonist, geboren zu Königsberg; sein Vater James, war Engländer, und hatte sich mit seiner Frau, der Tochter eines Schotten George Hay, in Königsberg niedergelassen', where he 'stand insbesondere mit Kant in Verkehr'. His 'englische Abstammung'

From the beginning of their acquaintance with the *Fairy Legends*, the Grimms had regarded them not only as a source of information on the folklore tradition of just another country in addition to the many others they had studied, but more especially as a means of acquiring some knowledge of Ireland. An impressive illustration of this fact is the letter which Jacob Grimm wrote towards the end of his life (12 April 1858) to Christian Adolf Helfferich, to thank him for a copy of his *Skizzen und Erzählungen aus Irland*, which had appeared in the same year:

> Erst spät kommt mein dank für die angenehme gabe. Ich wollte zuvor lesen und das buch wurde mir aus der hand genommen, so daß ich warten muste (sic). Mich hat nicht nur die einleitung vielfach belehrt, sondern die lebendigen erzählungen gefallen mir sehr wohl.

> Seit den elfenmärchen zieht mich auch die irische sprache an, ich habe mich aber auf bücher beschränken müssen, und bin der lebendigen sprache nicht gewarh worden, die Ihnen zu ohren gedrungen ist.[27]

We shall see that the Grimms knew still more of the books on Ireland written by Germans during the forties and fifties. Grimm's remark 'das buch wurde mir aus der hand genommen' may be interpreted as an illustration of the great interest with which those books met, an interest partly due to late Ossianic romanticism, but perhaps more to the popular interest in Celtic studies from which *Zeuss's Grammatica* Celtica sprang. Jacob Grimm was one of the first on the Continent to demand the linking of the book study of Celtic languages with the study of the living tradition of Gaelic. Similarly, Wilhelm Grimm, in his letter to Croker, had expressed his belief in the necessity of backing the book study of Irish folklore by autotopical knowledge of the living tradition.

In the Preface to the first volume of his collection, Croker had stated that he aimed at

> illustrating the superstitions of the Irish Peasantry, superstitions which the most casual observer cannot fail to remark powerfully influence their conduct and manner of thinking.

Croker's mentality reveals itself still more clearly in the note with which he concludes his notes:

> The Shefro, the Banshee and the other creations of imagination [will] melt into air as knowledge advances. When rational education shall be diffused among the misguided peasantry of Ireland, the belief in such supernatural beings must disappear in the country, as it has done in England.

With an eye on such pronouncements, and applying the present-day standards of Celtic scholarship and Irish nationalism, Dr. MacCarthy has recently represented Croker as nothing better than an amusing charlatan. It could be shown that Croker's political and philosophical ideas gradually became more mature. Is it not characteristic that the second volume of the *Fairy Legends* concludes with a poem in which Croker says that greater sorrow and evil have been worked in Ireland by the stormier spirits of 'our

---

expresses itself in his dress and habits of life. 'Er mache den Eindruck eines Gentleman.' In 1828 he had just published some works on English history. In later years Phillips made a curious contribution to folklore studies entitled Über den Ursprung der Katzenmusiken (Freiburg, 1849) (v. Schulte in Allg. Deutsche Biographie, xxvi (1888), 80 ff.)

27   Briefe der Brüder Grimm, 65f.

modern days' than by the fairies of olden times and that a prayer for the peace of the 'land beloved' concludes this poem? (In the third edition[28] this is the only epilogue.)

Regarding Croker's attitude to folklore in general, it was the sympathetic interpreter rather than the innocent foreigner who wrote in the *Vorrede zu Irische Elfenmärchen*:

> Man darf voraussetzen, daß der Verfasser ein geborener Irländer ist oder lang in Irland gelebt hat. Er zeigt genaue Kenntniß von Örtlichkeiten, Sitten und Denkweise und ist vertraut mit eigenthümlichen Ausdrücken, Gleichnissen, sprichwörtlichen Reden und anderen Kleinigkeiten dieser Art, die ... seine Darstellung beleben oder aus einem Buch sich nicht erlernen lassen.

In a certain measure it is correct to say both that Croker was Irish born and that he lived for a long time in this country. He was an offspring of the ascendency and, with various long interruptions, lived in the south of Ireland. To the trained modern folklorist his rambles through the countryside of Munster may appear as 'desultory' (MacCarthy). Grimm, however, attributed to them 'die Treue und Wahrheit seiner Sammlung'.[29]

Even more than the doubt whether Croker was really a born Irishman, the reference to Scott's influence on him (which Lachmann erroneously interpreted as a compliment to Scott) were expressive of the Grimms' awareness of Croker's shortcomings. 'Der Fehler des zu sorgsamen Ausmahlens', which distinguishes Croker's more sophisticated *Fairy Legends* from Grimm's *Hausmärchen*, is to be attributed to the influence 'den Walter Scotts Darstellungsart gegenwärtig in *England* ausübt'.[30] Still more characteristic of the *English* is, according to the Grimms' *Vorrede*, the irrelevance of many of his notes. While going into great length to render faithfully the twenty-seven fairy-tales, the Grimms reduced the notes to about one-fourth of what Croker offered.

Croker's work should be considered not only in the light of his own development but also in that of the history of folklore studies in general. In 1856 Wilhelm Grimm started an essay on Irish folklore studies with the words: 'Bei den Iren[31] brach T. C. Croker (1797-1854) mit seinen *Fairy Legends* ... zuerst Bahn.' This statement still holds good. Grimm's essay was reprinted by Bolte in vol. v of the *Anmerkungen zu Kinder- und Hausmärchen der Brüder Grimm*. (Stuttgart, 1932, p. 55 ff.):

> Der Inhalt seiner Sammlung ist echt,[32] und auf eine geschickte Weise sind in die Erzählungen seltsame, kühne, aber lebendige Anschauung verratende Redensarten, Bilder und Gleichnisse des Volkes eingewebt; man muß bedauern, daß die Darstellung zu dem ausgebildeten Geschmack der jetzigen Zeit sich etwas mehr zuneigt, als zuträglich ist, zumal wenn sie jene Ironie anwendet, die

---

28   Cf. below, p. 52, n.4.

29   Treue und Wahrheit is the title of the second part of the Vorrede to Deutsche Sagen (1816).

30   In his review of the Fairy Legends (see above) Wilhelm Grimm also described Brooke's illustrations as typically English. These illustrations indeed emphasize the non-Irish character of the spirit of Croker's collection.

31   Taylor (see p. 44, n. 3) gave it as his opinion that even in England Croker 'brach Bahn'.

32   In his letter of 20 April 1825 Jacob Grimm similarly described the Fairy Legends 'als "echte Volkssagen"'.

uns zu verstehen gibt, daß das Märchenhafte nur das Erzeugnis einer durch den Rausch erregten Phantasie sei, womit jede tiefere Bedeutung schwindet.

Grimm obviously quotes here from Croker's Epilogue to vol. I.[33]

Parenthetically, we may note an interesting illustration of this fundamental difference of opinion between the Grimms and Croker in the Grimms' note to no. 11 of Croker's collection:

> Leute, welche an Elfen glauben, werden die Erscheinung so auslegen, daß die Geister, welche sich den Augen der beiden jungen Leute nicht zeigen wollten, sich in Pilze verwandelt hätten, unter welchen sie ohnehin gerne hausen; und es ist nicht die Absicht der Sage, den Glauben daran lächerlich zu machen. Dahin deutet die Überschrift im Original: *fairies or no fairies?* die hier mit einer andern (Die vertauschten Elfen) ist vertauscht worden.

Similarly, Grimm's notes omit Croker's rationalist explanation of the water-phantoms (*Fairy Legends*, I, 327).

Wilhelm Grimm then refers to v. Killinger's *Irische Sagen und Märchen* (Stuttgart, 1847-9) 'wo auch benutzt ist was in den Popular tales and legends von S. Lover (1832-34) und in W. A. Thoms Märchen und Sagen aller Völker (Bd III, 1834) vorkommt'.[34]

The second part of Grimm's survey of the first generation of Irish fairy-tale studies consists of a general characterization of Irish fairy tales. 'Nichts kann besser die immer aufgeregte, mit einer gewissen Wildheit[35] behaftete, aber auch mit den geistigen Kräften ausgestattete Natur der Irländer schildern als diese Märchen.' Subsequently Grimm speaks of 'die behende Phantasie der Iren'.

There is a certain parallelism between Küttner's intensive study of the works of his friend Vallancey,[36] Goethe's study of O'Halloran, and the Grimms' occupation with Croker; of Küttner and the Grimms it will be said that they were fooled by charlatans. Yet should we have modern Celtic scholarship if two hundred years ago the greatest spirits of the Continent had not been fooled by the impostor Macpherson? Is it not a splendid example of the method of 'den Autor besser verstehen als er sich selbst' (of which, according to Dilthey, the Grimms were masters), when Croker's collection led the most eminent philologists of his time to recognize that to make a real study of

---

33 See above, p. 50. Croker's reference (I, 18) to 'the very extravagant imagination in which the Irish are so fond of indulging', the Grimms render by 'die wunderliche Einbildungskraft der Einwohner' (p. 157). In his preface to the second volume, Croker said that the Grimms' Einleitung deals with 'fairy superstitions'. The change from 'Fairy Legends' to 'Elfenmärchen' marks the difference in attitude to folklore tradition. On the reality of Märchen see the Vorrede to vol. II of Deutsche Mythologie.

34 Lover's Legends and Stories of Ireland (Dublin, 1831, 21832. 31834) and Popular Tales and Legends of Irish Peasantry (ibid. 1834). The bibliography added by Bolte at the end of the section written by Wilhelm Grimm includes only one work published during his life-time, namely, V.A. Huber's Skizzen aus Irland (Leipzig, 1850).

35 See above, p. 47, n. 2.

36 The Memoir of the Irish Bards (1786 and 1816), by Joseph Cooper Walker (see D.N.B.), one of Vallancay's school, is repeatedly referred to in Croker's notes. See below, p. 53, n. 1.

Celtic folklore would require a first-hand knowledge of Ireland and the Gaelic language?[37]

Considering the low standard of Continental knowledge of Ireland, the mere fact that through those twenty-seven Irish fairy-tales some sixty Irish place-names and some hundred Irish surnames (Gaelic and English) were conveyed to the Continent is significant. Regarding Croker's notes, the *Vorrede* said:

> Nichts was zur Erläuterung der Überlieferung selbst diente, ist von uns ausgelassen, wohl aber was ungehörig schien, darunter auch manche gerade nicht glückliche allgemeine Sprachbemerkung oder etymologische Ausführung.

What the Grimms regarded as essential in Croker's notes[38] was first of all everything relating to the geographical background, 'die Örtlichkeiten', a thorough knowledge of which even the most critical reader cannot deny to Croker. The notes to nos. 7, 10, 13, 14, 19 and 20 are particularly interesting in this respect.[39] In note 24 the Grimms rearrange the material offered by Croker, so that the geographical note comes first. A fine example is the beginning of the note to no. 9:

> Mourne liegt zwey Stunden südlich von Mallow und man sieht die Ruinen noch immer zwischen dem alten und neuen Weg von Cork nach jener Stadt, welche beide unter den Mauern herlaufen. Sonst gehörte es den Tempelherrn. *S. Archdale's Monasticon hibernicum* und *Smith's history of Cork.*
>
> Der Flaschenberg *(Bottle hill)* liegt in der Mitte zwischen Cork und Mallow und ist eine dürftig angebaute Strecke, auf der man nur zuweilen die nackten (Croker: roofless) Mauern verlassener Häuser (Croker: manufactories) erblickt, welche samt der Dürre und Unfruchtbarkeit einen unglaublich traurigen Eindruck macht *(Elfenmärchen,* 208 = *Fairy Legends,* I, 104).

I may note that the melancholy of the same district was also described by Küttner. Other books of general information on Ireland quoted in Croker's notes so far as preserved by the Grimms are Ryan's *Worthies,* Miss Brooke's *Reliques of Irish*

---

37 'Croker's initial success and the greater part of his literary reputation were based on his supposed knowledge of Irish history, Irish literature and the folklore...of the people. A true investigator would have needed a comprehensive knowledge of Irish history, of the Irish language, of Irish antiquities ... He considered Irish as a suspect tongue. He never speaks of the native Irish but as "peasants" ' [this is not correct; see for example, p. 51, n. 4] (MacCarthy, loc. cit. p. 541).

38 In the third edition (1834), in which vols. I and II of the second edition were combined, 'all superfluous annotations have been struck out, and a brief summary at the end of each section substituted'. P. 70 refers to Irische Elfenmärchen, p. 96 to 'the Brothers Grimms' Essay on the Nature of Elves'; p. 126, a 'MS. Communication from Dr. Wilhelm Grimm', including a reference to Deutsche Sagen; p. 152, the Grimms' note on Phooka; p. 240, a quotation from Journal des Sciences, 1826, 'communicated by Dr William Grimm'; p. 310, a reference to Grimm's Deutsch Sagen and to a French translation of Creuzer. In the Appendix the letter from Scott, but not that of Grimm.

39 The relationship between Croker's notes and the geographical descriptions given in Deutsche Sagen is obvious.

Poetry, and O'Brien's *Irish Dictionary*.[40] It would be interesting to ascertain whether any of those books were found in the Kassel Library.[41]

For many of the German readers of *Irische Elfenmärchen*, this will have been the first book to refer to the works of Sheridan, Thomas Moore, Lady Morgan and Miss. Edgeworth.[42]

Only of *The popular superstitions and festive amusements of the Highlanders of Scotland*, Edinburgh, 1823, by W. Grant Stewart, the chief source of the section *Die Elfen in Schottland* in the *Einleitung*, Grimm could claim that, though an important source of information on Celtic folklore, it was unknown not only in Germany but also to the 'Sammler der irischen Sagen'.

> Gleichwohl ist es äußerst schätzbar durch den Reichthum und die Vollständigkeit der darin aufbewahrten mündlichen Überlieferungen (Elfenmärchen, XIX).

Grimm's own property is also the reference to Aubrey's *De Miscellaneis* in the addition to the note to no. 14, where it replaces Croker's quotation from *The Witch of Fife*. Grimm says that this reference was obtained from another work of Scott's. I may note[43] that Aubrey's work had been quoted by Jean Paul (1840 edition, vol. XXVII, 22), as an authority for second-sight among the Irish. (Jean Paul gleaned this quotation from a German magazine.)

What the *Einleitung* has to say on the meanings of the words *Banshi, Shefro, Phooka, Thierna na oge, Leprechaun, Clunicaun, Lusmore* and *Bocough* is taken from Croker's

40 'The footnotes in the Fairy Legends in which he gives derivations of Irish words merely imply that he consulted Vallancey, O'Brien and others' (MacCarthy, loc. cit. p. 545)

41 Elfenmärchen 219: Croker's quotation from 'die Verhandlungen der königl. Irischen Academie'. This is the first reference made in German literature to the Royal Irish Academy. On 30 November 1825, Goethe had been elected Honorary Member.

On 19 November 1849, the Committee for Polite Literature (to which belonged John Anster, the translator of Faust) recommended the election as Honorary Members in the Department of Polite Literature of Jacob Grimm, Bopp, Lepsius, Guizot and Ranke. The actual election took place on 30 November. At the same time Alex. v. Humbolt was elected in the Department of Science.

At the meeting of the Royal Irish Academy on 14 January 1856, the Secretary, the Rev. J. H. Todd, read a letter from Dr Jacob Grimm, H.M.R.I.A., written in French to the R.I.A. on certain formulae – supposed to be written in a Celtic dialect – in the works of Marcellus, a pilgrim of the age of Theodosius the Great. In this letter Grimm stated that he had written on this subject a few years before. This letter, Todd said, never reached the Academy. Todd added that 'he hoped on some future occasion to lay before the Academy a more complete examination of this very interesting question. The thanks of the Academy are due to Dr Grimm for bringing the subject under the notice of Celtic scholars. It is deeply regretted that the apparent neglect of this former communication should have tended to discourage so eminent a scholar in a philological inquiry of such interest' (Proc. Royal Irish Academy, vi, 290 f.). Todd's paper on this subject did not appear.

42 On Croker and Maria Edgeworth see MacCarthy, loc. cit. p. 555 f.

43 See my article on 'Jean Paul and Ireland', in Modern Language Review, XL (1945), 190.

notes. In the note on *Miscaun marry* (to no. 19), a parallel drawn by Croker with the Greek was omitted by Grimm, as were also the notes on the use of the word *dia* (Croker, p. 33) and the remarks on modern Anglo-Irish usages (Croker, pp. 62, 75 and 207). Though, in his review of *Fairy Legends* in 1826, Wilhelm Grimm has suggested a comparison with 'Shackespears Elfenwelt', all the superficial notes of Croker's on this subject were omitted. While adding numerous notes on Nordic parallels, some unsuitable quotations of Croker's from Nordic sources, such as Olavus Magnus (p. 11) and Rüh's *Edda* (p. 63), were omitted. Irving (ibid.) and Young (p. 136) did not appear to Grimm as relevant interpreters of Irish life.

One of the few notes of Croker's which was incorporated into Elfenmärchen is that to no. 32, dealing with Irish hurling and the folklore of Bealtine (Mayday), a fine illustration of the Grimm's sound judgement as to what was genuine folklore tradition.

While in his letter to Croker Wilhelm Grimm had spoken of the difficulties to attain a perfect understanding of some expressions found in the original, Croker in his dedicatory letter referred to his difficulties in translating the German original to the *Einleitung*. As an example of their mutual difficulties he refers to Grimm's note on Ir. *boliaun* (to no. 15, *Elfenmärchen*, 218).

> Im Original steht boliaun, das Wort findet sich nicht in Nemnichs *Catholicon*, geschweige in einem Wörterbuch. Geborne Irländer, die ein Freund befragt hat, versichern, daß boliaun ein Stab oder Knüttel sey, doch dem Zusammenhang nach muß es nothwendig eine Pflanze bedeuten, wird auch daran ein beigesetztes *ragweed* erklärt, das zwar gleichfalls kein englischen Wort ist, worunter man aber nach Versicherung der Irländer ein Unkraut versteht.

Whether the 'Irländer' whom Grimm consulted belonged to that part of the Irish nation who 'noch in der eignen Sprache redet'[44] we do not know. More important is that he realized the necessity of consulting a 'native speaker', and that he knew scarcely any Irishmen personally (see p. 47).

Little is known of Croker's qualification to translate a difficult German text. The only indication of his knowledge of German is, apart from the excellent translation itself, a German poet quoted in the note to no. 27 and described in Grimm's shortened note as 'die deutsche Sage vom Auszug des Rodensteiners'. In his note to no. 5 Croker refers to a Thuringian folklore tradition; Grimm retained this note without giving an authority either (*Elf.* 203).

(Quelle: MLA 41, 42, 43, 1946, S. 44-45, 237-42, 92f) S. 44-54 vorliegendes Original)

---

44   Cf. above, p. 46.

Wilhelm v. Humboldt und John Charles Stapleton

In seinem Brief vom 3. Juli 1831 an Charlotte Diede sprach Wilhelm v. Humboldt von der wunderbaren Erneuerung seines Freundeskreises im hohen Alter: „Ich weiß nicht, durch welche Ideenverbindung mir dabei Stapleton einfällt, den Sie in Göttingen kannten. Wissen Sie, daß er mit den Einkünften einer Irländischen geistlichen Pfründe in London leben soll? Seine Stelle verwaltet, wie es dort Sitte ist, ein anderer. Ich denke auch gehört zu haben, daß er verheiratet ist."[1]

Stapleton wird in den „Briefen an eine Freundin" zuerst in Humboldts Brief vom 18. Juli 1817 aus Berlin erwähnt: „S[2] war noch nicht bei mir. Ich werde ihn mit großer Freude sehen, da mich, was Sie mir von ihm sagen, sehr interessiert." Charlotte Diedes Briefe an Humboldt sind mit Ausnahme von zweien nicht erhalten, aber wir haben andere Quellen, die uns über ihre Beziehung zu Stapleton unterrichten. Der Bitte entsprechend, die Humboldt in seinem zweiten Brief (14. 12. 1814) an sie gerichtet hatte, war sie von Holzminden nach Göttingen gezogen[3]. Am 14. 12. 1817 schrieb sie an ihre Schwester Dorothea, daß sie im Mai 1815 nach Göttingen zog und dort zwei Jahre wohnte. „Das zweite Jahr war trüber – trübe"[4]. Im Vorwort zu seiner Ausgabe von Charlotte Diedes Briefen an ihre Schwestern, ihren Schwager und ihre Nichte sagte O. Hartwig[5]: „Welche Anziehung die damals schon 45 Jahre alte Frau immer noch selbst auf verwöhnte junge Männer ausübte, dafür läßt sich ein merkwürdiger Beleg anführen. In das Haus, welches Charlotte vor dem Tore bewohnte, war ein junger vornehmer Engländer gezogen, der sich auf diese Weise dem Verkehr mit rohen Landsleuten besser entziehen zu können hoffte. Er gehörte der Familie Stapleton an, war ein Mündel des englischen Premiers Lord Castlereagh[6] und mit George Canning[7], dessen Sekretär

---

1 W. v. Humboldt, Briefe an eine Freundin, ed. A. L i e t z m a n n (Leipzig 1909) 2 S. 197. Während des 19. Jahrhunderts waren diese Briefe das meistgelesene Buch von W. v. Humboldt und, wie die englischen Übersetzungen daraus, „eine weltliche Bibel für viele". Für die von ihrer Freundin Therese v. Bacherach geb. v. Struve herausgebrachte Ausgabe richtete Charlotte Diede die Briefe zurecht, wobei sie viele, u. a. auch hier anzuführende, unterdrückte. Dieser erste Brief ist in der Erstausgabe auf den 2. Juli datiert (S. 134).

2 L i e t z m a n n s Ausgabe 1 S. 32 „S(tapleton)". Dieser Brief wurde zuerst von Lietzmann veröffentlicht.

3 Ebd. S. 31.

4 A. P i d e r i t und O. H a r t w i g , Charlotte Diede (Halle 1884) S. 226.

5 Ebd. S. 68 f.

6 In einem Brief an seine Gattin im Januar 1814 gab Humboldt von London aus eine Beschreibung von Castlereagh (Briefwechsel ed. A. S y d o w 4, Berlin 1910, S. 226). Im Februar schlug Caroline ihrem Gatten scherzhaft vor, „sich von Castlereagh eine Insel schenken zu lassen", wo sie ihren Lebensabend verbringen könnten, ein Vorschlag, auf den Humboldt mit Freuden einging (S. 259). Humboldt folgte Castlereagh nach Bar-sur-Aube und Wien. Caroline nahm besonderen Anteil an den Verhandlungen mit Castlereagh über die Teilung Sachsens. 1817 und 1818 hatte Humboldt noch ausgiebiger mit Castlereagh zu tun (s. Register zu Humboldts Tagebüchern 2 [Ges. Schriften 15]).

7 Begegnungen Humboldts mit Canning werden in den Tagebüchern 2 S. 495, 505, 510 und 514 erwähnt. In „Gabriele von Bülow" (Berlin 1893) S. 186 wird über Bülows Reaktion auf die

und Biograph ein Stapleton war, verwandt. Der gutmütige, leichtsinnige Mensch hatte sich wiederholt von seinen Landsleuten zum Spiel und anderen Torheiten verleiten lassen. Doch hatte er auch bessere Gelegenheiten gefunden, um sein Geld loszuwerden. Auf einer Auktion kaufte er einmal eine Menge Bücher, die er dann einem armen Studenten schenkte, dessen Lebensglück er dadurch begründete. Ein anderes Mal kam er zu einer Zwangsversteigerung einer dürftigen Familie und kaufte alles Hausgerät zurück, und schenkte es den alten Besitzern als ihr Eigentum zurück. – Dieser junge Mensch begegnete eines Tages Charlotte in der Nähe ihrer Wohnung und strich so nahe an ihr vorüber, daß sie ausweichen und in die Gosse treten mußte, wobei ihr weißes Kleid beschmutzt wurde. Dessen schämte sich doch der wohlerzogene Engländer, und ließ sich am folgenden Tage bei Charlotte melden, um sich zu entschuldigen. Diese nahm ihn an und bald war sie die Vertraute seines Herzens. Er beichtete ihr nach und nach, wie er ein verkehrtes Leben in Göttingen führe und von dort fort müsse, wenn er besser werden sollte. Charlotte durchschaute die Lage des jungen Menschen ganz klar, faßte sich ein Herz und schrieb an seinen Vormund, den Lord Castlereagh, einen ausführlichen französischen Brief [8].

Dieser sah die Richtigkeit ihrer Auseinandersetzungen und Gründe ein, antwortete sofort wiederholt verbindlichst[9], und der junge Mann wurde nach Heidelberg geschickt. Was aus ihm geworden, ist nicht sicher zu ermitteln gewesen; nach einer Version soll er in einem Duell geblieben sein."

Der letzte Satz beruht offenbar auf dem dritten Brief, in dem Humboldt von Stapleton sprach. In der Beantwortung von Charlottes Briefen vom 1. und 22. Februar, schrieb ihr Humboldt am 3. März 1832 von Tegel[10]: „Ich fange in meiner Erwiderung zuerst mit dem an, was Sie zuletzt geschrieben haben, mit dem Duell. Ich habe die erste Nachricht davon durch Sie erhalten. Ich lese die Zeitungen höchst unordentlich ... Ich habe bis jetzt nicht ergründen können, ob es derselbe Stapleton gewesen, den wir hier gekannt haben. Man vermuthet es nur, weil er solchen Zufällen nicht aus dem Wege

---

Nachricht von Cannings Tod berichtet (s. auch meine Notiz über Goethe und Canning in Modern Language Quarterly 10 (1949) S. 512-516).

8   Stapleton hatte offenbar wie andere junge Briten, die um diese Zeit nach Deutschland kamen, sich rechtzeitig eine genügende Kenntnis der deutschen Sprache angeeignet (s. meine Notiz „Irish descriptions of Goethe" in: Publications of the English Goethe Soc. 25; (1956) S. 114-124). Charlotte Diede konnte kein Englisch; am 6. 11. 1830 schrieb Humboldt an sie: „Soviel ich weiß, lesen Sie nicht Englisch." In demselben Brief empfahl ihr Humboldt, sich eine tiefere Kenntnis von England zu verschaffen: „Ich würde Ihnen rathen, mit Humes Geschichte anzufangen." Das entscheidende literarische Erlebnis von Charlotte Diede war Richardson, den sie auf Deutsch las. Ihre Begegnung mit Humboldt in Pyrmont stand unter dem Einfluß von „Clarissa" in einer Weise, die sich mit dem Einfluß Ossians auf Werther und Lotte vergleichen läßt (L i e t z m a n n 1 S. 19, 134, 228).

9   Weder Charlotte Diedes Brief noch Castlereaghs Antworten finden sich in „Castlereaghs Correspondence", die sein Bruder Charles 1848-1859 veröffentlichte. „Stapleton" kommt in P. T. F i t z g e r a l d , Political and private life of the Marquess of Londonderry (Dublin 1822) nicht vor.

10   Wieder erstmalig von L i e t z m a n n veröffentlicht (2, 217).

ging, vielmehr sich wenig in Acht nahm, sie selber herbeizuführen. Sonst weiß man aber nichts Bestimmtes davon. Ich werde Ihnen aber gewiß sichere Auskunft schaffen. Der Name Stapleton ist übrigens so selten nicht in England, und so braucht er nicht einmal einer der drei Brüder zu seyn. Der, an dem Sie Theil nehmen, hatte zuletzt eine geistliche Pfründe. Doch war er selbst nicht geistlich geworden. In seiner Herkunft war nichts Geheimnisvolles. Der Herzog v. Cumberland[11] hat sie mir einmal ausführlich erzählt. Ich habe sie wieder vergessen, aber es war nichts Ungewöhnliches. Ich habe ihn kaum gekannt. Er war hier, trotz mancher Extravaganzen, geliebt, und auch jetzt höre ich, daß die selbst noch ungewisse Nachricht Theilnahme erweckt. Mit den Duellen ist es übrigens eine eigene Sache. Viele, und deren mag Stapleton allerdings mehrere gehabt haben, sind bloße Jugendtorheiten."[12]

In diesem Brief sagt Humboldt nicht wieder, daß es sich bei der von Stapleton innegehabten Pfründe um eine irische gehandelt habe. Der verstorbene Kanonikus J. B. Leslie, der größte Kenner des Personals der Church of Ireland in jener Zeit, teilte mir mit, daß er den Namen Stapleton während der in Frage kommenden Jahre nicht finden konnte. Humboldt erwähnte Stapleton in seinen Briefen nicht wieder. Offenbar gelang es ihm nicht, sichere Auskünfte über die Duellanten zu erhalten, von denen Charlotte Diede wohl durch eine Zeitungsnotiz gehört hatte.

In der Matrikel der Universität Göttingen wird (nach freundlicher Mitteilung von Herrn Professor Gerhard v. Rad) am 12. Mai 1814 John Charles Stapleton, Vater: Lord Boringdon, Kent House, Knightsbridge, London für die juristische Fakultät, und am 14. Januar 1816 J. C. Stapleton, Vater: Graf Morley, Kent House, London, für die philosophische Fakultät aufgeführt. Die zweite Eintragung ist mit der Anmerkung „siehe auch 12. Mai 1814" versehen. Es handelt sich also um den gleichen Studenten. 1815 war John Parker, 2nd Baron Boringdon, erster Earl of Morley geworden. In der Matrikel der Universität Heidelberg erscheint Stapleton nicht.

In seiner Einleitung zu Humboldts Briefen an Charlotte Diede fügte Lietzmann nicht nur nichts zu Hartwigs Mitteilungen hinzu, sondern ließ auch Hartwigs Bezug auf Stapleton, den Sekretär und Biographen Cannings weg. Augustus Granville Stapleton wurde 1800 geboren und 1814 in das Register von Rugby als „Augustus Granby[13] son of John Stapleton Esq. and ward of the Rev. Yeoman, Barnstaple Devon." eingetragen. In einem Brief vom 15. März 1830 teilte Joseph Jekyll[14] mit, daß „Stapylton (the

---

11   Ernest Augustus war in Göttingen zur gleichen Zeit wie Humboldt Student gewesen.

12   1815 hatte Humboldt ein Duell mit Boyen gehabt (Brief an Karoline vom 5. 5. 1815, ed. v. S y d o w 4. 546). In seinem „Logbook of a rambler" (1830, s. meine in Anm. 8 zitierte Notiz) sprach Charles L e v e r von den Duellsitten deutscher Studenten und vom Studentenleben in Göttingen (s. auch seinen Roman „Arthur O'Leary", Kapitel 20).

13   „This presumably was altered to Granville by the Editor (des gedruckten Studentenverzeichnisses) ... on the authority of the Dictionary of National Biography from which the biographical details were derived [1809, Bd. 18, 94 f.] ... there is nothing to show the exact date of his admission to the School, except it was between mid-summer and Michaelmass, 1814" (briefliche Mitteilung des Bursar, Rugby School).

14   Correspondence with his sister-in-law Lady Gertrude Sloane-Stanley (London 1894) S. 226.

private secretary of Canning) was a natural son of Lord Morley", dem frühesten Anhänger und intimen Freund von Canning. Augustus Granville Stapleton wurde am 22. Februar 1817 in Trinity Hall, Cambridge eingetragen, bezog aber seine Wohnung dort nicht; am 14. Oktober 1818 wurde er als ‚pensioner' von St. John's College, Cambridge angenommen. Herr Dr. Venn, Registrar des letztgenannten Kollegs, teilte mir mit, daß „none of the local authorities (in Cambridge) give any details as to Stapleton's parentage or as to who paid his fees; but this is not unusual". Augustus Granville Stapleton heiratete 1825. Sein jüngster Sohn Edward J. setzte das literarische Werk seines Vaters fort, indem er (1887) „Some official correspondence of George Canning" herausgab.

Morley scheint somit zwei uneheliche Söhne gehabt zu haben, die beide den Familiennamen Stapleton trugen. Man darf also eine längere Assoziation mit einer Frau dieses Namens vermuten, welche vielleicht ein Grund für das Auseinandergehen von Morleys erster Ehe gewesen ist. John Charles war der ältere dieser beiden Söhne. Es entspricht dem Charakterbild, das wir aus Humboldts und Hartwigs Mitteilungen gewinnen, daß er sich im Frühjahr 1814 nach Göttingen schicken ließ, wozu angesichts der politischen Lage einiger Mut gehörte, und daß er das juristische Studium zu trocken fand. Hartwig sagt, daß Charlotte Diede (geb. 1769) 45 Jahre alt war, als sie Stapleton kennenlernte. Sie muß ihn also kurz nach seiner ersten Immatrikulation kennengelernt haben, und vielleicht erfolgte der Wechsel in die philosophische Fakultät schon unter ihrem Einfluß.

Der Eindruck, den der „junge vornehme Engländer" auf die wesentlich ältere Charlotte Diede machte, entspricht ganz dem Eindruck, den so viele junge Briten in jener Zeit auf die Weimarer Damen machten. Vor allem von Goethe und seiner Schwiegertochter wissen wir, welche Eigenschaften besonderen Eindruck machten: Natürlichkeit, Gesundheit, gepaart mit Offenheit und Gesittung. Aber auch von dem Leichtsinn dieser jungen Briten hören wir viel[15.] Den Nachrichten über John Charles Stapleton eigen sind einerseits die von Hartwig angeführten Beispiele von Nächstenliebe, andererseits die Mitteilung, Stapleton habe unter der Roheit seiner Landsleute gelitten. Er muß einer der ersten britischen Studenten gewesen sein, die nach den Napoleonischen Kriegen wieder die durch Anwesenheit der königlichen Prinzen ausgezeichnete Universität Göttingen bezogen.

Es entspricht auch dem Charakter Stapletons, daß er nach seinem Abgang aus Göttingen offenbar die Verbindung mit der älteren Vertrauten abreißen ließ und den von ihr eingefädelten Plan, nach Heidelberg zu gehen, nicht durchführte. Offenbar wandte er sich zuerst einmal nach Berlin, wo er vermutlich mit einem Empfehlungsschreiben von Charlotte Diede auch Humboldt seine Aufwartung machte und „trotz mancher Extravaganzen"[16] Freunde fand.

---

15 S. meine Anm. 8 zitierte Notiz sowie meine Notiz über Goethe und Charles Sterling in Modern Language Review 54 (1959) 76-79; es bestehen einige Parallelen zwischen Charlotte Diedes Verhältnis zu Stapleton und Ottilie v. Goethes zu Sterling.

16 In seiner Zusammenfassung von H a r t w i g s Mitteilungen über Stapleton änderte L i e t z - m a n n das Wort „Thorheiten" in „Laster"!

Die Abstammung von Morley (nach dem er wohl John genannt wurde) macht es erklärlich, daß Ernst August, der Herzog von Cumberland, Humboldt überhaupt „ausführlich" über Stapletons Herkunft erzählen konnte. Daß Humboldt so wenig Ungewöhnliches daran fand, und daher die Einzelheiten vergaß, ist nicht erstaunlich. Uneheliche Söhne gehören in jener Zeit in der deutschen Literatur (Wilhelm Meister, Jean Pauls „Hesperus" u. a.) zu einem rechten englischen Edelmann. Daß aber Charlotte Diede weder durch Stapleton noch mittelbar über seine Abkunft gehört hatte, ist bemerkenswert. Es ist nicht ausgeschlossen, daß Humboldt ihre Gefühle, deren mehr als mütterliche Natur ihm nicht verborgen geblieben war, schonen wollte. Das Gespräch zwischen Humboldt und dem Herzog fand wohl in London statt, wo Humboldt ja hauptsächlich über die geplante Heirat Ernst Augusts mit der Schwägerin des Königs von Preußen zu verhandeln hatte.

Humboldt kehrte von London wenige Tage nach Augustus Granvilles Eintritt in St. John's College, Cambridge, zurück. Aus der Bemerkung in seinem Brief vom 3. März 1832, daß „der Name Stapleton ... selten nicht in England" ist, kann man schließen, daß er selbst an einen Zusammenhang mit Cannings Sekretär dachte, der 1827, zu Ehren seines Meisters zum Commissioner of Customs ernannt worden war und dessen „Political Life of Canning" (1830) große Diskussionen hervorrief. Die Nachricht von den drei in ein Duell verwickelten Brüdern hatte sicher nichts mit den Söhnen Morleys zu tun; die Verwicklung Augustus Granvilles in eine solche Affäre hätte weitere Kreise gezogen.

Abgesehen davon, daß es Freude macht, einen Vergessenen zum Leben zu erwecken, bleibt an John Charles Stapleton erinnernswert das Licht, das durch ihn auf das Leben britischer Studenten in Deutschland fällt, insbesondere in Göttingen[17], und auf das – Goethe verwandte – Eingehen Humboldts auf seine Freunde und auf junge Menschen.

(Quelle: Archiv für Kulturgeschichte 46, 1964, S. 127-132)

Ireland's Place in Nineteenth-Century German Poetry

While forming a unit by their tradition over a thousand years, Irish-German literary relations are distinguished by the absence of that material foundation in geographical, political and social relations on which otherwise similar relations are based. A point of special interest in the study of these relations therefore is the amount of knowledge conveyed of one country to the other through these relations. In this respect, poetry seems to be least interesting, as it is not a likely carrier of material information. Yet, Ireland's place in German poetry is an important source of German knowledge of Ireland or subjects related with Ireland, illustrating the various moods through which interest in Ireland passed during the centuries and in particular the permanent romantic trend.

---

17 Vgl. meinen Artikel: John Stuart Blackie's translation of Goethe's Jahrmarktsfest zu Plundersweilern, Modern Language Quarterly 8 (1947) 92 und oben Anm. 12. Man darf auch an Goethes Bemerkung (in „Wilhelm Meisters theatralische Sendung", Weimarer Ausgabe I, 52, 173) von dem Hamletkult unter den Göttinger Studenten erinnern.

The first three phases of the tradition of Ireland's place in German literature have been described as hagiographical (900 to 1150), chivalresque (to the end of the Middle Ages) and military (up to 1750). In the first phase the most outstanding works of German poetry are Ratpert's *Lobgesang auf den Heiligen Gallus* and the Alemannic poem of *Patricius*. The transition to the second phase, represented of course by *Trisran* and *Kudrun*, is marked by the German versifications of *Tundalus*. In the third phase we have the poetic description of the Irish soldiers in the army of Gustavus Adolphus (on the Stettin 1631 broadsheets) and Neukirch's poems on the flight of James II after the battle of the Boyne and to the memory of Tyrconnell.

It was only in the fourth period, which may be described as that of the scholar, that Ireland's place in German literature was primarily based on poetry. In 1770 Goethe sent Herder some translations made by him from the 'Galic' original produced by Macpherson in support of his claim to the authenticity of his Ossianic poems. While Goethe's translation is the earliest known German version of a Gaelic text, the interest taken by the poets of the classical period has been the foundation of German studies in the language and literature of ancient Ireland. In his poem 'Die Fremdlinge', one of the *Legenden* (1787), Herder linked the new Ossianic interest in Ireland with the tradition of the early Irish missionaries, in particular Columbanus, Gall and Fridolin.[1]

Verklungen war die Harfe Ossians

Im fernen West, auf jenen Eilanden
Des sanften Galenstammes ... Nicht Ossians
Gesänge mehr; sie singen Davids Psalmen[2] ...
Die zu Schlachten ernst,
Zu Rettungen auf ferne Küsten zogen,
Errettend ziehen sie jetzt zu stillen Siegen aus.

Herder added some philological and historical notes, gleaned from Müller's *Geschichte der Schweiz,* and the main body of his poem is the story of St. Columbanus (based on Jonas) and St. Gall (based on Wetti). Finally Herder refers to the work done at St. Gallen in preserving the ancient writers. We owe

Sanct Gall und Mang und allen Schotten Dank,
Die *scotice* mit Bardenfleiss,
Die Bücher schrieben und bewahrten[3] ...

Gute Galen, euch,
Die bis gen Lappland, bis zur Lombardei
Die Völker lehrten, Bücher sicherten,
Nachkommen euch des menschlichesten der Helden,
Des menschlichsten der Sänger [note: 'Fingal und Ossian'] Ruhm und Dank.

---

1   The Irish associations with this Saint, now recognized as unhistorical, are also referred to in Scheffel's Trompeter von Säckingen.

2   Follow the two verses quoted at the end of the present paper.

3   These verses are quoted in one of the notes of Scheffel's Ekkehard.

Among the 1200 sonnets (written about 1833) found in the Nachlass of Wilhelm von Humboldt,[4] there were two entitled *Hibernia* and *Scotia*. The latter is among the few published in its entirety.[5]

> Auf deinen Hügeln Ossians Harfe tönte,
> dem Sturm, von dem der Felsen dumpf erdröhnte,
> mischend den Laut der seelenvollen Klage
> am Meeresstrand, an nebelvollem Tage ...
> Hattest du ihn nicht, Scotia, besessen,
> wär' in der Zeiten Nacht dein Ruhm vergessen
> in wüster Kämpfe dunklem Irrgewühle.

Of the poem *Hibernia* only a few lines have been published so far. 'Die Myrte und der Lorbeer bluhen heiter' – obviously influenced by *Mignon* – "blumige Gründe und trüben Himmel hast du' – a fact also referred to in Humboldt's letters.[6] The relationship with the sonnet on *Scotia* is established by the subsequent words: 'Trübe und verwirrt ist auch dein Volk und nebelhaft der Gesang deiner frühen Taten' The relationship between the climate and history of Ireland had been established twenty years earlier in Tieck's dramatization of *Fortunatus* (iv): 'O Irland! Irland! du trauriges finsteres Land!'

Apart from Fortunatus, Tristan was the most important literary tradition carrying information on Ireland through many centuries of German literature. Of the many modern German poets who were inspired by the Tristan-tradition (A. W. Schlegel, Platen, Rückert, Wagner), Immermann was the only one to treat of those parts of the story the scene of which is laid in Ireland, including the place-names of Dublin (accentuated on the last syllable), Leinster, Connaught, Ulster[7] and 'Mounster'. Immermann's references to 'Liffy-Strom', 'Liffy-Fluss' and the 'Königsschloss in Dublin' may have been influenced by Marike's poem *Die traurige Krönung* (1828), which is a late example of the long and venerable tradition of fictitious associations with Ireland in German literature:

> Es war ein König Milesint,
> von dem will ich euch sagen:
> der meuchelte sein Bruderskind,
> wollte selbst die Krone tragen.
> Die Krönung ward mit Prangen
> auf Liffey-Schloss begangen.
> 0 Irland! Irland! warst du so blind?

Also during the classical period of German literature, the third period of Irish-German literature relations was reflected again in German poetry. In *Wallensteins Tod*, Schiller did not refer to the nationality of 'Buttler', Gordon, Macdonald and Devereux, but in

---

4   See F.M. Wassermann, 'Die Alterssonette Wilhelm von Humboldts' in Monatshefte, LXII (1950), pp. 395-408.

5   A. Lietzmann, W.v.H. Gesammelte Schriften (Berlin 1903 ff), IX, p. 432.

6   Briefe an eine Freudin (ed. A. Lietzmann, Leipz. 1909): 12.1.1834.

7   Rhymed with 'Polster'.

the *Lager* 'der erste Dragoner' ('Buttlersche Dragoner') says: 'Weit aus Hibernien komm' ich' and in a later passage: 'Der Irländer folgt des Glöckes Stern.' In his poem *Schloss Eger* Fontane laid, eighty years later:

Da sieh, in Stahl,
Buttlersche Dragoner
dringen in den Saal.

About the time when Schiller wrote his *Wallenstein*, Goethe had visited the town hall at Eger, noting the portrait of Butler in the wall-painting illustrating the assassination of the Duke of Friedland.

There has been to this day scarcely any Continental writer who, while never crossing the English Channel, had a picture more comprehensive and more correct of Ireland than Goethe. While his extensive *Irlandkunde* is recorded mainly in his diaries, letters, conversations and prose-works, a conspicuous sign of this interest is also found in his poetry. *Klaggesang. Irisch* was chosen in 1818 from Caro Lamb's *Glenarvon* for translation, and insertion in the section *Aus fremden Sprachen,* because of its specific reference to Ireland. The original, Goethe's translation and Mangan's re-translation represent three pictures of Ireland, the romantic of condescending Anglo-Irish view, the sympathetic if cautious view of a conscientious Continental observer, and the bold nationalist interpretation leading up to Young Ireland. Goethe's translation is also of interest with regard to his several other contacts with the Gaelic language.

Goethe was one of the few Continental writers of the time who realized that the sequence from Catholic Emancipation to Repeal Movement, Disestablishment, Land Reform and Independence was inevitable. He could not see, and perhaps was right in doing so, that this sequence would lead to social revolution as was suggested by Marx (in *Das Kapital*), his friend Venedy (in his book on *Ireland)* and, in poetry, by Freiligrath and Weerth. The ruthlessness of this interpretation can be illustrated by comparing Goethe's *Klaggesang* with Freiligrath's *Die irische Witwe* (published in 1840). In the first line of his poem, Freiligrath said that the story of the Irish widow was one of the few really moving items lately reported in 'Zeitungsblättern'. (O'Connell, of course, was the first modern statesman to make full use of press publicity.)

Hört: weil ein irisch Weib in Wittwennöthen,
Den Zehenten nicht zeitig abgetragen,
Liess ihr den einz'gen Sohn ein Priester – tödten!
Fünf Pfund! – ein Priester! – einer Witwe Sohn!

This is one of Freiligrath's longest poems, and its main body is a free version of the deposition made by 'die Wittwe Ryan zu den Richtern'. Considering his poem as a source of popular information on conditions in Ireland the only relevant passage is the description of the actual police action. 'Der Mann im Chorrock drückt uns bis aufs Blut.' In his zeal to fight social and clerical reaction, Freiligrath missed the most aggravating point in his story, namely that the tithes were extracted not for a priest of the people's own church but for the minister of an alien establishment. The German news-paper apparently had rendered the word 'priest' by 'Priester', and this point fitted in with Freiligrath's conception of rapacious Catholic clergy (in this respect his poem no doubt influenced Liliencron's *Pidder Lüng).* During the subsequent years,

Freiligrath learnt more of Ireland, while he tried to eke out a living for himself and his young family as a clerk at Messrs. Huth & Co. in London. In February 1847 he wrote what to my knowledge is the first and only German poem to bear the simple title of *Irland*.

Before considering this poem, let us discuss in the chronological order *Gebet eines Irländers,* published in 1846 by Georg Weerth,[8] the first German to write a poem relating to Ireland after actually visiting that country. In his capacity as London correspondent of the *Cölnische Zeitung*, Weerth had attended the great O'Connell trial in Dublin, which, marking the climax of the Liberator's career, was reported verbatim by this and other Continental newspapers. Weerth forecast the conflict between the nationalist and religious traditions of Ireland, and, in spite of its Paddy-sentimentality, his poem has remained one of the best statements of the political situation of Ireland in German literature.

> Sankt Patrick, grosser Schutzpatron,
> Du sitzest auf dem warmen Himmelsthron;[9]
> O sieh mich an mit freundlichem Sinn,
> Dieweil ich ein armer Paddy bin!

> Sankt Patrick, sieh, die Nacht kommt bald,
> Von England herüber weht es so kalt;[10]
> O blicke auf meinen schäbigen Frack
> Und auf meinen löchrigen Bettelsack!

> Sankt Patrick, tu was dir gefällt:
> So gross und so schön ist ja die Welt –
> O lass mich werden, was du willt,
> Nur bleiben nicht solch ein Menschenbild!

> (Let me be a flower, a deer, a bear, a swan, a panther, a lion or)
> Einen Tiger! auf dass ich manch reichen Tyrann
> Mit rasselnden Tatzen zerreissen kann! –

> Doch, Patrick, ach! taub[11] bleibt dein Ohr;
> Der Paddy bleib ich wohl nach wie vor.
> 's bleibt doch alles wie sonst und die Nacht ist kalt,
> Und der Dan O'Connell wird dick und alt!

Irish misgivings at O'Connell's growing fat and senile were voiced through those rallying around *The Nation*. One of the many functions of this paper in the cultural development of modem Ireland was to give a realist note to earlier interest in German poetry. In his article on Freiligrath in *Dublin University Magazine*, 1843, Mangan had spoken only of the romantic poems such as *Der Löwenritt*. In 1846, however, *The Nation* published Mangan's translation of *Freiheit und Recht*. The poem *Irland* was

---

8   Kindly communicated to me by Prof. Georg Kaiser, Berlin.

9   Clearly inspired by Morolt's exclamation: 'Sankt Patrick, du sitzest warm' in Immermann's Tristan und Isolde.

10   'Frisch weht der Wind der Heimat zu', the Irish sailor's song opening Wagner's Tristan. Compare zur Linde's poem at the end of this paper.

11   'Was hilft es? Gott ist taub' (Hebbel, Das Haus am Meer).

never published in Ireland, and Justin McCarthy mentioned the political poems neither in his study on Freiligrath[12] nor in his account of his friendship with the poet in London.[13] In 1917, *Irische Blätter,* the organ of the Deutsch-Irische Gesellschaft, republished Freiligrath's poem. There is a considerable amount of concrete information on Ireland in this poem, such as the references to the fishing rights, the export of cattle continued during the Famine, and the lack of bog cultivation ('bogs' being rhymed with 'Ochs'; 'Ihr kennt sie ja: Irlands Moräste! ... Sumpf und Wildniss, vier Millionen Aecker!').

> Erin - da liegt sie auf den Knien,
> Bleich und entstellt, mit when'dem Haare,
> Und streut des Shamrocks welkend Grün
> Zitternd auf ihrer Kinder Bahre ...
> 'Die Niobe der Nationen'.[14]

In his description of absenteeism, Freiligrath, from rash inference of conditions in Germany, missed the most revolting feature, that it was not 'sein Volk' that the landlord neglected but a people oppressed, religiously, socially and politically, by an alien.

Freiligrath left it to Marxists to suggest efficacious means of redeeming Ireland. Weerth had seen deeper when realizing that despondent wisdom had immunized the Irish against the glaring phantom of improvement by revolution: 's bleibt alles wie sonst'. Herder seems to have felt that this wisdom was rooted in a cyclical conception of historical time by which Ireland has been distinguished, since her first literary records,[15] from the rest of Europe:

> Der Strom der Zeiten ändert seinen Lauf,
> Und bleibt derselbe. *(Die Fremdlinge,* ii, 3).

A contemporary German poet has suggested that gathering up the traditions of Ossian and St. Patrick, Ireland, by what she is rather than by what she does, has a message for the present world. The following poem by Otto zur Linde,[16] published in 1901, reflects the vision of the romantic tourist, but also summarizes the tradition of Ireland in German poetry (notably its expressions in W. v. Humboldt and Richard Wagner):

> Wenn über Meer ein Segel steht,
> Vom Lande her der Ostwind weht:
> So tut sich auf das blaue Tor,
> Weit, weit, und taucht mein Irland, grünes Irland, hervor.
> Über dem Blauen des Meeres
> Schwebe die Blüte der Mandel,
> Über des Rosmarins Blaue

---

12   Originally published in the London Quarterly Review, reprinted in Con Amore (1868).

13   Reminiscences, I (1899), pp. 146-151. See also Prof. Liddell's introduction to his edition of Freiligrath's poems (Blackwell, Oxford, 1949).

14   O'Connell's rhetorics had not failed to impress Freiligrath.

15   See my paper 'A feast of all the Saints of Europe', Speculum, XXI, (1946), p. 66.

16   Kindly communicated to me by Prof. Ernst Loewy, Dublin.

Sonne und goldenes Dach.
Neben der Erde gehe,
Wage der See, es fahre
Rund um den Himmel der Wind,
Stehe die Seele in Gott.

(Quelle: German Life and Letters, N.S. 8, 1955, S. 201-207)

Daniel O'Connell in the Opinion of Some German Poets of His Time

In my contribution 'Continental Opinion' to *Daniel O'Connell* (Dublin, 1949, 233-69) I referred on the one hand to the interest which Goethe took, during the last years of his life, in the political developments in Ireland and on the other hand to the poem 'Gebet eines Irländers' written in 1846 by Georg Weerth. In his review of Pückler's *Briefe eines Verstorbenen* (1839) Goethe said:[1]

> Er [Pückler] besucht den famosen O'Connell in seiner entfernten, kaum zugänglichen Wohnung und vollendet das Bild, das wir uns nach den bisherigen Schilderungen von diesem wundersamen Manne im Geiste entwerfen konnten. Dann wohnt er populären Zusammenkünften bei, hört den Genannten sprechen, sodann jenen merkwürdigen Shiel und andere wunderliche auftretende Personen ... An der großen irländischen Hauptangelegenheit nimmt er menschlich-billigen Antheil, begreift aber die Zustände in aller ihrer Verwickelung zu gut, als daß er sich zu heitern Erwartungen sollte hinreissen lassen.

Weerth's poem concluded with the line: 'Und der Dan O'Connell wird dick und alt.'[2]

The years between these two pronouncements have remained unparalleled in the history of Continental interest in Ireland. During that period more publications on Ireland appeared in French and German than during the rest of the nineteenth century. At no time did a greater number of eminent persons in various walks of life state their opinion on Ireland. No one realized more fully than O'Connell the importance of public opinion.

Ten weeks after Goethe wrote his review, Heine referred to Pückler's work in the introduction to the first book edition of his *Englische Fragmente*. After saying,

> Was Reisebeschreibungen betrifft, so gibt es, außer Archenholz und Göde, gewiß kein Buch über *England* [my italics], das uns die dortigen Zustände besser veranschaulichen könnte,

Heine subsequently quoted the full title of *Briefe eines Verstorbenen* including the word 'Irland':

> Es ist dieses noch in mancher anderen Hinsicht ein vortreffliches Buch und verdient in vollem Maße das Lob, das ihm Goethe und Varnhagen von Ense in den Berliner Jahrbüchern für wissenschaftliche Kritik gespendet haben.

---

1   Weimar edition I, xlii, 1, p. 58.

2   See my paper on 'Ireland's place in nineteenth-century German poetry' in German Life and Letters, VIII (1955), 205. At the end of chapter XX of Leben und Taten des berühmten Ritters Schapphahnski (1849, republished Berlin 1958) Weerth refers to the proceedings in the House of Commons.

It is quite possible that Heine heard of Pückler's work through Goethe's review, and his various references to Catholic Emancipation may have been influenced by Goethe. The fourth chapter of Heine's *Englische Fragmente*, entitled 'John Bull (übersetzt aus einer englischen Beschreibung Londons)', begins with the following passage:

> Es scheint, als ob die Irländer durch ein unveränderliches Gesetz ihrer Natur den Müßiggang als das echte, charakteristische Kennzeichen eines Gentleman betrachten; und da ein Jeder dieses Volkes, kann er auch aus Armuth nicht einmal sein gentiles Hintertheil bedecken, dennoch ein geborner Gentleman ist, so geschieht es, daß verhältnismässig wenige Sprößlinge des grünen Erin sich mit den Kaufleuten der City vermischen ...

Later 'John Bulls beharrliches Knurren, des Schotten nachgiebige Philosophie' are compared with 'das stürmische Feuer des Irländers'. That Heine considered this English appraisal of the sister-nations worth translating illustrates the background against which the development of Continental opinion of Ireland during the subsequent years must be studied.

Heine's eleventh fragment is entitled 'Die Emancipation'.[3]

> Burke, der große Renegat der Freiheit, konnte nicht soweit die Stimme des Herzens unterdrücken, daß er gegen Irland gewirkt hätte. Auch Canning, sogar damals, als er noch ein toryscher[4] Knecht war, konnte nicht ungerührt das Elend Irlands betrachten. Burke[5] und Canning konnten nimmermehr Partei nehmen gegen das arme grüne Erin; Irländer, die schreckliches Elend und namenlosen Jammer über ihr Vaterland verbreiten, sind Menschen wie der selige Castlereagh und der unselige Wellington.

Heine then translated from *Parliamentary History and Review During the Session of 1825-26* Lord King's reference (p. 31) to the

> sechs Millionen Katholiken jenseits des irländischen Kanals und die dortige schlechte Regierung. Der Großsultan hat sich bemüht, die Griechen zu bekehren, in derselben Weise wie das englische Gouvernement die Bekehrung der irländischen Katholiken betreibt, aber ohne Erfolg.

Heine felt that the comparison drawn by Lord King between Greece and Ireland showed

> daß die Völker Europas mit gleichem Rechte sich der irländischen Katholiken annehmen [as they intervene for the Greeks]. Freilich hatten Europas Völker das heiligste Recht, sich für die Leiden Irlands mit gewaffneter Hand zu verwenden, und dieses Recht würde auch ausgeübt werden, wenn nicht das Unrecht stärker wäre.

From the same source (p. 252) Heine translated from Spring Rice's speech of 26 May 1825:

---

3   Werke (Hamburg 1861), III, 116. In his description of a journey from Munich to Genoa (ibid. II, 132), Heine referred to 'die Emancipation der Irländer, Griechen, Frankfurter Juden und westindischen Schwarzen'.

4   Ibid. III, 96 f. Heine referred to the tradition of the Irish origin of the terms 'Whig' and 'Tory'. See also my paper on 'Goethe and Canning' in M.L.Q. x (1949), 512-16.

5   Heine's reference to Burke was not mentioned by Frieda Braune, Edmund Burke in Deutschland (Heidelberg, 1917).

Die Bedrückung ist es, wodurch Leute wie Herr O'Connell und Herr Sheil so einflußreich geworden sind. Die Nennung dieser Herren geschieht nicht, um sie verdächtig zu machen; im Gegenteil
man muß ihnen Achtung zollen, und sie haben sich um das Vaterland Verdienste erworben;
dennoch wäre es besser, wenn die Macht vielmehr in den Gesetzen als in den Händen der Individuen, seien diese auch noch so achtungswert, beruhen möchte.

While Goethe had taken a cautious view of the possibility of undoing the misfortunes
of Ireland by means of Catholic Emancipation, the younger generation considered this
possibility as an established fact. The literary movement, from what appeared as
reactionary romanticism to revolutionary liberalism, was first described, in a letter
written by Gutzkow in 1833, as 'das junge Deutschland', a term which, after it had
already been discarded, exercised some influence in Ireland.[6]

In 1835, that is just between his two monumental novels *Die Ritter vom Geist* and *Der
Zauberer von Rom,* Gutzkow wrote an essay on O'Connell, which in the Jena edition
of his works occupies ten closely printed pages.[7]

Das grüne Erin [the same term as used by Heine],[8] dreifach geschützt durch einen Kranz von
Untiefen, einen Wall von Klippen und im Inneren [!] durch ungebahnte Gebirgsstraßen ... mit
seiner Unruhe, seinen barocken Einfällen, seiner glühenden katholischen Andacht ..., mit seinem
Irish Bull[9] immer leichtsinnig, beweglich und bereit, oft für den Hauch eines Gerüchtes ... ins
Feuer zu gehen ... hoffte, der heilige Patrick[10] würde endlich auf einer Armada den katholischen
Himmel, von welchem es sich unter englischem Scepter ausgeschlossen fühlt, zuführen ... Der
irische Bauer erträgt den Reichtum neben sich und vermißt in der Lehmhütte, neben seinem
einzigen Besitztum, einem Ferkel und einem Mass Kartoffeln für den nächsten Tag, nichts von
dem Glanze, über den sein Vetter oder Sohn, der in London Schuhe putzt oder die Bettelkunst mit
witzigen Impromptus treibt, in ein schüchternes und uneigennütziges Erstaunen gerät.

– perhaps a reflexion from Heine's fourth fragment. Unlike Freiligrath,[11] Gutzkow realized that the tithes were collected for the clergy of the Established rather than of the
Catholic Church.

---

6   T. F. O'Sullivan, The Young Irelanders (Tralee, 1944).

7   IX, 84, preceded by an essay on Wellington.

8   See also 'Erin – des Shamrocks welkend Grün' in Freiligrath's poem 'Irland' (see my paper
      quoted in n. 2 above, p. 205).

9   See my papers 'Two Irish Bulls in Kant's Kritik der Urtheilskraft', M.L.Q., VIII (1947), 487 f.
      and 'Goethe and the Edgeworths', ibid. XV (1954), 366 f.

10   St Patrick is mentioned also in Immermann's Tristan und Isolde (see my paper in M.L.R. XLIV
      (1949), 246-52, and in Weerth's poem (see above n. 2). Later in his essay Gutzkow says that
      O'Connell is 'ein Enkel des Heiligen Patricius im Glauben des Volks' (p. 90).

11   See my paper quoted in n. 2 above, p. 206. Towards the end of the fifth chapter of Uli der
      Pächter, Jeremias Gotthelf said: 'Die Pachtherren haben es gar verschieden gegenüber ihren
      Pächtern. Es ist hier nicht von irländischen, nicht von englischen Pachtherren die Rede ...'.
      When reprinting this novel in the eleventh volume of Gotthelf's Gesammelte Werke (Erlenbach,
      1927), the editors made the following note: 'Irische [!] Pachtherren: In den vierziger Jahren,
      besonders 1843, führten die trostlosen ökonomischen Zustände der irischen Pächter zu revolu-
      tionären Bewegungen, infolge deren Hunderte von Landleuten den Pachtzins verweigerten. Im
      Jahre 1846 kam dazu noch die schreckliche Teuerung [!]. Die damaligen Zeitungen und

Gutzkow believed that the French Revolution and the Union had been the turning-points in Irish history; he obviously had no conception of Cromwell and the Penal Laws. Contemporary Ireland seemed to him to confirm the theory that history is the work of ideas rather than of material interests. He realized that the

> sogenannte prädiale Agitation [as represented by the 'Weißbuben', a subject on which ample information was then available in German literature][12] ist es, vor welcher die politische, der Demagogismus O'Connells in gesetzlichen Formen, immer so emphatisch zu warnen pflegt und welche doch der eigentliche Rückhalt und gefürchtete Bundesgenosse des letzteren ist:

– a prophetic statement. O'Connell, he said, has studied the history of demagogism,

> kann aber dem überlieferten System so viel Neues geben, daß wir einsehen, eine Agitation, wie die seinige, ist noch nicht dagewesen. Das Neue liegt bei ihm in seiner wunderbaren[13] Stellung, in dieser kron- und scepterlosen, aber darum nicht weniger anerkannten Herrschaft über Millionen, in diesem Vertrauen eines Volkes.

It was the realization of the novelty of this conception of demagogy which was the common basis of all Continental interest, whether Catholic, Conservative, Liberal or Socialist, in Daniel O'Connell, a point rarely considered in connexion with Ireland's position in, and attitude to, present-day world affairs.[14]

> Der Zweck seiner Agitation kann niemals die Devise: Dan I. sein, sondern das Ganze handelt sich sowohl darum die Zukunft zu befestigen, als sie zu beschleunigen. O'Connell sieht ein, daß sein System auf drei Grundsätze zurückkommen muß: auf die Notwendigkeit, die Wunde Irlands immer offen zu erhalten, auf den Schein der Gesetzmässigkeit und endlich auf die Sicherung seiner Person.

Gutzkow charged O'Connell with 'delphische Schlauheit', 'Scheingebung, die nahe an Satyre streift', 'Egoismus' and 'Scheinheiligkeit' and gave a magnificent analysis of his rhetorical methods. 'Das Privilegium der üblen Nachrede und Injurie. . .ist eine für den Demagogen unerläßliche Maßregel.'

Concluding his essay, Gutzkow summarized O'Connell's career with special reference to his parliamentary speeches and his trial:

> In London verwickelt er sich in die Intrigen der Parteien, die seine Stimme erobern möchten. In London strauchelt er hie und da auf dem schlüpfrigen Boden der Debatte ... Das Ministerium Grey ... ging an des Agitators Unbedachtsamkeit zu Grunde, da derselbe in Dublin unter den Seinigen immer das zu bereuen pflegt, was er in London zugelassen hat. Diese Unbehaglichkeit

---

namentlich die vielverbreiteten Pfennigmagazine schilderten die dortige Agrarbewegung in ausgiebigem Maße.' That this note was considered necessary and that such an inadequate explanation of Gotthelf's reference could be given, illustrates the deterioration of Continental knowledge of Ireland between the years 1848 and 1927. On two Swiss penny tracts on contemporary Ireland (Basle, 1840), see my article on 'Irische Frauengestalten in der Weltliteratur' in Basler Nachrichten, 23 May 1954.

12   See, for example, my paper on (the German translation of) Michael Whitty in Irish Bookman (February 1947), pp. 39-44.

13   Compare Goethe's description of O'Connell as 'wundersam'.

14   See the survey of the history of the Irish term taoiseach in my paper on 'The Literary Tradition of Moses in Ireland' in Traditio. VII (1949-51), 257-61.

einer unheimischen Stellung ist der Grund, warum O'Connell nie zu einer großen Macht im Unterhause gelangt.

On 2 June 1836, Bulwer procured for Grillparzer an admission ticket to the Commons. At the end of his autobiography, Grillparzer briefly referred to this visit:[15]

> Es war damals eben im Parlament die frische Zehentbill in Verhandlung. Ich versäumte keinen Tag, oder vielmehr keine Nacht, der Diskussion, die oft bis vier Uhr Morgens währte, beizuwohnen. Bei meinem für die Aussprache des Englischen ungeübten Ohre verstand ich zwar kaum die Hälfte der Reden, aber schon als Schauspiel war das Ganze hinreissend....Am besten, wenigstens am Lebhaftesten sprach Shirl [sic !]....O'Connell und die meisten Uebrigen hatten weniger Fluß der Rede, als ich voraussetzte und die gedruckten Verhandlungen glauben machen.

A more detailed account is found in Grillparzer's *Tagebuch aus dem Jahre 1836*:[16]

> Wir saßen rechts im vollen Anblick der ministeriellen Seite. O'Connell ganz schwarz gekleidet, mit kleiner vorstehender Hemdkrause. Ein starker Mann, schwarzes Haar, eine Papierrolle in der Hand, die er während der Rede der Gegenpartei wie eine Klarinette an den Mund hielt. Seine Züge konnte ich nicht ausnehmen. Er saß auf der zweiten Bank. Beinahe vor ihm auf der ersten Sheil. Hager, blond, lebhaft. Wie wir eintraten, hielt eben der Sekretär für Irland, Lord Morpeth, eine Rede.

The report on Morpeth's speech in *The Times* says that

> when the noble lord sat down, Mr O'Connell came up to the Treasury bench, and cordially shook hands with him, which was noticed on the opposite side of the house by cheering.

Grillparzer continued:

> Darauf Sir James Graham [the previous Secretary for Ireland] ... Endlich stand Sheil auf. Seine Stimme war wie ein zweischneidiges Schwert, von vornherein unangenehm, er selbst eine Feuerflamme. Die Lebhaftigkeit seiner Bewegungen, die Abwechslung der Stimme, die Bitterkeit seines Hohnes, das Donnern seiner Verwünschungen unbeschreiblich.

Although Grillparzer could not understand, he was greatly impressed, and this in one of the most extensive accounts of Sheil's art of speaking. A point not mentioned by Grillparzer was Sheil's reference in this speech to Graham's late 'continental tour' to study the financial position of the churches in Prussia after the late accession of Catholic Rhineland. 'He found in Prussia Catholicism mitigated by the precepts of Erasmus and Lutheranism mellowed by Melancthon *(sic)*' a reference, no doubt, to the accommodating attitude of the archbishop of Cologne. Sheil then referred to 'Poland, Russia's Ireland'.

While listening to Shell, Grillparzer thought:

> Die Engländer mögen nur ruhig sein. Sie kennen die andern Nationen vielleicht nicht genug, um ganz zu wissen, wie allmächtig sie sind. Wenn sie einmal ernsthaft wollen, wird alles vor ihnen zerstäuben, wie selbst Napoleon zerstäubte. Die Welt ist gesichert. Als Sheil ausgeredet hatte, brauchte es keine Auflösung der Sitzung, alles ging aus einander,

a point specially stressed in the press reports on this session.

---

15 Sämtliche Werke (Stuttgart, 1872), x, 205.

16 Ibid. pp. 393 ff. Compare the reference made to the tithes question in Ireland by Lamartine in bis speach 'L'Etat, l'Eglise et l'enseignement' (1843).

On 3 June Grillparzer again attended the Commons debate on the Irish Church Bill:

> Plötzlich Bewegung, alles drängt sich, die Zuseher stehen auf. O'Connell fängt an zu sprechen. Wenn je ein Mensch alle äußern Eigenschaften eines Redners vereinigte, so ist er's. Tüchtige Gestalt, tief klingendes Organ, leichte, treffende Bewegungen; im Spott wie im Donner des Ernstes gleich wirksam ... Er spie Invektiven auf Persönlichkeiten, so daß ihn der Sprecher zurückweisen musste. [*The Times* report says: 'The speaker interposed, saying that the hon. and learned member for Kilkenny was quite out of order if he meant to apply the word "men of blood" to any member of the house'] ... Die Irländer scheinen treffliche Deklamatoren....Am Ende seiner Rede eine ungeheure Bewegung unter den Mitgliedern, deren Ursache ich nicht abnehmen konnte.

O'Connell had concluded with a reference to a petition lately submitted to the Tory corporation of Bristol 'in favour of the emancipation of the Jews': 'The time has arrived when justice must be done, and when it will be impossible to trample upon the liberties and rights of men'. *The Times* reported: 'The hon. and learned member at the Conclusion of his speech was cheered from the Minister benches, and he then rose to quit the house, upon which great cheering and laughter ensued.'

On the following day, Grillparzer read in the two numbers of the *Morning Chronicle* the speeches he bad heard:

> Las jetzt bis zum Erblinden das Gehörte nach, und fand die Reden, mit Ausnahme der von Lord Morpeth, unbedeutender, als ich mir vorgestellt hatte.

Still he had become imbued with Irish nationalist views. Referring (under 9 June) to 'der protestantische Erzbischof über ganz Irland' he added in brackets: *'all Ireland,* Gott verdamm' ihn!' (Later he speaks of him as 'Erzbischof von Armagh (ein hochtoristischer Lord Beresford)'). Under 13 June Grillparzer recorded his meeting 'Mistress Courtenay mit ihrem 13- oder 14-jährigen Burschen, den sie für O'Connells Sohn ausgibt', an episode scarcely mentioned in the biographies of O'Connell.

Apart from Weerth, who in hin capacity of correspondent to the *Kölnische Zeitung* attended the Dublin trial, Grillparzer was the only one of the German writers here considered who actually saw O'Connell.

During the subsequent 120 years only two political leaders of Ireland have attained a stature comparable to that of O'Connell. The decline of continental interest in Ireland can be gauged by the fact that there is no outstanding German writer in whose works one could trace the names of Parnell or De Valera.

(Quelle: MLR 54, 1959, S. 76-79)

The Irish Widow

In connection with the centenary commemoration of Thomas Davis and the Young Ireland Movement, the Government recently held an exhibition of painting of Irish historical interest. The National Library held at the same time an exhibition of contemporary documents relating to Davitt and Parnell. An official collection of materials relating to the Famine is also being prepared. In this connection, documents of Continental reaction to conditions in Ireland may be of new interest. Of German writers, few did more to give wide publicity to the sufferings of Ireland than did Ferdinand Freiligrath.

Freiligrath's career as a poet began at a time when, already after Goethe's death, German poetry tried in vain to keep up the high level, which it had attained during the classical period. His early poems are characteristic of that curious second-hand Romanticism which turning away from the drabness of ordinary life drew its inspiration from far away countries, such as India, Asia Minor, Africa and even Ireland.

In the forties however, Freiligrath and many of his contemporaries discovered that there were subjects no less interesting nearer home. He became entangled in the democratic or Liberal movement. Soon he had to leave Germany, to escape prosecution by the reactionary authorities. For some time he eked out a living for himself and his young family as a clerk in Messrs. Ruth & Co in London. Then came the revolution of '48. Freiligrath returned to his native Rhineland, where he edited a democratic paper, but he had to flee again. This time James Oxford, a Jewish businessman at London, offered him a sanctuary. Later he became correspondent in the Swiss bank in London. Returning to Germany and living there for the last twenty years of his life, Freiligrath was one of the most popular poets of the period.

London of course was then the centre of political refugees from all parts of Europe, Poland, Italy, Hungary, Spain and France as well as Germany. Arriving there in 1846 Freiligrath praised England as the only democratic power in the world, though by that time he was well aware of the limitations of British democracy in the sister-island. Freiligrath had further, more personal reasons for returning to England. From his early twenties, he had been interested in English literature. He planned to publish a new periodical to spread knowledge of contemporary English literature in Germany, a plan which he did not succeed in realising until the year 1860. Few Germans of that period played a greater part than Freiligrath did in the propagation of contemporary English poetry. The greater part of Freiligrath's collected works is taken up by translations from Coleridge, Southey, Wordsworth, Charles Lamb, Keats, Thomas Campbell, Scott, Longfellow, Thackeray, Browning, Tennyson, Macauly and even less known poets such as John Wilson, Ebenezer Elliott, Felicia Hemans and Allan Cunningham. Freiligrath was the first to introduce the German public to Walt Whitman and Bret Harte.

However, in the first collection of Freiligrath's poems, no foreign poet is represented by a greater number of his works than Thomas Moore. This first collection included 26 poems of Moore's, mostly taken from "Sacred Songs", "Ballads and Songs" and "National Airs". There was not one of the "Irish Melodies" among those early translations. It was not until the time after his return from London, that Freiligrath translated just one of the "Irish Melodies", namely "Oh banquet not in those shining bowers", certainly one of the least characteristic and least Irish poems of that series. Still later, Freiligrath translated one of Moore's poems to Lord Byron.

There exist no less than ten studies on Freiligrath's translations of English poetry. The headline for all these investigations was set by Freiligrath himself when saying that "the Englishmen Byron, Moore, Scott, Coleridge, Wilson and Wordsworth gave me the first important impulse". The order in which these poets are listed is significant. Goethe too regarded Byron, Moore and Scott as the greatest poets of the period. Freiligrath's reading of the Englishman Moore's work must have started at an early age; long before publishing those translations, the influence of "Evenings in Greece" and of "Lalla Rookh" can be traced in Freiligrath's descriptions of Eastern scenes, which neither he nor Moore had even seen with their own eyes.

Introducing the Irish public to Freiligrath, Mangan, in the 18th instalment of his Anthologia Germanica (Dublin University Magazine, 1843[1]) confined himself to the early African poems, which he translated from the third edition of Freiligrath's works (Stuttgart 1840). Similarly Prof. Liddell, Professor of German in Trinity College, (who in two recent studies showed that, forgotten and despised though he may be nowadays, Freiligrath is a great poet), made just one casual reference to Freiligrath's "Verses on the Irish famine". One American investigator is said to have proved that in contrast to the usual assumption that Freiligrath's poetry was most strongly influenced by Byron, Moore's influence is still more prominent. Apart from Moore's poems, the only other work of Irish writing to be translated by Freiligrath is "The Irische Volkslied" Eileen Aroon. The choice of this poem is significant as there is a political note in it.

Freiligrath's political interest in Ireland followed the line taken by his democratic and liberal friends in Germany and France who regarded Ireland as the classical illustration of the effects of that system of tyranny against which they were fighting. This new interest, indirect though it was, exercised great influence on the promotion of Continental knowledge of this "minor British isle". How detailed this interest could occasionally become may be seen from Freiligrath's poem "The Irish widow", which appeared in the section "Terzinen" of the 1840 edition of his poems. This is one of the longest poems of Freiligrath's, occupying no less than nine pages. In the beginning of his poem Freiligrath tells us that it is a reflection of a news-item, which he found on one of the rare occasions on which he looked at a paper. Since Goethe's "Werther" the newspaper had frequently been a source of inspiration to poets. Freiligrath glanced at that paper, while sitting in a coffee house, one of the early literary cafes on the continent. Around him conversations were carried on in French, Danish and English; the scene is probably in Hamburg. Such international cafes used to keep not only German but also foreign, notably English, newspapers. Half reading, half listening to the chatting of some card-players beside him, Freiligrath suddenly feels something like a blow. "A cold shudder came over me. Am I dreaming? Is this a gag? No, it is true. It has really happened. Only a week ago. I still hear the horses galloping up to the cottage. Listen: An Irish woman, a distressed widow, not having paid the tithe in due course, her son was murdered by – a priest! Five pounds! – a priest! – the son of a widow! My lips begin to quiver, not in prayer though. I clench my fists. Futile rage –

---

1   In the book-edition of his German-Anthology, Mangan gave translations of no less than ten of Freiligrath's African poems, all unpolitical. One of Freiligrath's African poems was reprinted in the review of Mangan's Anthology in "The Nation", August 9th 1845. On April 4, 1846, "The Nation" published Mangan's translation of Freiligrath's poem "Freedom and Right", a general democratic song.

you may call it –, but have I not got the gift of words to chastise this system of slavery?"

"This news-sheet is but for the day. The poet however will be listened to by many generations. He who has been belasted by him, remains blasted for ever. I begin to picture to my mind that scene in all its details. There lies the son, stiff, every limb bleeding. The grey-haired mother kneeling by his side. I meant to describe this scene to you, but then I felt it would not do to give "publicity" to the poor widow. Thus I locked up this scene in my heart. A few months later however it came back to my mind. Going back to the cafe, I asked for that news sheet. I was shown the file. Finding that that issue had been thumbed to bits, I pushed the file back into its shelf. There was nobody who had kept that story in his heart, the shameful misdeed of the desecrator. I was ashamed of my silence while the screams of that mother were still ringing in my ears."

"Though the impression of that news has worn off, I will write this poem, lest the memory of that scene will be wiped out altogether. Indeed I cannot speak as the widow spoke when she stood before the jury. The rifles glitter around her cottage. Listen to the shame of a priest. The widow Ryan said to the judge: 'I had gone into the field. Dick said to me: I shall come after you. So I waited for him. Suddenly I heard shooting. Smoke rose between the roofs. I ran home struck with terror. In the village, "Black Bill" was raging, ordering the dragoons to punish all who were not giving the tithe. I was in his debt. I am poor. One year the crops had failed, another year they had been destroyed by a hail-storm. Then before Christmas two of our cows died. My husband is dead. Dick works hard in garden and fields, but still we had to owe those five pounds and eighteen shillings. I saw the soldiers stopping in front of our cottage. There was a man whose mouth is supposed to preach the Word – not to us though. He smashed the door of my hut. On my knees, I asked for patience, but he rebuked me, swearing he would not leave the village until he had been paid. I asked for my son. Why did he not speak to that hard-hearted man? The neighbours pointed towards the barn. There I found him on the thrashing floor, shot – by order of a priest." Now follows a long description of the widow's silent mourning. "I did not cry – oh Lord, I cannot cry: While the dragoons were rioting, I closed his eyes with my hand. Then I went into the house. Kneeling by the fire, I stirred the embers. A tear was hizzing in the fire."

I do not know whether the story of the widow Ryan is authentic. At any rate, Freiligrath pictured to his readers one of the heart-rending scenes, which certainly made them realise the sufferings of Ireland. Freiligrath's picture of the whole scene may be romantic, sentimental, exaggerated, even sensational. Still it would be unfair to accuse him of lack of that sincerity which makes a true poet, and which could be the only justification of treating poetically such a subject.

By using the word "Priester", Freiligrath at first suggests to the average German reader that the "man in the surplice" was a Catholic priest. The reference to is "preaching the Word - not to us though" was too casual to impart to his readers knowledge of the real background of the tithe system. Freiligrath was a Protestant and, like his fellow-Liberals, anticlerical. Whether in France or in Germany, these Liberal writers on

Ireland were in the rather awkward position of having to admit that catholics and even the catholic clergy were among the victims of tyranny. Religion to them was a political issue or a pure sentimentality. On Palm Sunday 1832 Freiligrath had written a poem "In an English Church", whether actually in England (where by that time he had not yet been) or in Germany (where in many cities the Anglican congregations owned fine churches), I do not know. Listening to the sermon, he asks himself: "Is this not the language, which Wakefield's Vicar spoke, o gentle Wakefield, paradise of dreams!" I wonder did Freiligrath realise that Goldsmith was an Irishman and that Wakefield was somewhere in Ireland?

While staying in London, Freiligrath like many of his fellow-refugees acquired a more material notion of conditions in Ireland. His friend Venedy actually came over here to make a study of the Repeal Movement. In 1847 Freiligrath wrote his poem "Irland", the only German poem to bear this title. In November 1917 the "Irische Blätter", the organ of the German-Irish Society in Berlin, reprinted this poem as an early record of German political interest in Ireland's fight against the Saxon. In this poem, Freiligrath describes the famine as a result of landlord policy in Ireland. The land, the cattle, fishing and hunting are owned by Ireland's masters. While huge exports of cattle and corn leave the country, while the landowners destroy the last meagre crops by hunting, "Paddy" is starving to death. Only the bogs – "you know the morasses of Ireland" – are left to the natives. There are four million acres of wilderness and bog-land in Ireland – the reference to this figure in a work of poetry is remarkable. In the last verse of this poem, there is a note reminiscent of "The West's Awake":

"From Connnacht (sic) to Leinster a dull rambling is heard, right to my widow. It is the voice of Erin, the voice of a dying nation, the Niobe among the nations".

Freiligrath had no message of hope for Ireland. He left it to Marx and Engels to suggest to Ireland ways end means of recovering her freedom. Ireland at that time was a subject hardly fit for poetical treatment. Still Freiligrath's poems have remained the most outstanding poems on this country written in any continental language. Embodied as they were in the collections of his works, his poems on Irish subjects carried some knowledge of contemporary Ireland to – one may say, millions, who would never bother to read a book on Ireland.

(nicht veröffentlicht, ohne Jahr)

Michael Whitty

One of the most interesting aspects of the history of English literature in Ireland is certainly the place held in it by Ireland and the Irish themselves. It was not until the late 18th century that English writing in Ireland made the life of the people of this country its definite and foremost subject. Maria Edgeworth is usually credited with having written the first novels dealing with the life of the Irish peasantry, but it is generally agreed that she did not really get under the skin of her countrymen. Gerald Griffin, the brothers Banim, William Carleton and, perhaps Thomas Crofton Croker are usually regarded as the first Irish writers who gave the world genuine descriptions of the life of the Irish people.

The predominance of the south in this early writing on Irish life is remarkable. The Banims were born in Kilkenny, Griffin in Limerick, Croker in Cork. It is curious that in this connection the name of Michael James Whitty of Wexford is hardly ever mentioned, though in his tales the Irish peasant came for the first time really alive on paper. That Whitty is so little known is probably due to the fact that it was not until 1900 that it was stated that he was the author of the two slim, smartly bound volumes of *Tales of Irish Life,* which had been published anonymously at London as early as 1824. When in 1873 the *Athenaeum* was the only literary periodical to take notice of Whitty's death, it confined itself to briefly reviewing his journalistic activities. Neither the British Museum nor Trinity College seem to own a copy of Whitty's *Tales*; the copy acquired in 1925 by the National Library of Ireland is rightly preserved among the rare books.

Carleton was born in 1794, Michael Banim in 1796, Whitty in 1795. It may be said that as a writer on Irish country life, Whitty had the twofold handicap of being neither of farmers' stock nor a Catholic. Yet his father's trade (that of malster) cannot have failed to bring young Whitty into contact with Irish farmers. In the preface to his *Tales,* Whitty says he felt qualified for his task as he had lived for twenty years in various parts of Ireland. Most of his later years, Whitty lived as a journalist in Liverpool in close contact with Irishmen. His firm stand for catholic emancipation originated from his aversion to any form of bigotry, one of the chief subjects of his stories.

The subtitle of Whitty's *Tales of Irish Life* describes the contents of this work as 'illustrative of the manners, customs and conditions of the people'. 'Less is actually known in this country', Whitty writes, 'of the real state of Ireland (the words 'real state of Ireland' are printed in capital letters) than of the regions beyond the Ganges or the Mississippi . ...

While native writers, from a false patriotism, have exaggerated and distorted facts, foreigners, from prejudice and ignorance, have dealt largely in misrepresentation.' Thus the author makes it clear that adopting the position of the unbiassed, though well-informed, outsider, he tries to give a true picture of Irish country-life for the information of Englishmen. He was the first to try deliberately to draw attention to the fact that while 'Irish affairs are acquiring growing importance on this side of the channel. many English readers are only pleased with representations of Irish life where nature, truth and commonsense are outraged and insulted.' Whitty was the first to publish genuine stories of Irish peasants with the definite aim of overcoming English ignorance and prejudice with regard to Irish affairs. In 1825 appeared the first volume of Banim's *O'Hara Tales*; in 1826 the first volume of Croker's *Fairy Legends of the South of Ireland* (incidentally both works were published anonymously like Whitty's *Tales*) and only five years later appeared Carleton's *Traits and Stories of the Irish Peasantry.*

Whitty's work consists of sixteen short stories, each of which deals with one particular aspect of Irish country life of that time, mainly political, economic and social. Whitty's statement: 'The author has witnessed most scenes here described', refers only to the scenic background of his stories, that is, life in Munster and south Leinster. As the subtitle of his work clearly says, he did not expect his readers to be primarily interested in the stories of love and revenge which occupy the foreground of most of his *Tales*; these stories are of course fiction. What Whitty could claim to have experienced himself was the general background, the importance of which he constantly emphasized by philosophical reflections and moral statements interrupting the actual narrative.

It is characteristic that the hero of the first of these stories is an Englishman, whose failure to settle in Ireland is due not to adversity shown by the natives, but to the hostile attitude of the ascendancy. There seems to be an autobiographical background in this story. The Whittys were, apparently, not cromwellian planters, but came to Wexford in the 18th century, buying there some property and setting up their trade, keeping aloof from party spirit. When Whitty left Ireland for London, he did not do so like Banim and Griffin to be trained as a journalist but because he felt that as a protestant in complete disagreement with his party, he could not live in Ireland. Like the hero of his first story, he returned to England intending to 'expose the nefarious policy which caused disaster and oppression in Ireland'. The actual subject of this story is a picture of the consequences of the disregard of law by the gentry and magistrates. There is no law in Ireland he states melancholically, 'not only for a catholic, but even for an Englishman accustomed to the standards of jurisdiction in England'.

In some respects, indeed, the hero of this story is a literary descendant of Mrs Leadbeater's Scotch ploughman. He believes in 'the improved English plan, using newly invented implements of husbandry', a subject to which Whitty repeatedly returns. However, unlike earlier writers, Whitty does not attribute Ireland's failure to adopt those improved methods to the innate sloth of the race but to 'the miscalculated pride with which the self-important and self-willed landowners have retarded improvement by ridicule and refused to follow example by denying its utility'. Whitty applauds the 'singular happiness of the Irish peasantry in lessening presumptuous importance (in their masters) by the ignominious brand of a characteristic nick-name such as bucker'.

Perhaps the most convincing proof of Whitty's genuineness is his admission that the real Irish remained a mystery to him.

'Few people on the globe', he says, 'have a greater suavity of manners than the Irish, and, as they want the insidious officiousness of the French, the stranger has no clue to discover whether their expressions are in unison with their feelings.'

Against the background of this admission the few instances where Whitty ventures upon general statements on the Irish are of special interest. The conscientiousness of these statements can be appreciated only by comparison with the superficiality of the sweeping statements passed on this subject by foreign travellers and other writers of that time.

'It is in societies, not equalized by polished manners, that original characters can still be found. Half barbarians, they have all the fidelity of unpractised savages.' – 'The Irishman's friendship, like premature products, is too quick in its growth to be durable and too extended to be strong.' – The homes of the better-class Irish 'show profusion without comfort, vanity without elegance'. – 'The spirit of revenge is common among the Irish peasantry.' – 'Personal courage is allowed in Irishmen in abundance.' 'It is a general failing in Ireland ... to consider education as a blessing, never referring to the sphere in which the scholar is destined by circumstances to move.'

Whitty, we see, had not kissed the stone of Blarney, but can he be accused of being just another abusive slanderer of Ireland? Let us consider the explanations which he offers for that characteristic of the Irish of which their English rulers complained most bitterly. What is the reason for the spirit of lawlessness among the catholic Irish? 'The inhumanity and bad policy of landlords and agents bringing ruin and infamy to thousands of Irish peasants.' 'The only means for a catholic farmer to get to money is illicit distillation.' 'Nothing less than rebellion, general and deep could hold out the prospect of greatness to a man whose religion was an incumbrance too large for admission to places of trust and emolument.' 'The Irish are not insensible to the degradation which the art of solicitation implies.' 'The cause of Irish misery and indolence lies in the facility of escaping front responsibility', due to the penal laws. I have picked up these statements almost at random from Whitty's *Tales,* because the continuity of the seriousness of Whitty's interest is thus illustrated.

It is not only by this conscientiousness that Whitty's *Tales* stand far above English and Anglo-Irish descriptions of Ireland at that time. The range of subjects dealt with by Whitty is equally astounding. He describes the Wicklow rising and its aftermath, the Whiteboys and similar movements, he speaks of the consequences of the Insurrection Act and traces the connection of the Irish rebels with the French revolution. We hear of Hoche's invasion and other continental influences, as *e.g.*, Austrian recruiting officers. Above all, however, Whitty deals with the effects of loyalism, orangeism, gentlemen's clubs and the yeomanry on the protestant and catholic element, with the land-question, rack-rent, agents, middle-men and absenteeism, with Revivalism amongst the protestants and catholic reaction to it, with hedge-schools, the education and life of protestant and catholic clergy and the effects of the education received at Trinity College by both protestants and catholics. The fight against bigotry is perhaps the most pronounced feature in Whitty's *Tales*. He praises a curate of the established church 'who, officiating for an absent rector, had strangled the coiling serpent of bigotry, and who was equally kind to catholics and protestants'. On the other hand, while recognising that the life of a catholic priest in Ireland is that of 'selfdenial and want', he denounces 'the bigoted superstition of the prejudiced countrymen' with regard to 'a spoilt priest'. Similarly, in the political sphere, the names of Derry, Boyne and Aughrim are for Whitty associated with no more glorious and inglorious memories than those of Limerick, Shannon and Wexford.

My interest in Whitty's *Tales of Irish Life* was evoked by early German and French translations of that work which I may claim to have discovered among the treasures of the National Library. The German translation of Whitty's *Tales* published as early as 1825 at Breslau is one of the first works of modern Irish literature published in a German translation, an interesting sign of the interest in Ireland spreading to eastern Germany, and – as the publisher was a leading catholic firm – an illustration of early German catholic interest in Ireland. The French translation on the other hand appeared together with a selection from Croker's *Fairy Legends* and illustrates the political interest taken by French liberalism in contemporary Ireland.

Both in these countries and on the continent, Whitty's tales were the first published work of literature giving a detailed and reliable picture of the wretched state in which the majority of the Irish people lived at that time. They also represent the first specifically Irish version of the trend then generally found in European literature towards stories of peasant life.

By comparison with many other works of this kind, Whitty's *Tales* are distinguished by the absence of patronising talking-down, by their wealth of material information and the author's high sense of responsibility. It was the purpose of this paper to plead that Whitty's work should be given in the history of English writing in Ireland that place which it deserves.

This omission is most remarkable in the 3rd chapter of Dr. Kran's *Irish Life in Irish Fiction* (New York, 1909). To my knowledge, the only Irish writer who referred to Whitty is Father Stephen Brown, S.J., who in his Ireland in Fiction (Dublin, 1916, p. 254) gave a brief description of his Tales, a work which consists of 'excellent stories by a journalist very well known in these days'.

(Quelle: Radio Eireann in September, 1946)

A Note in the First English Translation of Schiller's 'History of the Thirty Years War'

No German writer, without having been in Ireland or having professionally studied Irish things, has ever displayed a knowledge of Ireland more varied and profound than Goethe. In Schiller's works the only references to Ireland and the Irish are made in connection with the *Butlerische Dragoner* in *Wallensteins Lager* and *Geschichte des dreißigjährigen Krieges*. Goethe's personal relations with Irishmen were extensive[1] We do not know of one Irishman whom Schiller met. Irish contributions to the spreading of Goethe's works in the English-speaking well known, Des Voex's translation of *Tasso*, Anster's of *Faust* and Dowden's of the *West-östlicher Divan*. The numerous translations of Schiller's poems published by Mangan between 1833 and 1847 have been forgotten,[2] though many of them were included in his *German Anthology*,[3] a translation of *Wallensteins Lager*, appeared as instalment viii/ix of 'Anthologia Germanica' in the *Dublin University Magazine*, but neither Rae,[4] nor Bayard Morgan,[5] nor Nicolai has given Mangan credit for it.[6]

---

1   See my articles on Goethe's knowledge of Ireland (*Dt. Vjs. Literaturw.* xxxi (1957), 70-83) and his Irish friends (P.E.G.S. xxv (1957), 114-24). Schiller's wife resembled Goethe's daughter-in-law inasmuch as to her 'war die Liebe zu England angeboren ... und (sie) übertrug diese Zuneigung auch auf andere Teile der britischen Insel' (Muncker, 'Anschauungen vom englischen Staat', *Sitzungsber. Bayer. Akad.,* philol.-hist. Kl., 1918,97)

2   *German Literature in British Magazines* 1750-1860 (Madison, 1949). One of the very few Irish writers to treat of Schiller was Justin McCarthy, for whom we may quote with reference to the present paper: 'Schiller has not, indeed, influenced English literature to the same extent as Goethe, but he has far more nearly attained a thorough domestication among us' (*Con Amore (1868),* p. 112.

3   See my centenary article in *Irish Times,* 29 June 1945

4   *Schiller's Dramas and Poems in England* (1906), pp. 64, 146.

'Schiller became known as an historian for the first time in England in 1799 by a *History of the Thirty Years War*. The translator, a young officer named Blaquiere, in a preface dated from Dublin. ...' This statement by Violet Stockley, contains rather less than can be derived from the work itself.[7] On the title page the translator was described as 'Captain Blaquiere of the Royal Artillery'. This was William, second son of John, The Chief secretary of Ireland, and of Eleanor Dobson of Anne's Grove, Co. Cork. Born in 1778, he became in 1791 ensign in the Fifty-Sixth Foot and in 1798 major in the Twenty-Fifth Light Dragoons. Having served with gallantry in Flanders, at the Cape and in India, he became a general in 1841. He shot himself at Beulah Hill, Norwood, in 1851.[8]

The translators preface is dated 4 September 1799. The frontspiece, a reproduction of A. Smith's engraving from Graff's portrait of Schiller, bears the note 'published Nov. 1, 1799.' The Dublin edition (vol. I by Kelly, vol. II by Marchbanks) was published in 1800[9], the year when the translator's father was raised to the peerage of Ireland under the title of Baron de Blaquire of Ardkill.

When the Dublin edition of this translation was published, there existed already numerous Irish reprints of English translations of *Die Räuber*, *Don Carlos* and *Kabale und Liebe*. Within a year of its publication, Blaquire's translation was abstracted or reviewed in *Monthly Epitome, New London Review, Critical Review, Monthly Review, British Critic* and *Monthly Magazine*, a typical illustration of the efficiency of literary criticism at that time.[10] In Miss Stockley's work, abstracts of some of these reviews are preceeded by a critical examination of Blaquiere's translation summed up in the words: 'He neither knew enough German nor could he write good English'. No reference has ever been made to the notes which Blaquire added to his translation, but a brief examination of these notes may be justified for three reasons:

(1) They illustrate various points for which Schiller's work appeared to be of special interest to the translator and was regarded by him as being of interest to his readers.

(2) They illustrate various aspects of the translator's political views as a descendant of a Huguenot family resident (since 1732) in England and lately associated with Ireland, occupying a position of considerable significance at that time.

(3) It appears that some of Blaquire's mistranslations are expressive of these views.

5   *Bibliography of German Literature in English translation*, no. 8168, and list of translators.

6   *German Literature in British Magazines*, p. 103.

7   *German Literature in England* (1929), p. 162

8   Boase, *Modern English Biography*, v, 54.

9   Morgan, op. Cit. Pp. 8103 f. knows only the London edition, vol. 2 of which, he says, contains sixteen portraits (not found in the copy in the National Library of Ireland). According to Morgan, Blaquiere's translation was reprinted at Frankfurt a. M. in 1842.

10 To *Bibliography of German Literature in British Magazine* add the reference quoted by Stockley, loc. Cit.

The subjects of Blaquiere's notes can be listed under three headings.[11]

A. France

Blaquiere's attitude to the country of his forefathers is factional rather than national. In his first note to Wieland's preface he suggested that the Emperor Leopold was secretly murdered by the Jacobins. To Wieland's depreciation of Louis XIV he added a note saying that 'the victories of Louis XIV were less destructive to German liberties than the progress of French republicans'. In Great Britain and Ireland, the Huguenots generally espoused the cause of their former persecutors rather than that of the atheist Revolution.[12]

Blaquiere's notes relating to military history illustrate a Huguenot conception of French history. He referred to 'the memorable victory' at Rocroi, to the chivalry shown by Turenne and Condé to Mercy, their former adversary, and to 'the storming of Valenciennes by the celebrated Vauban'. Turning to more recent events, his attitude became hostile to France and favourable to her adversaries. To Schiller's account of the fall of 'Donauwerth' he noted that 'not far from that town Prince Eugene and Marlborough afterwards obtained the great victory of Blenheim'. With obvious pleasure Blaquiere dwelt on Schiller's comparison between the battles of Tuttlingen (1663) and Rossbach (1757): in these two battles the French supported one German party against another, but the defeat gave rise to all-German nationalism. 'The victory of Rossbach', Blaquiere remarked, 'excited as much joy amongst the Austrians as among the Prussians.'

B. Germany

At the end of his preface, Blaquiere had said:

> Should any degree of approbation be bestowed on it [the present translation], the translator intends to publish the history of a second war, more recent and more bloody(!), and by it to terminate the two most memorable epochs of German history.

He referred to Archenholtz's *Geschichte des Siebenjährigen Krieges*, a work praising Frederick of Prussia.[13] His note on the decay of the Spanish infantry concludes: 'The Dutch subsequently became famous for a discipline which has since been carried to the best perfection by the German infantry.' Blaquiere's knowledge of German and his preference for Germany may be due to a visit to that country. Or was his knowledge of the battlefield of Lützen derived from books only? 'The country about Lützen is dead flat. The trenches which the author mentions were small canals, intended to convey

---

11   Some of these notes were explanitory of German terms: I (I quote the London edition, henceforth abbreviated B), 39, 60, 65, 191; II, 28, 129, 143, 209, 143, 209, 249.

12   Froude, op.cit. II, 190 f. and III, 157. In 1797 'a country gentleman' dating his preface from Cork (identified as Captain Thomas Blaquiere, R.I.A.) published at Dublin *General Observations on the State of Affairs in Ireland in Defence against an invasion:* 'The difference of Religion would scarce be felt since the French revolution. Protestants are united with Catholics in charity and tolerance' (p 13).

13   In his note on the Battle of Rossbach, Blaquiere quoted an anecdote from p. 59 of the Mannheim 1788 edition of Archenholtz's work did not appear until 1843 (F.A. Catty, at Frankfurt).

timber to save land-carnage, and were impassable for cavalry and infantry.' This description is even more surprising when we consider that Blaquiere labours under a misunderstanding of the original text. Schiller spoke of 'die weite Ebene zwischen *dem* Floßgraben [Blaquiere:trenche*s*] und Lützen'[14]

In his preface, Blaquiere described himself as 'a young and unexperienced writer'. In spite of some mistranslations his work is quite good for a young man of twenty years without academic training.[15] His statement that 'German is the most vigorous and eloquent perhaps of all modem languages', while English is 'chaster', is at least worth considering. Some of his earlier critics said that his English was defective. Yet where he lets himself go, in his notes, it comes up to a high standard.[16] Blaquiere knew that Schiller's work had originally appeared in *Historischer Taschenkalender für Damen* (1791-3) and that it was 'received in Germany with great applause'. The expectation, expressed in the preface, that Schiller would continue his work up to the Peace Treaty[17] was repeated in Blaquiere's final note:

'A subject of such importance, treated by such ,a master, must be of infinitely more use than the most elaborate descriptions of battles and sieges, which in all ages and circumstances betray a sameness.'

C. England

> Although the transactions described in this History are more particularly interesting to German readers, they are not altogether foreign to English history.

Although it is dated from Dublin, Blaquiere's preface makes it quite clear that his work aimed at introducing Schiller to the English public. It expresses Blaquiere's personal position that he proposes his own interpretation of James I. At the first reference made by Schiller to James I, Blaquiere noted that the king failed to support his daughter in the sentiments he had inspired her with and that 'he shamefully abandoned her to her fate'.[18] To Schiller's remark, 'Ein angeborenes Grauen vor jeder bloßen Klinge schreckte ihn [James] auch vor dem gerechtesten Kriege zurück', Blaquiere added the note: 'This was owing to the fright, as is reported, which his mother received while pregnant of him, from the assassins of Rizzio, her favourite.' It is obvious that this note aims at ridiculing James. Blaquiere's antipathy to James expressed itself in his translation. Schiller described the king as 'das Spiel der österrei-

---

14 Schiller (Säkularausgabe xv, henceforth abbreviated S), 302 and 459; B, II, 143. Another Irish soldier who studied the Battle of Lützen was North Ludlow Beamish in his translation of Bismarck's *Lectures on the tactics of Cavalry* (London, 1827), p. 41.

15 The frequent misspellings or misprints of German place-names are remarkable: 'Eidu' for Eider (I, 14), 'Lutteron Baenburg' for 'Lutter-on-Barenberg' (I, 84), 'Griefswald' (I, 244; but then, how often in English literature do we find 'Wiemar'!).

16 See, e.g., his note on Mansfield, I, 186 f.

17 K.L.v. Woltmann's *Geschichte des Westphälischen Friedens* appeared in 1805 'ohne Wissen des Autors als Fortsetzung von Schillers *Geschichte*' (A.D.B.)

18 I, 123.

chischen Arglist', but Blaquiere renders these words by *'ever* the dupe of Austrian cunning', thus removing all blame from the Austrian diplomats. Schiller subsequently speaks of James's *'törichte* Geschäftigkeit'; Blaquiere translates: 'his *ridiculous* interference'. The British attempts at interceding for the Winter-king are minimized by Blaquiere's translating the words 'englische Gesandte' (plural) by 'an English envoy'; Blaquire apparently assumed that these attempts were made under James I, whereas in reality Charles I had ascended the throne by that time.

The contrast between Blaquiere's antipathy to James I and his sympathy for Charles I illustrates a Tory interpretation of British history. On Schiller's statement: 'Alle diese Schritte [of the rebellious Bohemians] geschahen zur Aufrechterhaltung der königlichen Macht ... die Sprache aller Rebellen, bis sich das Glück für sie entschie den hat', Blaquiere commented: 'This example was followed by Charles I. The article of using the king's name and authority against himself was not therefore a new expedient as Mr. Hume imagines.' Some pages previously Blaquiere censured Schiller's description of the Landstände of Austria speaking against Matthias 'eine Sprache, die Selbst im Londoner Parliament [Blaquiere added, on his own authority, 'even in Cromwell's time']: überrascht hätte':

> Had the author been more intimately acquainted with the English history, he would have found it difficult to say what sort of language would have appeared strange in one of Cromwell's parliaments: that of common sense was perhaps the scarcest.

Blaquiere's indignation is raised by Schiller's reference to 'die Untätigkeit und die widersinnige Politik des englischen Hofes, die den Eifer Gustav Adolfs [for Frederick] erkaltete':

> A poor excuse with the author's leave. The Swedish monarch might have known that Charles I then engaged in a quarrel with the rebellious fanatics of Scotland and his own Parliament...could not possibly interfere in foreign transactions ...

Similarly, when Schiller describes the arrival of six thousand English under Hamilton as 'alles, was die Geschichte von den Taten der Engländer im Dreißigjährigen Kriege zu berichten hat', Blaquiere commented:

> These auxiliaries were Scots and English, and offered the first example, perhaps, that ever occurred, of British troops performing nothing worthy of their native country in a foreign one. They were, however, commanded by a hypocrite and a coward, as his subsequent conduct, when opposed to Cromwell, showed him to be.[19]

D. Ireland

Blaquiere was quite unaware of the Irish contingent in the British auxiliary force fighting for the Swedes, and so was Schiller. On the other hand, they knew of the Irishmen serving in the Imperial and Wallenstein's armies. According to Schiller 'ein

---

19   To my article on 'Simplicius Simplicissimus' British relations' in M.L.R. XL (1945); 37 ff., I wish to add that, according to Poten (A.D.B. xxvii, 220), James Ramsay (Simplicius' uncle) arrived with this contingent. See also my note on 'Irish soldiers in the Thirty Years War' *in J.R. Soc. Antiq. Irel.* LXXXII (1952), 28-36.

Irländer, namens Leßley' [Blaquiere: 'Leslie, an Irishman '] disclosed[20] to 'Obersten Buttler' [Blaquiere: 'Colonel Butler'] und dem Oberleutnant [Blaquiere: 'Lieutenant-Colonel '] Gordon, zweien protestantischen Schottlandern,[21] alle schlimmen Anschläge des Herzogs'. Blaquiere noted: 'Here the author is mistaken. Butler was an Irishman and a Papist; he died a general in the Emperor's service. Though a murderer, he was a man of great piety, and founded at Prague a convent of Irish Franciscans.'[22]

Only once in his notes does Blaquiere mention Ireland. Schiller said: 'Der Haß zwischen zerfallen Freunden ist gewöhnlich der grimmigste und unversöhnlichste', whereupon Blaquiere noted : 'An observation confirmed by... the late rebellion in Ireland ... when near relatives fought on opposite sides, and neither gave nor took quarter.'[23] Biaquiere's annotated translation has remained the most outstanding contribution made by Ireland to the study of Schiller in the English-speaking world, but in Ireland it was scarcely acknowledged as such.[24] Reviewing the Goethe-Schiller correspondence, the *Dublin Literary Gazette* of 20 February 1830 referred to the *History of the Thirty Years War* as a 'work pretty generally known and read, especially since Mr. Constable's publication in his Miscellany'. When in 1836 the *Dublin University Magazine* reviewed a number of recent translations from Schiller's works it said that

> Schiller was fortunate above all other writers in his translators, and yet, we do not think him popular or likely to be very popular, in *England*. The style of German poets is evidenced in their triumph over some disadvantages of their language ... their prose writers are absolutely unreadable
> ...[25]

The *Geschichte des dreißigjährigen Krieges* is Schiller's largest work the full translation of it therefore was an important achievement. No other work of his was translated so soon after publication.

---

20 The parenthesis '(ob aus Pflichtgefühl oder aus niedrigen Antrieben, ist ungewiß)' was later omitted. Apart from Leslie, also 'Hauptmann Deveroux' was described by Schiller (p. 373) as 'Irländer'. Omitting Schiller's words 'der schon bereit gehaltene Mörder', Blaquire described him simply as 'Captain Deveroux (!) an Irishman' (II, 245). Schiller may be credited with having firmly established the spelling 'Irland' rather than 'Irrland'.

21 Blaquiere : 'Scotchmen'. Also with reference to Henderson, 'ein Schottländer' was rendered by 'a Scotchman' (II, 144), but, with reference to Hebron, 'ein tapferer Schottländer' by 'a brave Scotchman' (II, 127). Thus it would apppear that Blaquiere used the term 'Scotchman' in a derogatory sence.

22 II, 239. See M. Macken in *Studies* (Dublin), XXIII (1934), 608, and B. Jennings, ibid. XXVIII (1939), 210, also my paper in *Ir. Eccl. Rec.* VI, LXV (1945), 399 f.

23 S, 398; B, II, 278.

24 Another soldier in Ireland was among the earliest translators of *Fiesco*: Sir George Charles d'Aguilar translated it while on the staff of the Horse Guards in Dublin. This translation was published only in Dublin (in 1832) and was reviewed in *Dublin University Magazine* (1836)

25 A few months earlier (D.U.M. v (1835), 42), Mangan had written: '(Schiller's) prose productions are characterised by an originality essentially distinct from that of Goethe'; however, Mangan undoubtedly was thinking of Schiller's short stories.

These remarks on Blaquiere's translation and notes are a further addition to my studies of British-German literary relations. In this field the aesthetic and formalist point of view has been so prevalent that but little attention has been paid to translations of prose works.[26] Indeed it is scarcely realized that the investigation of translations of dramas and poems and that of translations of prose works has to follow different lines. 'Der realistische Tick' which according to Goethe was the basis of his relationship with Schiller has expressed itself primarily in Goethe's scientific and Schiller's historical works. Whether Blaquiere was right in treating Schiller's *Geschichte* as a work of historical writing. is irrelevant. In 'domesticating' this work through his notes, he at least showed that he took Schiller seriously.

(Quelle: MLR 55, 1960, S. 249-254)

---

26   See, e.g., my paper on earlier English translations of Goethe's essays on Bryon in M.L.R. XLIV (1949), 360-71, and, on the other hand mu numerous studies of Goethe's translations of British scientific texts (concluded by my study of his Newton translation in *Goethe*, xx (1958), 2250232).

528

Deutschlandkunde in James Clarence Mangans Prosawerken

In seinem Beitrag ‚James Clarence Mangan, Ireland's ‚German poet'' (in: Anglo-German and American-German Crosscurrents I. 1957. S. 65 f) sagte Eoin McKiernan:

„In passing – and only in passing, for little of it rises above good journalism – Mangan's prose might be mentioned. Influences in his fiction can be listed as allusions and settings that are German, references to German men of letters, and interspersions of phrases in German. The question of actual German influence upon Mangan's original work can be dealt with briefly. There seems to have been no borrowing and assimilation of themes. What influence there was remains extrinsic, employed as an embellishment, designed possibly as a lure for the enticement of readers whose taste for German writings had been whetted part by Mangan himself."

Daß es in der Literaturgeschichte Irlands jemanden gibt, der als „Ireland's German poet" bezeichnet wird, mag ebenso überraschen wie, daß sich bisher kein Deutsch-sprachiger monographisch mit ihm befaßt hat. Der als Herausgeber einer Jakob Boehme-Ausgabe erinnerte Josef Grabisch, der 1948 in Dublin starb[1], arbeitete noch bis in seine letzten, von schwerer Krankheit überschatteten Tage an einer Würdigung von Mangans Beitrag zur Verbreitung der Kenntnis deutscher Literatur im englischen Sprachbereich. Wenn unter diesem Gesichtspunkt hier – m.W. überhaupt erstmalig – Mangans Prosawerke betrachtet werden, so ist doch eine Vorbemerkung über Mangans Übersetzertätigkeit erforderlich.

Unter den ersten, die Werke von Goethe und Schiller ins Englische übersetzten, waren in Irland Geborene, aber, wie schon ihre Namen (de Blaquiere[2], Des Voeux[3], und Anster[4]) zeigen, Angehörige der fremden Herrenschicht. Mangan war der erste National- (oder katholische) Ire[5], der über deutsche Literatur schrieb, und, wie kritisch

---

1   S. mein Nachruf in: Irish Bookman. Juli 1948, S. 87-89. Die deutsche Beschäftigung mit Mangan wird illustriert durch die einzige Erwähnung Mangans in V. Stockley: German literature as known in England. 1929. S. 126 Anm., wo die Bemerkung in A. Dropp: Die Belesenheit P. B. Shelleys. 1905. S. 124, daß Mangans Übersetzung von Schubarts ‚Ewiger Jude' in ‚Dublin University Magazine' [hinfort: DUM] 1809 (Mangan wurde 1803 geboren und das DUM begann 1833 zu erscheinen) erschienen sei, zurückgewiesen wird. Tatsächlich handelt es sich bei Mangans Übersetzung von Schubarts ‚Ewiger Jude' um eine seiner letzten Arbeiten (C.P. Meehan: Vorrede zu Mangans ‚Anthologia Germanica'. 1884. S. I, IVf).

2   S. meine Arbeit: The first English translation of Schiller's ‚History of the Thirty Years' War', in: Modern Language Review [hinfort: MLR] 55. 1960. S. 249-54. Zu Mangans Übersetzung von ‚Wallensteins Lager' s.: German literature in British magazines 1750-1850. 1949. [hinfort: GL] S. 103 und Thomas Rae: Schiller's dramas and poems in England. 1906. S. 64, 146.

3   S. meine Arbeit: Irish descriptions of Goethe. In: Publications of the English Goethe Society 5. 1956. S. 115.

4   Edward Dowden in: Dict. Nat. Biography II. 1885. S. 38 und H.-G. Fiedler in: MLR 18. 1923. S. 61, 63.

5   Allerdings teilte Mangan nicht in allen Punkten die Ansichten der irischen Nationalisten, besonders nicht der späteren. In DUM VI. 1835. S. 401f. sagte er: „We once more bring down the volumes from the German shelf of our library…cull their choicest extracts and translate them into the language that, after all, is the language of our love. For though there be those who would cry shame upon us for the confession, we do confess that to our ear no language sounds as pleasing as that of England … Is it not the language of our homes? [damals sprach noch die

man auch seine Leistungen beurteilen mag, man muß zugeben, daß er bislang kaum von einem seiner Landsleute übertroffen worden ist. Die 1845[6] veröffentlichte ‚German anthology', eine Auswahl aus den zwischen 1835 und 1838 im ‚Dublin University Magazine' veröffentlichten Übersetzungen deutscher Gedichte, war trotz der schweren Zeiten ein finanzieller Erfolg und wurde 1884 und 1923 nochmals aufgelegt[7] und bis heute oft zitiert, das einzige Buch eines Iren, in dessen Titel das Wort ‚German' erscheint[8].

Mangans eigene Gedichte erschienen mehrfach in Buchform. Seine Prosaschriften wurden weit weniger beachtet[9]. In seiner – der maßgebenden – Sammlung von Man-

---

überwiegende Mehrzahl der Iren Gälisch] ... Yet we love the language of Germany and we admire her poetry."

6   Das Vorwort war June 1845 datiert. Nur mein Artikel in: The Irish Times 29. und 30. Juni hat an den 100. Jahrestag erinnert.

7   D.J. O'Donoghue: The life and writings of James Clarence Mangan. 1897 und P.S. O'Hegarty: The bibliography of J.C.M. 1941. Unergiebig John D. Sheridan: J.C.M. 1937. S. 46ff.; mir nicht zugänglich Henry E. Caen: J.C.M. 1930 (British Museum Catalogue). S. auch Cambridge Bibliography of English Literature III. 1940. S. 1051. Die Vorrede zu der Buchpublikation: Anthologia Germanica. German anthology. A series of translations from the most popular of the German authors. 1845, sagte: „The translations comprised in this volume have been selected from a series which have appeared at irregular intervals within the last ten years in the pages of the DUM. They are now published ... at the instance of some valued friends of mine, admirers, like myself, of German literature, and – as I am happy to believe, even more solicitous than I am to extend the knowledge of that literature through these kingdoms." Zum finanziellen Hintergrund dieser Publikation, insbes. die Subskriptionsgarantie durch Sir Charles Gavan Duffy, s. dessen: Four years of Irish history. 1883. S. 77f. Dort die interessante Mitteilung: „The public took ten years to buy one small edition of Anster's Faust [s.o. Anm. 4], a book which all at once occupies a very high position in the literary world" (Die 'Anthologia Germanica' verkaufte sich weit besser). S. 73 sagte Duffy: „In Ireland, literary men must be content with a limited celebrity and moderate reward, that they might endeavour to do for their country what Scott has done for Scotland, and what Goethe and Schiller had done for Germany". Um die Wirkung von Mangans Übersetzung zu würdigen, muß man die Abdrucke einzelner Übersetzungen an anderen Stellen, etwa von Gedichten Schillers in den verschiedenen Ausgaben von Mangans ‚Poems' (New York 1859 und 1870, Dublin 1886 und London 1903) in Betracht ziehen. Zu Mangans Übersetzungen ist auch zu rechnen ‚The story of the old wolf' (O'Donoghues Ausg. – s.u. Anm. 8, S. 319), eine freie Wiedergabe eines Grimmschen Märchens (zuerst in: Irish Penny Journal. 1840, eine der von GL nicht erfaßten Zeitschriften). Will man Patrick Kavanagh (Tarry Flynn. 1948. S. 1) glauben, so werden Mangans Gedichte heute noch auch vom irischen Landvolk gelesen.

8   Im XVIII. Jahrhundert waren schon mehrere Nachdrucke in Irland erschienen, in deren Titel das Wort ‚German' vorkommt (s. meine Arbeit: Irland und das friderizianische Preußen. In: Archiv für Kulturgeschichte 48. 1966. S. 281); sonst kenne ich nur Heinrich Becker: German songs of seven centuries. 1943.

9   Zunächst einiges in C.P. Meehan: Mangan's essays in prose and verse 1884. Meehans Interesse an Mangans Deutschlandkunde war ebenso gering wie seine Kenntnis der deutschen Sprache. Trotz der inzwischen erschienenen Berichtigung durch O'Donoghue (s.u.) enthielt die 2. Aufl. 1906 noch vor dem Essay ‚My bugle, and how I blow it' (ursprünglich in: Belfast Vindicator 27.3.1841, dann in: The Nation November 1844 – letzteres Organ von ‚Young Ireland' wurde in

gans Prosaschriften druckte O'Donoghue unter dem Titel ‚A German poet' den Essay über Tieck ab[10] und wies damit darauf hin, daß die Bemerkungen, die Mangan seinen Übersetzungen deutscher Gedichte in der Serie ‚Anthologia Germanica' im ‚Dublin University Magazine' beigegeben hatte, zu seinen Prosaschriften zu rechnen wären. In der Vorrede zu O'Donoghues Ausgabe sagte Lionel Johnson, daß in dem Tieckaufsatz Mangan „is seen at his gayest. This is the real Mangan, quizzical and yet critical, half-humorous, half serious"; Johnson ging aber nicht auf den Inhalt ein[12].

Was für Mangans Übersetzungen gilt, gilt auch für die Erläuterungen dazu: Sie sind weniger literarisch als literatur- oder geistesgeschichtlich interessant, insbesondere für die Geschichte der irischen Deutschlandkunde[13]. Die erste Lieferung von ‚Anthologia Germanica'[14] beginnt mit den Worten: „More than a century ago Fr. Bouhours[15] answered the question ‚Un Allemand peut-il avoir de l'esprit?' by ‚point du tout'". Francophilie und Germanophilie sind bis heute in Irland – tiefreichende – Gegensätze.

Deutschlandkunde in Mangans Erläuterungen in ‚Anthologia Germanica' kann durch folgende Zitate illustriert werden:

IV[16]: „We have presented our readers with many of those gems of the rich mine of German poesy ... The grand, albeit sometimes gloomy spirit that presides over the songs and legends of the land of Goethe ..." (Es folgt die Anm. 5 zitierte Stelle). Vgl.

GL nicht erwähnt!) die Zeilen „Ein Alphorn noch erschallen --- hör ich in süsSer qual". Mangans Übersetzung dieses Gedichts war 1836 erschienen (GL Nr. 3318). „SüsSer" ist eine amüsante Illustration des Gebrauchs „deutscher Schrift" in Irland (s. meine Notiz in: Irish Book Lover. 30. 1948. S. 89f.). Am Ende von ‚A sixty-drop dose of Laudanum' (von DUM März 1839, O'Donoghues Ausg. s.u. – S. 229) schrieb Mangan black letters vor. Von D.J. Donoghues: The prose writings of J.C.M. 1904. [hinfort: PW] besitze ich ein Exemplar mit handschriftlicher Widmung des Herausgebers an Dr. J. O'Brien.

10   PW. S. 254ff. GL Nr. 3395.

11   Der Titel ist offenbar dem von ‚Horae Germanicae' in ‚Blackwoods Edinburgh Magazine' (GL Nr. 2175 ff) nachgebildet.

12   PW. Viii. „Schneller Wechsel von Ernst und Scherz, von Anteil und Gleichgültigkeit, von Leid und Freude soll in dem irländischen Charakter liegen" (Goethe: Maximen und Reflexionen (1828), hierzu meine Arbeit: Goethes Irlandkunde. In DVjs 31. 1957. S. 74).

13   Einige meiner Arbeiten zu diesem Thema (bis zum Ende des 18. Jahrhunderts) wurden zusammengefaßt in meinem Forschungsbericht in DVjs. 35. 1961. S. 617-629. O' Donoghue: The life ... of Mangan. S. 72: „To Mangan's translations most Irish people may be said to owe whatever knowledge they possess of German poetry, and his ‚Anthologia Germaniae' ... would tempt many an indifferent student to study the original of his generally beautiful versions". Aber dass. (S. 117) sagte O' Donoghue im Bezug auf Mangans ‚Chapters in ghostcraft' (s.u.): „These are entirely devoted to German visions; consequently there is no temptation to deal with them here".

14   DUM 5. 1835. S. 39ff, s. GL Nr 3234.

15   Dominique B., S. J., +1702.

16   DUM 6. 1836. S. 401ff, s. GL Nr 3242.

auch XII[17]: „German poetry is mostly an affair of moonshine and fog" (entsprechend dem ‚Ossianischen' Landschaftsbild von Irland).

I: Nach einer Skizze der Geschichte der deutschen Literatur von Opitz über Gellert, Hagedorn, Haller und Rabener zu Klopstock[18] kommt Mangan zu Goethe und Schiller: „They are hackneyed, but one cannot help that. The land of Teutons has cradled no other two greater than those two". Zu der Frage, ob ‚Die Räuber' geschrieben worden wären, wenn 'Götz' nicht erschienen wäre: „Schiller has accomplished for the Drama, what Goethe with all his powers could never compass – he conferred upon it stability, definiteness, consistency, weight". Auch Schillers Prosawerke zeigen „an originality essentially different from that (Goethes) ... Schiller's mind was unpoisoned by any sympathy with the Ludicrous. 'Für eine Comödie hatte er einst einen Stoff gefunden (says one of his biographers), fühlte sich aber zu fremd für diese Gattung'" [ein so langes deutsches Zitat mutete Mangan seinen Lesern zu, wie er auch zu seinen Übersetzungen immer die Anfangszeilen des Originalgedichts beifügte].

II[19]: „No parallel to the ‚Lied von der Glocke' can be found in the anthology of any nation. It could only be produced by Schiller and by a German [das war also höchstes Lob]. Bürger and Uhland surpassed Schiller in ballads, but Schiller's ballads are invested with a grace ... occasionally a mystery rarely equalled in the most finished efforts of other writers". Das übliche Urteil, daß Schiller Mangans Lieblingsdichter war, muß insofern eingeschränkt werden, als er gerade bezüglich der Balladen in XII[20] zu einer anderen Bewertung gelangt: Die Mehrzahl der Schillerschen Balladen sind unübersetzbar „because they are dull, we merely echo the opinion of the best German critics. Great as the other powers of Schiller were, he wanted those which constitute the perfect ballad-singer. His genius, essentially dramatic and didactic, never accomodated itself gracefully to the realities". Die anschließende Kritik der einzelnen Hauptballaden kann man nur verstehen als Ausdruck des „Wechsels von Anteil zu Gleichgültigkeit"[21]. Vermutlich verlor Mangan das Interesse an der Serie, als er nicht mehr vorwiegend auf sie für seinen Lebensunterhalt angewiesen war. So erlaubt er sich denn auch, „im schnellen Wechsel von Ernst und Scherz" dem irischen Hang zu Sentenzen nachzugeben: „Schiller should have lived to see Canova, read Byron and

---

17   DUM II. 1838. S. 46ff, s. GL Nr 3461. Von Lieferung X an war die ‚Anthologia' beeinflußt von Wilhelm Klauer-Klatowski: Popular songs of the Germans. 1836 und seinen explanatory notes.

18   Zum Beginn meiner Arbeit: Jean Paul and Ireland. In: MLR 40. 1945. S. 190, möchte ich hinzufügen, daß in ‚An extraordinary adventure in the shades' (The Comet. January 1833; PW. S. 300) Mangan schrieb: „To spout Opitz, Canitz, Ugo, Wieland, and oh' above all, Richter – meines herz Richter, (ach wenn Ich ein Herz habe)", eine Stelle, mit der man die Stellen vergleichen mag, die ich erstmalig (in der oben Anm. 3 zitierten Arbeit) aus Charles Levers Erinnerungen an Deutschland zitierte. Nach O'Donoghue (The life. S. 18) verlor Lever seine Stelle als Herausgeber der ‚Dublin Literary Gazette' (nicht in GL), weil er 1830 Mangans Übersetzung von Schiller: ‚An die Freude' gebracht hatte.

19   DUM 5. 1835. S. 140ff, s. GL Nr 3235.

20   S.o. Anm. 17.

21   S.o. Anm. 12.

hear Paganini" oder: „Schiller as it happened was a good man as well as a great poet, but he might have been either one or the other alone". Immerhin – auch dies ist irisch – war sich Mangan wenigstens bewußt, daß er nun Schiller nicht mehr gerecht wurde: „Our task is complete ... Future translators will, we should fancy, do ample justice to all writings – including the ballads – of this distinguished man. A time will come when the name of Schiller alone shall be sufficient to awaken enthuasiasm on behalf of all that is pure in principle". Da der Inhalt von Mangans Urteilen[22] nicht Gegenstand unserer Betrachtung ist, genüge es zu sagen, daß im englischen Sprachbereich, geschweige denn in Irland, diese Zeit noch auf sich warten läßt.

Mangans Übersetzungen und seine Bemerkungen dazu sollten im Rahmen einer Darstellung der Beschäftigung mit deutscher Literatur im 19. Jahrhundert im englischen Sprachbereich – sein Werk wurde ja auch in Amerika, besonders auch unter den sonst nicht sonderlich gebildeten Iren bekannt – gewürdigt werden. Anzufangen wäre mit einem Studium der ‚Anthologia' unter den vielen anderen mit deutscher Literatur befaßten Beiträge in ‚Dublin University Magazine'[23]. Erwähnt sei nur, daß diese Zeitschrift die erste in Irland war, die Artikel von einem in Irland lebenden Deutschen brachte, nämlich von Zander, dem ersten Professor für Deutsch in Trinity College Dublin, in Bd I, S. 45 1 ff. über ‚German schools and universities' und in Bd II, S. 23 ff. über ‚Chivalrous romances'[24].

In ‚Anthologia' XII bietet Mangan auch die ersten Beispiele für eine bis heute im englischen Sprachbereich bekannte Unsitte, fremdsprachliche Worte in Erzählungen einzuflechten in einer Orthographie, deren Nachlässigkeit eher auf affectation als auf Unkenntnis beruht. So heißt es da bei Mangan: „the adorable Grafinn and Frau" oder: „Drey Worte nenn ich, innhaltschwer" (50, 53). In den Prosaerzählungen, die O'Donoghue in seine ‚Centenary edition' von Mangans Prosaschriften aufnahm, begegnet man wiederholt dem unidiomatischen „Mein Herr!", das sich Mangan so aneignete, daß er es nicht mehr, wie sonst fremdsprachliche Brocken, kursiv drucken ließ. In der ersten von O'Donoghue abgedruckten Geschichte ‚The thirty flasks' wird Grabbs dreiste Anbiederung an Van Rosenwald dadurch ausgedrückt, daß die ersten Worte eines von ihm gesprochenen Satzes in Deutsch, mit einer nachfolgenden pedantischen englischen Übersetzung geboten werden: „Vierzig, forty" – „Recht, right" – „Da, there" und natürlich „ja" und „nein". Sobald etwas mehr Deutsch zitiert wird, treten Fehler auf: „Er hat sich die Gurgel geschnitten", „Im Hause, at home". „The kropper" (Anmerkung: Croupier) in dem in dieser Geschichte vorkommenden „Spielhaus" sagt: „Thut euer Spiel, meine Hernn"[25].

---

22 Außer McKiernan (Beginn dieser Arbeit) auch O'Donoghue: The life. S. 73-83. Eine merkwürdige ‚Übersetzung' Mangans behandelte ich in: Klaggesang. Irisch. In: Monatshefte (Univ. of Wisconsin) 41. 1949. S. 71-76.

23 Eine Basis dafür bietet GL, S. 117f.: "DUM very friendly towards German literature; 33 references in the first three years of publication".

24 GL Nr 3100, s. auch 3099; McKiernan a.a.O.S. 48.

25 PW S. 38f, 70. Diese Erzählung erschien in DUM II. 1838. S. 408-424, 666-686 unter Mangans Pseudonym „An Out-and-Outer" (nicht in GL). Nach O'Donoghue: The life. S. 103 „by far the

‚The thirty flasks' wäre als Beispiel der deutschtümelnden romantischen Erzählungen zu würdigen, die zu jener Zeit im englischen Sprachbereich zu Dutzenden nachzuweisen sind. Ein typisches Beispiel in Buchform war ‚Kruitzner or the German's tale' von Harriet Lee (1823)[26]. Die deutsche Patina ist meist nur hauchdünn. Die Fabel von ‚The thirty flasks' ist verwandt mit der von Peter Schlemihl: Der Held verkauft seine Körpergröße Zoll um Zoll. Sein Name ist „Basil Theodore Von Rosenwald". Sein Bruder heißt „Rupert", seine Geliebte „Fraulein Aurelia Jacintha Wilhelmina Elsberg". Andere Namen in dieser Geschichte lauten „Heinrick Flemming", „Lichtenmark", „Prince von Lowenfeld-Schwarzbach" (angeblich ein Ort in „Pomerania"), „Steinhart", „Trigg", „Bubbell", „Grabb" (ein Pfandleiher, hier natürlich Shakespeares Einfluß), „Ullenbruck", „Lubeck"[27] (wobei Mangan wenigstens richtig die Häufigkeit deutscher Ortsnamen bei Juden erkennt), „Hartmann" („Schuh- und Steifelmacher"), „Lord Kanzler", „Klaus", „Slickwitz", ferner von Orten: „Berlin", „Dresden", „Konigsmark" (eins von Von Rosenwalds Gütern) und „Alberstadt" in „Saxony", wo die Geschichte spielt, mit „Platz", „Kaiserstrasse", „Vogelstrasse", „Bildstrasse", „Brunnengasse", „Dornensteg", „Brunhugel", „Grunthal", „Wildgasse". Grundsätzlich ist zu sagen, daß der Wegfall der Umlautzeichen nicht auf Fehlen der entsprechenden Typen bei den Druckern zurückzuführen ist[28].

In Mangans Vorstellung hat die spezifisch deutsche Spielart des Romantischen zwei Hauptaspekte, Gefühl („Aurelia prepares to greet her lover à la mode Germanorum") und Schreckcn („the effect of this apparently insignificant act was tremendously terrible and German. An explosion ... à qui mieux mieux")[29]. Seine ironische Einstellung zu diesen Aspekten ist ihrerseits Ausdruck seiner Verbundenheit mit der Romantik[30]. Der Sinn für wirkliche Komik fehlt ihm in einem für einen Iren erstaunlichen Maße; wenn sein Urteil über Schiller berechtigt ist, so war er Schiller hierin verwandt. Die gesuchte Drolligkeit, die sich in den deutschtümelnden Namen zeigt, ist für sein Bild von deutschem Leben charakteristisch. Auch hierin ist er für seine Landsleute maßgebend geblieben, aber diese können sich mit Recht darauf berufen, daß das traditionelle Bild des Iren auf dem Festland ähnlich oberflächlich ist. In ‚The thirty flasks' wird, ohne tiefere Begründung, auf „Rübezahl" und „Mephistopheles" Bezug genommen[31], im übrigen ist es aber eher deutsche Philosophie als deutsche Dichtung, die hier die deutsche Patina bestimmt.

---

best thing of its kind written by Mangan". Zu der Frage, ob Mangan oder LeFanu die deutschen Geistergeschichten verfaßte: Michael Sadleir in: Bibliographical Soc. of Ireland 5. 1938. S. 71.

26 Die Quelle von Byrons ‚Werner'.

27 In: DUM 3. 1834. S. 149ff. erschien: The wanderer, from Schmidt Von Lubeck (nicht: von Lübeck, wie GL Nr 3158 sagt).

28 S. meine Notiz: Zur Geschichte der englischen Aussprache des Namens „Goethe", in: Goethe 28. 1966. S. 270f.

29 PW. S. 26, 96.

30 GL NR 3236, 3317, 3395, 3400, 3462, 3530 ect.

31 PW. S. 93.

Von dem Helden wird erzählt, was wahrscheinlich Mangan selbst erfahren hatte[32]:

> „While at college, he had perused with some diligence certain abstruse treatises ‚Ueber die Natur des Geistes', but being completely satisfied with the great proficiency which these works had enabled him to make in the knowledge of nothing at all on the subject, he had thought it better to devote himself henceforth exclusively to studies of a mere practical description",

der Übergang von der Romantik zu Jungdeutschland und den ihm nicht nur terminologisch verbundenen ‚Young Ireland', für das Mangan einer der geistigen Führer wurde. Der Held in ‚The thirty flasks' fühlt daher nicht auf „the metaphysical subterfuge" herein, wenn ihm, nachdem er mit einer Droge „gedopt" worden ist, eingeredet wird[33]:

> „I repeat it, I have no existence whatever: I am the mere creature of your imagination, or rather of your volition, which has unconsciously operated to endow a thought with speech and appearance",

äußerlich eine Assoziation mit De Quinceys und Maginns Beschreibungen der Wirkung von Drogen[34], innerlich aber der Abhub von Lehren des deutschen Idealismus.

In ‚An extraordinary adventure in the shades'[35] heißt es denn auch:

> „There is, as some German metaphysicians maintain, idiosyncrasy in some individuals, endowing them with the possession of a sixth sense or faculty to which nomenclature has as yet affixed no distinct idea (for our ideas are in fewer instances derivable from things than from names)".

Dieser Aspekt wird weiter illustriert durch ‚The man in the cloak'[38]. Auch hier geben die Namen eine oberflächliche deutsche Ansicht: „Willibald", „Wilhelmina", „Johann Klaus Braunbrock" (man sieht, Mangans Liste deutscher Vornamen ist begrenzt), „Baron Querkopf", „Karl", „Kellenhofer" und „Rudolf Steiglitz", mit „a public Strass" als dem einzigen Ortsnamen. In dieser Geschichte gibt es nur einen deutschen Satz; am Ende heißt es: „Mein Gott, was ist denn das? Sind das Menschen [mit Tilde über dem letzten n] – oder vielleicht Troglodyten?"[37], aber daneben findet sich die wichtige Bemerkung: „I have a book in my pocket – Jacob Boehmen". In einer Anmerkung zu Kap.III ‚On ghostcraft' wird „Bohm" als Verfechter des „principle of Anstechungsem-

32   PW. S. 65.

33   PW. S. 50.

34   L. Johnson, Vorrede zu PW. S. VIII.

35   Aus: The Comet. 1833; PW. S. VIII.

36   Untertitel: A very German story. In: DUM 12. 1838. S. 552ff. (GL Nr 3468: „Unidentified; perhaps not a translation"). PW. S. 99ff. O'Donoghue: The life. S. 103, meinte, daß diese Geschichte von Spurzheim inspiriert gewesen sei, der 1815 und 1830 in Dublin Vorträge gehalten hatte, Ehrenmitglied der Royal Irish Academy wurde (wie Goethe) und viele Leute, einschl. Führender Ärzte z.B. A. Carmichael (s.u. Anm. 42), beeindruckte. The tartan princess, a tale from the German. In: DUM 4. 1834. S. 369ff ist vermutlich auch keine Übersetzung (entgegen GL Nr 3167). 1838 erschien in DUM (II. S. 646; GL Nr 3460) eine Übersetzung (nicht von Mangan) von Schillers ‚Eine grossmüthige Handlung'. Noch 1859 erschien in DUM (52. S. 687ff.; GL Nr 5299): The black chamber, a German ghost story (kaum eine Übersetzung).

37   PW. S. 134. Ich vermute Einfluß der deutschen Namen in Byrons ‚Werner'.

pfindlichkeit" erwähnt, während in Kap. X „the Jacobo-Boehmenical manner of delight in the true Inner Man" erwähnt wird.

In ‚Chapters on ghostcraft' werden die ersten Worte der deutschen Titel der besprochenen Werke von Justinus Kerner, G.H. Schubert, C. A. Eschenmayer, Johann Heinrich Jung-Stilling, A. Steinbeck, J. F. Von Meyer, die Namen dieser Autoren und der jeweiligen Verlagsorte genannt, ferner Suso und „Gorres"[39], sowie die termini technici „Herzgrube", „Hellschlafwachen ohne Schleier und Scheidewand", „Gnadensonne", „Nachfühlen", „Seligkeit in unserm Luftraum" und eine Übersetzung von Mme. Haufes ‚Dich, Lebenskreis, dich werd'ich (sic!) wieder finden'. In ‚An extraordinary adventure in the shades' sprach Mangan von der Untersuchung des Unterbewußten „Stückweisse [Anmerkung: „Bit by bit"], as they say at Vienna"[40]. In ‚The man in the cloak' wird berichtet, daß auf Baron Querkopfs Schnupftabaksdose zu sehen waren „three separate views of the head of Goethe, phrenology mapped out according to the very newest charts laid down by the most fashionable predecessors of his darling theory"[41]. Gerade weil, wie Eoin McKiernan an sich richtig erkannt hat, diese Bezugnahmen auf deutsches Geistesleben nebenbei vorkommen, sind sie wichtige Illustrationen irischer Deutschlandkunde, denn Mangan mußte voraussetzen, daß seine Leser nicht nut an derlei Dingen Interesse nahmen, sondern auch davon bereits eine gewisse Kenntnis besaßen. Auch hier wäre nun, ausgehend von ‚Dublin University Magazine', Mangan eher als typischer Vertreter denn als Wegbereiter zu ver-

---

38   PW. S. 330 irrtümlich als in DUM 1841 angegeben, in Wirklichkeit: 19. 1842. S. 1-17. O'Donoghue betrachtete diesen Aufs. wohl als Fortsetzung der Artikel: German ghosts and ghost-seers. In: DUM 17. 1841. S. 33-50 und 217-32. Letzere, sagte O'Donoghue, sind „certainly by Mangan". Sie sind aber signiert „Irys Herfner", während ‚Chapters in ghostcraft' als Verfasser „An Out-and-Outer" (s.o. Anm. 25) nennen. Beide Artikel befassen sich mit Kerner und Eschenmayer (vgl. GL Nr 3533). Mit Kerner befaßte sich Mangan in mehreren Lieferungen der ‚Anthologia' (GL Nr 3318 und 3400); er wird auch in dem Gedicht ‚Twenty golden years ago' (GL Nr 3613) erwähnt (daß „Selber" (GL. Index. S. 355!) hier eins von Mangans Pseudonymen war, stellte schon A.M. Sullivan fest, als er dieses Gedicht in seinen ‚Irish penny readings' abdruckte, und O'Donoghue bekräftigte dies). In seinem Aufs. ‚My bugle, and how I blow it' (s.o. Anm. 9) befaßte sich Mangan auch eingehend mit Kerner, den er Jean-Paulisierend als „a man of many accomplishments – poet, physician, metaphysician, hobgoblin-hunter, widower and weeper ... by birth a Swabian, or, perhaps I should say, a swab" (PW. S. 280) beschreibt.

39.   In ‚My bugle' nahm Mangan den Ausdruck ‚The man in the cloak' wieder auf, der ihm 1838 als Titel einer Erzählung gedient hatte: „The Germans call me Der Mensch mit dem Mantel, the Man with the Cloak: I lose my cloak and my consciousness both in the twinkling of a pair of tongs; I become what the philosophy of Kant (in opposition to the Cant of Philosophy) denominates a Nicht-ich, a Not-I, a Non-ego" (PW. S. 285f.). Vgl. ferner die Bezugnahme auf Reid, Malebranche, Schelling und „Leibnitz" in ‚A treatise on a pair of tongs' (von: The Comet. 1833; PW. S. 265).

40   PW. S. 293.

41   PW. S. 103. Zu Mangans Interesse an Lavater O'Donoghue: The life. S. 103ff. Lavaters ‚Aphorisms on Man' waren in Dublin 1790 abgedruckt worden. Zu Lavaters Aufnahme in der englisch sprechenden Welt s.V. Stockley: Recreption (s.o. Anm. I). S. 26ff.

stehen. Man bedenke nur, daß bereits im ersten Band von ‚Dublin University Magazine' Carmichaels Aufsatz über Spurzheims Philosophie erschien[42].

Zur gleichen Zeit wie Mangan arbeitete an ‚Dublin University Magazine' Joseph Sheridan LeFanu mit. Seine Erzählung ‚In a glass darkly'[43] stellt sich vor als

„translation from letters and papers left by Martin Hesselius, the German physicist of inner knowledge and intuition and to whom the author for more than twenty years, to his death in 1819, acted as secretary. They are written, some in English, some in French, but the greater part in German. I am a faithful, though I am conscious by no means a graceful translator",

also das Gegenstück zu Mangan. Browne meinte, daß „Dr. Hesselius, a German physician in mind and soul" nur den Father Purcell in LeFanus ‚Purcell Papers'[44] als „an invented character who acting as the editor of the series links the stories together" ersetzte, aber daß er als Deutscher bezeichnet wird, ist deutlich auf Mangans Einfluß zurückzuführen. In ‚The Familiar', die zweite Geschichte von ‚In a glass darkly'[45] fragt Captain Barton Dr. Hesselius:

„Is there any disease, which would have the effect of perceptibly contracting the stature and whole frame − causing the man to shrink in all his proportions, and yet to preserve his exact resemblance to himself ... ?",

deutlich eine Verbindung zu ‚The thirty flasks'. In ‚Green tea', der ersten Geschichte von ‚In a glass darkly' sagt Mr. Jennings: „I had met with a man who had some odd old books, German editions in mediaeval Latin", und der Inhalt dieser Bücher verursachte in Mr. Jennings die eigentümliche Geistesstörung, die diese Geschichte so meisterhaft beschreibt; es handelt sich um eine der frühesten Darstellungen des Leidens an der Bewußtheit besonders im religiösen Bereich[46]. Mr. Jennings „knew German, and had read Dr. Hesselius's ‚Essays on metaphysical medicine', which suggest more than they actually say". Das Zeitalter der L.S.D.-Philosophie könnte geneigt sein, diesen Ramifikationen des Einflusses der spätromantischen deutschen Philosophie im englischen Sprachbereich nachzugehen. Andererseits kann das gegenwärtige Interesse an der Geschichte der Vampirliteratur[47] kaum ‚Carmilla'[48], die letzte Ge-

---

42   S. o. Anm. 36.

43   1871 (Neudruck 1929). S. die Bibliographie in S.M. Ellis: Wilkie Collins, LeFanu and others. 1931, und Nelson Browne: Sheridan LeFanu. 1929. S. 77. Lefanu war von 1861-1872 Herausgeber von DUM.

44   Hier nehmen die Niederlande den Platz von Deutschland als Heimat des Spiritismus ein. In der Vorr. z. seiner Ausg. (1880) behandelte Alfred P. Graves LeFanus Beiträge zum DUM.

45   Ursprünglich: The watcher (1851). Abgedruckt in der zweisprachigen Serie: Sprachenpflege. S. 22f. (1912); die National Library of Ireland, Dublin besitzt ein Exemplar mit handschriftlicher Widmung des Herausgebers − Professor (Richard?) Kabisch − an Lyster, den damaligen Direktor.

46   S.o. Anm. 39. Die Quelle war vermutlich das Kapitel ‚Green Tea' in dem Artikel ‚German ghosts' (s.o. Anm. 38) in DUM 17. 1841. S. 43.

47   Karl Heinz Bohrer: Dracula (Besprechung einer soeben erschienenen Übersetzung des gleichnamigen ‚Vampir-Romans' (1897) des Iren Bram Stoker, welchen sich nun Irlandreisende als

schichte von ‚In a glass darkly', übersehen, die handelt von „the appalling superstition of vampires prevailing in Upper and Lower Styria, Moravia and Silesia"; der Ort der Handlung ist ein „Schloss occupied by an English nobleman and his daughter in Styria", eine der vielen Parallelen zu Mérimées ‚Colomba' (und Gottfried Kellers ‚Pankraz der Schmoller'). In 'Carmilla' werden deutsche Ortsnamen (einschl. „Gratz")[49] und Personennamen zitiert und unter der Literatur über Vampire werden die ‚Philosophicae et Christianae Cogitationes' eines John Christofer Herenberg (der frühe Drucker Johann Herenberck?) erwähnt.

LeFanus Werke, geschweige denn die darin enthaltene Deutschkunde, sind m. W. im deutschen Sprachbereich noch nicht gewürdigt worden. Hier sollte nur ihr Zusammenhang mit Mangan in Betracht gezogen werden. Bei Mangan war die Deutschlandkunde zwar breiter als bei LeFanu, aber äußerlicher[50]. LeFanu bezog daraus Kenntnis und Bewußtsein gewisser Grundzüge des modernen Geistes, ohne die das Werk von James Joyce[51] undenkbar wäre; der Aufsatz über Mangan aber war der Beginn von Joyces literarischer Laufbahn[52].

(Quelle: DVLG 44, 1970, S. 496-507)

Mangan's German Anthology

In last year's Leaving Certificate Examinations, 1,366 Irish boys and girls sat for French and 17 for German. There are few countries in Europe where the number of persons who have attained to a knowledge of German sufficient to enable them to enjoy the reading of works of German literature in the original is smaller than it is in Ireland.

---

passende Ferienlektüre mitnehmen, (Frankf. Allg. Ztg. 25. 7. 68 R I) in Frankf. Allg. Ztg. 8.8. u. 17.9.1967 und die sich anschließenden Leserbriefe zur Vampirtradition.

48 1871; eine Übersetzung durch Elizabeth Schnack erschien 1967 in Zürich.

49 S.o. Anm. 39: Leibnitz. In ‚Uncle Silas', dem ersten Werk LeFanus, das ins Deutsche übersetzt wurde, wird Teil I. Kapitel xxxiv eine Waldlandschaft als „the very spot in which to read a volume of German folk-tales" bezeichnet. In Teil II. Kapitel xvii wird vom Titelhelden gesagt: „He was something higher than the garrulous and withal feeble demon of Goethe. He was profoundly reticent Mephistopheles". In Teil I, Kapitel ii und iv wird „German" unter den Sprachen aufgeführt, die ein gebildetes Mädchen beherrschen sollte. Uncle Silas illustriert die oben erwähnte Tatsache, daß sich in Irland Germanophilie und Francophobie meist entsprechen (die jüngste Illustration dieser Tatsache ist der zweite Band von Frank O'Connors Autobiographie: My father's son. 1968). Nicht nur die widerwärtige französische Gouvernante, deren Sprache unbarmherzig verhöhnt wird, verleitet Milly dazu zu sagen: „I hate France" (Teil II, Kapitel ii).

50 Hierin Canon Sheehan vergleichbar, s. meine Notiz über dessen Interesse an deutscher Literatur, in: Modern Language Review 49. 1954. S. 352-355.

51 LeFanus ‚The horse by the churchyard' war eine Quelle von ‚Finnegans Wake' (Eire-Informationsblatt des irischen Außenministeriums – 29.1.1954).

52 S. meine Notiz in: The Bell II. 1945. S. 708 f.

A hundred years ago, at the end of the short period during which German poetry and philosophy produced works of world-wide significance, this was different. When in 1828 Goethe wrote to his friend Sulpiz Boisserée that of all the numerous foreigners visiting his house „the Irish were certainly the most popular," he had in mind not only a large number of occasional visitors from this country, but a series of Irish students of German language and literature who were staying for months, and even years, in Weimar. At the same time, Goethe was made an honorary member of the Royal Irish Academy; for the first time, also, a Professorship of German was established In Trinity College. This knowledge of German and this interest in German literature were naturally confined to the wealthy and cultured classes.

EARLY INTEREST

The first Irish Catholic who showed an active interest in German literature was James Clarence Mangan. In 1830, at the age of twenty-seven, he sent a translation of Schiller's poem, „To my Friends" to the *Dublin Literary Gazette,* then edited by Lever, who, it is said, was removed from the editorship for accepting it. A few months later, Mangan joined the Comet Club, originally an association advocating the abolition of tithes, but then engaged in the publication of a literary magazine. Still more important was the publication of Mangan's poems and translations in the *Dublin Penny Journal* edited by John O'Donovan, the great antiquarian.

From the very beginning of its publication, the *Dublin University Magazine* numbered Mangan among its regular contributors. In a series of almost twenty articles, Mangan published there his criticisms and translations of contemporary German poetry, the largest introduction to German literature ever published in this country. The fact that for ten years or so Mangan, was enabled to make a substantial part of his living from this series shows that the editor regarded these contributions not only as valuable, but as sufficiently popular.

FINANCIAL BACKING

In 1845 Mangan's friends suggested that this series should be published in book form. Among these friends the most important was Sir Charles Gavan Duffy, who promised to back the undertaking financially, with the result that McGlashan eventually declared himself prepared to publish the work. The Preface to Mangan's „German Anthology," which is dated „Dublin, June, 1845," says that „the translations comprised in these two volumes" were reprinted „at the instance of some valued friends, admirers, like myself, of German literature, and, as I am happy to believe, even more solicitious than I am, to extend the knowledge of that literature through these kingdoms."

The selection made by Mangan in both his articles in the *Dublin University Magazine* and his „Anthology" reflects his literary likes and dislikes. The sombre and melancholy note in the poetry of the German Romantics appealed to him so much that he included a large number of such poems, even at the cost of giving undue prominence to writers whose work, from a more objective viewpoint, appears not particularly valuable. On the other hand, he placed Schiller above all German poets, even above Goethe. It has often been said that in translating Schiller he was at his best. Yet there is hardly a finer translation of the description of an Ossianic scenery in „Mignon's Song," from Goethe's „Wilhelm Meister," than that given by Mangan:

Knowest thou the mountain's brow?
Its pathway clouds and shadows cover:
Amid the darkling mist the mule pursues his blind way over.
The dragon and his brood lurk in its thousand cavern hollows;
The rent rock topples down; the headlong sweep of waters follows.
That mountain dost thou know?
Thither our way lies. Father! let us go.

Mangan apparently acquired his knowledge of German by self-teaching. Books for learning German, such as those compiled by Klauer-Klatowsky, were reviewed in the *Dublin University Magazine.* Mangan also tells us that he took the originals, from which he translated, „from the shelves of the Library of Trinity College." There can be no doubt that he took greater liberties with them than a modern translator could afford to do; yet it should be remembered that, among the numerous translators of German poetry, he was one of the few who were poets themselves. By comparison with Anster's translation of Faust, his „German Anthology" has certainly more original vigour.

CRITICISM

It is hardly to be regretted that the critical remarks made in the *Dublin University Magazine* on the various German poets were not re-printed in the book edition of the translations. Most of these remarks were too casual to be of lasting significance. Still, the very fact that Mangan treasured Schiller's poems so much shows that he realised the philosophical background of classical German poetry, and what is said in the last stanza of the Schiller-section of his German Anthology may be regarded as a summary of his own idealist conviction preserved through the tragedy of his life:

Never deem it a Shibboleth phrase of the crowd,
Never call it the dream of a rhymer;
The instinct of Nature proclaims it aloud -
WE ARE DESTINED FOR SOMETHING SUBLIMER.
This truth, which the Witness within reveals,
The purest worshipper deepliest feels.

(Quelle: Irish Times 29/30.6.1945)

A Travel Book on Germany Published in Dublin

In I.B.L. xxx (1947), 55 I mentioned that the English translation of Risbeck's *Briefe (Travels through Germany)* was the first book on Germany ever published in Ireland. Published in 1787 in London, this translation (by Rev. Paul-Henry Maty, assistant-librarian of the British Museum) was re-printed a few months later at Dublin.

The first printed account by an Irishman of a journey to Germany was of course Carve's *Itinerarium.* A hundred years later, John Baptist de Burgo, abbot of Clare and Vicar Apostolic of Ireland, published his curious *Viaggio di cinque anni in Asia,*

Africa et Europa (Milan 1668), including an account of his journey via Hamburg to Ireland (see my paper in I.E.R. V, lxix. 139 (1947))

In 1795, the London edition of the *Journey made in the summer of* 1794 *through Holland and the Western parts of Germany by* Ann Radcliff (Countess Ruault de la Haye) was also reprinted within a few weeks in Dublin. The first travel-book on Germany written by an Irishman and published in Ireland was *Letters from Mecklenburg* (Dublin 1822) by George Downes, the friend of Goethe. The first original travel book covering virtually the whole of Germany, published in Ireland was *Travels/in/Germany/and the/Illyrian Provinces/Compiled from the most recent authorities*/Dublin/ Printed by P. Hayes, No. 134, Capel Street/1828, 180 pp. 120. The British Museum Catalogue also lists „another copy" of this work „Dublin 1825?" The exact wording of its title-page can no longer be established, as this copy was destroyed in May 1941. On pp. 26 and 175 of the 1828 edition it is stated that the author travelled in Germany from October 1825 to April 1826; his book therefore did not appear before 1826.

In the British Museum Catalogue, the name of the author has not been stated. On p. 21 of the 1828 edition the author clearly said that his name was Alexander Gordon, son of John Gordon, who after retiring from service in the 26th or Cameronians had settled near Edinburgh. The Principal Keeper of the Department of Printed Books of the British Museum kindly informed me that my suggestion that the author's name should be stated in the General Catalogue has been adopted.

Throughout his book, Gordon referred to Great Britain as his country. He frequently referred to Edinburgh, in particular in connection with childhood memories. On two occasions only he spoke of Ireland. P. 75 he compared what he considered a typical German funeral with what he „had witnessed in Ireland: but how different was the demeanour and conduct of those present, from what I had observed on that occasion!" This remark indicated that the author's attitude to Ireland was unsympathetic and based only on casual contacts. P. 81 he referred to the superiority of jurisdiction „in England and Ireland" over that in Germany.

Gordon was born abroad while his mother followed the regiment in which his father served, presumably in the Peninsular War. It seems that it was only after his retirement that his father settled in Scotland. Speaking of the peasants of Carinthia, Gordon stated that such „miserable hovels" as theirs could not be seen even in North Scotland. Later English writers, no doubt, would have referred to Ireland. It is curious that his book was published in Ireland, and in Ireland only. Both author and publisher seem to have speculated on the new interest in Germany which was then very lively indeed in Ireland.

Among the English travel books on Germany of that time, Gordon's work holds a special place, because the author visited the Continent (as, previously, North and South America) on a definite business, namely as confidential clerk of an Edinburgh firm, who had correspondents in all the important commercial centres of Central Europe. He wrote with the avowed aim of encouraging „those improvements in machinery, which send our manufactures cheaper into market than other countries can afford to dispose of theirs." Gordon travelled from Harwick via Heligoland and Hamburg to

Hanover, Berlin, Dresden, Leipzig, via Prague and Vienna down to the Illyrian provinces and returned via Frankfurt to Edinburgh. Everywhere he had excellent sources of information on aspects rarely dealt with in the usual travel-books.

It would be interesting to know whether also the other edition owned by the British Museum bore the misleading sub-title „compiled from the most recent authorities." With the exception of some lengthy quotations from private sources (especially on conditions in Hungary), Gordon's account is entirely first-hand. In some details, such as his descriptions of the Dresden *Vogelwiese* and the Leipzig Christmas-fair, I was in a position to check the veracity of Gordon's account down to the smallest detail. I am not aware of any English travel book of the early eighteenth century that has more to say on the actual life of the German people, including folklore and social customs, than has Gordon's. This is particularly surprising when we consider that Gordon's knowledge of German was limited; that of his printer was scarcely better. The 1828 edition abounds with misspellings of German names, but, with references to my note in I.B.L. xxx. 89 f., it is interesting that the printer had a special type for ü (not however for ä and ö), somewhat smaller than, and obviously not belonging to the same set as, his ordinary characters. Thus p. 77 we find „Grüne Gewolbe" (on the following page however „Rust Kammer") and p. 84 „Kugelchen" (in a curious account of the trial of the murderer of the painter, which is of interest as it fills the gap existing between the two principal parts of the autobiography of Kügelgen's son, the *Jugendererinnerungen* and the *Lebenserinnerungen eines alten Mannes,* perhaps the most beautiful autobiographical work of early nineteenth century literature). Gordon's work was a perfect supplement to the travel books on Germany published by Downes (the latter dwelling entirely on the literary and artistic spheres). Apart from Ennis's geographical cyclopedia (Dublin 1816, see my paper in *The Irish Bookman,* June 1947), these are important records of Irish information on and interest in Germany at that time.

A copy of Gordon's work (which is neither in the National Library of Ireland nor in the Library of Trinity College) was picked up on the 1*d.* shelf of a second-hand bookshop in Dublin.

(Quelle: Irish Book Lover 3, November 1951, S. 131f)

The Place of German Theology in the Works of Canon Sheehan

To the younger generation of Irish men and women, the works of Canon Sheehan, presumably, are as much a source of historical information as they have been at least to one newcomer to this country. Reading that grand passage in the seventeenth chapter of *My New Curate* which starts with the words: 'I have been now in touch with three generations of Irish priests,' we cannot fail to recognize that Canon Sheehan himself meant his works to become, in the course of time, historical records. To mention but one aspect of the eminent historical value of his works the early nineteenth century Irish novelists stored up much information on the tradition of the characteristics of Irish devotional life, but where should we find information as reliable, comprehensive and detailed as that embodied in *My New Curate* on Irish particularities in the administration of the Sacraments[1] and in the observance of the liturgical feasts,[2] on the spreading of May devotions[3] and of the First Fridays,[4] on the way in which the Office used to be recited by the older generation of Irish priests whom Canon Sheehan had known,[5] or on the attempts to introduce in Ireland the 'German' way of saying the Rosary ?[6]

Being of German descent, the first and principal biographer[7] of Cannon Sheehan duly pointed out his hero's special interest in Germany. Heuser did scarcely more than point out. He confined himself to a brief reference to Canon Sheehan's interest in Germany, leaving aside his intimate knowledge of German history, geography, politics, music, science, philosophy and, above all, theology. This extensive and varied interest in Germany was one of Canon Sheehan's idiosyncrasies; at his time it was not typical of Catholic Ireland, and to his modern readers its details have become largely incomprehensible, so much so that the reality of this interest is scarcely appreciated.

My interests in Canon Sheehan as a source on the tradition of liturgical and devotional life in Ireland and as a link in the tradition of Irish-German literature relations were equally evoked in the accounts of the clerical symposium and the diocesan conference in *My New Curate* where we learn something of the impact which nineteenth-century German theology,[8] both Protestant and Catholic, had on the younger generation of Irish clergy:

---

1   Penance (ch. xiv), Holy Eucharist (ch. xii and xiv), Matrimony' (ch. xxvi) and Extreme Unction (ch. ill).

2   Christmas (ch. xv), Corpus Christi (ch. xxv).

3   Ibid.

4   Ch. xiv and xvii

5   Ch. i and xii

6   Ch. ix and xvii, namely by inserting in every *Hail Mary,* after the Holy Name; a relative clause commemorating the mystery meditated upon in that decade.

7   H. J. Heuser, *Canon Sheehan of Doneraile* (London, 1913).

8   'The Germans entered the contest more soberly and seriously than the French but with more dangerous effect,' said the Rev. D. Hallinan in his paper 'Modern erroneous systems of Bible interpretation' in I. E. RECORD, iii, 3 (1882), p. 238, where Kant and Eichhorn (see below) are

They speak dreadful things about evolution and modern interpretation, and the new methods of hermeneutics. ... they laugh at the idea of the world's creation in six days, and make (the older generation) forecast a dismal future for Ireland when German metaphysics and coffee will first impair, and then destroy, the sacred traditions of Irish faith.

The word 'hermeneutics'[9] was one of the magic wands by which Germany has fascinated the intellectual world, from Kant's 'Vernunft' and Hegel's 'Geist' right down to Jaspers's *'Existenz'* 'Hermeneutics', or as in later years the great Dilthey said in German 'Verstehen,' is the method of scholarly interpretation of the objectivizations of the mind, a method more complicated than a mere co-ordination between perception and reasoning. In the early nineteenth century, German Catholics were unprepared for an understanding of the implications which this conception, initiated by Herder,[10] might have on the traditional structure of exegetics. The decisive question in this field was, of course, whether scholarly interpretation was to be enlightened by reason and Faith or by reason alone, indeed a reason deliberately rejecting from the very outset the possibility of enlightenment by Faith. The answer was on the one hand rank mysticism, such as 'the visions of Emmerich,'[11] and on the other hand rationalism in metaphysical disguise, such as the systems of Hermes, Günther and Frohschammer, who managed to rally Catholic followings so numerous and conspicuous that the highest authority of the Church had to issue detailed rejections of their tenets.[12]

The early Catholic exegetes who found their bearings in this apparent conflict between modern scholarship and authoritative tradition therefore deserve a special place in the history of Catholic theology. Significantly enough it was a convert, Ch. G. Wilke,[13] who wrote the first Catholic 'hermeneutics'. Hermes, Günther and Frohschammer were deeply indebted to the philosophy known as German Idealism, by which 'the German genius' not only reached 'its zenith and apogee,'[14] but kept the mind of the white race under its sway right to the year 1939 when Nazi-Fascism, Bolshevism and Anglo-American Liberalism equally claimed to be the true heirs of Hegel. Outside strictly philosophical literature, no Irish Catholic writer has shown himself more conversant with German idealist philosophy than Canon Sheehan.

---

contrasted with the Conservative Protestants such as Hengstenberg and Fritzsche. In the continuation of his paper (ibid. 4, 530), Father Hallinan spoke of Semler (see below).

9   The place of Catholic hermeneutics was established in J. Wach, *Das Verstehen* (Tübingen 1933; see the index complied by the present writer).

10   In *Parerga*, Spring vi ff, Canon Sheehan spoke of Herder. In particular he meditated on the sentence: 'Herder died of disappointment and of a broken heart, of a failed life,' which meditation may be connected with Father Dan's 'retrospect' *(My New Curate,* ch. ii) ending with the words: 'My life was a failure,' the most beautiful passage written by Canon Sheehan.

11   *Luke Delmege* ch. xvi, a subject earlier dealt with in the *Dublin University Magazine.*

12   Denzinger, *Enchiridion Symbolorum* no. 1618, 1655 and 1666.

13   *Biblische Hermeneutik nach katholischen Grundsätzen* (Würzburg, 1853), see K. Werner. *Geschichte der katholischen Theologie* (Munich, 1889), 533.

14   *Parerga,* Winter lxiv.

Wherever I went in my searches after, I will not say Truth, for I knew right well where Truth was to be found, but after high intellectuality, I found myself referred instantly to German thinkers. 'The Kantian antinomies', 'imbued with the spirit of Fichte', 'at that time Germans stood still under the spell of Schelling's teaching', 'the Hegelian theories of contradictories have coloured all modern thought,'– these were phrases continually crossing and recrossing not only high-toned works on history and science, but even the ordinary novel that is thumbed and wept over by the emancipated schoolgirl.

These words and many detailed references to the philosophical systems occur not in one of Canon Sheehan's philosophical essays, but in *The Triumph of Failure,*[15] of which I used a thumbed 1945-reprint borrowed from a County Library. It is in that novel too that we find an explanation of the whimsical reference made in *My New Curate* to the threat of 'German metaphysics and coffee':

The Germans imperilled your faith? If you took my silver and gold and turned them into suicidal weapons against yourself, you have no one but yourself to blame.

Mis-application of German idealism had its roots in Germany: 'The cause of Kant's popularity was that not twenty in Germany understood his speculations,'[16] a statement with which few Neo-Kantians will find fault. Is there any other 'ordinary novel' in Irish literature which dared to impose upon its readers an exposition of the systems of Kant and Fichte as concise as *The Triumph of Failure* (I, iv and ix) ? In *Under the Cedars and the Stars,* Autumn lxxxvii, Canon Sheehan compared, partly in German terms, the principal tenets of Hegel and Schelling, and in Winter ix f. he spoke of the personal relations between Kant and Fichte, while Hegel's relationship with Kant was discussed in *Parerga,* winter lxiv.

With regard to both German philosophy and German literature in general, Canon Sheehan adopted a different attitude when dealing with their material details and when expounding their intellectual and spiritual implications. Of individual works by Goethe, notably some of his poems, he spoke in the highest terms, but his general sizing up of the writer was devastating (as, incidentally, was his criticism of Shakespeare). Similarly, his benevolent attitude to individual representatives of German philosophy must be contrasted with the crushing passage in his *Sermon on Bad Books:*

In Germany, outside the Catholic Church, anyone that can read is a transcendental philosopher, in other words an atheist, and this is attributable to the pernicious writings of a few dreamers[17] who had substituted shadows of their own making for the shadow of Christianity left by the Reformers.

Yet, the new curate (ch. xiv) had been favourably referred to as 'a transcendentalist, desperately in earnest,' and Luke Delmege 'thought that German idealism and Celtic mysticism[18] were the same. 'His friend Father Casey jocosely hides his embarrassment 'when in his library a book on Kant[19] is discovered' exclaiming: 'Who the mischief was this Kant! What a name for a Christian!'

---

15 (1898), I, iv, also II, xvi.

16 I, ix

17 *Lisheen* iv : '*Erzträumer*'.

18 Ibid. : 'Irish *Nebelwelt*'

19 Ch. vii. Another reference to Kant's life is in *Tristram Lloyd,* ch. vi.

While Father Dan did not venture further on the dreaded ground of German literature than Jean Paul, his new curate was imbued with

> the great thinkers of Germany, Bahrdt, and Semler, and Eichhorn (who) had swept away all our preconceived ideas about the Bible. The Wolfian[20] ideas have been expanded and developed, and advanced by Catholic apologists have set themselves to the task of reconciling our ancient tradition with the discoveries of modern science.

In the 'eighties, Father Letheby's German authorities were slightly out-dated. Bahrdt, the Rationalist Bible explainer, died in 1792; no serious writer has ever regarded him as anything but scurrilous. Semler's 'Theological hermeneutics' appeared between 1760 and 1769, and Eichhorn's 'Introductions' to the Old and New Testaments between 1780 and 1810.[21] These writers moreover were very different indeed in both calibre and influence. Old Father Dan was more advanced than his curate when inserting in a bibliography he drew up for the latter 'Neander's Church History (8 vols.)'; this standard work had appeared in 1824. Luke Delmege (ch. v, viii and xvi) again and again referred to Wegscheider,[22] whose advocacy of Kant in theological matters was obsolete when he died in 1849. In one instance a connection is established between this 'fairly modern German' and the Monophysites, in another instance he is listed, along with 'Bunsen,[23] the great heathen', as a Sabellian. Of the early nineteenth century Catholic theologians only two are mentioned. Among Father Pat Casey's books[24] there was an Alzog, presumably *Explicatio de interpretatione literarum sacrarum* (1835),[25] and in the discussion in a Heidelberg hotel in the thirty-sixth chapter of *The Graves of Kilmorna,* Möhler's *Symbolik* (1832) is described as 'one of the books which everybody talks about and nobody reads.'

In the 'Battle of the giants' at the diocesan conference in *My New Curate,*[26] 'the whole course of German exegesis' is one of the subjects, discussed on the basis of a paper on the inspiration of Holy Scripture, in which paper

> by something called Ritschlian[27] interpretation, the whole Bible was knocked into a cocked hat.

Also the names of Wellhausen and Tischendorf are alluded to, and when the lecturer is asked whether

---

20 Of course Friedrich August Wolf's ideas on the origin of the Homeric epics.

21 See above, my note on Father Hallinan's paper, p. 380, n.2.

22 *Allgemeine Deutsche Biographie* 41, pp. 427-32. The reference in *Luke Delmege,* ch. xiv, would have delighted the author of *Finnegans Wake.*

23 The historian and diplomatist (died in 1860).

24 *Luke Delmege,* ch. vii

25 Alzog's *Church History,* edited by F. X. Kraus, appeared in an English translation.

26 Ch. xxiii.

27 Albrecht, R. (1822-1899), after Schleiermacher, the most influential Protestant theologian in nineteenth-century Germany. His 'Origins of the old Catholic Church' (Bonn, 1850) was an attack on the Tübingen 'historical' school.

we are to adopt the conclusions of the German rationalist schools and set aside completely the supernatural element of the Bible,

he produces an exposition of the then state of Catholic theology in Germany, where Kaulen[28] and Schanz represented[29] the conservative side and Aurelian Schoepfer[30] and Scholl[31] the revolutionary one. Father Duff, the lecturer, further reports that in his list of favourable reviews by Catholics of Schoepfer's *Bible and Science,* (Eduard) Koenig, a Protestant theologian,[32] also referred to Ireland; it would appear to be unlikely though that this review was published in the IRISH ECCLESIASTICAL RECORD. [33]

It is particularly with regard to this passage in what is undoubtedly Canon Sheehan's most popular novel that it is suggested that brief explanatory notes of the many references lost on the average modern reader might be useful.

In his reply to the daring lecturer, the new curate stated that 'but for all the learning stored up in those German universities, which you so much admire, I would not think as you appear to think on this sacred subject.' Earlier, in his conversations with Father Dan, he had asked: 'How do they manage in the German universities, I wonder'–namely with' theological faculties,' possibly Catholic and Protestant side-by-side, in the *Kulturkamf* atmosphere.[34] However, among the many points in which, in *The Graves of Kilmorna,* Ireland is unfavourably contrasted with Germany is that in the latter 'universities raised to the level of intellectual capitals even humble villages' and that 'the Germans' (artists and scholars) 'work under State patronage'. In 1886 Canon Sheehan gave his review of the Abbé Henri Didon's book on *The Germans* (English translation 1884) the title 'On German Universities,' and in this review[35] the most favourable picture is painted, though apart from the Rationalist Bible interpreters also

---

28   On Franz Kaulen's (died in 1907) Introductions to the Old and New Testaments (1879ff), see Werner, op. cit., pp. 532 and 542, and M. Grabmann, *Geschichte der katholischen Theologie* (1933), p. 329.

29   Paul V. Schanz (died 1905), equally versed in exegetics and in science, wrote commentaries on the Gospels and three volumes of Apologetics (Grabmann, op. cit. p. 288).

30   Brixen, 1894.

31   Unidentified.

32   See Herzog-Hauck's *Realencyclopaedie für protestantische Theologie* v, p.255.

33   Apart from Father Hallinan's paper (above), see the later Cardinal McRory's articles in I. E. RECORD, iii, xiii (1892), pp. 481 and 878 and xvi (1895), pp. 26 and 193, referring to Gesenius (died in 1842) and Ewald, his pupil (died 1875), the great Hebraists also mentioned in Canon Sheehan's review of Père Didon's book on the Germans. Other articles in I. E. RECORD, on modern Biblical studies in iii, xv (1894:), 682 and 769 and ix (1888), pp. 22-30.

34   Cannon Sheehan was one of the few Irish Catholic writers who expressed sympathy with Bismarck (*My New Curate,* ch. xi; also *Parerga,* Winter lxxxiv on Moltke).

35   This review occupied several instalments in I. E. RECORD, 1886. Only in 1902 a namesake of the Canon reported in the same periodical (iv, xi, pp. 481-94) on the 'Religious [scil. neo-pagan] mind of a German student,' at Bonn university, an account the veracity of which is even more striking in the historical perspective.

the more recent Materialist philosophy in Germany, represented by Vogt, Moleschott, Fischer and even Haeckel,[36] is mentioned.

With regard to the latter though, Canon Sheehan's attitude was of course entirely adverse. In *Luke Delmege* xii Father Elton says 'bitterly' :

> The ghost of Democritus has appeared in the nineteenth century; and he rattles his chains, like every decent ghost – 'atoms,' 'germs,' 'cells,' we hear it all *da capo,* only Weismann differs from Eimer ...[37]

Moreover, with regard to these Darwinists, Canon Sheehan was quite up-to-date. Eimer, the Swiss biologist, died in 1898, while Weismann died only a few years before Canon Sheehan.

It was a true reflection of the state of affairs in German philosophy and theology during the nineteenth century[38] that Canon Sheehan mentioned far more non-Catholics than Catholics. Similarly his interest in German literature was primarily concerned with Goethe and Jean Paul, while Novalis and Friedrich Schlegel, both converts, are referred to only in a few notes in *Under the Cedars and the Stars.* Only in his posthumous essay on 'The limitations and possibilities of Catholic literature' (which is still read with benefit) he spoke of 'the great intellectual activity of Catholic writers in Germany',[39] then indeed just arising from its two hundred years of sound sleep.[40]

Interest in German theology was largely a ramification of Canon Sheehan's general infatuation with 'the Fatherland.' Still, in this field, his interest was historically more representative of Ireland than in the literary or musical sphere. What Irish writer would nowadays insert in his novels of Irish life references to Martin Grabmann, Karl Adam, Peter Wust or, for that matter, even Karl Barth? Is it that if you said 'Mendelsohn,' 'Guercino' or 'Canova' in a drawing room today, you would be met by solemn silence, probably considered what is called 'bad form.' The people are decent enough not to pretend to know anything about art, science and literature,[41]

or is it that Germany's influence, both good and bad, has abated?

(Quelle: IER 80, 1953, S. 381-387)

---

36   On Haeckel see E. Gaynor, 'Modern Scientific Materialism' in I. E. RECORD, iv, ii (1897), p. 333 ff. and vi (1899), pp. 147-66, also J. Macken, 'Haeckel and the Existence of God,' ibid. xiv (1903), p. 194. A review of *Principles of Anthropology and Biology* by T. Hughes, S.J. (1890) appeared in iii, xii (1891), p. 286.

37   On Weismann see *Oath. Encycl.* v, 658, and on Eimer, *Allg. Deutsch. Biogr.* xxxxviii, p. 300.

38   Compare in this respect my article on 'Thomas Moore as Theologian' in *Irish Monthly* 1947, pp. 114-24.

39   Except for Canon Sheehan, no Irish Catholic writer of the time did more for Irish German literature relations than J. F. Hogan; see in particular his papers on 'The Spirit and Influence of Germany' (I. E. RECORD iii, xii (1891), pp. 289-307 and 'The Literary Organisation of German Catholics' (ibid. xvii (1896), p. 233 ff.).

40   See my paper on Canon Sheehan's opinions of German literature to be published in *Modern Language Review.*

41   *The Graves of Kilmorna,* ch. xxxiv.

A Note on Cannon Sheehan's Interest in German Literature

My paper on 'Jean Paul and Ireland' *(M.L.R.* XL (1945), 190) refers to the translation of "The New Year's night of a miserable man" in Mangan's *Anthologia Germanica.* It should be added that in the review of Mangan's work in *The Nation*[1] (9 August 1845) this translation was reprinted, though without Jean Paul's name. In its issue of 7 January 1843, the section on 'German literature' consisted of 'Bits from Jean Paul Richter's Shruelzle' (in Thomas Davis's copy, preserved in the Royal Irish Academy, this misspelling, repeated in the text, was corrected by Gavan Duffy), 'translated by Carlyle', with a brief biographical note on Jean Paul. In the issues for 6 and 20 September 1845 (the latter being the obituary issue on Thomas Davis) 'Thoughts from Jean Paul' were published. In the first instalment the first item was headed 'The atheist'; in the second instalment, where the first item is 'The genius', the words 'the atheist' were (erroneously) repeated and made an attribute to 'Jean Paul'.

Speranza's interest in Jean Paul was undoubtedly evoked by *The Nation,* and so was presumably Canon Sheehan's – no writer in these islands has shown himself a more ardent admirer of Jean Paul.[2]

Chapter xviii of *My new curate* (1899), Sheehan's most popular work, which is still reprinted, has been translated into German and other Continental languages and forms indeed one of the most genuine portraits of Catholic Ireland, is entitled 'The Kampaner Thal'. In chapter xv this work had been introduced in the conversation of Father Dan, an old parish priest in a remote village in the South of Ireland, with his new curate, as 'the very thing' to initiate the conversion of an atheist. However, both the curate and other confreres of Father Dan (ch. xvii f.) had to admit that they did not know whether the *Kampaner Thal* was 'bird, beast, fish or insect; whether it was a powerful drug or a new system of hypnotism', whether 'Greek, Latin or Irish'. They 'hunted up all encyclopaedias and could find no trace whatever of that thing'. Father Dan had to tell his young confreres that "'tis only a little book. I always carry it about me. It is really very beautiful' He owned a 'little duodecimo' edition (one of the two editions of the only English translation of this work by Gowa, 1848 and 1857), extensive quotations from which are embodied in chapter xviii.

In Ireland, the days had gone when Catholics followed the earlier example of their more fortunate Protestant countrymen in taking an interest in the language and literature of Germany. Also the numerous American readers of Canon Sheehan's works did not understand the reference to the *Kampaner Thal*[3] but his partiality for

---

1   It is curious that so far no comprehensive study of *The Nation's* work for the spreading of a knowledge of German literature among Irish nationalists has been published.

2   The reference by J. H. Heuser, the main biographer of Cannon Sheehan, to this subject is in-adequate and the description of Jean Paul as 'a satirist who loved little children ...' indeed ludicrous. In the popular summary of this biography published as an introduction to Sheehan's *Tristram Lloyd* (Dublin s.a.) this subject is scarcely mentioned.

3   Heuser (p. 164) stated that Sheehan explained his reference to the *Kampaner Thal* in a special article contributed to the *American Ecclesiastical Review.*

Jean Paul can be traced in many of his works. In *The Intellectuals* (1911, ch. xiv), one of the brilliant expositions of Sheehan's knowledge of world literature, Dickens's humour, 'burlesque and caricature', is contrasted with the 'genuine, delicate humour of Sterne and Richter'. One of the many points in which in *The Graves of Kilmorna* (1912) Ireland is unfavourably contrasted with Germany in that 'we have no Jean Paul now, and if we had, no such honour could be paid him' (ch. xxxvi). In *Geoffrey Austin,* the last novel published in Sheehan's lifetime, Herr Messing describes 'Richter's Siebenkäs' as 'divine' (ch. xx).

The most extensive information on Sheehan's attitude to Jean Paul is obtained from *Parerga,* the second collection of Sheehan's philosophical aphorisms and essays, where in Winter liii we find the remarkable statement:

> I am of the opinion that no modem writer approaches Shakespeare but one. Jean Paul affects the simple life of simple German people, except where, as in his *Titan,* he reflects the thoughts and manners of the nobility in rank and genius. Some [of his critics] who clearly have never read beyond *Flower, Fruit* and [sic] *Thorn-Pieces* are content to rank Richter with Sterne and Goldsmith. When you have read *Levana* you rank him with Bacon. When you have read *Titan* or *Hesperus* with Shakespeare.

Myles, the hero of *The Graves of Kilmorna,* found some comfort in the thought that 'his country's indifference' to national literature 'was shared by more favourite countries', and in *Parerga* (Winter lv) Sheehan stated:

> I find that in Germany Richter is no longer read ... Richter's abominable obscurity, that made a Richter-Lexikon[4] necessary even during his life-time, repels modern readers.

Canon Sheehan's interest in Jean Paul is the apex of his interest in German literature in general. There is practically none of his works in which he does not refer to Goethe. In *The blindness of Dr Gray* (1909), chapter xvi is entitled 'Röslein roth' and concludes with the chorus of *Heidenröslein.* The words 'Röslein, Röslein, Röslein roth' are repeated in chapters xix, xxi, and in chapter xviii a priest finds that these words 'would come to his lips when reading in the Matins the words: Sanctus, Sanctus, Sanctus, Dominus Deus Sabaoth'.[5] In *Tristram Lloyd,* Sheehan's last and unfinished work, the words '*Dichtung* and *Wahrheit*'[6] occur six times. In *The Triumph of Failure* we have a quotation from *Faust* in German, with the English translation in a footnote, while in *Parerga* (Spring xciv) the *Erdgeist*-scene is quoted. In the essay on 'The German and the Gallic muses' *(Ir. Eccl. Rec.,* 1887), 'the familiar lines from Mignon' are quoted.

In contrast to Sheehan's attitude to Jean Paul, his attitude to Goethe was ambiguous. In *Under the Cedars and the Star,* his first philosophical collection, Sheehan said (Winter lxxxii):

---

4   See my paper on 'Stephen Hero and William Meister in *German Life and Letters,* n.s., v (1951), 22 f.

5   In *The Graves of Kilmorna,* ch. xxxvi, Goethe and Wagner are described as not incompatible with the spirit of the Mass.

6   On Goethe's autobiography cf. also *Parerga,* Winter liii.

I confess I cannot whip my mind into enthusiasm about Goethe as I cannot bend the knee to Burns or other Philistine deities. I have read through Elective Affinities and Wilhelm Meister's Apprenticeship and the rest. It was weary work lightened only by the Ariel-presence and the ever-to-be remembered song of Mignon. The world will ever be grateful to Goethe for this. Goethe's masterpieces are in his lyrics.

Among the 'Philistine deities' rejected by Sheehan is also Shakespeare:

Goethe commenced to the lies about Shakespeare in that very silly and salacious book 'William Meister's Apprenticeship' (Autumn lxxxii).

Sheehan of course followed the usual trend of purely aesthetic appreciation of Goethe and of literature in general. He forgot the appalling biographical background of the Ariel-like presence of Mignon[7] and he professed at the end of the quoted passage his admiration of Shelley. In Winter lxxxii Sheehan also referred to *Faust* and *Iphigenie.* In Spring xvii he quoted Blackie[8] on Goethe's immorality and in xix (also Summer lxvii and *Parerga* Spring xxxvf.) Carlyle on Goethe. *Parerga* Winter lxii is entitled 'Goethe' and reference is made to the influence of the puppet-theatre and to *Faust I* and *II* including Retsch's illustrations.[9] In Spring xxviii we have Carlyle's translation and Goethe's original of *Symbolum (Die Loge).*

In *Under the Cedars and the Stars* (Winter lxxxi) Sheehan stated that 'Klopstock has long gone out of fashion in his native Germany' and in the subsequent chapter he spoke of Schiller[10]; in Summer xxiiiff. he discussed 'Novalis, the German Pascal', while Friedrich Schlegel was briefly referred to in Spring xxxii (and *Parerga* Winter Iv), where also Tieck is mentioned. Of Schiller and Goethe, we hear in *Parerga* Winter lxiii and in *Geoffrey Austin,* ch. xx, and of Heine and Goethe in *Parerga,* Summer xcix *(Atta Troll* is mentioned in *Luke Delmege,* ch. xvi). In *The Triumph of Failure,* chapter ii, Herr Messing's little son while protesting that he is an Irishman sings Koerner's *Schwertlied*[11], and in *The Graves of Kilmorna,* chapter xxxv, the tradition of 'Uhland, Rückert, Koerner, Arndt, not to speak of greater names' is contrasted with the then growing Irish indifference to Thomas Moore. Schiller, Bürger, Koerner and Uhland are again referred to in the essay on 'The German and the Gallic muses', with a quotation from Uhland's *Schloß am Meer.* In *Parerga,* Winter lxiv and lxvi, Sheehan discussed the characteristics of classicism and romanticism in German literature in general.

---

7   See my article on 'Stephen Hero and Wilhelm Meister', p. 27 f.

8   See my paper on 'John Stuart Blackie's translation of Goethe's *Jahrmarktsfest zu Plunders-weilern*' (which was published in the *Dublin University Magazine)* in *Mod. Lang. Quarterly* viii (1947), 91 ff.

9   On Goethe and Ret(z)sch see my paper on 'Goethe's relations with Hüttner' in M.L.R. xlvi (1951), 409.

10   *Geoffrey Austin* is prefaced by a motto from Schiller in German, and Herr Messing, the German teacher in that book, discusses Schiller with his pupils.

11   In *Geoffrey Austin,* ch.iv, Herr Messing also refers to 'Sword-song'. Sheehan was one of the few Irish Catholics who were in sympathy with Bismark's Germany.

Perhaps the most intimate contact with German literature that can be traced in the works of Canon Sheehan is the obvious relationship existing between his meditation upon the words 'Herder died of disappointment, of a broken heart and of a failed life' (*Parerga,* Spring vi-viii), extracted from a biography, and the undoubtedly autobiographical second chapter of *My new curate,* entitled 'A retrospect', ending in the words 'I had a dread consciousness that my life was a failure', this whole chapter being an unsurpassed description of the inevitable effects of the 'inertia of Ireland'.

Sheehan's interest in German literature is only part of his wider interest in 'the Fatherland', its geography, history, politics, musical tradition (right up to Wagner), philosophy (from Kant to Nietzsche) and theology (both Catholic and Protestant).[12] In all these fields Sheehan's opinions are less interesting than the scope of his interest and knowledge. In particular, it should be noted that, except for Mangan, no Irish writer has tried harder than Canon Sheehan to spread some knowledge of German literature. He surpassed Mangan in width of interest in German culture, and through his novels, to this day widely read throughout the English-speaking Catholic world, his references, however incomprehensible to many modern readers, have reached a wider public than Mangan's translations did or could do. (Even in such purely Irish novels as *Glenanaar,* Sheehan would not do without German words such as *heimweh.*)

Canon Sheehan's interest in German literature was the record of a passing phase in the intellectual history of Catholic Ireland.[13]

(Quelle: MLR 49, 1954, S. 352-355)

---

12   See my paper on 'The place of German theology in the works of Cannon Sheehan' in *Irish Ecclesiastical Record,* v, lxxv (1953), 379-387

13   See my surveys of Irish interest in German literature in my article quoted above, note 2, p. 354 and in my paper on 'Irish German Literary Relations' in *German Life and Letters,* n.s. III (1950), 102-10.

V.5 20. Jahrhundert

A Footnote to James Joyce

'Could anything have more fortified Joyce in his alienation from the Irish Revival than the treatment afforded *Dubliners* by Dubliners?' In these words, Mr. Herbert Gorman summed up, twenty-five years ago, what Joyce's failure with Irish publishers meant for his work. The famous letter which, ten years previously, Joyce had sent in 1911 from Trieste to Irish newspapers to complain of 'the scandalous state of authorship in Ireland', was published only by *Sinn Fein* in Dublin and *The Northern Whig* in Belfast. About the same time, two of the stories of *Dubliners* appeared in *the Irish Homestead*. These were the last occasions of any of Joyce's works being published in his native country. They were, however, not the first.

It was again in his book on Joyce's 'first forty years' that Mr. Gorman told us that 'Joyce declared that at the age of nine he had written a pamphlet on Parnell, of which, however, no copy is in existence'. In his 'definitive biography' of Joyce, Mr. Gorman omitted this reference.

Joyce's first published work, an essay on *Ibsen* which the eighteen years old student got published in the *Fortnightly* of 1900, was reprinted in 1930 by the Ulysses Book-shop. Irish reaction to this essay seems to have been summed up in George Moore's casual remark to Æ., describing it as 'preposterously clever'. Æ. himself did not bother to read the Ibsen essay, but passing on Moore's remark to W. B. Yeats, he recommended to him 'a young fellow named Joyce, who has all the intellectual equipment, the culture and education which our other clever friends here lack'.

The only work of Joyce's which may be said to have been published in book form in this country, is his essay entitled *The Day of the Rabblement*, which appeared, together with an essay by F. Skeffington (later Sheehy Skeffington) in a two-penny pamphlet dated Oct. 15, 1901, printed by Gerrard Bros., 37 Stephen's Green.* Joyce's essay takes only two pages in this pamphlet, which is now one of the curiosities of modern Irish book production.

Joyce obviously alludes to the significant place held by this essay in the history of his intellectual development when he writes in *Stephen Hero*: 'Stephen had begun to regard himself seriously as a literary artist. He professed scorn for the rabblement and contempt for authority.'

Mr. Gorman already stated that *The Day of the Rabblement* was originally written for *St. Stephen's*, the short-lived organ of University College, Dublin, at the beginning of the century. The history of that interesting periodical might be re-traced in connection with the history of *The National Student*, which, I understand, is at present being prepared.

> 'To parry the charge of obscurantism', Joyce tells us in *Stephen Hero*, 'a monthly review was started under the editorship of McCann. The new editor was in high spirits over the event:

---

* It was only a few months ago that Mssrs. Gerrard Bros. gave up the premises at 37 Stephen's Green.

'I have got nearly all the "copy" for the first number', he said to Stephen. 'I'm sure it will be a success. I want you to write us something for the second number – but something we can understand. Condescend a little. You can't say we are such barbarians now: we have a paper of our own. We can express our views. You will write us something, won't you?'

'Of course there is a censor?' said Stephen.

'Well', said McCann, 'the person who originated the idea of the paper in the first instance was Father Cummins.'

'The director of your sodality.'

'Yes. He originated the idea so you see he acts as a kind of sponsor to us.'

'He is the Censor then?'

'He has discretionary powers but he is not at all narrow-minded. You needn't be afraid of him.'

'I see. And tell me, will I be paid?'

'I thought you were an idealist', said McCann.

'Good luck to the paper', said Stephen waving his hand in adieu.

Then Joyce goes on to tell us of the contents of the first number. Strangely enough, he did not restate the history of the contribution which, after all, he sent in to the editor of *St. Stephen's*. Mr. Gorman reprinted *The Day of the Rabblement*, adding, with regard to its publication: 'Joyce reckoned without the Censor. His protest was refused.' The author's preface to *Two Essays* more clearly says: 'These two essays were commissioned by the Editor of *St. Stephen's* for that paper, but were subsequently refused insertion by the Censor.' Neither Mr. Gorman nor, apparently, any other writer on Joyce mentioned the justification which 'McCann' (*i.e.*, Hugh Kennedy, the first editor of *St. Stephen's* and at that time also Auditor of the Lit. and Hist.) subsequently gave for his (and the Censor's) refusal.

While summing up what to this day appears to be the official attitude towards Joyce in this country, Kennedy's review of *The Day of the Rabblement* is, so far as I am aware, the earliest criticism of Joyce published in Ireland. Moreover, this review is of interest with regard to recent criticism on the Abbey Theatre. What Gabriel (in 'The Dead', the final story of *Dubliners*), wanted to say, that 'literature was above politics', is the essential point of *The Day of the Rabblement*: –

'We have been favoured', says the Editorial in the issue of *St. Stephen's* of December, 1901 (vol. i, 3, p. 42), 'with a copy of a pamphlet containing two essays written by students of this college.
...

'The second essay is entitled *The Day of the Rabblement*, by James A. Joyce. The opening sentence describes his attitude towards the subject which he treats, the Irish Literary Theatre. He begins thus: "No man, said the Nolan, can be a lover of the true and good unless he abhors the multitude." In deference to the multitude, or, as Mr. Joyce prefers to say, the rabblement, of which "the Irish Literary Theatre must be considered the property", the directors have refrained from presenting Ibsen, Tolstoy, Hauptmann, Sudermann, Björnson, and Giacosa, "where even *Countess Cathleen* is pronounced vicious and damnable". Now, as we understand the Literary Theatre, its object was to educate a vulgarised public, in a word, to rescue the Irish rabblement from the influences which, from the point of view of the artist, were working havoc. But this rabblement clung to a standard of morality – the tradition of the Catholic Church, the ethical teaching of Christendom. For a spiritual life based thereon it had sacrificed material prosperity and well-being, and it now showed itself willing, in the same interest, to forgo all that art might add to the surroundings of life. So it happened that when the rabblement protested against *Countess Cathleen*, our fellow-students approved and supported the protest. Mr. Joyce alone, to our know-ledge, stood aloof. If Mr. Joyce thinks that the artist must stand apart from the multitude, and means that he must also sever himself from the moral and religious teachings which have, under Divine guidance, moulded its spiritual character, we join issue with him, and we prophesy but ill-success for any school which offers our Irish public art based upon such a principle.'

With reference to the support given by 'our fellow-students' to the 'rabblement', Lady Gregory speaks of

'Young men from the Catholic university being roused to come and make a protest against this insult to their faith. There was hooting and booing. In the end the gallery was lined with police, for an attack on the actors was feared. Some of the young men who hissed the play then, are our good supporters now.'

It is interesting to note that a few years later Joyce translated into Italian *Countess Cathleen* and Synge's *Riders to the Sea*. As early as summer, 1901, he had translated into English Hauptmann's *Vor Sonnenaufgang*, and later he also translated *Michael Kramer* (at the end of *The Day of the Rabblement* he speaks of the author of that play as the natural successor of Ibsen). It was not until 1908 that a play by Sudermann (translated by Lady Gregory) was produced in the Abbey, while as late as 1913 *Hanneles Himmelfahrt*, one of Hauptmann's tamest plays, was put on.

Was it Joyce's essay on the Irish Literary Theatre which Dr. Peter Kavanagh had in mind when, a few months ago, he wrote in a review of *An Gúm* publications: 'The officials of the *Gúm* seem never to have heard of Strindberg ... Chekov, Ibsen and all the other world-famous dramatists; instead they give us translations of plays by such people as ...'? The Editor of *St. Stephen's* was 'broadminded' enough to publish, five months after his adverse criticism of *The Day of the Rabblement*, Joyce's essay on *Mangan* (reprinted, in 1930, by the Ulysses Bookshop – the *Cambridge Bibliography of English Literature* erroneously says 'Dublin, 1930'). This essay concluded the first period of Joyce's literary career.

Joyce's interest in Mangan was apparently evoked not only by Mangan's work for the promotion of Irish appreciation of German literature, but – in still closer connection with the discussions on the Irish Literary Theatre and the Gaelic Revival – by his attitude to the language question: –

'Though there be those', Mangan had written sixty years ago in the *Dublin University Magazine* (vol. vi, 403 f), 'who would cry shame upon us for this confession, we do confess that to our ears no language sounds as pleasing as that of England. Is it not the language of our homes? Is it not that in which we remember the voices of our parents and the poems of our youth?'

While *The Day of the Rabblement* was mentioned neither by Lady Gregory in her book on *Our Irish Literary Theatre* nor by Miss Ellis-Fermor in her study of *The Irish Dramatic Movement*, Joyce's essay on *Mangan* has attained a firm place in the – scanty – literature on Mangan. Both of these essays are expressive of that 'honest egoism' with which *Stephen Hero* 'acknowledged to himself that he could not take to heart the distress of a nation, the soul of which was antipathetic to his own, so bitterly as the indignity of a bad line of verse.'

(Quelle: The Bell, 11, 1945, S. 704-709)

Dr Josef Grabisch

When a few months ago, Dr Josef Grabisch passed away, only a few of his intimate friends realised that one of the greatest experts on Irish-German cultural relations had gone from us. Dr Grabisch's interest in these relations dated back to the early days of his marriage to Miss Agatha Bullitt, an American lady of Irish extraction, who in the beginning of the European war held an appointment with the German foreign office, being particularly entrusted with the collecting of information on Irish affairs. On one occasion she answered an article by Lord Bryce on Belgium by drawing attention to the Irish question, then, in spite of Dr Bonn's books, still a chapter of world politics little known to the Continent. Sir Roger Casement was so much pleased with this article that he invited Mrs Grabisch for tea, and from this meeting dated the close association of Dr and Mrs Grabisch with this country.

Mrs Grabisch was made secretary to the German-Irish Society, presided over by Professor Kuno Meyer. She and her husband cooperated in editing the *Deutsch-Irische Blaetter*, devoted to the promotion of German-Irish cultural relations, chiefly through literary articles and translations of Irish and Anglo-Irish literature. At his Berlin home, Dr Grabisch had a fine collection of early German books on Ireland. In 1921 the Society discontinued its activities. The Grabischs then devoted themselves to promoting understanding between America and Germany. In connection with this work, they also visited Ireland. They became acquainted with many leaders of the national movement. Their home in Berlin continued to be the headquarters of the Irish nationalists visiting Germany.

In 1938, political conditions compelled the Grabischs to leave Germany. To their friends, both Irish and German, it can hardly appear as a mere accident that during the subsequent fateful years they should have resided in Ireland. Immediately after settling down in Dublin, the late Dr Grabisch engaged in a comprehensive study of the sources of Mangan's translations from the German, backed by a survey of Irish knowledge of Germany and her civilisation and its place in Irish cultural life during the first half of the nineteenth century.

Outside the wide circle of their personal friends, Dr Grabisch was, perhaps, best known among the second-hand booksellers in Dublin. For many years he toured every week the bookshops and book-barrows collecting from their penny shelves books and pamphlets. His collection on Irish-German cultural relations was unique not only for its external value, but even more so through the work which Dr Grabisch had put into its arrangement. After his death, this collection had to be broken up, but some of its treasures have found a home in some of our public libraries where Dr Grabisch had been a constant reader.

How often did I meet him at his book-haunts, in Nassau Street and along the Quays, with his well-known worn out leather bag under his arm bursting with books. Even when it was at half-past five, at O'Connell Bridge, he would start an argument, on some obscure German poet whose footsteps he had traced in Mangan's work, on some edition, so far unknown, of a German travel-book on Ireland, on some curious evidence of Irish interest in Germany. And he would make me forget everything, trams, buses, messages, lectures, pouring out with boundless generosity, his learning and thought, always enlightening, and above all, always demanding from his interlocutor the same genuine love of historical truth with which he radiated.

His interest in Ireland stood out against the background of his fervent attachment to the country of his birth. How delighted he was when I told him that the earliest German translations of works of nineteenth century Anglo-Irish literature (Whitty's *Irish tales* and Thomas Moore's *Captain Rock*) had been published at Breslau, where he had gone to school. He almost tore from my hands when I showed it to him in the National Library the only German book ever printed in Ireland, a translation published by Crooke in 1710 of the *Book of common prayer*. That translation was not made in these countries, but a reprint from that published six years earlier at Frankfurt-on-Oder, near his native town. Among his books I found the counterpart to this work, the only German translation from the English made in Ireland to have been published in this country, a fairy tale, entitled *Der goldene Faden*, the golden thread (1879).

At no time of history, were Irish-German literary relations closer than at Mangan's. In the forties more books on Ireland appeared in Germany than during the subsequent hundred years, and knowledge of German and classical German literature was then regarded as indispensable for a cultured Irishman. Many of the German books collected by Dr Grabisch bore owners' signatures or dedications from that time. From later periods, he had German books the character or dedications of which pointed to Irishmen following the usual track up the Rhine valley to Oberammergau or Salzburg, to Irish students in German universities, or to Irish girls in German convents. Dr Grabisch did not live to have his work ready for publication, but the few manuscripts of his preparatory to the study on Mangan may, perhaps, one day attract the interest of an Irish student who will then recall, in the most adequate manner, that great friend of Ireland.

(Quelle: Irish Bookman, 1948, S. 87-89)

Nietzsche, Jaspers and Christianity

One of the first books published by authority of the British Military Government in Germany was *Nietzsche and Christianity* by Karl Jaspers.[1] This was the first of a number of post-war publications through which Professor Jaspers became practically the spokesman of academic Germany. He had been one of the few outstanding university professors who, though not directly discriminated for racial, religious or political reasons, had never for a moment associated themselves with National Socialism. Apart from church dignitaries and scientific technicians, he was the first German intellectual to be invited after the war for lectures abroad. When the first

---

[1]   *Nietzsche und das Christentum*, Verlag der Buecherstube Fritz Seifert, Hameln 1946. See my articles 'Das neue Denken und das neue Glauben' in *Zeitschrift fuer Theologie und Kirche*, xvii (1936), p. 30-50, 'The measure of Man', *Catholic Biblical Quarterly*, viii (1946), p. 332 and 'Simplicius Simplicissimus's British associations' in *Modern Language Review*, xl (1945), p. 37.

German university was re-opened by the Allied Military Authorities at Heidelberg, he was not only restored to his professorship but appointed Rector. Fifteen years after the publication of his chief work, Jaspers has become perhaps the most influential figure in the intellectual life of Central and Western Europe. In Switzerland, the Low Countries, Scandinavia, England and France, his Existentialism is discussed even by those who used to take but little interest in philosophical pursuits.

In these countries, it is difficult to obtain genuine information on Jaspers's philosophy. Only one small book of his has been translated into English.

In 1931 the publishers of *Sammlung Goeschen* asked Jaspers to write the 1,000th volume of this series of popular text-books on all branches of learning. He gave his book the title *The spiritual Situation of our Time* which the Australian translators (E. and C. Paul) rendered by *Man in the Modern Age*. This book is long out of print.

Even more than Jaspers, Martin Heidegger is usually regarded as the initiator of Existentialism. Indeed Heidegger's chief work appeared as early as 1928, but he had been Jaspers's pupil and his work remained a grand torso. Through his close association with National Socialism Heidegger is now somewhat discredited; indeed for some years his philosophy was in fashion with the Spanish Falangists and some of the early 'idealist' followers of Hitler believed that Heidegger supplied them with a philosophical foundation of political dynamism. Jaspers is Heidegger's senior by fifteen years or so. While Heidegger is of South German Catholic origin, Jaspers comes from a Northern family with no Christian affiliations. Heidegger began his career by studies in scholastic philosophy. Jaspers was up to his forties a medical scientist rather than a professional philosopher. Amidst the turmoil caused by Spengler's prophecy of the 'Decay of the West', now fulfilled to an undreamt of extent in all its details, Jaspers published his *Psychology of Weltanschauung*, in which he showed that Weltanschauung had become the modern substitute for positive religion and was an attempt to shelter in ever new 'shells' from the onslaught of direct and vital experience.

It was in *Man in the Modern Age* that Jaspers first outlined the scope of Existential philosophy. I quote from the Paul's translation:

'Existence-philosophy is the thought, making use of or transcending all expertise, by means of which man would fain become himself. This thought does not cognise objects, but illuminates and elaborates the being of the thinker. Brought into a state of suspense by having transcended the cognitions of the world (as the adoption of the *philosophical attitude towards the world*), that fixate being, appeals to its own freedom (as the *illumination of existence*) and gains space for its own unconditioned activity through conjuring up transcedentalism (as *metaphysics*)'.

(The words in italics are the titles of the three volumes of Jaspers' *Philosophie*, the most comprehensive system of philosophy produced by our generation).

I cannot blame the translators for not even attempting to render Jaspers into idiomatic English. In fact the original Jaspers is perhaps even more difficult to read, because he, like Heidegger, has largely abandoned the traditional terminology of philosophy. It is a well known fact that right from the beginning German (vernacular) philosophy derived much of its inspiration from meditation upon the original meaning of words. Hegel's idea of dialectics, for example, loses much of its apparent arbitrariness when we con-

558

sider it as a result of a meditation upon the threefold meaning of the German word 'aufheben' (corresponding to English 'up' and 'heave'), namely 'to raise', 'to eliminate' and 'to preserve'. Heidegger and Jaspers, in analogy to contemporary poetry and prose-writing, raised this technique to the rank of a general method; ordinary life, what Hegel called 'dirty reality' supplied them with their raw material. In no respect is the relationship between 'modern art' and 'modern philosophy' more evident. The former claims to decompose natural forms into their essential components; the latter unfolds the components and aspects of vulgar and traditional usage. None of the traditional conceptions of philosophy is left its conventional meaning, though indeed none of them is completely deprived of it either. *Either* the original or literal meaning of the word is given preference, as e.g. in the word 'Existence' literally 'out-standing', therefore no longer meaning 'real being' (as in traditional studies *de existentia Dei* etc.) but those extra-ordinary moments in human life of complete truthfulness, sincerity and genuineness, for which – as every second modern novel tells us – our generation is craving. *Or* the traditional meaning is shaded by manifold meaning which words have in vulgar speech, especially through the various degrees of their figurative use (most noticeable in German, where one cannot escape into Latinism). Students of classical German philosophy will be aware of the fact that there is no English equivalent to the word 'erkennen', literally meaning 'to know thoroughly' also 'to beget', which Kant and Hegel used for the fundamental activity of the philosophical mind. The English translators of Jaspers followed the tradition to render this word by to 'cognise', which only shows how right Jaspers was in abandoning this word. He uses instead the expression 'es geht auf', literally 'it opens itself', which in German implies the following idioms: 'The sun rises', 'a door opens by itself', 'an equation dissolves itself', 'a blister bursts', 'it dawns upon me'. In each case where Jaspers uses this expression virtually all these meanings are implied, though in each case one of them is articulated. This expression points to the three essential characteristics attributed to 'Existential' (in contrast to what is described as 'objective') thinking, namely its spontaneity (not 'I recognise' but 'it acknowledges itself',) suddenness (in contrast to the slow labours of ratiocination) and completeness (the door was closed, and now it has been flung open). This use of words in their original (perhaps long forgotten or at least obsolete) or their rudimentary vulgar and material sense is not confined to Existential philosophy. Under the influence of his early German studies, James Joyce tried to apply it to the English language, with what success readers of his *Finnegan's Wake* may decide. In *Stephen Hero*, his earliest work, posthumously published, Joyce described 'epiphanies' as the only experience life was worth living for. In Existential philosophy 'transparence' is the most outstanding characteristic of 'existence'. The use of the word 'transparent' in modern Continental literature alone would suffice to show that Existential terminology is not the arbitrary invention of some queer German professors but the summary of a very deep and significant stratum of contemporary European thought.

As it is most difficult to translate Jaspers's *Philosophie*, those who realise the importance of Existentialism will welcome the publication of *Nietzsche and Christianity*, a series of lectures which Jaspers gave in 1938 to a meeting of Protestant clergy. Of Jaspers's numerous post-war publications this is the only one to be strictly philosophical, and also the only one which was written before the war. There are few books of this kind which could be reprinted without the slightest alteration after those eight years. Not only in Germany but also in Holland, Switzerland, Scandinavia and in these countries, Protestant clergy have been among the first students of Existential philosophy.

Nietzsche and Christianity would appear to be an avenue of approach to Jaspers's philosophy because it deals with a historical subject. In 1936 Jaspers had published a book on Nietzsche, implicitly a defence against the attempts then made to claim Nietzsche as a fore-runner of the 'philosophy' of Rosenberg, and a warning against the attempts made in subsequent years to list Nietzsche along with Treitschke, Bernardi, Houston Chamberlain etc. as an advocate of 'blood and iron' nationalism. In 1938 Jaspers warned his clerical listeners not to be misguided by the well-known ferocity of Nietzsche's onslaught on bourgeois Christianity. Indeed, even those who have a fairly good knowledge of Nietzsche might not be aware that right between those fierce condemnations we can hear him saying: 'Christianity has been the best piece of ideal life I have ever known. From childhood days I have sought it, and I firmly believe that I have never been mean against it in my heart.' 'The most noble type of man I have seen was the sincere Christian. I regard it as an honour to originate from families where Christianity was taken seriously in every respect.' 'The meek, the upright and chaste priest is not only the anointed and elect of the people, from whom he originated and to whom he belongs. He is sacrificed to the welfare of the people, and therefore can be trusted like no one else.' 'The self-denial which the Jesuits impose upon themselves and which is taught in their manuals, is beneficial to the laity even more than to the Society itself. Jesuitism is one of the few true forms of Christianity and indeed the only true form of democracy in the modern world.'

However, Jaspers is not really concerned with the ambiguity of Nietzsche's attitude towards Christianity. Both his hostility and his admiration are merely the superficial, outside expressions of his rational and his sentimental moods. Behind this ambiguity is his desperate search for truth, a keen awareness of the insufficiency of any position yet attained, characteristic, as Jaspers believes, of the spirit of learning proper to Christian Europe. Jaspers understands Nietzsche better than Nietzsche could understand himself. The very ambiguity of Nietzsche's attitude is expressive of the fundamental tenet of Existential philosophy that truth is not simply here and not there, unambiguous at any time and to anybody. Truth in general is not an objective position but rather a specific quality which, theoretically, can appear in any position, however 'incorrect' it may appear in the 'objective' sphere. The standard of truth is not the fitting of ideas upon things or facts but the full weight of existential perspicuity. So far as Nietzsche is concerned, one can certainly agree with Jaspers that neither in his hatred nor in his praise of Christianity Nietzsche was fully himself and that he is at his best, his deepest and perhaps his truest where he confines himself to urging upon us boundless love of truth.

It is hard to deal with Existential philosophy in the traditional forms of philosophical work. This philosophy does not claim to establish theories but to confine itself to descriptions. Dealing with history it somewhat transcends its boundaries. I believe that Existential philosophy has really discovered something which is peculiar to modern man, perhaps one of the very few things he can be proud of, namely his desire of perfect sincerity and almost Jansenist craving for personally living up to the greatness of truth. Former generations could find some peace in the distinction between *attritio* and *contritio* or of Probabilism and Probabiliorism. Modern man, in spite of his apparent weakness, has standards of truthfulness which sometimes appal the older generation. Unfortunately Existential philosophy has become what Jaspers would call a shell, an ism, by its doctrine that truth can be found *only* through existence, *only* in transparence, *only* in the fullness of sincerity. It is unaware of the tension characteristic of the modern Christian between a gigantic truth and our prayer for faith.

> NOTE. Since this article was written Professor Jaspers has gone to Basle, another work of his on the nature of truth has appeared, and his booklet on the conception of guilt has been translated into English.

(Quelle: Blackfriars 29, 1948, S. 476-480)

Katholisches Irland, heute und morgen

> Entgegen meiner Erwartung erscheint der vorliegende Artikel lange nach meinem später geschriebenen Artikel über "Irland und der Nationalsozialismus" (Oktoberheft 1947). Die Kritik an letzterem Artikel wäre vielleicht etwas milder ausgefallen, würde der vorliegende Artikel zuerst erschienen. Die Verzögerung seiner Veröffentlichung bietet Gelegenheit, die Richtigkeit meiner Ausführungen an der Entwicklung der letzten zwei Jahre, insbesondere der letzten Monate, zu prüfen. J. H.

Die *Schweizer Rundschau*, die durch Herrn Dr. Benziger, den hiesigen Chargé d'Affaires, in großzügigster Weise öffentlichen Bibliotheken in Dublin zugeleitet wurde, war nicht nur für Iren kontinentaler Abstammung, sondern auch für den kleinen Kreis deutschsprechender Iren während des ganzen Krieges eine Quelle zuverlässiger Information über politische, soziale und kulturelle Vorgänge auf dem Kontinent. Besonderes Interesse fanden natürlich Nachrichten aus und von einem Lande, mit dem Irland mehr als je verbunden ist durch das gemeinsame Schicksal einer Neutralität im Schatten der übermächtigen Propaganda des großen Nachbarn, ohne wie andere neutrale Nationen durch Sprachverschiedenheit dagegen geschützt zu sein. Irland ist sich, wie die Schweiz, in diesem Kampf der durch die Neutralität auferlegten geistigen Verantwortung den unzerstörbaren Werten der Menschheit gegenüber immer bewußter geworden.

Für Irland bildete die Neutralität ein größeres Wagnis als für die Schweiz. Es war das erste Mal in der Geschichte, daß Irland überhaupt die Möglichkeit hatte, neutral zu sein. Irlands Neutralität war nicht die selbstverständliche positive Fortsetzung einer in der ganzen Welt anerkannten und geschätzten Politik, sondern die negative Folge bitterster Erfahrungen. Wie die Schweiz war Irland fast völlig umgeben von *einer* der kriegführenden Mächtegruppen; aber diese Mächtegruppe war im Falle Irlands im Besitze eines bedeutenden Teils des nationalen Territoriums des Landes. Die während des Krieges und jetzt noch unvermindert andauernde Unterdrückung der katholischen Minorität in Nordirland (eine Minorität von nahezu 45%!) war und ist der Grund, warum selbst die Verurteilungen des Nationalsozialismus durch den Heiligen Stuhl in Irland zögernd aufgenommen werden. Mit einer in der katholischen Hierarchie seltenen Bitterkeit hat der verstorbene Kardinal McRory, der als Erzbischof von Armagh ein Bürger von Nordirland und damit des Vereinigten Königreiches war, immer wieder von der Scheinheiligkeit des britischen Anspruchs, Beschützer der kleinen und unterdrückten Nationen zu sein, gesprochen. Während in den protestantischen Kirchen offen oder versteckt für den Sieg der Alliierten gebetet wurde, machten viele Katholiken aus ihren pro-deutschen Gefühlen kaum ein Hehl. Ich hörte z.B. einen bekannten irischen Journalisten in Sinn Féin, der alten (jetzt verkalkten und verbitterten) nationalistischen Bewegung, auf einem Vortrag über das Thema «Irland und Deutschland» behaupten, er habe im Jahre 1937 bei einem Besuch in St. Kilians Bischofssitz, Würzburg, von der Fuldaer Bischofskonferenz zurückkehrende deutsche Geistliche gesprochen, die ihm mitgeteilt hätten, die Hierarchie habe unbeschränkte Unterstützung des Führers als Parole ausgegeben. Als der Redner das deutsche Wort «Führer», aussprach, brach die Zuhörerschaft in lauten Beifall aus. Noch heute erscheinen in den – ausschließlich von Katholiken bewohnten – *slums* neben den köstlichen vom Eucharistischen Kongreß überlebenden Inschriften «long live the Pope» oder «God bless Jesus Christ», «scrawls», wie «Hiel (sic) Hitler» oder «Up Germany».

Das eigentümlich enge Verhältnis zwischen Religion und Politik hierzulande ist durch den Krieg eher noch ausgeprägter geworden. Die Reformation war ja in kaum einem anderen Lande so rein politisch und materiell wie in Irland. Heute rangieren für den irischen Durchschnittskatholiken Protestantismus und Neuheidentum, zu denen einflußreiche katholische Schriftsteller noch Freimaurerei und Judentum hinzufügen, auf gleicher Ebene. Die spirituelle Grundlage der Episkopalkirche in Irland ist nach wie vor äußerst schmal, und man fragt sich mit Recht, ob ihre Anhänger wesentlich über die traditionelle Konzeption dieses Monumentes englischen Unterdrückungswillens hinausgekommen sind. In der irischen Sprache wird nach wie vor der Protestant als «Sachse», das traditionelle Schimpfwort für Engländer, bezeichnet.

Auf katholischer Seite liegt der Grund für die Verknüpfung von Religion mit Politik aber wohl tiefer. Der Glaube ist hier nicht eine rein geistige «Überzeugung», sondern eine physisch-materielle Realität im Nationalleben. Während seit dem Bürgerkrieg die Hierarchie jede politische Betätigung der Geistlichkeit untersagt hat, ist der Einfluss religiöser und kirchlicher Erwägungen auf das politische Leben noch enorm. Lesern von Joyce's *Portrait of the Artist as a young Man* wird die Unterhaltung im Elternhaus des Autors über Parnell und seinen auf den Einfluß der Kirche zurückgehenden Fall (wegen einer Ehescheidungsgeschichte) in Erinnerung sein. In einem ähnlichen Falle würde heute wohl die Mehrheit noch spontaner auf der Seite der Kirche sein, als sie es vor fünfzig Jahren war.

Die Eigentümlichkeiten des katholischen Charakters Irlands und seines Volkes lassen sich immer noch am besten an Anekdoten zeigen. Den ersten tiefen Eindruck empfing ich in dieser Hinsicht drei Stunden nach meiner Ankunft in diesem Lande, im Herbst des Jahres 1939. Als ich im Aufzug des Regierungsgebäudes zum Justizministerialdirektor hinauffuhr, bemerkte ich über der Tür ein mit einer Reißzwecke befestigtes Bildchen. Ich schaute näher zu. War das ein Porträt De Valeras oder eines der Nationalhelden? Nein, es war das mir nun aus fast allen irischen Häusern so wohl bekannte Bild des Allerheiligsten Herzens Jesu mit der Umschrift «Ich will jedes Haus segnen, wo mein Bild geehrt wird». Dieses Bild war nicht auf Befehl der Regierung im offiziellen Aufzug angebracht worden (wie im Schuschnigg-Österreich die Heiligenbilder in den Amtsstuben), sondern vom Aufzugführer. Auch in Trambahn-Wagen und in Autobussen kann man solche Bilder finden.

Ein paar Wochen später war ich in der Kapelle der Ewigen Anbetung am Merrion Square. Als ich wieder hinausging, bemerkte ich, daß außer den beiden weißen Nonnen vor dem Altar nur noch ein schwarz gekleideter älterer Herr mit mir in der Kapelle war. Er hatte hinter mir gekniet, und wir verließen gleichzeitig die Kirche. Draußen stand ein kleiner unscheinbarer Wagen. Als der Herr einstieg, erkannte ich ihn. *An Taoiseach*, Mr. De Valera. Drüben auf dem Parlamentsgebäude wehte die irische Trikolore. Ein paar Minuten später beantwortete dort im *Dail* De Valera einige die Neutralitätspolitik betreffende Fragen. Irische Freunde, denen ich mein Erlebnis erzählte, zuckten die Schultern und sagten: «Ja, was wollen Sie denn? ,Dev' geht jeden Tag vor der Arbeit in jene Kapelle.»

Ich hatte gelobt, wenn der Krieg zu Ende sei, die Wallfahrt nach Lough Derg zu machen. «St. Patricks Fegfeuer» ist seit Jahrhunderten die nationale Wallfahrt Irlands. Der erste deutschsprachige Pilger zu St. Patricks Fegfeuer, von dem wir wissen, war ein Schweizer. Heute verläßt der Pilger Dublin um acht Uhr morgens, nüchtern. Während des Krieges fuhr er im plombierten Zug durch eine Ecke von Nordirland, bis Pettigo, wo der Bahnhof auf nordirischem Boden, die Stadt aber auf «freistaatlichem» Boden liegt, eine kleine Illustration des wirtschaftlichen Unsinns dieser «Grenze». Gegen Mittag kommt man zu dem einsamen Bergsee in Donegal, in dem die «Heiligtum-Insel» liegt. Während der folgenden 48 Stunden muß man, barfuß über die scharfen Felsklippen der Insel wandernd, eine unglaubliche Menge von Gebeten sagen. Die erste Nacht wird im Gebet in der Kapelle zugebracht. An jedem Tage darf der Pilger einmal eine Mahlzeit, bestehend aus schwarzem Tee und trocknem harten Haferbrot zu sich nehmen. Erst am Morgen nach der Rückkehr nach Dublin darf das Fasten wieder gebrochen werden. Papst Pius XI sagte, daß dies die einzige Wallfahrt in der Welt sei, die ihren alten Bußcharakter rein bewahrt habe.

Ich erfuhr erst auf der Insel, daß ein paar Tage vorher Mr. De Valera die Wallfahrt gemacht habe, um Gott für die Errettung Irlands in Kriegsgefahren zu danken. Auf der Insel genoß er keinerlei Privilegien. Barfuß nahm der Pilger Eamonn DeValera an all den Bußübungen teil, fastend, wachend, betend. Die zweite Nacht ruhte er auf einem harten schmalen Lager unter einer Wolldecke in einer der winzigen Zellen, die durch einen Vorhang vom Korridor abgetrennt sind. Eine kleine Notiz in der Zeitung hatte mitgeteilt, daß der Staatschef für einige Tage Dublin verlassen werde.

Ein englischer Bekannter, dem ich diese Geschichte erzählte, sagte: «A very clever gesture». Ist es nur die Phantasie religiöser Schwärmer, die uns hier fühlen läßt, die Weltgeschichte würde anders aussehen, wenn die *Großen Drei*, oder besser die *Großen 200*, vor ihrer nächsten Weltfriedenskonferenz erst einmal zusammen drei Tage in der Grafschaft Donegal verbringen würden?

In Lough Derg sah ich Damen und Herren der ersten Kreise, elegante junge Mädchen und junge Intellektuelle zwischen Scharen kleiner Angestellter und der kompakten

grauen Masse «richtiger Iren» aus den wilden Bergtälern von Donegal und Connemara. Selbst an der Kommunionbank habe ich nie so vollkommene soziale Gleichheit
gesehen als unter diesen Barfüßlern, die sich in gleicher Weise um Gottes willen
harten physischen Bedingungen unterwarfen. Banken, Börsen, Weltmärkte, Flughäfen,
Pressekonferenzen, internationale Sicherheit und Atombomben, all das war in seine
gehörige Perspektive gerückt. Da waren Himmel, Wolken, Nebel, kahle Berge, der
See, das nackte Land, eine Kirche, ein Haus, Speise, Trank und Lager, und da waren
Menschen, die sich zu diesen Urformen zurückführen ließen, um Raum zu schaffen für
die Heiligung des Lebens in sich und um sich. Zwischen dem 1. Juli und dem 15.
August machen alljährlich etwa fünfzigtausend Iren diese Wallfahrt. Ich traf einen
Kleinbauern aus Mayo, der seit 45 Jahren jedes Jahr in Lough Derg gewesen war.

Den kontinentalen Konflikt zwischen Neuheidentum und Christentum kennen die Iren
nur vom Hörensagen, vor allem aus den Berichten gelegentlich, für ein paar Tage aus
der Emigration Heimkehrender. Kurz bevor diese Zeilen geschrieben wurden, hielt im
Radio einer der führenden katholischen Publizisten des Landes eine Vortragsreihe über
die Prinzipien katholischer Moral, in der er die Gegenstandslosigkeit der gegenwärtigen kontinentalen und angelsächsischen Häresien mit den handfesten Methoden der
alten Kontrovers-Theologie nachweist. Der Versuch, in diesen Häresien mehr als intellektuelle Kunststücke entarteter Demagogen zu sehen, wird hier katholischerseits
kaum gemacht. Natürlich, – denn hier sind Dinge wie Kritizismus, Historismus, Po-
sitivismus, Lebensphilosophie, Psychoanalyse, Existentialismus, Individualpsycho-
logie, Kommunismus, Faschismus usw. von geringerer Relevanz als z. B. Pelagia-
nismus und Jansenismus. Die inneren Realitäten, die jenen modernen -ismen entsprechen, sind nur indirekt zugänglich. Das Studium der Philosophie ist bei Protestanten
und Katholiken praktisch auf die Theologen beschränkt; beide folgen einer strikten
Schultradition, von der aus alles andere «widerlegt» wird.

Für die Laienschaft wurden zwei philosophische Handbüchlein veröffentlicht, das eine
von einem Dominikaner, das andere von einem Jesuiten; letzteres trägt den bezeich-
nenden Titel «Philosophie ohne Tränen». Das Fehlen tieferer Problematik ist am
ehesten erkenntlich in den Fragekästen der zahlreichen von geistlichen Orden herausgegebenen Zeitschriften; die dort behandelten Probleme betreffen ausschließlich die
äußeren Formen kirchlicher Disziplin oder historische Fakten.

Das Studium des irischen Zeitschriftenmarktes ist um so aufschlußreicher, als die
eigentliche Buchproduktion kümmerlich ist. Der Einfluß des Kinos (kein Land der
Welt hat eine höhere Zahl von Kinobesuchern per Kopf der Bevölkerung als Irland) ist
hier am auffallendsten. Junge Menschen sind nahezu unfähig geworden, noch ein
ernstes Buch zu lesen. Der durch die Kleinheit und Armut des Landes schon an sich
beschränkte Markt würde überhaupt keine seriöse Buchproduktion rechtfertigen, wenn
man nicht auf Export nach England und Amerika rechnen könnte. Zeitschriften dagegen werden viel gelesen und haben ein verhältnismäßig hohes Niveau. Die Jesuiten
publizieren *Studies*, die einzige wissenschaftliche Zeitschrift für die katholischen
Laien Irlands, und *The Irish Monthly*, die, ebenso wie der von den Dominikanern
herausgegebene *Irish Rosary* (weniger devotionell als der Titel andeutet) und die von
Laien herausgegebene Zeitschrift *Hibernia*, für Gebildete gedacht ist. Die zahlreichen

kleineren populären Magazine der verschiedenen religiösen Gemeinschaften halten sich im allgemeinen auf einem höheren Niveau als entsprechende Publikationen in Amerika. Von den katholischen Wochenzeitschriften repräsentiert *The Irish Catholic* die Konservativen, *The Standard* die soziale Bewegung und *The Leader* die irische Kulturbewegung. Eine eigentlich katholische Tagespresse existiert nicht.

Ausländische, insbesondere englische Beobachter beklagen immer wieder das Fehlen intellektueller Bewußtheit im katholischen Leben Irlands. Tatsächlich läßt sich kaum ein größerer Gegensatz denken als der historisch-emotionale Proletarierkatholizismus hier und der aristokratische hochkultivierte Katholizismus Englands (natürlich abgesehen von dem starken irischen Element dort). Der Schriftleiter des *Catholic Herald* wies vor einiger Zeit – nach einer mehrtägigen Reise durch Irland – auf das Fehlen einer liturgischen Bewegung in Irland hin. Auf Grund meiner ausgedehnten Studien über die Geschichte und den gegenwärtigen Stand des liturgischen Lebens in Irland darf ich sagen, daß in dieser Hinsicht das Verständnis des katholischen Irlands besondere Schwierigkeiten bietet. Der Gebrauch des Meßbuches hat sich zwar etwas ausgebreitet; aber die Zahl der Gläubigen, deren Meßandacht sich weiterhin an den Rosenkranz und private Gebetskompilationen hält, ist noch immer größer als in England oder auf dem Festland. Versuche, die Gläubigen zu aktiverer Teilnahme am heiligen Opfer heranzuziehen, scheitern meist schon am Widerstand der Geistlichkeit. Hochämter sind auf die Kathedralkirchen beschränkt und nicht sonderlich gut besucht. Liturgische Vesper und Komplet wurden in verschiedenen Kirchen wieder abgeschafft, da nur ein Viertel der den üblichen Andachten beiwohnenden Menge erschien. Die Andachten bestehen übrigens das ganze Jahr hindurch aus Rosenkranz, Lauretanischer Litanei und Segen.

Dagegen darf man darauf hinweisen, daß es kaum ein anderes Land geben dürfte, wo die Zahl der täglichen oder allsonntäglichen Kommunikanten größer, der Herz-Jesu-Freitag populärer, der Besuch der späten Wochentagsmessen in den größen Stadtkirchen besser und der allabendliche Familien-Rosenkranz üblicher ist.

Einen wesentlichen Beitrag zur Aktivierung der Laien leistet die *Legion of Mary*, die sich während der letzten zwanzig Jahre über die gesamte englisch sprechende Welt verbreitet hat. Ob ihr Einfluß wesentlich darüber hinausgehen wird, ist angesichts ihrer deutlich angelsächsischen Methodik zu bezweifeln. Die Parallelen hinsichtlich der Organisation und Abzweckung zwischen der *Legio Mariae* und der *Oxford-Group* sind schlagend. Auch darf nicht übersehen werden, daß die theologische Grundlage der Legion eine intensive mariologische Tradition ist, die, in Irland wenigstens, eine historisch bedingte antiprotestantische Note hat. Ebenso wie die *Oxford-Group* wird die *Legion* in Zukunft zu entscheiden haben, ob es ihr gelingen kann, wesentlich über die bürgerliche Mittelklasse hinauszudringen. In Irland ist der Einfluß der *Legion* außerordentlich groß. Selbst die liturgische Bewegung und die irische Kulturbewegung sind in den letzten Jahren angegliedert worden.

Da meine berufliche Tätigkeit mich mit allen Klassen der Jugend Irlands in Berührung gebracht hat, darf ich wohl mit der Bemerkung schließen, daß man Verbesserungen im katholischen Leben Irlands erwarten kann, wenn es der Jugend gestattet wird, ihre Ideale zu verwirklichen. Dabei denke ich vor allem an die jungen Menschen, die während des Krieges ihr Brot außerhalb Irlands verdienen mußten und die auch weiterhin in großer Zahl wenigstens für eine Reihe von Jahren im Ausland Ausbildung und Arbeit suchen müssen. Sie empfinden, daß es notwendig ist, daß der lebendige Glaube mehr bewußt, man darf wohl sagen, intellektuell, fundiert wird. Die hervorstechendsten Merkmale der Jugend dieses Landes sind ihre harmonische Gutmütigkeit, ihre ungebrochene Anhänglichkeit an die Kirche und ihr Sittengesetz, ihr aktives sakramentales und devotionelles Leben, ihre Einsicht in die Mängel des Gewohnheitskatholizismus und ihre wirkliche Bereitschaft, mit dem Leben für die Grundlagen des Glaubens einzustehen.

Sollte, man wagt es kaum zu hoffen, diesem Lande eine Periode ungestörter Entfaltung seiner fast ein Jahrtausend unterdrückten Geistesgaben vergönnt sein, so wird die weitere Entwicklung seines katholischen Nationalcharakters für die gesamte christliche Kultur von Bedeutung sein.

(Quelle: Schweizer Rundschau 48, 1948, S. 498-504)

Irland und der Nationalsozialismus

Die nachstehende Betrachtung zu einigen Problemen der irischen Politik wurde dadurch angeregt, daß der Schriftleiter der *Schweizer Rundschau* in einem Brief an mich erwähnte, daß die Schweiz wenig Verständnis für die Deutschlandfreundlichkeit Irlands habe. Diese Bemerkung brachte mir zum Bewußtsein, in welch eigentümlicher Lage ich mich befinde. Irland war im Frühjahr 1939 das einzige Land, das meiner aus Nazi-Deutschland fliehenden Familie Asyl gewährte. Während des Krieges habe ich innerhalb der mir durch meine Stellung gezogenen Grenzen oft versucht, bei den katholischen Nationalisten unter meinen irischen Freunden Kenntnis über den wahren Charakter des Nationalsozialismus zu verbreiten. Andererseits habe ich besonders seit Kriegsende versucht, aus meiner Perspektive heraus um Verständnis für das Land zu werben, das mir nunmehr neue Heimat geworden ist.

Über die offizielle Neutralitätspolitik Irlands unterrichten am besten die Reden De Valeras, die in verschiedener Form veröffentlicht worden sind. Das Buch von Henry Harrison *The Neutrality of Ireland* ist zu empfehlen. In mehreren Artikeln in der Schweizer Tageszeitung *Die Tat* habe ich über dieses Thema berichtet. Im vorliegenden Artikel habe ich mich nicht gescheut, von persönlichen Erfahrungen zu sprechen. Durch meine vielseitigen Beschäftigungen bin ich mit Hunderten von Iren aller Kreise in Berührung gekommen, so daß ich meinen Erfahrungen eine gewisse Allgemeingültigkeit zuschreiben kann.

Nur zweimal während der letzten neun Jahre dürften Nachrichten über Irland auf der ersten Seite der Weltpresse Platz gefunden haben. Bei Kriegsbeginn erklärte Irland als, wie es der Welt erschien, einziger Teil des Commonwealth, es werde neutral bleiben. Am Tage nach der Dönitz-Erklärung sprach der Regierungschef bei dem deutschen Gesandten in Dublin vor, um zum Ableben des Führers zu kondolieren. Nicht einmal der Tenno, der doch zum Tode Roosevelts sein Beileid ausgesprochen hatte, folgte De Valeras Beispiel. Kann man sich wundern, wenn Rußland jetzt Irlands Zulassung zur UNO vetiert mit der Begründung, Irland habe sich zu deutschfreundlich gezeigt?

Von der deutsch- oder vielmehr nazi-freundlichen Gesinnung eines sehr großen Teils der Iren hat kaum einer einen besseren Begriff, als wer als deutschstämmiger Nazigegner in Irland gelebt hat. Besonders den Katholiken unter uns ist es kaum je geglückt, unseren irischen Glaubensgenossen glaubhaft zu machen, wir könnten ernstlich nicht einen Sieg Hitlers wünschen. «Ihr Deutsche seid wundervoll» sagte man uns, als «wir» England coventrierten. Als der von einer deutschen Bombe – wohl versehentlich – zerstörte Häuserblock am Nordwall in Dublin abgerissen worden war (ein Dutzend Leute kamen dabei ums Leben), wurde die rauchgeschwärzte Mauer mit einem riesigen Hakenkreuz verziert. Unter den zwanzig Kollegen, die ich an einem von Geistlichen geleiteten Gymnasium hatte, war nur einer, der nicht den Sieg Deutschlands wünschte. Einer meiner Kollegen bekannte: «Es ist uns ganz recht, wenn die Deutschen möglichst viele englische Schiffe in den Grund bohren.» Meine Wirtin: «Wir werden schon dafür sorgen, daß die Briten nicht den Krieg gewinnen.» Ein hochgebildeter, aktiv im katholischen Leben stehender Herr: «Ich bete jeden Abend für den Sieg Hitlers.» Ein Ordensgeistlicher: «Wenn Hitler sich nicht an der Kirche vergriffe, wäre er ein ganz großer Mann.» Ein höherer Regierungsbeamter: «Hitler hat ganz recht; natürlich steckt er nur Kommunisten in die Konzentrationslager.» Ein Siebzehnjähriger in einem deutschen Schulaufsatz: «Die Juden sind ein Ungeziefer, man muß sie erlegen, wie Hitler es tut» (drei Monate später trat der Junge bei der R.A.F. ein).

Noch heute laufen junge Männer und Mädchen mit Hoheitsabzeichen und sogar echten Parteiabzeichen herum. In den Slums von Dublin sieht man immer noch einmal eine neue Kreideanschrift: «Hiel (sic!) Hitler». Als vor einigen Wochen der letzte der von den Deutschen hier während des Krieges abgesetzten Fallschirm-Spione deportiert werden sollte und daraufhin Selbstmord beging, folgte eine fanatische Menge dem Sarg, der mit einer Hakenkreuzfahne bedeckt war. Am Grabe betete man den Rosenkranz und erwies den Hitlergruß.

Noch in der letzten Auflage des sehr verbreiteten Werkes *The Mystical Body of Christ in the Modern World* von Dr. Denis Fahey C. S. Sp., einem bekannten Sozialwissenschaftler, kann man in dem Kapitel über Deutschland lesen, Judenverfolgungen seien «isolated incidents». Der irische Episkopat hat sich nie zu den Zuständen in Deutschland oder deutschbesetzten Gebieten geäußert, dagegen spontan und leidenschaftlich gegen kommunistische Kirchenverfolgungen in Sowjet-Polen und Jugoslawien protestiert. In einer Versammlung hörte ich im Jahre 1944 einen bekannten Journalisten berichten, er habe 1938 in Deutschland von Priestern, die gerade von Fulda zurückgekehrt waren, gehört, der Episkopat habe restlose Unterstützung Hitlers beschlossen. Rauschender Beifall. Eine von Ordensgeistlichen herausgegebene irische Zeitschrift schrieb, England habe sich durch seine Allianz mit dem atheistischen Rußland allen Respekt verscherzt, und das im Juli 1947.

Ich könnte Seiten füllen mit solchen Zeugnissen irischer Nazi-Freundlichkeit, und doch werden mich meine irischen Freunde der Einseitigkeit zeihen. Ebenso werden meine kontinentalen Leser mir Falschmünzerei vorwerfen, wenn ich jetzt versuche, diese ganze scheinbar so einseitige «Deutschfreundlichkeit» der Iren in ihre rechte Perspektive zu rücken.

Kaum ein Land in Europa ist so schwer zu verstehen wie Irland. Schon Goethe, der größte Irlandkenner seiner Zeit, stellte die fundamentale Zweideutigkeit des irischen Charakters fest. Gottfried Keller wußte darum, wie er seinen Pankraz mit seiner irischen Jugendgeliebten verfahren läßt. Im allgemeinen ist es richtig zu sagen, daß im persönlichen Gespräch der Ire prinzipiell nicht das meint, was er sagt, zumal dem Ausländer gegenüber. Natürlich heißt das nicht, daß er lügt. Es ist vielmehr eine anerkannte Spielregel intelligenter Gespräche, daß man etwas anderes sagt, als was der Partner erwarten könnte. Argumentieren ist dem Iren Lebenselement, selbst wenn es sich um Dinge handelt, die dem sentimentaleren Festländer zu wichtig sind, um darüber zu argumentieren.

Innerhalb der übermächtigen angelsächsischen Umgebung kann sich der Ire nur erhalten, wenn er um jeden Preis anders ist. Propaganda, ob geschäftlich oder politisch, besonders wenn sie in Englisch ist, ist an sich schon der Verlogenheit verdächtig. Gleichzeitig hat der Ire eine tiefe Abscheu gegen Heuchelei. Er hat nicht nur Furchtbares von anderen Nationen erlebt, sondern auch seine eigene Geschichte bis zur jüngsten Gegenwart ist von einer unglaublichen Wildheit. Durch seine dem Orient mehr als dem Westen verwandte Geschichtskonzeption sind ihm diese Furchtbarkeiten dauernd gegenwärtig. Mit Goethe hat er noch nie von einem Verbrechen gehört, das zu begehen er sich nicht selbst imstande fühlte. Seine romantische Ironie bewahrt ihn vor dem Fehler anderer kleiner Nationen, sich selbst zu ernst zu nehmen. Über nichts lacht er herzlicher als über seine eigenen Fehler. Nichts trennt ihn mehr vom Engländer und noch mehr vom Deutschen als dessen fundamentale, fast metaphysische Selbstgerechtigkeit.

Dem Festländer erscheint daher seine Einstellung zu den geistigen Dingen dieser Welt als leichtfertig. Nichts scheint Gegenstand, alles Werkzeug zu sein.

Diese Mentalität ist in der Geschichte wohl begründet. Irlands Vergangenheit und Gegenwart sind voll von Fiktionen. Es beginnt mit der Tradition, daß Irland die Insel der Heiligen sei, ein Mißverständnis des Ausdrucks *Insula Sacra* und des irischen Wortes *noemh* (das nicht «sanctus» sondern «illuster» heißt). Dann kam die anglo-normannische Legende von Irland dem Wunderland an der Grenze der bewohnten Welt, von der die europäische Literatur bis tief ins 19. Jahrhundert zehrte. Die ossianische Legende rief die moderne Keltologie hervor. Unzählige kontinentale Romantiker verbreiteten die Legende von der smaragdenen Insel, bis Karl Marx Irland zum Paradebeispiel kapitalistischer Ausbeutung erhob.

Die gegenwärtige politische Lage Irlands ist weitgehend von Fiktionen bestimmt, die eng mit jenen Legenden zusammenhängen. Die erste Fiktion entstand daraus, daß Irland den Vertrag mit England, nach dem es Dominion war, einseitig durch seine Verfassung außer Kraft setzte, in der König und Commonwealth nicht erwähnt werden. Die Nationalisten, auf deren Hilfe der deutsche Generalstab spekuliert hatte, verlangen immer wieder von ihrem früheren Führer De Valera, er solle die Fiktion der «Republik» Irland zur Wirklichkeit erheben. Der Kriegsausgang hat aber De Valera in der Überzeugung bestärkt, daß diese Fiktion die Grundlage der Politik Irlands bleiben muß. Für die wenigen Länder, mit denen Irland direkte diplomatische Beziehungen unterhält, werden seine Vertreter vom Präsidenten der «Republik» ernannt, aber ihre Beglaubigungsschreiben unterzeichnet der englische König, dessen «Dienste», wie es Mr. De Valera ausdrückte, Irland «in dieser Sache allein aus freien Stücken in Anspruch nimmt». Reist ein Ire nach England, so muß er ein Visum haben; fliegt er direkt nach Paris oder Brüssel und reist von da nach England ein, so geht er in Folkestone stolz durch die Sperre «For British Subjects», wo er kein Visum benötigt. Irland ist, wie Mr. De Valera neulich zur Überraschung seiner Gegner bekannte, zwar nicht *in* dem Commonwealth, aber mit ihm «assoziiert».

Die zweite Fiktion ist, daß das nationale Gebiet die gesamte Insel umfasse. Im Jahre 1921 hatten jedoch die von Mr. De Valera entsandten Bevollmächtigten in dem, was Lord Pakenham dann treffend *Peace by Ordeal* nannte, unterschrieben, daß die sechs nordöstlichen Grafschaften, in denen vorläufig noch die Protestanten und England-freunde die Mehrheit haben, im Vereinigten Königreich verbleiben sollten. Der durch die Verfassung vollzogene fiktive Anschluß der Irredenta wird mit der historischen Fiktion begründet, die in Nordostirland vor dreihundert Jahren Angesiedelten seien eigentlich gar keine Iren. Wieder sind es nur die extremen Nationalisten, die von Mr. De Valera verlangen, er solle die Konsequenzen aus seiner Fiktion ziehen, die nord-irischen nationalistischen Abgeordneten zu seinem Parlament zulassen oder gar die erste Gelegenheit wahrnehmen, die sechs Grafschaften zu befreien. Dies war einer der wenigen Punkte, in dem der deutsche Generalstab im letzten Kriege richtig sah. Er befahl seinen Agitatoren, sich auf Nordirland zu beschränken, denn er wußte, daß den Südiren ihre Selbsterhaltung und ihr Neutralitätswille noch über die sechs Graf-schaften ging.

Die dritte Fiktion, auf der das moderne Irland beruht, ist die, daß es virtuell ein gä-lischsprechendes oder wenigstens zweisprachiges Land sei. Die deutsche Wissenschaft hat ihren großen Beitrag zur Wiederbelebung der irischen Sprache oft dadurch in Frage gestellt, daß sie glaubte, damit politische Inspirationen verbinden zu können. Die irische Sprachbewegung verdient vollste Sympathie, weil sie fundamental unpo-litisch ist. Leider ist sie aber auch im rein Kulturellen von so wenig Erfolg begleitet, daß die offizielle Fiktion, Irland sei zweisprachig, zu fast grotesken Ergebnissen führt.

Wer von Irland so wenig weiß wie der Durchschnittsdeutsche (ich habe den Namen Dublin nie in der Schule gehört), ist in der Gefahr, die pro-deutschen Äußerungen der Iren für bare Münze zu nehmen und zu übersehen, daß sie Ausdruck der fiktiven Grundlage sind, auf der Irland historisch und politisch zu leben genötigt ist. Ein Blick auf die Karte und die Geschichte genügt, um zu sehen, daß die Beziehungen zwischen Deutschland und Irland so minimal sind, daß von irgendwelchen tieferen Gefühlen keine Rede sein kann. Ich darf sagen, daß meine zahlreichen Beiträge zur Geschichte der irisch-deutschen Kulturbeziehungen vor allem gezeigt haben, daß in diesen Bezie-hungen ein nahezu undurchdringliches Dunkel – auf beiden Seiten – herrscht. Im Jahre 1939 wurde in keinem Lande Europas so wenig Deutsch gelehrt wie in Irland. Selbst gebildeten Kreisen ist deutsche klassische Literatur (trotz zahlreicher ausgezeichneter Übersetzungen von Iren) nur minimal bekannt. Eine verschwindend kleine Zahl von Iren hat es zu einer Cooktour den Rhein herauf oder nach Oberammergau gebracht. In Irland hat nie eine größere deutsche Kolonie bestanden als heute, wo sich, die 300 oder 400 deutschen Ruhrkinder nicht mitgerechnet, etwa 250 deutschstämmige Personen befinden, davon 150 Refugiés, bis auf sechs oder sieben Ausnahmen Geschäftsleute (der ehemalige deutsche Gesandte schlägt sich mit Konditorei durch), die kein anderes Interesse haben, als nicht aufzufallen. Nur dann kann man von echter Deutschfreundlichkeit des Iren sprechen, wenn er im Deutschen einfach den leidenden Menschen sieht, ob es ein geächteter Jude oder ein hungerndes Ruhrkind ist. In solchen Fällen vergißt er aber auch dem Engländer gegenüber allen Haß.

Soweit die fiktive Nazi-Freundlichkeit der Iren nicht der ganz primitiven «We would back the devil against Britain» Haltung entspringt, ist sie vor allem auf Unwissenheit zurückzuführen. Irische Touristen kehrten von Deutschland meist als so begeisterte Nazis wieder wie deutsche Liberale von Italien als Anhänger Mussolinis. Die meisten dieser Touristen konnten kaum ein Wort deutsch. Deutsche Bücher sind hier schlechthin unbekannt. Um sich das ganze Ausmaß dieser Unwissenheit klarzumachen, bedenke man, daß diese Nazi-Freunde ausschließlich in fromm katholischen Kreisen zu finden sind. Die populäre katholische Presse tat wenig, um aufklärend zu wirken. Rassenhygienische Maßnahmen konnten schon aus moralischen Gründen nicht diskutiert werden. Ich arbeitete jahrelang mit einer der hiesigen katholischen Wochenzeitschriften und konnte aus nächster Nähe die entwaffnend unbewußte Selbstverständlichkeit beobachten, mit der Nachrichten über die antichristliche Politik in Deutschland durch Mitteilungen aus dem «schwarzen Norden» (d.h. von Katholikenverfolgungen in den sechs Grafschaften) überlagert wurden. Das vom englischen Episkopat herausgegebene Werk über die Kirche im Dritten Reich wurde verboten.

Es gibt kaum ein Land in Europa, das gegen das Gift des Autoritärismus besser gefeit ist als Irland. Das politische Leben von Irland ist so schwer zu verstehen, weil der rein menschliche Kampf um persönliche Freiheit immer wieder die Schranken der Gemeinschafts-Disziplin durchbricht. Nicht einmal die primitive Dorfgemeinschaft existiert in diesem Lande. Für außenpolitische Freiheit tritt der Ire vor allem deshalb ein, weil er weiß, daß sie der äußere Rahmen für persönliche Freiheit ist. Für Deutschland und Spanien verlangt man, daß sie die Freiheit haben sollen, sich ihrer Freiheit zu begeben. Aber für sich selbst ist der Ire stolz, daß er von dieser «Freiheit» nie Gebrauch machen würde.

Meine These ist also, daß die Nazi-Freundlichkeit entscheidender irischer Kreise nicht substantiell, sondern rein funktionell ist. Sie beruht auf Widerspruchsgeist, Fiktionalismus und Unwissenheit. Alle drei Faktoren sind Ausdruck des Minderwertigkeitskomplexes, an dem die Iren als Individuen und als Gemeinschaft leiden. Jahrhundertelang existierten sie für die Machthaber einfach nicht. Was die Machthaber taten oder sagten, mußte als Ausdruck ihres Unterdrückungswillens betrachtet werden. Alles was von England kommt, ist noch immer verdächtig. Objektive Kritik prallt an der existentiellen Tatsache ab, daß der Ire mit diesem Verdacht aufsteht und mit ihm zu Bett geht. Noch sind Sprache, Literatur, Kunst, Wissenschaft, Wirtschaft und Besitz in einer für ein freiheitsliebendes Volk unerträglichen Weise mit dem großen Nachbarn verstrickt. Sobald der Ire aus dem engsten Kreise heraustritt, stößt er an dessen materielle Überlegenheit.

Während des Krieges war die Zensur über politische Berichterstattung streng. Radio und Presse mußten sich auf die amtlichen Communiqués beschränken; nur militärwissenschaftlich getarnte Kommentare wurden zugelassen. Der B.B.C. schied wegen seines Oxford-Akzentes aus. Es blieb Lord Haw-Haw. Der Einfluß dieses Herrn Joyce aus Galway war groß, aber nicht tief. Er vermittelte auf der Grundlage eines Minimums von Fakten ein Maximum an Stimmungen und trug daher wesentlich zur Erhaltung irischer Unwissenheit über kontinentale Verhältnisse bei. Die primitivsten geographischen und historischen Grundbegriffe fehlten. Den Effekt britischer Propaganda auf Irland kann ich durch ein Erlebnis umschreiben, das ich im September 1945 in den Dubliner Bergen hatte. Ich besuchte eine mir bekannte Bauernfamilie und brachte dem kranken Söhnchen Plastilin mit. Um dem Kind den Gebrauch des Materials zu zeigen, knetete ich Männchen für ihn. «Oh, guck mal, wie lustig», rief seine Mutter, indem sie eines meiner Männchen aufhob, «die langen Beinchen, fast so drollig wie die Leute in den Konzentrationslager-Filmen.» Auschwitz? Der alte Ladenhüter (wie es eine Schweizer Zeitung kürzlich nannte), daß die Engländer die Konzentrationslager im Burenkrieg erfunden hätten, hat nirgends willigere Annahme gefunden als in Irland. «Die *Black and Tans*», die von den Engländern 1919 bis 1921 auf Irland losgelassene Zuchthäuslertruppe, «haben es hier noch viel schlimmer getrieben».

(Quelle: Schweizer Rundschau, Heft 7, 1946/47, S. 518-525)

VI. Auswahlbibliographie
John Hennigs Schriften zu deutsch-irischen Themen

Anmerkung:

Die mit einem * gekennzeichneten Artikel und Aufsätze sind in der von Severus OSB erstellten "Bibliographie Dr. phil. Dr. phil. h.c. John Hennig – 1932-1970", (*Archiv für Liturgiewissenschaft*, Bd. 13, 1971, S. 141-171) bzw. der 1978 und 1986 ergänzten Bibliographie von Angelus A. Häussling (*Archiv für Liturgiewissenschaft*, Bd. 19, 1978, S. 98-105 und *Archiv für Liturgiewissenschaft*, Bd. 28, Heft 2, 1986, S. 235-245) entnommen.

Die mit einer [1] versehenen Titel sind in der Sammlung *Literatur und Existenz – Ausgewählte Aufsätze* (Heidelberg: C. Winter 1980) enthalten, die mit einer [2] sind in *Goethes Europakunde* (Amsterdam: Rodopi 1987) zu finden, die mit einer [3] sind in *Goethe and the English Speaking World* (Bern/ Frankfurt u.a.: Peter Lang 1988) gesammelt, und die mit einer [4] sind in *Medieval Ireland, Saints and Martyrologies* (hrsg. v. M. Richter, Northampton: Variorum Reprints 1989) aufgenommen. Eine [5] kennzeichnet Beiträge, die in *Liturgie gestern und heute* (Bd. 1 u. 2, o.O. 1989) erschienen. Im Folgenden wird zwischen wissenschaftlichen Aufsätzen, Artikeln, die meist in Zeitungen und Wochenzeitschriften erschienen, und Rezensionen unterschieden:

Aufsatz (A), Artikel (Ar) und Rezensionen (R).

Zusätzlich zu den hier aufgeführten Arbeiten gab es weitere Vorträge im irischen Radio (1941-1956), im schweizerischen Radio und aktuelle Beiträge über Irland in *Die Tat* (1953-1956); zwischen 1960-1964 schrieb Hennig zahlreiche Beiträge zu irischen Ortsnamen und Heiligen für die 2. Auflage des Lexikons für Theologie und Kirche, ebenso für das Lexikon des Mittelalters, Bd. 1, 2, 3 (1979/83) und andere Sammelwerke und Lexica.

1941

St. Killian, Standard, 11. Juli (Ar)
In Memoriam James Joyce, Bell 2, 91-94 (R)*
Charles Hubert O'Hara, Standard, 19. September (Ar)
St. Gall, Standard, 10. Oktober (Ar)
F.Blanke, Columban and Gallus, Irish Historical Studies 3, 180-186 (R)*

1942

The Position of the Church in Germany, Standard, 27. März (Ar)
Irish Links with Much-Bombed Rostock, Standard, 1. Mai (Ar)
House and Home in Germany, Leader, 2. Mai (Ar)
Irish Monks Introduced Potatoes into Central Europe, Standard, 26. Juni (Ar)
Cologne has new Archbishop, Standard, 21. August (Ar)
Catholics under Germany, Standard, 28. August (Ar)
Swiss Catholics in Wartime, Standard, 4. September (Ar)
The Magic Flute, Radiobeitrag, 18. September
Swiss can make 'Hit' Films, Standard, 9. Oktober (Ar)

Irish Saints in the Liturgical and Artistic Tradition of Central Europe, Irish
Ecclesiastical Record 59, 181-192 (A)*

1943

Goethe's Personal Relationship with Ireland, Dublin Magazine, Vol. 18, 45-56 (A)* [3]
Salzburg, its Primate and Ireland, Standard, 16. April (Ar)
Irish Literature on the Continent, Irish Art Handbook, 107-113 (A)*
Irish footsteps along the Rhine [?], 17. August (Radiovortrag)

1944

Catholics and Protestants in Germany, Blackfriars 25, 336-341 (A)*
Goethe's friendship with Antony O'Hara, MLR 39, 146-151 (A)* [3]
Catholics and Protestants in Germany, Blackfriars 25, 336-341 (Ar)*
H. Bauersfeld, Entwicklung der keltischen Studien in Deutschland, Irish Historical
    Studies 4, 119-122, (R)*
L. Mühlhausen, Die kornische Geschichte von den drei Ratschlägen, Irish Historical
    Studies 4, 119-122, (R)*
L. Mühlhausen, Zehn irische Volkserzählungen, Irish Historical Studies 4, 119-122,
    (R)*
An Irishman Makes European History, The Leader, 30. Dezember (Ar)

1945

Jean Paul and Ireland, MLR 40, 190-96 (A)*
Sir Francis Cruise Street, Irish Times, 6. März (Ar)
Irish Links With Cologne, Irish Catholic, 8. März (Ar)
How I learned English, Irish Rosary March-April, 121-125 (Ar)
A Footnote on James Joyce, The Bell 11, 704-709 (Ar)*
Catholic Berlin, Irish Catholic, 19. April (Ar)
Mangan's German Anthology, Irish Times 29/30. Juni (Ar)
The Voice of German Catholics, The Tablet, 28. April, 197f (Ar)
My Early Irish Associations, Irish Rosary, Christmas, 366-370 (Ar)
Hamburg and its Catholic Story, Catholic Herald, 10. August (Ar)

1946

Goethe's translations of Ossians songs of Thelma, JEJP 45, 77-87 (A)*, [3]
Pestalozzi in Irland, Die Tat 18.5. (Ar)*
Living with books, Hibernia, May, 11f (Ar)
Moore's Influence on the Continent, Thomas Moore Society, Dublin (Vortrag)*
The Brothers Grimm and T.C. Croker, MLA 41, 42, 43, 44-45, 237-42, 92f (A)*
Thomas Moore and the Holy Alliance, Irish Monthly, July, 282-294 (A)*
Vincent Priessnitz and Father Matthew, Father Matthew Record (July) (Ar)*
Father Matthew through German eyes, Father Matthew Record (Sept) (Ar)*

Schoolboy in Germany, Irish Monthly, September, 384-392 (Ar)
Fruit, The Leader, September, 15f (Ar)
Forests, The Leader, September, 16f (Ar)
Anglo-Irish Literature on the Continent – R. Stamm, Three Anglo-Irish plays, Irish
    Book Lover 30, October (R)*
Michael Whitty, Radio Eireann, September
Remembering the Dead, The Leader, 23.11. (Ar)
Christmas in a German Home, The Leader, 14. Dezember, 7f (Ar)

1947

Beethoven and Ireland, Irish Monthly 75, 332-338 (A)*
Mozart and Ireland, Irish Monthly 75, 377-382 (A)*
Augustine Gibbon de Burgo: A Study in Early Irish Reaction to Luther, IER 69, 135-
    151 (A)*
Goethe's translations of McPhersons 'Berrathon' , Modern Language Review 42, 127-
    130 (A)* (3)
Goethe and Lord Bristol, Bishop of Derry, Ulster Journal of Archaeology 10, 101-109
    (A)* (3)
The Lough Derg Pilgrimage, The Leader, 21.6., 14f (Ar)
Irisch-Schweizerische Literaturbeziehungen, Die Tat, 24.6. (Ausstellungsbe-
    sprechung)*
Irish Saints in Early German Literature, Speculum 22, 358-374 (A)*
John Stuart's Blackie translation of Goethe's Jahrmarktsfest zu Plundersweilern,
    Modern Language Quarterly 8, 91-100 (A)*
Two Irish Bulls in Kants Kritik der Urteilkraft, Modern Language Quarterly 91, 487f
    (A)*
Irland und der Nationalsozialismus, Schweizer Rundschau 47, 518-525 (A)*
Swift in Switzerland, Irish Book Lover 30, November, 54f. (Ar)

1948

"German" Script in Irish Printing, Irish Book Lover, January, 89-92 (Ar)
Some Early German Accounts of Schombergs Irish Campaign, Ulster Journal of
    Archaology 11, 65-80 (A)*
Music in the home, Hibernia, February, 12f (Ar)
Dr. Josef Grabisch, Irish Bookman, 87-89 (Ar)*
The Love of Books, Irish Library Bulletin, April, 65-67 (Ar)
When I Started Writing, Hibernia, July, 9 (Ar)
Nietzsche, Jaspers and Christianity, Blackfriars 29, 476-480 (A)*
Katholisches Irland heute und morgen, Schweizer Rundschau 48, 498-504 (A)* (5)

1949

Continental opinion , Daniel O'Connell (Dublin 1949), 235-69 (A)*
Goethe's "Klaggesang, 'Irisch'", Monatshefte 41, 71-75 (A)* (3)

Some Thoughts on Examinations, Hibernia, May, 13f (Ar)
Immermann's Tristan und Isolde and Ireland, Modern Language Review 44, 246-252 (A)*

1950

Notes on Early Representations of Irish Men in German Books, Journal of the Royal Society of Antiquaries of Ireland 80, II, 158-163 (A)*
Ireland's Place in the Chivalresque Literature of Mediaeval Germany, Proceedings Royal Irish Academy 53 C, 279-298 (A)*
Fortunatus in Ireland, Ulster Journal of Archaology 13, 93-104 (A)*
Irish-German Literary Relations, German Life and Letter, N.S. 3, 102-110 (A)*
A Donegal family in Germany (and Switzerland), Donegal Annual 2, 315-318 (Ar)*
Recent German publication relating to Ireland, Irish Book Lover 31, 13f; 37 (R)*
A bibliographical note on the Schottenkloster of St. James, Ratisbon, Irish Book Lover 31, 79-81 (Ar)*
German literature on Napper Tandy, Irish Book Lover 31, 108f (Ar)*
A Saint Was Ireland's First Ambassador, Irish Digest (condensed from Father Matthew Record), October, 16-18 (Ar)
L. Bieler, The life and legend of St. Patrick, Scriptorium 4, 319-322 (R)*
H. Harder, Irische Heimkehr, Irish Book Lover 31, 112f (R)*

1951

A Note on Goethe and Charles Gore, Monatshefte 43, 27-37 (A)* [3]
Robert Emmet's Strategical Studies (with reference to Emmet's handwritten notes on a German book), Irish Sword 1, 148-150 (Ar)*
Irish minerals in the Vienna collection, Irish Naturalist's Journal 10, 195f (Ar)*
Stephen Hero and Wilhelm Meister , German Life and Letter, N.S. 5, 22-29 (A)* [3]
A Travel Book on Germany Published in Dublin, Irish Book Lover 3, November, 131f (Ar)*
German Literature on Napper Tandy, Irish Book Lover 31, 108f (Ar)

1952

Ireland and Germany in the Tradition of St. Kilian, Irish Ecclesiastical Record 78, 21-33 (A)*
My Tale of Three Cities (Leipzig, Aachen, Dublin), Irish Digest, April, 40-42 (Ar)
The Irish Background of St. Fursey, Irish Ecclesiastical Record 77, January-June, 18-28 (A)*
Irish Soldiers in the Thirty Years War, Journal of the Royal Society of Antiquaries of Ireland 82, 28-36 (A)*
Die Stellung der Schweiz in der hagiographischen und liturgischen Tradition Irlands, Zeitschrift für Schweizerische Kirchengeschichte 46, 204-216 (A)* [5]
A note on Ireland's place in the literary tradition of St. Brendan, Traditio 8, Washington, 397-402 (Ar)

1953

Goethe and 'Lalla Rookh', Modern Language Review 48, 445-450 (A)* (3)
The Place of German Theology in the Works of Canon Sheehan, Irish Ecclesiastical
    Record 80, 381-387 (A)*
Fáilte or: I Boarded the Boat for Ireland, Irish Rosary March/April, 71-76

1954

Irische Einflüsse auf die frühen Kalendarien von St. Gallen, Zeitschrift für Schweize-
    rische Kirchengeschichte 48, 17-30 (A)* (4)(5)
Irische Frauen in der Weltliteratur, Basler Nachrichten 23.5 (Ar)*
Zwei frühe Pestalozzi Schulen in Irland und Spanien, Basler Nachrichten 5.9. (Ar)*
Lacustrine objects from Ireland in the Museum Schwab at Biel, Journal of the Royal
    Society of Antiquaries of Ireland 84, 92f (Ar)*
Goethe and the Edgeworths, Modern Language Quarterly 15, 366-371 (A)* (3)
A Note on Canon Sheehan's Interest in German Literature, Modern Language Review,
    352-355 (A)*
Goethe's knowledge of Irish Scientists, Irish Book Lover 32, 84-87 (A)* (3)

1955

With Irish Saints along the Alps, Irish Rosary 59, 470-73 (Ar)*
Ireland's place in 19th century German Poetry, German Life and Letters, N.S. 8, 201-
    207 (A)*
The Auerbach Keller scene and 'She stoops to conquer', Comparat. Literature 7, 193-
    197 (A)* (3)

1956

Irish Descriptions of Goethe, Publications English Goethe Society 25, 114-124 (A)*
W. Delius Geschichte der irischen Kirche, Deutsche Literaturzeitung 77, Heft 6 (R)*

1957

The liturgical veneration of Irish Saints in Switzerland, Iris Hibernia, Fribourg Nr. 3,
    23-32 (A)*
Goethes Irlandkunde, Deutsche Vierteljahrsschrift für Literaturwissenschaft und
    Geistesgeschichte 31, 70-83 (A)* 2)

1958

The Irish Monastic Tradition on the Continent, Irish Ecclesiastical Record 87, 186-193
    (A)*

1959

Ireland, Europe and the Western world, Irish Rosary 63, 5-7 (Ar)*

A note on Goethe's relations with Charles Sterling, Modern Language Review 54, 76-79 (A)* [3]

Daniel O'Connell and the Opinion of Some German Poets of His Time, Modern Language Review 54, 573-578 (A)*

1960

A Note on the First English Translation of Schiller's 'History of the Thirty Years War', Modern Language Review 55, 249-254 (A)*

1961

Studien zur Geschichte der deutschsprachigen Irlandkunde, Deutsche Vierteljahrs-schrift für Literaturwissenschaft und Geistesgeschichte 35, 617-629 (A)* [1]

1962

Ulster Place-names in the Continental Tradition of St. Patrick, Seanchas Ardmacha, 76-86 (A)*

Frank O'Connor and Goethe, Goethe 24, 296-99 (A)*

A. Dodd Wessobrunner Kalenderblätter irischen Ursprungs, Archival. ZS 58, Nov-32, (Mitarbeit)*

L. Bieler, Irland - Wegbereiter des Mittelalters, Archiv für Liturgiewissenschaft 7, 2, 571f. (R)*

1964

Wilhelm von Humboldt und John Charles Stapelton, Archiv für Kulturgeschichte 46, 127-32 (A)*

1966

Kieran, Patrick (341-346), Kolumban, Gallus, Kilian, Rupert von Salzburg, Korbinian (379-390) in: Die Heiligen in ihrer Zeit, Mainz 1966, Bd 1 (Ar)* [5]

Irland und das friderizianische Preussen, Archiv für Kulturgeschichte 48, 278-86 (A)*

1967

R. McNally SJ (Hg.), Old Ireland, Dublin 1965, Archiv für Liturgiewissenschaft 10, 1, 306 (R)

1969

Zum Gebrauch des ir. 'fior' als Präfix, Sprache 15, 135-143 (A)*

1970

Deutschlandkunde in James Clarence Mangans Prosawerken, Deutsche Vierteljahrs-
schrift für Literaturwissenschaft und Geistesgeschichte 44, 496-507 (A)* [1]
Scottorum gloria gentis. Erwähnung irischer Heiliger in festländischen Liturgietexten
des frühen Mittelalters, Archiv für Kulturgeschichte 52, 1970, 222-234 (A)* [5]

1971

P. Gaechter, Die Gedächtniskultur in Irland, Institut für vergleichende Sprachwissen-
schaft Universität Innsbruck, Archiv für Kulturgeschichte 53, 200f, (R)*

1972

Deutsche Ortsnamen in der martyrologischen Tradition Irlands, Archiv für Kulturgeschichte 54, 223-240 (A)* [5]
Grundzüge der martyrologischen Tradition Irlands, Archiv für Liturgiewissenschaft
14, 1972, 71-98 (A)* [5]

1973

Studien zur deutschsprachigen Irlandkunde im 19. Jahrhundert, Deutsche Vierteljahrs-
schrift für Literaturwissenschaft und Geistesgeschichte 47, 617-629 (A)* [1]

1977

Die kulturgeschichtliche Bedeutung der Stellung Irlands in der hagiographischen Tradition, Archiv für Kulturgeschichte, 59, 222-234 (A)* [1][5]

1978

Die Heimat der Heiligen, Heiliger Dienst 32, 133-137 (Ar)* [5]

1979

Wendelin (409ff), Virgil von Salzburg (303), Fridolin von Säckingen (127ff), Pirmin
(424ff), In: H.J. Weisbender (Hg.), Heilige des Regionalkalenders, Leipzig 1979
(Ar)* [5]

1980

Ein Atlas von Irland, Dublin 1979, Neue Zürcher Zeitung 38, 16.4. (R)*

1982

Irlandkunde in der festländischen Tradition irischer Heiliger, In: H. Löwe (Hg.) Die
Iren und Europa im frühen Mittelalter, Stuttgart: Klett-Cotta, 686-696 (A)* [5]

1984

Löwe, Irlandkunde in der festländischen Tradition irischer Heiliger, In: H. Löwe (Hg.)
   Die Iren und Europa im frühen Mittelalter, Stuttgart: Klett-Cotta Archiv für Li-
   turgiewissenschaft 26, 408f, (R)*
Richter, Irland im Mittelalter, Archiv für Liturgiewissenschaft 26, 408, (R)*

1985

NiChatain, M. Richter, Irland und Europa , Zeitschrift für Kirchengeschichte 96, 96,
   (R)*

Ohne Datum

Irish Footsteps in Aachen, ohne Quelle (Ar)
Mile-stones of German-Irish Literary Relations, unveröffentlicht (A)
The Irish Widow (Ar)